EUROPEAN AND INTERNATI
MEDIA LAW

This book is the first to incorporate current academic literature and case law on European, transnational and international media law into a comprehensive overview intended primarily for students. It introduces the legal framework for globalised communication via mass media, and considers the transformative effect globalisation has had on domestic media law. Engaging case examples at the beginning of each chapter and questions at the end give students a clearer idea of legal problems and encourage them to think critically. A wide variety of topics – including media economics, media technology and social norms concerning media publications – are discussed in relation to media law and numerous references to case law and suggestions for further reading allow students to conduct independent research easily.

JAN OSTER is Assistant Professor for EU Law and Institutions in the Department of History at Leiden University. He is also a visiting lecturer for media law at the Mainz Media Institute and King's College London. He received the Carla Musterd Award for Teaching in 2014, and is the author of *Media Freedom as a Fundamental Right* (Cambridge University Press, 2015).

EUROPEAN AND INTERNATIONAL MEDIA LAW

JAN OSTER

Universiteit Leiden

CAMBRIDGE UNIVERSITY PRESS

CAMBRIDGE
UNIVERSITY PRESS

University Printing House, Cambridge CB2 8BS, United Kingdom

Cambridge University Press is part of the University of Cambridge.

It furthers the University's mission by disseminating knowledge in the pursuit
of education, learning, and research at the highest international levels of excellence.

www.cambridge.org
Information on this title: www.cambridge.org/9781107026582

First published 2017

Printed in the United Kingdom by Clays, St Ives plc

A catalogue record for this publication is available from the British Library.

Library of Congress Cataloguing in Publication Data
Names: Oster, Jan, 1978–
Title: European and international media law / Jan Oster, Universiteit Leiden.
Description: Cambridge [UK] : Cambridge University Press, [2017] |
Includes bibliographical references and index.
Identifiers: LCCN 2016026755| ISBN 9781107026582 (hardback : alk. paper) |
ISBN 9781107620766 (pbk. : alk. paper)
Subjects: LCSH: Mass media – Law and legislation. | Freedom of expression. |
Freedom of speech. | Mass media policy. | Mass media – Law and legislation – Europe.
Classification: LCC K4240 .O78 2017 | DDC 343.09/9–dc23
LC record available at https://lccn.loc.gov/2016026755

ISBN 978-1-107-02658-2 Hardback
ISBN 978-1-107-62076-6 Paperback

CONTENTS

Preface   *page* xvii
Table of Cases   xx
Treaties, Conventions, Declarations and Statutes   xliii
Reports and Other Documentary Sources   liv

1   Introduction   1
     Case Example   1
     I What is Media Law?   1
         1 What is 'the Media'?   2
         2 A Privileged Protection for the Journalistic Media?   5
         3 The Distinction between the Journalistic Media and Other Content
             Providers   9
         4 The Distinction between Media in a Technological Sense and Content
             Providers   13
         5 The Evaluation of Media Content   16
         6 Application of these Principles to the *Jersild* Case   18
     II The Transnational, European and International Dimensions of Media Law   20
         1 The Notion of Transnational Media Law   20
         2 Jurisdiction and the Choice of the Applicable Law   22
         3 European Media Law   23
             a The Council of Europe   23
             b The European Union   24
         4 International Media Law   25
     III Questions   26

2   Fundamental Rights and Principles   27
     Case Example   27
     I Introduction   27
     II The Legal Frameworks   28
         1 The Human Rights Framework   29
         2 The Economic Rights Frameworks   33
             a The Internal Market Provisions of the TFEU   34
             b The WTO   37
     III The Rights of Content Providers   39
         1 Freedom of Expression   39

v

a Freedom of Expression Theory   39

b Right to Impart Information and Ideas   42

c Choice of the Means and Forms of Expression   42

d The Internet as a Means of Communication   44

e The Protection of Anonymous and Pseudonymous Speech   46

2 Privileges of the Journalistic Media   50

a Independence of the Media   52

b Protection of Journalistic Research and Investigation   52

c Protection of Journalistic Sources   53

d Protection Against Interception of Communication, Surveillance, Searches, Seizures and Arrests   54

e Entitlements of the Media   54

f Non-Discrimination   55

g The Case Example   56

IV The Rights of Recipients   57

1 The Right to Receive Information   58

2 The Right of Access to Information   59

V The Rights of Intermediaries   64

VI Questions   67

VII Further Reading   67

3   Restrictions on Freedom of Expression and Media Freedom   68

Case Examples   68

I Introduction   69

II Personality Rights   71

1 The Taxonomy of 'Personality Rights'   71

2 The Balancing Exercise between Freedom of Expression and Personality Rights   73

a The Extent to which a Publication Contributed to a Debate of Public Concern   74

b The Position of the Person Concerned and the Extent to which he is Well-Known   76

c The Prior Conduct of the Person Concerned   77

d Content, Form and Consequences of the Publication   78

e Veracity of the Publication and the Prior Conduct of the Publisher   79

aa True Statements of Fact   80

bb Knowingly False Statements of Fact   83

cc Statements that Turn Out to be Untrue or Cannot be Proven to be True   83

dd Value Judgements   86

f Severity of the Sanction Imposed   87

g Application of these Principles to the Case Examples   87

III Intellectual Property and Other Exclusive Rights   89

IV Threats to Public Order Interests: National Security, Public Safety and Prevention
of Disorder and Crime   89

   1 The Balancing Exercise   91

   2 In Particular: The Disclosure of State Secrets   93

V Laws on Morality and Decency   95

VI Hate Speech   98

VII Religiously Offensive Speech   100

   1 The Notion of 'Defamation of Religions'   100

   2 The 'Right to Respect for One's Religious Feelings'   101

   3 Public Order Interests   103

   4 Margin of Appreciation   103

VIII Authority and Impartiality of the Judiciary   104

IX Commercial Speech   105

X Media Pluralism   105

   1 The Relationship between Media Freedom and Media Pluralism   106

   2 Policy Areas of Media Pluralism   107

XI Licensing of Journalists and Media Companies   108

XII Questions   110

XIII Recommended Reading   111

4   The Jurisdictional Question   112

   Case Examples   112

I Introduction   112

II The Notion of 'Jurisdiction'   114

III The Legal Framework   116

IV Establishing Jurisdiction in Transnational Media Law Cases   120

   1 Jurisdiction at the Place of Establishment   121

   2 Jurisdiction at the Place Where the Publication Originated   123

   3 Jurisdiction at the Country of Reception   125

   4 Limitation of the Country-of-Reception Principle by the 'Mosaic
Formula'   129

   5 The 'Centre of Interests' Analysis   132

   6 Alternative Approaches   133

     a 'Targeting Approach'   134

     b Quantitative Criteria   134

     c The 'Centre of Gravity of the Conflict' Analysis   135

     d Exclusive Country-of-Origin Principle   137

   7 Application of These Principles to the *Shevill* and the *Yahoo* Cases   138

V Recognition and Enforcement of Foreign Decisions   140

VI Questions   143

VII Further Reading   143

5   Broadcasting and Other Audiovisual Media Services   144
        Case Example   144
      I Introduction   145
     II International Law   145
    III The European Broadcasting Order   148
        1 The Legal Frameworks   150
          a The EU Framework: The AVMS Directive and Other Provisions   150
            aa Service   151
            bb Programme   151
            cc Provision of Programme is the Principal Purpose   153
            dd To the General Public   153
            ee In Order to Inform, Entertain or Educate   154
            ff Editorial Responsibility of a Media Services Provider   154
            gg Via Electronic Communication Networks   154
          b The Distinction between Television and On-Demand Services   155
          c Relationship to Other Provisions   156
          d The European Convention on Transfrontier Television   156
        2 Principles of the European Broadcasting Order   157
        3 The Establishment of, and Investment in, Audiovisual Media
          Companies   160
        4 The Country-of-Origin Principle   162
          a The AVMS Directive   162
          b The European Convention on Transfrontier Television   164
        5 Stricter Rules and their Circumvention   165
        6 Regulation of Audiovisual Commercial Communication   168
          a Terminology   168
          b Concepts   172
            aa Transparency Requirements   172
            bb Content-Based Restrictions   173
            cc Aggressive and Misleading Practices   175
            dd Editorial Independence and Principle of Separation   175
            ee Restrictions on the Time and Timing of Television Advertising
               and Teleshopping   176
        7 Content Regulation   179
        8 Restrictions on Exclusive Rights and Access to Content   181
          a Territorially Applicable Exclusive Rights   181
          b 'Events of Major Importance for Society'   184
          c Short News Reports   187
        9 Protection of Minors   189
       10 Promotion of European Productions   190
          a The Concepts of 'European Works'   191

b Promotion of European Works   192

11 Accountability   193

12 Access to Network Infrastructure and to Broadcasting Channels   194

13 Privileges Under Public Procurement Law   199

14 Commission Proposal for an Amendment of the AVMS Directive   200

IV Questions   201

V Further Reading   201

6 Internet Governance and Regulation   202

Case Example   202

I Introduction   202

II The Internet and the World Wide Web   203

III Schools of Thought   206

IV Global Internet Governance   214

1 Self-Regulating Organisations   214

2 ICANN   215

3 Internet Governance at the UN Level   216

V The European Legal Framework   219

1 Council of Europe   219

2 The European Union   221

a Scope   222

aa 'Service Normally Provided for Remuneration'   222

bb 'At a Distance'   223

cc 'By Electronic Means'   223

dd 'At the Individual Request'   223

ee Relationship to Other Provisions   223

b Country-of-Origin Principle   224

c Taking up an Activity as an Information Society Service Provider   227

d Commercial Communication   227

e Liability of Internet Intermediaries   227

aa Applicability   229

(1) Provision of Own Content or Adoption of Third-Party Content   229

(2) Editorial Control Over Third-Party Statements   230

(3) Absence of an 'Active Role'   231

bb Requirements to Obtain Immunity   232

cc No General Obligation to Monitor   234

dd One-Sided versus Full Harmonisation   236

ee Current Developments   237

ff The *Delfi* Case   238

VI Questions   241

VII Further Reading   241

7   Telecommunications   242

        Case Example   242

    I Introduction   243

    II Economics of Telecommunications   244

    III International Telecommunications Law   245

        1 The International Telecommunication Union   246

            a The ITU's Legal Framework and its Scope   246

            b Purposes of the ITU   247

            c ITU Organs   248

            d The ITU Sectors   248

                aa Radiocommunication Sector (ITU-R)   249

                bb Telecommunication Standardization Sector (ITU-T)   250

                cc Telecommunication Development Sector (ITU-D)   251

            e Substantive ITU Law   251

                aa Freedom and Equality of Correspondence versus Principle of Prior
                   Consent and Privileged Communications   251

                bb Secrecy of Telecommunications   252

                cc Principle of Technical Efficiency   252

                dd Special Provisions for Radio   252

                    (1) Principles of Efficient Use and Prohibition of Harmful
                        Interference   252

                    (2) International Radio-Frequency Management   253

            f Settlement of Disputes   255

        2 The World Trade Organization   255

            a The Annex on Telecommunication   256

                aa Scope   256

                bb Transparency   257

                cc Access to and Use of Networks and Services   257

            b The Reference Paper   258

                aa Scope   259

                bb Competitive Safeguards   259

                cc Interconnection   260

                dd Universal Services   260

                ee Allocation and Use of Scarce Resources   260

            c The WTO and EU Telecommunications Law   260

    IV The Council of Europe Legal Framework   261

    V The Legal Framework of EU Telecommunications Law   263

        1 Liberalisation and Harmonisation of the EU Telecommunications
          Sector   264

            a Liberalisation   264

            b Harmonisation   265

            c Historical Development   265

                aa First Phase 1987–1998   265

bb Second Phase 1998–2003   267

cc Third Phase, 2003–2011   268

2 Actors in EU Telecommunications Law   269

a Commission   270

b BEREC and IRG   270

c National Regulatory Authorities (NRAs)   271

3 Scope of the Regulatory Framework   271

a Transmission Services as Opposed to the Provision of Content   272

b Public Networks and Publicly Available Services   273

c Provided Against Payment   274

d Exclusion of Telecommunications Equipment   274

e Distinction between Sector-Specific Regulation and Competition Law   274

4 Objectives and Principles   275

a Principle of Non-Discrimination   276

b Necessity to Balance Conflicting Interests and the Principle of Proportionality   276

c Principles of Technology Neutrality and Service Neutrality   277

d Net Neutrality   277

VI Substantive EU Telecommunications Regulation   279

1 Access to Domestic Telecommunication Markets   279

2 *Ex Ante* Regulation   280

a Market Identification and Definition, and Market Analysis   282

aa Market Identification and Definition   283

bb Market Analysis   287

cc Procedure   287

b Imposition of a Specific Regulatory Obligation   289

aa Access Regulation, Article 12 Access Directive   290

bb Price Control and Cost Accounting Obligations, Article 13 Access Directive   294

cc Transparency, Article 9 Access Directive   296

dd Non-Discrimination, Article 10 Access Directive   296

ee Accounting Separation, Article 11 Access Directive   296

ff Functional Separation, Article 13a Access Directive   297

gg Regulatory Controls on Retail Services   297

c Access Obligation of Undertakings Without Significant Market Power, Article 5(1)(a) Access Directive   298

d Procedure   299

3 Frequency Allocation and Frequency Management   299

a EU Radio Spectrum Policy   300

b Authorisation Directive   301

c Framework Directive   302

VII Questions   302

VIII Further Reading   303

8   Data Protection   304
         Case Examples   304
      I Introduction   305
     II The Phenomenon of Big Data   307
    III The Public and Private Dimensions of Data Protection and their Threats to the
         Digital Sovereignty of the Individual   309
     IV Transnational Developments   312
      V Data Protection Philosophies in Europe and the US   313
     VI The European and International Legal Framework for Data Protection   317
         1 Council of Europe   318
         2 The EU Legal Framework   322
         3 Substantive Scope of the European Regulatory Regimes   325
           a Personal Data   325
           b Data Processing   329
           c Data Controllers and Data Processors   330
    VII Principles of European Data Protection Law   332
         1 Obligation to Notify   332
         2 Principles of Data Processing   333
           a Principle of Purpose Specification   334
           b Requirements on Data Quality   334
           c Consent   335
           d Justification of Data Processing in the Absence of Consent   337
           e Security and Confidentiality of Data Processing   340
           f Processing of Traffic Data and Location Data   341
         3 Rights of the Data Subject   343
           a Transparency and Access to Information   343
           b Data Rectification and Erasure   345
           c Right to Object to Processing   346
           d Rights in Relation to Automated Decision-Making   346
         4 Exceptions and Derogations   347
         5 Compatibility with Human Rights   348
         6 The Transfer of Personal Data to Third Countries   351
           a The Global and European Legal Framework   352
           b Adequacy Decision   353
           c Evaluation and Outlook   355
         7 Jurisdiction and International Applicability of European Data Protection
           Law   356
         8 The Case Examples   361
           a The Data Retention Directive Case   361
           b The *Google Spain* Case   364
   VIII Questions   367
     IX Further Reading   369

9   Copyright   370
    Case Examples   370
    I Introduction   371
    II Rationales for Protecting Copyright   373
      1 The Lockean Argument from Labour   373
      2 The Argument from Personality   374
      3 The Utilitarian Argument   374
      4 Economic Analysis of Intellectual Property   374
    III The International Copyright Framework   376
      1 WIPO   376
        a The Berne Convention and the Copyright Treaty   377
        b The Rome Convention and the Performances and Phonograms Treaty   379
      2 Article 27(2) UDHR   379
      3 WTO   380
      4 The Anti-Counterfeiting Trade Agreement (ACTA)   380
      5 Council of Europe   381
      6 European Union   382
        a Copyright and the Free Movement Provisions   383
        b Approximation and Harmonisation   385
          aa The Rental Rights Directive   386
          bb The Satellite and Cable Directive   387
          cc The Copyright Directive   388
          dd Current Developments   389
    IV Transnational Copyright Law   389
      1 Terminology   390
      2 Requirements for Copyright Protection   392
        a Subject-Matter of a Copyright   393
        b Originality   394
        c Fixation   395
        d Qualification   395
      3 Beneficiaries of Copyright Protection   395
      4 Rights of Copyright Owners and Holders of Related Rights   397
        a Moral Rights   397
        b Assignment and Licence   397
        c Economic Rights   398
          aa Fixation   398
          bb Reproduction   398
          cc Communication to the Public   399
            (1) The International Framework   400
            (2) The EU Framework   400
            (3) The Concepts of 'Communication' and 'Making Available' to the Public   403

dd Distribution   407

5 Infringements of Copyright   408

6 Exceptions and Limitations   409

a Temporary Acts of Reproduction   409

b Further Exceptions and Limitations   414

c The 'Three-Step Test'   421

7 Term of Copyright Protection   422

8 The Enforcement of Copyright   422

a The Legal Framework   423

b Protection of Personal Data   425

c Liability of Internet Intermediaries   427

V The Case Examples   431

1 The *Painer* Case   431

2 *Infopaq*   434

VI Jurisdiction and Applicable Law   436

1 The Establishment of Jurisdiction   437

2 The Choice of the Applicable Law   439

VII Questions   443

VIII Further Reading   444

10   Media Competition Law   445

Case Example   445

I Introduction   445

II The Aims of Antitrust Law   447

III International Antitrust Law   449

IV European Antitrust Law   450

1 General Aspects   450

a Jurisdiction   450

b Market Definition   452

aa Relevant Product Market   453

bb Relevant Geographic Market   454

c Undertaking   454

d Affecting Trade between Member States   455

e Enforcement   456

2 The Definition of Media Markets   458

a TV-Related Markets   459

aa Licensing and Acquisition of Broadcasting Rights   459

bb Wholesale Supply of TV Channels   461

cc Retail Supply of TV Services   462

b The Transmission Infrastructure   463

c Newspaper Markets   463

d Other Media Markets   464

e The Relevant Geographic Markets 465

3 Anti-Competitive Multilateral Behaviour 466

a Agreements, Decisions and Concerted Practices 466

b Distortion of Competition 467

c Exemptions 467

d Application to the Media 468

4 Abuse of a Dominant Position 470

a Dominant Position 470

b Abuse 471

c Application to the Media 472

5 Mergers, Acquisitions and Joint Ventures in Media Sectors 477

a Introduction 477

b Media Concentrations 480

6 The Case Example 485

V Unfair Competition 487

1 The International Framework 488

2 The Human Rights Dimension 489

3 Misleading Advertising 491

4 Comparative Advertising 492

VI Jurisdiction and Conflict of Laws 493

1 Unfair Competition 493

2 Antitrust and Concentration Law 499

VII Questions 500

VIII Further Reading 501

11 Media Law and State Aid 502

Case Example 502

I Introduction 503

II The Main Areas of Media State Aid 504

1 Funding of Public Service Broadcasters 505

2 Film Funding 506

3 Public Investment in Communication Infrastructure 507

III International Law 507

IV EU Law 509

1 Aid Granted by the EU 509

2 Definition of State Aid 510

a Aid 510

b Granted by a Member State or through State Resources 518

c Favouring Certain Undertakings 520

d Distorting or Threatening to Distort Competition 521

e Affecting Trade between Member States 522

3 The Commission Procedure in State Aid Cases 524

4 The Compatibility of State Aid with the Internal Market   529
   a The Compatibility of State Aid under Article 107(2) TFEU   529
   b The Compatibility of State Aid under Article 107(3) TFEU   530
   c The Compatibility of State Aid under Article 106(2) TFEU   536
   d Aids Approved by the Council under Article 108(2)3 TFEU   544
5 Recovery of an Unlawful Aid   545
6 The Case Example: Financing of Public Service Broadcasters in
   Germany   546
V Questions   548
VI Further Reading   549

References   550
Index   563

PREFACE

This book deals with European and international law on communication via mass media. That includes a lot, but it also excludes some things.

First, the book is about *law*. Lawrence Lessig, to whom we will return in more detail in Chapter 6, identified four modalities of 'regulation': law, norms, market and architecture. Applied to media communication, each of those factors would deserve an examination in its own right. This book will focus on the first of Lessig's modalities: the law. But it will not do so in isolation. It will refer to social norms concerning media publications, to media economics and to media technology in order to show the interaction of media law with those factors. For example, social norms play a significant role with regard to the 'ethics of journalism'. It will be shown in Chapter 3 that the Strasbourg Court has incorporated the 'ethics of journalism' as a factor in the balancing exercise in cases in which media publications presumably harm the rights of others. The economics of the media will play a particularly important role in Chapter 10 on media competition law. Lastly, mass communication is dependent on a particular infrastructure, or architecture. The regulation of this architecture, such as computer systems, is subject to information technology law or information and communication technology law (ICT law). In Chapters 6 and 7, this book will explain the architecture of communication to the extent that it is relevant to understand the legal problems and it will refer the reader to more in-depth literature that should also be digestible for technology laypersons. Other than that, the book will focus on the content of mass communication, that is, the 'I' and the 'C' of 'ICT'.

Second, the book deals with the law relating to *mass media communication*; that is, communication made accessible to an indefinite number of people. It excludes private communication between individuals, such as via e-mail or telephony. Moreover, it excludes the sale of goods and the provision of services other than the provision of information itself. Therefore, it will not deal with contract law and electronic commerce. Moreover, the book will focus on legal questions relating to the media in particular. In turn, general issues of law will only be mentioned briefly, even if they are of huge practical significance, such as questions of judicial review. References to case law and literature should help the reader to conduct further research into those topics, if necessary. Moreover, the book will focus on communication media, particularly the journalistic media, and it will largely exclude questions relating specifically to the entertainment industry.

Third, the book focuses on *European and international* law, and thus largely excludes domestic law. By doing so, the book aims to contribute to a truly transnational media law order. Its focus is on Europe, in particular on the EU as a postnational union that has to a large extent overcome the Westphalian boundaries of state sovereignty. The Europeanisation of media law has had a transformative effect on domestic media law. The book should contribute to thinking about media law in the first place from an international, especially European, perspective, and only in the second place from a domestic point of view.

The book is suitable as an introduction to the European and international dimension of media law. However, a basic understanding of domestic media law, such as the law of defamation and privacy, as well as of EU law, is a prerequisite. The book is therefore aimed at more advanced students, particularly Master's students.

Also, this book is mostly descriptively focused on the law as it is, and rarely prescriptively on the law as it should be. For more analytical approaches, it will frequently refer to academic literature.

The book builds on, and further develops, ideas of earlier articles and a monograph. Chapters 2 and 3 are largely based on my book *Media Freedom as a Fundamental Right* (Cambridge University Press), which itself was inspired by my work on 'Theory and Doctrine of "Media Freedom" as a Legal Concept', *Journal of Media Law* 5 (2013), 57. Chapter 4 is based on, and further develops, ideas I published in 'Rethinking *Shevill*: Conceptualising the EU Private International Law of Internet Torts Against Personality Rights', *International Review of Law, Computers & Technology* 26 (2012), 113, and in 'Public Policy and Human Rights', *Journal of Private International Law* 11 (2015), 542. Finally, Section V of Chapter 2 as well as parts of Chapter 6 build on my article 'Communication, Defamation and Liability of Intermediaries', *Legal Studies* 35 (2015), 348.

Three comments on the structure and style of this book: First, the chapters begin with one or two case examples that are based on judgments or decisions of the European Commission. They shall guide the reader through the chapter. The summaries of the facts are shortened to what is essential for understanding the gist of the case as far as it is relevant for the chapter. Those cases will be explained in detail at some stage in the chapters, applying the concepts discussed in previous sections. Therefore, keep those cases in mind while you study the chapters. Each chapter (except for the introduction) refers to literature that could not be considered in detail, but that the reader should consult if he or she wishes to delve deeper into the topics discussed. Second, directives require implementation by the Member States and thus do not directly grant rights to, or impose obligations on, individuals. However, for the sake of brevity, rather than repeating each time that 'according to Article XY of the Directive, Member States shall grant the right to everyone…', this book speaks of 'according to Article XY of the Directive, everyone has the right…'. This does not necessarily include a statement on the directive's direct applicability. Third, for reasons of legibility, the book uses generic masculine pronouns when making examples or when quoting a legal provision. This does not include any assumption on gender or biological sex.

I would like to thank many people who helped me to write this book: Marta Walkowiak and Valerie Appleby at Cambridge University Press for their strong support of this project; Katrina Simpson for her invaluable proofreading assistance and critical comments; Dan Svantesson and Ashwin van Rooijen for their critical comments; and the Institute for History at Leiden University for a grant of sabbatical leave.

All websites cited in this book have been last accessed on 19 February 2016. I have sought to state the law accurately up to March 2016. It was possible to include references to some later material in July 2016. Comments are gratefully received: j.s.oster@hum.leidenuniv.nl.

TABLE OF CASES

Human Rights Committee

Aduayom and others v. Togo [1996] Communication nos. 422–424/1990

A.K. and A.R. v. Uzbekistan [2009] Communication no. 1233/2003

Ballantyne and others v. Canada [1993] Communication no. 359, 385/89

Benhadj v. Algeria [2007] Communication no. 1173/2003

Bodrožić v. Serbia and Montenegro [2005] Communication no. 1180/2003

Coleman v. Australia [2006] Communication no. 1157/2003

Dissanayake v. Sri Lanka [2005] Communication no. 1373/2005

Faurisson v. France [1996] Communication no. 550/93

Fernando v. Sri Lanka [2005] Communication no. 1189/2003

Gauthier v. Canada [1999] Communication no. 633/95

Gryb v. Belarus [2011] Communication no. 1316/2004

Hertzberg and others v. Finland [1985] Communication no. 61/1979

J. R. T. and W. G. Party v. Canada [1984] Communication no. 104/1981

Kim v. Republic of Korea [1999] Communication no. 574/1994

Kivenmaa v. Finland [1994] Communication no. 412/1990

Marques de Morais v. Angola [2005] Communication no. 1128/2002

Mavlonov et al. v. Uzbekistan [2009] Communication no. 1334/2004

Mukong v. Cameroon [1994] Communication no. 458/91

Njaru v. Cameroon [2007] Communication no. 1353/2005

Park v. Republic of Korea [1998] Communication no. 628/1995

Pinkney v. Canada [1981] Communication no. 27/1978

Shchetko and others v. Belarus [2001] Communication no. 1009/2001

Shin v. Republic of Korea [2004] Communication no. 926/2000

Toktakunov v. Kyrgyzstan [2011] Communication no. 1470/2006

Velichkin v. Belarus [2001] Communication no. 1022/2001

Zalesskaya v. Belarus [2011] Communication no. 1604/2007

Permanent Court of International Justice

S.S. Lotus (France v. Turkey) [1927] PCIJ (Series A) No. 10

Special Court for Sierra Leone

Prosecutor v. Alex Tamba Brima and others, Decision on Prosecution appeal against decision on oral application for witness TF1-150 to testify without being compelled to answer questions on grounds of confidentiality, Case No. SCSL-2004-16-AR73 [2006] SCSL 2

WTO

WTO Panel

Japan – Taxes on alcoholic beverages [1996] WT/DS8/AB/R, WT/DS10/AB/R and WT/DS11/AB/R

Mexico – Measures affecting telecommunications services [2004] WT/DS204/R

WTO Appellate Body

Canada – Certain measures concerning periodicals [1997] WT/DS31/AB/R

China – Measures Affecting Trading Rights and Distribution Services for Certain Publications and Audiovisual Entertainment Products [2009] WT/DS363/AB/R

United States – Section 110(5) of the US Copyright Act [2000] WT/DS160/R

United States – Standards for Reformulated and Conventional Gasoline [1996] WT/DS2/AB/R

United States – Measures affecting the cross-border supply of gambling and betting services [2005] WT/DS285/AB/R

African Commission on Human and Peoples' Rights

Constitutional Rights Project, Civil Liberties Organisation and Media Rights Agenda v. Nigeria [1999] App. nos. 140/94, 141/94 and 145/95

Media Rights Agenda, Constitutional Rights Project, Media Rights Agenda and Constitutional Rights Project v. Nigeria [1998] App. nos. 105/93, 128/94, 130/94 and 152/96

Council of Europe

European Commission on Human Rights

Aral, Tekin and Aral v. Turkey [1998] App. no. 24563/94

B.H., M.W., H.P. and G.K. v. Austria [1989] App. no. 12774/87
Christie v. the United Kingdom v. United Kingdom [1994] App. no. 21482/93
Ediciones Tiempo S.A. v. Spain [1989] App. no. 13010/87
Glimmerveen and Hagenbeek v. Netherlands [1979] App. nos. 8348/78 and 8406/78
Haider v. Austria [1995] App. no. 25060/94
Huggett v. United Kingdom [1995] App. no. 24744/94
Kühnen v. Federal Republic of Germany [1988] App. no. 12194/86
Lenzing AG v. Germany [1998] App. no. 39025/97
Lindberg v. Norway [1997] App. no. 26604/95
Loersch and Nouvelle Association du Courrier v. Switzerland [1995] App. nos. 23868/94 and 23869/94
Nachtmann v. Austria [1998] App. no. 36773/97
Purcell and others v. Ireland [1991] App. no. 15404/89
Schimanek v. Austria [2000] App. no. 32307/96
Smith Kline and French Laboratories Ltd v. the Netherlands [1990] App. no. 12633/87
Tete v. France [1987] App. no. 11123/84
X v. United Kingdom [1982] App. no. 9702/82
X. Ltd. and Y. v. United Kingdom [1982] App. no. 8710/79

European Court of Human Rights

A. v. Norway [2009] App. no. 28070/06
A. Menarini Diagnostics S.R.L. v. Italy [2011] App. no. 43509/08
Ageyevy v. Russia [2013] App. no. 7075/10
Aksu v. Turkey [2012] App. nos. 4149/04 and 41029/04
Albert-Engelmann-Gesellschaft mbH v. Austria [2006] App. no. 46389/99
Aleksey Ovchinnikov v. Russia [2010] App. no. 24061/04
Alithia Publishing Company Ltd and Constantinides v. Cyprus [2008] App. no. 17550/03
Alkaya v. Turkey [2012] App. no. 42811/06
Amann v. Switzerland [2000] App. no. 27798/95
Anheuser-Busch Inc. v. Portugal [2007] App. no. 73049/01
Animal Defenders International v. United Kingdom [2013] App. no. 48876/08
Annen v. Germany [2015] App. no. 3690/10
Armellini and Others v. Austria [2015] App. no. 14134/07.
Armonienė v. Lithuania [2008] App. no. 36919/02
Ashby Donald and others v. France [2013] App. no. 36769/08
Association Ekin v. France [2001] App. no. 39288/98
Autronic AG v. Switzerland [1990] App. no. 12726/87
Axel Springer AG v. Germany (No. 1) [2012] App. no. 39954/08
Aydın Tatlav v. Turkey [2006] App. no. 50692/99

Balan v. Moldova [2008] App. no. 19247/03

Balsytė-Lideikienė v. Lithuania [2008] App. no. 72596/01

Banković and Others v. Belgium and Others [2001] App. no. 52207/99

Barfod v. Denmark [1989] App. no. 11508/85

B.B. v. France [2009] App. no. 5335/06

Ben El Mahi v. Denmark [2006] 5853/06D

Bergens Tidende and others v. Norway [2000] App. no. 26132/95

Bernh Larsen Holding AS and Others v. Norway [2013] App. no. 24117/08

Biriuk v. Lithuania [2008] App. no. 23373/03

Bladet Tromsø and Stensaas v. Norway [1999] App. no. 21980/93

Botta v. Italy [1998] App. no. 153/1996/772/973

Bowman v. United Kingdom [1998] App. no. 141/1996/760/961

Brasilier v. France [2006] App. no. 71343/01

Braun v. Poland [2014] App. no. 30162/10

Bremner v. Turkey [2015] App. no. 37428/06

Brosa v. Germany [2014] App. no. 5709/09

Bucur and Toma v. Romania [2013] App. no. 40238/02

Burghartz v. Switzerland [1994] App. no. 16213/90

Busuioc v. Moldova [2004] App. no. 61513/00

Campmany y Diez de Revenga and Lopez-Galiacho Perona v. Spain [2000] App. no. 54224/00

Casado Coca v. Spain [1994] App. no. 15450/89

Castells v. Spain [1992] App. no. 11798/85

Cemalettin Canlı v. Turkey [2008] App. no. 22427/04

Cengiz and others v. Turkey [2015] App. nos. 48226/10 and 14027/11

Centro Europa 7 S.r.l. and Di Stefano v. Italy [2012] App. no. 38433/09

Chauvy and others v. France [2004] App. no. 64915/01

Chorherr v. Austria [1993] App. no. 13308/87

Ciubotaru v. Moldova [2010] App. no. 27138/04

Copland v. United Kingdom [2007] App. no. 62617/00

Colombani and others v. France [2002] App. no. 51279/99

Cox v. Turkey [2010] App. no. 2933/03

Cumpănă and Mazăre v. Romania [2004] App. no. 33348/96

Dammann v. Switzerland [2006] App. no. 77551/01

De Haes and Gijsels v. Belgium [1997] App. no. 19983/92

Delfi AS v. Estonia [2015] App. no. 64569/09

Demuth v. Switzerland [2002] App. no. 38743/97

Dima v. Romania [2005] App. no. 58472/00

Eerikäinen and others v. Finland [2009] App. no. 3514/02

Egeland and Hanseid v. Norway [2009] App. no. 34438/04

Engel and others v. Netherlands [1976] App. nos. 5100/71, 5101/71, 5102/71, 5354/72 and 5370/72

Erdoğdu v. Turkey [2000] App. no. 25723/94

Faccio v. Italy [2003] App. no. 33/04

Fatullayev v. Azerbaijan [2010] App. no. 40984/07

Fayed v. United Kingdom [1994] App. no. 17101/90

Filatenko v. Russia [2007] App. no. 73219/01

Financial Times Ltd and others v. United Kingdom [2009] App. no. 821/03

Flinkkilä and others v. Finland [2010] App. no. 25576/04

Flux v. Moldova (No. 6) [2008] App. no. 22824/04

Frankowicz v. Poland [2008] App. no. 53025/99

Fressoz and Roire v. France [1999] App. no. 29183/95

Fuentes Bobo v. Spain [2000] App. no. 39293/98

Garaudy v. France [2003] App. no. 65831/01

Gardel v. France [2009] App. no. 16428/05

Gaskin v. United Kingdom [1989] App. no. 10454/83

Gawęda v. Poland [2002] App. no. 26229/95

Glas Nadezhda EOOD and Elenkov v. Bulgaria [2007] App. no. 14134/02

Goodwin v. United Kingdom [1996] App. no. 17488/90

Gough v. United Kingdom [2014] App. no. 49327/11

Groppera Radio AG and others v. Switzerland [1990] App. no. 10890/84

Gsell v. Switzerland [2009] App. no. 12675/05

Guerra and others v. Italy [1998] App. no. 116/1996/735/932

Guja v. Moldova [2008] App. no. 14277/04

Gül and others v. Turkey [2010] App. no. 4870/02

Gündüz v. Turkey [2003] App. no. 35071/97

Hachette Filipacchi Associés v. France [2007] App. no. 71111/01

Hachette Filipacchi Associés ('Ici Paris') v. France [2009] App. no. 12268/03

Hadjianastassiou v. Greece [1992] App. no. 12945/87

Haldimann and others v. Switzerland [2015] App. no. 21830/09

Halis Doğan and others v. Turkey [2006] App. no. 50693/99

Handyside v. United Kingdom [1976] App. no. 5493/72

Hashman and Harrup v. United Kingdom [1999] App. no. 25594/94

Heinisch v. Germany [2011] App. no. 28274/08

Hertel v. Switzerland [1998] App. no. 59/1997/843/1049

I v. Finland [2008] App. no. 20511/03

İ.A. v. Turkey [2005] App. no. 42571/98

Informationsverein Lentia and others v. Austria [1993] App. nos. 13914/88, 15041/89, 15717/89, 15779/89 and 17207/90

Issa and Others v. Turkey [2004] App. no. 31821/96

Janowski v. Poland (No. 1) [1999] App. no. 25716/94

Jersild v. Denmark [1994] App. no. 15890/89

Jerusalem v. Austria [2001] App. no. 26958/95

Jokitaipale and Others v. Finland [2010] App. no. 43349/05

July and SARL Liberation v. France [2008] App. no. 20893/03

Kaperzyński v. Poland [2012] App. no. 43206/07

Karataş v. Turkey [1999] App. no. 23168/94

Karhuvaara and Iltalehti v. Finland [2004] App. no. 53678/00

Karsai v. Hungary [2009] App. no. 5380/07

Kasabova v. Bulgaria [2011] App. no. 22385/03

Kayasu v. Turkey (No. 1) [2008] App. nos. 64119/00 and 76292/01

Kenedi v. Hungary [2009] App. no. 31475/05

Kennedy v. United Kingdom [2010] App. no. 26839/05

K.H. and others v. Slovakia [2009] App. no. 32881/04

Khelili v. Switzerland [2011] App. no. 16188/07

Khurshid Mustafa and Tarzibachi v. Sweden [2008] App. no. 23883/06

Klass and others v. Germany [1978] App. no. 5029/71

Klein v. Slovakia [2006] App. no. 72208/01

Kobenter and Standard Verlags GmbH v. Austria [2006] App. no. 60899/00

Kokkinakis v. Greece [1993] App. no. 14307/88

Köpke v. Germany [2010] App. no. 420/07

Kopp v. Switzerland [1998] App. no. 13/1997/797/1000

Krone Verlag GmbH & Co. KG v. Austria (No. 1) [2002] App. no. 34315/96

Krone Verlag GmbH & Co. KG v. Austria (No. 3) [2003] App. no. 39069/97

K.U. v. Finland [2008] App. no. 2872/02

Kudeshkina v. Russia [2009] App. no. 29492/05

Lavric v. Romania [2014] App. no. 22231/05

Leander v. Sweden [1987] App. no. 9248/81

Lehideux and Isorni v. France [1998] App. no. 55/1997/839/1045

Leroy v. France [2009] App. no. 36109/03

Leschiutta and Fraccaro v. Belgium [2008] App. nos. 58081/00, 58411/00

Liberty and Others v. United Kingdom [2008] App. no. 58243/00

Lindberg v. Sweden [2004] App. no. 48198/99

Lindon, Otchakovsky-Laurens and July v. France [2007] App. nos. 21279/02 and
    36448/02

Lingens v. Austria [1986] App. no. 9815/82

Lombardo and others v. Malta [2007] App. no. 7333/06

Malone v. United Kingdom [1984] App. no. 8691/79

Manole and others v. Moldova [2009] App. no. 13936/02

Marchenko v. Ukraine [2009] App. no. 4063/04

Markt intern Verlag GmbH and Klaus Beermann v. Germany [1989] App. no. 10572/83

Matky v. Czech Republic [2006] App. no. 19101/03

McGinley and Egan v. United Kingdom [1998] App. no. 10/1997/794/995–996

McVicar v. United Kingdom [2002] App. no. 46311/99

Megadat.com SRL v. Moldova [2008] App. no. 21151/04

Melnychuk v. Ukraine [2005] App. no. 28743/03

Meltex Ltd and Mesrop Movsesyan v. Armenia [2008] App. no. 32283/04
Menteş and Others v. Turkey [1997] App. no. 58/1996/677/867
M.G. v. United Kingdom [2002] App. no. 39393/98
MGN Ltd v. United Kingdom [2011] App. no. 39401/04
M.K. v. France [2013] App. no. 19522/09
M.S. v. Sweden [1997] App. no. 20837/92
Mladina d.d. Ljubljana v. Slovenia [2014] App. no. 20981/10
Mosley v. United Kingdom [2011] App. no. 48009/08
Mouvement raëlien suisse v. Switzerland [2012] App. no. 16354/06
Müller and others v. Switzerland [1988] App. no. 10737/84
Murphy v. Ireland [2003] App. no. 44179/98
Muscio v. Italy [2007] App. no. 31358/03
Mustafa Erdoğan and others v. Turkey [2014] App. nos. 346/04 and 39779/04
Nagla v. Latvia [2013] App. no. 73469/10
Neij and Sunde Kolmisoppi v. Sweden [2013] App. no. 40397/12
News Verlags GmbH & Co. KG v. Austria [2000] App. no. 31457/96
Niemietz v. Germany [1992] App. no. 13710/88
Nikowitz and Verlagsgruppe News GmbH v. Austria [2007] App. no. 5266/03
Nilsen and Johnsen v. Norway [1999] App. no. 23118/93
Nordisk Film & TV A/S v. Denmark [2005] App. no. 40485/02
Norwood v. United Kingdom [2004] App. no. 23131/03
Novaya Gazeta and Borodyanskiy v. Russia [2013] App. no. 14087/08
Oberschlick v. Austria (No. 1) [1991] App. no. 11662/85
Oberschlick v. Austria (No. 2) [1997] App. no. 20834/92
Observer and Guardian v. United Kingdom [1991] App. no. 13585/88
Orban and others v. France [2009] App. no. 20985/05
Österreichischer Rundfunk v. Austria [2004] App. no. 57597/00 (admissibility decision)
Österreichischer Rundfunk v. Austria [2006] App. no. 35841/02
Österreichische Vereinigung zur Erhaltung, Stärkung und Schaffung eines wirtschaftlich gesunden land- und forstwirtschaftlichen Grundbesitzes v. Austria [2013] App. no. 39534/07
Otto-Preminger-Institut v. Austria [1994] App. no. 13470/87
Özgür Gündem v. Turkey [2000] App. no. 23144/93
Öztürk v. Turkey [1999] App. no. 22479/93
P4 Radio Hele Norge ASA v. Norway [2003] App. no. 76682/01
Pasko v. Russia [2009] App. no. 69519/01
Pavel Ivanov v. Russia [2004] App. no. 35222/04
Peck v. United Kingdom [2003] App. no. 44647/98
Pedersen and Baadsgaard v. Denmark [2004] App. no. 49017/99
Pentikäinen v. Finland [2015] App. no. 11882/10
Perinçek v. Switzerland [2015] App. no. 27510/08

Perrin v. United Kingdom [2005] App. no. 5446/03

PETA Deutschland v. Germany [2012] App. no. 43481/09

Petrina v. Romania [2008] App. no. 78060/01

Pfeifer v. Austria [2007] App. no. 12556/03

P.G. and J.H. v. United Kingdom [2001] App. no. 44787/98

Polanco Torres et Movilla Polanco v. Spain [2010] App. no. 34147/06

Prager and Oberschlick v. Austria [1995] App. no. 15974/90

Print Zeitungsverlag GmbH v. Austria [2013] App. no. 26547/07

Radio France and others v. France [2004] App. no. 53984/00

Radio Twist a.s. v. Slovakia [2006] App. no. 62202/00

Raninen v. Finland [1997] App. no. 152/1996/771/972

Refah Partisi (the Welfare Party) and others v. Turkey [2003] App. nos. 41340/98, 41342/98, 41343/98 and 41344/98

Reklos and Davourlis v. Greece [2009] App. no. 1234/05

Renaud v. France [2010] App. no. 13290/07

Ricci v. Italy [2013] App. no. 30210/06

Ringier Axel Springer Slovakia, a. s. v. Slovakia [2011] App. no. 41262/05

Ristamäki and Korvola v. Finland [2013] App. no. 66456/09

Roche v. United Kingdom [2005] App. no. 32555/96

Roemen and Schmit v. Luxembourg [2003] App. no. 51772/99

Rotaru v. Romania [2000] App. no. 28341/95

Rumyana Ivanova v. Bulgaria [2008] App. no. 36207/03

Ruusunen v. Finland [2014] App. no. 73579/10

Růžový panter, o.s. v. Czech Republic [2012] App. no. 20240/08

S. and Marper v. United Kingdom [2008] App. nos. 30562/04 and 30566/04

Salumäki v. Finland [2014] App. no. 23605/09

Sanoma Uitgevers B.V. v. Netherlands [2010] App. no. 38224/03

SC Editura Orizonturi SRL v. Romania [2008] App. no. 15872/03

Schüssel v. Austria [2002] App. no. 42409/98

Schweizerische Radio- und Fernsehgesellschaft SRG v. Switzerland [2012] App. no. 34124/06

Sciacca v. Italy [2005] App. no. 50774/99

Seckerson v. United Kingdom and Times Newspapers Ltd v. United Kingdom [2012] App. nos. 32844/10 and 33510/10

Segerstedt-Wiberg and others v. Sweden [2006] App. no. 62332/00

Selistö v. Finland [2004] App. no. 56767/00

Şener v. Turkey [2000] App. no. 26680/95

Shabanov and Tren v. Russia [2006] App. no. 5433/02

Silver and others v. United Kingdom [1983] App. nos. 5947/72, 6205/73, 7052/75, 7061/75, 7107/75, 7113/75 and 7136/75

Skałka v. Poland [2003] App. no. 43425/98

Société Colas Est and Others v. France [2002] App. no. 37971/97

Société de Conception de Presse et d'Edition et Ponson v. France [2009] App. no. 26935/05

Soltész v. Slovakia [2013] App. no. 11867/09

Sorguç v. Turkey [2009] App. no. 17089/03

Sosinowska v. Poland [2011] App. no. 10247/09

Soulas and others v. France [2008] App. no. 15948/03

Stambuk v. Germany [2002] App. no. 37928/97

Standard Verlags GmbH v. Austria (No. 2) [2009] App. no. 21277/05

Standard Verlags GmbH v. Austria (No. 3) [2012] App. no. 34702/07

Steel and Morris v. United Kingdom [2005] App. no. 68416/01

Steur v. Netherlands [2003] App. no. 39657/98

Stoll v. Switzerland [2007] App. no. 69698/01

Sunday Times v. United Kingdom (No. 1) [1979] App. no. 6538/74

Sürek v. Turkey (No. 1) [1999] App. no. 26682/95

Sürek v. Turkey (No. 2) [1999] App. no. 24122/94

Sürek v. Turkey (No. 3) [1999] App. no. 24735/94

Sürek and Özdemir v. Turkey [1999] App. nos. 23927/94 and 24277/94

Tammer v. Estonia [2001] App. no. 41205/98

Tănăsoaica v. Romania [2012] App. no. 3490/03

Tanrıkulu, Çetin and Kaya v. Turkey [2001] App. no. 40160/98

Társaság a Szabadságjogokért v. Hungary [2009] App. no. 37374/05

Taylor-Sabori v. the United Kingdom [2002] App. no. 47114/99

Telegraaf Media Nederland Landelijke Media B.V. and others v. Netherlands [2012] App. no. 39315/06

Thoma v. Luxembourg [2001] App. no. 38432/97

Thorgeir Thorgeirson v. Iceland [1992] App. no. 13778/88

Tierbefreier e.V. v. Germany [2014] App. no. 45192/09

Tillack v. Belgium [2007] App. no. 20477/05

Times Newspapers Ltd v. United Kingdom (Nos. 1 and 2) [2009] App. nos. 3002/03 and 23676/03

Tolstoy Miloslavsky v. United Kingdom [1993] App. no. 18139/91

Tuşalp v. Turkey [2012] App. nos. 32131/08 and 41617/08

TV Vest AS & Rogaland Pensjonistparti v. Norway [2008] App. no. 21132/05

Tyrer v. United Kingdom [1978] App. no. 5856/72

Uzun v. Germany [2010] App. no. 35623/05

Unabhängige Initiative Informationsvielfalt v. Austria [2002] App. no. 28525/95

Ungváry and Irodalom Kft v. Hungary [2013] App. no. 64520/10

Vajnai v. Hungary [2008] App. no. 33629/06

Vereniging Weekblad Bluf! v. Netherlands [1995] App. no. 16616/90

Vereinigung Bildender Künstler v. Austria [2007] App. no. 68354/01

Vereinigung demokratischer Soldaten Österreichs and Gubi v. Austria [1994] App. no. 15153/89

Verlagsgruppe News GmbH v. Austria (No. 2) [2006] App. no. 10520/02

VgT Verein gegen Tierfabriken v. Switzerland (No. 1) [2001] App. no. 24699/94

Vides Aizsardzības Klubs v. Latvia [2004] App. no. 57829/00

Von Hannover v. Germany (No. 1) [2004] App. no. 59320/00

Von Hannover v. Germany (No. 2) [2012] App. nos. 40660/08 and 60641/08

Von Hannover v. Germany (No. 3) [2013] App. no. 8772/10

Wagner and JMWL v. Luxembourg [2007] App. no. 76240/01

Weber v. Switzerland [1990] App. no. 11034/84

Weber and Savaria v. Germany [2006] App. no. 54934/00

Węgrzynowski and Smolczewski v. Poland [2013] App. no. 33846/07

White v. Sweden [2006] App. no. 42435/02

Wille v. Liechtenstein [1999] App. no. 28396/95

Willem v. France [2009] App. no. 10883/05

Wingrove v. United Kingdom [1996] App. no. 17419/90

Wirtschafts-Trend Zeitschriften-Verlagsgesellschaft m.b.H. v. Austria (no. 3) [2005] App. nos. 66298/01 and 15653/02

Wizerkaniuk v. Poland [2011] App. no. 18990/05

Wojtas-Kaleta v. Poland [2009] App. no. 20436/02

Worm v. Austria [1997] App. no. 83/1996/702/894

Wypych v. Poland [2005] App. no. 2428/05

X and Y v. Netherlands [1985] App. no. 8978/80

Yıldırım v. Turkey [2012] App. no. 3111/10

Youth Initiative for Human Rights v. Serbia [2013] App. no. 48135/06

Z v. Finland [1997] App. no. 22009/93

European Court of Justice/Court of Justice of the EU

Opinion 2/13 [2014] 'EU Accession to the ECHR'

Opinion 1/94 [1994] 'WTO Accession'

Case C-435/12 [2014] ACI Adam BV and Others v. Stichting de Thuiskopie and Others

Case C-143/99 [2001] Adria-Wien Pipeline and Wietersdorfer & Peggauer Zementwerke

Joined Cases C-89/85, C-104/85, C-114/85, C-116/85, C-117/85, C-125/85, C-126/85, C-127/85, C-128/85, C-129/85 [1988] Ahlström Osakeyhtiö and Others v. Commission ('Wood Pulp I')

Joined Cases C-89/85, C-104/85, C-114/85, C-116/85, C-117/85, C-125/85, C-126/85, C-127/85, C-128/85, C-129/85 [1988] Ahlström Osakeyhtiö and Others v. Commission ('Wood Pulp I'), Opinion of Advocate-General Darmon

Case 66/86 [1989] Ahmed Saeed Flugreisen v. Zentrale zur Bekämpfung unlauteren Wettbewerbs

Joined Cases C-431/09 and C-432/09 [2011] Airfield NV and Canal Digitaal BV
Case C-62/86 [1991] AKZO v. Commission
Case C-280/00 [2004] Altmark Trans GmbH
Case C-205/99 [2001] Analir
Joined Cases C-264/01, C-306/01, C-354/01 and C-355/01 [2004] AOK Bundesverband
    and others
Case C-55/06 [2008] Arcor
Joined Cases C-152/07, C-154/07 and C-153/07 [2008] Arcor and others
Case T-158/00 [2003] ARD v. Commission
Case C-6/98 [1999] ARD v. ProSieben
Joined Cases C-468/10 and C-469/10 [2011] ASNEF and FECEMD
Case 229/83 [1985] Association des Centres distributeurs Édouard Leclerc
Case T-194/04 [2007] Bavarian Lager
Case C-337/06 [2007] Bayerischer Rundfunk and others v. GEWA
Case C-56/93 [1996] Belgium v. Commission
Case C-75/97 [1999] Belgium v. Commission
Case C-413/06 P [2008] Bertelsmann
Case C-348/13 [2014] BestWater International GmbH v. Mebes and Potsch
Case C-393/09 [2010] Bezpečnostní softwarová asociace – Svaz softwarové ochrany
Case 352/85 [1988] Bond van Adverteerders v. Netherlands
Case C-461/10 [2008] Bonnier Audio
Joined Cases C-399/10 P and C-410/10 P [2013] Bouygues Télécom SA
Case 41/83 [1985] British Telecommunications
Case C-302/94 [1996] British Telecommunications II
Case C-7/97 [1998] Bronner v. Mediaprint Zeitungs- und Zeitschriftenverlag
Case 127/73 [1974] BRT v. SABAM
Case T-289/03 [2008] BUPA and Others v. Commission
Joined Cases T-346/02 and T-347/02 [2003] Cableuropa
Case C-348/96 [1999] Calfa
Case C-156/96P [1997] Calvin Williams v. Court of Auditors
Case 15/74 [1974] Centrafarm v. Sterling Drug
Case C-380/05 [2008] Centro Europa 7 Srl.
Case C-212/97 [1999] Centros v. Erhvervs-og Selskabsstyrelsen
Joined Cases 60 and 61/84 [1985] Cinéthèque
Case C-283/10 [2011] Circul Globus Bucureşti v. Uniunea Compozitorilor şi
    Muzicologilor din România
Case C-218/00 [2002] Cisal
Case T-16/96 [1998] Cityflyer
Case C-279/13 [2015] C More Entertainment AB v. Sandberg
Case 62/79 [1980] Coditel v. Ciné Vog Films and others ('Coditel I')
Case 262/81 [1982] Coditel and others v. Ciné Vog Films and others ('Coditel II')

Case C-288/89 [1991] Collectieve Antennevoorziening Gouda
Case C-553/07 [2009] College van burgemeester en wethouders van Rotterdam v. M.E.E. Rijkeboer Joined Cases 56 and 58/64 [1966] Consten and Grundig
Case C-82/07 [2008] Comisión del Mercedo de las Telecomunicaciones
Case C-211/91 [1992] Commission v. Belgium
Case C-11/95 [1996] Commission v. Belgium
Case C-355/98 [2000] Commission v. Belgium
Case C-221/01 [2002] Commission v. Belgium
Case C-110/02 [2004] Commission v. Council
Case C-399/03 [2006] Commission v. Council
Case C-154/89 [1991] Commission v. France
Case C-262/02 [2004] Commission v. France
Case C-113/03 [2004] Commission v. France
Case C-104/04 [2005] Commission v. France
Case C-424/07 [2009] Commission v. Germany
Case C-518/07 [2010] Commission v. Germany
Case C-198/89 [1991] Commission v. Greece
Case C-180/89 [1991] Commission v. Italy
Case C-260/04 [2007] Commission v. Italy
Case C-97/01 [2003] Commission v. Luxembourg
Case C-33/04 [2005] Commission v. Luxembourg
Case C-353/89 [1991] Commission v. Netherlands
Case C-227/07 [2008] Commission v. Poland
Case C-222/94 [1996] Commission v. United Kingdom
Case 121/85 [1986] Conegate v. HM Customs and Excise
Case C-274/99P [2001] Connolly
Case C-280/11 P [2013] Council v. Access Info Europe
Case C-453/99 [2001] Courage Ltd. v. Crehan
Joined Cases C-34/95, C-35/95 and C-36/95 [1997] De Agostini (Svenska) Förlag AB and others
Case 8/74 [1974] Dassonville
Case C-201/13 [2014] Deckmyn v. Vandersteen
Case C-17/00 [2001] De Coster
Case C-234/89 [1991] Delimitis
Case C-256/97 [1999] Déménagements-Manutention Transport SA (DMT)
Case 78/70 [1971] Deutsche Grammophon v. Metro
Case C-262/06 [2007] Deutsche Telekom
Case C-280/08 P [2010] Deutsche Telekom v. Commission
Case C-543/09 [2011] Deutsche Telekom AG v. Germany
Joined Cases C-293/12 and C-594/12[2014] Digital Rights Ireland Ltd and Kärntner Landesregierung

Case C-516/13 [2015] Dimensione Direct Sales Srl and others v. Knoll International SpA

Joined Cases C-509/10 and C-161/10 [2011] eDate Advertising and Olivier Martinez, Robert Martinez v. MGN Ltd.

Case C-5/11 [2012] Donner

Joined Cases C-509/09 and C-161/10 [2011] eDate Advertising GmbH and Olivier Martinez and Robert Martinez, Opinion of Advocate-General Cruz Villalón

Case T-239/94 [1997] EISA v. Commission

Case C-293/98 [2000] Entidad de Gestión de Derechos de los Productores Audiovisuales (Egeda) v. Hostelería Asturiana SA (Hoasa)

Case C-260/89 [1991] ERT v. DEP and others

Joined Cases C-317/04 and C-318/04 [2006] European Parliament v. Council

Case T-8/06 [2009] FAB v. Commission

Case C-531/07 [2009] Fachverband der Buch- und Medienwirtschaft v. LIBRO Handelsgesellschaft mbH

Case C-368/95 [1997] Familiapress v. Heinrich Bauer Verlag

Case T-385/07 [2011] FIFA v. Commission

Case C-334/00 [2002] Fonderie Officine Meccaniche Tacconi SpA v. Heinrich Wagner Sinto Maschinenfabrik GmbH (HWS)

Case C-173/11 [2012] Football Dataco Ltd v. Sportradar

Case C-61/97 [1998] Foreningen af danske Videogramdistributører v. Laserdisken

Case C-212/13 [2014] František Ryneš

Case T-17/02 [2005] Fred Olsen

Case C-188/89 [1990] Foster and others v. British Gas

Case C-243/01 [2003] Gambelli

Case T-102/96 [1999] Gencor Ltd v. Commission

Case T-21/06 [2009] Germany v. Commission

Case C-544/09 P [2011] Germany v. Commission

Case C-380/03 [2006] Germany v. Parliament and Council ('Tobacco advertising II')

Joined Cases T-195/01 and T-207/01 [2002] Gibraltar v. Commission

Joined Cases C-236/08 to C-238/08 [2010] Google France SARL and others v. Louis Vuitton Malletier SA and others

Case C-131/12 [2014] Google Spain SL v. AEPD and others

Case C-131/12 [2014] Google Spain SL v. AEPD and others, Opinion of Advocate-General Jääskinen

Joined Cases C-403/08 and C-429/08 [2011] Football Association Premier League Ltd and others v. Karen Murphy and others

Case C-159/90 [1991] Grogan

Case 7/82 [1983] GVL v. Commission

Case 21/76 [1976] Handelskwekerij G.J. Bier B.V. v. Mines de Potasse d'Alsace S.A.

Case C-172/03 [2005] Heiser

Case C-441/13 [2015] Hejduk v. EnergieAgentur.NRW GmbH

Case 85/76 [1979] Hoffmann-La Roche v. Commission

Case C-71/02 [2004] Herbert Karner Industrie-Auktionen GmbH v. Troostwijk GmbH

Case C-572/13 [2015] Hewlett-Packard Belgium v. Reprobel

Case C-41/90 [1991] Höfner and Elser v. Macrotron GmbH

Case C-524/06 [2008] Huber v. Germany

Joined Cases C-392/04 and C-422/04 [2006] i-21 Germany GmbH and Arcor

Case 48/69 [1972] ICI v. Commission ('Dyestuffs')

Case C-418/01 [2004] IMS Health GmbH & Co. OHG v. NDC Health GmbH & Co. KG

Case C-5/08 [2009] Infopaq International A/S v. Danske Dagblades Forening ('Infopaq I')

Case C-302/10 [2012] Infopaq International A/S v. Danske Dagblades Forening ('Infopaq II')

Case T-33/01 [2005] Infront WM AG v. Commission

Case T-286/09 [2014] Intel v. Commission

Joined Cases 21–24/72 [1972] International Fruit Company NV

Case T-228/97 [1999] Irish Sugar v. Commission

Case C-303/88 [1991] Italy v. Commission

Case C-261/89 [1991] Italy v. Commission

Case C-298/00 P [2004] Italy v. Commission

Case C-400/99 [2005] Italy v. Commission

Case C-607/11 [2013] ITV Broadcasting Ltd v. TVCatchup Ltd

Case C-336/07 [2008] Kabel Deutschland v. Niedersächsische Landesmedienanstalt für privaten Rundfunk

Case 189/87 [1988] Kalfelis v. Bankhaus Schröder, Münchmeyer, Hengst and Co. and others

Joined Cases C-267/91 and C-268/91 [1993] Keck and Mithouard

Case C-272/09 P [2011] KME v. Commission

Case T-110/97 [1999] Kneissl

Case C-195/06 [2007] KommAustria v. ORF

Case C-52/09 [2011] Konkurrensverket v. TeliaSonera Sverige AB

Case C-168/02 [2004] Kronhofer

Case C-258/08 [2010] Ladbrokes Betting & Gaming and Ladbrokes International

Case C-192/04 [2005] Lagardère v. SPRE and GVL

Case C-24/95 [1997] Land Rheinland-Pfalz v. Alcan

Case C-412/93 [1995] Leclerc-Siplec v. TFI and M6

Case C-42/07 [2009] Liga Portuguesa de Futebol Profissional and Bwin International

Case C-101/01 [2003] Lindqvist

Case 31/80 [1980] L'Oréal v. De Nieuwe AMCK

Case C-324/09 [2011] L'Oréal SA and Others v. eBay International AG and Others

Case C-557/07 [2009] LSG-Gesellschaft zur Wahrnehmung von Leistungsschutzrechten GmbH

Case C-277/10 [2012] Luksan v. van der Let

Case T-112/99 [2001] M6

Joined Cases T-185/00, T-216/00, T-299/00 and T-300/00 [2002] M6 and others

Joined Cases C-295/04 to C-298/04 [2006] Manfredi and others

Case C-364/93 [1995] Marinari v. Lloyds Bank plc.

Case C-89/04 [2005] Mediakabel v. Commissariaat voor de Media

Case C-403/10 P [2011] Mediaset v. Commission

Cases C-244/10 and C-245/10 [2011] Mesopotamia Broadcast A/S METV and Roj TV A/S

Case C-200/96 [1998] Metronome Musik GmbH v. Music Point Hokamp GmbH

Case 322/81 [1983] Michelin v. Commission

Case T-201/04 [2007] Microsoft v. Commission

Case T-167/08 [2012] Microsoft v. Commission

Case T-395/13 [2015] Miettinen v. Council

Case C-222/04 [2006] Ministero dell'Economia e delle Finanze v. Cassa di Risparmio di Firenze SpA

Joined Cases C-544/03 and C-545/03 [2005] Mobistar and Belgacom

Case C-281/05 [2006] Montex Holdings Ltd v. Diesel SpA

Joined Cases T-231/06 and T-237/06 [2010] Netherlands and Nederlandse Omroep Stichting (NOS) v. Commission

Case C-347/14 [2015] New Media Online GmbH v. Bundeskommunikationssenat

Case C-339/04 [2006] Nuova società di telecomunicazioni SpA

Case C-281/02 [2005] Owusu v. Jackson

Case C-100/88 [1989] Oyowe and Traore v. Commission

Case C-145/10 [2012] Painer v. Standard Verlags GmbH and others

Joined Cases C 585/08 and C 144/09 [2010] Pammer and Hotel Alpenhof

Case C-291/13 [2014] Papasavvas

Case C-14/96 [1997] Paul Denuit

Joined Cases C-180/98 to C-184/98 [2000] Pavlov and Others

Case C-456/06 [2008] Peek & Cloppenburg KG v. Cassina SpA

Case C-730/79 [1980] Philip Morris Holland BV v. Commission

Joined Cases C-446/09 and C-495/09 [2011] Philips and Nokia

Case C-170/12 [2013] Pinckney v. KDG Mediatech AG

Joined Cases C-338/04, C-359/04 and C-360/04 [2007] Placanica

Case 25/62 [1963] Plaumann v. Commission

Case T-129/96 [1998] Preussag Stahl v. Commission

Case C-379/98 [2001] PreussenElektra AG v. Schleswag AG

Case C-3/14 [2015] Prezes Urzędu Komunikacji Elektronicznej and Telefonia Dialog sp. z o.o. v. T-Mobile Polska SA

Case C-360/13 [2014] Public Relations Consultants Association Ltd v. Newspaper Licensing Agency Ltd

Case 52/79 [1980] Procureur du Roi v. Debauve and others

Case C-275/06 [2008] Promusicae v. Telefónica de España SAU

Case C-44/94 [1995] R v. Minister of Agriculture, Fisheries and Food, ex p National Federation of Fishermen's Organisations and others and Federation of Highlands and Islands Fishermen and others

Case T-69/89 [1991] Radio Telefis Eireann v. Commission

Joined Cases C-465/00, C-138/01 and C-139/01 [2003] Rechnungshof v. Österreichischer Rundfunk and others

Case C-261/90 [1992] Reichert v. Dresdner Bank AG (No. 2)

Case C-38/98 [2000] Renault

Case C-51/97 [1998] Réunion Européenne v. Spliethoff's Bevrachtingskantoor

Case 120/78 [1979] Rewe v. Bundesmonopolverwaltung für Branntwein ('Cassis de Dijon')

Case C-391/12 [2013] RLvS Verlagsgesellschaft mbH v. Stuttgarter Wochenblatt GmbH

Case 223/85 [1987] RSV v. Commission

Joined cases C-241/91 P and C-242/91 [1995] P RTE and ITP v. Commission ('Magill')

Joined Cases C-320/94, C-328/94, C-329/94 and C-337/94 to C-339/94 [1996] RTI and Others

Case C-245/01 [2003] RTL v. Niedersächsische Landesmedienanstalt für privaten Rundfunk

Case C-245/01 [2003] RTL v. Niedersächsische Landesmedienanstalt für privaten Rundfunk, Opinion of Advocate-General Jacobs

Case C-18/88 [1991] RTT v. GB-Inno-BM

Case C-360/10 [2012] SABAM v. Netlog

Case 155/73 [1974] Sacchi

Case C-406/10 [2012] SAS Institute Inc.

Case C-325/14 [2015] SBS Belgium v. SABAM

Case C-70/10 [2011] Scarlet Extended v. SABAM and others

Case C-70/10 [2011] Scarlet Extended v. SABAM and others, Opinion of Advocate-General Cruz Villalón

Case C-112/00 [2003] Schmidberger v. Austria

Case C-362/14 [2015] Schrems v. Data Protection Commissioner

Case C-39/94 [1996] SFEI and Others

Case C-68/93 [1995] Shevill and others v. Presse Alliance

Case T-46/97 [2000] SIC – Sociedade Independente de Comunicação SA v. Commission

Case T-442/03 [2008] SIC v. Commission

Case C-234/12 [2013] Sky Italia

Case C-283/11 [2013] Sky Österreich v. Österreichischer Rundfunk

Case C-306/05 [2006] Sociedad General de Autores y Editores de España (SGAE) v. Rafael Hoteles SA Joined Cases C-514/07 P, C-528/07 P and C-532/07 P [2010] Sweden and others v. API and Commission

Case 56/65 [1966] Société Technique Minière v. Maschinenbau Ulm GmbH

Joined Cases C-278/92 to C-280/92 [1994] Spain v. Commission
Case C-342/96 [1999] Spain v. Commission
Case C-501/00 [2004] Spain v. Commission
Case C-203/08 [2010] Sporting Exchange Ltd, trading as 'Betfair'
Case 29/69 [1969] Stauder v. City of Ulm
Case C-288/89 [1991] Stichting Collectieve Antennevoorziening Gouda and others
    v. Commissariaat voor de Media,
Case C-466/12 [2014] Svensson and others v. Retriever Sverige AB
Case C-506/08 P [2011] Sweden v. MyTravel Group plc and Commission
Joined Cases C-39/05 P and C-52/05 P [2008] Sweden and Turco v. Council
Case C-334/00 [2002] Tacconi v. Wagner
Case C-117/13 [2014] Technische Universität Darmstadt v. Eugen Ulmer KG
Case C-192/08 [2009] TeliaSonera Finland Oyj
Case C-219/91 [1992] Ter Voort
Case C-12/03 P [2005] Tetra Laval
Case C-333/94 P [1996] Tetra Pak International SA
Case T-354/05 [2009] TF1 v. Commission
Case T-193/06 [2010] TF1 v. Commission
Case C-73/07 [2008] Tietosuojavaltuutettu v. Satakunnan Markkinapörssi Oy and
    Satamedia Oy
Case C-8/08 [2009] TMobile Netherlands and Others
Case C-28/04 [2005] Tod's SpA v. Heyraud
Case C-395/87 [1989] Tournier
Joined Cases T-309/04, T-317/04, T-329/04 and T-336/04 [2008] TV 2/Danmark A/
    S v. Commission
Case C-23/93 [1994] TV 10 SA v. Commissariaat voor de Media
Case T-55/08 [2011] UEFA v. Commission
Case C-148/04 [2005] Unicredito Italiano v. Commission
Case 27/76 [1978] United Brands v. Commission
Case C-66/04 [2005] United Kingdom v. Parliament and Council
Case C-250/06 [2007] United Pan-Europe Communications Belgium SA and others
    v. Belgium and others
Case C-475/12 [2014] UPC DTH Sàrl
Case C-518/11 [2013] UPC Nederland BV
Case C-314/12 [2014] UPC Telekabel Wien GmbH v. Constantin Film Verleih and others
Case C-314/12 [2014] UPC Telekabel Wien GmbH v. Constantin Film Verleih and
    others, Opinion of Advocate-General Cruz Villalón
Case C-128/11 [2012] UsedSoft GmbH v. Oracle International Corp.
Case C-222/07 [2009] UTECA
Case 33/74 [1974] Van Binsbergen
Case 35/67 [1968] van Eick v. Commission
Case 26/62 [1963] van Gend en Loos

Joined Cases C-43/82 and C-63/82 [1984] VBVB and VBBB v. Commission
Case C-148/91 [1993] Veronica Omroep v. Commissariaat voor de Media
Case C-167/00 [2002] VKI v. Henkel
Case C-58/08 [2010] Vodafone
Joined Cases C-92/09 and C-93/09 [2010] Volker und Markus Schecke GbR and Hartmut Eifert
Case C-56/96 [1997] VT4 Ltd v. Vlaamse Gemeenschap
Case C-523/10 [2012] Wintersteiger AG v. Products 4U Sondermaschinenbau GmbH
Case C-230/14 [2015] Weltimmo

EFTA Court

Case E-21/13 [2014] FIFA v. ESA
Joined Cases E-8/94 and E-9/94 [1995] Mattel Scandinavia A/S and Lego Norge A/S
Case E-8/97 [1998] TV 1000 Sverige AB

Inter-American Court of Human Rights

Advisory Opinion OC-5/85 of November 13, 1985: Compulsory Membership in an Association Prescribed by Law for the Practice of Journalism (cited as 'Advisory Opinion OC-5/85')
Claude Reyes and others v. Chile [2006] Case 12.108
Ivcher-Bronstein v. Peru [2001] Case 11.762
Ríos and others v. Venezuela [2009] Case 12.441

Inter-American Commission of Human Rights

Oscar Elías Biscet and others v. Cuba [2006] Case 12.476
Perozo and others v. Venezuela [2009] Case 12.442
Steve Clark and others v. Grenada [1996] Case 10.325
Tarciso Medina Charry v. Colombia [1998] Case 11.221

Australia

Dow Jones v. Gutnick [2002] HCA 56
Lange v. Australian Broadcasting Corporation [1997] HCA 25
Thompson v. Australian Capital TV Ltd [1996] HCA 38

Austria

Austrian Supreme Court (Oberster Gerichtshof)

'Natascha K'[2008] Case 4Ob170/07i
'Natascha K II' [2008] Case 4Ob102/08s
'Natascha K III'[2008] Case 4Ob92/08w
'Natascha K V' [2012] Case 4Ob104/11i

Austrian Federal Communications Senate (Bundeskommunikationssenat)

'KommAustria v. ORF' [2008] Case no. GZ 611.009/0042-BKS/2007

Canada

Bangoura v. Washington Post [2005] CanLII 32906 (ON CA)
Paulsson v. Cooper [2009] CanLII 38795 (ON SC)

France

Tribunal de Grande Instance de Paris

LICRA et UJEF v. Yahoo!, order of 22 May 2000

Cour de Cassation

Case no 11-20358 [2013] SNEP

Germany

Federal Constitutional Court (Bundesverfassungsgericht)

'6th broadcasting decision' [1991] Cases 1 BvF 1/85 and 1/88
'7th broadcasting decision' [1992] Cases 1 BvR 1586/89 and 487/92
'Censorship' [1972] Case 1 BvL 13/67
'Cicero' [2007] Cases 1 BvR 538/06 and 1 BvR 2045/06
'Lebach' [1973] Case 1 BvR 536/72
'NSU trial' [2013] Case 1 BvR 990/13
'Secret infiltration of an IT system' [2008] Case 1 BvR 595/07

Federal Court of Justice (Bundesgerichtshof)

'Announcement with map details' [2013] Case I ZR 39/12
'Auschwitz denial' [2000] Case 1 StR 184/00
'blogspot' [2011] Case VI ZR 93/10
'www.chefkoch.de' [2009] Case Az.: I ZR 166/07
'eDate Advertising' [2009] Case VI ZR 217/08
'Google's autocomplete function' [2013] Case VI ZR 269/12
'Hotel Maritime' [2004] Case I ZR 163/02
'New York Times' [2010] Case VI ZR 23/09
'Personality rights on the internet'[2011] Case VI ZR 111/10

Federal Administrative Court

'Axel Springer AG' [2014] Case 6 C 2.13

*Court of Appeals in Administrative Law (Oberverwaltungsgericht)
Schleswig-Holstein*

'Facebook' [2013] Case 4 MB 11/13

Hanseatic Higher Court of Appeal (Oberlandesgericht) Bremen

'Frieden mit Gott allein durch Jesus Christus' [1996] Case 1 W 49/95

Hong Kong

Oriental Press Group Ltd and others *v. Fevaworks* Solutions Ltd and others [2013]
   HKCFA 47

Israel

Attorney-General of the State of Israel v. Eichman [1962] 36 I.L.R. 277

United Kingdom

Berezovsky v. Michaels [2000] 1 WLR 1004 (HL)
Bin Mahfouz v. Ehrenfeld [2005] EWHC 1156

British Steel Corporation v. Granada Television Ltd [1981] 1 All ER 417
Campbell v. MGN [2004] UKHL 22
Chaplin v. Boys [1971] AC 356
Duke of Brunswick v. Harmer [1849] 14 QB 185
Durant v. Financial Services Authority [2003] EWCA Civ 1746
Euromarket Designs Ltd v. Peters Ltd [2001] F.S.R. 288
Flood v. Times Newspapers Ltd [2012] UKSC 11
Google Inc. v. Vidal-Hall and Others [2015] EWCA Civ 311
Harrods Ltd v. Dow Jones [2003] EWHC 1162
Hyde Park Residence v. Yelland [2001] Ch 143
Jameel v. Dow Jones [2005] EWCA Civ 75
Jameel v. Wall Street Journal Europe Sprl [2006] UKHL 44
John Terry (previously referred to as "LNS") v. Persons Unknown [2010] EWHC 119 (QB)
Kaschke v. Gray [2010] EWHC 690 (QB)
King v. Lewis [2004] EWHC 168 (QB)
King v. Lewis [2004] EWCA Civ 1329 (CA)
Ladbroke v. William Hill [1964] 1 All ER 465
L'Oréal SA v. Bellure NV [2007] EWCA Civ 968
McAlpine v. Bercow [2013] EWHC 981 (QB)
McAlpine v. Bercow [2013] EWHC 1342 (QB)
Newspaper Licensing Agency Ltd v. Marks & Spencer plc [2003] 3 WLR 1256
Norwich Pharmacal v. Customs & Excise Commissioners [1974] AC 133
Phillips v. Eire (1870) LR 6 QB 1
R (Davis) v. Secretary of State for the Home Department [2015] EWHC 2092 (Admin)
Red Sea Insurance Co Ltd v. Bouygues SA [1995] 1 AC 190
Reynolds v. Times Newspapers Ltd [2001] 2 AC 127
OBG Ltd. and others v. Allan and others [2007] UKHL 21
R v. Secretary of State for the Home Department, ex p Simms [2000] 2 AC 115
The Author of Blog v. Times Newspapers Ltd [2009] EMLR 22
The Law Society and others v. Kordowski [2011] EWHC 3182 (QB)
Totalise plc v. Motley Fool Ltd and Interactive Investor Ltd [2001] EWCA Civ 1897

United States

Abrams v. United States, 250 U.S. 616 (1919)
ACLU v. Clapper, Docket No. 14-42-cv (2015)
Associated Press v. United States, 326 U.S. 1 (1945)
Bachchan v. India Abroad Publications, 154 Misc. 2d 228, 585 N.Y.S.2d 661 (N.Y. Sup. Ct. 1992)
Barnes v. Yahoo! Inc., 570 F.3d 1096 (9th Cir. 2009)

Bartnicki v. Vopper, aka Williams, and others, 532 U.S. 514 (2001)

Blackmer v. United States, 284 U.S. 421 (1932)

Blumenthal v. Drudge, 992 F. Supp. 44, 49–53 (D.D.C. 1998)

Brandenburg v. Ohio, 395 U.S. 444 (1969)

Branzburg v. Hayes, 408 U.S. 665 (1972)

Briscoe v. Reader's Digest Association, 93 Cal.Rptr. 866 (1971)

Buckley, Secretary of State of Colorado v. American Constitutional Law Foundation, Inc., 525 U.S. 182 (1999)

Calder v. Jones 465 U.S. 783 (1984)

Campbell v. Acuff-Rose Music, 510 U.S. 569 (1994)

CBS, Inc. v. FCC, 453 U.S. 367 (1981)

Chaplinsky v. New Hampshire, 315 U.S. 568 (1942)

Christiansen v. Christiansen, 253 P.3d 153 (2011)

Citizens United v. FEC, 130 S. Ct. 876 (2010)

City of Erie v. Pap's A. M., 529 U.S. 277 (2000)

Cohen v. California, 403 U.S. 15 (1971)

Compuserve Inc. v. Patterson 89F.3d 1257 (6th Cir. 1996)

Curtis Publishing Co. v. Butts, 388 U.S. 130 (1967)

Feist Publications, Inc. v. Rural Tel. Service Co., 499 U.S. 340 (1991)

Firth v. State of New York (2002) NY Int 88

Gertz v. Robert Welch Inc., 418 U.S. 323 (1974)

Giboney v. Empire Storage & Ice Co., 336 U.S. 490 (1949)

Hartford Fire Insurance Co. v. California, 509 U.S. 764 (1993)

Hustler Magazine v. Falwell, 485 U.S. 46 (1988)

International Shoe v. Washington, 326 U.S. 310, 316–17 (1945)

Katz v. United States, 389 U.S. 347 (1967)

Klayman v. Obama, 957 F. Supp. 2d 1 (2013)

Lawrence v. Texas, 539 U.S. 558 (2003)

Lorain Journal Co. v. United States, 342 U.S. 143 (1951)

MCI Communications Corp. v. AT&T, 708 F2d 1081 (7th Cir. 1982)

McIntyre v. Ohio Elections Commission, 514 U.S. 334 (1995)

Mills v. Alabama, 384 U.S. 214 (1966)

National Archives & Records Administration v. Favish, 124 S. Ct. 1570 (2004)

New York Times Co. v. Gonzales, 382 F. Supp. 2d 457 (S.D.N.Y. 2005)

New York Times Co. v. Sullivan, 376 U. S. 254 (1964)

New York Times Co. v. United States, 403 U.S. 713 (1971)

O'Grady v. Superior Court, 44 Cal. Rptr. 3d 72 (Cal. Ct. App. 2006)

Otter Tail Power Co. v. United States, 410 U.S. 366 (1973)

Pell v. Procunier, 417 U.S. 817 (1974)

Reno v. ACLU 521 U.S. 844 (1997)

Revell v. Lidov, 317 F.3d 467 (5th Cir. 2002)

Saxbe v. Washington Post Co., 417 U.S. 843 (1974)

Sorrell v. IMS Health Inc., 131 S. Ct. 2653 (2011)
Talley v. California 362 U.S. 60 (1960)
Telnikoff v. Matusevitch, 347 Md. 561, 702 A.2d 230 (Md. 1997)
Timberlane Lumber Co. v. Bank of America, 549 F.2d 597 (9th Cir. 1976)
United States v. Aluminium Co. of America (Alcoa), 148 F.2d 416 (2d Cir. 1945)
United States v. Terminal Railroad Association, 224 U.S. 383 (1912)
Verizon v. Trinko, 540 U.S. 398 (2004)
Watchtower Society v. Village of Stratton, 536 U.S. 150 (2002)
Watts v. United States, 394 U.S. 705 (1969)
Whitney v. California, 274 U.S. 357 (1927)
Wolfson v. Syracuse Newspapers Inc. (1938) 279 NY 716
Young v. New Haven Advocate, 315 F.3d 256 (4th Cir. 2002)
Zeran v. America Online (AOL), Inc., 129 F3d 327 (4th Cir. 1997)

TREATIES, CONVENTIONS, DECLARATIONS AND STATUTES

United Nations and International Treaties

Convention against Torture and Other Cruel, Inhuman or Degrading Treatment or Punishment (United Nations Convention against Torture) (1984)

Convention against Transnational Organized Crime (2000)

Convention on the Rights of the Child (1989)

Convention on the Protection and Promotion of the Diversity of Cultural Expressions (2005)

International Convention on the Elimination of All Forms of Racial Discrimination (ICERD) (1965)

International Convention on the Elimination of Discrimination Against Women (CEDAW) (1979)

International Covenant on Civil and Political Rights (ICCPR) (1966)

International Covenant on Economic, Social and Cultural Rights (ICESCR) (1976)

Universal Declaration of Human Rights (UDHR) (1948)

Westphalian Peace Treaty (1648)

Vienna Convention on the Law of Treaties (1969)

International Telecommunications Union

Constitution and Convention of the International Telecommunications Union (2010)

International Telecommunications Regulations (1988)

Radio Regulations (2003)

WIPO Agreements

Berne Convention for the Protection of Literary and Artistic Works of 9 September 1886, completed at Paris on 4 May 1896, revised at Berlin on 13 November 1908, completed at Berne on 20 March 1914, revised at Rome on 2 June 1928, at Brussels on 26 June 1948, at Stockholm on 14 July 1967, and at Paris on 24 July 1971, and amended on 28 September 1979

Convention Establishing the World Intellectual Property Organization, signed at Stockholm on 14 July 1967 and as amended on 28 September 1979

Convention Relating to the Distribution of Programme-Carrying Signals Transmitted by Satellite, done at Brussels on 21 May 1974

Paris Convention for the Protection of Industrial Property of 20 March 1883, as revised at Brussels on 14 December 1900, at Washington on 2 June 1911, at The Hague on 6 November 1925, at London on 2 June 1934, at Lisbon on 31 October 1958, and at Stockholm on 14 July 1967, and as amended on 28 September 1979

Rome Convention: International Convention for the Protection of Performers, Producers of Phonograms and Broadcasting Organisations, done at Rome on 26 October 1961

WIPO Copyright Treaty (WCT), adopted in Geneva on 20 December 1996

WIPO Performances and Phonograms Treaty (WPPT), adopted in Geneva on 20 December 1996

World Trade Organization

Agreement on Trade-Related Aspects of Intellectual Property Rights (TRIPS) (1994)

General Agreement on Tariffs and Trade (GATT) (1947/1994)

General Agreement on Trade in Services (GATS) (1994)

African Union

African Charter on Human and Peoples' Rights (1981)

Council of Europe

Convention for the Protection of Human Rights and Fundamental Freedoms (European Convention on Human Rights – ECHR) (1950)

Convention for the Protection of Individuals with regard to Automatic Processing of Personal Data (1981)

Amendments to the Convention for the Protection of Individuals with regard to Automatic Processing of Personal Data (1999)

Convention on Access to Official Documents (2008)

Convention on Cybercrime (2001)

Additional Protocol to the Convention on Cybercrime, concerning the criminalisation of acts of a racist and xenophobic nature committed through computer systems (2003)

Convention on the Prevention of Terrorism (2005)

Convention on Transfrontier Television (1989)

European Union

Charter of Fundamental Rights of the European Union (2007)

Consolidated versions of the Treaty on European Union and the Treaty on the Functioning of the European Union (2012)

Protocol (No. 29) to the TEU and the TFEU on the system of public broadcasting in the Member States

Agreement between the European Community and the Kingdom of Denmark on jurisdiction and the recognition and enforcement of judgments in civil and commercial matters, OJ L 299/62

Convention of 27 September 1968 on jurisdiction and the enforcement of judgments in civil and commercial matters (Brussels Convention)

Convention of 16 September 1988 on jurisdiction and the enforcement of judgments in civil and commercial matters (Lugano Convention)

Commission Directive 88/301/EEC of 16 May 1988 on competition in the markets in telecommunications terminal equipment, OJ L 131/73

Commission Directive 90/388/EEC of 28 June 1990 on competition in the markets for telecommunications services, OJ L 192/10

Commission Directive 94/46/EC of 13 October 1994 amending Directive 88/301/EEC and Directive 90/388/EEC in particular with regard to satellite communications, OJ L 268/15

Commission Directive 95/51/EC of 18 October 1995 amending Directive 90/388/EEC with regard to the abolition of the restrictions on the use of cable television networks for the provision of already liberalized telecommunications services, OJ L 256/49

Commission Directive 96/2/EC of 16 January 1996 amending Directive 90/388/EEC with regard to mobile and personal communications, OJ L 20/50

Commission Directive 96/19/EC of 13 March 1996 amending Directive 90/388/EEC with regard to the implementation of full competition in telecommunications markets, OJ L 74/13

Commission Directive 2002/77/EC of 16 September 2002 on competition in the markets for electronic communications networks and services, OJ L 249/21

Commission Directive 2005/81/EC of 28 November 2005 amending Directive 80/723/EEC, OJ L 312/47

Commission Directive 2008/63/EC of 20 June 2008 on competition in the markets in telecommunications terminal equipment, OJ L 162/20

Commission Regulation (EC) No. 773/2004 of 7 April 2004 relating to the conduct of proceedings by the Commission pursuant to Articles 81 and 82 of the EC Treaty, OJ L 123/18

Commission Regulation (EC) No. 794/2004 of 21 April 2004 implementing Council Regulation (EU) 2015/1589 laying down detailed rules for the application of Article 108 of the Treaty on the Functioning of the European Union, OJ L 140/1

Commission Regulation (EC) No. 1627/2006 of 24 October 2006 as regards the standard forms for notification of aid, OJ L 302/10

Commission Regulation (EC) No. 1998/2006 of 15 December 2006 on the application of Articles 87 and 88 of the Treaty to de minimis aid, OJ L 379/5

Commission Regulation (EC) No. 800/2008 of 6 August 2008 declaring certain categories of aid compatible with the common market in application of Articles 87 and 88 of the Treaty (General block exemption Regulation), prolonged by Commission Regulation (EU) No. 1224/2013 of 29 November 2013 amending Regulation (EC) No. 800/2008 as regards its period of application, OJ L 320/22

Commission Regulation (EU) No. 330/2010 of 20 April 2010 on the application of Article 101(3) of the Treaty on the Functioning of the European Union to categories of vertical agreements and concerted practices, OJ L 102/1

Commission Regulation (EU) No. 360/2012 of 25 April 2012 on the application of Articles 107 and 108 of the Treaty on the Functioning of the European Union to de minimis aid granted to undertakings providing services of general economic interest, OJ L 114/8

Commission Regulation (EU) No. 316/2014 of 21 March 2014 on the application of Article 101(3) of the Treaty on the Functioning of the European Union to categories of technology transfer agreements, OJ L 93/17

Commission Regulation (EU) No. 651/2014 of 17 June 2014 declaring certain categories of aid compatible with the internal market in application of Articles 107 and 108 of the Treaty, OJ L 187/1

Council Directive 89/552/EEC of 3 October 1989 on the coordination of certain provisions laid down by law, regulation or administrative action in Member States concerning the pursuit of television broadcasting activities, OJ L 298/23

Council Directive 90/387/EEC of 28 June 1990 on the establishment of the internal market for telecommunications services through the implementation of open network provision, OJ L 192/1

Council Directive 92/44/EEC of 5 June 1992 on the application of Open Network Provision to leased lines, OJ L165/27

Council Directive 92/50/EEC of 18 June 1992 relating to the coordination of procedures for the award of public service contracts, OJ L 209/1

Council Directive 93/83/EEC of 27 September 1993 on the coordination of certain rules concerning copyright and rights related to copyright applicable to satellite broadcasting and cable retransmission, OJ L 248/15

Council Framework Decision 2002/475/JHA of 13 June 2002 on combating terrorism, OJ L 164/3, amended by Council Framework Decision 2008/919/JHA of 28 November 2008 amending Framework Decision 2002/475/JHA on combating terrorism, OJ L 330/21

Council Framework Decision 2005/214/JHA of 24 February 2005 on the application of the principle of mutual recognition to financial penalties, OJ L 76/16

Council Framework Decision 2008/909/JHA of 27 November 2008 on the application of the principle of mutual recognition to judgments in criminal matters imposing custodial sentences or measures involving deprivation of liberty for the purpose of their enforcement in the European Union, OJ L 327/27

Council Framework Decision 2008/913/JHA of 28 November 2008 on combating certain forms and expressions of racism and xenophobia by means of criminal law, OJ L 328/55

Council Framework Decision 2008/919/JHA of 28 November 2008 amending Framework Decision 2002/475/JHA on combating terrorism, OJ L 330/21

Council Regulation (EC) No. 40/94 of 20 December 1993 on the Community trademark, OJ L 11/1, now codified as Council Regulation (EC) No. 207/2009 of 26 February 2009 on the Community trademark, OJ L 78/1

Council Regulation (EC) No. 994/98 of 7 May 1998 on the application of Articles 92 and 93 of the Treaty establishing the European Community to certain categories of horizontal State aid, OJ L 142/1

Council Regulation (EC) No. 6/2002 of 12 December 2001 on Community designs, OJ L 3/1

Council Regulation (EC) No. 1/2003 of 16 December 2002 on the implementation of the rules on competition laid down in Articles 81 and 82 of the Treaty, OJ L 1/1

Council Regulation (EC) No. 510/2006 of 20 March 2006 on the protection of geographical indications and designations of origin for agricultural products and foodstuffs, OJ L 93/12

Council Regulation (EC) No. 1791/2006 of 20 November 2006 adapting certain Regulations and Decisions in the fields of free movement of goods, freedom of movement of persons, company law, competition policy, agriculture (including veterinary and phytosanitary legislation), transport policy, taxation, statistics, energy, environment, cooperation in the fields of justice and home affairs, customs union, external relations, common foreign and security policy and institutions, by reason of the accession of Bulgaria and Romania, OJ L 363/1

Council Regulation No. 1891/2006 of 18 December 2006 amending Regulations (EC) No. 6/2002 and (EC) No. 40/94 to give effect to the accession of the European Community to the Geneva Act of the Hague Agreement concerning the international registration of industrial designs, OJ L 386/14

Council Regulation (EC) No. 207/2009 of 26 February 2009 on the Community trademark (codified version), OJ 78/1

Council Regulation (EU) No. 517/2013 of 13 May 2013 adapting certain regulations and decisions in the fields of free movement of goods, freedom of movement for persons, company law, competition policy, agriculture, food safety, veterinary and phytosanitary policy, transport policy, energy, taxation, statistics, trans-European networks, judiciary and fundamental rights, justice, freedom and security, environment, customs union, external relations, foreign, security and defence policy and institutions, by reason of the accession of the Republic of Croatia, OJ L 158/1

Council Regulation (EU) No. 733/2013 of 22 July 2013 amending Regulation (EC) No. 994/98 on the application of Articles 92 and 93 of the Treaty establishing the European Community to certain categories of horizontal State aid, OJ L 204/1

Council Regulation (EU) 2015/1589 of 13 July 2015 laying down detailed rules for the application of Article 108 of the Treaty on the Functioning of the European Union (codification), OJ L 248/9

Decision of the European Central Bank of 4 March 2004 on public access to European Central Bank documents (2004/258/EC), OJ L 80/42

Directive 95/46/EC of the European Parliament and of the Council of 24 October 1995 on the protection of individuals with regard to the processing of personal data and on the free movement of such data, OJ L 281/31

Directive 96/9/EC of the European Parliament and of the Council of 11 March 1996 on the legal protection of databases, OJ L 77/20

Directive 97/13/EC on a common framework for general authorisations and individual licences in the field of telecommunications service, OJ L 117/15

Directive 97/33/EC of the European Parliament and of the Council of 30 June 1997 on interconnection in Telecommunications with regard to ensuring universal service and interoperability through application of the principles of Open Network Provision (ONP), OJ L 199/32

Directive 97/51/EC of the European Parliament and of the Council of the 6 October 1997 amending Council Directives 90/387/EEC and 92/44/EEC for the purpose of adaptation to a competitive environment in telecommunications, OJ L 295/23

Directive 97/66/EC of the European Parliament and the Council of 15 December 1997 concerning the processing of personal data and protection of privacy in the telecommunications sector, OJ L 24/1

Directive 98/10/EC of the European Parliament and of the Council of 26 February 1998 on the application of open network provision (ONP) to voice telephony and on universal service for telecommunications in a competitive environment, OJ L 101/24

Directive 98/84/EC of the European Parliament and of the Council of 20 November 1998 on the legal protection of services based on, or consisting of, conditional access, OJ L 320/54

Directive 1999/5/EC of the European Parliament and of the Council of 9 March 1999 on radio equipment and telecommunications terminal equipment and the mutual recognition of their conformity, OJ L 91/10

Directive 2000/31/EC of 8 June 2000 on certain legal aspects of information society services, in particular electronic commerce, in the Internal Market (Directive on electronic commerce), OJ L 178/1

Directive 2001/29/EC of the European Parliament and of the Council of 22 May 2001 on the harmonisation of certain aspects of copyright and related rights in the information society, OJ L 167/10

Directive 2001/83/EC of the European Parliament and of the Council of 6 November 2001 on the Community code relating to medicinal products for human use, OJ L 311/67

Directive 2001/84/EC of the European Parliament and of the Council of 27 September 2001 on the resale right for the benefit of the author of an original work of art, OJ L 272/32

Directive 2002/19/EC of the European Parliament and of the Council of 7 March 2002 on access to, and interconnection of, electronic communications networks and associated facilities (Access Directive), OJ L 108/7

Directive 2002/20/EC of the European Parliament and of the Council of 7 March 2002 on the authorisation of electronic communications networks and services (Authorisation Directive), OJ L 108/21

Directive 2002/21/EC of the European Parliament and of the Council of 7 March 2002 on a common regulatory framework for electronic communications networks and services (Framework Directive), OJ L 108/33

Directive 2002/22/EC of the European Parliament and of the Council of 7 March 2002 on universal service and users' rights relating to electronic communications networks and services (Universal Service Directive), OJ L 108/51

Directive 2002/58/EC of the European Parliament and of the Council of 12 July 2002 concerning the processing of personal data and the protection of privacy in the electronic communications sector (Directive on privacy and electronic communications), OJ L 201/37

Directive 2003/4/EC of the European Parliament and of the Council of 28 January 2003 on public access to environmental information and repealing Council Directive 90/313/EEC, OJ L 41/26

Directive 2003/33/EC of the European Parliament and of the Council of 26 May 2003 on the approximation of the laws, regulations and administrative provisions of the Member States relating to the advertising and sponsorship of tobacco products, OJ L 152/16

Directive 2003/98/EC of the European Parliament and of the Council of 17 November 2003 on the re-use of public sector information, OJ L 345/90

Directive 2004/48/EC of the European Parliament and of the Council of 29 April 2004 on the enforcement of intellectual property rights, OJ L 195/16

Directive 2005/29/EC of the European Parliament and of the Council of 11 May 2005 concerning unfair business-to-consumer commercial practices in the internal market and amending Directives 84/450/EEC, 97/7/EC, 98/27/EC and 2002/65/EC and Regulation (EC) No. 2006/2004 (Unfair Commercial Practices Directive), OJ L 149/22

Directive 2006/24/EC of the European Parliament and of the Council of 15 March 2006 on the retention of data generated or processed in connection with the provision of publicly available electronic communications services or of public communications networks and amending Directive 2002/58/EC, OJ L 105/54

Directive 2006/114/EC of the European Parliament and of the Council of 12 December 2006 concerning misleading and comparative advertising (codified version), OJ L376/21

Directive 2006/115/EC of the European Parliament and of the Council of 12 December 2006 on rental right and lending right and on certain rights related to copyright in the field of intellectual property, OJ L 376/28

Directive 2006/116/EC of the European Parliament and of the Council of 12 December 2006 on the term of protection of copyright and certain related rights (codified version), OJ L 372/12

Directive 2009/22/EC of the European Parliament and of the Council of 23 April 2009 on injunctions for the protection of consumers' interests (Codified version), OJ L 110/30.

Directive 2009/24/EC of the European Parliament and of the Council of 23 April 2009 on the legal protection of computer programs (Codified version), OJ L 111/16

Directive 2009/136/EC of the European Parliament and of the Council of 25 November 2009 amending Directive 2002/22/EC on universal service and users' rights relating to electronic communications networks and services, Directive 2002/58/EC concerning the processing of personal data and the protection of privacy in the electronic communications sector and Regulation (EC) No. 2006/2004 on cooperation between national authorities responsible for the enforcement of consumer protection laws, OJ L 337/11

Directive 2009/140/EC of the European Parliament and of the Council of 25 November 2009 amending Directives 2002/21/EC on a common regulatory framework for electronic communications networks and services, 2002/19/EC on access to, and interconnection of, electronic communications networks and associated facilities, and 2002/20/EC on the authorisation of electronic communications networks and services, OJ L 337/37

Directive 2010/13/EU of the European Parliament and of the Council of 10 March 2010 on the coordination of certain provisions laid down by law, regulation or administrative action in Member States concerning the provision of audiovisual media services (Audiovisual Media Services Directive), OJ L 95/1

Directive 2011/77/EU of the European Parliament and of the Council of 27 September 2011 amending Directive 2006/116/EC on the term of protection of copyright and certain related rights, OJ L 265/1

Directive 2011/92/EU of the European Parliament and of the Council of 13 December 2011 on combating the sexual abuse and sexual exploitation of children and child pornography, and replacing Council Framework Decision 2004/68/JHA, OJ L 335/1

Directive 2012/28/EU of the European Parliament and of the Council of 25 October 2012 on certain permitted uses of orphan works, OJ L 299/5

Directive 2013/40/EU of the European Parliament and of the Council of 12 August 2013 on attacks against information systems and replacing Council Framework Decision 2005/222/JHA, OJ L 218/8

Directive 2014/24/EU of the European Parliament and of the Council of 26 February 2014 on public procurement and repealing Directive 2004/18/EC, OJ L 94/65

Directive 2014/104/EU of the European Parliament and of the Council of 26 November 2014 on certain rules governing actions for damages under national law for infringements of the competition law provisions of the Member States and of the European Union, OJ L 349/1

Directive (EU) 2015/1535 of the European Parliament and of the Council of 9 September 2015 laying down a procedure for the provision of information in the field of technical regulations and of rules on Information Society services (codification), OJ L 241/1

Directive (EU) 2016/680 of the European Parliament and of the Council of 27 April 2016 on the protection of natural persons with regard to the processing of personal data by competent authorities for the purposes of the prevention, investigation, detection or prosecution of criminal offences or the execution of criminal penalties, and on the free movement of such data, and repealing Council Framework Decision 2008/977/JHA, OJ L 119/89

Regulation (EC) No. 2887/2000 of the European Parliament and of the Council of 18 December 2000 on unbundled access to the local loop, OJ L 336/4

Regulation (EC) No. 45/2001 of the European Parliament and of the Council of 18 December 2000 on the protection of individuals with regard to the processing of personal data by the Community institutions and bodies and on the free movement of such data, OJ L 8/1

Regulation (EC) No. 1049/2001 of the European Parliament and of the Council of 30 May 2001 regarding public access to European Parliament, Council and Commission documents, OJ L 145/43

Regulation (EC) No. 139/2004 of 20 January 2004 on the control of concentrations between undertakings, OJ L 24/1

Regulation (EC) No. 1924/2006 of the European Parliament and of the Council of 20 December 2006 on nutrition and health claims made on foods, OJ L 404/9

Regulation (EC) No. 717/2007 of the European Parliament and of the Council of 27 June 2007 on roaming on public mobile telephone networks within the Community and amending Directive 2002/21/EC, OJ L 171/32

Regulation (EC) No. 864/2007 of the European Parliament and of the Council of 11 July 2007 on the law applicable to non-contractual obligations (Rome II), OJ L 199/40

Regulation (EC) No. 1211/2009 of the European Parliament and of the Council of 25 November 2009 establishing the Body of European Regulators for Electronic Communications (BEREC) and the Office, OJ L 337/1

Regulation (EU) No. 1215/2012 of the European Parliament and of the Council of 12 December 2012 on jurisdiction and the recognition and enforcement of judgments in civil and commercial matters (recast), OJ L 351/1 ('Brussels Ia')

Regulation (EU) No. 1295/2013 of the European Parliament and of the Council of 11 December 2013 establishing the Creative Europe Programme (2014 to 2020) and repealing Decisions No. 1718/2006/EC, No. 1855/2006/EC and No. 1041/2009/EC, OJ L 347/221

Regulation (EU) 2015/2120 of the European Parliament and of the Council of 25 November 2015 laying down measures concerning open internet access and amending Directive 2002/22/EC on universal service and users' rights relating to electronic communications networks and services and Regulation (EU) No. 531/2012 on roaming on public mobile communications networks within the Union, OJ L 310/1

Organization of American States

American Convention on Human Rights (1969)

National Laws (all provisions as amended)

Germany

Act Against Unfair Competition (*Gesetz gegen den unlauteren Wettbewerb*) (2004)
Basic Law (*Grundgesetz*) for the Federal Republic of Germany (1949)
Civil Law Code (*Bürgerliches Gesetzbuch*) (1900)
Civil Procedure Code (*Zivilprozessordnung*) (1877)
Criminal Law Code (*Strafgesetzbuch*) (1872)
Criminal Procedure Code (*Strafprozessordnung*) (1877)
Interstate Treaty on Broadcasting and Telemedia (*Rundfunkstaatsvertrag*) (1991)
Telecommunications Act (*Telekommunikationsgesetz*) (2004)

United Kingdom

Communications Act (2003)
Contempt of Court Act (1981)
Copyright, Designs and Patents Act (1988)
Defamation Act (1996)
Defamation Act (2013)
Private International Law Act (1995)
Postal Services Act (2000)
Royal Charter on self-regulation of the press (2013)

United States

Communications Act (1934)
Communications Decency Act (1996)
Constitution of the United States (1789)
Securing the Protection of our Enduring and Established Constitutional Heritage (SPEECH) Act (2010)
Sherman Antitrust Act (1890)

Other Countries

Constitution of Belgium (1831)
Constitution of the Italian Republic (1947)
Swiss Federal Constitution 1999

United Nations

Commission on Human Rights

Report of the Special Rapporteur on the promotion and protection of the right to freedom of opinion and expression, Mr Abid Hussain, submitted pursuant to Commission Resolution 1997/27, E/CN.4/1998/40/Add.1

Resolution 1999/82: Defamation of religions of 30 April 1999, E/CN.4/1999/167

Commission on Human Rights, Resolution 2000/84: Defamation of religions of 26 April 2000, E/CN.4/RES/2000/84

Resolution 2001/4: Combating defamation of religions as a means to promote human rights, social harmony and religious and cultural diversity of 18 April 2001, E/CN.4/RES/2001/4

Resolution 2002/9: Combating defamation of religions of 15 April 2002, E/CN.4/RES/2002/9

Resolution 2003/4: Combating defamation of religions of 14 April 2003, E/CN.4/RES/2003/4

Resolution 2004/6: Combating defamation of religions of 13 April 2004, E/CN.4/RES/2004/6

Commission on Human Rights, Resolution 2005/3: Combating defamation of religions of 12 April 2005, E/CN.4/RES/2005/3

Economic and Social Council

Siracusa Principles on the Limitation and Derogation Provisions in the International Covenant on Civil and Political Rights, UN Doc. E/CN.4/1985/4, Annex (1985)

General Assembly

Document A/5000 of the sixteenth session, 5 December 1961

Resolution 1904 (XVIII): Declaration on the elimination of all forms of racial discrimination of 20 November 1963, A/RES/1904(XVIII)

Resolution 35/63 on restrictive business practices of 5 December 1980, A/RES/35/63

Resolution 45/95 Guidelines for the regulation of computerized personal data files of 14 December 1990, A/RES/45/95

Resolution 54/263, Optional protocols to the Convention on the Rights of the Child on the involvement of children in armed conflict and on the sale of children, child prostitution and child pornography of 25 May 2000, A/RES/54/263

Resolution 56/183, World Summit on the Information Society of 31 January 2002, A/RES/56/183

Resolution 60/150: Combating Defamation of Religions of 16 December 2005, A/RES/60/150

Resolution 61/164: Combating defamation of religions of 19 December 2006, A/RES/61/164

Resolution 62/154: Combating defamation of religions of 18 December 2007, A/RES/62/154

Resolution 63/171: Combating defamation of religions of 18 December 2008, A/RES/63/171

Resolution 64/156: Combating defamation of religions of 18 December 2009, A/RES/64/156

Resolution 65/224: Combating defamation of religions of 21 December 2010, A/RES/65/224

Human Rights Committee

General Comments

Short name	Reference
General Comment no. 16	Article 17 (Twenty-third session, 1988), reprinted in Compilation of General Comments and General Recommendations Adopted by Human Rights Treaty Bodies, U.N. Doc. HRI/GEN/1/Rev.6 at 142 (2003)
General Comment no. 22	Article 18 (Forty-eighth session, 1993), U.N. Doc. CCPR/C/21/Rev.1/Add.4 (1993), reprinted in Compilation of General Comments and General Recommendations Adopted by Human Rights Treaty Bodies, UN Doc. HRI/GEN/1/Rev.6 at 155 (2003)
General Comment no. 25	The right to participate in public affairs, voting rights and the right of equal access to public service (Art. 25), (Fifty-seventh session, 1996), UN Doc. CCPR/C/21/Rev.1/Add.7 (1996), reprinted in Compilation of General Comments and General Recommendations Adopted by Human Rights Treaty Bodies, U.N. Doc. HRI/GEN/1/Rev.6 at 168 (2003)

Short name	Reference
General Comment no. 31	Nature of the General Legal Obligation on States Parties to the Covenant, U.N. Doc. CCPR/C/21/Rev.1/Add.13 (2004)
General Comment no. 34	Article 19, Freedoms of opinion and expression, 12 September 2011, CCPR/C/GC/34

Concluding Observations

Short name	Reference
Concluding observations on Democratic People's Republic of Korea (CCPR/CO/72/PRK)	Concluding observations on Democratic People's Republic of Korea (CCPR/CO/72/PRK) of 27 August 2001
Concluding observations on Guyana (CCPR/CO/79/Add.121)	Concluding observations on Guyana (CCPR/CO/79/Add.121) of 25 April 2000
Concluding observations on Kuwait (CCPR/CO/69/KWT)	Concluding observations on Kuwait (CCPR/CO/69/KWT) of 27 July 2000
Concluding observations on Lesotho (CCPR/CO/79/Add. 106)	Concluding observations on Lesotho (CCPR/CO/79/Add. 106) of 8 April 1999
Concluding observations on Peru (CCPR/CO/70/PER)	Concluding observations on Peru (CCPR/CO/70/PER) of 15 November 2000
Concluding observations on the Republic of Moldova (CCPR/CO/75/MDA)	Concluding observations on the Republic of Moldova (CCPR/CO/75/MDA) of 5 August 2002
Concluding observations on the Russian Federation (CCPR/CO/79/RUS)	Concluding observations on the Russian Federation (CCPR/CO/79/RUS) of 1 December 2003
Concluding observations on Sri Lanka (CCPR/CO/79/LKA)	Concluding observations on Sri Lanka (CCPR/CO/79/LKA) of 1 December 2003
Concluding observations on Ukraine (CCPR/CO/73/UKR)	Concluding observations on Ukraine (CCPR/CO/73/UKR) of 12 November 2001
Concluding observations on the United Kingdom of Great Britain and Northern Ireland (CCPR/C/GBR/CO/6)	Concluding observations on the United Kingdom of Great Britain and Northern Ireland (CCPR/C/GBR/CO/6) of 30 July 2008
Concluding observations on Uzbekistan (CCPR/CO/83/UZB)	Concluding observations on Uzbekistan (CCPR/CO/83/UZB) of 26 April 2005

Human Rights Council

Report of the Special Rapporteur on the promotion and protection of the right to freedom of opinion and expression, David Kaye, 22 May 2015, A/HRC/29/32

Resolution 4/9: Combating defamation of religions of 30 March 2007, A/HRC/RES/4/9

Resolution 7/19: Combating defamation of religions of 27 March 2008, A/HRC/RES/7/19

Resolution 10/22: Combating defamation of religions of 26 March 2009, A/HRC/RES/10/22

Resolution 28/16: The right to privacy in the digital age, 1 April 2015, A/HRC/RES/28/16

International Law Commission

Articles on Responsibility of States for Internationally Wrongful Acts, Report of the International Law Commission on the Work of Its Fifty-third Session, 2001 (A/56/10)

Security Council

Resolution 1624 (2005) of 14 September 2005, S/RES/1624 (2005)

OECD Council

Best practices on Information Exchange (2005)

Recommendation on Competition Policy and Exempted or Regulated Sectors (1979)

Recommendation concerning Effective Action against Hard Core Cartels (1998)

Recommendation concerning Merger Review (2005)

Recommendation on Competition Assessment (2009)

Recommendation concerning International Co-operation on Competition Investigations and Proceedings (2014)

WTO

Ministerial Declaration WT/MIN(01)/DEC/1, 20 November 2001

Council of Europe

Committee of Ministers

Declaration on freedom of communication on the Internet (28 May 2003)

Declaration on the protection and promotion of investigative journalism (26 September 2007)

Declaration on enhanced participation of member states in Internet governance matters – Governmental Advisory Committee (GAC) of the Internet Corporation for Assigned Names and Numbers (ICANN) (26 May 2010)

Declaration on the Digital Agenda for Europe (29 September 2010)

Declaration on the management of the Internet protocol address resources in the public interest (29 September 2010)

Declaration on network neutrality (29 September 2010)

Declaration on Internet governance principles (21 September 2011)

Declaration on the protection of freedom of expression and information and freedom of assembly and association with regard to Internet domain names and name strings (21 September 2011)

Declaration on the protection of freedom of expression and freedom of assembly and association with regard to privately operated Internet platforms and online service providers (7 December 2011)

Declaration on the Desirability of International Standards dealing with Forum Shopping in respect of Defamation, "Libel Tourism", to ensure Freedom of Expression (4 July 2012)

Declaration on Risks to Fundamental Rights stemming from Digital Tracking and other Surveillance Technologies (11 June 2013)

Explanatory Report to the European Convention on Transfrontier Television, Text of the Report amended by the provisions of the Protocol (ETS No. 171), entered into force on 1 March 2002

Recommendation No. R (81) 19 on the access to information held by public authorities

Recommendation No. R(83) 10 on the protection of personal data used for scientific research and statistics

Recommendation No. R(85) 20 on the protection of personal data used for the purposes of direct marketing

Recommendation No. R(87) 15 regulating the use of personal data in the police sector

Recommendation No. R (91) 10 on the communication to third parties of personal data held by public bodies Recommendation No. R (97) 18 concerning the protection of personal data collected and processed for statistical purposes

Recommendation No. R (94) 13 on measures to promote media transparency

Recommendation No. R(95) 4 on the protection of personal data in the area of telecommunication services, with particular reference to telephone services

Recommendation No. R (96) 10 on the guarantee of the independence of public service broadcasting

Recommendation No. R(97) 5 on the protection of medical data

Recommendation No. R (97) 18 concerning the protection of personal data collected and processed for statistical purposes

Recommendation No. R (97) 20 on "hate speech"

Recommendation No. (97) 21 on the media and the promotion of a culture of tolerance

Recommendation No. R(99) 5 for the protection of privacy on the Internet

Recommendation No. R (2000) 7 on the right of journalists not to disclose their sources of information

Recommendation No. R (2000) 13 on a European policy on access to archives

Recommendation Rec(2000)23 on the independence and functions of regulatory authorities for the broadcasting sector

Recommendation Rec(2001)7 on measures to protect copyright and neighbouring rights and combat piracy, especially in the digital environment

Recommendation No. R(2002) 9 on the protection of personal data collected and processed for insurance purposes

Recommendation Rec(2003)13 on the provision of information through the media in relation to criminal proceedings

Recommendation Rec(2004)16 on the right of reply in the new media environment

Recommendation Rec(2002)2 on access to official documents

Recommendation CM/Rec(2007)2 on media pluralism and diversity of media content

Recommendation CM/Rec(2007)11 on promoting freedom of expression and information in the new information and communications environment

Recommendation CM/Rec(2007)16 on measures to promote the public service value of the Internet

Recommendation CM/Rec(2008)6 on measures to promote the respect for freedom of expression and information with regard to Internet filters

Recommendation CM/Rec(2009)5 on measures to protect children against harmful content and behaviour and to promote their active participation in the new information and communications environment

Recommendation CM/Rec(2010)13 on the protection of individuals with regard to automatic processing of personal data in the context of profiling

Recommendation CM/Rec(2011)7 on a new notion of media

Recommendation CM/Rec(2011)8 on the protection and promotion of the universality, integrity and openness of the Internet

Recommendation CM/Rec(2012)4 on the protection of human rights with regard to social networking services

Recommendation CM/Rec(2012)3 on the protection of human rights with regard to search engines

Recommendation CM/Rec(2015)6 on the free, transboundary flow of information on the Internet

Resolution (74) 26 on the right of reply – Position of the individual in relation to the press

Parliamentary Assembly

Resolution 1551 (2007): Fair trial issues in criminal cases concerning espionage or divulging state secrets

Resolution 1636 (2008): Indicators for media in a democracy

Resolution 1729 (2010): Protection of 'whistle-blowers'

Recommendation 1950 (2011): The protection of journalistic sources

European Union

Agency for Fundamental Rights and Council of Europe

Handbook on European data protection law, 2013

Council of the European Union

Council Decision 2000/278/EC of 16 March 2000 on the approval, on behalf of the European Community, of the WIPO Copyright Treaty and the WIPO Performances and Phonograms Treaty, OJ L 89/6

Council Decision No. 676/2002/EC of the European Parliament and of the Council of 7 March 2002 on a regulatory framework for radio spectrum policy in the European Community (Radio Spectrum Decision), OJ L 108/1

Council Decision 94/800/EC of 22 December 1994 concerning the conclusion on behalf of the European Community, as regards matters within its competence, of the agreements reached in the Uruguay Round multilateral negotiations (1986–1994), OJ L 336/1

Council Decision 97/838/EC of 18 December 1997 concerning the conclusion on behalf of the European Community, as regards matters within its competence, of the results of the WTO negotiations on basic telecommunications services, OJ L 347/45

Council Decision 1999/468/EC of 28 June 1999 laying down the procedures for the exercise of implementing powers conferred on the Commission, OJ L 184/23

Council Decision 2004/496/EC of 17 May 2004 on the conclusion of an Agreement between the European Community and the United States of America on the processing and transfer of PNR data by Air Carriers to the United States Department of Homeland Security, Bureau of Customs and Border Protection, OJ L 183/83 (corrigendum at OJ L 255/168)

Council Decision 2006/515/EC of 18 May 2006 on the conclusion of the Convention on the Protection and Promotion of the Diversity of Cultural Expressions, OJ L 201/15

Proposal for a Directive of the European Parliament and of the Council on the harmonisation of certain aspects of copyright and related rights in the information society, Addendum, 15 September 2000, 1997/0359 (COD)

Recommendation of the Council concerning Guidelines governing the Protection of Privacy and Transborder Flows of Personal Data (2013) [C(80)58/FINAL, as amended on 11 July 2013 by C(2013)79]

Resolution of the Council and of the Representatives of the Governments of the Member States, meeting within the Council of 25 January 1999 concerning public service broadcasting, OJ C 30/1

European Commission

Case No. IV/26.760 [1971] GEMA I
Case No. IV/26.760 [1972] GEMA II
Case No. IV/29.971 [1981] GEMA statutes
Case No. IV/27.394 [1988] Net Book Agreements
Case No. IV/31.734 [1989] Film purchases by German television stations
Case No. IV/M.110 [1991] ABC/Générale des Eaux/Canal+/W.H. Smith TV
Case No. IV/34.689 [1993] Sea Containers v. Stena Sealink
Case No. IV/M.410 [1994] Kirch/Richmond/Telepiù
Case No. IV/M.423 [1994] Newspaper Publishing
Case No. IV/M.469 [1994] MSG Media Service
Case No. IV/M.489 [1994] Bertelsmann/News International/Vox
Case No. IV/M.490 [1995] Nordic Satellite Distribution
Case No. IV/M.553 [1995] RTL/Veronica/Endemol
Case No. IV/M.584 [1995] Kirch/Richemont/Multichoice/Telepiù
Case No. IV/M.779 [1996] Bertelsmann/CLT
Case No. IV/M.877 [1997] Boeing/McDonnell Douglas
Case No. IV/M.993 [1998] Bertelsmann/Kirch/Premiere
Case No. IV/M.1027 [1998] Deutsche Telekom/Beta Research
Case No. IV/M.1081 [1998] Dow Jones/NBC – CNBC Europe
Case No. IV/36.237 [1999] TPS
Case No. IV/36.539 [1999] British Interactive Broadcasting/Open
Case No. COMP/M.1439 [1999] Telia/Telenor
Case No. IV/M.1574 [1999] Kirch/Mediaset
Case No. IV/32.150 [2000] Eurovision

Case No. COMP/JV.37 [2000] BSkyB/KirchPayTV

Case No. COMP/M.1958 [2000] Bertelsmann/GBL/Pearson TV

Case No. COMP/M.1978 [2000] Telecom Italia/News Television/Stream

Case No. COMP/M.2050 [2000] Vivendi/Canal+/Seagram

Case No. COMP M. 2211 [2000] Universal Studio Networks/De Facto 829 (NTL) Studio Channel Ltd. Case No. COMP/M.2220 [2001] General Electric/Honeywell

Case No. COMP/M.2300 [2001] YLE/TDF/Digita/JV

Case No. 37.576 [2001] UEFA's broadcasting regulations

Case No. COMP/C2/38.014 [2002] IFPI 'Simulcasting'

Case No. COMP/M.2876 [2003] News Corp/Telepiù

Case No. COMP/C.2–38.287 [2003] Telenor/Canal+/Canal Digital

Case No. COMP/C.2–38.287 [2003] Telenor/Canal+/Canal Digital

Case No. COMP/C.2–37.398 [2003] UEFA Champions League

Case No. COMP/C-3/37.792 [2004] Microsoft

Case No. COMP/M.2978 [2004] Lagardère/Natexis/VUP

Case No. COMP/C-2/37.214 [2005] Bundesliga

Case No. COMP/M.3178 [2005] Bertelsmann/Springer

Case No. COMP/M.3595 [2005] Sony/MGM

Case No. COMP/M.3752 [2005] Verizon/MCI

Case No. COMP/C-2/38.173 [2006] FA Premier League

Case No. COMP/C2/38.681 [2006] Cannes Extension Agreement

Case No. COMP/M.4504 [2007] SFR/Télé 2 France

Case No. COMP/M.4519 [2007] Lagardère/Sportfive

Case No. COMP/M.4547 [2007] KKR/Permira/ProSiebenSat.1

Case No. COMP/C2/38.698 [2008] CISAG

Case No. COMP/M.5121 [2008] News Corp/Premiere

Case No. COMP/M.5533 [2009] Bertelsmann/KKR/JV

Case No. COMP/M.5734 [2010] Liberty Global Europe/Unitymedia

Case No. COMP/M.5932 [2010] News Corp/BSkyB

Cases No. COMP/C-3/39.740, COMP/C-3/39.775 & COMP/C-3/39.768 [2010] Google

Case No. COMP/M.5900 [2011] LGI/KBW

Case No. COMP/M.6369 [2011] HBO/Ziggo/HBO Nederland

Case No. COMP/AT.39847 [2012] E-Books

Case No. COMP/M.6381 [2012] Google/Motorola Mobility

Case No. COMP/M.6866 [2013] Time Warner/CME

Case No. COMP/M.6880 [2013] Liberty Global/Virgin Media

Case No. COMP/M.6990 [2013] Vodafone/Kabel Deutschland

Case No. COMP/M.7288 [2014] Viacom/Channel 5 Broadcasting

Case No. COMP/M.7332 [2014] BSkyB/Sky Deutschland/Sky Italia

Code of Best Practice for the conduct of state aid control procedures of 16 June 2009, OJ C 136/13

Communication, Towards a new framework for electronic communications infrastructure and associated services — the 1999 Communications Review, COM(1999) 537 final and COM(1999) 539 final

Communication, Principles and guidelines for the Community's audiovisual policy in the digital age, COM (1999) 657 final

Communication, Certain legal aspects relating to cinematographic and other audiovisual works Review of the EU Regulatory Framework for electronic communications networks and services, 2002/C 43/04

Communication, Guidelines on market analysis and the assessment of significant market power under the Community regulatory framework for electronic communications networks and services, 2002/C 165/0

Communication, Guidelines on the assessment of horizontal mergers under the Council Regulation on the control of concentrations between undertakings (2004/C 31/03), OJ C 31/5.

Communication, Vademecum – Community law on State aid, 30 September 2008

Communication, Guidance on the Commission's enforcement priorities in applying Article 82 of the EC Treaty to abusive exclusionary conduct by dominant undertakings (2009/C 45/02)

Communication, The application of State aid rules to public service broadcasting, 2009/C 257/01

Communication, A Digital Agenda for Europe, COM(2010) 245 final

Communication, Europe 2020, A strategy for smart, sustainable and inclusive growth, COM(2010) 2020 final

Communication, The open internet and net neutrality in Europe, COM(2011) 222 final

Communication, A coherent framework for building trust in the Digital Single Market for e-commerce and online services, COM(2011) 942

Communication, A European Union framework for State aid in the form of public service compensation (2011), OJ C 8/15

Communication, The application of the European Union State aid rules to compensation granted for the provision of services of general economic interest, 2012/C 8/02

Communication, EU Guidelines for the application of State aid rules in relation to the rapid deployment of broadband networks, 2013/C 25/01

Communication, State aid for films and other audiovisual works, 2013/C 332/01

Communication, A Digital Single Market Strategy for Europe, COM(2015) 192 final

Comparative study on the situation in the 27 Member States as regards the law applicable to non-contractual obligations arising out of violations of privacy and rights relating to personality, JLS/2007/C4/028. Final Report

Declaration on protecting the dignity, security and privacy of children on the internet (20 February 2008)

Decision of 20 February 2004 C(2004)527final in Cases FI/2003/0024 and FI/2003/0027

Decision of 5 October 2004 C(2004)3682final in Case FI/2004/0082

Decision of 20 October 2004 C(2004)4070final in Case AT/2004/0090

Decision of 17 May 2005 C(2005)1442final in Case DE/2005/0144

Decision of 10 January 2007 C(2006)7300final in Cases PL/2006/0518 and PL/2006/0514

Decision of 4 January 2010 C(2010)10 in Cases PL/2009/1019 and PL/2009/1020

Decision of 10 August 2012 in Case CZ/2012/1322

Decision 94/119/EC of 21 December 1993, Port of Rødby (Denmark)

Decision 97/238/EC of 2 October 1996 concerning aid granted by the French State to the audiovisual production company Société française de Production

Decision of 24 February 1999, Aid No. NN 70/98, 'State aid to public broadcasting channels "Kinderkanal and Phoenix"'

Decision C(2003)3371fin of 14 December 1999, State aid No. NN 88/98– United Kingdom, Financing of a 24-hour advertising-free news channel out of the licence fee by the BBC

Decision 2000/520/EC of 26 July 2000 pursuant to Directive 95/46/EC of the European Parliament and of the Council on the adequacy of the protection provided by the safe harbour privacy principles and related frequently asked questions issued by the US Department of Commerce

Decision 2001/497/EC of 15 June 2001 [Set I] – Standard contractual clauses for the purposes of Article 26(2) of Directive 95/46/EC for the transfer of personal data to third countries which do not ensure an adequate level of protection (controller to controller transfers) (amended by Commission Decision C(2004) 5271)

Decision 2002/2/EC of 20 December 2001 pursuant to Directive 95/46/EC of the European Parliament and of the Council on the adequate protection of personal data provided by the Canadian Personal Information Protection and Electronic Documents Act

Decision C(2004)5721 of 27 December 2001, SET II – Standard contractual clauses for the transfer of personal data from the Community to third countries (controller to controller transfers)

Decision C(2002)1886fin of 22 May 2002, State aid No. N 631/2001 – United Kingdom, BBC licence fee

Decision 2002/627/EC of 29 July 2002 establishing the European Regulators Group for Electronic Communications Networks and Services

Decision C(2003)3371fin of 1 October 2003, State aid No. N 37/2003 – United Kingdom, BBC Digital Curriculum

Decision 2004/339/EC of 15 October 2003 on the measures implemented by Italy for RAI SpA

Decision 2005/406/EC of 15 October 2003 on ad hoc measures implemented by Portugal for RTP

Decision 2004/838/EC of 10 December 2003 on State aid implemented by France for France 2 and France 3

Decision C (2005)586 fin of 16 March 2005, State aid N 622/03 – Austria: Digitalisierungsfonds

Decision C(2005)1479 fin of 7 June 2005, State aid France – Chaîne française d'information internationale

Decision C(2005)1166 fin of 20 April 2005, State Aid E 10/2005 – France Redevance radiodiffusion

Decision 2006/513/EC of 9 November 2005 on the State Aid which the Federal Republic of Germany has implemented for the introduction of digital terrestrial television (DVB-T) in Berlin-Brandenburg

Decision of 10 November 2005 imposing a periodic penalty payment pursuant to Article 24(1) of Regulation No. 1/2003 on Microsoft Corporation (Case COMP/C-3/37.792 Microsoft)

Decision 2005/842/EC of 28 November 2005 on the application of Article 86(2) of the EC Treaty to State aid in the form of public service compensation granted to certain undertakings entrusted with the operation of services of general economic interest

Decision C(2006)5492 final of 22 November 2006, State Aid N 157/2006 – United Kingdom, South Yorkshire Digital Region Broadband Project

Decision C(2007)1761 of 24 April 2007, State aid E 3/2005 (ex-CP 2/2003, CP 232/2002, CP 43/2003, CP 243/2004 and CP 195/2004) – Financing of public service broadcasters in Germany

Decision C (2007)6072 final of 11 December 2007, State aid case C 53/2006, Investment by the city of Amsterdam in a fibre-to-the home (FttH) network

Decision of 27 February 2008 fixing the definitive amount of the periodic penalty payment imposed on Microsoft Corporation by Decision C(2005) 4420 final (Case COMP/C-3/37.792 Microsoft), C(2008) 764 final

Decision C (2008)1839 final of 20 May 2008, State aid N 537/2007 – Finland

Decision C(2010)593 of 5 February 2010 – Standard Contractual Clauses (processors) (repealing Decision 2002/16/EC)

Decision C(2010)888 of 8 February 2010, State aid N 596/2009 – Italy, Bridging the digital divide in Lombardia

Decision C (2010)4862 of 12 July 2010, State aid N 53/2010 – Germany, Federal framework programme on duct support

Decision C (2010)4941 final of 20 July2010, State aid E 4/2008 (ex-N 450/2008) – Sweden, Aid to the press

Decision C(2011)7285 final of 19 October 2010, State Aid N 330/2010 – France Programme national 'très haut debit' – Volet B

Decision C(2011)2612 of 20 April 2011 on the measures implemented by Denmark (C 2/03) for TV2/Danmark

Decision C(2011)8121 of 10 November 2011, State aid – SA.33438 (2011/N), SA.33440 (2011/N), SA.33441 (2011/N), SA.33439 (2011/N), SA 30851 (2011/N), Broadband network project in Eastern Poland

Decision 2012/365/EU of 20 December 2011 on the State aid C 85/01 on ad hoc measures implemented by Portugal in favour of RTP

Decision of 20 December 2011 on the application of Article 106(2) of the Treaty on the Functioning of the European Union to State aid in the form of public service compensation granted to certain undertakings entrusted with the operation of services of general economic interest, OJ L 7/3

Europe's Way to the Information Society – An Action Plan, Communication to the Council and the European Parliament and to the Economic and Social Committee and the Committee of the Regions, COM (94) 347 final (19.07.1994)

Green Paper on the development of the common market for telecommunications services and equipment, COM(87) 290

Green Paper: Damages actions for breach of the EC antitrust rules, COM(2005) 672 final

Green Paper Copyright in the Knowledge Economy, COM(2008) 466/3

Market definition in the media sector – Comparative legal analysis (Volume I), Report by Bird & Bird for the European Commission, Directorate-General for Competition, Information, communication and multimedia, December 2002

Media Market Definitions – Comparative Legal Analysis, Final Report (July/October 2003)

Media Market Definitions – Comparative Legal Analysis, Final Report (18 July 2005)

Notice on the definition of relevant market for the purposes of Community competition law (1997), OJ C 372/5.

Notice on agreements of minor importance which do not appreciably restrict competition under Article 101(1) of the Treaty on the Functioning of the European Union (De Minimis Notice) (2001), OJ C 291/1

Notice on cooperation within the Network of Competition Authorities (2004), OJ C 101/43

Notice – Guidelines on the effect on trade concept contained in Articles 81 and 82 of the Treaty (2004), OJ C 101/81

Notice on Immunity from fines and reduction of fines in cartel cases (2006), OJ C 298/17

Notice on a simplified procedure for treatment of certain types of state aid (2009), OJ C 136/3

Proposal for a Regulation of the European Parliament and the Council on the law applicable to non-contractual obligations ("Rome II"), COM(2003) 427 final

Proposal for a Directive of the European Parliament and of the Council amending Directives 2002/21/EC on a common regulatory framework for electronic communications networks and services, 2002/19/EC on access to, and interconnection of, electronic communications networks and services, and 2002/20/EC on the authorisation of electronic communications networks and services, COM(2007) 697 final

Proposal for a Regulation on the protection of individuals with regard to the processing of personal data and on the free movement of such data (General Data Protection Regulation), COM(2012) 11 final

Publication 2008/C 17/06 of the consolidated measures in accordance with Article 3a(2) of Directive 89/552/EEC on the coordination of certain provisions laid down by law, regulation or administrative action in Member States concerning the pursuit of television broadcasting activities, as amended by Directive 97/36/EC of the European Parliament and of the Council, OJ C 17/7

Recommendation 98/322/EC of 8 April 1998 on interconnection in a liberalised telecommunications market (Part 2 – accounting separation and cost accounting), C(1998) 960 final

Recommendation of 29 July1998 amending Recommendation 98/195/EC on interconnection in a liberalised telecommunications market (Part 1 – Interconnection pricing), C(1998) 2234 final

Recommendation of 24 November 1999 on Leased lines interconnection pricing in a liberalised telecommunications market, C(1999)3863

Recommendation C(2003) 497 of 11 February 2003 on relevant product and service markets within the electronic communications sector susceptible to *ex ante* regulation in accordance with Directive 2002/21/EC of the European Parliament and of the Council on a common regulatory framework for electronic communications networks and services

Recommendation 2003/561/EC of 23 July 2003 on notifications, time limits and consultations provided for in Article 7 of Directive 2002/21/EC of the European Parliament and of the Council on a common regulatory framework for electronic communications networks and services

Recommendation C(2007) 5406 of 17 December 2007 on relevant product and service markets within the electronic communications sector susceptible to *ex ante* regulation in accordance with Directive 2002/21/EC of the European Parliament and of the Council on a common regulatory framework for electronic communications networks and services

Recommendation 2014/710/EU of 9 October 2014 on relevant product and service markets within the electronic communications sector susceptible to *ex ante* regulation in accordance with Directive 2002/21/EC of the European Parliament and of the Council on a common regulatory framework for electronic communications networks and services

Report by Europe Economics for the European Commission, DG Competition, Market Definition in the Media Sector – Economic Issues, November 2002

Report on the application of Council Directive 93/83/EEC of 27 September 1993 on the coordination of certain rules concerning copyright and rights related to copyright applicable to satellite broadcasting and cable retransmission, COM(2002) 430 final

Report on the question of authorship of cinematographic or audiovisual works in the Community, COM(2002) 691 final

Report on the application of Directive 2001/29/EC on the harmonisation of certain aspects of copyright and related rights in the information society, SEC(2007) 1556

Report on the Implementation and Effect of the Resale Right Directive (2001/84/EC), COM(2011) 878 final

Staff Working Document, The treatment of Voice over Internet Protocol (VoIP) under the EU Regulatory Framework, 14 June 2004

Staff Working Document, Online services, including e-commerce, in the Single Market, SEC(2011) 1641 final

Staff Working Paper, Impact Assessment, COM(2012) 10 final

Staff Working Document, E-commerce Action plan 2012–2015, State of play 2013, SWD(2013) 153 final

Staff Working Document, A Digital Single Market Strategy for Europe – Analysis and Evidence, SWD(2015) 100 final

Working Document CC TVSF (97) 9/3, Implementation of Article 3A of Directive 89/552/EEC, as modified by Directive 97/36/EC: Evaluation of National Measures

European Parliament

Legislative resolution of 24 September 2008 on the proposal for a directive of the European Parliament and of the Council amending Directive 2002/21/EC on a common regulatory framework for electronic communications networks and services, Directive 2002/19/EC on access to, and interconnection of, electronic communications networks and associated facilities, and Directive 2002/20/EC on the authorisation of electronic communications networks and services (COM(2007)0697 – C6-0427/2007 – 2007/0247(COD))

Recommendation of the European Parliament and of the Council of 20 December 2006 on the protection of minors and human dignity and on the right of reply in relation to the competitiveness of the European audiovisual and on-line information services industry (2006/952/EC), OJ L 378/72

Report of 21 February 2014 on the US NSA surveillance programme, surveillance bodies in various Member States and their impact on EU citizens' fundamental rights and on transatlantic cooperation in Justice and Home Affairs, 2013/2188(INI)

Resolution of 4 September 2003 on Television without Frontiers, OJ C 76/453

Resolution of 22 April 2004 on the risks of violation, in the EU and especially in Italy, of freedom of expression and information (Article 11(2) of the Charter of Fundamental Rights), OJ C 104/1026

Resolution of 6 September 2005 on the application of Articles 4 and 5 of Directive 89/552/EEC (Television without Frontiers), as amended by Directive 97/36/EC, for the period 2001–2002, OJ C 193/117

Resolution of 9 July 2015 on the implementation of Directive 2001/29/EC of the
European Parliament and of the Council of 22 May 2001 on the harmonisation
of certain aspects of copyright and related rights in the information society, 2014/
2256(INI)

Session document A7-0070/2009 of 16.11.2009, III report on the joint text approved
by the Conciliation Committee for a directive of the European Parliament and of
the Council amending Directives 2002/21/EC on a common regulatory framework for electronic communications networks and services, 2002/19/EC on access
to, and interconnection of, electronic communications networks and associated
facilities, and 2002/20/EC on the authorisation of electronic communications networks and services (PE-CONS 3677/2009 – C7-0273/2009 – 2007/0247(COD))

Praesidium of the European Convention

Declaration concerning the explanations relating to the Charter of Fundamental
Rights of 16 December 2004, C-310

WP29

Explanatory Document on the Processor Binding Corporate Rules, Adopted on
19 April 2013, as last revised and adopted on 22 May 2015

Guidelines on the implementation of the Court of Justice of the European Union
judgment on Google Spain and Inc. v. Agencia Española de Protección de Datos
(AEPD) and Mario Costeja González C-131/12, Adopted on 26 November 2014

Opinion 4/2002 on the level of protection of personal data in Argentina; Opinion
6/2002 on transmission of Passenger Manifest Information and other data from
Airlines to the United States

Opinion 4/2004 on the Processing of Personal Data by means of Video Surveillance

Opinion 4/2007 on the concept of personal data

Opinion 1/2008 on data protection issues related to search engines

Opinion 5/2009 on online social networking

Opinion 6/2009 on the level of protection of personal data in Israel

Opinion 1/2010 on the concepts of "controller" and "processor"

Opinion 3/2010 on the principle of accountability

Opinion 6/2010 on the level of protection of personal data in the Eastern Republic
of Uruguay

Opinion 8/2010 on applicable law

Opinion 11/2011 on the level of protection of personal data in New Zealand

Opinion 15/2011 on the definition of consent

Opinion 04/2012 on Cookie Consent Exemption

Opinion 05/2012 on Cloud Computing

Opinion 03/2013 on purpose limitation

Opinion 02/2014 on a referential for requirements for Binding Corporate Rules submitted to national Data Protection Authorities in the EU and Cross Border Privacy Rules submitted to APEC CBPR Accountability Agents

Opinion 03/2014 on Personal Data Breach Notification

Opinion 05/2014 on Anonymisation Techniques

Opinion 06/2014 on the notion of legitimate interests of the data controller under Article 7 of Directive 95/46/EC

Opinion 07/2014 on the protection of personal data in Quebec

Statement on the impact of the development of big data on the protection of individuals with regard to the processing of their personal data in the EU, Adopted on 16 September 2004

Working Document Privacy on the Internet – An integrated EU Approach to On-line Data Protection, Adopted on 21st November 2000

Working document on determining the international application of EU data protection law to personal data processing on the Internet by non-EU based web sites, Adopted on 30 May 2002

Working Document on Functioning of the Safe Harbor Agreement, Adopted on 2 July 2002

Working Document on data protection issues related to intellectual property rights, 18 January 2005

Working document on a common interpretation of Article 26(1) of Directive 95/46/EC of 24 October 1995, Adopted on 25 November 2005

Working Document 1/2008 on the protection of children's personal data (General guidelines and the special case of schools)

Working Document 1/2009 on pre-trial discovery for cross border civil litigation

Working Document 02/2013 providing guidance on obtaining consent for cookies

Working document 01/2014 on Draft Ad hoc contractual clauses "EU data processor to non-EU sub-processor"

Working Document Setting Forth a Co-Operation Procedure for Issuing Common Opinions on "Contractual clauses" Considered as compliant with the EC Model Clauses, Adopted on 26 November 2014

Inter-American Commission on Human Rights

Office of the Special Rapporteur for Freedom of Expression with the Inter-American Commission on Human Rights, Inter-American Legal Framework Regarding the Right to Freedom of Expression, 2009, CIDH/RELE/INF. 2/09

1

Introduction

CASE EXAMPLE

Mr Jersild is a journalist working for a Danish broadcasting corporation and assigned to its *Sunday News Magazine*. The *Sunday News Magazine* is known as a serious television programme intended for a well-informed audience, dealing with a wide range of social and political issues, including xenophobia, immigration and refugees. The editors of the *Sunday News Magazine* decided to produce a documentary on the 'Greenjackets', a group of young people with racist attitudes. Subsequently Mr Jersild invited three representatives of that group, together with a social worker, to take part in a television interview. The interview lasted between five and six hours, of which between two and two-and-a-half hours were video-recorded. The applicant subsequently edited and cut the film of the interview down to a few minutes. The edited version of the interview included abusive and derogatory remarks about immigrants and ethnic groups in Denmark made by the Greenjackets, interrupted by explanations by the social worker on the reasons for the Greenjackets' attitude. It was then broadcast as a part of the *Sunday News Magazine*.

Following the broadcast, the three youths interviewed were prosecuted and convicted for disseminating statements threatening, insulting or degrading a group of persons according to the Danish Criminal Code. Mr Jersild was convicted of aiding and abetting the three youths.

(ECtHR, Jersild v. Denmark [1994] App. no. 15890/89)

I What is Media Law?

Media law is an established field of legal scholarship. Similar to other legal cross-sectoral areas, such as environmental law, energy law or construction law, the starting point of the analysis is not one particular set of rules – as is the case with, say, competition law or copyright law – or one particular level of rule-making, such as constitutional law or public international law. And neither does it fit into the public–private law dichotomy. Rather, it takes one particular phenomenon, in this case 'the media', and analyses the law with a view to its interpretation and application to this phenomenon.

The establishment of a legal cross-sectoral area requires justification. The question must be raised why this phenomenon deserves a distinct type of academic and practical treatment – which is certainly the case with media law, established in academic education at undergraduate as well as graduate level and as a specialised

1

legal area for practitioners. First, there are several sets of rules that apply exclusively to media institutions, such as the Audiovisual Media Services Directive (AVMS Directive) on the EU level and the implementing domestic broadcasting acts (see Chapter 5), as well as domestic press statutes and codes. Second, there are rules and regulations that do not apply exclusively to the media, but that are particularly relevant for media institutions, such as copyright law or the law of data protection (see Chapters 8 and 9), and where the media is treated distinctly from other actors, as is the case with regard to competition law (see Chapter 10). Third, the special treatment of the media is not limited to these fields of 'secondary law' or statutory law. The media is also treated in a special way in domestic constitutions and on the level of international human rights treaties and conventions. These fundamentals of media law (see Chapter 2) must be considered when interpreting 'secondary' media law.

1 What is 'the Media'?

In order to define the scope of media law, an explanation is required as to what 'the media' actually is. While many people use the term 'media' congruently with press and broadcasting, others regard any communication facility as 'media', including letters and telephones. Communication theorist Marshall McLuhan even defined 'media' as any extension of human senses, including, for example, spoken and written words, radio and broadcasting television, but also clothing, housing and money.[1] Yet, while a narrow definition reducing 'media' to traditional mass media excludes forms of 'new media', especially internet communication, McLuhan's broad definition cannot serve as a suitable basis for making media law workable as a distinct legal discipline either. Otherwise, legal fields such as financial law or construction law would have to be considered subdisciplines of media law.

Instead, media law focuses on media as a *means to disseminate information and ideas to a mass audience*, and the *persons disseminating such information and ideas*. Media law is thus intrinsically tied to the concept of communication. Any communication requires, first, content or a 'message' (1). This message stems from an information source (2), also named 'author' or 'sender'. The destination of the message (3) is usually another human being, but can also be, for instance, an animal or a machine. Finally, in order to communicate the message, the author or creator has to use a particular medium or media (4).[2] The choice of the medium or media may involve other individuals, companies and/or items in the communication process.

---

[1] See McLuhan (1964).
[2] Shannon (1948, pp. 379–423, 623–656); see also Shannon and Weaver (1949); Rogers (1994, pp. 434 ff).

As a consequence, 'media' are any communication intermediaries. Such communication intermediaries transmitting third-party information may be, for example, operators of broadcasting cables and internet service providers (ISPs). Those intermediaries are henceforth named 'media in a technological sense'.

Nevertheless, the term 'media' for *means* of mass communication has often been used interchangeably with the term 'media' for those information *sources* that use mass communication media regularly and on a professional basis, namely press and broadcasting. These 'media' encompass those persons or institutions that do not merely disseminate third-party information, but that are themselves authors of information; that is, sources within the meaning of communication theory. They regularly disseminate content via means of mass communication and usually commit themselves to certain standards of conduct in the information gathering and dissemination process. This understanding of media in a broader sense is often called 'old media', and it largely corresponds to the notion of traditional journalism and entertainment media. Those traditional 'media' were, technically speaking, not identical with 'media' as a concept of communication theory, but rather content providers *using* certain media. But since those institutions, until some 20 years ago, almost had a monopoly on addressing the general public via means of mass communication, they were treated interchangeably with the communication media they used in both linguistic and legal terms. For instance, the term 'press' has been used to describe both the printing press as a medium and the entire publishing industry, and both the content on the TV screen and the act of disseminating this content has been named 'broadcasting'. The most significant exception to the perceived unity of author and medium has arguably been the book publishing industry. Consequently, the law relating to book publishing has sometimes been treated as a distinct legal field. Furthermore, means of distant *individual* communication, such as telephone or letters, have been subject to distinct legal treatment too. But apart from that, media as a technology and media as content providers have mostly been regarded as one and the same.

As will be shown in Chapter 2, because of their important role in a democratic society, those to be considered *journalistic* media have indeed enjoyed certain privileges, such as the right to keep their sources of information confidential, and they have also been subject to enhanced duties and responsibilities. However, the media landscape has changed over the past few decades, hence also its legal assessment. Two factors can be identified as the major reasons for the change in media law: First, the rise of commercial broadcasting and the privatisation and liberalisation of electronic communication infrastructure and services in the late 1980s/early 1990s in Europe, and second, the development of the internet into a generally available mass medium from the late 1990s onwards.

The privatisation and liberalisation of electronic communication infrastructure and services has brought the actual separation of broadcasters from their transmission infrastructure into stronger focus. This separation was barely perceptible in the times in which traditional terrestrial television had been the dominant method of television delivery, which is arguably the reason why the term 'broadcasting' has been used interchangeably for both content providers and the medium they used. With the rise of cable television as a system of broadcasting television programming in the 1980s, the advent of commercial broadcasting and the subsequent privatisation of electronic communication network infrastructures in the EU,[3] broadcasters had to seek access to those networks and services in order to disseminate their content. It had then become the task of public authorities to regulate access to electronic communication networks, such as telephone networks and also cable television networks.

Another major change has been brought about by the evolution of the internet into a publicly available mass medium. Because of the internet, private individuals are now able to reach a mass – even a global – audience. In addition, traditional media corporations themselves use the internet to disseminate their information. Consumers are increasingly able to obtain multiple services on a single platform or device, such as online information services, or to obtain one single service on multiple platforms or devices, such as smartphones or smart television. Moreover, new players have entered the media content market, such as network operators and internet service providers.[4] The provision of transmission services and content is thus converging.

Due to this phenomenon of 'media convergence', the distinction between provision of own content and the mere dissemination of third-party content is thus difficult to draw in individual cases and subject to controversy. Because different forms of media content are being distributed via the same technological system (technological convergence), there is a convergence of the content (content convergence), which synergistically creates new efficiencies; services are no longer restricted to a particular technological infrastructure and vice versa.[5] Different media-related phenomena such as audio services, visual services, sounds, texts and data are being combined. Mass communication and individual communication merge and, thus, become indistinctive from one another. Examples for technological convergence are the distribution of broadcasting, radio, press services and voice telephony via broadband internet. The content convergences that are thereby created are, for instance, video clips (TV broadcasting) included in an article of an online newspaper (press), or written comments (press) accompanying a news podcast on the BBC website (radio broadcasting/online services). It is also to be expected that the distinction will become even more blurred with the development of automatically generated speech, such as a search engine's autocomplete function, and 'active intermediaries'.[6]

---

[3] In the US as well as in a few European countries, cable television networks had been provided by private operators from the outset.

[4] COM, Communication 2009/C 257/01 on the application of State aid rules to public service broadcasting [5].

[5] N. van Eijk, in Castendyk et al. (2008), Electronic Communications Regulatory Framework para. 4. For further reading on the legal challenges of media convergence, see, for example, Craufurd Smith (2007); Nehaluddin (2010).

[6] See Hurwitz (2013); ECtHR, Delfi AS v. Estonia [2015] App. no. 64569/09, Joint Dissenting Opinion of Judges Sajó and Tsotsoria [1].

However, these developments do not require giving up the distinction between communication intermediaries – media in a technological sense – and content providers, especially press and broadcasting. On the contrary, they require an even sharper distinction. The difference between provision of own content and the dissemination of third-party content still underlies the EU media law framework *de lege lata*. For example, Article 1(1)(c) and Recital 25 AVMS Directive as well as Article 2(c) of the Framework Directive (2002/21/EC) expressly refer to the notion of 'editorial control' or 'editorial responsibility' to distinguish between content providers (which, in the case of audiovisual media service providers, would fall under the AVMS Directive; see Chapter 5), and services that consist of the conveyance of signals on electronic communications networks (which, if they are electronic communications services, would fall under the regulatory framework of electronic communication; see Chapter 7).[7] Articles 12–14 E-commerce Directive only apply to merely passive hosting or conduit of information, and not to the generation of information itself (see Chapter 6). Nevertheless, a person might be a content provider in one case and an intermediary in another. For example, a company operating an electronic communications network may also provide broadcasting services. In such a case, the extent to which the company operates the network will be regulated by the framework on electronic communication, whereas the extent to which it provides broadcasting content will fall within the scope of the AVMS Directive.

2 A Privileged Protection for the Journalistic Media?

It is subject to considerable controversy in legal scholarship, reinforced by the emergence of non-professional 'citizen journalists', whether *journalistic* media should enjoy protection that differs from that afforded to other publishers. According to a point of view that is widespread in European legislation, case law and scholarship, content providers have to be distinguished into the journalistic media on the one hand, and individuals or institutions that also disseminate information to a mass audience via a communication medium, but that do not fulfil the legal standards for journalism, on the other hand. The latter may invoke freedom of expression protection, but they do not enjoy the privileged protection of journalists (called 'media freedom' or 'freedom of the press'). By contrast, many legal scholars, particularly from the United States, reject the notion that certain content providers, such as newspaper companies or broadcasters, should enjoy any privileges or be subject to any special duties distinct from other individuals or companies.[8] This has been named the 'equivalence model', since the protection of journalists should be equivalent to that of other individuals invoking freedom of expression,[9] the 'neutrality doctrine', because

---

[7] See CJEU, Case C-518/11 [2013] UPC Nederland BV [41]; Case C-475/12 [2014] UPC DTH Sàrl [36].
[8] See, for example, Lange (1975); Lewis (1979); Amar (1999, p. 714); Carter (1992, p. 874); Anderson (2002, p. 528); Baker (2007, p. 958; 2011, p. 230); Volokh (2012, pp. 538–539).
[9] Compare Fenwick and Phillipson (2006, p. 20).

the absence of special media rights follows from the state's obligation to be neutral in granting such rights,[10] or the 'press-as-technology model', as freedom of the press within the First Amendment to the US Constitution should be conceptualised as the mere right of every person to use communication technology, and not as a right belonging exclusively to Court's approach to the First Amendment. Although the Supreme Court has acknowledged the role of the press 'as a powerful antidote to any abuses of power by governmental officials',[11] it has 'consistently rejected the proposition that the institutional press has any constitutional privilege beyond that of other speakers'.[12] This point of view also finds support in UK legislation: According to Section 10 Contempt of Court Act 1981: 'No court may require a person to disclose, nor is any person guilty of contempt of court for refusing to disclose, the source of information contained in a publication for which he is responsible, unless it be established to the satisfaction of the court that disclosure is necessary in the interests of justice or national security or for the prevention of disorder or crime.' This provision thus guarantees the right to keep sources confidential, a right that many regard as one of the most formidable privileges for journalists (see Chapter 2), to every publisher.

Legislators and courts in continental Europe as well as scholars in both Europe and the US have taken a different approach. They argue that the difficulty of defining or identifying the media does not justify ignoring media protection clauses: press clauses, as provided in the First Amendment to the US Constitution, Article 21(2) of the Italian Constitution, Article 5(1)2 of the German Basic Law or Article 25(1) of the Belgian Constitution, and the media clauses in Article 17 of the Swiss Constitution or in Article 11(2) of the EU Charter of Fundamental Rights (EUChFR). And also secondary EU law builds on the distinction between journalists and other content providers: EU legislation acknowledges the importance of media freedom by providing exemptions for journalists from data protection (Article 9 of the Data Protection Directive) and copyright provisions (Article 5(3)(c) of the EU Copyright Directive). These clauses must mean something beyond free speech, otherwise they would be redundant.[13] Freedom of the press or of the media in general identifies, in the first

---

[10] Compare Bezanson (1977, p. 755); Rooney (1983, p. 54).

[11] Mills v. Alabama, 384 U.S. 214, 219 (1966); see also Estes v. Texas, 381 U.S. 532, 539 (1965): 'The free press has been a mighty catalyst in awakening public interest in governmental affairs, exposing corruption among public officers and employees and generally informing the citizenry of public events and occurrences.'

[12] Citizens United v. FEC, 130 S. Ct. 876, 905 (2010) (citations omitted). See, for instance, Associated Press v. United States, 326 U.S. 1, 7 (1945); Curtis Publishing Co. v. Butts, 388 U.S. 130, 150 (1967); Branzburg v. Hayes, 408 U.S. 665, 704 (1972); Pell v. Procunier, 417 U.S. 817, 834 (1974); Saxbe v. Washington Post Co., 417 U.S. 843, 848–49 (1974). The Supreme Court's approach stands in contrast to several judgments of District Courts; see, for instance, New York Times Co. v. Gonzales, 382 F. Supp. 2d 457, 501–03 (S.D.N.Y. 2005); O'Grady v. Superior Court, 44 Cal. Rptr. 3d 72 (Cal. Ct. App. 2006). Furthermore, 40 States and the District of Columbia have adopted shield laws; that is, legislation providing a journalist with the right to refuse to testify as to information and/or sources of information obtained during the newsgathering and dissemination process. For more details, see Oster (2015b, pp. 25–28).

[13] Fundamentally Stewart (1975, p. 633). See also, for example, Nimmer (1975, p. 640); Schauer (2005, pp. 1263–1264); Bezanson (2012, p. 1261).

place, the rights-holder, and not subject-matter of a freedom of expression right. It is freedom *of the* press and *of the* media, and not the freedom to publish something *with* certain media.

However, within this line of argument, it is controversial *which* special privileges the journalistic media should exactly enjoy. This question concerns the relationship between media freedom and freedom of expression. According to one point of view, media freedom is merely an instrumental right, subordinate to freedom of expression. This approach is reflected in the case law of the German Federal Constitutional Court, which regards 'broadcasting freedom' according to Article 5(1)2 of the Basic Law merely as a 'serving liberty' (*dienende Freiheit*).[14] Media freedom serves the values of freedom of speech in that it safeguards the absence of censorship and the promotion of a lively and vigorous public debate in which all have an opportunity to participate. But it does not go beyond.[15] In particular, the journalistic right to publish is based on the same freedom of expression guarantees as the right of private publishers.

Another approach regards media freedom not as a right subordinate to freedom of expression. Instead, media freedom is regarded as *lex specialis* to freedom of expression in the sense that a person or institution, by virtue of being a journalist and acting as a journalist, is governed by a different set of factors concerning the intensity of protected action. The fact that an impugned statement is 'media speech', rather than speech by any other individual or institution, adds to the burden of justifying its restrictions. This approach finds support in the case law of the European Court of Human Rights (ECtHR or 'the Strasbourg Court'). For example, in *Busuioc* v. *Moldova*, the applicant had been ordered to pay damages for the publication of a newspaper article containing allegations of favouritism against civil servants.[16] The respondent state referred to the Strasbourg Court's decision *Janowski* v. *Poland (No. 1)*, according to which 'civil servants must enjoy public confidence in conditions free of undue perturbation if they are to be successful in performing their tasks and it may therefore prove necessary to protect them from offensive and abusive verbal attacks when on duty'.[17] However, the Strasbourg Court highlighted that, in contrast to the statements made by the applicant as a private individual in the case of *Janowski*, the impugned article in *Busuioc* v. *Moldova* was written by the applicant in his capacity as a journalist, and thus fell within the scope of freedom of the press. Therefore the Court held that the Moldovan authorities enjoyed a less extensive margin of appreciation when deciding whether there was a 'pressing social need' to interfere with the applicant's freedom of expression.[18] By contrast, in the cited *Janowski* decision, the Court

---

[14] See, for example, German Federal Constitutional Court, Cases 1 BvF 1/85 and 1/88 [1991] '6th broadcasting decision'; Cases 1 BvR 1586/89 and 487/92 [1992] '7th broadcasting decision'.

[15] See, for example, Barendt (2015b, pp. 309–310).

[16] Busuioc v. Moldova [2004] App. no. 61513/00.

[17] Janowski v. Poland (No. 1) [1999] App. no. 25716/94.

[18] Busuioc v. Moldova [2004] App. no. 61513/00 [64] and [65].

observed that the applicant's critical remarks did not involve the issue of freedom of the press, since the applicant, 'although a journalist by profession, clearly acted as a private individual on this occasion'.[19]

In *Wojtas-Kaleta* v. *Poland*,[20] the applicant was a journalist employed by a public television company. He was reprimanded for publicly complaining about the lack of support for classical music, and the fact that the quality of public television programmes was negatively affected as a result of fierce competition from private broadcasters. The Strasbourg Court, 'having regard to the role played by journalists in society and to their responsibilities to contribute to and encourage public debate', considered that the obligation of discretion and constraint under general employment law 'cannot be said to apply with equal force to journalists, given that it is in the nature of their functions to impart information and ideas'.[21]

Finally, in his concurring opinion to the ECtHR's decision in *Vejdeland and others* v. *Sweden*, Judge Zupančič pointedly summarised the effect of the media speech privilege. The applicants – private citizens – were convicted for distributing homophobic leaflets in an upper secondary school. The ECtHR upheld this conviction, but Judge Zupančič observed: '[I]f exactly the same words and phrases were to be used in public newspapers such as *Svenska Dagbladet*, they would probably not be considered as a matter for criminal prosecution and condemnation'.[22] These examples explain how the Strasbourg Court distinguishes between journalists and private individuals (*Busuioc*), and how this distinction affects the application of both private law (*Wojtas-Kaleta*) and criminal law (*Vejdeland*).

Whether one regards media freedom as an instrumental right to freedom of expression, on the one hand, or as *lex specialis* to freedom of expression, on the other hand, gains significance when assessing the intensity of protection to be afforded to a particular publication and the duties and responsibilities to be abided by the publisher. The *lex specialis* approach justifies stronger protection of journalistic publications because journalists commit themselves to adhere to certain standards of diligence when preparing, issuing or distributing publications, and if they abided by these standards also in the particular case (even if the publication turned out to be inaccurate and defamatory).[23] By contrast, treating media freedom as an instrumental right applies the same freedom of expression standards to journalists and to private individuals or non-journalistic entities. But the *lex specialis* approach and the instrumental approach share large common ground in that they both protect the media not as publishers but as

---

[19] Janowski v. Poland (No. 1) [1999] App. no. 25716/94 [32].

[20] Wojtas-Kaleta v. Poland [2009] App. no. 20436/02.

[21] Wojtas-Kaleta v. Poland [2009] App. no. 20436/02 [46].

[22] Vejdeland and others v. Sweden [2012] App. no. 1813/07, concurring opinion by Judge Boštjan M. Zupančič [12]; see also Barthold v. Germany [1985] App. no. 8734/79 [42]: 'This is especially so since the publication prompting the restriction was an article written by a journalist and not a commercial advertisement.'

[23] See Chapter 3.II.2.e.

institutions. The institutional protection of the media guarantees rights that are not directly related to the content of a publication or the way in which it is presented, but are related to the media in its newsgathering, editorial or distribution process, or even to the mere existence of an independent media. These privileges of the journalistic media will be further dealt with in Chapter 2.

3 The Distinction between the Journalistic Media and Other Content Providers

If one agrees with view that freedom of the journalistic media (or freedom of the press) is a fundamental right distinct from freedom of expression – be it as *lex specialis* to freedom of expression, be it as an instrumental right – one question necessarily follows: What is a journalist? In the course of the evolution of the internet, the ability to reach a mass audience is no longer the privilege of traditional media corporations and, hence, not a clearly distinguishing element for the media–public divide anymore. Bloggers and other amateur journalists enrich public discourse by contributing to debates of general interest. As a consequence, the boundaries between the traditional media, especially the press, and non-media actors become more and more blurred. But it would go too far to argue that anyone reaching a mass audience should be considered to be a journalist, and should enjoy journalists' privileges.[24] Such an interpretation would be over-inclusive, as it encompasses virtually every internet publication. Internet publications do not only vary in their quality, but also in their appearance, ranging from political blogs to hotel evaluations. The distinguishing element of 'journalism' is that journalists have to act according to 'ethics of journalism' and principles of 'responsible journalism', and thus have to take considerable steps to verify published information. Moreover, the professional media is also subject to a right of reply and must make available certain information on the publisher, for example, under Article 5 AVMS Directive – a duty that is hardly compatible with the anonymity often practised on the internet. Furthermore, assume that a blogger publishes secret information on his website that someone else has obviously obtained by illegal means. Would the blogger, as a layperson, be obliged to reveal the name of his source, or would he, as a journalist, have the right to keep his sources confidential? These examples should illustrate that the concept of journalism should not be interpreted too extensively without further consideration. Journalists' right not to reveal sources is conceptualised as an exceptional privilege. This privilege is justified because journalists have a reputation for trust and credibility – at least more credibility than some obscure leaflet or conspiracy blog. If everyone with internet access and a blog or a social media account were considered to be a journalist, the exception would become the rule, which would severely impede the course of justice. As a result, the fact that a statement has been published online and so can be accessed by a mass audience does not *per se* make the publication a journalistic

---

[24] But see Human Rights Committee, General Comment no. 34, para. 44.

publication: the 'medium' internet must not be confused with 'the media' as a legal concept, just as the medium 'paper' does not automatically constitute the press. It is necessary to distinguish the diligent journalist engaged in informing the public from someone who seeks a privilege in media disguise. The increasing difficulty to draw a line between journalists and non-journalistic publishers seems to support the view that such a line should not be drawn in the first place.

But the line can arguably still be drawn, although one has to accept that controversial judgments will inevitably occur. As most ambiguous legal terms, the notion of 'journalism' should be approached from a practice-oriented, typological 'core-penumbra' perspective. Certain persons, institutions and publications are part of the uncontroversial, paradigmatic core of the notion of 'journalism', such as the *Guardian* newspaper, as well as Bob Woodward and Carl Bernstein when they investigated and reported on the Watergate scandal. Other persons, institutions and publications are clearly outside the notion of journalism, such as Mrs Bercow's Tweet, which will be dealt with further below. It can be assumed that the vast majority of court cases unambiguously fall under one of those clear categories. The remaining cases, 'hard cases' in a Dwokinian sense, either fall within the penumbra of the notion of 'journalism', or they have to be considered 'non-journalism'. This is a matter of argument based on relevant factors, three of which are:

1 A distinction based on formal criteria: accordingly, a journalist someone who underwent a journalistic education, who is affiliated to a news organisation and/or who is registered with a body of press self-regulation.
2 A distinction based on functional criteria: a journalist is someone who does journalistic work; that is, who regularly publishes contributions on matters of public concern to an undefined number of recipients and abides by certain standards of conduct.
3 Whether an actor describes himself as a journalist – thus claiming particular creditworthiness – or not.

Still an important factor to draw the line in the media–public divide is the requirement of professionalism. For example, that a publisher must be associated with a traditional media company or needs to undergo a journalistic education.[25] A requirement of professionalism for privileged protection of the media under Article 10 of the European Convention on Human Rights (ECHR) is supported by the ECtHR and the Committee of Ministers of the Council of Europe, which regularly refer to 'media professionals'.[26] If people provide

---

[25] See EComHR, Loersch and Nouvelle Association du Courrier v. Switzerland [1995] App. nos. 23868/94 and 23869/94 [3]; Council of Europe, Recommendation No. R (97) 20 on "hate speech", Principle 2; Recommendation Rec(2003)13 on the provision of information through the media in relation to criminal proceedings, para. 3; Parliamentary Assembly, Resolution 1636 (2008): Indicators for media in a democracy, no. 10.
[26] See Sürek and Özdemir v. Turkey [1999] App. nos. 23927/94 and 24277/94 [63]; Şener v. Turkey [2000] App. no. 26680/95 [42]; Wizerkaniuk v. Poland [2011] App. no. 18990/05 [68]; Kaperzyński v. Poland [2012] App. no. 43206/07 [70]; Council of Europe, Recommendation No. R (2000) 7 on the right of journalists

news reports on a professional basis, they have a stronger incentive not to spread false-hoods, lest they might lose readership and risk their source of income. In turn, private blog-gers who provide their information for free lack an economic incentive to provide accurate information.

Yet a requirement of 'professionalism' eliminates freelancers and anyone supplying news who does not receive remuneration; that is, most bloggers who do contribute to matters of general interest.[27] Therefore, 'professionalism' should be one, albeit not the only, factor for determining the difference between journalists and non-journalists. Another factor should be the actual work of a publisher. Private bloggers who regu-larly contribute to matters of public interest and act with a level of diligence com-parable to that of traditional news media organisations should also be considered 'journalists' in a legal sense.[28]

Finally, in its recent case law, the Strasbourg Court has revealed a stronger focus on the extent to which a contribution contributed to a matter of public interest and the prior conduct of the publisher rather than a strict categorisation into pro-fessional newspaper/broadcasting journalism enjoying media privileges on the one hand, and non-professional 'freedom of expression only' citizens who do not enjoy these privileges on the other hand. For example, the ECtHR decision *Fatullayev v. Azerbaijan* pertained to the applicant's blog, 'The Karabakh Diary', which concerned the Khojaly massacre of 26 February 1992. The applicant made certain statements that could be understood as differing from the commonly accepted version of the Khojaly events. According to the official version, hundreds of Azerbaijani civilians had been killed by the Armenian armed forces, with the reported assistance of the Russian army, during their assault on the town of Khojaly in the course of the war in Nagorno-Karabakh. It was not clear whether the applicant posted the impugned statements online in his capacity as a journalist or whether he expressed his per-sonal opinions as a citizen. For the Strasbourg Court, however, it was more impor-tant that 'the applicant … did not hide his identity' when posting the statements and 'that he publicly disseminated his statements by posting them on a freely accessible popular Internet forum, a medium which in modern times has no less powerful an effect than the print media'.[29] The Court thus granted significant freedom of expres-sion protection to the applicant.

Furthermore, *Růžový panter, o.s.* v. *Czech Republic*[30] concerned an online press release of the Czech anti-corruption NGO 'Pink Panther', in which the NGO asserted

---

not to disclose their sources of information, Appendix: 'For the purposes of this Recommendation [...] the term "journalist" means any natural or legal person who is regularly or professionally engaged in the collection and dissemination of information to the public via any means of mass communication'; Recommendation CM/Rec(2011)7 on a new notion of media, Appendix, para. 38.

[27] See Ugland (2008, p. 137); West (2011, p. 1068); Blocher (2012, p. 429); Oster (2015b, pp. 64–65).
[28] Anonymous (2007, p. 998); Oster (2013, p. 78).
[29] ECtHR, Fatullayev v. Azerbaijan [2010] App. no. 40984/07 [95].
[30] ECtHR, Růžový panter, o.s. v. Czech Republic [2012] App. no. 20240/08.

a connotation between a politician and people who allegedly committed fraud and plotted a murder. Since 'Pink Panther' could not prove these allegations, it had been ordered to pay damages. The Strasbourg Court did not find a violation of Article 10 ECHR. Although 'Pink Panther' did not conduct research-based journalism, the Court held against the NGO that the public regarded its website as serious and credible. Hence the Court made the NGO subject to duties of due diligence, which it usually only applies to journalists.

In *Růžový panter, o.s.* v. *Czech Republic* the ECtHR thus decided that non-journalists may have to meet responsibilities to no lesser degree than professional journalists, even if they contribute to a debate of general interest. Yet the Court did not have to address the question as to whether domestic authorities may even impose higher standards of diligence on non-journalists than on journalists. The Court had the opportunity to answer this question in the decision *Braun* v. *Poland*, which we will deal with in more detail in Chapter 3. In *Braun* v. *Poland*, the Court decided that imposing on a non-journalist higher demands of diligence than on a journalist violates Article 10 ECHR.[31]

These three judgments represent a paradigm shift in the case law of the Strasbourg Court. Certainly, the Court still emphasises the role of traditional journalistic media as 'public watchdog' (see Chapter 2). However, it is also discernible that the Court attaches significance to non-journalistic statements, which contribute to debates of general interest and are addressed to a mass audience, in a similar way to journalistic news reporting. It thus appears that the Court seems to understand the notion of 'press freedom' or 'media freedom' in a more functional, rather than categorical, way. Rather than deciding whether or not a person or institution is to be categorised as a 'journalist' – hence enjoys certain privileges and has to abide by standards of conduct – the question is whether a person or institution regularly contributes to public discourse and therefore should enjoy special privileges.[32] Journalistic privileges may thus extend to contributions to discussions of public affairs by actors of civil society (other than traditional media undertakings) if they act according to certain standards of conduct. Such actors may include, for instance, citizen-journalists, NGOs,[33] interest groups or credit rating agencies – especially when issuing sovereign ratings.[34]

---

[31] ECtHR, Braun v. Poland [2014] App. no. 30162/10.

[32] See Oster (2013).

[33] See Human Rights Committee, Toktakunov v. Kyrgyzstan [2011] Communication no. 1470/2006 [6.3]; Special Court for Sierra Leone, Prosecutor v. Alex Tamba Brima and others, Decision on Prosecution appeal against decision on oral application for witness TF1-150 to testify without being compelled to answer questions on grounds of confidentiality, Case No. SCSL-2004-16-AR73 [2006] SCSL 2 [33]. The Special Court acknowledged a privileged relationship between a human rights officer and his informants, as well as a public interest attached to the work of human rights officers gathering confidential information, and therefore protected researchers for NGOs similar to journalistic sources.

[34] See Oster (2012b, p. 211; 2015b, p. 65).

4. The Distinction between Media in a Technological Sense and Content Providers

A further distinction underlying media law is the distinction between content providers, including the journalistic media, and communication intermediaries (media in a technological sense). 'The media' as a content provider is to be characterised as persons or institutions generating information and ideas and disseminating them via facilities of mass communication to an undefined number of recipients.[35] By contrast, a communication medium is a mere speech facilitator that transmits or disseminates third-party content, but that is not part of the fabrication of the publication itself.[36] Examples for mere speech intermediaries are communication network and service providers, news aggregators, social networks and website operators, insofar as they host unredacted comments from users.

To be sure, the media in a broader sense can also operate the facilities for the dissemination of its content, and thus act as speech disseminator. But this is not necessarily the case. Electronic communication services or broadcasting networks are often run by operators other than the content providers. In turn, media content providers may, under certain circumstances, also act as mere intermediaries for third-party speech, for instance, if they are obliged to publish a reply.

The crucial difference between the media as 'author' or content provider, and a medium as a mere facilitator of communication, lies in the exercise of editorial control.[37] Editorial control describes the creation, selection or redaction of content before its publication.[38] Whoever exercises editorial control is fully liable for the published content. The author or creator of a statement has to abide by certain legal standards of conduct, or, in the words of Articles 19(2) of the International Covenant on Civil and Political Rights (ICCPR) and 10(2) ECHR, 'duties and responsibilities'. By the same token, the author or creator of a statement enjoys particularly strong freedom of expression protection. This is reflected, for example, in certain defences to defamation claims that are available to an author only, such as 'honest opinion' and 'publication on a matter of public interest'.[39]

By contrast, whoever transmits a third-party statement without editing it acts as a mere intermediary. Yet this does not mean that speech intermediaries are not protected at all. Freedom of expression includes the right to disseminate information and ideas of others. Speech intermediaries thus enjoy the right to impart information, but not the privileges afforded to the content-providing media in a broader sense,

---

[35] See Oster (2013, p. 68).

[36] Compare Luhmann (1996, p. 3).

[37] See Oster (2015b, p. 58), with further references.

[38] For more details on the concept of 'editorial control', see Council of Europe, Recommendation CM/Rec(2011)7 on a new notion of media, Appendix, paras 30–36.

[39] On honest opinion, see Flood v. Times Newspapers [2012] UKSC 12, now codified in Section 3 Defamation Act 2013; on publication on a matter of public interest, see Reynolds v. Times Newspapers Ltd [1999] 2 AC 127, now codified in Section 4 Defamation Act 2013.

such as the protection of its sources of information. In turn, those intermediaries do not have to abide by the traditional media's strict duties and responsibilities either, such as making attempts to verify the information they impart. Speech intermediaries cannot be held fully liable for a transmitted statement, because they may not even be aware of its content. As will be shown in Chapter 6, the law thus provides limited liability or even immunity to those speech facilitators, such as under Articles 12–15 of the E-commerce Directive and Section 230(c)(1) of the US Communications Decency Act 1996. But the privileges of 'media freedom', which will be further elaborated on in the next chapter, may only apply to content providers, and not to mere disseminators of third-party speech. This is relevant, for example, with regard to the question whether these intermediaries are obliged to identify subscribers who allegedly committed unlawful acts on the internet, such as copyright infringement or defamation. If intermediaries were considered journalistic media, and thus enjoyed journalistic privileges, they would be entitled to refuse to reveal the subscriber's identity because they would have the same privilege as journalists to not disclose their 'sources'.[40] However, since they cannot be categorised as journalistic media, internet intermediaries cannot rely on the privileges deriving from media freedom as a fundamental right.

Therefore, media in a technological sense are mere disseminators in the communication process, and not sources of information. In turn, a person involved in the communication process is not to be considered a mere intermediary if he provides own content, adopts third-party content, exercises editorial control over third-party content or initiates a publication.[41] The question of whether own content is being provided or third-party content is being adopted is a matter of legal evaluation. It depends on the perception of an ordinary reasonable person. Indications for the adoption of third-party content are, for instance, whether the publisher expressly approved them, or attached his brand name to them.[42] As a consequence, neither the provision of own content nor the adoption of third-party content requires an endorsement of a particular statement. A person may even be considered a content provider if the statement does not reflect his opinion at all.

Even if he does not adopt third-party content, an intermediary goes beyond mere dissemination if he exercises editorial control over the information concerned.[43] This is the case, first, with regard to the dissemination of a third-party statement by a traditional medium of 'one-to-many' mass communication, that is, broadcasting and print. If a newspaper or a broadcasting channel publishes third-party content, such as newsletters or interviews, it is not usually merely a subordinate publisher. Rather,

---

[40] See Chapter 2.
[41] See Oster (2015a, pp. 385 ff).
[42] See, for example, The Law Society and others v. Kordowski [2011] EWHC 3182 (QB); German Federal Court of Justice, Case Az.: I ZR 166/07 [2009], 'www.chefkoch.de'.
[43] Kaschke v. Gray [2010] EWHC 690 (QB) [86].

if it has the *ability* to edit the text or the programming but choses not to exercise editorial control over the content, then it has to be considered a primary publisher and not a mere disseminator of the statement concerned.[44] In turn, if a newspaper or broadcaster does not have the ability to edit content it is obliged to publish, then it does not to exercise editorial control, and hence is a mere disseminator. This is the case, for example, where a newspaper or a broadcaster has been ordered by a court to publish a particular apology or a reply. Furthermore, undertakings distributing television programmes by cable that are under a duty to broadcast certain predetermined radio and television programmes – so-called 'must carry' obligation[45] – do not exercise editorial control over the content they 'must carry' and are therefore mere disseminators.

Second, in contrast to 'one-to-many' mass communication, online services providing 'many-to-many' platforms of communication for third-party content do in principle not exercise editorial control over the content they publish. However, online platforms for user-generated content assume editorial control if they modify third-party content, even if this modification has been made in good faith. By modifying third-party content, the activity of the communication intermediary is not limited to the process of a mere dissemination of information.[46]

Finally, although he has neither created nor modified the text, a communication intermediary assumes content provider status if he initiates the publication of the information. This also applies if the intermediary directs a third-party statement to another audience; that is, a public that was not taken into account by the initial publisher when he authorised the initial communication to the public.[47] For example, in the ECtHR decision *Print Zeitungsverlag GmbH v. Austria*, a newspaper quoted verbatim an anonymous letter with defamatory content that had been sent to members of the supervisory board of a tourism association.[48] Although the applicant newspaper duly distanced itself from the content of the letter, the Court held that by reproducing the anonymous letter, the newspaper had disseminated it to a far larger audience than the restricted circle of initial recipients.[49] Therefore, the newspaper activated an entirely new communication process: one-to-many mass communication to an undefined number of recipients via the printed press rather than communication of a letter to a limited number of individuals.[50]

---

[44] See Thompson v. Australian Capital TV Ltd [1996] HCA 38; Oriental Press Group Ltd & Others v. Fevaworks Solutions Ltd & Others [2013] HKCFA 47 [57].

[45] See Article 31 Universal Service Directive.

[46] Oster (2015a, p. 361).

[47] Compare CJEU, Case C-466/12 [2014] Svensson et al. v. Retriever Sverige AB [24], concerning the concept of 'communication to the public' within the meaning of Article 3(1) of the Copyright Directive (see Chapter 9).

[48] Print Zeitungsverlag GmbH v. Austria [2013] App. no. 26547/07.

[49] Print Zeitungsverlag GmbH v. Austria [2013] App. no. 26547/07 [40–41].

[50] See Oster (2015a, p. 362).

5 The Evaluation of Communication Content

As has been stated before, any communication requires content or a 'message'. The subject of a message is information. Therefore, information is a central aspect of media law. Media law categorises and assesses information included in statements and publications. In order to analyse media publications, legal doctrine should be combined with speech act theory, known from linguistics and the philosophy of language. According to language philosopher J.L. Austin, utterances do not only convey information, but they may also have performative function.[51] Speech act theory distinguishes utterances into their locutionary, illocutionary and perlocutionary components. The locutionary component relates to the content of the utterance, the illocutionary component concerns its intended meaning, and the perlocutory component is the utterance's effect. The facts underlying the High Court case *McAlpine* v. *Bercow*[52] may serve as an example: in 2012, the BBC broadcast a news report linking an unnamed 'leading Conservative politician from the Thatcher years' to an allegation of child abuse. This led to a debate on social internet networks, including on Twitter, as to who this politician might be. In this context, the defendant, wife of the Speaker of the House of Commons and participant in several TV shows, tweeted 'Why is Lord McAlpine trending? *innocent face*'.[53] The claimant Lord McAlpine, formerly a close aide to Margaret Thatcher, brought a libel action against the defendant. Therefore, the High Court had to determine, *inter alia*, the meaning of the words complained of and whether they were defamatory of the claimant.[54] Regarding the locutory component of the defendant's tweet, the tweet implicitly stated that the claimant's name was 'trending' on Twitter; that is, that it was mentioned at a greater rate than other names. Moreover, taken at face value, the tweet conveyed the question as to why this was the case. Moreover, the words 'innocent face' were to be understood like a stage direction. Readers were to imagine the expression on the defendant's face was one of innocence; that is, that the defendant herself did not know the answer to the question.[55] The crucial questions were, therefore, what the defendant *intended* to say (illocutionary component) and whether this statement had a defamatory *effect* (perlocutory component). The defendant argued that the question she asked in her tweet was a neutral question that did not imply that the claimant might be involved in the child abuse case. However, the court held that the reasonable reader would understand the words 'innocent face' as being insincere and ironical; the defendant did not simply want to know the answer to a factual question.[56] Instead, a reasonable

---

[51] Austin (1962).
[52] [2013] EWHC 981 (QB) and [2013] EWHC 1342 (QB).
[53] In Twitter parlance, 'trending' describes a word, phrase or topic that is mentioned at a greater rate than others (https://en.wikipedia.org/wiki/Twitter).
[54] Possible defences and the award of damages are left out of the account here.
[55] McAlpine v. Bercow [2013] EWHC 1342 (QB) [7].
[56] McAlpine v. Bercow [2013] EWHC 1342 (QB) [84].

reader would understand the tweet to suggest that the defendant intended to picture the claimant as a paedophile who was guilty of child abuse. This message, in its perlocutory effect, was also defamatory of the claimant, as it referred to him and substantially affected in an adverse manner the attitude of other people towards him.[57]

What principles does media law apply to communication? First of all, media law distinguishes between factual information and opinions. Factual information can be defined as information that is susceptible to proof. While the existence of facts can be demonstrated, opinions (or comment or value judgements) are not susceptible of proof.[58] The distinction between factual information and value judgements gains particular significance in defamation and privacy cases as well as in cases of 'hate speech', which will be further discussed in Chapter 3. For example, in the above mentioned case of *McAlpine* v. *Bercow*, the conveyed message that the claimant was involved in child abuse was a statement of fact, and not an expression of an opinion.

The line between statements of fact and value judgements can be difficult to draw. The wording of utterances can be misleading in this concern. For example, if a publication states 'In my opinion, XY committed child abuse', it would still be a statement of fact. It is the task of courts to decide on the meaning of a statement; that is, whether it is to be regarded as a statement of fact or as a value judgement. For example, in *Salumäki* v. *Finland*, the impugned article was entitled: 'The Victim of the Vantaa Homicide Had Connections with K.U. [the name of a well-known Finnish businessman]?' The Strasbourg Court followed the domestic court's finding that this title, although formulated as a question, 'created a connection between K.U. and the homicide, implying that he was involved in it'.[59] The Strasbourg Court held that the article 'contained a false insinuation and that this false insinuation was capable of causing suffering to K.U.'[60] The Court found that the newspaper violated K.U.'s presumption of innocence, and thus decided against the newspaper.

Since factual information is susceptible to proof, it can be further distinguished along the following lines:

- information that has been proven to be true;
- information that has been proven to be untrue; and
- information that has neither been proven true nor untrue.

Media law presupposes that factual information can be verified.[61] For example, proving the truth of a defamatory statement is a defence in the English law of defamation

---

[57] McAlpine v. Bercow [2013] EWHC 1342 (QB) [36].
[58] See, for instance, ECtHR, Lingens v. Austria [1986] App. no. 9815/82 [46]; De Haes and Gijsels v. Belgium [1997] App. no. 19983/92 [42]; Jerusalem v. Austria [2001] App. no. 26958/95 [42]; Steel and Morris v. United Kingdom [2005] App. no. 68416/01 [87].
[59] Salumäki v. Finland [2014] App. no. 23605/09 [57].
[60] Salumäki v. Finland [2014] App. no. 23605/09 [58].
[61] This applies not only to media law, but to the law in general. For example, in many jurisdictions the crime of fraud requires 'pretending false facts or distorting or suppressing true facts' (see Section 263 of the German Criminal Law Code).

(see Chapter 3). Since the claimant in *McAlpine* v. *Bercow* was innocent of any child abuse crime, the defendant could thus not avail herself of that defence. Moreover, Article 12(b) Data Protection Directive stipulates a right to rectify, erase or block data 'in particular because of the … inaccurate nature of the data'. In addition, false information disseminated in advertising may mislead consumers and thus be subject to penalties under the law of unfair competition (Chapter 10). Finally, the European Court of Human Rights frequently indicates that the truthfulness of a statement is an important factor when balancing conflicting interests, such as in cases of 'hate speech' (see Chapter 3). 'The truth' or 'accuracy' of information is not to be understood as an absolute truth in a philosophical sense. Rather, it is sufficient that a court – the final arbiter that the philosophical notion of truth is lacking – is convinced that a statement corresponds to reality or not.

In addition, the law attributes certain characteristics to information, for example, whether it is confidential or secret (Chapter 3) or whether data can be considered 'personal' (Chapter 8). As will be shown in Chapter 9, copyright law does not protect information as such, but rather information *expressed in original works*. This does not only include factual information and opinions, but also fictional works.

Moreover, the law assesses the perlocutory effects of utterances. As has been shown with regard to the case of *McAlpine* v. *Bercow*, the defamatory meaning of a statement is to be established according to the effect it has on recipients. Under the law of England and Wales, a publication bears a defamatory meaning if it tends to lower another in the estimation of right-thinking members of society generally,[62] is likely to injure the reputation of another by exposing him to hatred, contempt or ridicule[63] or tends to make another be shunned and avoided.[64] Similarly, domestic and international law suppress certain speech if it elicits hatred, so-called 'hate speech' (see Chapter 3).

Finally, media law assesses the public value of information. One of the most difficult tasks for a media lawyer is to assess the extent to which information contributes to a matter of public concern. This is an important factor in the balancing exercise between freedom of expression and media freedom, on the one hand, and conflicting interests (such as privacy or public order) on the other hand (Chapter 3). Similarly, EU data protection legislation asks whether personal data is, or has ceased to be, 'relevant' or not.

6 Application of these Principles to the *Jersild Case*

Media law requires a distinction to be drawn between content providers and communication intermediaries. Content providers can be journalists, the entertainment

---

[62] Sim v. Stretch [1936] 2 All ER 1237, 1240.
[63] Parmiter v. Coupland [1840] 6 M & W 105.
[64] Youssoupouff v. MGM [1934] 50 TLR 581.

media, academics, artists and other individuals or institutions. Intermediaries are booksellers, newspaper vendors, operators of broadcasting cables and satellites, transmitters and hosts of internet content. In order to analyse the *Jersild* case, we thus need to ask, first, whether Mr Jersild was a content provider or a mere intermediary of the statements of the 'Greenjackets'. The 'Greenjackets' were undoubtedly content providers. By contrast, Mr Jersild neither made the objectionable statements himself nor did he adopt them, but merely assisted in their dissemination. However, he exercised editorial control over the statements, as he edited and cut the film of the interview down to a few minutes. Therefore, he has to be regarded as a content provider and not as a mere speech intermediary.

The second question that has to be raised is whether the activities of the 'Greenjackets' and of Mr Jersild were protected under Article 10 ECHR. To a certain extent this depends on whether their contributions to the programme have to be regarded as journalistic or not, on whether their remarks contributed to a matter of general interest, and on how they conveyed their message.[65] The 'Greenjackets' were clearly not journalists. Moreover, the Strasbourg Court found that 'the remarks of the "Greenjackets" were more than insulting to members of the targeted groups and did not enjoy the protection of Article 10'.[66] By contrast, Mr Jersild acted as a television journalist. Therefore, the ECtHR drew a distinction between the statements of the interviewees and the alleged violation of the law by Mr Jersild. Regarding the latter, the Strasbourg Court noted that he knew that racist statements were likely to be made during the interview, and that he even encouraged such statements. However, the Court did not agree with the national courts that the racist speech was presented without any attempt to counterbalance the extremist views expressed. Instead, the Court emphasised the fact that the piece was broadcast as part of a serious Danish news programme and was intended for a well-informed audience. Another important factor in the Court's evaluation was whether the interview appeared to have had as its purpose the propagation of racist views and ideas.[67] The TV presenter introduced the programme by referring to a recent public debate and press comments on racism in Denmark, thus inviting the audience to see the interview in that context. Taken as a whole, the feature sought to expose, analyse and explain this particular group of youths with criminal records, violent attitudes and frustrated by their social situation, thus dealing with a matter that was of great public concern.[68] In view of the journalist's discretion as to the form of expression used, the Court did not consider the absence of precautionary reminders as to 'the immorality, dangers and unlawfulness of the promotion of racial hatred' to be relevant.[69] Probably the most important

---

[65] On the factors to be considered in this balancing exercise, see Chapter 3.
[66] Jersild v. Denmark [1994] App. no. 15890/89 [35].
[67] Jersild v. Denmark [1994] App. no. 15890/89 [31].
[68] Jersild v. Denmark [1994] App. no. 15890/89 [33].
[69] Jersild v. Denmark [1994] App. no. 15890/89 [34].

aspect in the *Jersild* case was the Court's observation that news reporting based on interviews constitutes one of the most important means whereby the media is able to play its vital role of 'public watchdog'. Therefore, 'the punishment of a journalist for assisting in the dissemination of statements made by another person in an interview would seriously hamper the contribution of the press to discuss matters of public interest and should not be envisaged unless there are particularly strong reasons for doing so'.[70]

II The Transnational, European and International Dimensions of Media Law

Apart from local newspapers and radio stations, media activity almost invariably has a transnational dimension. Copies of national newspapers are – in varying quantities – available in many countries on the globe, broadcasting most often transcends national borders, and the internet is, by its very architecture, a global medium. Hardly any other human activity reifies Marshall McLuhan's vision of a 'global village' as vividly as communication via mass media. This internationalisation and globalisation of communication necessitates a transnational approach to media law.

1 The Notion of Transnational Media Law

The Peace Treaties of Westphalia in 1648 established principles relating to respecting the boundaries of sovereign states and non-interference in their domestic affairs, which became central to the world order that developed over the following centuries.[71] As a consequence, Western legal thought has, for a considerable time, associated law with the state. In the Westphalian model, nation-states are perceived as the dominant actors, with centralised powers and clearly defined and secured borders. However, the Westphalian perspective has become too static for the postmodern international system in general and the global phenomenon of the internet in particular. The 'transnational law' approach, which has been established by Philip Jessup in his Storrs Lectures at Yale Law School,[72] transcends the Westphalian territorial fragmentation. Transnational law encompasses the 'interdisciplinary discourse about the status and role of law in an increasingly inchoate, globe-spanning web of regulatory regimes, actors, norms and processes'.[73] It challenges the dichotomies of state versus society, international versus domestic law, public versus private law and the question of what law actually *is*.[74]

---

[70] Jersild v. Denmark [1994] App. no. 15890/89 [35]; see also July and SARL Liberation v. France [2008] App. no. 20893/03 [69].

[71] An English version of the Treaty is available at http://avalon.law.yale.edu/17th_century/westphal.asp.

[72] See Jessup (1956).

[73] Zumbansen (2012, p. 900).

[74] Zumbansen (2012, pp. 901–903); K. Tuorin and S. Sankari, in Maduro et al. (2014, Introduction, pp. 17 ff).

The content of the concept of 'transnational law' is controversial. Some see it as a theory, others as a method.[75] It is not the purpose of this book to espouse a particular definition of transnational law. Instead, the notion of 'transnational media law' that is underlying this book should be understood as a *perspective* on the phenomenon of distance and mass media communication that transgresses jurisdictional boundaries. A transnational perspective on media law is commendable for several reasons. First, communication via distance and mass media often crosses national frontiers. This necessitates the development of globally applicable legal principles. The internet will inevitably lead to a rise of transnational violations of reputation and privacy, resulting in an increasingly important role of private international law and questions of pre-scriptive jurisdiction (see Chapter 4). Moreover, this book aims at institutionalising transnationally applicable standards and limitations to media communication, thus contributing to the development of a global *ordre public* for torts and crimes committed by, or against, communication media, and to a harmonisation of regulatory principles.

Second, and related to the previous point, media law transcends the international–domestic dichotomy. EU legislation, such as the E-commerce Directive and the Audiovisual Media Services Directive; the case law of international adjudicators; and the challenges media communication poses for claims of jurisdiction blur the boundaries between domestic and international law. International media law increasingly becomes domestic law, and domestic media law influences the shaping of international law. To be sure, the domestic law, such as the law of defamation, remains directly applicable. However, the interpretation and application of domestic law has to be in compliance with international human rights standards. For example: Sections 3 and 4 of the UK Defamation Act 2013 on publication on a matter of public interest and the honest comment defence have to be applied in light of Articles 8 and 10 ECHR. So, international law can be decisive in each case and even for the development of the domestic law itself. The predecessor of the publication on a matter of public interest defence, the *Reynolds* defence, had been adopted in the light of Article 10 ECHR.[76]

Third, transnational law perceives the state not as an opponent to society, but as part of society.[77] Media law likewise transcends this state–society dichotomy. For example, public broadcasters are part of the state, but they also have to be independent from other state institutions. Furthermore, media law encompasses more than the relations between states and individuals. Not only states exercise power on media activity. Rather, individuals, corporations and other private groups may have a significant influence either *on* the media sector or on other people *via* the media. Examples of the former are private bodies regulating the media sector, such as the Internet

---

[75] On the concepts and conceptions of 'transnational law', see, for example, Ehrenzweig (1968); Calliess and Zumbansen (2010); Zumbansen (2012); Maduro et al. (2014).
[76] House of Lords, Reynolds v. Times Newspapers Ltd [2001] 2 AC 127.
[77] Zumbansen (2012, p. 902).

Corporation for Assigned Names and Numbers (ICANN) or the British Board of Film Classification. An example of the latter is the violation of the rights of others by individuals on online social networks.

Fourth, media law also transcends the public–private law dichotomy. For instance, 'hate speech' in a blog may constitute both a violation of public law, including criminal law, and a tort of defamation. Moreover, human rights significantly influence the interpretation of private law especially in media law via their 'indirect horizontal effect'.[78]

Fifth, transnational law transcends the hard law–soft law dichotomy, and so does media law. The Strasbourg Court regularly emphasises that the journalistic media has to act according to the principles of 'responsible journalism' and the 'ethics of journalism'; the violation of which may justify an interference with media freedom.[79] In addition, media law is strongly influenced by the normative power of factuality, such as the very architecture of the internet, where 'code is law' (see Chapter 6).

This book will focus on two approaches to the development of a transnational media law order: the establishment of jurisdiction as an allocation of competences and responsibilities in the area of media law, and European and international media law with their tendencies to harmonise media law.

2 Jurisdiction and the Choice of the Applicable Law

Rules on jurisdiction determine which state's authorities may decide a case with a transnational dimension, a question which can occur with regard to both private law and public law. In contrast to, for instance, a car accident, a defect product or a polluted river, media activities do usually not relate to a physically visible incident, but to elusive information. As a consequence, in a media-related case there may be several different geographical locations that may be regarded as the place where the harmful event occurs, and thus as decisive to establish jurisdiction.[80] For example, the harm inflicted by the upload of defamatory material onto an online social networking site may be seen as 'occurring' in the country from which the author uploaded the material, and thus establish jurisdiction of the authorities of this country. But it may also establish jurisdiction in the country where the material could be downloaded – which means essentially every country in the world from which the social networking site is accessible. Finally, one could also argue that jurisdiction is only established in the country where the victim of the publication lives, or in which the server of the social networking site is located.

---

[78] See Chapter 2.
[79] See, for example, ECtHR, Ricci v. Italy [2013] App. no. 30210/06 [57].
[80] As will be shown later, the 'place where the harmful event occurs' is the decisive criterion to establish jurisdiction under Article 7(2) of the Brussels Ia Regulation.

In the absence of a unified transnational legal media order, rules on jurisdiction play a decisive role for the outcome of a particular case, as different legal regimes may treat the same social conflict in different ways. This fragmentation of media law regimes is to a certain degree necessary to safeguard the plurality of values underlying the legal orders of different jurisdictions. Examples that will be further dealt with in this book are the outstanding position of freedom of speech in the First Amendment to the US Constitution, on the one hand, and the European emphasis on the equal protection of the right to respect for one's private life, on the other hand. At the same time, the fragmentation of media law regimes causes legal uncertainty, which can have a chilling effect on those who wish to provide international media-based services or to publish certain material that is of public concern, but may be regarded as unlawful in some countries. For example, the statements of the 'Greenjackets' in the *Jersild* case would arguably be protected under the First Amendment, as opposed to Article 10 ECHR. A US 'Greenjacket' would thus have to think twice before publishing similar statements on an online platform when travelling through Europe.

This necessitates an international approach to media law, which examines both regional harmonisation, especially in the European Union (EU), and international convergences, fostered particularly through international conventions and institutions.

3 European Media Law

The European media law order is fed from two sources of law: the public international law of the Council of Europe, and the law of the EU. Although the latter only applies to the Member States of the EU and the EU itself is not a member to the Council of Europe,[81] the media law orders of the Council of Europe and the EU are to a huge extent interrelated. The degree of harmonisation is more advanced in the EU than in the Council of Europe, but Council of Europe Conventions and especially the case law of the European Court of Human Rights have led to broad convergences among the Member States to the Council of Europe.

a The Council of Europe

The Council of Europe aims at protecting and promoting human rights, democracy, and the rule of law through its (now some 200) conventions and other treaties, including, for instance, the Convention on Cybercrime, the Convention on the Prevention of Terrorism, the Convention against Corruption and Organised Crime, the Convention on Action against Trafficking in Human Beings, and the Convention on Human Rights and Biomedicine. The most influential convention of the Council of Europe is the ECHR, which is supervised by the ECtHR in Strasbourg. The most

---

[81] With its Opinion 2/13 the CJEU has rendered accession to the ECHR difficult, if not impossible.

relevant media-related provisions in the Convention are Article 10 ECHR protecting freedom of expression and Article 8 ECHR on the right to respect for one's private life, respectively. With its case law, the ECtHR has strongly contributed to the
European media law order.

b The European Union

The media law jurisprudence and legislation of the former European Economic
Community (EEC), now European Union (EU), is to a significant degree characterised by the EU's focus on the development of a common market rather than by the
pursuit of human rights standards. Under EU law, media goods and services had, in
the first place, been perceived as economic commodities. In the seminal *Sacchi* decision, the then-European Court of Justice (ECJ)[82] held that broadcasting of television
signals, including those in the nature of advertisements, falls within the rules of the
Treaty relating to services.[83] In *Procureur du Roi* v. *Debauve*, the ECJ included transnational transmission of broadcasting signals by cable television within the rules of
the Treaty relating to services as well.[84] Later on, however, the EEC/EU also recognised the media as a factor of public interest with implications that go far beyond the
market, such as cultural diversity, the right to information, diversity of opinion and
media plurality, the protection of minors and consumer protection.

Furthermore, it was the ECJ that introduced human rights into the Community
legal order.[85] Since then, fundamental rights have formed an integral part of the general principles of law that the Court observes.[86] The ECJ case law on freedom of
expression in particular concerned statements of EU officials[87] and the relationship
between freedom of expression and the fundamental freedoms in the now-Treaty on
the Functioning of the European Union (TFEU), with freedom of expression either
bolstering a free movement claim[88] or constituting a legitimate interest capable of
justifying a restriction on the fundamental freedoms.[89] The principles established
by the Court's case law are now reaffirmed in Article 6(3) of the Treaty on European
Union (TEU). Furthermore, the EUChFR, which has the same legal status as the

---

[82] Court of Justice of the European Union (CJEU) since the Lisbon Treaty.
[83] Case C-155/73 [1974] Sacchi [6].
[84] Case 52/79 [1980] Procureur du Roi v. Debauve and others [15]. See also Case 62/79 [1980] Coditel and
others v. Ciné Vog Films and others ('Coditel I'): assignment of copyright limited to the territory of a
Member State is capable of constituting a restriction on freedom to provide services.
[85] The first decisions were Case 35/67 [1968] van Eick v. Commission and Case 29/69 [1969] Stauder v. City
of Ulm.
[86] See, for example, Case C-260/89 [1991] ERT v. DEP and others [41]; Case C-112/00 [2003] Schmidberger
v. Austria [71].
[87] Case C-156/96P [1997] Calvin Williams v. Court of Auditors; Case C-274/99P [2001] Connolly; see also
Case C-100/88 [1989] Oyowe and Traore v. Commission [16].
[88] Case C-159/90 [1991] Grogan [26]; Case C-260/89 [1991] ERT v. DEP and others [43]; Case C-219/91
[1992] Ter Voort [38]; Case C-368/95 [1997] Familiapress v. Heinrich Bauer Verlag [24]; Case C-71/02
[2004] Herbert Karner Industrie-Auktionen GmbH v. Troostwijk GmbH [50].
[89] Case C-112/00 [2003] Schmidberger v. Austria [74].

Treaties, has brought significant change with regard to human rights protection in the EU. Particularly remarkable is Article 11(2) EUChFR which protects freedom and pluralism of the media; a landmark in international media law.

4 International Media Law

Media law is harmonised to a much lesser degree on the global level than on the European level, thus leaving more space for transnational legal conflicts. The starting point for the analysis of a developing global media law order are Articles 19 and 12 of the Universal Declaration of Human Rights (UDHR),[90] protecting freedom of expression, on the one hand, and the right to respect for privacy, honour and reputation, on the other hand. The UDHR has been adopted as a declaration rather than an international treaty and is therefore not legally binding. However, in the preamble, governments commit themselves and their people to progressive measures that secure the universal and effective recognition and observance of the human rights set out in the Declaration, and the rights enumerated in the Declaration have acquired the status of customary international law.[91] The human rights enshrined in the UDHR have been further developed in subsequent international treaties, regional human rights instruments and national constitutions, and have served as the foundation for the ICCPR, the International Covenant on Economic, Social and Cultural Rights (ICESCR) and other international treaties.[92]

The ICCPR is monitored by the Human Rights Committee. The most relevant media-related provisions in the ICCPR are Article 19 on freedom of expression; Article 17 on the right to privacy, honour and reputation; and Article 20 requiring the prohibition of '[a]ny propaganda for war' and '[a]ny advocacy of national, racial or religious hatred that constitutes incitement to discrimination, hostility or violence'. A number of State Parties to the ICCPR have made reservations to, and interpretative declarations on, their application of the Covenant. Reservations to Article 19 ICCPR are, fortunately, relatively uncommon.[93] Some State Parties that are also members of the ECHR have included the reservation that Article 19 ICCPR shall be applied in accordance with Articles 10 and 11 ECHR.[94] Furthermore, some State Parties, including the USA, have made reservations regarding Article 20 ICCPR, holding this provision incompatible with, or at least endangering, freedom of speech.[95]

---

[90] Adopted by the United Nations General Assembly on 10 December 1948 in Paris.
[91] De Schutter (2010, p. 50), with further references.
[92] For example, the International Convention on the Elimination of All Forms of Racial Discrimination, the International Convention on the Elimination of Discrimination Against Women, the United Nations Convention on the Rights of the Child or the United Nations Convention Against Torture.
[93] See Keller (2011, pp. 210–212).
[94] Such as Belgium and France.
[95] States having made a reservation to Article 20 ICCPR also include Australia and Finland.

Another important contributor to a global media law order is the World Trade Organization (WTO), which supervises and liberalises international trade. The WTO was established in Marrakesh in April 1994 by the Agreement Establishing the World Trade Organization with Understanding on the Rules and Procedures Governing the Settlement of Disputes and Trade Policy Review Mechanism (hereinafter WTO Agreement), replacing the General Agreement on Tariffs and Trade (GATT) of 1947. The WTO's main functions are to liberalise trade by providing a forum for governments to negotiate trade agreements and settle trade disputes (Article III WTO Agreement). The current set of rules, including the revised GATT, the General Agreement on Trade in Services (GATS) and the Agreement on Trade-Related Aspects of Intellectual Property Rights (TRIPS), was the outcome of the 1986–1994 Uruguay Round negotiations. Similar to the early years of the European Economic Community, the WTO's contribution to media law has in the first place been focused on communication media as an economic factor, not as an instrument to realise human rights.

III Questions

1 Does the Strasbourg Court's case law in *Fatullayev* v. *Azerbaijan*, *Růžový panter, o.s.* v. *Czech Republic* and *Braun* v. *Poland* reveal a tendency towards the 'press-as-technology' model?
2 Is the distinction between content providers and mere intermediaries still defensible? To what extent has the digitalisation of communication blurred this distinction, or even made it impossible?
3 To what extent is the distinction between journalistic media and non-journalistic publishers still defensible? Should this distinction make any legal difference?

Fundamental Rights and Principles

CASE EXAMPLE

Interbrew, a Belgian brewing company, asked its investment bank advisers for a work on a potential association between Interbrew and South African Breweries plc (SAB), with a view to a possible takeover bid for SAB by Interbrew. The advisers produced a presentation and submitted it to Interbrew. The document was confidential and contained data that were likely to affect both Interbrew and SAB's share prices.

X, whose identity is unknown, sent a copy of the document to various news media organisations, including the *Financial Times*. The copy sent by X was almost identical to the original presentation, except for the following: it replaced the offer price for SAB shares of between 500 and 650 pence with a price between 400 and 550 pence; moreover, X's copy contained a timetable for making the offer that was not included in the original document.

The *Financial Times* contacted representatives from the investment bank and from Interbrew and told them that it had received the document and that it intended to publish it. The *Financial Times* subsequently published an article stating that Interbrew had been plotting a bid for SAB. The article did not state the proposed offer price but gave accurate codenames used for the advisers in the presentation and quoted from the document on the likely positive market reaction and with reference to potential rival bids. The impact of this press coverage on the market in shares of Interbrew and SAB was significant. Interbrew's share price fell, while the SAB share price rose.

Interbrew subsequently launched proceedings against the *Financial Times* in the High Court in order to establish X's identity and to bring claims for damages against X. Since the *Financial Times* itself was not aware of the identity of X, Interbrew lodged a claim for disclosure of the document received by the *Financial Times* from X. The High Court granted the application. The *Financial Times* complained that the decision of the High Court violated its right to freedom of expression.

(Based on ECtHR, Financial Times Ltd and others v.
United Kingdom [2009] App. no. 821/03)

I Introduction

This chapter provides a general overview on the fundamental rights and freedoms of those involved in the communication process via mass media. Based on the categories developed in Chapter 1, it distinguishes between the freedoms of content providers, intermediaries (media in a technological sense) and recipients. The rights of the intermediaries and of the recipients are not identical with those of the content providers, but to a large extent dependent on them. However, the provider of content enjoys particularly strong freedom of expression protection. Moreover, among those content providers, a distinction needs to be made between the journalistic media and non-journalistic individuals and entities.

The chapter will show that international conventions and their interpretation have led to the establishment of certain minimum standards for freedom of expression and media freedom, especially in Europe. However, due to the global divergences of values underlying freedom of expression and conflicting interests and the margin of appreciation that international adjudicators grant to Member States, the development of a transnational legal order of communication-related fundamental rights is still inchoate. Where media law regimes are fragmented, rules on jurisdiction and conflict of laws maintain their significance (see Chapter 4).

II The Legal Frameworks

The fundamental principles underlying the transnational media law order derive essentially from two sources: the economic dimension and the human rights dimension of communicative action. The human rights protection of expression was codified on an international level in the early post-WWII period. The applicable freedom of expression provisions will be explained in the first subsection. But communicative action may also have an economic dimension. Insofar as media services have a transnational character and are provided for remuneration, they participate in the economic freedoms underlying systems of international economic integration. These are regional systems of integration, such as the internal market of the EU, the North American Free Trade Agreement (NAFTA) and the Association of Southeast Asian Nations (ASEAN), as well as the global WTO. The EU's internal market and the WTO regime will be the focus of the second part of this section.

This dichotomy reflects the nature of the free flow of information as both a commercial commodity subject to international economic law (such as free movement provisions, state aid law, and competition law), and as a public good necessary for a democratic society and for individual self-fulfilment, and therefore protected by human rights. But the economic dimension and the human rights dimension should not be regarded in isolation. In the EU, the provisions on economic integration have been conceptualised to take on board the significance of media services for a democratic society. This has led to an integration of human rights concerns in the economic dimension of an integrated media market. Article 6(3) TEU expressly provides that fundamental rights, as guaranteed by the ECHR and as they result from the constitutional traditions common to the Member States, shall constitute general principles of EU law.

These are not just dead letters but an expression of the ECJ's practice: not only in its case law on media services does the European Court of Justice regularly refer to the case law from Strasbourg.[1] In addition, free movement provisions are structurally similar to human rights. Both prohibit unjustified interferences with their substantive guarantees. This has also led to a convergence of legal doctrines, such as the similar application of the principle of proportionality. Yet there are also differences: in contrast to human rights, the free movement provisions of the TFEU do not apply to activities whose relevant elements are confined within a single Member State.[2] Moreover, the free movement provisions only apply to economic activities; that is, activities provided for remuneration. Human rights, however, apply to all human beings within a particular jurisdiction.

By contrast to the EU, the integration of human rights into the economic framework is less developed within the WTO system. Unlike the European Court of Human Rights, the UN Human Rights Committee has not yet been able to provide a substantial body of human rights-related case law that could buttress the WTO Dispute Settlement Body's adjudication. Nevertheless, there have been tentative attempts by the WTO Appellate Body to integrate general principles of public international law into its adjudication. The WTO Appellate Body has acknowledged that the WTO rules are 'not to be read in clinical isolation from public international law'.[3] However, the WTO rules governing the settlements of disputes restrict the Body's competence to add to or diminish the rights and obligations provided in the WTO agreements.[4]

1 The Human Rights Framework

The main documents in the international human rights framework are the UN Universal Declaration of Human Rights (UDHR) and the ICCPR, both of which protect freedom of expression in their Article 19. Additionally, the ECHR guarantees freedom of expression in its Article 10 ECHR. Article 11(1) EUChFR corresponds to the first two sentences in Article 10(1) ECHR. Moreover, Article 11(2) EUChFR provides that the freedom and pluralism of the media shall be respected. In contrast to Article 11(1), Article 11(2) EUChFR does not have a directly equivalent provision in the ECHR. Yet the Explanations to the Charter indicate that 'Article 11', and not only Article 11(1), 'corresponds to Article 10 [ECHR]'.[5] The Explanations to the

---

[1] See, for example, ECJ, Case C-368/95 [1995] Familiapress v. Heinrich Bauer Verlag [26].
[2] ECJ, Case 52/79 [1980] Procureur du Roi v. Debauve and others [8].
[3] United States – Standards for Reformulated and Conventional Gasoline [1996] WT/DS2/AB/R, p. 17.
[4] Article 3(2) of the WTO Understanding on Rules and Procedures Governing the Settlement of Disputes; see Keller (2011, pp. 153–155).
[5] Declaration concerning the explanations relating to the Charter of Fundamental Rights of 16 December 2004, C-310, p. 432.

Charter further state that 'Paragraph 2 … spells out the consequences of paragraph 1 regarding freedom of the media, in particular on Court of Justice case law regarding television, particularly in *Stichting Collectieve Antennevoorziening Gouda*,[6] on the Protocol on the system of public broadcasting in the Member States annexed to the [TFEU][7] and on Council Directive 89/552/EEC'.[8]

In order to conceptualise Article 11 EUChFR, account must thus be taken of three factors. First, pursuant to Article 52(3) EUChFR, the meaning and scope of the rights stipulated in Article 11 EUChFR are the same as those guaranteed by the 'corresponding' Article 10 ECHR. Therefore, the case law of the ECtHR on Article 10 ECHR has to be considered, which the ECJ has already done in the past.[9] If not otherwise indicated, the remarks on the ECHR made in this book therefore equally apply to the interpretation of Article 11(1) EUChFR. Second, when construing Article 11(2) EUChFR, regard must be had to the EU documents cited in the Explanations to the Charter, that is, the Protocol on the system of public broadcasting in the Member States and Directive 89/552/EEC, which is now codified in the Audiovisual Media Services Directive (AVMS Directive).[10] Still, as secondary law, the AVMS Directive must in itself be in accordance with Article 11(2) EUChFR, and not vice versa. The Directive itself partly serves to codify the ECJ case law on TV broadcasting.[11] The third factor to be taken into consideration in order to conceptualise Article 11 EUChFR is the ECJ case law on television.[12]

Human rights and fundamental freedoms are binding on all branches of the state (executive, legislative and judicial) and all parts of federal states. The state is accountable for acts of all its organs, agents and servants, irrespective of their rank.[13] This includes private bodies if a state holds a dominant stake of such an entity or if they exercise elements of governmental authority.[14] Important examples in media law are domestic non-governmental organisations under a statutory requirement to classify

---

[6] ECJ, Case C-288/89 [1991] Stichting Collectieve Antennevoorziening Gouda and others v. Commissariaat voor de Media.

[7] See now Protocol (No. 29) on the system of public broadcasting in the Member States.

[8] Declaration concerning the explanations relating to the Charter of Fundamental Rights of 16 December 2004, C-310, p. 433.

[9] See, for example, ECJ, Case C-274/99P [2001] Connolly [40]; Case C-219/91 [1992] Ter Voort [38]; Case C-368/95 [1997] Familiapress v. Heinrich Bauer Verlag [26].

[10] Directive 2010/13/EU of the European Parliament and of the Council of 10 March 2010 on the coordination of certain provisions laid down by law, regulation or administrative action in Member States concerning the provision of audiovisual media services (Audiovisual Media Services Directive), OJ L 95/1.

[11] See Recitals 35, 40, 41 and 43 of the Directive.

[12] See Chapter 5.

[13] ECtHR, Wille v. Liechtenstein [1999] App. no. 28396/95 [46]. See, for example, Ageyevy v. Russia [2013] App. no. 7075/10 [174]: hospital under the authority of the Department of Healthcare of the City of Moscow.

[14] See International Law Commission, Articles on Responsibility of States for Internationally Wrongful Acts, Report of the International Law Commission on the Work of Its Fifty-third Session, 2001 (A/56/10), Articles 5 and 8.

videos, DVDs or video games, such as the British Board of Film Classification.[15] Furthermore, human rights place the state under obligations even when acting on the basis of private law.[16]

An interference with human rights is any impairment through the exercise of official authority, pressure or force.[17] First, an interference with freedom of expression may consist of any *legal* act against a particular publication, including administrative regulations or judicial decisions, such as prohibitions, civil or criminal liability. Second, the notion of interference also covers more subtle restrictions. Any direct or indirect *factual* restriction thus constitutes an interference too. Media-related examples from case law are attempts to uncover journalistic sources by search or seizure; abuse of control over equipment used in the dissemination of information; arbitrary and discriminatory granting of public subsidies or privileges, such as the placement of advertisements;[18] travel constraints for journalists;[19] the blocking of internet sites;[20] confiscation of journalistic equipment;[21] reprimands or dismissals;[22] obligations to publish a reply, an apology or a counterstatement;[23] the revocation of the citizenship of the director of a media outlet as a consequence of its editorial point of view;[24] harassment and intimidation;[25] and official statements creating a media-hostile environment.[26]

Moreover, a state must not only negatively abstain from interfering with human rights; the beneficiaries of these guarantees may also be entitled to positive state action in order to secure their rights and freedoms.[27] The obligation to protect is

[15] See ECtHR, Wingrove v. United Kingdom [1996] App. no. 17419/90 [36]; Human Rights Committee, Hertzberg and others v. Finland [1985] Communication no. 61/1979 [9.1].

[16] ECtHR, Vereinigung demokratischer Soldaten Österreichs and Gubi v. Austria [1994] App. no. 15153/89 [27].

[17] Oster (2015b, pp. 103–104).

[18] Office of the Special Rapporteur for Freedom of Expression with the Inter-American Commission on Human Rights, Inter-American Legal Framework Regarding the Right to Freedom of Expression, 2009, CIDH/RELE/INF. 2/09, para. 96.

[19] Human Rights Committee, Marques de Morais v. Angola [2005] Communication no. 1128/2002 [6.8]; Concluding observations on Democratic People's Republic of Korea (CCPR/CO/72/PRK), para. 23.

[20] ECtHR, Yıldırım v. Turkey [2012] App. no. 3111/10 [55].

[21] IAComHR, Oscar Elías Biscet and others v. Cuba [2006] Case 12.476 [211].

[22] See, for example, ECtHR, Wille v. Liechtenstein [1999] App. no. 28396/95 [50]; Fuentes Bobo v. Spain [2000] App. no. 39293/98 [38]; Steur v. Netherlands [2003] App. no. 39657/98 [29]; Frankowicz v. Poland [2008] App. no. 53025/99 [44]; Wojtas-Kaleta v. Poland [2009] App. no. 20436/02 [44]; Voorhoof and Humblet (2014, p. 3).

[23] See, for example, EComHR, Ediciones Tiempo S.A. v. Spain [1989] App. no. 13010/87, p. 253; ECtHR, Kaperzyński v. Poland [2012] App. no. 43206/07 [66]; from academic literature, see Ó Fathaigh (2012).

[24] IACtHR, Ivcher-Bronstein v. Peru [2001] Case 11.762 [152].

[25] See, for example, Human Rights Committee, Concluding observations on Uzbekistan (CCPR/CO/83/UZB), para. 20; Concluding observations on the Russian Federation (CCPR/CO/79/RUS), para. 22; Concluding observations on Guyana (CCPR/CO/79/Add.121), para. 19.

[26] IACtHR, Ríos and others v. Venezuela [2009] Case 12.441 [122]; IAComHR, Perozo and others v. Venezuela [2009] Case 12.442 [160].

[27] Oster (2015b, pp. 93 ff).

engaged in the following three situations: first, where individuals need to be protected from harming themselves; second, where individuals need to be protected from being attacked by others; and third, where the state has to enable individuals to exercise their rights in the first place.[28] A state violates its obligation to secure media freedom, for instance, where it does not protect journalists from threats and acts of violence as they carry out their journalistic work, and if it does not duly, promptly and exhaustively investigate such acts when they occur.[29] On the other hand, those affected by publications of others also have a right to be protected against interferences with their rights to reputation and privacy vis-à-vis the state.[30]

Human rights principally do not have a direct effect between individuals; they are not actionable *per se* between private parties. Human rights are not rules stipulating conditions for actionable claims, such as the right to damages or injunctions. As a consequence, the proposal to establish human rights between private individuals, such as a catalogue of 'human rights in cyberspace', is well intended, but does not add anything to existing doctrine. And the existing doctrine is sufficiently able to cope with the human rights challenges in cyberspace.

Human rights doctrine distinguishes between the direct and the indirect horizontal effect of human rights. Only in those few cases in which a human rights catalogue itself provides that certain rights apply between private individuals, are those human rights directly applicable.[31] Although human rights are, apart from those few exceptions, basically not *directly* applicable, they influence the interpretation and application of pre-existing law in a trial between private individuals.[32] In short, they may have an *indirect* horizontal effect. The legislator as creator of private law and the courts as adjudicators are obliged to protect individuals from fellow citizens within the private law order.[33] Examples are intrusions on the privacy and reputation of other individuals, or the reconciliation of the conflict between the right to disseminate information and intellectual property rights. The balancing of those conflicting principles may be accomplished either by interpreting existing private law rules in light of fundamental rights, or even through the extension of existing private law rules.[34] An example of

---

[28] See, for example, Human Rights Committee, Concluding observations on the Russian Federation (CCPR/CO/79/RUS), para. 22; Concluding observations on Sri Lanka (CCPR/CO/79/LKA), para. 18; General Comment no. 34, para. 32; General Comment no. 31, para. 8.

[29] See, for example, ECtHR, Özgür Gündem v. Turkey [2000] App. no. 23144/93 [38 ff]; UN Commission on Human Rights, Report of the Special Rapporteur on the promotion and protection of the right to freedom of opinion and expression, Mr Abid Hussain, submitted pursuant to Commission Resolution 1997/27, E/CN.4/1998/40/Add.1, para. 28.

[30] See, for example, ECtHR, Pfeifer v. Austria [2007] App. no. 12556/03 [35]; Petrina v. Romania [2008] App. no. 78060/01 [29].

[31] Article 13(3) and Article 14 ACHR of the American Convention on Human Rights (ACHR) are such directly actionable private law claims; see Oster (2015b, pp. 105–106). The same applies to Article 8(2)2 EUChFR, if the data controller is a private entity (see Chapter 8).

[32] See Oster (2015b, pp. 105 ff), providing further references.

[33] Oster (2015b, p. 106).

[34] Oster (2015b, pp. 106–107).

the former is the interpretation of open statutory clauses, such as 'morality' or 'public policy', in a human rights-friendly way.[35] An example of the latter is the particularly common law-based approach to extend or enrich existing rules with human rights-compatible components, such as the – now codified – *Reynolds* defence in the tort of defamation, or the considerable expansion of breach of confidence claims with a view to misuse of private information.[36]

The doctrine of indirect horizontal effect blurs the public–private law distinction, and with good reason: threats posed by private actors are equally as harmful as state action. Examples from media law are violations of intellectual property rights, the misuse of personal data by online companies, media intrusion into one's private sphere or the interests affected by the administration of bottleneck infrastructures by private actors, such as electronic communication networks or the DNS system by ICANN.[37]

2 *The Economic Rights Frameworks*

Systems of international economic integration, such as the EU's internal market and the WTO's free trade agreements, envisage media services primarily as economic products that participate in international economic integration and trade liberalisation. There are nonetheless significant differences between the EU and the WTO. The EU with its Economic and Monetary Union, which presupposes an internal market, is a further progressed system of international economic integration.[38] As such, it encompasses free trade, a customs union with a common commercial policy, a common market with free mobility of the factors of economic production, and even a partly common monetary policy. The EU thus pursues positive market integration, that is, not only the abolition of measures impeding trade between the Member States, but the creation of a single market based on harmonised regulation under the auspices of supranational institutions. The WTO, by contrast, is a system of negative international economic integration; that is, it merely requires participating states to abolish impediments to trade, in this case measures that discriminate between domestic and foreign products.[39] In short, measures that impede trade but apply to domestic and foreign products and services alike are problematic under EU law, but do not fall

---

[35] See German Federal Constitutional Court, Case 1 BvR 400/51 [1958] 'Lüth' with a view to the interpretation of Section 826 of the German Civil Law Code (Intentional damage contrary to public policy) in light of the fundamental right to freedom of opinion, Article 5 Basic Law.

[36] With regard to the '*Reynolds* defence', see House of Lords, Reynolds v. Times Newspapers Ltd [2001] 2 AC 127; Jameel v. Wall Street Journal Europe [2006] UKHL 44; now Section 4 Defamation Act 2013. On the extension of breach of confidence, see House of Lords, Campbell v. MGN [2004] UKHL 22; OBG Ltd. and others v. Allan and others [2007] UKHL 21.

[37] On ICANN and human rights, see Zalnieriute and Schneider (2014).

[38] On the stages of international economic integration, see El-Agraa (2011, pp. 1–2).

[39] The distinction between negative and positive international economic integration had been developed by Tinbergen (1954).

under the auspices of the WTO. Finally, by contrast to the free movement provisions of the TFEU, the WTO obligations do not confer rights on individuals or companies.[40]

a The Internal Market Provisions of the TFEU

According to Article 26(2) TFEU, the internal market shall comprise an area without internal frontiers in which the free movement of goods, persons, services and capital is ensured in accordance with the provisions of the Treaties. Of particular relevance for media communication are the free movement of goods and the freedom to provide services, as protected in Articles 34 and 56 TFEU, respectively. Moreover, media undertakings participate in the freedom of establishment, guaranteed in Article 49 TFEU. Finally, investment in media companies is protected by the free movement of capital, Article 63 TFEU.[41]

Whether information is protected as a 'good' or 'service' depends on its method of transmission. Information disseminated via intangible means have been considered as 'services': radio and TV broadcasting signals and the transmission of those signals via cable networks.[42] Moreover, the ECJ also regarded the publication of advertisements for which the content provider and/or the transmitter received remuneration as a service.[43] Tangible assets containing information, such as newspapers, CDs, DVDs and video cassettes, are 'goods' within the meaning of Article 34 TFEU.[44]

The TFEU entails, first, an abolition of any discrimination of goods or services because of their country of origin. National rules that discriminate between goods or services for reason of their origin are compatible with EU law only if they are justified by an express exemption, such as Articles 36 and 62 in conjunction with Article 52 TFEU.[45] Merely economic aims cannot constitute grounds of public policy within the meaning of these provisions.[46] Second, an interference with the freedoms guaranteed by the Treaty may arise from the application of indistinctly applicable rules; that is, rules that do not discriminate between goods or services because of their origin but that affect any product in the jurisdiction.[47] As the Court of Justice established in *Cassis de Dijon*, such restrictions need to be justified by overriding reasons relating to the public interest and they have to be proportionate.[48] Overriding reasons relating

---

[40] See ECJ, Joined Cases 21–24/72 [1972] International Fruit Company NV [27], in contrast to ECJ, Case 26/62 [1963] van Gend en Loos, p. 13.

[41] See, *mutatis mutandis*, ECJ, Case C-148/91 [1993] Veronica Omroep v. Commissariaat voor de Media [15].

[42] ECJ, Case C-155/73 [1974] Sacchi [6]; Joined Cases C-544/03 and C-545/03 [2005] Mobistar and Belgacom [26 ff].

[43] See, for example, ECJ, Case 352/85 [1988] Bond van Adverteerders v. Netherlands [16]; Joined Cases C-34/95, C-35/95 and C-36/95 [1997] De Agostini (Svenska) Förlag AB and others [48].

[44] ECJ, Joined Cases 60 and 61/84 [1985] Cinéthèque; Case C-368/95 [1995] Familiapress v. Heinrich Bauer Verlag.

[45] See, for example, ECJ, Case 352/85 [1988] Bond van Adverteerders v. Netherlands [32].

[46] ECJ, Case 352/85 [1988] Bond van Adverteerders v. Netherlands [34].

[47] ECJ, Case 8/74 [1974] Dassonville.

[48] ECJ, Case 120/78 [1979] Rewe v. Bundesmonopolverwaltung für Branntwein ('Cassis de Dijon') [8].

to the public interest that are relevant for the media include, for example: protection of intellectual property;[49] consumer protection;[50] the conservation of the national historic and artistic heritage;[51] and the widest possible dissemination of knowledge of the artistic and cultural heritage of a country.[52] Moreover, according to Article 167(1) TFEU, the EU 'shall contribute to the flowering of the cultures of the Member States, while respecting their national and regional diversity and at the same time bringing the common cultural heritage to the fore'. Article 167(4) TFEU requires the Union to take cultural aspects into account in its action under other provisions of that Treaty, in particular in order to respect and promote the diversity of its cultures. A cultural policy, such as the safeguarding of media pluralism, may therefore also constitute an overriding requirement relating to the general interest that justifies a restriction on the free movement of provisions.[53]

Third, according to the formula established in *Keck and Mithouard*, national measures restricting or prohibiting certain selling arrangements are not to be regarded as an interference, 'so long as those provisions apply to all relevant traders operating within the national territory and so long as they affect in the same manner, in law and in fact, the marketing of domestic products and of those from other Member States'.[54] The distinction between such mere selling requirements, which do not constitute an interference, and product-related requirements, which require justification, is particularly problematic with regard to restrictions on advertising. In *Leclerc-Siplec*, the Court held that legislation that prohibits a particular form of promotion (televised advertising) of a particular method of marketing products (distribution) concerns selling arrangements.[55] However, in *De Agostini*, the Court held that 'it cannot be excluded that an outright ban [on television advertising], applying in one Member State, of a type of promotion for a product which is lawfully sold there might have a greater impact on products from other Member States'.[56] This is even more relevant if television advertising is the only effective form of promotion enabling a product to penetrate a particular market. Therefore, an outright ban on advertising is to be considered a selling arrangement only if it is shown that the ban affects in the same way, in fact and in law, the marketing of national products and of products from other Member States.[57]

---

[49] ECJ, Case 62/79 [1980] Coditel and others v. Ciné Vog Films and others ('Coditel I') [15]; see Chapter 9.

[50] See, for example, ECJ, Case C-288/89 [1991] Collectieve Antennevoorziening Gouda [14]; Joined Cases C-34/95, C-35/95 and C-36/95 [1997] De Agostini (Svenska) Förlag AB and others [53].

[51] See ECJ, Case C-180/89 [1991] Commission v. Italy [20].

[52] ECJ, Case C-154/89 [1991] Commission v. France [17]; C-198/89 [1991] Commission v. Greece [21].

[53] ECJ, Case C-368/95 [1995] Familiapress v. Heinrich Bauer Verlag [18]; Case C-353/89 [1991] Commission v. Netherlands [30]; Case C-250/06 [2007] United Pan-Europe Communications Belgium SA and others v. Belgium and others [41].

[54] ECJ, Joined Cases C-267/91 and C-268/91 [1993] Keck and Mithouard [16].

[55] ECJ, Case C-412/93 [1995] Leclerc-Siplec v. TFI and M6 [22].

[56] ECJ, Joined Cases C-34/95, C-35/95 and C-36/95 [1997] De Agostini (Svenska) Förlag AB and others [42].

[57] ECJ, Joined Cases C-34/95, C-35/95 and C-36/95 [1997] De Agostini (Svenska) Förlag AB and others [44].

Freedom of expression and the free movement provisions of the TFEU may therefore interact in three ways:

1 The liberty to publish may align with a free movement claim. For example, in the case *Familiapress* v. *Heinrich Bauer Verlag*, Austrian law prohibited press periodicals from inviting consumers to take part in prize draw competitions.[58] Familiapress GmbH, an Austrian newspaper publisher, brought proceedings against Heinrich Bauer Verlag, a newspaper publisher established in Germany, asking the latter to cease selling publications in Austria offering readers the chance to take part in games for prizes. The ECJ observed that the Austrian prohibition did not only have to be compatible with the free movement of goods, but also with Heinrich Bauer Verlag's freedom of expression, as protected in Article 10 ECHR.

2 Freedom of expression or the need to safeguard domestic media pluralism may justify an interference with a free movement claim. For example, in the *Familiapress* case, the ECJ also advised the referring Austrian court that both Heinrich Bauer Verlag's freedom of expression and the free movement of goods permit derogations for the purposes of maintaining press diversity. The Austrian court thus had to establish, first, whether newspapers offering games of chance were competing with small newspapers, which were unable to offer comparable prizes and, second, whether the offering of those games brought about a shift in demand.

3 In the EU, economic rights themselves have become human rights. The main example is the freedom to conduct a business according to Article 16 EUChFR. While content providers' freedom of expression and media freedom usually eclipses economic human rights, the latter are particularly important for speech intermediaries. Burdensome obligations on internet service providers to monitor or block certain content do not only have to be measured against their freedom to provide services and their right to impart information under Article 11(1) EUChFR, but also have to be justified in light of their freedom to conduct a business.

Article 114 TFEU and Article 62 in conjunction with 52(2) TFEU provide the necessary competences for the EU to adopt legislation harmonising the markets for media services. Based on these provisions (or their predecessors), the EU has adopted, in particular, the Audiovisual Media Services Directive (AVMS Directive) and the Directive on Electronic Commerce (E-commerce Directive). However, when adopting legislation in the field of media services, the EU institutions have to take into consideration Article 167 TFEU. According to this provision, the EU has to respect the Member States' national and regional diversity and shall take cultural aspects into account in its action under other provisions of the Treaties, in particular in order to respect and to promote the diversity of its cultures. As far as the regulation of media content is concerned, the EU is thus only entitled to minimum harmonisation, as has

---

[58] ECJ, Case C-368/95 [1995] Familiapress v. Heinrich Bauer Verlag.

happened with the AVMS and the E-commerce Directive (see Chapters 5 and 6). In contrast, as far as the regulation of media transmission technology is concerned, the EU may fully harmonise the internal market (see Chapter 7).

In non-harmonised areas of media law, EU primary law, including the fundamental freedoms, remains applicable. Trade in products used for television broadcasting, such as DVDs, newspapers, magazines, books and CDs, is therefore subject to the rules on the free movement of goods,[59] while radio broadcasting and online gambling[60] are 'services' within the meaning of Articles 56, 57 TFEU.

b The WTO

The WTO trade regime is aimed at mere negative harmonisation by abolishing discrimination, but not positive integration through harmonisation, as is the case in the EU.[61] The distinction between the applicability of the GATS and of the GATT to the media is similar to the distinction between goods and services under the TFEU. The GATT covers tangible goods, such as newspapers, CDs and DVDs.[62] Information disseminated via intangible electronic transmission, such as broadcasting, is considered a service falling under the GATS. The same applies to the services transmitting this information. The exhibition of cinematographic works, although technically a service, is expressly mentioned in Article IV GATT 1994. But since it is a service, it also falls under the GATS regime.

Unlike the GATT, the GATS does not require across-the-board liberalisation. Instead, its disciplines only apply to those service sectors in which member states have made specific commitments. For example, by contrast to the US, the EU has not scheduled a commitment to free trade audiovisual services. Audiovisual services belong to those sectors in which the number of WTO members with commitments is the lowest.[63]

The basic WTO principles are the most-favoured-nation (MFN) principle, the national treatment obligation, the prohibition of quotas and other quantitative restrictions, and the transparency of instruments that restrict trade. Trade liberalisation on an MFN basis means that the lowest tariff applicable to one member must be extended

---

[59] ECJ, Case C-155/73 [1974] Sacchi [7]; Case C-260/89 [1991] ERT v. DEP and others [14]. For example, in Joined Cases 60 and 61/84 [1985] Cinéthèque, the ECJ held that an indistinctly applicable regulation ensuring the priority use in cinemas of cinematographic works of any origin in relation to other methods of broadcasting is compatible with the free movement of goods. With regard to the distribution of magazines, see Case C-368/95 [1997] Familiapress v. Heinrich Bauer Verlag.

[60] See ECJ, Case C-243/01 [2003] Gambelli; Joined Cases C-338/04, C-359/04 and C 360/04 [2007] Placanica; Case C-260/04 [2007] Commission v. Italy; Case C-42/07 [2009] Liga Portuguesa de Futebol Profissional and Bwin International; Case C-203/08 [2010] Sporting Exchange Ltd, trading as 'Betfair'; Case C-258/08 [2010] Ladbrokes Betting & Gaming and Ladbrokes International.

[61] Keller (2011, p. 152).

[62] See WTO Appellate Body, Canada – Certain measures concerning periodicals [1997] WT/DS31/AB/R.

[63] As of January 2009 there were only 30 commitments (www.wto.org/english/tratop_e/serv_e/audiovisual_e/audiovisual_e.htm).

to all members (Article I GATT, Article II GATS). This does not, however, apply to regional and bilateral trade agreements, such as the EU and NAFTA (Article XXIV GATT, Article V GATS). The national treatment obligation describes the absence of discrimination between foreign and domestic goods, services and, as far as services are concerned, also the service providers themselves (Article III GATT, Article XVII GATS). Related to this point, the WTO commitments prohibit quotas and other quantitative restrictions (Article XI GATT, Article XVI GATS). The WTO system is thus based on merely negative economic integration; that is, the absence of impediments on trade between participating nations, in this case in the form of discrimination. Yet the notion of discrimination is rather broad, encompassing discrimination both in law and in fact.[64] Therefore, restrictions intended to protect the cultural or social character of the domestic media are likely to violate the WTO obligations.[65] However, discrimination may be excluded from the WTO obligations by the exception provisions in Article XX GATT and Article XIV GATS. Of particular significance for the media are the public morals exceptions in Article XX(a) GATT and Article XIV(a) GATS. Notably, by contrast to the GATT, the GATS also provides a public order caveat in Article XIV(a). This exception may be invoked 'where a genuine and sufficiently serious threat is posed to one of the fundamental interests of society'.[66] The public order exception might develop into a gateway to take on board media-specific issues, such as the need to protect domestic media pluralism.[67] As the GATT lacks such an exception, China once employed a broad interpretation of the 'public morals' exception in Article XX(a) GATT in order to justify restrictions on the import of audiovisual products, sound recordings and publications – but to no avail.[68]

In the *United States – Gambling* case, the WTO Dispute Settlement Body had to decide on a complaint by Antigua and Barbuda regarding US federal and state prohibitions of online betting and gambling services that affected the cross-border supply of such services. According to Antigua and Barbuda, the measures at issue were inconsistent with the US obligations under the GATS. However, the Appellate Body accepted that these measures were 'necessary to protect public morals or to maintain public order' within the meaning of Article XIV(a) GATS. Acts adopted to address concerns such as those pertaining to money laundering, organised crime, fraud, underage gambling and pathological gambling served to protect public morals and/or to maintain public order within the meaning of Article XIV(a).[69]

---

[64] See, for example, WTO Panel, Japan – Taxes on alcoholic beverages [1996] WT/DS8/AB/R, WT/DS10/AB/R and WT/DS11/AB/R [6.33–6.34].

[65] Keller (2011, p. 155); see WTO Appellate Body, Canada – Certain measures concerning periodicals [1997] WT/DS31/AB/R.

[66] Fn. 5 to Article XIV GATS.

[67] See Keller (2011, pp. 441–442).

[68] See WTO Appellate Body, China – Measures Affecting Trading Rights and Distribution Services for Certain Publications and Audiovisual Entertainment Products [2009] WT/DS363/AB/R [337]; Delimatsis (2011).

[69] WTO Appellate Body, United States – Measures affecting the cross-border supply of gambling and betting services [2005] WT/DS285/AB/R.

Finally, instruments that restrict trade have to be published (Article X GATT, Article III GATS). This supports transparency in domestic regulation and thus public debate on such issues.

III The Rights of Content Providers

The right to impart (one's own) information and ideas is the most important human right of content providers, and will therefore be in the focus of the following explanations. As has been shown in Chapter 1, a distinction has to be made between the freedom to express oneself, which applies to all content providers, and media freedom, which only applies to the journalistic media. Although to a large extent overlapping, freedom of expression and media freedom are distinct concepts. Media freedom is a fundamental right that only applies to the journalistic media and not to all speakers alike. Other fundamental rights may apply in particular cases involving the media, such as freedom of the arts and sciences according to Article 13 EUChFR, the right to engage in work under Article 15 EUChFR or the freedom to conduct a business as codified in Article 16 EUChFR. As shown above, under EU law, freedom of expression may be bolstered by the content provider's freedom to provide services or the free movement of goods, if applicable.

1 Freedom of Expression

Freedom of expression includes the freedom to impart information and ideas without interference by public authorities and regardless of frontiers, as Article 19(2) ICCPR, Article 11(1) EUChFR and Article 10(1) ECHR almost identically stipulate. The clause 'regardless of frontiers' guarantees that cross-border speech, such as publications transmitted via broadcasting or the internet, enjoys the same freedom of expression protection as domestic speech.[70] Furthermore, freedom of expression prohibits any distinction between the protected freedom of expression of nationals and that of foreigners.[71]

a Freedom of Expression Theory

Freedom of expression may largely be based on three main conceptions: the argument from democracy; the argument from truth, including its subcategory, the 'marketplace of ideas'; and the argument from individual autonomy or 'self-fulfilment'.[72]

The free speech argument from democracy follows the idea that, in order for an electorate to be appropriately knowledgeable, there must be no constraints on

---

[70] Compare ECtHR, Association Ekin v. France [2001] App. no. 39288/98 [62]; Nowak (2005) Article 19 para. 16 fn. 37; Council of Europe, European Convention on Transfrontier Television (1989).

[71] ECtHR, Cox v. Turkey [2010] App. no. 2933/03 [31].

[72] There are further rationales and interests to explain freedom of expression, which are related to the conceptions mentioned before, such as suspicion of government intrusion, social interaction and community, or balance between stability and change; see Scanlon (1972); Wells (1997, p. 166); Emerson (1963, pp. 884–886). For a general overview, see Barendt (2005, pp. 6–30).

democratic deliberation and the free flow of information and ideas on matters of political concern.[73] Freedom of political debate lies at the heart of democracy and must therefore be afforded very strong protection. In a democratic society 'the actions or omissions of the Government must be subject to the close scrutiny not only of the legislative and judicial authorities but also of the press and public opinion'.[74] The right to scrutinise and to criticise one's government and its representatives is thus a fundamental principle prevailing throughout the application of any human rights convention. The argument from democracy has subsequently been developed further into an argument from 'public discourse'. Freedom of speech protects the public discussion on all matters of public concern. The ECtHR in particular has reiterated that 'there is no warrant in its case law for distinguishing between political discussion and discussion of other matters of public concern'.[75]

According to the argument from truth, freedom of expression serves the advancement of knowledge and the search for truth.[76] The argument from truth traces back to John Milton and John Stuart Mill.[77] It protects freedom of expression because truth is best achieved, and falsehood best suppressed, when they face each other through free expression. As Justice Holmes explained:

> [W]hen men have realized that time has upset many fighting faiths, they may come to believe even more than they believe the very foundations of their own conduct that the ultimate good desired is better reached by free trade in ideas – that the best test of truth is the power of the thought to get itself accepted in the competition of the market.[78]

As a consequence, the arguments from democracy, from public discourse and from truth, including the 'marketplace of ideas' rationale, share the focus on the societal effect of speech; that is, the progress of a democratic society, contributions to discourses on matters of importance for society in general, and the pursuit of truth.

These consequentialist approaches to freedom of speech stand in contrast to the argument from individual or private autonomy. According to this rationale, freedom of speech has to be regarded as valuable not because of its consequences, but because of its intrinsic value as an essential feature of a person's individual autonomy. It is based on the paradigm that individuals must *as such* be able to

---

[73] See in particular Meiklejohn (1948, 1961); Bork (1971, p. 20); Sunstein (1992, p. 263); Weinstein (2011).

[74] ECtHR, Castells v. Spain [1992] App. no. 11798/85 [46]; see also Kaperzyński v. Poland [2012] App. no. 43206/07 [64]; High Court of Australia, Lange v. Australian Broadcasting Corporation [1997] HCA 25.

[75] ECtHR, Thorgeir Thorgeirson v. Iceland [1992] App. no. 13778/88 [64].

[76] Emerson (1963, p. 881); Schauer (1982, p. 15).

[77] Milton (1644, p. 35); Mill (1869, p. 85).

[78] Abrams v. United States, 250 U.S. 616, 630 (1919) (Holmes J, dissenting). See also Whitney v. California, 274 U.S. 357, 375–78 (1927) (Brandeis J, concurring); Gertz v. Robert Welch, Inc., 418 U.S. 323, 339–40 (1974); House of Lords, R v. Secretary of State for the Home Department, ex p Simms [2000] 2 AC 115.

express themselves.[79] The argument from individual autonomy is thus focused on the speaker, not on the speaker's impact on society.[80]

These freedom of expression theories are not hermetically sealed off. Rather, they are intertwined, encompass different aspects of freedom of expression and complement each other.[81] In the seminal decision *Handyside* v. *United Kingdom*, the ECtHR established, and has since then reiterated: 'Freedom of expression constitutes one of the essential foundations of [a democratic] society, one of the basic conditions for its progress and for the development of every man.'[82] In cases following *Handyside*, the Court replaced the term 'the development of every man' with 'each individual's self-fulfilment'.[83] The Human Rights Committee and the Court of Justice of the EU (CJEU) established similar principles. The Human Rights Committee acknowledges that freedom of opinion and freedom of expression 'are indispensable conditions for the full development of the person'[84] and constitute the

> cornerstones in any free and democratic society. It is the essence of such societies that citizens must be allowed to inform themselves about alternatives to the political system/parties in power, and that they may criticize or openly and publicly evaluate their Governments without fear of interference or punishment by the Government, subject to certain restrictions set out in [Article 19(3) ICCPR].[85]

Furthermore, the Committee regularly reiterates that 'the right to freedom of expression is of paramount importance in any democratic society, and that any restrictions on its exercise must meet strict tests of justification'.[86] And the CJEU observed that '[t]he safeguarding of the freedoms protected under Article 11 of the Charter undoubtedly constitutes a legitimate aim in the general interest, the importance of which in a democratic and pluralistic society must be stressed in particular'.[87]

---

[79] See Oster (2015b, pp. 17–18), providing further references.

[80] Blasi (1977, p. 553).

[81] See Blasi (1977, p. 554); Barendt (2005, pp. 6–7); Marshall (1992, p. 44); Wragg (2013).

[82] Handyside v. United Kingdom [1976] App. no. 5493/72 [49]; reiterated in, among many other decisions, Sunday Times v. United Kingdom (No. 1) [1979] App. no. 6538/74 [65]; Lingens v. Austria [1986] App. no. 9815/82 [41]; Axel Springer AG v. Germany (No. 1) [2012] App. no. 39954/08 [78].

[83] See, for example, Lindon, Otchakovsky-Laurens and July v. France [2007] App. nos. 21279/02 and 36448/02 [45]; Frankowicz v. Poland [2008] App. no. 53025/99 [38].

[84] General Comment no. 34, para. 2.

[85] Benhadj v. Algeria [2007] Communication no. 1173/2003 [8.10]; see also Aduayom and others v. Togo [1996] Communication nos. 422–424/1990 [7.4]; Gryb v. Belarus [2011] Communication no. 1316/2004 [13.3]; General Comment no. 34, para. 2.

[86] See, for example, Park v. Republic of Korea [1998] Communication no. 628/1995 [10.3]; Shchetko and others v. Belarus [2001] Communication no. 1009/2001 [7.3]; Velichkin v. Belarus [2001] Communication no. 1022/2001 [7.3].

[87] CJEU, Case C-283/11 [2013] Sky Österreich v. Österreichischer Rundfunk [52], with further references.

b Right to Impart Information and Ideas

Articles 19(2) ICCPR and 10(1)2 ECHR distinguish between the freedom to hold opinions and to impart and receive *ideas*, on the one hand, and to receive and impart *information*, on the other hand, as subcategories of freedom of expression. The provisions thus protect both statements of fact ('information'), and value judgements (opinions, comments or 'ideas').

Freedom of expression is content-neutral regarding the information and ideas imparted or received. It is applicable not only to information or ideas 'that are favourably received or regarded as inoffensive or as a matter of indifference, but also to those that offend, shock or disturb. Such are the demands of that pluralism, tolerance and broadmindedness without which there is no "democratic society".'[88] Even false and defamatory statements and pornography are *basically* protected by freedom of expression as well. The focal point of the analysis thus lies in the question whether a restriction of the expression concerned is justified, in particular regarding the proper balancing of conflicting rights and interests. The 'duties and responsibilities' clauses in international conventions allow adjudicators to balance freedom of expression with conflicting rights and interests on an ad hoc basis. Hence the seminal question is whether an interference with speech may be justified for the protection of conflicting rights and interests. In contrast to the First Amendment, international conventions do not afford dominance to freedom of speech, but treat freedom of speech as a right with equal value to human rights of others, especially the right to respect for private life and its subcategories, privacy and reputation.[89]

c Choice of the Means and Forms of Expression

Article 19(2) ICCPR expressly protects all forms of expression and their means of dissemination. With a view to Article 10(1) ECHR, the Strasbourg Court decided that this provision does not only protect the substance of the ideas and information expressed, but also the form in which they are conveyed and the means of dissemination.[90] 'Means of expression' may thus include any publication medium, such as books,[91] the printed

---

[88] ECtHR, Handyside v. United Kingdom [1976] App. no. 5493/72 [49]; reiterated in, among many other decisions, Sunday Times v. United Kingdom (No. 1) [1979] App. no. 6538/74 [65]; Lingens v. Austria [1986] App. no. 9815/82 [41]; Axel Springer AG v. Germany (No. 1) [2012] App. no. 39954/08 [78]. See also US Supreme Court, Cohen v. California, 403 U.S. 15, 25 (1971): 'one man's vulgarity is another's lyric'.

[89] Oster (2015b, p. 73).

[90] See, for example, Autronic AG v. Switzerland [1990] App. no. 12726/87 [47]; Jersild v. Denmark [1994] App. no. 15890/89 [31]; De Haes and Gijsels v. Belgium [1997] App. no. 19983/92 [48]; Murphy v. Ireland [2003] App. no. 44179/98 [61]; Radio France and others v. France [2004] App. no. 53984/00 [39].

[91] See, for example Human Rights Committee, Concluding observations on Kuwait (CCPR/CO/69/KWT), para. 20; ECtHR, Chauvy and others v. France [2004] App. no. 64915/01 [68]; Éditions Plon v. France [2004] App. no. 58148/00 [43]; Lindon, Otchakovsky-Laurens and July v. France [2007] App. nos. 21279/02 and 36448/02 [47]; ECJ, Joined Cases 43/82 and 63/82 [1984] VBVB and VBBB v. Commission.

press,[92] radio or TV broadcasting [93] or text messages,[94] and also leaflets,[95] posters[96] or banners.[97] The freedom to choose the means of expression includes the right to confidentiality of the communication process, as the observation of one's communication or the retention of communication data could deter someone from using this means of communication.[98]

'Forms of expression' may include spoken, written and sign language, and non-verbal expression, such as images, objects of art and even public nudity as an expression of one's view on the human body.[99] Freedom of expression also includes the speaker's right to use the language of their choice to express themselves.[100] Finally, freedom of expression does not only protect speech in a literal sense, but also symbolic expression, such as wearing a badge[101] or actions impeding the activities of which the actors disapprove.[102] A Denial of Service Attack against a particular website can therefore be regarded as 'expression'.

One important method of expressing information and ideas is via the form of arts. This becomes relevant where the publication of satires, caricatures or poems is concerned. In contrast to Article 19(2) ICCPR and Article 13 EUChFR, the ECHR does not contain an express provision protecting the arts or artistic speech. The Strasbourg Court thus refused to afford protection to artistic expression *as such*, as was called for by Judges Spielmann and Jebens in their joint dissenting opinion in *Vereinigung*

---

[92] See, for example, ECtHR, Sunday Times v. United Kingdom (No. 1) [1979] App. no. 6538/74 [66]; Bergens Tidende and others v. Norway [2000] App. no. 26132/95 [60]; ECJ, Case C-368/95 [1997] Familiapress v. Heinrich Bauer Verlag [25].

[93] See, for example, EComHR, Purcell and others v. Ireland [1991] App. no. 15404/89; ECtHR, Jersild v. Denmark [1994] App. no. 15890/89 [31]; Radio France and others v. France [2004] App. no. 53984/00 [33]; ECJ, Case C-288/89 [1991] Stichting Collectieve Antennevoorziening Gouda and others v. Commissariaat voor de Media; Case C-23/93 [1994] TV 10 SA v. Commissariaat voor de Media.

[94] Compare ECJ, Case C-73/07 [2008] Tietosuojavaltuutettu v. Satakunnan Markkinapörssi Oy and Satamedia Oy [29].

[95] See, *mutatis mutandis*, Human Rights Committee, Kim v. Republic of Korea [1999] Communication no. 574/1994 [12.4]; Zalesskaya v. Belarus [2011] Communication no. 1604/2007 [10.2]; ECtHR, Chorherr v. Austria [1993] App. no. 13308/87; Tolstoy Miloslavsky v. United Kingdom [1995] App. no. 18139/91; Annen v. Germany [2015] App. no. 3690/10.

[96] ECtHR, PETA Deutschland v. Germany [2012] App. no. 43481/09 [42]; Mouvement raëlien suisse v. Switzerland [2012] App. no. 16354/06 [49].

[97] See Human Rights Committee, Kivenmaa v. Finland [1994] Communication no. 412/1990 [9.3].

[98] See CJEU, Joined Cases C-293/12 and C-594/12[2014] Digital Rights Ireland Ltd and Kärntner Landesregierung [28].

[99] See Human Rights Committee, Shin v. Republic of Korea [2004] Communication no. 926/2000 [7.2]; on public nudity, see ECtHR, Gough v. United Kingdom [2014] App. no. 49327/11 [147] and US Supreme Court, City of Erie v. Pap's A.M., 529 U.S. 277 (2000). In both cases the courts found no violation of freedom of expression.

[100] Human Rights Committee, Ballantyne and others v. Canada [1993] Communication no. 359, 385/89 [11.3]; ECJ, Case C-250/06 [2007] United Pan-Europe Communications Belgium SA and others v. Belgium and others [42]; De Varennes (1993, p. 163).

[101] ECtHR, Vajnai v. Hungary [2008] App. no. 33629/06 [47].

[102] Such as blowing a hunting horn and engagement in hallooing with the intention of disrupting the activities of a hunt; see ECtHR, Hashman and Harrup v. United Kingdom [1999] App. no. 25594/94 [28].

Bildender Künstler v. *Austria*.[103] Freedom of expression nonetheless protects the arts as a *form* of expression.[104] As the ECtHR noted in *Müller* v. *Switzerland*: 'Those who create, perform, distribute or exhibit works of art contribute to the exchange of ideas and opinions which is essential for a democratic society.'[105] The Strasbourg Court thus does not *categorically* afford less protection to 'artistic speech'. If speech on a debate of public concern is expressed in the form of arts, the Court grants extensive freedom of expression protection in favour of the artist.[106] The distinction of classes of speech that currently prevails in legal scholarship – the categories of political, commercial and artistic speech[107] – should thus be rejected. Artistic speech should not be perceived as a category of speech *content*, but rather as a *form* of speech.[108]

Except for Article 13 EUChFR, international human rights catalogues do not include an express provision protecting academic speech, such as research published in academic articles. However, freedom of expression also covers the publication of academic articles, teaching and speeches.[109]

d The Internet as a Means of Communication

Freedom of expression also protects speech via the internet.[110] The Strasbourg Court regularly emphasises that the ECtHR has to be interpreted 'in the light of present-day conditions'.[111] Therefore, any interpretation of the Convention 'must take into account the specific nature of the Internet as a modern means of imparting information ... In light of its accessibility and its capacity to store and communicate vast amounts of information, the Internet plays an important role in enhancing the public's access

---

[103] Vereinigung Bildender Künstler v. Austria [2007] App. no. 68354/01, joint dissenting opinion of Judges Spielman and Jebens [6]. Judges Spielman and Jebens nevertheless voted against finding a violation of Article 10, because they found the impugned painting in violation of human dignity.

[104] See ECtHR, Müller and others v. Switzerland [1988] App. no. 10737/84 [33]; Vereinigung Bildender Künstler v. Austria [2007] App. no. 68354/01 [26]; Leroy v. France [2009] App. no. 36109/03 [39]; Société de Conception de Presse et d'Edition et Ponson v. France [2009] App. no. 26935/05 [34]; Office of the Special Rapporteur for Freedom of Expression with the Inter-American Commission on Human Rights, Inter-American Legal Framework Regarding the Right to Freedom of Expression, 2009, CIDH/RELE/INF. 2/09, para. 23

[105] Müller and others v. Switzerland [1988] App. no. 10737/84 [33]; see also Vereinigung Bildender Künstler v. Austria [2007] App. no. 68354/01 [26]; Leroy v. France [2009] App. no. 36109/03 [44].

[106] Compare ECtHR, Karataş v. Turkey [1999] App. no. 23168/94; Vereinigung Bildender Künstler v. Austria [2007] App. no. 68354/01.

[107] See Cooper and Williams (1999, p. 603) and Fenwick and Phillipson (2006, pp. 38 fn. 3, 51ff).

[108] Oster (2015b, pp. 78–79).

[109] See, for example, ECtHR, Hertel v. Switzerland [1998] App. no. 59/1997/843/1049 [50]; Wille v. Liechtenstein [1999] App. no. 28396/95 [36 ff]; Sorguç v. Turkey [2009] App. no. 17089/03 [35]; Mustafa Erdoğan and others v. Turkey [2014] App. nos. 346/04 and 39779/04 [40].

[110] See Human Rights Committee, General Comment no. 34, paras. 12, 43; ECtHR, Times Newspapers Ltd v. United Kingdom (Nos. 1 and 2) [2009] App. nos. 3002/03 and 23676/03 [27]; Renaud v. France [2010] App. no. 13290/07 [28]; US Supreme Court, Reno v. ACLU 521 U.S. 844 (1997).

[111] See ECtHR, Tyrer v. United Kingdom [1978] App. no. 5856/72 [31].

to news and facilitating the dissemination of information generally.[112] Yet it is discernible from the Strasbourg Court's case law that the Court perceives the internet as a double-edged sword. In some decisions the Court hails the internet's capacity to inform the general public on matters of public interest,[113] whereas in others the Court has held *against* the applicant that placing information online has exacerbated its harmful effect.[114]

Communication via mass media has certain characteristics that have to be taken into account when balancing conflicting rights and interests. Mass communication has a more powerful effect than face-to-face communication, and thus a greater impact on public discourse. However, the communication of, for example, defamatory, confidential or obscene information to a mass audience has a more damaging effect than communication of the same information to just another individual. For example, in *Willem* v. *France*, a mayor had been fined for publishing on the municipality's website a call for a boycott of Israeli products in the municipality to protest against the anti-Palestinian policies of the Israeli Government. The Court found that incitement by the mayor to commit an act of discrimination does not contribute to a free discussion of a subject of general interest. Rather, the condemnable nature of his message had been aggravated by its publication on the internet.[115] The Court thus found no violation of Article 10 ECHR.

Moreover, in *Węgrzynowski and Smolczewski* v. *Poland*, the Court decided that a publisher can be requested to add an appropriate qualification to an article contained in an internet archive, where he has been informed that a libel action has been initiated against the article published in the written press. Yet such a request is a less intrusive, and therefore more proportionate, interference with freedom of expression and media freedom than requiring the removal of potentially defamatory articles from archives altogether, as it is not for courts to rewrite history and to treat articles as if they never existed.[116]

In the past, the possibility to impart information to a mass audience had to a large extent been the privilege of the journalistic and entertainment media. The traditional mass media thus enjoys certain privileges, insofar as it regularly contributes to public discourse, but it is also subject to enhanced duties and responsibilities. Only with

---

[112] ECtHR, Times Newspapers Ltd v. United Kingdom (Nos. 1 and 2) [2009] App. nos. 3002/03 and 23676/03 [27].

[113] See, for example, ECtHR, Wypych v. Poland [2005] App. no. 2428/05, p. 12; Times Newspapers Ltd v. United Kingdom (Nos. 1 and 2) [2009] App. nos. 3002/03 and 23676/03 [27]; Yıldırım v. Turkey [2012] App. no. 3111/10 [54].

[114] See, for example, ECtHR, Willem v. France [2009] App. no. 10883/05; Delfi AS v. Estonia [2015] App. no. 64569/09 [147].

[115] ECtHR, Willem v. France [2009] App. no. 10883/05 [38].

[116] ECtHR, Węgrzynowski and Smolczewski v. Poland [2013] App. no. 33846/07 [59–65].

the advent of the internet do private individuals have similar opportunities. Yet the impact of this development on *their* freedom of expression rights is far from being fully explored. In the balancing exercise between freedom of expression and conflicting rights and interests (see Chapter 3), freedom of expression on the internet is to be conceptualised along the following lines:

1 Both the contribution to public discourse and the enhanced harmful effect of mass communication have to be taken into account when balancing conflicting interests.
2 The fact that persons impart information and ideas via means of mass communication does not in itself make them journalists, and thus does not automatically afford them the privileges of the traditional news media.
3 Rather, private individuals or non-journalistic organisations publishing information via means of mass communication enjoy privileges similar to the traditional news media only if they contribute to matters of public concern and follow standards of due diligence when gathering and disseminating information and ideas.
4 In turn, private individuals or non-journalistic organisations publishing information via means of mass communication do not enjoy privileges similar to the traditional news media if they do not contribute to debates of public concern or if they do not adhere to standards of due diligence when gathering and disseminating information and ideas.

e The Protection of Anonymous and Pseudonymous Speech

Much commentary on the internet is done anonymously or by using unidentifiable pseudonyms. 'Anonymity' means that a speaker is at least not *immediately* identifiable. That a speaker may be identified after a protracted procedure with an uncertain outcome, such as a lawsuit against an internet service provider claiming the disclosure of a user's real name or at least his IP address, does not change the fact that the speech was made anonymously. Furthermore, 'anonymity' includes the use of unidentifiable pseudonyms. The online encyclopaedia Wikipedia is written mostly by authors using pseudonyms. Blogs are often written under a false name, and the same applies to participants in online social networks. Social media sites, such as Facebook and Google+, require users to sign in with their legal names. However, this policy is often circumvented and difficult to enforce. Moreover, it is even illegal in some countries; we will come back to this point later.

With the practice of anonymity many people try to avoid accountability for their speech. Rights of others, such as defamation and privacy laws, are difficult to be enforced against anonymous speakers. However, anonymous speech is neither a new phenomenon nor confined to the internet. The history (not only) of Great Britain and the United States reveals a tradition of anonymous political criticism, although – or because – anonymity had long been prohibited. Even today, the weekly magazine *The Economist* publishes its articles anonymously.

There is no general 'right to anonymity' as such. Rather, anonymity derives from other rights. Those rights are freedom of expression and the right to privacy. The privacy rationale for anonymity is the right to keep certain information secret, including one's own identity.[117] The freedom of expression rationale for the protection of anonymity is that speakers may be deterred from publishing statements under their real name for fear of harassment and prosecution. The 1960 landmark decision of the United States Supreme Court *Talley* v. *California* may serve as an example. The case concerned the prohibition of distributing unsigned handbills urging readers to boycott certain Los Angeles merchants who were allegedly engaging in discriminatory employment practices. After elaborating on the history of abusive press licensing laws and seditious libel prosecutions in Britain, Justice Black, who wrote the majority opinion for the Court, issued the following statements: '[T]here are times and circumstances when States may not compel members of groups engaged in the dissemination of ideas to be publicly identified. ... [I]dentification and fear of reprisal might deter perfectly peaceful discussions of public matters of importance.' The Court thus held that the impugned prohibition violated the First Amendment.[118] Upon closer examination, however, it becomes clear that the Court has not protected anonymous speech as absolutely as is sometimes purported. Justice Black's words suggest that the First Amendment does not protect anonymous speech *per se*. Rather, there are '*times and circumstances*' where freedom of speech requires such protection. However, this raises the question of when these 'times and circumstances' are existent. This is arguably only the case with regard to speech where fear of repression has been most prevalent. Justice Black thus highlighted: 'Anonymous pamphlets, leaflets, brochures and even books have played an important role in the progress of mankind. Persecuted groups and sects from time to time throughout history have been able to criticize oppressive practices and laws either anonymously or not at all.' Similarly, Justice Stevens noted in *McIntyre* v. *Ohio Elections Commission*:

> Under our Constitution, anonymous pamphleteering is not a pernicious, fraudulent practice, but an honorable tradition of advocacy and of dissent. Anonymity is a shield from the tyranny of the majority ... It thus exemplifies the purpose behind the Bill of Rights, and of the First Amendment in particular: to protect unpopular individuals from retaliation – and their ideas from suppression – at the hand of an intolerant society. The right to remain anonymous may be abused when it shields fraudulent conduct. But political

---

[117] See Human Rights Council, Report of the Special Rapporteur on the promotion and protection of the right to freedom of opinion and expression, David Kaye, 22 May 2015, A/HRC/29/32, paras. 16 ff.

[118] United States Supreme Court, Talley v. California 362 U.S. 60 (1960); see also Buckley, Secretary of State of Colorado v. American Constitutional Law Foundation, Inc., 525 U.S. 182 (1999); Watchtower Society v. Village of Stratton, 536 U.S. 150 (2002); Court of Appeal, Totalise plc v. Motley Fool Ltd and Interactive Investor Ltd [2001] EWCA Civ 1897 [25]; Human Rights Council, Report of the Special Rapporteur on the promotion and protection of the right to freedom of opinion and expression, David Kaye, 22 May 2015, A/HRC/29/32, paras. 22 ff.

speech by its nature will sometimes have unpalatable consequences, and, in general, our society accords greater weight to the value of free speech than to the dangers of its misuse.[119]

The Supreme Court nonetheless recognised that there may be legitimate interests in identification requirements to prevent abuses, such as defamation, invasions into privacy and fraudulent or false claims.[120] By way of concurrence in *McIntyre*, Justice Ginsburg thus succinctly observed, 'in for a calf is not always in for a cow'.[121] The fact that the Supreme Court recognised a constitutional right of anonymity related to the distribution of political and religious leaflets does not mean that anonymous speech cannot be regulated in other contexts: 'We do not thereby hold that the State may not in other, larger circumstances, require the speaker to disclose its interest by disclosing its identity.'[122] Justice Scalia, in a dissenting opinion, also once expressed the view that 'anonymity can still be enjoyed by those who require it, without utterly destroying useful disclosure laws'.[123]

Two rationales justifying the protection of anonymous speech may be identified. First, anonymity may be considered to place the argumentative force of an article in the forefront, and not the author's popularity or unpopularity. This rationale applied, for example, to the Federalist papers, and it still applies to the policy of *The Economist*. Second, and more importantly, anonymity requires protection where the speaker has to fear illegitimate harassment or repression for his speech. In addition to the general factors that apply in the balancing exercise between freedom of expression and conflicting rights and interests (see Chapter 3), three factors have to be considered with regard to anonymous speech:

1 the fact that the statement had been published anonymously;
2 the extent to which the speaker had to fear harassment or repression for his speech; and
3 whether the harassment or repression would have been illegitimate.

Regarding the first factor, a speaker who publishes a statement anonymously can basically not be traced, or at least it is more difficult for those affected by his speech to identify him. Therefore, the fact that a statement has been published anonymously is, as such, a factor that weighs against a speaker. In turn, it weighs in the speaker's favour if he does not publish anonymously, but allows himself to be identified by his name.

The ECtHR decision *Fatullayev* v. *Azerbaijan*, which has already been referred to in Chapter 1, hints to a particular problem, namely anonymity of the journalistic

---

[119] McIntyre v. Ohio Elections Commission, 514 U.S. 334, 357 (1995).
[120] Talley v. California, 362 U.S. 60, 71 (1960) (Black J); McIntyre v. Ohio Elections Commission 514 U.S. 334, 372 (1995) (Scalia J, dissenting).
[121] McIntyre v. Ohio Elections Commission 514 U.S. 334, 358 (1995) (Ginsburg J, concurring).
[122] McIntyre v. Ohio Elections Commission 514 U.S. 334, 358 (1995) (Ginsburg J, concurring).
[123] McIntyre v. Ohio Elections Commission 514 U.S. 334, 380 (1995) (Scalia J, dissenting).

media. Journalists enjoy certain privileges, as will be explained further below, but they are also subject to particular duties and responsibilities. Among their duties and responsibilities is transparency. The journalistic media is subject to a right of reply.[124] Therefore, in presumably all European countries, the professional media has to make available certain information about the publisher or editor – a duty that stands in stark contrast to a culture of anonymity often practised on the internet. While anonymity is part of freedom of expression, responsible journalism requires that at least the editor of a publication be immediately identifiable in order to facilitate effective protection against defamation and privacy violation.[125]

Fear of harassment or sanctions – the second factor – basically weigh in the speaker's favour. According to the 'marketplace of ideas' rationale for freedom of expression, everyone should have a voice in the public debate. If speech is either made anonymously or not at all, then it is preferable that it is being made anonymously. This applies even more given that fear of harassment or sanctions often – but of course not necessarily – arises in cases in which the speaker wants to contribute to a controversial matter of general interest, such as political or religious affairs.

However, fear of harassment or repression is in itself not sufficient to grant strong protection to anonymous speech. In addition, the harassment or sanctions must be illegitimate (third factor). Freedom of expression protects courage, not cowardice. Obnoxious statements that have been published anonymously for fear of a legitimate defamation lawsuit deserve no protection. Illegitimate harassment would be, for example, unjustified sanctions by an employer against an employee for leaking information of public concern, arbitrary criminal prosecution for the criticism of government policy, or humiliation for statements made in a support group.

This balancing exercise not only applies in the citizen–state relationship, but also between private individuals due to the indirect horizontal effect of human rights. Two questions should be raised here. First, it is the practice of online social networks to require their users to enter their real names rather than pseudonyms. This policy collides with provisions of some domestic laws. For example, Section 13(6) of the German Telemedia Act requires that a service provider must enable the anonymous or pseudonymous use of internet services where this is technically possible and reasonable. Yet German data protection authorities could not yet enforce this provision against Facebook due to the lack of jurisdiction (see Chapter 8).[126] Is the practice of social networks to prohibit the use of pseudonyms compatible with human rights

---

[124] See, for example, Article 28 AVMS Directive. See also EComHR, Ediciones Tiempo S.A. v. Spain [1989] App. no. 13010/87; Resolution (74) 26 of the Committee of Ministers of the Council of Europe on the right of reply – Position of the individual in relation to the press; Recommendation Rec(2004)16 of the Committee of Ministers to Member States on the right of reply in the new media environment.

[125] For audiovisual services, see Article 5 AVMS Directive; for information society services provider, see Article 6 E-commerce Directive.

[126] See Court of Appeals in Administrative Law (Oberverwaltungsgericht) Schleswig-Holstein, Case 4 MB 11/13 [2013] 'Facebook'.

in their indirect horizontal effect? The providers of social networks have a considerable commercial interest in knowing the identity of their users, which is protected in the EU by Article 16 EUChFR. This interest has to be balanced against the legitimate interest of users to remain anonymous. In addition, one has to consider the interest of other network participants who might have a legitimate interest in knowing the identity of other users in case they are a victim of cyber-mobbing. This leads to the second question: may access providers be required to reveal the IP address and thus help to identify users? One could argue that ISPs have a right to refuse the disclosure of their users' IP addresses, similar to journalists who do not have to disclose their sources. But this comparison is inapt; ISPs do not generate information similar to journalists, but they merely disseminate the content of others. ISPs are not responsible for the publications they transmit, so they do not enjoy the same privileges as journalists. Therefore, under domestic laws, a court order in civil proceedings, or the police in a criminal case, can usually compel an ISP to identify the subscriber from whose computer the message was sent. As a result, it has to be decided on a case-by-case basis whether it is legitimate for ISPs to protect a subscriber's identity.[127] With a view to copyright infringements in particular, this will be further discussed in Chapter 9.

2 Privileges of the Journalistic Media

'Freedom of the media' is now expressly mentioned in Article 11(2) EUChFR, and it can also be inferred from the Human Rights Committee's and the Strasbourg Court's case law on Article 19(2) ICCPR and Article 10(1) ECHR, respectively.[128] Many domestic constitutions[129] and courts applying international human rights conventions thus acknowledge a special role of the mass media in the framework of freedom of expression not only by granting special privileges, but also by imposing enhanced duties and responsibilities on journalists and media companies. As the Strasbourg Court regularly emphasises,

> Although the press[130] must not overstep certain bounds, in particular in respect of the reputation and rights of others, its duty is nevertheless to

---

[127] See, for example, The Author of Blog v. Times Newspapers Ltd [2009] EMLR 22. From academic literature, see Wells Branscomb (1995); Sandeen (2002); Barendt (2009); Hughes (2010).

[128] See, for example, ECtHR, Lingens v. Austria [1986] App. no. 9815/82 [42]; reiterated in, for example, Oberschlick v. Austria (No. 1) [1991] App. no. 11662/85 [58]; Thoma v. Luxembourg [2001] App. no. 38432/97 [45]; Cumpănă and Mazăre v. Romania [2004] App. no. 33348/96 [93]; Human Rights Committee, Bodrožić v. Serbia and Montenegro [2005] Communication no. 1180/2003 [7.2]; Gauthier v. Canada [1999] Communication no. 633/95 [13.4].

[129] Such as the First Amendment to the US Constitution, Article 5(1)2 of the German Basic Law, Article 21(2) of the Italian Constitution, Article 25(1) of the Belgian Constitution or Article 17 of the Swiss Constitution.

[130] The Court extends the protection afforded to the press to audiovisual media; see Jersild v. Denmark [1994] App. no. 15890/89 [31]; Radio France and others v. France [2004] App. no. 53984/00 [33].

impart – in a manner consistent with its obligations and responsibilities – information and ideas on all matters of public interest. Not only does the press have the task of imparting such information and ideas; the public also has a right to receive them. Were it otherwise, the press would be unable to play its vital role of 'public watchdog'.[131]

In addition, freedom of the media 'affords the public one of the best means of discovering and forming an opinion of the ideas and attitudes of political leaders. It is incumbent on the press to impart information and ideas on political issues and on other subjects of public interest.'[132]

The Human Rights Committee has also acknowledged the importance of journalists for a democratic society. In *Bodrožić* v. *Serbia and Montenegro*, the Committee observed 'that in circumstances of public debate in a democratic society, *especially in the media*, concerning figures in the political domain, the value placed by the Covenant upon uninhibited expression is particularly high'.[133] In this context, the Committee has also referred to the right to take part in the conduct of public affairs, as laid down in Article 25 ICCPR.[134] In order to ensure the full enjoyment of this right, the free communication of information and ideas about public and political issues between citizens, candidates and elected representatives is essential. This implies that a free press and other media are able to comment on public issues and inform public opinion.[135] According to the Committee, Article 25 ICCPR, read together with Article 19, implies 'that citizens, *in particular through the media*, should have wide access to information and the opportunity to disseminate information and opinions about the activities of elected bodies and their members'.[136]

Media freedom protects both media publications and the journalistic media as institutions fulfilling their role as 'public watchdog' and 'fourth estate'. In the former case, media freedom is *lex specialis* to freedom of expression in that a person or institution, by virtue of being a journalist and acting as a journalist, is governed by a different set of factors concerning the intensity of protection when issuing a publication, compared to freedom of expression afforded to private individuals or

---

[131] Axel Springer AG v. Germany (No. 1) [2012] App. no. 39954/08 [79]; Von Hannover v. Germany (No. 2) [2012] App. nos. 40660/08 and 60641/08 [102].

[132] Centro Europa 7 S.r.l. and Di Stefano v. Italy [2012] App. no. 38433/09 [131]; see, for example, Lingens v. Austria [1986] App. no. 9815/82 [41–42]; Sürek v. Turkey (No. 1) [1999] App. no. 26682/95 [59]; Thoma v. Luxembourg [2001] App. no. 38432/97 [45].

[133] Bodrožić v. Serbia and Montenegro [2005] Communication no. 1180/2003 [7.2] (emphasis added).

[134] Article 25 ICCPR reads: 'Every citizen shall have the right and the opportunity, without any of the distinctions mentioned in article 2 and without unreasonable restrictions: (a) To take part in the conduct of public affairs, directly or through freely chosen representatives; (b) To vote and to be elected at genuine periodic elections which shall be by universal and equal suffrage and shall be held by secret ballot, guaranteeing the free expression of the will of the electors; (c) To have access, on general terms of equality, to public service in his country.'

[135] General Comment no. 25, para. 25; see also Marques de Morais v. Angola [2005] Communication no. 1128/2002 [6.8].

[136] Gauthier v. Canada [1999] Communication no. 633/95 [13.4] (emphasis added).

non-media entities.[137] In the latter case, media companies and journalists are also protected against undue state interference that is not directly publication-related. Here, freedom of the media differs from general freedom of expression not only in terms of the *intensity* of protection, as is the case with media speech, but also in terms of the *scope* of protected action. The institutional protection of the journalistic media guarantees rights that are not directly speech-related, but related to the media in its newsgathering, editorial and distribution process and independence of the media in general. Media freedom as a fundamental right – this includes freedom of the press, freedom of broadcasters and any other journalistic activity, including writing a blog – finds its theoretical underpinning in the importance of the journalistic media for public discourse.[138]

a Independence of the Media

The journalistic media, as an institution, must not be unduly influenced by the government. The independence of the media is particularly relevant with regard to public broadcasting. As regards private media undertakings, governments must neither directly nor indirectly influence the editorial process in media undertakings, for example, by exerting pressure on board members or journalists, or by arbitrarily granting and withdrawing public subsidies or privileges.

b Protection of Journalistic Research and Investigation

Media freedom also prevents unjustified interferences with the media's newsgathering activities. Journalists enjoy the right to seek information, including the freedom to decide on the method for obtaining the information, such as by means of investigative journalism.[139] The Strasbourg Court stated that 'the law cannot allow arbitrary restrictions which may become a form of indirect censorship should the authorities create obstacles to the gathering of information[, which] is an essential preparatory step in journalism and [...] an inherent, protected part of press freedom'.[140] Media freedom thus protects all forms of newsgathering, such as undercover work.[141] Even measures that are indistinctly applicable to journalists and the general public may violate media freedom if they disproportionately hamper the exercise of

---

[137] Stewart (1975, p. 633). See also, among many other works, Bezanson (1977, p. 733); West (2011, p. 1032); Oster (2015b, pp. 84 ff).

[138] Oster (2015b, pp. 28 ff).

[139] ECtHR, Cumpănă and Mazăre v. Romania [2004] App. no. 33348/96 [96]; Dammann v. Switzerland [2006] App. no. 77551/01 [52]; Társaság a Szabadságjogokért v. Hungary [2009] App. no. 37374/05 [27]; Bremner v. Turkey [2015] App. no. 37428/06 [76]; Council of Europe, Declaration by the Committee of Ministers on the protection and promotion of investigative journalism (26 September 2007).

[140] ECtHR, Társaság a Szabadságjogokért v. Hungary [2009] App. no. 37374/05 [27]; see also Kenedi v. Hungary [2009] App. no. 31475/05 [43]: access to original documentary sources for historical research.

[141] See ECtHR, Nordisk Film & TV A/S v. Denmark [2005] App. no. 40485/02; Haldimann and others v. Switzerland [2015] App. no. 21830/09.

the journalist's profession.[142] However, media freedom does not give licence to illegal activity or violations of public safety rules that apply to everyone.[143] Yet media freedom protects the media's right to publish information, even if it has been obtained unlawfully, if the public interest in receiving the information supersedes the state's or an individual's interest in confidentiality.[144]

c Protection of Journalistic Sources

The right of journalists not to disclose information identifying a source is one of the most important rights deriving from media freedom and is widely recognised under domestic law as well as in several international documents.[145] In addition, there is a considerable body of case law and legal scholarship concerning the protection of journalistic sources.[146] Based on the seminal decision *Goodwin v. United Kingdom*, the ECtHR has consistently emphasised the right of journalists to protect their sources as an important safeguard of media freedom. The ECtHR explained that protection of journalistic sources 'is one of the basic conditions for press freedom. Without such protection, sources may be deterred from assisting the press in informing the public on matters of public interest'.[147] As a result, the ability of the press to provide accurate and reliable information, and thus its public-watchdog role, may be undermined. The protection of journalistic sources is 'a cornerstone of freedom of the press without which sources may be deterred from assisting the press in informing the public on matters of public interest'.[148] Therefore, an order for the disclosure of the identity of an anonymous source of information constituted an interference with a journalist's rights under Article 10 ECHR, even though the order had not been enforced.[149]

---

[142] ECtHR, Gsell v. Switzerland [2009] App. no. 12675/05 [49]: restrictions on road access to the World Economic Forum in Davos.

[143] Compare ECtHR, Pentikäinen v. Finland [2015] App. no. 11882/10 [114].

[144] US Supreme Court, New York Times Co. v. United States, 403 U.S. 713 (1971); Bartnicki v. Vopper, 532 U.S. 514 (2001); ECtHR, Radio Twist a.s. v. Slovakia [2006] App. no. 62202/00 [62]; Nagla v. Latvia [2013] App. no. 73469/10 [97].

[145] See, for example, Section 53(1) no. 5 of the German Criminal Procedure Code; Section 383(1) no. 5 of the German Civil Procedure Code. Under Swiss law, the protection of sources even has constitutional status; see Article 17(3) of the Swiss Constitution. From international documents, see UN Commission on Human Rights, Report of the Special Rapporteur on the promotion and protection of the right to freedom of opinion and expression, Mr Abid Hussain, submitted pursuant to Commission Resolution 1997/27, E/CN.4/1998/40/Add.1, paras. 17 and 22; Council of Europe, Recommendation No. R(2000) 7 on the right of journalists not to disclose their sources of information; Parliamentary Assembly, Recommendation 1950 (2011): The protection of journalistic sources.

[146] See Oster (2015b, p. 88), providing further references.

[147] Goodwin v. United Kingdom [1996] App. no. 17488/90 [39].

[148] Citation from Sanoma Uitgevers B.V. v. Netherlands [2010] App. no. 38224/03 [50]; see also, for example, Roemen and Schmit v. Luxembourg [2003] App. no. 51772/99 [57]; Telegraaf Media Nederland Landelijke Media B.V. and others v. Netherlands [2012] App. no. 39315/06 [127]. Under domestic law, see British Steel Corporation v. Granada Television Ltd [1981] 1 All ER 417.

[149] Financial Times Ltd and others v. United Kingdom [2009] App. no. 821/03 [56].

Yet, the protection of journalistic sources is not absolute. Whether a legitimate interest in a disclosure outweighs the media freedom right not to disclose information identifying a source depends, in particular, on the nature of the interest in the disclosure, especially the public interest in preventing and punishing criminal offences, the authenticity of the information, the conduct and good faith of the source and the availability of alternative, less intrusive means to obtaining the information.[150]

d Protection Against Interception of Communication, Surveillance, Searches, Seizures and Arrests

Searches of media premises and seizures of journalistic material are irreconcilable with media freedom if their sole or predominant purpose is the disclosure of journalistic sources. Such searches and seizures have an intolerable, chilling effect on journalistic work and may also deter informants from providing information that they are only willing to provide confidentially.[151] An order for search and seizure in the journalist's home or workplace is thus an even more drastic measure than an order to disclose the source's identity. The searches of a journalist's home and workplace undermine the protection of sources to an even greater extent than disclosure orders.

By contrast, searches and seizures that merely serve to gain material that does not relate to a journalistic source are not *per se* contrary to media freedom. However, there must be an overriding public or private interest in obtaining the information, and regard must be had to whether the public authorities have pursued alternative means of gathering the information.[152] In addition, even if searches prove unproductive, it does not deprive them of their purpose, namely to establish the identity of a journalist's source or the discovery of other journalistic information.[153] Therefore, the mere threat to carry out a search of journalistic premises already causes a 'chilling effect' and thus constitutes an interference with media freedom.[154]

e Entitlements of the Media

One of the main characteristics distinguishing media freedom from freedom of expression is that media freedom not only includes more defensive rights against the state, but also more positive entitlements to state action where these are necessary for the media to fulfil its role as 'public watchdog' and to inform the public on matters of general interest. These entitlements include: the right to enable a publisher to

---

[150] See ECtHR, Roemen and Schmit v. Luxembourg [2003] App. no. 51772/99 [58]; Financial Times Ltd and others v. United Kingdom [2009] App. no. 821/03 [67]; Oster (2015b, pp. 87 ff).

[151] See German Federal Constitutional Court, Cases 1 BvR 538/06 and 1 BvR 2045/06 [2007] 'Cicero' [44].

[152] ECtHR, Roemen and Schmit v. Luxembourg [2003] App. no. 51772/99 [60].

[153] ECtHR, Roemen and Schmit v. Luxembourg [2003] App. no. 51772/99 [57]; Tillack v. Belgium [2007] App. no. 20477/05 [64].

[154] ECtHR, Sanoma Uitgevers B.V. v. Netherlands [2010] App. no. 38224/03 [71]; German Federal Constitutional Court, Cases 1 BvR 538/06 and 1 BvR 2045/06 [2007] 'Cicero' [44].

distribute his publications by any appropriate means,[155] including the possibility to introduce a newspaper in a certain region;[156] privileged access to government information,[157] press conferences[158] or court trials;[159] and special obligations of the state to protect the media, especially to protect journalists from acts of violence as they exercise their journalistic work.[160] A further state obligation is to protect the media from undue influence by financially powerful groups.[161] The state has a duty to ensure 'that the public has access to impartial and accurate information through television and radio and a range of opinion and comment, reflecting *inter alia* the diversity of political outlook within the country'.[162] Hence the state has to protect independent media in order to safeguard media pluralism.

f Non-Discrimination

Finally, media freedom also has an equality dimension. It includes a right to non-discrimination in addition to the general right to equal protection under Articles 2 ICCPR, 14 ECHR and 20 EUChFR. Media freedom as an equality right is at stake when allocation of state resources among journalists and media companies is at issue. In order to deal with such situations, a distinction needs to be made between 'necessary choice situations' and 'unnecessary choice situations'.[163] A necessary choice situation exists when the resources to be allocated are scarce, such as broadcasting frequencies, places in a press conference or seats reserved for media representatives in a court trial.[164] In these situations, the state has to act on a transparent and non-discriminatory basis. This may be implemented, for example, by drawing lots or on a first-come, first-served principle. In particular, the state must abstain from making decisions based on content-related or personal preferences, and it must ensure that all representatives have equal access to the distribution mechanism. By contrast, if resources are not scarce, such as information, it is not necessary

---

[155] ECtHR, VgT Verein gegen Tierfabriken v. Switzerland (No. 1) [2001] App. no. 24699/94 [48].

[156] See ECtHR, Halis Doğan and others v. Turkey [2006] App. no. 50693/99 [24].

[157] Human Rights Committee, Gauthier v. Canada [1999] Communication no. 633/95 [13.4]; Toktakunov v. Kyrgyzstan [2011] Communication no. 1470/2006 [6.3]; ECtHR, Társaság a Szabadságjogokért v. Hungary [2009] App. no. 37374/05 [35]; Youth Initiative for Human Rights v. Serbia [2013] App. no. 48135/06 [24]; Österreichische Vereinigung zur Erhaltung, Stärkung und Schaffung eines wirtschaftlich gesunden land- und forstwirtschaftlichen Grundbesitzes v. Austria [2013] App. no. 39534/07 [34–36] and [41].

[158] Human Rights Committee, Gauthier v. Canada [1999] Communication no. 633/95 [13.4]; Anderson (2002, p. 432).

[159] See German Federal Constitutional Court, Case 1 BvR 990/13 [2013] 'NSU trial': Reservation of seats for media correspondents in a criminal trial.

[160] See, for example, ECtHR, Özgür Gündem v. Turkey [2000] App. no. 23144/93 [38 ff].

[161] See ECtHR, VgT Verein gegen Tierfabriken v. Switzerland (No. 1) [2001] App. no. 24699/94 [72]; Animal Defenders International v. United Kingdom [2013] App. no. 48876/08 [112].

[162] ECtHR, Manole and others v. Moldova [2009] App. no. 13936/02 [100].

[163] Schauer (1982, p. 118).

[164] Schauer (1982, p. 118). On the latter situation, see German Federal Constitutional Court, Case 1 BvR 990/13 [2013] 'NSU trial'.

to make choices, and states must not artificially and arbitrarily make such resources scarce in order to discriminate between media undertakings.[165]

In the case of *Vereinigung demokratischer Soldaten Österreichs and Gubi* v. *Austria*, the Strasbourg Court thus held that if a Convention State supports the dissemination of certain materials, it must not discriminate between types of publication based on the publication's content.[166] Therefore the applicant company was entitled to distribute their magazine on military life, *Der Igel* (*The Hedgehog*), which often contained critical information and articles, in the military barracks in the same way as the only other two military magazines published by private associations.

g The Case Example

The *Financial Times* claimed a violation of its rights out of Article 10 ECHR. But which Article 10 ECHR right had exactly been interfered with? The *Financial Times* undoubtedly conducts journalistic work, and hence enjoys freedom of the press. In this case, the journalistic privilege of not having to disclose sources of information could apply. The *Financial Times* was not required to disclose documents that would directly identify its journalistic source, but only to disclose documents that might, upon examination, lead to such identification. However, the Strasbourg Court did not consider this distinction to be crucial. Instead, a 'chilling effect' would arise 'wherever journalists are seen to assist in the identification of anonymous sources'.[167] As a result, the disclosure order interfered with the *Financial Times'* journalistic privilege to keep its sources confidential.

As has been stated before, the protection of journalistic sources is not absolute. Instead, a legitimate interest in a disclosure may outweigh the media's right not to disclose information identifying a source. This depends, in particular, on the nature of the interest in the disclosure, especially the public interest in preventing and punishing criminal offences, the authenticity of the information, the conduct and good faith of the source and the availability of alternative, less intrusive means to obtaining the information. In the *Financial Times* case, X had apparently fabricated the original document in order to influence the market value of Interbrew's or SAB's shares, or both. If this were true, X would have acted in bad faith – a factor that would weigh against the *Financial Times'* right to keep its source confidential. For the Strasbourg Court, these were too many 'ifs' and 'woulds'. The Court clarified: '[C]ourts should be slow to assume, in the absence of compelling evidence, that [circumstances where a source was clearly acting in bad faith with a harmful purpose and disclosed intentionally falsified information] are present in any particular case.'[168] This part of the

---

[165] Office of the Special Rapporteur for Freedom of Expression with the Inter-American Commission on Human Rights, Inter-American Legal Framework Regarding the Right to Freedom of Expression, 2009, CIDH/RELE/INF. 2/09, para. 96; Oster (2015b, p. 101).

[166] Nicol et al. (2009, para. 2.32).

[167] ECtHR, Financial Times Ltd and others v. the United Kingdom [2009] App. no. 821/03 [70].

[168] ECtHR, Financial Times Ltd and others v. the United Kingdom [2009] App. no. 821/03 [63].

Court's finding concerned the factual side of the source's alleged bad faith: it was for the claimant to prove that the source acted in bad faith, not for the defendant journalist to prove that this was not the case. But even if the claimant could prove that the source acted in bad faith, this was not a compelling legal factor in the balancing exercise: '[T]he conduct of the source can never be decisive in determining whether a disclosure order ought to be made but will merely operate as one, albeit important, factor to be taken into consideration in carrying out the balancing exercise required under Article [10(2) ECHR]'.[169] In this case, the legal proceedings against the *Financial Times* 'did not allow X's purpose to be ascertained with the necessary degree of certainty'.[170] This wiped X's alleged bad faith off the table.

But the question remained whether the *Financial Times* had violated its journalistic duties and responsibilities by publishing inaccurate information – a factor that would also weigh in favour of a disclosure order. In this regard, the Court also observed that it had not been established with a sufficient degree of certainty that the document had been doctored.[171]

The last point to examine was whether the interests of Interbrew in identifying and bringing proceedings against X were sufficient to override the public interest in the protection of journalistic sources. The *Financial Times* had notified Interbrew prior to publication of the article that a copy of the leaked document had been obtained and that there was an intention to publish the information it contained. However, Interbrew did not seek an injunction to prevent publication of the information.[172] In addition, the Court held that 'the aim of preventing further leaks will only justify an order for disclosure of a source in exceptional circumstances where no reasonable and less invasive alternative means of averting the risk posed are available and where the risk threatened is sufficiently serious and defined to render such an order necessary'.[173] In this case, Interbrew had not provided sufficient evidence that it had taken all reasonable steps to discover the source. Therefore, Interbrew's interests to bring proceedings against X in order to eliminate the threat of damage through future dissemination of confidential information and to obtain damages for past breaches of confidence were insufficient to outweigh the public interest in the protection of journalists' sources.[174] There had, accordingly, been a breach of Article 10 ECHR.

IV The Rights of Recipients

It is uncontroversial under any human rights catalogue that everyone has the right to receive information that others are willing to impart on him (see subsection 1 below).

---

[169] ECtHR, Financial Times Ltd and others v. the United Kingdom [2009] App. no. 821/03 [63].
[170] ECtHR, Financial Times Ltd and others v. the United Kingdom [2009] App. no. 821/03 [66].
[171] ECtHR, Financial Times Ltd and others v. the United Kingdom [2009] App. no. 821/03 [67].
[172] ECtHR, Financial Times Ltd and others v. the United Kingdom [2009] App. no. 821/03 [69].
[173] ECtHR, Financial Times Ltd and others v. the United Kingdom [2009] App. no. 821/03 [69].
[174] ECtHR, Financial Times Ltd and others v. the United Kingdom [2009] App. no. 821/03 [71].

It is highly controversial, however, whether freedom of expression also includes a right of access to information that others, in particular the government, are *not* willing to impart (see subsection 2).

1 The Right to Receive Information

The recipients of information and ideas, the 'destinations' under communication theory, have a right to receive information according to Articles 19(2) ICCPR, 10(1) ECHR and 11(1) EUChFR. Within the framework of the EU, the right to receive information originating from other EU Member States, such as broadcasting via a satellite dish, is also protected as a right to receive services within the meaning of Article 56 TFEU.[175]

The human right to receive information is a corollary of the right to freedom of expression. It is an original right to receive a speaker's expression alongside a speaker's right to express himself, and not a mere derivative right.[176] As a consequence, the right to receive information imposes on states the duty not to restrict a person from receiving information that others wish, or may be willing, to impart on him.[177] Therefore, speakers do not only have the right to impart information and ideas via means of mass and distance communication; the recipients also have a right to receive them.[178] In addition, states may even be under a positive obligation to enable potential recipients to receive information.

The right to receive information is interfered with even when measures merely make receiving information more cumbersome.[179] For example, the prohibition on receiving television programmes by means of a dish or other aerial inhibits the right to receive information.[180] In *Faccio* v. *Italy*, the Court decided that sealing off the applicants' television amounted to an interference with Article 10(1) ECHR, which, however, was justified because the applicant refused to pay his licence fee.[181] The Inter-American Commission of Human Rights held in *Tarciso Medina Charry* v. *Colombia* that the detainment of a person for merely carrying a communist newspaper violated his right to seek, receive and impart information and ideas.[182] Furthermore, an injunction to install an internet blocking system as a measure of enforcement of

---

[175] See ECJ, Case C-17/00 [2001] De Coster.

[176] See the analysis of Ramsay (2012), providing further references.

[177] Human Rights Committee, Mavlonov et al. v. Uzbekistan [2009] Communication no. 1334/2004 [8.4]; EComHR, Loersch and Nouvelle Association du Courrier v. Switzerland [1995] App. nos. 23868/94 and 23869/94 [3]; ECtHR, Faccio v. Italy [2003] App. no. 33/04.

[178] See, among many other authorities, Human Rights Committee, Mavlonov et al. v. Uzbekistan [2009] Communication no. 1334/2004 [8.4]; ECtHR, Sunday Times v. United Kingdom (No. 1) [1979] App. no. 6538/74 [65]; Observer and Guardian v. United Kingdom [1991] App. no. 13585/88 [59]; Bladet Tromsø and Stensaas v. Norway [1999] App. no. 21980/93 [62].

[179] ECtHR, Társaság a Szabadságjogokért v. Hungary [2009] App. no. 37374/05 [26].

[180] ECtHR, Autronic AG v. Switzerland [1990] App. no. 12726/87 [47]; Khurshid Mustafa and Tarzibachi v. Sweden [2008] App. no. 23883/06 [36].

[181] Faccio v. Italy [2003] App. no. 33/04.

[182] Tarciso Medina Charry v. Colombia [1998] Case 11.221 [77].

rights of others must also be measured against the rights of affected internet users to receive information.[183]

It should be noted that the right to receive information does not dispose of the requirement of 'standing' in a court trial. Under the case law of the Strasbourg Court, the right to receive information must not be conceptualised in a way that it allows an *actio popularis*. It would thus not be sufficient, for example, to claim a violation of one's right to receive information merely because a newspaper of which a person is a regular reader has been prohibited.[184] In the recent decision *Cengiz and others v. Turkey*, however, the Strasbourg Court decided that the right of two Turkish academics to receive information had been violated because a Turkish court order had requested to block access to YouTube.[185] This was because, according to the Court, the applicants had a particular professional interest in accessing videos posted on YouTube.[186] By comparison, the African Charter on Human and Peoples' Rights (AfChHPR) seems to conceptualise the right to receive information even as a right that may be invoked by way of an *actio popularis*. Article 9 AfCHPR locates the right to receive information in a paragraph prior to freedom of expression. The African Commission on Human and Peoples' Rights (AfComHPR) therefore scrutinises interferences with freedom of expression not only under Article 9(2) AfCHPR, but also under Article 9(1) AfCHPR. The Commission has held, for instance, that the proscription of a newspaper or the imprisonment of a journalist violates not only the publisher's right, but also the rights of the public to receive information protected by Article 9(1) AfCHPR.[187]

2 *The Right of Access to Information*

It is controversial whether there is a right of access to information that others, particularly the government, are *not* willing to impart. This controversy revolves around the question how the right of access to information, or 'freedom of information', should be conceptualised: as an intrinsic right or as an instrumental right. Conceptualised as an intrinsic right, access to information has to be granted without the applicant having to demonstrate a particular interest in, or purpose of doing something with, the information that is requested. Accordingly, freedom of information applies to everyone and for no specific purpose. Conceptualised as an instrumental right, access to information applies only under certain conditions: either under the right to respect

---

[183] CJEU, Case C-314/12 [2014] UPC Telekabel Wien GmbH v. Constantin Film Verleih and others [47].

[184] ECtHR, Tanrıkulu, Çetin and Kaya v. Turkey [2001] App. no. 40160/98.

[185] ECtHR, Cengiz and others v. Turkey [2015] App. nos. 48226/10 and 14027/11.

[186] ECtHR, Cengiz and others v. Turkey [2015] App. nos. 48226/10 and 14027/11 [49].

[187] AfComHPR, Media Rights Agenda, Constitutional Rights Project, Media Rights Agenda and Constitutional Rights Project v. Nigeria [1998] App. nos. 105/93, 128/94, 130/94 and 152/96 [57]; Constitutional Rights Project, Civil Liberties Organisation and Media Rights Agenda v. Nigeria [1999] App. nos. 140/94, 141/94 and 145/95 [38]; Scanlen & Holderness v. Zimbabwe [2009] App. no. 297/05 [108].

for private life if the applicant has a particular private interest in the information, or under freedom of expression if the applicant is a 'social watchdog' that wants to use the information to contribute to a debate of general interest, such as NGOs or the journalistic media.

EU primary and secondary law grant relatively generous intrinsic freedom of information rights. Article 42 EUChFR and – with some reservations – Article 15(3) TFEU stipulate that '[a]ny citizen of the Union, and any natural or legal person residing or having its registered office in a Member State, has a right of access to documents of the institutions, bodies, offices and agencies of the Union, whatever their medium'. Several pieces of secondary legislation further expatiate on this right.[188]

The first international human rights court to declare access to public information an aspect of freedom of expression was the Inter-American Court of Human Rights in its seminal judgment *Claude Reyes and others* v. *Chile*.[189] In this case, an NGO unsuccessfully requested information from the Chilean Committee on Foreign Investment on a deforestation project. The NGO wished to evaluate the commercial factors and also the environmental impact of this activity. In its decision, the Inter-American Commission on Human Rights held that the divulgence of state-held information plays a very important role in a democratic society, because it enables citizens to control the actions of the government to which it has entrusted the protection of its interests.[190] The Inter-American Court of Human Rights then observed:

> [A]ccess to public information is an essential requisite for the exercise of democracy, greater transparency and responsible public administration and that, in a representative and participative democratic system, the citizenry exercises its constitutional rights through a broad freedom of expression and free access to information.[191]

The Court therefore acknowledged access to information as a fundamental right, but it is subject to certain exceptions. In the instant case, the Court held that the restriction applied to the access to information was not based on a law, since there had been

---

[188] Regulation (EC) No. 1049/2001 of the European Parliament and of the Council of 30 May 2001 regarding public access to European Parliament, Council and Commission documents, L 145/43; Decision of the European Central Bank of 4 March 2004 on public access to European Central Bank documents (2004/258/EC), OJ L 80/42; Directive 2003/4/EC of the European Parliament and of the Council of 28 January 2003 on public access to environmental information and repealing Council Directive 90/313/EEC, OJ L 41/26; Directive 2003/98/EC of the European Parliament and of the Council of 17 November 2003 on the reuse of public sector information, OJ L 345/90. On the interpretation of these pieces of legislation, see, for example, ECJ, Joined Cases C-39/05 P and C-52/05 P [2008] Sweden and Turco v. Council; CJEU, Joined Cases C-514/07 P, C-528/07 P and C-532/07 P [2010] Sweden and others v. API and Commission; Case C-506/08 P [2011] Sweden v. MyTravel Group plc and Commission; Case C-280/11 P [2013] Council v. Access Info Europe; Case T-395/13 [2015] Miettinen v. Council. From academic literature, see Adamski (2014).

[189] Claude Reyes and others v. Chile [2006] Case 12.108.

[190] See Claude Reyes and others v. Chile [2006] Case 12.108 [58].

[191] Claude Reyes and others v. Chile [2006] Case 12.108 [84].

no legislation in Chile that regulated the issue of restrictions to access to state-held information.[192] Furthermore, the respondent state 'did not prove that the restriction responded to a purpose allowed by the American Convention, or that it was necessary in a democratic society, because the authority responsible for responding to the request for information did not adopt a justified decision in writing, communicating the reasons for restricting access to this information in the specific case.'[193]

Similarly, the Human Rights Committee interprets the right to seek and receive information rather broadly as a right of access to information.[194] In its General Comment on Article 19, the Committee stated that Article 19(2) ICCPR 'embraces a right of access to information held by public bodies. Such information includes records held by a public body, regardless of the form in which the information is stored, its source and the date of production.'[195] In *Toktakunov v. Kyrgyzstan*, the Committee held:

> [T]he right to freedom of thought and expression includes the protection of the right of access to State-held information, which also clearly includes the two dimensions, individual and social, of the right to freedom of thought and expression that must be guaranteed simultaneously by the State. In these circumstances, the Committee is of the opinion that the State party had an obligation either to provide the author with the requested information or to justify any restrictions of the right to receive State-held information under [Article 19(3) ICCPR].[196]

Freedom of information as an intrinsic right is based on the principles of openness and transparency of public authority.[197] Only well-informed citizens may discuss matters of public interest and contribute to the marketplace of ideas. However, the practical disadvantage of conceptualising freedom of information as an intrinsic right is obvious: If applicants do not have to show a particular interest in receiving the information, freedom of information is prone to abuse. Individuals may frequently file complicated freedom of information requests to the public administration merely to keep the civil servants busy. This is arguably the reason for ECtHR to refuse accepting an intrinsic right of access to information, although documents of the Council of Europe and international recommendations encourage Member States to establish such freedom of information acts.[198] In *Leander v. Sweden*, the

---

[192] Claude Reyes and others v. Chile [2006] Case 12.108 [94].
[193] Claude Reyes and others v. Chile [2006] Case 12.108 [95].
[194] See Gauthier v. Canada [1999] Communication no. 633/95 [13.4]; Toktakunov v. Kyrgyzstan [2011] Communication no. 1470/2006 [6.3].
[195] General Comment no. 34, para. 18.
[196] Toktakunov v. Kyrgyzstan [2011] Communication no. 1470/2006 [7.4].
[197] See Goldberg (2009); Oswald (2012); Recital 2 of Regulation 1049/2001 regarding public access to European Parliament, Council and Commission documents.
[198] See Council of Europe, Convention on Access to Official Documents, adopted on 27 November 2008; Recommendation No. R (81) 19 on the access to information held by public authorities;

Court held that 'Article 10 does not, [...] confer on the individual a right of access to a register containing information on his personal position, nor does it embody an obligation on the Government to impart such information to the individual'.[199] Instead, the Strasbourg Court has conceptualised access to information as an instrumental right; that is, as a right dependent on the applicant's particular interest in the information. The Strasbourg Court found in a number of cases that the authorities had an obligation under Article 8 ECHR to disclose certain data that was relevant for the applicant, such as information about risks to one's health and well-being resulting from environmental pollution,[200] information that would permit them to assess any risk resulting from their participation in nuclear tests,[201] tests involving exposure to toxic chemicals,[202] access to social service records containing information about their childhood and personal history[203] and access to copies of their medical records.[204] However, the Court had been reluctant to recognise that Article 10 ECHR guarantees a general and independent right of access to state-held information, and thus saw no obligation on governments to provide such data to the public.[205] Yet since 2006,[206] the Court has progressed towards a broader interpretation of the notion of 'freedom to receive information' and thereby towards the recognition of a general right of access to information. However, the cases that were brought to Strasbourg all involved NGOs and other organisations that had an interest in the information concerned, because they intended to use it in order to fulfil their particular role as 'social watchdogs'. In *Társaság a Szabadságjogokért* v. *Hungary*, an NGO concerned with the promotion and protection of human rights requested the Hungarian Constitutional Court to grant them access to a complaint pending at the court concerning drug-related offences. The court refused. The Strasburg Court, placing the NGO on equal footing with the journalistic media, held that 'the State's obligations in matters of freedom of the press include the elimination of barriers to the exercise of press functions where, in issues of public interest, such barriers exist solely because of an information monopoly held by the authorities'.[207] The Court considered that 'obstacles created in order to hinder access to information of public interest may discourage

---

Recommendation No. R (91) 10 on the communication to third parties of personal data held by public bodies; Recommendation No. R (97) 18 concerning the protection of personal data collected and processed for statistical purposes; Recommendation No. R (2000) 13 on a European policy on access to archives; Recommendation Rec(2002)2 on access to official documents.

[199] ECtHR, Leander v. Sweeden [1987] App. no. 9248/81 [74].

[200] Guerra and others v. Italy [1998] App. no. 116/1996/735/932 [60].

[201] McGinley and Egan v. United Kingdom [1998] App. no. 10/1997/794/995–996 [101].

[202] Roche v. United Kingdom [2005] App. no. 32555/96 [167].

[203] M.G. v. United Kingdom [2002] App. no. 39393/98 [27].

[204] K.H. and others v. Slovakia [2009] App. no. 32881/04 [50].

[205] See Leander v. Sweden [1987] App. no. 9248/81 [74]; Matky v. Czech Republic [2006] App. no. 19101/03, p. 10; Társaság a Szabadságjogokért v. Hungary [2009] App. no. 37374/05 [35].

[206] The first decision in which the ECtHR considered (but eventually rejected) to derive a right to access to public documents from Article 10 ECHR was Matky v. Czech Republic [2006] App. no. 19101/03.

[207] Társaság a Szabadságjogokért v. Hungary [2009] App. no. 37374/05 [35].

those working in the media or related fields from pursuing such matters'.[208] As a consequence, 'they may no longer be able to play their vital role as "public watchdogs" and their ability to provide accurate and reliable information may be adversely affected'.[209] As a result, the Court held that there had been a violation of the NGO's rights out of Article 10 ECHR.

In the case of *Youth Initiative for Human Rights* v. *Serbia*, the Strasbourg Court held that the refusal of an intelligence agency to provide the applicant NGO with information as to the use of electronic surveillance measures constituted an interference with the applicant's right to freedom of expression, as 'the applicant was obviously involved in the legitimate gathering of information of public interest with the intention of imparting that information to the public and thereby contributing to the public debate'.[210] But because of the factual peculiarities of the case, the precedential character of the decision for a general right of access to information should not be overrated: the intelligence agency first refused the request and then, after an order by the Information Commissioner that the information at issue be nevertheless disclosed, the intelligence agency notified the applicant that it did not hold that information. After very brief reasoning, the Court concluded that 'the obstinate reluctance of the intelligence agency of Serbia to comply with the order of the Information Commissioner was in defiance of domestic law [i.e., the Serbian Freedom of Information Act 2004] and tantamount to arbitrariness'.[211] However, *Youth Initiative for Human Rights* v. *Serbia* may be seen as a further step of the ECtHR to accept a general right of access to information out of Article 10 ECHR. Judges Sajó and Vučinić highlighted 'the general need to interpret Article 10 in conformity with developments in international law regarding freedom of information' in their concurring opinion.[212]

The Strasbourg Court then moved a step closer towards a general right of access to information, at least for the media and other associations involved in the legitimate gathering of information of public interest, in the case of *Österreichische Vereinigung zur Erhaltung, Stärkung und Schaffung eines wirtschaftlich gesunden land- und forstwirtschaftlichen Grundbesitzes* v. *Austria*.[213] In this case, the applicant association requested paper copies of all decisions issued by a public Real Property Transactions Commission from 1 January 2000 to mid-2005. It argued that the state had an obligation either to publish all decisions of the Commission in an electronic database, or to provide it with anonymised paper copies upon request, which the Commission

---

208 Társaság a Szabadságjogokért v. Hungary [2009] App. no. 37374/05 [38].
209 Társaság a Szabadságjogokért v. Hungary [2009] App. no. 37374/05 [38].
210 Youth Initiative for Human Rights v. Serbia [2013] App. no. 48135/06 [24].
211 Youth Initiative for Human Rights v. Serbia [2013] App. no. 48135/06 [26].
212 Youth Initiative for Human Rights v. Serbia [2013] App. no. 48135/06, concurring opinion of Judges Sajó and Vučinić.
213 Österreichische Vereinigung zur Erhaltung, Stärkung und Schaffung eines wirtschaftlich gesunden land- und forstwirtschaftlichen Grundbesitzes v. Austria [2013] App. no. 39534/07 [34–36] and [41].

refused. Although the Strasbourg Court did 'not consider that a general obligation of this scope can be inferred from its case law under Article 10', it nonetheless saw its task in the present case 'to examine whether the reasons given by the domestic authorities for refusing the applicant association's request were "relevant and sufficient" in the specific circumstances of the case and whether the interference was proportionate to the legitimate aim pursued'.[214] Yet this reasoning seems paradoxical: if a general obligation to provide access to information cannot be inferred from Article 10 ECHR, then there has been no interference with that right in the present case. To scrutinise whether the reasons given by the domestic authorities to justify 'the interference' were 'relevant and sufficient' is illogical if there has been no such interference. An examination of the justification of the refusal to grant access to information would only be necessary if access to information is a right encompassed by Article 10(1) ECHR.

The Court eventually found that the reasons relied on by the domestic authorities in refusing the applicant association's request were 'relevant', but not 'sufficient'. It decided that a complete refusal to give it access to any of its decisions was disproportionate, since the Commission held an information monopoly in respect of its decisions. This made it impossible for the applicant association to carry out its research and to participate in a meaningful manner in the legislative process concerning amendments of real estate transaction law. Much of the difficulty brought forward by the Commission was caused by its own choice not to publish any of its decisions.[215]

Howsoever access to information is conceptualised – as an intrinsic or an instrumental right, as a right applying to everyone or only to privileged rights-holders – it is not an unlimited right. It has to be balanced with conflicting rights and interests, such as the protection of personal data, intellectual property or national security.[216]

In contrast to access to public information, access to *private* information, such as information held by internet service providers, can only be based on statutory law. For example, Article 12 of the EU Data Protection Directive obliges Member States to guarantee every data subject the right to obtain from the controller certain information regarding the processing of data relating to him. But such a right cannot be derived from freedom of expression, because it does not have a direct effect between individuals.

V The Rights of Intermediaries

In order to communicate a message, an author or creator has to use a particular medium or media. The choice of the medium or media may involve other individuals

---

[214] Österreichische Vereinigung zur Erhaltung, Stärkung und Schaffung eines wirtschaftlich gesunden land- und forstwirtschaftlichen Grundbesitzes v. Austria [2013] App. no. 39534/07 [42].

[215] Österreichische Vereinigung zur Erhaltung, Stärkung und Schaffung eines wirtschaftlich gesunden land- und forstwirtschaftlichen Grundbesitzes v. Austria [2013] App. no. 39534/07 [46–47].

[216] See, for example, Human Rights Committee, Gauthier v. Canada [1999] Communication no. 633/95 [13.4]; Toktakunov v. Kyrgyzstan [2011] Communication no. 1470/2006 [7.5]; Article 4 of Regulation 1049/2001 regarding public access to European Parliament, Council and Commission documents. From academic literature, see, for example, Tiilikka (2013, p. 83); Oswald (2012).

or companies in the communication process. Such communication intermediaries may be, for instance, providers of noticeboards, booksellers, libraries, newspaper vendors or ISPs. By providing such media, intermediaries play an invaluable role for human communication. But by providing means of communication, intermediaries inevitably increase the risk of violations of public order interests or rights of others, albeit involuntarily.[217] For example, the CJEU emphasised with regard to search engines that 'the activity of a search engine can be distinguished from and is additional to that carried out by publishers of websites'.[218] By aggregating and structuring information published on the internet, search engines render webpages with personal information accessible, for instance, on the basis of a person's name, which internet users in many cases would not have found.[219] Search engines thus assist in making statements known to the public that otherwise would have been a needle in a haystack.

The treatment of speech intermediaries is the area of law that gained most significance in the development of modern communication technologies. While the law of speech intermediaries in the pre-internet age concerned book publishers, newspaper vendors and postal services, the liability of internet service providers is one of the core features of modern media law. A human rights-compliant approach to liability of communication intermediaries has to strike a proper balance between the socially beneficial function of such intermediaries and the individual harm they may contribute to. Section 230(c)(1) of the Communications Decency Act 1996[220] furnishes ISPs with total immunity from defamation actions. This approach is understandable within the context of the robust protection of free speech by the First Amendment to the US Constitution. However, in the realm of the ECHR and the EUChFR, such a sweeping immunity for ISPs – and for communication intermediaries in general[221] – would fail to achieve a proper balance between the conflicting rights and interests: the freedom to impart information of the content provider, the corollary right of other individual(s) or the general public to receive such information and the interests of the person whose rights (copyright, reputation, privacy, etc.) have been violated or the public order interest of the interfering state. Finally, speech intermediaries themselves have a right to impart third-party information under Articles 19(2) ICCPR, 10(1) ECHR and 11(1) EUChFR.[222] These provisions do not make an express distinction according to the role played by persons in the exercise of that freedom. Unlike, for instance, Article 5(1) of the German Basic Law, which only guarantees

---

[217] See Oster (2015a).

[218] Case C-131/12 [2014] Google Spain SL v. AEPD and others [35].

[219] Case C-131/12 [2014] Google Spain SL v. AEPD and others [36–37].

[220] 47 USC § 230.

[221] Total immunities for speech intermediaries are exceptional (see, for example, the UK Postal Services Act 2000, s 90).

[222] CJEU, Case C-70/10 [2011] Scarlet Extended v. SABAM and others, Opinion of Advocate-General Cruz-Villalón [85]; compare Case C-314/12 [2014] UPC Telekabel Wien GmbH v. Constantin Film Verleih and others.

the freedom to express one's *own* opinions, Articles 19(2) ICCPR, 10 ECHR and 11(1) EUChFR apply not only to the content provider of information, but also to the provider of means of dissemination. Even if speech disseminators do not associate themselves with the opinions expressed in the works they help to disseminate, they participate in the exercise of freedom of expression by providing authors with a medium.[223]

In addition, if intermediaries act on a professional basis, they enjoy the right to conduct a business according to Article 16 EUChFR.[224] Within the framework of the internal market, intermediaries also enjoy freedom to provide services according to Article 56 TFEU, if applicable.

At the same time, communication intermediaries are, according to Article 10(2) ECHR and 19(3) ICCPR, subject to 'duties and responsibilities'. Therefore, a human rights-compliant approach to liability of communication intermediaries has to strike a proper balance between the socially beneficial function of such intermediaries and the social or individual harm to which they may contribute. The limitations of the freedoms of intermediaries essentially correspond to the limitations on content providers. If a content provider is not allowed to disseminate certain information, such as 'hate speech' or copyright-infringing material, the intermediary may be subject to restrictions as well. However, the parameters for justifying an interference are slightly different. Unlike media freedom, which is applicable only to journalistic content providers, the right to impart third-party information does not afford privileged protection to speech intermediaries. For example, search engine operators may be obliged to delist certain content from their search results, although the content provider may still publish the content on his website. As the CJEU explained in its *Google Spain* decision:

> [T]he outcome of the weighing of the interests at issue ... may differ according to whether the processing carried out by the operator of a search engine or that carried out by the publisher of the web page is at issue, given that, first, the legitimate interests justifying the processing may be different and, second, the consequences of the processing for the data subject, and in particular for his private life, are not necessarily the same.[225]

However, if and because they are not aware of the content they disseminate, speech intermediaries sometimes lack accountability for the content they transmit. This is codified in secondary EU law and domestic law, for example, in Articles 12–14 of the E-commerce Directive, Section 1 of the UK Defamation Act 1996 and Section 5(2) of

---

[223] See ECtHR, Groppera Radio AG and others v. Switzerland [1990] App. no. 10890/84; Öztürk v. Turkey [1999] App. no. 22479/93 [49].

[224] See CJEU, Case C-314/12 [2014] UPC Telekabel Wien GmbH v. Constantin Film Verleih and others [47]. The ECHR protects only single aspects of businesses, such as property under Article 1 First Protocol ECHR or business premises as 'home' under Article 8(1) ECHR.

[225] CJEU, Case C-131/12 [2014] Google Spain SL v. AEPD and others [86]. This case will be further dealt with in Chapter 8.

the UK Defamation Act 2013. Intermediaries also have to observe data protection rules, and they may be under an obligation to grant access to their infrastructure and services, such as under 'must carry' obligations (see Chapters 5 and 7).

VI Questions

1 As can be seen from *Fatullayev v. Azerbaijan*, *Růžový panter, o.s.* v. *Czech Republic* and *Braun* v. *Poland*, which we discussed in Chapter 1, the ECtHR blurs the boundaries between freedom of the journalistic media and freedom of expression of non-journalistic individuals and entities. However, those cases only concerned the protection of speech. Should an NGO or a historian also be entitled to specific privileges of the journalistic media, such as keeping their sources of information confidential, and under what circumstances?

2 If the protection of speakers depends more on the extent to which they contribute to matters of public concern and the adherence to standards of due diligence, and less on their categorisation as journalists or 'freedom of expression only' citizens, what would be the impact on tabloid journalism? For example, would the government be entitled to prefer 'serious' journalists/bloggers to light entertainment media when distributing a limited number of seats for a press conference?

3 For whom is it to decide whether a publication contributes to a matter of public concern?

VII Further Reading

- E. Barendt, *Freedom of Speech*, 2nd edn, 2005
- O. Castendyk, E. Dommering and A. Scheuer (eds.), *European Media Law*, 2008
- D. Hunter, R. Lobato, M. Richardson and J. Thomas, *Amateur Media: Social, Cultural and Legal Perspectives*, 2012
- H. Fenwick and G. Phillipson, *Media Freedom under the Human Rights Act*, 2006
- D. Geradin and D. Luff, *The WTO and Global Convergence in Telecommunications and Audio-Visual Services*, 2004
- D. Goldberg, G. Sutter and I. Walden, *Media Law and Practice*, 2009
- P. Keller, *European and International Media Law*, 2011
- T. McGonagle and Y. Donders (eds.), *The United Nations and Freedom of Expression and Information: Critical Perspectives*, 2015
- J. Oster, *Media Freedom as a Fundamental Right*, 2015
- T. Voon, *Cultural Products and the World Trade Organization*, 2007
- S. Wunsch-Vincent, *The WTO, the Internet and Trade in Digital Products, EC–US Perspectives*, 2006

3

Restrictions on Freedom of Expression and Media Freedom

CASE EXAMPLES

X is a well-known television actor. Between 1998 and 2003 he played the part of a police superintendent, the hero of a television series. In 2003 the tabloid newspaper *Bild*, published by the Axel Springer AG, revealed that X had been convicted of unlawful possession of drugs. After receiving a warning from X, it undertook, on pain of an agreed penalty, to refrain from publishing information according to which four grams of cocaine had been found at X's home, for which he had been given a prison sentence, suspended for five months, and fined €5,000. On 23 September 2004, X was arrested at the Munich beer festival (*Oktoberfest*) for possession of cocaine. A journalist from Axel Springer AG declared that she had asked the police present at the scene whether X had been arrested and, if so, on what grounds. The police had confirmed that X had been arrested in an *Oktoberfest* tent in possession of cocaine, information that was subsequently confirmed by the public prosecutor's office of Munich. In its 29 September 2004 edition, the *Bild* newspaper published an article on X's arrest with a large-type headline on its front page. The article was accompanied by three photos of X. In its 7 July 2005 edition, *Bild* printed an article on the criminal trial against X for the unlawful possession of drugs. The article was accompanied by a photo of X.

Immediately after the articles appeared, X instituted proceedings against Axel Springer AG. The courts prohibited any further publication of almost the entire first article and of the second article and ordered Axel Springer AG to pay c. €1,500 in total as a penalty. According to the courts, the articles in question amounted to a serious interference with X's personality rights. Given that the crime at issue was not particularly serious, the right to protection of X's personality rights prevailed over the public's interest in being informed, even if the truth of the facts related by the daily had not been disputed.

(ECtHR, Axel Springer AG v. Germany (No. 1) [2012] App. no. 39954/08)

Mr Braun is a film director, historian, and author of press articles often commenting on current issues. In April 2007, he participated in a debate on a regional radio station and subsequently gave an interview on television. Both times he stated that J.M., a well-known linguistic professor, used to be an informer of the communist-era secret political police. J.M. brought a civil action against Mr Braun. The domestic courts examined the veracity of Mr Braun's statement, heard experts and researched the remaining files of the communist-era security services. Although they confirmed that the claimant had indeed been registered as a collaborator and in the past there had been a two-volume file on him, the file in question could no longer be found. The courts thus concluded that it could not be proven that the claimant had intentionally and secretly collaborated with the regime. Mr Braun's statement was therefore considered untrue and, as he was not a journalist, he could not benefit from the journalistic privilege to erroneously publish false statements, although he had conducted considerable research before he went public with his allegations. The courts ordered Mr Braun to pay a fine to a charity and to publish an apology.

(ECtHR, Braun v. Poland [2014] App. no. 30162/10)

I Introduction

Interferences with fundamental rights, and thus also with freedom of expression and media freedom, are allowed if such limitations are prescribed by law (principle of legality), pursue a legitimate aim (principle of legitimacy) and are necessary in pursuit of this aim (principle of proportionality). Legitimate aims are, in the first place, the aims mentioned in Articles 19(3) ICCPR, 10(2) ECHR and 52 EUChFR. Aims that are not expressly provided in those paragraphs may under certain circumstances nonetheless justify an interference with freedom of expression. With regard to media law, this may in particular be the aim of achieving a high level of media pluralism.

The proportionality test examines:

1 whether the interference was suitable to achieve the legitimate aim pursued (suitability);
2 whether the interference was the least intrusive instrument among those which might achieve the legitimate aim (necessity); and
3 whether the interference was strictly proportionate to the legitimate aim pursued (proportionality *sensu stricto*).[1]

However, an international adjudicator's task is not to take the place of the national authorities, but rather to *review* under the human rights convention the decisions they have taken.[2] Within this review, international adjudicators grant a margin of appreciation to the member states. The more this margin of appreciation is limited, the stricter the scrutiny an international adjudicator applies regarding the legal and factual circumstances of an application. A narrow margin of appreciation therefore

---

[1] See, among many other authorities, Human Rights Commitee, Ballantyne and others v. Canada [1993] Communication no. 359, 385/89 [11.4]; Coleman v. Australia [2006] Communication no. 1157/2003 [7.3]; ECtHR, Sunday Times v. United Kingdom (No. 1) [1979] App. no. 6538/74 [62]; Observer and Guardian v. United Kingdom [1991] App. no. 13585/88 [59] ECJ, Case C-331/88 [1990] R v. Minister for Agriculture, ex p Fedesa [13]; CJEU, Case C-283/11 [2013] Sky Österreich v. Österreichischer Rundfunk [48] and [50].
[2] ECtHR, Handyside v. United Kingdom [1976] App. no. 5493/72 [50]; Sunday Times v. United Kingdom (No. 1) [1979] App. no. 6538/74 [59].

leads to a higher degree of harmonisation of domestic laws. In turn, a broad margin of appreciation maintains a fragmentation of the legal regimes and strengthens the significance of jurisdictional rules (see Chapter 4). The scope of the margin of appreciation depends on the reason for the interference. There are situations where domestic authorities are better placed to make normative evaluations concerning issues that require knowledge of local sensitivities, such as the protection of morals, or a factual assessment, such as the necessity of measures to protect national security.[3]

Certain types of interferences are fundamentally contrary to freedom of expression and media freedom in a way that they destroy the essence of this right, and may thus under no circumstances be justified. Such interferences include attacks on journalists targeted at their profession, such as arbitrary arrest, torture, threats to life and killing.[4] Furthermore, statutory or administrative requirements to submit a publication to a public authority in advance in order to obtain permission to publish, such as licensing requirements for books and newspapers, cannot be reconciled with media freedom, and should therefore never be subject to a balancing exercise.[5]

If the interference is not unjustified in abstract terms, then the value attached to the exercise of freedom of expression or media freedom, on the one hand, and to the conflicting interest, on the other hand, must be estimated in *relative* terms with a view to the particular case. Neither freedom of expression/media freedom nor any other norm – apart from rights protected in absolute terms, such as human dignity[6] – enjoys precedence *per se* over the other. Both freedom of expression and media freedom are subject to 'duties and responsibilities' – notably, no other human right provides such a qualification. As a consequence, the intensity of protection afforded to freedom of expression and media freedom depends on the extent to which speakers abide by their duties and responsibilities, or whether they abuse their right to speak and publish freely. Where content providers do not act according to their duties and responsibilities, the relative importance of their protection is significantly lowered.

This chapter describes certain categories of limitations to freedom of expression and media freedom. Note that these labels are not mutually exclusive. The same expression, such as religiously offensive speech, may involve an attack on morality, incitement to hatred and an attack on a person's reputation.

---

[3] See, for more details, Oster (2015b, pp. 118 ff).

[4] See, for example, Human Rights Committee, Mukong v. Cameroon [1994] Communication no. 458/91 [9.7]; Marques de Morais v. Angola [2005] Communication no. 1128/2002 [6.8]; Njaru v. Cameroon [2007] Communication no. 1353/2005 [6.4].

[5] Compare Milton (1644); German Federal Constitutional Court, Case 1 BvL 13/67 [1972] 'Censorship'.

[6] See Article 1 EUChFR; Article 1(1) of the German Basic Law.

II Personality Rights

Articles 19(3)(a) ICCPR and 10(2) ECHR state that the exercise of freedom of expression may be subject to, *inter alia*, restrictions as are necessary for the protection of the rights of others. The most relevant 'rights of others' are the rights relating to one's personality: the right to respect for honour, reputation and privacy according to Article 17 ICCPR, and the right to private life according to Articles 8(1) ECHR and 7 EUChFR. A personality right in the broader sense is freedom of religion according to Articles 18 ICCPR and 9(1) ECHR. Further 'rights of others' are intellectual property rights and other exclusive rights.

1 The Taxonomy of 'Personality Rights'

The wording of international conventions is not coherent regarding the protection of honour, reputation and privacy. Article 17 ICCPR is the only provision expressly protecting privacy, honour and reputation. Articles 8 ECHR and 7 EUChFR use the term 'private life'. However, the ICCPR and the ECHR/EUChFR merely use different terms for the same legal concepts. Together with the right to privacy, honour and reputation are thus subcategories of the concept of 'private life'.[7]

Unlike Articles 12 UDHR and 17 ICCPR, Articles 8 ECHR and 7 EUChFR do not expressly provide for a right to protection against attacks on a person's honour and reputation. However, the ECtHR has, in recent cases, recognised reputation and also honour as part of the right to respect for private life.[8] The concept of 'honour' can be subcategorised into a person's self-esteem and a person's esteem by others; that is, a person's reputation. For instance, the tort of defamation protects a person's reputation and not just a person's honour, as it requires that at least one recipient of the defamatory statement is not identical to the defamed person. By contrast, the legal concept of 'insult'[9] also protects against a violation of a person's self-esteem by punishing derogatory statements made face-to-face.

Therefore, an individual's reputation and honour are not only protected as defensive rights against free speech, as Article 10(2) ECHR suggests. Rather, they have their own value as fundamental rights, namely as characteristics of the right

---

[7] On reputation, see, for example, ECtHR, Chauvy and others v. France [2004] App. no. 64915/01 [70]; Radio France and others v. France [2004] App. no. 53984/00 [31]; Pfeifer v. Austria [2007] App. no. 12556/03 [35]. On honour, see, for example, ECtHR, Polanco Torres et Movilla Polanco v. Spain [2010] App. no. 34147/06 [40]; A. v. Norway [2009] App. no. 28070/06 [64].

[8] ECtHR, Radio France and others v. France [2004] App. no. 53984/00 [31]; reiterated in, for example, Pfeifer v. Austria [2007] App. no. 12556/03 [35]; Alithia Publishing Company Ltd and Constantinides v. Cyprus [2008] App. no. 17550/03 [53]; A. v. Norway [2009] App. no. 28070/06 [64]. See also Fenwick and Phillipson (2006, p. 1069).

[9] See, for example, Section 185 of the German Criminal Law Code.

to respect for private life as guaranteed in Article 8(1) ECHR. However, in *Axel Springer AG v. Germany (No. 1)*, the Grand Chamber of the Court required that 'an attack on a person's reputation must attain a certain level of seriousness' in order for Article 8 ECHR to come into play.[10] Yet the Court did not clarify in later decisions what this 'level of seriousness' actually is.[11]

Although a precise definition of privacy is still lacking, several aspects have been identified as being encompassed by the notion of privacy. Privacy relates to both the ability to physically shield oneself from unwanted access (privacy as freedom from intrusion), especially Warren and Brandeis' 'right to be let alone',[12] and the right to conceal certain information from others (information privacy). In philosophical terms, privacy can be explained by both deontological and utilitarian arguments. From a deontological point of view, privacy has to be protected because lives of others must be considered as ends in themselves, not as means to other ends, such as to satisfy another person's curiosity. This reveals the dignitarian character of privacy. As a utilitarian argument, privacy has to be protected because of the importance of private space for the development of an individual and thus for society in general, whereas the lack of privacy would lead to conformity. In doctrinal terms, privacy encompasses the institutions mentioned in Article 8 ECHR and Article 17 ICCPR: family, home and correspondence;[13] furthermore, a person's name[14] or picture;[15] a person's physical intimacy, such as nakedness, illness or injury;[16] a person's sexuality, sexual life and orientation;[17] the personality of each individual in his relations with other human beings;[18] and personal data.[19] Privacy thus contradicts the idea of a general right to know everything about everybody. Yet privacy is a relative term, which is in the first place defined by the rights-holder himself. While some people voluntarily abandon their privacy, for instance, by exhibiting their intimate life on

---

[10] Axel Springer AG v. Germany (No. 1) [2012] App. no. 39954/08 [83]; confirmed in Tănăsoaica v. Romania [2012] App. no. 3490/03 [37] and Lavric v. Romania [2014] App. no. 22231/05 [31]: 'a certain level of gravity'.

[11] Compare ECtHR, Soltész v. Slovakia [2013] App. no. 11867/09; Brosa v. Germany [2014] App. no. 5709/09.

[12] Warren and Brandeis (1890).

[13] These areas are not mutually exclusive; a measure can simultaneously interfere with both private and family life and the home or correspondence (Menteş and others v. Turkey [1997] App. no. 58/1996/677/867 [73]).

[14] See Articles 24(2) ICCPR, 18 ACHR and 7 and 8 of the UN Convention on the Rights of the Child; ECtHR, Burghartz v. Switzerland [1994] App. no. 16213/90 [24]; Standard Verlags GmbH v. Austria (No. 3) [2012] App. no. 34702/07 [36].

[15] ECtHR, Schüssel v. Austria [2002] App. no. 42409/98; Von Hannover v. Germany (No. 1) [2004] App. no. 59320/00 [50 ff]; Eerikäinen and others v. Finland [2009] App. no. 3514/02 [61].

[16] ECtHR, X and Y v. Netherlands [1985] App. no. 8978/80 [22]; Raninen v. Finland [1997] App. no. 152/1996/771/972 [63]; Biriuk v. Lithuania [2008] App. no. 23373/03 [43].

[17] ECtHR, Peck v. United Kingdom [2003] App. no. 44647/98 [57]; Biriuk v. Lithuania [2008] App. no. 23373/03 [34]; Ruusunen v. Finland [2014] App. no. 73579/10 [50].

[18] ECtHR, Botta v. Italy [1998] App. no. 153/1996/772/973 [32]; Von Hannover v. Germany (No. 1) [2004] App. no. 59320/00 [50].

[19] See Chapter 8.

social internet networks, others wish to protect their private sphere, and have a right to have it respected.

But rather than delving in more detail into the substantive notions of reputation and privacy, which would certainly go beyond the scope of this book, the following sections analyse personality rights externally; that is, with a view to possible *interferences* with these rights. They will show how the gathering or revelation of certain information can violate singular aspects of personality rights. In this context, the distinction between reputation and privacy is based on the dichotomy of factual information and comment, and the further distinction between true and false factual information. False statement of facts (which includes 'leaving out true facts which, had they been stated, could have significantly altered the perception of the matter'[20]) and defamatory comment may tarnish a person's reputation. By contrast, privacy is usually engaged where true but private information is being gathered or disclosed.[21]

2 The Balancing Exercise between Freedom of Expression and Personality Rights

The ECtHR summarised the criteria laid down in its case law for the balancing exercise between freedom of expression and the right to respect for private life in *Axel Springer AG* v. *Germany* (No. 1). The Court established the following six criteria:[22]

1 Whether the publication contributed to a debate of general interest.
2 How well known the person concerned is and what the subject of the report is.
3 The prior conduct of the person concerned.
4 The method of obtaining the information and its veracity.
5 The content, form and consequences of the publication.
6 The severity of the sanction imposed.

The Court subsequently applied those criteria rather statically to both privacy and defamation cases. Later on, however, the Court applied those criteria to defamation cases in moderated ways.[23] As has been stated previously, the crucial difference between cases related to information privacy and defamation cases usually lies in

---

[20] ECtHR, Shabanov and Tren v. Russia [2006] App. no. 5433/02 [36].
[21] Compare Marshall (1992, p. 54); ECtHR, Markt intern Verlag GmbH and Klaus Beermann v. Germany [1989] App. no. 10572/83 [35]. But see also John Terry (previously referred to as 'LNS') v. Persons Unknown [2010] EWHC 119 (QB) [96]: 'the law of privacy gives rise to an overlap with the law of defamation', albeit 'only in limited classes of cases'. For example, under US law, the publication of untrue facts that are not defamatory, but that portray a person in a 'false light', may give rise to a tort of invasion of privacy; see Prosser (1960, p. 400). In turn, under German law, a violation of a person's reputation may occur despite proof of truth if the defamation results from the circumstances under which the statement was made (Section 192 German Criminal Law Code). From academic literature, see Barendt (2015a).
[22] ECtHR, Axel Springer AG v. Germany (No. 1) [2012] App. no. 39954/08 [89–95]; reiterated in, for example, Satakunnan Markkinapörssi Oy and Satamedia Oy v. Finland [2015] App. no. 931/13 [62].
[23] See, for example, ECtHR, Armellini and others v. Austria [2015] App. no. 14134/07.

the veracity of the information concerned. As a consequence, the factors 'contribution to a debate of general interest', the publicity of the person concerned and the subject-matter of the publication, the prior conduct of the person concerned, the content, form and consequences of the publication and the severity of the sanction imposed are roughly the same in privacy and defamation cases. However, the criterion 'method of obtaining the information and its veracity' varies significantly between privacy and defamation.

Taking into consideration the Strasbourg Court's case law preceding and succeeding *Axel Springer AG*, the following – slightly amended – criteria provide the appropriate framework to approach both privacy and defamation cases:

1 The extent to which a publication contributes to a debate of public concern.
2 The position of the person concerned and the extent to which he is well known.
3 The prior conduct of the person concerned.
4 The content, form and consequences of the publication.
5 The veracity of the information and the prior conduct of the publisher.
6 The severity of the sanction imposed.

With regard to the margin of appreciation to be granted in cases of violations of personality rights, the Strasbourg Court has highlighted, first, that 'bearing in mind the diversity of the practices followed and the situations obtaining in the Contracting States' the requirements of the notion of 'respect' in Article 8 ECHR 'will vary considerably from case to case'.[24] Second, because of 'their direct and continuous contact with the vital forces of their countries', the ECtHR considers the state authorities 'in a better position than the international judge to give an opinion on how best to secure the right to respect for private life within the domestic legal order'.[25]

a The Extent to which a Publication Contributed to a Debate of Public Concern

Contributions to matters of public concern are strongly protected under any free speech theory. If, however, publications are not of public concern, they tend to enjoy less protection, and they may even constitute an abuse of freedom of expression if relating to exclusively private or even intimate matters. The term 'public concern' should be preferred to the more frequently used 'general interest' or 'public interest', which can be too easily confused with 'interest to the public'. 'Interest' is a subjective term, whereas 'concern' is an objective concept. This emphasises the fact that 'public concern' is a qualitative and normative, rather than an empirical or quantitative, criterion.[26]

'Public concern' is a vague concept. Nevertheless, three factors should provide guidance for both content providers and courts to establish 'public concern' in a particular

---

[24] Mosley v. United Kingdom [2011] App. no. 48009/08 [108].
[25] Mosley v. United Kingdom [2011] App. no. 48009/08 [108]. Critically Oster (2015b, pp. 152–153).
[26] Oster (2015b, p. 37).

case.[27] First, rather than asking the binary question if or if not a matter is of public concern, it has to be established *to what extent* it is of public concern. The more a publication pertains to a matter of public concern, the stronger the protection it deserves in the balancing exercise. For example, the alleged marital difficulties of the president of the Republic of Austria may, to a certain extent, pertain to the most intimate aspects of the President's private life.[28] On the other hand, they may also affect the exercise of his office and thus, to a certain extent, be of public concern. A further example is the alcohol problems of a famous actor. These are *to a certain degree* of public concern, because they may affect the public's awareness of, and attitude towards, consumption of alcoholic beverages. However, this issue is at the same time a significantly private matter, as it relates to a person's health.

Second, the attempt to establish the extent to which a publication contributes to a matter of 'public concern' might be facilitated by contrasting the concept of public concern to its counterpart: the degree to which a matter is of private concern. The concepts of 'public concern' and 'private concern' merge into one another. They should not be perceived as a 'binary opposition'.[29] The crucial question, therefore, is to what degree a matter is of public concern, and to what degree it is of private concern. Just like the term public concern, 'private concern' is not susceptible to an exhaustive definition. A matter is of private concern if it concerns a person's privacy. In the words of the Strasbourg Court, sensational and lurid news 'intended to titillate and entertain, which are aimed at satisfying the curiosity of a particular readership regarding aspects of a person's strictly private life',[30] serving only to 'entertain' and not to 'educate', would be of private but not of public concern.[31] Examples from case law are reportings of details of the private life of an individual who does not exercise public functions,[32] the love affair between a noblewoman and a banker[33] and the financial difficulties of a famous singer.[34]

Third, journalists and courts should always consider applicable precedences. Case law and international resolutions provide a variety of examples for publications that have been recognised as 'matters of public concern' or 'matters of public or general interest'. These include political reporting;[35] reporting on public

---

[27] See Oster (2015b, pp. 37 ff).

[28] See ECtHR, Standard Verlags GmbH v. Austria (No. 2) [2009] App. no. 21277/05.

[29] Moosavian (2014, p. 243).

[30] ECtHR, Mosley v. United Kingdom [2011] App. no. 48009/08 [114]; see also, for example, Von Hannover v. Germany (No. 1) [2004] App. no. 59320/00 [65]; Hachette Filipacchi Associés ('Ici Paris') v. France [2009] App. no. 12268/03 [40]; MGN Ltd v. United Kingdom [2011] App. no. 39401/04 [143]; Alkaya v. Turkey [2012] App. no. 42811/06 [35].

[31] ECtHR, Mosley v. United Kingdom [2011] App. no. 48009/08 [131].

[32] ECtHR, Von Hannover v. Germany (No. 1) [2004] App. no. 59320/00 [63].

[33] ECtHR, Campmany y Diez de Revenga and Lopez-Galiacho Perona v. Spain [2000] App. no. 54224/00, p. 8.

[34] ECtHR, Hachette Filipacchi Associés ('Ici Paris') v. France [2009] App. no. 12268/03 [43].

[35] See, among many further decisions, ECtHR, Lingens v. Austria [1986] App. no. 9815/82 [42]; Bowman v. United Kingdom [1998] App. no. 141/1996/760/961 [42]; Éditions Plon v. France [2004] App. no. 58148/00 [44]; Cumpănă and Mazăre v. Romania [2004] App. no. 33348/96 [101].

administration[36] and the justice system;[37] reporting on businesses and the economy in general;[38] the search for historical truth and debates between historians that shape public opinion as to historical events;[39] the prevention, investigation and prosecution of crimes;[40] and many further examples.[41]

b The Position of the Person Concerned and the Extent to which he is Well Known

With regard to the person who is the subject of a publication, a distinction has to be made between private individuals and persons acting in the public sphere. People who expose themselves by virtue of their role as a 'public figure', as a participant in a public debate on a matter of public concern, or by otherwise entering the public scene, may claim weaker protection of their personality rights than a private person. By contrast, private individuals unknown to the public may claim strong protection of their personality rights.[42] This might require the professional media, for example, to blur the image of a private person when broadcasting investigative news reporting.[43]

Public figures *per se* are professional politicians acting in their public capacity[44] and trading companies.[45] Civil servants who are not politicians are entrusted with the execution of public authority. However, even when acting in an official capacity, civil servants do not lay themselves open to the same scrutiny as politicians, and

---

[36] ECtHR, Thorgeir Thorgeirson v. Iceland [1992] App. no. 13778/88; Nilsen and Johnsen v. Norway [1999] App. no. 23118/93 [44]; Sürek v. Turkey (No. 2) [1999] App. no. 24122/94 [37].

[37] See, for example, ECtHR, Prager and Oberschlick v. Austria [1995] App. no. 15974/90 [34]; De Haes and Gijsels v. Belgium [1997] App. no. 19983/92 [37]; Mustafa Erdoğan and others v. Turkey [2014] App. nos. 346/04 and 39779/04 [40].

[38] ECtHR, Fressoz and Roire v. France [1999] App. no. 29183/95 [50]; Steel and Morris v. United Kingdom [2005] App. no. 68416/01.

[39] See, for example, ECtHR, Radio France and others v. France [2004] App. no. 53984/00 [34]; Chauvy and others v. France [2004] App. no. 64915/01 [69]; Perinçek v. Switzerland [2015] App. no. 27510/08 [223].

[40] See ECtHR, White v. Sweden [2006] App. no. 42435/02 [29]; Egeland and Hanseid v. Norway [2009] App. no. 34438/04 [58]; Salumäki v. Finland [2014] App. no. 23605/09 [54].

[41] See, for example, ECtHR, Sunday Times v. United Kingdom (No. 1) [1979] App. no. 6538/74: the Thalidomide scandal; Bergens Tidende and others v. Norway [2000] App. no. 26132/95 [51]: surgery errors; Bladet Tromsø and Stensaas v. Norway [1999] App. no. 21980/93, VgT Verein gegen Tierfabriken v. Switzerland (No. 1) [2001] App. no. 24699/94 [70], PETA Deutschland v. Germany [2012] App. no. 43481/09 [47] and Animal Defenders International v. United Kingdom [2013] App. no. 48876/08 [102]: protection of animals; Selistö v. Finland [2004] App. no. 56767/00 [52]: problem of alcohol consumption while working; Société de Conception de Presse et d'Edition et Ponson v. France [2009] App. no. 26935/05 [55]: sports issues.

[42] See, for example, ECtHR, Armonienė v. Lithuania [2008] App. no. 36919/02 [47]; Ageyevy v. Russia [2013] App. no. 7075/10 [217].

[43] ECtHR, Bremner v. Turkey [2015] App. no. 37428/06 [80].

[44] See, for example, ECtHR, Lingens v. Austria [1986] App. no. 9815/82; Oberschlick v. Austria (No. 1) [1991] App. no. 11662/85 [59]; High Court of Australia, Lange v. Australian Broadcasting Corporation [1997] HCA 25.

[45] See ECtHR, Fayed v. United Kingdom [1994] App. no. 17101/90 [75]; Steel and Morris v. United Kingdom [2005] App. no. 68416/01 [94]; Verlagsgruppe News GmbH v. Austria (No. 2) [2006] App. no. 10520/02 [36]; Oster (2011, p. 269).

should therefore not be treated equally with the latter when it comes to the criticism of their actions or investigations into their private conduct.[46] Special considerations apply to judges and the judiciary. The administration of justice is *per se* a matter of public concern, and must therefore be subject to public scrutiny. However, the judiciary in general, as 'the guarantor of justice', must enjoy public confidence if it is to be successful in carrying out its duties.[47] Furthermore, the individual judges are subject to a duty of discretion that precludes them from replying to criticism, and hence, as opposed to politicians, they are not at liberty to discuss their decisions in public.[48] This imbalance has to be evened out by an enhanced protection of their professional reputation. While the public has a right to scrutinise and criticise a court's judicial reasoning, it must refrain from personal attacks on the judges themselves or comments calculated to bring the judiciary into disrepute.[49]

c The Prior Conduct of the Person Concerned

The prior conduct of the person concerned as a further criterion for balancing freedom of expression against rights of others may cut both ways: public figures may receive stronger protection of their personality rights if they shield their private lives from public attention, and the lives of private persons may become matters of public interest if those persons have entered the public scene. Even if persons are known to the public and had been in the media on account of their function, they may nonetheless claim strong protection of their personality rights if they had not disclosed details of their private life prior to a publication.[50] This applies particularly where public figures expressly request that details of their private life should not be published, or if they have taken legal steps to prevent such publications.[51] Yet, even if public figures sought to avoid public attention on a private matter, they may nonetheless provoke legitimate public scrutiny because of their prior behaviour. This may be the case where public figures voluntarily open aspects of their private life to a public audience, or if they publicly deny facts relating to their private life.[52]

---

[46] See ECtHR, Steur v. Netherlands [2003] App. no. 39657/98 [40–41]; Pedersen and Baadsgaard v. Denmark [2004] App. no. 49017/99 [80]; *mutatis mutandis*, July and SARL Liberation v. France [2008] App. no. 20893/03 [74].

[47] See, for example, ECtHR, Prager and Oberschlick v. Austria [1995] App. no. 15974/90 [34]; De Haes and Gijsels v. Belgium [1997] App. no. 19983/92 [37]; Skałka v. Poland [2003] App. no. 43425/98 [34]. From scholarship, see Addo (1998, 2000).

[48] See, for example, ECtHR, Prager and Oberschlick v. Austria [1995] App. no. 15974/90 [34]; De Haes and Gijsels v. Belgium [1997] App. no. 19983/92 [37]; Skałka v. Poland [2003] App. no. 43425/98 [34]; Kobenter and Standard Verlags GmbH v. Austria [2006] App. no. 60899/00 [31].

[49] Compare ECtHR, Barfod v. Denmark [1989] App. no. 11508/85 [35].

[50] Compare ECtHR, Print Zeitungsverlag GmbH v. Austria [2013] App. no. 26547/07 [37].

[51] See ECtHR, Von Hannover v. Germany (No. 3) [2013] App. no. 8772/10 [55].

[52] See, for example, ECtHR, MGN Ltd v. United Kingdom [2011] App. no. 39401/04 [147].

In turn, persons who seek the limelight of public attention by laying open details regarding their own private lives expose themselves to scrutiny and must therefore bear the consequences, even if they have not been known to the public before. Private individuals become subject to legitimate public interest 'when they enter the arena of public debate', although they do not fulfil official functions.[53] Particularly persons who publicly express extremist views lay themselves open to public scrutiny.[54]

Furthermore, private individuals may become subject to legitimate public interest if they have been involved in criminal investigations or proceedings, as crimes and criminal investigations are *per se* a matter of public concern.[55] Finally, private persons enter the public domain if their conduct pertains to a matter of public concern. In *Flinkkilä and others* v. *Finland*, for instance, the person concerned ('B') had developed a relationship with a married senior public figure. The Strasbourg Court thus found that the prohibition to disclose B's identity in the reporting violated Article 10 ECHR.[56]

d Content, Form and Consequences of the Publication

Freedom of expression protects both the substance of the ideas and information expressed and the form in which they are conveyed, including a certain degree of provocation and exaggeration,[57] immoderate statements,[58] the use of strong terms[59] or polemic formulation,[60] vulgar phrases or a satirical style.[61] In particular, it is for journalists and not for courts to decide on the methods and techniques of their reporting.[62] However, freedom of expression brings with it duties and responsibilities. The Court has regularly emphasised that the safeguard afforded by Article 10

---

[53] See, for instance, ECtHR, Nilsen and Johnsen v. Norway [1999] App. no. 23118/93 [52]; Karsai v. Hungary [2009] App. no. 5380/07 [35]; Jerusalem v. Austria [2001] App. no. 26958/95 [38].

[54] ECtHR, Österreichischer Rundfunk v. Austria [2006] App. no. 35841/02 [65].

[55] ECtHR, White v. Sweden [2006] App. no. 42435/02 [29]; Egeland and Hanseid v. Norway [2009] App. no. 34438/04 [58]; Salumäki v. Finland [2014] App. no. 23605/09 [54]. However, the fact that a person has been the subject of criminal proceedings does not fully deprive him from his right to respect for private life; see subsection e.aa.

[56] Flinkkilä and others v. Finland [2010] App. no. 25576/04 [85].

[57] ECtHR, Prager and Oberschlick v. Austria [1995] App. no. 15974/90 [38]; De Haes and Gijsels v. Belgium [1997] App. no. 19983/92 [46]; Bladet Tromsø and Stensaas v. Norway [1999] App. no. 21980/93 [59]; Fressoz and Roire v. France [1999] App. no. 29183/95 [45]; Thoma v. Luxembourg [2001] App. no. 38432/97 [46].

[58] ECtHR, Mladina d.d. Ljubljana v. Slovenia [2014] App. no. 20981/10 [40].

[59] ECtHR, Thorgeir Thorgeirson v. Iceland [1992] App. no. 13778/88 [67]; July and SARL Liberation v. France [2008] App. no. 20893/03 [75]. Compare US Supreme Court, Cohen v. California, 403 U.S. 15 (1971), where the appellant wore a jacket bearing the words 'Fuck the Draft' in a county courthouse.

[60] ECtHR, Oberschlick v. Austria (No. 2) [1997] App. no. 20834/92 [33]; Unabhängige Initiative Informationsvielfalt v. Austria [2002] App. no. 28525/95 [43].

[61] ECtHR, Tuşalp v. Turkey [2012] App. nos. 32131/08 and 41617/08 [48].

[62] See ECtHR, Jersild v. Denmark [1994] App. no. 15890/89 [31]; Bladet Tromsø and Stensaas v. Norway [1999] App. no. 21980/93 [63]; Stoll v. Switzerland [2007] App. no. 69698/01 [146]; Schweizerische Radio- und Fernsehgesellschaft SRG v. Switzerland [2012] App. no. 34124/06 [64].

ECHR to journalists in relation to reporting on issues of general interest is subject to the proviso, *inter alia*, to provide information 'in accordance with the ethics of journalism'.[63] As a consequence, the way in which a photo or report is published and the manner in which the person concerned is represented in the photo or report are factors to be taken into consideration.[64] The search for less intrusive, alternative methods of publication is part of the media's duties and responsibilities. This may include, for example, that the report may be basically published, but has to omit certain expressive terms, or can only be published after a certain lapse of time.[65] Where the publication of a privacy-related photo in addition to an article is concerned, one has to ask whether the publication of this photo was necessary to ensure the credibility of the story. The – newsworthy – fact that a famous actor has been the victim of a burglary does not need to be corroborated by the publication of her home address.[66]

Moreover, a publisher has to consider the consequences of his publication. In *Armonienė v. Lithuania*, the biggest Lithuanian daily newspaper had published an article on the applicant's late husband's infection with HIV. The Court noted that the publication of the article about the state of health of the applicant's husband as well as the allegation that he was the father of two children by another woman who was also suffering from AIDS, were of a purely private nature. The Court highlighted that the family lived in a village, which increased the possibility that the husband's illness would be known by his neighbours and his immediate family, thereby causing public humiliation and exclusion from village social life.[67] The Court thus found a violation of the applicant's Article 8 ECHR right.

e Veracity of the Publication and the Prior Conduct of the Publisher

With regard to the veracity of the publication or the statement, the distinction between factual statements on the one hand, and opinions, comments and value judgements on the other, gains particular significance. The most important factor relevant to the balancing exercise between freedom of expression and the protection of a person's reputation or privacy with regard to a *factual* statement is the authenticity of the information disclosed. Therefore, a distinction must be made between four categories of statements of fact:[68]

---

[63] See, for example, ECtHR, Fressoz and Roire v. France [1999] App. no. 29183/95 [54]; Pedersen and Baadsgaard v. Denmark [2004] App. no. 49017/99 [78]; Stoll v. Switzerland [2007] App. no. 69698/01 [103]; Axel Springer AG v. Germany (No. 1) [2012] App. no. 39954/08 [93].

[64] ECtHR, Wirtschafts-Trend Zeitschriften-Verlagsgesellschaft m.b.H. v. Austria (no. 3) [2005] App. nos. 66298/01 and 15653/02 [47]; Reklos and Davourlis v. Greece [2009] App. no. 1234/05 [42]; and Jokitaipale and others v. Finland [2010] App. no. 43349/05 [68]; Axel Springer AG v. Germany (No. 1) [2012] App. no. 39954/08 [94].

[65] See ECtHR, Éditions Plon v. France [2004] App. no. 58148/00 [51].

[66] ECtHR, Alkaya v. Turkey [2012] App. no. 42811/06 [36].

[67] ECtHR, Armonienė v. Lithuania [2008] App. no. 36919/02 [42].

[68] See Oster (2015b, pp. 167 ff).

Category I: true statements.

Category II: statements that are untrue and that the publisher knew to be untrue.

Category III: statements that the publisher believed to be true when issued, but that later turned out to be untrue.

Category IV: statements that have neither been proven true nor untrue.

aa True Statements of Fact   If statements of fact are found to be true (Category I), then there is usually no room left for a violation of a person's honour, since honour may only be affected by untrue statements and derogatory opinions.[69] However, the gathering and dissemination of true information may violate a person's right to privacy, because the concept of 'privacy' includes the right to control the release and circulation of information about oneself.[70] The seminal test is, therefore, whether the victim had a 'reasonable' or 'legitimate' expectation of privacy outweighing the public interest in receiving the information. Particular vigilance is called for where privacy of minors is concerned.[71]

The right to privacy encompasses, in particular, the individual's right to control the taking and use of an image, including the right to refuse its publication.[72] The publication of photos or video recordings has thus led to some of the most delicate balancing exercises between the right of the media to gather and publish information, on the one hand, and the right to privacy, on the other hand.[73] The proliferation of smartphones, smart glasses, video drones and online street view and the opportunity to instantly upload photos or videos on the internet have further increased this problem. The balancing exercise between the right to take and publish a photo and a person's right to privacy has to be based on a three-step test.

---

[69] This is at least the approach of English law, where the truth of a statement constitutes an absolute defence. Under German law, by contrast, Section 192 of the Criminal Law Code states that '[p]roof of truth of the asserted or disseminated fact shall not exclude punishment [for insult] if the insult results from the form of the assertion or dissemination or the circumstances under which it was made' (translation provided by M. Bohlander, juris GmbH, 2009).

[70] Compare Warren and Brandeis (1890); Prosser (1960, p. 392); Solove (2002, p. 1109); Hughes (2012, p. 809); Volokh (2000, p. 1050).

[71] See Article 16 of the UN Convention on the Rights of the Child; Council of Europe, Recommendation Rec(2003)13 on the provision of information through the media in relation to criminal proceedings, Principle 8; ECtHR, S. and Marper v. United Kingdom [2008] App. nos. 30562/04 and 30566/04 [124]; see also Aleksey Ovchinnikov v. Russia [2010] App. no. 24061/04 [51]; Ageyevy v. Russia [2013] App. no. 7075/10 [175].

[72] See ECtHR, Von Hannover v. Germany (No. 2) [2012] App. nos. 40660/08 and 60641/08 [96].

[73] See, in particular, ECtHR, Von Hannover v. Germany (No. 1) [2004] App. no. 59320/00; Von Hannover v. Germany (No. 2) [2012] App. nos. 40660/08 and 60641/08; Von Hannover v. Germany (No. 3) [2013] App. no. 8772/10.

First, one needs to examine the content of the pictures, especially whether the images contain very personal or even intimate information about an individual.[74] The non-consensual publication of pictures of nakedness, wardrobe malfunctions, sexual activity, ill or dead persons usually violates this person's privacy or even dignity.[75] In addition, even if a person consented to certain pictures, there may be an implicit agreement of confidentiality in personal relations. The phenomenon of 'revenge porn' – the sharing of sexually explicit pictures of an ex-partner online without the consent of the pictured individual – is therefore a breach of confidentiality and a violation of privacy.[76]

Second, where the news media is concerned, the publication of a photo in addition to an article has to be necessary to ensure the credibility of the story.[77] For example, the publication of the photograph of a murdered politician is usually not necessary to prove that he is in fact dead. The possibly newsworthy information that a child was born does not require visual proof that his mother was in labour. A report may also not be used as a pretext to publish photos of a person that are unrelated to the content of the text.[78]

Third, one must examine the circumstances under which the pictures have been taken. Under the Strasbourg Court's case law, even the fact that pictures have been taken in a public place or in relation to an event in public does not automatically exclude a violation of a person's privacy.[79] By contrast, the idea that a person can be private in public is alien to US law. Consequently, in a transnational dimension, such cases are particularly susceptible to conflicts.

In turn, even if the information concerned is private, an individual may have a lesser expectation of privacy because the person consented to the intrusion into his private sphere. This is the case, for instance, with regard to so-called 'home stories' or if individuals intentionally and ostentatiously conduct private activities in public places. Moreover, a person's privacy is less protected if the information concerned refutes prior public statements of the person, which served to build a positive

---

[74] See, for example, ECtHR, Von Hannover v. Germany (No. 1) [2004] App. no. 59320/00 [59]; Mosley v. United Kingdom [2011] App. no. 48009/08 [115]; see also, *mutatis mutandis*, Krone Verlag GmbH & Co. KG v. Austria (No. 1) [2002] App. no. 34315/96 [37]; Eerikäinen and others v. Finland [2009] App. no. 3514/02 [62].

[75] See, for example, ECtHR, Hachette Filipacchi Associés v. France [2007] App. no. 71111/01 [46]; US Supreme Court, National Archives & Records Administration v. Favish, 124 S. Ct. 1570 (2004).

[76] Compare ECtHR, Ruusunen v. Finland [2014] App. no. 73579/10 [50].

[77] See ECtHR, Fressoz and Roire v. France [1999] App. no. 29183/95 [54]; MGN Ltd v. United Kingdom [2011] App. no. 39401/04 [151].

[78] See, *mutatis mutandis*, ECtHR, Von Hannover v. Germany (No. 3) [2013] App. no. 8772/10 [49–52].

[79] See ECtHR, Peck v. United Kingdom [2003] App. no. 44647/98 [62]; Von Hannover v. Germany (No. 1) [2004] App. no. 59320/00 [61]; Egeland and Hanseid v. Norway [2009] App. no. 34438/04 [61]; Moreham (2006).

reputation. Privacy is a shield against unjustified intrusion, but not a cover for a false reputation.

When publishing on crimes and criminal proceedings, the journalistic media in particular has to carefully balance the public's interest in information against the interests of victims, their relatives and other people involved. Furthermore, Articles 17(1) ICCPR and 6(1) ECHR recognise that the principle of open justice may have to yield to privacy under certain circumstances. Therefore courts have to balance the interest of the media and of the public against those of the persons involved in the court proceedings.[80] Both the media and the general public also have to observe that a person has a right to be presumed innocent of any criminal offence until proven guilty.[81]

Freedom of expression may also be legitimately restricted with regard to publications on the criminal history of a person in order to facilitate the reintegration of the person into society.[82] The transnational relevance of this question has been highlighted by the CJEU decision *eDate Advertising*, which will be further elaborated on in Chapter 4:[83] an Austrian website had published the names of two men convicted of the murder of a German actor. The Court of Justice then had to rule, *inter alia*, whether German courts had jurisdiction to decide the case. The conflict between the public's right to be informed about another person's criminal history, on the one hand, and the former convict's right to respect for privacy, on the other hand, has also gained particular topicality with the so-called 'right to be forgotten' decision of the Court of Justice in *Google Spain SL* v. *AEPD and others* (see Chapter 8).

Yet this conflict is not susceptible to a clear yes/no answer. Rather, the conflicting rights should be balanced in a way that each right can be realised to the optimal extent. The ECtHR decision *Österreichischer Rundfunk* v. *Austria*, which concerned a broadcaster's publication of a picture of a convicted person after his release on parole, provides commendable guidance for this balancing exercise. The Strasbourg Court considered the degree of notoriety of the person concerned, the lapse of time since the conviction and the release, the nature of the crime, the connection between the contents of the report and the picture shown and the completeness and correctness of the accompanying text.[84]

---

[80] See, for example, ECtHR, Eerikäinen and others v. Finland [2009] App. no. 3514/02; Egeland and Hanseid v. Norway [2009] App. no. 34438/04; News Verlags GmbH & Co. KG v. Austria [2000] App. no. 31457/96.

[81] Articles 14(2) ICCPR and 6(2) ECHR. See, for example, ECtHR, Bladet Tromsø and Stensaas v. Norway [1999] App. no. 21980/93 [65]; Pedersen and Baadsgaard v. Denmark [2004] App. no. 49017/99 [78]; White v. Sweden [2006] App. no. 42435/02 [21]; Axel Springer AG v. Germany (No. 1) [2012] App. no. 39954/08 [96]; Council of Europe, Recommendation Rec(2003)13 on the provision of information through the media in relation to criminal proceedings.

[82] See ECtHR, Österreichischer Rundfunk v. Austria [2004] App. no. 57597/00 (admissibility decision); but see also Österreichischer Rundfunk v. Austria [2006] App. no. 35841/02 [68].

[83] CJEU, Joined Cases C-509/09 and C-161/10 [2011] eDate Advertising GmbH and Olivier Martinez and Robert Martinez.

[84] Österreichischer Rundfunk v. Austria [2006] App. no. 35841/02 [68]. See also ECtHR, Österreichischer Rundfunk v. Austria [2004] App. no. 57597/00 (admissibility decision); Oster (2015b, pp. 177 ff).

bb Knowingly False Statements of Fact If the publisher knew that a defamatory statement was false (Category II), then there is little room for freedom of expression protection, and even less room for media freedom. As a consequence, the Strasbourg Court regularly upholds interferences with a false defamatory statement made in bad faith, which cannot be reasonably perceived as satire or parody.[85] Similarly, even under First Amendment doctrine, public figures succeed in a defamation lawsuit if they can prove that the defamatory statement was made with 'actual malice' – that is, with knowledge that it was false or with reckless disregard of whether it was false or not.[86] As a consequence, transnational conflicts should rarely occur in such cases.

cc Statements that Turn Out to be Untrue or Cannot be Proven to be True The most difficult cases of statements of fact are those where neither the truth nor the falsity of the statement could be established (Category IV), and those where the publisher believed the statement to be true when issued, but that later turned out to be untrue (Category III). In these categories, the First Amendment jurisprudence of the US Supreme Court differs most significantly from the approaches taken by the Human Rights Committee, the Strasbourg Court and also domestic European courts. According to the US Supreme Court, public figures succeed in a defamation lawsuit *only* if they can prove that the defamatory statement was made with 'actual malice'.[87] By contrast, international adjudicators have accepted it as principally compatible with freedom of expression to place the onus of proving the truth of defamatory statements even concerning a public figure on a defendant in libel proceedings.[88] Under international human rights conventions, the right to respect for one's reputation is in itself protected as a human right with equal value to freedom of expression and media freedom. Therefore, Categories III and IV can be treated equally with regard to civil liability. Both a publisher who cannot prove the truth of his statement and a publisher who unintentionally issued a false statement may be subject to civil liability. But they must have the opportunity to establish a defence, because to impose the burden of proof regarding the full veracity of a factual statement on the defendant would not only be contrary to the general rule that the claimant in civil proceedings, or the state in criminal proceedings, has the burden of proving that a wrongful act has been committed.[89] In addition, such a reversal of the burden of proof would have an intolerable chilling effect on public discourse. Consequently,

---

[85] ECtHR, Alithia Publishing Company Ltd and Constantinides v. Cyprus [2008] App. no. 17550/03 [67]; see also Pedersen and Baadsgaard v. Denmark [2004] App. no. 49017/99 [78].

[86] New York Times Co. v. Sullivan, 376 U.S. 254, 279–280 (1964).

[87] New York Times Co. v. Sullivan, 376 U.S. 254, 279–280 (1964).

[88] See Human Rights Committee, Marques de Morais v. Angola [2005] Communication no. 1128/2002 [6.8]; General Comment no. 34, para. 47; ECtHR, McVicar v. United Kingdom [2002] App. no. 46311/99 [87]; Steel and Morris v. United Kingdom [2005] App. no. 68416/01 [93].

[89] See Pasqualucci (2006, p. 406).

there can be no *absolute* obligation on a defendant in libel proceedings to establish the truth of his publication.[90] Instead, the publisher has to establish that he abided by his duties and responsibilities by attempting to verify factual statements that are defamatory.[91] The Strasbourg Court regularly emphasises that 'the protection of the right of journalists to impart information on issues of general interest requires that they should act in good faith and on an accurate factual basis and provide "reliable and precise" information in accordance with the ethics of journalism'.[92] In *Braun* v. *Poland*, the Court highlighted that the same principles apply to others who engage in public debate. As a consequence, private individuals must not be required to fulfil a standard more demanding than that of due diligence of journalists.[93]

Within the European media law order, the Strasbourg Court has established several factors that have to be taken into account when balancing freedom of expression and the right to respect for one's reputation if defamatory statements turn out to be untrue or cannot be proven to be true:

- Whether the publisher communicated remaining doubts.[94]
- Whether the publisher has taken all reasonable steps to verify the factual basis of the allegations. Which steps have to be regarded as 'reasonable' depends on several factors, such as:
  - The extent to which the publisher can regard his sources as reliable.[95] In particular, publishers are entitled to rely on the contents of official reports[96] or investigations by professionals specialised in a certain area[97] without having to undertake independent research.

---

[90] See, for example, ECtHR, Thorgeir Thorgeirson v. Iceland [1992] App. no. 13778/88 [65]; Human Rights Committee, General Comment no. 34, para. 47.

[91] See, for example, ECtHR, De Haes and Gijsels v. Belgium [1997] App. no. 19983/92 [39]; Pedersen and Baadsgaard v. Denmark [2004] App. no. 49017/99 [78]; Karsai v. Hungary [2009] App. no. 5380/07 [32]; Kaperzyński v. Poland [2012] App. no. 43206/07 [64].

[92] See, for example, ECtHR, Fressoz and Roire v. France [1999] App. no. 29183/95 [54]; Bladet Tromsø and Stensaas v. Norway [1999] App. no. 21980/93 [59]; Prager and Oberschlick v. Austria [1995] App. no. 15974/90 [37].

[93] ECtHR, Braun v. Poland [2014] App. no. 30162/10 [40] and [50].

[94] ECtHR, Pedersen and Baadsgaard v. Denmark [2004] App. no. 49017/99 [77 ff]; Wizerkaniuk v. Poland [2011] App. no. 18990/05 [66].

[95] See, for example, ECtHR, Bladet Tromsø and Stensaas v. Norway [1999] App. no. 21980/93 [66]; McVicar v. United Kingdom [2002] App. no. 46311/99 [84]; Pedersen and Baadsgaard v. Denmark [2004] App. no. 49017/99 [78 ff]; Ringier Axel Springer Slovakia, a. s. v. Slovakia [2011] App. no. 41262/05 [97].

[96] ECtHR, Bladet Tromsø and Stensaas v. Norway [1999] App. no. 21980/93 [68]; Colombani and others v. France [2002] App. no. 51279/99 [65]; Selistö v. Finland [2004] App. no. 56767/00 [60]; Tănăsoaica v. Romania [2012] App. no. 3490/03 [50]; *mutatis mutandis*, Rumyana Ivanova v. Bulgaria [2008] App. no. 36207/03 [65].

[97] ECtHR, Ungváry and Irodalom Kft v. Hungary [2013] App. no. 64520/10 [75].

- The seriousness of the defamation in question. The more serious the allegation is, the more solid the factual basis has to be.[98]
- Whether the defamed persons had the opportunity to defend themselves prior to publication.[99]
- The topicality, because news is a perishable commodity.[100] However, journalists must not focus in a sensationalist fashion on being the first paper to print the story.[101]
- Authors of historical texts are required to respect the fundamental rules of historical method.[102]
- Where allegations of having committed a crime are at issue, the presumption of innocence has to be respected.[103]
- Whether the publisher corrected false statements of fact after he learned of their falsity.[104]
- The context of the allegations: in 'the course of a lively political debate', publishers should enjoy a wide freedom to criticise the actions of public officials, even where the statements may lack a clear factual basis.[105] This applies especially to statements that have been issued in live broadcasting, where a person has but a limited possibility of reformulating, refining or retracting any statements before they are made public.[106]
- The tone of the publication. Publications should observe a minimum degree of moderation and propriety. They should consider different points of view, in particular those of the person concerned.[107] Facts have to be presented in an objective and reasonably balanced manner and not with recourse to excessive language.[108]

In *Braun* v. *Poland*, the Court found a violation in Article 10 ECHR by the mere fact that the domestic courts imposed higher demands on the applicant than on

---

[98] ECtHR, Pedersen and Baadsgaard v. Denmark [2004] App. no. 49017/99 [78]; Rumyana Ivanova v. Bulgaria [2008] App. no. 36207/03 [64]; Kasabova v. Bulgaria [2011] App. no. 22385/03 [65].

[99] ECtHR, Bergens Tidende and others v. Norway [2000] App. no. 26132/95 [58]; *mutatis mutandis*, Flux v. Moldova (No. 6) [2008] App. no. 22824/04 [29].

[100] ECtHR, Observer and Guardian v. United Kingdom [1991] App. no. 13585/88 [60].

[101] ECtHR, Novaya Gazeta and Borodyanskiy v. Russia [2013] App. no. 14087/08 [37]; Ageyevy v. Russia [2013] App. no. 7075/10 [227].

[102] ECtHR, Chauvy and others v. France [2004] App. no. 64915/01 [77].

[103] Articles 14(2) ICCPR and 6(2) ECHR. See ECtHR, Flux v. Moldova (No. 6) [2008] App. no. 22824/04 [31]; Salumäki v. Finland [2014] App. no. 23605/09 [58].

[104] See ECtHR, Ristamäki and Korvola v. Finland [2013] App. no. 66456/09 [57].

[105] ECtHR, Lombardo and others v. Malta [2007] App. no. 7333/06 [60].

[106] Compare ECtHR, Fuentes Bobo v. Spain [2000] App. no. 39293/98 [46]; Gündüz v. Turkey [2003] App. no. 35071/97 [49]; Filatenko v. Russia [2007] App. no. 73219/01 [41].

[107] ECtHR, Bladet Tromsø and Stensaas v. Norway [1999] App. no. 21980/93 [63]; Bergens Tidende and others v. Norway [2000] App. no. 26132/95 [58]; Selistö v. Finland [2004] App. no. 56767/00 [62] and [66].

[108] ECtHR, Bergens Tidende and others v. Norway [2000] App. no. 26132/95 [57]; Lindon, Otchakovsky-Laurens and July v. France [2007] App. nos. 21279/02 and 36448/02 [66]; Kaperzyński v. Poland [2012] App. no. 43206/07 [64].

journalists. Therefore, the Court did not go into the details whether Mr Braun did actually fulfil those standards; for example, whether he communicated remaining doubts, whether he has taken all reasonable steps to verify the facts of his allegations or whether he gave the victim the opportunity to defend himself before he went public with his allegations. The Strasbourg Court decided that domestic courts must not impose *higher* standards on utterances of private individuals who contribute to a debate of general interest. But, as has been shown in Chapter 1, in *Růžový panter, o.s.* v. *Czech Republic* the Court also indicated that the standards should not be *lower* either.[109] In practice, however, it seems that these demands can normally be fulfilled by journalists only.

dd Value Judgements   Freedom of expression also encompasses the right to impart 'ideas', that is, to issue value judgements. And also the media's freedom to publish goes beyond the mere dissemination of factual information. The task of the media is not to merely impart information, the interpretation of which must be left to the reader: 'Freedom of the press [...] affords the public one of the best means of discovering and forming an opinion of the ideas and attitudes of political leaders and on other matters of general interest.'[110]

Freedom of expression and media freedom even protect defamatory statements of opinion if they constitute fair comment and do not overstep the boundaries of acceptable criticism. However, the requirements for 'fair comment' under domestic law vary among jurisdictions. Yet again, within the European media law order, the Strasbourg Court has established several factors that have to be taken into account when balancing the freedom to impart value judgements and the right to respect for one's reputation. The factors the Strasbourg Court has established for a fair comment defence are:

- Whether the comment was based on a sufficiently factual basis to support it, since a value judgement without any factual basis to support it may be excessive.[111]
- The facts on which the value judgement is founded must be true, or there must have been at least sufficient efforts to establish the truth.
- Even if the factual basis of a value judgement is correct, a true statement, coupled with additional comments or innuendo, may create a false image to the public and may thus go beyond the limits of acceptable criticism.[112]

---

[109] ECtHR, Růžový panter, o.s. v. Czech Republic [2012] App. no. 20240/08; see also Braun v. Poland [2014] App. no. 30162/10 [40].

[110] ECtHR, Lingens v. Austria [1986] App. no. 9815/82 [42]; reiterated in, for example, Oberschlick v. Austria (No. 1) [1991] App. no. 11662/85 [58]; Thoma v. Luxembourg [2001] App. no. 38432/97 [45]; Cumpănă and Mazăre v. Romania [2004] App. no. 33348/96 [93].

[111] See, for example, ECtHR, De Haes and Gijsels v. Belgium [1997] App. no. 19983/92 [47]; Unabhängige Initiative Informationsvielfalt v. Austria [2002] App. no. 28525/95 [47]; Lindon, Otchakovsky-Laurens and July v. France [2007] App. nos. 21279/02 and 36448/02 [55].

[112] ECtHR, Vides Aizsardzības Klubs v. Latvia [2004] App. no. 57829/00 [45]; Růžový panter, o.s. v. Czech Republic [2012] App. no. 20240/08 [32].

- The tone of the publication: whether the value judgement constituted insult rather than criticism.[113] However, the use of strong polemical terms is allowed where the impugned statement constitutes a reaction to a provocative statement by the allegedly defamed person in a robust and heated public discussion.[114] Offensive language may, however, not be protected by freedom of expression if it amounts to wanton denigration, for example 'where the sole intent of the offensive statement is to insult'.[115] The precise words used in the precise context are thus of crucial importance.[116]
- The way facts and comments are presented to the public and the impression they could produce in the reader.[117]

A singular area of value judgement is the stylistic device of satire and caricature. Freedom of expression and media freedom cover a certain degree of exaggeration and even provocation, including vulgar phrases and a satirical style. Satire may contribute to debates of general interest in a particular way by using wit as a weapon, yet its capability to ridicule is often more distinct compared to an unvarnished comment. Acceptable satirical comment seeks to make a critical contribution to an issue of general concern rather than insulting the other person, and the humorous character must be cognisable for the average reader.[118]

f Severity of the Sanction Imposed

The nature and severity of the sanctions imposed are also factors to be taken into account when assessing the proportionality of an interference with the exercise of freedom of expression. Where criminal sanctions for media wrongdoing are still enforced, they must be applied with the utmost reservation, and mere civil liability has to be considered as a less intrusive remedy. The mere existence of laws criminalising publications has a dissuasive effect on anyone who intends to contribute to a matter of general interest, but has to consider the risk of criminal liability, even if the imposed fine is rather low.[119]

g Application of these Principles to the Case Examples

In the case example *Axel Springer AG*, the Court indicated that the fact that X played the role of a police superintendent, 'whose mission is law enforcement and crime

---

[113] See ECtHR, Mustafa Erdoğan and others v. Turkey [2014] App. nos. 346/04 and 39779/04 [44].

[114] See, for example, ECtHR, Oberschlick v. Austria (No. 2) [1997] App. no. 20834/92 [33] and [34]; Nilsen and Johnsen v. Norway [1999] App. no. 23118/93 [52]; Unabhängige Initiative Informationsvielfalt v. Austria [2002] App. no. 28525/95 [43].

[115] ECtHR, Tuşalp v. Turkey [2012] App. nos. 32131/08 and 41617/08 [48]; see also Skałka v. Poland [2003] App. no. 43425/98 [34].

[116] See, for example, ECtHR, Tammer v. Estonia [2001] App. no. 41205/98 [68]; Karhuvaara and Iltalehti v. Finland [2004] App. no. 53678/00 [45]; Kobenter and Standard Verlags GmbH v. Austria [2006] App. no. 60899/00 [31].

[117] ECtHR, Růžový panter, o.s. v. Czech Republic [2012] App. no. 20240/08 [31].

[118] See ECtHR, Nikowitz and Verlagsgruppe News GmbH v. Austria [2007] App. no. 5266/03 [25].

[119] See, for instance, ECtHR, Brasilier v. France [2006] App. no. 71343/01 [43]: one 'symbolic franc'; Fatullayev v. Azerbaijan [2010] App. no. 40984/07 [102].

prevention', increased the public's interest in being informed of his arrest.[120] This reasoning, however, is unconvincing: *mutatis mutandis*, one could conclude that there is less public interest in the arrest of an actor who usually plays the role of the 'bad guy'. What was more relevant was the fact that the case concerned criminal prosecution, which – within the boundaries of the presumption of innocence –is *per se* of public concern. Moreover, the facts stated by the *Bild* newspaper had been found to be true (Category I). The articles did not reveal details about X's private life, but mainly concerned the circumstances of, and events following, his arrest. They contained no disparaging expression or unsubstantiated allegation. Having regard to the nature of the offence committed by X, the degree to which X is well known to the public, the circumstances of his arrest and the veracity of the information in question, the applicant company – having obtained confirmation of that information from the prosecuting authorities themselves – did not have sufficiently strong grounds for believing that it should preserve X's anonymity. Finally, although the sanctions imposed on the applicant company were lenient, they were capable of having a chilling effect on the applicant company. The Court thus found a violation of Article 10 ECHR.

Braun v. *Poland* concerned the search for historical truth, which is also a matter of public interest. Mr J.M. was neither a politician nor a famous actor, but at least a well-known Polish linguistic professor. Mr Braun's allegations were a serious attack on Mr J.M.'s good name. The domestic courts had concluded that it could not be proven that the claimant had collaborated with the regime; therefore, the statements have neither been proven true nor untrue (Category IV). The protection of the right of *journalists* to impart information on issues of general interest requires that they act in good faith and on an accurate factual basis, and provide reliable and precise information in accordance with the ethics of journalism. However, in the absence of bad faith, Article 10 ECHR requires that journalists cannot be expected to fully prove the veracity of their statements if they have all reasonable steps to verify the factual basis of their allegations. But Mr Braun was not a journalist. Therefore, the Polish courts decided that he could not benefit from the journalistic privilege to erroneously disseminate false allegations made in good faith and based on diligent research. However, in *Braun* v. *Poland*, the Strasbourg Court decided that the principles applicable to journalists also apply to others who engage in public debate. As a consequence, private individuals must not be required to fulfil a standard more demanding than that of due diligence of journalists.[121] This fact was sufficient for the Court to find a violation of Article 10 ECHR. However, as can be discerned from *Růžový panter, o.s.* v. *Czech Republic*, the standards of due diligence applied to non-journalistic publishers are not lower than those applied to journalists. Yet the Court did not engage in an in-depth analysis as to whether Mr Braun actually met the

---

standards of due diligence. Mr Braun was a historian, the author of press articles and television programmes, and someone who actively and publicly commented on current affairs. He had considerable professional experience, for which he was invited to the interviews. Most importantly, he had conducted considerable research before he went public with his allegations. One can thus conclude that he actually met the standards that would normally be applied to professional journalists.

III Intellectual Property and Other Exclusive Rights

A special category of 'rights of others' preventing the dissemination of information is the protection of intellectual property rights and other exclusive rights. Intellectual property rights, especially copyright, impose limitations on others who want to publish certain information by granting the creator of an original work exclusive rights to it. Intellectual property rights thus do not fall squarely into the fact–opinion dichotomy, but pertain to creative work, which is often fictional in nature.

But intellectual property rights are not absolute. Provisions restricting the use of copyright-protected material and their enforcement may constitute an interference with the user's right of freedom of expression or media freedom and must thus be in accordance with the conditions for restrictions of these rights.[122] Restrictions based on intellectual property rights are not justified if the use of the protected information contributes to a debate of general concern.[123] As a consequence, legislation protecting intellectual property has to provide mechanisms for conflicting rights and interests to be duly balanced, especially by providing exemptions for journalists from copyright provisions. An example is Article 5(3)(c) Copyright Directive, which allows Member States to provide for exceptions or limitations to copyright. A more detailed analysis of intellectual property will be provided in Chapter 9.

Furthermore, access of broadcasting services to telecommunications networks and services may conflict with intellectual property rights of the regulated provider. The domestic regulatory authorities must therefore duly balance and reconcile conflicting interests, as is the case, for example, under Article 12(2) of the EU Access Directive (see Chapter 7).

IV Threats to Public Order Interests: National Security, Public Safety and Prevention of Disorder and Crime

Article 19(3)(b) ICCPR allows restrictions on freedom of expression for the protection of national security or public order. Similarly, Article 10(2) ECHR may justify an

---

[122] ECtHR, Ashby Donald and others v. France [2013] App. no. 36769/08 [34]; Neij and Sunde Kolmisoppi v. Sweden [2013] App. no. 40397/12; CJEU, Case C-70/10 [2011] Scarlet Extended v. SABAM and others [43]; Volokh (2003a); see also Volokh (2003b).

[123] See, *mutatis mutandis*, ECtHR, Ashby Donald and others v. France [2013] App. no. 36769/08; Neij and Sunde Kolmisoppi v. Sweden [2013] App. no. 40397/12.

interference in the interests of national security, territorial integrity or public safety, and for the prevention of disorder or crime.[124] The concept of 'public order' involves, in particular, the fight against crimes – particularly terrorism – in order to ensure public safety. Various international and EU documents condemn incitement to commit terrorist acts and the glorification of such acts.[125]

Nevertheless, the Strasbourg Court has also emphasised that it is 'incumbent on the press to convey information and ideas on political issues, even divisive ones'.[126] In the same vein, UN Security Council Resolution 1624 recalls the right to freedom of expression reflected in Article 19 UDHR and Article 19 ICCPR, and 'that any restrictions thereon shall only be such as are provided by law and are necessary on the grounds set out in [Article 19(3) ICCPR]'. States must avoid any use of the notion of 'threat to the State security' that would repress freedom of expression.[127] Eventually, Recital 10 of the EU Framework Decision on combating terrorism highlights that nothing in the Framework Decision may be interpreted as being intended to reduce or restrict fundamental rights or freedoms, including freedom of expression. In addition, Recital 14 of the Framework Decision amending the Framework Decision on combating terrorism[128] re-emphasises that the Framework Decision may not be interpreted as being intended to reduce or restrict the dissemination of information for scientific, academic or reporting purposes. Thus, 'the expression of radical, polemic or controversial views in the public debate on sensitive political questions, including terrorism, falls outside the scope of this Framework Decision and, in particular, of the definition of public provocation to commit terrorist offences [according to Article 3(1)(a) of the amended Framework Decision]'. Moreover, the amending Framework Decision stipulates in Article 2 that it

> shall not have the effect of requiring Member States to take measures in contradiction of fundamental principles relating to freedom of expression, in particular freedom of the press and the freedom of expression in other media as

---

[124] The French version speaks of 'à la défense de l'ordre *et* à la prévention du crime' (emphasis added). However, the Court's interpretation tends towards the English version, thus seeing 'prevention of disorder' and 'prevention of crime' as two different concepts; see ECtHR, Engel and others v. Netherlands [1976] App. nos. 5100/71, 5101/71, 5102/71, 5354/72 and 5370/72 [98]. 'Prevention of disorder' and 'prevention of crime' therefore do not have to be invoked cumulatively, as suggested by the French version.

[125] See, for example, Article 1(a) of Resolution 1624 (2005), adopted by the Security Council at its 5261st meeting, on 14 September 2005, S/RES/1624 (2005); Article 5 of the Council of Europe Convention on the Prevention of Terrorism; Article 4(1) of the EU Council Framework Decision 2002/475/JHA of 13 June 2002 on combating terrorism, OJ L 164/3, amended by Council Framework Decision 2008/919/JHA of 28 November 2008 amending Framework Decision 2002/475/JHA on combating terrorism, OJ L 330/21.

[126] Özgür Gündem v. Turkey [2000] App. no. 23144/93 [58]; Şener v. Turkey [2000] App. no. 26680/95 [41]; see also Human Rights Committee, General Comment no. 34, para. 46.

[127] Human Rights Committee, Concluding observations on Democratic People's Republic of Korea (CCPR/CO/72/PRK), para. 23.

[128] Council Framework Decision 2008/919/JHA of 28 November 2008 amending Framework Decision 2002/475/JHA on combating terrorism, OJ L 330/21.

they result from constitutional traditions or rules governing the rights and responsibilities of, and the procedural guarantees for, the press or other media where these rules relate to the determination or limitation of liability.

As a consequence, the aforementioned pieces of legislation all confirm that there is little scope for restrictions on political publications or on other debates on matters of public concern, even in the interest of national security or public order.

1 The Balancing Exercise

As a general rule, speech that is likely to cause harm may be restricted. However, both the necessary degree of likeliness and the extent to which speech potentially causes harm is subject to controversy. Hence the question is: what are the allowed dangers to be accepted as the price to be paid for freedom of expression and a free media?[129] This requires a balancing exercise between suppression of speech that would, if allowed, be harmless, and speech that, having been allowed, causes unlawful action.[130] On the one hand, in a democratic society, the limits of permissible criticism are wider with regard to the government and public officials than in relation to private individuals. The actions or omissions of governments and politicians must be subject to the close scrutiny of public opinion. On the other hand, due to historical experiences, international conventions are also based on the idea of democracies that must be able to defend themselves. A democratic society must be tolerant, but also vigilant and not inert. It has to be in a position to fight against abuses that are directed at democratic values themselves. As a consequence, the Strasbourg Court has granted a rather broad margin of appreciation for the State authorities 'to adopt, in their capacity as guarantors of public order, measures, even of a criminal-law nature, intended to react appropriately and without excess to [remarks that] incite to violence against an individual or a public official or a sector of the population'.[131] By doing so, the Court has maintained territorial fragmentation with regard to the legality of interferences with speech threatening national security and public safety. Nevertheless, the following factors can be regarded as the minimum standard for the balancing exercise between freedom of expression protection and public order interests in the European media law order:[132]

- The extent to which the publication contributes to a matter of public concern.
- Whether the publication is directed to inciting or producing lawless action. The content of publications may vary along the following spectrum:[133]

---

[129] Compare Schauer (1982, p. 141).
[130] Schauer (1982, p. 142).
[131] ECtHR, Sürek v. Turkey (No. 1) [1999] App. no. 26682/95 [61]; Şener v. Turkey [2000] App. no. 26680/95 [40]; Erdoğdu v. Turkey [2000] App. no. 25723/94 [62]; see also Human Rights Committee, A.K. and A.R. v. Uzbekistan [2009] Communication no. 1233/2003 [7.2].
[132] Oster (2015b, pp. 201–202).
[133] Schauer (1982, pp. 192–195).

- Non-inflammatory criticism, which is always permitted.
- Publications that do not incite lawless action, but the tone and context of the criticism may encourage disobedience to the law. Such publications are usually permitted.
- General criticism coupled with incitement to violate the criticised laws. The criticism should be allowed, but the admonition can be prohibited. This corresponds to the general principle that the search for less intrusive alternative ways of publication is part of the media's duties and responsibilities.
- Publications specifically, directly and exclusively devoted to inciting disobedience. Such publications may be prohibited based on public order concerns.
- The probability of causing harm. Courts should examine whether there is room for public discourse to separate truth from error, or whether lawless action is imminent. The Strasbourg Court required in a decision that the impugned expression represent a 'clear and imminent danger' in order for an interference to be justified.[134] This requirement moves the Court close to the US Supreme Court's 'imminent lawless action' test, as established in *Brandenburg v. Ohio*.[135]
- The degree of potential harm to be caused: the more serious the effect, the less likelihood is required.
- Timing and place of the publication: the history, geopolitical situation or instability of a country or a region.[136]
- Whether a criminal penalty, if imposed, was proportionate.

Because of its special duties and responsibilities, the journalistic media is under a general obligation not to advocate the use of violence, glorify war or intend to stigmatise one side of a conflict, for example, by the use of labels such as 'fascists' or 'murder gang'.[137] The media must also take account of the particular situation of the region a publication refers to.[138] Conversely, a use of terms that does not in itself incite unlawful action, but is merely unpalatable for the government, may not justify an interference with media freedom.[139] Moreover, offences such as 'encouragement

---

[134] Gül and others v. Turkey [2010] App. no. 4870/02 [42].

[135] Brandenburg v. Ohio, 395 U.S. 444 (1969). Compare Murray (2009, p. 340).

[136] Keller and Sigron (2010, p. 160).

[137] Compare ECtHR, Sürek v. Turkey (No. 1) [1999] App. no. 26682/95 [62]; Sürek v. Turkey (No. 3) [1999] App. no. 24735/94 [40]; Özgür Gündem v. Turkey [2000] App. no. 23144/93 [70]; Balsytė-Lideikienė v. Lithuania [2008] App. no. 72596/01 [79].

[138] See, for example, ECtHR, Şener v. Turkey [2000] App. no. 26680/95 [35]; Özgür Gündem v. Turkey [2000] App. no. 23144/93 [65] regarding south-east Turkey; Balsytė-Lideikienė v. Lithuania [2008] App. no. 72596/01 [78] concerning the situation after the re-establishment of the independence of the Republic of Lithuania on 11 March 1990.

[139] See, for example, ECtHR, Sürek v. Turkey (No. 3) [1999] App. no. 24735/94 [40]; Şener v. Turkey [2000] App. no. 26680/95 [45]; Erdoğdu v. Turkey [2000] App. no. 25723/94 [64]; Özgür Gündem v. Turkey [2000] App. no. 23144/93 [63]; see also Human Rights Committee, Kim v. Republic of Korea [1999] Communication no. 574/1994 [12.4]: distribution of material that was 'seen as coinciding' with the policy statements of the DPRK (North Korea).

of terrorism'[140] and 'extremist activity',[141] as well as offences of 'praising', 'glorifying' or 'justifying' terrorism, should be clearly defined in order to ensure that they fulfil the requirement of being 'prescribed by law'. Furthermore, states must specify the exact nature of the threat that the speaker's exercise of freedom of expression allegedly poses for national security.[142] Even legitimate objectives of national security or public order may not justify attempts 'to muzzle advocacy of multi-party democracy, democratic tenets and human rights'.[143]

2 In Particular: The Disclosure of State Secrets

Publishers may come into conflict with state authorities if they reveal classified information. This has been the case, for example, with the publication of US diplomatic cables and classified files by several newspapers and WikiLeaks, or following Edward Snowden's leak of details regarding top-secret US and British government mass surveillance programmes to the press.

The disclosure of state secrets makes the distinction between media in a technological sense and media in a journalistic sense particularly relevant: unredacted information dumped on a website will receive less protection than information that has been diligently redacted and selected before publication, thereby taking into account the interests of presumably endangered persons. If investigative journalists are prevented from, or punished for, disclosing information considered confidential or secret, it prevents them from informing the public on matters of public security, and thus inhibits public discourse on matters of paramount public concern. As a result, the ability of the press to provide accurate and reliable information is diminished, and journalists are no longer able to play their role as 'public watchdog'.[144] In particular, a state interfering with a disclosure of information that has been officially declared as confidential or even as a state secret may not automatically rely on 'national security' or 'public safety'.[145] This would imply too broad a margin of appreciation for the state. Rather, the state has to ensure that its powers to suppress the release of certain information are restricted to matters that have been *proven* to

---

[140] Human Rights Committee, Concluding observations on the United Kingdom of Great Britain and Northern Ireland (CCPR/C/GBR/CO/6), para. 26.

[141] Human Rights Committee, Concluding observations on the Russian Federation (CCPR/CO/79/RUS), para. 20.

[142] Human Rights Committee, Park v. Republic of Korea [1998] Communication no. 628/1995 [10.3]; Kim v. Republic of Korea [1999] Communication no. 574/1994 [12.4]; Shin v. Republic of Korea [2004] Communication no. 926/2000 [7.2].

[143] Human Rights Committee, Mukong v. Cameroon [1994] Communication no. 458/91 [9.7].

[144] ECtHR, Stoll v. Switzerland [2007] App. no. 69698/01 [110]; see also Goodwin v. United Kingdom [1996] App. no. 17488/90 [39]; US Supreme Court, New York Times Co. v. United States, 403 U.S. 713, 717 (1971) (Black J, concurring).

[145] See ECtHR, Hadjianastassiou v. Greece [1992] App. no. 12945/87; Human Rights Committee, Concluding observations on the United Kingdom of Great Britain and Northern Ireland (CCPR/C/GBR/CO/6), para. 24.

be necessary for the protection of national security.[146] The burden of proof for secrecy of certain information is on the state; it is not for the media to prove that the disclosure of the information was of public concern. Secrecy can hence only be justified in those few cases where the public interest in the non-disclosure of certain information outweighs the public interest in its publicity.

A number of different aspects thus need to be considered in order to ascertain whether a state measure aimed at preventing a disclosure of, or punishing for, revealing classified information was 'necessary in a democratic society':[147]

- The extent to which the publication was of general concern.
- Whether the information in question had already been known to the public. If this is the case, the information had ceased to be confidential, and it becomes unnecessary to prevent its disclosure.[148]
- The gravity of the repercussions of a publication and the degree of secrecy of an official document.[149]
- The manner in which the information in question had been obtained:[150] whether the content provider himself leaked the documents, whether he obtained them by illegal means, or whether he acted in good faith. However, a journalist cannot be punished merely because he published information that someone else had obtained illegally.[151]
- Whether a criminal penalty, if imposed, was proportionate.

Regarding the protection of the whistle-blower himself, the public interest in the disclosure of the confidential information has to be balanced with the whistle-blower's duty of loyalty and discretion as well as the public interest in keeping certain information confidential. The following factors are to be taken into consideration in this balancing exercise:[152]

- The extent to which the information is of public concern, especially – but not exclusively – whether the information concerns misconduct or an illegal activity of public officials.[153]

---

[146] See Human Rights Committee, Concluding observations on the United Kingdom of Great Britain and Northern Ireland (CCPR/C/GBR/CO/6), para. 24; ECtHR, Stoll v. Switzerland [2007] App. no. 69698/01 [54].

[147] See Oster (2015b, p. 206).

[148] See, for example, ECtHR, Weber v. Switzerland [1990] App. no. 11034/84 [51]; Observer and Guardian v. United Kingdom [1991] App. no. 13585/88 [69]; Vereniging Weekblad Bluf! v. Netherlands [1995] App. no. 16616/90 [45]; Dammann v. Switzerland [2006] App. no. 77551/01 [53]; Council of Europe, Parliamentary Assembly, Resolution 1551 (2007): Fair trial issues in criminal cases concerning espionage or divulging state secrets; *mutatis mutandis*, ECtHR, Pasko v. Russia [2009] App. no. 69519/01 [85].

[149] ECtHR, Stoll v. Switzerland [2007] App. no. 69698/01 [136]; Vereniging Weekblad Bluf! v. Netherlands [1995] App. no. 16616/90 [41].

[150] ECtHR, Stoll v. Switzerland [2007] App. no. 69698/01 [140].

[151] ECtHR, Radio Twist A.S. v. Slovakia [2006] App. no. 62202/00 [62].

[152] See Oster (2015b, pp. 210–211).

[153] See ECtHR, Guja v. Moldova [2008] App. no. 14277/04; Kayasu v. Turkey (No. 1) [2008] App. nos. 64119/00 and 76292/01 [93]; Kudeshkina v. Russia [2009] App. no. 29492/05 [94]; Sosinowska v. Poland [2011]

- Whether the whistle-blower was the only person, or part of a small group of persons, who were aware of the occurrences at their workplace, and 'thus best placed to act in the public interest by alerting the employer or the public at large'.[154]
- Whether any other effective means to remedy the wrongdoing was available to the whistle-blower, especially whether it was practicable to report to the person's superior or any other competent authority or body.[155]
- The authenticity of the information disclosed.[156] Where the information turns out to be false, it is decisive whether the whistle-blower acted in good faith and whether he attempted to verify, to the extent permitted by the circumstances, that the information is accurate and reliable.[157]
- Whether the damage inflicted upon the state's interest outweighs the interest of the public in having the information revealed.[158]
- Whether a sanction, if imposed, was proportionate.[159]

V Laws on Morality and Decency

Articles 19(3)(b) ICCPR and 10(2) ECHR provide that the exercise of freedom of expression may be subject to restrictions for the protection of, *inter alia*, morals. International courts and tribunals allow Member States a wide margin of discretion in this field.[160] By doing so, they maintain territorial fragmentation and potential for transnational conflicts. One and the same publication may be tolerated in its country of origin but considered indecent in a country of reception. The Strasbourg Court explained the reason for its self-restraint in *Handyside* v. *United Kingdom*:

> [I]t is not possible to find in the domestic law of the various Contracting States a uniform European conception of morals. The view taken by their respective

---

App. no. 10247/09 [83]; Bucur and Toma v. Romania [2013] App. no. 40238/02 [101]; *mutatis mutandis*, Tierbefreier e.V. v. Germany [2014] App. no. 45192/09 [54].

[154] ECtHR, Guja v. Moldova [2008] App. no. 14277/04 [72]; Marchenko v. Ukraine [2009] App. no. 4063/04 [46].

[155] ECtHR, Guja v. Moldova [2008] App. no. 14277/04 [73]; Bucur and Toma v. Romania [2013] App. no. 40238/02 [97]; Council of Europe, Parliamentary Assembly, Resolution 1729 (2010): Protection of 'whistle-blowers', para. 6.2.3.

[156] ECtHR, Guja v. Moldova [2008] App. no. 14277/04 [75]; Frankovicz v. Poland [2008] App. no. 53025/99 [50]; Sosinowska v. Poland [2011] App. no. 10247/09 [81]; Bucur and Toma v. Romania [2013] App. no. 40238/02 [105].

[157] ECtHR, Guja v. Moldova [2008] App. no. 14277/04 [75]; Bucur and Toma v. Romania [2013] App. no. 40238/02 [105]; Council of Europe, Parliamentary Assembly, Resolution 1729 (2010): Protection of 'whistle-blowers', para. 6.2.4.

[158] ECtHR, Guja v. Moldova [2008] App. no. 14277/04 [76]; Pasko v. Russia [2009] App. no. 69519/01 [86]; Bucur and Toma v. Romania [2013] App. no. 40238/02 [114].

[159] ECtHR, Guja v. Moldova [2008] App. no. 14277/04 [95]; Bucur and Toma v. Romania [2013] App. no. 40238/02 [119]; Kayasu v. Turkey (No. 1) [2008] App. nos. 64119/00 and 76292/01 [106]; Kudeshkina v. Russia [2009] App. no. 29492/05 [99].

[160] Critically Oster (2015b, pp. 215 ff.).

laws of the requirements of morals varies from time to time and from place to place, especially in our era which is characterised by a rapid and far-reaching evolution of opinions on the subject. By reason of their direct and continuous contact with the vital forces of their countries, State authorities are in principle in a better position than the international judge to give an opinion on the exact content of these requirements as well as on the 'necessity' of a 'restriction' or 'penalty' intended to meet them.[161]

Similar to the Strasbourg Court, the Human Rights Committee observed that the notion of public morals differs widely and that there is no universally applicable common standard: '[T]he concept of morals derives from many social, philosophical and religious traditions; consequently, limitations [...] for the purpose of protecting morals must be based on principles not deriving exclusively from a single tradition.'[162] In the same vein, in *Conegate* v. *HM Customs and Excise*, the ECJ observed that Member States, in the absence of arbitrary discrimination, are permitted to make their own assessment relating to public morality within their territory.[163]

Despite the broad margin of appreciation in *Vereinigung Bildender Künstler* v. *Austria*, the Strasbourg Court granted strong Article 10 ECHR protection, although the impugned picture was allegedly obscene. The painting showed, among other persons, Mother Teresa, an Austrian cardinal and several politicians in sexual positions. One politician, Mr Meischberger, was shown gripping the ejaculating penis of another politician while at the same time being touched by two other politicians and ejaculating on Mother Teresa. The naked bodies of these figures were painted, but the heads and faces were depicted using photos taken from newspapers. The eyes of some of the persons were hidden under black bars. Although the Court found that Mr Meischberger was depicted 'in a somewhat outrageous manner', the Court nonetheless emphasised that he, in his capacity as a politician, had to expose a wider degree of tolerance against criticism.[164] Furthermore, the Court followed the view taken by the court of first instance that the scene in which Mr Meischberger was portrayed could be understood to constitute some sort of counterattack against his political party, whose members had strongly criticised the painter's work.[165] The Court thus found that the injunction against the applicant association prohibiting it from continuing to exhibit the painting violated Article 10 ECHR. This is similar to the US Supreme Court's findings in *Hustler Magazine* v. *Falwell*.[166]

---

[161] Handyside v. United Kingdom [1976] App. no. 5493/72 [48]. See also Müller and others v. Switzerland [1988] App. no. 10737/84 [36].

[162] General Comment no. 22; see also Hertzberg and others v. Finland [1985] Communication no. 61/1979 [10.3]; UN Economic and Social Council, Siracusa Principles on the Limitation and Derogation Provisions in the International Covenant on Civil and Political Rights, U.N. Doc. E/CN.4/1985/4, Annex (1985), no. 27.

[163] ECJ, Case 121/85 [1986] Conegate v. HM Customs and Excise [14–15].

[164] Vereinigung Bildender Künstler v. Austria [2007] App. no. 68354/01 [34].

[165] Vereinigung Bildender Künstler v. Austria [2007] App. no. 68354/01 [34].

[166] Hustler Magazine v. Falwell, 485 U.S. 46 (1988).

By contrast to adult pornography, child pornography is prohibited in absolute terms by several international conventions and an EU directive.[167] Likewise, the US Supreme Court excludes child pornography from First Amendment protection.[168] It is therefore safe to speak of a global legal order as far as the condemnation of child pornography is concerned. However, differences still exist with regard to details, especially the enforcement of child pornography rules.

The leading case of the European Court of Human Rights on obscene internet publications is *Perrin v. United Kingdom*. In this case, a French national living in the United Kingdom had published scatological photographs. The website was operated and controlled by a company based in the US that complied with US laws. The applicant was charged in the UK with publishing an obscene article, contrary to the Obscene Publications Act 1959. The applicant essentially raised four arguments: first, that there should not be a wide margin of appreciation for the British authorities because that would amount to imposing moral standards on publishers of a webpage that are not regarded as necessary in the US. Second, he argued that prosecution under the Obscene Publications Act 1959 was unlikely to have any significant impact on the protection of morals because similar material was available on other sites. Third, he submitted that other measures would be more effective to achieve the aims in question, such as parental control software packages, making the accessing of the sites illegal and requiring internet service providers to block access. Fourth, he pointed out that websites were rarely accessed by accident. Yet the Strasbourg Court rejected all arguments. Referring to *Handyside*, the Court stated that the fact that dissemination of the images in question may have been legal in the United States does not mean that a Convention State exceeds its margin of appreciation in proscribing such dissemination within its own territory. Moreover, the fact that the 1959 Act may provide only limited protection to vulnerable people is no reason why a responsible government should abandon the attempt to protect them. In particular, the Court distinguished the facts of *Perrin* from a situation in which confidential material is being disseminated. While the first publication of confidential material compromises its secrecy, each publication of morally harmful material causes harm at any time at which a person is confronted with the material. Furthermore, the fact that there may be other measures available to protect against the harm does not render it disproportionate for a government to resort to criminal prosecution, particularly when those other measures have not been shown to be more effective. The applicant's websites were freely available to anyone surfing the internet, and might thus have been sought out by young persons whom the national authorities were trying to protect.[169]

---

[167] See, for example, Article 34(c) of the UN Convention on the Rights of the Child; Directive 2011/92/EU of the European Parliament and of the Council of 13 December 2011 on combating the sexual abuse and sexual exploitation of children and child pornography, and replacing Council Framework Decision 2004/68/JHA, OJ L 335/1. From legal scholarship, see Akdeniz (2008).

[168] US Supreme Court, New York v. Ferber, 458 U.S. 747 (1982).

[169] ECtHR, Perrin v. United Kingdom [2005] App. no. 5446/03.

VI Hate Speech

Many international and EU provisions and documents deal with incitement to hatred.[170] A clear and generally accepted definition of what 'hate speech' actually is has not yet been found.[171] In *Mesopotamia Broadcast A/S METV and Roj TV A/S*, the CJEU defined 'incitement to hatred' within the meaning of (now) Article 6 AVMS Directive as follows:

> As regards the words 'incitation' and 'hatred', ... they refer, first, to an action intended to direct specific behaviour and, secondly, a feeling of animosity or rejection with regard to a group of persons. Thus, the Directive, by using the concept 'incitement to hatred', is designed to forestall any ideology which fails to respect human values, in particular initiatives which attempt to justify violence by terrorist acts against a particular group of persons.[172]

Based on this definition, hate speech has two dimensions: it may cause harm against an individual person or a group of persons, and it may cause harm to public order interests. Hate speech bans may therefore be motivated by the idea of countering harm to individuals or by countering harm to public order.

But rather than arguing how to define 'hate speech' and whether this label can be placed on an impugned publication or not, it is more important to identify the content and context of this particular expression and apply the underlying rationales of media freedom and its limitations. All those attempts to define 'hate speech' share a common thread, namely the idea that hate speech is a speech act that elicits hatred. Therefore, hate speech is significant not because of what language *says*, but because of what it *does*.[173]

In practice, 'hate speech' belongs to the subjects where the differences between the US Supreme Court's jurisprudence and the approaches by international organisations and adjudicators are most obvious. Transnational 'hate speech' may thus provoke conflicts between the legal regimes of Europe, on the one hand, and the US, on the other hand. One of the earliest internet-related cases raising questions of jurisdiction concerned the sale of Nazi memorabilia, which is allowed in the US but prohibited in France and Germany.[174]

---

[170] See, for example, Article 20 ICCPR; General Assembly, Resolution 1904 (XVIII): United Nations Declaration on the elimination of all forms of racial discrimination of 20 November 1963; International Convention on the Elimination of All Forms of Racial Discrimination (ICERD); Council of Europe, Recommendation (97) 20 on "hate speech"; Recommendation No. (97) 21 on the media and the promotion of a culture of tolerance; Article 7(1)(b) of the Convention on Transfrontier Television; Council Framework Decision 2008/913/JHA of 28 November 2008 on combating certain forms and expressions of racism and xenophobia by means of criminal law, OJ L 328/55.

[171] See, for example, Committee of Ministers of the Council of Europe, Recommendation No. R (97) 20 on "hate speech"; ECtHR, Gündüz v. Turkey [2003] App. no. 35071/97 [40]; Weber (2009).

[172] CJEU, Cases C-244/10 and C-245/10 [2011] Mesopotamia Broadcast A/S METV and Roj TV A/S [42–43].

[173] See Oster (2015b, pp. 223 ff).

[174] Tribunal de Grande Instance de Paris, LICRA et UJEF v. Yahoo!, order of 22 May 2000 (see Chapter 4).

The US Supreme Court permits content-based restrictions on hateful speech only under narrowly defined circumstances: advocacy intended, and likely, to incite imminent lawless action, defamation, speech integral to criminal conduct, true threats and 'fighting words'.[175] The Supreme Court considers as a 'bedrock principle underlying the First Amendment' that the state may not prohibit the expression of an idea 'simply because society finds the idea itself offensive or disagreeable'.[176] The US approach is based on the confidence that the best remedy against hate speech is more speech, and that falsehoods are best encountered by true speech, which is at the heart of the 'marketplace of ideas' rationale.

By contrast, particularly because of their historical experience, European jurisdictions do not share this optimism. Attacks on the underlying values of the European Convention – equality, anti-discrimination, tolerance and democracy – are regarded as sufficient to justify an interference with freedom of expression, or even to exclude speech from the protection of Article 10 ECHR altogether. In contrast to the US approach, it is not necessary that the speech incites *lawless* action; instead, the ECtHR also allows for the *harmful effect* on social peace and political stability at large to justify an interference with freedom of expression.[177] Based on Articles 5(1) ICCPR and Article 17 ECHR, respectively, the Human Rights Committee as well as both the European Commission on Human Rights and the Strasbourg Court excluded the denial of the Holocaust,[178] incitement to hatred or racial discrimination[179] and justifications and glorifications of a pro-Nazi or fascist policy[180] from freedom of expression protection.

Within the European media law order, the Strasbourg Court has established basic principles for the balancing exercise in hate speech cases. The factors for this balancing exercise are:

- The extent to which the publication contributes to a matter of public concern.
- Whether the publication reflects the speaker's own opinion, or whether it is a journalistically edited third-party statement.

---

[175] See Brandenburg v. Ohio, 395 U.S. 444 (1969) on imminent lawless action; Giboney v. Empire Storage & Ice Co., 336 U.S. 490 (1949) on criminal conduct; Watts v. United States, 394 U.S. 705 (1969) on true threats; Chaplinsky v. New Hampshire, 315 U.S. 568 (1942) on fighting words.

[176] United States v. Eichman, 110 S. Ct. 2404, 2410 (1990).

[177] ECtHR, Perinçek v. Switzerland [2015] App. no. 27510/08 [205].

[178] Human Rights Committee, Faurisson v. France [1996] Communication no. 550/93 [9.6]; ECtHR, Lehideux and Isorni v. France [1998] App. no. 55/1997/839/1045 [47]; Garaudy v. France [2003] App. no. 65831/01; Witzsch v. Germany [2005] App. no. 7485/03.

[179] See, for example, Human Rights Committee, J. R. T. and the W. G. Party v. Canada [1984] Communication no. 104/1981; ECtHR, Norwood v. United Kingdom [2004] App. no. 23131/03, p. 4; Pavel Ivanov v. Russia [2004] App. no. 35222/04, p. 4, Aksu v. Turkey [2012] App. nos. 4149/04 and 41029/04 [44].

[180] EComHR, Nachtmann v. Austria [1998] App. no. 36773/97; see also Glimmerveen and Hagenbeek v. Netherlands [1979] App. nos. 8348/78 and 8406/78, p. 197; B.H., M.W., H.P. and G.K. v. Austria [1989] App. no. 12774/87; Kühnen v. Federal Republic of Germany [1988] App. no. 12194/86; Schimanek v. Austria [2000] App. no. 32307/96; ECtHR, Lehideux and Isorni v. France [1998] App. no. 55/1997/839/1045 [53].

- The tone of the publication: whether it is composed in a balanced manner, merely 'shocking' or 'disturbing', or gratuitously offensive.[181]
- The victims of the publication, particularly whether they constitute a disadvantaged and vulnerable social group.[182]
- Whether less offensive means would have been available to get the message across.
- Timing and place.[183]
- Whether the publisher ensured, to the broadest extent possible, the veracity of the underlying facts of its story.[184]
- The social and historical context of the publication concerned: where historical debates are concerned, the lapse of time between the historical event and the publication plays a significant role.[185]

VII Religiously Offensive Speech

The particular methods of opposing or denying religious beliefs may require states to balance the right to peaceful enjoyment of one's faith or public order interests with freedom of expression. Although freedom of expression is also applicable to information or ideas that shock, offend or disturb, the 'duties and responsibilities' include a duty to avoid, as far as possible, an expression that is gratuitously offensive to others or profanatory.[186]

Much disagreement in the debate about 'religiously offensive speech' has been caused by not properly distinguishing between the following kinds of 'offences' caused:

- offence caused to religions, or 'beliefs', as such (see subsection 1 below);
- offence caused to individual religious believers (see subsection 2 below); and
- offence caused to public order interests (see subsection 3 below).

1 The Notion of 'Defamation of Religions'

In April 1999, the UN Human Rights Commission approved a resolution entitled 'Defamation of Religions', which had originally been brought before the Commission by Pakistan under the draft title 'Defamation of Islam'.[187] On the initiative particularly of

---

[181] ECtHR, Soulas and others v. France [2008] App. no. 15948/03 [43].
[182] See, for example, ECtHR, Aksu v. Turkey [2012] App. nos. 4149/04 and 41029/04 [44]: Sinti and Roma.
[183] See, for example, ECtHR, Gündüz v. Turkey [2003] App. no. 35071/97 [49]: live broadcasting debate.
[184] Compare ECtHR, Aksu v. Turkey [2012] App. nos. 4149/04 and 41029/04 [72].
[185] Compare ECtHR, Vajnai v. Hungary [2008] App. no. 33629/06 [49]; Orban and others v. France [2009] App. no. 20985/05 [49].
[186] Compare ECtHR, Otto-Preminger-Institut v. Austria [1994] App. no. 13470/87 [49]; Wingrove v. United Kingdom [1996] App. no. 17419/90 [52].
[187] UN Commission on Human Rights, Resolution 1999/82: Defamation of religions of 30 April 1999.

countries with a predominantly Muslim population, the Human Rights Commission and subsequently the UN Human Rights Council adopted several resolutions in opposition to 'defamation of religions'.[188] Similar resolutions were adopted between 2005 and 2010 by the UN General Assembly.[189]

However, the concept of 'defamation of religions' is problematic, for two reasons.[190] First, it seems unjustifiable to distinguish 'religion' as particularly worthy of protection, as opposed to, say, ethnic origins or nationalities. Second, the notion of 'defamation of religions' is at odds with human rights doctrine, because human rights serve to protect individuals, not religions. Thus freedom of religion protects believers, not beliefs. The tort of defamation in particular serves to protect a person's reputation as a subcategory of the right to respect for private life.[191] Similar considerations apply to laws protecting the 'honour' of public authorities and to the prohibition of criticism of public institutions, such as, for instance, 'the army' or 'the administration': the individuals working in and for those institutions are worthy of protection, but not the institutions as such.[192] The concept of 'defamation of religions' has thus been widely rejected.

2 The 'Right to Respect for One's Religious Feelings'

It is controversial whether freedom of religion, as protected by Article 9 ECHR, includes a right not to be offended in one's religious beliefs.[193] In their joint dissenting opinion to *Otto-Preminger-Institut* v. *Austria*, Judges Palm, Pekkanen and Makarczyk wrote: 'The Convention does not, in terms, guarantee a right to protection of religious feelings. More particularly, such a right cannot be derived from the

---

[188] UN Commission on Human Rights, Resolution 2000/84: Defamation of religions of 26 April 2000; Resolution 2001/4: Combating defamation of religions as a means to promote human rights, social harmony and religious and cultural diversity of 18 April 2001; Resolution 2002/9: Combating defamation of religions of 15 April 2002; Resolution 2003/4: Combating defamation of religions of 14 April 2003; Resolution 2004/6: Combating defamation of religions of 13 April 2004; Resolution 2005/3: Combating defamation of religions of 12 April 2005; UN Human Rights Council, Decision 1/107: Incitement to racial and religious hatred and the promotion of tolerance of 30 June 2006; Resolution 4/9: Combating defamation of religions of 30 March 2007; Resolution 7/19: Combating defamation of religions of 27 March 2008; Resolution 10/22: Combating defamation of religions of 26 March 2009.

[189] UN General Assembly, Resolution 60/150 of 16 December 2005, Resolution 61/164 of 19 December 2006, Resolution 62/154 of 18 December 2007, Resolution 63/171 of 18 December 2008, Resolution 64/156 of 18 December 2009 and Resolution 65/224 of 21 December 2010, all titled 'Combating defamation of religions'.

[190] For a more detailed analysis, see Parmar (2009).

[191] See, for example, ECtHR, Chauvy and others v. France [2004] App. no. 64915/01 [70]; Pfeifer v. Austria [2007] App. no. 12556/03 [35]; Print Zeitungsverlag GmbH v. Austria [2013] App. no. 26547/07 [31].

[192] Economic and Social Council, Siracusa Principles on the Limitation and Derogation Provisions in the International Covenant on Civil and Political Rights, U.N. Doc. E/CN.4/1985/4, Annex (1985), no. 37; Office of the Special Rapporteur for Freedom of Expression with the Inter-American Commission on Human Rights, Inter-American Legal Framework Regarding the Right to Freedom of Expression, 2009, CIDH/RELE/INF. 2/09, para. 134 ff: *desacato* laws in Latin America.

[193] From academic literature, see, for example, Letsas (2012).

right to freedom of religion, which in effect includes a right to express views critical of the religious opinions of others.'[194] This view finds support in academic literature.[195] By contrast, the majority in *Otto-Preminger-Institut* v. *Austria* held that the purpose of the Austrian authorities when prohibiting the religiously offensive film *Das Liebeskonzil* 'was to protect the right of citizens not to be insulted in their religious feelings by the public expression of views of other persons'. The Court therefore accepted that the impugned measures pursued 'the protection of the rights of others' within the meaning of Article 10(2) ECHR.[196]

The debate on the 'right to respect for one's religious feelings' is still going. Here are but a few thoughts on how such a right could be properly conceptualised. First, the 'right to respect for one's religious feelings' is not identical with the interest that one's religion should not be offended. As has been shown before, a concept of 'defamation of religions' has to be rejected. Second, however, the notion of offence to beliefs has to be distinguished from offence caused by speech to individual believers. To be sure, there is no 'right not to be offended' as such. However, where offence consists of insult or causes legally cognisable harm, as is the case with defamation, it interferes with a person's reputation. Just as with honour, reputation and privacy, freedom of religion and thus the protection of one's religious feelings have to be conceptualised as one aspect of an individual's personality rights. Freedom of thought, conscience and religion is 'in its religious dimension, one of the most vital elements that go to make up the identity of believers and their conception of life'.[197] Hence, similar to the 'legitimate expectation of privacy', an individual's 'legitimate expectation of respect for one's religious feelings' has to be weighed against freedom of expression on a case-by-case basis. As 'an attack on a person's reputation must attain a certain level of seriousness' in order for Article 8 ECHR to come into play,[198] an attack on a person's religious beliefs also has to attain a 'certain level of seriousness' in order for Article 9 ECHR to come into play. These are cases that are usually covered by the law of defamation and insult, harassment, the protection of privacy, etc. Thus conceptualised, the 'right not to be offended in one's religious feelings' is to be accepted but at the same time significantly limited in its scope. In particular, the right not to be offended in one's religious feelings should not serve to stifle criticism

---

[194] Otto-Preminger-Institut v. Austria [1994] App. no. 13470/87, joint dissenting opinion of Judges Palm, Pekkanen and Makarczyk [6]. From legal scholarship, see, for example, Ahdar and I. Leigh (2005, pp. 395–396); Temperman (2008); Khan (2012).

[195] See, for example, Ahdar and I. Leigh (2005, pp. 395–396); Letsas (2012).

[196] Otto-Preminger-Institut v. Austria [1994] App. no. 13470/87 [48]; Wingrove v. United Kingdom [1996] App. no. 17419/90 [48]; see already EComHR, X. Ltd. and Y v. United Kingdom [1982] App. no. 8710/79 [11]; see also Keller (2011, p. 204); Oliva (2007, p. 85).

[197] ECtHR, Kokkinakis v. Greece [1993] App. no. 14307/88 [31]; reiterated, for example, in Otto-Preminger-Institut v. Austria [1994] App. no. 13470/87 [47]; Refah Partisi (the Welfare Party) and others v. Turkey [2003] App. nos. 41340/98, 41342/98, 41343/98 and 41344/98 [90].

[198] ECtHR, Axel Springer AG v. Germany (No. 1) [2012] App. no. 39954/08 [83] (emphasis added).

of church dignitaries or religious debates that are of considerable interest to the concerned religious community.[199] High-ranking church officials are in their influence and public perception – at least in religious communities – comparable to politicians in general. Therefore, similar freedom of expression standards should apply to speech about religious figures.[200]

3 Public Order Interests

Publications that insult religious feelings might not only violate the interests of individual persons, but also of society as a whole. Such speech can have a harmful effect on social peace in general by generating or reinforcing hatred in the community, leading to hateful attitudes, discrimination, suppression and exclusion of particular groups, or even physical violence.[201] The duties codified in Article 19(3) ICCPR and Article 10(2) ECHR include a duty to avoid, as far as possible, an expression that is 'gratuitously offensive to others or profane'.[202] The particular methods of opposing or denying religious beliefs are thus crucial for the balancing exercise between the interest in a peaceful enjoyment of religious beliefs with the right to freedom of expression.[203]

4 Margin of Appreciation

A uniform global or even regional conception of the significance of religion in society does not exist. Hence, it is not possible to define in abstract terms what constitutes a permissible interference with freedom of expression where a publication hurts the religious feelings of others.[204] Therefore, even in Europe the protection of religious interests differs from country to country due to the margin of appreciation granted by the Strasbourg Court to the Convention States. In *Otto-Preminger-Institut v. Austria*, the Strasbourg Court held that the Austrian courts did not overstep their margin of appreciation when they ordered the seizure and subsequently the forfeiture of the 1982 film *Council in Heaven*, which portrayed 'God as old, infirm

---

[199] Compare ECtHR, Albert-Engelmann-Gesellschaft mbH v. Austria [2006] App. no. 46389/99 [30].

[200] See, for example, ECtHR, Klein v. Slovakia [2006] App. no. 72208/01 [52].

[201] See Post (1991); Jaoude (2003); Hare (2006); Simpson (2006).

[202] Compare ECtHR, Otto-Preminger-Institut v. Austria [1994] App. no. 13470/87 [49]; Wingrove v. United Kingdom [1996] App. no. 17419/90 [52]; İ.A. v. Turkey [2005] App. no. 42571/98 [24]; Soulas and others v. France [2008] App. no. 15948/03 [43].

[203] See ECtHR, İ.A. v. Turkey [2005] App. no. 42571/98 [29]; Aydın Tatlav v. Turkey [2006] App. no. 50692/99 [28]; Giniewski v. France [2006] App. no. 64016/00 [51].

[204] See EComHR, X. Ltd. and Y. v. United Kingdom [1982] App. no. 8710/79 [12]; ECtHR, Otto-Preminger-Institut v. Austria [1994] App. no. 13470/87 [50]; Wingrove v. United Kingdom [1996] App. no. 17419/90 [58]; Murphy v. Ireland [2003] App. no. 44179/98 [81]; İ.A. v. Turkey [2005] App. no. 42571/98 [25].

and ineffective, Jesus Christ as a "mummy's boy" of low intelligence and the Virgin Mary, who is obviously in charge, as an unprincipled wanton'. The domestic courts acted to ensure religious peace in a particular Austrian region (Tyrol) and preventing people from feeling that they are the object of attacks on their religious beliefs in an unwarranted and offensive manner. 'It is,' the Strasbourg Court stated, 'in the first place for the national authorities, who are better placed than the international judge, to assess the need for such a measure in the light of the situation obtaining locally at a given time.'[205]

VIII Authority and Impartiality of the Judiciary

The 'authority and impartiality of the judiciary' justify interferences with freedom of expression and media freedom to protect the functioning of the courts and the judicial procedure,[206] the protection of the rights of the litigants,[207] the confidentiality of judicial deliberations of jurors[208] and the reputation of the judiciary itself, especially of judges. Unlike Article 10(2) ECHR, Article 19(3) ICCPR does not provide a qualification of 'maintaining the authority and impartiality of the judiciary'. This notwithstanding, provisions protecting order and dignity in court are encompassed by the public order caveat in this provision.[209] The purpose of 'maintaining the authority and impartiality of the judiciary' is closely linked to the obligations under Articles 14 ICCPR and 6 ECHR to ensure a fair trial.

When 'authority of the judiciary' is invoked as a reason for justifying an interference with freedom of expression or media freedom, courts have to balance the public interest in the impugned reporting with the public interest in the fair administration of justice. The public has a legitimate interest in the reception of information about proceedings in order to exercise scrutiny over the functioning of the criminal justice system.[210] Consequently, especially the journalistic media must be able to freely report and comment on such proceedings. 'The press is one of the means by which politicians and public opinion can verify that judges are discharging their heavy responsibilities in a manner that is in conformity with the aim which is the basis of the task entrusted to them.'[211]

---

[205] Otto-Preminger-Institut v. Austria [1994] App. no. 13470/87 [56]; critically Oster (2015b, pp. 245–246).
[206] ECtHR, Sunday Times v. United Kingdom (No. 1) [1979] App. no. 6538/74 [55].
[207] ECtHR, Sunday Times v. United Kingdom (No. 1) [1979] App. no. 6538/74 [56]; Observer and Guardian v. United Kingdom [1991] App. no. 13585/88 [56]; Weber v. Switzerland [1990] App. no. 11034/84 [44].
[208] ECtHR, Seckerson v. United Kingdom and Times Newspapers Ltd v. United Kingdom [2012] App. nos. 32844/10 and 33510/10 [43].
[209] Human Rights Committee, Fernando v. Sri Lanka [2005] Communication no. 1189/2003 [9.2]; Dissanayake v. Sri Lanka [2005] Communication no. 1373/2005 [8.2].
[210] ECtHR, July and SARL Liberation v. France [2008] App. no. 20893/03 [66].
[211] ECtHR, July and SARL Liberation v. France [2008] App. no. 20893/03 [66].

However, court proceedings, especially criminal trials, may have a damaging effect on the accused person, family members and third parties' personality rights. The limits of permissible comment by journalists on pending criminal proceedings must, in particular, not extend 'to statements which are likely to prejudice, whether intentionally or not, the chances of a person receiving a fair trial or to undermine the confidence of the public in the role of the courts in the administration of criminal justice'.[212] Furthermore, the media – and the public in general – may under certain specified circumstances be excluded from court proceedings. Articles 14(1) ICCPR and 6(1) ECHR provide such exceptions to the principle of public hearing. In addition, the Strasbourg Court upheld a general prohibition of broadcasting in court proceedings.[213]

IX Commercial Speech

Speech that is primarily disseminated for commercial or financial interests rather than with the aim of contributing to a debate of general concern, often named 'commercial speech', enjoys less protection.[214] However, instead of categorising certain forms of speech under labels, in this case as 'commercial speech', one should apply a contextual approach, scrutinising the particular impugned statement.[215] A distinction between 'commercial speech' and 'publications on matters of public concern' is not as clear-cut as it seems at first glance. Even advertising, arguably the purest form of 'commercial speech', may relate to matters of public concern, because the public needs to be informed about the availability and characteristics of products and services on the market. The label 'commercial speech', which allegedly deserves less protection than speech on matters of public concern, should thus be applied with reservation. Further reference to case law on 'commercial speech' will be provided in the context of broadcasting (Chapter 5) and unfair competition (Chapter 10).

X Media Pluralism

Article 11(2) EUChFR codifies that the freedom and pluralism of the media 'shall be respected'. Under the ICCPR, the obligation to secure media pluralism is closely

---

[212] ECtHR, Worm v. Austria [1997] App. no. 83/1996/702/894 [50]; Ageyevy v. Russia [2013] App. no. 7075/10 [225].

[213] P4 Radio Hele Norge ASA v. Norway [2003] App. no. 76682/01.

[214] See ECtHR, Markt intern Verlag GmbH and Klaus Beermann v. Germany [1989] App. no. 10572/83; Hertel v. Switzerland [1998] App. no. 59/1997/843/1049 [47]; but see also, *mutatis mutandis*, VgT Verein gegen Tierfabriken v. Switzerland (No. 1) [2001] App. no. 24699/94 [66]; ECJ, Case C-245/01 [2003] RTL v. Niedersächsische Landesmedienanstalt für privaten Rundfunk [73]; Case C-71/02 [2004] Herbert Karner Industrie-Auktionen GmbH v. Troostwijk GmbH [51]. For analyses of commercial speech in academic scholarship, see Munro (2003); Randall (2006); Johnson and Youm (2009).

[215] Oster (2015b, pp. 249 ff); see also Ballantyne and others v. Canada [1993] Communication no. 359, 385/89 [11.3].

connected to Article 27 ICCPR, which provides: 'In those States in which ethnic, religious or linguistic minorities exist, persons belonging to such minorities shall not be denied the right, in community with the other members of their group, to enjoy their own culture, to profess and practice their own religion, or to use their own language.' Finally, the Strasbourg Court expressed that '[i]t is of the essence of democracy to allow diverse political programmes to be proposed and debated, even those that call into question the way a State is currently organised, provided that they do not harm democracy itself'.[216] As a consequence, states are not just compelled not to harm existing media pluralism, rather, they are under a positive obligation to safeguard media pluralism.[217] But what is 'media pluralism'? It essentially requires that as many different voices as possible shall be heard in the marketplace of ideas, such as different political, moral, cultural and religious opinions.[218]

1 The Relationship between Media Freedom and Media Pluralism

As the ECJ observed, media pluralism is a 'cultural policy' aiming at safeguarding 'the freedom of expression of the various – in particular social, cultural, religious and philosophical – components of a Member State in order that that freedom may be capable of being exercised in the press, on the radio or on television'.[219] In turn, media pluralism is not a subjective right that individuals may invoke in a court.

The relationship between the right to media freedom and media pluralism as a policy is twofold. On the one hand, media pluralism may serve as a value *supporting* media freedom. This is especially the case where media companies seek access to a particular market. Consequently, the aim of achieving a high level of media pluralism may require states to take measures breaking up existing media monopolies or oligopolies.[220] Furthermore, the state has to protect an independent media in order to guarantee media pluralism.[221]

---

[216] Manole and others v. Moldova [2009] App. no. 13936/02 [95]; reiterated in Centro Europa 7 S.r.l. and Di Stefano v. Italy [2012] App. no. 38433/09 [129].

[217] See, for example, Human Rights Committee, Concluding observations on Sri Lanka (CCPR/CO/79/LKA), para. 17; Concluding observations on the Russian Federation (CCPR/CO/79/RUS), para. 18; Mavlonov et al. v. Uzbekistan [2009] Communication no. 1334/2004 [8.6]; ECtHR, Informationsverein Lentia and others v. Austria [1993] App. nos. 13914/88; 15041/89; 15717/89; 15779/89; 17207/90 [32–34]; VgT Verein gegen Tierfabriken v. Switzerland (No. 1) [2001] App. no. 24699/94 [77]; Manole and others v. Moldova [2009] App. no. 13936/02 [99]; Article 10*bis* of the European Convention on Transfrontier Television (1989). See also Garry (1989); Komorek (2009).

[218] For a more detailed analysis, see Oster (2015b, pp. 256 ff).

[219] Case C-288/89 [1991] Stichting Collectieve Antennevoorziening Gouda and others v. Commissariaat voor de Media [22–23]; Case C-353/89 [1991] Commission v. Netherlands [29–30]; Case C-148/91 [1993] Veronica Omroep v. Commissariaat voor de Media [9]; Case C-23/93 [1994] TV 10 SA v. Commissariaat voor de Media [18].

[220] Compare Case C-260/89 [1991] ERT v. DEP and others [20].

[221] See Garry (1989); Komorek (2009). See also ECtHR, Informationsverein Lentia and others v. Austria [1993] App. nos. 13914/88; 15041/89; 15717/89; 15779/89; 17207/90 [32–34]; TV Vest & Rogaland Pensjonistparti v. Norway [2008] App. no. 21132/05 [78].

On the other hand, a high level of media pluralism may constitute an unwritten legitimate aim *justifying an interference* with media freedom. This observation finds support in the case law of both the ECJ and the ECtHR. With regard to the freedom to provide services under EC/EU law, the Luxembourg Court has recognised media pluralism as an overriding requirement relating to the general interest, capable of justifying a restriction on the freedom to provide media services by powerful broadcasting companies.[222] Moreover, in the 1993 decision *Informationsverein Lentia and others* v. *Austria*, the Strasbourg Court had to decide whether the Austrian public broadcasting monopoly was in accordance with Article 10(2) ECHR. The Court thereby underlined that the state is the ultimate guarantor for media pluralism.[223] A public broadcasting monopoly may constitute a justified measure to guarantee media pluralism; however, it also imposes restrictions on the freedom of expression of other potential broadcasters. The Court found that there is no longer a 'pressing social need' to maintain a public broadcasting monopoly, in particular because technological progress made a number of frequencies and channels available.[224] The Court also rejected the government's argument that the Austrian market was too small to sustain a sufficient number of stations to avoid the constitution of 'private monopolies': private and public stations coexist in several European states of a comparable size to Austria, but the development of private monopolies could nonetheless be prevented there.[225]

2 Policy Areas of Media Pluralism

How a pluralist media can be realised nowadays is one of the main challenges contemporary media law is facing. The tools to safeguard media pluralism include different aspects, such as diversity of ownership, variety in the sources of information as well as in the range of contents available and so-called 'internal pluralism', providing diversity of output or content. Three areas of external media pluralism policy will be sketched in other chapters of this book: media competition policy, which will be further elaborated on in Chapter 10; the provision of public broadcasting, which will be

---

[222] See, for example, Case C-288/89 [1991] Stichting Collectieve Antennevoorziening Gouda and others v. Commissariaat voor de Media [23]; Case C-353/89 [1991] Commission v. Netherlands [30]; Case C-148/91 [1993] Case C-23/93 [1994] TV 10 SA v. Commissariaat voor de Media [19]; Case C-250/06 [2007] United Pan-Europe Communications Belgium SA and others v. Belgium and others [41]. See also Case 352/85 [1988] Bond van Adverteerders v. Netherlands [38]: the maintenance of a pluralistic broadcasting system may constitute a justification for an indistinctly applicable measure, but not for discrimination. On EU media pluralism policy, see Valcke et al. (2010).

[223] Informationsverein Lentia and others v. Austria [1993] App. nos. 13914/88, 15041/89, 15717/89, 15779/89 and 17207/90 [38]; see also VgT Verein gegen Tierfabriken v. Switzerland (No. 1) [2001] App. no. 24699/94 [73]; Manole and others v. Moldova [2009] App. no. 13936/02 [99].

[224] Informationsverein Lentia and others v. Austria [1993] App. nos. 13914/88, 15041/89, 15717/89, 15779/89 and 17207/90 [39].

[225] Informationsverein Lentia and others v. Austria [1993] App. nos. 13914/88, 15041/89, 15717/89, 15779/89 and 17207/90 [42].

explained in Chapter 5; and governmental support of media pluralism by subsidising private companies, which will be the subject of Chapter 11. In addition, media pluralism also requires the protection of internal media pluralism; that is, pluralism within a particular media organisation. Internal media pluralism requires that journalists must not be obliged to self-censorship when approaching delicate subjects – in particular when issues are delicate for the owners of the media company that employs them, or when they work for state broadcasters.[226] Media freedom applies to every journalist, both self-employed and employed. Although human rights do not have a direct effect between private individuals, employment law has to be legislated and interpreted in a media-freedom and pluralism-friendly way. Media freedom does not only foster discourse *between* media undertakings, but also *within* them. At the same time, owners of media organisations should be able to determine the strategy of their companies, including an editorial line and a certain political slant. These two conflicting interests might have to be balanced when applying, for example, domestic employment law in litigation procedures between media employees and media employers.

XI Licensing of Journalists and Media Companies

This section deals with *ex ante* licensing regimes for journalists and broadcasters, as opposed to content-based interferences with media freedom that have been set out in the previous sections. A licensing requirement for journalists that is based on the fulfilment of particular prerequisites, such as quotas, qualifications or content, are *per se* a disproportionate interference with media freedom. Such requirements would impede the exercise of journalistic activity. Based on the 'press-as-technology' argument,[227] everyone should be entitled to such activity. Therefore, according to the Human Rights Committee and the Strasbourg Court,[228] compulsory official registration of journalists is compatible with media freedom only if the requirements for the registration are purely formal.

The Inter-American Court in its 'Advisory Opinion on Compulsory Membership in an Association Prescribed by Law for the Practice of Journalism' went even one step further: the Court distinguished journalists from the organisation of other professions. While the organisation of professions in general by means of professional 'colegios' is not *per se* contrary to the Convention by reasons of public order,

---

[226] ECtHR, Manole and others v. Moldova [2009] App. no. 13936/02 [100].

[227] See Chapter 1.

[228] Human Rights Committee, Concluding observations on Lesotho (CCPR/CO/79/Add. 106), para. 23; compare Mavlonov et al. v. Uzbekistan [2009] Communication no. 1334/2004 [8.4]; General Comment no. 34, para. 39; Nicol et al. (2009, para. 11.19). In Gawęda v. Poland [2002] App. no. 26229/95 [48], the Strasbourg Court held that a Polish registration scheme for periodicals was not 'prescribed by law'.

this rationale does not apply to the media. Such regulation 'would have the effect of permanently depriving those who are not members of the right to make full use of the rights that Article 13 [ACHR] grants to each individual. Hence, it would violate the basic principles of a democratic public order on which the Convention itself is based.'[229] The compulsory licensing of journalists is unnecessary, because 'the establishment of a law that protects the freedom and independence of anyone who practices journalism is perfectly conceivable without the necessity of restricting that practice only to a limited group of the community'.[230]

A voluntary accreditation scheme is basically compatible with media freedom, if the registration merely serves practical purposes, such as the receipt of a press card. However, the receipt of a press card should not be constitutive of being a journalist and the disadvantages of not having been registered must not be arbitrary. In those cases where a state applies limited accreditation schemes to provide journalists with privileged access to certain places or events, these schemes must not be applied in a discriminatory manner and they must provide a legal remedy to determine the legality of denying certain journalists access.[231]

By contrast to individual journalists, compulsory licensing requirements for broadcasting companies do not *per se* violate media freedom. Such licensing may be justified by the need to manage scarce resources, such as the electromagnetic wavelength spectrum.[232] Sentence 3 of Article 10(1) ECHR states that freedom of expression shall not prevent states from requiring the licensing of broadcasting, television or cinema enterprises. Under the ICCPR, licensing of broadcasters is covered by the reference to 'public order' in Article 19(3).[233] However, licensing requirements interfere with media freedom and are therefore subject to the requirements for the justification of an interference as stipulated in Articles 19(3) ICCPR and 10(2) ECHR.[234] Hence, the compulsory licensing of broadcasters must be 'prescribed by law' and necessary in a democratic society for one of the legitimate purposes mentioned in the human rights catalogues. For a licensing regime to be 'prescribed by law', the applicant for a licence must be made aware on what basis the national authority exercises its discretion to deny such a licence. Domestic law must also afford a measure

---

[229] IACtHR, Advisory Opinion OC-5/85 [68–76].
[230] IACtHR, Advisory Opinion OC-5/85 [79].
[231] Human Rights Committee, Gauthier v. Canada [1999] Communication no. 633/95 [13.7]; see also General Comment no. 34, para. 44. On the right of the media not to be discriminated against, see Chapter 2.III.2.f.
[232] Council of Europe, Recommendation CM/Rec(2011)7 on a new notion of media, Appendix, para. 77.
[233] See General Assembly Document A/5000 of the sixteenth session, 5 December 1961, para. 23; see also ECtHR, Groppera Radio AG and others v. Switzerland [1990] App. no. 10890/84 [61].
[234] See, for example, ECtHR, Groppera Radio AG and others v. Switzerland [1990] App. no. 10890/84 [61]; Informationsverein Lentia and others v. Austria [1993] App. nos. 13914/88, 15041/89, 15717/89, 15779/89 and 17207/90 [29]; Demuth v. Switzerland [2002] App. no. 38743/97 [33]; Glas Nadezhda EOOD and Elenkov v. Bulgaria [2007] App. no. 14134/02 [44].

of legal protection against an arbitrary refusal to grant a licence. The Council of Europe Recommendation Rec(2000)23 on the independence and functions of regulatory authorities for the broadcasting sector[235] provides further guidance for the Convention States and, finally, the Strasbourg Court. Against this background, the ECtHR found a violation of Article 10 ECHR in several decisions because the process in which the licence had been denied was not sufficiently transparent.[236]

XII Questions

1 'The notion of "hate speech" is under-conceptualised and has in no way contributed to the content and limits of freedom of expression. It is a confusing label that should be abandoned.' Do you agree?

2 Article 1 of the EU Council Framework Decision on combating racism and xenophobia requires Member States to take the measures necessary to ensure that certain behaviours are punishable as criminal offences. These behaviours include public incitement to violence or hatred directed at a group of persons or a member of such a group defined by reference to race, colour, religion, descent or national or ethnic origin. Article 1(3) of the Framework Decision then explains that the reference to religion in Article 1 of that Framework Decision 'is intended to cover, at least, conduct which is a pretext for directing acts against a group of persons or a member of such a group defined by reference to race, colour, descent, or national or ethnic origin'.

    What is the impact of Article 1(3) of the Council Framework Decision on religiously offensive speech, particularly the notion of 'defamation of religions'?

3 What are the rationales and arguments for and against the prohibition of denials of 'clearly established historical facts'? Read the ECtHR decision *Perinçek v. Switzerland*.[237] Do you think that this judgment heralds a change in the ECtHR's approach to denials of historical facts?

4 'Criminal trials take place in public, but not for the public.' Critically discuss this statement and explain its significance for media reporting on criminal trials.

5 The Strasbourg Court also regards the motive behind the actions of a whistle-blower as a determinant factor in deciding whether a particular disclosure should be protected or not.[238] Accordingly, an act motivated by a personal grievance,

---

[235] Council of Europe, Recommendation Rec(2000)23 on the independence and functions of regulatory authorities for the broadcasting sector.

[236] Glas Nadezhda EOOD and Elenkov v. Bulgaria [2007] App. no. 14134/02 [50]; Meltex Ltd and Mesrop Movsesyan v. Armenia [2008] App. no. 32283/04 [83]; Centro Europa 7 S.r.l. and Di Stefano v. Italy [2012] App. no. 38433/09 [154].

[237] ECtHR, Perinçek v. Switzerland [2015] App. no. 27510/08.

[238] ECtHR, Guja v. Moldova [2008] App. no. 14277/04 [77]; Kudeshkina v. Russia [2009] App. no. 29492/05 [95].

personal antagonism or the expectation of personal advantage should weaken the protection of whistle-blowers. Do you agree?

XIII Recommended Reading

- R. Clayton and H. Tomlinson, *Privacy and Freedom of Expression*, 2nd edn, 2010
- L. McNamara, *Reputation and Defamation*, 2007
- D. Milo, *Defamation and Freedom of Speech*, 2008
- J.L. Mills, *Privacy: The Lost Right*, 2008
- P. Mitchell, *The Making of the Modern Law of Defamation*, 2005
- D. Rolph, *Reputation, Celebrity and Defamation Law*, 2008
- P. Tweed, *Privacy and Libel Law: The Clash with Press Freedom*, 2012
- R. Wacks, *Privacy and Media Freedom*, 2013
- M. Warby, N. Moreham and I. Christie (eds.), *The Law of Privacy and the Media*, 2nd edn, 2011
- R.L. Weaver, A.T. Kenyon, D.E. Partlett and C.P. Walker, *The Right to Speak Ill*, 2006

4

The Jurisdictional Question

CASE EXAMPLES

Fiona Shevill is a British national residing in Yorkshire, England. Presse Alliance SA is a company incorporated under French law whose registered office is in Paris. In its newspaper *France-Soir*, Presse Alliance published an allegedly defamatory newspaper article about Ms Shevill. It is estimated that more than 237,000 copies of the issue of *France-Soir* in question were sold in France and approximately 15,500 copies distributed in the other European countries, of which 230 were sold in England and Wales (five in Yorkshire). The parties sought to establish whether English or French courts would have jurisdiction to hear an action for damages for the harm allegedly caused to Ms Shevill by the publication of the article.

(ECJ, Case C-68/93 [1995] Shevill and others v. Presse Alliance SA)

Yahoo! Inc., a company based in California, provides online auction services. These services were used for the sale of Nazi memorabilia and could also be accessed in France. Upon application by the Ligue contre le racisme et l'antisémitisme et Union des étudiants juifs de France (LICRA), a court in Paris decided in an interim judgment of 22 May 2000 that the offerings were illegal under French law. Yahoo had been ordered to take all appropriate measures to deter and prevent access to auctions of Nazi memorabilia on its site by French residents. Yahoo argued that these auctions were conducted under the jurisdiction of the United States, where they were protected under the First Amendment to the US Constitution. Moreover, Yahoo claimed that their servers were located on US territory and their services were primarily aimed at US residents. Therefore, French courts had no jurisdiction to hear the case. Finally, Yahoo argued that it was technically impossible to comply with the order of the French court. After receiving an expert opinion, the French court found that Yahoo was capable of complying with the order. The court subsequently rendered an injunction against Yahoo on 10 November 2000. It ruled that there were sufficient links with France to give it full jurisdiction to hear the complaint.

(Tribunal de Grande Instance de Paris, Ligue contre le racisme et l'antisémitisme et Union des étudiants juifs de France c. Yahoo! Inc. et Société Yahoo! France (LICRA v. Yahoo!), No. RG 00/05308)

I Introduction

Shevill and *Yahoo* would never have made it to the annals of transnational media law if their outcomes had been the same, disregarding whether English, French or American courts adopted the decision. However, this was not the case. *Shevill* and

Yahoo, and many other cases of transnational media law, have come to certain fame because media law is not one and the same around the globe.

Chapter 2 has already explained the – mainly European – convergences in media human rights law. Nevertheless, there are still many discrepancies, even among EU Member States. This applies even more on the global stage, in spite of multilateral cooperation, international organisations such as the WTO and adjudicators such as the Human Rights Committee.

Insofar as the substantive law has not been harmonised, the jurisdictional question plays a significant role for publishers and litigants. US media law is well-known for its robust protection of free speech under the First Amendment to the US Constitution, whereas London, by reference to a Johnny Cash song sometimes nicknamed 'A Town Named Sue', has been perceived as the libel capital of the world. Continental Europe prohibits the exposition of Nazi memorabilia, which is allowed in the US. Further examples of global divergences are laws on blasphemy, defamation of public officials and *lèse-majesté* and rules on hate speech. Within the area of private law, the different outcomes among different jurisdictions invite forum shopping, especially 'libel tourism'.[1] Although forum shopping has a negative connotation within the academic debate, it is neither illegal nor illegitimate. On the contrary, contemplating comparative law and the question of jurisdiction is obligatory for any legal consultant.

However, providing predictability and legal certainty is particularly important for the human rights-sensitive activity of transnational media publications. Jurisdictional rules do not operate independently of human rights commitments. Instead, the interpretation and application of provisions on jurisdiction in transnational media law cases has to strike a balance between conflicting interests: on the one hand, society in general and a publisher in particular have an interest in freedom of speech and the free exchange of information and ideas. On the other hand, the receiving country has an interest in protecting its citizens' privacy and reputation (the *Shevill* scenario) and in safeguarding public order interests (the *Yahoo* scenario).

This chapter scrutinises legal frameworks on jurisdiction in order to distil common themes. It will focus on the public law dimension and on the jurisdictional question in private international law regarding torts, and largely exclude questions relating to the choice of law as well as contractual matters. However, many of the questions related to aspects of public law jurisdiction and court jurisdiction equally apply to the choice of law. It is often a matter of coincidence whether a case arises as a public or a

---

[1] On the phenomenon of 'libel tourism', see, for example, Council of Europe, Declaration on the Desirability of International Standards dealing with Forum Shopping in respect of Defamation, 'Libel Tourism', to ensure Freedom of Expression (4 July 2012); Garnett and Richardson (2009); Hartley (2010); Nielsen (2013).

private law case. The notorious *Google Spain* case, which will be further dealt with in Chapter 8, could have equally appeared as a private law case. Similarly, the *Yahoo* case was a private law litigation between *LICRA* and *Yahoo*, but it could equally have been an administrative or even criminal procedure against *Yahoo*. Likewise, cases involving hate speech, defamation or violations of privacy often involve both a public and a private law dimension. In such cases, the guiding principles are often the same, namely to strike a proper balance between the free speech rights of the publisher and its domestic legal values.

II The Notion of 'Jurisdiction'

Jurisdiction has essentially two meanings. The term 'jurisdiction' is often synonymous with territory. For example, Article 1 ECHR provides: 'The High Contracting Parties shall secure to everyone *within their jurisdiction* the rights and freedoms defined in Section I of this Convention.'[2] Understood as a legal term, 'jurisdiction' is generally divided into three subcategories: prescriptive jurisdiction, adjudicative jurisdiction and enforcement jurisdiction. Prescriptive jurisdiction, also referred to as legislative jurisdiction, describes a state's authority to promulgate rules applicable to persons or activities.[3] 'Jurisdiction to adjudicate' refers to a state's authority to subject persons or things to its judicial process. 'Jurisdiction to enforce' means a state's power to give effect to its rules and decisions by means of implementing measures, usually through courts or administrative agencies.[4] Prescriptive and adjudicative jurisdiction can be further divided into personal and subject-matter jurisdiction. Subject-matter jurisdiction describes the power of a court to hear and decide cases of a class.[5] This form of jurisdiction can be left aside for the purpose of this book. Personal jurisdiction describes the power of a legislator or a court to exercise authority over persons.

In 1935 the Harvard Law School published its 'Research in International Law, Jurisdiction with Respect to Crime'.[6] It contained a set of principles to establish jurisdiction, which are today widely recognised under international law:

1 The territorial principle.
2 The nationality principle.

---

[2] Emphasis added. On the interpretation of this provision, see ECtHR, Banković and others v. Belgium and others [2001] App. no. 52207/99 [59–65]; Issa and others v. Turkey [2004] App. no. 31821/96 [65–71]; Ben El Mahi v. Denmark [2006] 5853/06.

[3] ECJ, Joined Cases C-89/85, C-104/85, C-114/85, C-116/85, C-117/85, C-125/85, C-126/85, C-127/85, C-128/85, C-129/85 [1988] Ahlström Osakeyhtiö and others v. Commission ('Wood Pulp I'), Opinion of Advocate-General Darmon [28].

[4] Compare ECJ, Joined Cases C-89/85, C-104/85, C-114/85, C-116/85, C-117/85, C-125/85, C-126/85, C-127/85, C-128/85, C-129/85 [1988] Ahlström Osakeyhtiö and others v. Commission ('Wood Pulp I'), Opinion of Advocate-General Darmon [28].

[5] See Supreme Court of Wyoming, Christiansen v. Christiansen, 253 P.3d 153 (2011) [4].

[6] 29 *American Journal of International Law* 443 (Supp. 1935).

3 The protective principle.
4 The passive personality principle.
5 The universality principle.

Territorial jurisdiction is based on the presence of a person, a good or an event within a territory. For the EU, the application of the territoriality principle is codified in Articles 52 TEU and 355 TFEU. The territoriality principle can be further subdivided into subjective and objective territoriality. Subjective territoriality describes the capacity of states to exercise jurisdiction over acts originating within its territory, even though they were completed abroad. Objective territoriality means that states may exercise jurisdiction to regulate activity that originated abroad but that was completed within its territory.[7] According to the nationality principle, states may exercise prescriptive and adjudicative jurisdiction over their own nationals, even when they are located outside national territory.[8] The protective principle implies that states may exercise prescriptive and adjudicative jurisdiction over certain conduct outside their territory that is directed against certain important state interests. In transnational media law, the protective principle could apply, for example, in cases of high treason or revelation of state secrets published in a newspaper or on a website from abroad.[9] According to the passive personality principle, states may exercise prescriptive and adjudicative jurisdiction with regard to an act committed outside its territory when a national is the victim of the act.[10] Depending on the domestic laws, a state may apply the passive personality principle, for example, to offences committed abroad against a journalist of that state's nationality, if the act is a criminal offence in the country where it is committed or if that locality is not subject to any criminal jurisdiction.[11] Finally, the universality principle prescribes that any state may exercise prescriptive and adjudicative jurisdiction in relation to a certain act that is widely condemned by the international community.[12] Acts that might be prosecuted under the universality principle are offences committed abroad against internationally protected legal interests, such as distribution of child pornography.[13]

However, of those principles, the territorial principle is the most important one. Territoriality is the rule, the other principles are the exception. Every state has, in principle, personal jurisdiction over persons within its territory. Conversely, a state

---

[7] ECJ, Joined Cases C-89/85, C-104/85, C-114/85, C-116/85, C-117/85, C-125/85, C-126/85, C-127/85, C-128/85, C-129/85 [1988] Ahlström Osakeyhtiö and others v. Commission ('Wood Pulp I'), Opinion of Advocate-General Darmon [20]; Schultz (2008, pp. 800, 812).

[8] See, for example, US Supreme Court, Blackmer v. United States, 284 U.S. 421 (1932); Section 7(2)(1) of the German Criminal Law Code.

[9] See, for example, Section 5(2) and (3) of the German Criminal Law Code.

[10] See, for example, Article 15(2)(a) of the UN Convention against Transnational Organized Crime.

[11] See, for example, Section 7(1) of the German Criminal Law Code.

[12] See, for example, Israeli Supreme Court, Attorney-General of the State of Israel v. Eichman, 36 I.L.R. 277 (1962).

[13] See, for example, Article 3 of the Optional Protocol to the Convention on the Rights of the Child on the sale of children, child prostitution and child pornography.

can basically not exercise personal jurisdiction outside its territory unless the persons have manifested some relevant contact with the state. As the Permanent Court of International Justice already explained in the *S.S. Lotus* case:

> [T]he first and foremost restriction imposed by international law upon a State is that – failing the existence of a permissive rule to the contrary – it may not exercise its power in any form in the territory of another State. In this sense jurisdiction is certainly territorial; it cannot be exercised by a State outside its territory except by virtue of a permissive rule derived from international custom or from a convention.[14]

III The Legal Framework

For an overview of the legal framework on jurisdiction, one has to distinguish between private law cases on the one hand, and public law cases (including criminal law) on the other hand. In private law, one has to sharply distinguish between the establishment of a court's jurisdiction and the determination of the applicable law. In tort cases in which the defendant is domiciled in an EU Member State, as was the case in *Shevill and others* v. *Presse Alliance*, the Brussels Ia Regulation[15] applies. If the defendant is not established in an EU Member State, as was the case in *LICRA* v. *Yahoo*, domestic rules on jurisdiction apply. This will not be discussed further here. In order to understand the *LICRA* v. *Yahoo* case, it is sufficient to assume that the relevant French rules on jurisdiction correspond to those of the Brussels Ia Regulation.

According to Article 4(1) Brussels Ia Regulation, persons domiciled[16] in an EU Member State (with the exception of Denmark)[17] shall principally be sued in the courts of that State. However, Article 7(2) establishes a special jurisdiction, providing that a person may be sued in matters relating to tort, delict or quasi-delict in the courts for the place where the harmful event occurred or may occur. Article 7(2) therefore has two requirements for a court to establish jurisdiction: First, the subject matter of the claim must be 'relating to tort, delict or quasi-delict'. Article 7(2) of

---

[14] S.S. Lotus (France v. Turkey) [1927] PCIJ (Series A) No. 10, pp. 18–19.

[15] Regulation (EU) No. 1215/2012 of the European Parliament and of the Council of 12 December 2012 on jurisdiction and the recognition and enforcement of judgments in civil and commercial matters (recast), OJ L 351/1 ('Brussels Ia'). When referring to the Brussels Ia Regulation, this chapter means to refer to the Convention of 16 September 1988 on jurisdiction and the enforcement of judgments in civil and commercial matters (Lugano Convention) that applies to Iceland, Norway and Switzerland at the same time.

[16] According to Article 62(1) Brussels Ia Regulation, a legal person or association of natural or legal persons is domiciled at the place where it has its statutory seat, central administration or principal place of business.

[17] Recital 41 Brussels I Regulation. The Convention of 27 September 1968 on jurisdiction and the enforcement of judgments in civil and commercial matters (Brussels Convention) continues to apply to Denmark; see also the Agreement between the European Community and the Kingdom of Denmark on jurisdiction and the recognition and enforcement of judgments in civil and commercial matters, OJ L 299/62.

the Brussels Ia Regulation requires an autonomous interpretation.[18] Yet the provisions on special jurisdiction enumerated in Articles 7 et seq., which derogate from the general principle in Article 4, should, according to the CJEU, not be construed unduly widely.[19] As Recital 15 of the Brussels Ia Regulation emphasises, the rules of jurisdiction must be 'highly predictable and founded on the principle that jurisdiction is generally based on the defendant's domicile and jurisdiction must always be available on this ground *save in a few well-defined situations* in which the subject-matter of the litigation or the autonomy of the parties warrants a different linking factor' (emphasis added). However, as the ECJ established in its *Kalfelis* decision, 'torts' within the meaning of (now) Article 7(2) encompass an 'independent concept covering all actions which seek to establish the liability of a defendant and which are not related to a "contract" within the meaning of [Article 7(1)]'.[20] The concept of 'tort' includes, for example, violations of privacy, violations of intellectual property rights, unfair competition and defamation. Therefore, second, the decisive question is: what is the place 'where the harmful event occurred', with regard to transnational torts committed by means of mass communication?

Once a court has established its jurisdiction in a private law dispute, it has to decide which law applies to this case. By contrast to public law cases, in private law cases this is not necessarily the law of the country in which the court is situated (the *lex fori*). In order to determine the applicable law for non-contractual obligations in civil and commercial matters, courts of EU Member States (again with the exception of Denmark)[21] have to apply the Rome II Regulation[22] in the first place. The Rome II Regulation provides conflict of laws rules with regard to, for example, claims of unfair competition in Article 6 (see Chapter 10) and infringement of intellectual property rights in Article 8 (see Chapter 9). However, Article 1(2)(g) of the Rome II Regulation excludes violations of personality rights from its scope. The provision stipulates that 'non-contractual obligations arising out of violations of privacy and rights relating to personality, including defamation', shall be excluded from the scope of this Regulation. Despite the European Parliament's effort, the Commission and the Council rejected an inclusion of a choice of law rule for violation of personality

---

[18] Case 189/87 [1988] Kalfelis v. Bankhaus Schröder, Münchmeyer, Hengst and Co. and others [16]; Case C-334/00 [2002] Fonderie Officine Meccaniche Tacconi SpA v. Heinrich Wagner Sinto Maschinenfabrik GmbH (HWS) [19].

[19] Case 189/87 [1988] Kalfelis v. Bankhaus Schröder, Münchmeyer, Hengst and Co. and others [19]; Case C-168/02 [2004] Kronhofer [14]; Stone (2010, p. 77).

[20] Case 189/87 [1988] Kalfelis v. Bankhaus Schröder, Münchmeyer, Hengst and Co. and others [17]; see also Case C-261/90 [1992] Reichert v. Dresdner Bank AG (No. 2) [19]; Case C-51/97 [1998] Réunion Européenne v. Spliethoff's Bevrachtingskantoor; Case C-334/00 [2002] Tacconi v. Wagner; Case C-167/00 [2002] VKI v. Henkel; Case C-334/00 [2002] Fonderie Officine Meccaniche Tacconi SpA v. Heinrich Wagner Sinto Maschinenfabrik GmbH (HWS) [21].

[21] Article 1(4) Rome II Regulation.

[22] Regulation (EC) No. 864/2007 of the European Parliament and of the Council of 11 July 2007 on the law applicable to non-contractual obligations (Rome II), OJ L 199/40.

matters.[23] Article 73m of the EC Treaty, as amended by the Treaty of Amsterdam, which is now Article 81 TFEU, was accompanied by a declaration that the provision 'shall not prevent any Member State from applying its constitutional rules relating to freedom of the press and freedom of expression in other media'. It was therefore contested whether the Community had a legal basis to regulate matters concerning freedom of expression and personality rights.[24] Article 30(2) of the Rome II Regulation has obliged the European Commission to submit until 31 December 2008 a study on the situation in the field of the law applicable to non-contractual obligations arising out of violations of privacy and rights relating to personality, taking into account freedom of expression in the media and conflict-of-law issues related to the Data Protection Directive. The Commission complied in February 2009.[25]

The interpretation of Article 1(2)(g) Rome II Regulation is in many cases problematic. For example, does this provision also cover defamation of legal persons, such as companies? Commentators have argued that it should not make a difference for the application of Article 1(2)(g) whether, for example, a defamation claim is raised by a natural or a legal person.[26] However, the provision speaks of 'obligations arising out of violations of ... rights relating to personality, *including* defamation' (emphasis added). This suggests that defamation – to be more precise: a defamation claim – is an obligation arising out of personality rights. It is questionable whether companies have such 'personality rights'. Instead, it seems more convincing to argue that companies' rights to sue for defamation arise out of their property rights, but not their personality rights.[27] On the other hand, it would indeed seem artificial to exclude companies from the scope of Article 1(2)(g) Rome II Regulation. The history of this provision suggests that the legislators did not have the victims of the claims mentioned in this provision in mind when drafting the legislation, but the alleged offenders, especially the news media. And for the news media it does not make a difference whether it allegedly defames a natural or a legal person. Therefore, Article 1(2)(g) Rome II Regulation should basically be applied to defamation of companies. In Chapter 10 it will be argued that this shall not be the case if the defamation of a company constitutes an act of unfair competition, which would fall under Article 6 Rome II Regulation.

Another problematic example on the interpretation of Article 1(2)(g) is the disclosure of confidential information. If the confidential information relates to a private person, then the Data Protection Directive and subsidiarily Article 1(2)(g) apply. But what about the disclosure of business secrets? It is controversial whether this could

---

[23] On the legislative history of Article 1(2)(g), see I. Bach, in Huber (2011, Art. 1 Rome II para. 53 ff).

[24] Dickinson (2008, para. 3.217).

[25] See COM, Comparative study on the situation in the 27 Member States as regards the law applicable to non-contractual obligations arising out of violations of privacy and rights relating to personality, JLS/2007/C4/028. Final Report.

[26] Dickinson (2008, para. 3.227).

[27] See Oster (2011).

be subsumed under the notion of 'privacy' within the meaning of Article 1(2)(g) Rome II Regulation.[28] A small hint is given by Article 30(2) Rome II Regulation: this provision refers to the Data Protection Directive, which the European Commission had to take into account for its study. Unlike the E-privacy Directive, to which Article 30(2) does *not* refer, the Data Protection Directive only applies to natural, but not to legal persons. This might allow the very tentative inference that confidential business information is not covered by Article 1(2)(g) of the Rome II Regulation. In any case, these two examples show that Article 1(2)(g) is rather misconceived.

As a consequence of Article 1(2)(g) Rome II Regulation, the applicable law in cases of alleged violations of personality rights has to be determined according to domestic choice of law rules.[29] In contrast to jurisdictional rules, conflict of laws provisions are mostly *loi uniforme*; that is, they may not only refer to the application of domestic law, but also of foreign law. The domestic court would in such cases usually have to consult a legal expert on the foreign law. Rules on jurisdiction, however, are usually one-sided; that is, they either confirm or deny jurisdiction of the domestic court, but in cases that they deny jurisdiction of the domestic court, they do not inform the court which other foreign court has jurisdiction.

Public law cases with a transnational dimension work similarly to the establishment of jurisdictional claims in private law cases in that they are one-sided. But unlike private law cases, prescriptive jurisdiction and adjudicative jurisdiction are usually concomitant in public law cases with a transnational dimension; if a regulatory authority regards its own country's public law as applicable, then it sees itself entitled to decide on the matter. The same applies vice versa: if a regulatory authority claims to have jurisdiction, it would only apply its domestic public law to this case. By contrast, private international law rules often allow the claimant a freedom to choose between several potentially applicable laws.[30] This does not apply within the area of public law.

This chapter will therefore treat prescriptive jurisdiction and adjudicative jurisdiction synonymously as the power of a state's court or any other public agency both to try, or to exercise regulatory authority in, cases involving a foreign element and to apply the law of its state to such cases. For the sake of brevity, it will largely exclude questions of the applicable law. These are usually similar to questions underlying the

---

[28] See I. Bach, in Huber (2011, Art. 1 Rome II para. 58); Dickinson (2008, para. 3.227).

[29] This is, for example, the Introductory Act to the Civil Code (Einführungsgesetz zum Bürgerlichen Gesetzbuche) in Germany, the 10th Book to the Civil Code in the Netherlands (Boek 10 van het Burgerlijk Wetboek), and the Private International Law Act 1995 in the UK. Note, however, that Section 13 of the UK Private International Law Act 1995 excludes defamation claims from the application of the Act. As a consequence, the common law rules, especially the requirement of 'double actionability' (deriving from Phillips v. Eire (1870) LR 6 QB 1 at 18–19 (per Willes J), modified by the House of Lords in Chaplin v. Boys [1971] AC 356 and the Privy Council in Red Sea Insurance Co Ltd v. Bouygues SA [1995] 1 AC 190), still apply to defamation claims.

[30] See, for example, Article 14 of the Rome II Regulation. Note, however, that the law applicable under Article 8 (infringement of intellectual property rights) and Article 6 (unfair competition) may not be derogated from by an agreement pursuant to Article 14.

rules on jurisdiction, such as Article 7(2) Brussels Ia Regulation: what is the place which gives rise to the damage, and what is the place where the damage occurred? Conflict of laws rules on data protection, copyright and competition law will be dealt with in Chapters 8, 9 and 10, respectively. Moreover, where broadcasts or commercial internet publications from within the EU are concerned, the impact of the country-of-origin principle enshrined in the AVMS Directive and in the E-commerce Directive has to be taken into consideration.

IV Establishing Jurisdiction in Transnational Media Law Cases

The challenges transnational media law is facing with regard to the establishment of jurisdiction can be best understood against the backdrop of the 1976 decision of the European Court of Justice in the case of *Bier*.[31] In this case, a French company running potash mines in Alsace was alleged to have discharged chlorides into the river Rhine and caused damage to a Dutch company engaged in the business of nursery gardening that used water from the Rhine. Since the claimant sued the defendant at a Dutch court, the European Court of Justice had to interpret what is now Article 7(2) of the Brussels Ia Regulation. Therefore, the Court had to decide whether the Netherlands was the 'place where the harmful event occurred' within the meaning of this provision. The particular challenge of *Bier* was that the alleged tortuous act was committed from a distance: the pollution of the river took place in France, and the damage to the gardens in the Netherlands. Technically speaking, the *locus actus* and the *locus damni* were not identical. The ECJ decided that (now) Article 7(2) Brussels Ia Regulation has to be interpreted in a way that the claimant may choose to sue the defendant either in the courts for the place where the damage occurred or in the courts for the place of the event which gives rise to that damage – the so-called 'ubiquity principle'.

The application of the *Bier* ubiquity formula to torts committed by means of mass communication poses significant difficulties. Media law has to rise to three challenges. First, torts committed via communication media are mostly committed via a distance, often crossing national borders. The place where a tortuous act has been performed and the place where the damage occurs are not identical in such cases. For example, the publication of a newspaper or the upload of a video in the United States may violate personality rights or intellectual property rights in the UK. Second, transnational media law pertains to information, personality rights and intellectual – hence not physical – property. In turn, it does not involve tangible, visible incidents such the pollution of a river, an air crash or a defective product. As a consequence, the 'place where the harmful event occurs' is more difficult to establish with regard to torts omitted via media of mass communication compared to most other torts. Third,

---

[31] ECJ, Case 21/76 [1976] Handelskwekerij G.J. Bier B.V. v. Mines de Potasse d'Alsace S.A.

torts committed via means of *mass* communication often cause damage not only in one single territory, but in several different jurisdictions. For example, a person defamed by a newspaper article may be well-known in several countries, and a video may violate intellectual property rights in different jurisdictions.

Transnational media law has to find an answer to the question: where can a violation of rights be geographically located that has been committed in an internationally sold newspaper, via broadcasting frequencies or online? Transnational media law has to allocate activities via mass communication media to particular territories, and thus to particular jurisdictions. The following sections will explain the approaches that are commonly applied.

1 Jurisdiction at the Place of Establishment

According to the principle *actor sequitur forum rei* (the plaintiff must follow the forum of the defendant),[32] many European and domestic private international law codifications establish a general jurisdiction at the place where the defendant has his domicile, residence or head office. This is mostly identical with the jurisdiction where the defendant has acted (see subsection 2 below), but not necessarily. For mobile and flexible bloggers, for example, it is not uncommon that they upload their publications at another place than their place of domicile. The reason for the *actor sequitur forum rei* principle is that the defendant should basically not be drawn into a jurisdiction other than his domestic one. Exceptions to this principle have to be predictable for the defendant.[33] An example for a codification of *actor sequitur forum rei* is Article 4 of the Brussels Ia Regulation. Examples of domestic codifications of this principle are Section 12 of the German Civil Procedure Code and Article 18 of the Italian Civil Procedure Code.[34]

In EU media regulation, the EU Member State in which a media service provider is established shall have jurisdiction to regulate this provider (country-of-origin principle). According to Article 3(1) of the E-commerce Directive, each Member State shall ensure that internet services provided by a service provider *established on its territory* comply with the national provisions that fall within the field coordinated by the Directive. In compliance with the definition of the ECJ, a service provider is

---

[32] The phrase is often also translated as 'The plaintiff must follow the forum of the thing in dispute'. 'Rei' is the genitive of both 'reus' (defendant, accused) and 'res' (thing). As far as immovable property is concerned, it is indeed correct to say that the claimant has to sue at the courts of the Member State in which the property is situated (see, for example, Article 24 Brussels Ia Regulation). But apart from this exclusive jurisdiction, the general jurisdiction is usually established at the forum of the defendant.

[33] Recital 15 Brussels Ia Regulation.

[34] Since the Brussels Ia Regulation is only applicable if the defendant is domiciled in an EU Member State (with the exception of Denmark), domestic rules on international jurisdiction remain applicable for all cases in which the defendant is not domiciled in an EU Member State.

'established' in a Member State if he 'effectively pursues an economic activity using a fixed establishment for an indefinite period' (Article 2(c)). According to Recital 22 of the Directive, the rationale behind this rule is that information society service providers 'should be supervised at the source of the activity'. This is supposedly 'the Member State where the services originate'. However, the place of establishment is not necessarily the 'source of the activity' and the place where the services originate. The Directive thus seems to confuse the place of establishment with the place from where a person has acted. To be sure, these places are usually identical, but this is not necessarily the case.

The place at which the technology supporting the website is located does not, in itself, constitute an establishment of the provider.[35] If a provider has several places of establishment, the place of establishment from which the service concerned is provided is relevant.[36] Here the E-commerce Directive moves slightly towards a *locus actus* jurisdiction. However, in cases in which it is difficult to determine from which of several places of establishment a given service is provided, the place where the provider has the centre of his activities relating to this particular service is decisive.[37]

Similarly, the establishment of jurisdiction under the AVMS Directive and the European Convention on Transfrontier Television is also to a certain extent dependent on where a media service provider is established. According to Article 2(1) of the AVMS Directive and the similarly worded Article 5 of the European Convention on Transfrontier Television, each Member State shall ensure that all audiovisual media services transmitted by media service providers under its jurisdiction comply with the rules in that Member State. The media service providers under the jurisdiction of a Member State are primarily 'those established in that Member State' (Article 2(2)(a) AVMS Directive, comparable to Article 5(3)(a) European Convention on Transfrontier Television). The AVMS Directive's predecessor, the Television Without Frontiers Directive, merely required that broadcasters were 'under the jurisdiction' of a Member State. However, case law on that Directive already required 'establishment' of the media service provider in order to fall under a Member State's jurisdiction *ratione personae*.[38] A media service provider shall be deemed to be established in a Member State if the media service provider has its head office in that Member State *and* the editorial decisions about the audiovisual media service are taken in that Member State (Article 2(3)(a) AVMS Directive, Article 5(3)(a) European Convention on Transfrontier Television). Accordingly, the AVMS Directive and the Convention on Transfrontier Television establish jurisdiction based on both the country of establishment and the country in which the editorial decisions are taken.

---

[35] Recital 19 of the E-commerce Directive.
[36] Recital 19 of the E-commerce Directive.
[37] Recital 19 of the E-commerce Directive.
[38] See ECJ, Case C-222/94 [1996] Commission v. United Kingdom; Case C-14/96 [1997] Paul Denuit [23]; Joined Cases C-34/95, C-35/95 and C-36/95 [1997] De Agostini (Svenska) Förlag AB and others [29].

By contrast to the E-commerce Directive, the AVMS Directive and the Convention thus acknowledge that these countries are not necessarily identical. In case of a divergence between these two places, the media service provider 'shall be deemed to be established in the Member State where a significant part of the workforce involved in the pursuit of the audiovisual media service activity operates'.[39] This criterion serves to avoid the risk that more than one Member State would have jurisdiction over the same broadcaster.[40] If a media service provider has its head office in a Member State but decisions on the audiovisual media service are taken in a non-EU country, or vice versa, it shall be deemed to be established in that Member State if a significant part of the workforce involved in the pursuit of the audiovisual media service activity operates there (Article 2(3)(c) AVMS Directive, Article 5(3)(c) European Convention on Transfrontier Television).

By contrast, the origin of the programmes broadcast by the television broadcaster or their conformity with the AVMS Directive are irrelevant in determining the Member State having jurisdiction over such a broadcaster.[41] The same applies to the territory from which the broadcast is transmitted.[42] This was different in an earlier version of Article 5 of the Convention on Transfrontier Television, but the Convention text has been aligned with the Directive in 1998.[43]

2 Jurisdiction at the Place Where the Publication Originated

Moreover, in EU private international law, jurisdiction in matters relating to tort can be established at 'the place where the harmful event occurred or may occur' (Article 7(2) Brussels Ia Regulation). According to the above-mentioned *Bier* formula, this includes both the place of the event that gives rise to a damage – that is, the place where the claimant has acted – and the place at which the damage occurred. If initial damage occurs at several places, the claimant may vindicate the entire damage at the forum of the *locus actus*. Accepting a *locus actus* jurisdiction finds its theoretical underpinning in the subjective territoriality principle, as outlined above. In transnational media law, the *locus actus* is the place where the editorial decision to distribute the information is being taken. For example, as has been shown above, the AVMS Directive is partly based on the *locus actus* principle, as it basically requires both the establishment of the head office and the editorial decision-making to be located in the same Member State in order to establish jurisdiction in that state. However, places where merely preparing activities took place are not to be taken into account. For example, if the research for the

---

[39] Article 2(3)(b) AVMS Directive and Article 5(3)(b) European Convention on Transfrontier Television, which then provide further rules for ambiguous cases.

[40] Compare ECJ, Case C-222/94 [1996] Commission v. United Kingdom [57–58].

[41] ECJ, Case C-14/96 [1997] Paul Denuit [27].

[42] ECJ, Case C-222/94 [1996] Commission v. United Kingdom [28–29].

[43] Article 7 of Protocol amending the European Convention on Transfrontier Television of 1 October 1998 (ETS No. 171). On previous discrepancies between the Convention and the Directive, see ECJ, Case C-222/94 [1996] Commission v. United Kingdom [43–53].

allegedly defamatory article in the *Shevill* case took place in Italy, but the newspaper is published from France, Italy cannot be considered the *locus actus*. But if the preparing activity itself constituted a tortuous action, then an *additional* jurisdiction can be established at the place where this action occurred. For example, if a tabloid magazine paparazzo surreptitiously takes a photograph of a French celebrity during a private event in France and publishes the picture in a German magazine, then there are two possible *loca actus*: France, where the intrusion to privacy took place, and Germany, where the publication of the picture originated. Violation of privacy may already occur with the intrusion into the private sphere, which may therefore constitute a 'harmful event' in its own right. A publication of a photograph would, for that reason only, manifest a merely additional violation of privacy.[44]

The place of the event that gave rise to the violation of the law is also to be distinguished from the place in which the publisher uses communication media. This distinction is important if the communication media are located in a different jurisdiction to the one in which the editorial decisions were taken. This might be the case, for example, if a newspaper company located in France prints the actual newspapers across the border in Belgium, or if a website of a German blogger is hosted by a server located in Ireland. In such cases, the place of the event that gave rise to the damage is the one at which the editorial decisions were taken, and not the location of the communication medium.[45] The location of the printing press or the server would only provide a rather fortuitous connection, which would be either coincidental or prone to abuse. In particular, servers may be located in one or more countries other than where the hosting provider is established, without its clients being aware of it.[46]

However, there are exceptions to this principle. One exception has to be made in those cases in which actual physical access to those communication media is necessary. In such cases, the jurisdiction depends on mere territorial location of the facility. In the above-mentioned examples, only Belgian authorities would be legitimised to searches and seizures of the printing press located in Belgium, and only Ireland would have jurisdiction to enter the premises of the server located in Ireland. Another exception is provided in the EU Data Protection Directive with regard to the choice of the applicable law. According to its Article 4(1)(c), the Directive shall be applicable to controllers of the processing of personal data not established on EU territory if they make use of equipment situated on the territory of a Member State. Among other things, this equipment may consist of a web server.

---

[44] Oster (2012a, p. 116).
[45] See, for example, ECJ, Case C-222/94 [1996] Commission v. United Kingdom [28–29] and now Article 2(3) AVMS Directive; Recital 19 of the E-commerce Directive.
[46] ECJ, Case C-101/01 [2003] Lindqvist [59].

Finally, since the AVMS Directive is supposed to apply to services offered to the general public in the EU, Article 2(4) of this Directive grants jurisdiction to regulate the programme of a media service provider if the provider uses a satellite up-link situated in that Member State or if they use satellite capacity appertaining to that Member State. A similar provision is included in Article 5(4) of the Convention on Transfrontier Television. However, Article 2(4) only applies to media service providers for which no EU Member State has jurisdiction. This has already been established in earlier case law of the ECJ[47] and now follows expressly from Article 2(4). Yet Article 2(4), read together with Article 2(1), does not merely allow the EU Member State to regulate third-country audiovisual media services but even obliges it to do so. If an EU Member State fails to make media service providers from third countries subject to its law, although they come under its jurisdiction under Article 2(4), it would be in violation of the Directive.[48] The Member States are also precluded from the application of a less stringent regulatory regime to non-domestic satellite services than to domestic satellite services.[49] Moreover, jurisdiction according to Article 2(4) AVMS Directive can only be established if the conditions of this provision are fulfilled; that is, if the provider uses a satellite up-link situated in an EU Member State or if they use satellite capacity appertaining to that Member State. Conversely, providers from third countries can avoid the rules of the AVMS Directive altogether if they use other technology to disseminate their audiovisual content in Europe, such as the internet. In this case, the AVMS Directive would not apply if the providers are not established in an EU Member State.[50] Then they would be subject to the rules of each individual Member State in which they offer their content, provided that Member State bases its jurisdiction on a country-of-reception principle.

3 Jurisdiction at the Country of Reception

Courts and regulatory authorities often claim jurisdiction of the country that receives media content, even if the publisher is not located in this country. This is based on the ubiquity principle: media content is perceived to potentially violate the law and to cause damage everywhere a broadcast programme can be watched, a newspaper can be bought or a website can be accessed. This is not to be confused with the universality principle. Applying the universality principle to media publications would entail that a country may claim jurisdiction even if illegal content cannot be received or accessed in a particular country.

The main rationale for the country-of-reception principle is the desire of the receiving country to protect its domestic population: either to protect society as a

---

[47] ECJ, Case C-222/94 [1996] Commission v. United Kingdom [38].
[48] ECJ, Case C-222/94 [1996] Commission v. United Kingdom [66–68].
[49] ECJ, Case C-222/94 [1996] Commission v. United Kingdom [74].
[50] Wagner (2014, p. 295).

whole against perceived harmful content, such as blasphemous speech or pornography, or individuals domiciled or at least known in the jurisdiction, for example, against defamation or violation of privacy. The country-of-reception principle therefore appears in both private international law and public law, including criminal law and administrative regulation. Its theoretical foundation is the objective territoriality principle, as outlined above.

In the above-mentioned *Bier* decision, the Court of Justice established the country-of-reception principle under (now) Article 7(2) Brussels Ia Regulation. Accordingly, the claimant may sue the defendant in matters relating to tort not only at the place at which the defendant has acted, but also at the place at which the damage occurred (the *locus damni*). This only includes the initial damage; the place where the victim claims to have suffered financial damage following initial damage arising, and suffered by him, in another Member State has to be left out of account.[51]

The country-of-reception principle has been applied in transnational defamation cases inside and outside the EU. The *locus classicus* on transnational defamation via the internet is the High Court of Australia 2002 decision *Dow Jones v. Gutnick*. In *Gutnick*, the claimant, who lived in Victoria/Australia, sued the US-based publishing and financial information firm Dow Jones in Australian courts over an allegedly defamatory article posted on Dow Jones' US-based website. Dow Jones contended that the statements were published in the US and that, therefore, only US courts had jurisdiction to decide on the case. If other courts claimed jurisdiction because of the mere fact that material could be downloaded there, a publisher would have to take into account the law of every country on earth. However, the High Court of Australia held that Australian law does not locate the place of publication of defamatory material necessarily, and only, at the place of the publisher's conduct.[52] Instead, defamation is also to be located at the place where the damage to reputation occurs. As the publication was accessible from Victoria, Mr Gutnick lived in Victoria and he was well-known there, the Australian courts had jurisdiction and Australian defamation law would govern this action.[53] Because Mr Gutnick sought to vindicate his reputation in Victoria, and only in Victoria, the High Court had no reason to deal with the question as to whether Australian courts had jurisdiction to decide on damages caused to Mr Gutnick in other countries. However, the High Court also indicated that it would not have dealt with the case if Mr Gutnick had no reputation to defend in Australia. Referring to Dow Jones' main argument, the Court noted:

> [T]he spectre which Dow Jones sought to conjure up in the present appeal, of a publisher forced to consider every article it publishes on the World Wide Web against the defamation laws of every country from Afghanistan to Zimbabwe is seen to be unreal when it is recalled that in all except the most unusual

---

[51] ECJ, Case C-364/93 [1995] Marinari v. Lloyds Bank plc.
[52] Dow Jones v. Gutnick [2002] HCA 56 [42].
[53] Dow Jones v. Gutnick [2002] HCA 56 [48].

of cases, identifying the person about whom material is to be published will readily identify the defamation law to which that person may resort.[54]

In the same vein, Justice Kirby noted: 'In a cause of action framed in defamation, the publication of the material which damages the reputation of the plaintiff is essential. Merely creating and making the material available is insufficient. The material has to be accessed or communicated in a jurisdiction where the plaintiff has a reputation.'[55]

English courts subsequently adopted decisions similar to *Gutnick*. As the claimants were well known (although not necessarily residents) in England and Wales and thus had a reputation to defend there, the courts rejected to stay the proceedings based on the doctrine of *forum non conveniens* just because the publication originated from abroad.[56] In the well-known exceptional case *Jameel* v. *Dow Jones*, Justice Eady stayed the defamation action as an abuse of process because only five people had accessed the impugned online publication in England and Wales, three of which were 'members of the claimant's camp': his solicitor, a consultant who has worked for his company and the director of an associated company.[57] In the similar, but less well-known decision of the Ontario Court of Appeal in *Bangoura* v. *Washington Post*, a former UN employee brought an action against the *Washington Post* for an allegedly defamatory article that the newspaper published and then uploaded on its website. The Ontario Court of Appeal ruled in favour of the newspaper. It distinguished *Gutnick* on the grounds that Mr Bangoura did not live in Ontario at the time the article was published. Moreover, Dow Jones had some 1,700 subscribers in Australia, whereas there were only seven subscribers to the *Washington Post* in Ontario. Evidence was that only one person – the claimant's counsel – had accessed the article online.[58]

The country-of-reception principle also influences the jurisdictional rules of the AVMS Directive and the E-commerce Directive. As has been shown above, these directives establish a country-of-origin principle: The reception of the programme, if it originates in another EU Member State, is basically irrelevant for determining jurisdiction over a broadcaster.[59] However, the receiving Member States may, under exceptional circumstances, derogate from this principle and impose their own measures on media service providers (Article 3(2–4) AVMS Directive, Article 3(4) E-commerce Directive).[60] This is essentially a codification of the written justifications of the TFEU and the 'mandatory requirements' doctrine as established in *Cassis de*

---

[54] Dow Jones v. Gutnick [2002] HCA 56 [54].
[55] Dow Jones v. Gutnick [2002] HCA 56 [151] (Kirby J).
[56] *Forum non conveniens* is a doctrine applicable in common law jurisdictions. Having been served with a claim form, upon application of the defendant, courts have discretion to stay actions on the basis that their jurisdiction is a clearly inappropriate forum (so the formula in Australia), or that there is another more appropriate forum (so the formula in England). See, for example, King v. Lewis [2004] EWHC 168 (QB); Richardson v. Schwarzenegger [2004] EWHC 2422.
[57] Jameel v. Dow Jones [2005] EWCA Civ 75 [17].
[58] Bangoura v. Washington Post, 2005 CanLII 32906 (ON CA).
[59] ECJ, Case C-222/94 [1996] Commission v. United Kingdom [63–64].
[60] See Chapters 5 and 6.

Dijon, which permit interferences with the free movement provisions for mandatory reasons.

Furthermore, within the AVMS Directive, the country-of-reception principle also applies to services offered to the general public in the EU by a media service provider that neither has its head office nor makes its editorial decisions in an EU Member State. Member States may take measures they deem appropriate with regard to audiovisual media services coming from third countries that do not satisfy the conditions of domestic and EU law.[61] Such a provider shall be deemed to be under the jurisdiction of a Member State if it uses a satellite up-link situated in, or satellite capacity appertaining to, that Member State (Article 2(4)). In turn, the AVMS Directive does not apply to audiovisual media services intended exclusively for reception in third countries and that are not received with standard consumer equipment directly or indirectly by the public in one or more Member States (Article 2(6)).[62] By contrast, the E-commerce Directive does not include a comparable rule. Therefore, internet content from a publisher established in a non-EU country is subject to the jurisdictional rules of the Member States themselves. Practice has shown that Member States' regulatory authorities acknowledge their own country-of-reception jurisdiction rather swiftly.

However, the country-of-reception principle raises significant problems. In the *Yahoo* case, Yahoo would be subject to any jurisdiction in the world in which the sale of Nazi memorabilia is prohibited, maybe even criminalised, although it was legal under US law. Moreover, if the country-of-reception principle would be applied without any qualification in private international law, the defendant-publisher could potentially be sued in any jurisdiction in which he distributes his publication and in which he potentially causes harm to the claimant. Applied to the internet, the country-of-reception would entail that the publisher could be drawn to any jurisdiction from which his website is accessible, which mostly means any jurisdiction in the world.

One might of course argue that this is justified due to the fact that anyone who uses the internet benefits from its ubiquity and therefore has to bear the consequences.[63] However, this conclusion would be in conflict with Article 19 ICCPR, Article 10 ECHR and Article 11 EUChFR. Applying the country-of-reception principle to transnational offences committed via the internet leads to unpredictable and limitless jurisdiction and gives incentives to extensive 'forum shopping'.[64] This creates a risk of severe chilling effects on online publications. Prudent website operators

---

[61] Recital 54 AVMS Directive.

[62] The Directive has left the definition of 'standard consumer equipment' to the national authorities (Recital 39).

[63] Cf. Dow Jones v. Gutnick [2002] HCA 56 [39], [192] (Callinan J).

[64] CJEU, Joined Cases C-509/09 and C-161/10 [2011] eDate Advertising GmbH and Olivier Martinez and Robert Martinez, Opinion of Advocate-General Cruz Villalón [56]; German Federal Court of Justice, Case VI ZR 23/09 [2010] 'New York Times' [17]; Smith (2007b, para. 6–031); Maier (2010, p. 150).

would have to adjust to the standards of the most restrictive jurisdiction; that is, the lowest common denominator for freedom of expression.[65] Rather than asking *where* to publish certain information, internet publishers have to decide *if* to publish certain information at all.

In private international law, it is therefore widely accepted that the country-of-reception principle requires qualification. It is controversial, however, *how* this has to be done. The following sections will provide an overview. By comparison, in the public law area, calls for limitations of the country-of-reception principles are uttered in a rather low voice. There are apparently two reasons for this: first, within the private international law discourse, the main tool to limit ubiquitous jurisdictional claims is the size of the damage to be awarded (see subsection 4 below). By contrast, administrative regulation and criminal law are mostly binary procedures: either a publisher is subject to an administrative cease-and-desist order, or he is not. Likewise, either a content provider may be punished under domestic criminal law, or he may not. Second, administrative regulation and criminal prosecution need to find a balance not between two conflicting private interests, such as freedom of speech and reputation, but between freedom of speech and public order interests, such as public morals and national security. From a receiving country's point of view, the desire and, in fact, the obligation to protect their state's interest and their own population usually supersedes the content provider's interest in not being subject to this jurisdiction.

4 Limitation of the Country-of-Reception Principle by the 'Mosaic Formula'

In private international law, the 'mosaic rule' provides at first that the claimant may either sue before the courts of the state where the publisher is established, or before the courts of each state in which the publication was distributed and is alleged to have caused damage (see subsections 1 to 3 above).[66] However, the mosaic formula then derogates from the country-of-reception principle: Only the courts of the state from which the publisher has acted shall have jurisdiction to award damages for all the harm caused by the publication, whereas the courts of each state in which the publication was distributed shall have jurisdiction to rule solely in respect of the harm caused in the state of the court seised.[67] In addition, the claimant may sue for damages in full before the courts of the state where the publisher is established. Within the EU, these courts always have jurisdiction according to Article 4 Brussels Ia Regulation.[68] This is mostly, but not necessarily, the country whence the publication originated. As a result, the mosaic rule provides several alternative jurisdictions for the claimant to choose from. The claimant may sue for all the harm caused in the

---

[65] Mensching (2010, p. 284); Kuipers (2011, p. 1686); Oster (2012a, p. 117).
[66] ECJ, Case C-68/93 [1995] Shevill and others v. Presse Alliance SA [61].
[67] ECJ, Case C-68/93 [1995] Shevill and others v. Presse Alliance SA [61].
[68] Apart from cases of exclusive jurisdiction, such as in Article 24 Brussels Ia Regulation.

jurisdiction where the publisher is established or where the publication took place, or he may sue in each state in which the publication was distributed with regard to the harm caused in that jurisdiction.

The mosaic formula has a particularly significant role in the area of media law, namely in cases in which one publication is claimed to violate rights in several countries. The mosaic formula applies, first, with regard to copyright violations. As will be shown in Chapter 9, substantive copyright law is based on the territoriality principle. This means that the scope of copyright is restricted to the territory of state that grants that copyright. Thus, a claim of violation of copyright can only be raised with regard to a particular jurisdiction in which this copyright is purportedly protected (*lex loci protectionis*). Consequently, the claimant has to vindicate a violation of his copyright in each jurisdiction that protects his copyright and in which the copyright has been violated, unless he sues the defendant at the place of his domicile or where he has acted ('copyright mosaic').

Second, as will be shown in Chapter 10, the mosaic formula also applies in competition law. In cases of unfair competition, claims for injunctions and damages may be brought in each jurisdiction, and the law of each country applies, in which an allegedly unfair publication can be received and affects competitors' or consumers' interests. However, this applies only with a view to the damage caused in this particular country. In antitrust cases, if one anti-competitive behaviour leads to immediate damages in more than one jurisdiction, the claimant could sue the defendant in each jurisdiction in which damage occurred, but only for the loss suffered in that jurisdiction.

Third, since the seminal *Shevill* decision, the mosaic formula is also applied to torts against personality rights committed by the mass media.[69] In *Shevill and others* v. *Presse Alliance*, the ECJ decided that the claimant may either sue before the courts of the state where the publisher is established, or before the courts of each state in which the publication was distributed, when the claimant was known in these places.[70] However, the Court also stated that only the courts of the state where the publisher is established shall have jurisdiction to award damages for all the harm caused by the defamation, whereas the courts of each state in which the publication was distributed shall have jurisdiction to rule solely in respect of the harm caused in the state of the court seised.[71]

The mosaic formula therefore considers the necessity to concentrate lawsuits aiming at full compensation to just one – or maximally two – jurisdiction(s). However, it also allows the claimant to bring a lawsuit where his rights have been violated, but the lawsuit is then limited to the harm caused in this jurisdiction. For traditional forms of communication, such as printed newspapers and broadcasts, the mosaic formula

[69] The following explanations are based on Oster (2012a, pp. 115 ff).
[70] ECJ, Case C-68/93 [1995] Shevill and others v. Presse Alliance SA [61].
[71] ECJ, Case C-68/93 [1995] Shevill and others v. Presse Alliance SA [61].

thus seems to strike a fair balance between the interests of the publisher-defendant and of the claimant: the publisher may choose the country to establish his business in and where to publish his information, and may calculate the risk of running into a lawsuit in these places. The claimant, on the other hand, may vindicate his rights everywhere he suffers primary damage. The mosaic formula is also practicable, as the place of publication can be easily recognised by ascertaining the number of newspaper copies sold in a particular country or by establishing where a certain TV programme has been broadcast.

However, the impact of the mosaic formula is more complex than that. In theory, it seems to strike an appropriate balance between the claimant's and the defendant's interest. If the claimant wants to avoid the jurisdiction(s) in which the defendant is located and/or from where the publication originated, he has to collect the 'tesserae' of his damage in every jurisdiction in which publication took place and in which his rights appear to have been violated. In practical terms, however, the mosaic formula is quite advantageous for the claimant. Two things have to be considered. First, it is the courts of each jurisdiction itself that estimate the damage that occurred in this particular jurisdiction. For example, in the *Shevill* case example, an English court may decide that the damage *France-Soir* inflicted upon Ms Shevill in England and Wales alone amounted to, say, £30,000, whereas a French court could have tallied the *entire* damage to, say, €10,000. Second, defamation cases in particular are more often a matter of principle than of money. For claimants who can afford 'libel tourism', the actual size of the awarded damage is often of secondary nature. What is more important is the fact that a court decides that the defendant was not entitled to publish a particular statement that is defamatory of them. The mosaic formula furnishes such claimants with a voucher for forum shopping, which can have a considerable chilling effect on any media defendant.

Moreover, it is questionable whether the mosaic formula should be applied to internet publications. To be sure, according to the principle of technology neutrality, the criteria for the establishment of jurisdiction must not focus exceedingly on the communication technology, but should be applicable to all forms of communication media.[72] However, there is one significant difference between 'old media' and internet publications that has to be taken into account. 'Old media' publishers could choose where to sell their newspapers or where to broadcast their programme. By contrast, internet websites can technically be accessed almost everywhere in the world. An internet publication is by default ubiquitous and would necessitate an 'opt out' decision regarding particular countries via means of geo-blocking (if available at all), whereas the distribution of newspapers requires an 'opt in' decision to sell copies in a particular country. If the mosaic formula is applied to internet publications, a

---

[72] CJEU, Joined Cases C-509/09 and C-161/10 [2011] eDate Advertising GmbH and Olivier Martinez and Robert Martinez, Opinion of Advocate-General Cruz Villalón [53]; see also Dow Jones v. Gutnick [2002] HCA 56 [125] (Kirby J).

publisher would be subject to 28 jurisdictions in the EU alone, depending on where the claimant is known. In addition, the Brussels Ia Regulation provides for an almost automatic recognition of judgments within the EU. Finally, with a view to personality rights, even the requirement that the claimant must be known in the jurisdiction where he wants to sue does not properly limit the mosaic formula's extent: particularly in the internet age, it might be the defamation or the violation of a person's privacy *itself* that makes a person known in a jurisdiction. Nevertheless, in *eDate Advertising and Martinez*, the Court of Justice established a 'centre of interest' jurisdiction in addition to the *Shevill* mosaic formula.

5 The 'Centre of Interests' Analysis

In *eDate Advertising and Martinez and Martinez v. MGN*, the CJEU offered the claimant an additional jurisdiction in which he may sue for the entire damage, namely the place at which the claimant had his centre of interest.[73] The facts of the joined cases can be summarised as follows: eDate Advertising, an Austrian website operator, had published information about a German citizen who had been convicted for the murder of a well-known German actor. Upon his request, eDate Advertising removed the publication about the convict. He then successfully sued for an injunctive relief requiring eDate Advertising to refrain from publishing any information about him. eDate Advertising lodged an appeal at the German Federal Court of Justice, questioning the jurisdiction of German courts. *Olivier Martinez, Robert Martinez v. MGN Ltd* pertained to a publication of the British newspaper the *Sunday Mirror* suggesting that the French citizen Olivier Martinez and the singer/actress Kylie Minogue had recommended their relationship. The article included details about their meeting in Paris, thereby ascribing statements mentioned in the article to Martinez' father Robert Martinez. Olivier and Robert Martinez sued MGN Ltd, the owner of the *Sunday Mirror*, at the Tribunal de grande instance de Paris. Both the German Federal Court of Justice and the Tribunal de grande instance de Paris requested a preliminary ruling of the Court of Justice of the EU, essentially asking whether in cases of violations of personality rights on a website the 'place where the harmful event occurred' might be any place where the website can be acceded to, or whether there should be a special connection to the jurisdiction that goes beyond the mere accessibility of the website. The courts further asked for the criteria determining this connection, if such a special connection is required.[74]

The CJEU located the relevant connecting criterion to establish jurisdiction for awarding full damages at the place where the alleged victim has his 'centre of interests'.

---

[73] The following explanations are based on Oster (2012a, pp. 118 ff). However, note that the article treated the 'centre of interest' analysis and the 'centre of gravity of the conflict' analysis interchangeably. This is differentiated in this book.

[74] The Federal Court of Justice further asked whether the E-commerce Directive lays down a conflict of laws rule. This question will be addressed in Chapter 6.

The CJEU decided that the 'centre of interests' criterion is an additional criterion to the mosaic formula.[75] According to the Court, the 'centre of interests' is generally the place where a person has his habitual residence. However, a person may also have the centre of his interests in a Member State in which he does not habitually reside, insofar as other factors, such as the pursuit of a professional activity, may establish the existence of a particularly close link with that state.[76] The defendant, on the other hand, should be in a position to know the centres of interests of the persons who are the subject of the published content.[77] The centre of interests criterion should thus allow both the claimant to identify the court in which he may sue, and the defendant to foresee before which court he may be sued.[78] The place where the owner of the personality right has the 'centre of his interests' is similar to the *Shevill* criterion 'place where the claimant is known', but not identical. It is not sufficient that the claimant is known in a place; it has to be the *main* place of his self-fulfilment. Moreover, it is not necessarily identical with the claimant's main place of residence.

The Court's case law in *Shevill* and *eDate Advertising* on jurisdiction for damage claims against violations of personality rights can thus be summarised as follows:

1 The claimant may sue in the forum of the defendant's place of domicile or establishment for the entire damage (Article 4(1) Brussels Ia Regulation).
2 The claimant may sue in the forum of the place where the defendant has acted for the entire damage, if this place is not identical with the place of domicile or establishment anyway (Article 7(2) Brussels Ia Regulation).
3 The claimant may sue in the forum in which he has the 'centre of his interests' for the entire damage, if this is not identical with the fora 1. or 2. (Article 7(2) Brussels Ia Regulation (*eDate Advertising*)).
4 The claimant may sue in each forum in which the publication has been distributed and in which the claimant is known, but only for the damage that the claimant incurred in each respective forum (Article 7(2) Brussels Ia Regulation (*Shevill*)).

6 Alternative Approaches

Shevill and *eDate Advertising and Martinez* combined reflect the current state of the CJEU's interpretation of Article 7(2) Brussels Ia Regulation. Yet there are alternative approaches suggested in legal scholarship and taken by courts when interpreting rules on jurisdiction.[79] A few of them will be outlined in this section: the jurisdiction

---

[75] CJEU, Joined Cases C-509/10 and C-161/10 [2011] eDate Advertising and Olivier Martinez, Robert Martinez v. MGN Ltd [52].

[76] CJEU, Joined Cases C-509/10 and C-161/10 [2011] eDate Advertising and Olivier Martinez, Robert Martinez v. MGN Ltd [49].

[77] CJEU, Joined Cases C-509/10 and C-161/10 [2011] eDate Advertising and Olivier Martinez, Robert Martinez v. MGN Ltd [50].

[78] CJEU, Joined Cases C-509/10 and C-161/10 [2011] eDate Advertising and Olivier Martinez, Robert Martinez v. MGN Ltd [50].

[79] Note that domestic rules on jurisdiction still apply if the defendant is not domiciled in an EU Member State.

that the defendant has 'targeted' with his publication (see subsection a below), the jurisdiction in which the publication received most attention (see subsection b) and the 'centre of gravity of the conflict' analysis (see subsection c). An exclusive country-of-origin approach, which is practiced in the US, cuts the Gordian knot of the ubiquity principle rather than trying to disentangle it (see subsection d).

a 'Targeting Approach'

The so-called 'targeting approach' is a 'third way' between a subjective and an objective territoriality principle.[80] The court seised has jurisdiction if the content provider *intended* to aim at an audience in this country. This approach is applied by the German Federal Court of Justice in cases of transnational trademark infringements[81] and is also applicable in the EU with regard to consumer contracts: Article 17(1)(c) Brussels Ia Regulation determines jurisdiction if the person the contract has been concluded with 'direct [commercial or professional] activities' to the Member State of the consumer.[82] It also finds support in academic literature.[83] In a more recent decision, the Court of Justice applied a targeting approach to the establishment of the applicable law in a transnational data protection case.[84]

However, it is questionable whether this doctrine can be properly applied to other torts committed via mass media, such as violations of personality rights.[85] Targeting requires, at least to a certain extent, a subjective intention on behalf of the publisher.[86] Unlike directing commercial activities or trademark use to another state, violations of personality rights or copyright may occur without the publisher even knowing if and where harm might be caused to the defendant's rights.[87]

b Quantitative Criteria

Another way to establish jurisdiction for torts committed via transnational mass media would be through the application of quantitative criteria: The country has jurisdiction in which a particular website has been accessed most often, in which most copies of a particular newspaper have been sold, or in which the largest audience watched a particular TV programme.[88] However, at least with regard to the

---

[80] See Smith (2007b, para. 6–055); Kohl (2007, pp. 24–26); Wagner (2014, p. 291).

[81] See German Federal Court of Justice, Case I ZR 163/02 [2004] 'Hotel Maritime'; see also from the UK Euromarket Designs Ltd v. Peters Ltd [2001] F.S.R. 288 (Jacob J).

[82] On the interpretation of this provision, see CJEU, Joined Cases C-585/08 and C-144/09 [2010] Pammer and Hotel Alpenhof.

[83] Schultz (2008, pp. 800, 816); Michel (2012/2013); see also WP29, Opinion 8/2010 on applicable law, p. 24.

[84] CJEU, Case C-230/14 [2015] Weltimmo [41].

[85] See Oster (2012a, p. 118).

[86] King v. Lewis [2004] EWCA Civ 1329 (CA) [34]. However, it should be noted that 'targeting' and 'intention' are not identical concepts; see Smith (2007b, para. 6–053).

[87] German Federal Court of Justice, Case VI ZR 23/09 [2010] 'New York Times' [18]; Edwards (2004, p. 109).

[88] Compare Tribunal de grande instance de Paris, Reference for a preliminary ruling, made by decision of 6 July 2009, declared inadmissible by the Court on 20 November 2009, Case C-278/09.

accession of internet websites, this solution is hardly practicable: for reasons of data protection and for technical reasons it is not entirely measurable how often a website has been visited, and from where.[89] Furthermore, such an approach would be suscep-tible to abuse, as both the claimant and the defendant could influence the number of accessions.[90] The number of times a website has been accessed may therefore only serve as an indication for the website's influence in a particular country, but it may not be used as the sole criterion to establish jurisdiction.[91]

c The 'Centre of Gravity of the Conflict' Analysis

In 2010, the German Federal Court of Justice had to decide on an online publication of the *New York Times* alleging the involvement of the claimant in criminal activi-ties and connections to the Russian mafia.[92] The Federal Court of Justice ruled that if, according to the circumstances of the case, the website content objectively refers to a certain 'receiving' country and if that may lead to a collision of the conflicting interests – the protection of the claimant's personality right on the one hand, the protection of the defendant's interest to freely create his internet appearance and coverage on the other hand – within this jurisdiction, the courts of the 'receiving' country have jurisdiction to decide upon the case.[93] This shall be the case when, first, notice of the website content in the 'receiving' jurisdiction is 'likely'; mere accessibility of the website is not sufficient. Second, the alleged infringement of the claimant's personality right has to occur within this jurisdiction, but not necessarily exclusively within this jurisdiction.[94] In this particular case, the Federal Court of Justice decided that German courts had jurisdiction: the claimant was mentioned by name, he had residence in Germany, the article referred to information of German security authorities and 14,484 German internet users visited the website in June 2001.[95] The Court rejected the argument that the article lacked the necessary refer-ence to Germany because it was published in the NYT's local news 'Metropolitan Desk', since readers of a newspaper's online version may search for articles referring to Germany with the aid of a search engine.[96] The German Federal Court of Justice

---

[89] German Federal Court of Justice, Case VI ZR 23/09 [2010] 'New York Times' [19].

[90] See Jameel v. Dow Jones [2005] EWCA Civ 75.

[91] German Federal Court of Justice, Case VI ZR 23/09 [2010] 'New York Times' [19]; Case VI ZR 217/08 [2009] 'eDate Advertising' [16]; CJEU, Joined Cases C-509/09 and C-161/10 [2011] eDate Advertising GmbH and Olivier Martinez and Robert Martinez, Opinion of Advocate-General Cruz Villalón [50]; Oster (2012a, p. 117).

[92] German Federal Court of Justice, Case VI ZR 23/09 [2010] 'New York Times'.

[93] German Federal Court of Justice, Case VI ZR 23/09 [2010] 'New York Times' [20].

[94] German Federal Court of Justice, Case VI ZR 23/09 [2010] 'New York Times' [20]; see also Case I ZR 163/02 [2004] 'Hotel Maritime', p. 7; Case 1 StR 184/00 [2000] 'Auschwitz denial'.

[95] German Federal Court of Justice, Case VI ZR 23/09 [2010] 'New York Times' [21–22].

[96] German Federal Court of Justice, Case VI ZR 23/09 [2010] 'New York Times' [24].

confirmed its approach in later decisions, such as the ruling on Google's 'autocomplete function'.[97]

Advocate-General Cruz Villalón followed and enhanced the Court's approach in his opinion preceding the CJEU's decision in the cases of *eDateAdvertising and Martinez*.[98] He suggested that in cases of violations of personality rights, in addition to the *Shevill* criteria, jurisdiction should be established at the 'centre of gravity of the conflict'. He located the 'centre of gravity of the conflict' where a court can decide upon a conflict between the 'information freedom' and the 'right to one's own image' under the most favourable circumstances.[99] The country of the 'centre of gravity of the conflict' is, according to the Advocate-General, the country where the potential infringement of the personality rights and the dissemination of information are most 'visible' or manifested.[100] It is in this country where the owner of the personality right would suffer particularly broad and intensive damage. This would also be the country where the publisher could have foreseen the damage to occur and, hence, to be sued. The courts of the 'centre of gravity of the conflict' shall have jurisdiction to award damages for the entire harm caused.[101]

Thus, in order to determine the location of the 'centre of gravity of the conflict', a number of circumstances have to be established. One criterion is the claimant's 'centre of interest', but it is not the only one. Another criterion is that the information published must be 'objectively relevant' in a certain territory. The contested information must have been published in a way that arouses interest in a certain territory and incites the readers in this territory to actively access the information; it must be 'newsworthy'.[102] Whether information is 'objectively relevant' in a country depends on the content of the information, such as the country of residence of the person to whom the information pertains, or the country where the alleged actions took place.[103] The court may also consider further indications, such as the intention of

---

[97] German Federal Court of Justice, Case VI ZR 269/12 [2013] 'Google's autocomplete function' [7], see also Case VI ZR 111/10 [2011] 'Personality rights on the internet'; Case VI ZR 93/10 [2011] 'blogspot' [11].

[98] CJEU, Joined Cases C-509/09 and C-161/10 [2011] eDate Advertising GmbH and Olivier Martinez and Robert Martinez, Opinion of Advocate-General Cruz Villalón [55 ff].

[99] CJEU, Joined Cases C-509/09 and C-161/10 [2011] eDate Advertising GmbH and Olivier Martinez and Robert Martinez, Opinion of Advocate-General Cruz Villalón [58]. The French version says: '[L]e lieu du "centre de gravité du conflit" serait celui où une juridiction peut statuer dans les conditions les plus favorables sur un conflit entre la liberté d'information et le droit à l'image.'

[100] CJEU, Joined Cases C-509/09 and C-161/10 [2011] eDate Advertising GmbH and Olivier Martinez and Robert Martinez, Opinion of Advocate-General Cruz Villalón [58].

[101] CJEU, Joined Cases C-509/09 and C-161/10 [2011] eDate Advertising GmbH and Olivier Martinez and Robert Martinez, Opinion of Advocate-General Cruz Villalón [57], [66].

[102] CJEU, Joined Cases C-509/09 and C-161/10 [2011] eDate Advertising GmbH and Olivier Martinez and Robert Martinez, Opinion of Advocate-General Cruz Villalón [64]. See also German Federal Court of Justice, Case VI ZR 23/09 [2010] 'New York Times' [20]; Dow Jones v. Gutnick [2002] HCA 56 [154]; Harrods Ltd v. Dow Jones [2003] EWHC 1162 [32 ff].

[103] Compare CJEU, Joined Cases C-509/09 and C-161/10 [2011] eDate Advertising GmbH and Olivier Martinez and Robert Martinez, Opinion of Advocate-General Cruz Villalón [64].

the publisher, the domain name, the language of the website, a categorisation of the website's content into different countries or advertising, if available.[104]

However, one should also see the disadvantages of the 'centre of gravity of the conflict' analysis. It is based on the balancing of different factors rather than offering a clear structure. Hence it may be difficult for the publisher to predict what the 'centre of conflict' will actually be, and this might lead to significant legal uncertainty. Instead of objective and factual criteria such as the claimant's residence, the physical publication of a newspaper as under *Shevill* or quantitative criteria, the 'centre of gravity of the conflict' doctrine introduces an evaluating interest analysis considering different criteria in order to establish the appropriate forum most suitable for the interests of all the parties – an approach that is strikingly similar to the *forum (non) conveniens* doctrine in common law countries. In *Owusu* v. *Jackson*, the ECJ decided that the *forum non conveniens* doctrine is inapplicable under the (now) Brussels Ia Regulation – because it fails to provide legal certainty.[105]

d Exclusive Country-of-Origin Principle

The rules suggested thus far are all based on the presumption that a newspaper that is purchasable in different countries, or an internet publication that can be accessed all over the globe, can lead to a violation of the laws of different countries, which may thus claim jurisdiction because of the effect a publication has on their territory. Each approach to curtailing the ubiquity principle is met with strong objections. This might call for an attempt to think outside the box: to do away with the ubiquity principle in general. A possible solution might be an exclusive country-of-origin approach: to subject a publisher exclusively to the law of the forum from which the flow of information stems.[106] This corresponds to the approach taken by US courts in the area of defamation law.

The ubiquity principle is based on the assumption that each country in which a newspaper has been sold or from which a website can be accessed represents a new 'publication', which is a necessary requirement for a successful defamation claim. The quintessence of the above-mentioned rules is therefore the so-called 'multiple publication rule'. According to this rule, whenever and wherever a new publication or republication of a defamatory statement takes place, each publication gives rise to a separate cause of action.[107] In the UK, this rule had been established long before the rise of the internet, namely with regard to the limitation period of defamation claims, which is renewed with each sale of a book, magazine or newspaper.[108] The application

---

[104] CJEU, Joined Cases C-509/09 and C-161/10 [2011] eDate Advertising GmbH and Olivier Martinez and Robert Martinez, Opinion of Advocate-General Cruz Villalón [65].

[105] ECJ, Case C-281/02 [2005] Owusu v. Jackson; for a detailed analysis, see Kruger (2008, paras 5.55, 564 ff); Fawcett and Carruthers (2008, p. 323).

[106] Schultz (2008, pp. 800, 811).

[107] Smith (2007b, para. 4–006); Murray (2013, p. 169).

[108] Duke of Brunswick v. Harmer [1849] 14 QB 185. In Times Newspapers Ltd v. United Kingdom (Nos. 1 and 2) [2009] Application Nos. 3002/03 and 23676/03, the ECtHR held that the application of the multiple publication rule to internet archives does not constitute a breach of Article 10 ECHR.

of this rationale to the rules on jurisdiction entails that a newspaper constitutes a separate publication in every jurisdiction in which it is sold, a broadcasting programme is a publication in every jurisdiction in which it can be watched and a website that is globally accessible constitutes a separate publication in every jurisdiction in the world, and may theoretically lead to actions or interferences by public authorities in any jurisdiction. However, in defamation claims, US courts have applied the so-called 'single publication rule' instead of the 'multiple publication rule' – at first with regard to the limitation period of defamation claims, and later to conflict of laws problems.[109] The single publication rule allows jurisdiction for a defamation claim only in the state where the publisher initially produced the newspaper, broadcast the TV programme or uploaded the communication on a web-server.[110]

An exclusive country-of-origin principle has the advantage of providing a precise connecting factor that makes jurisdictional claims predictable. However, it is also heavily in favour of the defendant and susceptible to abuse.[111] In practice, publishers would take advantage of jurisdictions more favourable to free speech to the detriment of the claimant's rights. The introduction of a single publication rule has therefore received strong opposition in countries other than the US.[112] It would lead to an under-protection of values in other countries in which the publication has a negative effect for an individual (*Shevill*) or society in general (*Yahoo*). However, a stronger emphasis of a country-of-origin principle is justifiable the more the substantive law of states has been harmonised. This is the case in the EU under the E-commerce Directive and the AVMS Directive, which allow exceptions to the country-of-origin principle only under very narrow circumstances.

7 Application of These Principles to the Shevill and the Yahoo Cases

In *Shevill*, the defendant had its registered office, thus presumably its head office, in France. Therefore, the Brussels Ia Regulation was applicable. According to its Article 4, Ms Shevill would have to sue Presse Alliance in France, unless she could avail herself of a special jurisdiction. Article 7(2) Brussels Ia regulation provides such a special jurisdiction in matters relating to tort at 'the place where the harmful event occurred or may occur'. This covers, according to the *Bier* decision, both the place of the event that gave rise to Ms Shevill's alleged damage and the place in which that damage occurred. The allegedly defamatory article originated in France. Moreover, it had to be established whether a constituent element of the tort of defamation had

---

[109] See Section 577A Restatement (Second) of Torts (1976). The rule was originally formulated in Wolfson v. Syracuse Newspapers Inc. (1938) 279 NY 716, and applied to Internet cases in Firth v. State of New York (2002) NY Int 88.

[110] Barendt (2005–2006, p. 733); see Compuserve Inc. v. Patterson 89F.3d 1257 (6th Cir. 1996).

[111] Svantesson (2012, p. 338).

[112] Berezovsky v. Michaels [2000] 1 WLR 1004 (HL) (Lord Steyn); Dow Jones v. Gutnick [2002] HCA 56 [133] (Kirby J.); Barendt (2005–2006, p. 734); Smith (2007a).

been committed in England. That was the case, as a few copies of the newspaper in question had been distributed in England, which is necessary for the notion of 'publication' as a prerequisite for a defamation claim. Ms Shevill could thus establish jurisdiction in England, albeit under the application of the mosaic rule, limited to the damage she suffered in England and not for the entire damage the publication caused to her worldwide. This would be different today in light of the *eDate Advertising and Martinez* 'centre of interest' analysis, provided that its rule would also be applied to offline publications. The CJEU has not yet had the opportunity to clarify this question, but the principle of technology neutrality speaks for such an application. In the absence of any indications that Ms Shevill has the centre of her interests outside Yorkshire, it can be assumed that the centre of her interests is England and Wales. Applying the 'centre of interests' analysis, Ms Shevill could sue for the entire damage caused to her in England and Wales.

The outcome would presumably be different if alternative approaches were applied. The application of quantitative criteria would clearly lead to the result that France alone is the appropriate jurisdiction. Then: Was *France-Soir*'s article 'targeted' at England and Wales? Selling 230 copies in England and Wales means that the English jurisdiction was at least not avoided. But the main target was certainly France: the article was written in French and most copies were sold in France. What would be the outcome of a 'centre of gravity of conflict' analysis, provided again that this analysis would be applied to a newspaper publication? This analysis involves several of the above-mentioned factors. Ms Shevill had the 'centre of her interests' in England, so Presse Alliance could foresee that the damage to Ms Shevill would occur in England. On the other hand, the article was written in French, and only 230 copies were sold in England and Wales. The dissemination of the information was thus most 'visible' in France. It was unlikely that particular notice of the article would be taken in Yorkshire, where only five copies were sold. As a result, there is good reason to argue that the 'centre of gravity of the conflict' was France, not the UK. Finally, if the country-of-origin principle would be applied exclusively, only French courts would have jurisdiction to decide the case.

In the *Yahoo* case, the defendant had its head office in the United States, thus outside the EU. Therefore, French rules on jurisdiction were applicable. Article 46 of the French Code of Civil Procedure corresponds to the CJEU's interpretation of Article 7(2) Brussels Ia Regulation in that it provides jurisdiction of French courts at the place of the event causing liability or the one in whose district the damage was suffered. The information on the Nazi memorabilia could be downloaded in France, and the Tribunal de Grande Instance thus assumed that the damage had been suffered in France. As *LICRA* v. *Yahoo* was not a claim for damages but an application for an injunction, the *Shevill* formula could not be applied. It is highly unlikely that most customers accessed the auction website from France, so a quantitative approach would have denied French jurisdiction. Yahoo claimed that their services were primarily aimed at US residents. It can thus be presumed that they were at least not 'targeted' at French residents.

To which outcome would a hypothetical application of the 'centre of interests' and 'centre of gravity of the conflict' analysis lead? This is a particularly interesting question as these two doctrines were developed with regard to civil lawsuits. To be sure, *LICRA* v. *Yahoo* is a civil lawsuit, but, as has been stated before, it could equally have been brought as an administrative procedure or even as a criminal prosecution. The broader question is, therefore, whether the 'centre of interests' and 'centre of gravity of the conflict' analyses are suitable frameworks to approach cases in which a value of public interest (such as public order or morals) instead of a private right (such as reputation or privacy) is concerned. It is in the interest of the French Republic that Nazi memorabilia cannot be accessed there, so there is a strong argument that the centre of LICRA's interest is in France. But this shows that the 'centre of interests' analysis, if applied to public and criminal law cases, always leads to the jurisdiction of the receiving country, as the authorities of the receiving country have an interest to defend the domestic values against foreign speech. So where would the 'centre of gravity of the conflict' be? There are arguments for both sides. The criteria 'targeted audience' and 'quantitative criteria' speak in favour of the US; LICRA's interest in protecting French values speaks for France as the 'centre of gravity'. Finally, an exclusive country of origin approach would lead to the clearest – but not necessarily most reasonable – outcome: under a single publication rule, only a US court would have jurisdiction.

V Recognition and Enforcement of Foreign Decisions

Any judgment or administrative decision adopted in a transnational media law case must eventually be enforced.[113] Recognition and enforcement of judgments is strictly attached to the notion of territory. A state can enforce its laws and judgments only against actors or assets present in the state. The recognition and enforcement of foreign judgments or administrative decisions is basically for the national state to decide. There is no general obligation under public international law to recognise and enforce a decision of a foreign authority, unless states have agreed to a system of mutual recognition and reciprocity via international agreements.

In the EU, rudimentary systems of mutual recognition of criminal judgments and of administrative decisions are in place.[114] This is better developed in the area of private international law. An example is Article 36 of the Brussels Ia Regulation. However, private international law usually provides exemptions to the recognition of foreign judgments if the recognition of the foreign judgment would be contrary to

---

[113] This section is based on Oster (2015c).

[114] See, for example, Council Framework Decision 2005/214/JHA of 24 February 2005 on the application of the principle of mutual recognition to financial penalties, OJ L 76/16; Council Framework Decision 2008/909/JHA of 27 November 2008 on the application of the principle of mutual recognition to judgments in criminal matters imposing custodial sentences or measures involving deprivation of liberty for the purpose of their enforcement in the European Union, OJ L 327/27.

the public policy of the state where recognition is sought. The key question underlying the application of public policy clauses is, therefore, to what extent states have to mutually trust each other's legal systems, and to what extent they may invoke their own legal principles if they do not trust the home state control.[115]

Recognition of public policy clauses, such as Article 45(1)(a) of the Brussels Ia Regulation, serve two functions. First, they control the potential offence to the *procedural* public policy of the forum, in that the foreign litigation procedure has not been conducted according to the fundamental standards of the enforcing state. Second, they relate to the potential offence to the forum's public policy because of the merits of a foreign court's decision whose recognition is sought (*substantive* public policy).[116] Public policy includes 'the fundamental moral convictions or policies' of a society that are 'of such paramount importance that [their] non-application to the facts of the case would be intolerable'.[117] It encompasses those rules of law that are 'regarded as essential in the legal order' of the state concerned.[118] In any democratic society, the respect for human rights ranks among those fundamental principles.[119] Among those human rights that influence the interpretation and application of a public policy clause are, of course, freedom of expression, media freedom and right to respect for private life. For example, in the US, the SPEECH Act 2010 refuses recognition of foreign defamation judgments that are incompatible with the First Amendment to the Constitution of the United States.[120] With the SPEECH Act, Congress reacted to the perceived threat to free speech protection by applications seeking to enforce foreign defamation judgments in the US. Moreover, the Act allows US citizens and residents and corporations in the US to bring an action for a declaration that a foreign judgment would not be enforceable because of the Act. The background of this clause was a litigation between a US counterterrorism researcher, Rachel Ehrenfeld, and a Saudi billionaire, Khalid bin Mahfouz. In her book, *Funding Evil: How Terrorism is Financed and How to Stop It*, Ehrenfeld accused bin Mahfouz of having financed Al-Qaeda. Bin Mahfouz successfully sued against Ehrenfeld in London,[121] whereupon Ehrenfeld applied for a judgment in New York declaring that the English decision would not be enforced in the United States and that her book was not actionable under United States defamation law. As the New York Court of Appeals decided that it lacked personal jurisdiction over bin Mahfouz, the New York State legislature took

---

[115] See Peers (2011, p. 685). Compare CJEU, Opinion 2/13 [2014] Accession to the ECHR [191–192]; Oster (2015c, p. 544).

[116] Oster (2015c, p. 545).

[117] Kahn-Freund (1954, p. 40).

[118] ECJ, Case C-38/98 [2000] Renault [34].

[119] Oster (2015c, pp. 546 ff).

[120] 'Securing the Protection of our Enduring and Established Constitutional Heritage Act', 124 STAT. 2380 PUBLIC LAW 111–223 – AUG. 10, 2010, amending title 28, United States Code (Judiciary and Judicial Procedure). See also Bachchan v. India Abroad Publications, 154 Misc. 2d 228, 585 N.Y.S.2d 661 (N.Y. Sup. Ct. 1992); Telnikoff v. Matusevitch, 347 Md. 561, 702 A.2d 230 (Md. 1997), preceding the SPEECH Act.

[121] Bin Mahfouz v. Ehrenfeld [2005] EWHC 1156.

immediate action and passed the 'Libel Terrorism Protection Act 2008', which provided a 'Rachel's law' similar to that now included in the SPEECH Act. Decisions such as *von Hannover* v. *Germany* (No. 1),[122] *Standard Verlags GmbH* v. *Austria*[123] or *Delfi AS* v. *Estonia,*[124] in which the Strasbourg Court decided in favour of the privacy or reputation of what would be a 'public figure' under US free speech doctrine,[125] would thus certainly be refused recognition in the US in light of the SPEECH Act 2010.

Conversely, European jurisdictions would arguably object to the recognition of US judgments allowing hate speech or defamation. In recognition proceedings, a court of an enforcing European country would have to review whether the outcome of the foreign judgment is compatible with the result of a balancing exercise between human rights applicable in this country. For example, if a German court recognises an Australian defamation judgment, it might be in violation of the defendant's freedom of expression by refusing to consider Article 10 ECHR as part of German public policy. In turn, if a German court refuses to recognise an Australian defamation judgment based on public policy, it might violate the claimant's right to respect for private life (Article 8 ECHR).[126]

A case from Europe in which freedom of expression as domestic public policy became relevant was the 2004 decision *Lindberg* v. *Sweden.*[127] The applicant, a seal hunting inspector, had been ordered to pay compensation for the publication of allegations to the effect that certain seal hunters had violated Norwegian seal hunting regulations. Mr Lindberg's application to the former European Commission of Human Rights against the *Norwegian* court's judgment alleging violations of Articles 6, 10 and 13 of the Convention had been lodged out of time.[128] Therefore, the applicant lodged an application against the decision of the *Swedish* authorities not to refuse the enforcement of the Norwegian defamation judgment in Sweden, where he lived. The ECtHR held that the Swedish courts had not violated Article 10 ECHR.[129] Most notably, in the related case of *Bladet Tromsø and Stensaas* v. *Norway*, the Strasbourg Court decided that a defamation judgment against a newspaper that published statements from the applicant's report violated the newspaper's right out of Article 10 ECHR.[130] The rejection of Mr Lindberg's application against Sweden is arguably due

---

[122] ECtHR, von Hannover v. Germany (No. 1) [2004] App. no. 59320/00.

[123] ECtHR, Standard Verlags GmbH v. Austria (No. 2) [2009] App. no. 21277/05.

[124] ECtHR, Delfi AS v. Estonia [2015] App. no. 64569/09.

[125] See US Supreme Court, New York Times Co. v. Sullivan, 376 U. S. 254 (1964).

[126] Compare ECtHR, Wagner and JMWL v. Luxembourg [2007] App. no. 76240/01: Violation of Article 8 ECHR because the receiving state refused to recognise a judicial decision concerning full adoption of a child by a single woman; Leschiutta and Fraccaro v. Belgium [2008] App. nos. 58081/00, 58411/00: Violation of Article 8 ECHR because the receiving state did not immediately enforce a foreign judgment on handing over custody of a child.

[127] ECtHR, Lindberg v. Sweden [2004] App. no. 48198/99.

[128] EComHR, Lindberg v. Norway [1997] App. no. 26604/95. In Lindberg v. Sweden, the application number is mistakenly referred to as 26604/94.

[129] ECtHR, Lindberg v. Sweden [2004] App. no. 48198/99, p. 11.

[130] ECtHR, Bladet Tromsø and Stensaas v. Norway [1999] App. no. 21980/93.

to the Strasbourg Court's reduced scope of judicial review. The mere coincidence that the applicant lived in Sweden, and not in Norway, should not open a back door for the applicant to *de facto* have his inadmissible application against the Norwegian judgment reviewed.[131] It is not the function of public policy clauses to circumvent the admissibility rules of the Strasbourg Court's procedure.

However, had the judgment originated from a non-Convention state, such as China, this rationale would not have applied. The argument that redress to the Strasbourg Court should be sought against an original judgment does not apply in such cases. Rather, it would be the court of the Convention state that would be the first one in violation of Convention rights by recognising and enforcing a third-country judgment in violation of the ECHR.

VI Questions

1 In *Dow Jones* v. *Gutnick*, Justice Callinan wrote (para. 200): 'what the appellant [i.e., Dow Jones] seeks to do ... is to impose upon Australian residents ... an American legal hegemony in relation to Internet publications'. Do you agree with this statement? Or does *Gutnick* impose on US residents an Australian hegemony in relation to internet publications?

2 Assume your client is a Swedish politician who wants to file a defamation lawsuit against a US online journal with no presence or assets in the EU. What would you have to consider when advising your client regarding:
   a) the choice of the jurisdiction?
   b) the possibility of enforcing a judgment in his favour?

3 To what extent has the territorial principle itself become part of the problem in transnational media-related cases? Is it too parochial? Would you have suggestions for alternatives to territoriality-based conceptions of jurisdiction?[132]

4 According to Article 3(2) of the General Data Protection Regulation, a data controller not established in the EU will be subject to the General Data Protection Regulation as far as he processes personal data of data subjects residing in the EU, where the processing activities are related to the offering of goods or services to such data subjects in the EU or the monitoring of their behaviour as far as that behaviour takes place within the EU. Critically evaluate this provision.

VII Further Reading

- U. Kohl, *Jurisdiction and the Internet: Regulatory Competence over Online Activity*, 2007
- D.J.B. Svantesson, *Private International Law and the Internet*, 2nd edn, 2012

---

[131] Oster (2015c, p. 565).
[132] See, for example, Schiff Berman (2012); Mills (2014); Scott (2014).

Broadcasting and Other Audiovisual Media Services

CASE EXAMPLE

Roj TV is a Danish company with its registered office in Denmark providing a television channel. It broadcasts programmes by satellite, mainly in Kurdish, throughout Europe (including Germany) and the Middle East. In 2006 and 2007, government authorities in Turkey lodged complaints with the Danish Radio and Television Board, which ensures the application of the national rules implementing the provisions of the AVMS Directive in Denmark. The Turkish authorities complained that, by its programmes, Roj TV supported the objectives of the Kurdistan Workers Party (PKK), which is classified as a terrorist organisation by the European Union. The Danish Radio and Television Board gave a ruling on those complaints by decisions of 3 May 2007 and 23 April 2008. It held that Roj TV had not infringed the Danish rules implementing (now) Articles 27 and 6 of the Directive. The Board observed, in particular, that Roj TV's programmes did not incite hatred on grounds of race, sex, religion or nationality. It took the view that Roj TV's programmes merely broadcast information and opinions and that the violent images broadcast reflected the real violence in Turkey and the Kurdish areas.

According to Article 9(2) of the German Basic Law as well as the German law governing the public law of associations (*Vereinsgesetz*), associations whose purposes or activities conflict with the principles of international understanding are prohibited. By a decision of 13 June 2008, addressed to Roj TV, the German Federal Interior Ministry, taking the view that the operation of Roj TV conflicts with the 'principles of international understanding' within the meaning of the Vereinsgesetz prohibited Roj TV from carrying out any activities falling within the scope of the *Vereinsgesetz*, i.e. the Federal Republic of Germany. On 9 July 2008, Roj TV brought an action before the Federal Administrative Court seeking to have that decision set aside. The Federal Administrative Court found that Roj TV's programmes were biased in favour of the PKK, reflecting to a large extent the militaristic and violent approach. Roj TV attempted to justify the armed struggle led by the PKK. It did not report the conflict impartially but supports the PKK's use of guerrilla units and terrorist attacks by adopting the latter's point of view and propagating a cult of heroes and martyrs with respect to fallen combatants. Roj TV thereby played a role in inciting violent confrontations between persons of Turkish and Kurdish origin in Turkey and to exacerbating tensions between Turks and Kurds living in Germany. The Federal Administrative Court decided to stay proceedings and referred to the Court of Justice for a preliminary ruling on the interpretation of Articles 3 and 6 of the AVMS Directive.

(CJEU, Joined Cases C-244/10 and C-245/10 [2011]
Mesopotamia Broadcast A/S METV and Roj TV A/S v. Germany)

I Introduction

The narrative of transnational broadcasting law began with a conflict that emerged soon after World War II and that has influenced the transnational broadcasting order ever since. In the negotiations preceding the GATT 1947, the US with its economically powerful entertainment industry had – and still has – a strong interest in free trade in film and broadcasting productions. The endeavour to disseminate such productions to a preferably broad, ideally global audience has found ideological support in the free speech clause in the First Amendment to the US Constitution. In contrast, particularly countries of the then-Economic Community wanted to protect their comparatively weaker, subsidised domestic industry from Hollywood productions. Yet it would be wrong to perceive this position as mere economic protectionism. Instead, the EEC countries have traditionally regarded broadcasting content and films as important factors for domestic cultural policy, national identity as well as social cohesion and, at the same time, as potentially endangering public policy concerns, such as the development of minors and consumer protection. Thus, broadcasting and film were explicitly not considered purely economic commodities. The European appreciation of the broadcasting media had been most distinctly expressed by the existence of public broadcasters, which once had a broadcasting monopoly and now still coexist alongside commercial broadcasting.

Transnational broadcasting law has thus constantly oscillated between the principle of 'free flow of information', which is supported by the arguments from free trade and freedom of speech, and the need to protect domestic cultural values and public policy interests. This is now best visible in the European broadcasting order, which is based on a country-of-origin principle and yet allows states to derogate from European harmonisation if overriding domestic concerns so require (see Section III below). The conflict between cultural policy and free trade interests is also discernible in global law. But it will be shown that the current state of the law is rather rudimentary and incoherent, hence far from being a fully developed global broadcasting order (see Section II below).

II International Law

The European countries were successful in the negotiations for the GATT 1947. To be sure, the GATT does cover trade in media hardware, such as newspapers, video tapes, CDs and DVDs. However, Article IV of the GATT 1947, which later became part of the GATT 1994, allows quotas for the exhibition of cinematographic films of national origin, applying to both cinemas and television.[1] The provision thus

---

[1] On this provision, see Grant (1995); Chao (1996).

exempts the exhibition of films from the national treatment clause in Article III GATT 1994. Article IV thus serves as the basis for the quotas on European productions in the European Convention on Transfrontier Television and the Audiovisual Media Services Directive. However, it only applies to the *exhibition* of films. In turn, measures that do not relate to the exhibition of films but that otherwise discriminate against foreign films are fully subject to the GATT, particularly the most-favoured-nation clause, the national treatment clause and the elimination of quantitative restrictions.[2] In addition, Article IV is only applicable to films of 'national origin', a term that the GATT itself unfortunately does not define. Given the trade-related background of the GATT, it is probable that the origin of the producer is the relevant factor.[3] In any case, a preferential treatment of *foreign* productions would not be covered by Article IV and would therefore violate the most-favoured-nation clause in Article I GATT 1994. Yet this does not apply to the European Union, which, as a customs union, falls under the exception of Article XXIV. Hence the favourable treatment of European productions in the AVMS Directive is permissible. However, since Article XXIV does not apply to the Council of Europe, the quota for European products stipulated in Article 10 of the European Convention on Transfrontier Television (see Section III below) is arguably impermissible.

After the conclusion of the Uruguay Round, exhibition quotas remained in Article IV GATT 1994 and did not migrate to the GATS.[4] Yet the GATS is also applicable to the exhibition of films as a service as well as to other media services: motion picture and video tape distribution services, radio and television distribution services, sound recording services and broadcasting services.[5] However, the GATS is based on a compromise: because of the initiative particularly of the United States, audiovisual services are basically covered by the GATS. But due to the pressure of the European Union, Members have to schedule a commitment to each service sector, and audiovisual services belong to those sectors in which the number of WTO members with commitments is the lowest.[6] The EU itself has, as expected, not scheduled a commitment to free trade audiovisual services, whereas the US has. The EU's adamant refusal to open its markets for third-country – especially US – productions has to be seen against the backdrop of the rise of commercial satellite broadcasting in the 1980s. The European Commission has regularly emphasised that audiovisual products are 'privileged mediums of identity, pluralism and integration' and 'not an industry like any other'.[7] The global availability

---

[2] See Chapter 2.

[3] See Filipek (1992, p. 358).

[4] O. Castendyk, in Castendyk et al. (2008, Article 4 TVWF para. 43).

[5] Services Sectoral Classification List (MTN.GNS/W/120), sub-sector 2.D. See WTO, Audiovisual Services, Background Note by the Secretariat, 15 June 1998, S/C/W/40.

[6] As of January 2009 there were only 30 commitments (www.wto.org/english/tratop_e/serv_e/audiovisual_ e/audiovisual_e.htm).

[7] COM, Europe's Way to the Information Society – An Action Plan, Communication to the Council and the European Parliament and to the Economic and Social Committee and the Committee of the Regions,

of broadcasting content via satellite – and now also via the internet – also trig-gered the inclusion of a quota for European productions in Article 4 of the 1989 Television Without Frontiers Directive, which is now Article 16 of the Audiovisual Services Directive. Without such an EU-wide harmonised quota, a third-country broadcaster could transmit all its content from one EU Member State to the others because of the 'country of origin' principle.[8]

As has been shown in Chapter 2, the WTO trade regime is aimed at mere negative harmonisation by abolishing discrimination, but not positive integration through harmonisation, as is the case in the EU.[9] Just as under EU law, such discrimination can be justified. Under the GATT, importing states may adopt measures necessary to protect public morals (Article XX lit. a)), for example, to prevent the import of certain sexually explicit material.[10] Such measures are only permissible if they are not applied in a discriminatory manner. By contrast, the exception clause in Article XX lit. c) GATT protecting national treasures of artistic, historic or archaeological value is arguably not applicable to media products, as this provision has to be applied narrowly.[11] The general exceptions clause in Article XIV GATS includes measures necessary to protect public morals or to maintain public order. But how do those provisions have to be interpreted? Unlike in the EU, the exceptions to the GATT and GATS commitments are based on public policy considerations that are not tightly interwoven with human rights or the notion of media pluralism. In the *Canada – Periodicals* decision, Canada had imposed an import prohibition on periodicals containing advertisements that were primarily directed to a market in Canada and did not appear in identical form in all editions of that issue of the periodical that were distributed in the periodical's country of origin. Canada argued that this meas-ure was 'designed to provide Canadians with a distinctive vehicle for the expression of their own ideas and interests'. Canada thus invoked, in essence, the need to safe-guard media pluralism. But the Panel did not even consider whether this argument could fit under the 'public morals' exception in Article XX(a) GATT 1997.[12] Unlike the European broadcasting order, the GATT does therefore not acknowledge media pluralism as an exception to its obligations.[13]

It is questionable whether media pluralism would be acceptable as a reason to deviate from the GATS obligations, which allows measures aiming at maintaining public order in addition to those protecting public morals. Such a case will still have

---

COM (94) 347 final (19.07.1994), p. 14; Communication to the Council, the European Parliament, the Economic and Social Committee and the Committee of the Regions: Principles and guidelines for the Community's audiovisual policy in the digital age, COM (1999) 657 final, p. 8.

[8] See Section III.4 in this volume.

[9] Keller (2011, p. 152).

[10] On the protection of morals, see Chapter 3.

[11] See, however, Cahn and Schimmel (1997, p. 284).

[12] WTO Appellate Body, Canada – Certain measures concerning periodicals [1997] WT/DS31/AB/R.

[13] See Keller (2011, p. 441).

to be decided. The footnote to Article XIV(a) GATS highlights that the public order exception may be invoked 'only where a genuine and sufficiently serious threat is posed to one of the fundamental interests of society', and thus underlines the provision's narrow interpretation.[14]

Finally, both the GATT and the GATS allow Member States to prevent the disclosure of information that it considers contrary to its essential security interests.[15] The interpretation of this provision can be built on general principles of media law, especially the obligation not to imprudently disclose state secrets.[16]

A global broadcasting order is thus a long way from being fully developed, not only because of the weak commitment to free trade in audiovisual services and the restriction of trade rules to discriminatory measures, but also due to the fragmentation of global legal regimes relating to broadcasting. Similar to the European Union, such a transnational broadcasting order could be built on an interaction between economic freedoms, human rights and cultural policy. On a global scale, these positions could be taken by the WTO regime, Article 19 ICCPR and the UNESCO Convention on the Protection and Promotion of the Diversity of Cultural Expressions, respectively. Article 19 ICCPR protects freedom of expression through any media of one's choice. Moreover, the UNESCO Convention emphasises that 'cultural activities, goods and services have both an economic and a cultural nature, because they convey identities, values and meanings, and must therefore not be treated as solely having commercial value'.[17] The Convention could thus serve as a reference point to take on board cultural concerns in the application of trade law. However, the construction of a global broadcasting order currently meets several obstacles. Article 19 ICCPR would need further refinement through an adjudicative institution. The Human Rights Committee is far from being able to provide such a body of case law, unlike the European Court of Human Rights. In addition, the WTO Dispute Settlement Body would have to consider the principles of international law, such as those codified in the ICCPR and the UNESCO Convention, in its decision-making. However, The Dispute Settlement Body lacks the mandate to develop such a case law itself.[18]

III The European Broadcasting Order

The European legal order on broadcasting has been influenced by many factors and actors. The main institutions for the shaping of the European broadcasting order

---

[14] See WTO Appellate Body, United States – Measures affecting the cross-border supply of gambling and betting services [2005] WT/DS285/AB/R [298].
[15] Article XXI(a) GATT 1994, Article XIV*bis*(1)(a) GATS.
[16] See Chapter 3.
[17] See Burri (2013).
[18] Article 3(2) of the WTO Understanding on Rules and Procedures Governing the Settlement of Disputes; see Keller (2011, pp. 153–155).

are, first, the Council of Europe with its European Convention on Transfrontier Television and the ECtHR with its interpretation of Article 10 ECHR. Second, the internal market provisions, the decisions of the European Court of Justice and the Television Without Frontiers Directive as well as its successor, the Audiovisual Media Services Directive (AVMS Directive), have shaped the transnational broadcasting order in the EU.[19] Third, the Court of the European Free Trade Association (EFTA) has contributed to a European broadcasting order with its decisions on the interpretation of the Television Without Frontiers Directive and the AVMS Directive.[20]

In 1989, the Council of Europe adopted the European Convention on Transfrontier Television.[21] The Convention had been drafted and adopted in parallel to and in coordination with the Television Without Frontiers Directive, which had been based on what are now Articles 53(1) and 62 TFEU.[22] Both documents were thus very similar. Due to several amendments to the Television Without Frontiers Directive and its codification as the Audiovisual Media Services Directive in 2010, the Convention and the Directive now reveal a few differences. In particular, the AVMS Directive applies to all audiovisual media services, including on-demand services, while the Convention only applies to television broadcasting.[23] Furthermore, the AVMS Directive sets out many requirements of the Convention in more detail. Nonetheless, both codifications are based on the same principles and overlap to a huge degree.

The following explanations will therefore focus on the more refined EU broadcasting order, but they will refer to the Convention to highlight convergences and differences. The chapter thus tries to develop the common principles and concepts of a transnational pan-European broadcasting order, in which legal texts are coordinated and actors regularly refer to each other.[24] As of 14 January 2015, 33 Convention States

---

[19] See also the resolutions of the European Parliament: Resolution of 4 September 2003 on Television without Frontiers (OJ C 76/453); Resolution of 22 April 2004 on the risks of violation, in the EU and especially in Italy, of freedom of expression and information (Article 11(2) of the Charter of Fundamental Rights) (OJ C 104/1026); Resolution of 6 September 2005 on the application of Articles 4 and 5 of Directive 89/552/EEC (Television without Frontiers), as amended by Directive 97/36/EC, for the period 2001–2002 (OJ C 193/117).

[20] See EFTA Court, Joined Cases E-8/94 and E-9/94 [1995] Mattel Scandinavia A/S and Lego Norge A/S; Case E-8/97 [1998] TV 1000 Sverige AB; Case E-21/13 [2014] FIFA v. ESA.

[21] Text amended according to the provisions of the Protocol (ETS No. 171), which entered into force, on 1 March 2002. The European Convention on Transfrontier Television will subsequently be named 'the Convention' for the purposes of this chapter.

[22] Council Directive 89/552/EEC of 3 October 1989 on the coordination of certain provisions laid down by law, regulation or administrative action in Member States concerning the pursuit of television broadcasting activities, OJ L 298/23. In 2007, the Directive was named 'Directive 89/552/EEC of the European Parliament and of the Council of 3 October 1989 on the coordination of certain provisions laid down by law, regulation or administrative action in Member States concerning the provision of audiovisual media services (Audiovisual Media Services Directive)'. On the EU competence to regulate the broadcasting sector, see Harrison and Woods (2007, pp. 62 ff).

[23] See subsection 3.

[24] See, for example, ECJ, Joined Cases C-320/94, C-328/94, C-329/94 and C-337/94 to C-339/94 [1996] RTI and others [33]; Case C-6/98 [1999] ARD v. ProSieben [9]; Case C-245/01 [2003] RTL [63]; Case C-89/

and the Holy See have ratified the Convention. Parties to the Convention that are also EU Member States[25] shall apply EU rules and shall not apply the rules arising from the Convention except insofar as there is no EU rule governing the particular subject concerned.[26] The AVMS Directive has been incorporated into the EEA Agreement on 15 June 2012.[27]

1 The Legal Frameworks

The Convention had been adopted in 1989 and has been barely amended ever since. By contrast, the current AVMS Directive has been adopted in 2010. These 21 years have brought about significant changes to broadcasting technology and viewers' habits. While the Convention is only applicable to television broadcasting in a traditional sense, the more recently adopted AVMS Directive applies to both broadcasting and on-demand services. The following explanations will begin with the Directive, as its more detailed definition of broadcasting, the delimitation of broadcasting to on-demand services (and other forms of mass communication) and the case law thereto pertaining allow drawing conclusions on the Convention, which is based on a similar terminology but less elaborate interpretive guidance.

a The EU Framework: The AVMS Directive and Other Provisions

The Directive applies to 'audiovisual media services'. Article 1(1)(a) AVMS Directive offers a convoluted definition, which is quite difficult to digest: accordingly, 'audiovisual media service' means

(i) a service as defined by Articles 56 and 57 [TFEU] which is under the editorial responsibility of a media service provider and the principal purpose of which is the provision of programmes, in order to inform, entertain or educate, to the general public by electronic communications networks ... Such an audiovisual media service is either a television broadcast ... or an on-demand audiovisual media service ...;
(ii) audiovisual commercial communication.

The best way to unlock this definition is to resolve the term 'audiovisual media service' into its components, to define these components and to exclude what is *not* encompassed by this term. An audiovisual media service is constituted of the following cumulative criteria:

---

04 [2005] Mediakabel v. Commissariaat voor de Media [41]; Recital 3 of the AVMS Directive; Council of Europe, Explanatory Report to the European Convention on Transfrontier Television, para. 39; EFTA Court, Joined Cases E-8/94 and E-9/94 [1995] Mattel Scandinavia A/S and Lego Norge A/S [52].

[25] As of 14 January 2015, these are all EU Member States except for Belgium, Denmark and Ireland. Greece, Luxembourg, the Netherlands and Sweden have signed but not yet ratified the Convention.

[26] Article 27(1) of the European Convention on Transfrontier Television.

[27] EEA Joint Committee Decisions of 15 June 2012.

1 A service as defined by Articles 56, 57 TFEU;
2 providing programmes;
3 the provision of those programmes is the principal purpose of the service;
4 to the general public;
5 in order to inform, entertain or educate;
6 under the editorial responsibility of a media services provider;
7 via electronic communication networks.

aa Service An audiovisual media service is, first, a 'service'. As Article 1(1)(a)(i) AVMS Directive re-emphasises, the term is congruent with 'service' as defined in Article 56 and 57 TFEU. Consequently, an audiovisual media service has to be a service that is normally provided for remuneration and on a self-employed basis. User-generated video clips on channels such as YouTube and Vimeo are thus not covered by the Directive, insofar as they are not provided on a commercial basis. Yet if such content is provided on a commercial basis, for instance, because it includes advertising, then it is to be perceived of as a 'service' within the meaning of Articles 56, 57 TFEU.[28] Provided that the following requirements are also fulfilled, it constitutes on-demand services and falls within the scope of the AVMS Directive. Those having editorial responsibility for the content – which is usually not the video platform itself – are then to be regarded as audiovisual media services providers.

In turn, the AVMS Directive does not cover goods, such as DVDs, video tapes or products used for the diffusion of television signals. Such hardware is subject to the rules relating to the free movement of goods.[29] Nor does it encompass non-economic activities, such as private websites and 'services consisting of the provision or distribution of audiovisual content generated by private users for the purposes of sharing and exchange within communities of interest'.[30] Finally, the law applicable to media employees is not covered by the Directive either.

bb Programme Article 1(1)(b) defines 'programme' as 'a set of moving images with or without sound constituting an individual item within a schedule or a catalogue established by a media service provider and the form and content of which are comparable to the form and content of television broadcasting'. This definition is as cryptic as it is important. Accordingly, a programme is 'a set of moving images'. This distinguishes audiovisual media services from radio services, as is already indicated by the term audio*visual*, and from electronic versions of newspapers and magazines, the images of which are usually not 'moving'. The additional specification 'with or without sound' effectuates that silent films are also encompassed by the Directive – which renders its denomination as *Audio*visual Media Service Directive somewhat misleading.

---

[28] Compare ECJ, Case 352/85 [1988] Bond van Adverteerders v. Netherlands [16].
[29] ECJ, Case C-155/73 [1974] Sacchi [7]; Joined Cases 60 and 61/84 [1985] Cinéthèque.
[30] Recital 21 AVMS Directive.

But more importantly, a programme has to constitute 'an individual item within a schedule or a catalogue' established by a media service provider. That refers to a very important distinction the Directive is built on, namely the way in which a programme is presented. The Directive distinguishes between 'television broadcasting' (so-called 'linear audiovisual media services') and on-demand audiovisual media services (so-called 'non-linear audiovisual media services').

Finally, Article 1(1)(b) requires that the form and content of the programme should be comparable to the form and content of television broadcasting ('television-like'). The criteria for the 'television-likeness' are whether the service competes for the same audience as television broadcasts and whether the user may reasonably expect regulatory protection within the scope of this Directive.[31] Yet, due to the principle of technology neutrality, the way of transmission is not a suitable criterion. The requirement of 'television likeness' reveals the Directive's pedigree as the successor to the Television Without Frontiers Directive. The legislator recognised the challenges posed by the internet and noticed that if the Directive would merely cover old-fashioned broadcasting television, then a regulatory gap would occur.

The notion of 'television-likeness' had been a crucial issue in the CJEU decision *New Media Online*. An online newspaper that mainly featured press articles provided a link to a subdomain that led to a page on which it was possible to access more than 300 videos. The videos included edited reports and readers' videos selected by the editors concerning various topics, such as local politics, economics, sport issues, of varying lengths, from 30 seconds to several minutes. Very few of the videos that appeared in the videos subdomain had a connection to the articles featured on the newspaper website. The CJEU had to decide whether such a service can be categorised as 'programme', in this case as an on-demand video service, with the consequence that it would be subject to the AVMS Directive (including, in particular, its rules on advertising). The Court acknowledged that the short video clips did not correspond to the portfolio that is usually offered by a traditional television broadcaster. Nevertheless, Article 1(1)(b) requires that 'the set of moving images', and not the entire programme schedule, be comparable to television broadcasting. The Court of Justice thus inferred that the video clips have to be comparable to the form and content of television broadcasting, and not that the complete compilation of the short videos can be compared to a complete schedule established by a television broadcaster. In addition, Article 1(1)(b) does not contain any requirement relating to the length of the set of images concerned. Television broadcasting also offers, alongside programmes of long to medium length, programmes of short length. Moreover, the Court held that, like a television broadcast programme, the videos at issue were aimed at a mass audience and were likely to have an impact on that audience. Furthermore, the Court observed that New Media Online competes with

---

[31] Compare Recital 24 AVMS Directive.

traditional television broadcasters for the same audience. As a result, and contrary to the Advocate-General's opinion, the Court classified New Media Online's video clips as on-demand services.[32]

The *New Media Online* decision can be expected to have a major impact on the European broadcasting landscape. It set a rather low threshold for video clips to be subjected to the regulatory framework of the AVMS Directive, if they are provided on a commercial basis and not merely incidental. Such on-demand services would have to observe the provisions of the AVMS Directive, ranging from the transparency requirements in Article 5 over the regulation of advertising in Article 9 to the content regulation in Article 12 and the promotion of European works in Article 13. It is difficult to estimate whether the Member States' broadcasting regulatory authorities will be able to cope with the task of enforcing the provisions of the Directive. The intention of the CJEU to subject forms of new media to the existing regulatory framework might thus backfire into a structural enforcement deficit, which would impede the efficacy of the Directive in general.

cc Provision of Programme is the Principal Purpose The provision of programmes has to be the principal purpose of the service. In turn, as Recital 28 AVMS Directive elucidates, the Directive excludes audiovisual content that is merely incidental or ancillary to the service and not its principal purpose, such as video clips in electronic versions of newspapers and magazines. For that reason, in the *New Media Online* case, the Austrian authorities had decided not to classify the videos as an audiovisual media service. The Court of Justice rejected this assessment: an audiovisual service must not be 'systematically be excluded from the scope of [the AVMS Directive] solely on the ground that the operator of the website of which that service is part is a publishing company of an online newspaper'.[33] Instead, the notion of the 'principle purpose' has to be assessed on a case-by-case basis. This depends on whether the videos have 'form and content which is independent of that of the written press articles', or whether they are 'indissociably complementary to the journalistic activity of that publisher, in particular as a result of the links between the audiovisual offer and the offer in text form'.[34] This requirement of a case-by-case analysis will certainly not contribute to reducing the workload that domestic broadcasting regulatory authorities, and eventually domestic courts, are now facing.

dd To the General Public Furthermore, Article 1(1)(a)(i) AVMS Directive makes clear that the Directive only covers mass communication: the programmes have to be provided 'to the general public'. This means that the service has to be intended for reception by, and could have a clear impact on, a significant proportion of the general

---

[32] CJEU, Case C-347/14 [2015] New Media Online GmbH v. Bundeskommunikationssenat [19–24].
[33] CJEU, Case C-347/14 [2015] New Media Online GmbH v. Bundeskommunikationssenat [28].
[34] CJEU, Case C-347/14 [2015] New Media Online GmbH v. Bundeskommunikationssenat [34].

public.[35] The 'general public' has to be understood as an indeterminate number of potential television viewers.[36] Hence the Directive excludes private correspondence, such as e-mails sent to a limited number of recipients.[37] As will be shown later in context with on-demand services, this distinction is difficult to define.

ee In Order to Inform, Entertain or Educate   The service must have an editorial content. This requirement distinguishes audiovisual media services from merely incidental broadcasts. The Directive thus excludes, for example, webcam videos disseminated via the internet.

ff Editorial Responsibility of a Media Services Provider   The service has to be a *media* service. As has been explained in Chapter 1, the notion of 'media' is rather broad. It encompasses both the medium through which information is being disseminated, such as electronic communication networks or broadcasting frequencies, and the content providers who disseminate their content via such a medium. Article 1(1) (a)(i) AVMS Directive clarifies that the Directive only covers the latter. It requires editorial responsibility of a media service provider for the provision of programmes.

The programme has to be provided by a media service provider. Article 1(1)(d) AVMS Directive defines 'media service provider' as 'the natural or legal person who has editorial responsibility for the choice of the audiovisual content of the audiovisual media service and determines the manner in which it is organised'. Lit. (c) of the same provision then defines 'editorial responsibility' as 'the exercise of effective control both over the selection of the programmes and over their organisation either in a chronological schedule, in the case of television broadcasts, or in a catalogue, in the case of on-demand audiovisual media services'. Article 1(1)(c) thus re-emphasises the distinction between linear audiovisual media services ('chronological schedule') and non-linear audiovisual media services ('catalogue'). As has already been indicated, the requirement of editorial responsibility excludes those service providers who merely disseminate third-party content. The concept of 'effective control' shall be further specified by the Member States when adopting measures to implement this Directive.[38]

gg Via Electronic Communication Networks   Regarding the medium of dissemination, Article 1(1)(a)(i) AVMS Directive refers to 'electronic communications networks' within the meaning Article 2(a) of the Framework Directive 2002/21/EC. The provision thus confirms the distinction between the provision of content, which shall

---

[35] Recital 21 AVMS Directive.
[36] ECJ, Case C-89/04 [2005] Mediakabel v. Commissariaat voor de Media [30]; Case C-347/07 [2008] Kabel Deutschland v. Niedersächsische Landesmedienanstalt für privaten Rundfunk [64].
[37] Recital 22 AVMS Directive.
[38] Recital 25 AVMS Directive.

be covered by the AVMS Directive, and the transmission of this content, which is subject to the regulatory framework on electronic communication.

b The Distinction between Television and On-Demand Services

Television broadcasting is an audiovisual media service 'for simultaneous viewing of programmes on the basis of a programme schedule' (Article 1(1)(e) AVMS Directive). Since the viewing of the programme is simultaneous or quasi-simultaneous to its dissemination, television broadcasting is also called 'linear audiovisual media service'. Television broadcasting includes, in particular, analogue and digital television, live streaming, webcasting and near-video-on-demand.[39] To make it simple, television broadcasting is what happens when we switch on our television, but also when we switch on our computer to watch TV real-time. This is what Article 1(1) (b) refers to when it requires a programme to constitute an individual item 'within a schedule'. The AVMS Directive itself names as examples for television broadcasting 'feature-length films, sports events, situation comedies, documentaries, children's programmes and original drama'. Moreover, a pay-per-view television service that comprises only programmes selected by the broadcaster and is broadcast at times set by the broadcaster is covered by the concept of 'television broadcasting'. The fact that the service is accessible only to a limited number of subscribers using a personal code is not relevant in this respect, because the subscribing public all receive the broadcast at the same time.[40]

However, the development of the internet has made it possible to watch a TV programme in a time-delayed manner; that is, not simultaneous to its dissemination via television broadcasting. Examples are iTunes, the BBC iPlayer, the ITV player, and many more. Such audiovisual media services that can be viewed 'at the moment chosen by the user and at his individual request' (Article 1(1)(g) AVMS Directive) are called 'on-demand audiovisual media services' or 'non-linear audiovisual media services'. On-demand services are what Article 1(1)(b) refers to when it requires a programme to constitute an individual item 'within ... a catalogue'. On-demand services are, as information society services, not only covered by the E-commerce Directive,[41] but also by the AVMS Directive.

The AVMS Directive distinguishes between linear and non-linear audiovisual media services. This is because it presumes on-demand audiovisual media services to have a less harmful impact on society than television broadcasting because of the users' increased choice and control.[42] This should justify imposing lighter regulation on on-demand audiovisual media services. Such services only have to comply with the basic rules of the AVMS Directive, particularly Article 6 on content-based

---

[39] Recital 27; on near-video-on-demand in particular, see ECJ, Case C-89/04 [2005] Mediakabel v. Commissariaat voor de Media [41].

[40] ECJ, Case C-89/04 [2005] Mediakabel v. Commissariaat voor de Media [32].

[41] Recital 18 E-commerce Directive.

[42] Recital 58 and 79.

regulation and Article 9 on commercial communications, as well as the rather general provisions in Chapter IV of the Directive. In turn, the stricter rules of the Directive on, for example, advertising in Chapter VII, only apply to television broadcasting, not to on-demand services. Since the rules on television broadcasting are stricter than those for on-demand services, television programmes that are also offered as on-demand audiovisual media services by the same media service provider shall be regarded as fulfilling the requirements to on-demand services, if they fulfil those on television broadcasting.[43] At the same time, the legislator of the AVMS Directive attaches greater social importance to the free flow of television broadcasting than to on-demand services. This is discernible from the fact that it is easier for a receiving Member State to justify derogation from the country-of-origin principle with regard to on-demand services than to television broadcasting.

In practice, the distinction between broadcasting services and information society services, including on-demand services, can be difficult to draw. In addition, it is questionable whether the policy of imposing lighter regulation on on-demand services is indeed justified with a view to the technological development and changing viewing habits. With the increasing convergence of television and internet, the distinction between linear and non-linear media services seems to become more and more artificial.[44]

c Relationship to Other Provisions

The AVMS Directive is without prejudice to generally applicable provisions covering commercial practices, such as Directive 2005/29/EC concerning unfair business-to-consumer commercial practices in the internal market and Directive 2006/114/EC concerning misleading and comparative advertising. Furthermore, rules on the protection of intellectual property remain applicable, such as the Conditional Access Directive 98/84/EC, the Satellite Broadcasting Directive, the Related Rights Directive and the Copyright Directive. Those provisions, which play an important role for audiovisual media services, will be dealt with in Chapter 9 on copyright and Chapter 10 in the context of unfair commercial practices. Finally, the legal frameworks on state aid, competition law and data protection, which will also be dealt with in separate chapters, may significantly affect the activity of broadcasters, too.

d The European Convention on Transfrontier Television

The Convention, which was adopted in 1989, only applies to broadcasting in a traditional sense. According to Article 3, the Convention 'shall apply to any programme service transmitted or retransmitted by entities or by technical means within the jurisdiction of a Party ... and which can be received, directly or indirectly, in one or more other Parties'. A 'programme service' means 'all the items within a single service

---

[43] Recital 27.
[44] For a more detailed analysis, see Lutz (2006); Ridgway (2008); Dizon (2012).

provided by a given broadcaster' (Article 2(d)). According to Article 2(c), 'broad-caster' means 'the natural or legal person who has editorial responsibility for the composition of television programme services for reception by the general public and transmits them or has them transmitted, complete and unchanged, by a third party'. Accordingly, the notion of 'broadcasting' under the Convention is based on the same concepts as the AVMS Directive, namely the notions of 'programme' and 'editorial responsibility'. Moreover, the Convention also delineates broadcasters from commu-nication services operating on individual demand, as can be seen from the definition of 'transmission' in Article 2(a).[45] It thus excludes video-on-demand and interactive services such as video conferencing, videotext, telefacsimile services, electronic data banks and similar communication services from the scope of the Convention.[46] By contrast, subscription television services, pay-per-view or near video-on-demand services and teletext services are not communication services operating on individ-ual demand, and are therefore covered by the Convention.[47]

2 Principles of the European Broadcasting Order

The European broadcasting order is based on the following six principles, which run as common threads through all regulatory areas. First, broadcasting is of utmost importance for the right to disseminate and to receive information and ideas as well as for media pluralism. All measures taken in the European broadcast-ing order have to be in accordance with Articles 10 ECHR and 11(1) EUChFR: the Convention, the AVMS Directive, measures serving to implement those codifica-tions and domestic measures derogating from them.[48] The obligation to respect media pluralism is required by Article 11(2) EUChFR as well as Article 10*bis* of the Convention and accepted by both the ECJ and the ECtHR.[49] This principle may also justify a derogation of Member States from the provisions of the Convention and the Directive.[50]

---

[45] Accordingly, 'transmission' means 'the initial emission by terrestrial transmitter, by cable, or by satellite of whatever nature, in encoded or unencoded form, of television programme services for reception by the general public. It does not include communication services operating on individual demand.'

[46] Council of Europe, Explanatory Report to the European Convention on Transfrontier Television, para. 83.

[47] Council of Europe, Explanatory Report to the European Convention on Transfrontier Television, para. 84; see ECJ, Case C-89/04 [2005] Mediakabel v. Commissariaat voor de Media [41].

[48] See, for example, CJEU, Joined Cases C-244/10 and C-245/10 [2011] Mesopotamia Broadcast A/S METV and Roj TV A/S v. Germany [33].

[49] See, for example, ECJ, Case C-288/89 [1991] Stichting Collectieve Antennevoorziening Gouda and others v. Commissariaat voor de Media [27]; Case C-353/89 [1991] Commission v. Netherlands [30]; Informationsverein Lentia and others v. Austria [1993] App. nos. 13914/88, 15041/89, 15717/89, 15779/89 and 17207/90 [38]; see also VgT Verein gegen Tierfabriken v. Switzerland (No. 1) [2001] App. no. 24699/94 [73]; Manole and others v. Moldova [2009] App. no. 13936/02 [99].

[50] See, for example, ECJ, Case C-288/89 [1991] Stichting Collectieve Antennevoorziening Gouda and others v. Commissariaat voor de Media [27]; Case C-353/89 [1991] Commission v. Netherlands [30]; Case C-23/93 [1994] TV 10 SA v. Commissariaat voor de Media [25].

The second principle is the internal market of the EU with its country-of-origin principle, which is similar to the 'free flow of information' principle under the Convention. The AVMS Directive serves to safeguard the freedom to provide audiovisual media services and to codify the internal market-related case law of the European Court of Justice in this field. In *Sacchi*, the ECJ held that broadcasting of television signals, including those in the nature of advertisements, falls within the rules of the Treaty relating to services.[51] Rights of broadcasters under the freedom to provide services, as well as their limitations, have subsequently been further defined in the case law of the ECJ.[52] This case law has, in 1989, been codified in the Television Without Frontiers Directive and later in the Audiovisual Media Services Directive, respectively. Therefore, Member States' derogations that the AVMS Directive basically allows still have to be in accordance with the free movement provisions. They must, in particular, not discriminate between domestic and foreign media service providers. Arguably the most important aspect of the internal market is the country-of-origin principle, which, in the context of media services, serves to enable a free flow of information. The free flow of information is not only codified in Articles 2 and 3 of the AVMS Directive, but also expressed in the preamble and Articles 4 and 5 of the Convention. It will be dealt with in more detail further below.

The third principle, which is to a certain extent in conflict with the 'free flow of information', is the significance of broadcasting for the domestic and pan-European culture. By virtue of Article 167 TFEU, the EU has to allow Member States certain discretion to derogate from the provisions of the AVMS Directive to protect domestic cultural interests, as is codified in Article 4(1) AVMS Directive. The AVMS Directive thus only provides minimum harmonisation. Moreover, the importance of broadcasting for culture, language and social cohesion also serves to justify the promotion of European works.

Fourth, and related to the previous point, stands the coexistence of private and public broadcasting as another significant feature that distinguishes the European audiovisual media market and the European broadcasting order. Such 'broadcasting dualism' may contribute to the quality and balance of programmes.[53] However, there is no obligation

---

[51] Case C-155/73 [1974] Sacchi [6].

[52] See, for example, ECJ, Case 52/79 [1980] Procureur du Roi v. Debauve and others; Case 352/85 [1988] Bond van Adverteerders v. Netherlands; Case C-260/89 [1991] ERT v. DEP and others; Case C-288/89 [1991] Stichting Collectieve Antennevoorziening Gouda and others v. Commissariaat voor de Media; Case C-353/89 [1991] Commission v. Netherlands; Case C-211/91 [1992] Commission v. Belgium; Case C-148/91 [1993] Veronica Omroep v. Commissariaat voor de Media; Case C-23/93 [1994] TV 10 SA v. Commissariaat voor de Media; Case C-412/93 [1995] Leclerc-Siplec v. TF1 and M6; Case C-17/00 [2001] De Coster; Case C-262/02 [2004] Commission v. France.

[53] See Protocol (No. 29) to the TEU and the TFEU on the system of public broadcasting in the Member States; Council of Europe, Recommendation CM/Rec(2007)2 on media pluralism and diversity of media content: 'Recalling the importance of transparency of media ownership so as to ensure that the authorities in charge of the implementation of regulations concerning media pluralism can take informed decisions, and that the public can make its own analysis of the information, ideas and opinions expressed by the media.'

to install a public broadcasting service if other means can be used to the same end. *If a state decides to create a public broadcasting system, the domestic law and practice has to safeguard that the public broadcaster provides a pluralistic programme.*[54]

In the *Sacchi* decision, the Court of Justice held that Member States may remove certain radio and television broadcasters from the field of competition by conferring on them a broadcasting monopoly, if this is based on considerations of a non-economic nature relating to the public interest and not discriminatory.[55] Given the limited number of channels available when *Sacchi* was decided in 1974, this rule appeared justified in order to safeguard media pluralism.[56] However, in 1993, the European Court of Human Rights then had to decide in *Informationsverein Lentia and others* v. *Austria* whether the Austrian public broadcasting monopoly was in compliance with Article 10(2) ECHR. The Court found that there was no longer a 'pressing social need' to maintain a public broadcasting monopoly in order to safeguard media pluralism, in particular because technological progress made available a number of frequencies and channels.[57] *Informationsverein Lentia and others* v. *Austria* thus denied the justification of public broadcasting monopolies and confirmed the coexistence of public and private broadcasting. In the EU, this coexistence is re-emphasised by the 1997 Amsterdam Protocol on the System of Public Broadcasting in the EU Member States (now Protocol No. 29 to the Lisbon Treaty).

Because of their special role in disseminating information and ideas, and because they do not – and must not be used to – exercise governmental powers, media freedom and freedom to provide services also applies to public broadcasters. States that have established public broadcasters, such as the BBC in Britain, ARD and ZDF in Germany, or RAI in Italy, must respect the media freedom of such broadcasters. Where a state decides to create a public broadcasting system, 'the domestic law and practice must guarantee that the system provides a pluralistic audiovisual service'.[58] Being both media entities and part of the state, public broadcasters are yet not only beneficiaries, but also addressees, of human rights. Therefore, public broadcasting services also have to respect the human rights of others. In particular, given their influential role in society, they have to be neutral. Competing views, including those of political parties opposed to government policy, must be appropriately reflected in the broadcaster's transmissions.[59] Moreover, public broadcasters have to safeguard

---

[54] ECtHR, Manole and others v. Moldova [2009] App. no. 13936/02 [101]. See also Council of Europe, Recommendation No. R (96) 10 on the guarantee of the independence of public service broadcasting; Recommendation No. R (94) 13 on measures to promote media transparency; Katsirea (2012, p. 420).

[55] ECJ, Case C-155/73 [1974] Sacchi [14]; reiterated in Case C-260/89 [1991] ERT v. DEP and others [10].

[56] See ECJ, Case C-260/89 [1991] ERT v. DEP and others [25].

[57] Informationsverein Lentia and others v. Austria [1993] App. nos. 13914/88, 15041/89, 15717/89, 15779/89 and 17207/90 [39].

[58] ECtHR, Wojtas-Kaleta v. Poland [2009] App. no. 20436/02 [47].

[59] Human Rights Committee, Concluding observations on Republic of Moldova (CCPR/CO/75/MDA), para. 14; Concluding observations on Togo (CCPR/CO/76/TGO), para. 17; Concluding observations on Peru (CCPR/CO/70/PER), para. 17.

'internal editorial freedom'. Employees of public broadcasters are therefore under a less strict obligation to observe their duties of loyalty and discretion when publicly criticising the programming policy of their employer.[60]

Fifth, the EU broadcasting order is not organised in an exclusively top-down regulatory approach, but encourages co-regulation and/or self-regulatory regimes as a complementary method of implementing certain provisions of the Directive at national level.[61] For example, Member States and the Commission shall encourage media service providers to develop codes of conduct regarding inappropriate audiovisual commercial communications in children's programmes of foods and beverages (Article 9(2) AVMS Directive). This has been implemented in several Member States by codes of conduct for HFSS ('high in fat, salt and sugar') foods.

Lastly, as has been indicated in Chapters 1 and 2, European media law is based on the distinction between content and transmission. This principle is also valid for the European broadcasting order. Both the Convention and the AVMS Directive only apply to audiovisual content, not to its transmission. Within the EU, the transmission is covered by the regulatory framework on electronic communication, which will be therefore dealt with in a separate chapter of this book.[62] An exception to this principle are the provisions on 'must carry', which apply with a view to the broadcasting content to be transmitted and will therefore be treated in this chapter. Related to the separation of content from transmission is the principle of technology neutrality. Accordingly, the manner in which audiovisual images are transmitted is not a determining factor for their treatment in the European broadcasting order. For example, Article 3 of the Convention explains that the Convention shall apply to programme services transmitted by any technical means, such as by cable, terrestrial transmitter or satellite. Furthermore, already in the 1980 decision *Procureur du Roi* v. *Debauve*, the ECJ included transnational transmission of broadcasting signals by cable television within the rules of the Treaty relating to services.[63] *Debauve* was thus an early expression of the principle of technology neutrality applied to the transmission of broadcasting.

3. The Establishment of, and Investment in, Audiovisual Media Companies

Articles 49 to 55 TFEU lay down the freedom of establishment, which of course also applies to commercial audiovisual service providers. Therefore, they are basically at liberty to choose the Member States in which they establish themselves, even if they do not offer their services there.[64] However, as will be shown below, broadcasters'

---

[60] ECtHR, Wojtas-Kaleta v. Poland [2009] App. no. 20436/02 [47].
[61] See Article 4(7) and Recital 44 AVMS Directive; Harrison and Woods (2007, pp. 50–51).
[62] See Chapter 7.
[63] Case 52/79 [1980] Procureur du Roi v. Debauve and others [15]. See also, for example, Case C-89/04 [2005] Mediakabel v. Commissariaat voor de Media [43].
[64] ECJ, Case C-56/96 [1997] VT4 Ltd v. Vlaamse Gemeenschap [22]; Case C-212/97 [1999] Centros v. Erhvervs-og Selskabsstyrelsen; see also: Case C-11/95 [1996] Commission v. Belgium; Case C-14/96 [1997] Paul Denuit.

freedom to provide their services in another country may be restricted if their establishment abroad merely serves to circumvent stricter rules applicable in this country.

Unlike the E-commerce Directive, neither the Convention nor the AVMS Directive prohibits a domestic authorisation requirement.[65] This corresponds to Article 10(1) ECHR, which 'shall not prevent States from requiring the licensing of broadcasting, television or cinema enterprises'.[66] EU law merely prohibits making the transmission of television programmes of broadcasting services *from other Member States* subject to a prior authorisation to which conditions are attached.[67] However, any such licensing regime has to be in accordance with the requirements of Article 10(2) ECHR; that is, they have to be prescribed by law and necessary in a democratic society for one of the purposes defined in this provision (see Chapter 3).

Furthermore, both the Convention and the AVMS Directive impose transparency requirements on broadcasters when they establish themselves, as users should be able to know exactly who is responsible for the content of the services provided.[68] The European broadcasting order thus contradicts any notion of anonymity in the provision of audiovisual media services within the scope of the Directive and the Convention. Instead, Article 5 AVMS Directive requires audiovisual media service providers to make easily, directly and permanently accessible to the recipients of a service certain information, such as the name of the service provider, its address and contact details and the competent regulatory or supervisory bodies. Similarly, Article 6(2) of the Convention requires certain information about the broadcaster to be made available upon request, such as the broadcaster's name or denomination, seat and status, the name of the legal representative, the composition of the capital and the nature, purpose and mode of financing of the programme service the broadcaster is providing or intends to provide.

Audiovisual media service providers benefit not only from freedom of establishment, but also from free movement of capital, as guaranteed by Article 63(1) TFEU. As a consequence, Member States may not reserve a certain percentage of the capital of television broadcasting companies to particular investors.[69] Yet, as with the other free movement provisions, broadcasting organisations – or potential investors in broadcasting companies – may only avail themselves of the free movement of capital insofar as there are no overriding requirements justifying an interference with this freedom. Such an overriding requirement may consist of, for instance, the need to ensure broadcasting pluralism. For example, in *Veronica Omroep* v. *Commissariaat voor de Media*, Dutch legislation prohibited a broadcasting organisation established

---

[65] See Recital 19 AVMS Directive and Article 6(1) of the Convention.

[66] On this provision, see ECtHR, Demuth v. Switzerland [2002] App. no. 38743/97.

[67] Case C-211/91 [1992] Commission v. Belgium [16] (emphasis added).

[68] See Recital 45 AVMS Directive.

[69] See ECJ, Case C-211/91 [1992] Commission v. Belgium, in which Belgium reserved 51 per cent of the capital of a non-public television broadcasting company that serves the entire Flemish Community to publishers of Dutch-language daily and weekly newspapers whose registered office is situated in the Dutch-speaking region or in the bilingual Brussels region.

in the Netherlands and financed by public funds from investing in a commercial television company established in another Member State but providing services directed towards the Netherlands. By doing so, the legislation sought to prevent national broadcasting organisations from evading their obligations under national law, namely to ensure a pluralistic and non-commercial broadcasting system. The Court of Justice held the interference by the Dutch legislation with the free movement of capital and the freedom to provide services to be justified.[70]

4 The Country-of-Origin Principle

The country-of-origin principle, which serves to enable the 'free flow of information', is a core principle of both the AVMS Directive and the Convention. The following sections will again begin with the more elaborate Directive, which allows inferences for the interpretation of the Convention.

a The AVMS Directive

Articles 2–3 codify the principles of 'country of origin' and 'mutual recognition' for the purposes of the AVMS Directive.[71] According to Article 2(1), each Member State 'shall ensure that all audiovisual media services transmitted by media service providers under its jurisdiction comply with the rules of the system of law applicable to audiovisual media services intended for the public in that Member State'. The domestic 'system of law applicable to audiovisual media services' includes, in the first place, the national rules implementing the AVMS Directive.

Basically only the Member State of origin should have jurisdiction over the audiovisual media service provider. It has to ensure that audiovisual media services disseminated by this provider comply with the Directive, or more precisely, with the national law as coordinated by the Directive. Member States in which the programme can be received shall basically not exercise secondary control for reasons that fall within the fields coordinated by the Directive (Article 3(1) AVMS Directive).[72] Receiving Member States may only provisionally, under specific conditions and after a particular procedure suspend the retransmission of televised broadcasts. Article 3 AVMS Directive stipulates those narrow conditions for the fields coordinated by the Directive, thereby distinguishing between television broadcasting and on-demand services. The provision thus serves to codify the case law of the ECJ on the right of Member States to derogate from the country-of-origin principle.[73]

---

[70] ECJ, C-148/91 [1993] Veronica Omroep v. Commissariaat voor de Media [15].
[71] For a detailed analysis of those provisions, see Craufurd Smith (2011).
[72] See, for example, ECJ, Joined Cases C-34/95, C-35/95 and C-36/95 [1997] De Agostini (Svenska) Förlag AB and others [56].
[73] See, for example, Case 52/79 [1980] Procureur du Roi v. Debauve and others [15 ff]; Case 352/85 [1988] Bond van Adverteerders v. Netherlands [31 ff]; Case C-288/89 [1991] Stichting Collectieve Antennevoorziening Gouda and others v. Commissariaat voor de Media [14 ff].

With regard to television broadcasting coming from another Member State (Article 3(2)), a Member State may provisionally derogate from the prohibition of secondary control if:

- the broadcast manifestly, seriously and gravely infringes Article 27(1) or (2) (protection of minors)[74] and/or Article 6 (prohibition of incitement to hatred);[75]
- the broadcaster has infringed one or more of those provisions on at least two prior occasions during the previous 12 months;
- the receiving Member State concerned has notified the broadcaster and the Commission of the alleged infringements and of the measures it intends to take should any such infringement occur again; and
- consultations with the transmitting Member State and the Commission have not produced an amicable settlement within 15 days of the notification, and the alleged infringement persists.

If the Commission decides, within two months following notification, that the measures taken by the Member State are incompatible with EU law, the Member State will be required to put an end to the measures in question as a matter of urgency.

If the requirements of Article 3(2) AVMS Directive are not fulfilled, then the receiving Member State is barred from taking any measures, even if the programme violates other provisions of the Directive or of EU law in general. A Member State may not unilaterally adopt measures designed to correct other Member States' breaches of EU law, even if such measures serve to protect the receiving Member State's population.[76] The mechanism provided by the TFEU for such cases is the infringement procedure in Article 259 TFEU.

With regard to on-demand audiovisual media services (Article 3(4)), a Member State may take measures to derogate from the prohibition of secondary control if the following conditions are fulfilled:

- the measures are taken for reasons of public policy, public health, public security or consumer protection;
- the measures are taken against an on-demand audiovisual media service that prejudices those objectives referred or that presents a serious and grave risk of prejudice to those objectives;
- the measures are necessary and proportionate;[77] and
- before taking the measures in question, the Member State has asked the Member State of origin to take measures, but without avail, and notified the Commission and the Member State of origin of its intention to take such measures.[78]

---

[74] As will be shown further below (subsection 9), it is, in the first place for the receiving Member State to assess what it considers to be to the detriment of minors.

[75] See subsection 7 below.

[76] ECJ, Case C-11/95 [1996] Commission v. Belgium [37]; Case C-14/96 [1997] Paul Denuit [35].

[77] As a general principle of EU law, the codification of the principle of proportionality was not necessary.

[78] The proceedings under Article 3(4) are without prejudice to court proceedings, including preliminary proceedings and acts carried out in the framework of a criminal investigation. Furthermore, Member States may, in urgent cases, derogate from those procedural conditions (Article 4(5)).

If the European Commission finds that the measures are incompatible with EU law, it shall ask the receiving Member State in question to refrain from taking any proposed measures or urgently to put an end to the measures in question (Article 4(6)).

Article 3(4) AVMS Directive is thus a codification of the written justifications under the TFEU as well as of consumer protection as an unwritten justification. It should be noted that economic aims cannot constitute grounds of public policy within the meaning of the Treaty,[79] and thus arguably fall outside the scope of Article 3(4) as well.

On a final note, in contrast to the E-commerce Directive with its Article 1(4), the AVMS Directive is silent on whether the country-of-origin principle codified in Article 3 AVMS Directive provides a conflict-of-law rule. In *Martinez and eDate Advertising*, the CJEU had to decide whether the country-of-origin principle codified in the E-commerce Directive has a conflict-of-laws character or whether it operates as a corrective at a substantive law level. The Court's reasoning in *eDate*, which will be further elaborated on in Chapter 6, can be transferred to transnational private law litigation under the AVMS Directive, for example, in cases of defamation in a television programme.

b The European Convention on Transfrontier Television

The Convention provides a similar, but slightly less refined, system of home state control and free flow of information. According to Article 5, each Convention State shall ensure that all programme services transmitted by broadcasters within its jurisdiction comply with the terms of the Convention. Furthermore, similar to Article 4(1) AVMS Directive, Article 28 of the Convention allows Convention States to apply stricter or more detailed rules than those provided for in the Convention. And, just as Article 3(1) AVMS Directive, Article 4 prevents the Convention States, *inter alia*, from restricting the retransmission on their territories of programme services that comply with the terms of the Convention.

If a Convention State finds a violation of the Convention, it shall communicate to the country of origin the alleged violation and the two states shall endeavour to overcome the difficulty on the basis of a cooperation, conciliation and arbitration procedure akin to Article 3(2) AVMS Directive, which is set out in Articles 19, 25 and 26 of the Convention.[80] In particular, if the alleged violation is 'of a manifest, serious and grave nature which raises important public issues' and concerns particular responsibilities of broadcasters, the receiving Party may suspend provisionally the retransmission of the incriminated programme service two weeks after it has communicated the infringement to the country of origin.[81] Finally, Article 24*bis* of the Convention provides a clause similar to Article 4(2) AVMS Directive,

---

[79] ECJ, Case 352/85 [1988] Bond van Adverteerders v. Netherlands [34].
[80] Article 24 of the Convention.
[81] Article 24 of the Convention sets out further details.

addressing alleged abuses of rights conferred by the Convention, namely the circumvention of domestic rules by a broadcaster that establishes itself in another Convention State and then 'wholly or principally' directs its programme to the other state. Article 16 of the Convention includes a special clause for circumvention of domestic provisions with regard to advertising and teleshopping in particular.[82]

5 Stricter Rules and their Circumvention

As has been indicated before, Article 167(4) TFEU requires the Union to respect and promote the diversity of its Member States' cultures. The AVMS Directive thus does not completely harmonise the rules relating to all areas to which it applies, but provides only minimum harmonisation.[83] Consequently, Member States may, according to Article 4(1) of the AVMS Directive, require media service providers under their jurisdiction to comply with more detailed or stricter rules in the fields coordinated by the AVMS Directive, provided that such rules are in compliance with EU law. These may, for instance, be rules on consumer protection, on public order, public morality, public security or public health, on the protection of minors, on cultural policy such as the promotion of the official language(s) of a state, or measures to ensure a pluralistic domestic broadcasting system or a certain level of programme quality.[84] The Court of Justice and the EFTA Court have accepted, for example, the exclusion of the distribution sector from televised advertising,[85] a ban on television advertising for alcoholic beverages,[86] a prohibition of advertisements broadcast during commercial breaks designed to attract the attention of children under 12 years of age,[87] the imposition of shorter hourly television advertising limits for pay-TV broadcasters than those set for free-to-air broadcasters,[88] the requirement that television operators earmark a percentage of their operating revenue for the pre-funding of European cinematographic films and films made for television, particularly for the production of works of which the original language is one of the official languages of that

---

[82] On this provision, see EFTA Court, Joined Cases E-8/94 and E-9/94 [1995] Mattel Scandinavia A/S and Lego Norge A/S [52].

[83] See ECJ, Case C-222/07 [2009] UTECA [19]; CJEU, Joined Cases C-244/10 and C-245/10 [2011] Mesopotamia Broadcast A/S METV and Roj TV A/S [34].

[84] For broadcasting-related cases, see, for example, ECJ, Case C-288/89 [1991] Stichting Collectieve Antennevoorziening Gouda and others v. Commissariaat voor de Media [27]; Case C-353/89 [1991] Commission v. Netherlands [30]; Case C-412/93 [1995] Case C-262/02 [2004] Commission v. France [30]; EFTA Court, Joined Cases E-8/94 and E-9/94 [1995] Mattel Scandinavia A/S and Lego Norge A/S [40].

[85] ECJ, Case C-412/93 [1995] Leclerc-Siplec v. TFI and M6.

[86] ECJ, Case C-262/02 [2004] Commission v. France.

[87] ECJ, Joined Cases C-34/95, C-35/95 and C-36/95 [1997] De Agostini (Svenska) Förlag AB and others [56]; see also EFTA Court, Joined Cases E-8/94 and E-9/94 [1995] Mattel Scandinavia A/S and Lego Norge A/S [40].

[88] CJEU, Case C-234/12 [2013] Sky Italia [14].

Member State,[89] and the prescription of the 'net principle' in derogation from Article 20(2) AVMS Directive.[90]

Furthermore, the Directive does not preclude a Member State from applying *general* legislation; that is, legislation that is not specifically targeted at audiovisual media services, provided that those measures do not prevent the retransmission *per se*.[91] This includes, first, rules that pursue a domestic public policy objective. For instance, in our case example *Roj TV*, the CJEU held that the German law governing the public law of associations constituted such a permissible general legislation, provided that it did not prevent retransmission *per se* (which was for the domestic court to establish).[92] Second, it encompasses provisions implementing EU legislation, such as Directive 2005/29/EC concerning unfair business-to-consumer commercial practices in the internal market, and Directive 2006/114/EC concerning misleading and comparative advertising.[93] Finally, several provisions of the Directive leave the Member States discretion to implement or not to implement certain rules as well as to implement stricter rules, such as Article 11(3) on the admissibility of certain forms of product placement and Article 26 on television advertising.

However, those additional or derogating rules have to be in compliance with EU law, especially Article 11 EUChFR and the provisions on the internal market, and they have to be proportionate to the aim pursued. This means, in particular, that they must not discriminate between foreign and domestic audiovisual services.[94] For example, while Member States may impose a complete ban on advertising on a particular product, as was the case in *Commission* v. *France*,[95] they must not discriminate between domestic and foreign advertisements. Furthermore, Member States may not prohibit the transmission of programmes in a language other than that of the country in which the broadcaster is established, and they may not define in a discriminatory manner own cultural productions that constitute a compulsory part of the programmes of non-public television broadcasting companies.[96] Nor may Member States impose an obligation on broadcasters to use the technical resources (recording studios, set workshops, technicians, etc.) of a particular domestic company for the production of their programmes.[97]

---

[89] ECJ, Case C-222/07 [2009] UTECA [40].

[90] ECJ, Case C-6/98 [1999] ARD v. ProSieben [43]; see subsection 7 below.

[91] ECJ, Joined Cases C-34/95, C-35/95 and C-36/95 [1997] De Agostini (Svenska) Förlag AB and others [38].

[92] CJEU, Joined Cases C-244/10 and C-245/10 [2011] Mesopotamia Broadcast A/S METV and Roj TV A/S [50].

[93] See EFTA Court, Joined Cases E-8/94 and E-9/94 [1995] Mattel Scandinavia A/S and Lego Norge A/S [58].

[94] See ECJ, Case 52/79 [1980] Procureur du Roi v. Debauve and others [13]; Case C-288/89 [1991] Stichting Collectieve Antennevoorziening Gouda and others v. Commissariaat voor de Media [11]; Case C-211/91 [1992] Commission v. Belgium [11].

[95] ECJ, Case C-262/02 [2004] Commission v. France.

[96] ECJ, Case C-211/91 [1992] Commission v. Belgium [31].

[97] ECJ, Case C-353/89 [1991] Commission v. Netherlands.

The country-of-origin principle seems to offer a great opportunity for audiovisual media service providers who want to disseminate certain content in a particular country, but who are prevented from doing so because of a stricter set of rules in that country: they may simply locate themselves in a country with less strict rules – which of course still have to be in compliance with the AVMS Directive – and retransmit their programmes to the country that they initially intended to reach. This receiving country would, because of Article 3, basically be prohibited from imposing its own regulatory standards on the service provider. Such 'forum shopping' for the most favourable jurisdiction became particularly attractive with the advent of commercial satellite broadcasting in the 1980s, and it is still attractive today for audiovisual media service providers from third countries that do not have an affiliation with a particular EU Member State.[98]

The legislator of the European framework has recognised this problem and has therefore codified provisions on circumvention of national rules in (now) Article 4(2) to (5) AVMS Directive with regard to broadcasters. Accordingly, a Member State may adopt appropriate measures against the broadcaster concerned in cases in which:

- it has exercised its freedom under Article 4(1) to adopt more detailed or stricter rules;
- it assesses that a broadcaster under the jurisdiction of another Member State provides a television broadcast that is 'wholly or mostly directed towards its territory';
- the broadcaster in question has established itself in the Member State of origin in order to circumvent the stricter rules;
- the receiving Member State has, without avail, contacted the Member State of origin with a view to achieving a mutually satisfactory solution;
- it has notified the Commission and the Member State of origin of its intention to take such measures while substantiating the grounds on which it bases its assessment; and
- the Commission has decided that the measures are compatible with EU law.

This provision codifies the decisions of the ECJ on the circumvention of national rules by broadcasters that establish themselves in another Member State.[99] The Court has held that a Member State may take measures to prevent the exercise of the freedoms guaranteed by the Treaty by a service provider whose activity is entirely or principally directed towards its territory, and who thus avoid the rules that would be applicable were the provider established in that Member State.[100] This case law

---

[98] See Wagner (2014).

[99] See Case C-212/97 [1999] Centros v. Erhvervs-og Selskabsstyrelsen; Case 33/74 [1974] Van Binsbergen; Case C-23/93 [1994] TV 10 SA v. Commissariaat voor de Media. From media-specific literature, see Le Goueff (2007).

[100] See ECJ, Case C-211/91 [1992] Commission v. Belgium [12]; Case C-148/91 [1993] Veronica Omroep v. Commissariaat voor de Media [12]; Case C-23/93 [1994] TV 10 SA v. Commissariaat voor de Media [21]. Based on ECJ, Case 33/74 [1974] Van Binsbergen [13].

can thus be referred to when interpreting Article 4(2–5). Indicators as to whether a broadcast is 'wholly or mostly directed' towards a particular Member State are: the origin of the television advertising and/or subscription revenues, the main language of the service or the existence of programmes or commercial communications targeted specifically at the public in the Member State where they are received.[101] Yet the exception from the country-of-origin principle has to be interpreted restrictively.[102]

Yet Article 4(2) applies only to broadcasters, not to on-demand services. Non-linear audiovisual media services have thus to be treated according to the general framework provided by the Court of Justice. This can be inferred from Recital 57 of the E-commerce Directive. As has been shown before, non-linear audiovisual media services are not only subject to the AVMS Directive, but also to the E-commerce Directive.

6 Regulation of Audiovisual Commercial Communication

Chapter 3 has explained that commercial speech usually enjoys less protection than other forms of speech, such as political reporting. This applies even more to the audiovisual media, which has a particular power not only to shape, but also to mislead public opinion.[103] Limitations on duration, frequency and harmful content of advertisements as well as restrictions enabling viewers not to confuse advertising with other parts of the programme may thus be justified by overriding reasons relating to the general interest. Such reasons may be, for instance, consumer protection, editorial independence of the programme provider and the maintenance of a certain level of programme quality. Both Chapter III of the Convention on advertising and teleshopping and the AVMS Directive with its regulatory regime on 'audiovisual commercial communication' have taken these concerns on board. This section will first introduce the terms and relevant provisions applicable to such commercial communication, and will then provide an overview on the regulatory concepts underlying all these provisions together.

a Terminology

The first alternative of the definition of an audiovisual media service, that is, Article 1(1)(a)(i) of the Directive, only covers services 'the principal purpose of which is the provision of programmes, in order to inform, entertain or educate'. Article 1(1)(a)(ii) extends the applicability of the AVMS Directive to media services that do not have as their *principal* purpose to inform, entertain or educate (although these factors may be significant components of those services), but to promote goods, services or images in return for payment or for self-promotional purposes. Such 'audiovisual

---

[101] Recital 42.
[102] ECJ, Case C-355/98 [2000] Commission v. Belgium [28]; Case C-348/96 [1999] Calfa [23].
[103] Compare ECtHR, Demuth v. Switzerland [2002] App. no. 38743/97 [43] and [44].

commercial communication' is defined by Article 1(1)(h) as 'images with or without sound which are designed to promote, directly or indirectly, the goods, services or image of a natural or legal entity pursuing an economic activity'. Audiovisual commercial communication may accompany or be included in a programme 'in return for payment' or for similar consideration or for self-promotional purposes'. 'In return for payment' underlines the commercial character of the advertisement, which is constitutive for being covered by the internal market provisions in the first place; the broadcasters are paid by the advertisers for the service that they perform for them in scheduling their advertisements.[104] In turn, the Directive shall not apply to public service announcements and charity appeals broadcast free of charge.[105] Self-promotional activities do not include payment or similar consideration, and would thus basically not be covered by the Directive. However, such activities are a particular form of advertising in which the broadcaster promotes its own products, services, programmes or channels; hence they are sufficiently commercial to fall within the scope of the internal market provisions, and thus the Directive.[106]

Article 9 AVMS Directive establishes the general rules for audiovisual commercial communication, applicable to both television broadcasters and on-demand services. These include, for instance, that audiovisual commercial communications shall be readily recognisable as such, they shall not prejudice respect for human dignity, promote discrimination or cause physical or moral detriment to minors. In particular, surreptitious advertising, advertising for tobacco products and for medicinal products as well as medical treatment available only on prescription in the Member State of origin shall be prohibited.

The Directive then further distinguishes four forms of audiovisual commercial communication: sponsorship, product placement, television advertising and tele-shopping. These forms of audiovisual commercial communication are not only subject to the general provision of Article 9, but also to specific provisions, which set out the principles of Article 9 in more detail or add further principles.

Sponsorship is 'any contribution made by ... undertakings or natural persons not engaged in providing audiovisual media services or in the production of audiovisual works, to the financing of audiovisual media services or programmes with a view to promoting their name, trademark, image, activities or products' (Article 1(1)(k)). In addition to the general requirements for audiovisual commercial communication in Article 9, services or programmes that are sponsored have to meet the requirements of Article 10 of the Directive. For example, the sponsoring must not affect the responsibility and editorial independence of the media service provider, it shall not directly encourage the purchase or rental of goods or services, and viewers shall be clearly informed of the existence of a sponsorship agreement.[107]

---

[104] Compare ECJ, Case 352/85 [1988] Bond van Adverteerders v. Netherlands [16].
[105] Recital 31; see also Article 12(4) of the Convention.
[106] Recital 96.
[107] On Ofcom's regulatory treatment of sponsorship in particular, see Brown (2010).

Product placement is 'any form of audiovisual commercial communication consisting of the inclusion of or reference to a product, a service or the trademark thereof so that it is featured within a programme, in return for payment or for similar consideration' (Article 1(1)(m)). The difference between product placement and sponsorship is the fact that in product placement the reference to a product is built into the plot, which is expressed by the words 'within a programme' in Article 1(1)(m). In contrast, sponsor references may be shown during a programme but are not part of the action of a programme.[108] Arguably the best-known examples for product placement are those for watches, cars and other gadgets in the *James Bond* movies.

Article 11 basically prohibits product placement in programmes produced after 19 December 2009. Yet Article 11(3) declares certain forms of product placement admissible: product placement in cinematographic works (which would include the *James Bond* movies), films and series made for audiovisual media services, sports programmes and light entertainment programmes other than children's programmes, as well as in cases in which there is no payment but only the provision of certain goods or services free of charge for their inclusion in a programme.[109] However, the provision leaves the Member States discretion to opt out of these derogations; that is, to declare even those forms of product placement partially or totally inadmissible.

The entire Chapter VII of the AVMS Directive is concerned with television advertising and teleshopping. Television advertising encompasses any form of announcement broadcast in return for payment, for similar consideration or for self-promotional purposes 'in connection with a trade, business, craft or profession in order to promote the supply of goods or services, including immovable property, rights and obligations, in return for payment' (Article 1(1)(i)). Teleshopping is defined as 'direct offers broadcast to the public with a view to the supply of goods or services, including immovable property, rights and obligations, in return for payment' (Article 1(1)(l)). In turn, teleshopping does not include conventional programme elements such as news, sports, films, documentaries and drama.[110]

The Court of Justice had the opportunity to further define the concepts of 'television advertising' and 'teleshopping' in *KommAustria* v. *ORF*.[111] The broadcaster ORF broadcast a programme named 'Quiz-Express', in which the public could participate in a prize game by dialling a premium-rate telephone number in return for the payment of €0.70 to the telephone provider, which had an agreement with ORF. The game fell into two parts: the first involved an element of chance, namely that, in order to be put through to the programme, the caller had to reach a particular telephone line; in the second part, the selected caller had to answer a question on the programme. Callers who are not put through to the programme participated

---

[108] Recital 91.
[109] The provision of goods or services free of charge should only be considered to be product placement in the first place if the goods or services involved are of significant value (Recital 91).
[110] Recital 101.
[111] Case C-195/06 [2007] KommAustria v. ORF.

in a 'weekly prize' draw. For the ECJ, the decisive criterion to establish whether the 'Quiz-Express' constituted *teleshopping* was whether ORF pursued an economic activity in its own right involving the supply of a service in the gambling sector, or whether the programme was restricted to a mere offer of entertainment within the broadcast to make it more interactive.[112] For this purpose, the national court should take into account the purpose of the broadcast of which the game forms part, the time spent on the game within the broadcast as a whole, the anticipated economic effects of the game in relation to the broadcast in general and whether the questions that the candidates are asked are related to an economic activity.[113] To establish whether the game constituted *television advertising*, it was necessary to examine whether it consisted of an announcement that encouraged viewers to buy the goods and services presented as prizes to be won or promoted the programmes of the broadcaster in question in the form of self-promotion.[114] This should be determined according to the purpose and content of that game, the circumstances in which the prizes to be won were presented and whether the questions given to the candidates related to their knowledge of other broadcasts by that body and thus encouraged potential candidates to watch them.[115] Following the judgment of the ECJ, the Austrian Federal Communications Senate eventually decided that 'Quiz-Express' did indeed constitute teleshopping.[116]

The Convention is based on concepts of commercial communication similar to the AVMS Directive. However, due to its more limited scope, it applies only to television advertising, teleshopping and sponsoring of television programmes, but not to commercial communication in on-demand services. Furthermore, it does not regulate product placement. Under the Convention, 'advertising' means 'any public announcement in return for … consideration or for self-promotional purposes, which is intended to promote the sale, purchase or rental of a product or service, to advance a cause or idea, or to bring about some other effect desired by the advertiser or the broadcaster itself' (Article 2(f)). 'Teleshopping' (or 'tele-shopping' in the spelling of the Convention) means 'direct offers broadcast to the public with a view to the supply of goods or services … in return for payment' (Article 2(g)). Finally, Article 2(h) defines 'sponsorship' as 'the participation of a natural or legal person, who is not engaged in broadcasting activities or in the production of audiovisual works, in the direct or indirect financing of a programme with a view to promoting the name, trademark, images or activities of that person'.

The rules for advertising and teleshopping are set out in Chapter III of the Convention. Similar to Article 9 of the AVMS Directive, Article 11 of the Convention

---

[112] Case C-195/06 [2007] KommAustria v. ORF [37 f].
[113] Case C-195/06 [2007] KommAustria v. ORF [36].
[114] Case C-195/06 [2007] KommAustria v. ORF [47].
[115] Case C-195/06 [2007] KommAustria v. ORF [45].
[116] Austrian Federal Communications Senate (Bundeskommunikationssenat), Case no. GZ 611.009/0042-BKS/2007 [2008] KommAustria v. ORF.

establishes the general standards that apply to advertising and teleshopping. Accordingly, such commercial communication shall be fair, honest, not mislead and not prejudice the interests of consumers. Advertising and teleshopping addressed to or using minors 'shall avoid anything likely to harm their interests and shall have regard to their special susceptibilities'. Furthermore, teleshopping shall not exhort minors to contract for the sale or rental of goods and services. Finally, the advertiser shall not exercise any editorial influence over the content of programmes.

Article 18*bis* declares that the Convention shall apply *mutatis mutandis* to programme services devoted exclusively to self-promotion. Chapter IV and Article 18*ter* apply to sponsorship.

b Concepts

Rather than going through each provision individually, which would be a rather dull exercise, the following sections will explain the common concepts the regulatory regimes for audiovisual commercial communication in the AVMS Directive and the Convention are built on:

- Transparency requirements.
- Content-based regulation.
- Aggressive or misleading practices.
- Regulation with a view to the impact on editorial independence.
- Restrictions on the time and timing of such communication.

aa Transparency Requirements According to Article 9(1)(a) and (b) AVMS Directive, which apply to both television broadcasting and on-demand services, audiovisual commercial communications shall be readily recognisable as such, they shall not use subliminal techniques and surreptitious audiovisual commercial communication is generally prohibited. 'Surreptitious audiovisual commercial communication' consists of three components:

- Goods, services, the name, the trademark or the activities of a producer of goods or a provider of services are presented in programmes.
- The presentation is intended by the media service provider to serve as advertising, which is particularly the case if it is done in return for payment or for similar consideration.
- It might mislead the public as to its nature as advertising (Article 1(1)(j)). Surreptitious audiovisual commercial communication is a practice prohibited by the Directive because of its misleading effect on consumers. Yet illegal surreptitious audiovisual commercial communication has to be distinguished from legal product placement. Product placement is legal if one of the cases of Article 11(3) subpara. 1 is applicable, if the Member State of origin has not decided for the inadmissibility of product placement, and if the requirements of Article 11(3) subpara. 3 are fulfilled. These requirements include, in particular, that viewers are clearly

informed of the existence of such product placement at the start and the end of the programme and when a programme resumes after an advertising break.[117] If this is not the case, then product placement constitutes illegal surreptitious advertising.

If channels not exclusively devoted to teleshopping include teleshopping windows in their broadcasting, those windows have to be clearly identified as such by optical and acoustic means at the beginning and the end of the window and shall be of a minimum uninterrupted duration of 15 minutes (Article 24 and Recital 100 AVMS Directive). This should enable the viewer to distinguish between the programme and teleshopping.

Akin to Article 9(1)(a) and (b) AVMS Directive, Article 13 of the Convention requires advertising and teleshopping to be clearly distinguishable as such and recognisably separate from the other items of the programme service by optical and/or acoustic means. Advertising and teleshopping shall not use subliminal techniques, and surreptitious advertising and teleshopping shall not be allowed. Going beyond the AVMS Directive, the Convention also requires advertising and teleshopping not to feature persons regularly presenting news and current affairs programmes (Article 13(4)). Just as Article 24 AVMS Directive, Article 12(3) of the Convention requires windows devoted to teleshopping programmes broadcast within programme services to be clearly identified by optical and acoustic means. Finally, according to Article 17(1), sponsored programmes or series of programmes 'shall clearly be identified as such by appropriate credits at the beginning and/or end of the programme'.

bb Content-Based Restrictions Audiovisual commercial communication is also subject to certain content-based restrictions. Those restrictions may apply because of the product that is being promoted, the way it is being presented or both.

Product-related restrictions apply to advertising for tobacco products, medicinal products, medical treatment and alcoholic beverages. Under both the Directive and the Convention, any forms of audiovisual commercial communication for tobacco products or for medicinal products and medical treatment available only on prescription in the Member State of origin are prohibited without exception.[118] Within the EU, this policy harmonises with Directive 2003/33/EC relating to the advertising and sponsorship of tobacco products,[119] which prohibits advertising and sponsorship for cigarettes and other tobacco products in printed media, information society services and radio broadcasting, and Article 88(1) of Directive 2001/83/EC on

---

[117] Similar to the transparency requirements for product placement, Article 10(1)(c) requests that viewers shall be clearly informed of the existence of a sponsorship agreement.

[118] See Articles 9(1)(d) and (f), 10(2) and (3), and 11(4) AVMS Directive; Articles 15(1) and (3) and 18(1) and (2) of the Convention.

[119] Directive 2003/33/EC of the European Parliament and of the Council of 26 May 2003 on the approximation of the laws, regulations and administrative provisions of the Member States relating to the advertising and sponsorship of tobacco products, OJ L 152/16. The ECJ in Case C-380/03 [2006] Germany v. Parliament and Council dismissed an action for annulment of this Directive.

medicinal products for human use,[120] which prohibits advertising to the general public of certain medicinal products. In addition, Article 15(4) of the Convention requires advertising for all other medicines and medical treatment to be 'clearly distinguishable as such, honest, truthful and subject to verification and [to] comply with the requirement of protection of the individual from harm'. Furthermore, under both the Convention and the Directive, any teleshopping for medicines and medical treatment shall not be allowed.[121]

Audiovisual commercial communication for alcoholic beverages is not entirely prohibited, but significantly restricted. Audiovisual commercial communications in general shall not encourage immoderate consumption of alcoholic beverages (Article 9(1)(e) AVMS Directive). More specifically, television advertising and teleshopping for alcoholic beverages shall, according to Article 22 AVMS Directive and the similarly worded provision in Article 15(2) of the Convention, comply with the following criteria: they shall not link the consumption of alcohol to enhanced physical performance or to driving; they shall not create the impression that the consumption of alcohol contributes towards social or sexual success; they shall not claim that alcohol has therapeutic qualities or that it is a stimulant, a sedative or a means of resolving personal conflicts; they shall not encourage immoderate consumption of alcohol or present abstinence or moderation in a negative light, or place emphasis on high alcoholic content as being a positive quality of the beverages. Yet since both the Convention and Article 22 AVMS Directive only apply to television advertising and teleshopping, this means, in turn, that such practices are – within the general framework provided by Article 9(1)(e) AVMS Directive – allowed for commercial communication in on-demand services. This seems inconsistent, but is apparently intended by the European Parliament and the Council. Recital 79 of the AVMS Directive emphasises that the 'availability of on-demand audiovisual media services increases consumer choice. Detailed rules governing audiovisual commercial communication for on-demand audiovisual media services thus appear neither to be justified nor to make sense from a technical point of view.'

Furthermore, under the AVMS Directive, audiovisual commercial communications shall not cause physical or moral detriment to minors.[122] In particular, audiovisual commercial communications for alcoholic beverages shall not be aimed specifically at minors or depict minors consuming these beverages.[123]

Lastly, under the AVMS Directive, audiovisual commercial communications shall not, *inter alia*, prejudice respect for human dignity, include or promote discrimination, encourage behaviour prejudicial to health, safety and the protection of

---

[120] Directive 2001/83/EC of the European Parliament and of the Council of 6 November 2001 on the Community code relating to medicinal products for human use, OJ L 311/67.

[121] Article 21 AVMS Directive (referring to 'medicinal products which are subject to a marketing authorisation within the meaning of Directive 2001/83/EC') and Article 15(5) of the Convention.

[122] Article 9(1)(g) AVMS Directive.

[123] Articles 9(1)(e) and 22(a) AVMS Directive; see also Article 15(2)(a) of the Convention.

the environment (Article 9(1)(c)). Similar to the interpretation of Article 6 AVMS Directive,[124] Article 9(1)(c) reveals the conundrum that occurs when the legislator expressly mentions several reasons for discrimination, but omits others. Does this allow the conclusion that discrimination based on reasons that are not mentioned in the provisions is allowed? Article 9(1)(c)(ii) prohibits audiovisual commercial communications from including or promoting 'any discrimination based on sex, racial or ethnic origin, nationality, religion or belief, disability, age or sexual orientation'. Consequently, discrimination based on social origin, genetic features, language, political or any other opinion, membership of a national minority, property or birth (all of which are included in Article 21 EUChFR and some of which are included in Article 19 TFEU) is apparently allowed under Article 9. Yet it is questionable whether such a policy is intended.

cc Aggressive and Misleading Practices   Under the general provision of Article 11(2) of the Convention, advertising and teleshopping shall not be misleading and shall not prejudice the interests of consumers. In the EU, the AVMS Directive is without prejudice to Directive 2005/29/EC concerning unfair business-to-consumer commercial practices in the internal market, which applies to unfair commercial practices, such as misleading and aggressive practices occurring in audiovisual media services. Furthermore, Regulation (EC) No 1924/2006 on nutrition and health claims made on foods and Directive 2006/114/EC concerning misleading and comparative advertising also apply.[125]

In addition to those regulatory frameworks, both the AVMS Directive and the Convention prohibit audiovisual media services or programmes that are sponsored or that contain product placement to directly encourage the purchase or rental of goods or services, in particular by making special promotional references to those goods or services. In addition, product placements shall not give undue prominence to the product in question.[126]

dd Editorial Independence and Principle of Separation   Both the AVMS Directive and the Convention also contain specific rules safeguarding editorial independence from undue influence by advertisers. In addition, the AVMS Directive includes a principle of separation between editorial content and advertising that, however, is only applicable to television advertising and teleshopping.

The content and scheduling of sponsored audiovisual media services or of programmes that contain product placement shall not affect the responsibility and editorial independence of the media service provider.[127] Furthermore, news and current

---

[124] See subsection 7 below.
[125] Compare ECJ, Joined Cases C-34/95, C-35/95 and C-36/95 [1997] De Agostini (Svenska) Förlag AB and others [37].
[126] Articles 10(1)(b) and 11(3) AVMS Directive; Article 17(3) of the Convention (applies to sponsoring only).
[127] Articles 10(1)(a) and 11(3) AVMS Directive; Article 17(2) of the Convention (applies to sponsoring only).

affairs programmes shall not be sponsored.[128] This reflects the generally higher estimation of speech on political and social affairs compared with entertainment programmes.[129]

Article 19 stipulates that TV advertising and teleshopping shall be readily recognisable and distinguishable from editorial content. They are to be kept distinct from other parts of the programme by optical and/or acoustic and/or spatial means. Isolated advertising and teleshopping spots, other than in transmissions of sports events, shall remain the exception.

By contrast to the programme-related independence of editorial content from advertising, in its parallel decisions *Stichting Collectieve Antennevoorziening Gouda* and *Commission* v. *Netherlands*, the ECJ declared incompatible with EU law a national rule requiring a *structural* separation between the producers of advertisements and the producers of programmes. The Dutch authorities had argued that such a rule is necessary to guarantee the non-commercial nature and independence of broadcasting and broadcasting pluralism. However, the ECJ held that there is not necessarily a connection between such a cultural policy and the structure of broadcasting bodies.[130] But the Court also decided that a limitation of the duration or frequency of advertisements and restrictions designed to enable listeners or viewers not to confuse advertising with other parts of the programme may basically be justified by overriding reasons relating to the general interest, such as consumer protection or the maintenance of a certain level of programme quality.[131] The Court thus acknowledged that restrictions on the time and timing of advertising may be justified. This will be dealt with in the next section.

ee Restrictions on the Time and Timing of Television Advertising and Teleshopping

Both the Convention and the AVMS Directive include rules for the time and timing of advertising and teleshopping, disregarding their content. These provisions from Chapter III of the Convention and Chapter VII of the Directive apply only to television broadcasting, unless it is exclusively devoted to advertising, teleshopping or self-promotion anyway,[132] but not to on-demand services.

According to Article 20(1) AVMS Directive and Article 14(1) of the Convention, television advertising or teleshopping inserted *during* programmes – that is, not *between* programmes – shall not prejudice the integrity of the programmes and

---

[128] Article 10(4) AVMS Directive and Article 18(3) of the Convention.
[129] See Chapter 3.
[130] Case C-288/89 [1991] Stichting Collectieve Antennevoorziening Gouda and others v. Commissariaat voor de Media [24]; Case C-353/89 [1991] Commission v. Netherlands [42].
[131] ECJ, Case C-288/89 [1991] Stichting Collectieve Antennevoorziening Gouda and others v. Commissariaat voor de Media [27]; Case C-353/89 [1991] Commission v. Netherlands [45]. However, since the provisions of the Dutch law at issue restricted the competition to which the Dutch public broadcasting advertising foundation STER was exposed, the Court held that the restriction in this case was not justified by overriding requirements relating to the general interest.
[132] See Article 25.

the rights of the rights-holders. Television advertising or teleshopping must not be inserted during religious services (Article 20(2) AVMS Directive and Article 14(5) of the Convention). In addition, Article 14(2) of the Convention requires, as did Article 11(2) of the Directive on Transfrontier Television, that advertising and teleshopping spots shall be inserted in programmes consisting of autonomous parts or intervals only between the parts or in the intervals. The AVMS Directive does not include such a rule anymore.

The transmission of films made for television, cinematographic works and news programmes may only be interrupted by television advertising and/or teleshopping once for each scheduled period of at least 30 minutes (Article 20(2) AVMS Directive) or 45 minutes (Article 14(3) of the Convention), respectively.[133] In addition, Article 14(4) of the Convention requires, as did the Television Without Frontiers Directive, that where programmes are interrupted by advertising or teleshopping spots, a period of at least 20 minutes should elapse between each successive advertising or teleshopping break.

In *ARD* v. *ProSieben*, the ECJ had to decide whether the calculation of the number of advertising interruptions in feature films has to be calculated according to 'the gross principle' or the 'the net principle'.[134] According to the gross principle, which had been brought forward by the commercial broadcasters as it permits a greater number of interruptions, the duration of the advertisements themselves must be included in the period of time in relation to which the permissible number of interruptions is calculated. By contrast, according to the net principle, which was supported by the public broadcaster involved in the case, only the duration of the films themselves is to be included. The ECJ decided that (now) Article 20(2) AVMS Directive is to be construed as prescribing the gross principle, but (now) Article 4 AVMS Directive allows Member States to prescribe, for television broadcasters under their jurisdiction, the net principle.[135]

There are several exceptions to the rules established by Article 20(2) AVMS Directive and Article 14(3) of the Convention. First, they both exclude series, serials and documentaries.[136] The reason for singling out these productions for special treatment is arguably that they require less sustained concentration of viewers as opposed to other films made for television.[137] In the case of *RTL*, a private broadcaster broadcast *The Revenge of Amy Fisher*, a film lasting 86 minutes, interrupting it four times with advertising. It did the same a week later during the broadcasting of *Cries in the*

---

[133] Unlike Article 11(3) of the Television Without Frontiers Directive and Article 14(3) of the Convention, Article 20 AVMS Directive allows interruptions for advertising not only for audiovisual works whose scheduled duration is more than 45 minutes.

[134] ECJ, Case C-6/98 [1999] ARD v. ProSieben.

[135] ECJ, Case C-6/98 [1999] ARD v. ProSieben [31] and [43].

[136] In addition, the Convention also excludes 'light entertainment programmes', as did Article 11(3) of the Television Without Frontiers Directive.

[137] ECJ, Case C-245/01 [2003] RTL, Opinion of Advocate-General Jacobs [51].

Forest, a film lasting 90 minutes. Both films were broadcast as part of a sequence entitled 'Dangerous Liaisons'.[138] They had the same broadcasting slot, both scripts were based on novels and they had as common themes love, passion and family relationships. Apart from that, however, they were entirely self-standing, did not share a common plot and were staged by different actors. The broadcaster RTL nonetheless argued that this sequence was a 'series' within the meaning of Article 20(2) AVMS Directive, and thus excluded from the maximum amount of advertising allowed by this provision, which it otherwise would have clearly infringed. The Court did not follow the RTL's arguments, as such an interpretation would enable a broadcaster to circumvent the rule in (now) Article 20(2).[139] Tenuous links between films based on formal criteria such as those suggested by RTL can therefore not be regarded as sufficient for the definition of the term 'series'. Instead, the concept of 'series' requires 'links of substance, that is to say, common elements that relate to the content of the films concerned', such as 'the development of the same story from one episode to another or the reappearance of one or more characters in different episodes'.[140]

As a second exception to the rules on the scheduling of advertising, the transmission of children's programmes[141] may be interrupted once for each scheduled period of at least 30 minutes only if the scheduled duration of the programme is greater than 30 minutes. Third, according to Article 26 AVMS Directive, Member States may derogate from Article 20(2) in respect of television broadcasts intended solely for their national territory, which cannot be received directly or indirectly by the public in one or more other Member States. However, Article 20 does not allow a *prohibition* by a Member State of televised advertising in the distribution sector.[142] Such a prohibition could only be based on Article 4 AVMS Directive.

The proportion of television advertising spots and teleshopping spots within a given clock hour shall not exceed 12 minutes (Article 23(1) AVMS Directive and Article 12(2) of the Convention).[143] Yet Article 23 AVMS Directive does not apply to announcements made by the broadcaster in connection with its own programmes and ancillary products directly derived from those programmes, sponsorship announcements and product placements (Article 23(2)). The term 'ancillary' refers to products intended specifically to allow the viewing public to benefit fully from, or to interact with, these programmes.[144] Furthermore, the Member States may also derogate from

---

[138] ECJ, Case C-245/01 [2003] RTL.
[139] ECJ, Case C-245/01 [2003] RTL [103].
[140] ECJ, Case C-245/01 [2003] RTL [105] and [108].
[141] Plus news and current affairs programmes, documentaries and religious programmes according to the Convention.
[142] ECJ, Case C-412/93 [1995] Leclerc-Siplec v. TF1 and M6 [36].
[143] The Convention further requires in Article 12(1) that the proportion of teleshopping spots, advertising spots and other forms of advertising, with the exception of teleshopping windows, shall not exceed 20 per cent of the daily transmission time. The transmission time for advertising spots shall not exceed 15 per cent of the daily transmission time.
[144] Recital 98.

Article 23 in respect of television broadcasts intended solely for their national territory, which cannot be received in other Member States (Article 26). Finally, under the conditions of Article 4(1) AVMS Directive, Member States may impose shorter hourly television advertising limits for pay-TV broadcasters than for free-to-air broadcasters.[145] The Court of Justice held in *Sky Italia* that this was not an unlawful discrimination, as pay-TV and free-to-air broadcasters are not in a comparable situation: while pay-TV broadcasters generate revenue from subscriptions taken out by viewers, free-to-air broadcasters do not benefit from such a direct source of financing and must finance themselves by generating income from television advertising.[146]

The legislator of the AVMS Directive abstained from regulating the insertion of spot advertising.[147] Such advertising is part of the hourly amount of admissible advertising, but otherwise broadcasters are at liberty to insert such advertising under the conditions of Article 20(1).

7 Content Regulation

Article 6 AVMS Directive, which is drafted along the lines of Article 7 of the Convention, is the central provision of the Directive regulating audiovisual content. It applies to both television broadcasting and on-demand services. Accordingly, Member States' audiovisual media services must not contain any incitement to hatred based on race, sex, religion or nationality. Similar to Article 9 AVMS Directive, Article 6 is an example of sloppy legislative workmanship. It reveals the problem that occurs when legislators protect certain victims, but thereby omit to include others. For example, Article 6 does not expressly prohibit incitement to hatred based on sexual orientation, age or disability. Is such incitement therefore allowed *argumentum e contrario*? Such an argument would even find support in the Directive itself: according to Article 9(1)(c)(ii), audiovisual commercial communication shall not include or promote any discrimination 'based on sex, racial or ethnic origin, nationality, religion or belief, disability, age or sexual orientation'. One could thus conclude that since the legislator expressly prohibited discrimination based on disability, age or sexual orientation in Article 9, but omitted these terms from Article 6, incitement to hatred based on those reasons shall *not* be prohibited. Yet there is no warrant in freedom of expression doctrine for such a result, and it also falls short of the EU's obligations under Article 10 TFEU, Article 1 and Article 7 EUChFR. The dignity and reputation of those affected by such forms of hate speech may even require the Member States to go beyond the requirements of Article 6. Unlike Recital 60 of the AVMS Directive suggests, human dignity is protected in absolute terms and cannot 'be carefully balanced with ... freedom of expression'.

---

[145] CJEU, Case C-234/12 [2013] Sky Italia [14].

[146] CJEU, Case C-234/12 [2013] Sky Italia [20]. The Court indicated that the principle of proportionality has to be observed, which was for the national court to decide.

[147] Recital 85.

Neither the Directive nor its drafting history contains any definition of what 'incitement to hatred' actually means.[148] To interpret this provision's predecessor was the task of the Court of Justice in the case of *Roj TV*, our case example. The CJEU first established that 'the scope of [now] Article 6 of the Directive must be determined by considering the usual meaning in everyday language of the terms used in that article, while also taking into account the context in which they occur and the purposes of the rules of which they are part'. As regards the words 'incitement' and 'hatred', the Court then observed 'that they refer, first, to an action intended to direct specific behaviour and, second, a feeling of animosity or rejection with regard to a group of persons'. Thus, the Directive, by using the concept 'incitement to hatred', aimed at forestalling 'any ideology which fails to respect human values, in particular initiatives which attempt to justify violence by terrorist acts against a particular group of persons'.[149] The Court found that a broadcasting programme that stirs up violent confrontations between persons of Turkish and Kurdish origin in Turkey and exacerbates the tensions between Turks and Kurds living in Germany is covered by the concept of 'incitement to hatred'. The Court did not engage in more detail with the argument of the Danish Radio and Television Board that Roj TV's programmes merely broadcast information and opinions and that the violent images broadcast reflected the real violence in Turkey and the Kurdish areas. This would have given rise to refer to the ECtHR's decision *Jersild* v. *Denmark*, our case example from Chapter 1. Recall that in *Jersild*, the Strasbourg Court decided that news reporting based on interviews constitutes one of the most important means whereby the media is able to play its vital role of 'public watchdog'. Therefore, 'the punishment of a journalist for assisting in the dissemination of statements made by another person in an interview would seriously hamper the contribution of the press to discussion of matters of public interest and should not be envisaged unless there are particularly strong reasons for doing so'.[150] Similar considerations apply to news reporting based on images. Yet in *Roj TV* there were arguably 'particularly strong reasons' for such interference, as the news was apparently presented without any attempt to counterbalance the views expressed and with the purpose of propagating militaristic and violent views.

However, the Danish broadcasting authority did not find a violation of the Danish rules implementing the Directive, presumably because the television programme did not incite to hatred in Denmark itself. The question was, therefore, whether Denmark was also under an obligation to ensure compliance of a broadcaster with (now) Article 6 AVMS Directive with regard to the programme's effect in other states.

---

[148] See also Chapter 3 on 'hate speech'.
[149] See CJEU, Joined Cases C-244/10 and C-245/10 [2011] Mesopotamia Broadcast A/S METV and Roj TV A/S [40–42].
[150] ECtHR, Jersild v. Denmark [1994] App. no. 15890/89 [35].

The Court of Justice decided that the Member State having jurisdiction has to ensure compliance Article 6 AVMS Directive,

> irrespective of the presence in that Member State of the ethnic or cultural communities concerned. The application of the prohibition laid down in Article 6 does not depend on the potential effects of the broadcast in question in the Member State of origin or in one Member State in particular, but only on the combination of the two conditions stipulated in that article, namely incitement to hatred and grounds of race, sex, religion or nationality.[151]

8 Restrictions on Exclusive Rights and Access to Content

The licensing of broadcasting rights is, in the first place, subject to the autonomy of the rights-holder. He may decide whether or not he wants to grant licences in the first place, and under which conditions. This autonomy is, under certain circumstances, restricted in order to safeguard broader public interests, particularly media pluralism. As we will see in Chapter 10, one general tool to override the refusal to permit the use of copyright-protected works is competition law. Three further instruments apply more specifically to broadcasting. First, territorially applicable exclusive rights have to be compatible with the free movement provisions. This was one of the main questions of the *Karen Murphy* decision (see subsection a below). Second, even within the same jurisdiction, if exclusive rights pertain to the broadcasting of events of high interest to the public, the AVMS Directive and the Convention ensure that the exclusivity of the broadcasting rights does not work to the detriment of media pluralism and the right of the public to be informed on such events. Article 14 AVMS Directive, which is drafted along the lines of Article 9*bis* of the Convention, thus ensures that the public has the opportunity to watch the entire event live or deferred in free-TV (see subsection b below).[152] And Article 15 AVMS Directive, which is built on Article 9 of the Convention, furnishes competing broadcasters with a right to inform the public on such events via short news reports (see subsection c below).

a Territorially Applicable Exclusive Rights

In the 1980 decision *Coditel* v. *Ciné Vog Films I*, the Court held that it is in principle compatible with the internal market for parties to agree in a contract of assignment of intellectual property rights on geographical limits for such an assignment, even if those geographical limits coincide with the frontiers of the Member States. The

---

[151] See CJEU, Joined Cases C-244/10 and C-245/10 [2011] Mesopotamia Broadcast A/S METV and Roj TV A/S [45].

[152] The notion of 'free' television does not exclude modes of funding of public service broadcasting, such as a licence fee.

parties may thus prevent television broadcasting companies from communicating a work to the public without authorisation by the rights-holder.[153]

The application – or rather, the applicability – of these principles was one of the main problems in the seminal case *Football Association Premier League Ltd and others* v. *Karen Murphy and others*, which the Court decided in 2011. The Football Association Premier League Ltd ('FAPL') holds the television broadcasting rights for Premier League football matches. Based on a tender procedure, the FAPL grants licences in respect of those broadcasting rights for live transmission on a territorial basis and for three-year terms. That territorial basis is usually national since there is only a limited demand from bidders for global or pan-European rights. In order to protect the territorial exclusivity of all broadcasters, each successful bidder obliges itself to prevent the public, by means of encryption, from receiving its broadcasts outside the area for which it holds the licence. Moreover, they have to ensure that no decoding device is knowingly authorised to enable viewing their transmissions outside the country concerned. As a result, by contrast to the *Coditel I* case, in *Karen Murphy* the broadcasters had obtained broadcasting rights from the FAPL and had paid remuneration to them.

In the UK, the licensee for live Premier League broadcasting was BSkyB. However, certain restaurants and bars used foreign decoding devices to access Premier League matches from abroad, in this case from Greece, where subscription was cheaper than BSkyB's subscription. The FAPL feared that this practice undermined the valuable exclusivity of the rights granted by licence in a given territory and hence threatened its commercial interests. It thus brought actions both against suppliers of equipment that enabled the reception of programmes of foreign broadcasters, and against operators of public houses that screened live Premier League matches by using such a foreign decoding device.

Three aspects were at the heart of this case. First, the FAPL claimed a violation of both the Conditional Access Directive because of the use of 'illicit devices' within the meaning of the Directive and Section 298 of the UK Copyright, Designs and Patents Act because of the unlawful use of an apparatus designed to circumvent conditional access technology. Second, the FAPL argued that its intellectual property rights have been breached. Third, the question arose whether the FAPL's licensing practice violated EU competition law. While the second and the third question will be the subject of Chapters 9 and 10, respectively, the first question triggered some groundbreaking responses by the Court of Justice with a view to territorial exclusive rights.

The Conditional Access Directive has as its purpose to protect broadcasting and information society services the access to which is dependent on prior authorisation by the service provider and secured by technical means ('conditional access'). Article

---

[153] ECJ, Case 62/79 [1980] Coditel and others v. Ciné Vog Films and others ('Coditel I') [16]; reiterated in CJEU, Joined Cases C-403/08 and C-429/08 [2011] Football Association Premier League Ltd and others v. Karen Murphy and others [118–119]. See Chapter 9.

4 of the Conditional Access Directive therefore prohibits various forms of use of 'illicit devices', including their distribution and possession. 'Illicit devices' are defined as 'any equipment or software designed or adapted to give access to a protected service in an intelligible form without the authorisation of the service provider' (Article 2(e) Conditional Access Directive). The Court thus had to decide, first, whether foreign decoding devices, including those used in breach of a contractual limitation, constituted 'illicit devices' within the meaning of Article 2(e) of the Conditional Access Directive. The Court decided that this was not the case: Article 2(e) of the Conditional Access Directive defines 'illicit device' as any equipment or software 'designed' or 'adapted' to give access to a protected service. The concept of an 'illicit device' is thus limited to equipment 'that has been manufactured, manipulated, adapted or readjusted', but it does not cover the mere use of foreign decoding devices, even if the use is in breach of a contractual arrangement.[154] Therefore, neither the suppliers of the equipment – although they had obtained the devices under false names and addresses and used them in breach of contractual agreements – nor the pub owners were in violation of the Conditional Access Directive. However, Section 298 of the UK Copyright, Designs and Patents Act prevents the import, sale and use of foreign decoding devices in general and is thus broader than the Conditional Access Directive. The Luxembourg Court thus had to answer the question of whether the application of this provision was precluded by the Conditional Access Directive. Under Article 3(2) of the Conditional Access Directive, Member States may not restrict the free movement of protected services and conditional access devices for reasons falling within the field coordinated by that Directive. Since the devices in the case at hand did not constitute 'illicit devices', they did not fall in the field coordinated by the Directive. Therefore, Article 3(2) of the Directive did not preclude the application of the domestic law.[155] As a result, the Court had to address the question whether the domestic prohibition on the import, sale and use of foreign decoding devices that give access to an encrypted satellite broadcasting service from another Member State was compatible with the internal market. In this case the Court applied the freedom to provide services, as the supply of the equipment was of a 'purely secondary manner'.[156] The restriction on the freedom to provide services, the Court decided, was not justified. According to the Court, the FAPL was not able to successfully claim copyright in the Premier League matches themselves, as they could not be classified as 'works' within the meaning of copyright law.[157] Particularly with a view to Article

---

[154] CJEU, Joined Cases C-403/08 and C-429/08 [2011] Football Association Premier League Ltd and others v. Karen Murphy and others [64].

[155] CJEU, Joined Cases C-403/08 and C-429/08 [2011] Football Association Premier League Ltd and others v. Karen Murphy and others [74].

[156] CJEU, Joined Cases C-403/08 and C-429/08 [2011] Football Association Premier League Ltd and others v. Karen Murphy and others [80].

[157] CJEU, Joined Cases C-403/08 and C-429/08 [2011] Football Association Premier League Ltd and others v. Karen Murphy and others [96]; see Chapter 9.

165(1) TFEU, the UK was nevertheless permitted to protect sporting events by recognising agreements concluded between the rights-holders and the broadcasters, including by affording intellectual property rights.[158] However, the Court then held that the interference with the freedom to provide services in the particular case was disproportionate. According to the Court, intellectual property law does not guarantee the opportunity to demand the *highest* possible remuneration, but only *appropriate* remuneration.[159] The absolute territorial exclusivity of the broadcasting rights has led to artificial price differences between the partitioned national markets, a fact that the Court regarded as irreconcilable with the internal market.[160] Consequently, the payment of such a premium goes beyond what is necessary to ensure appropriate remuneration for rights-holders. Therefore, the prohibition on using foreign decoding devices could not be justified for the protection of exclusive rights. Finally, the Court rather swiftly rejected the argument that the restriction on the freedom to provide services could be justified by the objective of encouraging the public to attend football stadiums.[161]

Karen Murphy was expected to have a major impact on international licensing of broadcasting rights on sporting events, particularly with a view to the pricing policy of rights-holders in sport events. When licensing broadcasting rights, they would have to take into account not only the audience in the Member State of the licensee, but also the potential audience in other Member States. It was even compared with the seminal *Bosman* decision on the transfer of football players.[162] However, it seems that *Karen Murphy* has not changed the licensing practice as significantly as initially expected. This might be due to the copyright-related questions involved in *Karen Murphy*: While football matches are as such not susceptible to copyright protection, many of the related aspects that make watching a football match on TV an actual event – opening video sequences, broadcasting anthems, various graphics, etc. – can be copyright-protected. And copyright protection is still confined to national boundaries. This will be dealt with in more detail in Chapter 9.

b 'Events of Major Importance for Society'

Article 14 AVMS Directive authorises each Member State to draw up a list of designated events, national or non-national, which it considers to be of 'major importance for society', and notify the Commission. Within a period of three months from the notification, the Commission shall 'verify' that such measures are compatible

---

[158] CJEU, Joined Cases C-403/08 and C-429/08 [2011] Football Association Premier League Ltd and others v. Karen Murphy and others [102].
[159] CJEU, Joined Cases C-403/08 and C-429/08 [2011] Football Association Premier League Ltd and others v. Karen Murphy and others [108].
[160] CJEU, Joined Cases C-403/08 and C-429/08 [2011] Football Association Premier League Ltd and others v. Karen Murphy and others [115].
[161] CJEU, Joined Cases C-403/08 and C-429/08 [2011] Football Association Premier League Ltd and others v. Karen Murphy and others [124].
[162] Hyland (2012); Wood (2012).

with EU law and communicate them to the other Member States. If the Commission decides that the list is compatible with EU law, the Member State may take measures to ensure that such events are accessible on free television. Furthermore, Member States shall ensure that broadcasters under their jurisdiction do not exercise their exclusive rights in a way that a substantial proportion of the public in *another* Member State is deprived of the possibility of following events that are designated by that other Member State as events of major importance for society. The purpose of Article 14 is thus the mutual recognition of lists of events of major importance. States must ensure that broadcasters under their jurisdiction respect the lists of other Member States that are notified to the Commission.[163]

The crucial and most controversial aspect of Article 14 is the concept of an 'event of major importance for society'.[164] Whether an event can be regarded as being of 'major importance for society' decides on whether a pay-TV provider may broadcast this event on an exclusive basis or not. It goes without saying that this has a significant impact on the value of such exclusive rights: pay-TV broadcasters have less interest in, and less willingness to pay for, 'exclusive' broadcasting rights for events that they then may not broadcast exclusively. This lowers the prices for such exclusive rights. The declaration of an event as being of 'major importance for society' thus affects not only the business model of pay-TV broadcasters themselves, but also of the event organisers who are entitled to sell the rights pertaining to those events. Ironically, such organisers therefore have an economic interest in *not* having their event being declared of major importance for society. So what is an event of major importance for society? These should 'be outstanding events which are of interest to the general public in the Union or in a given Member State or in an important component part of a given Member State'.[165] The Directive itself does not provide a harmonised list of events of major importance. Instead, the Directive is based on the idea that considerable social and cultural differences exist between the Member States as regards the importance of certain events for the general public.[166] Hence it is, in the first place, for the Member States themselves to decide what they consider as being of major importance. They enjoy broad discretion when notifying their list to the European Commission. Given this discretion, the Commission's power of review is limited to an assessment of a 'manifest error' in designating an event of major importance.[167]

The European Commission has issued guidelines to assess whether an event may be considered to be of major importance to the society in question.[168] These guidelines

---

[163] See EFTA Court, Case E-21/13 [2014] FIFA v. ESA [29].
[164] From academic literature, see Lefever et al. (2010).
[165] Recital 52.
[166] See EFTA Court, Case E-21/13 [2014] FIFA v. ESA [30].
[167] See EFTA Court, Case E-21/13 [2014] FIFA v. ESA [35].
[168] COM Working Document CC TVSF (97) 9/3, Implementation of Article 3A of Directive 89/552/EEC, as modified by Directive 97/36/EC: Evaluation of National Measures.

include four indicators to assess if an event is of major importance, the fulfilment of at least two of which suffices for including an event on the list:

1 The event and its outcome have a general resonance and are not simply significant to those who ordinarily follow the sport or activity concerned.
2 The event has a generally recognised, distinct cultural importance for the population, in particular as a catalyst of its cultural identity.
3 In the case of a sport event, the event involves the national team in the sport concerned in a major international tournament.[169]
4 It has traditionally been broadcast on free television and has commanded large television audiences.

The Directive itself names the Olympic Games, the Football World Cup and the European Football Championship as such events.[170] Other events that Member States have successfully listed include, for example: the Vienna Philharmonic Orchestra's New Year concert and the Vienna Opera Ball in Austria, the men's Ice Hockey World Championships for Finland, the San Remo music festival in Italy, the Derby in the UK or the Nations Cup at the Dublin Horse Show in Ireland.[171]

The Commission has to examine whether the listing of events notified by the Member State is in compliance with EU law, especially Article 11 EUChFR, the rules on the freedom to provide services and competition law. As a consequence, it is not sufficient that the events are of major importance for society, such as the Football World Cup or the Olympic Games. In addition, the listing itself must be clear and transparent, based on objective criteria that are known in advance by the parties concerned, it must not discriminate between undertakings established in the national territory and undertakings established in other Member States, it must be appropriate to protect the right to information and to ensure wide public access to television broadcasts of events of major importance for society and it must not go beyond what is necessary in order to achieve this objective.[172]

The 'verification' of the European Commission has the legal nature of a 'decision' according to Article 288 TFEU. As a decision, it is legally binding, it has to comply

---

[169] As a consequence, the fact that the tournament does not involve the national team does not affect the States' ability to designate the tournament as a whole as an event of major importance, if at least two other criteria are fulfilled; see, to that effect, CJEU, Case T-55/08 [2011] UEFA v. Commission [103]; EFTA Court, Case E-21/13 [2014] FIFA v. ESA [65].

[170] Recital 49; see also CJEU, Case T-385/07 [2011] FIFA v. Commission [72] and EFTA Court, Case E-21/13 [2014] FIFA v. ESA [70]: Football World Championship; CJEU, Case T-55/08 [2011] UEFA v. Commission [125]: European Football Championship.

[171] See Publication 2008/C 17/06 of the consolidated measures in accordance with Article 3a(2) of Directive 89/552/EEC on the coordination of certain provisions laid down by law, regulation or administrative action in Member States concerning the pursuit of television broadcasting activities, as amended by Directive 97/36/EC of the European Parliament and of the Council, OJ C 17/7.

[172] ECJ, Case T-33/01 [2005] Infront WM AG v. Commission [97]; Case T-385/07 [2011] FIFA v. Commission [56] and [152]; Case T-55/08 [2011] UEFA v. Commission [50] and [64]; EFTA Court, Case E-21/13 [2014] FIFA v. ESA [34].

with the rules on the adoption of decisions, especially Article 296 TFEU, and it is subject to an action for annulment under Article 263 TFEU.[173] Furthermore, the Court of Justice has decided that both undertakings that sell exclusive rights to broadcast an event that has been listed as one of 'major importance for society' and those that have acquired those rights are directly and individually concerned by the Commission's approving decision, and thus have standing within the meaning of Article 263(4) TFEU to challenge the decision.[174]

c Short News Reports

Article 15 AVMS Directive does not relate to the coverage of the full event, but to the right of competitors of exclusive rights-holders to short news reports of 'events of high interest to the public'. As a basic rule, the Member States shall ensure that for the purpose of short news reports (not exceeding 90 seconds[175]) any broadcaster established in the EU has access on a fair, reasonable and non-discriminatory basis to events that are transmitted on an exclusive basis by a broadcaster under their jurisdiction. Such short extracts may solely be used for general news programmes, not for programmes serving entertainment purposes.[176] Furthermore, they may be used in on-demand audiovisual media services only if the same programme is offered on a deferred basis by the same media service provider (Article 15(5)). This should enable media service providers to provide their news programmes in the on-demand mode after live transmission without having to omit the short extracts.[177]

Article 15 leaves the Member States two ways to implement this rule; in addition, broadcasters may conclude more detailed contracts.[178] First, Member States may allow broadcasters to freely choose short extracts from the transmitting exclusive broadcaster's signal (Article 15(3)).[179] This 'signal access' solution, which furnishes broadcasters with a claim against the exclusive rights-holder, has been implemented by most Member States. It provides a right to broadcast the short news report within the entire EU, not only in the Member State of origin.[180] In a transnational case, the country-of-origin principle applies to both the access to and the transmission of the short extracts.[181] This means that the law of the Member State where the broadcaster supplying the initial signal is established applies to the access, and the law of the

---

[173] ECJ, Case T-33/01 [2005] Infront WM AG v. Commission [111]; Case T-385/07 [2011] FIFA v. Commission [69]; EFTA Court, Case E-21/13 [2014] FIFA v. ESA [89 ff].
[174] ECJ, Case T-33/01 [2005] Infront WM AG v. Commission [111]; Case T-385/07 [2011] FIFA v. Commission [45]; Case T-55/08 [2011] UEFA v. Commission [38].
[175] Recital 55.
[176] Recital 55.
[177] Recital 57.
[178] Recital 56.
[179] If the broadcaster seeking access is established in the same Member State as an exclusive broadcaster, access shall be sought from that broadcaster, Article 15(2).
[180] Recital 55.
[181] Recital 55.

Member State where the broadcaster transmitting the short extracts is established applies to the transmission.

Second, Article 15(4) allows Member States to 'establish an equivalent system which achieves access on a fair, reasonable and non-discriminatory basis through other means'. Recital 56 mentions as such an equivalent means granting access to the venue of the events itself.[182] Yet for two reasons it is questionable whether this 'physical access' solution does indeed constitute an 'equivalent system' to signal access. First, 'signal access' is economically much more interesting for a broadcasting provider than 'physical access'. Especially small providers prefer to eschew the costs and efforts to send their own team of reporters and their equipment to the venue of an event. Hence 'physical access' contradicts the basic idea of the AVMS Directive itself, namely to promote media pluralism and wide access to information in the EU. Second, the 'physical access' alternative has a different geographical scope than the 'signal access' solution, leading to significant regulatory gaps. A claim to 'physical access' can only be enforced against a Member State if the venue of the event is located in the Member State itself. Yet a domestic broadcaster seeking to present short news reports would not have a right against any EU Member State if the event takes place outside the European Union, which is the case for most Olympic Games and Football World Championships. By contrast, under a 'signal access' regime, a broadcaster would have a right of access to the television signal against the domestic exclusive rights-holder or, in the second degree, against a rights-holder located in another EU Member State, even if the event takes place outside the EU. As a consequence, in those constellations in which one or more broadcasters in the EU have exclusive rights to broadcast an event, but the venue of the event is outside the EU, a 'physical access' solution is not equivalent to a 'signal access' solution.

The right to broadcast short news reports would be valueless if the exclusive rights-holder could levy any payment for compensation. Article 15(6) AVMS Directive thus requires that where Member States provide for compensation, it shall not exceed the additional costs directly incurred in providing access to the signal. In the 2013 case of Sky Österreich, the Court of Justice of the EU had to examine the validity of this – for the rights-holder quite disadvantageous – provision.[183] Although rights on exclusive transmission have an asset value, the Court held that such contractually acquired rights cannot confer an established legal position on a broadcaster protected by Article 17(1) EUChFR.[184] However, since Article 15 AVMS Directive curtails the contractual freedom of the holder of exclusive broadcasting rights to enter into an agreement regarding the right to make short news reports, the Court held

---

[182] This is the way Germany has chosen to implement the Directive; see Section 5 of the Interstate Treaty on Broadcasting and Telemedia. Sections 9 and 10 allow for a right to signal access only under exceptional circumstances.

[183] CJEU, Case C-283/11 [2013] Sky Österreich v. Österreichischer Rundfunk. On this decision, see Anagnostaras (2014); Hins (2014).

[184] CJEU, Case C-283/11 [2013] Sky Österreich v. Österreichischer Rundfunk [38].

that this constituted an interference with Article 16 EUChFR (freedom to conduct a business).[185] But the CJEU held that interference to be justified. Article 15 AVMS Directive puts any broadcaster in a position to be able to make short news reports and thus to inform the general public of events of high interest, irrespective of their commercial power and financial capacity. Furthermore, since short news reports on the event being exclusively retransmitted may be produced only for general news programmes, Article 15 AVMS Directive ensures 'that the extent of the interference with the freedom to conduct a business and the possible economic benefit which broadcasters might draw from making a short news report are confined within precise limits'.[186] In the light of the importance of safeguarding the right to receive information and the freedom and pluralism of the media guaranteed by Article 11 EUChFR, the CJEU thus held that the EU legislature was entitled to adopt Article 15 AVMS Directive.

9 Protection of Minors

The protection of the physical, mental and moral development of minors is an important aspect of public morality.[187] In this area, it is not possible to determine a uniform European conception, as the conceptions of morals vary from time to time and from place to place.[188] As a consequence, it is, in the first place, for the Member States to assess what they consider to be to the detriment of minors. Such an assessment, however, must not discriminate between domestic and foreign content.[189]

Nevertheless, the AVMS Directive includes several articles harmonising the protection of minors. Article 12 provides the regulatory framework for the protection of minors against harmful content in on-demand services, while Article 27 applies to television broadcasts. In addition, Directive 2011/92/EU on combating the sexual abuse and sexual exploitation of children and child pornography prohibits the dissemination of child pornography. According to Article 12 AVMS Directive, Member States shall ensure that on-demand audiovisual media services that might seriously impair the physical, mental or moral development of minors are only made available in a way that minors will not normally hear or see such services. As can be inferred from Article 27, harmful services are in particular those that involve pornography or gratuitous violence. Measures preventing minors from receiving such services may include, for example, the use of personal identification numbers (PIN codes), filtering systems or

---

[185] CJEU, Case C-283/11 [2013] Sky Österreich v. Österreichischer Rundfunk [44].
[186] CJEU, Case C-283/11 [2013] Sky Österreich v. Österreichischer Rundfunk [61–62].
[187] EFTA Court, Case E-8/97 [1998] TV 1000 Sverige AB [26]; Council of Europe, Recommendation CM/Rec(2009)5 on measures to protect children against harmful content and behaviour and to promote their active participation in the new information and communications environment; Declaration on protecting the dignity, security and privacy of children on the internet (20 February 2008).
[188] ECtHR, Handyside v. United Kingdom [1976] App. no. 5493/72 [48].
[189] EFTA Court, Case E-8/97 [1998] TV 1000 Sverige AB [26].

labelling.[190] The Recommendation on the protection of minors and human dignity and on the right of reply already recognised the importance of filtering systems and labelling. It includes a number of possible measures for the benefit of minors, such as systematically supplying users with an effective, updatable and easy-to-use filtering system when they subscribe to an access provider or equipping the access to services specifically intended for children with automatic filtering systems.[191]

By contrast to on-demand services, harmful television programmes may not only 'not be made available' to minors. Rather, according to Article 27(1), broadcasters must not *include* such programmes in the first place.[192] Moreover, the Member States shall also ensure that television broadcasts do not include any programmes that are 'likely' to impair development of minors. Unlike Articles 12 and 27(1), the mere likeliness of harm is therefore sufficient to justify suppression of such programmes. However, unlike Article 27(1) and similar to Article 12, Articles 27(2) and (3) allow television broadcasters to disseminate their programme if they select the time of the broadcast or apply technical measures in a way that minors will not normally hear or see such broadcasts. When such programmes are broadcast in unencoded form, they have to be preceded by an acoustic warning or identified by the presence of a visual symbol throughout their duration.

To summarise, the AVMS Directive provides the following system for the protection of minors:

- Television programmes that might seriously impair the development of minors must not be broadcast at all.
- On-demand services that might seriously impair the development of minors may only be made available if it is ensured that minors will not normally hear or see such services.
- Television programmes that are likely to impair the development of minors may only be broadcast if it is ensured that minors will not normally hear or see such broadcasts.
- On-demand services that are likely to impair the development of minors are not restricted at all.

10 Promotion of European Productions

European audiovisual works are important for the culture and social cohesion in European countries and for Europe in general. One kind of measure to promote

---

[190] Recital 60.
[191] Recommendation 2006/952/EC of the European Parliament and of the Council of 20 December 2006 on the protection of minors and human dignity and on the right of reply in relation to the competitiveness of the European audiovisual and on-line information services industry, L 378/72.
[192] See also EFTA Court, Case E-8/97 [1998] TV 1000 Sverige AB [27]: it is not sufficient that, through selection of the time of broadcast or technical measures, it is ensured that minors will not normally hear or see such broadcasts.

European works are national support schemes for the development of European productions. Such measures will be covered in Chapter 11. Another measure is the privileged consideration of European audiovisual works within the transmission time of broadcasters; that is, content quotas. Those quotas are enshrined in both the Convention and the AVMS Directive. In addition, due to its broader scope, the AVMS Directive also includes a provision on the promotion of European works in on-demand services.

The main purpose of such quotas, as has been indicated before, is the protection and promotion of cultural values and social cohesion in Europe, such as the fostering of minority languages. However, it should not be ignored that such quotas also distort competition between European and third-country producers. In addition, they reduce consumer choice and impede the free flow of information.[193] With a view to WTO law, they are nonetheless justified by Article IV GATT 1994.

a The Concepts of 'European Works'

Both pieces of legislation are based on similar concepts of European works, with the AVMS Directive having a broader notion of such works: Article 2(e) of the Convention defines 'European audiovisual works' as 'creative works, the production or co-production of which is controlled by European natural or legal persons'. By comparison, for the purposes of the AVMS Directive, 'European works' means works 'originating' in Member States or in European third States party to the Convention.[194] Yet, as has been shown, the inclusion of works originating in Convention States that are not Member States to the European Union is problematic under Article IV GATT 1994. But when do works 'originate' in a state? Article 1(3) AVMS Directive answers this question with a rather intricate definition:

- The works have to be mainly made with authors and workers residing in one or more of those states; and
- they are made by producers established in those states, or the production of the works is supervised and actually controlled by producers established in those States, or the contribution of co-producers of those States to the total co-production costs is preponderant and the co-production is not controlled by producers established outside those states.

The second part of this definition ensures compliance with Article IV GATT 1994, which – as has been argued before – determines the origin of the work by the origin of its producer. Yet the first part of the definition further narrows down the definition of European works by adding a 'cultural' to the economic requirement: the authors and workers involved in the production have to reside in one or more EU or Convention States.

---

[193] For a more detailed analysis, see Katsirea (2003).
[194] See Article 1(1)(n) AVMS Directive.

Moreover, works co-produced within the framework of agreements related to the audiovisual sector concluded between the EU and third countries are to be regarded as 'European works' if they fulfil the conditions defined in each of those agreements and if works originating in EU Member States are not subject to discrimination in the third country concerned (Article 1(1)(n)(iii)).

Works that are produced within the framework of bilateral co-production agreements concluded between Member States and third countries shall be deemed European works if the co-producers from the EU supply a majority share of the total cost of production and if the production is not controlled by producers established outside the Member States.[195] Lastly, EU Member States may lay down a more detailed definition of 'European works' as regards media service providers under their jurisdiction, in compliance with EU law and account being taken of the objectives of the AVMS Directive.[196] Yet such a definition also has to be in accordance with Article IV GATT 1994, otherwise it may be challenged under the WTO dispute resolution procedure.

b Promotion of European Works

With regard to the promotion of European works in television broadcasting, Article 16(1) AVMS Directive and Article 10 of the Convention almost identically require Member States to ensure that broadcasters shall reserve for European works a majority proportion of their transmission time, excluding the time allotted to news, sports events, games, advertising, teletext services and teleshopping. Yet this only applies 'where practicable and by appropriate means', which merely requires Member States' reasonable efforts rather than strict compliance.[197]

In addition, Article 17 AVMS Directive requires Member States to ensure that broadcasters reserve at least 10 per cent of their transmission time or at least 10 per cent of their programming budget for European works created by producers *who are independent of broadcasters*.[198] The relevant criteria to establish independence of producers are the ownership of the production company, the amount of programmes supplied to the same broadcaster and the ownership of secondary rights.[199] Furthermore, the Court of Justice has held that the Member States are allowed to adopt additional measures under Article 4(1) AVMS Directive to promote European, and especially domestic works, such as requiring television operators to reserve a percentage of their operating revenue for the pre-funding of European films.[200]

The fulfilment of those quotas can be difficult for certain 'new media' service providers qualifying as television broadcasters, such as near-video-on-demand service

---

[195] Article 1(4) AVMS Directive.
[196] Recital 32 AVMS Directive.
[197] Keller (2011, p. 461).
[198] Article 17 AVMS Directive; see Castendyk (2006).
[199] Recital 71 AVMS Directive.
[200] ECJ, Case C-222/07 [2009] UTECA [40].

providers. Yet the mere difficulties for a service provider to comply with the obligations under Articles 16 and 17 AVMS Directive do not preclude the application of these provisions to such a provider.[201] Only channels broadcasting entirely in a foreign language should not be covered by Articles 16 and 17 of the AVMS Directive. If such a language merely represents a part of the channel's transmission time, Articles 16 and 17 should apply to the transmission time in the European language.[202]

Cultural content obligations in 'new media' services not qualifying as television broadcasters are still subject to debate. The E-commerce Directive merely stipulates that it 'does not affect measures ... in order to promote cultural and linguistic diversity and to ensure the defence of pluralism'.[203] In accordance with the generally less strict approach to on-demand services compared with television services, Article 13(1) AVMS Directive merely requires that on-demand audiovisual media services shall 'promote, where practicable and by appropriate means, the production of and access to European works'. Hence Article 13 does not expressly require a quota for European works. To be sure, support for European works might take the form of a quota of European works in video-on-demand catalogues. Yet it may also consist of, for example, financial contributions to the production of and acquisition of rights in European works, or a certain prominence of European works in electronic programme guides.[204]

11 Accountability

According to general principles, accountability in the European broadcasting order has to distinguish between the liability of the content provider and the liability of the transmitter.[205] With regard to audiovisual media, this distinction runs along the following lines: European law provides a right of reply against broadcasters for their content, but includes no provision on liability of mere transmitters of broadcasting signals. With regard to on-demand services, it is exactly the other way round: European law does not regulate liability of content service providers, but Articles 12 to 14 E-commerce Directive are applicable to the internet service providers transmitting or hosting such content.

The European broadcasting order includes provisions on a right of reply against television broadcasters in Article 8 of the Convention and Article 28 AVMS Directive. In turn, claims other than a right of reply against television broadcasters, against on-demand services and against third parties that merely transmit audiovisual content have to be established according to domestic law. In particular, 'editorial responsibility' within the meaning of the AVMS Directive does not necessarily imply legal

---

[201] ECJ, Case C-89/04 [2005] Mediakabel v. Commissariaat voor de Media [47 ff].
[202] See Recital 72 AVMS Directive.
[203] Article 1(6) E-commerce Directive.
[204] Article 13(1)2 AVMS Directive; Recital 69 AVMS Directive.
[205] See Chapters 1 and 2.

liability under national law for the content or the services provided (Article 1(1)(c) AVMS Directive). Domestic law may, for example, stipulate that broadcasters shall be responsible for their own programmes. Unless transmitters are excluded from liability, measures may be taken against them if measures against those responsible for programme services cannot be enforced.[206]

Articles 12–14 of the E-commerce Directive apply only to information society services; that is, services provided at the individual request of a recipient. Therefore, they apply to on-demand services, but not to television broadcasting.

12 Access to Network Infrastructure and to Broadcasting Channels

Audiovisual content – more precisely, the electronic communication service that conveys the broadcasting signals – needs access to electronic communications networks, such as cable, satellite and terrestrial broadcasting networks. Communication networks thus have the character as a 'bottleneck infrastructure' for the dissemination of such content. In the EU, the regulatory framework for such access is set out in the provisions on electronic communication networks and services, especially Article 12 of the Access Directive. This Directive defines 'access' as 'the making available of facilities and/or services to another undertaking ... for the purpose of providing electronic communications services, including when they are used for the delivery of information society services or broadcast content services' (Article 2(a)). Under the regulatory framework, access to networks is at the regulatory discretion of the National Regulatory Agency; network operators 'may have to' carry certain content.[207]

However, audiovisual content is of particular importance for a pluralistic democratic society, media freedom and the right of the public to receive information. Consequently, operators of a broadcasting infrastructure may be put under an obligation to grant access for the transmission of specified radio and television broadcast channels; in short, they 'must carry' such content. The relevant provision for such 'must carry' obligations is Article 31 of the Universal Services Directive as a *lex specialis* to Article 12 Access Directive. In derogation from the regulatory framework of the Access Directive, this provision allows Member States to oblige network operators to offer different terms and conditions for the transmission of specified broadcast channels than to other undertakings seeking access.[208] Article 31 of the Universal Services Directive thus interferes with the operator's freedom to conduct a business and his right to property under Articles 16 and 17(1) EUChFR, respectively. Yet it is supposed to be justified as it aims at preserving a pluralist range of programmes

---

[206] See, for example, Section 52a(2) of the German Interstate Treaty on Broadcasting and Telemedia; see, *mutatis mutandis*, Thompson v. Australian Capital TV Ltd [1996] HCA 38; Oriental Press Group Ltd and others v. Fevaworks Solutions Ltd and others [2013] HKCFA 47 [57].

[207] See Chapter 7. See also Harrison and Woods (2007, pp. 115 ff.).

[208] See Recital 2 Access Directive.

available on television distribution networks, and ensure that all television viewers have access to a wide range of programmes.[209] This is stipulated within the regulatory framework on electronic communications itself, as Article 1(3) of the Framework Directive provides: 'This Directive as well as the Specific Directives are without prejudice to measures taken at [EU] or national level, in compliance with [EU] law, to pursue general interest objectives, in particular relating to content regulation and audiovisual policy.' Furthermore, with a view to *voluntary* agreements between network operators and undertakings seeking access, Article 31(1) limits the right of network operators to choose which channels to broadcast.[210] Article 31 of the Universal Service Directive is thus an expression of the EU's obligation to respect the Member States' culture, national and regional diversity deriving from Article 167 TFEU.

'Must carry' obligations affect market participants in two ways: Network operators are obliged to carry certain content; they 'must carry'. On the other side, broadcasters have a significant interest in receiving the status of providers whose content 'must be carried'. The guiding decisions on the imposition of 'must carry' obligations and the granting of a 'must be carried' status are *United Pan-Europe Communications Belgium SA and others* v. *Belgium and others* and *Kabel Deutschland* v. *Niedersächsische Landesmedienanstalt für privaten Rundfunk.*[211] Although *United Pan-Europe Communications* had been decided with a view to Article 49 EC Treaty (now Article 56 TFEU) and not Article 31 of the Universal Service Directive, the criteria established by the Court in this decision are still relevant for the interpretation of the latter provision. According to Article 31 of the Universal Service Directive, read together with these two decisions and with Recital 43 of the Directive, the imposition of a 'must carry' obligation on network operators and the granting of a 'must be carried' status to a particular broadcaster are based on the following requirements:

1 The infrastructure operator provides electronic communications networks used for the distribution of radio or television broadcast channels to the public.
2 A significant number of end-users use such networks as their principal means to receive radio and television broadcast channels.
3 The broadcasting channels that 'must be carried' have to be specified.
4 The imposition of a 'must carry' obligation and granting of a 'must be carried' status pursue an aim in the general interest.
5 The relevant provisions should be based on objective criteria, applied in a transparent procedure and the criteria should be known in advance.
6 They must be non-discriminatory.
7 They must not be disproportionate in relation to that objective.

---

[209] Oster (2015b, p. 82).
[210] Case C-336/07 [2008] Kabel Deutschland v. Niedersächsische Landesmedienanstalt für privaten Rundfunk [34].
[211] ECJ, Case C-250/06 [2007] United Pan-Europe Communications Belgium SA and others v. Belgium and others.

8 The imposition of 'must carry' obligations and the granting of a 'must be carried' status is subject to periodical review.

In detail: with regard to the first criterion, the infrastructure operator has to provide electronic communications networks used for the distribution of radio or television broadcast channels to the public. Electronic communications networks are defined in Article 1(a) Framework Directive. As regards the second point, the ECJ decided in *Kabel Deutschland* that the coverage of around 57 per cent of households by an analogue cable network fulfils the condition of reaching a 'significant' number of end-users.[212] Third, the ECJ also held in the *Kabel Deutschland* decision that Article 31 of the Universal Service Directive does not seek to lay down a quantitative condition by requiring that the television channels to be broadcast be 'specified'. It is sufficient that the cable operator is required to provide access to programmes broadcast terrestrially and to set aside all channels still available on its network for transmission of the selected programmes, in accordance with an order of priority established by the competent authority.[213]

Fourth, the imposition of a 'must carry' obligation and granting of a 'must be carried' status have to pursue an aim of general interest, which is to be defined by the Member States in conformity with EU law. In this context, the case law on general interest objectives in the audiovisual media can be referred to.[214] Such objectives may be, for instance, the maintenance of the pluralistic character of the television programmes available in the country or in a particular territory. However, the status of a 'must be carried' broadcaster must be strictly limited to those channels providing content that is appropriate for the purpose of attaining such an objective, and the number of channels reserved to broadcasters having that status 'must not manifestly exceed what is necessary in order to attain that objective'.[215]

The fifth criterion refers to the transparency and the procedural aspects. In particular, broadcasters must be able to determine in advance the nature and scope of the conditions to be satisfied to obtain 'must be carried' status. Mere principles and general policy objectives set out in the reasons for the national legislation are not sufficient.[216]

Sixth, the requirements on the basis of which a 'must be carried' status is awarded must be non-discriminatory. In the first place, they must not discriminate in law.

---

[212] Case C-336/07 [2008] Kabel Deutschland v. Niedersächsische Landesmedienanstalt für privaten Rundfunk [23].

[213] Case C-336/07 [2008] Kabel Deutschland v. Niedersächsische Landesmedienanstalt für privaten Rundfunk [26].

[214] See *supra* on Article 4(1) AVMS Directive.

[215] ECJ, Case C-250/06 [2007] United Pan-Europe Communications Belgium SA and others v. Belgium and others [47]; Case C-336/07 [2008] Kabel Deutschland v. Niedersächsische Landesmedienanstalt für privaten Rundfunk [42].

[216] ECJ, Case C-250/06 [2007] United Pan-Europe Communications Belgium SA and others v. Belgium and others [46].

Insofar as those requirements discriminate in fact – that is, are capable of being more easily satisfied by broadcasters established on the national territory – they must be essential for the attainment of the legitimate objective that is being pursued.[217] Yet the award of a 'must be carried' status must neither in law nor in fact be subject to a requirement of establishment on the national territory.[218]

The imposition of 'must carry' obligations on a network operator must be proportionate in relation to the legitimate objective (seventh criterion). Network operators have to be protected from unreasonable and arbitrary obligations, also with a view to the resulting economic consequences.[219] They must not be prevented from performing their obligations in conditions that are economically acceptable in the light of all their activities.[220] To prevent a disproportionate interference with the operator's property rights, Article 31(2) of the Universal Service Directive allows Member States to determine an appropriate remuneration.

If the channels on the network are insufficient to transmit all television programmes, Member States may draw up an order of priority for the allocation of the remaining channels available on the network on the basis of the applicants' contribution to the diversity of the service on that network.[221] Yet there is no such obligation.

No human rights catalogue has established a right to express oneself through a *particular* medium owned by another person, such as a broadcasting channel.[222] In addition, freedom of expression and media freedom include the right of broadcasters *not* to disseminate certain information and ideas. However, under very narrow circumstances, providers of broadcasting services may be under an obligation to grant time slots to third persons.[223] This is the case, first, with regard to the right of reply. Second, broadcasters may have to grant time slots to campaign groups or political parties in order to safeguard a high level of plurality in the media. This is the case, for example, under Section 312(a)(7) of the US Communications Act 1934. Accordingly, the FCC 'may revoke any station license or construction permit [...] for willful or repeated failure to allow reasonable access to or to permit purchase of reasonable amounts of time for the use of a broadcasting station, other than a non-commercial

---

[217] ECJ, Case C-250/06 [2007] United Pan-Europe Communications Belgium SA and others v. Belgium and others [49].

[218] ECJ, Case C-250/06 [2007] United Pan-Europe Communications Belgium SA and others v. Belgium and others [48].

[219] Case C-336/07 [2008] Kabel Deutschland v. Niedersächsische Landesmedienanstalt für privaten Rundfunk [41].

[220] Case C-336/07 [2008] Kabel Deutschland v. Niedersächsische Landesmedienanstalt für privaten Rundfunk [46].

[221] Case C-336/07 [2008] Kabel Deutschland v. Niedersächsische Landesmedienanstalt für privaten Rundfunk [51].

[222] Human Rights Committee, Hertzberg and others v. Finland [1985] Communication no. 61/1979 [10.2]; see also EComHR Tete v. France [1987] App. no. 11123/84, p. 69; Huggett v. United Kingdom [1995] App. no. 24744/94; Haider v. Austria [1995] App. no. 25060/94; ECtHR, VgT Verein gegen Tierfabriken v. Switzerland (No. 1) [2001] App. no. 24699/94 [75].

[223] These explanations are based on Oster (2015b, pp. 81–82).

educational broadcast station, by a legally qualified candidate for Federal elective office on behalf of his candidacy'.[224]

In the seminal ECtHR case *VgT Verein gegen Tierfabriken* v. *Switzerland (No. 1)*, the applicant NGO sought to broadcast a nationwide TV commercial for the protection of animals on Swiss Radio and Television Company (*Schweizerische Radio- und Fernsehgesellschaft*) programmes. The Commercial Television Company (*AG für das Werbefernsehen*, now called *Publisuisse*), a company established under Swiss private law and responsible for television advertising, refused to broadcast the commercial because of its 'clear political character'. The Court observed that the applicant association had no other means available for its purpose than the national television programmes.[225] The Court thus applied the 'bottleneck' rationale, and held that the prohibition of the applicant to broadcast the advertisement violated Article 10 ECHR.

In contrast to *VgT Verein gegen Tierfabriken (No. 1)*, the Court then refused the right of access to broadcasting in *Murphy* v. *Ireland*, where the applicants asked for the transmission of a religious advertisement.[226] This decision, however, could be regarded as an exception to the rule because of the margin of appreciation granted to the Convention States when religious concerns are at issue.[227] To be specific, in *TV Vest* v. *Norway*, the Strasbourg Court confirmed the *VgT (No. 1)* ruling when reviewing the application of a Norwegian blanket-ban on political advertising. The First Section held that the blanket-ban, as applied to the advertisement of a pensioners' political party, and the fine imposed on a broadcaster for broadcasting the advertisement, violated Article 10 ECHR. Following *VgT (No. 1)*, the Court applied a 'strict scrutiny' standard of review. The Court unanimously held that the applicant party did not belong to the 'primary targets' of the disputed prohibition, namely those that, because of their financial strength, might have obtained an unfair advantage over those with fewer resources by being able to spend more on television advertising.[228]

However, the Strasbourg Court then changed its standard of scrutiny in the case *Animal Defenders International* v. *United Kingdom*, decided in 2013. In this case, the applicant NGO submitted an advertisement for a TV broadcast describing ill-treatment of primates.[229] The Broadcast Advertising Clearance Centre concluded that the advertisement breached the Communications Act 2003, which prohibits advertisements 'directed towards a political end'. Although *TV Vest* and especially the nearly identical case *VgT* v. *Switzerland (No. 1)* would have been expected to be the guiding authorities, the majority opinion departed from the Court's previous case law on political advertising and presented a new standard for reviewing the proportionality of such blanket-bans: a distinction between 'general measures' and

---

[224] On the enforcement of this provision, see US Supreme Court, CBS, Inc. v. FCC, 453 U.S. 367 (1981).

[225] ECtHR, VgT Verein gegen Tierfabriken v. Switzerland (No. 1) [2001] App. no. 24699/94 [77].

[226] ECtHR, Murphy v. Ireland [2003] App. no. 44179/98.

[227] See Chapter 3.

[228] ECtHR, TV Vest AS & Rogaland Pensjonistparti v. Norway [2008] App. no. 21132/05 [72].

[229] ECtHR, Animal Defenders International v. United Kingdom [2013] App. no. 48876/08.

prior restraints. According to the Court, 'general measures' are rules 'which apply to pre-defined situations regardless of the individual facts of each case even if this might result in individual hard cases'.[230] The Court then laid down a three-step test to determine the proportionality of a 'general measure': (a) the legislative choices underlying the general measure, (b) the quality of the parliamentary and judicial review of the necessity of the measure and (c) the risk of abuse if a general measure is relaxed.[231] The more convincing the general justifications for the general measure are, the less importance the Court will attach to its impact in the particular case.[232] The Court then held that the

> central question as regards such measures is not, as the applicant suggested, whether less restrictive rules should have been adopted or, indeed, whether the State could prove that, without the prohibition, the legitimate aim would not be achieved. Rather the core issue is whether, in adopting the general measure and striking the balance it did, the legislature acted within the margin of appreciation afforded to it.[233]

The Court eventually concluded that the reasons brought forward by the domestic authorities justified the rejection of the applicant's advertisement.

13 Privileges Under Public Procurement Law

The award of public contracts by or on behalf of Member States' authorities has to comply with free movement provisions of the TFEU and the principles deriving therefrom, such as equal treatment, non-discrimination, mutual recognition, proportionality and transparency.[234] For public contracts above a certain value, the EU Public Procurement Directive coordinates procurement procedures to ensure that those principles are observed and public procurement is opened up to competition.[235] The Directive requires, for example, that tender proceedings are transparent and open to bidders from the entire single market on a non-discriminatory basis. In *Bayerischer Rundfunk*, the Court of Justice decided that public broadcasters are in principle also to be regarded as 'contracting authorities' within the meaning of an earlier version of the Directive, hence they would also be obliged to conduct such proceedings when awarding a contract.[236] However, the strict application of

---

[230] Animal Defenders International v. United Kingdom [2013] App. no. 48876/08 [106], with further references.

[231] Animal Defenders International v. United Kingdom [2013] App. no. 48876/08 [108].

[232] Animal Defenders International v. United Kingdom [2013] App. no. 48876/08 [109].

[233] Animal Defenders International v. United Kingdom [2013] App. no. 48876/08 [110]. Critically Animal Defenders International v. United Kingdom [2013] App. no. 48876/08, joint dissenting opinion of Judges Ziemele, Sajó, Kalaydjieva, Vučinić and De Gaetano [8]; Oster (2015b. pp. 122–123).

[234] See Recital 1 Public Procurement Directive.

[235] Directive 2014/24/EU of the European Parliament and of the Council of 26 February 2014 on public procurement and repealing Directive 2004/18/EC, OJ L 94/65.

[236] ECJ, Case C-337/06 [2007] Bayerischer Rundfunk and others v. GEWA.

that Directive to audiovisual media services would lead to inappropriate outcomes. Production contracts would have to be awarded to the economically best offer rather than to the company that would serve the interest of the particular audience. Therefore, Article 10 of the Public Procurement Directive excludes public service contracts, awarded *by* audiovisual and radio media service providers, regarding the acquisition, development, production or co-production of programme material, as well as contracts for broadcasting time or programme provision that are awarded *to* audiovisual or radio media service providers. This allows audiovisual and radio media services to take into account aspects of cultural or social significance when awarding public contracts. The exclusion does not apply to the supply of technical equipment necessary for the production, co-production and broadcasting of such programmes.[237]

14 *Commission Proposal for an Amendment of the AVMS Directive*

In May 2016, the European Commission published a proposal for a Directive amending the AVMS Directive 'in view of changing market realities'. According to the proposal, video-sharing platform services (such as YouTube) would be included in the scope of the AVMS Directive, but only with regard to the regulation of hate speech and the protection of minors (Article 1(1)(a)(aa) and Articles 28a and 28b of the proposal). These provisions would most certainly raise problems with regard to Article 15 e-commerce-Directive, which prohibits Member States from imposing a general obligation on host providers to monitor user-generated content. Moreover, under Article 14 of that Directive services are, in principle, exempt from liability for any illegal information that they host.

The rules for linear and non-linear services would to a certain extent be aligned, particularly with regard to the protection of minors, but the basic distinction between these two kinds of services would be maintained. Article 6 AVMS Directive would be aligned to the Framework Decision 2008/913/JHA on combating certain forms and expressions of racism and xenophobia and would prohibit 'any incitement to violence or hatred directed against a group of persons or a member of such a group defined by reference to sex, racial or ethnic origin, religion or belief, disability, age or sexual orientation.' A new Article 6a would oblige audiovisual media service providers to provide information to viewers about content which may impair the development of minors. The proposal furnishes broadcasters with slightly more flexibility with regard to advertising, product placement and sponsorship (Articles 11 and 23 of the proposal). A new Article 12 would replace Article 27 AVMS Directive, requiring everything that may 'impair'—and not, as under Article 27, 'seriously impair'—the development minors to be restricted on all services. The proposal for a new Article 13 imposes a European works quota requirement of 20% on on-demand service provider, and these works should be given prominence.

---

[237] Recital 23 Public Procurement Directive.

A new Article 30 would oblige Member States to designate independent national regulatory authorities, and Article 30a would codify the European Regulators Group for Audiovisual Media Services (ERGA).

The principle of minimum harmonisation would be maintained, but an amended Article 4(1) AVMS Directive would limit the issues in respect of which Member States may impose stricter rules. In turn, issues which would not be mentioned in the new Article 4(1) AVMS Directive would be subject to full harmonisation. This would include, in particular, the new rules on video-sharing platforms.

The country-of-origin principle would also be maintained, and linear and non-linear services would be aligned as far as exceptions are concerned—but different procedural rules would apply.

The proposal generally encourages the development of self- and co-regulatory codes of conduct, and the European Commission shall facilitate the development of EU-wide codes of conduct.

IV Questions

1 Assume that your client is a US company providing on-demand audiovisual media services. It wants to offer its products on the European market. Which regulatory aspects do you have to consider when advising your client on establishing a subsidiary in a Member State of the European Union? What would be the regulatory consequence of not establishing a subsidiary in the EU?

2 Recall Article 2(4) AVMS Directive, which has been elaborated on in Chapter 4. According to Article 3(2)(a) of the General Data Protection Regulation, a data controller not established in the EU will be subject to the General Data Protection Regulation as far as he processes personal data of data subjects residing in the EU, where the processing activities are related to the offering of goods or services to such data subjects. Would you recommend a similar provision for the AVMS Directive along the line that, for example, the Directive should apply to any audiovisual media services that are offered to residents of an EU Member State from a provider established in a third country?

3 Do you agree with the regulatory distinction between linear and non-linear audiovisual media services? Do you have suggestions for alternative approaches?

4 Critically evaluate the 'general measure' doctrine, as applied in *Animal Defenders International*, with a view to the principles of legality and proportionality.

V Further Reading

• J. Harrison and L. Woods, *European Broadcasting Law and Policy*, 2007
• I. Katsirea, *Public Broadcasting and European Law: A Comparative Examination of Public Service Obligations in Six Member States*, 2008

6

Internet Governance and Regulation

CASE EXAMPLE

Delfi AS is the owner of an internet news portal that publishes up to 330 news articles per day. Following the news articles, Delfi provides fields for readers' comments, the commenter's name and his or her e-mail address (optional). The comments are uploaded automatically under the article and are, as such, not edited or moderated by Delfi, which Delfi indicates in its 'Rules of comment'. However, there is a system of notice-and-take-down in place: any reader could mark a comment as insulting or inciting hatred and the comment would be removed expeditiously. Furthermore, Delfi runs a system of automatic deletion of comments that includes certain obscene words. In addition, a victim of a defamatory comment could directly notify the applicant company, in which case the comment would be removed immediately. The articles receive about 10,000 readers' comments daily, the majority posted under pseudonyms. Delfi has a notorious history of publishing defamatory and degrading readers' comments.

In January 2006, the Delfi portal published an article under the heading 'SLK Destroyed Planned Ice Road'. Ice roads are public roads over the frozen sea, which are open between the Estonian mainland and some islands in winter. The abbreviation 'SLK' stands for a shipping company providing a public ferry transport service between the mainland and certain islands. The article attracted 185 comments. About 20 of them contained personal threats and offensive language directed against L., a member of the supervisory board of SLK and a company's shareholder. Those comments included, *inter alia*: 'bloody shitheads', 'burn in your own ship, sick Jew!', 'go ahead, guys, [L.] into the oven!', 'knock this bastard down once and for all', '[L.] very much deserves [lynching], doesn't he', 'I pee into [L.'s] ear and then I also shit onto his head', and further comments of that sort. In March 2006, six weeks after the publication, L.'s lawyers requested Delfi to remove the offensive comments and claimed approximately €32,000 in compensation for non-pecuniary damage. Delfi complied immediately with the request for removal, but refused the claim for damages. Upon L.'s lawsuit, the Estonian courts awarded €320 in compensation for non-pecuniary damage.

(Based on ECtHR, Delfi AS v. Estonia [2015] App. no. 64569/09)

I Introduction

Delfi raises several important questions that help us to understand approaches to internet regulation. The internet, particularly Web 2.0, has made it possible to communicate one's thoughts to a mass audience. The internet complemented the traditional one-to-many information via the bottleneck communication infrastructures of professional media organisations with opportunity for each individual to be part of a larger public discourse. The internet has thus fulfilled a dream of mankind. But sometimes the dream turns into a nightmare: The internet does not only provide the opportunity to make sophisticated contributions to matters of public concern; it is also a tool to let off steam, to destroy people's lives by way of cyber-mobbing, defamation or divulging private information, especially because it enables the providers of obnoxious content to hide behind a shield of anonymity. Should this entail liability of those who provide the infrastructure of the internet; that is, internet network operators and internet service providers? More broadly speaking, what is the idea of the internet? Should it be a forum of liberty where everybody is entitled to say anything about anyone, or should there be restrictions? Would such restrictions amount to censorship? Is there such as thing as an 'idea of the internet' in the first place?

This chapter deals with the governance and regulation of the internet architecture and neglects the actual content being disseminated; for this purpose, Chapters 2 and 3 should be consulted. Moreover, this chapter does not deal with aspects of data protection (see Chapter 8). Finally, the ubiquity of the internet is addressed in Chapter 4 on jurisdiction. Pursuant to the general theme of this book, the chapter will focus on the internet as a medium for communication, and it will largely exclude cybercrime, such as hacking and phishing, as well as commercial aspects of the internet, such as electronic contracts, the problem of spam e-mails and online advertising.

II The Internet and the World Wide Web

Contrary to its literal meaning, 'the internet' is not one single network. Rather, it is a system of different interconnected computer networks. The internet originated as a research project of the Advanced Research Projects Agency, funded by the US Department of Defense, to build communication via computer networks in the 1960s that could withstand a nuclear first strike. This led to the internet's foundation, the Advanced Research Projects Agency Network (ARPANET), a network that, by the end of 1969, connected four host computers from universities into the initial ARPANET. More computers were subsequently added to the network, and the ARPANET grew into the internet. Early protocols of the internet were the FTP (file transfer protocol) and the SMTP (simple mail transport protocol).

Several components of the internet's early design are still key to its functioning. First, internet communication is based on packet-switching instead of circuit-switching. With the traditional circuit-switching method, networks would interconnect at the circuit level, passing individual bits on a synchronous basis between end locations.[1] By comparison, packet-switching is more efficient. The Transmission Control Protocol (TCP) breaks the information to be transmitted into data packages and internet service providers transfer the data packages to the internet backbone. Once in the network, those packages could take any route to their destination, where they would be reassembled. Most notably, only the sender and the recipient would have to take notice of the content of the information in the data packages. The network would merely have to know the IP address of the recipient and technical information about the data packages in order to recompose them.

Second, the internet is based on open architecture networking. The internet consists of multiple independent interconnected networks of various designs, such as Wireless Local Area Networks (WLAN), satellite networks and fibre optic cables. The network technology can be selected freely by a network operator.[2] Network Service Providers connect to each other to exchange data packages through Network Access Points. The hardware device that forwards data packets between computer networks is called a router. Routers forward data packages through the networks until they reach their destination node. Data packages are being sent based on a best-effort principle; that is, via the most efficient route, not because of geographical parameters. An e-mail from Amsterdam to Berlin might thus be fragmented into data packages of which one is transmitted via Frankfurt and another via New York.

Third, in order to function, the internet needs a protocol able to meet the needs of an open-architecture network environment. This protocol eventually became the Transmission Control Protocol/Internet Protocol (TCP/IP), developed by Vint Cerf and Bob Kahn in the 1970s. Four rules were essential to the TCP/IP:

1 Each distinct network would have to stand on its own and no internal changes to any such network could be required to connect it to the internet.
2 Communications would be on a best-effort basis. If a packet did not make it to the final destination, it would shortly be retransmitted from the source.
3 Black boxes would be used to connect the networks, gateways and routers. There would be no information retained about the individual flows of packets passing through the gateways and routers, thereby keeping them simple and avoiding complicated adaptation and recovery from various failure modes.
4 There would be no global control at the operations level.[3]

Fourth, the philosophy underlying the internet's design has been the end-to-end principle.[4] A network should be kept as simple as possible. By contrast to a broadcasting

---

[1] Internet Society (2012, p. 3).
[2] Internet Society (2012, p. 3).
[3] Internet Society (2012, p. 4).
[4] Saltzer et al. (1984).

network and similar to a mail delivery network, the intelligence on the internet has been placed in its ends, not in its core. This principle has also been considered in the TCP/IP. The TCP/IP is based on the principle of best-effort delivery of data packages. Since the content of the message is irrelevant for the process of its transmission, the TCP/IP is not 'aware' of the content of the message. This has an important consequence: Since the TCP/IP does not relate to the data packages' content, it does not discriminate between different forms of data, such as e-mails or a video stream. This initially 'neutral' conception of the TCP/IP still plays a role today in the debate on network neutrality.

Fifth, the internet was 'not designed for just one application, but as a general infrastructure on which new applications could be conceived'.[5] Moreover, the software implementing these protocols was open; that is, the source code for the software was freely accessible. Therefore, people can contribute to the network by adding a service application to the use of the TCP/IP protocol. The best-known examples for such applications are internet telephony (voice over IP) and the emergence of the World Wide Web.

The infrastructure of the internet consists of its hardware components and a system of protocols. The most detailed model for describing those software layers is the open systems interconnect (OSI) reference model by the International Organization for Standardization (ISO). It describes seven layers, each representing a function performed when data is transferred between cooperating applications across the network.[6] Other descriptions define three to five levels in the protocol architecture. The best-known computer networking model is the Internet Protocol Suite, commonly known as TCP/IP, named after its most important protocols. The TCP/IP model provides four layers of protocol that constitute the networking architecture of the internet.[7] For the purposes of this book, it is sufficient to visualise a simplified version of the three key environmental layers:[8]

1 The physical infrastructure layer.
2 The logical infrastructure layer.
3 The content layer.

The physical infrastructure layer consists of the network hardware, such as cables, computers and routers. The logical infrastructure layer describes the software that

---

[5] Internet Society (2012, p. 6).
[6] These are, from bottom to top: the physical layer, the data link layer, the network layer, the transport layer, the session layer, the presentation layer and the application layer.
[7] These are, from the bottom to the top: the link layer, the internet or network layer, the transport layer and the application layer.
[8] See Benkler (2000); Murray (2013, pp. 32–33).

interconnects networks, enables computers to identify and locate each other, and routes their traffic via networks. The logical infrastructure encompasses, in particular, the TCP/IP protocol, network application protocols, such as the File Transfer Protocol (FTP), the Simple Mail Transfer Protocol (SMTP), the Domain Name System (DNS), the Post Office Protocol (POP), the Hypertext Transfer Protocol (HTTP) and the Internet Message Access Protocol (IMAP). The content layer includes all materials stored, transmitted and accessed online. The content layer is essentially what is considered as 'cyberspace'. According to the *Oxford Dictionary*, Cyberspace is the '*notional* environment in which communication over computer networks occurs'.[9] Cyberspace thus describes the 'life' and experience online.

The early 1990s saw the advent of the World Wide Web, or simply the Web. Although many people use the terms 'internet' and 'World Wide Web' interchangeably, they are not identical. The World Wide Web is but one application, although arguably the best known, that people use on the internet. However, the internet provides many other services, such as e-mail and internet telephony. In 1991, CERN researchers Tim Berners-Lee and Robert Cailliau developed the HTTP, a protocol to publish and read hypertext documents across the web, and HTML (hypertext markup language), which constituted the World Wide Web. The HTTP is the main access protocol of the World Wide Web. Browser software, such as Mozilla Firefox, Microsoft's Internet Explorer and Google Chrome, and search engines, such as Google Search and Yahoo, are all built on the Web's protocols.

III Schools of Thought

This book is about ideas, not people. This also applies to this chapter. It is not about bringing *people* into schools of thought, such as 'Lawrence Lessig is a Cyberrealist'. Those who contributed a particular idea to one school of thought might even deny membership in that school, as great thinkers in general do not appreciate being labelled. Rather, this chapter is about bringing *ideas* into schools of thought. It is about schools of thought, not schools of thinkers. Thus, Lawrence Lessig's idea on the regulability of the internet, which can be summarised in his famous dictum 'Code is law', is certainly enrolled in the Cyberrealist school.

By and large, two schools of thought concerning regulation and governance of the internet can be distinguished. They shall henceforth be named 'Cyberidealism' and 'Cyberrealism'. These schools of thought largely correspond to the notions of 'Cyberlibertarianism' and 'Cyberpaternalism'[10] or the 'Cyberspace Exceptionalists' and the 'Cyberspace Unexceptionalists',[11] but it is suggested that 'idealism' and 'realism' are the best terms to grasp the epistemological premises of those approaches.

---

[9] www.oxforddictionaries.com/us/definition/american_english/cyberspace (emphasis added).
[10] Murray (2013, pp. 56, 60).
[11] Post (2008).

In 1996, the American poet, cattle rancher and former lyricist for the rock band Grateful Dead, John Perry Barlow, wrote his famous 'Declaration of the Independence of Cyberspace'. He exclaimed, *inter alia*:

> Governments of the Industrial World, you weary giants of flesh and steel, I come from Cyberspace, the new home of Mind. ... I declare the global social space we are building to be naturally independent of the tyrannies you seek to impose on us. You have no moral right to rule us nor do you possess any methods of enforcement we have true reason to fear.[12]

This brief excerpt of the Declaration of Independence for Cyberspace reflects three ideas that became core tenets of the Cyberidealist, or Cyberlibertarian, school:

1 Cyberspace is a separate place, or space: 'I declare the global social space we are building to be naturally independent of the tyrannies you seek to impose on us.'
2 As a consequence, no traditional government has the *legitimacy* to regulate cyberspace: 'You have no moral right to rule us.'
3 As a further consequence, no traditional government has the *power to enforce laws* in cyberspace: 'nor do you possess any methods of enforcement we have true reason to fear.'

The eloquent and slightly romanticised 'Declaration of Independence' drove the narrative and arguments of the Cyberidealist school.[13] External regulation of cyberspace is perceived to be not only illegitimate, but even impossible, as there is no regulatory arbiter. So where should regulation in cyberspace come from, in case we want to avoid anarchy? The answer of the Cyberidealist school is that the only legitimate form of regulation comes from within the cyberspace community itself. The application of law to cyberspace is therefore preceded by a conflict of laws between state laws and cyberspace's laws, a conflict in which the laws of cyberspace will prevail. If we look back at Chapter 4, the *Yahoo* and *Gutnick* case should, from a Cyberidealist perspective, not have been decided as a conflict between French and US jurisdiction or Australian and US jurisdiction, but between the jurisdiction of cyberspace and the jurisdiction of – in Barlow's words – 'fleshly' governments.

What are the laws of cyberspace according to the Cyberidealist school? Apart from the norms that have been, or would have been, adopted by the cyberspace community, the Cyberidealist school implicitly accepts that a certain normative framework already exists, and this is the architecture, or infrastructure, of the internet itself. As has been shown above, the internet has been constructed as an open end-to-end infrastructure with no centralised control. The Cyberidealist school elevated those technical conditions to norms, identifying them as the nature, or the 'idea', of the internet (which is why 'Cyberidealism' seems to be the proper denomination for this

---

[12] Barlow (1996).
[13] See, for example, Johnson and Post (1996).

school of thought). The internet enables anonymous behaviour, which is why the Cyberidealist school argues against identification controls. The internet enables perfect and free copies of content, which is why the Cyberidealist school argues in favour of copyright limitations online. The internet does not require centralised control of the information that is disseminated, which is why internet content is equal and free. The Cyberidealist school of thought can thus be summarised as being largely based on the following principles:

1 Cyberspace is a separate place.
2 External regulation is illegitimate.
3 External regulation is unfeasible.
4 The internet is transnational, ubiquitous, borderless, global.
5 All bits are equal.
6 The internet is free.

John Perry Barlow wrote his Declaration of Independence of Cyberspace in response to the enactment of the US Communications Decency Act 1996. The Act was an attempt by the US legislator to regulate pornographic material on the internet.[14] The Communications Decency Act represented what the Cyberidealist feared most: an intrusion of the weary giants of flesh and steel into cyberspace.

The ideas of Cyberidealism have hitherto been challenged by the school of Cyberrealism, well-represented in academic literature, by courts and legislators. Cyberrealism questions the very foundation of the Cyberidealist school, namely the assumption, or at least the fiction, that cyberspace is a separate place, naming it the 'cyberspace fallacy argument'.[15] Accordingly, it is a fallacy to say that people 'travel' to cyberspace. The individual remains physically domiciled in the 'real world', thus within the control of the jurisdiction of the place where they are. The internet is a mere means of communication. Acts 'in cyberspace' are committed by people living and present in the physical sphere, and they have an effect on other people in the physical sphere who might not even be 'in cyberspace': authors whose works are unlawfully published, celebrities who are insulted, pupils who are victims of cyber-mobbing. Since there is no separate place called cyberspace, governments are entitled to regulate those in the physical sphere who act online. Moreover, there might be separate cyberspace *communities*, such as people participating in Second Life or joining Facebook or a particular Facebook group. But in these communities, they are mostly customers, not members. However, there is no macro-community of cyberspace that could take decisions there.[16] One could also speak of many *cyberspaces* rather than one *cyberspace*.

---

[14] In Reno v. ACLU 521 U.S. 844 (1997), the US Supreme Court struck down the anti-indecency provisions of the Act.

[15] Reed (2004, pp. 1–2, 218); Goldsmith and Wu (2008); on the 'space' metaphor, see Hunter (2003); Lemley (2003, p. 521); Cohen (2007).

[16] Stein (1998).

Arguably the most powerful claim of the Cyberidealist school was its third one: it is not feasible to regulate behaviour 'in cyberspace'. This point has been taken up most powerfully by Lawrence Lessig. He developed an argument that Cyberidealists have initially employed for their side: the internet's architecture. This architecture, its hardware and software, both enables and constraints behaviour online; but this architecture is subject to change.[17] More generally, Lessig devises four interacting modalities that constrain or empower – hence, in Lessig's terms, regulate – human behaviour: norms, law, market and architecture.[18] To begin with, it is best to explain Lessig's model with an offline example (an example that Lessig has not chosen himself, but that aptly explains his model). Assume that the speed limit on a motorway is 60mph. Why would people not drive faster than 60mph? Lessig's model would explain it the following way: because they think it is dangerous, and thus morally wrong, to drive faster (norms); because they are afraid of punishment if they are caught speeding (law); or because driving faster is more costly due to the higher fuel consumption (market). But many people still drive faster than the allowed 60 mph. How can this behaviour be addressed? The above-mentioned modalities offer the instruments, such as: an advertisement campaign on the dangers of speeding and that it is wrong to endanger other road users (norms), by increasing the threat of punishment for speeding (law) or by increasing the fuel prices (market). But there is another tool: one could also change the architecture of driving to make it impossible to transgress the speed limit, for example, by building cars that cannot drive faster than 60 mph or by placing speed bumps on the road. In this case, people would be physically barred from transgressing the speed limit by the cars' or streets' architecture, just as burglars are physically barred from entering a house by a lock.

Likewise, online behaviour is regulated by social norms, by laws, by market constraints or incentives, and by the internet's architecture. The internet's architecture is its 'code'. The notion of 'code' corresponds to the logical infrastructure layer of the internet, as set out in the previous section. This code is not heaven-sent, but made by human beings. The internet is not something that has an innate character, but it is constructed by humans. Hence human beings can also change this code. Certainly, the internet is by default anonymous – but it enables locating the IP address. The TCP/IP protocol does not require identifying the content carried in data packets – but it does not exclude such applications either. The location of a user is irrelevant for access to the internet – which did not prevent Cyril Houri from developing IP address geolocation technologies.

Lessig argues that the code is part of the regulation of the internet itself, thus understanding the notion of 'regulation' rather broadly. Those who regulate the code regulate the internet. The code may be influenced by the law, but not necessarily. It

---

[17] Lessig (2006); see also Lessig (1996, 1999); Reidenberg (1998).

[18] Lessig (2006, pp. 122 ff., 234, 340 ff.). But see also the critiques of single aspects of Lessig's narrative: Post (2000) and Mayer-Schönberger (2008), both criticising Lessig's market and technological determinism.

may be, and it has often been, influenced by the commercial aims of private companies. For example, the internet's architecture in 1995 made users basically untraceable. When users switched from one website to the next, the operator of the following website could not know from which site the user came. This was unsuitable for website operators who either wanted to know where a user came from, for example, in order to provide targeted advertising, or who even needed to know the content of the previous site in order to provide their services. If Amazon were not able to trace the content of a site a user visited previously, it would simply not be possible to pay for the book one has just ordered: the payment facilities would not 'know' which books the user selected on the previous sites. Service providers' response to the untraceability of online behaviour was the programming of web cookies: a small piece of data sent from a website and stored in a user's web browser while the user is browsing that website.

Another example for the internet's changeability, and hence regulability, is CAPTCHA. CAPTCHA is an acronym for 'Completely Automated Public Turing test to tell Computers and Humans Apart'. A CAPTCHA is the blurred image consisting of a sequence of letters or digits that often appears on the screen if you want to sign up to an online service, join an e-mail list or become a member in a social network. Unlike computers, human beings are (or should be) able to decipher them, hence they have to type in the correct text in a provided field. The CAPTCHA test thus serves to distinguish human beings from machines trying to enter a system. CAPTCHA has not solved the problem how to distinguish human beings from dogs surfing the internet.[19] But at least CAPTCHA helps to distinguish between human beings and machines.

The incentive to change the code does not necessarily have to be market-caused, but it can also be legally imposed: governments may adopt laws (note: the second factor of Lessig's model of regulation) compelling ISPs, for example, to store information longer than needed for the actual transaction, to provide identification facilities, to monitor content, etc. But in any case, if the internet does not enable control over certain information or behaviour, such as a user's identity or the indecency of a website's content, it is not necessarily because it is in the internet's immutable nature. It is a mere imperfection of the internet's code. Many of those initial 'imperfections' of the internet's code have been mended over time by means of geolocation, face recognition, cookies and many more.

The internet's code, its hardware and software, is thus the means of its regulatory control. As Lessig succinctly summarised it: 'Code is law.'[20] Yet this catchphrase is often misunderstood. Lessig does not use the term 'law' in this context as law imposed by a parliament, but rather as a modularity facilitating or restricting people's

---

[19] In 1993, the magazine *New Yorker* printed a now-famous cartoon featuring two dogs: one dog, sitting on a chair in front of a computer, tells the other dog, 'On the Internet, nobody knows you're a dog.'

[20] Lessig (2006, p. 5).

behaviour. He thus distinguishes between 'West Coast code', the code of the internet developed by companies particularly from the Silicon Valley, and 'East Coast code', laws enacted by Congress in Washington, DC. Both East Coast code and West Coast code produce regulatory effects, albeit in different ways: the former legally, the latter factually. The term 'code is law' is thus better to be understood as 'code is regulation in a broader sense', or even more awkwardly, 'code has an impact on behaviour similar to, although not identical with, acts adopted by a legislator'. But 'code is law' sounds, of course, much better.

The core Cyberrealist argument is, therefore, that the internet is not unregulable. Going even further, the internet is not just regulable, but it might even be the best regulable facility in the world.[21] Somewhat ironically, Cyberrealists thus see the term 'cyberspace' closer to its etymological meaning than Cyberidealists: 'Cyberspace' is derived from 'cybernetics', a term introduced by the American mathematician and philosopher Norbert Wiener for his work on regulatory systems, their structures, constraints and possibilities. 'Cybernetics' has its origins in the Ancient Greek term κυβερνήτης, which means both steersman and governor. Hence 'cyberspace' is literally a space that is steered and governed. According to Cyberrealists, the question of cyberspace regulation is not whether or not cyberspace can be regulated. Instead, the question is *to what extent* is Cyberspace regulable – in other words, to what extent is the regulation of the code efficient? To be sure, internet-savvy users might circumvent almost any internet code. But this does not change the fact that restrictions can be imposed and will restrict many, if not most, internet users. In legal terms, regulability of the internet is thus a question of the suitability of the means chosen to achieve the regulatory aim. Yet suitability does not mean certainty. Nor is the internet *necessarily* global: code, in this case technologies of geo-blocking and geo-targeting, enables sending or receiving operators to target or avoid certain jurisdictions, thus allowing for the protection of local norms and values. True, answers to jurisdictional challenges of the internet might be difficult to find; but it is not impossible (see Chapter 4).[22]

Yet the regulability of the internet raises two further questions. First, *who* regulates the code, who are the architects of the internet? This is the question of legitimacy. The first internet architects were researchers who built the network, as described in the previous section. Now the internet architecture seems to be mainly driven by the commercial sector.[23] European governments have missed the opportunity to shape the code of the internet themselves due to the privatisation of electronic communication technologies in the 1990s, and in the US those networks had mostly been private anyway. States occasionally disrupt the stride of private internet companies

---

[21] Compare Lessig (2006, p. 310); Reed (2004, p. 2).

[22] Stein (1998, p. 1191). The continued relevance of borders, law, national governments and physical coercion is the core claim of Goldsmith and Wu's influential book (Goldsmith and Wu (2008)).

[23] Yet this is subject to controversy; see Mayer-Schönberger (2008).

by way of legislation, such as the US Communications Decency Act in 1996 or the EU E-commerce Directive in 2000, or by unfavourable court decisions, such as the CJEU's *Google Spain* judgment.[24] But John Perry Barlow was arguably wrong when he warned of intrusion of states into cyberspace. Instead, it was multinational private companies who conquered cyberspace in the first place. Even worse, the internet has shown a tendency to facilitate monopolies. To be sure, because of its architecture, the internet is decentralised. But it caused a network effect with a first-mover advantage: The value of a network grows with the number of its participants, and if someone becomes a dominant player in a network early enough, it will be very difficult for competitors to draw even. The internet has thus become very centralised by the GAAF companies (Google, Apple, Amazon and Facebook) and their unimaginable data treasures that other companies will hardly be able to catch up with. But who should control the code in the future? The commercial sector, governments, or might there be a stronger role for civil society, as is already the case on Wikipedia?

Second, *how* should the internet be regulated in substantive terms? What is the online environment we want to live in? The factual basis of the claims of the Cyberidealist school have been largely eclipsed by reality. Internet service providers are now able to discriminate between different data sets, and they wish to favour their own integrated services to products of competitors. Hence all bits might be *created* equal, but some *are* obviously preferred to others. Moreover, the Great Firewall of China and recently disclosed surveillance activities of Western intelligence agencies have shattered the dream of a free internet. One commentator spoke of the surveillance activities as the 'fourth major blow against human vanity'.[25] The reality of cyberspace also proved those wrong who thought that everything in the internet is *for* free. To be sure, many products do not require financial remuneration (now with the exception of several newspapers who recognised – some of them too late – that the 'for free' mentality of the internet infancy did not match with the costs of quality journalism). However, even those services that are available 'for free' require remuneration in the form of data.

Yet these technological, political and socio-economic developments should not conceal the prescriptive force of Cyberidealist arguments. The claim that internet service providers *should* not discriminate between data they transmit is at the heart of the debate concerning net neutrality.[26] This will be further explained in Chapter 7. The surveillance activities of intelligence services and the data-gathering of private companies will be the subject of Chapter 8 on data protection. The market power of online services will be scrutinised in Chapter 10 on competition law.

How would the Cyberidealist and the Cyberrealist school approach the *Delfi* case? Cyberidealists would argue that the Estonian courts and the European Court of

---

[24] See Chapter 8.

[25] Lobo (2014). The three (other) major blows, as established by Freud, are Copernican cosmology, Darwinian evolutionary theory and Freud's own discoveries on the role played by unconsciousness.

[26] See, for example, Berners-Lee (2006).

Human Rights lack jurisdiction to adjudicate the matter. They would also point to the risk that an assumption of jurisdiction would include, for example, L. being able to file lawsuits not just in Estonia, but in any other jurisdiction in which he is known. Taking a Cyberrealist approach to the case, it was clear at the outset that the crux of the matter was code. It was obvious that the comments violated both social norms and Estonian defamation law and that the commentators' freedom of expression lost in the balancing exercise with Article 8 ECHR.[27] Market constraints did not play any role for Delfi's commentators: the costs of publishing the comments in terms of expenditure of time and money were almost zero (by contrast to, for example, a printed and stamped letter to the editor). As far as Delfi itself was concerned, the market might even have created an incentive to allow comments in the first place, as it attracted more readers to its site. But Delfi had not posted the comments itself. So what about code? The code underlying Delfi's website allowed the Delfi users to post comments pseudonymously. To be sure, Delfi required their readers to enter their names before publishing a comment. But the code itself did not enforce compliance with this obligation; readers could also enter 'Donald Duck'. Moreover, the code enabled users to post defamatory comments. True, Delfi had a system of automatic deletion of comments that included certain obscene words, but this left the possibility to enter other defamatory terms or moderately edited terms (just as we receive spam e-mails advertising the sale of 'Via6ra'). Did Delfi's code comply with the law? Or, put in other words, can the law require Delfi to change its code to prevent or remove such speech? Was Delfi protected by Article 10 ECHR by providing the comments section in the first place, by not preventing pseudonymous comments, by not preventing or removing defamatory speech or by not monitoring the comment section?

These questions will be dealt with further below. At this stage, the *Delfi* example shows two things. First, the factors of regulation (understood in a broader sense) – norms, law, market and code – are not mutually exclusive; rather, they complement and influence each other. Second, regulation in general and regulation of cyberspace in particular should not be conceived of as a merely static, legal top-down issue. The law is but one factor of many to influence online behaviour. To be sure, the law is arguably still the most important of those factors, as it can influence the other three factors significantly. For example, the law of state aid determines whether the government may contribute to a campaign on proper behaviour online; the law of defamation (or copyright, or privacy) determines the extent to which people are deterred from violating rights of others; and finally, the law determines the extent to which legislators, adjudicators and courts may influence the code of the internet. This is why the law relating to internet service providers – those who have the power over the code, such as Delfi – is the focus of this chapter.

Nevertheless, one should not neglect the other factors that shape online behaviour, such as social norms ('netiquette'), market-driven incentives or restrictions

---

[27] See ECtHR, Delfi AS v. Estonia [2015] App. no. 64569/09 [140].

(economies of scope, economies of scale, etc.) and, in particular, non-governmentally induced changes to the code by way of self-regulation and co-regulation.[28] From the users' perspective it is in the first place irrelevant *who* changes the code; whether the industry acts on its own incentive, or whether it has been ordered to do so by the government.

IV Global Internet Governance

As the internet consists of interconnected but autonomous networks, each constituent network sets and enforces its own policies. But in order to ensure interoperability, the internet requires cooperation, coordination and common standards among the network operators and service providers. However, the internet has no centralised governance. The current governance of the internet is a curious, unprecedented hybrid of decentralised international organisational structures, informal voluntary contributions and governmental influence. While the hardware components in the internet infrastructure are subject to generally applicable property laws and specific network infrastructure regulation (see Chapter 7), the design of its software is subject to self-regulatory regimes (see subsection 1 below). Moreover, ICANN, a not-for-profit public-benefit corporation, governs the internet's Domain Name System (DNS) (see subsection 2). By contrast, despite many initiatives, organisations of public international law have thus far played hardly any role with regard to the making of hard law (see subsection 3).

1 Self-Regulating Organisations

Throughout the development of the internet, there has been a growing international community working on internet issues.[29] In 1991, Vint Cerf and Bob Kahn founded the Internet Society (ISOC), an international, non-profit organisation, setting as its mission to 'promote the open development, evolution, and use of the Internet for the benefit of all people throughout the world'. The ISOC has its headquarters in Reston, Virginia, and offices in Geneva, Switzerland, as well as several regional bureaus. Its membership today is composed of more than 145 organisations and more than 65,000 members and supporters, organised in regional chapters. Its governing body is the Board of Trustees.[30]

The aims of the ISOC are to provide leadership in internet-related standards, policy and education. The ISOC is the parental organisation of standards-settings bodies, such as the Internet Engineering Task Force (IETF). The IETF develops internet standards, in particular the architectural design that comprises the internet protocol

---

[28] For the latter, see Marsden (2011).
[29] Internet Society (2012, p. 12).
[30] www.internetsociety.org/who-we-are/board-trustees.

suite (TCP/IP). Standards are published as Request for Comments (RFC) documents on the IETF website. The internet protocol suite, for example, has been originally documented in RFC 1122 and RFC 1123. The IETF is an open standards organisation based on voluntary contributors with no formal membership or membership requirements. With regard to policy-making, the ISOC cooperates with governments, international organisations, civil society, the private sector and other parties to promote policies about the internet. For example, the ISOC has an Observer Status in the Council of Europe Consultative Committee of the Convention for the Protection of Individuals with regard to Automatic Processing of Personal Data (T-PD), as well as the Steering Committee on Media and Information Society (CDMSI). It also regularly contributes to the work of ICANN and is involved in the World Summit on the Information Society (WSIS) and Internet Governance Forum (IGF). Finally, under the heading of education, the ISOC organises training, seminars and conferences on topical internet issues.

The development of the World Wide Web has brought with it a new community. In 1994, Tim Berners-Lee, one of the developers of the Web, founded the World Wide Web Consortium (W3C). The W3C has set itself the task to develop the protocols and standards associated with the Web. It is open to all types of organisations, including commercial, educational and governmental entities, as well as individuals. As of 4 August 2015, the World Wide Web Consortium (W3C) has 387 Members.[31]

2 ICANN

The management of the internet's technological underpinning has to be distinguished from the governing of its Domain Name System (DNS). The DNS provides a mechanism for distributing host names into an internet address. In 1998, the US government adopted a White Paper calling for the establishment of a non-profit organisation charged with deciding the policy questions relating to the administration of the DNS. This policy was effected through the creation of the ICANN, headquartered in Los Angeles. ICANN is a not-for-profit public-benefit corporation under Californian law. Its tasks are based on agreements between ICANN and the US Department of Commerce. In a Memorandum of Understanding from 1998, the Department of Commerce entrusted ICANN with the administration of the DNS and the root server, which had hitherto been the US government's task.[32] After the Memorandum expired, it was followed by a Joint Project Agreement in 2006 and an Affirmation of Commitments in 2009.[33] ICANN's structure is enshrined in its Bylaws.[34] Accordingly, ICANN is governed by a Board of Directors.[35] The Board of

---

[31] www.w3.org/Consortium/Member/List.

[32] Available at www.icann.org/resources/unthemed-pages/icann-mou-1998-11-25-en.

[33] Available at www.icann.org/resources/pages/affirmation-of-commitments-2009-09-30-en.

[34] Available at www.icann.org/resources/pages/governance/bylaws-en.

[35] Article VI of the Bylaws; see www.icann.org/resources/pages/board-of-directors-2014-03-19-en.

Directors consists of 16 voting Directors and four non-voting Liaisons. The President is a voting Director *ex officio*, six Directors are selected by ICANN sub-organisations, one Director is selected by the 'At-Large Community', a community of individual internet users, and the remaining eight Directors are selected by the Nominating Committee, which mainly consists of representatives of industrial stakeholders.

ICANN has three central tasks. First, it assigns globally unique identifiers on the internet, such as IP addresses. This is mainly overseen by the Internet Assigned Numbers Authority (IANA), a department of ICANN. Second, ICANN administers the top-level domain names: the country codes (such as '.nl' for the Netherlands) and the generic top-level domains, such as '.com' or '.edu'. Third, ICANN manages the operation of the 13 root name servers via the DNS Root Server System Advisory Committee. However, the National Telecommunications and Information Administration, an agency of the US Department of Commerce, must approve all changes to the root zone file requested by ICANN.

Both ICANN's status and the exercise of its functions have been subject to criticism. ICANN's status as a private corporation under contract to the US government created controversy among other governments at the World Summit on the Information Society, particularly with a view to the NSA surveillance scandal. Moreover, the US Department of Commerce can unilaterally terminate the Memorandum of Understanding with ICANN, and thus ICANN's authority of DNS administration.[36] Other commentators take issue with ICANN's legitimacy, seeing ICANN as an independent agency outside the democratic process and not committed to any human rights standards.[37]

In March 2014, the US National Telecommunications and Information Administration (NTIA) announced its intent to transition key internet domain name functions, the IANA functions, to the global multistakeholder community. It asked ICANN to convene global stakeholders to develop a proposal to transition the current role played by NTIA in the coordination of the internet's domain name system.[38] Shortly thereafter, ICANN launched a multistakeholder process for the transition of NTIA's stewardship of the IANA functions.

3 Internet Governance at the UN Level

According to the now prevailing Cyberrealist perspective, generally applicable provisions of public international law, such as Articles 17 and 19 of the ICCPR and

---

[36] Memorandum of Understanding, Article VII.

[37] Weinberg (2000); Froomkin (2000); Lessig (2006, p. 321).

[38] www.ntia.doc.gov/press-release/2014/ntia-announces-intent-transition-key-internet-domain-name-functions.

the Optional Protocol to the Convention on the Rights of the Child on the sale of children, child prostitution and child pornography,[39] also apply to online activities. However, international organisations have thus far not played a major role in shaping hard law *specifically* applicable to the internet. In simplified terms, the core conflict among states lies in the role that governments should play within an internet regulatory framework. While the US insists on maintaining the largely private actor-driven self-governance, other countries and the EU argue in favour of a stronger role of governments in the regulation of the internet. Therefore, institutions of international organisations, especially of the United Nations, have adopted declarations and principles in great profusion, but so far no binding legal commitments. The internet is thus a highly interesting object for the study of international relations, but barely so for the study of international law.[40] The decision-making in terms of hard internet governance policy still remains with the domestic governments. Therefore, it is too early to speak of a truly supranational internet governance order.

Upon the initiative of the International Telecommunications Union, in 2001 the United Nations General Assembly adopted a resolution to hold a World Summit on the Information Society (WSIS) in two phases, the first in Geneva in 2003 and the second in Tunis in 2005.[41] In 2003, the number of participants was 11,000, representing 175 countries, and in 2005 the number of participants was more than 19,000, representing 174 countries. The objective of the Geneva phase was 'to develop and foster a clear statement of political will and take concrete steps to establish the foundations for an Information Society for all, reflecting all the different interests at stake'.[42] However, an agreement on what internet governance comprised could not be reached. In particular, the US commitment to private sector involvement collided with the desire of other governments to be more heavily involved in internet governance. WSIS thus initiated a Working Group on Internet Governance (WGIG) to clarify the issues and report before the Tunis summit.

A couple of months before the Tunis summit, the WGIG had defined internet governance as 'the development and application by Governments, the private sector and civil society, in their respective roles, of shared principles, norms, rules, decision-making procedures, and programmes that shape the evolution and use of the Internet'.[43] Moreover, the WGIG set out 13 'issues of highest priority' for the attention of the WSIS: administration of the root zone files and system, uneven distribution of interconnection costs, internet stability, security and cybercrime, spam, meaningful participation in global policy development, capacity-building, allocation of domain names, IP addressing, intellectual property rights, freedom of expression,

---

[39] Adopted and opened for signature, ratification and accession by General Assembly Resolution A/RES/54/263 of 25 May 2000, entered into force on 18 January 2002.

[40] See A. Taubman, in Edwards and Waelde (2009, p. 3).

[41] UN General Assembly, Resolution 56/183, World Summit on the Information Society.

[42] www.itu.int/net4/wsis/forum/2015/About/Background.

[43] Report of the Working Group on Internet Governance, June 2005, para. 10.

data protection and privacy rights, consumer rights and multilingualism.[44] In addition to reaching agreements on those issues of internet governance, further objectives of the Tunis phase were to put Geneva's Plan in action,[45] to agree on financing mechanisms and to follow-up and implement of the Geneva and Tunis documents.[46] The Tunis WSIS established the Internet Governance Forum, an open and inclusive multistakeholder forum about the future of internet governance.[47] Moreover, since the two phases of the WSIS, a cluster of WSIS-related events was held on an annual basis. In 2009, the cluster of WSIS-related events was rebranded as WSIS Forum. However, similar to the Geneva and the Tunis summit, the IGF and the WSIS Forum have thus far made little progress in developing policy.

Although international organisations have so far not succeeded in adopting hard policy, the conferences and fora since 2003 have at least paved the way for future global internet governance by establishing the applicable discourse mechanisms. A snap-shot moment of the summer of 2015 promises that the 'internet governance ecosystem' will be shaped by bottom-up multistakeholder processes rather than top-down governmental regulation. The most recent effort to establish a global governance framework for the internet has been the NetMundial Initiative. This initiative was proposed at the Global Multistakeholder Meeting on the Future of Internet Governance (GMMFIG) conference in April 2014 in Brazil. The meeting was attended by some 850 government officials, academics, campaigners and technical experts.[48] The conference adopted the NETmundial Multistakeholder Statement, hailed as the 'Magna Carta of internet governance'.[49] The non-binding Statement has been signed by more than 100 governments, the most influential internet companies and many actors of civil society. It provides principles of internet governance, such as the respect for human rights, protection of intermediaries, culture and linguistic diversity, internet security, open internet architecture and internet governance process principles. The latter include, in particular, a multistakeholder process, open, participative, consensus-driven governance, transparency, government accountability and inclusiveness. The Statement also provides a roadmap for the future evolution of internet governance, calling for a strengthening of the IGF, transition of the stewardship of IANA functions and a rejection of mass surveillance. The multistakeholder inaugural Coordination Council meeting of the NETmundial Initiative convened on 30 June 2015.

If Foucault was right and discourse is an instrument of power,[50] then civil society is quite powerful in shaping internet governance. Whether this power will translate into binding and enforceable rules is yet to be seen.

---

44 Report of the Working Group on Internet Governance, June 2005, paras. 15–27.
45 WSIS, Document WSIS-03/GENEVA/DOC/5-E, 12 December 2003.
46 www.itu.int/wsis/basic/about.html.
47 Paragraph 72 of the Tunis Agenda for the Information Society, Document: WSIS-05/TUNIS/DOC/6(Rev.1)-E, 18 November 2005.
48 www.bbc.com/news/technology-27108869.
49 The Statement can be found at http://netmundial.br/netmundial-multistakeholder-statement.
50 See Foucault (1978).

V The European Legal Framework

The European legal framework on internet regulation is to a lesser degree influenced by the Council of Europe. The Strasbourg Court has not yet had the opportunity to develop a coherent body of case law on this subject matter. Declarations and resolutions of the Committee of Ministers provide helpful guidance, but are not legally binding. By contrast, the EU with its E-commerce Directive has adopted one of the first pieces of internet-specific legislation worldwide. Its provisions on liability of internet intermediaries – or rather, their exemptions from liability – will be the focus of this section. Yet it will also be seen that the Directive from 2000, the era of the Web 1.0, is in need of an update.

1 Council of Europe

Apart from the generally applicable Articles 8 and 10 ECHR, the most important Council of Europe document specifically tailored to the internet is the 2001 Convention on Cybercrime.[51] The main aim of the Convention is to 'deter action directed against the confidentiality, integrity and availability of computer systems, networks and computer data as well as the misuse of such systems, networks and data by providing for the criminalisation of such conduct'. Provisions on online hate speech were moved to an additional protocol.[52] This ensured that the US became one of the non-Council of Europe signatories to the Convention. Moreover, the Council of Europe Committee of Ministers adopted a plethora of declarations and recommendations on internet governance and regulation.[53]

Furthermore, the Strasbourg Court's case law provides first insights into the Court's stance on internet technology regulation. In *Muscio* v. *Italy*, the applicant, chairman

---

[51] ETS No. 185.

[52] Additional Protocol to the Convention on Cybercrime, concerning the criminalisation of acts of a racist and xenophobic nature committed through computer systems of 28 January 2003, ETS No. 189.

[53] See, for example, Recommendation CM/Rec(2015)6 on the free, transboundary flow of information on the Internet; Recommendation CM/Rec(2012)4 on the protection of human rights with regard to social networking services; Recommendation CM/Rec(2012)3 on the protection of human rights with regard to search engines; Declaration on the protection of freedom of expression and freedom of assembly and association with regard to privately operated Internet platforms and online service providers (7 December 2011); Declaration on the protection of freedom of expression and information and freedom of assembly and association with regard to Internet domain names and name strings (21 September 2011); Declaration on Internet governance principles (21 September 2011); Recommendation CM/Rec(2011)8 on the protection and promotion of the universality, integrity and openness of the Internet; Declaration on the management of the Internet protocol address resources in the public interest (29 September 2010); Declaration on the Digital Agenda for Europe (29 September 2010); Declaration on enhanced participation of member states in Internet governance matters – Governmental Advisory Committee (GAC) of the Internet Corporation for Assigned Names and Numbers (ICANN) (26 May 2010); Recommendation CM/Rec(2008)6 on measures to promote the respect for freedom of expression and information with regard to Internet filters; Recommendation CM/Rec(2007)16 on measures to promote the public service value of the Internet; Recommendation CM/Rec(2007)11 on promoting freedom of expression and information in the new information and communications environment; Declaration on freedom of communication on the Internet (28 May 2003).

of an association of Catholic parents, had received spam e-mails of a pornographic nature. However, the domestic authorities refused to act on his complaint against persons unknown. The Court agreed the applicant that the reception of the spam e-mails constituted an interference with his right to respect for private life. However, once connected to the internet, users could not claim a right to be protected against unwanted, unsolicited communication. Many countries faced difficulties in combating the phenomenon of spam e-mails due to the lack of technical resources. Therefore, the Italian government could not be found to have violated its positive obligation to protect the applicant's Article 8 ECHR rights.[54] The inconvenience caused by spam e-mails could be reduced by installing spam filters.

The Court took a stricter stance on governments' obligation to protect against unwanted intrusion via the internet in the case of *K.U.* v. *Finland*. In this case, an unknown individual had posted an advertisement of a sexual nature about a 12-year-old boy on an internet dating site.[55] At the time the material was uploaded, Finnish law did not permit the internet service provider to be required to identify the person who had posted the advertisement. The Court held that the domestic law did not provide sufficient protection for the applicant. The Court thus found that the Finnish law did not properly balance the competing interests, as it was too strongly in favour of the confidentiality of communications to the disadvantage of the applicant's Article 8 ECHR rights. The difference between *Muscio* and *K.U.* was thus that, in the former case, the government did not have the means available to protect the applicant's private life, whereas in the latter case the Convention State actively prevented the applicant from vindicating his Article 8 ECHR rights.

In the 2012 decision *Yıldırım* v. *Turkey*, the Court then decided on the legality of an internet blockage order. The applicant published content allegedly insulting the memory of Atatürk on his website, which was hosted by 'Google Sites'. The domestic court did not only order the restriction of access to the applicant's website, but of all of Google's sites. According to the court, this was the only means of blocking the offending website, as its owner did not have a server certificate and lived abroad. The measure was to remain in place until a decision was given on the merits or the illegal content of the site hosted by Google Sites was removed. As the act on which the Turkish court based its decision did not satisfy the 'foreseeability' requirement[56] and did not afford the applicant the degree of protection to which he was entitled by the rule of law in a democratic society, the Court found that the interference was not 'prescribed by law' within the meaning of Article 10(2) ECHR.[57]

---

[54] ECtHR, Muscio v. Italy [2007] App. no. 31358/03.
[55] ECtHR, K.U. v. Finland [2008] App. no. 2872/02.
[56] On the requirement of 'foreseeability', see ECtHR, Sunday Times v. United Kingdom (No. 1) [1979] App. no. 6538/74 [49]; Hashman and Harrup v. United Kingdom [1999] App. no. 25594/94 [41]; Glas Nadezhda EOOD and Elenkov v. Bulgaria [2007] App. no. 14134/02 [45]; Sanoma Uitgevers B.V. v. Netherlands [2010] App. no. 38224/03 [81].
[57] ECtHR, Yıldırım v. Turkey [2012] App. no. 3111/10 [67].

Therefore, the Court did not deal with the legality of blocking access to websites in principle. This was done by Judge Pinto de Albuquerque in his Concurring Opinion. Referring to documents adopted by the Committee of Ministers and previous case law of the Strasbourg Court on online speech, the judge established minimum criteria for Convention-compatible legislation on internet blocking measures. These can be summarised as follows:[58]

1 A definition of the categories of persons and institutions liable to have their publications blocked, such as national or foreign owners of illegal content, websites or platforms, users of these sites or platforms and persons providing hyperlinks to illegal sites or platforms which have endorsed them;
2 a definition of the categories of blocking orders, such as blocking of entire websites, IP addresses, ports, network protocols or types of use, like social networking;
3 a definition of the authorities competent to issue a reasoned blocking order;
4 a procedure to be followed for the issuance of that order, including notification of the blocking order and the grounds for it to the person or institution affected;
5 a judicial appeal procedure against the blocking order.
6 a provision on the territorial ambit of the blocking order, which may have region-wide, nationwide or even worldwide effect;
7 a limit on the duration of the blocking order; and
8 observance of the principle of proportionality.

In any case, the judge argued, blocking access to the internet, or parts of the internet, indiscriminately and for whole populations or segments of the public can never be justified.

2 The European Union

In the EU, the E-commerce Directive[59] lays down the framework to cover legal aspects of electronic commerce in the internal market. The objective of the Directive is to ensure the free movement of information society services between Member States.[60] Yet the Directive only provides minimum harmonisation. It encourages the Member States to take into account the various social and cultural implications of the information society.[61] In particular, it does not prevent the Member States from adopting measures 'to achieve social, cultural and democratic goals taking into account their linguistic diversity, national and regional specificities as well as their cultural

---

[58] See ECtHR, Yıldırım v. Turkey [2012] App. no. 3111/10, Concurring Opinion by Judge Pinto de Albuquerque (footnotes and redundancies omitted).
[59] Directive 2000/31/EC of the European Parliament and of the Council of 8 June 2000 on certain legal aspects of information society services, in particular electronic commerce, in the Internal Market ('Directive on electronic commerce'), OJ L 178/1.
[60] Recital 8 E-commerce Directive.
[61] Recital 63 E-commerce Directive.

heritage'.[62] However, it is controversial whether Articles 12–14 on liability privileges of internet intermediaries provide full harmonisation, or whether the Member States may derogate from those provisions to the advantage of such intermediaries.

a Scope

According to its Article 1(2), the E-commerce Directive approximates certain national provisions on information society services, the establishment of service providers, commercial communications, electronic contracts, the liability of intermediaries, codes of conduct, out-of-court dispute settlements, court actions and cooperation between Member States. The Directive thus regulates providers – both natural and legal persons – of information society services established on the territory of an EU Member State (Article 3(1) E-commerce Directive). In turn, domestic law remains fully applicable to the regulation of services from service providers established in a third country.[63]

'Information society services' are, according to Article 2(a) E-commerce Directive, services within the meaning of the former Article 1(2) of Directive 98/34/EC (now Article 1(1)(b) of the codifying Directive 2015/1535).[64] This definition covers:

- any service normally provided for remuneration;
- at a distance;
- by electronic means; and
- at the individual request of a recipient of a service.

aa 'Service Normally Provided for Remuneration'   The concept of a 'service normally provided for remuneration' reflects the notion of 'service' within the meaning of Article 56 TFEU. In accordance with the Treaty, a 'service' within the meaning of the E-commerce Directive is thus an economic activity. The remuneration for the service does not necessarily have to be provided by the recipient of the service. It is sufficient if the service providers are remunerated by those offering online information or commercial communications, such as advertisements posted on a website.[65]

'Information society services' thus include, for example: online bookstores, news websites, online social networks, search engines, online intermediary services, such as services consisting of the transmission of information via a communication network, or hosting services. By contrast, the delivery of goods is not covered by the Directive, as this activity would not be regarded as a 'service'; under EU primary law,

---

[62] Recital 63 E-commerce Directive.
[63] Recital 58 E-commerce Directive.
[64] Directive (EU) 2015/1535 of the European Parliament and of the Council of 9 September 2015 laying down a procedure for the provision of information in the field of technical regulations and of rules on Information Society services (codification), OJ L 241/1.
[65] Recital 18 E-commerce Directive; CJEU, Case C-291/13 [2014] Papasavvas [30]; compare ECJ, Case 352/85 [1988] Bond van Adverteerders v. Netherlands [16].

it would fall under the free movement of goods. The use of e-mail services by natural persons acting outside their trade, business or profession is not an information society service, as it would lack the economic dimension required by the notion of 'services'.[66]

bb 'At a Distance'   The services have to be provided at a distance. 'At a distance' means that the service is provided without the parties being simultaneously present (Article 1(1)(b)(i) of Directive 2015/1535).

cc 'By Electronic Means'   'By electronic means' means that 'the service is sent initially and received at its destination by means of electronic equipment for the processing (including digital compression) and storage of data, and entirely transmitted, conveyed and received by wire, by radio, by optical means or by other electromagnetic means' (Article 1(1)(b)(ii) of Directive 2015/1535).

dd 'At the Individual Request'   The service has to be provided 'at the individual request of a recipient' of that service. The requirement of the 'individual request' distinguishes information society services from radio and television broadcasting services. As has been shown in Chapter 5, television broadcasting is a media for simultaneous viewing of programmes on the basis of a programme schedule. Yet these 'linear audiovisual media services' have to be distinguished from 'non-linear audiovisual media services', which can be watched at the moment chosen by the user. These 'on-demand services' are therefore covered by both the AVMS Directive and the E-commerce Directive.

A 'recipient of the service' is any natural or legal person who uses an information society service, in particular for the purposes of seeking information or making it accessible (Article 2(d) E-commerce Directive). The notion of 'recipient of a service' within the meaning of the E-commerce Directive is thus not identical with the concept of 'recipients of information' within the meaning of communication theory. According to Article 2(d) of the E-commerce Directive, a recipient of an information society service is a person who uses an information society service, in particular for the purposes of seeking information *or making it accessible*. A recipient of an information society service can thus be either a recipient of information or a content provider using an information society service.

ee Relationship to Other Provisions   According to Article 1(5), the Directive excludes from its scope:

- the field of taxation;
- questions relating to agreements or practices governed by cartel law;

---

[66] Recital 18 E-commerce Directive.

- the activities of notaries or equivalent professions to the extent that they involve a direct and specific connection with the exercise of public authority;
- the representation of a client and defence of his interests before the courts; and
- gambling activities that involve wagering a stake with monetary value in games of chance, including lotteries and betting transactions. This does not cover promotional competitions or games encouraging the sale of goods or services and where payments serve only to acquire the promoted goods or services.[67]

However, questions relating protection of individuals with regard to the processing of personal data, the free movement of personal data between Member States and the confidentiality of communications, which are covered by Directive 95/46/EC and (now) Directive 2002/58/EC (see Chapter 8), remain fully applicable to information society services (Article 1(5)(b) E-commerce Directive).[68] Moreover, the E-commerce Directive applies in parallel to EU legislation on consumer protection and tobacco advertising.

b Country-of-Origin Principle

According to Article 3(1) E-commerce Directive, each Member State shall ensure that the information society services provided by a service provider established on its territory comply with the national provisions applicable in the Member State in question, which fall within the field coordinated by the Directive. In turn, Member States may not, for reasons falling within the coordinated field, restrict the freedom to provide information society services from another Member State (Article 3(2) E-commerce Directive). This includes restrictions both of a public law – including criminal law – and private law nature.[69] However, the Directive provides two exceptions to the country-of-origin principle. First, it does not apply to the fields referred to in the annex to the E-commerce Directive, including copyright. Second, Member States may derogate from the country-of-origin principle under the conditions provided by Article 3(4) e-commerce-Directive. The derogating measures have to be:

- necessary for one of the objectives mentioned in more detail Article 3(4): public policy, the protection of public health, public security and the protection of consumers;
- taken against a given information society service that prejudices at least one of those objectives or that presents a serious and grave risk of prejudice to those objectives; and
- in accordance with the principle of proportionality.

---

[67] Recital 16 of the E-commerce Directive.
[68] See ECJ, Case C-275/06 [2008] Promusicae v. Telefónica de España SAU [57].
[69] Recital 25 E-commerce Directive; CJEU, Joined Cases C-509/09 and C-161/10 [2011] eDate Advertising GmbH and Olivier Martinez and Robert Martinez [58].

Article 3(4) E-commerce Directive thus codifies the ECJ's case law on the principle of mutual recognition under EU primary law, especially the 'mandatory requirements' doctrine established in *Cassis de Dijon*.

Moreover, before taking the restricting measures, the Member State has to unavailingly ask the Member State of origin to take adequate measures and undertake to notify the Commission as well as the Member State of origin of its intention to take such measures. However, this procedural requirement does not apply to court proceedings, including preliminary proceedings and acts carried out in the framework of a criminal investigation. Furthermore, Member States may, in the case of urgency, derogate from these procedural requirements. Where this is the case, the measures shall be notified in the shortest possible time to the Commission and to the Member State of origin, indicating the reasons for which the receiving Member State considers that there is urgency (Article 3(5) E-commerce Directive).

Since the E-commerce Directive provides only minimum harmonisation, Member States may in principle impose stricter rules than those stipulated in the Directive, provided that these are compatible with EU law, especially Article 11 EUChFR. However, unlike Article 4(2) of the AVMS Directive, the E-commerce Directive does not provide a rule on the circumvention of stricter domestic legislation. Yet the ECJ's case law on circumvention nevertheless applies, as is clarified in Recital 57 of the E-commerce Directive.

It has long been controversial whether the country-of-origin principle in Article 3(2) E-commerce Directive provides a private international law rule. Article 1(4) E-commerce Directive expressly provides that the Directive 'does not establish additional rules on private international law nor does it deal with the jurisdiction of Courts'. Recital 23 E-commerce Directive underlines that the Directive 'neither aims to establish additional rules on private international law relating to conflicts of law nor does it deal with the jurisdiction of Courts; provisions of the applicable law designated by rules of private international law must not restrict the freedom to provide information society services as established in this Directive'. In *Martinez and eDate Advertising*, the CJEU had to decide, *inter alia*, whether Articles 3(1) and (2) of the E-commerce Directive have a conflict-of-laws character or whether they operate at the level of the substantive law. If they have a conflict of laws character, they would require the exclusive application of the law applicable in the country of origin. Articles 3(1) and (2) would then constitute a *lex specialis* to the provisions of the Rome II Regulation, something that Article 27 of that Regulation allows. If Articles 3(1) and (2) E-commerce Directive operate at a substantive law level, the applicable conflict of laws rule would first have to determine the applicable law. If the applicable substantive law is not identical with the law of the country of origin, the outcome of the application of that law would have to be altered and reduced to the legal requirements governing the country of origin. Recall that in *eDate Advertising* an Austrian website had published the names of two men convicted of the murder of a German actor, which was at this time presumed to be illegal in Germany but allowed in Austria. Had the Luxembourg Court decided that Articles 3(1) and (2) of the E-commerce Directive have a conflict-of-laws character, the German court would – in the absence of an exception under Article 3(4) E-commerce Directive – have had to apply Austrian law to the case.[70] If the CJEU decided that the country-of-origin principle operates as a corrective at a substantive law level, the German court would first have to apply German private international law in order to determine the applicable law, as Article 1(2)(g) of the Rome II Regulation excludes violations of personality rights from its scope. Under German law, the claimants in this case could choose between the application of German law and of Austrian law.[71] If the claimants chose the application of Austrian law, then the German court would have to decide the case based on Austrian law. If, however, the claimants chose the application of German law, then the Federal Court would have to apply German law but in compliance with the requirements of Austrian law. So if German law prohibited the publication of the men's names, but Austrian law allowed it, then German law would have to be applied in compliance with Austrian law.

The CJEU decided solomonically that Article 3 of the E-commerce Directive 'does *not require* transposition in the form of a specific conflict-of-laws rule'.[72] This is a broader reading of Article 3 than Article 1(4) E-commerce Directive actually suggests. Article 1(4) provides that the Directive 'does not *establish* additional rules on private international law'. Yet the Court of Justice clarified that the Directive does not *prohibit* such an implementation either. It is therefore left to the Member States to decide whether they either implement Article 3(1) and (2) E-commerce Directive as a conflict-of-laws rule leading to the application of the country-of-origin laws,[73] or whether they maintain the application of their domestic private international law, but apply their domestic substantive law in accordance with the law of the country-of-origin. What is important is that the substantive outcome of the case must not lead to the information society service provider being subject to stricter substantive rules in the receiving Member State than in the state in which they are established.[74] On a side note, the decision of the Court of Justice can be transferred to the AVMS Directive, which also provides a country-of-origin rule in Article 3. This provision can, for the purposes of private law, thus be implemented as a conflict-of-laws rule as well as a correction on substantive law level.

---

[70] Remember from Chapter 4 that the application of foreign law by a domestic court is not an unusual outcome of a conflict-of-laws rule.

[71] See Article 40 of the Introductory Code to the German Civil Law Code.

[72] CJEU, Joined Cases C-509/09 and C-161/10 [2011] eDate Advertising GmbH and Olivier Martinez and Robert Martinez [63] (emphasis added).

[73] This is the case, for example, in Austria.

[74] CJEU, Joined Cases C-509/09 and C-161/10 [2011] eDate Advertising GmbH and Olivier Martinez and Robert Martinez [66].

To conclude the *eDate* case: upon this response of the Court of Justice, the German Federal Court of Justice applied German private international law, came to the application of German law and already found in favour of the claimant based on German law. Hence, it was not necessary to apply German law in compliance with Austrian law.

c Taking Up an Activity as an Information Society Service Provider

Pursuant to Article 4 E-commerce Directive, the taking up and pursuit of the activity of an information society service provider may basically not be made subject to prior authorisation or any other requirement having equivalent effect. However, an information society service provider shall render easily, directly and permanently accessible to the recipients of the service and competent authorities certain information set out in Article 5 E-commerce Directive, such as his name, address, e-mail address and the trade register in which the service provider is entered and his registration number.

d Commercial Communication

Similar to the AVMS Directive, the E-commerce Directive provides a regulatory regime for commercial communication. This encompasses 'any form of communication designed to promote, directly or indirectly, the goods, services or image of a company, organisation or person pursuing a commercial, industrial or craft activity or exercising a regulated profession', such as discounts, promotional offers and promotional competitions or games (Article 2(f) and Recital 29). Different from the AVMS Directive, the regulatory regime of the E-commerce Directive on commercial communications essentially consists of transparency requirements. In addition to other information requirements established by EU law, commercial communications that are part of, or constitute, an information society service must comply as a minimum with the following conditions:

1 The commercial communication shall be clearly identifiable as such;
2 the person on whose behalf the commercial communication is made shall be clearly identifiable;
3 permitted promotional offers shall be clearly identifiable as such, and the conditions that are to be met to qualify for them shall be easily accessible and be presented clearly and unambiguously; and
4 permitted promotional competitions or games shall be clearly identifiable as such, and the conditions for participation shall be easily accessible and be presented clearly and unambiguously.

e Liability of Internet Intermediaries

The liability of internet intermediaries seems to be built on a paradox. On the one hand, the internet has led to a process called disintermediation: digitalised products such as electronic books, music, films and newspapers are delivered directly from the producer to the consumer. Intermediaries or 'middlemen', such as booksellers, newspaper vendors or music stores, are removed from the supply chain. Those human intermediaries play a significant role in the offline communication process, as they distribute the tangible goods that encode the information, such as books, CDs, DVDs or newspapers. However, at least in democratic societies where the publishing process is usually transparent and the source of information is known, those middlemen have rarely been subject to litigation or regulatory action, because it has mostly been possible to get hold of the content providers themselves. Section 1 of the UK Defamation Act 1996 even excludes speech intermediaries expressly from defamation claims, as does Section 90 of the UK Postal Services Act 2000 for postal services.

On the other hand, in order to function properly, the internet itself is based on a system of intermediaries who disseminate the information from one user to the other by providing transmission or host services. Although they are more automatically than consciously involved in the communication processes, they have often been subject to litigation: as it has proven to be difficult to establish the identity of the content providers themselves in the global and often anonymous net, internet intermediaries are convenient tactical targets for claimants in, for example, defamation or copyright lawsuits. The disintermediation of online transactions has thus led to an increased legal risk for the communication intermediaries.

Legislators in both the US and Europe have not only recognised the importance of internet service providers for the communication process on the internet, but also the chilling effect of lawsuits against them. In the US, Section 230(c)(1) of the Communications Decency Act 1996 exempts ISPs from defamation actions.[75] Title II of the Digital Millennium Copyright Act 1998, the Online Copyright Infringement Liability Limitation Act (OCILLA), exempts online service providers and access providers from copyright infringement liability for third-party content if they comply with a notice-and-take-down procedure.

By contrast to the fragmented US regime that distinguishes between defamation and copyright infringements, the EU has chosen to adopt Articles 12–14 of the E-commerce Directive as cross-section 'filters' or 'layers' preceding all claims against internet society service providers, such as defamation, copyright infringements, administrative regulation and criminal prosecution. Yet the EU has decided in favour of a gradual model similar to OCILLA and not a full exclusion from liability like Section 230(c)(1) of the Communications Decency Act 1996. In the realm of the ECHR and EUChFR, such a sweeping immunity for internet intermediaries would fail to achieve a proper balance between the conflicting rights and interests (see Chapter 3). Note, however, that Articles 12–14 of the E-commerce Directive do not constitute a basis for a legal claim against an internet intermediary. Any such claim

---

[75] See Zeran v. America Online (AOL), Inc., 129 F3d 327 (4th Cir. 1997); Blumenthal v Drudge 992 F. Supp. 44, 49–53 (D.D.C. 1998); Barnes v. Yahoo! Inc., 570 F.3d 1096 (9th Cir. 2009).

would have to pass scrutiny under Articles 12–14 *in addition* to the requirements for such a claim under domestic or international law.

aa Applicability   Articles 12–14 of the E-commerce Directive apply only to actions of dissemination via the internet rather than creation: mere conduit (Article 12), caching (Article 13) and hosting (Article 14).[76] The exemptions from liability only cover cases in which

> the activity of the information society service provider is limited to the technical process of operating and giving access to a communication network over which information made available by third parties is transmitted or temporarily stored, for the sole purpose of making the transmission more efficient; this activity is of a mere technical, automatic and passive nature, which implies that the information society service provider has neither knowledge of nor control over the information which is transmitted or stored.[77]

In turn, an ISP is thus not to be considered a mere intermediary under the law if at least one of the following questions can be answered in the affirmative: Did the ISP

- provide own content or adopt third-party content;
- exercise editorial control over third-party content; or
- play an active role of such a kind as to give it knowledge of, or control over, the data stored or transmitted?[78]

(1) Provision of Own Content or Adoption of Third-Party Content   The distinction between content providers and mere intermediaries has already been explained in Chapter 1. The question of whether own content is being provided or third-party content is being adopted depends not on the intention of the ISP, but on the perception of an ordinary reasonable person.[79] Consequently, a newspaper publishing company that posts an online version of a newspaper on its website cannot be considered to be an 'intermediary service provider' within the meaning of Articles 12 to 14 of the E-commerce Directive.[80]

The E-commerce Directive was adopted in 2000. Hence Articles 12–14 of the Directive do not cover recent forms of internet service, such as news aggregators, and the enhanced functions of search engines. Therefore, it is left to courts and legal scholarship to accommodate those services within the system of intermediary immunity.[81] The question of whether communication intermediaries are to be perceived as content providers has become particularly relevant with regard to automatically

---

[76] McEvedy (2013).
[77] Recital 42 of the E-commerce Directive.
[78] Compare Oster (2015a, p. 358).
[79] Oster (2015a, p. 358).
[80] CJEU, Case C-291/13 [2014] Papasavvas [45].
[81] On the free speech protection of search engines, see Volokh and Falk (2012); on Google's liability for autocomplete suggestions, see Coors (2013).

generated content, such as terms suggested by a search engine's autocomplete function.[82] Search engines are 'location tool services' and 'tools allowing for search of data' within the meaning of Article 21(2) and Recital 18 E-commerce Directive, and thus information society services. Since automatically generated terms are based on an algorithm instead of human activity, one could argue that such content is not provided as the operator's own content. On the other hand, all automatically generated content requires a human being to program the algorithm, which then generates the terms. As with all communication on the internet, a search engine's algorithm is based on code. The software engineer – or the company he works for – is the architect of that code. Since the code generates the information, there is good reason to argue that the architect has to be regarded as the information source within the communication process, and hence as the content provider of the automatically generated terms.[83]

By contrast, the publication of snippets of internet forum material by a search engine cannot be seen as the search engine's own publication. In this case, it is apparent from the perception of an ordinary, reasonable person that the search engine merely repeats the website operator's content.[84] Certainly, search engines are more than mere publication facilitators of the content providers. As the CJEU emphasised in its *Google Spain* decision, 'the activity of a search engine can be distinguished from and is additional to that carried out by publishers of websites'.[85] But this does not change the fact that search engine operators may avail themselves of the defences provided in Articles 12–14. In addition, the liability of a search engine operator for unlawful content has to be distinguished from its responsibility as a 'controller' processing personal data, as the CJEU established in the *Google Spain* decision (see Chapter 8).

(2) Editorial Control Over Third-Party Statements As has been indicated in Chapter 1, an intermediary goes beyond mere dissemination if he exercises editorial control over the information concerned. This is also reflected in Articles 12(1) (c) and 13(1)(a) of the E-commerce Directive, which state that the service provider is not liable for the information transmitted or temporarily stored, respectively, provided that he does not modify the information. However, online platforms for user-generated content assume editorial control if they modify third-party content, even if this modification has been made in good faith. By modifying third-party content, the activity of the communication intermediary is not limited to the process of mere dissemination of information.[86]

---

[82] See Cour de Cassation, Case no 11-20358 [2013] SNEP; German Federal Court of Justice, Case no. VI ZR 269/12 [2013] 'Google's autocomplete function'.

[83] See Oster (2015a, p. 359).

[84] Oster (2015a, p. 359).

[85] CJEU, Case C-131/12 [2014] Google Spain SL v. AEPD and others [35]. See, by contrast, WP29, Opinion 1/2008 on data protection issues related to search engines, p. 5, which regards search engines as content providers.

[86] Oster (2015a, p. 361).

(3) Absence of an 'Active Role' Although he has neither created nor modified the text, an internet service provider is to be treated like a content provider if he initiates the publication of the information. This rule is codified for access providers in Articles 12(1)(a) and (b) of the E-commerce Directive. Accordingly, the service provider is not liable for the information transmitted only if he does not initiate the transmission or select the receiver of the transmission. The latter is essentially the same as initiation of transmission, because by selecting the receiver of the transmission, the intermediary triggers a new communication process.

In its *Google France* v. *Louis Vuitton* decision, the Court of Justice adopted a similar rule for host providers within the meaning of Article 14 E-commerce Directive. Accordingly, a host providing service – in this case the Google AdWords referencing service – is to be exempted from the privileges of Article 14 E-commerce Directive if the service provider has 'played an active role of such a kind as to give it knowledge of, or control over, the data stored'.[87] In turn, the host provider enjoys the privilege of Article 14 if his role was neutral in the sense that its conduct is merely technical, automatic and passive, pointing to a lack of knowledge or control of the data that it stores.[88] The provider is not deprived of the exemptions from liability merely because the service is subject to payment, the provider sets the payment terms or it provides general information to its clients.[89] By contrast, it is relevant which role the provider played in the drafting of a commercial message that accompanies an advertising link or in the establishment or selection of keywords.[90]

In *L'Oréal and others* v. *eBay and others*, the CJEU applied that test to the operator of an online marketplace on which transactions infringing intellectual property rights were carried out. That the operator stored offers for sale on its server, set the terms of its service, was remunerated for that service and provided general information to its customers did not deprive him of the exemptions from liability provided for in Article 14. However, if the operator 'has provided assistance which entails, in particular, optimising the presentation of the offers for sale in question or promoting those offers, it must be considered not to have taken a neutral position between the customer-seller concerned and potential buyers'. Instead, it has 'played an active role of such a kind as to give it knowledge of, or control over, the data relating to those offers for sale'.[91] In such a case, it cannot benefit from the immunities of the E-commerce Directive.

---

[87] CJEU, Joined Cases C-236/08 to C-238/08 [2010] Google France SARL and others v. Louis Vuitton Malletier SA and others [120].

[88] CJEU, Joined Cases C-236/08 to C-238/08 [2010] Google France SARL and others v. Louis Vuitton Malletier SA and others [114]; see also Case C-324/09 [2011] L'Oréal SA and others v. eBay International AG and others [113].

[89] CJEU, Joined Cases C-236/08 to C-238/08 [2010] Google France SARL and others v. Louis Vuitton Malletier SA and others [116]; Case C-324/09 [2011] L'Oréal SA and others v. eBay International AG and others [115].

[90] CJEU, Joined Cases C-236/08 to C-238/08 [2010] Google France SARL and others v. Louis Vuitton Malletier SA and others [118].

[91] CJEU, Case C-324/09 [2011] L'Oréal SA and others v. eBay International AG and others [115–116].

bb Requirements to Obtain Immunity   If the intermediary did not provide own content, did not adopt or modify third-party content and did not play an 'active role' in the dissemination of content, then he acted as a mere communication intermediary and benefits from the immunities in Articles 12–14, provided the requirements from these provisions are fulfilled. Articles 12–14 of the E-commerce Directive apply to mere conduits, caching services and host providers, respectively. The main distinction between those services is the duration of the storage of information: the transient storage of information in order to transmit the information concerned is covered by Article 12, the temporary storage of information falls under Article 13 and the permanent storage is covered by Article 14. This also explains the rationale of those provisions: the longer a service provider stores information, the closer he is to the unlawful content and the heavier his obligations are. In essence, the 'exemptions from the exemptions of liability' are expressions of the intermediaries' 'duties and responsibilities' within the meaning of Article 10(2) ECHR.

Article 12 E-commerce Directive applies to mere transmitters of, and providers of access to, third-party content. Those mere conduits are not liable for the information transmitted if they do not initiate the transmission, do not select the receiver of the transmission and do not select or modify the information contained in the transmission. Unlike under Articles 13 and 14 E-commerce Directive, knowledge of the transmitted content alone is irrelevant for the availability of Article 12 E-commerce Directive. Therefore, a mere conduit is not liable for failing to take steps to prevent access to another site that he is aware carries defamatory material.

The acts of transmission and of provision of access within the meaning of Article 12 only include the automatic, intermediate and transient storage of the information transmitted for the sole purpose of carrying out the transmission in the communication network and only so long as it is necessary for the transmission. If the transmission includes a temporary storage of that information in order to make the information's onward transmission more efficient (caching), Article 13 E-commerce Directive is applicable. This provision is practically most relevant in cases of alleged copyright infringements, since the process of 'caching' can be regarded as a 'reproduction' of protected work within the meaning of Article 2 Copyright Directive (see Chapter 9). However, the transmitter is not liable for the storage of that information on condition that he

- does not modify the information (Article 13(1)(a));
- complies with conditions on access to the information (Article 13(1)(b));
- complies with rules regarding the updating of the information, specified in a manner widely recognised and used by industry (Article 13(1)(c));
- does not interfere with the lawful use of technology, widely recognised and used by industry, to obtain data on the use of the information (Article 13(1)(d)); and
- acts expeditiously to remove or to disable access to the information it has stored upon obtaining actual knowledge of the fact that the information at the initial source of the transmission has been removed, or access to it has been disabled, or that a court or an administrative authority has ordered such removal or disablement (Article 13(1)(e)).

Where the storage of information is permanent, Article 14 comes into play. This provision concerns the immunity of host providers. Where an information society service consists of the storage of third-party information, the service provider is not liable for the information stored at the request of a recipient of the service, on condition that:

- he does not have actual knowledge of illegal activity or information (Article 14(1) (a) Var. 1); and
- as regards claims for damages, he is not aware of facts or circumstances from which the illegal activity or information is apparent (Article 14(1)(a) Var. 2); or
- upon obtaining such knowledge or awareness, he acts expeditiously to remove or to disable access to the information (Article 14(1)(b)).

The privilege contained in Article 14(1) shall not apply if the author using the service is acting under the authority or the control of the provider (Article 14(2)). In this case, the internet intermediary would be fully accountable for the information like a content provider.

Article 14(1)(a) Var. 2 applies only to claims for damages, i.e., in cases of private law. For all the other cases, such as fines imposed by a regulatory authority or criminal prosecution, the stricter Var. 1 of Article 14(1)(a) is applicable. However, the immunities of intermediary service providers do not affect the possibility of injunctions that may be issued independently of the intermediary's knowledge. According to Articles 12(3), 13(2) and 14(3), courts and administrative authorities may require internet intermediaries to terminate or prevent an infringement. In addition, host providers may be required to establish procedures governing the removal or disabling of access to information.

Article 13(1)(e) and Article 14(1)(b) of the E-commerce Directive thus oblige transmitters providing caching services and host providers to act 'expeditiously to remove or to disable access to the information' upon obtaining actual knowledge, so-called 'notice and take down' procedure. However, these rules provide little guidance regarding the scope of knowledge of the caching host provider concerning the unlawful character of the information. For example, with regard to defamatory content, it is unclear whether awareness of its mere defamatory character is sufficient, or whether knowledge of the absence of defences is required. Article 14 requires knowledge or awareness of facts or circumstances from which the *illegal* activity or information is apparent, thus indicating that knowledge or awareness of lack of defences is required.

Moreover, in *L'Oréal SA* v. *eBay*, the Court regarded it as sufficient for the notion of 'awareness' if the intermediary was aware of facts or circumstances on the basis of which 'a diligent economic operator' should have realised the illegality in question.[92] This covers situations in which, for example, the intermediary detects an illegal activity or illegal information. It may cover a situation in which the intermediary is

---

[92] CJEU, Case C-324/09 [2011] L'Oréal SA and others v. eBay International AG and others [120].

notified of the existence of such an activity or such information. A notification does not automatically preclude the exemption from liability, because such a notification may turn out to be insufficiently precise or inadequately substantiated. However, the Court regards a notification as one factor to establish whether the operator was aware of facts or circumstances on the basis of which a diligent economic operator should have identified the illegality.[93]

Even if knowledge or awareness of an internet intermediary has been established, the obligations imposed have to be in compliance with the human rights of the parties involved: the content provider's freedom of expression, the right of the intermediary to impart information and ideas as well as his freedom to conduct a business, the public's right to receive information and ideas and the rights of persons concerned: reputation, privacy, copyright, etc. Neither of these conflicting principles takes precedence *per se*. Rather, they have to be balanced against each other on a case-by-case basis based on the principle of proportionality (see Chapter 3). Holding a communication intermediary liable or issuing an injunction is not 'necessary' according to the proportionality analysis if there was another measure available to protect the conflicting interests that would have been less restrictive but nonetheless equally effective. A less intrusive means that a court would have to consider before awarding damages against an intermediary is the liability of the content provider himself, who, in the absence of a valid defence, is fully liable for the statements he authored.[94] In order to establish the identity of an anonymous or pseudonymous primary publisher, a court may have to issue an injunction, such as a *Norwich Pharmacal* order under English law.[95] Yet intermediary liability is still 'necessary' if it is not possible for the claimant to establish the identity of the primary publisher and if the intermediary fails to remove or block access to the unlawful content.

cc No General Obligation to Monitor   It follows from Article 15 of the E-commerce Directive that Member States shall not impose a general obligation on internet service providers to monitor the information that they transmit or store, nor a general obligation actively to seek facts or circumstances indicating illegal activity. Member States may merely impose obligations on service providers to inform the public authorities of alleged illegal activities or to communicate to the competent authorities, at their request, information enabling the identification of recipients of their service (Article 15(2)). However, this provision does not require the Member States to lay down an obligation to communicate personal data in the context of civil proceedings. Such an obligation has to be compatible with the provisions on the protection of personal data and the fundamental rights of the parties involved.[96] But Member States may require

---

[93] CJEU, Case C-324/09 [2011] L'Oréal SA and others v. eBay International AG and others [120–122].
[94] Oster (2015a, p. 352).
[95] Established in Norwich Pharmacal v. Customs & Excise Commissioners [1974] AC 133, 175.
[96] ECJ, Case C-275/06 [2008] Promusicae v. Telefónica de España SAU [58–59], [61] and [70].

host providers to apply duties of care, which can reasonably be expected from them and that are specified by national law, in order to detect and prevent certain types of illegal activities.[97]

The Court of Justice of the EU provided guidance on the interpretation of Article 15 and the 'duties of care' in the cases of *L'Oréal* v. *eBay*, *Scarlet Extended* v. *SABAM and others* and *SABAM* v. *Netlog*. In *L'Oréal* v. *eBay*, the Court was asked whether holders of intellectual property rights have a right to injunctions requiring an operator of a website on which their rights have been infringed to take measures to prevent future infringements. According to Article 18 E-commerce Directive, 'Member States shall ensure that court actions available under national law concerning information society services' activities allow for the rapid adoption of measures, including interim measures, designed to terminate any alleged infringement and to prevent any further impairment of the interests involved'. The Court decided that this provision, in this case read together with the third sentence of Article 11 Enforcement Directive,[98] does not only allow injunctions aimed at prohibiting the *continuation* of an infringement, but also the prevention of *further* infringements.[99] At the same time, it follows from Article 15(1) E-commerce Directive 'that the measures required of the online service provider concerned cannot consist in an active monitoring of all the data of each of its customers in order to prevent any future infringement of intellectual property rights via that provider's website'.[100] However, in order to ensure that there is an effective remedy against persons who have used an online service to infringe intellectual property rights, the service operator may be ordered to take measures to facilitate the identification of its users.[101] Those measures must strike a fair balance between the various rights and interests concerned.[102]

The Court then further elaborated on this balancing exercise in *Scarlet Extended* v. *SABAM* and *SABAM* v. *Netlog*.[103] The Société belge des auteurs, compositeurs et éditeurs SCRL (SABAM), a management company representing authors, composers and publishers of musical works, ordered the access provider *Scarlet Extended* and the social network platform *Netlog* to install a system for indiscriminately filtering all electronic communications that use file-sharing software ('peer-to-peer'), with the purpose of preventing the copyright infringing practice of file-sharing. In both cases, the Court held that national authorities and courts have to strike a fair balance between the protection of the intellectual property right enjoyed by copyright holders and the freedom to conduct a business enjoyed by the ISPs pursuant to Article 16

---

[97] Recital 48 E-commerce Directive.
[98] We will come back to Article 11 Enforcement Directive in Chapter 9.
[99] CJEU, Case C-324/09 [2011] L'Oréal SA and others v. eBay International AG and others [131–134].
[100] CJEU, Case C-324/09 [2011] L'Oréal SA and others v. eBay International AG and others [139].
[101] CJEU, Case C-324/09 [2011] L'Oréal SA and others v. eBay International AG and others [142].
[102] CJEU, Case C-324/09 [2011] L'Oréal SA and others v. eBay International AG and others [143].
[103] CJEU, Case C-70/10 [2011] Scarlet Extended v. SABAM and others and Case C-360/10 [2012] SABAM v. Netlog.

EUChFR.[104] However, an injunction could not be made against an internet intermediary that requires it to install a system for filtering all information passing via its services or stored on its servers, exclusively at its expense and for an unlimited period, in order to detect violations of copyright. Such an injunction would be incompatible with both Article 15 E-commerce Directive and the fundamental rights of the parties involved, such as Article 16 EUChFR of the internet service providers and Articles 8 and 11 EUChFR of the users.

dd One-Sided versus Full Harmonisation   It is uncontroversial that Articles 12–15 E-commerce Directive harmonise the liability of internet intermediaries insofar as Member States must not go below the level of protection for such intermediaries. However, it is controversial whether the Member States may provide stronger protection for intermediaries. For example, going beyond Article 14 of the E-commerce Directive, the UK Defamation Act 2013 in its Section 5 includes a special provision for actions for defamation brought against a website operator, which is a subcategory of a host provider, in respect of statements posted on his website. Section 5(2) furnishes the operator with a defence if he shows that it was not he who posted the statement on the website. The provision thus goes beyond the immunity provision for host providers in Article 14 E-commerce Directive. By contrast, for example, both the German legislator and the German Federal Court of Justice assume that Articles 12–15 E-commerce Directive provide full harmonisation that cuts both ways; that is, with a view to both rules in favour and to the disadvantage of intermediaries. Consequently, the Member States must not provide a stronger protection of internet intermediaries either.[105] The Federal Court of Justice refers to Recitals 6 and 40 of the E-commerce Directive, which indicate that the Directive aims at coordinating national laws on information society service providers and service providers acting as intermediaries in particular. According to the German understanding, Section 5 Defamation Act 2013 would be in violation of EU law.

However, there is good reason to argue that Articles 12–15 only provide full harmonisation insofar as the Member States must not go *below* the protection afforded to internet intermediaries. But they may afford *stronger* protection to such intermediaries. The reference to Recitals 6 and 40 of the E-commerce Directive can be refuted by reference to Recital 63. Here the E-commerce Directive explains that

> [t]he adoption of this Directive will not prevent the Member States from taking into account the various social, societal and cultural implications which are inherent in the advent of the information society; in particular it should not hinder measures which Member States might adopt in conformity with

---

[104] CJEU, Case C-70/10 [2011] Scarlet Extended v. SABAM and others [47–49]; Case C-360/10 [2012] SABAM v. Netlog [44–47].

[105] See Bundestags-Drucksache 14/6098, p. 22; German Federal Court of Justice, Case I ZR 39/12 [2013] 'Announcement with map details' [19].

Community law to achieve social, cultural and democratic goals taking into
account their linguistic diversity, national and regional specificities as well as
their cultural heritage, and to ensure and maintain public access to the widest
possible range of information society services.

Moreover, the Court of Justice has made clear that Articles 12–15 'do not concern
the conditions in which judicial remedies for civil liability may be exercised against
those service providers, which, in the absence of any specific provision of EU law,
come under the sole competence of the Member States, subject to the principles of
equivalence and of effectiveness'.[106] Therefore, it is for the Member States to establish the conditions for liability of intermediaries on a substantive level, such as via
domestic tort law. Those conditions necessarily make it more difficult to successfully
sue intermediaries. To be sure, this extension of the freedom of intermediaries from
liability would operate on a substantive level and not on the 'filter level' provided
by Articles 12–15 of the E-commerce Directive. But the outcome of the case would
be that intermediaries are better protected under domestic law than under the E-
commerce Directive. If Articles 12–15 aimed at full harmonisation and a fully coordinated framework for intermediary liability, they would also have to stipulate the
substantive conditions for liability themselves, which the EU cannot do due to the
lack of competence. Otherwise the claimant would 'receive' something at the 'filter
level' – the fact that the Member States must not provide a stronger 'filter' in favour
of intermediaries – which would be taken from him at the substantive level, which
provides further conditions for his claim to be fulfilled in order to be successful.

Finally, it can also be inferred from the CJEU's case law that Articles 12–15 only
aim at harmonisation in that the Member States must not derogate from those provisions to the disadvantage of intermediaries. In *L'Oréal* v. *eBay*, the Court emphasised:

> Articles 12 to 15 [E-commerce Directive] seek to *restrict* the situations in
> which intermediary providers of information society services may be held
> liable pursuant to the applicable national law. It is therefore in the context
> of national law that the conditions under which such liability arises must be
> sought, it being understood, however, that, by virtue of Articles 12 to 15 [E-
> commerce Directive], *certain situations cannot give rise to liability on the part
> of intermediary service providers.*[107]

The Court thus only reasoned in a way that Articles 12–15 E-commerce Directive
seek to restrict intermediary liability. Yet there is no argument of the Court indicating that liability of intermediaries must not be restricted even further.

ee Current Developments   On 11 January 2012, the European Commission published a Communication on a Digital Single Market for e-commerce and online

---

[106] CJEU, Case C-291/13 [2014] Papasavvas [53].
[107] Case C-324/09 [2011] L'Oréal SA and others v. eBay International AG and others [107] (emphasis added).

services.[108] Based on a public consultation, this Communication reflects the vision of the Commission on the potential of online services regarding growth and employment, names the most significant obstacles for the development of electronic commerce and online services and identifies priorities. The Communication was accompanied by an Action Plan and a Working Paper.[109] The Working Paper analyses, *inter alia*, aspects of the liability privilege of internet intermediaries and the necessity of a 'notice and action procedure'. The Commission has subsequently dealt with 'notice and action' in the context of Article 14 E-commerce Directive in more detail and conducted a further consultation.[110] On 23 April 2013, the Commission presented a Working Document with an 'E-commerce Action Plan' in which the Commission announced a horizontal initiative for a notice and action procedure amending Article 14 E-commerce Directive.[111] On 6 May 2015, the European Commission published its Communication 'A Digital Single Market Strategy for Europe'.[112] Among other issues, the Commission engages in detail with the legal framework of intermediary liability in this Communication. The Communication was also accompanied by a Working Document, in which the Commission sets out the questions raised in the Communication in more detail.[113] The Commission refers to the fragmentation of national rules and describes its plans for an amendment of the current legal framework. In May 2016, the Commission then published its Communication titled 'Online Platforms and the Digital Single Market', in which it formulates its policy approach to online platforms. Emphasising the key role of online platforms in innovation and growth in the Digital Single Market, the Commission outlined an approach that focusses, in particular, on self- and co-regulation that should tackle copyright violations and hate speech online.

ff The *Delfi* Case   How is the *Delfi* case to be judged under the current scheme of Articles 12–15 E-commerce Directive and in light of Articles 8 and 10 ECHR/Articles 7 and 11 EUChFR? The Strasbourg Court was merely empowered to give the final ruling on whether the domestic courts' interpretation was reconcilable with Article 10 ECHR. However, it was not entitled to review the right application of the E-commerce

---

[108] COM, Communication to the European Parliament, the Council, the Economic and Social Committee and the Committee of the Regions, A coherent framework for building trust in the Digital Single Market for e-commerce and online services, COM(2011) 942.

[109] COM, Staff Working Document, Online services, including e-commerce, in the Single Market, SEC(2011) 1641 final.

[110] The Commission's roadmap is available at http://ec.europa.eu/smart-regulation/impact/planned_ia/docs/2012_markt_007_notice_and_takedown_procedures_en.pdf.

[111] COM, Staff Working Document, E-commerce Action plan 2012–2015, State of play 2013, SWD(2013) 153 final.

[112] Communication from the Commission to the European Parliament, the Council, the Economic and Social Committee and the Committee of the Regions, A Digital Single Market Strategy for Europe, COM(2015) 192 final.

[113] COM, Staff Working Document, A Digital Single Market Strategy for Europe – Analysis and Evidence, SWD(2015) 100 final.

Directive. The right addressee to review whether the case had been correctly decided in light of the E-commerce Directive and the EUChFR would have been the Court of Justice of the EU. Therefore, the Estonian courts should have referred this question to Luxembourg under Article 267 TFEU.

Delfi could only benefit from the immunity rules of the E-commerce Directive – in this case Article 14 – if it merely stored information provided by its users as a host provider. This provision would not apply if Delfi had provided own content, exercised editorial control over third-party content or played an 'active role' of such a kind as to give it knowledge of, or control over, the data stored. Delfi itself did not author the comments. However, Delfi had integrated the comment environment into its news portal, inviting visitors to the website to complement the news with their own comments. Moreover, it exercised control over the comment section as such. Delfi's activity with regard to the comments was thus not of a merely technical, automatic and passive nature. Delfi played an 'active role' of such a kind as to give it knowledge of, or control over, the data stored within the meaning of *Google France v. Louis Vuitton*.[114] Therefore, it could not avail itself of Article 14 E-commerce Directive.

However, the application of the law on intermediary liability also has to be in compliance with the human rights of the persons involved: Article 7 EUChFR (and Article 8 ECHR) on behalf of L., and Article 11 EUChFR (and Article 10 ECHR) on behalf of Delfi. The Strasbourg Court identified the following aspects as relevant for its analysis:

- The context of the comments.
- The liability of the actual authors of the comments as an alternative to the applicant company's liability.
- The measures applied by the applicant company in order to prevent or remove defamatory comments.
- The consequences of the domestic proceedings for the applicant company.[115]

As regards the context of the comments, the Court accepted that the article was a balanced one and contained no offensive language. However, Delfi was a professionally managed internet news portal run on a commercial basis, which sought to attract a large number of comments on news articles that it published. Delfi actively called for comments on the news items appearing on the portal, and it exercised a substantial degree of control over the comments published on its portal. Moreover, the Court observed that holding the actual authors of the comments liable was not a sensible alternative to holding Delfi liable, as they were anonymous. The effectiveness of measures establishing the identity of the authors of the comments was uncertain. Regarding the measures applied by Delfi in order to prevent or remove defamatory

---

[114] Compare ECtHR, Delfi AS v. Estonia [2015] App. no. 64569/09 [146].
[115] ECtHR, Delfi AS v. Estonia [2015] App. no. 64569/09 [143].

comments, Delfi removed the comments in question some six weeks after they were uploaded on the website, upon notification by the injured person's lawyers to the applicant company. However, according to the ECtHR, it should have removed comments that amounted to hate speech and incitements to violence from its website without delay right after publication. Lastly, concerning the consequences of the domestic proceedings, Delfi was obliged to pay the injured person the modest sum of €320 in compensation for non-pecuniary damage. Therefore, the Strasbourg Court concluded that there had been no violation of Article 10 ECHR.

What are the ramifications of the *Delfi* decision for online communication? The Joint Concurring Opinion to Delfi rightly remarked that the Court 'should have stated more clearly the underlying principles leading it to find no violation of Article 10. Instead, the Court has adopted case-specific reasoning and at the same time has left the relevant principles to be developed more clearly in subsequent case law'.[116] Consequently, one has to be careful to complain about 'collateral censorship' because of the Delfi ruling.[117] First, the internet service providers affected by the Delfi decision constitute a smaller circle than it seems at first glance. Delfi is a commercial news portal that initiates and invites comments on certain articles it publishes. Therefore, its activity could be distinguished from online social media platforms in which people comment on topics that have not been brought up by the service provider (Facebook, Twitter, etc.) itself.[118] Second, the Strasbourg Court did not impose an obligation on news portals such as Delfi to censor content in their comment sections. Rather, Delfi should have created a more effective system that would have ensured rapid removal of unlawful comments from the portal rather than leaving this to other users or potential victims. In particular, the impugned comments in the *Delfi* case constituted hate speech and speech that directly advocated acts of violence. '[T]he establishment of their unlawful nature did not require any linguistic or legal analysis since the remarks were on their face manifestly unlawful'.[119] It can be inferred from this that where such a 'linguistic or legal analysis' is required, Article 10 ECHR will weigh stronger in favour of the internet service provider. Third, one always has to consider the interests of those affected by defamatory comments online. Articles 7 EUChFR and 8 ECHR oblige the states to actively protect an individual's reputation against abominable comments. For this reason alone, comparisons of the *Delfi* decision with licensing regimes and arbitrary arrests of printers of political pamphlets in the seventeenth and eighteenth century are highly problematic.[120] Rather, since comments in news portals usually come

---

[116] ECtHR, Delfi AS v. Estonia [2015] App. no. 64569/09, Joint Concurring Opinion of Judges Raimondi, Karakas, De Gaetano and Kjølbro [8].

[117] See ECtHR, Delfi AS v. Estonia [2015] App. no. 64569/09, Joint Dissenting Opinion of Judges Sajó and Tsotsoria.

[118] ECtHR, Delfi AS v. Estonia [2015] App. no. 64569/09 [116].

[119] ECtHR, Delfi AS v. Estonia [2015] App. no. 64569/09 [117].

[120] See, however, ECtHR, Delfi AS v. Estonia [2015] App. no. 64569/09, Joint Dissenting Opinion of Judges Sajó and Tsotsoria [3] and Annex.

along with anonymity that renders litigation against the authors useless, adjudicators have no other option than to regulate those who control the code in order to fulfil their duties under Articles 7 EUChFR and 8 ECHR.

VI Questions

1 On which one of the two schools of thought – Cyberrealism or Cyberidealism – is the case law on jurisdiction in online cases in Chapter 4 based?
2 In *Delfi*, a third-party intervener argued that authors should be accountable for their defamatory comments and that the state should provide a regulatory framework making it possible to identify and prosecute online offenders. At the same time, the intervener emphasised that the possibility of publishing anonymously on the internet should be regarded as a value.[121] Are these two positions reconcilable? Do also reconsider the section on anonymous speech in Chapter 2.
3 What are the incentives set by Articles 12–15 of the E-commerce Directive and the CJEU's case law on these provisions on the *voluntary* monitoring of third-party content by internet intermediaries?
4 What are the incentives set by the Strasbourg Court in the *Delfi* judgment for providers of news portals whether or not to provide a comments section? What is the impact of the *Delfi* decision on public discourse?

VII Further Reading

- L.A. Bygrave and J. Bing (eds.), *Internet Governance: Infrastructure and Institutions*, 2009
- M. Collins, *The Law of Defamation and the Internet*, 3rd edn, 2010
- J. Goldsmith and T. Wu, *Who Controls the Internet? Illusions of a Borderless World*, 2008
- D. Lindsay, *International Domain Name Law: ICANN and the UDRP*, 2007
- C.T. Marsden, *Internet Co-Regulation: European Law, Regulatory Governance and Legitimacy in Cyberspace*, 2011
- E. Morozov, *The Net Delusion: The Dark Side of Internet Freedom*, 2011
- A.D. Murray, *The Regulation of Cyberspace: Control in the Online Environment*, 2007
- C. Reed, *Making Laws for Cyberspace*, 2012
- G. Smith, *Internet Law and Regulation*, 4th edn, 2007

---

[121] ECtHR, Delfi AS v. Estonia [2015] App. no. 64569/09 [95].

Telecommunications

CASE EXAMPLE

The former Soviet Union broadcast uncoded television programmes. These were transmitted to a Soviet satellite, which sent them back to receiving earth stations on Soviet territory, and these in turn distributed them to users. The satellite was a telecommunications satellite and not a direct-broadcasting one: it provided a fixed point-to-point radiocommunication service using the frequencies allotted to radiocommunications. It also transmitted telephone conversations, telexes or telegrams and data. The signals could also be received in Switzerland.

Autronic AG was a Swiss company specialising in electronics, which sold 90cm-diameter dish aerials for home use. Autronic applied to the national Telecommunications Authority requesting permission to give a showing at a public exhibition on electronics of the public television programme that it received directly from the Soviet satellite by means of a private dish aerial. The object of Autronic was to give a demonstration of the technical capabilities of the equipment in order to promote sales of it. The Telecommunications Authority wrote to the Soviet embassy in Berne, but did not receive a reply. It thus informed Autronic that without the express consent of the Soviet authorities, it could not allow reception of the broadcasts and that the ITU Radio Regulations required it to prevent such reception. Therefore, Autronic applied for a declaratory ruling that reception for private use of uncoded television programmes from satellites should not require the consent of the broadcasting state's authorities. The Telecommunications Authority rejected the applicant company's application, stating that it could not grant a receiving licence without the consent of the broadcasting state's authorities. According to Autronic, the fact that the permission to receive uncoded television broadcasts for general use from a telecommunications satellite was subject to the consent of the broadcasting state infringed its right to receive information as guaranteed in Article 10(1) ECHR.

The relevant ITU provisions read as follows:
Article 37 of the ITU Constitution:

Secrecy of Telecommunications

(1) Member States agree to take all possible measures, compatible with the system of telecommunication used, with a view to ensuring the secrecy of international correspondence.
(2) Nevertheless, they reserve the right to communicate such correspondence to the competent authorities in order to ensure the application of their national laws or the execution of international conventions to which they are parties.

Article 6(1) of the ITU Constitution:

(1) The Member States are bound to abide by the provisions of this Constitution, the Convention and the Administrative Regulations in all telecommunication offices and stations established or operated by them which engage in international services or which are capable of causing harmful interference to radio services of other countries, except in regard to services exempted from these obligations in accordance with the provisions of Article 48 of this Constitution.

The ITU Radio Regulations:

1.1 For the purposes of these Regulations, the following terms shall have the meanings defined below. …

1.21 *fixed-satellite service:* A *radiocommunication service* between *earth stations* at given positions, when one or more *satellites* are used; the given position may be a specified fixed point or any fixed point within specified areas; in some cases this service includes satellite-to-satellite links, which may also be operated in the *inter-satellite service*; the fixed-satellite service may also include *feeder links* for other *space radiocommunication services.*

1.39 *broadcasting-satellite service:* A *radiocommunication service* in which signals transmitted or retransmitted by *space stations* are intended for direct reception by the general public.
In the broadcasting-satellite service, the term "direct reception" shall encompass both *individual reception* and *community reception.*

4.17 Any administration may assign a frequency in a band allocated to the fixed service or allocated to the fixed-satellite service to a station authorized to transmit, unilaterally, from one specified fixed point to one or more specified fixed points provided that such transmissions are not intended to be received directly by the general public.

17.1 In the application of the appropriate provisions of the Constitution and the Convention, administrations bind themselves to take the necessary measures to prohibit and prevent:

17.2 *a)* the unauthorized interception of radiocommunications not intended for the general use of the public;

17.3 *b)* the divulgence of the contents, simple disclosure of the existence, publication or any use whatever, without authorization of information of any nature whatever obtained by the interception of the radiocommunications mentioned in No. 17.2.

(based on ECtHR, Autronic AG v. Switzerland [1990] App. no. 12726/87)

I Introduction

Telecommunications law is a subset of media law. It pertains to technical aspects of the transmission of signals, whereas other media law deals with questions of media content. Telecommunications law thus plays a significant role for the distribution and reception of speech and information. Without the technical platform to effectively disseminate opinions and points of view, freedom of speech provisions would be ineffective in many cases. To put it in a simple yet colourful way: without telecommunications infrastructure and services, radio and TV broadcasting and online services can be compared to having a newspaper without the paper. Therefore, media law cannot be properly comprehended without a basic understanding of the legal framework regulating the paths and means of transmission; that is, telecommunications networks and services.

II Economics of Telecommunications

The main rationale for regulating telecommunications network operators and service providers is market failure. Similar to railroad services or energy supply, the field of telecommunications is characterised by a particular feature: it is a network-related industry.[1] Network infrastructures are subject to economic peculiarities that justify a distinctive regulatory treatment compared to other fields of business regulation. These have long been considered natural monopolies or, at least, facilities that are predisposed to becoming monopolies.[2] A natural monopoly arises when one supplier has an overwhelming cost advantage over other actual and potential competitors. This tends to be the case in network industries where fixed costs, as opposed to marginal ones, predominate. It is very expensive to build transmission networks such as telephone lines (i.e., the initial fixed costs). However, once the initial investment is complete, the company incurs relatively low marginal expenses, mainly the cost of serving each customer. This characteristic of network infrastructures creates so-called economies of scale and, hence, high barriers that impede entrance to the market. It is usually more efficient for an incumbent monopolist to expand than for new firms to become established in the market. Thus, it is unlikely that a potential competitor would be willing to make the capital investment needed to even enter the monopolist's market.

In addition, communication infrastructures particularly benefit from network externalities. Network externalities, also called network effect, describe the effect that one user of a good or service has on the value of that product to other people. By contrast to economies of scale, network externalities result from the interoperability of the network rather than business size of the provider.[3] When network effect is present, the value of a product or service increases as more people use it. For example, the more people that own a telephone connection, the more valuable the telephone connection becomes for each customer of the same telephone network provider, even if a new user does not intend to create value for other users (positive externality).[4]

---

[1] The following explanations provide a brief and comprehensive overview of the topic. For further reading on network economics, see, for example, Katz and Shapiro (1985); Shy (2010).

[2] Lust (2003, p. 5).

[3] Energy networks, for instance, are characterised by economies of scale, but very little to no network effects, since they lack interoperability.

[4] Online social networks, such as Facebook or Twitter, are based on the same principles. The more users join, the more this raises the value of this social network for other users.

Therefore, the value of an interoperable network increases with every new customer the network operator gains. This causes difficulties for new market entrants, since they need to establish a sizable number of customers in order to create an incentive for new customers to join.

These characteristics cause significant consequences for the regulation of both networks and services. First, different operators may be needed to interconnect their networks, as this could not only increase the value of each network but permits both operators to function in an economically viable way. Assume that network operator A has 100,000 customers and network operator B has 20,000 customers, and their networks are not interconnected (that is, customers of each network can only reach users of the same network). Operator A's network is, due to its externalities, more valuable than operator B's; and it is probable that B's customers will eventually switch to A in order facilitate contact with its customers. If, however, A and B are legally forced to interconnect, all customers will benefit because they will be connected to a combined network of 120,000 contacts. Moreover, B could continue to run its business.[5]

Second, network economics have significant consequences for service providers. Since the provision of telecommunications services, such as telephone services or internet access, is only possible through an infrastructure (for example a cable infrastructure or wireless frequencies), they often turn out to be 'bottleneck resources'. In order to reach customers, service providers who do not operate their own network infrastructures need access to network facilities of network operators. This includes the risk that the network operator, aware of his power, either declines network access to other providers, or charges exorbitant prices. Therefore, regulation is necessary in order to both guarantee equitable access to the telecommunications network infrastructure, as well as to oversee accompanying aspects such as price determination and a sufficient level of transparency.

III International Telecommunications Law

The two most influential organisations in the field of telecommunications on an international stage are the International Telecommunication Union (ITU) and the WTO. While the ITU aims at promoting the efficient use of telecommunications services and coordinating the radio spectrum, the WTO provides a well-established forum for negotiations and agreements on market access.[6]

---

[5] Yet the main question of interconnection is in fact always whether the costs associated with interconnection are so high that society would be better off with a monopoly than with interconnection.

[6] Burri Nenova (2007, p. 835); Bronckers and Larouche (1997, pp. 6–7). However, the distinction between the work of the ITU and the WTO is not always clear-cut; see C. Koenig and A. Braun, in Koenig et al. (2009, pp. 33–38).

1 The International Telecommunication Union

The most important international institution that coordinates information and communication technology issues is the ITU. The history of the ITU dates back to 1865, when it was founded by 20 European countries as the International Telegraph Union in Paris. The ITU is one of the oldest intergovernmental organisations. In 1932, with the merger of the Telegraph and Radiotelegraph Conventions, the organisation changed its name from International Telegraph Union to International Telecommunication Union. In 1947, the ITU became a United Nations agency based in Geneva, Switzerland. Its membership includes 193 Member States[7] and more than 700 Private Sector Members and Associates[8] including broadcasting and telephone companies and NGOs.[9]

Private Sector Members are entitled to participate fully in the activities of their sectors, take part in the development of questions and recommendations, and be involved in decision-making relating to the working methods and procedures of their sectors (Article 3(3) ITU Constitution). Sector Members do not have the right to vote; however, they may act on behalf of a Member State (Article 19(9) ITU Convention). Contrastingly, Member States can both participate and vote in conferences, are eligible for election to the Council, and have the right to nominate candidates for election as officials of the Union or as members of the Radio Regulations Board (Article 3(2) ITU Constitution).

The EU exercises its influence in the ITU in three ways. First, all EU Member States are Members States of the ITU. Second, the EU is itself a member of all three ITU Sectors. Third, and most importantly, the European Conference of Postal and Telecommunications Administrations (CEPT), which consists of 48 European countries (including all EU Member States) and thus represents almost the whole European continent, plays a significant role as Sector Member on the ITU stage.

a The ITU's Legal Framework and its Scope

The legal framework of the ITU includes the Constitution, the Convention and two Administrative Regulations – the Radio Regulations[10] and the International Telecommunications Regulations.[11] In the case of inconsistency between these provisions, the Convention shall prevail over the Administrative Regulations and the Constitution shall prevail over both (Article 4(4) of the Constitution). As

---

[7] For a list of the Member States, see www.itu.int/cgi-bin/htsh/mm/scripts/mm.list?_search=ITUstates&_languageid=1. Non-members are, for example, Cook Islands or Palau, and states with limited recognition.
[8] www.itu.int/net/about/index.aspx.
[9] For example, British Telecom and the BBC are Sector Members.
[10] Signed on 4 July 2003 in Geneva; the majority of the provisions entered into force on 1 January 2005.
[11] Signed on 9 December 1988 in Melbourne, entered into force on 1 July 1990.

international treaties, they must be interpreted according to Articles 31–33 of the Vienna Convention on the Law of Treaties.[12] In the event of any discrepancy among the various language versions[13] of the Constitution and the Convention, the French text shall prevail (Article 58(5) ITU Constitution).[14]

Article 6 ITU Constitution obliges Member States to abide by the legal framework of the ITU in all their telecommunication offices and stations. Additionally, it compels their telecommunications agencies that engage in international services or that are capable of causing harmful interference to radio services of other countries to observe these provisions. An international telecommunications service is thereby defined as the 'offering of a telecommunication capability between telecommunication offices or stations of any nature that are in or belong to different countries'.[15]

Except for the principle of priority of emergency communications, military radio installations within the meaning of Article 48 ITU Constitution are exempted from the Member States' obligations stated in Article 6 ITU Constitution. However, neither Article 48 ITU Constitution nor any other provision of the ITU legal framework defines the term 'military radio installations', which then needs to be interpreted on a case-by-case basis according to the Vienna Convention on the Law of Treaties.

b Purposes of the ITU

The purposes of the ITU are set out in Article 1 ITU Constitution. The most important aims are to foster international cooperation and harmonious action among all its Member States for the improvement and rational use of telecommunications, to promote and offer technical assistance to developing countries in the field of telecommunications and to promote the development of technical facilities and their most efficient operation. The ITU shall, in particular, administrate the international radio-frequency spectrum of both terrestrial and geostationary nature. Furthermore, the ITU shall facilitate the worldwide standardisation of telecommunications. Hence, the ITU has to work in fields that its Member States are unable to manage, and not even bilaterally or multilaterally, but that need a global approach. The radio-frequency spectrum, for instance, is a scarce resource that needs rational and efficient allocation

---

[12] Vienna Convention on the Law of Treaties, done at Vienna on 23 May 1969, 1155 U.N.T.S. 331.

[13] Arabic, Chinese, English, French, Russian and Spanish.

[14] Article 58(5) ITU Constitution does not deal with language discrepancies regarding the Administrative Regulations. Since the provisions of the Administrative Regulations form an integral part of the Constitution and the Convention (see Articles 4(3) and 54(2) ITU Constitution), it should be concluded that Article 58(5) ITU Constitution applies to these provisions the same way.

[15] See the Annex to the ITU Constitution.

and use.[16] Due to their ubiquity and boundlessness, radio frequencies require, at least as a first step, a worldwide management.

c ITU Organs

The supreme policy-making body of the ITU is the Plenipotentiary Conference, composed of delegations representing ITU Member States and convened every four years. It establishes the strategic plan as well as the basis for the budget for the Union. It elects the Council, the Secretary-General and the Deputy Secretary-General, the Directors of the Bureaux of the Sectors and the members of the Radio Regulations Board. It makes decisions about proposals for amendments to the Constitution and the Convention put forward by Member States.[17]

The Council (see Article 4 of the Convention) is composed of Member States elected by the Plenipotentiary Conference. It comprises a maximum of 25 per cent of the total number of Member States, which are elected with due regard to the need for equitable distribution of Council seats among the five world regions. The current Council has 48 members. In the interval between Plenipotentiary Conferences, the Council shall act as governing body of the Union on behalf of the Plenipotentiary Conference within the limits of the powers delegated to it by the latter. It is responsible for ensuring the day-to-day running of the Union, coordinating work programmes, approving budgets and controlling finances and expenditures. The Council facilitates the implementation of the provisions of the ITU legal framework by the Member States.

A permanent General Secretariat, headed by the Secretary-General[18] (see Article 5 of the Convention), manages the day-to-day work of the Union and its sectors. The Secretary-General acts as the legal representative of the Union.

d The ITU Sectors

The ITU is comprised of three sectors, each managing a different aspect of the matters handled by the Union, which reflects the complexity of its responsibilities: Radiocommunication (ITU-R, Chapter II of the ITU Constitution), Standardization (ITU-T, Chapter III of the ITU Constitution) and Development (ITU-D, Chapter IV of the ITU Constitution). In addition, ITU Telecom as part of the ITU General Secretariat organises major events for the world's ICT community, such as ITU Telecom World, which is attended by governments, industry representatives and regulators.

The members of the sectors are the administrations of all Member States as well as any entity or organisation which becomes a Sector Member in accordance with the provisions of the Convention. The sectors, whose competences differ from sector to

---

[16] See Article 44 ITU Constitution.
[17] See Article 8 of the Constitution, Articles 1 ff of the Convention.
[18] On 23 October 2014, Houlin Zhao was elected 19th Secretary-General of the ITU.

sector, work through both world and regional conferences[19] and assemblies. In addition, the Radiocommunication Sector includes the Radio Regulations Board. These institutions are supported by Study Groups, an Advisory Group and Bureaus headed by the Director. Study Groups shall examine particular questions upon instruction by conferences or assemblies and prepare draft recommendations.[20] The Advisory Group of each Sector shall review the priorities and strategies, monitor progress and provide guidance for the work of the Study Groups, and recommend measures to foster cooperation and coordination with other organisations as well as with the other ITU Sectors.[21] Ultimately, the Bureau of each sector is responsible for organising and coordinating the work of their respective sector.[22]

aa Radiocommunication Sector (ITU-R) The Radiocommunication Sector is responsible for ensuring the rational, equitable, efficient and economical use of the radio-frequency spectrum by all radiocommunication services, including those using the geostationary-orbit or other satellite orbits, and carrying out studies and adopting recommendations on radiocommunication matters (Article 12(1) ITU Constitution). The radio-frequency spectrum is necessary for telecommunications services such as fixed and mobile communications, broadcasting, emergency telecommunications, global positioning systems and environmental monitoring. The ITU-R's primary objective is to ensure interference-free operations of radiocommunication systems by implementing the Radio Regulations and Regional Agreements. Furthermore, it establishes 'Recommendations' intended to ensure the necessary performance and quality in operating radiocommunication systems. It also seeks ways and means to conserve the spectrum and ensure flexibility for future expansion and new technological developments. ITU-R manages the coordination and recording procedures for space systems and earth stations. It processes and publishes data and carries out the examination of frequency assignment notices submitted by administrations. ITU-R also develops and manages space-related assignments and allotment plans and provides mechanisms for the development of new satellite services by locating suitable orbital slots.[23]

The two most significant institutions within the Radiocommunication Sector are the Radiocommunication Conference as the 'legislative branch', which shall normally be convened every three to four years, and the Radio Regulations Board as the 'executive branch'. Presumably, the most important function of the

---

[19] Except for ITU-T.

[20] See Article 11 ITU Convention (ITU-R), Article 14 ITU Convention (ITU-T) and Article 17 ITU Convention (ITU-D).

[21] Article 11A ITU Convention (ITU-R), Article 14A ITU Convention (ITU-T) and Article 17A ITU Convention (ITU-D).

[22] Article 12 ITU Convention (ITU-R), Article 15 ITU Convention (ITU-T) and Article 18 ITU Convention (ITU-D).

[23] For further details, see Chapter 5.

Radiocommunication Conference is the revision of the Radio Regulations. In addition, the Radiocommunication Conference may deal with any question of a worldwide nature within its competence and related to its agenda (Article 13(1) and (2) ITU Constitution). For this purpose, it may give instructions to the Radio Regulations Board and the Radiocommunication Bureau regarding their activities, review those activities (Article 7(1) ITU Convention) and set up radiocommunication Study Groups (Article 11(1) ITU Convention). In contrast to the world Radiocommunication Conferences, regional conferences only deal with specific radiocommunication questions of a regional nature, including instructions to the Radio Regulations Board and the Radiocommunication Bureau regarding their activities in the region concerned (Article 9 ITU Convention). The necessary technical bases for the work of the world Radiocommunication Conferences shall be provided by Radiocommunication Assemblies, which may be convened concurrently with world Radiocommunication Conferences (Article 13(3) ITU Constitution; see also Article 8 ITU Convention). They are responsible for the structure, programme and approval of radiocommunication studies.

The Radio Regulations Board consists of 12 members elected by the Plenipotentiary Conference, which shall be independent from the Union and from their Member State. In particular, the Radio Regulations Board approves the Rules of Procedure, which include technical criteria and shall be used by the Director and the Bureau in the application of the Radio Regulations to register frequency assignments made by Member States (Article 14(1) ITU Constitution). The Director of the Radiocommunication Bureau organises and coordinates the work of the Radiocommunication Sector (Article 12 ITU Convention).

bb Telecommunication Standardization Sector (ITU-T)   The Telecommunication Standardization Sector is responsible for developing communication standards on network functionalities, such as voice telephony, emergency communications and video messages, and the interoperability of networks. After examination in Study Groups, the World Telecommunication Standardization Assembly issues recommendations (ITU-T Recs) on specific standardisation matters. ITU-T Recs are given non-mandatory status until they are adopted as national laws. There are more than 3,000 recommendations in force on topics ranging from service definition to network architecture and security, from broadband DSL to Gbit/s optical transmission systems to next-generation networks (NGN) and IP-related issues. Recommendations are marked with a letter, which refers to the technical area, and a number. The letter H, for example, stands for audiovisual and multimedia systems, the letter I for integrated services digital network (ISDN) and V for data communication over the telephone network.[24] Significant recommendations are, for example, H.310 for broadband audiovisual

---

[24] For further information, see www.itu.int/en/ITU-T/publications/Pages/recs.aspx.

communication systems and terminals, V.2 on power levels for data transmission over telephone lines and V.153 on IP peering for real-time facsimile services.

cc Telecommunication Development Sector (ITU-D) The Telecommunication Development Sector aims at achieving access to infrastructure and information and communications services for all inhabitants of the planet. ITU-D assists countries in facilitating the mobilisation of technical, human and financial resources in the field of information and communication technologies (ICTs), participates in actions that assist in narrowing the digital divide and develops and manages programmes that facilitate information flow geared to the needs of developing countries. Unlike ITU-T conferences (see Article 31(3) third indent ITU Convention), ITU-D conferences do not produce Final Acts (Article 22(4) ITU Constitution). Their conclusions shall take the form of resolutions, decisions, recommendations and reports.

e Substantive ITU Law

Chapters VI and VII ITU Constitution include substantive provisions for telecommunications. Chapter VI contains general provisions, whereas Chapter VII provides special rules for radio, which are complemented by the Radio Regulations.

aa Freedom and Equality of Correspondence versus Principle of Prior Consent and Privileged Communications According to Article 33 ITU Constitution, Member States recognise the right of the public to correspond by means of international public telecommunications services. The services, charges and safeguards shall be the same for all users in each category of correspondence without priority or preference. However, these principles – freedom and equality of correspondence – are subject to restrictions, namely the principle of prior consent and the principle of priority of certain telecommunication correspondence.

First, freedom of correspondence is restricted by the Member States' right to suspend, in accordance with their national law, private telecommunications that may appear dangerous to the security of the State or contrary to its laws, public order or decency (Article 34 ITU Constitution). In addition, Article 35 ITU Constitution allows Member States to suspend the international telecommunications services, without having to provide explanations and without responsibility to users, provided that the Member State immediately notifies other Member States of such action through the Secretary-General. In its practical application, the principle of prior consent established by Articles 34 and 35 ITU Constitution supersedes the freedom of correspondence proclaimed in Article 33 ITU Constitution.

Second, Articles 40 et seq. ITU Constitution deviate from the principle of equality of correspondence. For good reasons, Article 40 prioritises telecommunications concerning safety of life at sea, on land, in the air and in outer space, as well as epidemiological telecommunications of exceptional urgency of the World Health

Organization.[25] Furthermore, Article 41 ITU Constitution gives priority to government telecommunications over other telecommunication correspondence.[26]

bb Secrecy of Telecommunications   Member States shall, according to Article 37 ITU Constitution, take all technically possible measures to ensure the secrecy of international correspondence. However, they reserve the right to communicate such correspondence to the appropriate authorities in order to ensure the application of their national laws or the execution of international conventions to which they are parties.

cc Principle of Technical Efficiency   To carry on the rapid and uninterrupted exchange of international telecommunications, Member States shall take all necessary steps to ensure the establishment, under the best technical conditions, of the necessary channels and installations. Whenever possible, these channels and installations must be operated by the methods and procedures that practical operating experience has shown to be the most effective. They must be safeguarded, maintained in proper operating condition and kept abreast of scientific and technical progress (Article 38 ITU Constitution).

dd Special Provisions for Radio   The ITU provisions for radio are based on the principles of efficient use and prohibition of harmful interference (see (1)). The administration and enforcement of the international frequency management is, in particular, regulated by the Radio Regulations (see (2)).

(1) Principles of Efficient Use and Prohibition of Harmful Interference   Radio frequencies and any associated orbits, including the geostationary-satellite orbit, are limited natural resources. Article 44 ITU Constitution thus establishes the principle that the number of frequencies and the spectrum used should be limited to only the minimum needed to provide the necessary services in a satisfactory manner. To that end, they shall endeavour to apply the latest technical advances as soon as they are available. This provision is also applicable to military radio installations (see Article 48(2) ITU Constitution).

According to Article 45 ITU Constitution, all stations must be established and operated in such a manner so as not to cause 'harmful interference' to the radio services or communications of other Member States or duly authorised operating agencies that operate a radio service. Member States have to take all practicable steps

---

[25] Article 46 ITU Constitution re-emphasises this principle for radio stations: they shall be obliged to accept, with absolute priority, distress calls and messages regardless of their origin, to reply in the same manner to such messages and immediately to take such action in regard thereto as may be required. This provision is also applicable to military radio installations; see Article 48(2) ITU Constitution.

[26] Government Telecommunications includes telecommunications with any head of state, head of government or members of a government, commanders-in-chief of military forces, diplomatic or consular agents, the Secretary-General of the United Nations; heads of the principal organs of the United Nations, the International Court of Justice, or replies to government telecommunications mentioned above (No. 1014 of the Annex to the ITU Constitution).

to prevent the operation of electrical apparatus and installations of any kind from causing harmful interference to radio services or communications.

'Harmful interference' is one of the most crucial terms in ITU law, as the question of whether there is a harmful interference in a particular case might be the subject of international disputes.[27] According to the Annex to the ITU Constitution, 'harmful interference' is defined as any '[i]nterference which endangers the functioning of a radionavigation service or of other safety services or seriously degrades, obstructs, or repeatedly interrupts a radiocommunication service operating in accordance with the Radio Regulations'. Articles 15 and 16 Radio Regulations further elaborate on the identification and consequences of interferences from radio stations.

(2) International Radio-Frequency Management   The international frequency management is based on Article 1(2)(a) ITU Constitution and, in particular, the Radio Regulations. In order to avoid harmful interference between radio stations of different countries, the ITU maintains a three-step procedure:

- The allocation of bands of the radio-frequency spectrum (step 1: allocation);
- the allotment of radio frequencies (step 2: allotment); and
- the registration of radio-frequency assignments (step 3: assignment).

The enforcement of these obligations is explained in greater detail in the Radio Regulations, as amended by the Radiocommunication Conference.[28] The allocation of a frequency band includes the entry of a frequency band between 9kHz and 1000GHz[29] in the Table of Frequency Allocations[30] for the purpose of its use by a particular service (see No. 1.16 Radio Regulations). Allotment of a radio frequency means the entry of a designated frequency channel in an agreed plan that is adopted by a competent conference for use by administrations for a radiocommunication service in one or more identified countries or geographical areas and under specified conditions (see No. 1.17 Radio Regulations). Assignment of a radio frequency or radio frequency channel ultimately means the authorisation given by an administration for a radio station to use a radio frequency or radio frequency channel under specified conditions (see No. 1.18 Radio Regulations). Consequently, the ITU does not assign radio frequencies directly to operators of radio stations, but to its Member States, which then distribute them further (Article 7 et seq. Radio Regulations).

---

[27] For the ITU dispute settlement mechanism, see subsection f below.

[28] In several provisions, the Radio Regulations refer to the World Radiocommunication Conference in which the respective provision has been amended. For example, provision No. 5.415 regulating the use of the bands 2500–2690MHz in Region 2 and 2500–2535MHz and 2655–2690MHz in Region 3 by the fixed-satellite service ends with the addendum '(WRC-07)', thus indicating that this provision has been amended by the World Radiocommunication Conference 2007 in Geneva.

[29] Including newly available spectrum, such as the spectrum within the UHF band that has traditionally been used by broadcasters, but that became available due to terrestrial television shifting from analogue to broadband signals; so-called 'digital dividend'.

[30] See Section IV of Article 5 Radio Regulations.

For the allocation of frequencies, the Radio Regulations divide the world into three regions.[31] Region 1 includes Europe, Middle East, Africa, the former Soviet Union and Mongolia; Region 2 encompasses the Americas and the Pacific east of the International Date Line; and Region 3 includes the rest of Asia not covered by Region 1, Australia, and the Pacific Rim west of the International Date Line. The heading of the Table of Frequency Allocations contains three columns, each of which corresponds to one of the regions. When an allocation occupies the whole of the width of the Table or only one or two of the three columns, it indicates a worldwide allocation or a regional allocation, respectively. The categories of services,[32] such as broadcasting, amateur services or radio astronomy services, are then allocated to certain frequencies. When, in a box of the Table of Frequency Allocations, a band is allocated to more than one service, 'primary services' are printed in all capital letters (for example: FIXED) and 'secondary services' are printed in normal characters (for example: Mobile). Primary services take priority over secondary services, and stations that provide a secondary service must not cause harmful interference to those that provide primary services. Furthermore, secondary service stations can only claim protection from harmful interference from stations of the same priority (see Nos. 5.28 to 5.31 Radio Regulations). Particular regard has to be given to the footnotes included in the boxes that refer to exceptions or special rules. The footnote references that appear in the Table *below* the allocated service or services apply to more than one of these services or to the entirety of the allocation. The footnote references which appear *to the right* of the name of a service are applicable only to that particular service (Nos. 5.51 and 5.52).

As an illustration, the table allocating frequency band 135.7–137.8kHz in Region 3 reads as follows:

> **135.7–137.8**
> FIXED
> MARITIME MOBILE
> RADIONAVIGATION
> Amateur 5.67A
> 5.64 5.67B

This implies, first, that fixed, maritime mobile and radionavigation services take priority over amateur services. Second, footnote reference 5.67A is only applicable to amateur services,[33] whereas footnote references 5.64 and 5.67B are applicable to all of the mentioned services.[34]

---

[31] As shown on the map under No. 5.2. and described in Nos. 5.3. to 5.9. Radio Regulations.
[32] See Article 1 Section III Radio Regulations.
[33] 5.67A says: 'Stations in the amateur service using frequencies in the band 135.7–137.8 kHz shall not exceed a maximum radiated power of 1 W (e.i.r.p.)' – i.e., equivalent isotropically radiated power – 'and shall not cause harmful interference to stations of the radionavigation service operating in countries listed in No. 5.67.'
[34] 5.67 says: 'Additional allocation: in Mongolia, Kyrgyzstan and Turkmenistan, the band 130–148.5 kHz is also allocated to the radionavigation service on a secondary basis. Within and between these countries

The assignment of a radio frequency or radio frequency channel usually implies that a national administrative agency has given a radio station permission to use that frequency or frequency channel (see, for example, Sections 301 et seq. US Communications Act 1934, Sections 52 ff German Telecommunications Act, and the UK Wireless Telegraphy Act 2006).

f Settlement of Disputes

Article 56 ITU Constitution provides a mechanism for the settlement of disputes in ITU-related matters, i.e., questions relating to the interpretation or application of the Constitution, the Convention or the Administrative Regulations. The provision is only applicable to Member States, not private parties.[35] Member States may principally settle their disputes by negotiation, through diplomatic channels, according to procedures established by bilateral or multilateral treaties for the settlement of international disputes or by any other method mutually agreed upon.

However, if none of these methods of settlement is adopted, any Member State involved in a dispute may have the option to begin arbitration procedures in accordance with Article 41 ITU Convention. The parties involved shall mutually agree whether the arbitration is to be entrusted to individuals, administrations or governments (Article 41(2) ITU Convention). If within one month following notice to submit the dispute to arbitration the parties have been unable to resolve their conflict, the arbitration shall be entrusted to the governments. The choice of the arbitrators and further procedural aspects are regulated in Article 41(3) through (10) ITU Convention. Each party shall bear the expenses incurred during the investigation and presentation of the arbitration. The costs of arbitration other than those incurred by the parties themselves shall be divided equally between the parties to the dispute (Article 41(11) ITU Convention).

2 The World Trade Organization

As an integral part of the WTO Agreement, the GATS consists of a number of articles in its main body and several annexes including an Annex on Telecommunications (the 'Annex').[36] Many Members also made additional commitments in the form of a 'Reference Paper', which contains a set of regulatory principles applicable to the telecommunications sector.[37] Both the main body of the GATS and the Annex are

---

this service shall have an equal right to operate.' 5.67B reads as follows: 'The use of the band 135.7–137.8 kHz in Algeria, Egypt, Iran (Islamic Republic of), Iraq, Libyan Arab Jamahiriya, Lebanon, Syrian Arab Republic, Sudan and Tunisia is limited to the fixed and maritime mobile services. The amateur service shall not be used in the above-mentioned countries in the band 135.7–137.8 kHz, and this should be taken into account by the countries authorizing such use.'

[35] Depending on the respective domestic approach of incorporating public international law, private undertakings may invoke ITU law as part of their national legal order.

[36] See Article XXIX GATS.

[37] www.wto.org/english/tratop_e/serv_e/telecom_e/tel23_e.htm.

applicable to every WTO Member. In addition, each Member has attached its own schedule to the GATS, which contain individual, specific commitments on market access and national treatment as well as additional obligations. These commitments are inscribed by service sector and mode of supply of the service and may be subject to limitations on market access and national treatment.

a The Annex on Telecommunication

The Annex on Telecommunications applies to all measures of a Member that affect access to and use of public telecommunications transport networks and services (Section 2(a) of the Annex). It includes obligations regarding transparency on conditions affecting access to and use of networks and services (Section 4), as well as the actual access to and use of those networks and services (Section 5). In addition, Member States shall encourage and endorse technical cooperation, particularly with developing countries (Section 6).

aa Scope   According to Section 3(d) of the Annex, 'public telecommunications transport network' means the public telecommunications infrastructure, which permits telecommunications between and among defined network termination points. Telecommunications services include any services that transmit and receive signals by electromagnetic means (see Section 3(a)), encompassing both basic telecommunications services and value-added telecommunications services.[38] The distinction between basic and value-added services originates from US telecommunications law.[39] Basic telecommunications services merely provide the transmission of information, for example, telegraph, telephone or telex services,[40] whereas value-added, or non-basic, telecommunications services include those that go beyond a basic transmission service (such as voice mail, e-mail, online information or data processing).[41]

The Annex does not apply to measures that affect the cable or broadcast distribution of radio or television programming (Section 2(b) of the Annex). This exception clause was created to prohibit foreign broadcasters from getting free access to domestic markets via telecommunications without having to fulfil national requirements of diversity of opinion or media pluralism.[42] However, the distinction between the transmission of customary telecommunications services and broadcasting is difficult to isolate. According to Section 3(a), 'telecommunications' means the transmission and reception of signals by any electromagnetic means. This definition

---

[38] WTO Panel, Mexico – Measures affecting telecommunications services [2004] WT/DS204/R [7.278].

[39] See C. Koenig and A. Braun, in Koenig et al. (2009, p. 17); Burri Nenova (2007, p. 840), providing further references.

[40] As can be inferred from Section 3(b) Annex on Telecommunication.

[41] No. 2C of the Services Sectoral Classification List, Note by the Secretariat, Document MTN.GNS/W/120. Note that under the EU regulatory framework, many of these services would fall under customary (basic) electronic communications services; see Section V below.

[42] Cahn and Schimmel (1997, p. 301).

also applies to the transmission of broadcasting. Even the – anyway outdated – distinction between point-to-point communication (i.e., telecommunications) and point-to-multipoint communication (i.e., broadcast) could not be invoked, since Section 3(b) stipulates that public telecommunications transport service include 'the real-time transmission of customer-supplied information between two *or more* points' (emphasis added). With regard to the convergence of the media, it is worthy of consideration whether the distinction between the contents to be transmitted should be abandoned and substituted by a harmonised approach regarding the requirements of broadcast content.

bb Transparency   Section 4 of the Annex obliges Member States to ensure transparency, i.e., to publish all relevant information on conditions affecting access to and use of public telecommunications transport networks and services. This information includes, *inter alia*, tariffs and other terms and conditions of service, specifications of technical interfaces with such networks and services, and any applicable notifications, registration or licensing requirements.

cc Access to and Use of Networks and Services   According to Section 5(a) of the Annex, each Member shall ensure that any service supplier of any other Member may have access to and use of public telecommunications transport networks and services on reasonable and non-discriminatory terms and conditions.[43] 'Non-discriminatory' thereby refers to most-favoured-nation treatment (Article II GATS) and national treatment (Article XVII GATS), as well as to terms and conditions no less favourable than those accorded to any other user of like networks or services under similar circumstances. It should be noted that Section 5 only requires Members to ensure right of access to, and use of, *existing* networks and services, but does not oblige them to authorise a foreign service supplier to establish its own networks or services in its country.[44] In particular, Members shall ensure that service suppliers of any other Member

- have access to and use of networks and services, including the purchase or lease of equipment that interfaces with the network, the interconnection of networks, and the use of operating protocols of the service supplier's choice in the supply of any service (Section 5(b));
- may use these networks and services for the movement of information and for access to information, subject to national security and confidentiality regulations (Section 5(c) and (d)); and

---

[43] Section 5(g) establishes an exception for developing country Members that may place conditions on access to and use of networks and services necessary to strengthen their domestic telecommunications infrastructure and service capacity and to increase their participation in international trade in telecommunications services.

[44] See Section 2(c).

- are not facing conditions imposed upon them that limit access to and use of net-works and services other than as necessary[45] to safeguard public service responsi-bilities, to protect the technical integrity of networks or services, or to ensure that service suppliers of any other Member do not supply services unless permitted pursuant to commitments in the Member's schedule (Section 5(e)).[46] Pricing ele-ments, such as rates charged for access to and use of networks and services, are encompassed by the word 'terms', but not by conditions.[47] This means that pricing measures are not 'conditions' permitted under Section 5(e).

Section 5(f) of the Annex then enumerates the content conditions may include, such as restrictions on resale or shared use of such services, a requirement to use specified technical interfaces or requirements for notification, registration and licensing. Since pricing measures are neither explicitly mentioned in Section 5(f) nor similar to any of the conditions included in this paragraph, they are not justifiable under this provision.[48]

The question of whether rates charged for access and use are 'reasonable' was sub-ject to the WTO Panel Decision *Mexico – Measures Affecting Telecommunications Services*. The Panel concluded that rates may be 'reasonable' even if they are higher than cost-oriented rates.[49] However, if the rates charged 'exceed cost-oriented rates by a substantial margin', thus excluding price competition in the relevant market, as was the case in this particular issue, they are not 'reasonable'.[50]

b The Reference Paper

The Reference Paper was adopted as an additional commitment incorporated into the Members' schedules. Although it is only six sections long, scholars regard the Reference Paper as a significant step forward in the opening of telecommunications markets.[51] In its decision *Mexico – Measures Affecting Telecommunications Services*, the WTO Panel took first steps to concretise the Reference Paper's provisions.[52] Similar to the Annex' provisions, many of the sections of the Reference Paper also draw from and add to existing obligations of the GATS, such as Articles III, VI, VIII and IX, and the Annex on Telecommunications itself. Accordingly, the obligations in both the Annex and the Reference Paper overlap in certain respects. However, there are differences in scope, level of obligation and specific detail provided between the

---

[45] On the interpretation of the term 'necessary' (whether it means 'indispensable', 'reasonable' or just 'mak-ing a contribution to'), see WTO Panel, Mexico – Measures affecting telecommunications services [2004] WT/DS204/R [7.338–43].

[46] On the interpretation of Article 5, see WTO Panel, Mexico – Measures affecting telecommunications services [2004] WT/DS204/R [7.306ff].

[47] WTO Panel, Mexico – Measures affecting telecommunications services [2004] WT/DS204/R [7.325].

[48] WTO Panel, Mexico – Measures affecting telecommunications services [2004] WT/DS204/R [7.326].

[49] The reference to cost-orientation derived from Article 2(2)(b) of the Reference Paper, which was applica-ble in the particular case.

[50] WTO Panel, Mexico – Measures affecting telecommunications services [2004] WT/DS204/R [7.334-5].

[51] Drake and Noam (1997, p. 806); Burri Nenova (2007, p. 853).

[52] WTO Panel, Mexico – Measures affecting telecommunications services [2004] WT/DS204/R.

two instruments. The obligations in the Reference Paper include both competition rules and sector specific regulations. According to Section 5 of the Reference Paper, the regulatory body has to be separate from, and not accountable to, any supplier of basic telecommunications services.

aa Scope The Annex sets out general obligations for access to and use of networks and services, applicable to *all* Members and *all* sectors in which specific commitments have been undertaken. By contrast, the Reference Paper as an Additional Commitment under Article XVIII GATS is only applicable to Members that have included them in their schedules. Furthermore, the Reference Paper is limited to basic telecommunications services. While the Annex applies to all operators of public telecommunications transport networks and services within Members, regardless of their competitive situation, the Reference Paper obligations on interconnection apply only to 'major suppliers'. The Annex broadly deals with 'access to and use of' public telecommunications transport networks and services, while the Reference Paper focuses on specific 'competitive safeguards' and interconnection.[53]

Therefore, the Annex on Telecommunications remains relevant:

1 for a WTO Member which has made no commitments under the Reference Paper (in contrast to the Reference Paper, the Annex on Telecommunications is applicable to all Members);
2 for issues falling outside the scope of the Reference Paper, in particular value-added telecommunications services; and
3 when a Member has committed to a service sector other than telecommunications, for foreign service suppliers in that sector when dealing with the incumbent telecommunications operator.[54]

bb Competitive Safeguards The Members shall maintain appropriate measures for the purpose of preventing a 'major supplier' from engaging in or continuing anti-competitive practices. According to the definition catalogue, a major supplier is a one who has the ability to materially affect the terms of participation (having regard to price and supply) in the relevant market for basic telecommunications services as a result of control over essential facilities or use of its position in the market.[55] In particular, the anti-competitive practices include engaging in anti-competitive cross-subsidisation, using information obtained from competitors with anti-competitive results and not making available to other service suppliers technical information about essential facilities and commercially relevant information necessary for them to provide services.

---

[53] On the interpretation of the term 'interconnection' within the meaning of the Reference Paper, see WTO Panel, Mexico – Measures affecting telecommunications services [2004] WT/DS204/R; Peng (2007, pp. 313–315).

[54] Burri Nenova (2007, p. 845).

[55] WTO Panel, Mexico – Measures affecting telecommunications services [2004] WT/DS204/R [7.145], [7.159] and [7.226–7.228] provides guidance on the concept of 'major supplier'.

cc Interconnection   Section 2.2 of the Reference Paper obliges Members to ensure interconnection[56] with a 'major supplier'

(a)   under non-discriminatory terms, conditions, and rates and of a quality no less favourable than those provided for its own like services or for like services of non-affiliated service suppliers or for its subsidiaries or other affiliates,

(b)   in a timely fashion, on terms, conditions and cost-oriented rates[57] that are transparent, reasonable, economically feasible, and sufficiently unbundled so that the supplier need not pay for unnecessary network components or facilities, and

(c)   upon request, at points in addition to the network termination points offered to the majority of users, subject to charges that reflect the cost of construction of necessary additional facilities.[58]

dd Universal Services   According to Section 3 of the Reference Paper, any Member has the right to define the kind of universal service obligation it wishes to maintain. Such obligations will not be regarded as anti-competitive *per se*, provided they are administered in a transparent, non-discriminatory and competitively neutral manner and are not more burdensome than necessary for the kind of universal service defined by the Member.

ee Allocation and Use of Scarce Resources   Any procedures for the allocation and use of scarce resources, including frequencies, numbers and rights of way, must be carried out in an objective, timely, transparent and non-discriminatory manner (Section 6 of the Reference Paper).

c The WTO and EU Telecommunications Law

WTO law, and thus the GATS, is binding upon the EU and their Member States as signatories to the WTO Agreements.[59] The EU Schedule of Specific Commitments[60] is

---

[56]   Section 2.1 of the Reference Paper defines interconnection as 'linking with suppliers providing public telecommunications transport networks or services in order to allow the users of one supplier to communicate with users of another supplier and to access services provided by another supplier'.

[57]   See WTO Panel, Mexico – Measures affecting telecommunications services [2004] WT/DS204/R [7.160 ff].

[58]   Section 2.3 requires the public availability of the procedures for and Section 2.4 the transparency of interconnection arrangements. Section 2.5 obligates to establish a dispute settlement mechanism.

[59]   Council Decision 94/800/EC of 22 December 1994 concerning the conclusion on behalf of the European Community, as regards matters within its competence, of the agreements reached in the Uruguay Round multilateral negotiations (1986–1994), OJ L 336/1; Council Decision 97/838/EC of 18 December 1997 concerning the conclusion on behalf of the European Community, as regards matters within its competence, of the results of the WTO negotiations on basic telecommunications services, OJ L 347/45. In Opinion 1/94 [1994] WTO Accession, the European Court of Justice decided on the legality of the EC accession to the WTO. As the successor of the EC (Article 1 subpara. 3 TEU) and having legal personality (Article 47 TEU), the EU has been a Member of the WTO since 1 December 2009.

[60]   European Communities and their Member States, Schedule of Specific Commitments, Trade in Services, Supplement 3, GATS/SC/31/Suppl. 3 (97–1526), 11 April 1997.

almost fully committed to both basic and value-added telecommunications services, including a commitment to the Reference Paper. It should be noted that the EU schedule explicitly excludes broadcasting[61] and any other form of content provision from the definition of telecommunications services, thereby implementing the EC (now EU) approach of distinguishing between transmission services and the content being transmitted.[62]

The EU regulatory framework on electronic communications is influenced by the WTO commitments and vice versa.[63] The EU telecommunications rules frequently refer to the need to comply with both international commitments in general as well as with the WTO in particular.[64] The concepts introduced at the Union level are, to a broad extent, similar to those of the WTO.[65] This includes regulatory instruments and principles contained in both the GATS and the EU rules, such as 'interconnection',[66] 'non-discrimination',[67] 'transparency',[68] 'reasonable terms and conditions'[69] and the concepts of 'major supplier' and 'significant market power'.[70]

IV The Council of Europe Legal Framework

Apart from Article 10 ECHR and the Declaration of the Committee of Ministers on network neutrality,[71] the Council of Europe has contributed little to the development of a European legal order for telecommunications. Arguably the most important contribution by an institution of the Council of Europe was the Strasbourg Court's decision in *Autronic AG* v. *Switzerland* (our case example). Contrary to the argument

---

[61] Broadcasting is thereby defined as 'the uninterrupted chain of transmission required for the distribution of TV and radio programme signals to the general public, but does not cover contribution links between operators'.

[62] For further details on this approach and its implementation in the EU regulatory framework, see Section V.3.a.

[63] C. Koenig and A. Braun, in Koenig et al. (2009, p. 10). For a detailed analysis of both coherences and differences between the WTO and the EU telecommunications regime, see Burri Nenova (2007, pp. 866 ff); Peng (2007, p. 305).

[64] See, for example, Article 8(3) Access Directive, Article 5(3) Authorisation Directive, Recital 29 Framework Directive, or Recital 3 Universal Service Directive.

[65] Burri Nenova (2007, p. 866).

[66] Section 5(b)(ii) GATS Annex on Telecommunications and Section 2 of the Reference Paper, as well as Articles 5(1)(a) and 12(1)(i) Access Directive. WTO Panel, Mexico – Measures affecting telecommunications services [2004] WT/DS204/R [7.111], referred to the definition of 'interconnection' as contained in Article 2(b) Access Directive.

[67] See Section 5(a) GATS Annex on Telecommunications and Section 2.2(a) of the Reference Paper; concerning the EU commitment to non-discrimination, see Section VI.2.b.dd, and in particular Article 10 Access Directive.

[68] See, for example, Section 4 GATS Annex on Telecommunications and Section 2.4 of the Reference Paper, as well as, for example, Article 9 Access Directive.

[69] See Section 5(a) GATS Annex on Telecommunications and Section 2.2(a) of the Reference Paper, as well as Articles 12(1), 13 Access Directive.

[70] Burri Nenova (2007, p. 866).

[71] Adopted on 29 September 2010.

of the Swiss government, the Strasbourg Court held that Article 10 ECHR was applicable in this particular case. The Court decided that Article 10 ECHR applies not only to the content of information, but also to the means of transmission or reception, since any restriction imposed on the means necessarily interferes with the right to receive and impart information.[72] For the majority of the Court, it was immaterial that Autronic had not attached any importance to the content of the transmission (programmes in Russian) and was pursuing purely economic and technical interests.[73]

As the decisions of the Telecommunications Authority prevented Autronic from lawfully receiving the Soviet transmissions, they amounted to an interference with Autronic's right to receive information. This argument was supported by Article 4 of the European Convention on Transfrontier Television, which guarantees freedom of reception and of retransmission of programme services that comply with the terms of the Convention. The Strasbourg Court found that the interference of the Swiss Telecommunications Authority was in pursuance of two aims mentioned in Article 10(2) ECHR, namely the prevention of disorder in telecommunications and the need to prevent the disclosure of confidential information. The Court then had to decide whether the interference was justified. The Swiss Government had emphasised the distinction between direct-broadcasting satellites and telecommunications satellites; they claimed that international telecommunications law was designed to afford the same legal protection to broadcasts from the latter as to telephone communications. Broadcasting satellites transmitted radio and television programmes to an undefined number of receiving stations within a given area, on frequencies expressly reserved for direct reception, while telecommunications satellites were covered by the secrecy of broadcasts which all Member States were obliged to ensure under Article 37 of the ITU Constitution and Articles 17.1–17.3 of the Radio Regulations. Yet the Court rejected the government's submission, which was based on the special characteristics of transmission. Instead, the nature of the broadcasts in issue – uncoded broadcasts intended for television viewers in the Soviet Union – in itself precluded describing them as 'not intended for the general use of the public' within the meaning of Articles 17.1–17.3 of the ITU Radio Regulations. There was therefore no need to prohibit reception of these broadcasts.[74] The Court thus concluded that the interference in question violated Article 10 ECHR. Contrary to the argument of the Swiss authorities, the decisive factor was thus the content of the radiocommunication transmitted, in this case a television programme, but not the mode of its transmission.[75]

Although – or maybe even because – the Autronic case was quite out of the ordinary, it combined many of the core aspects that determine the European media law

---

[72] ECtHR, Autronic AG v. Switzerland [1990] App. no. 12726/87 [47].
[73] But see also the Dissenting Opinion of Judges Bindschedler-Robert and Matscher, para. 1.
[74] ECtHR, Autronic AG v. Switzerland [1990] App. no. 12726/87 [63].
[75] For the purposes of copyright protection, see now Recital 6 of the Satellite and Cable Directive: 'a distinction is currently drawn for copyright purposes between communication to the public by direct satellite

order until today, especially the Court's interpretation of Article 10 ECHR as a right to receive information disregarding the information's content as well as the distinction between content and the means of dissemination. The Court thus paved the way for the principle of technology neutrality, which underlies the European media law order today. Although technological and, in particular, political developments since 1990 would prevent this case from reoccurring today, it is still instructive for the understanding of the transnational law of telecommunications.

Moreover, in *Megadat.com SRL* v. *Moldova*, the ECtHR decided that a licence for internet access provision constitutes 'possession' within the meaning of Article 1 of the First Protocol to the ECHR.[76] In this case, the applicant company's telecommunications licences had been invalidated because it had not informed the competent supervisory authority of a change of address. It had been the only one out of 91 companies to have been penalised by such a sanction. As a result the company had to discontinue its activity. The Court noted that the examination carried out by the Moldovan courts appeared to have been 'very formalistic', lacking any balancing exercise.[77] The Court thus found the domestic proceedings to be arbitrary, the treatment of the applicant company discriminatory and the measure taken by the domestic authorities disproportionately harsh. The authorities had not followed any consistent policy considerations when invalidating the applicant company's licences.[78] Consequently, there had been a violation of Article 1 of Protocol No. 1.

V The Legal Framework of EU Telecommunications Law

Over the past decades the European telecommunications[79] sector has moved from a tradition of strong public service monopolies to a position of increased privatisation and competition. As a consequence of this privatisation and liberalisation of network infrastructures and services, the former governmental responsibility to *provide* network-related services has transformed into a responsibility to *ensure* that private companies provide these services, and maintain and, respectively, extend the existing infrastructures. Instead of providing telecommunications services, the Member States have to supervise and regulate companies in order to guarantee the

---

and communication to the public by communications satellite; ... since individual reception is possible and affordable nowadays with both types of satellite, there is no longer any justification for this differing legal treatment'.

[76] ECtHR, Megadat.com SRL v. Moldova [2008] App. no. 21151/04 [63].

[77] ECtHR, Megadat.com SRL v. Moldova [2008] App. no. 21151/04 [74].

[78] ECtHR, Megadat.com SRL v. Moldova [2008] App. no. 21151/04 [79].

[79] EU documents usually apply the terms 'communications' or 'electronic communications'. Together with 'telecommunications', the terms may be used interchangeably. However, 'communications' is slightly misleading, because taken literally it might suggest that it also covers the regulation of communication content. As will be shown below, this is in fact not the case. Therefore the term 'telecommunications', describing the process of transmitting content more commonly, is used here.

availability of adequate and appropriate telecommunications services throughout their territories.[80]

1 Liberalisation and Harmonisation of the EU Telecommunications Sector

The primary driver of change in the telecommunications sector has been the dramatic increase in the use of information technologies, which has revolutionised the industry.[81] The regulatory process for telecommunications stands as an example for the broader process of economic integration in Europe. The Commission's main policy has been the move towards a single market for telecommunications services and equipment that progressively removes barriers to pan-European operation and supply.[82] This policy has seen an evolving interaction between different elements. In addition to competition law rules,[83] the two main instruments applied to introduce a single market for telecommunications services were:

1 liberalisation of former monopolies, and
2 accompanying harmonisation measures.

It is important to distinguish between the areas of 'harmonisation' and 'liberalisation'. First, they are based on different Treaty provisions. Under the principle of conferral, now explicitly fixed in Article 5(2) TEU, the Union shall act only within the limits of the competences conferred upon it by the Member States in the Treaties to attain the objectives set out therein. The EU therefore needs an authorisation by the Treaties to liberalise and harmonise the telecommunications sector. These provisions are 106(3) TFEU (formerly Article 86(3) EC) for liberalisation and Article 114(1) TFEU (ex Article 95(1) EC) for harmonisation. Second, liberalisation measures based on 106(3) TFEU/ex Article 86(3) EC may be adopted by the Commission, whereas the adoption of harmonising measures falls within the competence of the Council and the European Parliament (Article 114(1) TFEU/ex Article 95(1) EC). Third, the initiatives for liberalisation and harmonisation originate from different departments of the European Commission. While harmonisation measures reside with the Information Society Directorate-General, liberalisation has been the responsibility of the Competition Directorate-General.

a Liberalisation

Article 106(3) TFEU (formerly Article 86(3) EC) mandates that the Commission must ensure the application of these provisions and address appropriate Directives or Decisions to Member States. With regard to the telecommunications sector, Article

---

[80] In the US, by contrast, the provision of telecommunications services has always been the task of private companies that have been supervised by regulatory agencies, in particular the Federal Communications Commission (FCC). Although EU legislative documents do not explicitly refer to US regulation, it is discernible that the US regulatory instruments served in many aspects as role models for EU legislation, for instance regarding universal services according to Section 254 US Telecommunications Act 1934.

[81] See http://ec.europa.eu/information_society/policy/ecomm/doc/history/index_en.htm.

[82] http://ec.europa.eu/information_society/policy/ecomm/doc/history/index_en.htm.

[83] Articles 101, 102 TFEU (ex Articles 81, 82 EC). See Case 41/83 [1985] British Telecommunications.

86(3) EC conferred upon the Commission the authority to liberalise the telecommunications sector and to end monopolies. The main mechanisms to promote liberalisation were directives that abolished the special rights of certain public enterprises to produce or supply telecommunications equipment and services, which then breached competition and internal market rules. These Directives required Member States to allow competition in the market for telecommunications services but did not require the privatisation of national public services.

b Harmonisation

Complementing the liberalisation of the telecommunications sector, the Commission's strategy aimed at harmonising the national regulations in order to facilitate the access of competitors to telecommunications markets to create an internal market for telecommunications services in the long term. For this purpose, Article 114(1) TFEU (ex Article 95(1) EC) authorises the responsible EU institutions to adopt the measures for the approximation of the provisions in Member States that have as their objective the establishment and functioning of the internal market.[84] The Directives based on Article 95(1) EC aimed at harmonising the principles and conditions for the access to public telecommunications networks and services.[85]

c Historical Development

The Commission's telecommunications policy programme can be historically distinguished into three phases.

aa First Phase 1987–1998   In its Green Paper 1987, the Commission called for the complete liberalisation of the telecommunications sector with the exception of voice

---

[84] According to ECJ case law, Article 95 EC [now Article 114 TFEU] is used as a legal basis only 'where it is actually and objectively apparent from the legal act that its purpose is to improve the conditions for the establishment and functioning of the internal market' (see, for example, Case C-66/04 [2005] United Kingdom v. Parliament and Council [44]). The Court also pointed out that by using the expression 'measures for the approximation' in Article 95 EC [now Article 114 TFEU] the Treaty 'intended to confer on the Community legislature a discretion, depending on the general context and the specific circumstances of the matter to be harmonised, as regards the method of approximation most appropriate for achieving the desired result, in particular in fields with complex technical features'.

[85] See Council Directive 90/387/EEC of 28 June 1990 on the establishment of the internal market for telecommunications services through the implementation of open network provision, OJ L 192/1; Directive 97/33/EC of the European Parliament and of the Council of 30 June 1997 on interconnection in Telecommunications with regard to ensuring universal service and interoperability through application of the principles of Open Network Provision (ONP), OJ L 199/32; Council Directive 92/44/EEC of 5 June 1992 on the application of Open Network Provision to leased lines, OJ L 165/27; Directive 97/51/EC of the European Parliament and of the Council of the 6 October 1997 amending Council Directives 90/387/EEC and 92/44/EEC for the purpose of adaptation to a competitive environment in telecommunications, OJ L 295/23; Directive 97/66/EC of the European Parliament and the Council of 15 December 1997 concerning the processing of personal data and protection of privacy in the telecommunications sector, OJ L 24/1; Directive 98/10/EC of the European Parliament and of the Council of 26 February 1998 on the application of open network provision (ONP) to voice telephony and on universal service for telecommunications in a competitive environment, OJ L 101/24.

telephony.[86] Based on Article 86(3) EC (now Article 106(3) TFEU), the Commission adopted Directive 88/301/EEC on competition in the markets in telecommunications terminal equipment[87] and Directive 90/388/EC on competition in the markets for telecommunications services.[88] With the amendment of the latter Directive by Directives 94/46/EC (satellite communications),[89] 95/51/EC (cable television networks),[90] Directive 96/2/EC (mobile communications)[91] and 96/19/EC (competition),[92] the Commission required the Member States to fully liberalise the telecommunications sector in the EU beginning 1 January 1998. Furthermore, by virtue of Directive 90/387/EEC, the telecommunications industry was subjected to sector-specific regulation. The Directive established the principle of Open Network Provision (ONP), which was aimed at harmonising open network access for alternative providers. To adapt to the evolving competitive environment, the ONP Directive was complemented by further Directives such as the Directive 92/44/EEC on leased lines,[93] Directive 97/33/EC on interconnection,[94] Directive 97/51/EC on competition,[95] Directive 97/66/EC on privacy[96] and Directive 98/10/EC on voice telephony.[97]

[86] COM, Towards a Dynamic European Economy – Green Paper on the development of the common market for telecommunications services and equipment, COM(87) 290.

[87] Commission Directive 88/301/EEC of 16 May 1988 on competition in the markets in telecommunications terminal equipment, OJ L 131/73. The Directive was repealed and codified by Commission Directive 2008/63/EC of 20 June 2008 on competition in the markets in telecommunications terminal equipment, OJ L 162/20.

[88] Commission Directive 90/388/EEC of 28 June 1990 on competition in the markets for telecommunications services, OJ L 192/10. The Directive was repealed by Commission Directive 2002/77/EC of 16 September 2002 on competition in the markets for electronic communications networks and services, OJ L 249/21.

[89] Commission Directive 94/46/EC of 13 October 1994 amending Directive 88/301/EEC and Directive 90/388/EEC in particular with regard to satellite communications, OJ L 268/15.

[90] Commission Directive 95/51/EC of 18 October 1995 amending Directive 90/388/EEC with regard to the abolition of the restrictions on the use of cable television networks for the provision of already liberalised telecommunications services, OJ L 256/49.

[91] Commission Directive 96/2/EC of 16 January 1996 amending Directive 90/388/EEC with regard to mobile and personal communications, OJ L 20/59.

[92] Commission Directive 96/19/EC of 13 March 1996 amending Directive 90/388/EEC with regard to the implementation of full competition in telecommunications markets, OJ L 74/13.

[93] On the interpretation of Article 7 Leased Lines Directive, which provides that that minimum set of leased lines must be provided by one or more telecommunications organisations in each of the Member States, see Case C-302/94 [1996] British Telecommunications II.

[94] On the interpretation of this Directive, see ECJ, Case C-221/01 [2002] Commission v. Belgium; Case C-33/04 [2005] Commission v. Luxembourg; Joined Cases C-152/07, C-154/07 and C-153/07 [2008] Arcor and others; Case C-113/03 [2004] Commission v. France.

[95] Directive 97/51/EC of the European Parliament and of the Council of the 6 October 1997 amending Council Directives 90/387/EEC and 92/44/EEC for the purpose of adaptation to a competitive environment in telecommunications, OJ L 295/23.

[96] Directive 97/66/EC of the European Parliament and the Council of 15 December 1997 concerning the processing of personal data and protection of privacy in the telecommunications sector, OJ L 24/1.

[97] Directive 98/10/EC of the European Parliament and of the Council of 26 February 1998 on the application of open network provision (ONP) to voice telephony and on universal service for telecommunications in a competitive environment, OJ L 101/24.

Accompanied by Commission Recommendations,[98] these Directives made up the '1998 package' of legislation establishing the basis for fully liberating EU telecommunications markets by 1 January 1998.

bb Second Phase 1998–2003   The '1998 package' was primarily designed to manage the transition in the telecommunications sector from monopoly to competition. Due to the challenges of rapidly changing technology, media convergence and successfully liberalised markets, a new framework of regulation covering all electronic communication, including broadcasting networks, was developed since 1998.[99] The reform ended in 2002 when 20 Directives were reduced to six so that all transmission networks and associated services would be subject to the same regulatory framework: Competition Directive (2002/77/EC),[100] Framework Directive (2002/21/EC),[101] Authorisation Directive (2002/20/EC),[102] Access Directive (2002/19/EC),[103] Universal Service Directive (2002/22/EC)[104] and E-privacy Directive (2002/58/EC).[105] The Member States were required to implement the so-called Common Regulatory Framework (CRF) until 24 July 2003 and the E-privacy Directive until 31 October 2003, respectively.[106]

---

[98] For example, COM, Recommendation of 29 July 1998 amending Recommendation 98/195/EC on interconnection in a liberalised telecommunications market (Part 1 – Interconnection pricing), C(1998) 2234 final; Recommendation of 8 April 1998 on interconnection in a liberalized telecommunications market (Part 2 – Accounting separation and cost accounting), C(1998) 960 final; Recommendation of 24 November 1999 on Leased lines interconnection pricing in a liberalised telecommunications market, C(1999)3863.

[99] In November 1999, the Commission presented a communication to the European Parliament, the Council, the Economic and Social Committee and the Committee of the Regions entitled 'Towards a new framework for electronic communications infrastructure and associated services – the 1999 Communications Review', COM(1999) 537 final and COM(1999) 539 final. In that communication, the Commission reviewed the existing regulatory framework for telecommunications, in accordance with its obligation under Article 8 Directive 90/387/EEC. The Lisbon European Council of 23 and 24 March 2000 highlighted the potential for growth, competitiveness and job creation of the shift to a digital, knowledge-based economy. In particular, it emphasised the importance for Europe's businesses and citizens of access to an inexpensive, world-class communications infrastructure and a wide range of services.

[100] Commission Directive 2002/77/EC of 16 September 2002 on competition in the markets for electronic communications networks and services, OJ L 249/21.

[101] Directive 2002/21/EC of the European Parliament and of the Council of 7 March 2002 on a common regulatory framework for electronic communications networks and services (Framework Directive), OJ L 108/33.

[102] Directive 2002/20/EC of the European Parliament and of the Council of 7 March 2002 on the authorisation of electronic communications networks and services (Authorisation Directive), OJ L 108/21.

[103] Directive 2002/19/EC of the European Parliament and of the Council of 7 March 2002 on access to, and interconnection of, electronic communications networks and associated facilities (Access Directive), OJ L 108/7.

[104] Directive 2002/22/EC of the European Parliament and of the Council of 7 March 2002 on universal service and users' rights relating to electronic communications networks and services (Universal Service Directive), OJ L 108/51.

[105] Directive 2002/58/EC of the European Parliament and of the Council of 12 July 2002 concerning the processing of personal data and the protection of privacy in the electronic communications sector (Directive on privacy and electronic communications), OJ L 201/37.

[106] See, for example, the German Telecommunications Act (Telekommunikationsgesetz – TKG) of 22 June 2004 and the UK Communications Act 2003 (c. 21).

The Framework Directive includes general provisions for the CRF, which are specified and complemented by the other Directives. The Framework Directive regulates, *inter alia*, the scope and general aims of the regulatory framework, the national regulatory authorities and procedural aspects and judicial review. The Authorisation Directive encompasses the harmonisation and simplification of authorisation rules and conditions concerning electronic communications networks and services in order to facilitate their provision throughout the EU. The Access Directive provides conditions for regulatory measures ordering access to communications networks and services. The Universal Service Directive can be divided into three parts: scope and financing of universal service obligations, *ex ante* regulation of retail services and end-user rights. Finally, the E-privacy Directive aims at harmonising the provisions protecting the right to privacy with respect to the processing of personal data in the electronic communication sector. The Directive particularises and complements the generally applicable Directive 95/46/EC on the protection of individuals with regard to the processing and the free movement of personal data (see Chapter 8).

In 2000, the Commission additionally decided to open the local loops for competition. Regulation (EC) No. 2887/2000 on unbundled access to the local loop[107] obligated certain operators to offer unbundled access to their local loops and related facilities. Within the meaning of this Regulation, the 'local loop' included only the physical twisted metallic pair circuit in the fixed public telephone network that connected the network termination point at the subscriber's premises to the main distribution frame; that is, the 'classic' local telephone network. Under the 2002 framework, national regulatory authorities have a duty to analyse the market for wholesale unbundled access to these metallic loops and sub-loops for the purpose of providing broadband and voice services. Since all Member States have analysed this market at least once and the appropriate obligations are in place, Regulation (EC) No. 2887/2000 has become unnecessary and was therefore repealed by Article 4 of the 'Better Regulation Directive'. However, case law of the ECJ concerning the interpretation of the Local Loop Regulation is still valid as far as it pertains to general regulatory principles.[108]

cc Third Phase, 2003–2011   On 13 November 2007, the Commission published a bundle of new draft Directives in order to reform the legal framework for electronic communications.[109] This revision was an attempt to bring the telecommunications framework up-to-date for the fast-developing telecommunications sector in a Union

---

[107] Regulation (EC) No. 2887/2000 of the European Parliament and of the Council of 18 December 2000 on unbundled access to the local loop, OJ L 336/4.

[108] See, for example, Case C-55/06 [2008] Arcor, concerning the calculation of the charges that can be applied by a dominant incumbent telecoms operator for access to its local network.

[109] The Commission presented its initial findings in its Communication of 29 June 2006 on the review of the EU Regulatory Framework for electronic communications networks and services, COM(2006) 334 final. Recitals 2 and 3 Better Regulation Directive: '(2) [...] On the basis of these initial findings, a public

that then had 27 Member States.[110] The revised rules focus regulation on those market sectors where competition is still lacking, and develop stronger EU-level regulation to foster the development of the internal market. In November 2009, the European Parliament and the Council adopted the Directives 'Citizens' Rights'[111] and 'Better Regulation'[112] amending (but not repealing) the existing Directives composing the regulatory framework, as well as the Regulation establishing the BEREC. The Member States are required to enforce these Directives until 25 May 2011.

In addition, the European Parliament and Council adopted the Roaming Regulation in 2007, which concerns the prices payable by users of public mobile telephone networks when using their mobile telephones for voice calls, SMS and MMS when travelling abroad within the EU.[113]

2 Actors in EU Telecommunications Law

The most influential actors in the enforcement of EU telecommunications law are the Commission, the Body of European Regulators for Electronic Communications (BEREC), the Independent Regulators Group (IRG) and the national regulatory authorities (NRAs). In addition, decisions of national courts and the European Court of Justice (ECJ; now Court of Justice of the European Union) have contributed significantly to the interpretation of the legal framework.

---

consultation was held, which identified the continued lack of an internal market for electronic communications as the most important aspect needing to be addressed. In particular, regulatory fragmentation and inconsistencies between the activities of the national regulatory authorities were found to jeopardise not only the competitiveness of the sector, but also the substantial consumer benefits from cross-border competition. (3) The EU regulatory framework for electronic communications networks and services should therefore be reformed in order to complete the internal market for electronic communications by strengthening the Community mechanism for regulating operators with significant market power in the key markets.'

[110] http://ec.europa.eu/information_society/policy/ecomm/doc/history/index_en.htm.

[111] Directive 2009/136/EC of the European Parliament and of the Council of 25 November 2009 amending Directive 2002/22/EC on universal service and users' rights relating to electronic communications networks and services, Directive 2002/58/EC concerning the processing of personal data and the protection of privacy in the electronic communications sector and Regulation (EC) No. 2006/2004 on cooperation between national authorities responsible for the enforcement of consumer protection laws, OJ L 337/11.

[112] Directive 2009/140/EC of the European Parliament and of the Council of 25 November 2009 amending Directives 2002/21/EC on a common regulatory framework for electronic communications networks and services, 2002/19/EC on access to, and interconnection of, electronic communications networks and associated facilities, and 2002/20/EC on the authorisation of electronic communications networks and services, OJ L 337/37.

[113] Regulation (EC) No. 717/2007 of the European Parliament and of the Council of 27 June 2007 on roaming on public mobile telephone networks within the Community and amending Directive 2002/21/EC, OJ L 171/32, as amended by Regulation (EU) 2015/2120 of the European Parliament and of the Council of 25 November 2015 laying down measures concerning open internet access and amending Directive 2002/22/EC on universal service and users' rights relating to electronic communications networks and services and Regulation (EU) No. 531/2012 on roaming on public mobile communications networks within the Union, OJ L 310/1. The CJEU confirmed the validity of this Regulation in Case C-58/08 [2010] Vodafone.

a Commission

The Commission is more than a mere 'watchdog' of Member States' telecommunications regulation. It also has significant influence on the national regulatory processes themselves. Telecommunications law thus stands as a prime example for the
increasing interdependence of national and European administrative procedures,
or the 'Europeanisation of administrative law'. The Commission's powers include,
inter alia, the adoption of recommendations and guidelines, which have a significant
impact on market definition and market analysis, the power of veto (under certain
circumstances) in market definition and market analysis procedures, and a suspend-
ing veto right when Member States adopt particular regulatory measures. Apart from
that, the regulatory framework provides a number of situations in which the Member
States are obligated to notify the Commission, for example, regarding the imposition of *ex ante* regulatory obligations. The Commission is furthermore empowered
to adopt implementing measures to update Annexes I and II to the Access Directive
(see Recital 76 Better Regulation Directive). Commission measures necessary for
the implementation of the regulatory framework have to be adopted in accordance
with Council Decision 1999/468/EC laying down the procedures for the exercise of
implementing powers conferred on the Commission.[114]

b BEREC and IRG

The Body of European Regulators for Electronic Communications (BEREC) and the
Independent Regulators Group (IRG) also stand as paradigms for the Europeanisation
of administrative law. BEREC is a forum for cooperation among national regulatory
authorities and between these authorities and the Commission to ensure the consistent
application of the EU regulatory framework for electronic communications networks
and services in all Member States. BEREC and its office (with the simple and somewhat Kafkaesque name 'the Office') were established by Regulation (EC) No. 1211/
2009 ('BEREC Regulation').[115] BEREC is not an EU agency nor does it have legal personality. By contrast, the Office, which supports BEREC, is established as a Union body
with legal personality (see Recital 11 BEREC Regulation). BEREC is comprised of a
Board of Regulators consisting of the heads of the 28 national regulatory authorities.
The EU Commission, the EFTA states Switzerland, Norway, Iceland and Liechtenstein,
and the EU candidate states Turkey and the Former Yugoslav Republic of Macedonia
participate as observers to the Board of Regulators. As the successor of the European
Regulators Group (ERG),[116] BEREC's functions are merely advisory and its decisions

---

[114] OJ L 184/23.
[115] Regulation (EC) No. 1211/2009 of the European Parliament and of the Council of 25 November 2009
establishing the Body of European Regulators for Electronic Communications (BEREC) and the Office,
OJ L 337/1.
[116] The Commission established the European Regulators Group (ERG) as an advisory group pursuant to
COM, Decision 2002/627/EC of 29 July 2002 establishing the European Regulators Group for Electronic
Communications Networks and Services.

have no binding force. BEREC's main tasks are to provide assistance to national regulatory authorities and the Commission on regulatory matters, and to issue opinions on draft measures of national regulatory authorities concerning market definition, the designation of undertakings with significant market power and the imposition of remedies, in accordance with Articles 7 and 7a Framework Directive. According to Article 3(3) BEREC Regulation, both national regulatory authorities and the Commission 'shall take the utmost account of any opinion, recommendation, guidelines, advice or regulatory best practice adopted by BEREC'.

Established in 1997, the Independent Regulators Group (IRG) is an informal network of European telecom regulators who share experiences and points of view among its members on issues relating to the regulation and development of the European telecommunications market. IRG is registered as a not-for-profit organisation under Belgian law (ASBL) and has a Brussels-based secretariat.

c National Regulatory Authorities (NRAs)

The main actors within the field of telecommunications regulation are the national regulatory authorities (NRAs) such as the Office of Communications (Ofcom) in the United Kingdom, the Onafhankelijke Post en Telecommunicatie Autoriteit (Opta) in the Netherlands and the Bundesnetzagentur (BNetzA) in Germany.

According to Article 3(2) Framework Directive, the Member States have to guarantee the independence of the NRAs 'by ensuring that they are legally distinct from and functionally independent of all organisations providing electronic communications networks, equipment or services'. Thus 'independence' within the context of the European regulatory framework denotes functional independence from both the regulated industry and governmental institutions retaining ownership or control of undertakings that provide electronic communications networks or services.[117] However, the European lawmaker considered the tenet of agency accountability by including a caveat in sentence 2 that '[t]his shall not prevent supervision in accordance with national constitutional law'.

3 Scope of the Regulatory Framework

The scope of the regulatory framework extends to, but is also limited to, public transmission networks and services, and therefore excludes the regulation of content. In accordance with general principles of the internal market, the services have to be provided for remuneration. Finally, the regulatory framework excludes terminal equipment.

---

[117] See Case C-82/07 [2008] Comisión del Mercedo de las Telecomunicaciones [14]: 'Where Member States retain ownership or control of undertakings providing electronic communications networks and/or services, they are to take care, specifically, to ensure effective structural separation of the regulatory function, on the one hand, from activities associated with ownership or control of those undertakings, on the other.'

a Transmission Services as Opposed to the Provision of Content

According to Article 2(a) Framework Directive, an electronic communications network is defined as

> transmission systems and [...] other resources [...], which permit the conveyance of signals by [...] electromagnetic means, including satellite networks, fixed (circuit- and packet-switched, including internet) and mobile terrestrial networks, electricity cable systems, to the extent that they are used for the purpose of transmitting signals, networks used for radio and television broadcasting, and cable television networks, irrespective of the type of information conveyed.

In addition, Article 2(d) Framework Directive defines public communications networks as electronic communications networks 'used wholly or mainly for the provision of electronic communications services available to the public which support the transfer of information between network termination points'.[118] Ultimately, an electronic communications service is, according to Article 2(c) Framework Directive, 'a service normally provided for remuneration which consists wholly or mainly in the conveyance of signals on electronic communications networks, including telecommunications services and transmission services in networks used for broadcasting'. The provision explicitly excludes services providing content that do not consist wholly or mainly in the conveyance of signals on electronic communications networks.[119]

The regulatory framework thus does not cover the *content* of services transmitted over electronic communications networks, such as broadcasting and information society services. Consequently, Article 1(3) Framework Directive confirms that the regulatory framework on electronic communications is 'without prejudice to measures [...] to pursue general interest objectives, in particular relating to content regulation and audio-visual policy'. The regulatory framework on electronic communications does not, in particular, require providers to monitor information transmitted over their networks or to bring legal proceedings against their customers because of such information, nor does it make providers liable for that information. As Recital 31 Citizen Rights Directive emphasises, '[i]t is a task for the Member States, not for providers of electronic communications networks or services, to decide [...] whether content, applications or services are lawful or harmful'. The distinction between transmission services and the transmitted content, notably broadcasting, is due to the EU's commitment to protect cultural values, which are perceived as being reflected by, in particular, the domestic broadcasting landscape. Therefore, as we have

---

[118] Article 2(da) defines 'network termination point' (NTP) as the physical point at which a subscriber is provided with access to a public communications network; in the case of networks involving switching or routing, the NTP is identified by means of a specific network address, which may be linked to a subscriber number or name.

[119] See, *mutatis mutandis*, CJEU, Case C-518/11 [2013] UPC Nederland BV [43]; Case C-475/12 [2014] UPC DTH Sàrl [37].

seen in Chapter 5, the EU keeps the audiovisual sector out of the liberalisation and harmonisation procedures that take place in the field of electronic communications.

Due to the phenomenon of converging media technology and content, the distinction between electronic communications services on one side and content-related services, notably information society services, on the other, is often difficult to establish. This is further complicated by the wording 'wholly *or mainly*' in Article 2(c) Framework Directive. In individual cases it can be rather difficult to decide whether the conveyance of signals is the main service provided or whether a simultaneously provided content-related service preponderates. In Recital 10 Framework Directive, the European lawmaker assumes that voice telephony, the provision of internet access and e-mail conveyance services are covered by the electronic communications framework. For instance, publicly available voice over IP (VoIP) services allowing access to and from the public switched telephone networks (PSTN) are electronic communications services, assuming there is no content-related service attached.[120] By contrast, the offering of a VoIP software programme on a website does not constitute a communications service, but rather a wholly content-related one.

If the same undertaking offers both an electronic communications service and a service providing content, the undertaking has to meet obligations in relation to its activities as both a transmitter and a content provider. Cable operators, for instance, may offer the conveyance of television signals and television broadcasting content services. They must therefore abide by the regulatory framework on electronic communications, for example, the 'must carry' obligations for the transmission of specified radio and television broadcast channels according to Article 31 Universal Service Directive as well as the AVMS Directive.[121] Another example is an internet service provider that offers both an electronic communications service, such as access to the internet, and web-based content as information society service. Most information society services are covered by the E-commerce Directive.

b Public Networks and Publicly Available Services

In addition, the regulatory provisions, notably those concerning access to networks and services, usually refer to *public* communications networks and *publicly available* electronic communications services (see Article 4(2) Authorisation Directive and Article 2(c) Access Directive). Networks used for the provision of services only available for certain users, for instance corporate networks used to provide internal communications, are not subject to the rules contained in the Access Directive. Specifically to guarantee the protection of privacy, private communications networks are nevertheless subject to the Authorisation Directive.

---

[120] See COM, Staff Working Document, The treatment of Voice over Internet Protocol (VoIP) under the EU Regulatory Framework, 14 June 2004, p. 6.
[121] See Chapter 5.

c Provided Against Payment

To be covered by the scope of the regulatory framework, an electronic communications service must be 'normally provided for remuneration' (Article 2(c) Framework Directive; see also Recital 5 Authorisation Directive). The conferral of Union competences in Article 114 TFEU (ex Article 95 EC) refers to measures that have as their objective the establishment and functioning of the internal market. The internal market comprises an area without internal frontiers in which the free movement of, *inter alia,* services is ensured (Article 26(2) TFEU). Yet, the internal market only concerns those services where remuneration is paid in consideration of their provision (Article 57(1) TFEU). As a consequence, harmonisation measures under Article 114 TFEU may only include services provided against payment.[122]

For instance, direct internet telephony between users of voice over IP software without access to the public switched telephone network (so-called peer-to-peer or P2P applications) is usually free of charge and is therefore not an electronic communications service under the regulatory framework.

d Exclusion of Telecommunications Equipment

Furthermore, according to Article 1(4) Framework Directive, the regulatory framework does not cover equipment within the scope of Directive 1999/5/EC on radio equipment and telecommunications terminal equipment.[123] But it does cover consumer equipment used for digital television (Article 18 Framework Directive, Article 24 and Annex VI Universal Services Directive).

e Distinction between Sector-Specific Regulation and Competition Law

Finally, the regulatory framework on telecommunications needs to be distinguished from general competition law. Telecommunications law is sector-specific competition law and is based on the idea of the essential facilities doctrine, which we will look at in more detail in Chapter 10. By contrast to competition law, telecommunications regulation (specifically access regulation) does not apply the essential facilities doctrine on a case-by-case basis, but for a whole group of cases; that is, petitioners demanding access to communications networks or services owned or provided by a dominant incumbent. Telecommunications regulation therefore does not require an abuse of the dominant position as would normally be mandatory under competition law. With its forward-looking approach, telecommunications regulation aims at creating competition by changing the market structure, instead of reacting to an abuse that has occurred.

Although many principles of competition law are applicable in the field of telecommunications regulation – for instance, the designation of an undertaking of

---

[122] A. Brandenberg, in Koenig et al. (2009, p. 485).
[123] Directive 1999/5/EC of the European Parliament and of the Council of 9 March 1999 on radio equipment and telecommunications terminal equipment and the mutual recognition of their conformity, OJ L 91/10.

having significant market power under Article 7 Framework Directive – the most distinctive feature between telecommunications regulation and competition law is the fact that competition law applies to principally functioning competition, whereas telecommunications regulation needs to create competition in the first place. Thus, competition law is interventive, whereas telecommunications regulation is creative. So long as competition rules alone are not sufficient to ensure sustainable competition, regulation is necessary. However, as soon as competition law ensures sustainable competition, *ex ante* regulation becomes redundant and the antitrust rules are applicable.[124] In the field of telecommunications regulation, this principle is reflected by the fact that once effective competition is established on a particular market, the Commission and, subsequently, the Member States release this respective market from regulation. When examining whether markets should be subject to regulation, the Commission and the regulatory authorities ask, *inter alia*, whether the market in question lacks a tendency towards effective competition and whether the application of competition law alone would not adequately address the market failure(s) concerned. Only if the answer to both questions is in the affirmative can the investigations into whether the market should be regulated proceed. In practice, the difficult distinction between a functioning and a not-yet functioning market requires close cooperation and coordination between the regulatory authorities and the authorities entrusted with the implementation of competition law.

4 Objectives and Principles

The fundamental reason and justification for the regulation of the telecommunications sector, and many other fields of network infrastructure regulation, is market failure. Regulation usually occurs when the operator, left to his own devices, behaves in a way that is detrimental to general policy objectives. With regard to telecommunications services, it is commonly agreed upon that adequate and appropriate telecommunications services must be available throughout the country. A telecommunications monopoly or oligopoly would be contrary to this objective. For historical and economic reasons, functioning competition does not yet exist in many telecommunication markets, therefore regulation is considered necessary.

Article 8 Framework Directive lays down several objectives to be pursued by the national regulatory authorities. They shall

- promote competition in the provision of electronic communications networks, electronic communications services and associated facilities and services (para. 2);
- contribute to the development of the internal market (para. 3); and
- promote the interests of the citizens of the European Union (para. 4).

---

[124] See, for example, CJEU, Case C-280/08 P [2010] Deutsche Telekom v. Commission; Case C-52/09 [2011] Konkurrensverket v. TeliaSonera Sverige AB.

When carrying out their regulatory duties, regulatory agencies have to consider both the fundamental principles of EU law in general, as well as the Common Regulatory Framework in particular. These principles particularly include non-discrimination, the necessity to balance conflicting interests, the principle of proportionality and the principles of technology and service neutrality.

a Principle of Non-Discrimination

The principle of non-discrimination does not only oblige the national and European authorities not to discriminate against certain people or undertakings, as is already required by Article 2 TEU, Article 18 TFEU and Article 21 EUChFR. In telecommunications regulation, the principle of non-discrimination[125] shall ensure that undertakings with market power do not distort competition by favouring certain companies or customers over others, in particular when they are vertically integrated undertakings that supply services to undertakings with whom they compete on downstream markets (see Recital 17 and Article 10 Access Directive). Operators have to instead apply equivalent conditions in equivalent circumstances to undertakings providing equivalent services, and provide services and information to others under the same conditions and of the same quality as they provide for their own services or those of their subsidiaries or partners.[126] To detect discrimination and to enforce regulatory obligations of non-discrimination, undertakings may be bound to transparency requirements, such as Article 9 Access Directive.

b Necessity to Balance Conflicting Interests and the Principle of Proportionality

Typically, telecommunications regulation is not a conditionally determined way of reasoning consisting of 'if–then' clauses, but a complex process of balancing different aspects in order to reach certain, sometimes even irreconcilable, aims. The general aim of network infrastructure regulation, for instance, is the achievement of effective competition. However, ordering network operators to grant access to their networks affects their property rights and may spoil incentives for further investments in their infrastructure. Furthermore, telecommunications infrastructure can have adverse effects on the environment and the landscape. Finally, access to telecommunications services may conflict with data protection concerns or intellectual property rights of the regulated undertaking. It is therefore the duty of the national regulatory authority to duly balance and, whenever possible, to reconcile these conflicting interests. This re-emphasises the regulatory discretion the European regulatory framework has conferred on national regulatory authorities: it is for the agencies and not for national legislation to conduct this balancing process.[127]

---

[125] See, for example, Article 8(5) Framework Directive, Article 7(3) Authorisation Directive, or Article 3(2) Universal Service Directive.
[126] See Article 10(2) Access Directive.
[127] Case C-424/07 [2009] Commission v. Germany [92–94].

However, any regulatory action is subject to the principle of proportionality.[128] Under the principle of proportionality, the content and form of regulatory action shall not exceed what is necessary to achieve the objectives of the regulatory framework.

c Principles of Technology Neutrality and Service Neutrality

The principles of technology neutrality and service neutrality[129] derive from the rapid technological development and the phenomenon of media convergence. The technology used to provide services or to disseminate content is not a distinctive feature anymore, since different services may be provided by the same technology, and different technologies are capable of providing the same service.[130] Convergence between different electronic communications networks and services and their technologies therefore requires the establishment of a regulatory regime that covers all comparable services in a similar way regardless of the technologies used. Technology neutrality thus means that authorities must neither impose nor discriminate in favour of the use of a particular type of technology.[131] Article 2(a) Framework Directive therefore indicates that the existence of an electronic communications network is 'irrespective of the type of information conveyed'. For instance, whether a voice telephony service is based on customary circuit-switching or on modern packet-switching technology (voice over IP) must affect neither the regulatory classification of VoIP as a telephone service nor of the transmitting network as an electronic communications network.[132]

d Net Neutrality

As has been shown in Chapter 6, the internet – more precisely, the TCP/IP – has initially been conceived as neutral. Since it does not take notice of the content the network disseminates, it does not discriminate between distinct forms of content, such as e-mails or video streaming. This descriptive feature of the internet has been elevated to a prescriptive principle: the Cyberidealist claim that internet transmission *should* remain neutral. 'Net neutrality' describes the open and neutral character of the internet, which does not distinguish between different contents and the modes of communication. However, the proliferation of broadband as well as the increased demand for large contents (such as audio and video services) have led to conflicts between content providers and network operators.[133] Modern routers

---

[128] In Primary EU Law, the principle of proportionality is rooted in Article 5(4) TEU. For the EU communications framework, see Article 8(1) subpara. 2 and (5) Framework Directive, or Article 3(2) Universal Service Directive.

[129] See, for example, Article 8(1) subpara. 2 Framework Directive; Recital 18 Framework Directive; Recital 13 Citizens Rights Directive; Recital 34 Better Regulation Directive.

[130] From legal scholarship on technology neutrality, see, for example, Kamecke and Korber (2008); Maxwell and Bourreau (2015).

[131] See Recital 18 Framework Directive.

[132] See Recital 13 Citizen's Rights Directive.

[133] Dods et al. (2010, p. 106).

enable networks to prioritise some internet traffic over others in order to optimise network capacity and prevent congestion that, however, causes other content to be restricted.

The Better Regulation Directive has established that net neutrality is an additional principle and objective of telecommunications regulation. The European Commission maintains the view that the open and neutral character of the internet should be preserved.[134] Accordingly, the new Article 8(4)(g) Framework Directive obliges the national regulatory authorities to promote the ability of end-users to access and distribute information and run applications and services of their choice. This mandate is accompanied by related transparency requirements for network operators and service providers towards their subscribers (Articles 20(1)(b) and 21(3)(c) and (d) Universal Service Directive). Furthermore, national regulatory authorities are to be enabled to set minimum quality of service requirements on network operators in order to prevent the degradation of service and the obstruction or slowing down of traffic over networks (Article 22(3) Universal Service Directive). Eventually, in November 2015, the EU legislator adopted a Regulation concerning open internet access.[135] According to Article 3(3) of that Regulation, access providers shall treat all internet traffic equally without discrimination, restriction or interference, and irrespective of the sender and receiver, the content accessed or distributed, the applications or services used or provided or the terminal equipment used. But this provision is not absolute. According to the second subparagraph, access providers are not prevented 'from implementing reasonable traffic management measures', a concept that is then further set out in the paragraph and in Recitals 9ff of the Regulation. Although such measures are subject to conditions of proportionality and transparency, the clause leaves a 'back door' for preferential treatment of certain content and services, and will thus certainly lead to controversies in its practical application.

The controversial debate on net neutrality shapes an important aspect of how we will experience the internet in the future. The arguments are certainly more complex than the over-simplified reduction to a battle between good (open and neutral internet) versus evil (internet only for the rich).[136] Service providers argue that prioritisation of certain traffic enables them to run the network more efficiently, whereas supporters of net neutrality fear that providers may discriminate between their own integrated services and products of competitors.

---

[134] COM, Communication to the European Parliament, the Council, the Economic and Social Committee and the Committee of the Regions, The open internet and net neutrality in Europe, COM(2011) 222 final.

[135] Regulation (EU) 2015/2120 of the European Parliament and of the Council of 25 November 2015 laying down measures concerning open internet access and amending Directive 2002/22/EC on universal service and users' rights relating to electronic communications networks and services and Regulation (EU) No. 531/2012 on roaming on public mobile communications networks within the Union, OJ L 310/1.

[136] For further information on the net neutrality debate, see, for example, Wu (2003); Yoo (2006, p. 1847); Wu and Yoo (2007, p. 575); Newman (2008); Marsden (2010).

VI Substantive EU Telecommunications Regulation

The Common Regulatory Framework provides a broad set of regulatory tools for the national regulatory authorities.[137] However, the EU telecommunications framework does not provide a coherent enumeration of regulatory measures. Instead, the obligations that may be imposed on telecommunications undertakings are spread across the directives. The most important measures include the regulation of market access, *ex ante* regulatory measures (notably access regulation and price control) and frequency-related provisions.

1 Access to Domestic Telecommunication Markets

The freedom to provide services, as guaranteed by Article 56 TFEU, principally prohibits Member States to prevent foreign undertakings from providing electronic communications networks or services on its territory. Article 3 Authorisation Directive re-emphasises this right.[138] The provisions of electronic communications networks and electronic communications services may principally be subject to a 'general authorisation' only. A general authorisation is a legal framework established by the Member State that ensures rights for the provision of electronic communications networks or services and lays down obligations that may apply to all or to specific types of electronic communications networks and services (Article 2(2) Authorisation Directive). The term 'authorisation' is slightly misleading, as it suggests that a licensing regime is in place. Quite the opposite is true. An undertaking providing such services is not required to obtain an administrative act by the national regulatory authority before exercising its rights. By contrast to the preceding Directive 97/13/EC on a common framework for general authorisations and individual licences in the field of telecommunications service,[139] the Member States must no longer demand a *specific* individual licence. The undertaking only needs to fulfil its obligations in order to be covered by the *general* authorisation. The undertaking concerned may be required to merely submit a notification (Article 3(2) Authorisation Directive).[140] Upon this notification, the undertaking may commence. Undertakings

---

[137] It should be noted that the EU Directives regularly do not address the national agencies directly, but require implementing acts by the domestic legislative. However, for the sake of clarity and in order to ease the understanding, the following passages refer to the Directives as 'authorising' or 'obliging' the regulatory authorities to issue a regulatory measure. This means that the Directives oblige the Member States to authorize or oblige the agencies to issue a measure.

[138] See Case C-104/04 [2005] Commission v. France [36], regarding the preceding Directive 97/13/EC on a common framework for general authorizations and individual licences in the field of telecommunications services.

[139] OJ L 117/15. On the interpretation of this Directive, see Joined Cases C-392/04 and C-422/04 [2006] i-21 Germany GmbH and Arcor; Case C-339/04 [2006] Nuova società di telecomunicazioni SpA; Joined Cases C-544/03 and C-545/03 [2005] Mobistar and Belgacom; Case C-104/04 [2005] Commission v. France.

[140] Article 3(3) Authorisation Directive illustrates the content of this notification in more detail.

providing cross-border electronic communications services to undertakings located in several Member States are not obliged to submit more than one notification per Member State concerned.

With the general authorisation, an undertaking is fully admitted to the telecommunications market in the Member State.[141] This authorisation entitles undertakings providing public communications networks or publicly available electronic communications service, *inter alia*, to negotiate access and interconnection under the conditions of the Access Directive, in particular Article 4 Access Directive.[142] Undertakings providing electronic communications networks and services other than to the public must negotiate interconnection on commercial terms (Recital 10 Authorisation Directive).

However, the rights under the general authorisation are not unlimited. In accordance with the Treaty provisions, Article 3(1) Authorisation Directive re-emphasises that Member States may prevent an undertaking from providing electronic communications networks or services when necessary for the reasons set out in Article 46(1) EC (now Article 52(1) TFEU); that is, on grounds of public policy, public security or public health. Furthermore, the general authorisation may be subject to certain conditions stipulated in Annex A to the Authorisation Directive that are specific to the electronic communications sector. Such conditions are, *inter alia*, financial contributions to the funding of universal services, interoperability of services and interconnection of networks in conformity with the Access Directive, consumer protection rules, personal data and privacy protection, environmental, town and country planning requirements, and restrictions on the transmission of illegal content in accordance with the E-commerce Directive.

When a national regulatory authority finds that an undertaking does not comply with these conditions, it shall notify the undertaking of those findings, may require the cessation of the breach and take measures aimed at ensuring compliance (Article 10 Authorisation Directive). Undertakings have the right to appeal these measures in accordance with Article 4 Framework Directive.

2 Ex Ante *Regulation*

The *ex ante* measures provided by the EU to regulate telecommunications markets can be divided into two separate groups. The first group consists of regulatory obligations that may be imposed independently of significant market power. The other group, which will be the focus of this section, consists of obligations requiring significant market power (SMP) of the addressee of the regulatory measure.

---

[141] A. Brandenberg, in Koenig et al. (2009, p. 486); Nikolinakos (2006, p. 275).
[142] See Article 4 Authorisation Directive.

The most important regulatory measures independent of significant market power are:

- Access obligation on undertakings without significant market power controlling access to end-users, Article 5(1)(a) Access Directive.
- Obligations on operators to provide access to application programme interfaces (APIs) or electronic programme guides (EPGs), Article 5(1)(b) Access Directive.[143]
- Conditional Access System, Article 6 Access Directive.[144]
- Rights of way, Article 11 Framework Directive.[145]
- Co-location and facility sharing, Article 12 Framework Directive.
- Accounting separation and financial reports, Article 13 Framework Directive.
- 'Must carry' obligations for the transmission of radio and TV broadcast channels and services, Article 31 Universal Service Directive.[146]

Remedies based on SMP include regulatory controls on retail services (Article 17 Universal Service Directive) and access regulation on wholesale markets. Measures to regulate wholesale markets encompass, in particular:

- Obligation of access to, and use of, specific network facilities, Article 12 Access Directive.
- Price regulation, Article 13 Access Directive.
- Transparency obligations, Article 9 Access Directive.
- Obligations of non-discrimination, Article 10 Access Directive.
- Obligations of accounting separation, Article 11 Access Directive.
- Functional separation, Article 13a Access Directive.

Those measures will be explained in more detail in this section.

Apart from access obligations on undertakings controlling access to end-users (see subsection gg), the EU regulatory regime for access to electronic communications networks and services is based on the principle of asymmetric regulation. *Ex ante* regulatory obligations should be imposed only if there is no effective competition, i.e., in markets in which there are one or more undertakings with significant market power, and where national and EU competition law remedies are not sufficient to address the problem.[147] The addressee of an *ex ante* obligation is therefore generally an operator designated as having significant market power on a specific market.[148]

Such measures imposed on undertakings with significant market power are characterised by a two-step procedure. The first step, a market definition and market analysis, is determining the lack of competition on a particular market. The second step

---

[143] See Recital 31 and Article 18 Framework Directive.
[144] See Recital 10 and 11 Access Directive.
[145] See Recital 41 Better Regulation Directive; Case C-97/01 [2003] Commission v. Luxembourg.
[146] For detailed information, see the Chapter 5.
[147] This principle was introduced by the Directive 97/51/EC.
[148] An exception to the principle of asymmetric regulation is provided by Article 5(1)(a) Access Directive.

is the determination of regulatory remedies.[149] Thus, market definition and market analysis determine the 'if' of regulation, whereas the remedies constitute the 'how' of regulation. When a national regulatory authority concludes that the market *is* effectively competitive, it shall not impose or maintain any regulatory obligation (Article 16(3) Framework Directive). In cases in which sector-specific regulatory obligations already exist, the agency must withdraw such obligations placed on undertakings in that relevant market. In turn, when a national regulatory authority determines that a relevant market *is not* effectively competitive because one or more undertaking(s) enjoy(s) significant market power on that market, it must impose appropriate specific regulatory obligations on the undertaking(s) or maintain or amend such obligations where they already exist (Article 16(4) Framework Directive).[150] The agency thereby has considerable discretion over which measure(s) to choose ('toolbox approach'[151]).

By following this approach, the regulatory framework rejects a regime of mere self-regulation. If the regulatory agency concludes in its market definition and market analysis that an undertaking has significant market power, it must impose at least one regulatory obligation. However, following the principle of proportionality, the regulatory remedies themselves may include elements of 'regulated self-regulation': The regulatory agency may, for instance, require undertakings with significant market power to negotiate in good faith with undertakings requesting access (see Article 12(1)(b) Access Directive). Therefore, undertakings asking for access and undertakings receiving those requests should, in the first place, negotiate and conclude such agreements on a commercial basis. Regulatory authorities should only step in and impose further obligations on the incumbent operator when commercial negotiation fails.[152]

a Market Identification and Definition, and Market Analysis

The question of whether an undertaking has significant market power has to be assessed on the basis of a market definition and market analysis carried out in accordance with Articles 14–16 Framework Directive. According to Article 14(2) Framework Directive, an undertaking 'shall be deemed to have significant market power if, either individually or jointly with others, it enjoys a position equivalent to dominance, that is to say a position of economic strength affording it the power to behave to an appreciable extent independently of competitors, customers and ultimately consumers'.[153] This definition is equivalent to the concept of dominance as

---

[149] These steps can be divided into further intermediate steps. The establishment of significant market power requires a market definition and market analysis, and regulatory remedies may consist of several cumulative or consecutive regulatory measures.

[150] See Case C-424/07 [2009] Commission v. Germany [97].

[151] N. van Eijk, in Castendyk, Dommering and Scheuer (2008) Electronic Communications Regulatory Framework para. 15.

[152] See Galtung (2001).

[153] Two or more undertakings can be found to have a joint dominant position not only where there exist structural or other links between them but also where the structure of the relevant market is conducive

defined in the case law of the European Court of Justice[154] and further concretised by Commission Guidelines. In order to be able to determine the need to regulate a market according to each situation on a case-by-case basis, the NRAs have broad discretion when carrying out the market definition and market analysis. This discretion must not be limited through statutory pre-structuring by national legislation.[155]

Article 16(6) Framework Directive specifies the date when national regulatory authorities must finalise a definition and analysis of the relevant market. First, they shall complete a market definition and market analysis within three years from the adoption of a previous measure relating to that market. That period may be extended for up to three additional years, if the national regulatory authority has submitted a reason for the proposed extension to the Commission and the Commission has not objected within one month of the notification. Second, if the Commission adopts a revised Recommendation on relevant markets, the regulatory agency must perform a market definition and market analysis for markets not previously reported to the Commission within two years of their adoption. Third, Member States that have newly joined the EU must carry out a market definition and market analysis within two years from their accession.

If a national regulatory authority has not completed its analysis of a relevant market identified in the Recommendation within this time limit, BEREC shall, upon request, provide assistance to the national regulatory authority concerned to complete the analysis of the specific market and the specific obligations to be imposed. With this assistance, the national regulatory authority concerned shall notify the draft measure to the Commission within six months.

In the case of transnational markets, the national regulatory authorities concerned shall jointly conduct the market analysis and, in a concerted fashion, decide on any imposition, maintenance, amendment or withdrawal of regulatory obligations (Article 15(5) Framework Directive).

aa Market Identification and Definition   In order to assess whether an undertaking enjoys significant market power on a particular market, the first step to be taken by the NRA is to define the relevant market. The applicable method for this examination is, to a broad extent, determined by EU law. The NRAs shall take into the 'utmost account' the Commission Guidelines on market analysis and the assessment of significant market power pursuant to Article 15 Framework Directive.[156] These Guidelines

---

to coordinated effects; that is, it encourages parallel or aligned anti-competitive behaviour on the market; see Recital 26 Framework Directive. See also Annex II Framework Directive.

[154] See, for example, Case 27/76 [1978] United Brands v. Commission; Case 322/81 [1983] Michelin v. Commission [6]; Case T-83/91 [1994] Tetra Pak International v. Commission [122]; Case 85/76 [1979] Hoffmann-La Roche v. Commission [38].

[155] Case C-424/07 [2009] Commission v. Germany [61].

[156] COM, Guidelines on market analysis and the assessment of significant market power under the Community regulatory framework for electronic communications networks and services, 2002/C 165/03.

specifically address the market definition, the assessment and designation of significant market power and procedural issues related to all of these subjects. Based on the Guidelines, national regulatory authorities should analyse whether a given product or service market is effectively competitive in a given geographical area. An analysis of effective competition should include an examination of whether the market is prospectively competitive and, thus, whether any lack of effective competition is durable.[157] The Guidelines also address the issue of newly emerging markets, where *de facto* the market leader is likely to have a substantial market share but should not be subjected to inappropriate obligations.

According to No. 38 of the Guidelines, the extent to which the supply of a product or the provision of a service in a given geographical area constitutes the relevant market depends on the existence of competitive constraints on the price-setting behaviour of the producer(s) or service provider(s) concerned. The two main competitive constraints to consider in assessing the behaviour of undertakings on the market are the demand-side and the supply-side substitutions. Demand-side substitutability is used to measure the extent to which consumers are prepared to replace other services or products for the service or product in question in the event of a price increase. Supply-side substitutability indicates whether suppliers, other than those offering the product or services in question, would immediately or in the short term switch their line of production or offer relevant products or services without incurring significant additional costs.

In practice, the national regulatory authorities usually refer to the Commission's Recommendation on relevant product and service markets within the electronic communications sector.[158] This Recommendation identifies those product and service markets within the electronic communications sector, the characteristics of which may justify the imposition of regulatory obligations set out in the regulatory framework. Both the Commission and the national regulatory authorities thereby have recourse to the so-called 'three-criteria test', examining whether

1 there are high and non-transitory entry barriers of either structural, legal or regulatory nature;[159]

---

[157] Recital 27 Framework Directive.

[158] COM, Recommendation 2014/710/EU of 9 October 2014 on relevant product and service markets within the electronic communications sector susceptible to *ex ante* regulation in accordance with Directive 2002/21/EC of the European Parliament and of the Council on a common regulatory framework for electronic communications networks and services, replacing Recommendation C(2007) 5406 of 17 December 2007 on relevant product and service markets within the electronic communications sector susceptible to *ex ante* regulation in accordance with Directive 2002/21/EC of the European Parliament and of the Council on a common regulatory framework for electronic communications networks and services, OJ L 344/65, replacing the first Commission Recommendation C(2003) 497 of 11 February 2003 on relevant product and service markets within the electronic communications sector susceptible to *ex ante* regulation in accordance with Directive 2002/21/EC of the European Parliament and of the Council on a common regulatory framework for electronic communications networks and services.

[159] However, given the dynamic character and functioning of electronic communications markets, solutions to overcome barriers within a relevant time horizon also must be considered when carrying out a prospective analysis to identify the relevant markets for possible *ex ante* regulation.

2 there is no tendency towards effective competition within the relevant time horizon; and

3 the application of competition law alone would not adequately address the market failure(s) concerned.[160]

On 28 December 2007, the Commission published its new market Recommendation, thereby reducing the hitherto defined 18 markets to seven markets susceptible to *ex ante* regulation:

Retail level	
Old market Recommendation[161]	*New market Recommendation*
Market 1 Access to the public telephone network at a fixed location for residential customers	*Markets combined to new market 1*
Market 2 Access to the public telephone network at a fixed location for non-residential customers	*Access to the public telephone network at a fixed location for residential and non-residential customers*
Market 3 Publicly available local and/or national telephone services provided at a fixed location for residential customers	*Repealed*
Market 4 Publicly available international telephone services provided at a fixed location for residential customers	*Repealed*
Market 5 Publicly available local and/or national telephone services provided at a fixed location for non-residential customers.	*Repealed*
Market 6 Publicly available international telephone services provided at a fixed location for non-residential customers.	*Repealed*

(*continued*)

---

[160] Recital 11 of Recommendation 2014/710/EU.

[161] COM, Recommendation C(2003) 497 of 11 February 2003 on relevant product and service markets within the electronic communications sector susceptible to *ex ante* regulation in accordance with Directive 2002/21/EC of the European Parliament and of the Council on a common regulatory framework for electronic communications networks and services.

Market 7	*Repealed (see Recital 19 Citizens'*
The minimum set of leased lines	*Rights Directive)*
to end users	

Wholesale level

Old market Recommendation	*New market Recommendation*
Market 8	*New market 2*
Call origination on the public telephone network provided at a fixed location	
Market 9	*New market 3*
Call termination on individual public telephone networks provided at a fixed location	
Market 10	*Repealed*
Transit services in the fixed public telephone network	
Market 11	*New market 4*
Wholesale unbundled access (including shared access) to metallic loops and sub-loops for the purpose of providing broadband and voice services	
Market 12	*New market 5*
Wholesale broadband access	
Market 13	*New market 6*
Wholesale terminating segments of leased lines	
Market 14	*Repealed*
Wholesale trunk segments of leased lines	
Market 15 – public mobile telephone networks	*Repealed*
Access and call origination	
Market 16 – individual mobile networks	*New market 7*
Voice call termination	
Market 17 – public mobile networks	*Repealed – now covered by the*
Wholesale national market for international roaming	*Roaming Regulation*
Market 18	*Repealed*
Broadcasting transmission services	

In its most recent Recommendation of 9 October 2014, the Commission identified only the following four markets under the three-criteria test:

Market 1: Wholesale call termination on individual public telephone networks provided at a fixed location.

Market 2: Wholesale voice call termination on individual mobile networks.

Market 3: (a) Wholesale local access provided at a fixed location, (b) Wholesale central access provided at a fixed location for mass-market products.

Market 4: Wholesale high-quality access provided at a fixed location.

However, NRAs may continue *ex ante* regulatory intervention on the markets identified in at wholesale level provided that the three-criteria test is satisfied in the 2007 Recommendation, provided that the three-criteria test is satisfied in the national circumstances.[162]

Although recommendations have, according to Article 288(5) TFEU, no binding force, the national regulatory shall take 'the utmost account' of the Market Recommendation when defining relevant markets (Article 15(3) Framework Directive). Deviation from the Commission's Market Recommendation is, therefore, only justified in exceptional circumstances, and has rarely occurred in practice. The Commission's Market Recommendation can appropriately be described as a 'decision in disguise'.[163] It is, in particular, prohibited for national legislation to preclude markets from scrutiny, which, under the EU regulatory framework, would be subject to regulation.[164]

bb Market Analysis   To determine whether an undertaking has significant market power, national regulatory authorities shall, as a second step, carry out an analysis of the relevant markets, taking the 'utmost account' of the Guidelines, in particular No. 70 et seq. A dominant position is found by reference to a number of criteria of which market share plays the most significant role, even though it alone is not decisive.[165] In this context, similar criteria like those under competition law (see Chapter 10) apply: undertakings with market shares of no more than 25 per cent are not likely to enjoy a (single) dominant position in the market concerned. Single dominance concerns normally arise in situations with market shares of more than 40 per cent, although the Commission may, in some cases, have concerns about dominance even with lower market shares. Very large market shares (those in excess of 50 per cent) are themselves, save in exceptional circumstances, evidence of the existence of a dominant position.

cc Procedure   The market definition and market analysis are subject to the consultation and consolidation procedures provided in Articles 6 and 7 Framework Directive.[166] If a national regulatory authority intends to take measures in accordance

---

[162] COM, Recommendation 2014/710/EU, Recital 25.

[163] J.-D. Braun and R. Capito, in Koenig et al. (2009, p. 351).

[164] ECJ, Case C-424/07 [2009] Commission v. Germany.

[165] COM, Guidelines on market analysis and the assessment of significant market power under the Community regulatory framework for electronic communications networks and services, 2002/C 165/03, para. 75 ff.

[166] See COM, Recommendation 2003/561/EC of 23 July 2003 on notifications, time limits and consultations provided for in Article 7 of Directive 2002/21/EC of the European Parliament and of the Council on a common regulatory framework for electronic communications networks and services.

with the regulatory framework that have a significant impact on the relevant market, it has to give interested parties the opportunity to comment on the draft measure within a reasonable period of time (consultation procedure, Article 6 Framework Directive). It has to take account of these comments before adopting a final decision and make the results of the procedure publicly available.[167] If the intended measure affects trade between Member States, the national regulatory authority shall inform the Commission, BEREC and other national regulatory authorities of the draft measure and, together with the reasoning on which the measure is based, make it accessible to them. Foreign national regulatory authorities, BEREC and the Commission may all make comments to the national regulatory authority within a non-extendable one-month period (consolidation procedure, Article 7 Framework Directive). The national consultation provided for under Article 6 Framework Directive should be conducted prior to the consolidation in order to allow the views of interested parties to be reflected. This would also eliminate the need for a second consolidation procedure in the event of changes to a planned measure as a result of the national consultation.[168]

Articles 7(4) through (6) Framework Directive pertain to the Commission's right to veto the national market definition and market analysis. The provision is one of the rare cases in which the Commission immediately addresses a national agency directly and not the Member State, as is usually the case. Between 2002 and 2012, the Commission has issued seven veto decisions covering ten cases.[169] In addition, there have been several cases in which national regulatory authorities have decided to withdraw their proposed measures to avoid a veto decision.[170]

The procedural and substantive requirements for the exercise of the veto right are as outlined in the following statement. If

1   the national regulatory authority intends to assess a market definition of a relevant market which differs from those in the Commission's market Recommendation (market definition level) or decides whether or not to designate an undertaking as having significant market power (market analysis level), and
2   that assessment would affect trade between Member States, and
3   the Commission has indicated to the national regulatory authority that it considers that the draft would create a barrier to the single market, or it has serious

---

[167] The results of the consultation procedure shall not be made publicly available in the case of confidential information in accordance with EU and national law on business confidentiality.
[168] See Recital 17 Better Regulation Directive.
[169] COM, Decision of 20 February 2004 in Cases FI/2003/0024 and FI/2003/0027; Decision of 5 October 2004 in Case FI/2004/0082; Decision of 20 October 2004 in Case AT/2004/0090; Decision of 17 May 2005 in Case DE/2005/0144; Decision of 10 January 2007 in Cases PL/2006/0518 and PL/2006/0514; Decision of 4 January 2010 in Cases PL/2009/1019 and PL/2009/1020; Decision of 10 August 2012 in Case CZ/2012/1322.
[170] Commission Press Release MEMO/10/226 of 1 June 2010, Telecoms: how the Article 7 consultation and notification mechanism works: frequently asked questions.

doubts as to its compatibility with EU law, the draft shall not be adopted for a non-extendable period of two months.

4 Within this period, the Commission may make a decision requiring the national regulatory authority concerned to withdraw the draft measure, and/or make a decision to lift its reservations in relation to the draft measure. Before issuing a decision, the Commission shall take 'utmost account' of the opinion of BEREC. The decision shall be accompanied by a detailed and objective analysis of why the Commission considers that the draft measure should not be adopted, together with specific proposals for amending it.

5 If the Commission adopts a decision requiring the national regulatory authority to withdraw the draft measure, the national regulatory authority must amend or withdraw the draft measure within six months of the date of the Commission's decision. When the draft measure is amended, the national regulatory authority shall again undertake a public consultation and shall re-notify the Commission of the amended draft measure. However, when the Commission has adopted a decision lifting its reservations, the national regulatory agency may finally adopt its market definition and market analysis. Article 7(9) Framework Directive allows a national regulatory authority in exceptional circumstances to adopt provisional measures.

The notion of 'affecting trade between Member States' under Article 7 Framework Directive is analogous to that for the purposes of Articles 101 TFEU and 102 TFEU.[171] According to Recital 38 Framework Directive, measures that could affect trade between Member States are 'measures that may have an influence, direct or indirect, actual or potential, on the pattern of trade between Member States in a manner which might create a barrier to the single market'. They include, *inter alia*: measures that affect prices for users in other Member States; measures that affect the ability of an undertaking established in another Member State to provide an electronic communications service; and measures that affect market structure or access, leading to repercussions for undertakings in other Member States. Moreover, the effect must be appreciable and not be insignificant.[172]

b Imposition of a Specific Regulatory Obligation

When a national regulatory authority concludes that one or more undertakings have significant market power, it has to impose regulatory obligations ('remedies') on such undertakings or maintain or amend such obligations if they already exist. It thereby enjoys considerable discretion, limited only by the rather vague requirement that the measure has to be 'appropriate' (Article 16(4) Framework Directive) and subject to

---

[171] See CJEU, Case C-3/14 [2015] Prezes Urzędu Komunikacji Elektronicznej and Telefonia Dialog sp. z o.o. v. T-Mobile Polska SA [50].

[172] See CJEU, Case C-3/14 [2015] Prezes Urzędu Komunikacji Elektronicznej and Telefonia Dialog sp. z o.o. v. T-Mobile Polska SA [52–53].

the principle of proportionality. To ensure a consistent and harmonised approach of all national regulatory agencies to the application of remedies by NRAs, the ERG has adopted a Common Position on the approach to appropriate remedies in the ECNS regulatory framework, the so-called 'Remedies document'.[173] Although this document is not legally binding, it may serve as a guideline for national regulatory agencies.

Ex ante obligations for undertakings having significant market power may be split into two sets of remedies. First, Article 8 Access Directive authorises national regulatory authorities to adopt measures set out in Articles 9 through 13a Access Directive. These remedies concern wholesale markets (see subsections aa–ff below). If a national regulatory authority intends to impose obligations for access or interconnection other than those set out in these Articles, it shall submit this request to the Commission, which then makes a decision either authorising or preventing the national regulatory authority from taking such measures (Article 8(3) subpara. 2 Access Directive). Second, Article 17 Universal Service Directive empowers national regulatory authorities to adopt regulatory measures concerning retail services (see subsection gg below).

aa Access Regulation, Article 12 Access Directive   The most important regulatory measure on wholesale markets is the obligation to allow access to and use of specific network facilities according to Article 12 Access Directive. Competition in the provision of telecommunications services may only develop if new providers have access to customers under conditions similar to those of incumbent dominant undertakings. Therefore, a provider of telecommunications services might need access to the network facilities or services of competitors because it is usually not economically viable for new market entrants to duplicate the incumbent's network. Mandating access to the networks, such as the local loop or sub-loop of operators enjoying significant market power, may facilitate market entry and increase competition in service markets such as retail broadband services. The Access Directive aims at harmonising the way in which Member States regulate both access to and interconnection of electronic communications networks and associated facilities. The purpose of the Access Directive is to establish a regulatory framework for the relationships between suppliers of networks and services that will result in sustainable competition, interoperability of electronic communications services and consumer benefits.[174]

According to Article 2(a) Access Directive, 'access' describes 'the making available of facilities and/or services to another undertaking, under defined conditions, on either an exclusive or non-exclusive basis, for the purpose of providing electronic

---

[173]   Revised ERG Common Position on the approach to Appropriate remedies in the ECNS regulatory framework, Final Version May 2006. See http://erg.eu.int/doc/meeting/erg_06_33_remedies_common_position_june_06.pdf.

[174]   Compare Article 1(1) Access Directive.

communications services, including when they are used for the delivery of information society services or broadcast content services'. Therefore, access can roughly be divided into access to facilities and access to services. Those facilities include, *inter alia*, networks or network elements such as the local loop[175] or other physical infrastructure such as buildings, ducts and masts. Accessible services may be, for example, number translation systems, systems offering equivalent functionality or virtual network services. An important subcategory of access is interconnection. Interconnection means, according to Article 2(b) Access Directive, 'the physical and logical linking of public communications networks [...] in order to allow the users of one undertaking to communicate with users of the same or another undertaking, or to access services provided by another undertaking'.

It should be noted that access within the meaning of the Directive does not include access by end-users (see Article 1(2) Access Directive). The right of end-users to claim access to communications networks and services is covered by the Universal Services Directive.

According to Article 12(1) Access Directive, an NRA may impose obligations on operators to meet reasonable requests for access to and use of specific network elements and associated facilities. This applies, for example, in situations in which the NRA considers that denial of access or unreasonable terms and conditions having a similar effect would hinder the emergence of a sustainable competitive market at the retail level, or would not be in the end-user's interest. Operators may be required, *inter alia*:[176]

- To give third parties access to specified network elements and/or facilities (Article 12(1)(a) Access Directive), and not to withdraw access to facilities already granted (Article 12(1)(c) Access Directive). This includes access to network elements that are not active and unbundled access to the local loop. Article 12(1)(a) Access Directive has been amended by the Better Regulation Directive and now includes the former obligation of Article 19 Universal Service Directive to allow carrier selection or pre-selection.[177]

---

[175] 'Local loop', also referred to as subscriber line or 'last mile', is the physical circuit connecting the network termination point to a distribution frame or equivalent facility in the fixed public electronic communications network'; see Article 2(e) Access Directive as amended by the Better Regulation Directive.

[176] When national regulatory authorities impose one of the following obligations, they may attach conditions covering fairness, reasonableness and timeliness to those obligations. When imposing obligations on an operator to provide access in accordance with Article 12(1) Access Directive, national regulatory authorities may lay down technical or operational conditions to be met by the provider and/or beneficiaries of such access where this is necessary to ensure normal operation of the network, Article 12(3) Access Directive. Obligations to follow specific technical standards or specifications shall be in compliance with the standards and specifications laid down in accordance with Article 17 Framework Directive.

[177] According to the former Article 19 Universal Service Directive, carrier selection and pre-selection is access to services of any interconnected provider on a call-by-call basis by dialling a carrier selection code, or with a facility to override any pre-selected choice on a call-by-call basis by dialling a carrier selection code.

- To negotiate in good faith with undertakings requesting access (Article 12(1) (b) Access Directive). This provision represents the principle of 'regulated self-regulation' in *ex ante* access regulation: undertakings are obligated (i.e., 'regulation') to negotiate with undertakings requesting access (i.e., 'self-regulation'),[178] but if these negotiations fail, the regulatory agency may impose further obligations such as those according to Article 12(1)(a) Access Directive.
- To provide specified services on a wholesale basis for resale by third parties (Article 12(1)(d) Access Directive).
- To grant open access to technical interfaces, protocols or other key technologies that are indispensable for the interoperability of services or virtual network services (Article 12(1)(e) Access Directive).
- To provide co-location or other forms of associated facilities sharing (Article 12(1) (f) Access Directive). 'Associated facilities' are those services, physical infrastructures and other facilities or elements associated with an electronic communications network/service that enable and/or support the provision of services via that network/service or have the potential to do so. They include, for example, buildings or entries to buildings, building wiring, antennae, towers and other supporting constructions, ducts, conduits, masts, manholes and cabinets (Article 2(e) Framework Directive).
- To provide specified services needed to ensure interoperability of end-to-end services to users, including facilities for intelligent network services or roaming on mobile networks (Article 12(1)(g) Access Directive).
- To provide access to operational support systems or similar software systems necessary to ensure fair competition in the provision of services (Article 12(1)(h) Access Directive).
- To interconnect networks or network facilities (Article 12(1)(i) Access Directive).[179]
- To provide access to associated services such as identity, location and presence service (Article 12(1)(j) Access Directive). Article 2(ea) Framework Directive defines 'associated services' as those services associated with an electronic communications network/service that enable and/or support the provision of services via that network/service or have the potential to do so. They include, for example, number translation or systems offering equivalent functionality, conditional access systems and electronic programme guides, as well as other services such as identity, location and presence service.

---

[178] With regard to interconnection, this obligation exists for all operators of public communications networks, not only for those having significant market power; see Article 5(1) Access Directive. On the interpretation and implementation of this provision, see Case C-227/07 [2008] Commission v. Poland; Case C-192/08 [2009] TeliaSonera Finland Oyj.

[179] For details, see Case C-227/07 [2008] Commission v. Poland [23]. For interconnection in the mobile telecommunications, see Lust (2003).

If national regulatory authorities consider imposing the obligations provided by Article 12(1) Access Directive, they must take particular account of the factors listed in Article 12(2) Access Directive:

1 The technical and economic viability of using or installing competing facilities, in the light of the rate of market development, taking into account the nature and type of interconnection and/or access involved, including the viability of other upstream access products such as access to ducts.

2 The feasibility of providing the access proposed, in relation to the capacity available. It should be noted that, contrary to the wording of the provision, the technical feasibility is not merely an aspect 'to be taken into account', but a necessary requirement to provide access at all. Technically unfeasible access simply cannot be granted by the operator and, therefore, cannot be part of a regulatory obligation.[180]

3 The initial investment by the facility owner, taking account of any public investment made and the risks involved in making such an investment. The passage 'taking account of any public investment made' was inserted by the Better Regulation Directive, due to the fact that large parts of the network facilities still originate from former governmental undertakings; that is, built with taxpayer's money.

4 The need to safeguard competition in the long term, with particular attention to economically efficient infrastructure-based competition. The imposition by national regulatory authorities of mandated access that increases competition in the short term should not reduce incentives for competitors to invest in alternative facilities that will secure more competition in the long term.[181]

5 Where appropriate, any relevant intellectual property rights. Article 12 Access Directive thus allows balancing intellectual property rights with conflicting interests, as required by the Strasbourg Court (see Chapter 9), rather than giving strict priority to the former.

6 The provision of pan-European services.

Thus, when imposing one or more access obligations, the national regulatory authorities have to consider a number of factors. First, the measures have to be justified in the light of the objectives laid down in Article 8 Framework Directive. Second, they must take into account the above-mentioned factors of Article 12(2) Access Directive. Third, they have to consider the general principles of EU (telecommunications) law, in particular the principle of proportionality. Access regulation is therefore not a conditionally determined way of reasoning consisting of 'if–then' clauses, but a complex process of balancing different aspects in order to reach certain objectives. The

---

[180] See also Recital 19 Access Directive: 'An operator with mandated access obligations cannot be required to provide types of access which are not within its powers to provide.'

[181] Recital 19 Access Directive.

factors named in Article 8 Framework Directive and Article 12(2) Access Directive are different in nature and may even be irreconcilable in certain cases. Mandating access to network infrastructure, for instance, can be justified as a means of increasing competition, but NRAs need to balance the rights of an infrastructure owner and the rights of other service providers to access facilities that are essential for the provision of competing services.

This entails considerable discretion for the national regulatory authorities to be considered by both the legislative and the judicial branch. It is discernible from those provisions that it is the regulatory agency, and not the legislature, that is required to promote the regulatory objectives when carrying out the regulatory tasks. A statutory pre-structuring or anticipation of this balancing process by national legislation, for example, by attaching more importance to certain regulatory aims at the expense of other goals, is therefore prohibited.[182] The judicial branch, on the other hand, must acknowledge the fact that a complex act of reconciling conflicting interests for the purposes of reaching certain aims includes considerable elements of agency policy, and therefore courts may have to grant deference to the agency's decision.

bb Price Control and Cost Accounting Obligations, Article 13 Access Directive
Access regulation would be of no avail if the pricing was left to the obligated undertaking. Thus, Article 13(1) Access Directive authorises national regulatory authorities to impose obligations relating to cost recovery and price controls for the provision of access if a lack of effective competition means that the operator concerned may sustain prices at an excessively high level, or may apply a price squeeze,[183] to the detriment of end-users.

For three reasons, Article 13 is a rather complicated provision. First, the clause 'to the detriment on end-users' must not be understood as saying that Article 13 Access Directive is applicable to retail markets, as would be contrary to the scope of the Access Directive. This passage merely indicates that competition on wholesale markets is not in and of itself an end, but should serve the benefit of end-users. Second, it commingles the aims, the standards and the methods of price regulation. Third, it does not provide an exclusive catalogue with regulatory instruments to conduct the price control, but only includes a few indications.

Article 13(1) Access Directive stipulates that price controls may include obligations for 'cost orientation of prices' (which is a standard of price control). Yet the Directive does not define what 'cost orientation' means. Article 13(2) only requires regulatory authority to ensure that 'any cost recovery mechanism or pricing methodology that is mandated serves to promote efficiency and sustainable competition and

---

[182] Compare Case C-424/07 [2009] Commission v. Germany [91].

[183] A prize-squeeze exists when the difference between an undertaking's retail prices and the interconnection prices charged to competitors who provide similar retail services is not adequate to ensure sustainable competition; see Recital 20.

maximise consumer benefits'. As the term 'serves to promote' shows, the provision sets an aim of price control. Article 13(2) sentence 2, in turn, implies that national regulatory authorities may 'also take account of prices available in comparable competitive markets' (which is a method of price control). Furthermore, Article 13(3) Access Directive maintains that an operator that has an obligation regarding the cost orientation of its prices has the burden of proof 'that charges are derived from costs including a reasonable rate of return on investment', again providing a standard of price control. These costs must be, as the next sentence indicates, costs of 'efficient provision of services'. However, the Directive does not define what costs of efficient provision of services actually are, but authorises national regulatory authorities to use 'cost accounting *methods* independent of those used by the undertaking'[184] in order to calculate these costs.

The vagueness and openness of Article 13 Access Directive leaves much discretion to Member States' legislative and regulatory agencies to implement their own price control policies. The scale of regulatory intervention reaches from relatively light measures, such as an obligation that prices have to be reasonable, to heavier burdens, such as an obligation that prices must be cost-oriented, or the mandate to implement a cost accounting system.[185]

One of the main practical problems inherent in price regulation is that most costs for providing a network-related service are fixed, for instance the costs of installing and maintaining the network, whereas the costs for providing the service itself, such as establishing a phone call connection, are rather negligible. Therefore, the main difficulty is how to distribute the huge amount of fixed costs among the users.[186]

Similar to access obligations, price regulation requires a balancing of conflicting interests and the consideration of the principle of proportionality. To encourage investments by the operator, national regulatory authorities shall take into account the investment made by the operator and allow him a reasonable rate of return on adequate capital employed, such as appropriate labour and building costs, taking into account any risks specific to a particular new investment network project (see Article 13(1) sentence 2 Access Directive). Investments into new access networks may involve risks if they support products for which demand is uncertain.[187]

Although they have been repealed, it is enlightening to consult ECJ case law on the ONP Directive[188] and the Local Loop Regulation[189] for details on price regulation.

---

[184] Emphasis added.
[185] Compare Revised ERG Common Position on the approach to Appropriate remedies in the ECNS regulatory framework, Final Version May 2006, p. 47. For more details on the models and methods of price regulation, see Lust (2003, pp. 26–37).
[186] Lust (2003, p. 26).
[187] Better Regulation, Recital 57.
[188] Case C-221/01 [2002] Commission v. Belgium; Case C-33/04 [2005] Commission v. Luxembourg; Case C-262/06 [2007] Deutsche Telekom; Joined Cases C-152/07, C-154/07 and C-153/07 [2008] Arcor and others.
[189] Case C-55/06 [2008] Arcor.

cc Transparency, Article 9 Access Directive   Article 9(1) Access Directive authorises national regulatory authorities to impose obligations for transparency in relation
to access, requiring operators to make public specified information. This information
may include accounting information, technical specifications, network characteristics, terms and conditions for supply and use[190] and prices. The transparency requirement aims at speeding-up negotiations, avoiding disputes and giving confidence to
market players that a service is not being provided on discriminatory terms (Recital
16 Access Directive). If an operator has obligations under Article 12 Access Directive
concerning wholesale network infrastructure access, national regulatory authorities
shall, according to Article 9(4) Access Directive, ensure the publication of a reference
offer containing at least the elements set out in Annex II Access Directive.

dd Non-Discrimination, Article 10 Access Directive   A national regulatory
authority may impose obligations of non-discrimination in relation to interconnection and access. Those obligations shall ensure, in particular, that the operator applies
equivalent conditions in equivalent circumstances to other undertakings providing
like services, and provides services and information to others under the same conditions and of the same quality as it provides for its own services, or those of its subsidiaries or partners. If an operator has obligations of non-discrimination, national
regulatory authorities may, according to Article 9(2) Access Directive, require that
operator to publish a reference offer that shall be sufficiently unbundled to ensure that
undertakings are not required to pay for facilities that are not necessary for the service
requested, giving a description of the relevant offerings broken down into components
according to market needs and the associated terms and conditions including prices.

ee Accounting Separation, Article 11 Access Directive   A national regulatory
authority may impose obligations for accounting separation in relation to specified
activities related to access. This allows internal price transfers to be rendered visible
and allows national regulatory authorities to check compliance with obligations for
non-discrimination where applicable (Recital 18 Access Directive).[191] In particular,
a national regulatory authority may require a vertically integrated company to make
transparent its wholesale prices and its internal transfer prices, *inter alia*, to ensure
compliance where there is a requirement for non-discrimination under Article 10
Access Directive or, where necessary, to prevent unfair cross-subsidy. National regulatory authorities may specify the format and accounting methodology to be used.
Furthermore, they are empowered to require that accounting records, including
data on revenues received from third parties, are provided on request (Article 11(2)

---

[190] Including any conditions limiting access to and/or use of services and applications where such conditions
     are allowed by Member States in conformity with EU law.
[191] See COM, Recommendation 98/322/EC of 8 April 1998 on interconnection in a liberalised telecommu-
     nications market (Part 2 – accounting separation and cost accounting).

Access Directive). They may publish such information that contributes to an open and competitive market while still respecting national and EU rules on commercial confidentiality.

ff Functional Separation, Article 13a Access Directive Article 13a Access Directive was inserted by the Better Regulation Directive. It allows regulatory agencies to impose an obligation on vertically integrated undertakings to place activities related to the wholesale provision of relevant access products in an independently operating business entity (functional separation). The then-independently operating business entity shall supply products and services to all undertakings on the same timescales, terms and conditions, including those relating to price and service levels, and by means of the same systems and processes.

In practice, Article 13a Access Directive does not have a broad scope of application.[192] First, it may only be applied as *ultima ratio*; that is, if obligations under Articles 9 through 13 have persistently failed to achieve their aims.[193] Second, Articles 13a(2) through (4) require a complex and multipolar procedure, involving the European Commission and BEREC, which is susceptible to mistakes.[194] Third, the obligation of a functional separation may be at odds with property rights protected by Article 17 EUChFR and Article 1 of the First Protocol to the ECHR.[195]

gg Regulatory Controls on Retail Services End-users depend on the provision of access and services by network operators and service providers. There is a risk that an undertaking with significant market power providing such 'bottleneck' resources and services to end-users may abuse its position by charging excessive prices, inhibiting market entry of competitors or distorting competition.[196] Hence, Article 17 Universal Service Directive obligates Member States to ensure regulatory controls on retail services, i.e., access of end-users and the regulation of retail prices. National regulatory authorities shall impose 'appropriate regulatory obligations' on undertakings identified as having significant market power on a given retail market. Regulatory controls of retail services are subsidiary to *ex ante* regulation of wholesale markets according to the Access Directive (see Article 17(1)(b) Universal Service Directive).[197]

The obligations imposed under Article 17 Universal Service Directive include prohibitions of excessive prices, inhibition of market entry, predatory prices, undue preference to specific end-users and unreasonable bundling of services. NRAs may apply to such undertakings appropriate retail price cap measures, measures to control individual tariffs or measures to orient tariffs towards costs or prices on comparable

---

[192] See also the critical remarks of K.E. Winkler and G. Baumgarten, in Koenig et al. (2009, p. 469).
[193] See Recital 61 Better Regulation Directive.
[194] For details, see Articles 8(3) and 13a(2) to (4) Access Directive.
[195] K.E. Winkler and G. Baumgarten, in Koenig et al. (2009, p. 469).
[196] Recital 26 Universal Service Directive.
[197] In turn, the Access Directive is not applicable to end-user's access.

markets. In order for national regulatory authorities to fulfil their regulatory duties, they shall ensure, according to Article 17(4) Universal Service Directive, that the necessary and appropriate cost accounting systems are implemented. They may also specify the format and accounting methodology to be used.

Following the strong request of the European Parliament,[198] the new so-called 'internet freedom provision' in Article 1(3a) Framework Directive requires that measures taken by Member States regarding end-users' access to or use of services and applications through electronic communications networks 'shall respect the fundamental rights and freedoms of natural persons', as guaranteed by the ECHR and general principles of Community (now Union) law. Any of these measures, for example, those that fight child pornography or copyright infringements, 'may only be imposed if they are appropriate, proportionate and necessary within a democratic society, and their implementation shall be subject to adequate procedural safeguards in conformity with the [ECHR] and general principles of [Union] law, including effective judicial protection and due process'. These measures have to respect the presumption of innocence and the right to privacy. A prior fair and impartial procedure has to be guaranteed, including the right to be heard and the right to an effective and timely judicial review.

Despite its solemn wording, the internet freedom provision should not be perceived as a groundbreaking achievement.[199] Rather, it summarises and concretises the legal situation already in existence. In particular, the provision cannot be understood as creating a right for end-users to have internet access in the first place.[200] Nevertheless, the internet freedom provision may at least serve as a warning for Member States that intend to restrict internet access.

c Access Obligation of Undertakings Without Significant Market Power, Article 5(1)(a) Access Directive

Article 5(1)(a) Access Directive derogates from the principle of asymmetric regulation, as it explicitly does not require the addressed undertaking to have significant market power. The provision authorises national regulatory authorities to impose obligations on undertakings that control access to end-users, including the obligation to interconnect their networks, if this is necessary to ensure end-to-end connectivity.[201] Control of access may consist of ownership or control of the physical

---

[198] See European Parliament, Session document A7-0070/2009 of 16.11.2009, III report on the joint text approved by the Conciliation Committee for a directive of the European Parliament and of the Council amending Directives 2002/21/EC on a common regulatory framework for electronic communications networks and services, 2002/19/EC on access to, and interconnection of, electronic communications networks and associated facilities and 2002/20/EC on the authorisation of electronic communications networks and services (PE-CONS 3677/2009 – C7-0273/2009 – 2007/0247(COD)), p. 6.

[199] But see also Dods et al. (2010, p. 106), calling it a 'dramatic legislative development which fundamentally alters the legal landscape'.

[200] Dods et al. (2010, p. 104).

[201] In Case C-227/07 [2008] Commission v. Poland, the ECJ had to decide on the implementation of this provision in Poland.

link to the end-user (either fixed or mobile).[202] This would be the case, for example, if network operators were to unreasonably restrict end-user choice for access to internet portals and services.

The omission of the significant market power requirement is justified by the fact that the undertaking controls access to end-users. This may be, for example, a network operator controlling the local loop or a mobile phone network as a 'bottleneck resource'.

d Procedure

When a national regulatory authority intends to impose a regulatory remedy that falls within the scope of either Article 5 Access Directive or Article 8 in connection with Articles 9 through 13a Access Directive and could affect trade between Member States, the agency must carry out a further consolidation procedure according to Article 7(3) Framework Directive. However, by contrast to the consolidation procedure required for the market definition and market analysis, the Commission has no veto right concerning the specific regulatory measure(s): Article 7(4) Framework Directive only refers to measures aiming at defining a relevant market within the meaning of Article 15 Framework Directive or designating an undertaking as having significant market power under Article 16 Framework Directive. In the legislative procedure concerning the telecommunications review 2007, the European Parliament refused to extend the Commission's veto power to the specific regulatory remedies.[203] The Commission only has the possibility to suspend the measure for three months (Article 7a Framework Directive). In addition, the Commission may open an infringement procedure according to Article 258 TFEU against the Member State if it finds that the imposed or omitted measure violates EU law.

The consultation and consolidation procedures for market definition/analysis and for the regulatory remedy may be conducted simultaneously as well as successively.

3 Frequency Allocation and Frequency Management

As already illustrated, the management of frequencies is, to a large extent, a matter of global concern. Therefore, frequencies are at first allocated by the ITU to their

---

[202] Compare Recital 6 Access Directive.
[203] See European Parliament legislative resolution of 24 September 2008 on the proposal for a directive of the European Parliament and of the Council amending Directive 2002/21/EC on a common regulatory framework for electronic communications networks and services, Directive 2002/19/EC on access to, and interconnection of, electronic communications networks and associated facilities and Directive 2002/20/EC on the authorisation of electronic communications networks and services (COM(2007)0697 – C6-0427/2007 – 2007/0247(COD)), P6_TA(2008)0449, p. 31, as opposed to COM, Proposal for a Directive of the European Parliament and of the Council amending Directives 2002/21/EC on a common regulatory framework for electronic communications networks and services, 2002/19/EC on access to, and interconnection of, electronic communications networks and services and 2002/20/EC on the authorisation of electronic communications networks and services, COM(2007) 697 final, p. 29.

Member States. As a further step, national administrations must assign these frequencies to individual users, for instance through an auction.[204] In the EU, frequency management thus remains within the competence of the Member States. Since the EU is not a Member of the ITU, it has no direct influence on the allocation process. However, policy coordination and, where appropriate, harmonisation at EU level should help ensure that spectrum users derive the full benefits of the internal market and that EU interests can be effectively defended on a global stage.[205] The EU Radio Spectrum Decision No. 676/2002/EC[206] therefore established a framework for a coordinated and harmonised approach to EU frequency policy (see subsection a below). Furthermore, the Authorisation Directive (see subsection b below) and the Framework Directive (see subsection c below) establish general rules for the management of the radio spectrum at a national level. In practice, the switchover from analogue to digital terrestrial television with its superior transmission efficiency has recently increased the availability of valuable spectrum in the EU, commonly known as the 'digital dividend', and thus attached even more importance to the EU-wide coordination of domestic frequency management.

a EU Radio spectrum policy

Radio spectrum policy in the EU should 'contribute to freedom of expression, including freedom of opinion and freedom to receive and disseminate information and ideas, irrespective of borders, as well as freedom and plurality of the media'.[207] For the development and adoption of technical implementing measures, as well as with a view to contributing to the formulation, preparation and implementation of EU radio spectrum policy, the Commission is assisted by the Radio Spectrum Committee (Article 3(1) Radio Spectrum Decision). The Radio Spectrum Committee (RSC) is composed of representatives of the Member States and chaired by a representative of the Commission.

The RSC is not to be confused with the Radio Spectrum Policy Group (RSPG), a consultative group established by Decision 2002/622/EC,[208] comprised of governmental experts from the Member States and a representative of the Commission. In contrast to the more technology-focused RSC, the RSPG shall take into account 'not only technical parameters but also economic, political, cultural, strategic, health and social considerations, as well as the various potentially conflicting needs of radio

---

[204] The idea of auctions rather than licensing as a regime for distributing frequencies goes back to Coase (1959).

[205] Recital 28 Better Regulation Directive.

[206] Decision No. 676/2002/EC of the European Parliament and of the Council of 7 March 2002 on a regulatory framework for radio spectrum policy in the European Community (Radio Spectrum Decision), OJ L 108/1.

[207] Recital 3 Radio Spectrum Decision.

[208] COM, Decision 2002/622/EC of 26 July 2002 establishing a Radio Spectrum Policy Group, OJ L 198/49, as amended by COM, Decision 2009/978/EU of 16 December 2009amending Decision 2002/622/EC establishing a Radio Spectrum Policy Group, OJ L 336/50.

spectrum users with a view to ensuring that a fair, non-discriminatory and propor-tionate balance is achieved' (Recital 4 Decision 2002/622/EC).

Another organisation involved in European frequency policy-making is the European Conference of Postal and Telecommunications Administrations (CEPT). CEPT was established in 1959 by 19 countries and now has 48 European countries as members.[209] CEPT's activities include cooperation on commercial, operational and regulatory issues. It offers a European forum for discussions on regulatory issues in the field of post and telecommunication, such as developing common positions in ITU-related matters, or drafting technical measures with the objective of harmonising the use of radio spectrum. In 1988, CEPT created the European Telecommunications Standards Institute (ETSI) to take over all of CEPT's telecommunication standardisa-tion activities. In some cases, EU legislation adopted measures by CEPT and made it compulsory for Member States.[210]

b Authorisation Directive

Article 5(1) Authorisation Directive provides an exception to the general rule that the provision of services and networks as well as spectrum use should be subject to general authorisations only. When necessary, Member States may grant individual rights of use in order to avoid harmful interference, to ensure technical quality of service, to safeguard efficient use of spectrum or to fulfil other objectives of general interest as defined by Member States. In accordance with the general scope of the regulatory framework, Article 5 Authorisation Directive applies only if the use of radio frequencies involves the provision of an electronic communications network or service, normally for remuneration. The self-use of radio terminal equipment, based on the non-exclusive use of specific radio frequencies by a user and not related to an economic activity, such as use of a citizen's band by radio amateurs, is not covered by the Authorisation Directive.[211] Such use falls within the scope of Directive 1999/5/EC on radio equipment and telecommunications terminal equipment.

The pre-conditions for the granting of the rights of use are provided by Article 5(2) subpara. 2 Authorisation Directive.[212] The rights of use are principally transferable (Article 9b Framework Directive). Against the background of the need to ensure effi-cient use of radio spectrum, Article 7 Authorisation Directive allows Member States to limit the number of rights of use in certain situations.

The rights of use may be subject to the conditions listed in Part B of the Annex to the Authorisation Directive (as amended by the Better Regulation Directive). Conditions that may be attached to rights of use for radio frequencies may require,

---

[209] www.cept.org.
[210] For instance, Commission Directive 96/2/EC adopted CEPT's European Radiocommunications Committee Decision ERC/DEC/(97)01 on the publication of national tables of radio spectrum allocations.
[211] Recital 5 Authorisation Directive.
[212] Regarding compatibility of the criteria with Article 49 EC (now Article 56 TFEU), see Case C-380/05 [2008] Centro Europa 7 Srl.

inter alia, the obligation to actually provide a service or to use a type of technology for which the rights of use has been granted (and not merely to 'reserve' the scarce resource for future purposes), to abide by obligations under relevant international agreements relating to the use of frequencies or the effective and efficient use of frequencies in conformity with the Framework Directive.

c Framework Directive

Article 9 Framework Directive, as amended by the Better Regulation Directive, pertains to the Member States' frequency management. They shall ensure that spectrum allocation and the issuance of general authorisations or individual rights of use are based on objective, transparent, non-discriminatory and proportionate criteria, thereby respecting international agreements[213] and taking into account public policy considerations. According to Article 9(2) Framework Directive, Member States shall promote the harmonisation of use of radio frequencies across the EU, consistent with the need to ensure effective and efficient use thereof and in pursuit of benefits for the consumer. In so doing, they shall act in accordance with the Radio Spectrum Decision.

Articles 9(3) and (4) Framework Directive emphasise the principles of technology and service neutrality for the Member States' National Frequency Allocation Plans (see Recital 35 Better Regulation Directive). Member States shall ensure that all types of electronic communications services may be provided in the available radio frequency bands, and that all types of technology may be used, respectively. Restrictions on the technologies used may be justified, *inter alia*, to avoid harmful interference, to protect public health against electromagnetic fields or to ensure technical quality of service (Article 9(3) subpara. 2 Framework Directive). Restrictions on the services are justified if they are necessary to ensure the fulfilment of a general interest objective such as safety of life, the avoidance of inefficient use of radio frequencies or the promotion of cultural and linguistic diversity and media pluralism (Article 9(4) subpara. 2 Framework Directive).

VII Questions

1 Critically discuss the following statement: 'The predominant aim of sector-specific regulation must be to render itself superfluous.'
2 Article 10 ECHR states: '[Freedom of expression] shall include freedom to hold opinions and to receive and impart information and ideas.' By comparison, Article 5(1) of the German Basic Law states: 'Every person shall have the right freely to express and disseminate his opinions in speech, writing and pictures ... Freedom of the press and freedom of reporting by means of broadcasts and films shall be guaranteed.'[214] What conclusion does this comparison allow with a view to the freedom of expression protection of telecommunication network providers?

---

[213] Such as the ITU Radio Regulations.
[214] Translated by C. Tomuschat, D.P. Currie and D.P. Kommers in cooperation with the Language Service of the German Bundestag.

3 Critically discuss the following statement: 'Those who control the networks control the media.'

VIII Further Reading

- L. Garzaniti and M. Oregan (eds.), *Telecommunications, Broadcasting and the
  Internet: EU Competition Law and Regulation*, 3rd edn, 2010
- C. Koenig, A. Bartosch, J.-D. Braun and M. Romes (eds.), *EC Competition and
  Telecommunications Law*, 2nd edn, 2009
- P. Nihoul and P. Rodford, *EU Electronic Communications Law, Competition &
  Regulation in the European Telecommunications Market*, 2nd edn, 2011
- I. Walden (ed.), *Telecommunications Law and Regulation*, 4th edn, 2012

Data protection

CASE EXAMPLES

Google Search is an online search engine operated by Google Inc., which has its seat in the United States. Google Search is offered worldwide through the website www.google.com. In numerous states, a local version adapted to the national language exists, including the Spanish version www.google.es. Google Search indexes websites throughout the world. The information indexed is stored temporarily on servers whose location is kept secret. Google Spain, which is seated in Spain, is a Google Inc. subsidiary for the purpose of promoting and selling advertising space on the search engine in Spain. In 2010, Mr González, a Spanish national resident in Spain, lodged a complaint with the Spanish Data Protection Agency against Google Spain and Google Inc. The complaint was based on the fact that, when an internet user entered Mr González' name in the Google search engine, he would obtain links to two pages of a newspaper's website from 1998, on which Mr González' name appeared for a real-estate auction connected with attachment proceedings for the recovery of social security debts. Mr González requested that Google Spain or Google Inc. be required to remove or conceal the personal data relating to him so that they ceased to be included in the search results and no longer appeared in the links to the newspaper. Mr González stated in this context that the attachment proceedings concerning him had been fully resolved for a number of years and that reference to them was now entirely irrelevant.

(CJEU, Case C-131/12 [2014] Google Spain SL v. AEPD and others)

On 15 March 2006, the European Parliament and the Council adopted Directive 2006/24/EC on the retention of data generated or processed in connection with the provision of publicly available electronic communications services or of public communications networks and amending Directive 2002/58/EC (Data Retention Directive). The main objective of the Data Retention Directive is to harmonise obligations on providers of publicly available electronic communications services or providers of public communications networks to retain certain traffic and location data as well as related data necessary to identify subscribers or users. This data includes, for example, the date, time, duration and type of communication, the identification of the users' communication equipment, the location of mobile communication equipment, the name and address of the subscriber or registered user, the calling telephone number, the number called and IP addresses for internet services. The Directive stipulates that the providers must retain that data for a minimum of six months and, at most, two years. Competent national authorities would be able to request access to these details for the purposes of investigation, detection and prosecution of serious crime, such as organised crime and terrorism.

However, the Directive does not apply to the content of electronic communications, including information consulted using an electronic communications network. Ireland duly implemented the Data Retention Directive into domestic law. The NGO Digital Rights Ireland Ltd. brought an action before the Irish courts in which it claimed that it owned and used a mobile phone. It challenged the legality of national legislative and administrative measures implementing the Data Retention Directive. The Constitutional Court referred to the Court of Justice of the EU to examine the validity of the Data Retention Directive.

(CJEU, Joined Cases C-293/12 and C-594/12 [2014]
Digital Rights Ireland Ltd and Kärntner Landesregierung)

I Introduction

Data protection relates to human communication in various ways. First, it may protect those who communicate. As has been explained in Chapter 2, certain comments can be made only anonymously and unobserved, or they will not be made at all. Second, data protection laws protect the confidentiality of the information that has been communicated. As will be shown further below, communication content itself has become data. Third, communication generates metadata; that is, information about the communication process rather than the content of the communication. Metadata contains information about who communicated with whom, when and where. It does not reveal what has been communicated, but somewhat ironically, this knowledge is in most cases irrelevant and even inefficient to store, unless the content itself has been datafied. The interest in metadata rather than communication content is one of the most striking differences between the 'Big Data' and the 'small data' world. Until slightly more than 25 years ago, agents of the State Security (*Stasi*) of the German Democratic Republic spent hours eavesdropping on citizens, a highly personnel-intensive and time-consuming system (watch the film *The Lives of Others*). The gathering and evaluation of communication metadata that is possible today allows similar insights to the *Stasi's* analogue surveillance, but in a much more efficient way, on a vastly larger scale, and therefore it is even more threatening than the *Stasi's* one-to-one or one-to-few surveillances. If a dictatorial government such as the former GDR got hold of the communication metadata that is generated each day nowadays, the consequences would be inconceivable. The surveillance of just a person's smartphone would not only reveal most of his internet-based communication (and thus arguably most of his communication anyway) but in addition, smartphones are the most effective personal tracking devices in history. But it is not even necessary to summon the ghosts of the previous century to illustrate the threats involved in the gathering of metadata. For journalists communicating with their sources, the confidentiality of the communication process is as important as the confidentiality of the information itself; this applies even in democratic societies. This makes the protection of communication metadata a necessary prerequisite for uninhibited human communication.

Fourth, however, the safeguards provided by data protection laws may also restrict access to, and the communication of, protected information. The *Google Spain* case may serve as an example: Mr González wants to restrict Google from communicating information about him, because he regards this information as his personal data, which is to be protected.

For the sake of brevity and focus, this chapter will not deal in detail with many other interesting aspects of data protection that are not directly related to human communication. The chapter excludes, for example, security-related data transfers, such as the Passenger Name Record Agreement on data of flight passengers[1] and the SWIFT Agreement (on data regarding financial transactions), the generation and exploitation of data in electronic commerce, the challenges raised by the 'internet of things' and problems related to the collection and processing of health-data and the 'quantified self'. Moreover, the chapter will largely exclude the challenges posed by criminal breaches of data security, such as phishing and hacking.[2] However, the chapter will refer to such examples where necessary to explain the legal doctrine.

Finally, the chapter will focus on the *law* of data protection. It will largely exclude social privacy norms, market constraints and incentives and the significance of code. However, note that every solution to a social conflict, such as threats to a person's data autonomy, requires a mix of several modalities of regulation.[3] As far as data protection online is concerned, code has a particularly important role, which has already been referred to in Chapter 6. The importance of code for data protection is reflected in the use of privacy-enhancing technologies (PETs) and in the debate on 'privacy by design', a concept that was developed by the former Information and Privacy Commissioner of Ontario in the 1990s.[4]

---

[1] Council Decision 2004/496/EC of 17 May 2004 on the conclusion of an Agreement between the European Community and the United States of America on the processing and transfer of PNR data by Air Carriers to the United States Department of Homeland Security, Bureau of Customs and Border Protection, OJ L 183/83 (corrigendum at OJ L 255/168), and COM, Decision 2004/535/EC of 14 May 2004 on the adequate protection of personal data contained in the passenger name record of air passengers transferred to the United States Bureau of Customs and Border Protection, OJ L 235/11, both annulled by the ECJ in Joined Cases C-317/04 and C-318/04 [2006] European Parliament v. Council.

[2] See Directive 2013/40/EU of the European Parliament and of the Council of 12 August 2013 on attacks against information systems and replacing Council Framework Decision 2005/222/JHA, OJ L 218/8.

[3] Lessig (2006, p. 223).

[4] www.ipc.on.ca/english/privacy/introduction-to-pbd. On technical approaches to data protection, see, for example, Reidenberg (2000, p. 1331), providing further references.

II The Phenomenon of Big Data

Data protection has been on policy-makers' agendas since the 1970s. However, with the prevalence of digital technologies, society has created the ability 'to harness information in novel ways to produce useful insights or goods and services of significant value' – a phenomenon commonly known as 'Big Data'.[5] Big Data essentially consists of three distinct features. First, the sheer mass of information that is nowadays generated and stored. This includes, for example, Google search entries, purchases on Amazon, personal information divulged on Facebook, tweets and many more. Researchers estimate that Google receives some 3 billion search queries and produces more than 24 petabytes of data per day, which is more than thousands of times the quantity of all printed material in the Library of Congress.[6] The mass of information available distinguishes Big Data from 'small data': small data is based on inferences from samples of a population, such as surveys among 1,000 British citizens in order to draw conclusions on the entire British population. Big Data is aiming at completeness: not merely a representative sample of the population, but ideally the entire population. So where does this mass of information come from? It is not only the process of digitisation that has given birth to Big Data. This was merely a (necessary) prerequisite. It took a second step to generate the amount of data that is available today: the datafication of information. Datafication describes the phenomenon of taking all information that is available and transforming it into a quantified data format.[7] This includes not only information we are used to referring to as data, such as a person's birthday. It also includes any other information that is quantifiable. With regard to communication, it encompasses, for example, the corresponding parties, their location and even the content of their communication. Google is arguably the company that has best understood the value of not merely *digitised* words, but of *datafied* words.[8] The *Google Spain* case is an illuminative example: Google's search engine processes the information about Mr González' bankruptcy not for its content value, but for its data value.

The second feature of Big Data is the ability to store and process the mass of information on computer systems. This data is not 'lost' after it has fulfilled its primary purpose, such as leading to an online search result or concluding a book purchase. Instead, it will be stored and used for further purposes, such as refining a search result, making recommendations for further book purchases, suggesting new 'friends', and so on.

---

[5] Mayer-Schönberger and Cukier (2013, p. 2); see WP29, Statement on the impact of the development of big data on the protection of individuals with regard to the processing of their personal data in the EU, Adopted on 16 September 2004.

[6] Mayer-Schönberger and Cukier (2013, p. 8).

[7] Mayer-Schönberger and Cukier (2013, pp. 15, 76, 78).

[8] Mayer-Schönberger and Cukier (2013, p. 86).

The third notable characteristic of Big Data is the ability to draw conclusions from the data that is available. While our intuition searches for explanation and causation, Big Data is based on probability and correlation. For example, if a person bought five books on media law, it is likely that this person is interested in a sixth one, which the online bookstore will therefore suggest. But Big Data cannot explain why the person is likely to buy the book, whether he needs it for his academic work or as a birthday present. As a further example, if 80 per cent of someone's circle of social network 'friends' overlaps with someone else's 'friends', Big Data will infer that the latter is likely to 'befriend' some of the remaining 20 per cent as well. But it cannot say, for example, whether he actually likes them or not.

Big Data poses significant challenges to communication privacy, three examples of which shall be further highlighted in this chapter. First, the question as to when data is 'personal' data. As will be shown below, data is to be considered 'personal' if an individual is identified or identifiable. Yet with a sufficient amount of data available, each person is identifiable, even if his name has been anonymised. Second, one of the most important principles of data protection is the principle of purpose specification. Purpose specification means that data processing has to be carried out for explicit and legitimate purposes which must have been specified in advance. Big Data, however, is based on the principle that every data set may have an intrinsic value that has not been discovered yet. While according to current data protection law, data may be used to serve primary purposes for which the data subject has given his consent, companies and governments have an interest to store this data for further purposes that have not been conceived of as yet and for which the data subject has not given his consent. Third, as has been indicated before, more information than ever before is becoming datafied. Location, communication participants, the length of communication – all this has become data, and more importantly, personal data.

On a final note, consider how Big Data might inform the future of journalism. This is arguably more a social than a legal problem, but it is in any case noteworthy. Big Data makes it possible to quantify the interest a person takes in certain journalistic products. The time a person spends reading certain newspaper articles online, the topics to which those articles relate, the articles he ignores, his feedback on articles, whether or not he recommends certain articles to friends (and to whom specifically) and whether someone recommends particular articles to him – this is all measureable. It will change the perception of news, and the way news is presented, in two ways: The first change will occur at the receiving end of news. People will increasingly be served with articles that match their preferences. This means, in turn, they will to a lesser degree be exposed to articles that do not correspond to their interests, their mindset or their opinions. Hence they are less likely to be engaged in a pluralistic debate, to the detriment of public discourse.[9] The second change will be taking place at the source's end. Given that what people like to read is measurable, and since

---

[9] This problem has been presented by Sunstein (2007).

journalists want people to read their stories, Big Data will increasingly influence the content of products. Take e-books as an example. E-books generate data on how long it takes readers to read certain pages (conclusion: the faster the reader, the more exciting the page) and on which pages most readers finish the book prematurely (conclusion: until this point, the book must have been boring). If e-books feed this information back to their producers and they sell it to publishing houses, it would considerably influence the way books will be written in the future.[10] That a publisher accepts Tolstoy's *War and Peace* for publication is arguably less likely under these circumstances than it was in 1869. While Big Data tries to measure everything, the impact of Big Data on the ways news (and literature) are presented is unmeasurable.

III The Public and Private Dimensions of Data Protection and their Threats to the Digital Sovereignty of the Individual

Data protection is a prime example of the increasingly blurred public–private law divide. The 'Big Brother' of the twenty-first century might not be the government, but multinational internet companies. More significantly, private economic and public security interests are intertwined, albeit for different motivations. Both sides share a common interest in gathering and saving as much data as possible. More significantly, government institutions help themselves to data gathered by private companies in order to fulfil their tasks – the above-mentioned case on the Data Retention Directive gives ample proof of that. Sometimes the private and the governmental interests in data-gathering are even identical. For example, health data is of equal value for both private and public health insurance. With reasonable foresight, the Council of Europe Convention 108 and the EU data protection legislation do not strictly separate the processing of data by private or governmental actors, but address all 'data controllers'.

Yet there is good reason to argue that the distinction between data processing by private and public actors, and thus between private and public data protection law, is still significant. This does not mean that the one form of data collection is worse than the other; rather, they pose *different* threats to liberty. The *Google Spain* case and the *Digital Rights Ireland* case are exemplary. First, private companies and governmental agencies process personal data for different purposes. Therefore, second, the threat posed by such data processing varies significantly between private and public agents. Third, as a result, the legal requirements for such processing still differ.

Regarding the first point, private companies collect data mostly for commercial purposes. They provide services that seemingly make life more convenient, and gather data in return. For them, data is an economic asset; it is both raw material and currency of the internet age. Governmental surveillance, on the other hand, has many purposes, ranging from national security in democratic states to the maintenance of

[10] See Mayer-Schönberger and Cukier (2013, pp. 132–133).

power in dictatorships. However, it hardly ever has a commercial purpose. To be sure, these two scenarios can be overlapping. Private data-gathering can be (mis) used by public sector entities for governmental purposes, and states may collect data for economic purposes, such as industrial espionage. But the threats are nonetheless different.

This leads to the second point. What are those threats? With regard to private data-gathering, consumers are led to the false belief that they are receiving services 'for free', while they, in reality, pay with their personal data. By contrast, governmental data-gathering has no transaction character. For the public sector, data is usually not an economic asset, but mostly a surveillance and control tool. Surveillance – even the mere fear of being watched – has severe chilling and de-individualising effects. Surveillance and control are psychological interferences with freedom of expression and lead to conformist behaviour. Moreover, the conclusions drawn from data-gathering are based on probability, not certainty. If the government draws wrong conclusions from someone buying a significant amount of hydrogen peroxide, the person would spend some time in custody.

Threats by private companies to the data sovereignty of individuals should of course not be underestimated, but they are different. Conclusions private companies draw from gathered data might also be more than just inconvenient. A person might not receive a loan from his bank because of an automatically generated but false credit rating; a private insurance company might be able to infer details of a person's strictly intimate life because of a combination of data gathered from his health-tracking wearables and his car's data transfer; in general, companies might know more about us than we do ourselves. Nevertheless, it is still the government's power to prosecute, arrest or detain a person because of data.

As a consequence of the residual, but nonetheless significant, public–private distinction in data privacy, one of the main arguments brought forward in favour of governmental surveillance is flawed. Supporters of state surveillance often argue that citizens present personal information quite generously in blogs, on social networks, etc. Irresponsible as this might be, it is done voluntarily, and it only stretches to data that someone *wants* to give away because he promises himself a certain benefit or satisfaction from it. Moreover, everyone is at liberty to join and to leave Facebook, to use or not use Google. This does not apply to data gathered by the state. Government surveillance does not provide an opt-out.

Third, what are the legal consequences of the threats posed to data-gathering by private and public actors? In order for data to be handed over voluntarily to private companies, an important aspect of private data protection law is the notion of 'informed consent' – what does the company use my data for, and for how long? In short, users need to know the transaction character of their online behaviour. By contrast, state surveillance has to be justified in light of the vertical effect of human rights, in particular the principle of proportionality. Governmental data-gathering has to pursue a legitimate aim with suitable, necessary and proportionate means. In recent years, the fight against terrorism has mostly been brought forward in order to justify large-scale state surveillance. However, it is already questionable whether the data masses thus gathered are suitable to achieve the aim. Just as too little data can be problematic, too much data can be a problem as well. In order to find the needle in the haystack, it is counterproductive to increase the size of the haystack. Moreover, the success of state surveillance in the fight against terrorism has not yet been proven. Since data gathered to prevent a crime is usually kept secret, it is often impossible for the public to scrutinise the behaviour of security services. Even if considered necessary, the gathering of data has to be proportionate. An argument brought forward in this context is that secret services usually do not gather the content of internet communication, but 'only' metadata. However, this argument underestimates the fact that metadata facilitates the creation of comprehensive personal profiles. As a former director of the NSA and the CIA once expressed in the context of the use of drones: 'We kill people based on metadata.'[11]

Another argument often brought forward in the surveillance discourse is the 'nothing to hide, nothing to fear' narrative. Yet this argument misjudges that everyone has something to hide, with the exception of hopeless narcissists. This does not necessarily have to be information endangering public security, but intimate details of one's private life or exceptional psychological circumstances. Moreover, information that may today be considered harmless, such as political party affiliation and religious conviction, can be vitally important tomorrow. The tenet of state surveillance is thus not whether someone has something to hide, but rather that everyone has the right to hide certain information.

This does not mean that state surveillance is generally and always prohibited. These arguments should merely show that the legality of state surveillance requires careful balancing of the conflicting rights and interests. The arguments are more complex than they seem at first glance and, unfortunately, they are not always analysed with the sober view of legal doctrine. The argument has often been raised that mass surveillance leads to a reversal of the presumption of innocence. Indeed, Article 14(2) ICCPR, Article 6(2) ECHR and Article 48(1) EUChFR provide that everyone who has been charged shall be presumed innocent until proved guilty. However, legal doctrine distinguishes between the prevention of crime and the prosecution of a crime. The prevention of crime allows for a broader discretion than the prosecution of a crime. The police might ultimately even be allowed to shoot a person in order to prevent a crime, but not in order to prosecute or punish him (at least not in most countries). Yet it should also be clear that the undertaking of crime prevention has its own limits; the ends do not as such justify the means. Measures to prevent crimes can stigmatise a person or make his life more difficult, such as the public arrest or the freezing of financial assets. But it would be inaccurate to argue that any surveillance is a violation of the presumption

---

[11] See www.nybooks.com/blogs/nyrblog/2014/may/10/we-kill-people-based-metadata.

of innocence. In the first place, it would have to be established whether the surveillance serves to prevent a crime or to prosecute it. Moreover, one would also have to inquire in each individual case whether information gathered in the surveillance process for crime prevention may be used as evidence in criminal prosecutions and trials. But mere surveillance, in spite of the negative consequences it may have, does not as such make a person a suspect and violate the presumption of innocence.

IV Transnational Developments

In 1980, the OECD Council adopted the Guidelines on the Protection of Privacy and Transborder Flows of Personal Data (OECD Guidelines), which were last updated in 2013.[12] The 1980 Guidelines have been the first internationally agreed-upon set of privacy principles. Although the Guidelines are not binding for the OECD Member Countries, they have influenced privacy legislation and policy in OECD Member Countries. Similar to the EU legal framework, which will be addressed further below, the Guidelines envisage both the concerns for privacy arising from the use of personal data and the risk to global trade resulting from restrictions to the flow of information across borders. The Guidelines provide eight principles as minimum standards for the protection of personal data in both the public and in the private sector. These principles are: collection limitation, data quality, purpose specification, use limitation, security safeguards, openness, individual participation and accountability. Moreover, the Guidelines also deal with the transfer of personal data between states. The Guidelines strongly influenced the making of European data protection legislation. They will therefore be further referred to below in the context of European data protection law. The Working Party on Security and Privacy in the Digital Economy (SPDE), formerly known as Working Party on Information Security and Privacy (WPISP), is an OECD forum developing public policy analysis and recommendations on digital security and privacy.

On the UN level, both Article 12 UDHR and Article 17 ICCPR protect the right to privacy and correspondence. The Human Rights Committee has not yet had the opportunity to develop an in-depth body of information privacy law. Nevertheless, in its General Comment No. 16 on Article 17 ICCPR (Right to privacy), the Committee recognised rather succinctly some core aspects of information privacy law: the fact that personal information has to be protected against both public authorities or private individuals or bodies, the need for data security, the right of data subjects to be informed about the processing of their personal data and the right to rectification or elimination of unlawfully obtained or inaccurate data.[13] Moreover, the Human

---

[12] Recommendation of the Council concerning Guidelines governing the Protection of Privacy and Transborder Flows of Personal Data (2013) [C(80)58/FINAL, as amended on 11 July 2013 by C(2013)79].
[13] General Comment no. 16 on Article 17 ICCPR (Right to privacy), Thirtysecond session (1988), para. 10.

Rights Committee decided on individual communications alleging interferences with correspondence.[14]

In 1990, the UN General Assembly adopted the Guidelines for the Regulation of Computerized Personal Data Files (UN Guidelines).[15] The UN Guidelines stipulate minimum guarantees that (merely) 'should' be provided in national legislation: as a UN General Assembly resolution, the Guidelines are not legally binding. Their principles include the lawfulness, fairness, accuracy, purpose-specification, relevance and adequacy of data collection and processing, the principle of consent, the right to know whether information concerning oneself is being processed, the principle of non-discrimination and data security. Paragraph 6 allows the states to depart from some of those principles for reasons of national security, public order, public health or morality and the rights and freedoms of others. Paragraph 9 deals with transborder data flows. Except for the principle of non-discrimination, which is codified in EU primary law anyway, these principles have all been taken up by, and codified in more detail in, EU data protection legislation. They will therefore be dealt with further below in this chapter.

In its 29th session in June/July 2015, the Human Rights Council appointed Joseph Cannataci from Malta as the first Special Rapporteur on the Right to Privacy. The Special Rapporteur is mandated, *inter alia*, to collect information on the promotion and protection of the right to privacy, to submit proposals and recommendations to the Human Rights Council, to report on alleged violations of privacy and to submit an annual report to the Human Rights Council and to the General Assembly.[16]

V Data Protection Philosophies in Europe and the US

Europe and the US have significantly different data protection philosophies that inform transnational debates on privacy. The following paragraphs will introduce some of the core conflicts of US and European information privacy approaches. However, one has to be careful not to replace a thorough comparative analysis with over-simplified dichotomies.

The European, and especially the EU, data protection regime is based on an omnibus approach. It encompasses both data processing in the public and in the private sector, and it does, in principle, not distinguish between the type of information concerned, although there are exceptions concerning communication data and sensitive data. By contrast, the US has a rather fragmented legal regime on data protection. It has about 20 federal privacy laws and hundreds of such laws among its states. These laws either concern the public sector only or they are information-specific or medium-specific. They regulate individually, for example, health information, use

---

[14] See, for example, Human Rights Committee, Pinkney v. Canada [1981] Communication no. 27/1978 [34]; J. R. T. and W. G. Party v. Canada [1984] Communication no. 104/1981 [8].

[15] UN General Assembly, Resolution 45/95 of 14 December 1990.

[16] Human Rights Council, Resolution 28/16: The right to privacy in the digital age, 1 April 2015, A/HRC/ RES/28/16.

of credit reports, marketing communications, personal information collected online from children under 13, video privacy or electronic communications. Moreover, most US states impose security breach notification obligations. The US does not have an official data protection authority, and apart from the Health Insurance Portability and Accountability Act of 1996 and state laws there are no statutory requirements to appoint a data protection officer. Privacy laws are either enforced by the Federal Trade Commission (FTC), State Attorneys General, the regulatory authority for the industry sector in question or by civil lawsuits, often through class action lawsuits. The FTC uses its competence to adjudicate on unfair or deceptive trade practices to punish companies that fail to implement minimal data security measures or fail to meet its privacy policies.

As a consequence of this fragmentation, there is no coherent definition of personal data in the US. Some privacy laws provide a definition of 'personal information' that includes information that, on its own, does not actually identify a person. The FTC considers information that can reasonably be used to contact or distinguish a person, including IP addresses and device identifiers, as personal data. Moreover, the notion of sensitive personal data varies among the federal and state laws. US privacy law is also to a large extent based on best practices and self-regulation, such as the Safe Harbour Principles. Finally, there are no restrictions on the transfer of personal data by private entities in the US.

However, as a US author rightly emphasised: 'It is simply false to say that privacy doesn't matter to Americans.'[17] Rather, for various reasons, Americans and continental Europeans perceive privacy differently. It is best summarised as the contrast between the European perception of privacy as an aspect of dignity, and the US perception of privacy as an aspect of liberty.[18] Joel R. Reidenberg astutely described the data protection philosophies as the liberal, market-based governance in the US and the socially protective, rights-based governance in Europe.[19] The core Article 8 ECHR rights are rights to one's image, name and information privacy rights, which are protected against everyone, including – via the doctrine of indirect horizontal effect – other private individuals.[20] By contrast, the US approach is primarily based on the suspicion of government intrusion into one's private sphere. But this contrast is certainly not absolute, and the outcome of information privacy cases is often the same. In fact, there has long been a dialogue between US and European courts, academics and policy-makers on issues of privacy, most notably with regard to the OECD Guidelines themselves.[21]

---

[17] Whitman (2004, p. 1158).
[18] Whitman (2004, p. 1161). On the privacy as liberty and privacy as dignity rationales, see Post (2001).
[19] Reidenberg (2000).
[20] See Chapter 3.
[21] Schwartz (2013, pp. 1970–1971). See US Supreme Court, Lawrence v. Texas, 539 U.S. 558, 573 (2003); ECtHR, Von Hannover v. Germany (No. 1) [2004] App. no. 59320/00, concurring opinion by Judge Boštjan M. Zupančič: 'Privacy … is the right to be left alone.'

However, the view often taken in US scholarship is that the European concept of privacy is primarily focused on protection of one's public image, especially against intrusion by the media, whereas in the US the government is regarded as the prime enemy of privacy.[22] While the relatively little focus on privacy protection in the private sector corresponds to the outstanding value attached to freedom of speech in the US,[23] the suggestion that European privacy law is less focused on government intrusion does not seem entirely accurate. Rather, the European approach can best be explained with an example that has been brought forward in a comparative analysis.[24] The argument was that US citizens would be astonished by the European practice that governments prohibit the use of certain baby names. However, this state interference with the parents' liberty is only justified by the protection of another person's privacy: the baby's. To put it mildly, a boy would face a difficult time if he introduced himself at his first school day with 'My name is Blitzkrieg', or 'My name is Peace With God Through Jesus Christ Alone'.[25] In such a case, the necessity to protect the child's privacy trumps the parents' liberty to name their child as they like. For a lack of alternatives, the only agent capable of such protection is, whether we like it or not, the government. This example shows that Europe takes a holistic view on privacy protection within both the public and the private sector, even against one's own parents. At the same time, the example also illustrates that European jurisdictions have a greater trust in the government's capability to act as an arbiter of such a balancing exercise than the US. However, even the trust in the government's capabilities is not unlimited in Europe: various decisions of the European Court of Human Rights on Article 8 ECHR and the invalidation of the Data Retention Directive by the Court of Justice of the EU are ample proof of that. With a view to post-9/11 surveillance measures and particularly the NSA surveillance activities revealed by Edward Snowden, it even appears that the US has more confidence in the government as the arbiter of the 'liberty versus security balance' than Europe.[26]

Another conflict between the European and the US approach to data protection lies in the perception of data as a transaction commodity. As has been explained before, the philosophy in the US is in the first place focused on threats to information privacy by the government. Yet as far as processing of privacy in the private sector is concerned, the US approach relies heavily on market mechanisms and consumer choice. This leaves companies relatively broad leeway to practice innovative forms of

---

[22] See, for example, Whitman (2004, pp. 1161–1162).

[23] Wolf (2014, p. 255).

[24] Whitman (2004, pp. 1158–1159).

[25] For the latter, see the Hanseatic Higher Court of Appeal (Oberlandesgericht) Bremen, Case 1 W 49/95 [1996] 'Frieden mit Gott allein durch Jesus Christus'.

[26] But see also US Court of Appeals (2nd Cir), ACLU v. Clapper, Docket No. 14-42-cv (2015), ruling that Section 215 of the Patriot Act did not authorise the bulk collection of metadata; Klayman v. Obama, 957 F. Supp. 2d 1 (2013), ruling ruled that bulk collection of American telephone metadata likely violates the Fourth Amendment to the Constitution of the United States.

data-gathering and data-processing. The fact that the most influential internet service providers today have their origins in the US is certainly not a coincidence. By comparison, Europe has a stronger human rights-related approach to data protection, which includes both the indirect horizontal effect of human rights between private persons and the obligation of the governments to protect human rights against interferences by other individuals. Nevertheless, it would be over-simplified to argue that the market is irrelevant for the EU regulatory framework. On the contrary, European provisions regularly emphasise that they both aim at the protection of the right to privacy and ensure the free flow of personal data between Member States.[27]

Without over-simplifying the socio-legal philosophies underlying the European and US approaches to data protection, one can summarise the core aspects as follows: the underlying idea of EU data protection law is to protect against threats to data autonomy posed by both the government and private persons. US information privacy laws, by comparison, are mainly informed by concerns about government intrusion, while data protection laws applying to the private sector mostly focus on specific information or technologies. The main tool to address information privacy concerns in Europe is the law, enforced by independent data protection authorities. The US, by contrast, relies mostly on self-regulation, market mechanisms and consumer choice. The EU provides an omnibus legal framework concerning the protection of data in both the public and the private sector, basically disregarding the technology used or the information concerned. By contrast, the US provides a rather fragmented legal framework on both federal and state levels. In Europe, personal data may only be processed pursuant to a legal basis, in other words: the processing of personal data is prohibited unless it is permitted by law. In the US, the processing of personal data is allowed unless it is prohibited. EU data protection law has a significant extraterritorial effect: first, by establishing prescriptive jurisdiction of the EU data protection regime on companies established outside the EU if they process personal data in the EU using equipment there; and second, by allowing the transfer of personal data to countries outside the EU only if the third country provides adequate protection.[28] By contrast, US law does not limit data exports to other countries.

Any explanation on data protection philosophies would be incomplete without reference to postmodern philosophies of privacy protection. In Chapter 3 and in this chapter it is taken for granted that privacy is essential for self-development and for a democratic society, and thus deserves legal protection.[29] Privacy is regarded not merely as a 'social construction', but as an innate state of human beings, comparable to life and health. By contrast, in 1999 Scott McNealy, the chief executive officer of Sun Microsystems, was quoted with the words: 'You have zero privacy anyway. Get

---

[27] See, for example, Article 1 Data Protection Directive; Article 1(1) E-privacy Directive.
[28] See Section VII.6 in this chapter.
[29] See Schwartz (1999).

over it.'[30] To put it in a more complex setting, McNealy's words can be understood as the essential summary of the notion of post-privacy. Post-privacy encompasses both the descriptive view that we live in a 'transparency society' in which privacy is no longer the 'social norm',[31] and the prescriptive view that privacy laws *should* be abolished for the sake of freedom of speech and the right to receive information. A way to conceptualise the latter approach is the notion of 'privacy commons', in which privacy is viewed 'as a social and not merely an individual good'.[32] Here it will be left to the reader to think on both the descriptive and the prescriptive argument. However, as far as the *current* state of European law is concerned, this chapter will show that the protection of information privacy is alive and well.

VI The European and International Legal Framework for Data Protection

The first data protection statutes were adopted in 1970 by the Parliament of the German federal state of Hesse. Other German federal states, the Federal Republic itself (in 1977) and other European countries (such as Sweden in 1973, Austria, Denmark, France and Norway in 1978) subsequently adopted their own information privacy codifications. In 1981, the Council of Europe adopted Convention 108 for the Protection of Individuals with regard to Automatic Processing of Personal Data.[33] The Convention, which has been ratified by 48 States,[34] entered into force in October 1985. The European Communities acceded to the Convention in June 1999.[35] In July 2004, the Additional Protocol to Convention 108 regarding supervisory authorities and transborder data flows entered into force.[36]

In 1995, the then-EC adopted the EU Data Protection Directive 95/46/EC.[37] The E-privacy Directive 2002/58/EC[38] has been adopted in the context of the

---

[30] http://archive.wired.com/politics/law/news/1999/01/17538.

[31] These words are attributed to Facebook founder Mark Zuckerberg; see www.theguardian.com/technology/2010/jan/11/facebook-privacy. On the 'transparency society', see Han (2015).

[32] See Solove and Schwartz (2011, p. 59).

[33] Convention 108 of 28 January 1981 for the Protection of Individuals with regard to Automatic Processing of Personal Data.

[34] As of 23 July 2015; for a list of ratifications, seehttp://conventions.coe.int/Treaty/Commun/ChercheSig.asp?NT=108&CM=&DF=&CL=ENG.

[35] Amendments to the Convention for the Protection of Individuals with regard to Automatic Processing of Personal Data approved by the Committee of Ministers, in Strasbourg, on 15 June 1999.

[36] CETS No.: 181.

[37] Directive 95/46/EC of the European Parliament and of the Council of 24 October 1995 on the protection of individuals with regard to the processing of personal data and on the free movement of such data, OJ 281, 31.

[38] Directive 2002/58/EC of the European Parliament and of the Council of 12 July 2002 concerning the processing of personal data and the protection of privacy in the electronic communications sector (Directive on privacy and electronic communications), OJ L 201/37, as amended by Directive 2006/24/EC of the European Parliament and of the Council of 15 March 2006 on the retention of data generated or processed in connection with the provision of publicly available electronic communications services or of public communications networks and amending Directive 2002/58/EC, OJ L 105/54 and Directive 2009/

telecommunications package of 2002 and amended by the Citizen's Rights Directive in 2009.[39] In May 2016, the General Data Protection Regulation was published in the Official Journal.[40] The Regulation repeals Directive 95/46/EC with effect from 25 May 2018. The main aims of the Regulation are twofold: first, it should adapt EU data protection legislation to the requirements of the technological development age; note that the Data Protection Directive from 1995 had been adopted just about the time when the internet became available to the general public. Second, as a regulation, the General Data Protection Regulation leaves the Member States little discretion as to its application and enforcement, and it will thus reduce the legal fragmentation concerning data protection standards within the EU. The provisions of the General Data Protection Regulation are often more detailed than those of the Data Protection Directive it will replace. However, knowledge of the Data Protection Directive is still relevant, because the Regulation builds on many concepts of the Directive and because the Regulation takes effect only in 2018. Therefore, this chapter will focus on Directive 95/46/EC, but it will refer to the General Data Protection Regulation, where appropriate. The General Data Protection Regulation does not apply to the specific obligations set out in Directive 2002/58/EC.

1 Council of Europe

Convention 108 applies to data processing in the public as well as the private sector, but its scope is limited to automatic processing (Article 3). The basic principles of the Convention include provisions on data quality (Article 5), special categories of data (Article 6), data security (Article 7), additional safeguards for the data subject (Article 8) and sanctions and remedies (Article 10). Moreover, Article 12 provides rules on transborder data flows. These provisions will be dealt with further below. Convention 108 is also frequently referred to by the Strasbourg Court.[41]

In addition, the Committee of Ministers adopted several declarations, resolutions and recommendations on data protection. They usually relate to the processing of

---

136/EC of the European Parliament and of the Council of 25 November 2009 amending Directive 2002/22/EC on universal service and users' rights relating to electronic communications networks and services, Directive 2002/58/EC concerning the processing of personal data and the protection of privacy in the electronic communications sector and Regulation (EC) No. 2006/2004 on cooperation between national authorities responsible for the enforcement of consumer protection laws, OJ L 337/11.

[39] See Chapter 7.
[40] Regulation (EU) 2016/679 of the European Parliament and of the Council of 27 April 2016 on the protection of natural persons with regard to the processing of personal data and on the free movement of such data, and repealing Directive 95/46/EC (General Data Protection Regulation), OJ L 119/1.
[41] See, for example, ECtHR, Amann v. Switzerland [2000] App. no. 27798/95 [65]; Rotaru v. Romania [2000] App. no. 28341/95 [43]; Cemalettin Canlı v. Turkey [2008] App. no. 22427/04 [34].

data in specific sectors, such as medical services, insurances and social security; to the use of specific technologies, such as the internet, electronic payment or direct marketing; or to specific categories of data, such as biometric data.[42]

Finally, the Council of Europe data protection regime is strongly influenced by the case law of the Strasbourg Court on Article 8 ECHR. Although Article 8 ECHR, in contrast to Article 8 EUChFR, does not expressly protect personal data as such, it is protected as an aspect of 'private life' and 'correspondence' within the meaning of that provision. The notion of personal data under the 'private life' branch is a broad concept that encompasses the processing of any information relating to an identified or identifiable individual.[43] The Court and the European Commission on Human Rights thus adopted decisions on the protection of a person's name[44] or picture,[45] data collected in a census,[46] police or secret service registers on a person,[47] records of a person's voice,[48] monitoring of the actions of an individual by a CCTV camera and the disclosure of respective video footage,[49] interception of communication,[50] various forms of surveillance,[51] protection against storage of personal data by

---

[42] See, for example, Declaration on Risks to Fundamental Rights stemming from Digital Tracking and other Surveillance Technologies (11 June 2013); Declaration on the protection of freedom of expression and freedom of assembly and association with regard to privately operated Internet platforms and online service providers (7 December 2011); Recommendation CM/Rec(2010)13 on the protection of individuals with regard to automatic processing of personal data in the context of profiling (23 November 2010); Recommendation No. R(2002) 9 on the protection of personal data collected and processed for insurance purposes (18 September 2002); Recommendation No. R(99) 5 for the protection of privacy on the Internet (23 February 1999); Recommendation No. R(97) 18 on the protection of personal data collected and processed for statistical purposes (30 September 1997); Recommendation No. R(97) 5 on the protection of medical data (13 February 1997); Recommendation No. R(95) 4 on the protection of personal data in the area of telecommunication services, with particular reference to telephone services (7 February 1995); Recommendation No. R(91) 10 on the communication to third parties of personal data held by public bodies (9 September 1991); Recommendation No. R(87) 15 regulating the use of personal data in the police sector (17 September 1987); Recommendation No. R(85) 20 on the protection of personal data used for the purposes of direct marketing (25 October 1985); Recommendation No. R(83) 10 on the protection of personal data used for scientific research and statistics (23 September 1983) [replaced by Recommendation No. R(97) 18 with regard to statistics].

[43] ECtHR, Amann v. Switzerland [2000] App. no. 27798/95 [65].

[44] ECtHR, Burghartz v. Switzerland [1994] App. no. 16213/90 [24]; Standard Verlags GmbH v. Austria (No. 3) [2012] App. no. 34702/07 [36]. See also Articles 24(2) ICCPR, 18 ACHR and 7 and 8 of the UN Convention on the Rights of the Child.

[45] ECtHR, Schüssel v. Austria [2002] App. no. 42409/98; Von Hannover v. Germany (No. 1) [2004] App. no. 59320/00 [50 ff]; Eerikäinen and others v. Finland [2009] App. no. 3514/02 [61].

[46] EComHR, X v. United Kingdom [1982] App. no. 9702/82.

[47] ECtHR, Leander v. Sweden [1987] App. no. 9248/81 [59] and [67]; Amann v. Switzerland [2000] App. no. 27798/95 [67]; Rotaru v. Romania [2000] App. no. 28341/95 [43]; Segerstedt-Wiberg and others v. Sweden [2006] App. no. 62332/00.

[48] ECtHR, P.G. and J.H. v. United Kingdom [2001] App. no. 44787/98 [59].

[49] ECtHR, Peck v. United Kingdom [2003] App. no. 44647/98 [59].

[50] See, for example, ECtHR, Malone v. United Kingdom [1984] App. no. 8691/79; Kopp v. Switzerland [1998] App. no. 13/1997/797/1000; Copland v. United Kingdom [2007] App. no. 62617/00.

[51] See, for example, ECtHR, Klass and others v. Germany [1978] App. no. 5029/71; Uzun v. Germany [2010] App. no. 35623/05.

public authorities,[52] medical data,[53] access to social service records containing information about a person's childhood and personal history,[54] access to copies of medical records[55] and DNA samples.[56] With regard to the notion of 'correspondence', the Court and the Commission had to decide on the interception of letters,[57] telephone conversations,[58] telexes,[59] pager messages[60] and e-mail and internet usage.[61] The Court emphasised that the mere existence of legislation that allows secret monitoring of communications amounts to an interference with Article 8 ECHR.[62] The Court also highlighted that each processing action (collection, storage and transmission) amounts to a separate interference.[63] Moreover, Article 8(1) ECHR protects not only the content of correspondence, but also traffic data such as the numbers dialled and the time and duration of each call.[64]

Interferences with the rights enshrined in Article 8(1) ECHR have to be justified under Article 8(2) of that provision. They need to be in accordance with the law, have a legitimate aim (national security, public safety or the economic well-being of the country, the prevention of disorder or crime, the protection of health or morals or the protection of the rights and freedoms of others) and they must be necessary in a democratic society. In order to establish 'interference' with regard to surveillance measures, it is not necessary for an applicant to prove that public authorities have in fact acquired their communications data. As the Strasbourg Court held in *Weber and Saravia* v. *Germany*:

> [T]he mere existence of legislation which allows a system for the secret monitoring of communications entails a threat of surveillance for all those to whom the legislation may be applied. This threat necessarily strikes at freedom of communication between users of the telecommunications services

---

[52] See, for example, ECtHR, Leander v. Sweden [1987] App. no. 9248/81; S. and Marper v. United Kingdom [2008] App. no. 30562/04 and 30566/04.

[53] ECtHR, Biriuk v. Lithuania [2008] App. no 23373/03 [39]; I v. Finland [2008] App. no. 20511/03 [38]; Z v. Finland [1997] App. no. 22009/93 [96].

[54] ECtHR, M.G. v. United Kingdom [2002] App. no. 39393/98 [27].

[55] ECtHR, K.H. and others v. Slovakia [2009] App. no. 32881/04 [50].

[56] ECtHR, S. and Marper v. United Kingdom [2008] App. nos. 30562/04 and 30566/04 [41].

[57] ECtHR, Silver and others v. United Kingdom [1983] App. nos. 5947/72; 6205/73; 7052/75; 7061/75; 7107/75; 7113/75; 7136/75.

[58] ECtHR, Klass and others v. Germany [1978] App. no. 5029/71 [41]; Malone v. United Kingdom [1984] App. no. 8691/79 [64]; Liberty and others v. United Kingdom [2008] App. no. 58243/00 [56].

[59] EComHR, Christie v. the United Kingdom v. United Kingdom [1994] App. no. 21482/93.

[60] ECtHR, Taylor-Sabori v. the United Kingdom [2002] App. no. 47114/99.

[61] ECtHR, Copland v. United Kingdom [2007] App. no. 62617/00.

[62] ECtHR, Klass and others v. Germany [1978] App. no. 5029/71 [41]; Malone v. United Kingdom [1984] App. no. 8691/79 [64]; Liberty and others v. United Kingdom [2008] App. no. 58243/00 [56].

[63] ECtHR, Rotaru v. Romania [2000] App. no. 28341/95 [43]; P.G. and J.H. v. United Kingdom [2001] App. no. 44787/98 [59]; Peck v. United Kingdom [2003] App. no. 44647/98 [59]; Weber and Savaria v. Germany [2006] App. no. 54934/00 [79].

[64] ECtHR, Malone v. United Kingdom [1984] App. no. 8691/79 [84]; Copland v. United Kingdom [2007] App. no. 62617/00 [43].

and thereby amounts in itself to an interference with the exercise of the applicants' rights under Article 8, irrespective of any measures actually taken against them.[65]

The ECtHR explained the notion of 'accordance with the law' as follows:

> The requirement that any interference must be 'in accordance with the law' under [Article 8(2) ECHR] will only be met where three conditions are satisfied. First, the impugned measure must have some basis in domestic law. Second, the domestic law must be compatible with the rule of law and accessible to the person concerned. Third, the person affected must be able to foresee the consequences of the domestic law for him.[66]

In the context of secret measures of surveillance, the notion of 'foreseeability' 'cannot mean that an individual should be able to foresee when the authorities are likely to intercept his communications so that he can adapt his conduct accordingly'. However, it is necessary 'to have clear, detailed rules' on such surveillance measures, 'especially as the technology available for use is continually becoming more sophisticated'. Therefore, the domestic law 'must be sufficiently clear in its terms to give citizens an adequate indication as to the circumstances in which and the conditions on which public authorities are empowered to resort to any such measures'.[67] Moreover, the principle of legality does not only require that the data processing is prescribed by a legally binding statute, but also that the data subject is protected against arbitrary interferences.[68] For example, in *Rotaru v. Romania*, the Court held with a view to the secret collection and storage of personal data that domestic law has to limit the exercise of those powers by defining the kind of information that may be recorded, the categories of people against whom surveillance measures may be taken, the circumstances in which such measures may be taken, the procedure to be followed and the length of time for which the information may be kept.[69]

The Court conceptualised the protection of personal data under Article 8 ECHR not only as a negative right against state interference, but also as a positive obligation on the state to protect personal data. In this regard, the decision *K. U. v. Finland*, which has already been mentioned in Chapter 6, is of particular significance. Moreover, the Court has also obliged defendant states to take positive steps to adequately secure personal data.[70] The Court also held in other decisions that Article 8 ECHR in principle guarantees a right of access to information about one's personal data held or used

---

[65] ECtHR, Weber and Saravia v. Germany [2006] App. no. 54934/00 [78].

[66] ECtHR, Kennedy v. United Kingdom [2010] App. no. 26839/05 [151], providing further references.

[67] ECtHR, Weber and Saravia v. Germany [2006] App. no. 54934/00 [93], with further references.

[68] See, for example, ECtHR, Malone v. United Kingdom [1984] App. no. 8691/79 [67]; Kopp v. Switzerland [1998] App. no. 13/1997/797/1000 [64]; Amann v. Switzerland [2000] App. no. 27798/95 [56]; Segerstedt-Wiberg and others v. Sweden [2006] App. no. 62332/00 [76]; Cemalettin Canlı v. Turkey [2008] App. no. 22427/04 [38]; Liberty and others v. United Kingdom [2008] App. no. 58243/00 [69].

[69] ECtHR, Rotaru v. Romania [2000] App. no. 28341/95 [57].

[70] See, for example, ECtHR, I v. Finland [2008] App. no. 20511/03 [36].

by others.[71] This right may have to be balanced against conflicting rights of others, such as contributors to the data files, or legitimate state interests.

2 The EU Legal Framework

Like most Council of Europe documents, Convention 108 is strongly focused on human rights-related aspects, in this case of data protection (Article 1 of Convention 108). By contrast, EU legislation has in mind both the human rights dimension, and the relevance for the internal market, of personal data. EU data protection thus faces the conflict that, on the one hand, the internal market requires (personal) data to be able to flow freely from one Member State to another, but, on the other hand, the EUChFR requires the fundamental right to data protection to be safeguarded.

More specifically, Article 16(1) TFEU and Article 8 EUChFR expressly codify a right to protection of one's personal data. However, in contrast to Article 16(1) TFEU, Articles 8(2)1 and 52(1) of the Charter provide limitations to that right. One could thus argue that Article 16(1) TFEU offers more protection than Article 8 EUChFR. Yet, since the obliged addressees of these rights are the same – compare Article 51(1) EUChFR with Article 16(2) TFEU – Article 8(2) would be rendered redundant. On the other hand, applying the limitations of Article 8(2) and 52(1) EUChFR to Article 16 TFEU would be in conflict with Article 52(2) of the Charter, which provides that rights recognised by the Charter for which provision is made in the Treaties 'shall be exercised under the conditions and within the limits defined by those Treaties', and thus not vice versa. The relationship between Article 16 TFEU and Article 8 EUChFR, has, as apparent, not yet been addressed by the Court of Justice. Yet in *Volker und Markus Schecke GbR and Hartmut Eifert*, the Court, by reference to Article 52(1) EUChFR, indicated that '[t]he right to the protection of personal data is not ... an absolute right, but must be considered in relation to its function in society'.[72]

Based on (now) Article 114 TFEU, the EU institutions adopted the EU Data Protection Directive 95/46/EC in 1995 and the E-privacy Directive 2002/58/EC in 2002. The EU Data Protection Directive 95/46/EC covers all forms of processing of data, but its scope is restricted to data concerning natural persons only. The same applies to the General Data Protection Regulation. The E-privacy Directive 2002/58/EC is in substantive terms restricted to data processed in electronic communication, but it also includes data concerning legal persons. As far as the relationship between these pieces of legislation is concerned, the E-privacy Directive translates the principles set out in the Data Protection Directive into specific rules for the telecommunications sector. As Article 1(2) of the E-privacy

---

[71] ECtHR, Leander v. Sweden [1987] App. no. 9248/81 [48]; Gaskin v. United Kingdom [1989] App. no. 10454/83 [49]; Segerstedt-Wiberg and others v. Sweden [2006] App. no. 62332/00 [76]; M.G. v. United Kingdom [2002] App. no. 39393/98 [27]; K.H. and others v. Slovakia [2009] App. no. 32881/04 [50].

[72] CJEU, Joined Cases C-92/09 and C-93/09 [2010] Volker und Markus Schecke GbR and Hartmut Eifert [48–50].

Directive expresses it, the provisions of the E-privacy Directive 'particularise and complement Directive 95/46/EC' for the processing of personal data in the electronic communication sector. The E-privacy Directive is thus *lex specialis* to the Data Protection Directive, which means that the provisions of the latter Directive, such as the underlying definitions, in principle also apply within the field of application of the former.

As far as the relationship of EU data protection law to other fields of relevance for this book is concerned, the E-commerce Directive does not apply to questions relating to EU data protection law because of its Article 1(5)(b). Internet intermediaries can thus not claim an exemption from the EU regulatory regime on data protection because of their privileges under Articles 12 to 14 E-commerce Directive.[73] Moreover, it follows from Article 9 of Directive 2001/29 and Article 8(3)(e) of Directive 2004/48 that the protection of intellectual property shall not affect the requirements of the protection of personal data.[74]

Yet the scope of EU data protection legislation is limited to the fields for which the EU has a competence. Both Article 3(2) Data Protection Directive and Article 1(3) E-privacy Directive therefore stipulate that the Directives do not apply to the processing of personal data in the course of an activity that falls outside the scope of areas harmonised in 1995 and 2002, such as criminal law and Common Foreign and Security Policy (CFSP), public security, defence and state security. As a consequence, any activity that is carried out for one of those purposes does not come within the scope of this legislation, such as video surveillance for the purposes of preventing or prosecuting criminal offences,[75] or the transfer of passenger name records from the EU to the US for public security and law-enforcement purposes.[76] Similarly, the OECD Guidelines include a 'sovereignty clause' in Paragraph 4, stating that issues relating to national sovereignty, national security and public policy ('*ordre public*') shall be excluded from the scope of the Guidelines.

Yet the competences of the EU have significantly changed since 1995 and 2002. The Lisbon Treaty abolished the former three-pillar structure of the EU. The supranational competences now also stretch to police and judicial cooperation in criminal matters. By contrast, CFSP is still subject to intergovernmental policy-making. Article 39 TEU authorises the Council to adopt a decision on the protection of individuals with regard to the processing of personal data by the Member States when carrying out activities within the scope of CFSP and the free movement of such data.

Furthermore, activities that are purely personal or domestic, such as private correspondence and the holding of records of addresses, are also excluded from the scope of the data protection framework even if they incidentally concern the private life of other

---

[73] This will be maintained under the General Data Protection Regulation; see Article 2(2) thereof.
[74] On this balancing exercise, see ECJ, Case C-275/06 [2008] Promusicae v. Telefónica de España SAU.
[75] Recital 16 E-privacy Directive; see also WP29, Opinion 4/2004 on the Processing of Personal Data by means of Video Surveillance.
[76] ECJ, Joined Cases C-317/04 and C-318/04 [2006] European Parliament v. Council [55–60].

persons.[77] Those activities would not be relevant for the internal market. However, in light of the other rationale of the EU data protection regime – protecting the fundamental rights and freedoms of natural persons, and in particular their right to privacy – the exception has to be construed narrowly. As the Court of Justice emphasised in *Lindqvist*, publishing personal data on an internet website, even if for charitable and religious but not economic purposes, cannot be considered a mere personal or domestic activity, as a publication on the internet makes such data accessible to an indefinite number of people.[78] As a result, users of social networks or bloggers who disclose personal data of other individuals to an undefined number of recipients act as 'data controllers' and are thus, in principle, subject to the obligations under the Directive.[79] Moreover, in *František Ryneš*, the Court decided that a private video surveillance system that recorded the entrance to the owner's home, the public footpath and the entrance to the house opposite could not be considered a 'purely personal or household' activity.[80]

Finally, although the Data Protection Directive is based on the internal market competence contained in (now) Article 114 TFEU, its applicability does not depend on whether the specific data processing at issue has a link with the exercise of the fundamental freedoms guaranteed by the Treaty. Rather, since any personal data *can* move between Member States, the Data Protection Directive requires compliance with its rules with respect to *any* processing of data that does not expressly fall under one of the excluding provisions.[81] The same will apply under the General Data Protection Regulation.

As far as the relevant actors in EU data protection law are concerned, apart from the usual suspects – European Commission, European Parliament, Council and the Member States – the 'Article 29 Working Party' (WP29) has to be taken into account. It is an independent advisory body composed of representatives of the Member States' supervisory authorities set up according to Article 29 of the Data Protection Directive (hence the name), which advises the Commission and the Member States on issues of data protection. The opinions and recommendations of the WP29 are often helpful for the interpretation of EU data protection law. Eventually, the European Data Protection Supervisor (EDPS) is an independent authority supervising the protection of personal data and privacy in the EU institutions and bodies. He monitors the

---

[77] Recital 12 Data Protection Directive; Article 2(2)(c) General Data Protection Regulation; CJEU, Case C-212/13 [2014] František Ryneš [32].

[78] ECJ, Case C-101/01 [2003] Lindqvist [47].

[79] COM, Staff Working Paper, Impact Assessment, COM(2012) 10 final, p. 21; WP29, Opinion 5/2009 on online social networking, pp. 6–7; WP29, Opinion 1/2010 on the concepts of 'controller' and 'processor', p. 21.

[80] CJEU, Case C-212/13 [2014] František Ryneš [33]. However, the Court also indicated that the applicant, who had been attacked several times in his home, could have a legitimate interest in the data processing based on Article 7(f) Data Protection Directive.

[81] Cf. ECJ, Joined Cases C-465/00, C-138/01 and C-139/01 [2003] Rechnungshof v. Österreichischer Rundfunk and others [40–46].

EU institutions' and bodies' processing of personal data, advises on policies and legislation that affect privacy, and cooperates with other authorities to ensure consistent data protection.[82] Since 2014, the EDPS is Giovanni Buttarelli from Italy.

3 Substantive Scope of the European Regulatory Regimes

European data protection law applies to the processing (see subsection b below) of personal data (see subsection a). Obliged addressees of data protection laws are data controllers and data processors (see subsection c).

a Personal Data

Data protection law concerns data. Data means any information. Yet the Convention 108, the Data Protection Directive and also the OECD Guidelines are restricted to the processing of *personal* data. 'Personal data' means 'any information relating to a data subject'. 'Data subjects' are identified or identifiable natural persons (Article 2(a) Data Protection Directive, Article 4(1) General Data Protection Regulation, Article 2(a) Convention 108 and Paragraph 1(b) OECD Guidelines).

Personal data thus consists of three parts:

- Information: the notion of personal data may contain any information, both factual and value-based and both accurate and inaccurate facts, disregarding the format or medium in which the information is contained. It is irrelevant whether the information relates to a private or professional activity, whether the information communicated is of a sensitive character or whether the persons concerned have been inconvenienced in any way.[83]
- The information has to relate to a natural person: legal entities are thus excluded from the scope of the Convention 108 and the Data Protection Directive. However, the Court of Justice decided in *Volker und Markus Schecke GbR and Hartmut Eifert* that the name of a legal person is to be considered personal data if the official title of the legal person identifies one or more natural persons (in this case Volker and Markus Schecke).[84] Recital 14 of the General Data Protection Regulation expressly claims that this should not be the case anymore under the Regulation. By contrast, the E-privacy Directive also protects legal persons, but especially 'users'. Article

---

[82] See the Regulation (EC) No. 45/2001 of the European Parliament and of the Council of 18 December 2000 on the protection of individuals with regard to the processing of personal data by the Community institutions and bodies and on the free movement of such data, OJ L 8/1.

[83] ECJ, Joined Cases C-465/00, C-138/01 and C-139/01 [2003] Rechnungshof v. Österreichischer Rundfunk and others [73–75]; CJEU, Joined Cases C-293/12 and C-594/12 [2014] Digital Rights Ireland Ltd and Kärntner Landesregierung [33]; Joined Cases C-92/09 and C-93/09 [2010] Volker und Markus Schecke GbR and Hartmut Eifert [59–60]; *mutatis mutandis*, Case T-194/04 [2007] Bavarian Lager [119]; compare ECtHR, Niemietz v. Germany [1992] App. no. 13710/88 [29].

[84] CJEU, Joined Cases C-92/09 and C-93/09 [2010] Volker und Markus Schecke GbR and Hartmut Eifert [54].

2(a) E-privacy Directive defines a 'user' as 'any natural person using a publicly available electronic communications service'. Moreover, the Strasbourg Court also protects the business premises and the confidentiality of a legal person's correspondence under Article 8 ECHR.[85] Finally, European data protection law protects only *living* human beings.[86] A deceased person's privacy may nonetheless be protected under Article 7 EUChFR and Article 8 ECHR.[87]

- The person has to be identified or identifiable: a person is identified if all the elements that describe a person in such a way that he is distinguishable from all other persons and recognisable as an individual are available; a person is identifiable if additional information needed to identify the person can be obtained without unreasonable effort.[88] Identification may occur, for example, by reference to an identification number, by factors specific to this person's physical, physiological, mental, economic, cultural or social identity or by any other means. This means, in turn, that the principles of data protection do not apply to anonymised or pseudonymised data.[89] Yet anonymising and pseudonymising require more than merely deleting or replacing a person's name; data does not cease to be personal data as long as there are sufficient elements available that could, by exercising reasonable effort, serve to reidentify the person concerned.[90] A file that states that 'Person no XY2476 served as President of the European Commission between 2004 and 2014' is thus not a successful pseudonymisation. But even less obvious cases may give rise to data protection concerns. Big Data facilitates the reidentification of individuals contained in pseudonymised data sets, for example, if the information on a person in an online social network, in an internet auction platform and in an online payments system are being matched.

However, the legal definitions of personal data do not further clarify *by whom* a person is considered to be identified: is it required that the *particular data controller* is able to identify the data subject (narrow or relative approach), or is it sufficient that *anyone*, including persons who are not the data processor, would be able to identify the data subject (broad or absolute approach)? Under the absolute approach, data is much more likely to be 'personal' data than under the relative approach. Recital

---

[85] ECtHR, Niemietz v. Germany [1992] App. no. 13710/88 [29]; Bernh Larsen Holding AS and others v. Norway [2013] App. no. 24117/08 [106].

[86] WP29, Opinion 4/2007 on the concept of personal data, p. 22.

[87] ECtHR, Éditions Plon v. France [2004] App. no. 58148/00 [53].

[88] Recital 26 Data Protection Directive; European Union Agency for Fundamental Rights and Council of Europe, Handbook on European data protection law, 2013, pp. 36–37, 40; WP29, Opinion 4/2007 on the concept of personal data, pp. 12, 17.

[89] Recital 26 Data Protection Directive.

[90] WP29, Opinion 05/2014 on Anonymisation Techniques; Opinion 4/2007 on the concept of personal data, p. 18; European Union Agency for Fundamental Rights and Council of Europe, Handbook on European data protection law, 2013, p. 46.

26 Data Protection Directive seems to opt for the absolute approach: accordingly, to determine whether a person is identifiable, account should be taken of all the means likely reasonably to be used either by the controller *or by any other person* to identify the said person. The aim of the Directive to protect personal data also speaks for this approach. This problem has not been clarified in the General Data Protection Regulation: The Commission proposal included a reference to identifiability 'by the controller or by any other natural or legal person' in the definition of 'personal data' in Article 4(1) General Data Protection Regulation, but the European Parliament requested the deletion of this clause.

The notion of 'personal data' may include the following information, provided that the information relates to a natural person: a person's name, postal address, e-mail address and telephone number;[91] a person's date and place of birth;[92] biometric data, such as fingerprints;[93] photos, video footage or the record of a person's voice;[94] a person's bank account number, credit card numbers, social security number and driving licence number;[95] a person's hobbies;[96] a person's workplace;[97] a supervisor's assessment of an employee's work performance;[98] a person's income, salary and pensions.[99]

As has been described in Chapter 6, the internet has initially been conceived as a facility for anonymous communication. However, the Internet Protocol enables web servers to trace the computer that accessed certain web pages via the computer's IP address.[100] For some time it has been controversial whether IP addresses constitute personal data.[101] IP addresses merely allow the identification of a computer, but not of its user. They are thus not *per se* personal data. However, an IP address may help to

---

[91] ECJ, Case C-101/01 [2003] Lindqvist [24]; Case T-194/04 [2007] Bavarian Lager [104]; ECJ, Case C-553/07 [2009] College van burgemeester en wethouders van Rotterdam v. M.E.E. Rijkeboer [42]; CJEU, Case C-543/09 [2011] Deutsche Telekom v. Germany [53].

[92] European Union Agency for Fundamental Rights and Council of Europe, Handbook on European data protection law, 2013, p. 40.

[93] European Union Agency for Fundamental Rights and Council of Europe, Handbook on European data protection law, 2013, p. 40; see also ECtHR, M.K. v. France [2013] App. no. 19522/09 [26].

[94] European Union Agency for Fundamental Rights and Council of Europe, Handbook on European data protection law, 2013, p. 40; see, *mutatis mutandis*, Data Protection Directive, Recitals 16 and 17; compare ECtHR, P.G. and J.H. v. United Kingdom [2001] App. no. 44787/98 [59]; Peck v. United Kingdom [2003] App. no. 44647/98; Von Hannover v. Germany (No. 1) [2004] App. no. 59320/00; Sciacca v. Italy [2005] App. no. 50774/99; Köpke v. Germany [2010] App. no. 420/70; CJEU, Case C-212/13 [2014] František Ryneš [22].

[95] ECJ, Case T-194/04 [2007] Bavarian Lager [104].

[96] ECJ, Case C-101/01 [2003] Lindqvist [24].

[97] ECJ, Case C-101/01 [2003] Lindqvist [24].

[98] European Union Agency for Fundamental Rights and Council of Europe, Handbook on European data protection law, 2013, p. 42.

[99] ECJ, Joined Cases C-465/00, C-138/01 and C-139/01 [2003] Rechnungshof v. Österreichischer Rundfunk and others [64]; Case C-73/07 [2008] Satakunnan Markkinapörssi Oy and Satamedia Oy [35]; CJEU, Joined Cases C-92/09 and C-93/09 [2010] Volker und Markus Schecke GbR and Hartmut Eifert [58].

[100] By way of reference to Chapter 6, note that although anonymity was a default of the internet, the traceability of computers is part of the Internet Protocol, hence the internet's code.

[101] For the various approaches in the EU Member States, see COM, Staff Working Paper, Impact Assessment, COM(2012) 10 final, pp. 14–15.

identify a user if the access provider assigning the IP address has more information available to identify the user. Therefore, if and insofar as access providers are able to identify internet users to whom they have attributed an IP addresses, IP addresses are considered personal data.[102]

Moreover, any information stored on terminal equipment of users of electronic communications networks is personal data. Web bugs, devices that enter the users' terminal in order to gain access to information, to store hidden information or to trace the activities of the user thus constitute processing of personal data.[103] Therefore, they are basically prohibited, unless the user has given his consent or any other justification is applicable. Article 5(3) E-privacy Directive now expressly states that devices that serve to analyse the effectiveness of website design and advertising, such as cookies, are in principle only allowed if the user has given his informed consent. The 2009 Citizens' Rights Directive has turned the former 'opt-out' model of the E-privacy Directive with regard to the use of cookies into an 'opt-in' model: the user has to agree to the use of cookies before they are used. However, this raises questions as to the practical implementation. According to Article 5(3) E-privacy Directive, the consent shall not be required in cases of technical storage or access for the sole purpose of carrying out the transmission of a communication, or as strictly necessary in order for the provider of an information society service explicitly requested by the subscriber or user to provide the service (so-called session cookies). Where this is not the case, the user's consent to processing may be expressed by using the appropriate settings of a browser or other application, where it is technically possible and effective.[104]

Another form of personal data generated by the use of electronic communication networks is traffic data.[105] Traffic data is any data processed for the purpose of the conveyance of a communication on an electronic communications network or for the billing thereof (Article 2(b) E-privacy Directive). Traffic data may, *inter alia*, consist of data referring to the routing, duration, time or volume of a communication, to the protocol used, to the network on which the communication originates or terminates, to the beginning, end or duration of a connection. They may also consist of the format in which the communication is conveyed by the network.[106]

---

[102] See Recital 30 General Data Protection Regulation; WP29, Opinion 1/2008 on data protection issues related to search engines, p. 8; WP29, Opinion 4/2007 on the concept of personal data, pp. 16–17; ECJ, Case C-275/06 [2008] Promusicae v. Telefónica de España SAU [58]; CJEU, Case C-70/10 [2011] Scarlet Extended v. SABAM and others [51]; Case C-461/10 [2008] Bonnier Audio [52].

[103] Recitals 24 and 25 E-privacy Directive, WP29, Opinion 1/2008 on data protection issues related to search engines, p. 9; Google Inc. v. Vidal-Hall and others [2015] EWCA Civ 311 [115].

[104] Recital 66 Citizens' Rights Directive. See also WP29, Opinion 04/2012 on Cookie Consent Exemption; Working Document 02/2013 providing guidance on obtaining consent for cookies.

[105] See CJEU, Joined Cases C-293/12 and C-594/12 [2014] Digital Rights Ireland Ltd and Kärntner Landesregierung [36].

[106] Recital 15 E-privacy Directive.

A particular form of traffic data is location data. Location data is any data processed in an electronic communications network or by an electronic communications service indicating the geographical position of the terminal equipment of a user of a publicly available electronic communications service (Article 2(c) E-privacy Directive). Location data may refer to the latitude, longitude and altitude of the user's terminal equipment, to the direction of travel, to the level of accuracy of the location information, to the identification of the network cell in which the terminal equipment is located at a certain point in time and to the time the location information was recorded.[107]

b Data Processing

'Processing' of personal data encompasses 'any operation or set of operations which is performed upon personal data' (Article 2(b) Data Protection Directive, Article 4(2) General Data Protection Regulation, compare Article 2(c) Convention 108). The Directive, the Regulation and the Convention name examples for data processing: collection, recording, organisation, storage, adaptation or alteration, retrieval, consultation, use, disclosure by transmission, dissemination or otherwise making available, alignment or combination, blocking, erasure or destruction. The notion of 'processing' is basically independent of the technology used.[108] Moreover, processing also includes the re-publication of data that has already been in the public domain.[109]

The E-privacy Directive in particular applies to the processing of personal data in connection with the provision of publicly available electronic communications services in public communications networks (Article 3 E-privacy Directive).[110] The 2009 Citizens' Rights Directive inserted the clause 'including public communications networks supporting data collection and identification devices' in order to clarify the application of the Directive to Radio Frequency Identification Devices (RFIDs).[111] In turn, the Directive does not apply to non-public electronic communications services, closed user groups and corporate networks.[112] These are subject to the Data Protection Directive only. Moreover, the E-privacy Directive excludes information conveyed as part of a broadcasting service to the public, except to the extent that the information can be related to the identifiable subscriber or user receiving the

---

[107] Recital 14 E-privacy Directive.

[108] Manual processing is only covered under EU law if it forms part of a filing system or is intended to form part of a filing system; read Article 3(1) together with Article 2(c). On the interpretation of these provisions, see Durant v. Financial Services Authority [2003] EWCA Civ 1746 [46–51]. Convention 108 basically applies only to automatic processing of personal data, but the Member States may give notice by a declaration that it will also apply this convention to personal data files that are not processed automatically (Article 3(2)(c) of the Convention).

[109] ECJ, Case C-73/07 [2008] Satakunnan Markkinapörssi Oy and Satamedia Oy [37].

[110] On the definition of these terms, see Chapter 6.

[111] Recitals 56 and 66 Citizens' Rights Directive.

[112] Recital 55 Citizens' Rights Directive.

information, for example with video-on-demand services (Article 2(d) and Recital 16 E-privacy Directive).

c Data Controllers and Data Processors

The obliged addressees of European data protection law are those who determine the purposes and means of the processing of personal data: data controllers.[113] A data *controller* can be any natural or legal person, public authority, agency or any other body. It may act alone or jointly with other controllers. A data *processor* is thus someone who processes personal data on behalf, and on instruction of, the controller.[114] Hence, a data processor can be identical with a data controller, but this is not necessarily the case. In groups of companies, each affiliate, if they are separate legal persons and do not act under the direct authority of the parent company, count as separate controllers or processors.[115] But note that the definitions of 'data controller' vary among the European frameworks. While Convention 108 defines 'controller of the file' as the person who is *competent* according to the national law to decide what should be the purpose of the automated data file, the Data Protection Directive regards as data controller the one who *determines* the purposes and means of the data processing. The definition of data controller and data processor under the EU framework is thus functional rather than formal, serving to allocate responsibility according to the factual influence. By contrast to the Convention 108, the main element for the distinction between data controllers and mere processors within the EU framework is therefore the factual control, which is ideally but not necessarily identical with the legal competence.[116]

By way of example: WorldWeb Ltd. provides internet access services, BestFriends plc runs the online social network BestFriends.com and Paul is a WorldWeb customer who publishes personal information about his friends and colleagues on BestFriends.com. WorldWeb Ltd. has to be considered controller for traffic and billing data, but not for Paul's data which it transmits. If a message containing personal data is transmitted by means of a transmission service, the controller in respect of the personal data contained in the message is normally considered to be the person from whom the message originates, rather than the service provider. The service providers are usually considered controllers in respect of the processing of the additional personal data necessary for the operation of the service.[117] As a consequence, Paul himself is to be considered controller of personal data of his friends and colleagues,

---

[113] Article 2(d) Data Protection Directive; see also Article 2(d) Convention 108 and Paragraph 1(a) of the OECD Guidelines.

[114] Articles 2(e) and 17 Data Protection Directive. The relationship between controller and processor is explained in more detail in Article 17(2)–(4) Data Protection Directive.

[115] European Union Agency for Fundamental Rights and Council of Europe, Handbook on European data protection law, 2013, pp. 50, 55.

[116] WP29, Opinion 1/2010 on the concepts of 'controller' and 'processor', pp. 9–11.

[117] Recital 47 E-privacy Directive.

as far as the household exception in Article 3(2) Data Protection Directive does not apply.[118] As regards BestFriends.com, it has to be distinguished between its activity of merely hosting Paul's content and the processing of that content for its own purposes. Insofar as BestFriends.com merely provides the platform for hosting Paul's content, it is to be considered a data processor (with Paul being the data controller). Insofar as BestFriends processes this data for its own purposes, such as targeted advertising, BestFriends has to be considered data controller with regard to that specific processing.[119]

The notion of 'processing' of personal data includes, for example:

- publishing personal data on an internet page[120] or via a text message service;[121]
- the communication of personal data to third parties;[122]
- video surveillance that is stored on a recording device;[123]
- loading personal data on an internet page.[124]

Operations must also be classified as such processing where they exclusively concern data that has already been published in unaltered form in the media.[125] Furthermore, the transfer of data between different controllers, even if they are members of the same company, is a transfer to a 'third-party recipient' (Articles 2(f) and (g) Data Protection Directive, Article 4(9) and (10) General Data Protection Regulation) and has as such to be authorised by the EU legal framework. The transfer of data between an EU-based affiliate and a non-EU-based affiliate or parent company even constitutes a transfer of data to a third country, which is subject to a special legal regime. There is, in principle, no privilege permitting the exchange of personal data between separate legal entities within a company group.

As has been seen before, the definition of a data controller and its distinction from a data processor can be crucial in the search for the applicable law. Moreover, the data controller, not the data processor, is the main addressee of the EU data protection framework. The concept of 'processor' is, however, significant with regard to confidentiality and security of processing (Articles 16–17 Data Protection Directive, Articles 28 and 32 General Data Protection Regulation). Furthermore, the notion of 'data processing', which presupposes a 'data processor', is crucial for the definition of a 'data controller' in the first place, as a data controller is someone who determines the purposes and means of data processing.

---

[118] See ECJ, Case C-101/01 [2003] Lindqvist.

[119] WP29, Opinion 1/2010 on the concepts of 'controller' and 'processor', pp. 11, 25.

[120] ECJ, Case C-101/01 [2003] Lindqvist [26]; CJEU, Joined Cases C-92/09 and C-93/09 [2010] Volker und Markus Schecke GbR and Hartmut Eifert [58].

[121] ECJ, Case C-73/07 [2008] Satakunnan Markkinapörssi Oy and Satamedia Oy [37].

[122] ECJ, Joined Cases C-465/00, C-138/01 and C-139/01 [2003] Rechnungshof v. Österreichischer Rundfunk and others [74]; Case T-194/04 [2007] Bavarian Lager [105].

[123] CJEU, Case C-212/13 [2014] František Ryneš [25]; WP29, Opinion 4/2004 on the Processing of Personal Data by means of Video Surveillance.

[124] ECJ, Case C-101/01 [2003] Lindqvist [25].

[125] ECJ, Case C-73/07 [2008] Satakunnan Markkinapörssi Oy and Satamedia Oy [49]; CJEU, Case C-131/12 [2014] Google Spain SL v. AEPD and others [30].

Multinational companies with a complex organisational structure, cloud computing and the subcontracting and outsourcing of services can make it difficult to establish who is/who are controller(s) and/or processor(s) in a particular case.

VII Principles of European Data Protection Law

European, especially EU, data protection law consists of a rather confusing accumulation of harmonising rules and derogations, leaving a quite significant fragmentation of European data protection regimes. Nevertheless, certain basic principles can be extracted. The generally applicable General Data Protection Regulation will, however, contribute to more legal certainty and harmony in European data protection law.

1 Obligation to Notify

Pursuant to Article 18 Data Protection Directive, the controller must notify the supervisory authority before carrying out any automatic processing operation or set of such operations intended to serve a single purpose or several related purposes.[126] The obligation to notify is subject to exemptions in cases in which processing is unlikely to affect the rights and freedoms of data subjects. Article 19 provides further details regarding the contents of the notification. According to Article 20, the supervisory authority shall determine the processing operations likely to present specific risks to the rights and freedoms of data subjects, and shall check that these processing operations are examined prior to the start thereof.[127] Operations likely to present specific risks are, for example, those that exclude individuals from a right, benefit or contract.[128] Pursuant to Article 21, Member States shall take measures to ensure that processing operations are publicised, and the supervisory authority shall provide a register of notified processing operations, which may be inspected by any person demonstrating a legitimate interest.[129]

Under Article 35 General Data Protection Regulation, the controller shall, prior to the processing, carry out an impact assessment of the envisaged processing operations on the protection of personal data where a type of processing is likely to result in a high risk to the rights and freedoms of natural persons. The controller will have to consult the supervisory authority prior to processing where a data protection impact assessment indicates that the processing would result in a high risk in the absence of measures taken by the controller to mitigate the risk (Article 36(1) General Data Protection Regulation).

---

[126] See CJEU, Joined Cases C-92/09 and C-93/09 [2010] Volker und Markus Schecke GbR and Hartmut Eifert [95–101].
[127] CJEU, Joined Cases C-92/09 and C-93/09 [2010] Volker und Markus Schecke GbR and Hartmut Eifert [102–108].
[128] Recital 53 Data Protection Directive.
[129] See Recital 50 Data Protection Directive.

2 Principles of Data Processing

The basic principle of European data protection law is that any data processing has to be lawful.[130] The notion of 'lawfulness' reiterates that any data processing has to be in accordance with primary law, especially fundamental rights, and with secondary law, especially the data protection framework itself. But the principle of lawfulness expresses more than the obvious: it means that any data processing has to be *justified* in order to be legal. The main reason to justify data processing is the consent of the data subject; in the absence of consent, other reasons have to justify data processing. In essence, the principle of lawfulness expresses that in Europe, unlike in the US, any data processing is illegal unless it is justified. Besides, the European data protection framework emphasises that personal data must be processed fairly. The notion of 'fairness' means that data controllers may have to go beyond the mandatory legal minimum requirements of service to the data subject, should the legitimate interests of the data subject so require.[131]

The following sections will elaborate on the requirements for data processing to be lawful:

- It has to comply with EU secondary law, in particular the demands of the data protection framework on purpose specification (see subsection a below) and data quality (see subsection b);
- it has to be justified either by consent of the data subject (see subsection c) or, in the absence of consent, for another reason explicitly mentioned in the legal framework (see subsection d);
- it has to meet the demands of data security and confidentiality (see subsection e).
- Particular requirements apply to the processing of traffic data (see subsection f) and to the transfer of data to third countries (see subsection g).

Unlawful data processing may trigger claims of the data subject to rectification or erasure of personal data or claims for damages (see subsection 3 below). But note that the Member States may exercise their discretion to derogate from the principles codified in the EU data protection framework (see subsection 4). Moreover, like any other application of secondary law, the enforcement of the data protection provisions – including the authorisations to derogate from the framework – has to be compatible with the fundamental rights of the persons involved (see subsection 5).

---

[130] See Article 8(2) EUChFR, Article 6(1)(a) Data Protection Directive, Article 5(a) of Convention 108, Article 5 General Data Protection Regulation. See also paragraphs 7–10 of the OECD Guidelines, paragraph 1 of the UN Guidelines.

[131] European Union Agency for Fundamental Rights and Council of Europe, Handbook on European data protection law, 2013, p. 78.

a Principle of Purpose Specification

Data processing has to be carried out for specified, explicit and legitimate purposes and must not be incompatible with those purposes.[132] In turn, processing of personal data is not allowed for undefined purposes. The purpose must have been specified and notified by the controller to the supervisory authority before processing the data.[133] In human rights-doctrinal terms, the purpose of the data processing determines the 'legitimate aim' in the proportionality analysis.

With the exception of data processing for historical, statistical or scientific purposes, every new purpose for the processing of available data has to find its own legal basis, such as the consent of the data subject. The principle of purpose specification is thus at odds with one of the most fundamental aspects of Big Data: the concept of Big Data includes the idea that data is being stored even though there is currently no purpose for this data available, because there might be a purpose for it in the future, a purpose that has not been conceived of yet. However, the principle of purpose specification prohibits the storage of data for other purposes than the initial one. Any further processing of data requires a renewed expression of consent of the data subject or another justification. The principle of purpose specification is thus contrary to the 'option value' of data.[134]

b Requirements on Data Quality

The European as well as the OECD and UN frameworks on data protection impose obligations on data controllers regarding the quality of the data they process or let process. First, the data has to be adequate, relevant and not excessive in relation to the purposes for which it is collected and/or further processed (relevance principle).[135] The categories of data chosen for processing must be necessary in order to achieve the declared purpose of the processing operations.[136] Second, the data has to be accurate and, where necessary and possible, kept up-to-date (accuracy principle).[137] The more sensitive the data is, the more effort can be expected from the data controller to keep the information up-to-date. The accuracy principle is subject to the caveat that an update of the information has to be legally and factually feasible. The accuracy

---

[132] See Article 8(2) EUChFR, Article 6(1)(b) Data Protection Directive, Article 5(1)(b) of Convention 108, paragraph 9 of the OECD Guidelines, Article 5(1)(b) General Data Protection Regulation, paragraph 3 of the UN Guidelines.

[133] Article 18(1) Data Protection Directive; see the extensive elaborations by the WP29, Opinion 03/2013 on purpose limitation.

[134] See Mayer-Schönberger and Cukier (2013, pp. 102–111, 153).

[135] See Article 6(1)(c) Data Protection Directive, Article 5(c) of Convention 108, paragraph 7 of the OECD Guidelines, Article 5(1)(c) General Data Protection Regulation.

[136] European Union Agency for Fundamental Rights and Council of Europe, Handbook on European data protection law, 2013, p. 72.

[137] Article 6(1)(d) Data Protection Directive, Article 5(d) of Convention 108, paragraph 8 of the OECD Guidelines, Article 5(1)(d) General Data Protection Regulation, paragraph 2 of the UN Guidelines.

principle may not serve as a legal basis for a data controller to obtain information, for example, about his customers, which he would otherwise not receive.

Third, the data must not be excessive in relation to, and kept for no longer than is necessary for, the purposes for which the data was collected or for which it is further processed (the limitation, also known as minimisation, principle).[138] If it is possible to avoid using personal data, or to use pseudonymised or anonymised data, this solution should be preferred as the less intrusive means. The limitation principle is an important counterweight to companies' and governments' interest to retain data for longer than necessary. Just like the purpose specification principle, the limitation principle can be derogated from for data stored for longer periods for historical, statistical or scientific use.

c Consent

The most important reason to justify data processing is the data subject's consent. As a basic rule (but subject to many exceptions), the processing of personal data is basically prohibited unless the data subject has given his consent.[139] Moreover, the data subject can withdraw his consent at any time.[140] The principle of consent is the most significant expression of an individual's data autonomy. Any exception to the principle of consent curtails the sovereignty of an individual to determine the use of his own personal data, and is thus in need of justification.

The requirement of consent even has fundamental rights status via Article 8(2) EUChFR. However, that provision itself does not define the notion of 'consent'. For this purpose, the Charter Explanations refer to EU secondary legislation, such as the Data Protection Directive, but it should be kept in mind that secondary law has to be interpreted in compliance with primary law, and not vice versa. According to Article 2(h) Data Protection Directive, to which Article 2(f) E-privacy Directive refers, 'the data subject's consent' means 'any freely given specific and informed indication of his wishes by which the data subject signifies his agreement to personal data relating to him being processed'. The notion of 'consent' thus includes several requirements: First, it must be given freely; that is, without deception, intimidation or in a situation of dependence from the data controller combined with the threat of significant negative consequences for the data subject if consent is refused.[141]

---

[138] Article 6(1)(c) and (e) Data Protection Directive, Recitals 9 and 30 and Article 9(3) E-privacy Directive, Article 5(d) of Convention 108, Article 5(1)(c) General Data Protection Regulation, paragraph 3(c) of the UN Guidelines.

[139] See, for example, Articles 7(a), 8(2)(a), 26(1)(a) Data Protection Directive, Articles 6(3) and 9 E-privacy Directive, Article 7 General Data Protection Regulation.

[140] This is expressly codified only in Articles 6(3) and 9(1) E-privacy Directive and in Article 7(3) General Data Protection Regulation, but it is also implied in the Data Protection Directive; see WP29, Opinion 15/2011 on the definition of consent, p. 13; European Union Agency for Fundamental Rights and Council of Europe, Handbook on European data protection law, 2013, p. 62.

[141] WP29, Opinion 15/2011 on the definition of consent, p. 12; European Union Agency for Fundamental Rights and Council of Europe, Handbook on European data protection law, 2013, p. 58.

The latter would be the case, for example, in employment relationships, and it has also been discussed in cases in which important goods or services can be obtained only and exclusively if certain personal data are disclosed, as was the case with the Passenger Name Record Agreement.[142] It is questionable whether this thought can be transferred to cases in which a social media network rejects the membership of applicants who refuse to consent to the data processing by the network. Since social media networks neither establish a situation of dependence nor provide sufficiently important services, the consent to their data processing has to be regarded as free, although the refusal to consent and thus to become a member of the network may have negative personal consequences.

Second, the consent must be specific: it is not sufficient that the data subject is merely informed or otherwise made aware of the fact that his personal data will be processed.[143] Consent means more than mere knowledge. Moreover, a *carte blanche* consent allowing all possible processing of one's personal data without further details would not be sufficient. The data subject must give his consent again if processing operations are to be added to or changed in a way that could not reasonably have been foreseen when the initial consent was given.[144]

Third, the consent must be informed: the obligation to inform the data subject serves to compensate for the asymmetrical distribution of knowledge about the data processing. The data subject must generally have been provided with clear and comprehensive information about the purposes of the processing. The EU legal framework further details the notion of informed consent for specific forms of processing, such as the processing of location data (Article 9(1) E-privacy Directive) and of traffic data (Article 6(4) E-privacy Directive). The notion of 'informed' consent raises significant concerns with regard to the practice of many service providers to inundate potential users with verbose 'privacy terms and conditions'. To be sure, customers who fail to read those terms and conditions are to be blamed in the first place. However, since reality shows that only very few people actually read those provisions or are at least aware of the dimensions of data processing, the question should be raised whether consent given to such volumes is to be considered 'informed'.[145] An alternative might be to require companies to provide a concise version of information.

Fourth, the consent must be given in the appropriate form. In this context, European data protection law distinguishes between consent to the processing of ordinary personal data and of sensitive personal data (or, in the words of the General Data Protection Regulation: 'special categories of personal data'). Sensitive personal data reveals racial or ethnic origin, political opinions, religious or philosophical beliefs, trade-union membership and the

---

[142] See European Union Agency for Fundamental Rights and Council of Europe, Handbook on European data protection law, 2013, p. 59.

[143] CJEU, Joined Cases C-92/09 and C-93/09 [2010] Volker und Markus Schecke GbR and Hartmut Eifert [63].

[144] WP29, Opinion 15/2011 on the definition of consent, p. 17; CJEU, Case C-543/09 [2011] Deutsche Telekom v. Germany [64]; European Union Agency for Fundamental Rights and Council of Europe, Handbook on European data protection law, 2013, p. 60.

[145] See WP29, Opinion 15/2011 on the definition of consent, p. 18; Lessig (2006, pp. 226–228).

processing of data concerning one's health or sex life.[146] The ECJ has held, for example, that a website that refers to the fact that an individual has injured her foot and is on half-time on medical grounds is a publication of sensitive personal data.[147] In turn, ordinary personal data encompasses all other forms of personal data. The processing of ordinary personal data requires the data subject's 'unambiguous consent' (Article 7 Data Protection Directive), whereas the processing of sensitive personal data is only allowed if the data subject grants his 'explicit consent' (Article 8 Data Protection Directive). Unambiguous consent means that there is no doubt as to the data subject's intention to consent.[148] It might thus include cases in which the individual remains passive or silent, whereas explicit consent must always be given expressly. Consent may be given by any appropriate method enabling a freely given specific and informed indication of the user's wishes, including by ticking a box when visiting an internet website.[149] By contrast, neither the omission to untick a box nor the mere use of a service can be regarded as an unambiguous consent.[150] Aware of the legal uncertainty involved in the dichotomy of 'unambiguous' and 'explicit' consent, the General Data Protection Regulation will only allow explicit consent 'either by a statement or by a clear affirmative action' (Article 4(11)). It further elaborates on the conditions for consent in its Articles 7–9.

Since the current EU data protection framework does not stipulate a provision on legal capacity, the legal possibility to provide consent has to be determined by the Member States. Once the General Data Protection Regulation applies, the relevant provision on the conditions applicable to a child's consent applying throughout the EU will be Article 8 of that Regulation.

d Justification of Data Processing in the Absence of Consent

Yet the principle of consent is subject to many exceptions, whereby exceptions to the prohibition of the processing of sensitive personal data are narrower than those applying to ordinary personal data. Ordinary personal data may be processed without the data subject's consent if processing is based on at least one enumerated reason for justification from which the Member States must not derogate to the disadvantage of the data controller.[151] Accordingly, even in the absence of the data subject's consent, the processing of ordinary personal data is lawful, first, for the performance of a contract to which the data subject is party or in order to take steps at the request of the data subject prior to entering into a contract (Article 7(b) Data Protection Directive). This clause may justify, for example, processing the address of the data subject so that goods purchased online can be delivered, or processing credit card details in order to effect payment.[152]

---

[146] Article 8 Data Protection Directive, Article 6 Convention 108, Article 9 General Data Protection Regulation.

[147] ECJ, Case C-101/01 [2003] Lindqvist [51].

[148] WP29, Opinion 15/2011 on the definition of 'consent', p. 21.

[149] Compare Recital 17 E-privacy Directive; Recital 32 General Data Protection Regulation.

[150] See WP29, Opinion 15/2011 on the definition of consent, pp. 23–24.

[151] CJEU, Joined Cases C-468/10 and C-469/10 [2011] ASNEF and FECEMD [32].

[152] WP29, Opinion 06/2014 on the notion of legitimate interests of the data controller under Article 7 of Directive 95/46/EC, p. 16.

Second, data processing may be justified if it is carried out for compliance with a legal obligation (Article 7(c) Data Protection Directive). This provision applies, for example, to physicians and hospitals that are under a legal obligation to store data about the treatment of patients, or to employers who must process data about their employees for reasons of social security. Third, data processing is legitimate in order to protect the vital interests of the data subject (Article 7(d) Data Protection Directive). This provision may apply, for example, to health data of the data subject. Fourth, data may be processed for the performance of a task carried out in the public interest or in the exercise of official authority vested in the controller or in a third party to whom the data are disclosed (Article 7(e) Data Protection Directive). In *Huber* v. *Germany*, the Court of Justice decided that this provision may justify a Member State having a central register of foreign nationals, including nationals of another Member State, for the purposes of establishing their right of residence.[153] However, the register, which did not contain personal data relating to German nationals, had also been used for the purposes of fighting crime. As regards this purpose, the Court observed that the prosecution of crimes and offences is irrespective of the nationality of their perpetrators, hence the register unjustifiably discriminated between nationals and non-nationals of the Member State, and was thus in violation of Article 18 of the TFEU. Fifth, data may be processed for the purposes of the legitimate interests pursued by the controller or by the third party or parties to whom the data is disclosed, except where such interests are overridden by the interests or fundamental rights[154] and freedoms of the data subject that require protection under Article 1(1) (Article 7(f) Data Protection Directive). In practice, Article 7(f) Data Protection Directive is a very significant ground for justifying data processing. The notion of 'legitimate interest' includes any interest that is in accordance with the law. It may comprise, for example, business interests, such as the interest in marketing and advertisement, non-commercial interests, such as political campaigning and charitable fundraising, the prevention of criminal activity, the enforcement of legal claims including debt collection via out-of-court procedures, whistle-blowing schemes, IT and network security, processing for historical, scientific or statistical purposes or processing for research purposes.[155] In our case example *Google Spain*, the Court of Justice accepted that data processing carried out by the operator of a search engine is necessary for the legitimate interest of the controller.[156]

Whether the interest of the controller or the third party will ultimately prevail over the interests and rights of the data subjects depends on the balancing exercise between

---

[153] ECJ, Case C-524/06 [2008] Huber v. Germany [66].

[154] Note that Article 7(f) contains a typing error; it should read 'or fundamental rights' rather than 'for fundamental rights': WP29, Opinion 06/2014 on the notion of legitimate interests of the data controller under Article 7 of Directive 95/46/EC, p. 29.

[155] WP29, Opinion 06/2014 on the notion of legitimate interests of the data controller under Article 7 of Directive 95/46/EC, p. 25.

[156] CJEU, Case C-131/12 [2014] Google Spain SL v. AEPD and others [73].

those interests.[157] In this context, it is of significance whether the interest of the data controller or the third party is in itself protected by human rights, such as freedom of expression or the right to receive information (see subsection 5 below). Yet as far as the exercise of freedom of expression by the journalistic media is concerned, Article 9 Data Protection Directive is the more specific provision, as it excludes 'the processing of personal data carried out solely for journalistic purposes or the purpose of artistic or literary expression' from the scope of Article 7 in the first place if the application of this provision is not necessary to reconcile the right to privacy with the rules governing freedom of expression.

The data subject has the right, at least in the cases referred to in Articles 7(e) and (f) Data Protection Directive, to object on compelling legitimate grounds to the processing of data relating to him, save where otherwise provided by national legislation (Article 14(a) Data Protection Directive).

Sensitive personal data may be processed without the data subject's explicit consent only if the processing

- is necessary for the purposes of carrying out the obligations and specific rights of the controller in the field of employment law insofar as it is authorised by national law providing for adequate safeguards (Article 8(1)(b) Data Protection Directive);
- is necessary to protect the vital interests of the data subject or of another person where the data subject is physically or legally incapable of giving his consent (Article 8(1)(c) Data Protection Directive);
- is carried out by a foundation, association or any other non-profit-seeking body with a political, philosophical, religious or trade union aim and concerns the organisation's members (Article 8(1)(d) Data Protection Directive);
- relates to data that is manifestly made public by the data subject or is necessary for the establishment, exercise or defence of legal claims (Article 8(1)(e) Data Protection Directive); or
- is required by a health professional subject to rules of professional secrecy for the purposes of preventive medicine, medical diagnosis, the provision of care or treatment or the management of health-care services (Article 8(3) Data Protection Directive).

In addition, Member States may introduce further purposes for which sensitive data may be processed, under the conditions of Article 8(4) Data Protection Directive. However, unlike in the case of processing general data, a contractual relationship with the data subject alone cannot serve as a justification for the processing of sensitive data. Therefore, if sensitive data is to be processed in the context of a contract with the data subject, use of this data requires the data subject's separate explicit consent.[158]

---

[157] See, for example, ECJ, Case T-194/04 [2007] Bavarian Lager [107] (with regard to Regulation No. 45/2001).

[158] European Union Agency for Fundamental Rights and Council of Europe, Handbook on European data protection law, 2013, p. 90.

e Security and Confidentiality of Data Processing

The OECD Guidelines highlight that data controllers need to have effective privacy management programmes in place, and thus re-emphasise the notion of 'accountability' of data controllers. Core aspects of the principle of accountability, as stipulated in paragraph 14 and Part III of the OECD Guidelines, are requirements on security and confidentiality of data processing.[159] International and European data protection law thus imposes duties on data controllers and its subordinates, as well as on the Member States themselves, to safeguard the confidentiality and security of the data.[160] International standards for safe processing of data include, for example, the European Privacy Seal (EuroPriSe). The European Network and Information Security Agency (ENISA) regularly publishes on current security threats and advises how to address them. The human rights relevance of data security and confidentiality rules has become most visible in the ECtHR decision *I v. Finland*.[161] The applicant suspected that her health records had been accessed illegitimately by other employees of the hospital where she worked. As she was unable to provide sufficient proof, her claim was rejected by the domestic courts. However, the Strasbourg Court observed that the hospital's health records system was not in accordance with the legal requirements contained in domestic law. Since this had not been sufficiently taken into account by the domestic courts, the ECtHR concluded that there had been a violation of Article 8 ECHR.

In case of a particular risk of a breach of the security of a communication network, the communications service provider must inform the subscribers concerning such risk. Where the risk lies outside the scope of the measures to be taken by the service provider, he has to inform the subscribers of any possible remedies, including an indication of the likely costs involved.[162]

According to Article 5 E-privacy Directive, Member States are under an obligation to ensure the confidentiality of communications and the related traffic data by means of a public communications network and publicly available electronic communications services. They shall prohibit listening, tapping, storage or other kinds of interception or surveillance of communications and the related traffic data by persons other than users, without the consent of the users concerned, subject to exceptions under EU data protection law. For example, network operators and service providers are permitted to automatically, intermediately and transiently store information for the sole purpose of carrying out the transmission in an electronic communications network and provided

---

[159] On the notion of 'accountability', see also WP29, Opinion 3/2010 on the principle of accountability.

[160] Paragraph 7 of the UN Guidelines, paragraph 11 OECD Guidelines, Article 16 and 17 Data Protection Directive, Article 4 E-privacy Directive, Article 7 Convention 108, Article 32 General Data Protection Regulation.

[161] ECtHR, I v. Finland [2008] App. no. 20511/03.

[162] Article 4(2) E-privacy Directive; Articles 33 and 34 General Data Protection Regulation; WP29, Opinion 03/2014 on Personal Data Breach Notification. See also the elaborations on Data security breach notification in the OECD Guidelines.

that the information is not stored for any period longer than is necessary for the transmission and for traffic management purposes.[163] Moreover, communications may be recorded for the purpose of providing evidence of a commercial transaction.[164] Finally, Article 13(1) Data Protection Directive and Article 15(1) E-privacy Directive authorise the Member States to adopt measures to restrict the confidentiality of personal data where that restriction is necessary for the protection of state interests or the rights and freedoms of others. The provisions play an important role in cases in which internet intermediaries are requested to disclose personal data in the context of civil proceedings, particularly claims of copyright infringements.[165]

f Processing of Traffic Data and Location Data

The E-privacy Directive provides a special regulatory regime for the protection of personal data generated in the course of communication via an electronic communications network. In this context, three main categories of data have to be distinguished.

First, the content of the messages sent during communication. The EU regulatory framework on data protection does not allow the interception of the content of communication. This is also implied in the definition of 'data controller': According to Recital 47 of the Data Protection Directive,

> where a message containing personal data is transmitted by means of a telecommunications or electronic mail service, the sole purpose of which is the transmission of such messages, the controller in respect of the personal data contained in the message will normally be considered to be the person from whom the message originates, rather than the person offering the transmission services; [...] those offering such services will normally be considered controllers in respect of the processing of the additional personal data necessary for the operation of the service.

The provider of electronic communications services – hence the addressee of the E-privacy Directive – should therefore be considered controller only for traffic and billing data, and not for any data being transmitted. Since the interception of telecommunication content falls outside the EU legal framework, the Member States have the competence to adopt such measures, in particular for the prevention and prosecution of crimes. However, these measures must be compatible with human rights.[166] Second, communication via an electronic communication network requires

---

[163] Recital 22 E-privacy Directive; ECJ, Case C-275/06 [2008] Promusicae v. Telefónica de España SAU [47].
[164] Recital 23 E-privacy Directive.
[165] See Chapter 9.
[166] See, for example, ECtHR, Klass and others v. Germany [1978] App. no. 5029/71; Malone v. United Kingdom [1984] App. no. 8691/79; Kopp v. Switzerland [1998] App. no. 13/1997/797/1000; Liberty and others v. United Kingdom [2008] App. no. 58243/00; Uzun v. Germany [2010] App. no. 35623/05; German Federal Constitutional Court, Case 1 BvR 595/07 [2008] 'Secret infiltration of an IT system', in which the Court created a fundamental right to the guarantee of the confidentiality and integrity of IT systems; US Supreme Court, Katz v. United States, 389 U.S. 347 (1967).

and generates the data necessary for establishing and maintaining the communication, so-called traffic data. This data includes, for example, information about the communication partners, time and duration of the communication. Third, location data, which is a subcategory of traffic data, relates to the location of the communication device. Location data is particularly relevant when establishing the location of the users of mobile communication devices.

By contrast to the content of information, traffic data – including location data – is subject to the regulatory regime of the E-privacy Directive. Although traffic data only concerns connections and the transmission of information and not the content of the information itself, they may facilitate inferences on the private life of natural persons or the correspondence of legal persons. The E-privacy Directive therefore imposes restrictions on the extent and the time of storage of such information. According to Articles 6(1) and (2) E-privacy Directive, traffic data relating to subscribers and users processed and stored by a communications network or service provider must basically be erased or made anonymous when it is no longer needed for the purpose of the transmission of communication or for billing purposes. This obligation does not conflict with such procedures on the internet as the caching in the domain name system of IP addresses, the caching of IP addresses to physical address bindings or the use of log-in information to control the right of access to networks or services.[167] Location data relating to users may, according to Article 9 E-privacy Directive, only be processed when it is made anonymous, or with the consent of the users to the extent and for the duration necessary for the provision of a value-added service. Even in cases in which subscribers have given their consent, they should have a simple means to temporarily deny the processing of location data, free of charge.[168]

The internet architecture does not require service providers to store transmission data for longer than the transmission process. As a consequence, a network operator may store traffic data for a longer period of time than the transmission process only for billing purposes. This has changed because of the widespread use of flat rates. In addition, digital mobile networks may have the capacity to process location data that is more precise than is necessary for the transmission of communications.[169] But both private companies and governmental agencies may have an interest in a longer storage of such information for a variety of reasons.

Within the EU framework, Article 15(1) of the E-privacy Directive sets out the conditions under which Member States may restrict the scope of the rights and obligations provided for, *inter alia*, in Articles 5, 6 and 9 of the E-privacy Directive. Member States may, *inter alia*, adopt legislative measures providing for the retention of data for a limited period. Such measures must be necessary, appropriate and proportionate within a democratic society for specific public order purposes,

---

[167] Recital 28 E-privacy Directive.
[168] Recital 35 E-privacy Directive.
[169] Recital 35 E-privacy Directive.

such as national and public security and the prevention and prosecution of criminal offences. Consequently, the E-privacy Directive does not in principle affect the ability of Member States to allow, or even to order, a longer storage of traffic data or location data to safeguard the public interest. Against this backdrop, several Member States have adopted legislation providing for the retention of data by service providers for the prevention and prosecution of criminal offences. However, those national provisions vary considerably regarding the types of traffic and location data to be retained and the conditions and periods of retention.[170] EU legislators perceived this as an obstacle to the internal market and thus adopted the Data Retention Directive, which aimed at harmonising obligations on providers of publicly available electronic communications services or of public communications networks to retain certain traffic and location data.[171] Yet the Court of Justice invalidated the Data Retention Directive (see *infra*). To be sure, data retention and other measures still remain possible under Article 15(1) E-privacy Directive in conjunction with Article 13(1) of the Data Protection Directive, which continue to apply. Yet those measures have to operate within the narrow confines allowed by the Luxembourg Court.

Articles 16 and 17 of the Council of Europe Cybercrime Convention also empower State Parties to adopt measures to enable the retention of data, especially traffic data. However, such measures have to be subject to conditions and safeguards providing for the adequate protection of human rights (Article 15(1) of the Cybercrime Convention).

3 Rights of the Data Subject

European and international data protection law furnishes data subjects with rights, the breach of which is subject to a judicial remedy, including the entitlement to compensation.[172] In addition, under EU law, persons may lodge a claim at the supervisory authority concerning the protection of their rights and freedoms in regard to the processing of personal data (Article 28(4) Data Protection Directive; Article 77 General Data Protection Regulation). However, just like the obligations of data controllers, the rights of data subjects are subject to many exemptions.

a Transparency and Access to Information

Paragraph 12 of the OECD principles already established that there 'should be a general policy of openness about developments, practices and policies with respect to

---

[170] Recitals 5 and 6 of the annulled Data Retention Directive.

[171] Directive 2006/24/EC of the European Parliament and of the Council of 15 March 2006 on the retention of data generated or processed in connection with the provision of publicly available electronic communications services or of public communications networks and amending Directive 2002/58/EC, OJ L 105/54.

[172] Article 22 and 23 Data Protection Directive, Article 15(2) E-privacy Directive, Article 10 Convention 108, Article 82 General Data Protection Regulation. On the question whether 'damage' in Article 23 Data Protection Directive includes non-pecuniary loss, see Google Inc. v. Vidal-Hall and others [2015] EWCA Civ 311.

personal data. Means should be readily available of establishing the existence and nature of personal data, and the main purposes of their use, as well as the identity and usual residence of the data controller.' Moreover, under paragraph 13(a), individuals should have the right to obtain from a data controller confirmation of whether or not the data controller has data relating to them. This right has been taken up by paragraph 4 of the UN Guidelines.

According to Article 8(2) EUChFR, everyone has the right of access to data that has been collected concerning him. As stated before, this right has already been accepted in the Article 8 ECHR case law of the Strasbourg Court. The right is further specified in Articles 10 and 11 Data Protection Directive as well as in Article 8(d) of Convention 108, and it will be further developed in Articles 13 and 14 of the General Data Protection Regulation. Accordingly, the data controller must furnish the data subject with certain information, such as the fact that data about the data subject has been stored, the purposes of the processing for which the data is intended and the recipients of the data, as far as the circumstances require such information. Moreover, Article 12(a) Data Protection Directive establishes a freedom of information claim of every data subject against any data controller on whether or not the data controller processes information about the data subject, the categories of data concerned and the recipients to whom the data are disclosed. To be sure, this right of access to information must not adversely affect trade secrets or intellectual property and in particular the copyright protecting the software. However, these considerations must not result in the data subject being refused all information.[173] From May 2018 on, Article 15 General Data Protection Regulation will provide such a claim.

Article 12(a) does not explain whether that right concerns the past and, if so, what period in the past. This question was addressed by the Court of Justice decision in *Rijkeboer*. Mr Rijkeboer requested the local government body, the College of Rotterdam, to notify him of all disclosures of his personal data from the local authority personal records to third parties in the previous two years. He wished to know the identity of those persons and the content of the data disclosed to them. Mr Rijkeboer, who had moved to another municipality, wished to know to whom his former address had been disclosed. The College complied with that request, but limited the disclosure to data relating to the year preceding his request. According to Dutch legislation, basic data, such as a person's name and address, may be stored for a long time. By contrast, information on recipients or categories of recipients to whom those basic data is disclosed is stored for only one year.

The Court of Justice decided that the right of access 'must of necessity relate to the past', since it is necessary to enable the data subject to exercise the rights set out in Article 12(b) and (c) and Article 14 of the Directive.[174] The exact time-limit for storage of that information and for providing access to that information is for

---

[173] Recital 41 Data Protection Directive.
[174] ECJ, Case C-553/07 [2009] College van burgemeester en wethouders van Rotterdam v. M.E.E. Rijkeboer [54].

the Member State to fix; it has to fairly balance the interest of the data subject in protecting his privacy and the burden that the obligation to store that information represents for the controller. Regarding the *Rijkeboer* case in particular, the Court decided that rules limiting the storage of the relevant information to a period of one year (and correspondingly limiting access to that information), while the basic data is stored for a much longer period, do not constitute a fair balance of the interests at issue. This applies unless it can be shown that longer storage of that information would constitute an excessive burden on the controller.

b Data Rectification and Erasure

As stated above, data controllers are subject to certain requirements concerning data quality. Article 8(2) EUChFR, Article 12(b) Data Protection Directive and Article 8(c) Convention 108 establish corresponding rights to rectification, erasure or blocking of incomplete, irrelevant or inaccurate data.[175] Article 12(b) Data Protection Directive is thus the corollary to the requirements on data quality in Article 6(1)(c) to (e) of the same Directive. Furthermore, pursuant to Article 12(c) Data Protection Directive, the data controller is under an obligation to notify third parties to whom the data has been disclosed of any rectification, erasure or blocking, unless this proves impossible or involves a disproportionate effort.

The European Court of Human Rights also inferred a right to rectify or delete inaccurate, irrelevant or incomplete data from Article 8 ECHR.[176] For example, in *Cemalettin Canlı v. Turkey*,[177] the applicant had twice been involved in criminal proceedings because of alleged membership in illegal organisations, but he was never convicted. The police records nevertheless listed the applicant as a member of two illegal organisations. The applicant unsuccessfully requested to have the police records amended. The Court found that there had been a violation of Article 8 ECHR. Furthermore, in *Khelili v. Switzerland*, the applicant carried cards that read: 'Nice, pretty woman, late thirties, would like to meet a man to have a drink together or go out from time to time. Tel. no. [...]'. Following a police check, the police entered her name in their records as a prostitute, an occupation that she denied. The applicant unsuccessfully requested that the word 'prostitute' be deleted from the police records. The ECtHR decided that allegation of unlawful prostitution appeared too vague and general and was not supported by concrete facts since she had never been convicted of unlawful prostitution. The Court concluded that retention of the word 'prostitute' in the police files for years had not been necessary in a democratic society in order to justify an interference with Article 8 of the ECHR.[178]

---

[175] See Articles 16 and 17 General Data Protection Regulation.
[176] See, for example, ECtHR, Ciubotaru v. Moldova [2010] App. no. 27138/04 [59]; *mutatis mutandis*, B.B. v. France [2009] App. no. 5335/06 [61]; Gardel v. France [2009] App. no. 16428/05 [62], both decisions concerning the French national automated register of sex offenders.
[177] ECtHR, Cemalettin Canlı v. Turkey [2008] App. no. 22427/04.
[178] ECtHR, Khelili v. Switzerland [2011] App. no. 16188/07.

The right to have inaccurate data erased or blocked was a major issue for the CJEU's construction of the 'right to be forgotten' in its *Google Spain* decision (see *infra*).

c Right to Object to Processing

If there are reasons justifying the processing of personal data without the data subject's consent, there is no general right of data subjects to object to such processing.[179] However, Article 14(1)(a) Data Protection Directive entitles the data subject, at least in the cases referred to in Articles 7(e) and (f) (data processing in the public interest or for the legitimate interests of the controller or a third party) to object 'on compelling legitimate grounds relating to his particular situation' to the processing of data relating to him. Moreover, according to Article 14(b) Data Protection Directive, the data subject has a right to object to the use of his data for the purposes of direct marketing.

Furthermore, pursuant to Article 14(b) Data Protection Directive, the data subject has the right to object to the processing of personal data relating to him that the controller intends to process for the purposes of direct marketing, to be informed before personal data is disclosed for the first time to third parties or used on their behalf for the purposes of direct marketing and to be offered the right to object to such disclosures or uses.

d Rights in Relation to Automated Decision-Making

Many decisions are nowadays not taken by human beings anymore but by algorithms. Such decisions are often simple, such as switching on a coffee machine at a particular time of the day. But there are also automatically generated decisions without any human intervention that may affect a person's life significantly, for example, whether or not a loan should be granted to a particular individual. This scenario is envisaged by Article 15(1) Data Protection Directive. Based on this provision, every person has a right not to be subject to a decision that produces legal effects concerning him or significantly affecting him if this decision is based solely on automated data processing intended to evaluate certain personal aspects relating to him, such as his performance at work, creditworthiness, reliability, conduct, etc. But this provision alone would be one-sided. For example, if a bank would not be permitted to base its decision on automated processing of data intended to evaluate the customer's creditworthiness, it might not grant the loan at all. This is not in the customer's interest. Therefore, Article 15(2) Data Protection Directive stipulates that the right provided by paragraph 1 does not apply if:

- the decision is taken in the course of the entering into or performing under a contract, the data subject requested entering into or performing under the contract, and this request has been satisfied;

---

[179] European Union Agency for Fundamental Rights and Council of Europe, Handbook on European data protection law, 2013, p. 118; see ECtHR, Leander v. Sweden [1987] App. no. 9248/81; M.S. v. Sweden [1997] App. no. 20837/92 [44].

- there are suitable measures to safeguard the data subject's legitimate interests, such as arrangements allowing him to present his point of view (for example, on the presumed lack of his creditworthiness); or
- the decision is authorised by a law that also lays down measures to safeguard the data subject's legitimate interests.

4 Exceptions and Derogations

International and European data protection provisions allow for significant exceptions to data protection obligations and corresponding rights of data subjects because of conflicting public or private interests. Paragraph 6 of the UN Guidelines authorises states to depart from the data protection principles in the Guidelines to protect national security, public order, public health or morality, as well as the rights and freedoms of others.

Article 5 of the Data Protection Directive rather bluntly expresses that it is for the Member States to determine 'more precisely the conditions under which the processing of personal data is lawful'. The Directive includes many rules that provide a certain degree of flexibility and leave to the Member States the task of deciding the details or choosing between options. However, the margin of discretion that Member States have can be used only in accordance with the objective pursued by the Data Protection Directive of maintaining a balance between the free movement of personal data and the protection of private life.[180]

EU data protection law allows the processing of personal data for historical, statistical or scientific purposes 'provided that Member States provide appropriate safeguards' (Article 6(1)(b) Data Protection Directive).[181] Member States may, for reasons of substantial public interest, lay down exemptions to the prohibition of sensitive personal data processing (Article 8(4) Data Protection Directive). Moreover, they may adopt measures to restrict the scope of the obligations and rights provided for in EU data protection law when such a restriction is necessary to safeguard, *inter alia*, national and public security, the prevention and investigation of criminal offences, an important economic or financial interest of a Member State and the protection of the rights and freedoms of others.[182] The rights of others may become relevant, for example, where a data subject requires access to his personal data from a controller, which would include the disclosure of the identity of other people.[183] In any case, the application of Article 13 Data Protection Directive has to be in compliance with the human rights of all persons involved.

---

[180] CJEU, Joined Cases C-468/10 and C-469/10 [2011] ASNEF and FECEMD [34–35].
[181] These safeguards must in particular rule out the use of the data in support of measures or decisions regarding any particular individual (recital 29 Data Protection Directive).
[182] Article 13 Data Protection Directive, Article 15 E-privacy Directive, Article 9 of Convention 108 and Article 23 General Data Protection Regulation.
[183] See, for example, Durant v. Financial Services Authority [2003] EWCA Civ 1746 [53].

5 *Compatibility with Human Rights*

The application of the rules as well as the exceptions and derogations included in data protection law has to be in accordance with human rights. In addition, the EU data protection framework also has to be applied in compliance with EU primary law, including the free movement provisions and the provisions on citizenship.[184]

The relationship between human rights and data protection can cut both ways. On the one hand, in light of Articles 7 and 8 of the Charter and Article 8 ECHR, the provisions protecting personal data have to be applied broadly, and exemptions and derogations from data protection provisions thus narrowly.[185] For example, Article 7(f) Data Protection Directive allows data processing without the data subject's consent if the controller or third party to whom the data is disclosed pursues a legitimate interest, except where such interests are overridden by the interests or fundamental rights and freedoms of the data subject. Moreover, Article 15 of the E-privacy Directive allows restrictions on the data protection provisions, but only if those measures are in accordance with the general principles of EU law, including the fundamental rights referred to in Article 6(1) and (2) TEU. Although Article 13 Data Protection Directive provides no such express 'gateway' to take on board the data subject's human rights, this provision has to be applied in light of Articles 7 and 8 EUChFR as well.

On the other hand, the data protection provisions themselves have to be applied in accordance with conflicting human rights, such as freedom of expression, intellectual property, access to information or conflicting principles, such as transparency (Articles 1 TEU and 10 TEU and Article 15 TFEU) and national security and public order interests. This is expressed, for example, in Article 9 Data Protection Directive for the processing of personal data carried out for solely journalistic purposes or the purpose of artistic or literary expression. This provision applies, for instance, to the processing of personal data in the audiovisual field and in news archives and press libraries.[186] For example, in *Tietosuojavaltuutettu* v. *Satakunnan Markkinapörssi Oy and Satamedia Oy*, two companies disseminated publicly available tax data on 1.2 million Finnish citizens to their subscribers via a text-messaging system. Having verified that this constituted 'processing of personal data', the Court of Justice had to examine whether this data processing had to be considered as an activity carried out solely for journalistic purposes. The Court decided that such an activity may be

---

[184] See, for example, ECJ, Case C-524/06 [2008] Huber v. Germany [81].

[185] See, for example, ECJ, Joined Cases C-465/00, C-138/01 and C-139/01 [2003] Rechnungshof v. Österreichischer Rundfunk and others [68]; CJEU, Joined Cases C-92/09 and C-93/09 [2010] Volker und Markus Schecke GbR and Hartmut Eifert [64 ff]; Case C-212/13 [2014] František Ryneš [29]; compare Article 1(1) Data Protection Directive.

[186] Recital 17 Data Protection Directive; Recital 153 General Data Protection Regulation. Article 85 General Data Protection Regulation corresponds to Article 9 Data Protection Directive. From academic literature, see Erdos (2013).

classified as 'journalistic' if its object is the disclosure to the public of information, opinions or ideas, irrespective of the medium used to transmit them.[187] The Court also ruled that journalistic activities are not limited to media undertakings and may be undertaken for profit-making purposes. However, Article 9 of the Data Protection Directive has as its objective the balancing of freedom of expression with the right to privacy. Which one of those rights prevailed was for the Finnish courts to decide. The Finnish Supreme Administrative Court held that the publication of the database collected for journalistic purposes could not be regarded as a journalistic activity. Therefore, its reasoning considered the applicant's freedom of expression, but not its privileges as journalistic media. The Supreme Administrative Court eventually found that the right to respect for private life of the taxpayers prevailed over the applicant companies' Article 10 ECHR right. The applicants complained at the European Court of Human Rights, but the Fourth Section of the Strasbourg confirmed the decision of the Finnish court.[188] The applicants have appealed to the Grand Chamber. With a view to the fine distinction between freedom of expression and freedom of the journalistic media, which have been developed in Chapter 2, it would only be welcomed if the Grand Chamber looked more carefully into the Finnish court's assessment whether the applicants' activity does really not qualify as journalistic.

Moreover, the obligation to balance conflicting interests is codified in Article 13(1) (g) Data Protection Directive. Accordingly, Member States may restrict the scope of the obligations of data controllers and the corresponding rights of data subjects when such a measure is necessary to safeguard the protection of the data subject or of the rights and freedoms of others. An example from the Court's case law is *Promusicae* v. *Telefónica de España SAU*: If a collecting society claims disclosure of personal data from an access provider of users infringing copyright, the application of the relevant provisions – domestic legislation implementing Directive 2001/29/EC and Directive 2004/48/EC, on the one hand, and the EU data protection legislation, on the other hand – has to strike a fair balance between the conflicting fundamental rights involved.[189] This will be further dealt with in Chapter 9.

Furthermore, the protection of personal data may restrict a right of access to public information. For example, Article 4(1)(b) of Regulation No. 1049/2001 restricts the right of access to European Parliament, Council and Commission documents, *inter alia*, 'if a disclosure would undermine the protection of privacy and the integrity of the individual, in particular in accordance with Community legislation regarding the protection of personal data'. This provision has to be applied not only in light of

---

[187] ECJ, Case C-73/07 [2008] Satakunnan Markkinapörssi Oy and Satamedia Oy [61].

[188] ECtHR, Satakunnan Markkinapörssi Oy and Satamedia Oy v. Finland [2015] App. no. 931/13 [72]. However, the Court also held that the applicants were violated in their rights enshrined in Article 6 ECHR for different reasons.

[189] ECJ, Case C-275/06 [2008] Promusicae v. Telefónica de España SAU [68–70]; confirmed in ECJ, Case C-557/07 [2009] LSG-Gesellschaft zur Wahrnehmung von Leistungsschutzrechten GmbH [28]; CJEU, Case C-461/10 [2008] Bonnier Audio [56].

Articles 7 and 8 EUChFR, but also in compliance with Article 42 EUChFR on the right of access to documents.[190] An interesting example of this conflict is the ECtHR decision *Wypych* v. *Poland*. In this case, town councillors were obliged to disclose details concerning their financial situation and property. The declarations were to be published in a bulletin available to the general public via the internet. The applicant councillor complained that the publication might make him and his family a target for criminal acts. The Court held that the measure interfered with the applicant's private and family life, it was nevertheless necessary in a democratic society for the prevention of crime, in this case corruption in politics. The use of the internet for the publication of such information was a safeguard to ensure that the obligation to declare was subject to public scrutiny. The Court observed:

> The general public has a legitimate interest in ascertaining that local politics are transparent and Internet access to the declarations makes access to such information effective and easy. Without such access, the obligation would have no practical importance or genuine incidence on the degree to which the public is informed about the political process.[191]

The tool to reconcile conflicting rights and interests is the principle of proportionality.[192] Factors in the balancing exercise are:

- the sensitivity of the information for the data subject's private life and the interest of the public in having that information;[193]
- whether the data in question already appears in public sources;[194]
- whether the information is topical or concerns the distant past;[195]
- the data subject concerned – for example, whether the data subject plays a significant role in public life[196] or whether the data subject is a child;[197]
- in the context of alleged violations of intellectual property by the data subject: whether there is clear evidence that the data subject violated intellectual

---

[190] ECJ, Case T-194/04 [2007] Bavarian Lager [111–139].

[191] ECtHR, Wypych v. Poland [2005] App. no. 2428/05, p. 12.

[192] See Chapter 3. Compare, for example, ECJ, Joined Cases C-465/00, C-138/01 and C-139/01 [2003] Rechnungshof v. Österreichischer Rundfunk and others [77 ff]; Case C-275/06 [2008] Promusicae v. Telefónica de España SAU [68 ff]; Case C-557/07 [2009] LSG-Gesellschaft zur Wahrnehmung von Leistungsschutzrechten GmbH [29]; CJEU, Joined Cases C-92/09 and C-93/09 [2010] Volker und Markus Schecke GbR and Hartmut Eifert [65 ff]; Case C-461/10 [2008] Bonnier Audio [59].

[193] ECJ, Case C-101/01 [2003] Lindqvist [89]; ECJ, Case T-194/04 [2007] Bavarian Lager [125]; CJEU, Joined Cases C-468/10 and C-469/10 [2011] ASNEF and FECEMD [45].

[194] CJEU, Joined Cases C-468/10 and C-469/10 [2011] ASNEF and FECEMD [44]; compare Article 8(2)(e) Data Protection Directive.

[195] ECtHR, Rotaru v. Romania [2000] App. no. 28341/95 [43]; Segerstedt-Wiberg and others v. Sweden [2006] App. no. 62332/00 [90]; Cemalettin Canlı v. Turkey [2008] App. no. 22427/04 [33]; M.K. v. France [2013] App. no. 19522/09 [42].

[196] CJEU, Case C-131/12 [2014] Google Spain SL v. AEPD and others [81].

[197] See ECtHR, S. and Marper v. United Kingdom [2008] App. no. 30562/04 and 30566/04; Article 8 General Data Protection Regulation; WP29, Working Document 1/2008 on the protection of children's personal data (General guidelines and the special case of schools).

property rights, and whether the information on the data subject can be regarded as facilitating the investigation into such an infringement;[198]

- whether the confidentiality of personal data is abused to anonymously commit criminal offences;[199]
- whether less intrusive means, such as processing of anonymous rather than personal data, would have been available to achieve the legitimate aim;[200]
- whether the information has been processed by a content provider or by an intermediary;[201]
- whether the information has been processed for journalistic purposes or the purpose of artistic or literary expression, as expressed by Article 9 Data Protection Directive;[202] and
- the duration of the breach of the data protection rules.[203]

Member States may, in the exercise of their discretion under Article 5 Data Protection Directive, establish guidelines in respect of that balancing exercise. However, national legislation must not definitively prescribe the result of the balancing exercise for certain categories of data; instead, national rules must always allow a different result by virtue of the particular circumstances of each individual case.[204]

6 The Transfer of Personal Data to Third Countries

The transnational flow of personal data is an important aspect of international trade. Hardly any other phenomenon describes the transnational dimension of modern media law, and the necessity to find transnational solutions, better than the 'transborder data flow'. The flow of personal data across borders is arguably *the* driving force for international convergence of data protection standards. The transfer of personal data to a third country is a subcategory of processing of personal data. However, due to its economic importance and human rights-related sensitivity European – and international – data protection law provides a regulatory regime to monitor the transfer of data to third countries that complements the general regime concerning the lawfulness of processing of personal data. As will be shown in more detail below, in the absence of consent or any other justification, European data protection law allows the transfers of personal data to third countries only if those countries guarantee an 'adequate level of protection'. But

---

[198] CJEU, Case C-461/10 [2008] Bonnier Audio [58–60]; see Chapter 9.
[199] See ECtHR, K.U. v. Finland [2008] App. no. 2872/02 [49].
[200] ECJ, Joined Cases C-465/00, C-138/01 and C-139/01 [2003] Rechnungshof v. Österreichischer Rundfunk and others [77]; CJEU, Joined Cases C-92/09 and C-93/09 [2010] Volker und Markus Schecke GbR and Hartmut Eifert [81].
[201] CJEU, Case C-131/12 [2014] Google Spain SL v. AEPD and others [86].
[202] ECJ, Case C-73/07 [2008] Satakunnan Markkinapörssi Oy and Satamedia Oy [58].
[203] ECJ, Case C-101/01 [2003] Lindqvist [89].
[204] CJEU, Joined Cases C-468/10 and C-469/10 [2011] ASNEF and FECEMD [47].

note that EU data protection searches for an *adequate*, and not for an *equal*, level of data protection.

a The Global and European Legal Framework

Paragraph 9 of the UN Guidelines stipulates that when countries concerned by a transborder data flow offer 'comparable safeguards for the protection of privacy, information should be able to circulate as freely as inside each of the territories concerned. If there are no reciprocal safeguards, limitations on such circulation may not be imposed unduly and only insofar as the protection of privacy demands.' According to Article 12(2) of Council of Europe Convention 108, a Contracting State shall not, for the sole purpose of the protection of privacy, prohibit or subject to special authorisation transborder flows of personal data going to the territory of *another Contracting State*. The rationale for this provision is that all Contracting States, having subscribed to the principles on data protection set out in the Convention, offer a certain minimum level of protection.[205] However, pursuant to Article 12(3)(b), a State Party may, for the purpose of the protection of privacy, prohibit or subject to special authorisation transborder flows of personal data going to *third countries*.

EU data protection law does not define the expression 'transfer to a third country'. Paragraph 1(e) of the OECD Guidelines defines 'transborder flows of personal data' as 'movements of personal data across national borders'. Article 2(1) of the Additional Protocol to Convention 108 describes transborder data flow as the transfer of personal data to a recipient who or which is subject to a foreign jurisdiction. This includes, for example, data transmissions between businesses or governments, cloud computing services and outsourcing of data processing operations. In *Lindqvist*, the Court of Justice decided, however, that merely making available personal data on a website, which can be accessed in third countries, does not constitute a 'transfer' of that data to third countries.[206]

EU law distinguishes between transfer of personal data between Member States and transfer to third countries. Restrictions on the free flow of data between EU and EEA Member States for reasons of data protection are prohibited by Article 1(2) Data Protection Directive. Transborder data flows to third countries, however, are subject to a special legal regime. This legislation is particularly relevant for data transfers to the US. Many US internet companies have subsidiary branches in the EU, which are subject to EU legislation. Under EU data protection legislation, the flow of data transfers to third countries is basically restricted. Yet the Data Protection Directive does not prohibit the transfer of personal data to a third country if:

1 the subject-matter is not covered by the Data Protection Directive in the first place, such as national security;

---

[205] Council of Europe, Explanatory Report to Convention 108, para. 67.
[206] ECJ, Case C-101/01 [2003] Lindqvist [70].

2 the third country in question ensures an 'adequate level of protection' (see *infra*);[207] or
3 at least one of the conditions of Article 26 Data Protection Directive is fulfilled:[208]
   • The data subject has given his consent unambiguously to the proposed transfer.
   • The transfer is necessary for contractual or pre-contractual reasons.
   • The transfer is necessary or legally required on important public interest grounds.
   • The transfer is necessary for the establishment, exercise or defence of legal claims.[209]
   • The transfer is necessary in order to protect the vital interests of the data subject.
   • The transfer is made from a register that is intended to provide information to the public and that is open to consultation either by the public in general or by any person with a legitimate interest, to the extent that the conditions laid down in law for consultation are fulfilled in the particular case.
   • The controller adduces adequate safeguards with respect to the protection of the fundamental rights and freedoms of individuals and the exercise of these rights. Such safeguards may in particular result from appropriate contractual clauses, such as the standard contractual clauses for data transfers issued by the European Commission. The European Commission issued two sets of standard contractual clauses for transfers from data controllers to data controllers established outside the EU/EEA and one set for the transfer to processors established outside the EU/EEA.[210] These standard contractual clauses are presumed to offer sufficient safeguards as required by EU data protection law.

b Adequacy Decision

According to Article 25(2), the Member States shall assess the adequacy of the level of protection afforded by a third country 'in the light of all the circumstances surrounding a data transfer operation or set of data transfer operations'. The Member States have to consider, in particular:

• the nature of the data;
• the purpose and duration of the proposed processing operation or operations;

---

[207] Article 25 Data Protection Directive; Article 45 General Data Protection Regulation. Similarly, under paragraph 17 of the OECD Guidelines, a Member Country should refrain from restricting transborder flows of personal data between itself and another country where the other country substantially observes these Guidelines or sufficient safeguards exist, to ensure a continuing level of protection consistent with these Guidelines.

[208] For more detailed explanations, see WP29, Working document on a common interpretation of Article 26(1) of Directive 95/46/EC of 24 October 1995, Adopted on 25 November 2005. These provisions have been codified in Articles 46-49 General Data Protection Regulation.

[209] On international data transfers in litigation, see WP29, Working Document 1/2009 on pre-trial discovery for cross border civil litigation.

[210] See COM, Decision 2001/497/EC of 15 June 2001 [Set I] – Standard contractual clauses for the purposes of Article 26(2) of Directive 95/46/EC for the transfer of personal data to third countries that do not ensure an adequate level of protection (controller to controller transfers) (amended by Commission

- the country of origin and country of final destination;
- the rules of law, both general and sectoral, in force in the third country in question; and
- the professional rules and security measures which are complied with in that country.

The Member States and the Commission shall inform each other if they consider that a third country does not ensure an adequate level of protection (Article 25(3)). The Commission may then issue a binding decision that a third country ensures an adequate level of protection by its domestic law or international commitments it has entered into, particularly upon agreements between the EU and the third country (Article 25(6)). The European Commission may also confine its adequacy decision to parts of a country's legal system or to singular topics, as has happened, for example, with regard to Canada's private commercial legislation, or with the US's Safe Harbour Principles.[211]

Where the Commission finds that a third country does not ensure an adequate level of protection, Member States shall take the measures necessary to prevent any transfer of data of the same type to the third country in question (Article 25(5)). In this context, the opinions provided by the WP29 are of high practical significance.[212]

As has been shown above, Europe and the US have significantly different data protection philosophies. The EU has thus not yet found the US as such to provide 'adequate' protection. However, in a decision issued in 2000, the European Commission found that the US 'Safe Harbour Privacy Principles', a voluntary self-regulatory Code of Conduct supervised by the Federal Trade Commission, provide 'adequate protection' within the meaning of Article 25 of the Data Protection Directive.[213] By contrast, in 2014, the European Parliament adopted a non-binding statement declaring the Safe Harbour as not providing

---

Decision C(2004) 5271); Decision C(2004)5721 of 27 December 2001, SET II – Standard contractual clauses for the transfer of personal data from the Community to third countries (controller to controller transfers); Decision C(2010)593 of 5 February 2010 – Standard Contractual Clauses (processors) (repealing Decision 2002/16/EC); all available at http://ec.europa.eu/justice/data-protection/document/international-transfers/transfer/index_en.htm; see also WP29, Working document 01/2014 on Draft Ad hoc contractual clauses 'EU data processor to non-EU sub-processor'; Working Document Setting Forth a Co-Operation Procedure for Issuing Common Opinions on 'Contractual clauses' Considered as compliant with the EC Model Clauses, Adopted on 26 November 2014; Explanatory Document on the Processor Binding Corporate Rules, Adopted on 19 April 2013, as last revised and adopted on 22 May 2015; Opinion 02/2014 on a referential for requirements for Binding Corporate Rules submitted to national Data Protection Authorities in the EU and Cross Border Privacy Rules submitted to APEC CBPR Accountability Agents.

[211] COM, Decision 2002/2/EC of 20 December 2001 pursuant to Directive 95/46/EC of the European Parliament and of the Council on the adequate protection of personal data provided by the Canadian Personal Information Protection and Electronic Documents Act. See also WP29, Opinion 07/2014 on the protection of personal data in Quebec.

[212] See, for example, Opinion 4/2002 on the level of protection of personal data in Argentina; Opinion 6/2002 on transmission of Passenger Manifest Information and other data from Airlines to the United States; Opinion 6/2010 on the level of protection of personal data in the Eastern Republic of Uruguay; Opinion 6/2009 on the level of protection of personal data in Israel; Opinion 11/2011 on the level of protection of personal data in New Zealand.

[213] COM, Decision 2000/520/EC of 26 July 2000 pursuant to Directive 95/46/EC of the European Parliament and of the Council on the adequacy of the protection provided by the safe harbour privacy principles and

adequate protection for EU citizens.[214] Moreover, the Commission decision has been challenged in *Schrems* v. *Data Protection Commissioner* with regard to data transfers to the US by Facebook because of widespread data access by US intelligence services. The applicant in this case, an Austrian privacy activist, challenged a decision by the Irish Data Protection Commissioner not to investigate his claims relating to these data transfers. The High Court of Ireland referred to the CJEU, essentially asking whether the national data protection supervisory authorities[215] are absolutely bound by a Commission adequacy decision, or whether they may conduct their own investigations into the adequacy of data protection. In its answer, the Court affirmed the second alternative: Article 25(6) of the Data Protection Directive, read in the light of Articles 7, 8 and 47 EUChFR, allows the domestic data protection supervisory authorities to examine whether the law and practices in a third country to which personal data is transferred ensure an adequate level of protection.[216] In the same decision, the CJEU invalidated the Commission Decision on the adequacy of the protection provided by the Safe Harbour privacy principles.

In February 2016, the European Commission and the US Government reached an agreement on a new framework for transatlantic exchanges of personal data for commercial purposes: the EU-US Privacy Shield. The Commission finalised the adoption procedure in July 2016. It remains to be seen whether the Privacy Shield really 'reflects the requirements' set out by the CJEU, as stated by the European Commission.

c Evaluation and Outlook

What role does the European regime on transborder data flows play in the development of a transnational information privacy law? Anu Bradford conceived of the EU's influence in establishing global norms and values as the 'Brussels Effect'.[217] She names the Data Protection Directive's regulations on transfer of data to third countries as one example for the 'Brussels Effect'. Multinational corporations have to adjust their global data management systems to reduce their compliance costs with multiple regulatory regimes, tending to apply the strictest standard: the EU standard.[218] Put in the broader context of international relations theory, the notion of the 'Brussels Effect' is an aspect of the idea of 'Normative Power Europe': Lacking significant military power, the EU has established itself as a legitimate civilian power spreading its norms – democracy, rule of law, social justice and also its understanding of respect for human rights – in its external relations.[219]

related frequently asked questions issued by the US Department of Commerce; see also WP29, Working Document on Functioning of the Safe Harbor Agreement, Adopted on 2 July 2002. For a detailed analysis of the Safe Harbour Principles, see Reidenberg (2001); Wolf (2014).

[214] 2013/2188(INI), para. 30.

[215] On data protection supervisory authorities see Article 28 Data Protection Directive and Chapter VI of the General Data Protection Regulation. On the independence of these authorities, see CJEU, Case C-518/07 [2010] Commission v. Germany; Case C-362/14 [2015] Schrems v. Data Protection Commissioner [41ff]. See also paragraph 8 of the UN Guidelines.

[216] CJEU, Case C-362/14 [2015] Schrems v. Data Protection Commissioner.

[217] Bradford (2012, pp. 22–26).

[218] See Greenleaf (2012, p. 77).

[219] Manners (2002).

By contrast, Paul M. Schwartz regards Anne-Marie Slaughter's concept of 'harmonisation networks' as the more appropriate theoretical framework to describe the process. The EU has not succeeded in *imposing* its norm on foreign actors, in this case the US; instead, an EU–US privacy collision was averted through a collaborative approach rather than European unilateralism.[220] Article 50 General Data Protection Regulation seems to prove Paul M. Schwartz' assumption right: this provision will oblige the European Commission and supervisory authorities to develop effective international cooperation mechanisms to facilitate the enforcement of legislation for the protection of personal data.

What is the impact of the EU's approach to international data transfer on data privacy protection worldwide? On the one hand, in a globalised economy the knee-jerk reaction to high regulatory standards, such as the data protection standards in the EU, is the fear of a 'race to the bottom'. Companies will select the jurisdiction with the lowest regulatory standards, which will lead other jurisdictions to follow suit in lowering their standards to prevent being outdistanced in global competitiveness. The EU will thus have to lower its own privacy standards in order to remain attractive to data-intense global players.[221] On the other hand, the EU is too important a market to be ignored. Because of the EU's rather broad assumption of prescriptive jurisdiction, which will be extended further under the General Data Protection Regulation, companies that aim at gathering data in the EU will in most cases have to adapt to European standards. But by imposing high standards not only on data processing within the EU, but also on the transfer of data to third countries, the EU indirectly requires – be it by way of unilateral imposition, be it through bilateral cooperation – third countries to provide 'adequate' data protection; that is, data protection not too dissimilar from the European standards. Other jurisdictions will thus not only face internal pressure to enhance their data privacy standards, for example, because of their own human rights commitments. They will also face indirect external pressure by the EU, because they have to adapt their information privacy standards in a way that is 'adequate' to the EU to prevent disruption of international data flows. It is thus safe to speak of an *extraterritorial effect* of EU data protection law; with its strict data transfer rules, the EU seems to have caused a 'race to the top' in information privacy.[222] The title of the European Data Protection Supervisor's recently published privacy strategy for the years 2015–2019 succinctly summarises the EU's understanding of its role in the development of transnational data protection: It is called 'Leading by Example'.

7 Jurisdiction and International Applicability of European Data Protection Law

According to Article 28(6) of the Data Protection Directive, each domestic supervisory authority shall have jurisdiction on the territory of its own Member State.

---

[220] See Schwartz (2013, p. 1986), referring to A.-M. Slaughter (2004, pp. 59-61).
[221] Compare Swire and Litan (1998, p. 151).
[222] Compare Swire (1998, p. 1002).

However, the authorities shall have jurisdiction 'whatever the national law applicable to the processing in question'. Hence, under the Data Protection Directive, not only for the courts in private law matters, but even for the supervisory authorities, the notion of adjudicative jurisdiction is not identical with the choice of the applicable law. As a *lex specialis* to the Rome I and Rome II Regulations, Article 4 Data Protection Directive provides a two-tiered system of data protection conflict of laws rules. These rules are also applicable within the framework of the E-privacy Directive.[223]

First, each Member State shall apply its national provisions to the processing of personal data 'carried out in the context of the activities of an establishment of the controller on the territory of the Member State' (Article 4(1)(a) Data Protection Directive). Article 4 thus establishes a country-of-origin principle for controllers of personal data established in the EU. A data controller shall in principle be subject to the law of only one EU Member State. There is one exception to this principle, and this is where a data controller establishes subsidiary branches in other Member States. The data processing by these branches is then subject to the law of the Member State in which they are established. However, it is not relevant in which other EU countries the company actually processes its data if it does not have an establishment there; note that data processing may be carried out through different operations in different countries. Conversely, if a data controller has several establishments, only those Member States of establishment are relevant in which an establishment of the controller is involved in activities relating to the data processing in question. This is the meaning of the words 'context of activities' in Article 4(1)(a) Data Protection Directive. By way of example: an online magazine has its headquarters in Madrid and branches in Paris and Brussels. The office in Paris is responsible for collecting personal data of the magazine's subscribers, but delegates the analysis of this data, which is stored on a server in Frankfurt, to the Brussels office, which works exclusively on instructions from Paris. In this case, the data collection and further processing would be carried out 'in the context of the activities' of the French establishment. Therefore, French law would apply. Spanish law would not apply, because the headquarters in Madrid is not involved in the data processing at all, nor Belgian law (because Brussels is the host of a mere processor), nor German law (because the location of the server is irrelevant for the application of Article 4(1)(a)), nor would Italian or Austrian or any other country's law apply, even though the magazine is also accessible from there. The Belgian data processor would thus be subject to French law, except for the requirements of Belgian law with regard to the security measures applicable to data processors (Article 17(3) Data Protection Directive).

The notion of 'establishment' is further explained in the preamble to the Directive. Recital 19 explains that establishment 'implies the effective and real exercise of activity through stable arrangements'. The legal form of such an establishment, however,

---

[223] More details on the conflict of laws within the EU data protection framework are provided in WP29, Opinion 8/2010 on applicable law.

'whether simply branch or a subsidiary with a legal personality, is not the determining factor in this respect'.

The country-of-origin principle is in theory justified because of the harmonising effect of the Data Protection Directive. But this does not fully match reality; in practice there are huge differences between the Member States in terms of both the regulatory standards of the applicable legislation and its enforcement, with Germany arguably being the most restrictive Member State and Ireland the most lenient one.[224] It is therefore not surprising that many US internet companies have their main European branch in Ireland. This difference between domestic levels of data protection is owed to the derogations the Data Protection Directives allows, and agreeing to common standards was one of the most controversial aspects in the legislative proceedings to the General Data Protection Regulation. Germany wanted to retain its high level of data protection, whereas Ireland did not want to jeopardise its attractiveness for foreign companies.

The Court of Justice provided further guidance on the interpretation of Articles 28 and 4 Data Protection Directive in the case of *Weltimmo*.[225] A company registered in Slovakia (Weltimmo) ran a property-dealing website concerning Hungarian properties, thereby processing personal data of advertisers. Weltimmo did not carry out any activity in Slovakia. Two of its property-dealing websites were written exclusively in Hungarian, it had a Hungarian bank account and it used a Hungarian letterbox. Weltimmo was made up of only one or two persons, and it had a representative in Hungary who sought to negotiate the settlement of the unpaid debts with advertisers. It was uncertain where Weltimmo's servers were located. Some advertisers lodged complaints against Weltimmo's data processing practice with the Hungarian data protection authority. The Luxembourg Court had to address questions regarding the applicable law and the powers of the Hungarian data protection authority.

With a view to the applicable law, the Court highlighted that Article 4(1)(a) Data Protection Directive refers to the notion of 'establishment' and not 'registration'. The concept of 'establishment' has to be interpreted broadly and with a view to the aims of the Directive, namely to ensure effective protection of the right to privacy and to avoid any circumvention of national rules.[226] It was therefore relevant whether Weltimmo's activity was 'mainly or entirely directed' at a Hungarian audience.[227] The relevant factors for this examination are: the degree of stability of the arrangements, the effective exercise of activities in the Member State concerned and the specific nature of the economic activities and the provision of services concerned.[228] Even the presence of only one representative can suffice to constitute a 'stable arrangement'

---

[224] On the implementation of the provisions of the Data Protection Directive in national law, see COM, Staff Working Paper, Impact Assessment, COM(2012) 10 final.
[225] CJEU, Case C-230/14 [2015] Weltimmo.
[226] CJEU, Case C-230/14 [2015] Weltimmo [27] and [30].
[227] CJEU, Case C-230/14 [2015] Weltimmo [41].
[228] CJEU, Case C-230/14 [2015] Weltimmo [29].

if he 'acts with a sufficient degree of stability through the presence of the necessary equipment for provision of the specific services concerned in the Member State in question'.[229] With a view to the facts of the case at hand – the language of the website, the location of the properties and Weltimmo's arrangements in Hungary (bank account and letterbox) – the Court held that Weltimmo pursued a 'real and effective activity' in Hungary.[230] As a result, subject to further assessments by the domestic courts, Weltimmo could be regarded as being 'established' in Hungary. Moreover, since Weltimmo processed personal data 'in the context of the activities' of that establishment, Hungarian law could be declared applicable.[231]

But, as has been stated before, the assessment of Weltimmo's establishment, and hence of the applicable law, was subject to further examination by the domestic courts. What if the domestic courts concluded that Hungarian law was not applicable? As we have seen before, the jurisdiction of the data protection authority under Article 28(6) Data Protection Directive is independent from the applicable law, so the Hungarian data protection authority may have jurisdiction even if Hungarian data protection law was not applicable. However, would the Hungarian data protection authority be able to impose penalties on a company established in another Member State? The CJEU decided that data protection authorities may exercise the powers conferred on them in Article 28(3) Data Protection Directive (investigative powers, powers of intervention and the power to engage in legal proceedings). But they may not exercise all of the powers conferred on them by the law of their own Member State, such as the imposition of a penalty, outside the territory of their Member State.[232] Instead, they have to cooperate with the supervisory authority of the Member State of establishment, as laid down in Article 28(6) Data Protection Directive.[233]

Second, if the data controller is not established on EU territory, each Member State in which the data controller for purposes of processing personal data makes use of equipment shall apply their national provisions (Article 4(1)(c) Data Protection Directive). The reason behind this provision is that the Data Protection Directive also aims at protecting EU citizens against data processing carried out by an entity established in a third country. By contrast to the regulatory regime applying to the transfer of data to a third country, Article 4(1)(c) does not consider whether the third countries have an adequate level of protection of personal data or not. However, the criterion that the data controller has to make use of equipment located in an EU Member State has proven to be difficult to apply with the rise of the internet. A broad definition of the concept of 'equipment' would lead to significant extraterritorial effects of the Data Protection Directive. A narrow definition, however, might deprive EU citizens of the protection afforded by the Directive. The WP29 has favoured a broad interpretation

---

229 CJEU, Case C-230/14 [2015] Weltimmo [30].
230 CJEU, Case C-230/14 [2015] Weltimmo [32–33].
231 CJEU, Case C-230/14 [2015] Weltimmo [39].
232 CJEU, Case C-230/14 [2015] Weltimmo [55].
233 CJEU, Case C-230/14 [2015] Weltimmo [57].

of the notion of 'equipment', including human and/or technical intermediaries, the collection of information using questionnaires, terminals and servers located in the EU that are used by a third-country controller.[234] Consequently, if a website stores information on an internet user's hard disk that can be read back by the website that deposited it, such as by way of cookies, the user's computer would have to be considered 'equipment' within the meaning of the Directive.[235]

Particularly problematic is the notion of 'equipment located on the territory in an EU Member State' with regard to information stored in data 'clouds'. The term 'cloud' is already an unfortunate metaphor. It suggests an amorphous, intangible concept. However, the data has to be physically stored somewhere. As James Gleick aptly put it, the cloud is the 'avatar' of servers.[236] And if the server on which the 'cloud' data is stored is located in the EU, all data controllers using this infrastructure would have to comply with the law of that EU Member State. Moreover, the WP29 has even argued that the law of that Member State should not only be applied to the part of the data processing that is carried out on the EU-based server, but to all the stages of the processing of the same data, even those taking place in a third country. However, one could also argue that the legal regime on transfer of personal data with its 'adequacy' requirement seems to be the more appropriate framework to deal with such cases.[237]

The notion of 'equipment' does not cover equipment used only for the purposes of transit through the territory of the EU (Article 4(1)(c) Data Protection Directive), such as a mere telephone connection to a server outside the EU. Moreover, it does not cover websites hosted on a server located in a third country that asks users to enter personal data.

The territorial scope of EU data protection law will partly change under the General Data Protection Regulation. First, the Regulation will apply to the processing of personal data in the context of the activities of an establishment of a controller *or a processor* in the EU (Article 3(1)). Second, it will also apply to the processing of personal data of data subjects residing in the EU by a controller not established in the Union, where the processing activities are related to the offering of goods or services to such data subjects in the EU, or the monitoring of their behaviour as far as that behaviour takes place within the Union (Article 3(2)). This will significantly extend the territorial scope of the EU data protection regime.

Relevant factors to determine whether a controller or processor envisages 'offering' goods or services are the use of a language or a currency generally used in one or more

---

[234] WP29, Opinion 8/2010 on applicable law; Opinion 1/2008 on data protection issues related to search engines, p. 11; Working document on determining the international application of EU data protection law to personal data processing on the Internet by non-EU based web sites, Adopted on 30 May 2002, p. 9.

[235] WP29, Opinion 8/2010 on applicable law, p. 21; Working Document Privacy on the Internet – An integrated EU Approach to On-line Data Protection, Adopted on 21st November 2000, p. 28; Working document on determining the international application of EU data protection law to personal data processing on the Internet by non-EU based web sites, Adopted on 30 May 2002, p. 11.

[236] Gleick (2012, p. 396).

[237] WP29, Opinion 8/2010 on applicable law, pp. 24–25; Opinion 05/2012 on Cloud Computing, p. 7. See also from academic literature Hon et al. (2012).

Member States, or the mentioning of customers or users who are in the EU. By contrast, the mere accessibility of the controller's, processor's or an intermediary's website in the EU, of an e-mail address or of other contact details, or the use of a language generally used in the third country where the controller is established, is insufficient to ascertain such intention (Recital 23). The requirement of 'offering' in Article 3(2)(a) General Data Protection Regulation is thus based on the 'targeting approach' that also applies to the establishment of jurisdiction for consumer contracts according to Article 17(1)(c) Brussels Ia Regulation (see chapter 4).

Whether a processing activity can be considered a 'monitoring' of the behaviour of data subjects according to Article 3(2)(b) General Data Protection Regulation, it should be established 'whether natural persons are tracked on the internet including potential subsequent use of personal data processing techniques which consist of profiling a natural person, particularly in order to take decisions concerning her or him or for analysing or predicting her or his personal preferences, behaviours and attitudes' (Recital 24).

8 The Case Examples

One of the most significant cases involving the balancing of data sovereignty of the individual and public security interests, often stylised as the 'liberty versus security' conflict, was the 2014 decision of the Court of Justice on the validity of the Data Retention Directive (see subsection a below). But human rights are not only relevant for public data-gathering; data protection provisions also have to be applied in light of the conflicting human rights where private data-gathering is concerned. This was the subject-matter of *Google Spain* (see subsection b).

a The Data Retention Directive Case

The Data Retention Directive aimed at harmonising obligations on providers of publicly available electronic communications services or of public communications networks to retain certain traffic and location data. The Court identified two distinct interferences with the right to respect for private life: First, the obligation imposed by the Data Retention Directive on network and service providers to retain data relating to a person's private life and to his communications. Second, the access of the competent national authorities to the data constitutes an additional interference with Articles 7 and 8 EUChFR.[238] This corresponded to the jurisprudence of the ECtHR, which has held that each processing action (collection, storage and transmission) amounts to a separate interference with Article 8 ECHR.[239] The CJEU decided that, although the Directive pursued a legitimate aim, namely the prevention and prosecution of serious

---

[238] CJEU, Joined Cases C-293/12 and C-594/12 [2014] Digital Rights Ireland Ltd and Kärntner Landesregierung [34–35].

[239] ECtHR, Rotaru v. Romania [2000] App. no. 28341/95 [43]; P.G. and J.H. v. United Kingdom [2001] App. no. 44787/98 [59]; Peck v. United Kingdom [2003] App. no. 44647/98 [59]; Weber and Savaria v. Germany [2006] App. no. 54934/00 [79].

crime, it was disproportionate to achieve that aim. The proportionality analysis raised many important questions:

- Is the retention of data suitable to achieve the aim pursued? The Court of Justice decided that retained data is 'a valuable tool for criminal investigations'.[240] However, studies question the success of data retention in the fight against crime and terrorism.[241] Moreover, the tools provided by data retention can be circumvented by methods of electronic communication that allow anonymous communication. On the other hand, 100 per cent certainty cannot be required for the 'suitability' of a measure; it should be regarded as sufficient that the measure actually helps to achieve the legitimate aim.
- Are there less intrusive means available to achieve the aim pursued? In this context, one has to take into consideration that the retention of traffic and location data is already a 'less intrusive means', namely compared to the surveillance and retention of communication content. One could also consider whether data retention for six months is necessary, or whether three months would be sufficient, or whether one should distinguish the length of the retention according to the data at issue. There would also be other less intrusive means, such as a system of expedited preservation (quick freeze) and targeted collection of traffic data as agreed in Article 16(2) of the Cybercrime Convention.
- Is data retention strictly proportionate to the aim pursued? The case of the Data Retention Directive illustrated once more that the ends, legitimate as they may be, do by themselves not justify the means. Although the Directive did not permit the retention of data revealing the content of the communication, the traffic and location data alone enable the authorities to establish the identity of the person with whom a subscriber or registered user has communicated and to identify the time, place and frequency of the communication(s) with certain persons.[242] Those data facilitate a profile concerning individuals, such as the habits of everyday life, places of residence, movements, the activities carried out and their social relationships.[243] The fact that data is retained and subsequently used without the subscriber or registered user being informed might give the persons concerned the feeling of constant surveillance.[244] Moreover, the retention of the data alone might have an effect on the use, by subscribers or registered users, of the means of communication covered by that directive and, consequently, on their exercise of the freedom of expression guaranteed by Article 11 of the Charter.[245] Furthermore, the Court of Justice

---

[240] CJEU, Joined Cases C-293/12 and C-594/12 [2014] Digital Rights Ireland Ltd and Kärntner Landesregierung [49].

[241] See, for example, Albrecht et al. (2012).

[242] CJEU, Joined Cases C-293/12 and C-594/12 [2014] Digital Rights Ireland Ltd and Kärntner Landesregierung [26].

[243] CJEU, Joined Cases C-293/12 and C-594/12 [2014] Digital Rights Ireland Ltd and Kärntner Landesregierung [27].

[244] CJEU, Joined Cases C-293/12 and C-594/12 [2014] Digital Rights Ireland Ltd and Kärntner Landesregierung [37].

[245] CJEU, Joined Cases C-293/12 and C-594/12 [2014] Digital Rights Ireland Ltd and Kärntner Landesregierung [28].

highlighted that the Data Retention Directive did not provide sufficient substantive and procedural safeguards to effectively protect their personal data against the risk of abuse and against any unlawful access and use of that data.[246] In particular, the Directive did not require the data in question to be retained within the European Union, with the result that it cannot be held that the control required by Article 8(3) EUChFR is fully ensured.[247] Finally, one should not forget the rights of the providers that have to retain data. The Data Retention Directive did not provide a compensation scheme for the electronic communication network and service providers' cost of storing the data. This conflicts with the freedom to conduct a business, as enshrined in Article 16 EUChFR.

To conclude, the Court of Justice invalidated the Data Retention Directive, but the judges did not decide that any form of data retention is prohibited. Article 15(1) E-privacy Directive in conjunction with Article 13(1) Data Protection Directive, which provide exceptions to the obligation to erase unnecessary data, are still in place. However, the Court narrowed down the options for data retention significantly. Member States may adopt data retention laws, but within the narrow framework provided by the Court of Justice. Such legislation has to:

- restrict retention to data that relates to public security;
- restrict retention to a particular time period, a geographical area and suspects or persons whose data would contribute to the prevention, detection or prosecution of serious criminal offences;
- provide for exceptions for persons whose communications are subject to an obligation of professional secrecy, including Members of Parliament, lawyers and journalists;
- restrict access and use of the data for the purposes of prevention, detection or prosecution of defined, sufficiently serious crimes;
- ensure that an independent administrative or judicial body carries out a prior review of decisions regarding access to the data on the basis of what is strictly necessary;
- ensure destruction of the data when it is no longer required; and
- ensure the data is kept within the EU.[248]

Against this background, the High Court of England and Wales found in July 2015 that section 1 of the Data Retention and Investigatory Powers Act 2014 (DRIPA) was

---

[246] CJEU, Joined Cases C-293/12 and C-594/12 [2014] Digital Rights Ireland Ltd and Kärntner Landesregierung [61–66]. On the importance of procedural safeguards under Article 8 ECHR, compare ECtHR, Leander v. Sweden [1987] App. no. 9248/81 [59] and [67]: parliamentary and administrative control of secret scrutiny of persons applying for employment in posts of importance for national security; Rotaru v. Romania [2000] App. no. 28341/95 [59]: 'interference by the executive authorities with an individual's rights should be subject to effective supervision, which should normally be carried out by the judiciary'.

[247] CJEU, Joined Cases C-293/12 and C-594/12 [2014] Digital Rights Ireland Ltd and Kärntner Landesregierung [68].

[248] CJEU, Joined Cases C-293/12 and C-594/12 [2014] Digital Rights Ireland Ltd and Kärntner Landesregierung [58 ff].

inconsistent with EU law.[249] Moreover, in May 2015, the Stockholm Administrative Court of Appeals in the case *Tele2 Sverige AB* referred questions relating to the Swedish Data Retention Act to the CJEU.[250]

b The *Google Spain* Case

First of all, *Google Spain* raised an interesting jurisdictional question: does the Data Protection Directive apply to Google Inc., Google Spain, or even to both? Therefore, the Court had to establish, in the first place, whether a search engine operator could be characterised as a data controller. A search engine finds information placed online, indexes it, stores it temporarily and makes it available to internet users. The Court observed that in exploring the internet automatically, constantly and systematically in search of the information, the operator of a search engine 'collects', 'retrieves', 'records' and 'organises' data, 'stores' it on its servers and subsequently 'discloses' and 'makes [it] available' to its users in the form of lists of search results. As those operations are referred to in Article 2(b) of the Data Protection Directive, they must be classified as 'processing' within the meaning of that provision, regardless of the fact that the operator of the search engine also carries out the same operations in respect of other types of information and does not distinguish between the latter and personal data.[251] This is not affected by the fact that that data has already been published on the internet and is not altered by the search engine.[252] Although a search engine operator does not exercise control over the personal data published on the webpages of third parties, he is nonetheless to be qualified as a 'controller' processing personal data.[253] Once more, the Court referred to the necessity of protecting citizens from the privacy-threatening functions of search engines.[254] Most notably, with its literal and human rights-oriented approach to the Directive, the Court disagreed with the Advocate-General who had based his opinion on a historical interpretation and teleological reduction. The Advocate-General referred to the fact that the Data Protection Directive was drafted before the emergence of the internet, so it was difficult to apply the concepts of the Directive to search engine operators as to any other intermediaries. Were it otherwise, users who simply download files containing personal data could be held liable as controllers.[255] The Advocate-General therefore construed the notion of 'controller' as meaning someone who is *responsible* for data processing, 'in

---

[249] R (Davis) v. Secretary of State for the Home Department [2015] EWHC 2092 (Admin).
[250] Case C/203/2015. The Advocate General delivered his opinion on 19 July 2016, arguing that a general obligation to retain data may be compatible with EU law, but within strict safeguards (Opinion of Aqdvocate General Saugmandsgaard Øe, Joined Cases C-203/15 and C-698/15).
[251] CJEU, Case C-131/12 [2014] Google Spain SL v. AEPD and others [28]; see also WP29, Opinion 1/2008 on data protection issues related to search engines.
[252] CJEU, Case C-131/12 [2014] Google Spain SL v. AEPD and others [29].
[253] CJEU, Case C-131/12 [2014] Google Spain SL v. AEPD and others [33].
[254] CJEU, Case C-131/12 [2014] Google Spain SL v. AEPD and others [38].
[255] CJEU, Case C-131/12 [2014] Google Spain SL v. AEPD and others, Opinion of Advocate-General Jääskinen [81].

the sense that the *controller* is aware of the existence of a certain defined category of information amounting to personal data and the controller processes this data with some intention which relates to their processing *as* personal data'.[256] This is not the case with mere automatic processing operations on the internet.

Then, the Court had to interpret Article 4 Data Protection Directive. The Google search engine is run by Google Inc. in the US, whereas it is the purpose of the subsidiary Google Spain to merely promote and sell advertising space offered by that engine in Spain. The Court of Justice highlighted that Article 4(1)(a) of the Data Protection Directive does not require the processing of personal data in question to be carried out 'by' the establishment concerned itself, but only that it be carried out 'in the context of the activities' of the establishment.[257] This, the Court held, was the case with regard to Google Spain. The Court thus accepted prescriptive jurisdiction of the Data Protection Directive under Article 4(1)(a) Data Protection Directive, and it thus did not have to deal with the question whether Google Inc. used 'equipment' located in the EU within the meaning of Article 4(1)(c) Data Protection Directive. However, the case made obvious that the jurisdictional rules of the Directive from 1995 are, as the Advocate-General expressed it, 'not very helpful' to cope with ubiquitous data-gathering by an internationally operating search engine.[258] The Court thus relied more on the Directive's desired effectiveness and the fundamental rights relevance of the case to justify European jurisdiction.[259]

In substantive terms, the Court of Justice decided that Articles 12(b) and 14(1)(a) Data Protection Directive, interpreted in light of Articles 7 and 8 EUChFR, furnish a data subject with a right against a search engine operator to be delisted from search results, popularly known as a 'right to be forgotten'.[260] Article 12(b) Data Protection Directive provides that every data subject has a right against a data controller to rectify, erase or block data the processing of which does not comply with the provisions of the Data Protection Directive, 'in particular because of the incomplete or inaccurate nature of the data'. Article 14(a) Data Protection Directive entitles the data subject to object 'on compelling legitimate grounds relating to his particular situation' to the processing of data relating to him. A significant aspect of the *Google Spain* decision was that the information concerning Mr González was lawfully published and neither inaccurate nor incomplete, but simply contrary to his interests. It was thus difficult to subsume the information under either Article 12(b) or Article 14(a) Data Protection Directive. In disagreement with the Advocate-General, the

---

[256] CJEU, Case C-131/12 [2014] Google Spain SL v. AEPD and others, Opinion of Advocate-General Jääskinen [82] (emphasis in the original).

[257] CJEU, Case C-131/12 [2014] Google Spain SL v. AEPD and others [52].

[258] CJEU, Case C-131/12 [2014] Google Spain SL v. AEPD and others, Opinion of Advocate-General Jääskinen [63].

[259] CJEU, Case C-131/12 [2014] Google Spain SL v. AEPD and others [58].

[260] CJEU, Case C-131/12 [2014] Google Spain SL v. AEPD and others [89–99]; on this decision, see Lindsay (2014). The 'right to be forgotten' will be codified in Article 17 General Data Protection Regulation. On the concept of the 'right to be forgotten', see Mayer-Schönberger (2009); Sartor (2015).

Court of Justice decided to acknowledge a right to be delisted against a search engine operator: Article 12(b) referred to the accuracy principle contained in Article 6(1)(d) Data Protection Directive merely by way of example ('in particular'). Further reasons to justify a right of the data subject to erase or block data are hence not excluded. Regarding the right to object in Article 14(a) Data Protection Directive, the Court concluded that the assessment of 'compelling legitimate grounds' requires a balancing exercise that 'enables account to be taken in a more specific manner of all the circumstances surrounding the data subject's particular situation'.[261] Most importantly, the Court highlighted that the case had to be decided in light of the human rights involved, and the Court's emphasis was clearly on Articles 7 and 8 EUChFR. The Court concluded that a data subject may request from a search engine operator that information about the data subject no longer be made available to the general public by its inclusion in such a list of results, but with one caveat: unless 'it appeared, for particular reasons, such as the role played by the data subject in public life, that the interference with his fundamental rights is justified by the preponderant interest of the general public in having, on account of inclusion in the list of results, access to the information in question.'[262] Given the fact that the initial publication had taken place 16 years earlier, the Court found no preponderant interest of the public in having, in the context of such a search, access to that information.[263]

Remarkably, in contrast to the Advocate-General, the Court of Justice referred only marginally to the importance of freedom of expression in the *Google Spain* case, without even mentioning Article 11(1) EUChFR.[264] Article 11(1) EUChFR would have applied not only to Google Search itself, which has a right to impart information, but also to the users of Google Search, who have a right to receive that information which Google is willing to impart to them. Disregarding whether one agrees with the result of the Google Spain ruling or not, the Court has to be criticised for not properly balancing Mr González' 'right to be forgotten' against the public's 'right to remember' him.

How does the *Google Spain* decision shape the information and communication environment we live in? Within a few weeks of the Court ruling, Google enabled people to submit removal requests, and soon after that began delisting search results. Google did not even wait for the final decision of the Spanish court (recall that *Google Spain* was a reference for a preliminary ruling). Within the first year of the Court's decision, Google received 255,143 blocking requests and removed 381,049 URLs.[265] The impact of the *Google Spain* judgment is therefore difficult to estimate. Given the sheer number of requests and the fact that the burden of proving the preponderant

---

[261] CJEU, Case C-131/12 [2014] Google Spain SL v. AEPD and others [76].
[262] CJEU, Case C-131/12 [2014] Google Spain SL v. AEPD and others [97].
[263] CJEU, Case C-131/12 [2014] Google Spain SL v. AEPD and others [98].
[264] CJEU, Case C-131/12 [2014] Google Spain SL v. AEPD and others [81] and [97]; CJEU, Case C-131/12 [2014] Google Spain SL v. AEPD and others, Opinion of Advocate-General Jääskinen [121].
[265] Heise Online (www.heise.de), 15 May 2015.

public interest is on the internet service provider, the company arguably has an incentive to delete, rather than not to delete. On the other hand, the internet service provider has a business interest in having as much data available and published as possible, so it might have an internal incentive not to block the information. In this context, it is also important to note that Google can be taken to court for refusing to delist certain information, but it cannot be sued by anyone for delisting it.

Arguably the most controversial aspect of the 'right to be forgotten' concerns the criminal history of a person. Several courts have prohibited publishing information about criminal convictions of people who have served their sentence.[266] The rationale for those prohibitions is the fact that such reporting may threaten to jeopardise the released person's social rehabilitation. Having served a sentence means that the person has paid for his crime and should receive a chance to reintegrate into society.[267] On the other hand, one should consider that the commission of crimes is *per se* a matter of public concern (see Chapter 3). Furthermore, one might also argue that members of society have a right to have such information available in order to get an undistorted picture of a person.[268]

The very last point pertains to an oddity of the *Google Spain* case, which is less of doctrinal than of practical significance. The broader public knows exactly one thing about Mr González: the fact that he was bankrupt almost 20 years ago – the information he so dearly wanted to keep secret. This so-called 'Streisand Effect'[269] appears particularly paradoxical in a case that involved the protection of personal data and the right to privacy. The first person to whom the Court of Justice granted a 'right to be forgotten', a formerly unknown ex-bankrupt, will remain in the memory of law students with the same presence as the Princess of Monaco, Max Mosley and Naomi Campbell.

VIII Questions

1 In Europe, privacy as a personality right is largely based on the notion of human dignity. Which practical difference would it make to conceptualise privacy primarily as a property right? Would this degrade privacy to a mere transaction asset?

2 This chapter has focused on information privacy as a legal problem. How would you estimate the impact of the market on privacy? To what extent is privacy a factor in weakening an internet business model, and to what extent does the market set incentives to guarantee a stronger protection of privacy?

---

[266] See, for example, Supreme Court of California, Briscoe v. Reader's Digest Association, 93 Cal.Rptr. 866, 873 (1971); German Federal Constitutional Court, Case 1 BvR 536/72 [1973] 'Lebach'.

[267] Oster (2015b, pp. 176–177).

[268] See Volokh (2000, p. 1091).

[269] The 'Streisand effect' is named after US entertainer Barbra Streisand, whose attempt to suppress photographs of her residence inadvertently drew further public attention to it.

3 Is the rigid Data Protection Directive the proper framework to address the question raised in *Google Spain*? Is it to be welcomed that the Court decided the case more with an emphasis on human rights rather than the literal meaning of the Directive?

4 Does the *Google Spain* decision open the floodgates for internet censorship and suppress the 'marketplace of ideas'? Is there a 'marketplace' against the power of search engines in the first place?

5 For whom is it to decide whether information is 'relevant'? Can Google – or internet service providers in general – be trusted to make the 'right' decision in each case? And if not, then who else can be trusted? A regulatory agency perhaps? Critically evaluate the following suggestion: The challenge to properly implement the right to be delisted provokes thinking outside the traditional private versus public framework in favour of hybrid adjudicators composed of representatives of the company, the government and civil society.

6 Assume someone had a Facebook account when he was an adolescent. Although he left Facebook five years ago, personal information about him is still circulating on Facebook (digital photos posted on his former 'friends' pages, references to his activities, etc.). Does he have a right against Facebook to have his data erased? Or is it valid to argue that once you have joined Facebook, you have to live with it as part of your digital past?

7 On 12 June 2015, the French data protection agency CNIL requested Google to apply delisting on all the search engine's domain names.[270] However, on 30 July 2015, Google's Global Privacy Counsel published a blog article titled 'Implementing a European, Not Global, Right to be Forgotten'.[271] According to the article, Google delists personal information that can be deemed inadequate, irrelevant, no longer relevant or excessive, and not in the public interest, from all *European* versions of Google Search. However, the right to be delisted 'may now be the law in Europe, it is not the law globally'. Therefore, Google refuses to remove such information from all versions of Google Search around the world, such as Google.com. Does this comply with the wording and spirit of the CJEU's judgment? Did the CJEU have jurisdiction to decide on Google.com or Google.ca (Canada)?[272] How can this question be analysed in the Cyberidealism versus Cyberrealism framework provided in Chapter 6?

---

[270] See www.cnil.fr/linstitution/actualite/article/article/cnil-orders-google-to-apply-delisting-on-all-domain-names-of-the-search-engine; on 21 September 2015, CNIL rejected Google's informal appeal: www.cnil.fr/english/news-and-events/news/article/right-to-delisting-google-informal-appeal-rejected.

[271] Available at http://googlepolicyeurope.blogspot.de/2015/07/implementing-european-not-global-right.html. By contrast, see WP29, Guidelines on the implementation of the Court of Justice of the European Union judgment on Google Spain and Inc. v. Agencia Española de Protección de Datos (AEPD) and Mario Costeja González C-131/12, Adopted on 26 November 2014, p. 9.

[272] Svantesson (2015).

IX Further Reading

- P. Bernal, *Internet Privacy Rights: Rights to Protect Autonomy*, 2014
- L.A. Bygrave, *Data Privacy Law: An International Perspective*, 2014
- P. Carey, *Data Protection: A Practical Guide to UK and EU Law*, 4th edn, 2015
- European Union Agency of Fundamental Rights/Council of Europe, *Handbook on European Data Protection Law*, 2013
- C. Kuner, *European Data Protection Law: Corporate Regulation and Compliance*, 2nd edn, 2007
- C. Kuner, *Transborder Data Flows and Data Privacy Law*, 2013
- V. Mayer-Schönberger, *Delete: The Virtue of Forgetting in the Digital Age*, 2009
- V. Mayer-Schönberger and K. Cukier, *Big Data: A Revolution That Will Transform How We Live, Work and Think*, 2013
- D.J. Solove and P.M. Schwartz, *Information Privacy Law*, 4th edn, 2011
- D.J.B. Svantesson, *Extraterritoriality in Data Privacy Law*, 2013

9

Copyright

CASE EXAMPLES

In 1998, a ten-year old Austrian girl (N.) was abducted and held in a secret cellar by her kidnapper for more than eight years. The abduction and her escape in 2006 were the subject of major media and public attention.

Ms Painer is a freelance photographer, photographing, in particular, children in nurseries and day homes. In the course of that work, she took several photographs of N. before her abduction, designing the background, deciding the position and facial expression, and producing and developing them ('the contested photographs'). Ms Painer has labelled the photographs she produces with her name. That labelling has been done in different ways that have varied over the years, by stickers and/or impressions in decorative portfolios or mounts. Those indications have always stated her name and business address. Ms Painer sold the photographs that she produced, but without conferring on third parties any rights over them and without consenting to their publication. The price she charged for photographs corresponded solely to the price of the prints. After N. was abducted in 1998, the competent security authorities launched a search appeal in which the contested photographs of N. were used.

The defendants are publishing houses producing newspapers and magazines: *Der Standard* is a daily newspaper established and distributed in Austria; *Süddeutsche Zeitung* is a newspaper established in Germany and distributed in Austria and Germany; *Express* is a newspaper established in Germany and distributed in Germany; *Die Welt* is a newspaper established in Germany, distributed in Austria and Germany and running a website on the internet. Following N.'s escape and prior to her first public appearance, the defendants published the contested photographs without indicating the name of the photographer, or indicating a name other than Ms Painer's as the photographer. The defendants claim that they received the contested photographs from a news agency without Ms Painer's name being mentioned or with a name other than Ms Painer's name being indicated as the photographer's. Several of those publications also published a portrait, created by computer from the contested photographs, which, since there was no recent photograph of N. until her first public appearance, represented the supposed image of N. ('the contested photo-fit'). Ms Painer sought an order from a court in Vienna that the defendants immediately cease the reproduction and/or distribution without her consent and without indicating her as author of the contested photographs and the contested photo-fit. She also applied for an order against the defendants for payment of appropriate remuneration.

(CJEU, Case C-145/10 [2011] Painer v. Standard VerlagsGmbH and others)

Infopaq International A/S operates a media monitoring and analysis business that consists primarily of drawing up summaries of selected articles from Danish daily newspapers and other periodicals. The articles are selected on the basis of certain subject criteria agreed with customers and the selection is made by means of a 'data capture process'. The data capture process comprises the following five phases: first, the relevant publications are registered manually by Infopaq employees in an electronic registration database. Second, once the spines are cut off the publications so that all the pages consist of loose sheets, the publications are scanned. When scanning is completed, the file is transferred to an OCR ('Optical Character Recognition') server. Third, the OCR server translates the file into data that can be processed digitally. During that process, the image of each letter is translated into a character code that tells the computer what type of letter it is. These data are saved as a text file that can be understood by any text processing program. The OCR process is completed by deleting the file. Fourth, the text file is processed to find a search word defined beforehand. Each time a match for a search word is found, data is generated, giving the publication, section and page number on which the match was found, together with a value expressed as a percentage between 0 and 100 indicating how far into the text it is to be found, in order to make it easier to read the article. Also, in order to make it easier to find the search word when reading the article, the five words that come before and after the search word are captured ('extract of 11 words'). At the end of the process the text file is deleted. Fifth, at the end of the data capture process, a cover sheet is printed out in respect of all the pages where the relevant search word was found. The following is an example of the text of a cover sheet:

4 November 2005 – *Dagbladet Arbejderen*, page 3:
TDC: 73 per cent 'a forthcoming sale of the telecommunications group TDC which is expected to be bought'.

The summaries are sent to customers by e-mail.

Danske Dagblades Forening (DDF) is a professional association of Danish daily newspaper publishers, which assists its members with copyright issues. DDF became aware that Infopaq was scanning newspaper articles for commercial purposes without authorisation from the relevant rights-holders. Taking the view that such consent was necessary for processing articles using the process in question, DDF complained to Infopaq about this procedure. It argued that the data capture process led to four acts of reproduction of newspaper articles.

(ECJ, Case C-5/08 [2009] Infopaq International A/S v. Danske Dagblades Forening ('Infopaq I') and Case C-302/10 [2012] Infopaq International A/S v. Danske Dagblades Forening ('Infopaq II'))

I Introduction

Copyright laws grant authors of copyrighted works certain exclusive rights to prevent others from performing acts in relation to those works. Therefore, some say that copyright refers to ownership of information. This is not entirely accurate. Copyright law protects information and ideas only insofar as the information or idea is included in a work or in another expression. The distinction between idea and expression is thus an important tenet of copyright law: Copyright protects the original expression of ideas, but not ideas as such. This is expressed in Article 2 of the WIPO Copyright Treaty 1996 and Article 9(2) TRIPS Agreement, which state: 'Copyright protection extends[1] to expressions and not to ideas, procedures, methods of operation or mathematical concepts as such.' It is thus imprecise to say that copyright protects information. Rather, copyright protects information originally expressed in the form of works.[2]

---

[1] Article 9(2) TRIPS Agreement: 'shall extend'.
[2] See Hyde Park Residence v. Yelland [2001] Ch 143 [55] (per Aldous LJ).

This very brief introduction already reveals the relevance of copyright law for the media. On the one hand, people articulating themselves via means of mass communication, such as authors of poems or of novels, might have an interest in having the expression of their ideas protected. If they do not receive such protection, they might be deterred from creating works in the first place, which would entail a loss for cultural and informational pluralism. On the other hand, copyright laws may restrict those who wish to express the same idea or disseminate the original author's expression, and could thus inhibit free expression and the free flow of information. Moreover, the enforcement of national copyright laws may interfere with the free movement of goods and the freedom to provide services in the internal market. Just as with data protection rules, copyright can thus be both a shield and a sword in mass communication. Therefore, copyright laws have to strike a fair balance between rewarding and incentivising those who create intellectual works, on the one side, and the legitimate interests of individuals to republish certain works or the preservation of a public domain where exclusive rights should not operate at all, on the other side. These lines have to a certain extent been approximated and even harmonised on an international and EU level, but they are still largely left to domestic legislation. Copyright is thus an area of media law in which domestic provisions conflict particularly often in transnational disputes.

The internet has significantly increased the importance of copyright law for the media. As noted above, the subject-matter of copyright protection is intangible information expressed in works. In the analogue offline world, this information needs a carrier medium, such as paper or a music record. The carrier medium of information is usually a rivalrous good; that is, the consumption by one consumer prevents simultaneous consumption by other consumers. Only one person (or very few persons) is able to read the same newspaper at the same time, and only one person (or a limited number thereof) can enjoy the same music record at the same time. Each reproduction of the information stored on this carrier medium would lead to a loss of quality: letters on a copied or scanned version of printed paper are less sharp than those on the original, and music rerecorded on a tape does not have the same sound quality as the original record. The quality of the visible or audible information would further decrease with each reproduction, hence there is a strong incentive to buy the original carrier medium in the first place. However, the digitisation of information has led to a separation of content from carrier. For example, users of online peer-to-peer file-sharing services can indefinitely reproduce information, such as music or an audiobook, without any loss of quality. Similar considerations apply to texts or broadcasts published online, which can in principle be accessed simultaneously from everywhere on the globe. In economic terms, formerly rivalrous goods thus became non-rivalrous goods.[3] Information can be reproduced for an unlimited, indefinite number of persons. The consumption of this information by one person does not prevent the consumption of the same information by another person. The incentive

---

[3] Murray (2013, pp. 11–12).

to buy the 'original' has decreased; information piracy has experienced its heyday. Dissemination happens much more quickly and easily. It is no longer restricted by the difficulty or imperfections of copying but instead it is restricted almost uniquely by (copyright) law. Copyright laws thus face significant challenges not only regarding the adjustment of the scope and intensity of their protection with regard to new media, but also with a view to their enforcement.

This chapter will focus on copyright and related rights as the most relevant intellectual property rights for media communication. It also considers trademarks insofar as their protection and enforcement is relevant for mass media communication; the prerequisites for the protection of a trademark, namely registration and grounds for refusal thereof are, however, beyond the scope of this chapter.

Copyright laws confer, at least to a certain extent, a monopoly right to their owner. This may lead to tensions between copyright and competition law, namely in those cases in which invoking an exclusive right is considered an abuse of a dominant position. This will be further dealt with in Chapter 10.

II Rationales for Protecting Copyright

The exact reasons for the protection and the scope of copyright (and intellectual property in general) are controversial.[4] This has led to different approaches among nations in their protection of copyright, and thus to conflicts in cases with a transnational dimension. The following rationales can be identified as the main reasons justifying the protection of copyright:

1 The Lockean Argument from Labour

The argument from natural rights traces back to John Locke and his Second Treatise on Civil Government. He wrote:

> The labour of his body, and the work of his hands, we may say, are properly his. Whatsoever then he removes out of the state that nature hath provided, and left it in, he hath mixed his labour with, and joined to it something that is his own, and thereby makes it his property. It being by him removed from the common state nature hath placed it in, it hath by this labour something annexed to it, that excludes the common right of other men: for this labour being the unquestionable property of the labourer, no man but he can have a right to what that is.[5]

Although Locke's explanations deal with property of tangible assets rather than intellectual property, the gist of his argument can be transferred to intellectual property as well. Intellectual property might not be based on 'the work of [one's] hands', but on

---

[4] From academic literature, see, for example, Hughes (1988–1989); Hettinger (1989); Drahos (1997); Tamura (2009).

[5] Locke (1689, Ch. V, Sec. 27).

the work of one's mind. Therefore, the fruits of this intellectual labour should be the property of the labourer.

2 The Argument from Personality

The argument from personality can be traced back to natural rights philosophers of the enlightenment, particularly Kant, Fichte and Hegel. The personality rationale is similar to the Lockean theory in its approach, but it focuses on the significance of intellectual creation for the author's personality rather than his labour. The main argument against the personality theory is that it is not able to explain all facets of intellectual property protection. While literary and artistic works, such as poems and paintings, may constitute strong expressions of their author's personality, the same does not apply to scientific and technological creations, such as computer programs.

3 The Utilitarian Argument

The Lockean and the personality theory of intellectual property thus focus on the creator and the reward for his intellectual labour, and the significance of his work for his personality, respectively, but less on the beneficial impact of an intellectual creation for society in general. This distinguishes the natural rights-based approaches from the utilitarian justifications of intellectual property rights. The utilitarian justification of intellectual property rights leads back to Jeremy Bentham, the intellectual founder of modern utilitarianism. The idea of utilitarianism in general posits that the best moral action is the one that brings the greatest happiness to the greatest number of people. A utilitarian approach thus explains the existence of intellectual property rights with its beneficial impact on society in general. Intellectual property rights, and copyright in particular, incentivise authors to create literary, artistic or scientific works that contribute to the intellectual welfare of a society in general.

While the idea of intellectual property rights as incentive and encouragement to create intellectual work is intuitively appealing, it is – like all other intellectual property rationales – also subject to criticism. In particular, there is no empirical evidence showing that authors would not create works in the absence of intellectual property rights. On the contrary, literary and artistic works were already created without the protection of intellectual property – although many artists, such as Mozart, would arguably have been better off with their works being protected.

4 Economic Analysis of Intellectual Property

Broadly speaking, the law and economics approach asks for an economically efficient allocation of resources. Applied to intellectual property, an economic analysis would ask not for a maximal but an optimal protection of intellectual property. Optimal protection of intellectual property would have to consider both the necessity to incentivise the creation of intellectual works and the necessity to limit those rights in order to meet the needs of the market. It would then have to bring those conflicting interests to a Pareto-efficient balance.[6]

These theories on intellectual property are not mutually exclusive, but they overlap to a certain extent and complement each other. As a consequence, legislators and courts do not usually expressly avow themselves to one particular rationale, although tendencies can be discerned. The utilitarian justification of intellectual property rights is emphasised in the US in particular. Article I Section 8 of the US Constitution states: 'The Congress shall have Power … To promote the Progress of Science and useful Arts, by securing for limited Times to Authors and Inventors the exclusive Right to their respective Writings and Discoveries'. Similarly Article 7 of the TRIPS Agreement provides that the 'protection and enforcement of intellectual property rights should contribute to the promotion of technological innovation and to the transfer and dissemination of technology, to the mutual advantage of producers and users of technological knowledge and in a manner conducive to social and economic welfare, and to a balance of rights and obligations'. By contrast, the stronger consideration of the personality aspect of intellectual property – more precisely, of copyright – in continental jurisdictions is already discernible from the translations for 'copyright': The French *droit d'auteur*, the Dutch *auteursrecht* and the German *Urheberrecht* all include a reference to the author or creator.

EU intellectual property law takes a balanced approach. By way of example, Recital 9 of the EU Copyright Directive states:

> Any harmonisation of copyright and related rights must take as a basis a high level of protection, since such rights are crucial to intellectual creation. Their protection helps to ensure the maintenance and development of creativity in the interests of authors, performers, producers, consumers, culture, industry and the public at large. Intellectual property has therefore been recognised as an integral part of property.

By referring to both the interest of authors and the public at large, the Directive thus acknowledges both the natural rights-based and the utilitarian conception of intellectual property.

Arguably the major impact of the personality theory is the acceptance of 'moral rights' deriving from intellectual property. As will be explained in more detail below, moral rights protect the personality rights of the author rather than his economic interests. Moral rights are particularly widespread in civil law jurisdictions and included in international treaties such as the Berne Convention for the Protection of Literary and Artistic Works, the WIPO Copyright Treaty and the WIPO Performances and Phonograms Treaty. However, they are barely accepted in common law jurisdictions and are also excluded from the scope of the EU Copyright Directive.[7] The vindication

---

[6] Compare Landes and Posner (2003).
[7] Recital 19 Copyright Directive.

of moral rights may thus be subject to conflicting legal provisions in conflicts with a transnational dimension.

III The International Copyright Framework

With the increase of international trade towards the end of the nineteenth century, national governments realised the transnational dimension of copyright protection (and the protection of intellectual property in general), the need to approximate or even to harmonise rules and to guarantee their enforcement across national borderlines.

1 WIPO

The first multilateral treaties dealing with the protection of intellectual property were the Paris Convention for the Protection of Industrial Property, signed in 1883,[8] and the Berne Convention for the Protection of Literary and Artistic Works, concluded in 1886.[9] These Conventions have been amended over the course of time, but they are still in force today and as set out in the global framework for the protection of copyright (Berne Convention) and patents, trademarks and designs (Paris Convention), respectively.

The Madrid Agreement of 1891 Concerning the International Registration of Marks established a system for the international protection of trademarks. Further agreements that are relevant for this chapter are the Rome Convention for the Protection of Performers, Producers of Phonograms and Broadcasting Organisations,[10] the Brussels Convention Relating to the Distribution of Programme-Carrying Signals Transmitted by Satellite,[11] the WIPO Copyright Treaty (WCT)[12] and the WIPO Performances and Phonograms Treaty (WPPT).[13]

The first international organisation administering intellectual property protection was established in 1893: the United International Bureaux for the Protection of

---

[8] Paris Convention for the Protection of Industrial Property of 20 March 1883, as revised at Brussels on 14 December 1900, at Washington on 2 June 1911, at The Hague on 6 November 1925, at London on 2 June 1934, at Lisbon on 31 October 1958 and at Stockholm on 14 July 1967, and as amended on 28 September 1979.

[9] Berne Convention for the Protection of Literary and Artistic Works of 9 September 1886, completed at Paris on 4 May 1896, revised at Berlin on 13 November 1908, completed at Berne on 20 March 1914, revised at Rome on 2 June 1928, at Brussels on 26 June 1948, at Stockholm on 14 July 1967 and at Paris on 24 July 1971, and amended on 28 September 1979.

[10] Rome Convention: International Convention for the Protection of Performers, Producers of Phonograms and Broadcasting Organisations, done at Rome on 26 October 1961.

[11] Convention Relating to the Distribution of Programme-Carrying Signals Transmitted by Satellite, done at Brussels on 21 May 1974.

[12] WIPO Copyright Treaty (WCT), adopted in Geneva on 20 December 1996.

[13] WIPO Performances and Phonograms Treaty (WPPT), adopted in Geneva on 20 December 1996.

Intellectual Property (*Bureaux Internationaux Réunis pour la Protection de la Propriété Intellectuelle*, BIRPI) was set up to administer the Berne Convention and the Paris Convention. The BIRPI was the predecessor of the World Intellectual Property Organization (WIPO), a specialised agency of the United Nations based in Geneva (Switzerland), created in 1967. According to Article 3 of the WIPO Convention,[14] the objectives of WIPO are:

(i) to promote the protection of intellectual property throughout the world through cooperation among States and, where appropriate, in collaboration with any other international organization,

(ii) to ensure administrative cooperation among the Unions.

a The Berne Convention and the Copyright Treaty

The Berne Convention provides for rights of authors in their literary and artistic works. These works shall enjoy protection in all State Parties to the Berne Convention, which constitute the 'Union for the protection of the rights of authors in their literary and artistic works', or the Berne Union. As of September 2015, the Berne Convention had 168 Contracting Parties, or Berne Union States. Berne Union States may exclude works that have not been fixed in some material form (Article 2(2) Berne Convention) and political speeches, speeches delivered in the course of legal proceedings (Article 2*bis*(1)) from the protection provided by the Convention. Moreover, the Convention States themselves may determine the conditions under which lectures, addresses and other works of the same nature that are delivered in public may be reproduced by the press, broadcast, communicated to the public by wire and made the subject of public communication, and when such use is justified by the informatory purpose (Article 2*bis*(2)). The Berne Convention shall not apply to news of the day or to miscellaneous facts having the character of mere items of press information (Article 2(8) Berne Convention).

Article 5 stipulates the main principles of protection granted by the Berne Convention. Accordingly, authors shall enjoy, in respect of works for which they are protected under the Berne Convention, in countries of the Berne Union other than their country of origin:

- the rights that their respective laws grant to their nationals (principle of national treatment); and
- the rights granted by the Berne Convention (principle of minimum rights).
- Moreover, the 'enjoyment and the exercise of these rights shall not be subject to any formality'.
- Finally, the extent of protection is governed exclusively by the laws of the country where protection is claimed (*lex loci protectionis* principle).

---

[14] Convention Establishing the World Intellectual Property Organization, signed at Stockholm on 14 July 1967 and as amended on 28 September 1979.

The principle of national treatment implies that any Berne Union state has to provide the same rights for authors of other Union States as it confers on nationals from its own country. As a consequence, the host Union State may even have to confer rights on the author that are only available in this state, but not in the country of origin.[15] There are three exceptions to the principle of national treatment: protection of works of applied art and industrial designs and models (Article 2(7)); the duration of protection (Article 7(8)); and the *droit de suite*, a right to an interest in any sale of a work of arts and manuscripts subsequent to the first transfer by the author of the work (Article 14*ter*(2)).

The principle of minimum rights is self-explanatory: Berne Union States may go beyond (Article 19 Berne Convention), but they must not go below the protection of authors' rights as those stipulated in the Convention. However, note that the principle of minimum rights only applies to authors of all Union States except for the host country itself. As a consequence, host countries might in theory even confer the rights of the Berne Convention to authors from other countries, but bar their own nationals from enjoying these rights in their own country of origin – a scenario that hardly occurs in practice. Therefore, within the framework of those rights, a truly transnational copyright order does indeed exist.

The absence of any formality distinguishes copyright protection from rights that do require such registration, such as trademarks and patents. The *lex loci protectionis* principle has an important impact on transnational conflicts involving alleged copyright violations, as will be explained further below.

The Berne Convention is administered by the WIPO. Moreover, it provides an optional dispute settlement mechanism in Article 33, under which disputes can be brought to the International Court of Justice (ICJ). However, this mechanism has, thus far, not been used. The practically more important dispute settlement mechanism has been brought about by the incorporation of the Berne Convention in the WTO TRIPS (see *infra*).

The Diplomatic Conference held under the auspices of the WIPO in December 1996 led to the adoption of the WIPO Copyright Treaty, together with the WIPO Performances and Phonograms Treaty. Those treaties updated the international protection for copyright and related rights significantly, particularly with a view to new technological developments.

The Copyright Treaty is a special agreement within the meaning of Article 20 of the Berne Convention. This provision reserves the right of Berne Union states to enter into special agreements among themselves, insofar as such agreements grant authors more extensive rights than those granted by the Berne Convention, or contain other provisions not contrary to this Convention. As of September 2015, 93 states participate in the Copyright Treaty. In terms of the scope of copyright protection, the Copyright Treaty includes provisions on the protection of computer programs (Article 4) and

---

[15] A definition of 'country of origin' can be found in Article 5(4) Berne Convention.

databases (Article 5). Article 11 of the WIPO Copyright Treaty aims at preventing the circumvention of effective technological measures that are used by authors that restrict acts infringing their copyright. Article 12 imposes obligations concerning rights management information. Within the EU, these provisions are implemented in Articles 6 and 7 of the Copyright Directive.

b The Rome Convention and the Performances and Phonograms Treaty

The International Convention for the Protection of Performers, Producers of Phonograms and Broadcasting Organisations (Rome Convention) from 1961 sought to fill a gap that has been left open by the Berne Convention, namely the protection of producers who disseminated works via more recent technologies: sound recordings ('phonograms' in intellectual property parlance) and, with particular relevance for this book, broadcasting. Neither the producers of sound recordings nor broadcasters nor live performances disseminated via broadcasting were protected at an international level until 1961, because they were not considered 'authors of literary and artistic works' within the meaning of the Berne Convention. Therefore, it has been the purpose of the Rome Convention to protect those 'related rights' and their owners.

Like the Berne Convention, Article 30 of the Rome Convention provides a settlement mechanism at the ICJ, which has not been used yet. Moreover, similar to the Berne Convention, the principles of national treatment and minimum protection lie at the heart of the Rome Convention. However, in contrast to the Berne Convention, the Rome Convention does not include a provision on moral rights.

The rights of performers – mainly film actors – and their relationship to broadcasting rights have been further defined in the Beijing Treaty on Audiovisual Performances, concluded in 2012. In order to enter into force, 30 states need to ratify the treaty. As of September 2015, only nine states have ratified – or acceded to – the Treaty.

The WIPO Performances and Phonograms Treaty complements the Rome Convention for the Protection of Performers, Producers of Phonograms and Broadcasting Organisations with a view to the rights of performers (actors, singers, musicians, etc.) and producers of phonograms, particularly in the digital environment.

2 Article 27(2) UDHR

While the UN framework thus has a wide range of copyright-related provisions in store, UN human rights law is relatively scarce as far as intellectual property is concerned. The ICCPR includes neither a provision on intellectual property nor on property in general under which intellectual property could be subsumed (unlike Article 1 of the First Protocol in the ECHR, which we will come back to later). However, Article 27(2) of the non-binding UDHR provides: 'Everyone has the right to the protection of the moral and material interests resulting from any scientific, literary or artistic production of which he is the author.' This provision might thus serve at least as a starting point for the development of intellectual property as a human right in global law.

3 WTO

Although the WIPO has contributed significantly to approximation and harmonisation of intellectual property protection, it lacks enforcement mechanisms in cases of violations of its rules. Therefore, especially upon request by developed countries (that is, net exporters of intellectual property), the protection of intellectual property had also been brought under the jurisdiction of the WTO. The Agreement on Trade-Related Aspects of Intellectual Property Rights (TRIPS) was concluded in the Uruguay Round of the negotiations that resulted in the signature in April 1994 of the WTO Agreements in Marrakesh. The aim of the TRIPS Agreement is to integrate the international system of intellectual property protection into the framework of trade regulation administered by the WTO. The agreement covers four broad issues:

- The standards of minimum protection of intellectual property rights by the Paris and the Berne Convention (with the exception of the protection of moral rights), and other international intellectual property provisions.
- The application of the basic principles of WTO system (national treatment, Article 3, and most-favoured-nation treatment, Article 4).
- The enforcement of those rights in the Member States' territories (Part III of the TRIPS).
- Dispute settlement procedures between members of the WTO (Article 64 TRIPS). As of September 2015, 34 requests for consultation have been brought with regard to the TRIPS Agreement have been submitted to the WTO.[16]

The TRIPS Agreement has had a harmonising effect on intellectual property law, but it is far from being a fully harmonised transnational intellectual property order.[17] However, since the TRIPS Agreement also incorporates the Berne Convention – with the exception of moral rights – it provides a gateway for the indirect enforcement of the Berne Convention via the WTO's dispute settlement mechanism.

The TRIPS Agreement was approved on behalf of the European Community by Council Decision 94/800/EC concerning the conclusion on behalf of the European Community, as regards matters within its competence, of the agreements reached in the Uruguay Round multilateral negotiations (1986–1994).[18]

4 The Anti-Counterfeiting Trade Agreement (ACTA)

Article 20 of the Berne Convention allows Berne Union States to enter into special agreements granting authors more extensive rights than those granted by the Berne Convention. One of the most controversial of such multilateral agreements has been the Anti-Counterfeiting Trade Agreement (ACTA), a treaty for the purpose of

---

[16] www.wto.org/english/tratop_e/dispu_e/dispu_agreements_index_e.htm?id=A26#.
[17] See, from academic literature, Blakeney (1996); Correa (2007); Kur and Levin (2011).
[18] OJ 1994 L 336/1.

establishing international standards for intellectual property rights enforcement. The agreement aims to establish an international legal framework for targeting counterfeit goods, generic medicines and copyright infringement in the digital environment. The provisions of the Agreement would be enforced by criminal penalties. The Agreement had been signed by eight countries in October 2011,[19] and in 2012 the EU and 22 EU Member States signed as well. In order to enter into force, six countries would have to ratify the agreement. Thus far, there has only been one ratification (by Japan). The ACTA Agreement has been subject to heavy criticism, especially because of the secret nature of its negotiations (documents were leaked during the negotiation process on WikiLeaks), the alleged influence of the entertainment industry and its presumed threat to civil liberties, such as freedom of expression and privacy. On 4 July 2012, the European Parliament refused to give its consent to the Agreement, and it will thus not enter into force across the EU.[20]

5 Council of Europe

Council of Europe material on copyright, and on intellectual property in general, is relatively scant. The ECHR does not contain a provision protecting intellectual property as such. Nevertheless, following several decisions of the European Commission of Human Rights on cases involving intellectual property rights,[21] in its judgment in *Anheuser-Busch Inc.* v. *Portugal*, the Strasbourg Court found that Article 1 of the First Protocol to the ECHR, which protects 'the peaceful enjoyment of [one's] possessions', applies to intellectual property.[22] As regards moral rights, in *SC Editura Orizonturi SRL* v. *Romania*, the Court found that the right to publish the translation of a novel falls within the scope of Article 1 of the First Protocol.[23]

The scope of protection of intellectual property is to a large extent dependent on the protection under domestic law, as it is the domestic law that decides on the existence and the lawful or unlawful use of that right in the first place. Where domestic law grants intellectual property protection, unlawful uses of protected works do, at the same time, constitute interferences with Article 1 First Protocol.[24] Yet, the ECtHR also observed that intellectual property rights are not absolute. As the Strasbourg Court highlighted in two more recent decisions involving alleged infringements of copyright, *Ashby Donald and others* v. *France* and *Neij and Sunde Kolmisoppi*

---

[19] Australia, Canada, Japan, Morocco, New Zealand, Singapore, South Korea and the United States.

[20] For further reading on ACTA, see Geiger (2012); McManis (2009–2010); Weatherall (2011).

[21] EComHR, Smith Kline and French Laboratories Ltd v. the Netherlands [1990] App. no. 12633/87 (patents); Aral, Tekin and Aral v. Turkey [1998] App. no. 24563/94 (copyright); Lenzing AG v. Germany [1998] App. no. 39025/97 (patents).

[22] ECtHR, Anheuser-Busch Inc. v. Portugal [2007] App. no. 73049/01 [72]; see also Melnychuk v. Ukraine [2005] App. no. 28743/03, p. 7; Dima v. Romania [2005] App. no. 58472/00, p. 20; Balan v. Moldova [2008] App. no. 19247/03 [34]. From academic literature, see Helfer (2008).

[23] ECtHR, SC Editura Orizonturi SRL v. Romania [2008] App. no. 15872/03 [70].

[24] See, for example, ECtHR, Balan v. Moldova [2008] App. no. 19247/03 [37–40].

v. *Sweden*, provisions restricting the use of protected material and their enforcement may constitute an interference with the user's right of freedom of expression and must thus be in accordance with the conditions for restrictions of these rights.[25] Although the Court eventually decided against the applicants who had violated copyright provisions – fashion photographers in the case of *Ashby Donald* and the providers of the file-sharing service 'The Pirate Bay' in *Neij and Sunde Kolmisoppi* – the Court also indicated that restrictions based on intellectual property rights may not be justified if the use of the protected information contributes to a debate of general concern.[26]

The Convention on Cybercrime codifies offences to infringements of copyright and related rights in its Article 10. Accordingly, each State Party shall adopt such legislative and other measures as may be necessary to establish criminal offences under its domestic law for the infringement of copyright and related rights, as defined under the law of that party, pursuant to its international obligations where such acts are committed wilfully, on a commercial scale and by means of a computer system. However, as the EU legal framework, the Cybercrime Convention excludes moral rights from its scope.

In September 2001, the Committee of Ministers adopted a Recommendation on measures to protect copyright and neighbouring rights and combat piracy, especially in the digital environment.[27]

6 European Union

Similar to other areas of media law, the EU approaches copyright law from two perspectives: on the one hand, the enforcement of such exclusive rights may interfere with the free movement provisions constituting the internal market. On the other hand, the EU also considers the human rights dimension of copyright.[28] Intellectual property itself is protected as a fundamental right under Article 17(2) EUChFR, but the vindication of such rights may at the same time interfere with the freedom of expression of others. This is most significantly underlined by the press exception to the exclusive reproduction and communication rights as stipulated in Article 5(3) (c) Copyright Directive. In addition to competition law, which will be looked at in Chapter 10, three further factors have shaped EU copyright law: the free movement provisions, the approximation and harmonisation of domestic laws by secondary EU law and fundamental rights.

---

[25] ECtHR, Ashby Donald and others v. France [2013] App. no. 36769/08 [34]; Neij and Sunde Kolmisoppi v. Sweden [2013] App. no. 40397/12.

[26] See, *mutatis mutandis*, ECtHR, Ashby Donald and others v. France [2013] App. no. 36769/08; Neij and Sunde Kolmisoppi v. Sweden [2013] App. no. 40397/12. See also, from a US perspective, Volokh (2003a).

[27] Recommendation Rec(2001)7 on measures to protect copyright and neighbouring rights and combat piracy, especially in the digital environment (5 September 2001).

[28] See Griffiths (2013).

a Copyright and the Free Movement Provisions

Copyright is in principle tied to a particular territory; that is, within the EU to each Member State individually. Where domestic copyright law allows the exercise of an owner's exclusive rights, this might constitute an interference with the free movement of goods (where tangible carriers of protected works are concerned) or the freedom to provide services (where information carried by signals is concerned). This was first decided, with regard to the free movement of goods, in the case of *Deutsche Grammophon* v. *Metro*.[29] Deutsche Grammophon is a company that produces gramophone records, which it distributes directly or through its subsidiaries established in several (now) EU and EFTA states. A subsidiary of Deutsche Grammophon marketed its sound records in France. The retail company Metro sought to import records that it bought in France into Germany. Deutsche Grammophon invoked its copyright protection under German law and objected to the sale of its records by Metro. Upon reference for a preliminary ruling, the ECJ had to provide guidance on the interpretation of (now) Article 36 TFEU, which states:

> The provisions of Articles 34 and 35 [TFEU] shall not preclude prohibitions or restrictions on imports, exports or goods in transit justified on grounds of … the protection of industrial and commercial property. Such prohibitions or restrictions shall not, however, constitute a means of arbitrary discrimination or a disguised restriction on trade between Member States.

By doing so, the Court confirmed that the exercise of copyright excluding others from importing copyright-protected material created an impediment to the free movement of goods within the meaning of (now) Article 34 TFEU. The Court observed that (now) Article 36 TFEU only admits derogations from the free movement of goods 'to the extent to which they are justified for the purpose of safeguarding rights which constitute the specific subject-matter of [industrial and commercial] property'.[30] The Court continued:

> If a right related to copyright is relied upon to prevent the marketing in a Member State of products distributed by the holder of the right or with his consent on the territory of another Member State on the sole ground that such distribution did not take place on the national territory, such a prohibition, which would legitimize the isolation of national markets, would be repugnant to the essential purpose of the Treaty, which is to unite national markets into a single market. That purpose could not be attained if, under the various legal systems of the Member States, nationals of those States were able to partition the market and bring about arbitrary discrimination or disguised restrictions on trade between Member States.[31]

---

[29] ECJ, Case 78/70 [1971] Deutsche Grammophon v. Metro.
[30] ECJ, Case 78/70 [1971] Deutsche Grammophon v. Metro [11].
[31] ECJ, Case 78/70 [1971] Deutsche Grammophon v. Metro [12].

As a result, the Court held that it would be incompatible with the internal market if an owner of an industrial and commercial property right – which includes different forms of intellectual property rights[32] – 'to exercise the exclusive right to distribute the protected articles, conferred upon him by the legislation of a Member State, in such a way as to prohibit the sale in that State of products placed on the market by him or with his consent in another Member State solely because such distribution did not occur within the territory of the first Member State.'[33] The ECJ thus established the so-called exhaustion doctrine. The exhaustion doctrine implies that the first sale in the EU of a product by the rights-holder or with his consent exhausts the right to control resale of that product in the EU. The exhaustion doctrine has been confirmed in later decisions of the Court of Justice,[34] and it is now part of EU secondary copyright law with regard to the distribution of work incorporated in a tangible article (Article 4(2) Copyright Directive).[35] Thus conceptualised, the exhaustion right is limited to work incorporated in tangible carriers and to the first sale of products within the EU. On a side note, the Court of Justice extended the exhaustion doctrine to certain downloaded contents not distributed on physical carriers, notably computer programs.[36] This is controversial, as the exhaustion doctrine was thought to apply only to the distribution right (which in turn applies only to works fixed on physical carriers) and not to the reproduction right. However, the electronic copies of computer programs are reproduced and not distributed.

In turn, copyright does not exhaust, first, in respect of the original or of copies thereof sold by the rights-holder or with his consent outside the EU or the EEA.[37] To apply an exhaustion doctrine to that effect is left to the Member States. The issue of exhaustion of intellectual property rights has not been addressed by the TRIPS Agreement either, see Article 6 thereof.

Second, the question of exhaustion does not arise in the case of intangible carriers; that is, in the case of services and online services in particular.[38] In the case of *Coditel* v. *Ciné Vog Films I*, a cinematographic film distribution company (Ciné Vog) had acquired the exclusive right to show a particular film in Belgium in all its versions, including in the form of cinema performances and television broadcasts. A German television broadcasting station had acquired the right to broadcast the film on television in Germany. The Belgian cable television company Coditel picked up directly on their aerial at their reception sites in Belgium that film broadcast in Germany and distributed it by cable to their subscribers. Ciné Vog claimed an infringement of its copyright. The Court of Justice distinguished cinematographic films made available

---

[32] See, for example, ECJ, Case 78/70 [1971] Deutsche Grammophon v. Metro: copyright; Case 15/74 [1974] Centrafarm v. Sterling Drug: patents.

[33] ECJ, Case 78/70 [1971] Deutsche Grammophon v. Metro [13].

[34] See, for example, ECJ, Case 15/74 [1974] Centrafarm v. Sterling Drug.

[35] The same applies under Article 7(1) Trade Mark Directive.

[36] CJEU, Case C-128/11 [2012] UsedSoft GmbH v. Oracle International Corp.

[37] See Recital 28 Copyright Directive.

[38] See Recital 29 and Article 3(3) Copyright Directive.

to the public by performances that may be infinitely repeated from works that are inseparable from the material form of their carrier, as in the case of books or records.[39] By doing so, the Court differentiated between the free movement of goods, for which the exhaustion doctrine applied, and the freedom to provide services, for which this doctrine did not apply. With a view to the exhibition of films, the Court held that the owner of the copyright and his assigns 'have a legitimate interest in calculating the fees due in respect of the authorization to exhibit the film on the basis of the actual or probable number of performances and in authorizing a television broadcast of the film only after it has been exhibited in cinemas for a certain period of time'.[40] As a result, restrictions of the freedom to provide services may be justified for the protection of intellectual property rights, unless this constitutes an arbitrary discrimination or a disguised restriction on trade between Member States.[41]

b Approximation and Harmonisation

There is no unitary EU legislation on copyright yet. Copyright legislation is thus left to the Member States, but within the boundaries provided by harmonising EU legislation. The EU has adopted several directives aiming at harmonising or at least approximating the laws of the Member States on intellectual property. As far as copyright is concerned, these pieces of legislation can be systemised as follows:

- directives focusing on a particular subject matter, namely software[42] and databases;[43]
- directives dealing with certain rights following from copyright: the transmission of broadcasts across frontiers by satellite and cable,[44] the rental and lending[45] and the resale[46] of copyright-protected works;
- a directive dealing with one single, but important aspect of copyright protection, namely the term of protection;[47] and

---

[39] ECJ, Case 62/79 [1980] Coditel and others v. Ciné Vog Films and others ('Coditel I') [12].

[40] ECJ, Case 62/79 [1980] Coditel and others v. Ciné Vog Films and others ('Coditel I') [13].

[41] ECJ, Case 62/79 [1980] Coditel and others v. Ciné Vog Films and others ('Coditel I') [15]; reiterated in, for example, CJEU, Joined Cases C-403/08 and C-429/08 [2011] Football Association Premier League Ltd and others v. Karen Murphy and others [94].

[42] Directive 2009/24/EC of the European Parliament and of the Council of 23 April 2009 on the legal protection of computer programs (Codified version), OJ L 111/16.

[43] Directive 96/9/EC of the European Parliament and of the Council of 11 March 1996 on the legal protection of databases, OJ L 77/20.

[44] Council Directive 93/83/EEC of 27 September 1993 on the coordination of certain rules concerning copyright and rights related to copyright applicable to satellite broadcasting and cable retransmission, OJ L 248/15.

[45] Directive 2006/115/EC of the European Parliament and of the Council of 12 December 2006 on rental right and lending right and on certain rights related to copyright in the field of intellectual property (codified version) OJ L 376/28.

[46] Directive 2001/84/EC of the European Parliament and of the Council of 27 September 2001 on the resale right for the benefit of the author of an original work of art, L 272/32; see COM, Report on the Implementation and Effect of the Resale Right Directive (2001/84/EC), COM(2011) 878 final.

[47] Directive 2006/116/EC of the European Parliament and of the Council of 12 December 2006 on the term of protection of copyright and certain related rights (codified version), OJ L 372/12, as amended by

- the comprehensive Copyright Directive,[48] which concerns most legal aspects of copyright in the framework of the internal market which are not covered by the other directives.

Moral rights remain outside the scope of these directives.[49]

Article 1(2) Copyright Directive sets out the relationship between the different directives in the EU copyright framework. Accordingly, the Copyright Directive 'shall leave intact and shall in no way affect existing [EU] provisions relating to:

(a)   the legal protection of computer programs;
(b)   rental right, lending right and certain rights related to copyright in the field of intellectual property;
(c)   copyright and related rights applicable to broadcasting of programmes by satellite and cable retransmission;
(d)   the term of protection of copyright and certain related rights;
(e)   the legal protection of databases.'

The directives covering these areas, such as the Rental Rights Directive and the Satellite and Cable Directive are therefore *leges speciales* to the Copyright Directive, providing their own, self-standing rights and exceptions with a view to copyright and related rights.[50] Nevertheless, as Recital 20 of the Copyright Directive expresses, the Copyright Directive 'is based on principles and rules already laid down in the Directives currently in force in this area', such as the Satellite and Cable Directive and the Rental Rights Directive, 'and it develops those principles and rules and places them in the context of the information society'. Moreover, the requirements of unity and coherence of the EU legal order demand that the terms and concepts used by the directives 'must have the same meaning, unless the European Union legislature has, in a specific legislative context, expressed a different intention'.[51]

aa The Rental Rights Directive   Directive 2006/115/EC on rental rights and lending rights and on certain rights related to copyright in the field of intellectual property codified and replaced Directive 92/100/EEC. The Rental Rights Directive covers, first, exclusive rights to authorise or prohibit the rental and lending of both works subject to copyright and to related rights (Articles 1–6). Member States can derogate from the exclusive public lending right, provided that authors at least obtain remuneration

---

Directive 2011/77/EU of the European Parliament and of the Council of 27 September 2011 amending Directive 2006/116/EC on the term of protection of copyright and certain related rights, OJ L 265/1.

[48]   Directive 2001/29/EC of the European Parliament and of the Council of 22 May 2001 on the harmonisation of certain aspects of copyright and related rights in the information society, OJ L 167/10.

[49]   Recital 19 Copyright Directive.

[50]   See Aplin (2005, p. 102); Woods (2012, p. 197).

[51]   CJEU, Joined Cases C-403/08 and C-429/08 [2011] Football Association Premier League Ltd and others v. Karen Murphy and others [188]. See also CJEU, Joined Cases C-431/09 and C-432/09 [2011] Airfield NV and Canal Digitaal BV [44].

for such lending (Article 6). Second, it provides for a harmonisation of certain related rights and their limitations: the right of fixation, broadcasting and communication to the public, and distribution (Articles 7–10). The distribution right is limited by the principle of Union-wide exhaustion (Article 9(2)). In turn, Member States are prevented from applying international exhaustion. In conformity with Article 1(5) Satellite and Cable Directive, Article 2(2) of the Rental Rights Directive provides that the principal director of a cinematographic or audiovisual work shall be considered as its author or one of its authors.

bb The Satellite and Cable Directive   The Television Without Frontiers Directive, now Audiovisual Media Services Directive, has contributed to the establishment of a common market for broadcasting by harmonising certain rules on, for example, advertising and sponsorship, the protection of minors and the right of reply. Yet the Directive is almost silent on copyright and related rights. It merely obliges the Member States in its Article 8 to ensure that media service providers under their jurisdiction do not transmit cinematographic works outside periods agreed with the rights-holders. However, until the early 1990s, long before the Copyright Directive was established, the establishment of a common market with a view to cross-border satellite broadcasting and the cable retransmission of programmes from other Member States was obstructed by national rules of copyright and by legal uncertainty.[52] Moreover, a distinction was still drawn for copyright purposes between communication to the public by direct satellite and communication by communications satellite.[53] But as a result of technological development of satellites and of aerials for use by the general public, it had become possible to broadcast direct to the public on non-public frequency bands. Even though the latter were not, under the telecommunications legislation, formally reserved for communication to the public, programme-carrying signals could already *de facto* be received by the public direct from satellites using those frequency bands.[54] As a consequence, there was no longer any justification for this differing legal treatment of these two types of satellite.[55] In order to address these issues, in 1993 the Council adopted the Satellite and Cable Directive.

The Satellite and Cable Directive has brought several innovations. It does not harmonise copyright on a substantive level, but it has introduced a country-of-origin principle for the copyright protection of works disseminated via satellite broadcasts (Article 1(2)(b)). Then, it has harmonised the treatment of the transmission of programmes by communications satellites among the Member States with a view to copyright. The relevant test established by the Directive is whether works and other protected subject matter are 'communicated to the public' (Recital 13 and Article 2;

---

[52] Recital 5 Satellite and Cable Directive.
[53] Compare the case example of Chapter 7.
[54] See ECJ, Case C-192/04 [2005] Lagardère v. SPRE and GVL [29].
[55] Recital 6 Satellite and Cable Directive.

see *infra*). Moreover, the Directive provides a definition on 'communication to the public by satellite' in Articles 1(1) and (2)(a) applicable to frequency bands reserved for both the broadcast of signals for reception by the public and closed, point-to-point communication. Yet Article 1(1) adds that in the latter case of the non-public frequency bands, the circumstances in which individual reception of the signals takes place must be comparable to those that apply in the case of public frequency bands.[56]

Finally, the Directive harmonises the rules on the acquisition of rights on a contractual basis, including mediation (Article 11) and obligations that prevent rightsholders to refuse without valid reason to negotiate on the acquisition of the rights necessary for cable distribution or allowing such negotiations to fail (Article 12).

In cases in which the Satellite and Cable Directive does not apply, the Copyright Directive as the *lex generalis* becomes applicable. The Satellite and Cable Directive provides for minimal harmonisation in the case of communication to the public *by satellite or cable retransmission* of programmes from other Member States. In turn, it does not apply to terrestrial broadcasting or broadcasting via the internet, which is therefore subject to the Copyright Directive.[57] Moreover, the Satellite and Cable Directive applies to *communication to the public* by satellite or cable retransmission, but it does not cover acts of reproduction, such as those performed by a television set to which a satellite or terrestrial television signal is sent or within the memory of a satellite decoder.[58] These acts fall under by the Copyright Directive.

cc The Copyright Directive   Directive 2001/29/EC on the harmonisation of certain aspects of copyright and related rights in the information society is a subsidiary piece of EU legislation on the protection of copyright. Adopted in 2001, it aims at reflecting technological developments and at transposing into EU law the main international obligations arising from the 1996 WIPO Treaties: the Copyright Treaty and the Performances and Phonograms Treaty.[59] The commonly used abbreviations of the Directive vary: Scholars and practitioners mostly refer to the 'InfoSoc' Directive, thus highlighting the aim of the Directive to address the challenges of the information society. Nevertheless, the term 'Copyright Directive' is preferred here: to be sure, the challenges of the information society might have set the incentive to adopt the Directive, but they do not confine the scope of its application. Instead, the Directive represents the first comprehensive *lex generalis* on EU copyright law, as it is applicable to all copyright-related questions that are not regulated in another directive. Its field of application includes not only modern forms of reproduction, such as 'caching', but also (almost) old-fashioned photocopying.

---

[56] On the interpretation of this provision, see ECJ, Case C-192/04 [2005] Lagardère v. SPRE and GVL.

[57] See CJEU, Joined Cases C-431/09 and C-432/09 [2011] Airfield NV and Canal Digitaal BV [44–47]; Woods (2012, p. 197).

[58] ECJ, Case C-293/98 [2000] Entidad de Gestión de Derechos de los Productores Audiovisuales (Egeda) v. Hostelería Asturiana SA (Hoasa) [25–26]; Case C-306/05 [2006] Sociedad General de Autores y Editores de España (SGAE) v. Rafael Hoteles SA [31]; CJEU, Joined Cases C-403/08 and C-429/08 [2011] Football Association Premier League Ltd and others v. Karen Murphy and others [209].

[59] Recitals 5 and 15 Copyright Directive.

dd Current Developments   As part of its Digital Single Market Strategy, the European Commission has proposed a modernised copyright framework.[60] This should 'further reduce national discrepancies, encourage wider access, promote cultural diversity and ensure that everyone respects the rules of the game'.[61] In June 2015, the European Parliament already adopted a non-binding report, named 'Reda report' after its rapporteur, suggesting guidelines on the Commission proposal.[62] The most controversial issues of the new legislation can be expected to include portability and geo-blocking, further harmonisation of limitations and exceptions, liability of internet intermediaries, an extension of the terms of protection and the copyright protection of works exhibited in the public domain.

IV Transnational Copyright Law

Notwithstanding the various international treaties and increasing harmonisation at the EU level, copyright law is, to a large extent, still shaped by national laws. This makes a transnational perspective on copyright law difficult. Nevertheless, since conflicts on copyright protection, to an increasing extent, have a transnational dimension, a transnational and comparative perspective on copyright law is indispensable. The international framework on copyright has to a certain extent harmonised singular aspects of copyright protection, such as the notion of 'work', the beneficiaries of copyright protection and the rights of copyright owners. Other aspects of copyright law are still left to national law. The requirements for subsistence of a copyright or the notion of an infringement of copyright can only be understood against the background of national laws. This section will therefore take a comparative perspective where this is necessary to understand certain concepts.

The EU law on copyright will also be considered in this section and not separately, because international and EU copyright law are closely interconnected. The EU is not a party to the Berne Convention. However, it has approved the WIPO Copyright Treaty and the TRIPS Agreement.[63] Under Article 1(4) of the Copyright Treaty and Article 9 of the TRIPS Agreement, the Contracting Parties are to comply with Articles 1 to 21 of the Berne Convention. Consequently, the EU is also obliged to

---

[60] On the Digital Single Market Strategy, see COM, Communication to the European Parliament, The Council, the Economic and Social Committee and the Committee of the Regions of 6 May 2015, COM(2015) 192 final – A Digital Single Market Strategy for Europe.

[61] See https://ec.europa.eu/digital-agenda/en/copyright.

[62] European Parliament resolution of 9 July 2015 on the implementation of Directive 2001/29/EC of the European Parliament and of the Council of 22 May 2001 on the harmonisation of certain aspects of copyright and related rights in the information society (2014/2256(INI)).

[63] Council Decision 94/800/EC of 22 December 1994 concerning the conclusion on behalf of the European Community, as regards matters within its competence, of the agreements reached in the Uruguay Round multilateral negotiations (1986–1994), OJ L 336/1.

implement those provisions.[64] Moreover, the application of the EU copyright framework should be exercised in accordance with international obligations.[65]

1 Terminology

For a better understanding of the transnational copyright framework, we need to clarify certain aspects of copyright terminology. The Convention of 14 July 1967 creating the World Intellectual Property Organisation enumerates the rights covered by the notion of *intellectual property*: literary and artistic works, performances, inventions, scientific discoveries, industrial designs, trademarks, service marks, commercial names, etc. *Copyright* describes a set of exclusive rights in relation to creative literary and artistic works. Article 2(1) of the Berne Convention, which is frequently consulted when interpreting international and European conventions and legislation on copyright, provides an illuminative definition of the notion of 'literary and artistic works'. Accordingly, the concept of 'literary and artistic works' shall include 'every production in the literary, scientific and artistic domain, whatever may be the mode or form of its expression'. The provision then names examples for literary and artistic works:

> books, pamphlets and other writings; lectures, addresses, sermons and other
> works of the same nature; dramatic or dramaticomusical works; choreographic
> works and entertainments in dumb show; musical compositions with or without words; cinematographic works to which are assimilated works expressed
> by a process analogous to cinematography; works of drawing, painting, architecture, sculpture, engraving and lithography; photographic works to which
> are assimilated works expressed by a process analogous to photography; works
> of applied art; illustrations, maps, plans, sketches and three-dimensional works
> relative to geography, topography, architecture or science.

By contrast to, for example, patents and trademarks, copyright is an unregistered right. A person thus obtains a copyright on a certain creative work without having to register the copyright. This makes the acquisition of a copyright less expensive and less formal than that of a registered right, but it also makes it more difficult to prove the requirements for subsistence of a copyright in a particular case. The exact requirements for subsistence of a copyright vary from jurisdiction to jurisdiction, and they have only been harmonised on a transnational level to a limited extent. To be sure, international law, such as Article 2(1) Berne Convention, mentions certain works that can be copyright-protected. However, these are merely *subject-matters* of copyright. But it is usually dependent on domestic law to define *when* and *how* a certain work

---

[64] See Recital 19 Copyright Directive; CJEU, Joined Cases C-403/08 and C-429/08 [2011] Football Association Premier League Ltd and others v. Karen Murphy and others [198]; Case C-277/10 [2012] Luksan v. van der Let [59].

[65] See Recital 44 Copyright Directive; CJEU, Joined Cases C-403/08 and C-429/08 [2011] Football Association Premier League Ltd and others v. Karen Murphy and others [189].

is copyright-protected. Moreover, the copyright protection of new technologies has often been subject to territorial fragmentation. Take software as an example: while European and international copyright law acknowledges that computer programs can benefit from copyright protection, a transnational definition of the notion of a 'computer program' does not exist.[66]

Particularly in civil law jurisdictions, copyright law distinguishes between authors' rights and related rights, although the exact definition and delineation of those concepts vary from country to country. The term 'authors' rights' (*droit d'auteur* in French, *auteursrecht* in Dutch and *Urheberrecht* in German) is usually applied to the person whose creativity led to the protected work being created, such as book authors, composers and artists. Related rights (*verwandte Schutzrechte* in German), or neighbouring rights (*droits voisins* in French, *naburige rechten* in Dutch), are similar to authors' rights, but are not connected with the work's actual author and independent of any authors' rights. They include the rights of performers, phonogram producers and broadcasting organisations. Both authors' rights and related rights are considered copyrights in the sense of English or US law. However, the Berne Convention for the Protection of Literary and Artistic Works mainly protects authors' rights; related rights are mostly protected by other conventions, such as the Rome Convention for the Protection of Performers, Producers of Phonograms and Broadcasting Organisations and the WIPO Performances and Phonograms Treaty. EU copyright law also draws a distinction between authors' rights and related rights, as can be seen from, for example, Articles 3(1) and (2) and Article 4 of the Copyright Directive.

An example for the distinction between author's rights and related rights that is highly relevant for media law is the protection of photographs. Article 6 of the Term of Protection Directive regulates the duration of protection of photographs 'which are original in the sense that they are the author's own intellectual creation'. In addition, Member States may provide for the protection of 'other photographs', hence photographs that are not original in the sense that they are the author's own intellectual creation. This corresponds to the dichotomy applicable under German law, which distinguishes between 'photographic works' as copyright-protected works and mere 'photographs', which receive the slightly weaker protection (particularly regarding the terms of protection) of 'related rights'.[67] In order to receive protection as an author's right, a 'photographic work' requires a certain artistic expression, such as an arrangement of the background, whereas random snapshots are mere 'photographs'. To draw the exact line can of course be very difficult in detail. This has been the subject of our first case example, the *Painer* decision, which will be further discussed below.

---

[66] See Article 4 of the WIPO Copyright Treaty 1996, Article 10(1) of the TRIPS Agreement and Article 1(1) of the EU Software Directive. On the interpretation of the notion of a 'computer program' under the Software Directive, see CJEU, Case C-406/10 [2012] SAS Institute Inc.

[67] See Sections 2(1)(5), 18, 19, 26, 44, 58 and 62 of the German Copyright Act on photographic works; Section 72 on photographs.

As a consequence, one and the same production can be subject to different sets of rules. For example, under EU law, the participants in the production of a film would be protected in the following ways:

- The scriptwriter: author's rights (Articles 2(a), 3(1) and 4 Copyright Directive).
- The principal director: author's rights (Article 1(5) Satellite and Cable Directive; Article 2(2) Rental Rights Directive).
- The producer: related rights (Article 2(d) Copyright Directive).
- The actors: related right (see Articles 2(b), 3(2)(a) Copyright Directive).

Moreover, parts of what is apparently one and the same 'work' can be protected in different ways. Take the broadcasting of football matches as an example. In the decision *Football Association Premier League Ltd and others* v. *Karen Murphy and others*, which has already been referred to in Chapter 5, the Court of Justice held that football matches themselves cannot be classified as 'works', because they are 'subject to rules of the game, leaving no room for creative freedom for the purposes of copyright'.[68] However, the opening video sequence of a television broadcast of a football match, broadcasting anthems, pre-recorded films showing highlights of football matches, or various graphics, can be copyright-protected.[69]

A further set of exclusive rights that neither qualify as authors' rights nor as related rights – although the exact definition varies between the jurisdictions – are *sui generis* rights. These include, for example, the database right. Although many databases do not require a creative activity comparable to literary and artistic works, they nevertheless receive legal protection equivalent to copyright.[70] Databases are eligible for protection under two regimes: *sui generis* (based in effect on significant labour/investments) and copyright, but the latter only where the arrangement/selection of the database reflects originality or is the author's own intellectual creation.

2 Requirements for Copyright Protection

The prerequisites for copyright protection have only been harmonised at an international level to a very limited extent. They vary among the jurisdictions. International law presupposes the existence of the copyright, but it does not define when copyright exists. The most basic requirements to acquire copyright that apply in most jurisdictions are subject-matter, originality, fixation and qualification.[71] Within the EU, the Court of Justice has made use of its authority to interpret EU copyright legislation to

---

[68] CJEU, Joined Cases C-403/08 and C-429/08 [2011] Football Association Premier League Ltd and others v. Karen Murphy and others [97–99].

[69] CJEU, Joined Cases C-403/08 and C-429/08 [2011] Football Association Premier League Ltd and others v. Karen Murphy and others [149].

[70] See, for example, Directive 96/9/EC of the European Parliament and of the Council of 11 March 1996 on the legal protection of databases, OJ L 77/20.

[71] Aplin and Davis (2013, pp. 62 ff.).

an extent that it also influenced the requirements for subsistence that apply in the EU Member State; a harmonisation through the back door that has not been universally welcomed.[72] It is based on the rationale that EU law must be given an autonomous and uniform interpretation throughout the EU.[73]

a Subject-Matter of a Copyright

As has been stated before, Article 2(1) of the Berne Convention mentions works that are to be protected by members of the Berne Union. Yet, whether the list of possible works that can be copyright-protected is open or closed varies between states, including EU Member States. For example, Section 2(1) of the German Copyright Act stipulates:

Protected works in the literary, scientific and artistic domain include, in particular:

1. Literary works, such as written works, speeches and computer programs;
2. Musical works;
3. Pantomimic works, including works of dance;
4. Artistic works, including works of architecture and of applied art and drafts of such works;
5. Photographic works, including works produced by processes similar to photography;
6. Cinematographic works, including works produced by processes similar to cinematography;
7. Illustrations of a scientific or technical nature, such as drawings, plans, maps, sketches, tables and three-dimensional representations.[74]

By comparison, Section 1(1) of the UK Copyright, Designs and Patents Act 1988 (CDPA) provides:

> Copyright is a property right which subsists in accordance with this Part in
> the following descriptions of work—
> (a) original literary, dramatic, musical or artistic works,
> (b) sound recordings, films or broadcasts, and
> (c) the typographical arrangement of published editions'.

As a consequence, under UK law, a work can only be copyright-protected if it falls under one of the eight categories mentioned in Section 1(1) CDPA; a 'closed list approach'. By contrast, German copyright law protects *in particular* those works

---

[72] See Derclaye (2010); Woods (2012, p. 197); Rosati (2013).
[73] ECJ, Case C-5/08 [2009] Infopaq International A/S v. Danske Dagblades Forening ('Infopaq I')[27]; CJEU, Case C-201/13 [2014] Deckmyn v. Vandersteen [14].
[74] Translation provided by Ute Reusch, juris GmbH, 2014.

mentioned in Section 2(1) Copyright Act, hence the list is merely illustrative, but not comprehensive. Therefore, works in the literary, scientific and artistic domain can also be copyright-protected if they do not correspond to one of those examples mentioned in the Copyright Act; the Act thus applies an 'open list' approach. It is questionable whether the 'closed list' approach can be sustained with a view to the case law of the Court of Justice. Rather than categorising works as particular types of work, the Court merely asked whether the work was 'a subject-matter which is original in the sense that it is its author's own intellectual creation'.[75] This allows the tentative conclusion *argumentum e contrario* that the Court of Justice is not in favour of a 'closed list' approach, but allows every work that expresses the author's own intellectual creation as being capable of copyright protection. Yet a definitive decision of the Court on this matter is yet to be made.

b Originality

There is broad agreement that copyright protection requires originality, although this is expressed in different ways among international and domestic legal documents. Article 2(5) of the Berne Convention speaks of 'intellectual creations', Section 2(2) of the German Copyright Act of 'personal intellectual creations', the US Supreme Court requires a 'minimal level of creativity'[76] and the House of Lords, the author's 'labour, skill and judgment'.[77] One can discern from those varying definitions the underlying rationales for copyright protection, which have been explained in the previous section: the expression of one's personality in civil law jurisdictions, and the reward for the author's labour under the House of Lords' definition.

EU law expects 'the author's own intellectual creation'. This formula is borrowed from EU secondary copyright law, namely Article 1(3) Software Directive, Article 6 Term of Protection Directive and Article 3 Database Directive. Yet since the *Infopaq I* decision in 2009, the Court applies this formula to copyright in general, thus shaping an EU-wide interpretation of originality that was apparently not intended by the drafters of the Copyright Directive in the first place.[78] In *Painer*, the Court went on to explain that an intellectual creation is an author's own 'if it reflects the author's personality. That is the case if the author was able to express his creative abilities in the

---

[75] ECJ, Case C-5/08 [2009] Infopaq International A/S v. Danske Dagblades Forening ('Infopaq I')[37]; CJEU, Case C-393/09 [2010] Bezpečnostní softwarová asociace – Svaz softwarové ochrany [45]; Joined Cases C-403/08 and C-429/08 [2011] Football Association Premier League Ltd and others v. Karen Murphy and others [97]; see also Case C-406/10 [2012] SAS Institute Inc. [65].

[76] Feist Publications, Inc. v. Rural Tel. Service Co., 499 U.S. 340, 358 (1991).

[77] Ladbroke v. William Hill [1964] 1 All ER 465, 469 (per Lord Reid). From an international perspective, see Rahmatian (2013).

[78] ECJ, Case C-5/08 [2009] Infopaq International A/S v. Danske Dagblades Forening ('Infopaq I')[37]; CJEU, Case C-393/09 [2010] Bezpečnostní softwarová asociace – Svaz softwarové ochrany [45]; Joined Cases C-403/08 and C-429/08 [2011] Football Association Premier League Ltd and others v. Karen Murphy and others [97].

production of the work by making free and creative choices.'[79] On several occasions the Court applied its 'own intellectual creation' formula, and came to the conclusion, for example, that newspaper articles,[80] computer manuals,[81] portrait photographs[82] and graphic user interfaces[83] can fulfil this criterion, whereas sporting events cannot.[84] In practice, the required level of originality is fairly low, as has been demonstrated by the *Infopaq* judgments.

c Fixation

Article 2(2) of the Berne Convention allows Union Members to prescribe that works shall not be protected unless they have been fixed in some material form. Many Union Members have adopted such a fixation requirement; for example, Section 3(2) of the UK Copyright, Designs and Patents Act 1988 (CDPA), whereas others, such as France, have not. Moreover, for many works, such as phonograms, fixation is part of the definition of the work (Article 3(b) Rome Convention, Article 2(b) WIPO Performances and Phonograms Treaty). By contrast, broadcasting includes the transmission by *wireless* means (Article 3(f) Rome Convention). Therefore, the protection of broadcasting does not necessarily have a fixation requirement.

d Qualification

A work will be copyright-protected only if the author qualifies for such protection at the material time. These are mostly nationals or bodies incorporated under the law of the country in which copyright protection is claimed (see, for example, Section 154(1) CDPA, Section 120 German Copyright Act). This protection may (but does not have to) be extended to nationals of other countries that are members of the Berne Union, of the EU, or based on bilateral agreements.

3 Beneficiaries of Copyright Protection

The beneficiaries of the Berne Convention are set out in Articles 3 and 4: the protection of the Berne Convention shall apply to:

- authors who are nationals of one of the countries of the Berne Union, for their published or unpublished works (Article 3(1)(a));
- authors who are not nationals of one of the countries of the Berne Union but who have their habitual residence in one of them, for their published or unpublished works (Article 3(2));

---

[79] CJEU, Case C-145/10 [2012] Painer v. Standard Verlags GmbH and others [88–89].
[80] ECJ, Case C-5/08 [2009] Infopaq International A/S v. Danske Dagblades Forening ('Infopaq I').
[81] CJEU, Case C-406/10 [2012] SAS Institute Inc. [67].
[82] CJEU, Case C-145/10 [2012] Painer v. Standard Verlags GmbH and others [94].
[83] CJEU, Case C-393/09 [2010] Bezpečnostní softwarová asociace – Svaz softwarové ochrany.
[84] CJEU, Joined Cases C-403/08 and C-429/08 [2011] Football Association Premier League Ltd and others v. Karen Murphy and others [98].

- authors who are not nationals of one of the countries of the Berne Union, for their works first published in one of those countries, or simultaneously in a country outside the Union and in a country of the Union (Article 3(1)(b));[85]
- authors of cinematographic works, the maker of which has his headquarters or habitual residence in one of the countries of the Berne Union (Article 4(a));
- authors of works of architecture erected in a country of the Berne Union or of other artistic works incorporated in a building or other structure located in a country of the Union (Article 4(b)).

The beneficiaries of copyright protection are therefore, first and foremost, the work's author or authors. The notion of 'author' is not defined by international law, but left to the states. By way of example, Section 9(1) CDPA and Section 7 German Copyright Act define the author as the 'creator of a work'. Nevertheless, the notion of author is in two ways influenced by international, and especially European, law. First, Article 2 Term of Protection Directive and Article 1(5) Satellite and Cable Directive expressly state that the principal director of a cinematographic or audiovisual work shall be considered as its author or one of its authors.[86] Second, under EU law, the notion of 'creation' is usually determined by reference to the contribution to the work's originality.[87]

The first owner of a copyright in a work is its author (see, for example, Section 11(1) CDPA). In civil law systems, such as France and Germany, this also applies where the work is created by an employee in the context of their employment. This stands in contrast to the legal situation in the UK. According to Section 11(2) CDPA, where a literary, dramatic, musical or artistic work or a film is made by an employee in the course of their employment, their employer is the first owner of any copyright in the work subject to any agreement to the contrary. Similarly, according to Article 2(3) Software Directive, where a computer program is created by an employee in the execution of their duties or following the instructions given by their employer, the employer shall exclusively be entitled to exercise all economic rights in the program so created, unless otherwise provided by contract. Within the EU, the uses of works for which the copyright owner cannot be identified or located, so-called 'orphan works', are covered by a specific Directive.[88]

Owners of related rights are, for example, performers, producers of phonograms and broadcasting organisations (Article 3 Rome Convention, Article 2 Copyright Convention). Performers include 'actors, singers, musicians, dancers, and other

---

[85] A work shall be considered as having been published simultaneously in several countries if it has been published in two or more countries within 30 days of its first publication (Article 3(4) Berne Convention).

[86] On the background and impact of these provisions, see COM, Report on the question of authorship of cinematographic or audiovisual works in the Community, COM(2002) 691 final. On their interpretation, see CJEU, Case C-277/10 [2012] Luksan v. van der Let.

[87] Aplin and Davis (2013, p. 111).

[88] Directive 2012/28/EU of the European Parliament and of the Council of 25 October 2012 on certain permitted uses of orphan works, OJ L 299/5.

persons who act, sing, deliver, declaim, play in, or otherwise perform literary or artistic works' (Article 3(a) Rome Convention).

4 Rights of Copyright Owners and Holders of Related Rights

Copyright is a property right.[89] It is therefore a right to exploit the fruits of one's creative work. This is expressed in the economic rights and in the assignment and licence rights of copyright owners. Moreover, the Berne Convention and civil law jurisdictions also recognise the expression of the author's personality in his work.

a Moral Rights

'Moral rights' protect not the creator's economic rights, but his personality interests. Moral rights are non-pecuniary. They include, for example, the author's right to determine whether and how his work shall be published, the right to communicate or describe the content of his work to the public, the right to be recognised as author and the right to protect the integrity of the work against distortion or any other derogatory treatment (see Sections 12–14 of the German Copyright Act). Article 6*bis* Berne Convention provides that 'the author shall have the right to claim authorship of the work and to object to any distortion, mutilation or other modification of, or other derogatory action in relation to, the said work, which would be prejudicial to his honor or reputation'. This applies independently of the author's economic rights, and even after the transfer of the said rights. The moral rights shall in principle be maintained after the author's death, at least until the expiry of the economic rights. Article 6*bis*(3) declares the *lex loci protectionis* principle applicable to moral rights, too. Article 5 WIPO Performances and Phonograms Treaty protects moral rights of performers.

The concept of moral rights is particularly widespread in civil law jurisdictions, but it is at odds with the understanding of copyright in common law systems. The EU Copyright Directive excludes moral rights from its scope.[90] Outside the scope of Article 6*bis* Berne Convention, the vindication of moral rights thus bears significant potential for conflict in cases with a transnational dimension, even within the EU.

b Assignment and Licence

Copyright law allows the owner to commercially exploit the marketing of the protected work, particularly in the form of licences granted in return for payment of royalties.[91] A licence does not include the transfer of copyright ownership but is rather a mere permission to carry out acts that are otherwise reserved for the owner. The possibility to *license* the use of copyright-protected works exists, as apparent, globally.

---

[89] See CJEU, Case C-277/10 [2012] Luksan v. van der Let [68].

[90] Recital 19 Copyright Directive; see also Recital 28 Satellite and Cable Directive.

[91] See, for example, CJEU, Joined Cases C-403/08 and C-429/08 [2011] Football Association Premier League Ltd and others v. Karen Murphy and others [107].

By contrast, the (im)possibility to *transfer* ownership of one's copyright is another area where the differing rationales for the protection of copyright become visible. Common law jurisdictions emphasise the economic aspect of copyright. Therefore, they allow the partial or whole transfer of ownership of copyright (see Section 90 CDPA).

In contrast to common law jurisdictions, civil law countries also consider the personality aspect of copyright protection. Yet personality rights are not transferrable. As a consequence, Section 29 of the German Copyright Act excludes the transferability of copyright, unless it is transferred in execution of a testamentary disposition or to co-heirs as part of the partition of an estate.

c Economic Rights

The economic rights deriving from copyright and related rights entitle their owner to exploit their work in various ways. The exact economic rights flowing from copyright depend on the copyright laws of each individual state,[92] subject to a certain degree of international harmonisation.

aa Fixation   According to Article 7(1)(b) Rome Convention, Article 6 Performances and Phonograms Treaty and Article 7 Rental Rights Directive, performers shall have the exclusive right to authorise or prohibit the fixation of their performances. Moreover, broadcasting organisations shall have the exclusive right to authorise or prohibit the fixation of their broadcasts, whether these broadcasts are transmitted by wire or over the air, including by cable or satellite (Article 7 Rental Rights Directive, Article 13(b) Rome Convention).

bb Reproduction   The exclusive right to reproduce is arguably the oldest entitlement of rights-holders, and yet it has gained particular significance in the digital age. Pursuant to Article 9(1) Berne Convention, authors shall have the exclusive right of authorising the reproduction of their works, in any manner or form. Under Article 7(1)(c) Rome Convention, performers may prevent the reproduction, without their consent, of a fixation of their performance. According to Article 7 Performances and Phonograms Treaty, performers have the exclusive right of authorising the reproduction of their performances fixed in phonograms. And under Article 11 Performances and Phonograms Treaty, producers of phonograms enjoy the exclusive right of authorising the reproduction of their phonograms. These provisions are implemented by Article 2 of the EU Copyright Directive.

Article 2 Copyright Directive furnishes both authors and owners of certain related rights with the exclusive right of reproduction, or copying, of their works, fixations of performances, phonograms, fixations of films and fixations of broadcasts.[93] The

---

[92] See, for example, Section 16 CDPA, Section 15 German Copyright Act.

[93] Compare Article 9(1) Berne Convention (reproduction rights of authors of literary and artistic works); Article 14 TRIPS (protection of performers against fixation of their performance on a phonogram and producers of phonograms against reproduction of their phonograms).

notion of 'reproduction' in Article 2 of the Copyright Directive, which was specifically tailored to meet the challenges of the information society, is conceptualised broadly. It includes 'direct or indirect, temporary or permanent reproduction by any means and in any form, in whole or in part'. With the exception of Article 7 WIPO Performances and Phonograms Treaty 1996, the Copyright Directive is thus more advanced than any international copyright treaty.[94]

As can be inferred from Article 5(1) Copyright Directive, reproduction includes automatically generated, transient and incidental copies. By providing an exemption from the reproduction right in Article 2, the provision indirectly confirms that the acts mentioned *are* acts of reproduction in the first place. For example, browsing an internet webpage involves copying, as transient copies are made in the Random Access Memory (RAM) of one's computer.[95] The same applies to caching of computer webpages.[96] In *Karen Murphy*, the Luxembourg Court decided that the creation of transient sequential fragments of a work within the memory of a satellite decoder and on a television screen which are immediately effaced and replaced by the next fragments also constitutes a 'reproduction' within the meaning of Article 2(a) Copyright Directive.[97]

On a side note: recall that football matches as such are not susceptible to copyright protection. So what was the work in question that was possibly 'reproduced' here? The work in question was FAPL's contribution to the broadcasting of the football matches, namely the opening video sequence, the Premier League anthem, pre-recorded films showing highlights of recent Premier League matches and various graphics. By contrast to the football matches themselves, these contributions could be copyright-protected provided they were expressions of the authors' own intellectual creation, which was for the domestic court to decide.[98]

cc Communication to the Public The concepts of 'communication to the public' and 'making available to the public' have been at the core of a broad international debate on whether international, European and domestic copyright provisions are suited to cope with the implications of digital dissemination.[99]

---

[94] See Aplin (2005, p. 100). Article 7 WIPO Performances and Phonograms Treaty states: 'Performers shall enjoy the exclusive right of authorizing the direct or indirect reproduction of their performances fixed in phonograms, in any manner or form.'

[95] Aplin and Davis (2013, p. 162); S. von Lewinski and M.M. Walter, in von Lewinski and Walter (2010, para. 11.5.15); CJEU, Case C-360/13 [2014] Public Relations Consultants Association Ltd v. Newspaper Licensing Agency Ltd.

[96] See Recital 33 Copyright Directive; Council of the European Union, Proposal for a Directive of the European Parliament and of the Council on the harmonisation of certain aspects of copyright and related rights in the information society, Addendum, 15 September 2000, 1997/0359 (COD), p. 2.

[97] CJEU, Joined Cases C-403/08 and C-429/08 [2011] Football Association Premier League Ltd and others v. Karen Murphy and others [159].

[98] CJEU, Joined Cases C-403/08 and C-429/08 [2011] Football Association Premier League Ltd and others v. Karen Murphy and others [152] and [159].

[99] See Aplin (2005, pp. 127 ff), providing further references.

(1) The International Framework   Article 11 Berne Convention furnishes authors of dramatic, dramatico-musical and musical works with the exclusive right of authorising the public performance of their works and any communication to the public of the performance of their works. Article 11*bis*(1) grants authors the exclusive right of authorising the communication of their work to the public by wire or wireless means, including broadcasting and rebroadcasting. Finally, authors have the exclusive right of public recitation of their work under Article 11*ter* Berne Convention. The owner of copyright in a cinematographic work shall enjoy the same rights as the author of an original work (Article 14*bis*).

Article 8 WIPO Copyright Treaty 1996 was the first provision on international level to provide for an explicitly broad right of communication to the public and a right of making available to the public. Supplementing the rules of the Berne Convention on the right of communication to the public, it states that 'authors of literary and artistic works shall enjoy the exclusive right of authorizing any communication to the public of their works, by wire or wireless means, including the making available to the public of their works in such a way that members of the public may access these works from a place and at a time individually chosen by them.' It thus stipulates the right of communication to the public also with a view to communication by wire, such as cable transmission. Moreover, it includes an exclusive right on the making available to the public of works by way of on-demand services.

(2) The EU Framework   Within the EU framework, one has to distinguish at first between communication to the public via satellite and cable, and all other means of communication. The Satellite and Cable Directive provides an exclusive right for authors and holders of related rights to authorise the communication to the public by satellite of protected works, thus ensuring an appropriate remuneration. With a view to authors, it has established a self-standing right in Article 2; regarding holders of related rights, Article 4 refers to the rights provided by the Rental Rights Directive. According to Article 2 Satellite and Cable Directive, authors have the exclusive right to authorise the communication to the public by satellite of copyright works. Article 1(2)(a) of the Directive defines 'communication to the public by satellite' as 'the act of introducing, under the control and responsibility of the broadcasting organization, the programme-carrying signals intended for reception by the public into an uninterrupted chain of communication leading to the satellite and down towards the earth'.[100] Normal technical procedures relating to the programme-carrying signals should not be considered as interruptions to the chain of broadcasting.[101] If the programme-carrying signals are encrypted, then there is communication to the public by satellite on the condition that the means for decrypting the broadcast are provided to the public

---

[100] On the notion of 'communication to the public by satellite', see CJEU, Joined Cases C-431/09 and C-432/09 [2011] Airfield NV and Canal Digitaal BV.
[101] Recital 14 Satellite and Cable Directive.

by the broadcasting organisation or with its consent (Article 1(2)(c)). The authorisation to communicate to the public copyright works by satellite may be acquired only by agreement, including collective agreements between a collecting society and a broadcasting organisation (Article 3).

Moreover, the Directive provides an exclusive right for authors and holders of related rights to authorise the cable retransmission of programmes from other Member States (Recital 27, Article 8(1), Article 1(3)). At the same time, the Directive restricts the exercise of this right: the right to grant or refuse authorisation to a cable operator for a cable retransmission may be exercised only through a collecting society (Article 9(1)). Article 9 serves to ensure that the smooth operation of contractual arrangements is not called into question by the intervention of outsiders holding rights in individual parts of the programme.[102] While Article 9 thus defines the *exercise* of the right to authorise cable retransmission, the *right* to authorise itself remains with the rights-holders. As a consequence, it can still be assigned under domestic rules.[103] Moreover, the mandatory transfer of rights to a collecting society does not apply to the rights exercised by a broadcasting organisation in respect of its own transmission with a view to both its own rights and rights transferred to them by other rights-holders (Article 10 and Recital 29). This is owed to the fact that broadcasting organisations can be both holders of exclusive rights to their own programmes and acquirers of rights for programmes from third parties. Therefore, Article 10 intends to give them latitude to negotiate the acquisition of rights for the retransmission of programmes without rights-holders being mandatorily represented by a collecting society.[104] A broadcasting organisation may acquire all cable retransmission rights and be the sole party dealing with the cable operator. In other words, although the cable operator remains legally responsible for the acquisition of rights, in practice it is often the broadcasters that manage the cable acquisition rights on behalf of the cable operator.[105]

As far as owners of related rights are concerned, their right to *communicate to the public* is covered by the Rental Rights Directive, whereas the right to *make available to the public* falls under the Copyright Directive. Pursuant to Article 8(1) Rental Rights Directive, performers have the exclusive right to authorise or prohibit the broadcasting by wireless means and the communication to the public of their performances, except where the performance is itself already a broadcast performance or is made from a fixation. Since producers of phonograms – that is, the music industry – are not mentioned in this provision, they do not, *argumentum e contrario*, enjoy an

---

[102] Recital 28 Satellite and Cable Directive.
[103] Recital 28 Satellite and Cable Directive.
[104] COM, Report on the application of Council Directive 93/83/EEC of 27 September 1993 on the coordination of certain rules concerning copyright and rights related to copyright applicable to satellite broadcasting and cable retransmission, COM(2002) 430 final, p. 5.
[105] COM, Report on the application of Council Directive 93/83/EEC of 27 September 1993 on the coordination of certain rules concerning copyright and rights related to copyright applicable to satellite broadcasting and cable retransmission, COM(2002) 430 final, pp. 5–9.

exclusive right of communication to the public.[106] Instead, they 'only' enjoy a right to equitable remuneration according to Article 8(2) Rental Rights Directive. According to Article 8(3) Rental Rights Directive, broadcasting organisations have the exclusive right to authorise or prohibit the rebroadcasting of their broadcasts by wireless means. In concomitance with Article 13(d) Rome Convention, broadcasters have a right of communication to the public of their broadcasts only if such communication is made in places accessible to the public against payment of an entrance fee. These provisions also apply to the communication to the public by satellite (Article 4 Satellite and Cable Directive). Article 4(2) Satellite and Cable Directive thus clarifies that 'broadcasting by wireless means' in the Rental Rights Directive shall be understood as including communication to the public by satellite. Member States may provide for more far-reaching protection for holders of related rights than that required by Article 8 Rental Rights Directive.[107]

With a view to 'making available', according to Article 3(2) Copyright Directive, owners of related rights have an exclusive right to authorise or prohibit the making available to the public, by wire or wireless means, in such a way that members of the public may access them from a place and at a time individually chosen by them:

1 for performers, of fixations of their performances;
2 for phonogram producers, of their phonograms;
3 for the producers of the first fixations of films, of the original and copies of their films;
4 for broadcasting organisations, of fixations of their broadcasts, whether these broadcasts are transmitted by wire or over the air, including by cable or satellite.

Remarkably, phonogram producers thus enjoy the exclusive right to make their works available to the public, but, as has been stated above, not to communicate them. This shows the practical importance of the distinction between 'making available' from other forms of communication, and it raises the question whether this distinction is indeed justified. As regards Article 3(2)(d), the Court of Justice held in *C More Entertainment AB* v. *Sandberg* that Member States may extend the exclusive right of the broadcasting organisations to transmissions of broadcast live on the internet, provided that such an extension does not undermine the protection of copyright.[108]

In cases in which no special directive applies, such as the Satellite and Cable Directive, the right of authors both to communicate to the public and to make available their works follows from Article 3(1) Copyright Directive. This provision applies, for example, to live streaming of works and on-demand services making works available online, as these are not covered by the Satellite and Cable Directive.[109] Moreover,

---

[106] S. von Lewinski and M.M. Walter, in von Lewinski and Walter (2010, para. 11.3.21).
[107] Compare Article 6(1) Satellite and Cable Directive.
[108] Case C-279/13 [2015] C More Entertainment AB v. Sandberg.
[109] On the relevance of copyright for streaming, see Borghi (2011).

the reception by a hotel establishment of satellite or terrestrial television signals and their distribution by cable to the various rooms of that hotel is not an 'act of communication to the public' or 'reception by the public' within the meaning of the Satellite and Cable Directive. This would fall under Article 3(1) Copyright Directive as well.[110]

Article 3(1) Copyright Directive precludes the Member State from giving wider protection to copyright holders by laying down that the concept of communication to the public includes a wider range of activities than those referred to in that provision.[111]

(3) The Concepts of 'Communication' and 'Making Available' to the Public The line between 'communication' and 'making available' is not always simple to draw. But the difference is important in legal practice, because, as has been shown before, different provisions apply to these activities. The problem is exacerbated by the unclear definition of the notion of 'public'.

As Article 11*bis*(1)(iii) of the Berne Convention expressly indicates, the concept of 'communication' encompasses communication by loudspeaker or any other instrument transmitting, by signs, sounds or images. Therefore, the concept of communication includes any transmission of the protected works, irrespective of the technical means or process used.[112] However, it only covers communication to the public not present at the place where the communication originates.[113] The main example for the notion of 'communication to the public' is broadcasting. As will be explained in the next section, it is more precisely 'linear broadcasting'.

'Communication to the public' does not cover the concept of 'public performance' within the meaning of Article 11(1) of the Berne Convention; that is, the representation or performance of a work before the public that is in direct physical contact with the actor or performer.[114] However, it follows from Article 8(3) of the Related Rights Directive and Articles 2(g) and 15 of the Performance and Phonograms Treaty that communication includes 'making the sounds or representations of sounds fixed in a phonogram audible to the public' and that it encompasses broadcasting or 'any communication to the public'.

As can be inferred from Article 3(1) Copyright Directive ('communication ..., including making available'), 'making available' of protected works is a subcategory of communication to the public. Like communication to the public in general, the concept of 'making available' includes a distance element.[115] It is specific

---

[110] See ECJ, Case C-293/98 [2000] Entidad de Gestión de Derechos de los Productores Audiovisuales (Egeda) v. Hostelería Asturiana SA (Hoasa) [28].

[111] CJEU, Case C-466/12 [2014] Svensson et al. v. Retriever Sverige AB [41].

[112] CJEU, Joined Cases C-403/08 and C-429/08 [2011] Football Association Premier League Ltd and others v. Karen Murphy and others [191–193].

[113] Recital 24 Copyright Directive; S. von Lewinski and M.M. Walter, in von Lewinski and Walter (2010, para. 11.3.19).

[114] CJEU, Joined Cases C-403/08 and C-429/08 [2011] Football Association Premier League Ltd and others v. Karen Murphy and others [201]; Case C-283/10 [2011] Circul Globus București v. Uniunea Compozitorilor și Muzicologilor din România [35].

[115] S. von Lewinski and M.M. Walter, in von Lewinski and Walter (2010, para. 11.3.28).

in that members of the public may access the material from a place and at a time individually chosen by them.[116] But is that a valid distinction from broadcasting? Broadcasting programmes can also be accessed from a place and at a time chosen by the viewer. But there is of course one difference: the notion of 'communication' in general includes traditional forms of linear dissemination where transmission and access to the material is simultaneous. 'Making available' specifically refers to the separation of transmission and access. As a result, with a view to broadcasting in particular, 'communication' includes those phenomena that qualify as linear audio-visual media services (i.e., television), whereas 'making available' refers to non-linear services. 'Making available' thus includes, for example, video-on-demand services, whereas live streaming, webcasting and near-video-on-demand have to be qualified as 'communication'.

The application of provisions on 'communication to the public' and 'making available to the public' is further complicated by the difficulties involved in the notion of 'public'. The Court of Justice has indicated that the term 'public' refers to 'an indeterminate number of potential recipients and implies, moreover, a fairly large number of persons'.[117] This sounds simple and straightforward but, as the case law reveals, the problems are in the details.

In the case *SGAE*, a hotel owner used television sets in its hotel that broadcast, *inter alia*, copyright-protected works. The Court of Justice thus had to decide whether the installation of television sets in hotel rooms and the distribution of a signal through television sets to customers in hotel rooms constitutes 'communication to the public' within the meaning of Article 3(1) of the Copyright Directive. The hotel owner had argued that a hotel room constitutes a private sphere in which each customer could watch the programme only individually. Hence, television did not constitute a communication 'to the public'. The ECJ disagreed. It observed that hotel customers quickly succeed each other. Taking into account not only the actual but also the potential occupants of a hotel room, 'a fairly large number of persons' and hence a 'public' was involved in this case.[118] The Court thus concluded that a hotel proprietor carries out an act of communication when he gives his customers access to the broadcast works via television sets. Such intervention is not just a technical means to ensure or improve reception of the original broadcast in the catchment area, but an act without which those customers are unable to enjoy the broadcast works, even if they are physically within that area. By contrast, it is irrelevant that customers who leave the television switched off have not had access to the works.[119] On a final note, the Court emphasised that the mere

---

[116] See Article 3(2) Copyright Directive; Article 10 WIPO Performances and Phonograms Treaty.

[117] ECJ, Case C-306/05 [2006] Sociedad General de Autores y Editores de España (SGAE) v. Rafael Hoteles SA [37–38]; CJEU, Case C-466/12 [2014] Svensson v. Retriever Sverige AB [21].

[118] ECJ, Case C-306/05 [2006] Sociedad General de Autores y Editores de España (SGAE) v. Rafael Hoteles SA [38].

[119] ECJ, Case C-306/05 [2006] Sociedad General de Autores y Editores de España (SGAE) v. Rafael Hoteles SA [42–43].

installation of television sets in hotel rooms did not in itself constitute a communication to the public. In accordance with Article 8 of the WIPO Copyright Treaty, Recital 27 of the Copyright Directive states that the 'mere provision of physical facilities for enabling or making a communication does not in itself amount to communication within the meaning of [the Copyright] Directive'.[120] Instead, it is the distribution of a signal by means of those television sets that constitutes communication to the public.[121]

The notion of 'communication to the public' was also an important aspect of the *Karen Murphy* decision. The referring court asked whether 'communication to the public' within the meaning of Article 3(1) of the Copyright Directive must be interpreted as covering transmission of the broadcast works, via a television screen and speakers, to the customers present in a public house. In its reasoning, the Court separated the two requirements 'communication' and 'to the public'. As regards the 'communication' requirement, the Court observed that the proprietor of a public house 'intentionally gives the customers present in that establishment access to a broadcast containing protected works via a television screen and speakers'. Accordingly, the Court held that the proprietor of a public house 'effects a communication'.[122] The Court then proceeded to the 'to the public' limb. The Court regarded this requirement as fulfilled only if the work is being transmitted to a 'new public'; that is, to an audience that was not taken into account by the authors of the protected works when they authorised their use by the initial communication.[123] This was the case in *Karen Murphy*: the FAPL authorised the broadcasting of its works only for the owners of television sets who follow the broadcasts in private. Where a broadcast is transmitted in a place accessible to the public, such as a restaurant or a bar, it is communicated to a new public, because the customers constitute an additional public that was not considered by the authors when they authorised the broadcasting of their works.[124]

The notion of 'communication to the public', more specifically, of communication to a *new* public, has proven to be particularly problematic with regard to hyperlinks. In *Svensson* v. *Retriever Sverige AB*, the website operator Retriever Sverige provided its clients with hyperlinks redirecting them to articles published by other websites. Several journalists who also published their articles both on paper and on a freely accessible website claimed compensation from Retriever Sverige on the ground that it had

---

[120] See ECJ, Case C-306/05 [2006] Sociedad General de Autores y Editores de España (SGAE) v. Rafael Hoteles SA [45].

[121] ECJ, Case C-306/05 [2006] Sociedad General de Autores y Editores de España (SGAE) v. Rafael Hoteles SA [46].

[122] CJEU, Joined Cases C-403/08 and C-429/08 [2011] Football Association Premier League Ltd and others v. Karen Murphy and others [196].

[123] CJEU, Joined Cases C-403/08 and C-429/08 [2011] Football Association Premier League Ltd and others v. Karen Murphy and others [197], providing references to earlier case law; confirmed in CJEU, Case C-607/11 [2013] ITV Broadcasting Ltd v. TVCatchup Ltd [39]; Case C-466/12 [2014] Svensson v. Retriever Sverige AB [24].

[124] CJEU, Joined Cases C-403/08 and C-429/08 [2011] Football Association Premier League Ltd and others v. Karen Murphy and others [198–199].

communicated their articles without their authorisation. Following its two-step analysis in *Karen Murphy*, the Court distinguished between the notion of 'communication' and 'to the public'. Since the public was able to access the newspaper articles via the hyperlinks, there was a 'communication'. Notably, the Court indicated that this applied irrespective of whether someone availed themselves of that opportunity.[125] Yet it was more problematic whether there was a communication 'to the public', more precisely, to a 'new public'. The Court denied this point. It held that making available works by means of a hyperlink does not lead to the work in question being communicated to a new public. The public targeted by the initial communication, the publication of the newspaper articles on the website, consisted of all potential visitors to the site, because access to that site was not restricted. Since internet users could access the article directly on the newspaper's website without any involvement of Retriever Sverige, the latter's users were potential recipients of the initial communication and thus part of the public taken into account by the copyright holders when they authorised the initial communication.[126] This would be different if the hyperlink made it possible to circumvent restrictions put in place by the site of origin, such as a 'subscribers only' gate.[127] The Court came to the same conclusion with regard to the 'framing' of a video, that is, the embedding of another person's work within one's own website. Referring to the *Svensson* decision, the Court held that the framing of a work is not a communication to a 'new public' if the original work is freely available on a publicly accessible website.[128]

In its decision *SBS Belgium* v. *SABAM*, the Court had to explain whether the notion of 'communication to the public' applies to the transmission technique of 'direct injection'.[129] This is a process by which a broadcaster transmits its programme-carrying signals 'point to point' via a private line to its distributors, which then send the signals to their subscribers. The signals cannot be received by the general public during 'point to point' transmission. Therefore, the Court held that while there was 'communication', it was, in principle, not 'to the public'.[130] In particular, the distributors could not be regarded as 'public'.[131] Nevertheless, the Court did not entirely rule out that the subscribers of the distributors might, in some situations, be considered the 'public' in relation to the original transmission made by the broadcasting organisation.[132] That would be the case if the distributor is not independent from the broadcasting organisation and its distribution service is purely technical.[133]

The EU framework does not expressly require a commercial activity for there to be a 'communication to the public'. The Court of Justice has confirmed 'that a profit-making

---

[125] CJEU, Case C-466/12 [2014] Svensson et al. v. Retriever Sverige AB [19].

[126] CJEU, Case C-466/12 [2014] Svensson et al. v. Retriever Sverige AB [25–27].

[127] CJEU, Case C-466/12 [2014] Svensson et al. v. Retriever Sverige AB [31].

[128] CJEU, Case C-348/13 [2014] BestWater International GmbH v. Mebes and Potsch [19].

[129] CJEU, Case C-325/14 [2015] SBS Belgium v. SABAM.

[130] CJEU, Case C-325/14 [2015] SBS Belgium v. SABAM [23].

[131] CJEU, Case C-325/14 [2015] SBS Belgium v. SABAM [26].

[132] CJEU, Case C-325/14 [2015] SBS Belgium v. SABAM [25].

[133] CJEU, Case C-325/14 [2015] SBS Belgium v. SABAM [32].

nature is not necessarily an essential condition for the existence of a communication to the public'. However, the Court has also frequently indicated that 'it is not irrelevant' that a communication 'is of a profit-making nature'.[134] Yet it is still unclear what the exact relevance of the 'profit-making nature' of the communication is.

dd Distribution The distribution right applies to work incorporated in a tangible article.[135] The concept of 'distribution to the public' covers the sale of the original of a work or a copy thereof and acts that entail a transfer of the ownership of that object.[136] Moreover, the Luxembourg Court held that acts preceding the conclusion of a contract of sale, such as advertisements on a website targeted at an audience in a Member State in which advertised product is copyright-protected, may also fall within the concept of distribution and thus be reserved to the holders of copyright.[137]

According to Article 14(1)(i) Berne Convention, authors shall have the exclusive right of authorising the cinematographic adaptation and reproduction of these works, and the distribution of the works thus adapted or reproduced. Pursuant to Article 6 WIPO Copyright Treaty 1996, authors shall enjoy the exclusive right of authorising the making available to the public of the original and copies of their works through sale or other transfer of ownership. Similarly, Article 4 Copyright Directive confers on authors the exclusive right to authorise or prohibit any form of distribution of their works to the public. The notion of 'distribution to the public ... by sale' in Article 4(1) Copyright Directive has the same meaning as the expression 'making available to the public ... through sale' in Article 6(1) of the WIPO Copyright Treaty.[138]

Article 6(2) WIPO Copyright Treaty leaves the establishment of provisions on exhaustion to the states. Article 4(2) Copyright Directive regulates the exhaustion of the distribution right that has already been referred to in the context of primary law: the distribution right shall be exhausted within the EU where the first sale or other transfer of ownership in the EU of that object is made by the rights-holder or with his consent.

Rental and lending rights have been established in Article 7 WIPO Copyright Treaty, Article 9 Performances and Phonograms Treaty and in a separate EU Directive.[139] The exhaustion doctrine does not apply to rental and lending rights.[140]

---

[134] CJEU, Joined Cases C-403/08 and C-429/08 [2011] Football Association Premier League Ltd and others v. Karen Murphy and others [204]; Case C-607/11 [2013] ITV Broadcasting Ltd v. TVCatchup Ltd [42].

[135] Recital 28 Copyright Directive.

[136] ECJ, Case C-456/06 [2008] Peek & Cloppenburg KG v. Cassina SpA [36].

[137] CJEU, Case C-516/13 [2015] Dimensione Direct Sales Srl and others v. Knoll International SpA [26].

[138] CJEU, Case C-5/11 [2012] Donner [24]; Case C-516/13 [2015] Dimensione Direct Sales Srl and others v. Knoll International SpA [24].

[139] Directive 2006/115/EC of the European Parliament and of the Council of 12 December 2006 on rental right and lending right and on certain rights related to copyright in the field of intellectual property (codified version), OJ L 376/28.

[140] ECJ, Case C-200/96 [1998] Metronome Musik GmbH v. Music Point Hokamp GmbH [18]; Case C-61/97 [1998] Foreningen af danske Videogramdistributører v. Laserdisken [18].

The distribution right with regard to related rights is set out in Articles 8(1) and 12(1) Performances and Phonograms Treaty and Article 9 Rental Rights Directive. Accordingly, performers in respect of fixations of their performances, phonogram producers in respect of their phonograms, producers of the first fixations of films in respect of the original and copies of their films and for broadcasting organisations in respect of fixations of their broadcasts have the exclusive right to make these objects available to the public. According to Article 9(2) Rental Rights Directive, the exhaustion doctrine shall apply to the first sale in the EU of that object made by the rights-holder or with his consent.

5 Infringements of Copyright

The notion of infringement of copyright is largely determined by national law. In the UK, copyright law distinguishes between primary and secondary infringement. Primary infringement occurs where a person does – or authorises another person to do – one of the acts for which the copyright owner has an exclusive right without the owners' permission. Secondary infringement occurs where a person facilitates primary infringing activities or deals in infringing copies of a work.[141] By contrast to primary infringement, secondary infringement requires knowledge of the infringement. Continental jurisdictions, such as Germany, apply legal concepts known from criminal law, such as aiding and abetting. Yet the outcome is often the same, as aiding and abetting under German law also requires knowledge on behalf of the abettor.

By way of example, under UK law, primary infringement is based on the following requirements:

1 a person has carried out one of the exclusive acts or authorised the doing of one of them;
2 the infringing act occurs within the UK;
3 the infringing activity does not fall within the scope of an express or implied licence;
4 there is a causal connection between the copyright-protected work and the infringing work; and
5 the act must be done in relation to the whole or substantial part of the work.[142]

Since copyright is a territorially limited right, copyright infringements must occur within the jurisdiction under the law of which the infringement is claimed. This has an impact on the establishment and jurisdiction and the choice of the applicable law in transnational cases (see *infra*). The notion of a 'causal connection' essentially expresses that there has to be a *copy* of the original work. Creating the same or similar work independently and by coincidence does not constitute a copyright infringement. The notion of substantiality (fifth requirement) has been subject to

---

[141] Aplin and Davis (2013, p. 181).
[142] Aplin and Davis (2013, p. 182).

considerable case law, a detailed analysis of which would go beyond the scope of this book.[143]

6 Exceptions and Limitations

As rights-holders have an exclusive right on reproduction, communication and dissemination; these acts are in principle impermissible without their consent. However, both international and EU law provide certain exceptions and limitations to the exclusive copyright, and thus influence domestic legislation. Exceptions are provisions allowing a person to carry out an exclusive act without having to pay remuneration to the owner, whereas limitations allow such acts only against remuneration.[144] These provisions, such as Article 10 Berne Convention, Article 15 Rome Convention, Article 10 WIPO Copyright Treaty 1996, Article 5 Copyright Directive and Article 10 Rental Rights Directive, should safeguard a fair balance of rights and interests between the rights-holders and users of protected subject-matter. In particular, those provisions serve as a gateway to take on board conflicting human rights and interests of society in general. Exceptions and limitations are thus central to copyright's balancing act of incentives to create versus the right to reproduce and disseminate.

a Temporary Acts of Reproduction

Article 5(1) Copyright Directive provides an exception for 'temporary acts of reproduction' that are 'transient or incidental'. But it is a controversial provision, as it indirectly confirms that those acts are to be considered acts of reproduction in the first place. Therefore, both internet service providers and users always sail close to the wind of a possible copyright infringement. This became particularly visible, although in a different context, in the second case example for this chapter, which will be discussed further below. As a derogation from the general rule that the copyright holder must authorise any reproduction of his protected work, Article 5(1) must be interpreted strictly.[145] Scholars have argued to reduce the scope of the notion of 'reproduction' within the meaning of Article 2 to human acts and exclude the automatic acts in Article 5(1) altogether. But under the current legal circumstances, users distributing content over the internet run the risk of violating copyright twice, as distribution over the internet often involves both acts of reproduction and of communication to the public (see *infra*); hence a double authorisation would be required.[146]

---

[143] See Aplin and Davis (2013, pp. 184 ff).
[144] Aplin and Davis (2013, p. 202).
[145] ECJ, Case C-5/08 [2009] Infopaq International A/S v. Danske Dagblades Forening ('Infopaq I') [56–57]; CJEU, Joined Cases C-403/08 and C-429/08 [2011] Football Association Premier League Ltd and others v. Karen Murphy and others [162]; Case C-360/13 [2014] Public Relations Consultants Association Ltd v. Newspaper Licensing Agency Ltd [23].
[146] IViR (2007, p. 25).

Article 5(1) is based on the following cumulative conditions:

1 The act is temporary,
2 it is transient or incidental,
3 it is an integral and essential part of a technological process,
4 its sole purpose is to enable a transmission in a network between third parties by an intermediary or a lawful use, of a work or other subject-matter, and
5 the act has no independent economic significance.[147]

Moreover, the act of reproduction has to satisfy the generally applicable 'three-step test' in Article 5(5) Copyright Directive. Yet the Court of Justice has held that if acts of reproduction fulfil the conditions of Article 5(1) Copyright Directive, they do not conflict with the normal exploitation of the work or unreasonably prejudice the legitimate interests of the rights-holder.[148]

The first condition of Article 5(1) Copyright Directive is that the act of reproduction must be temporary. By way of example, if internet users visit particular websites, copies of those websites are being made on the user's computer screen and in the internet 'cache' of that computer's hard disk. While this constitutes a reproduction within the meaning of Article 2 Copyright Directive, the reproduction is temporary, because the on-screen copies are deleted when the internet user moves away from the website viewed and the cached copies are normally automatically replaced by other content after a certain time.[149] The second condition comprises alternative criteria: The act of reproduction has to be transient or incidental. An act of reproduction is 'transient' if its duration is limited to what is necessary for that process to work properly; that process must be automated inasmuch as it deletes the reproduction automatically once its function of enabling the completion of such a process has come to an end.[150] In turn, it must not be dependent on discretionary human intervention, particularly by the user of protected works.[151] However, an act of reproduction does not lose its transient nature merely because the deletion of the copy is preceded by the intervention of the user designed to terminate the technological process concerned.[152] An act of

---

[147] See CJEU, Joined Cases C-403/08 and C-429/08 [2011] Football Association Premier League Ltd and others v. Karen Murphy and others [161]; Case C-360/13 [2014] Public Relations Consultants Association Ltd v. Newspaper Licensing Agency Ltd [22].

[148] CJEU, Joined Cases C-403/08 and C-429/08 [2011] Football Association Premier League Ltd and others v. Karen Murphy and others [181]; Case C-302/10 [2012] Infopaq International A/S v. Danske Dagblades Forening ('Infopaq II') [57].

[149] CJEU, Case C-360/13 [2014] Public Relations Consultants Association Ltd v. Newspaper Licensing Agency Ltd [26].

[150] ECJ, Case C-5/08 [2009] Infopaq International A/S v. Danske Dagblades Forening ('Infopaq I') [64]; CJEU, Case C-360/13 [2014] Public Relations Consultants Association Ltd v. Newspaper Licensing Agency Ltd [40].

[151] ECJ, Case C-5/08 [2009] Infopaq International A/S v. Danske Dagblades Forening ('Infopaq I') [62] and [64].

[152] CJEU, Case C-360/13 [2014] Public Relations Consultants Association Ltd v. Newspaper Licensing Agency Ltd [42].

reproduction is 'incidental' if it neither exists nor has a purpose independent from the technological process of which it forms part.[153]

The third condition requires that two criteria be fulfilled: first, the acts of reproduction are an 'integral part' of the technological process. This means that they are carried out entirely in the context of the implementation of a technological process. However, it is irrelevant that the process in question has been activated and completed by human intervention, such as browsing the internet.[154] Second, the reproduction has to be an 'essential part' of the process. The completion of those acts of reproduction has to be necessary in that the technological process could not function correctly and efficiently without those acts. It is thus not necessary to establish that the technological process could not function at all without the reproduction. Instead, it is sufficient that the act of reproduction, such as caching, facilitates the technological process, such as browsing on the internet.[155]

A use should be considered lawful within the meaning of the fourth condition where it is authorised by the rights-holder or where it is not restricted by the law.[156] The notion of 'lawful use' is not determined by the question as to whether the use of the work constitutes a copyright infringement. Such reasoning would be circular, as it is the purpose of Article 5(1) to determine a copyright violation in the first place. Instead, the question is whether the use is lawful aside from copyright protection.

According to the fifth condition, the act of reproduction must have no independent economic significance. The significance has to go beyond the economic advantage of the reproduction itself, otherwise Article 5(1) Copyright Directive would be rendered redundant.[157] Acts of reproduction do not have an independent economic significance if they do not enable the generation of an additional profit going beyond that derived from lawful use of the protected work and if they do not lead to a modification of that work.[158]

In *Karen Murphy*, it was particularly problematic whether the ephemeral reproduction performed within the memory of the satellite decoders and on the television screens complied with fourth and fifth conditions. Since the acts of reproduction concerned were not intended to enable transmission in a network between third

---

[153] CJEU, Case C-360/13 [2014] Public Relations Consultants Association Ltd v. Newspaper Licensing Agency Ltd [43].

[154] ECJ, Case C-5/08 [2009] Infopaq International A/S v. Danske Dagblades Forening ('Infopaq I') [61]; CJEU, Case C-360/13 [2014] Public Relations Consultants Association Ltd v. Newspaper Licensing Agency Ltd [30].

[155] See CJEU, Case C-360/13 [2014] Public Relations Consultants Association Ltd v. Newspaper Licensing Agency Ltd [35].

[156] Recital 33 Copyright Directive; CJEU, Joined Cases C-403/08 and C-429/08 [2011] Football Association Premier League Ltd and others v. Karen Murphy and others [168].

[157] CJEU, Joined Cases C-403/08 and C-429/08 [2011] Football Association Premier League Ltd and others v. Karen Murphy and others [175].

[158] CJEU, Case C-302/10 [2012] Infopaq International A/S v. Danske Dagblades Forening ('Infopaq II') [54].

parties by an intermediary, the Court had to examine whether their sole purpose was to enable a lawful use to be made of a work or other subject-matter. Since the use of the works at issue were not authorised by the copyright holders, it had to be determined whether the acts in question were intended to enable a lawful use of works. The Court decided that they were: the acts of reproduction enabled the satellite decoder and the television screen to function correctly and hence the broadcasts to be received. The mere reception of these broadcasts, however, was neither restricted by EU law nor by domestic legislation. To be sure, domestic legislation prohibited the use of foreign decoding devices. However, as has been shown in Chapter 5, this legislation could not be applied as it was at variance with the freedom to provide services. The reproduction of the protected work thus enabled a 'lawful use'.[159] As far as the fifth requirement of Article 5(1) – the lack of an economic significance – was concerned, the Court observed that the protected works as such had an economic value. However, the temporary acts of reproduction did not generate an *additional* economic advantage going beyond the advantage derived from mere reception of the broadcasts at issue, hence they had no independent economic significance. As a result, the reproduction performed within the memory of the satellite decoders and on the television screens fulfilled the conditions of Article 5(1) of the Copyright Directive and did not require the authorisation of the FAPL.

In *Public Relations Consultants Association Ltd* v. *Newspaper Licensing Agency Ltd*, the Court of Justice decided that on-screen copies and cached copies made by an internet user in the course of viewing a website satisfy the conditions of Articles 5(1) and (5) Copyright Directive.[160] In this case, a media monitoring service (Meltwater) created online monitoring reports, compiled on the basis of keywords provided by the customers, on press articles published on the internet. Meltwater itself had obtained a licence from the newspaper companies. However, the newspaper companies argued that Meltwater's *customers* were also required to obtain their authorisation for receiving the media monitoring service, because the activity of viewing the reports online led to copies being made on the user's computer screen and in the internet 'cache' of that computer's hard disk. They contended that those copies constitute 'reproductions' within the meaning of Article 2 Copyright Directive (a point the Court of Justice agreed with) that do not fall under the exemption provided for in Article 5(1) of that Directive (a point the Court of Justice did not agree with). Somewhat unfortunately, the Court did not have to address the question how the legal situation would have been if Meltwater had not obtained a licence and would thus be in violation of the Copyright Directive. Would the customers' temporary act of reproduction then be exempted by Article 5(1)? Would it make a difference

---

[159] CJEU, Joined Cases C-403/08 and C-429/08 [2011] Football Association Premier League Ltd and others v. Karen Murphy and others [172].

[160] CJEU, Case C-360/13 [2014] Public Relations Consultants Association Ltd v. Newspaper Licensing Agency Ltd. On this decision, see Liu (2013).

whether or not they would have been aware of the fact that Meltwater published the information in violation of copyright? These are two of the most urgent questions for internet users that still await a decision by the Luxembourg Court. The distinction between copying from lawful versus unlawful sources comes up in the context of the private copying exception in Article 5(2)(b) Copyright Directive, which requires that the rights-holders receive fair compensation for reproductions.

Article 5(1) Copyright Directive and Articles 12–14 E-commerce Directive over-lap to a certain extent. To be sure, they regulate very different things. Article 5(1) Copyright Directive carves out rights-holders' exclusive rights, whereas the provisions of the E-commerce Directive immunise intermediaries from liability, *inter alia*, in cases of a copyright violation. Nevertheless, the end result of application of either or both sets of provisions is the same: a 'no liability' finding. So how do these provisions relate to each other? There are considerable differences in their scope of application. First, as regards the beneficiaries of those provisions, Article 5(1) Copyright Directive applies to *any* temporary and transient or incidental reproduction, including by internet users. By contrast, Articles 12 to 14 E-commerce Directive benefits only internet intermediaries. Second, with a view to the activity concerned, Article 5(1) Copyright Directive concerns only *temporary and either transient or incidental* acts of reproduction. Similarly, Articles 12 and 13 E-commerce Directive apply to the 'automatic, intermediate and transient storage' of information. Article 14 E-commerce Directive, however, applies to the *permanent* storage, the 'hosting', of information. An overlap between Article 5(1) Copyright Directive and Article 14 E-commerce Directive is thus barely conceivable, although not entirely impossible. Yet it is much more likely that Article 14 E-commerce Directive is relevant in cases of communication to the public rather than reproduction. Moreover, Article 5(1) Copyright Directive applies only to acts of *reproduction*. By contrast, Articles 12–14 E-commerce Directive have to be regarded as 'filters' that exempt intermediaries horizontally from any liability, including for reproduction, but also, for example, for communication to the public. Third, as regards the scope of the exemption, Articles 12–14 E-commerce Directive exempts intermediaries from any liability except for injunctions, as can be seen from Articles 12(3), 13(2) and 14(3). By contrast, Article 5(1) Copyright Directive also extends to protection against injunctive relief under Article 8(3) Copyright Directive.

As a result, Article 5(1) Copyright Directive and Articles 12 and 13 – and to a very limited extent also Article 14 Commerce Directive – overlap in cases in which:

- an internet intermediary
- is subject to a legal remedy other than an injunction
- for temporarily and either transiently or incidentally
- reproducing copyright-protected work or related subject matter.

So which provisions would apply in such cases, Article 5(1) Copyright Directive or Articles 12, 13 or 14 E-commerce Directive? This is not entirely clear. Recital 16

Copyright Directive states that the Copyright Directive is without prejudice to provisions relating to liability in the E-commerce Directive. This suggests that the E-commerce Directive has to be applied as *lex specialis* in cases of an overlap.[161] Yet one could also argue that in those cases Article 5(1) Copyright Directive and Articles 12, 13 or 14 E-commerce Directive both apply by way of concurrence of laws. In any case, the distinction is of no practical relevance, and the legal practitioner is well advised to consider both sets of rules.

b Further Exceptions and Limitations

Article 10(1) Berne Convention provides a mandatory exception – the only mandatory exception of the Convention. Accordingly, it shall be permissible to make quotations from a work that has already been lawfully made available to the public, provided that their making is compatible with fair practice, and their extent does not exceed that justified by the purpose, including quotations from newspaper articles and periodicals in the form of press summaries. All other Berne Convention exceptions are permissive. For example, pursuant to Article 10(2), the Union States may permit the utilisation, to the extent justified by the purpose, of literary or artistic works by way of illustration in publications, broadcasts or sound or visual recordings for teaching, provided such utilisation is compatible with fair practice. Where use is made of works in accordance with Articles 10(1) or (2), the source, and the name of the author if it appears thereon has to be mentioned (Article 10(3)). Article 10*bis* provides exceptions that are particularly important for the news media. Under Article 10*bis*(1), Union States may permit the reproduction by the press, the broadcasting or the communication to the public by wire of articles published in newspapers or periodicals on current economic, political or religious topics, and of broadcast works of the same character, in cases in which the reproduction, broadcasting or such communication thereof is not expressly reserved. The source of the article must always be clearly indicated; the legal consequences of a breach of this obligation shall be determined by the legislation of the country where protection is claimed. Article 10*bis*(2) permits Union States to determine the conditions under which works may be reproduced and made available to the public for the purpose of reporting current events.

Moreover, pursuant to Article 15 Rome Convention, any Contracting State may provide for exceptions to the protection guaranteed by the Convention as regards:

- private use;
- use of short excerpts in connection with the reporting of current events;
- ephemeral fixation by a broadcasting organisation by means of its own facilities and for its own broadcasts;
- use solely for the purposes of teaching or scientific research.

---

[161] See Aplin (2005, p. 109).

In addition, any Contracting State may provide for the same kinds of limitations with regard to the protection of broadcasting organisations, as it provides for in connection with the protection of copyright in literary and artistic works. However, compulsory licences may be provided for only to the extent to which they are compatible with the Convention.

In the EU copyright framework, exceptions and limitations have to be found, at first, in specific legislation. Article 10 of the Rental Rights Directive provides limitations to the exclusive right conferred on owners of related rights in Articles 7–9 Rental Rights Directive. Member States may provide for limitations to these rights in respect of:

- private use;
- use of short excerpts in connection with the reporting of current events;
- ephemeral fixation by a broadcasting organisation by means of its own facilities and for its own broadcasts;
- use solely for the purposes of teaching or scientific research.

Exceptions and limitations to exclusive rights conferred on authors and holders of related rights under the Copyright Directive can be found in Article 5 of that Directive. Consider the following general aspects when reading and applying this provision. First, as an exception that derogates from a general principle established by the same Directive, in this case the exclusive rights in Articles 2–4, Article 5 has to be interpreted strictly.[162] Second, Articles 5(1) and (2) only apply to the reproduction right in Article 2 Copyright Directive, whereas Article 5(3) provides exceptions and limitations to both Article 2 and the right to disseminate and make available in Article 3. Where the Member States may provide for an exception or limitation to the right of reproduction, they may provide similarly for an exception or limitation to the right of distribution as referred to in Article 4 'to the extent justified by the purpose of the authorised act of reproduction' (Article 5(4)). Third, many exceptions apply only under the caveat that the act of reproduction or dissemination is not commercial, such as Articles 5(2)(b) and 5(3)(a). Fourth, Articles 5(2) and (3) leaves discretion to the Member States as to their implementation, whereas Article 5(1) does not.[163] It is for the Member States to decide which of the exceptions provided in Articles 5(2) and (3) they implement. This deference of the EU legislation can be explained against the background of diverging copyright philosophies in the Member States, namely whether they conceptualise copyright as an instrument of control or to ensure financial remuneration.[164] Copyright is an exclusive right. Those who hold a copyright over particular content may determine whether it may be used, particularly whether it is published or not. Copyright is thus, in the first place, an

---

[162] See, for example, ECJ, Case C-5/08 [2009] Infopaq International A/S v. Danske Dagblades Forening ('Infopaq I') [56–58]; CJEU, Case C-201/13 [2014] Deckmyn v. Vandersteen [22].

[163] Nevertheless, the exceptions in Articles 5(2) and (3) are exhaustive, hence the Member States may not introduce other exceptions and limitations (Recital 32 Copyright Directive).

[164] Compare Woods (2012, p. 211).

instrument of control. The more exceptions to the exclusive copyright a jurisdiction provides, the less control over his content the rights-holder may exercise.

Fifth, the exceptions in Articles 5(2) and (3) are exhaustive, hence the Member States may not introduce other exceptions and limitations (Recital 32 Copyright Directive). Article 5 Copyright Directive thus provides a 'closed' list of exceptions and limitations, in contrast to, for example, the 'fair use' in the US.

Sixth, in certain cases in which Member States decide to limit the control of the rights-holder as provided by Articles 5(2) and (3), they may have to allow for an obligation to fair compensation, such as Article 5(2)(a) and Article 5(2)(e). In addition, the Member States may provide for fair compensation for rights-holders also when applying the optional provisions on exceptions or limitations that do not require such compensation.[165] In those cases, copyright ceases to be an instrument of control and becomes an instrument to ensure financial compensation. Needless to say that the decision between copyright as an instrument of control, on the one hand, and copyright as an instrument to ensure remuneration (including the level of remuneration), on the other hand, is subject to political conflicts.

Recital 35 of the Copyright Directive establishes relevant factors for the establishment of the level of compensation: the possible harm to the rights-holders resulting from the act in question, whether rights-holders have already received payment in some other form (for instance as part of a licence fee) and the degree of use of technological protection measures.[166] The European Commission took the view that no obligation for payment may arise regarding certain single, temporary acts of copying a broadcast work or other subject matter that are undertaken solely for the purpose of enabling it to be viewed and/or listened to at a more convenient time ('time-shifting').[167]

Finally, the exceptions and limitations provided for in Article 5 Copyright Directive shall only be applied in certain special cases that do not conflict with a normal exploitation of the work or other subject-matter and do not unreasonably prejudice the legitimate interests of the rights-holder. This follows from Article 5(5) and applies on the international level by virtue of Article 10 WIPO Copyright Treaty 1996.

Article 5(2) concerns exceptions and limitations only to the reproduction right provided for in Article 2 Copyright Directive. These exceptions and limitations include cases of reprography; reproductions for private use;[168] the preservation of ephemeral recordings of works made by broadcasting organisations in official archives; and reproductions of broadcasts made by social institutions pursuing non-commercial purposes, such as hospitals or prisons.

---

[165] Recital 35 Copyright Directive.

[166] On the application of those factors, see CJEU, Case C-572/13 [2015] Hewlett-Packard Belgium v. Reprobel [36 ff].

[167] Council of the European Union, Proposal for a Directive of the European Parliament and of the Council on the harmonisation of certain aspects of copyright and related rights in the information society, Addendum, 15 September 2000, 1997/0359 (COD), p. 2.

[168] See CJEU, Case C-435/12 [2014] ACI Adam BV and others v. Stichting de Thuiskopie and others.

Article 5(2)(c) is an important provision for the information society. It allows 'specific acts of reproduction made by publicly accessible libraries, educational establishments or museums, or by archives, which are not for direct or indirect economic or commercial advantage'. This covers, for example, certain acts of digitisation necessary for the preservation of works in library catalogues. However, as the provision permits only 'specific acts of reproduction', the exception does not furnish libraries and the other beneficiaries with a blanket exception from the exclusive right of reproduction.[169] Moreover, it does not cover uses made in the context of online delivery of protected works or other subject-matter.[170] Finally, private entities, such as Google with its 'Google Books' project, are not covered by this exception.

Article 5(3) stipulates exceptions or limitations to both the reproduction right in Article 2 and the communication as well as making-available right in Article 3 Copyright Directive. These include, for example, cases of illustrations for teaching or scientific research; uses for the benefit of people with a disability; use during religious celebrations; and analogue uses in certain other cases of minor importance where exceptions or limitations already exist under national law, provided that they do not affect the free circulation of goods and services within the EU.

Article 5(3)(c) Copyright Directive reflects the ideas of Article 10*bis* Berne Convention. It provides two exceptions: the first one applies to published articles specifically, and the second one to works and other subject-matter in general, such as photographs. Published articles may be reproduced by the press, communicated to the public or made available:

1 on current economic, political or religious topics or of broadcast works or other subject-matter of the same character;
2 where such use is not expressly reserved; and
3 and as long as the source, including the author's name, is indicated.

Other works or subject-matter, such as photographs, may be used:

1 in connection with the reporting of current events;
2 to the extent justified by the informatory purpose; and
3 as long as the source, including the author's name, is indicated, unless this turns out to be impossible.

Article 5(3)(c) is an important and remarkable provision. It includes an exception for 'the press', thus raising the problem we discussed in Chapter 1: How shall 'the press' be defined? Moreover, is it justified to exclude other contributors to matters of

---

[169] COM, Report on the application of Directive 2001/29/EC on the harmonisation of certain aspects of copyright and related rights in the information society, SEC(2007) 1556, p. 5; Green Paper Copyright in the Knowledge Economy, COM(2008) 466/3, p. 8.
[170] Recital 40 Copyright Directive.

general interest that would not have to be considered 'press' in a formal sense, such as NGOs, from the exception provided by this provision? Then, Article 5(3)(c) applies to 'current events' and 'current economic, political or religious topics'. The interpretation of the notion of 'current' has been subject to litigation in the Member States, but there is no decision of the Court of Justice available yet.[171] According to the leading commentary on the Copyright Directive, events are to be regarded as 'current' if they 'take place close to the time of use and, within this time frame, still have an informatory value and interest for the public'.[172]

Like the other exceptions and limitations codified in Article 5(2) and (3), Article 5(3)(c) Copyright Directive is merely optional for the Member States to implement. But it is questionable whether this also applies in light of Articles 10 ECHR and 11(2) EUChFR. Copyright imposes limitations on others who want to publish certain information included in a work by granting its creator exclusive rights. Therefore, provisions restricting the use of copyright-protected material and their enforcement may constitute an interference with the user's right of freedom of expression or media freedom and must thus be in accordance with the conditions for restrictions of these rights.[173] As the ECtHR indicated, restrictions based on intellectual property rights are not justified if the use of the protected information contributes to a debate of general concern.[174] As a consequence, legislation protecting copyright has to provide mechanisms for conflicting rights and interests to be duly balanced, particularly by providing exemptions for journalists from copyright provisions. Article 5(3)(c) of the Copyright Directive fulfils exactly this function. There is thus good reason to conclude that, in light of Articles 10 ECHR and 11 EUChFR, Member States are under an obligation to implement Article 5(3)(c) Copyright Directive.

Article 5(3)(d) Copyright Directive provides an exception for quotations for purposes such as criticism or review.[175] The Member States may, under the following requirements, exempt the use of a work from the author's exclusive right to reproduction and communication:

1 if the use of the work consists of a quotation for purposes such as criticism or review;

---

171 See Hyde Park Residence v. Yelland [2001] Ch 143; Newspaper Licensing Agency Ltd v. Marks & Spencer plc [2003] 3 WLR 1256. From academic literature, see Kelly (2012).

172 Von Lewinski and Walter (2010, paras. 11.5.56–57).

173 ECtHR, Ashby Donald and others v. France [2013] App. no. 36769/08 [34]; Neij and Sunde Kolmisoppi v. Sweden [2013] App. no. 40397/12; CJEU, Case C-70/10 [2011] Scarlet Extended v. SABAM and others [43]; Volokh (2003a), see also Volokh (2003b).

174 See, *mutatis mutandis*, ECtHR, Ashby Donald and others v. France [2013] App. no. 36769/08; Neij and Sunde Kolmisoppi v. Sweden [2013] App. no. 40397/12.

175 See also Article 10(1) of the Berne Convention: 'It shall be permissible to make quotations from a work which has already been lawfully made available to the public, provided that their making is compatible with fair practice, and their extent does not exceed that justified by the purpose, including quotations from newspaper articles and periodicals in the form of press summaries.'

2 if it relates to a work or other subject-matter that has already been lawfully made available to the public;

3 if the source, including the author's name, is indicated, unless this turns out to be impossible; and

4 if the use is in accordance with fair practice, and to the extent required by the specific purpose.

Note that the purposes of criticism or review are merely examples for the exception provided in this paragraph. The Commission has thus considered Article 5(3)(d) as a possible exception for the notion of 'transformative use'; that is, the creation of a derivative work using a source work in new ways.[176] While the notion of 'transformative use' has been considered, for example, in the United States as a possible justification qualifying for the 'fair use' doctrine,[177] the EU copyright framework does not provide an explicit exception for transformative use, except for the parody clause in Article 5(3)(k). Article 5(3)(d) Copyright Directive played a crucial role in the case of *Painer*, our first case example.

Article 5(3)(f) Copyright Directive permits the use of political speeches as well as extracts of public lectures or similar works or subject-matter:

1 to the extent justified by the informatory purpose; and

2 provided that the source, including the author's name, is indicated, except where this turns out to be impossible.

Article 5(3)(k) allows Member States to establish an exception for use for the purpose of caricature, parody or pastiche. As with Article 5(3)(c) Copyright Directive, there are strong arguments that Article 5(3)(k) is not merely optional for the Member States to implement, but that such a provision is necessary as a gateway for the balancing exercise between freedom of expression and conflicting copyright protection.

The provision was at the heart of the 2014 decision *Deckmyn* v. *Vandersteen*. A politician of a Flemish nationalist political party handed out calendars in which he was named as the editor. On the cover page of those calendars appeared a drawing resembling that appearing on the cover of a *Suske en Wiske* comic book,[178] which was completed in 1961 by the late Willy Vandersteen. The book's title was *De Wilde Weldoener*, which the CJEU roughly translated as *The Compulsive Benefactor*. The original drawing was a representation of one of the comic book's main characters wearing a white tunic and throwing coins to people who are trying to pick them up. In the drawing of Mr Deckmyn's calendar, that character was replaced by the Mayor of the City of Ghent and the people picking up the coins were replaced by people wearing veils and people of colour. Mr Vandersteen's heirs claimed that the drawing at issue and its communication to the public constituted an infringement of their

---

[176] COM, Green paper Copyright in the Knowledge Economy, COM(2008) 466/3, p. 20.

[177] See US Supreme Court, Campbell v. Acuff-Rose Music, 510 U.S. 569 (1994).

[178] *Bob et Bobette* in French, known as *Spike and Suzy* in Britain and as *Willy and Wanda* in the US.

respective copyrights. Mr Deckmyn argued that his version of the drawing fell under the parody exception in Article 5(3)(k) Copyright Directive.

At first, the Court decided – not unexpectedly – that the concept of 'parody' within the meaning of the Directive has to be regarded as an autonomous concept of EU law and interpreted uniformly throughout the EU.[179] The Court then went on to explain the characteristics of the notion of 'parody':

1 It has to evoke an existing work while being noticeably different from it, and
2 it has to constitute an expression of humour or mockery.[180]

In its reply to the referring Belgian court, the European Court also noted which requirements on parody Article 5(3)(k) does *not* impose: that parody had to display an original character of its own, other than that of displaying noticeable differences with respect to the original parodied work; that it had to be attributed to a person other than the author of the original work itself; or that it had to relate to the original work itself or mention the source of the parodied work. As a result, the Court interpreted the notion of 'parody' broadly, including both the parody 'on' and the parody 'with' an original work, the latter being applicable in this case.

But the Court then observed that Article 5(3)(k) of the Copyright Directive serves to balance the conflicting fundamental rights and interests of copyright and freedom of expression as well as the public interest.[181] Within this balancing exercise, the Court noted that Mr Deckmyn's parody was capable of conveying a discriminatory message, which had the effect of associating the protected work with such a message. The parody thus also conflicted with Article 21(1) EUChFR on the prohibition of discrimination.[182] Although the balancing exercise was eventually for the Belgian courts, the Court indicated that the Vandersteen heirs had a legitimate interest in ensuring that the work protected by copyright is not associated with such a message.[183]

Finally, Article 5(3)(n) permits the 'communication or making available, for the purpose of research or private study, to individual members of the public by dedicated terminals on the premises of establishments referred to in [Article 5(2)(c)] of works and other subject-matter not subject to purchase or licensing terms which are contained in their collections'. This provision envisages the same beneficiaries as Article 5(2)(c), such as public libraries and archives. By contrast to that provision, Article 5(3)(n) allows the 'communication or making available to the public'. However, this is restricted to the premises of the library or archive, hence the material could not be made available online. In the case of *Technische Universität Darmstadt v. Eugen Ulmer KG*, the Court of Justice decided that Member States may permit the

---

[179] CJEU, Case C-201/13 [2014] Deckmyn v. Vandersteen [15].
[180] CJEU, Case C-201/13 [2014] Deckmyn v. Vandersteen [20].
[181] CJEU, Case C-201/13 [2014] Deckmyn v. Vandersteen [27].
[182] CJEU, Case C-201/13 [2014] Deckmyn v. Vandersteen [29–30].
[183] CJEU, Case C-201/13 [2014] Deckmyn v. Vandersteen [31]. From academic literature on *Deckmyn*, see, for example, European Copyright Society (2015).

users of a library to print the works out on paper or store them on a USB stick from dedicated terminals. However, it is necessary that fair compensation in particular be paid to the rights-holders.[184]

c The 'Three-Step Test'

According to Article 9(2) of the Berne Convention, national legislation may permit the reproduction of works under a three-step test:

1 There has to be a 'certain special case'.
2 The reproduction does not conflict with a normal exploitation of the work.
3 The reproduction does not unreasonably prejudice the legitimate interests of the author.

Although Article 9(2) Berne Convention only applies to reproduction, the three-step test has been extended by Article 13 of the TRIPS Agreement to all exclusive rights covered by this Agreement, as well as by Article 10 WIPO Copyright Treaty and Article 16 of the WIPO Performances and Phonograms Treaty to the minimum rights established by those Treaties. The EU has included this test in Article 5(5) Copyright Directive, Article 10(2) Rental Rights Directive and partly also in Article 6(3) Software Directive and in Article 6(3) Database Directive. The three-step test can thus be considered one of the cornerstones of international copyright law.[185] It is to be understood as an order to the national legislature to draft exceptions and limitations only for certain special cases, thereby considering the conflicting interests.[186]

But it is questionable whether the three-step test under Article 5(5) Copyright Directive has any additional significance to Articles 5(1) to (4).[187] The Court of Justice's case law is not entirely clear on the legal significance of the three-step test in the Copyright Directive. The Court has indicated that the exceptions and limitations must be interpreted 'in the light of Article 5(5)'.[188] Article 5(5) does not define the substantive content of the different exceptions and limitations, 'but takes effect only at the time when they are applied by the Member States'.[189] But the Court also held that the requirements of Article 5(5) are fulfilled if the requirements of the exception, in this case Article 5(1), are fulfilled.[190] That reasoning appears circular. The Copyright Directive itself indicates that the exceptions or limitations, when implemented by the Member States, should reflect the increased economic impact they may have in

---

[184] See CJEU, Case C-117/13 [2014] Technische Universität Darmstadt v. Eugen Ulmer KG.
[185] See, for example, WTO Panel, United States – Section 110(5) of the US Copyright Act [2000] WT/DS160/R [6.97 ff]. From academic literature, see Senftleben (2004).
[186] Von Lewinski and Walter (2010, para. 11.5.78).
[187] Bently and Sherman (2014, p. 222).
[188] ECJ, Case C-5/08 [2009] Infopaq International A/S v. Danske Dagblades Forening ('Infopaq I') [58].
[189] CJEU, Case C-435/12 [2014] ACI Adam BV and others v. Stichting de Thuiskopie and others [25].
[190] See CJEU, Joined Cases C-403/08 and C-429/08 [2011] Football Association Premier League Ltd and others v. Karen Murphy and others [181].

the new electronic environment. As a consequence, 'the scope of certain exceptions or limitations may have to be even more limited when it comes to certain new uses of copyright works and other subject-matter'.[191]

7 Term of Copyright Protection

The term of copyright protection is in principle determined by each state individually, but it is to a certain extent harmonised by international agreements. The term of protection granted by the Berne Convention shall be the life of the author and 50 years after his death (Article 7(1)). In the case of cinematographic works, the countries of the Union may provide that the term of protection shall expire 50 years after the work has been made available to the public with the consent of the author, or, failing such an event within 50 years from the making of such a work, 50 years after the making (Article 7(2)). The term of protection to be granted for broadcasts under the Rome Convention shall last at least until the end of a period of 20 years computed from the end of the year in which the broadcast took place (Article 14(c)).

Within the EU, the term of protection is largely harmonised by the Term of Protection Directive.[192] Accordingly, the rights of an author of a literary or artistic work within the meaning of Article 2 of the Berne Convention shall run for the life of the author and for 70 years after their death (Article 1(1)). The term of protection of cinematographic or audiovisual works shall expire 70 years after the death of the last of the following persons to survive, whether or not these persons are designated as co-authors: the principal director, the author of the screenplay, the author of the dialogue and the composer of music specifically created for use in the cinematographic or audiovisual work (Article 2(2)). Unlike these author's rights, the term of protection of related rights, such as the rights granted to performers, phonograms, films and broadcasts, does not depend on the life of the creator, but rather of the first performance, publication, fixation or transmission, depending on the related right in question. Moreover, the protection lasts in principle only for 50 years (Article 3). This has been made subject to several exceptions in the 2011 amendment to the Term of Protection Directive: under certain circumstances, the protection of performers and phonograms shall extend to 70 years.

8 The Enforcement of Copyright

Legislation on intellectual property litigation is largely left to states. Nevertheless, international law and particularly EU law provide a range of rules on the

---

[191] Recital 44 Copyright Directive.
[192] Directive 2006/116/EC of the European Parliament and of the Council of 12 December 2006 on the term of protection of copyright and certain related rights (codified version), OJ L 372/12, as amended by Directive 2011/77/EU of the European Parliament and of the Council of 27 September 2011 amending Directive 2006/116/EC on the term of protection of copyright and certain related rights, OJ L 265/1.

enforcement of copyright and intellectual property rights in general, such as rules on evidence[193] and rights on information.[194] After a brief introduction into the international and European legal framework, this section will focus on aspects that are particularly relevant for modern mass media communication, namely the protection of personal data of those infringing copyright online and the liability of internet intermediaries for providing access to, or hosting of, copyright-infringing content.

a The Legal Framework

According to Article 14 WIPO Copyright Treaty and Article 41 TRIPS Agreement, the Contracting Parties shall ensure that enforcement procedures are available under their law so as to permit effective action against any act of infringement of rights covered by these treaties, including expeditious remedies to prevent infringements and remedies that constitute a deterrent to further infringements. These procedures shall be applied in such a manner as to avoid the creation of barriers to legitimate trade and to provide for safeguards against their abuse. The TRIPS Agreement then specifies the remedies: civil and administrative proceedings, including injunctions (Article 44), claims for damages (Article 45) and provisional measures (Articles 50 ff) and also criminal proceedings (Article 61). According to Article 46, the judicial authorities shall have the authority to order that goods that they have found to be infringing intellectual property rights be disposed of or destroyed in order to create an effective deterrent to infringement. Pursuant to Article 16 Berne Convention, infringing copies of a work shall be liable to seizure in any country of the Union where the work enjoys legal protection.

According to Article 8 Copyright Directive, Member States shall provide and apply appropriate sanctions and remedies in respect of copyright infringements. They shall ensure that rights-holders whose interests are affected by an infringing activity carried out on its territory can bring an action for damages, apply for an injunction and apply for the seizure of infringing material. The Directive 2004/48/EC on the enforcement of intellectual property rights concerns the measures, procedures and remedies necessary to ensure the enforcement of intellectual property rights in general, including copyright.[195] However, criminal sanctions are not included in the scope of the Directive; such measures are left for the Member States to legislate. Persons entitled to seek application of the measures, procedures and remedies referred to in the Directive are not only the holders of intellectual property rights themselves. All other persons authorised to use those rights, in particular licensees, intellectual property collective rights-management bodies as

---

[193] See Articles 6 and 7 Enforcement Directive; Article 43 TRIPS Agreement.
[194] See Article 8 Enforcement Directive; Article 47 TRIPS Agreement.
[195] Directive 2004/48/EC of the European Parliament and of the Council of 29 April 2004 on the enforcement of intellectual property rights, OJ L 195/16.

well professional defence bodies that are regularly recognised as having a right to represent holders of intellectual property rights, shall have standing under the Directive, insofar as permitted by and in accordance with the provisions of the applicable law (Article 4 Enforcement Directive).

The first problem of any copyright owner to enforce their copyright is thus to prove that he is the owner of that right. This is because copyright is not a registered right. Therefore, according to Article 15 of the Berne Convention, a person shall be regarded as the author of a literary or artistic work, and consequently be entitled to institute infringement proceedings in the countries of the Union, if their name or pseudonym appears on the work. The Enforcement Directive adopted the rule laid down in Article 15 of the Berne Convention, which establishes the presumption whereby the author of a literary or artistic work is regarded as such if his name appears on the work. A similar presumption applies to the owners of related rights (Article 5 Enforcement Directive).

Article 9 of the Enforcement Directive provides rules on provisional and precautionary measures, such as interim injunctions and the seizure of goods suspected of infringing an intellectual property right. Article 10 Enforcement Directive empowers judicial authorities to order that measures be taken with regard to goods that they have found to be infringing an intellectual property right, including their removal from the channels of commerce and their destruction. Moreover, where a judicial decision is taken finding an infringement of an intellectual property right, the judicial authorities may issue against the infringer an injunction aimed at prohibiting the continuation of the infringement (Article 11). Article 13 Enforcement Directive furnishes the rights-holder with a claim for damages against the infringer. Article 3(2) Enforcement Directive may cause some irritation in continental jurisdictions, because it requires remedies to be 'dissuasive'. This raises the question whether the Directive requires punitive damages, a concept that is largely rejected in continental legal systems. But Article 13, together with Recital 26, of the Enforcement Directive explains how the amount of damages to be awarded to the rights-holder can be established: either by considering all appropriate aspects, such as the loss of earnings incurred by the rights-holder or the unfair profits made by the infringer and the moral prejudice caused to the rights-holder by the infringement, or by a hypothetical assessment of the royalties or fees that would have been due if the infringer had requested authorisation to use the intellectual property right in question – the so-called licence analogy. Recital 26 clarifies that it is not the aim of the Enforcement Directive to introduce an obligation to provide for punitive damages.

Pursuant to Article 3 Enforcement Directive and Article 8 Copyright Directive, those measures, procedures and remedies shall not only be effective and dissuasive, but also proportionate. Therefore, domestic courts also have to consider the rights of the (alleged or actual) infringer and other persons concerned, such as internet service providers and internet users. This balancing exercise has to take place within the framework provided by fundamental rights, such as Article 17(2) EUChFR, Articles 7 and 8 EUChFR and Article 11(1) and (2) EUChFR. The relationship between the Copyright Directive and the Enforcement Directive, on the one hand, and the E-commerce Directive as well as the EU rules on the protection of personal data, on the other hand, has been subject to considerable case law by the CJEU.

b Protection of Personal Data

Article 8(1) of the Enforcement Directive stipulates that the competent judicial authorities may order that information on the origin and distribution networks of the goods or services that infringe an intellectual property right on a commercial scale be provided. Therefore, domestic courts may order internet service providers to disclose information to intellectual property claimants which is necessary to identify a wrongdoer, such a names, addresses, IP addresses, connection and traffic data of their customers. Under UK law, this would be conducted by way of a so-called *Norwich Pharmacal* order.[196] Such an order requires a delicate balancing exercise between conflicting rights and interests. On behalf of copyright holders these are notably Article 17(2) EUChFR, Article 47 EUChFR (right to an effective remedy), Article 8 Copyright Directive and Articles 41, 42 and 47 of the TRIPs Agreement, which require the effective protection of intellectual property rights and the institution of judicial remedies for their enforcement. Internet users may invoke Articles 7 and 8 EUChFR as well as the protection of personal data under EU secondary law in the Data Protection Directive and the E-privacy Directive (see Chapter 8). Article 1(5)(b) of the E-commerce Directive, Article 9 of the Copyright Directive and Article 8(3)(e) of the Enforcement Directive clarify that the protection of copyright does not affect the requirements of the protection of personal data.

The *locus classicus* on the reconciliation of these interests is the ECJ decision in the case of *Promusicae* v. *Telefónica de España SAU*. Promusicae, which represented music and film producers, applied for a court order against the internet access provider Telefónica to disclose the identities and physical addresses of certain persons whom it provided with internet access services, whose IP address and date and time of connection were known. According to Promusicae, those persons used a peer-to-peer file-exchange programme involving music in which the members of Promusicae held the exploitation rights. The Court distinguished three questions, which can be summarised as follows:[197]

1 Do the data protection directives *preclude* the Member States from imposing an obligation on an access provider to communicate personal data which will enable the copyright holder to bring civil proceedings against the infringer?

---

[196] Named after Norwich Pharmacal Co v. Customs and Excise Commissioners [1974] AC 133.
[197] ECJ, Case C-275/06 [2008] Promusicae v. Telefónica de España SAU [46].

2 If this is not the case, does the copyright framework *require* Member States to lay down such an obligation?

3 What reading of the applicable directives does the EUChFR require?

Regarding the first question, Article 5(1) of the E-privacy Directive protects the confidentiality of communications by means of a public communications network and publicly available electronic communications services, and of the related traffic data. Therefore, the storage of that data without the consent of the users concerned is basically prohibited. However, under Article 15(1) of that Directive, the Member States may adopt legislative measures necessary to safeguard public order interests, such as national security and the prevention and prosecution of criminal offences. Yet none of the exceptions mentioned in Article 15(1) relates to civil proceedings.[198] However, Article 15(1) also refers to Article 13(1) of the Data Protection Directive. As we saw in Chapter 8, that provision also allows measures necessary, *inter alia*, for the protection of the rights and freedoms of others. This also includes intellectual property rights. Therefore, the European legislative framework on data protection does not *per se* preclude the possibility for the Member States of laying down an obligation to disclose personal data in the context of civil proceedings.[199]

It is thus necessary to address the second question. As the data protection directives do not *preclude* the Member States from imposing an obligation on access providers to communicate personal data, does the copyright framework even *require* Member States to lay down an obligation that will enable copyright holders to bring civil proceedings against infringers? As has been stated before, Article 1(5)(b) of the E-commerce Directive, Article 9 of the Copyright Directive and Article 8(3)(e) of the Enforcement Directive clarify that the protection of copyright does not affect the requirements of the protection of personal data. Therefore, it cannot follow from Article 8(1) of the Enforcement Directive that it requires the Member States to lay down an obligation to communicate personal data in the context of civil proceedings in disregard of applicable data protection provisions. Nor can this follow from Articles 15(2) and 18(1) E-commerce Directive, from Article 8(1) and (2) of the Copyright Directive or from and Articles 41, 42 and 47 of the TRIPs Agreement.[200]

---

[198] ECJ, Case C-275/06 [2008] Promusicae v. Telefónica de España SAU [51].

[199] ECJ, Case C-275/06 [2008] Promusicae v. Telefónica de España SAU [54]; confirmed in Case C-557/07 [2009] LSG-Gesellschaft zur Wahrnehmung von Leistungsschutzrechten GmbH [29].

[200] ECJ, Case C-275/06 [2008] Promusicae v. Telefónica de España SAU [58–59]. Article 15(2) E-commerce Directive reads: 'Member States may establish obligations for information society service providers promptly to inform the competent public authorities of alleged illegal activities undertaken or information provided by recipients of their service or obligations to communicate to the competent authorities, at their request, information enabling the identification of recipients of their service with whom they have storage agreements.' Article 18(1) E-commerce Directive states: 'Member States shall ensure that court actions available under national law concerning information society services' activities allow for the rapid adoption of measures, including interim measures, designed to terminate any alleged infringement and to prevent any further impairment of the interests involved.'

As an intermediate result, neither does the data protection framework prohibit an obligation of access providers to communicate personal data in copyright proceedings nor does the copyright framework require such an obligation. However, as secondary EU law, those directives have to be interpreted in light of primary EU law, especially fundamental rights. Which interpretation do Articles 17(2) and 47 EUChFR, on the one hand, and Articles 7 and 8 EUChFR, on the other hand, require? As has been shown in Chapter 8, the gateway to take on board these human rights concerns is Article 15(1) E-privacy Directive in conjunction with Article 13(1) Data Protection Directive, which permit restrictions on the communication intermediaries' obligation to protect the confidentiality of communications in order to safeguard, *inter alia*, the protection of the rights and freedoms of others. The Court of Justice did not itself decide which outcome this balancing exercise requires, but left this to the Member States. However, the Court indicated that the Member States' institutions must, when transposing and applying the directives, rely on an interpretation of the directives that strikes a fair balance between the fundamental rights involved.[201] It would thus be incompatible with EU law if, for example, a Member State would implement the EU directives in a way that copyright legislation would compel courts to issue an order against internet service providers to disclose information to intellectual property claimants that is necessary to identify a wrongdoer. Nor could a fair balance be struck if Member States' data protection legislation would *per se* preclude such an order. Instead, administrative authorities and courts have to balance, and they have to be in a position to balance, the conflicting interests on a case-by-case basis. The key analytical tool for this balancing exercise is the principle of proportionality, which has already been dealt with in Chapter 3.

c Liability of Internet Intermediaries

In many cases of online infringement of intellectual property – especially copyright, but also trademarks – it is not possible or is too costly to identify the person who has committed the infringing act. In such cases, internet intermediaries seem to be best placed to bring such infringing activities to an end. Therefore, Article 8(3) Copyright Directive stipulates that Member States shall ensure that rights-holders are in a position to apply for an injunction against intermediaries whose services are used by a third party to infringe a copyright or related right. This possibility should be available even where the acts carried out by the intermediary are exempted under Article 5 Copyright Directive.[202]

At the same time, Article 8(3) Copyright Directive has to be reconciled with the regime guaranteeing the immunity from liability of internet intermediaries in the

---

[201] ECJ, Case C-275/06 [2008] Promusicae v. Telefónica de España SAU [68]. See also WP29, Working document on data protection issues related to intellectual property rights, 18 January 2005.
[202] Recital 59 Copyright Directive.

E-commerce Directive. According to its Article 2(3)(a), the Enforcement Directive 'shall not affect ... [the E-commerce Directive], in general, and Articles 12 to 15 of [the E-commerce Directive] in particular'. As we have seen in Chapter 6, Articles 12 to 15 E-commerce Directive address liability for activities in the network environment, including IP rights, horizontally. Notably, however, Article 13 of the E-commerce Directive has been specifically tailored to copyright infringements.[203] This provision basically exempts the activity of 'caching' from liability. As has been shown before, the process of 'caching' can be regarded as an act of reproducing protected work within the meaning of Article 2 Copyright Directive.

Google France v. *Louis Vuitton* concerned Google's 'AdWords' services operating in Google's internet search engine results. Louis Vuitton brought proceedings against Google with a view to obtaining a declaration that Google had infringed its trademarks by offering 'sponsored links' to sites offering imitation versions of Vuitton's products. Moreover, Google had offered advertisers the possibility of selecting not only keywords that correspond to Vuitton's trademarks, but also those keywords in combination with expressions indicating imitation, such as 'imitation' and 'copy'. As has been set out in Chapter 6, the Court of Justice had to decide this case in light of Article 14 E-commerce Directive, which essentially exempts host providers from liability. In this context, the Court established its 'active role' doctrine: Article 14 E-commerce Directive only applies if the service provider has 'played an active role of such a kind as to give it knowledge of, or control over, the data stored'.[204] In turn, the host provider enjoys the privilege of Article 14 if his role was neutral in the sense that its conduct is merely technical, automatic and passive, pointing to a lack of knowledge or control of the data that it stores.[205] Whether this was the case was for the domestic court to decide.

L'Oréal and others v. *eBay and others* then involved an injunction against an online marketplace. eBay had displayed listings of goods offered for sale by its customers, some of which allegedly infringed L'Oréal's trademark rights. L'Oréal brought an action against eBay, arguing that eBay and several of eBay's customers were liable for sales of 17 items made by those individuals through eBay's website. L'Oréal also claimed that, even if eBay was not liable for the infringements of its trademark rights, it should be granted an injunction against eBay by virtue of Article 11 Enforcement of Directive. According to Article 11 Enforcement Directive, the judicial authorities may issue against the infringer of an intellectual property right an injunction aimed at prohibiting the continuation of the infringement. Referring to the *Google France* judgment, the CJEU decided that if eBay

---

[203] L. Edwards, in Edwards and Waelde (2009, p. 64).

[204] CJEU, Joined Cases C-236/08 to C-238/08 [2010] Google France SARL and others v. Louis Vuitton Malletier SA and others [120].

[205] CJEU, Joined Cases C-236/08 to C-238/08 [2010] Google France SARL and others v. Louis Vuitton Malletier SA and others [114]; see also Case C-324/09 [2011] L'Oréal SA and others v. eBay International AG and others [113].

has provided assistance which entails, in particular, optimising the presenta-tion of the offers for sale in question or promoting those offers, it must be considered not to have taken a neutral position between the customer-seller concerned and potential buyers but to have played an active role of such a kind as to give it knowledge of, or control over, the data relating to those offers for sale.[206]

In such a case it cannot benefit from Article 14 E-commerce Directive. Moreover, the Court had to decide whether the third sentence of Article 11 Enforcement Directive requires the Member States to afford proprietors of intellectual property rights the right to obtain against the operator of a website, such as the operator of an online marketplace by means of which their rights have been infringed, injunctions requiring the operator to take measures to prevent future infringements of those rights. According to the first sentence of Article 11, Member States shall ensure that the judicial authorities may issue against the infringer of an intellectual property right an injunction aimed at prohibiting the continuation of the infringement. The third sentence of Article 11 then stipulates that Member States shall also ensure that rights-holders are in a position to apply for an injunction against intermedi-aries whose services are used by a third party to infringe an intellectual property right. The Court highlighted the difference between the first and the third sentence: while the first sentence allows for an injunction aimed at prohibiting the *continu-ation* of the infringement, the third sentence speaks of injunctions against inter-mediaries, but without reference to a continuation of an infringement. The third sentence thus needs to have a meaning distinct from the first sentence, otherwise it would be redundant. However, by reference to Article 18 E-commerce Directive, the Court decided that the third sentence has to be understood as allowing national courts to order an online service provider to take measures that contribute not only to bringing to an end infringements committed through that marketplace, but also to preventing further infringements.[207] While Article 15(1) E-commerce Directive and Article 3 Enforcement Directive prevent online service providers from being required to undertake active monitoring of all the data of each of its customers in order to prevent any future infringement of intellectual property rights, the opera-tor of an online marketplace may be ordered to take measures to make it easier to identify its customer-sellers.[208] Those measures must strike a fair balance between the various rights and interests concerned.[209] The Court then further elaborated on the notion of this 'fair balance' in *Scarlet Extended* v. *SABAM* and *SABAM* v. *Netlog* (see Chapter 6).[210]

---

[206] CJEU, Case C-324/09 [2011] L'Oréal SA and others v. eBay International AG and others [115–116].
[207] CJEU, Case C-324/09 [2011] L'Oréal SA and others v. eBay International AG and others [131–134].
[208] CJEU, Case C-324/09 [2011] L'Oréal SA and others v. eBay International AG and others [139–142].
[209] CJEU, Case C-324/09 [2011] L'Oréal SA and others v. eBay International AG and others [143].
[210] CJEU, Case C-70/10 [2011] Scarlet Extended v. SABAM and others and Case C-360/10 [2012] SABAM v. Netlog.

In *UPC Telekabel* v. *Constantin Film Verleih*, two film production companies applied, based on Article 8(3) Copyright Directive, for an order enjoining an internet service provider to block access of its customers to the website 'kino.to' on which some of the films the claimants had produced could be downloaded. The Luxembourg Court established, first, that even a mere internet access provider has to be regarded as an intermediary 'whose services are used by a third party to infringe a copyright or related right' within the meaning of Article 8(3) Copyright Directive.[211] To be sure, Article 12 E-commerce Directive basically exempts access providers from liability. However, due to Article 12(3), that provision does not affect the possibility for a court or administrative authority of requiring the service provider to terminate or prevent an infringement. Therefore, an access provider could be made subject to an injunction according to Article 8(3) Copyright Directive.[212]

However, such an injunction has to be compatible with the fundamental rights of the persons affected: the rights-holders, the access provider and customers seeking access to 'kino.to'. In this case, a balance had to be struck between copyrights and related rights, which are protected under Article 17(2) EUChFR, the access provider's freedom to conduct a business under Article 16 EUChFR, and the freedom of information of internet users according to Article 11(1) EUChFR. By contrast to the Advocate-General,[213] the Court ignored the right to impart information according to Article 11(1) EUChFR. Yet, as has been shown in Chapter 2, imparting information is protected under freedom of expression even if the information disseminated is not the publisher's own information.

The Court held the restriction on the freedom to conduct a business to be minor, as the access provider may choose the specific measures in order to block access to the website, and he could avoid liability by proving that he has taken all reasonable measures.[214] With a view to the internet users' right to receive information, the Court held that 'the measures adopted by the internet service provider must be strictly targeted, in the sense that they must serve to bring an end to a third party's infringement of copyright or of a related right but without thereby affecting internet users who are using the provider's services in order to lawfully access information'.[215]

UPC Telekabel concerned an 'outcome prohibition' (*Erfolgsverbot*), meaning that the access provider had to safeguard the outcome of the injunction; that is, blocking access to the website. However, the injunction order did not set out *which* measures the access provider should actually take. So what if Telekabel's blocking measures can be circumvented? The Court merely stated that:

---

[211] CJEU, Case C-314/12 [2014] UPC Telekabel Wien GmbH v. Constantin Film Verleih and others [32].

[212] CJEU, Case C-314/12 [2014] UPC Telekabel Wien GmbH v. Constantin Film Verleih and others [32]; confirming its holding in Case C-557/07 [2009] LSG-Gesellschaft zur Wahrnehmung von Leistungsschutzrechten GmbH [46].

[213] CJEU, Case C-314/12 [2014] UPC Telekabel Wien GmbH v. Constantin Film Verleih and others, Opinion of Advocate-General Cruz Villalón [82].

[214] CJEU, Case C-314/12 [2014] UPC Telekabel Wien GmbH v. Constantin Film Verleih and others [52–53].

[215] CJEU, Case C-314/12 [2014] UPC Telekabel Wien GmbH v. Constantin Film Verleih and others [56].

the measures which are taken by the addressee of an injunction ... must be sufficiently effective to ensure genuine protection of [Article 17(2) EUChFR], that is to say that they must have the effect of preventing unauthorised access to the protected subject-matter or, at least, of making it difficult to achieve and of seriously discouraging internet users who are using the services of the addressee of that injunction from accessing the subject-matter made available to them in breach of that fundamental right.[216]

V The Case Examples

This section discusses the substantive law issues regarding our case examples in *Painer* and *Infopaq*. *Painer* also raised questions of jurisdiction and conflict-of-laws, which will be treated separately in the subsequent section.

1 The Painer Case

In the *Painer* case, it has to be decided, first, whether the photographs are protected as copyright. This had to be decided, in the first place, by Austrian law. However, as has been shown in this chapter, international and EU law significantly influence domestic copyright law, including the requirements for establishing copyright. With a view to the copyright protection of photographs, Article 2(1) of the Berne Convention provides that the notion of literary and artistic works' includes 'photographic works'. Similarly, Article 6 of the Term of Protection Directive regulates the duration of protection of photographs 'which are original in the sense that they are the author's own intellectual creation'. In addition, Member States may provide for the protection of 'other photographs', hence photographs that are not original in the sense that they are the author's own intellectual creation. Austrian law thus distinguishes between copyright-protected 'photographic works' (*Lichtbildwerke*) and mere 'photographs' (*Lichtbilder*) as 'related rights'.[217] In the view of the Austrian Supreme Court, the contested photograph was a photographic work protected by copyright.[218] This was not disputed by the Court of Justice. It reiterated its case law, according to which copyright is liable to apply only in relation to a subject-matter, such as a photograph, which is original in the sense that it is its author's own intellectual creation.[219] This is the case if it reflects the author's personality; that is, whether he 'was able to express his creative abilities in the production of the work by making

---

[216] CJEU, Case C-314/12 [2014] UPC Telekabel Wien GmbH v. Constantin Film Verleih and others [62].

[217] See Sections 2(1)(5), 18, 19, 26, 44, 58 and 62 on photographic works; Section 72 on photographs.

[218] CJEU, Case C-145/10 [2012] Painer v. Standard Verlags GmbH and others [41]; Austrian Supreme Court (Oberster Gerichtshof), Case 4Ob170/07i [2008] 'Natascha K' [5.1]; Case 4Ob102/08s [2008] 'Natascha K II'.

[219] CJEU, Case C-145/10 [2012] Painer v. Standard Verlags GmbH and others [87], providing further references.

free and creative choices'.[220] As regards a portrait photograph, the Court observed that the photographer can make free and creative choices in several ways: he could choose the background, the subject's pose and the lighting, the framing, the angle of view and the atmosphere created.[221] By making those choices, a portrait photographer can stamp the work created with his 'personal touch'.[222] Therefore, a portrait photograph can be protected by copyright if it is an intellectual creation of the author reflecting his personality and expressing free and creative choices in the production of that photograph.[223] Whether or not this is the case is for the national courts to determine. Yet it should be noted that 'originality' is an objective test; that is, the author has made choices that are his own (as opposed to someone else's, or choices that are dictated by external considerations). The term 'personality' used by the Court does not imply that the work has to genuinely reflect subjective values held by the author.

However, the referring Austrian court also asked the CJEU to consider whether the allegedly minor 'creative effort' in making the contested portrait photographs reduced its protection compared to other works, such as artistic photographic works. In other words, did the allegedly minor degree of creative freedom in making a portrait photograph increase the possibility of its free use by the media? The Luxembourg Court denied that, observing that no provision in the EU copyright framework, such as Article 6 Term of Protection Directive and Article 2(a) Copyright Directive, supports that view.[224]

As a consequence, the newspapers would have needed Ms Painer's consent to publish the photographs, as they reproduced the photographs and communicated them to the public within the meaning of Articles 2 and 3 Copyright Directive. Moreover, Article 12 of the Berne Convention expressly states that authors 'shall enjoy the exclusive right of authorising adaptations, arrangements and other alterations of their works'. The question was, therefore, whether these acts where covered by an exception or limitation. One could think of Article 5(3)(c) Copyright Directive. Accordingly, 'use of works … in connection with the reporting of current events, to the extent justified by the informatory purpose', may be exempted from Articles 2 and 3. This depended, of course, on whether Austria had actually implemented Article 5(3)(c) Copyright Directive into domestic law – which it had. However, the Austrian Supreme Court decided that the Austrian provision implementing Article 5(3)(c) Copyright Directive did not apply here. The 'current event' (*Tagesereignis*) was the escape of N. from her kidnapper. The published photos of N. as a child may have informed the reader about N.'s looks before her abduction. However, it did not

---

[220] CJEU, Case C-145/10 [2012] Painer v. Standard Verlags GmbH and others [88–89]; see also Recital 16 Term of Protection Directive.

[221] CJEU, Case C-145/10 [2012] Painer v. Standard Verlags GmbH and others [90–91].

[222] CJEU, Case C-145/10 [2012] Painer v. Standard Verlags GmbH and others [92].

[223] CJEU, Case C-145/10 [2012] Painer v. Standard Verlags GmbH and others [94].

[224] CJEU, Case C-145/10 [2012] Painer v. Standard Verlags GmbH and others [97].

contribute to informing the public about the 'current event' of N.'s reappearance. Therefore, the publication of the photos was, according to the Austrian Supreme Court's opinion, not covered by Article 5(3)(c) Copyright Directive.[225] The referring Austrian Court, the Commercial Court in Vienna, did thus not ask the Court of Justice for an interpretation of that provision in this case.

However, the Commercial Court in Vienna did ask for an interpretation of Article 5(3)(e) Copyright Directive. The provision states that Member States may provide for an exception or limitation to the rights provided for in Articles 2 and 3 in the case of a use of a protected work, *inter alia*, for the purposes of public security. The Vienna Court asked whether the media can rely on that provision should they decide, of their own volition, without a search request being issued, to publish a photograph in the interests of public security. The European Court denied that. It held that the media cannot confer on itself the role of protection of public security. Only states are responsible for the fulfilment of that objective by appropriate measures including, for example, assistance with a search appeal.[226] Therefore, newspapers may, under specific circumstances, be requested by a state to publish a photograph of a searched person. However, the initiative for such a publication should be taken by the public authorities, which was not the case here.[227] The purpose of Article 5(3)(e) of the Copyright Directive is not to strike a balance between the protection of intellectual property and the freedom of the press, but to ensure the protection of public security.[228]

By contrast, striking a fair balance between freedom of expression and the protection of copyright is the purpose of the provision on quotation in Article 5(3)(d) Copyright Directive, which was then subject to the Luxembourg Court's scrutiny. The Austrian court had already ruled that the contested photographs were used for the purpose of quotation.[229] Therefore, the Court of Justice did not have to address this question. In this context, note that Article 5(3)(d) Copyright Directive speaks of 'purposes *such as* criticism or review'. Hence, criticism or review, both of which were not applicable in this case, are only mentioned as examples for a quotation. The photographs were also lawfully made available to the public, namely by the police authorities (or so, at least, the Court assumed) under Article 5(3)(e) Copyright Directive.[230] As has just been shown, by contrast to the newspapers, the national police authorities could avail themselves of that provision. The problem was, however, that Ms Painer's name was not indicated on the press photos. So was it impossible for the newspapers to mention her name, as the caveat in third requirement of

---

[225] Austrian Supreme Court (Oberster Gerichtshof), Case 4Ob92/08w [2008] 'Natascha K III' [3.3]; Case 4Ob104/11i [2012] 'Natascha K V' [3.3].

[226] CJEU, Case C-145/10 [2012] Painer v. Standard Verlags GmbH and others [111].

[227] CJEU, Case C-145/10 [2012] Painer v. Standard Verlags GmbH and others [113].

[228] CJEU, Case C-145/10 [2012] Painer v. Standard Verlags GmbH and others [114].

[229] CJEU, Case C-145/10 [2012] Painer v. Standard Verlags GmbH and others [123].

[230] CJEU, Case C-145/10 [2012] Painer v. Standard Verlags GmbH and others [144].

Article 5(3)(d) stipulates? Unlike Article 5(3)(d) Copyright Directive, Article 5(3)(e) does *not* require the author's name to be indicated. Therefore, the newspapers could not know who the author of the photographs was, as they did not include any indication in this regard. As a result, the newspapers had to name the source of the photos, namely the police authorities, but it turned out to be impossible for them to indicate the author's name.[231] That the use of the photos was in accordance with fair practice, and to the extent required by the specific purpose, was not disputed in this case.

2 Infopaq

As in *Painer*, in *Infopaq* it had to be established, first, whether the newspaper articles constituted 'work' within the meaning of Article 2(a) Copyright Directive. In *Infopaq I*, the Court established its seminal dictum that copyright within the meaning of Article 2(a) applies only in relation to a subject-matter that is original in the sense that it is its author's own intellectual creation.[232] As regards the newspaper articles themselves, it was clear for the Court that these were their authors' own intellectual creations because of their form, the manner in which the subject was presented and the linguistic expression.[233] Newspaper articles are thus 'literary works' within the meaning of the Copyright Directive. This corresponds to Article 2(1) of the Berne Convention, which includes books, pamphlets and other writings within the notion of 'literary and artistic works'.

Article 2(a) of the Copyright Directive provides that authors have the exclusive right to authorise or prohibit reproduction, in whole or in part, of their works. The Court had to address whether Infopaq reproduced parts of the newspaper articles within the meaning of Article 2(a) Copyright Directive by processing and showing 11 consecutive words thereof. This gave rise to the following observation of the Court:

> considered in isolation, [words] are not as such an intellectual creation of the author who employs them. It is only through the choice, sequence and combination of those words that the author may express his creativity in an original manner and achieve a result which is an intellectual creation. Words as such do not, therefore, constitute elements covered by the protection.[234]

On the other hand, the Court reasoned that if an entire work, in this case a newspaper article, is copyright-protected, then the protection must also apply to parts of the work. Hence the decisive question in *Infopaq* was whether the isolated extracts shown by Infopaq were 'suitable for conveying to the reader the originality of a

---

[231] CJEU, Case C-145/10 [2012] Painer v. Standard Verlags GmbH and others [148].
[232] ECJ, Case C-5/08 [2009] Infopaq International A/S v. Danske Dagblades Forening ('Infopaq I') [37]. From academic literature on the *Infopaq* decisions, see, for example, Derclaye (2010); Vousden (2010); Rosati (2011).
[233] ECJ, Case C-5/08 [2009] Infopaq International A/S v. Danske Dagblades Forening ('Infopaq I') [44].
[234] ECJ, Case C-5/08 [2009] Infopaq International A/S v. Danske Dagblades Forening ('Infopaq I') [45–46].

publication such as a newspaper article, by communicating to that reader an element which is, in itself, the expression of the intellectual creation of the author of that article'.[235] The Court left it for the national court to decide this question. Nevertheless, the Court also indicated that Infopaq's particular data capture technique allowed for the reproduction of multiple extracts of protected works. This increased the likelihood that Infopaq would make reproductions in part within the meaning of Article 2(a) of the Copyright Directive because 'the cumulative effect of those extracts may lead to the reconstitution of lengthy fragments which are liable to reflect the originality of the work in question, with the result that they contain a number of elements which are such as to express the intellectual creation of the author of that work'.[236]

As the Danish court came to the conclusion that the acts by Infopaq constituted reproduction within the meaning of Article 2 Copyright Directive, the consent of the newspaper publishers was in principle required. This would not apply, however, if the reproduction fell under the exceptions and limitations in Article 5 Copyright Directive. In this case, only Article 5(1) came into consideration. It had to be decided whether the five steps of the data capture process were covered by Articles 5(1) and (5) Copyright Directive in order to be excluded from the authors' exclusive reproduction right. As regards the first four steps of the data capture process, the Court decided that these acts of reproduction were temporary, transient and constituted 'an integral and essential part of a technological process', despite the fact that they involved human intervention.[237] As the acts of reproduction did not have as their sole purpose the enabling of a transmission in a network between third parties by an intermediary, the Court had to assess whether they had as their purpose the enabling of a 'lawful use' of the articles. Infopaq had not been authorised by the authors of the article. Nevertheless, nothing under Danish or EU law prevented the use of the articles (despite copyright itself, which, as has been shown before, has to be excluded from this analysis in order to avoid circular reasoning). The use was thus not unlawful.[238]

Moreover, the acts of reproduction must have had no independent economic significance. The articles themselves had an economic value. However, the acts of reproduction need to have an *independent* economic significance. The acts of temporary reproduction in the *Infopaq* case did not have independent economic significance, as the economic advantages derived from their application only materialised during the use of the reproduced subject matter, so that they were neither distinct nor separable from the advantages derived from its use.[239] Finally, since the acts of temporary

---

[235] ECJ, Case C-5/08 [2009] Infopaq International A/S v. Danske Dagblades Forening ('Infopaq I') [47].

[236] ECJ, Case C-5/08 [2009] Infopaq International A/S v. Danske Dagblades Forening ('Infopaq I') [50].

[237] ECJ, Case C-5/08 [2009] Infopaq International A/S v. Danske Dagblades Forening ('Infopaq I') [61–71]; CJEU, Case C302/10 [2012] Infopaq International A/S v. Danske Dagblades Forening ('Infopaq II') [30–39].

[238] CJEU, Case C-302/10 [2012] Infopaq International A/S v. Danske Dagblades Forening ('Infopaq II') [45].

[239] CJEU, Case C-302/10 [2012] Infopaq International A/S v. Danske Dagblades Forening ('Infopaq I') [51].

reproduction fulfilled the conditions laid down in Article 5(1) Copyright Directive, they did not conflict with a normal exploitation of the work or unreasonably prejudice the legitimate interests of the rights-holder within the meaning of Article 5(5) Copyright Directive.

However, by the last act of reproduction in the data capture process, namely the printing of the information on a paper medium, Infopaq had been making a reproduction outside the sphere of computer technology. Once the reproduction has been affixed onto such a medium, it disappears only when the paper itself is destroyed.[240] This last act in the data capture process can thus not be regarded as a transient act within the meaning of Article 5(1) of the Copyright Directive. Hence the reproduction was not covered by Article 5(1) and required the consent of the rights-holders.

VI Jurisdiction and Applicable Law

The establishment of jurisdiction and the determination of the applicable law in transnational copyright conflicts are strongly influenced by the singularities of substantive copyright law, especially the territoriality principle. The territoriality principle describes a notion that has been referred to before in this chapter, namely that the scope of domestic copyright law is limited to the territory of a particular state. As a consequence of the territoriality principle, an author is confronted with a bundle of national rules with – at times significantly – differing scope and intensity of copyright protection.

The substantive territoriality principle that has been described in the previous sections has, as such, not a conflict-of-laws character. However, it has a significant impact on the choice of the applicable law, and indirectly on the establishment of jurisdiction, in that it entails the *lex loci protectionis* principle. According to this principle, the existence of a copyright, its content and its limitations are determined by the law of the country for whose territory protection is being claimed. This leads to the 'copyright mosaic formula' that has already been dealt with in Chapter 4. Because of the close connection between the territoriality principle and the *lex loci protectionis* principle, a change of the latter would require giving up the former: a replacement of domestic copyright laws with a transnational, ideally global, copyright law. However, as has been seen before, even the international conventions administered by the WIPO and the TRIPS agreement could not establish such an all-encompassing transnational copyright order. Instead, those agreements aimed at harmonisation of substantive law, but they left the territoriality principle and hence the *lex loci protectionis* principle untouched.

---

[240] ECJ, Case C-5/08 [2009] Infopaq International A/S v. Danske Dagblades Forening ('Infopaq I') [67–68].

1 The Establishment of Jurisdiction

In the EU, the establishment of jurisdiction in transnational copyright cases follows the general rules. If the defendant is domiciled in an EU Member State, jurisdiction is determined by the Brussels Ia Regulation. The exclusive jurisdiction rule in Article 24(4) Brussels Ia Regulation only applies in proceedings concerned with the registration of intellectual property rights, such as trademarks.[241] Jurisdiction in cases of alleged copyright violation has to be determined under Articles 4 and 7(2), respectively. Article 7(2) Brussels Ia Regulation leads to the application of the 'copyright mosaic': rights-holders can only vindicate a violation of their copyright in a country in which they claim their copyright has been infringed. But they merely have to *claim* a copyright violation. For the purpose of establishing jurisdiction, it is not required to prove that the copyright has actually been violated. Instead, it is sufficient that the Member State in which that court is situated protects the copyrights relied on by the claimant and that the harmful event alleged may occur within that jurisdiction.[242] With a view to alleged copyright violations committed online, in *Pinckney v. KDG Mediatech*, the Court of Justice regarded it as sufficient for the establishment of jurisdiction that it is possible to obtain a reproduction of the work from an internet site accessible within the jurisdiction of the court seised.[243]

The establishment of jurisdiction in transnational copyright cases under the Brussels Ia Regulation can be illustrated with our first case example, the *Painer* case. Regarding the Austrian newspaper *Der Standard*, Ms Painer could establish jurisdiction of Austrian courts according to Article 4 Brussels Ia Regulation. With a view to the German newspapers *Süddeutsche Zeitung* and *Die Welt*, Ms Painer could have established jurisdiction in Germany under Article 4 Brussels Ia Regulation. Moreover, regarding their publications in Austria, she could – and she did – establish jurisdiction in Austria according to Article 7(2) Brussels Ia Regulation. Here the 'copyright mosaic' principle applies: Ms Painer could sue *Süddeutsche Zeitung* and *Die Welt* in Austria only with a view to their interference with her copyright in Austria, but not in Germany. The fact that the newspapers were printed in Germany was irrelevant for the jurisdiction of the Austrian courts. The same applies to *Die Welt*'s online publications: Ms Painer could sue *Die Welt* regarding those publications in Austria only with a view to the damage she suffered in Austria.[244] Finally, the German *Express* newspaper could only be sued in Germany according to Article 4 Brussels Ia Regulation, because it did not distribute its newspaper in Austria (that was at least the finding in this case).

---

[241] On the establishment of jurisdiction in cases of alleged violation of trademarks, see CJEU, Case C-523/10 [2012] Wintersteiger AG v. Products 4U Sondermaschinenbau GmbH.

[242] CJEU, Case C-170/12 [2013] Pinckney v. KDG Mediatech AG [43].

[243] CJEU, Case C-170/12 [2013] Pinckney v. KDG Mediatech AG [44].

[244] Compare CJEU, Case C-441/13 [2015] Hejduk v. EnergieAgentur.NRW GmbH [38].

But there was a special twist in this case. Article 8 of the Brussels Ia Regulation provides a special jurisdiction. Accordingly, a person domiciled in a Member State who is one of a number of defendants may also be sued in the courts for the place where any one of the defendants is domiciled, 'provided the claims are so closely connected that it is expedient to hear and determine them together to avoid the risk of irreconcilable judgments' resulting from separate proceedings'. In this case, the publisher of *Der Standard* was domiciled in Austria. Therefore, Ms Painer argued that the German newspapers could be sued in Austria as well under the rule of Article 8(1) Brussels Ia Regulation. Article 8(1) Brussels Ia Regulation has as its purposes facilitating of a sound administration of justice, minimising the possibility of concurrent proceedings and avoiding irreconcilable outcomes if cases are decided separately.[245] However, Article 8(1) cannot be applied so as to allow an applicant to make a claim against a number of defendants with the sole object of ousting the jurisdiction of the courts of the state where one of those defendants is domiciled.[246] The problem in the *Painer* case was the following: because of the Rome II Regulation, which we will come back to in a moment, German law would apply to the alleged infringements committed in Germany, whereas Austrian law would apply to the claims of copyright infringement in Austria.

As a consequence, the Austrian court asked the CJEU whether Article 8(1) of the Brussels Ia Regulation can be applied in a case in which actions against several defendants for substantially identical copyright infringements are brought on national legal grounds that vary according to the Member States concerned, in this case Austrian law and German law. The Court found nothing in the wording of Article 8(1) Brussels Ia Regulation requiring that the actions brought against different defendants should have identical legal bases.[247] To be sure, the identical legal bases of the actions brought might be one relevant factor speaking for the application of that provision, but it is not an indispensable requirement.[248] Other factors for deciding whether or not Article 8(1) can be applied are the following:

- whether the defendants acted independently from each other;[249]
- whether it was foreseeable by the defendants that they might be sued in the Member State where at least one of them is domiciled;[250] and
- the fact that the national laws on which the actions against the various defendants were based were to a large extent identical.[251]

---

[245] Recital 21 Brussels Ia Regulation; CJEU, Case C-145/10 [2012] Painer v. Standard Verlags GmbH and others [77].

[246] CJEU, Case C-145/10 [2012] Painer v. Standard Verlags GmbH and others [78], providing further references.

[247] CJEU, Case C-145/10 [2012] Painer v. Standard Verlags GmbH and others [75], providing further references.

[248] CJEU, Case C-145/10 [2012] Painer v. Standard Verlags GmbH and others [80].

[249] CJEU, Case C-145/10 [2012] Painer v. Standard Verlags GmbH and others [83].

[250] CJEU, Case C-145/10 [2012] Painer v. Standard Verlags GmbH and others [81]; compare Recital 16 Brussels Ia Regulation.

[251] Compare CJEU, Case C-145/10 [2012] Painer v. Standard Verlags GmbH and others [82].

As a result, the application of Article 8(1) Brussels Ia Regulation is not *per se* precluded solely because actions against several defendants for substantially identical copyright infringements are brought on national legal grounds that vary according to the Member States concerned. Rather, it is for the domestic courts to assess, based on the above-mentioned factors, whether there is a risk of irreconcilable judgments if those actions were determined separately.[252] Particularly with a view to the third factor, the degree of harmonisation of substantive copyright laws in the EU plays a significant role. At the moment, Member States enjoy considerable discretion when implementing the copyright framework, but this might change with the Commission's announced proposal on a copyright reform as a part of the Digital Single Market Strategy.

2 The Choice of the Applicable Law

International agreements, such as the Berne Convention, the WIPO Copyright Treaty and the TRIPS Agreement, arguably do not contain any rule on the applicable law. In particular, a conflict of laws rule does not follow from the national treatment clauses included in those treaties.[253] Moreover, the country-of-origin principle in Article 3 E-commerce Directive has no bearing on the conflict of laws in transnational copyright cases, because Article 3(2) E-commerce Directive expressly excludes intellectual property from the scope of the country-of-origin principle. In addition, no other piece of EU legislation, such as the Copyright Directive or the Enforcement Directive, provides a conflict of laws rule.[254] Therefore, in cases of transnational violations of copyright, courts have to apply their domestic conflict of laws rules or, within the EU, Article 8 Rome II Regulation.

This provision applies to intellectual property in a broad sense, including, for instance, copyright, related rights, the *sui generis* right for the protection of databases and industrial property rights.[255] According to Article 8 Rome II Regulation, the law applicable to a non-contractual obligation arising from an infringement of an intellectual property right shall be the law of the country for which protection is claimed. Article 8(1) Rome II Regulation thus codifies the *lex loci protectionis* principle for the choice of the applicable law; note that the law of the country *for* which the claimant claims protection applies, not the law of the country *in* which protection is claimed. The claimant thus has to vindicate his intellectual property rights according to the laws of each country individually in which he claims his rights have been violated, leading to a 'copyright mosaic' on the level of the applicable law.[256] Therefore, the jurisdiction and the applicable law correspond often, but not always. For example, if

---

[252] CJEU, Case C-145/10 [2012] Painer v. Standard Verlags GmbH and others [84].

[253] ECJ, Case C-28/04 [2005] Tod's SpA v. Heyraud [32]; Dickinson (2008, para. 8.05); M. Illmer, in Huber (2011, Art. 8 Rome II para. 21).

[254] See Recital 11 Enforcement Directive.

[255] Recital 26 Rome II Regulation.

[256] Note that Article 8(3) Rome II Regulation expressly excludes a choice of law by the parties.

the claimant establishes jurisdiction based on the defendant's domicile according to Article 4 Brussels Ia Regulation, the court may nonetheless have to apply the law of a foreign country for which the claimant claims protection. In the *Painer* scenario, this would have been the case, for example, if Ms Painer had sued the Süddeutsche Zeiung and Die Welt in Germany for their alleged copyright infringements in Austria.

Article 8 Rome II Regulation is a conflict rule for 'infringements' of intellectual property rights. In turn, this provision does not, as such, determine the applicable law with regard to questions of status, such as the existence of a copyright protection, its limitations, its transferability, the terms of its protection, etc. These questions are not regulated by Article 8 Rome II Regulation itself.[257] However, it covers those questions as far as they are logically prior to a question of infringement; for example, if the defendant claims that he has not infringed the claimant's copyright because the copyright protection did not exist in the first place. This follows from Article 15 Rome II Regulation, which explains that the law applicable to non-contractual obligations under the Rome II Regulation shall also govern preliminary questions, such as the basis and extent of liability, the grounds for exemption from liability, any limitation of liability and any division of liability.[258] Moreover, according to Article 13 Rome II Regulation, Article 8 shall apply to non-contractual obligations arising from an infringement of an intellectual property right. This serves to clarify that all claims related to an infringement of IP rights, including not only claims for damages, but also, for example, from unjust enrichment, are covered by the rule in Article 8.[259]

As has been shown before, the *lex loci protectionis* principle is a self-suggesting, albeit not a compelling,[260] consequence of the territoriality principle. The territoriality principle itself exists due to the lack of globally – and even regionally – harmonised rules on the protection of intellectual property. This even applies to the extent that intellectual property rights have been harmonised by EU directives, such as the Copyright Directive, because those directives have to be implemented by the Member States and leave them certain discretion in their implementation. Conversely, the *lex loci protectionis* principle is not preconditioned in those cases in which a transnationally, fully harmonised intellectual property right is the subject of the dispute. This is expressed in Article 8(2) Rome II Regulation. Accordingly, in the case of a non-contractual obligation arising from an infringement of a unitary EU intellectual property right, such as the Community Trade Mark and the Community Design, the applicable law has to be determined, in the first place, according to the

---

[257] Dickinson (2008, para. 8.18).

[258] M. Illmer, in Huber (2011, Art. 8 Rome II paras. 46 ff).

[259] Dickinson (2008, para. 8.20); M. Illmer, in Huber (2011, Art. 8 Rome II para. 14).

[260] See Dickinson (2008, para. 8.08): 'it would have been possible, in theory at least, for the Community to adopt a solution … other than the one favoured in Art 8(1) …, for example in favour of the law of the country of infringement'; M. Illmer, in Huber (2011, Art. 8 Rome II para. 3).

relevant EU legislation.[261] For any question that is not governed by the special legislation, the law of the country in which the act of infringement was committed applies, hence not (necessarily) the country for which protection is claimed. This is justified because the rights mentioned in Article 8(2) Rome II Regulation are one and the same throughout the EU.

Article 8(1) Rome II Regulation thus provides a conflict-of-laws rule regarding copyright infringements. However, the provision does not expressly codify whether the law of the place giving rise to the damage or the law of the place in which the damage occurred is applicable. Nonetheless, this follows indirectly from the territoriality principle and the *lex loci protectionis* principle. As far as protection of intellectual property for a particular country is being claimed, this country has to be the place of the action giving rise to the damage: the *lex loci delicti commissi* and the *lex loci protectionis* have to be identical. The territoriality principle and the *lex loci protectionis* principle neither permit the application of the law of the habitual residence of both claimant and defendant according to Article 4(2) nor a derogation by an agreement pursuant to Article 14 Rome II Regulation. The decisive questions are, therefore, how the place of the action that gave rise to the damage has to be localised in transnational cases and whether this place is identical with the place for which protection is being claimed. The answer to this question, which has already been raised in Chapter 4, has to be found by way of interpretation of the substantive domestic intellectual property law whose violation is being claimed.

For example, a violation of the reproduction right according to Article 2 Copyright Directive already takes place in one country even if the reproduction is made with a view to a later dissemination of that material in another country. With a view to the concept of 'communication to the public' or 'making available to the public' within the meaning of Article 3 Copyright Directive, two lines of argument can be distinguished.[262] According to the emission theory, only the law of the country from which the communication originates shall be regarded as the *locus actus*. Regarding internet publications, this raises the subsequent question of which country the country of origin is: the place of the upload or the place where the server is located? As has already been developed in Chapter 4, the place of the upload is to be preferred, as the location of the server is too random, prone to abuse and often not known anyway. This observation is confirmed by Recital 27 Copyright Directive, which states that '[t]he mere provision of physical facilities for enabling or making a communication does not in itself amount to communication within the meaning of this Directive'.

---

[261] See Council Regulation (EC) No. 40/94 of 20 December 1993 on the Community trademark, OJ L 11/1, now codified as Council Regulation (EC) No. 207/2009 of 26 February 2009 on the Community trademark, OJ L 78/1; Council Regulation (EC) No. 6/2002 of 12 December 2001 on Community designs, OJ L 3/1, amended by Council Regulation No. 1891/2006 of 18 December 2006 amending Regulations (EC) No. 6/2002 and (EC) No. 40/94 to give effect to the accession of the European Community to the Geneva Act of the Hague Agreement concerning the international registration of industrial designs, OJ L 386/14.

[262] See Aplin and Davis (2013, p. 179); Aplin (2005, pp. 131f, providing further references).

The emission theory has the advantage of providing legal certainty for those who fear that they might be in violation of copyright. They only have to adhere to the law of the country in which they act. Moreover, as will be seen in the next paragraph, the Satellite and Cable Directive itself is based on the emission theory. The counterargument against the emission theory is that it seems to contradict the notions of 'communication' and 'making available', which are based on reception, or at least the possibility of reception. Therefore, the so-called communication theory argues that both the country of emission and the country of reception – that is, the country where the work is accessed or accessible – shall be regarded as the places where the defendant has acted. Within the communication theory, a separate line of argument can be discerned that reduces the countries of reception to the one country at which the communication was targeted.

Football Dataco v. *Sportradar*, a decision related to the interpretation of the Database Directive, indicates that the Luxembourg Court follows the communication theory, refined with a targeting approach. The Court had to interpret the notion of 're-utilisation' within the meaning of the Database Directive, a concept that is similar to 'making available to the public' of copyright-protected works.[263] The Court decided that that the sending of data from a protected database by means of a web server located in Member State A to a computer in Member State B constitutes an act of 're-utilisation' of the data. That act, the Court held, 'takes place, at least, in Member State B, where there is evidence from which it may be concluded that the act discloses an intention on the part of the person performing the act to target members of the public in Member State B'.[264]

Article 1(2)(b) of the Satellite and Cable Directive – *lex specialis* to Article 3 Copyright Directive with regard to communication to the public by satellite – stipulates that the act of communication occurs solely in the Member State where, under the control and responsibility of the broadcasting organisation, the programme-carrying signals are introduced into an uninterrupted chain of communication leading to the satellite and down towards the earth.[265] This substantive country-of-origin principle seems to suggest that the act of communicating to the public has to be seen as occurring in that Member State. As a consequence, this Member State of origin has to be treated as the *locus actus*, and not the Member State(s) in which the signals can be received. By contrast, according to the so-called 'Bogsch theory' (named after a former Director General of the WIPO), the laws of those countries at which the programmes are targeted do also have to be considered.[266] This idea is to a certain extent reflected by Article 1(2)(d) of the Satellite Broadcasting and Cable Retransmission

---

[263] Article 7(2)(b) Database Directive defines 're-utilisation' as 'any form of making available to the public all or a substantial part of the contents of a database by the distribution of copies, by renting, by on-line or other forms of transmission.'

[264] CJEU, Case C-173/11 [2012] Football Dataco Ltd v. Sportradar [47].

[265] See ECJ, Case C-192/04 [2005] Lagardère v. SPRE and GVL.

[266] See, for example, B. Hugenholtz and J. Kirchherr, in Castendyk et al. (2008, Directive 93/83/EEC para. 15).

Directive. Accordingly, communications to the public by satellite from third countries will under certain conditions be deemed to occur within an EU Member State if the non-EU country does not provide the level of protection provided for under the Directive. Hence, unlike the conflict-of-law rule in data protection law (see Chapter 8), it does make a difference in private international copyright law whether or not the third country is able to provide a comparable level of protection.

Finally, as has been shown before, the concept of 'distribution to the public' within the meaning of Article 4 Copyright Directive covers the sale of the original of a work or a copy thereof and acts that entail a transfer of the ownership of that object.[267] As the Court of Justice explained in the *Donner* decision:

> distribution to the public is characterised by a series of acts going, at the very least, from the conclusion of a contract of sale to the performance thereof by delivery to a member of the public. Thus, in the context of a cross-border sale, acts giving rise to a 'distribution to the public' may take place in a number of Member States. In such a context, such a transaction may infringe on the exclusive right to authorise or prohibit any forms of distribution to the public in a number of Member States.[268]

Therefore, the place of the action that gave rise to the damage can be localised, for example, in both the country to which protected works have been imported and the country from which protected works have been exported. In turn, a country cannot be regarded as the place of distribution if the works merely transited through that country.[269]

VII Questions

1 Do you agree with the Court's interpretation of the parody exception in *Deckmyn* v. *Vandersteen* that the rights-holders may have a legitimate interest in opposing a parody they dislike to be associated with? How much scope does this interpretation leave of the parody exception?

2 To what extent may the rulings on the enforcement of intellectual property rights against internet intermediaries be transferred to the vindication of other rights, such as reputation and privacy? To what extent do they apply to the enforcement of public interest concerns, such as morals and the fight against racism or xenophobia?

3 Critically evaluate the case law of the Court of Justice on the enforcement of intellectual property rights against internet intermediaries. To what extent has the Court contributed to legal certainty in this area?

---

[267] ECJ, Case C-456/06 [2008] Peek & Cloppenburg KG v. Cassina SpA [36].

[268] CJEU, Case C-5/11 [2012] Donner [26].

[269] See, *mutatis mutandis*, ECJ, Case C-281/05 [2006] Montex Holdings Ltd v. Diesel SpA [27]; CJEU, Joined Cases C-446/09 and C-495/09 [2011] Philips and Nokia [51 ff]; both decisions with a view to alleged trademark violations.

4 To what extent has the Copyright Directive contributed to harmonisation of EU copyright law, given its long list of exceptions and limitations that are merely optional and may thus differ per Member State?

5 In *UPC Telekabel*, the CJEU stated: '[T]he national procedural rules must provide a possibility for internet users to assert their rights before the court once the implementing measures taken by the internet service provider are known.'[270] How can this be implemented in practice?

6 Reconsider Chapter 5 and the distinction between linear and non-linear audiovisual media services. In light of the questions raised in this context, do you agree with the distinction of 'making available to the public' as a special category of 'communication to the public'? Would you have suggestions for alternative approaches?

VIII Further Reading

- T. Aplin, *Copyright Law in the Digital Society*, 2005
- E. Derclaye (ed.), *Research Handbook on the Future of EU Copyright*, 2008
- J.C. Ginsburg, 'The Private International Law of Copyright in an Era of Technological Change', *Collected Courses of the Hague Academy of International Law* 273 (1998) 239
- P. Goldstein and P.B. Hugenholtz, *International Copyright*, 3rd edn, 2012
- L. Lessig, *Free Culture: How Big Media Uses Technology and the Law to Lock Down Culture and Control Creativity*, 2004
- S. von Lewinski, *International Copyright Law and Policy*, 2008

[270] CJEU, Case C-314/12 [2014] UPC Telekabel Wien GmbH v. Constantin Film Verleih and others [57].

10

Media Competition Law

CASE EXAMPLE

The German Football Association (Deutscher Fußball-Bund, DFB) is the governing body of football in Germany.[1] It has jurisdiction on the German football league system, including the first and the second football league (Bundesliga and 2. Bundesliga).[2] One of the members of the DFB is the League Association. The League Association's members are the licensed clubs in the first and second football league. The clubs are also, via regional associations, indirectly members of the DFB.

The DFB has entrusted the League Association with the organisation of the football matches in the first and the second league as well as the marketing and exploitation of the broadcasting rights in respect of these matches. This joint central marketing scheme covers all types of broadcasting rights, including television and radio, free-TV and pay-TV, terrestrial broadcasting, cable and satellite broadcasting, live and deferred broadcasting, showing of the entire event and of extracts, and existing and future technical facilities. The League Association determines the price as well as the nature and scope of exploitation. The clubs are prevented from dealing independently with television and radio operators as well as sports-rights agents and from marketing their rights independently. They are, in particular, prevented from taking independent commercial decisions about the price.[3]

The European Commission is concerned that the exclusive selling of the commercial broadcasting rights by the League Association could restrict competition between the clubs in the first and second league. Should the European Commission take action?

(Based on the Commission Decision of 19 January 2005, Case COMP/C-2/37.214 –
Joint selling of the media rights to the German Bundesliga)

I Introduction

Press and broadcasting companies are usually commercial institutions, and as such subject to competition law rules. But what is competition law? This chapter understands competition law in two ways: competition law in a traditional sense is

---

[1] The DFB is comparable with, for example, the Football Association (FA) in England or the Koninklijke Nederlandse Voetbal Bond (KNVB) in the Netherlands.

[2] The leagues are comparable with the Premier League and the Football League Championship in England or the Eredivisie and the Eerste Divisie in the Netherlands.

[3] For the sake of simplicity, this is treated as a fact. In the original case it was merely part of the Commission's preliminary assessment.

concerned with safeguarding the competitive process. One of the first – and until today, arguably the best known – competition law statutes was the US Sherman Act of 1890. It prohibited restrictions of competition by large companies and trusts, particularly in the railroads and in the oil sector. In the EU, the functional equivalent to the Sherman Act is Articles 101 and 102 TFEU. In order to avoid confusion, this chapter will henceforth name this part of competition law 'antitrust law'. Antitrust law encompasses anti-competitive multilateral agreements, anti-competitive unilateral behaviour and mergers and acquisitions.

The second subcategory of competition law is the law on unfair competition. The law on unfair competition has three objectives: it protects competitors (horizontal dimension), consumers and the public in general (vertical relations).[4] To distinguish it from antitrust law, one could also name it the 'modern competition law'. This chapter will speak of the law on unfair competition.

Both antitrust law and the law on unfair competition are highly relevant for the media. Antitrust law is, at least indirectly, an important instrument for safeguarding media pluralism.[5] This implies control of mergers between media conglomerates as well as restrictions on multilateral agreements and abuses of dominant positions in the media market. By maintaining competition between media undertakings, antitrust law also safeguards that a variety of publishers, hence a variety of points of view, are represented on the media markets. The notion of a 'marketplace of ideas', which we already encountered in Chapter 2, can thus be taken literally in the context of media antitrust law. As a result, antitrust law affects media companies, as economic actors, on the markets for advertising and audience. Presumably all antitrust philosophies, which will be presented in the next section, would agree on this point. But it is subject to controversy whether the demands of a democratic society justify *additional*, sector-specific antitrust rules and policies; for example, those specifically tailored to the media in order to safeguard media pluralism.

The rules on unfair competition are relevant to media law in two ways: they are relevant for content providers, such as companies (which can also be media companies themselves), when they publish content *with* means of mass communication in violation of rules on unfair competition. Examples that will be the focus of this chapter are misleading and comparative advertisements, calls for boycott and the disparagement of competitors. Moreover, the law of unfair competition is also relevant for the media, namely in cases in which newspapers or broadcasters publish statements, particularly advertisements, by order of third parties. In such cases, the media publisher should usually not be liable under the laws of unfair competition itself, as these laws are addressed to the businesses that are responsible for the content.[6] Nevertheless,

---

[4] Recital 21 Rome II Regulation; COM, Proposal for a Regulation of the European Parliament and the Council on the law applicable to non-contractual obligations ('Rome II'), COM(2003) 427 final, p. 15.

[5] See, for example, Baker (2009); Craufurd Smith and Tambini (2012).

[6] See CJEU, Case C-391/12 [2013] RLvS Verlagsgesellschaft mbH v. Stuttgarter Wochenblatt GmbH [39 ff].

newspapers and broadcasters are indirectly affected by such rules because advertisements are an important source of income for the media. Section V of this chapter should therefore provide a brief introduction to the international and European legal framework on unfair competition with a focus on media-related problems, particularly misleading and comparative advertising.

II The Aims of Antitrust Law

The aims of antitrust law have long been subject to dispute. In essence, the approaches can be divided along the following question: does antitrust law pursue any other purpose than safeguarding the competitive process as such?[7] In other words: is antitrust law a deontological or a utilitarian, instrumentalist concept? According to the ordoliberalist approach, antitrust law has no other purpose than to safeguard the competitive process as such. Further aims, such as protecting individual competitors, promoting domestic industries, protecting the environment or safeguarding media pluralism, could neither expand nor restrict the application of antitrust law rules. By contrast, a utilitarian understanding would also consider antitrust law aims other than safeguarding the competitive process as such. This approach can be bifurcated into two further lines of argument, which disagree on *which* aims antitrust law may pursue. According to a purely economic reading, antitrust law serves to safeguard economic aims, namely economic efficiency and consumer welfare. Only these aspects have to be considered when applying antitrust law rules. By contrast, another school of thought allows antitrust law also to be applied in order to attain non-economic ambitions, such as safeguarding media pluralism.

These schools of thought are not only represented in economic and legal academic scholarship, such as the 'Harvard School', the 'Chicago School' and the 'post-Chicago School', but also in antitrust law enforcement. By way of example, the ordoliberalist approach was particularly popular in the 1950s and 1960s in the Federal Republic of Germany, where it made a significant contribution to the German *Wirtschaftswunder*. It also influenced the beginnings of then-EEC antitrust policy in the 1960s.

This very brief overview introduces the challenges of transnational media antitrust law. The application of antitrust law provisions, such as Articles 101 and 102 TFEU and the US Sherman Act, are to a certain extent a matter of policy rather than law. The provisions do not exactly determine which policy considerations may, or may not, inform the enforcement decision. Due to the lack of international harmonisation of antitrust law and policy, the fragmented approaches by domestic/European antitrust authorities led to transnational conflicts in cross-border antitrust law cases. This general problem affects the media in particular. Depending on the antitrust law rationales the responsible competition authorities adhere to, media pluralism may, or

---

[7] For more details on competition theory, see Niels et al. (2011); Jones and Sufrin (2014, pp. 4 ff); Whish and Bailey (2015, 4 ff).

may not, influence the decision-making process. For example, Articles 101 and 102 TFEU are entirely silent as to whether safeguarding media pluralism may be considered as an aspect of antitrust law enforcement. Media pluralism is therefore not a compelling reason at least to be taken into account when applying those provisions. This is also reflected in the Commission's policy of the 'more economic approach', which describes the trend 'to ensure that competition policy is fully compatible with economic learning'.[8] Contrastingly, Article 21(4) of the EU Merger Regulation[9] states that '*Member States may* take appropriate measures to protect legitimate interests other than those taken into consideration by this Regulation ... [P]lurality of the media ... shall be regarded as legitimate interests within the meaning of the first sub-paragraph' (emphasis added). It is therefore left to the Member States whether or not they consider media plurality as a legitimate interest to be taken into account when applying the Merger Regulation.

The Commission's and the EU legislators' reluctance to consider media plurality as an aim of antitrust law is not only based on policy considerations. It also has a legal underpinning. According to Article 167(1) TFEU, the EU shall respect the national and regional diversity of the Member States. To be sure, the Union shall also 'contribute to the flowering of the cultures of the Member States' and even bring 'the common cultural heritage to the fore'. However, Article 167(5) TFEU expressly prevents the European Parliament and the Council from harmonising the laws and regulations of the Member States. This supports the argument that the EU lacks the competence to consider media pluralism as an aspect of competition policy.

But there is good reason to argue that it is insufficient to approach EU media anti-trust policy only with purely market-based considerations. Rather, media pluralism may require media-specific restrictions on media cartels and on mergers in order to avoid media ownership or control concentration.[10] Article 11(2) EUChFR stipulates that the pluralism of the media shall be respected. Of course, the Charter does not confer new competences to the EU (Article 51(2)). Nevertheless, media pluralism, as codified in Article 11(2), is a principle that the EU has to 'recognise' (Preamble of the Charter) and to 'observe' (Article 51(1)). According to Article 52(5) EUChFR, principles 'may be implemented by legislative and executive acts taken by institutions, bodies, offices and agencies of the Union ... in the exercise of their respective powers'. Therefore, the EU institutions should not be legally prevented from taking media pluralism into account when legislating or applying EU antitrust rules. On the contrary, they are even obliged to do so. The Enforcement Regulation in Recital 37 and the Merger Regulation in Recital 36 state almost identically: 'This Regulation[11] respects the fundamental rights and observes the principles recognised in particular

---

[8] Monti (2004, p. 2).

[9] Council Regulation (EC) No. 139/2004 of 20 January 2004 on the control of concentrations between undertakings, OJ L 24/1. See Part 5 Chapter 2 of the UK Communications Act 2003.

[10] For more details on this debate, see Craufurd Smith (2004); Bania (2013).

[11] The Merger regulation speaks of 'The Community'.

by the Charter of Fundamental Rights of the European Union. Accordingly, this Regulation should be interpreted and applied with respect to those rights and principles.' Against this backdrop, public authorities are required, for example, to apply the antitrust rules on significant market power considering the dominance of a cartel or a company with regard to the influence on public opinion. This can be estimated based on the average audience or reader share, thereby considering broadcasting time allocated to independent third parties.[12] Moreover, media ownership has to be transparent to ensure that the regulatory authorities and the public can take informed decisions.[13]

III International Antitrust Law

The need for a truly global antitrust law in a globalised economy is widely recognised, but its development is still in a nascent state.[14] The United Nations Conference on Trade and Development (UNCTAD) administers the non-binding 'Set of Multilaterally Agreed Equitable Principles and Rules for the Control of Restrictive Business Practices', adopted by the UN General Assembly.[15] Between 1985 and 2000, four United Nations Conferences to Review All Aspects of the Set have taken place under the auspices of UNCTAD. The OECD Council has adopted several non-binding recommendations on competition law and policy.[16] In addition, the OECD Competition Committee has adopted Best Practices.[17] Arguably the most suitable international organisation to administer globally applicable competition law rules would be the WTO. However, a Draft International Antitrust Code, negotiated in 1993, failed to receive enough support. A Ministerial Declaration, adopted in 2001, included three paragraphs on the interaction between trade and competition policy, thereby recognising 'the case for a multilateral framework to enhance the contribution of competition policy to international trade and development'.[18] However, subsequent meetings were not able to come to decisions on common competition policy.[19] While attempts to establish global competition law rules have thus failed, the International Competition Network, established in 2001 by domestic competition

---

[12] Compare, for example, Section 26 of the German Interstate Treaty on Broadcasting and Telemedia; Section 375 of the UK Communications Act 2003.

[13] Council of Europe, Recommendation CM/Rec(2007)2 on media pluralism and diversity of media content, para. III; compare Sunstein (2000, pp. 506, 531–538).

[14] For more details, see Jones and Sufrin (2014, pp. 1292 ff).

[15] Resolution 35/63 of 5 December 1980.

[16] See, for example, Recommendation on Competition Policy and Exempted or Regulated Sectors (1979); Recommendation concerning Effective Action against Hard Core Cartels (1998); Recommendation concerning Merger Review (2005); Recommendation on Competition Assessment (2009); Recommendation concerning International Co-operation on Competition Investigations and Proceedings (2014).

[17] See, for example, Best practices on Information Exchange (2005).

[18] WT/MIN(01)/DEC/1, 20 November 2001, para. 23.

[19] Jones and Sufrin (2014, p. 1294).

authorities (including the EU), 'provides competition authorities with a specialised yet informal venue for maintaining regular contacts and addressing practical competition concerns'.[20]

IV European Antitrust Law

This section will provide a very short introduction to EU antitrust law in general and a more expansive introduction to media antitrust law in particular. Section 1 will explain general aspects of EU antitrust law that apply across the board for multilateral and unilateral anti-competitive behaviour as well as mergers. It will also refer to media-specific aspects, except for the complex theme of the definition of media markets, which will be dealt with in Section 2. Sections 3, 4 and 5 will then look into anti-competitive behaviour and concentrations with a view to both general aspects and media-specific questions. The sixth section will then provide the solution to the case example.

1 General Aspects

This subsection begins with the question that arises first in any transnational case: the search for jurisdiction. Subsection a will be confined to the jurisdiction regarding the *public* enforcement dimension of EU antitrust and merger law vis-à-vis the law and jurisdiction of *third countries*. The jurisdiction of the European Commission will be delineated from the jurisdiction of EU *Member States'* competition authorities further below in subsection d. Moreover, questions of jurisdiction and applicable law in *private* enforcement cases will be dealt with in Section VI.

Subsection b deals with the crucial definition of the relevant markets. This part is of decisive importance in any antitrust case. Subsection e briefly summarises the enforcement practice of the European Commission.

a Jurisdiction

Jurisdiction of competition authorities to decide antitrust cases is, in the first place, based on the territoriality principle. For the European Commission, this follows from Article 52 TEU and Article 355 TFEU.[21] Therefore, if distortion of competition (agreement under Article 101, abuse under Article 102 TFEU) was committed on a Member State's territory, or if a concentration involves companies located in EU Member States, then Articles 101 and 102 TFEU and the Merger Regulation apply, and either the Commission or a National Competition Authority (NCA) has jurisdiction. Moreover, in the *Dyestuffs* case, the Court of Justice established that it is sufficient for the application of (now) Article 101 TFEU if an undertaking with its headquarters outside

---

[20] www.internationalcompetitionnetwork.org/about.aspx.
[21] Note that in this public law dimension jurisdiction and applicable law are concomitant.

the EU 'brought the concerted practice into being within the Common Market' via a subsidiary – this is the so-called 'single economic entity doctrine'.[22]

But does EU antitrust law also apply – and do the Commission or an NCA have jurisdiction – in cases in which anti-competitive behaviour or mergers involve companies having no presence in the EU?[23] This problem has gained relevance with the increase of global trade, multinational companies and global communication. In the absence of a harmonised global competition framework, and with a view to diverging competition laws and philosophies, this jurisdictional question bears significant importance. Neither Articles 101 and 102 TFEU nor the Merger Regulation contain an express provision on whether they apply extraterritorially. The first court decisions addressing antitrust cases with a transnational dimension came from the United States. US courts began to assume US jurisdiction if anti-competitive conduct in a foreign state had an *effect* in the United States.[24] Accordingly, the state subjected to harmful effects has jurisdiction, even if no constituent element of the offence has taken place within the territory of that state. The application of the 'effects doctrine' has been subject to controversy, even among US courts.[25] Nevertheless, in the *Wood Pulp I* decision, the Court of Justice adopted an approach similar to the effects doctrine. The Court observed that an infringement of (now) Article 101 TFEU consists of two elements:

> the formation of the agreement, decision or concerted practice and the implementation thereof. If the applicability of prohibitions laid down under competition law were made to depend on the place where the agreement, decision or concerted practice was formed, the result would obviously be to give undertakings an easy means of evading those prohibitions. The decisive factor is therefore the place where it is implemented.[26]

The seminal question under Article 101 TFEU – and the same applies arguably also to Article 102 TFEU[27] – is, therefore, what constitutes an 'implementation' of an anti-competitive agreement or anti-competitive unilateral behaviour. In the *Wood Pulp I* case itself, the Court explained that it is irrelevant whether or not the undertaking had recourse to subsidiaries, agents, sub-agents or branches within the EU in order to make their contacts with purchasers within the EU.[28] Instead, the criterion as to the 'implementation' of an agreement is satisfied by mere sale within the EU.[29]

---

[22] ECJ, Case 48/69 [1972] ICI v. Commission ('Dyestuffs') [141].

[23] For more details, see Jones and Sufrin (2014, pp. 1258 ff); Whish and Bailey (2015, pp. 518 ff).

[24] See United States v. Aluminium Co. of America (Alcoa), 148 F.2d 416 (2d Cir. 1945); US Supreme Court, Hartford Fire Insurance Co. v. California, 509 U.S. 764 (1993).

[25] See Timberlane Lumber Co. v. Bank of America, 549 F.2d 597 (9th Cir. 1976); Griffin (1998, p. 68).

[26] ECJ, Joined Cases C-89/85, C-104/85, C-114/85, C-116/85, C-117/85, C-125/85, C-126/85, C-127/85, C-128/85, C-129/85 [1988] Ahlström Osakeyhtiö and others v. Commission ('Wood Pulp I') [16].

[27] Jones and Sufrin (2014, p. 1277 fn. 93); see CJEU, Case T-286/09 [2014] Intel v. Commission [241].

[28] ECJ, Joined Cases C-89/85, C-104/85, C-114/85, C-116/85, C-117/85, C-125/85, C-126/85, C-127/85, C-128/85, C-129/85 [1988] Ahlström Osakeyhtiö and others v. Commission ('Wood Pulp I') [17].

[29] See CJEU, Case T-286/09 [2014] Intel v. Commission [241]. From academic literature, see, for example, van Gerven (1989).

The Merger Regulation applies to 'concentrations with a Community [now: EU] dimension' (Article 1). This provision serves not only to distinguish the Commission's adjudicative jurisdiction from the jurisdiction of NCAs, but also to establish the Commission's jurisdiction in cases with an extraterritorial effect.[30] The determining factor for the EU dimension is the worldwide and EU-wide turnover. However, the Regulation is silent on whether a concentration can also have an EU dimension even if the companies involved are not located in the EU. The Court of Justice addressed this question in the *Gencor* case. The Court held that application of the Merger Regulation 'is justified under public international law when it is foreseeable that a proposed concentration will have an immediate and substantial effect' in the EU.[31]

In the 2014 *Intel* judgment, the General Court then set out the relationship between the 'implementation doctrine' in *Wood Pulp I* and the qualified 'effects doctrine' in *Gencor*. The Court held 'in order to justify the Commission's jurisdiction under public international law, it is sufficient to establish either the qualified effects of the practice in the European Union or that it was implemented in the European Union'.[32] The two approaches may thus serve as alternatives.

b Market Definition

The definition of the relevant market has a central role in all three areas of antitrust law. For example, in order to determine whether a company abused its dominant position, it has to be determined whether it has a dominant position in the first place. And for that, it needs to be established *on which market* it occupies that dominant position. The definition of the relevant market is thus a highly controversial aspect in almost any antitrust law case. The conflicting interests are as follows: the smaller the relevant market, the easier it is for the competition authority to prove that the relevant firm enjoys market power or even significant market power, and thus the greater the potential for that firm's conduct to impede competition.[33] Conversely, the more competitors the market includes, the less likely is an anticompetitive effect of an agreement or the existence of a dominant position of an undertaking on that market. Therefore, undertakings have an interest to define the relevant market as broadly a possible, playing down their role on that market. This applies to no lesser degree on media markets, which often require a particularly complex assessment. As the Commission explained in the merger case of *Vivendi/ Canal+/Seagram*:

---

[30] Two of the most famous extraterritorial cases in which the Commission assumed jurisdiction were the Boeing/McDonnell Douglas merger (Case No. IV/M.877 [1997] Boeing/McDonnell Douglas [7]) and the General Electric/Honeywell merger (Case No. COMP/M.2220 [2001] General Electric/Honeywell [7]).

[31] ECJ, Case T-102/96 [1999] Gencor Ltd v. Commission [90].

[32] CJEU, Case T-286/09 [2014] Intel v. Commission [244].

[33] On the burden of proof in competition cases, see Article 2 Enforcement Regulation.

The structure of the media industry is multidimensional and complex. Indeed, different players such as content providers, right-holders, content distributors, operate in the value chain from the production of content such as films, pay-TV programming, and music, to its delivery via theatres, pay-TV channels or Internet 'portals'.[34]

In 1997, the European Commission published a notice on the definition of relevant markets for the purposes of EU antitrust law.[35] Accordingly, the market definition is composed of the relevant product market and the relevant geographic market. In addition, the Commission commissioned a report on market definition in the media sector and extensive studies on media markets in the EU Member States.[36]

However, note that the application of competition law in general, and the definition of the relevant market in particular, are inherently case-specific. For example, merger control involves a *prospective* analysis, whereas the application of Articles 101 and 102 TFEU concerns *past* behaviour. This might lead to the result that different geographic markets are defined for the same products.[37] Because of the complex economic assessments involved, the Court of Justice's scope of judicial review is limited to examining manifest errors when reviewing market definitions by the Commission.[38]

aa Relevant Product Market The relevant product market is defined, in the first place, by the notion of demand substitutability. Two products (or services) belong to the same market if they are, from a consumer's perspective, viewed as substitutes. This is the case if the consumer regards them 'as interchangeable or substitutable ... by reason of the products' characteristics, their prices and their intended use'.[39] There are various economic models to determine demand substitutability. One example is a hypothetical small but permanent increase in prices of a certain product:[40] the more likely it is that consumers switch to another product in case of a price increase, the more likely is the substitutability of those products, hence the competition of the producers of those products on the same market. If consumers would still purchase the

---

[34] COM, Case No. COMP/M.2050 [2000] Vivendi/Canal+/Seagram [14].

[35] COM, Notice on the definition of relevant market for the purposes of Community competition law (1997), OJ C 372/5.

[36] See Report by Europe Economics for the European Commission, DG Competition, Market Definition in the Media Sector – Economic Issues, November 2002, which can be found at http://ec.europa.eu/competition/sectors/media/documents/european_economics.pdf. The studies on media markets can be found at http://ec.europa.eu/competition/sectors/media/documents/index.html.

[37] COM, Notice on the definition of relevant market for the purposes of Community competition law, para. 12.

[38] See, for example, ECJ, Joined Cases T-346/02 and T-347/02 [2003] Cableuropa [118]; Case C-12/03 P [2005] Tetra Laval [38].

[39] COM, Notice on the definition of relevant market for the purposes of Community competition law, para. 7. See, for example, ECJ, Case 31/80 [1980] L'Oréal v. De Nieuwe AMCK [25]; Case C-62/86 [1991] AKZO v. Commission [51]; Case C-7/97 [1998] Bronner v. Mediaprint Zeitungs- und Zeitschriftenverlag [33].

[40] Also known as the SSNIP test: 'small but significant and non-transitory increase in price'.

product the price of which has been (hypothetically) increased, then the products are more likely to operate on different markets.

An additional factor for assessing the relevant market is supply-side substitutability. Supply-side substitutability examines the extent to which other suppliers could switch production to a relevant product without incurring significant additional costs or risks and thus become competitors.[41] The fewer impediments they face, the more likely is their operation on the same relevant product market.

bb Relevant Geographic Market   According to the Commission's notice, the relevant geographic market 'comprises the area in which the undertakings concerned are involved in the supply and demand of products or services, in which the conditions of competition are sufficiently homogeneous and which can be distinguished from neighbouring areas because the conditions of competition are appreciably different in those areas'.[42] The models used to determine the relevant geographic market are to a certain extent similar to those applied to determine the relevant product market. The initial question is whether companies in different geographical areas constitute a real alternative source of supply for consumers.[43] In the case of a (hypothetical) change of a particular product's price, would customers buy products from companies located elsewhere? If this is the case, then the two companies are operating on the same geographic market. Moreover, with a view to the supply side, to what extent would companies located in different geographic areas face impediments in developing their sales on competitive terms throughout a whole geographic market? The more obstacles – such as logistical, linguistic, regulatory and technical barriers – they would face, the less likely is their competition on the same market. Against this background, the geographic market can be global, regional (such as EU-wide), national or just local.

c Undertaking

EU antitrust rules apply to undertakings. The concept of an 'undertaking' in EU antitrust law covers any entity engaged in economic activity, regardless of the legal status of the entity or the way in which it is financed.[44] With a view to media law in particular, the notion of 'undertaking' includes, for example, football clubs,[45] public broadcasters[46] and collecting societies.[47] The UEFA and the European Broadcasting

---

[41] COM, Notice on the definition of relevant market for the purposes of Community competition law, para. 20.

[42] COM, Notice on the definition of relevant market for the purposes of Community competition law, para. 8; see, for example, ECJ, Joined Cases T-346/02 and T-347/02 [2003] Cableuropa [115].

[43] COM, Notice on the definition of relevant market for the purposes of Community competition law, para. 29.

[44] ECJ, Case C-41/90 [1991] Höfner and Elser v. Macrotron [21]; Case C-218/00 [2002] Cisal [22]; Joined Cases C-264/01, C-306/01, C-354/01 and C-355/01 [2004] AOK Bundesverband and others [46].

[45] COM, Case No. 37.576 [2001] UEFA's broadcasting regulations [47]; Case No. COMP/C-2/37.214 [2005] Bundesliga [21].

[46] COM, Case No. IV/31.734 [1989] Film purchases by German television stations [38].

[47] See, for example, COM, Case No. COMP/C2/38.014 [2002] IFPI 'Simulcasting' [59].

Union (EBU) are 'associations of undertakings'.[48] The concept of undertaking may also apply to state-owned companies, if they are engaged in an economic activity.[49]

d Affecting Trade between Member States

The agreement, decision or concerted practice within the meaning of Article 101 TFEU, or the abuse of a dominant position under Article 102 TFEU, has to be capable of affecting trade between Member States. The concept of interstate trade, which is also included in the free movement provisions, is in its doctrinal core a conflict-of-laws rule, and indirectly also a jurisdictional rule. It distinguishes the application of EU competition law, and hence the competence of the European Commission to decide a case, from Member States' antitrust law and the competence of the national competition authorities. More specifically, Article 103(2)(e) TFEU empowers the Council to legislate on the relationship between national laws and the EU antitrust law provisions. The division of competences between the European Commission and the national competition authorities is set out in the Enforcement Regulation. Essentially, the NCAs shall have the competence to decide on cases with and without a transnational dimension. However, according to Article 3 Enforcement Regulation, if the competition authorities of the Member States apply national antitrust law to behaviour that may affect trade between Member States, they shall also apply Articles 101 and 102 TFEU. The application of national antitrust law may not lead to the prohibition of agreements that would be allowed under Article 101 TFEU. However, Member States are not precluded from adopting and applying on their territory stricter laws than Article 102 TFEU. Moreover, Member States may implement on their territory national legislation that pursues objectives different from that of protecting competition, such as sanctions on acts of unfair trading practice.[50]

If the behaviour in question is capable of affecting trade between Member States, the Commission may also decide to investigate the issue and to adopt a decision. In such a case, the sole competence to decide the case is with the European Commission, unless the Commission refers the case to a domestic competition authority. Moreover, according to Article 16 Enforcement Regulation, national competition authorities must not adopt decisions based on Articles 101 and 102 TFEU that run counter to a prior decision taken by the Commission on the same issue. In order to safeguard the uniform application of Articles 101 and 102 TFEU, the Enforcement Regulation includes several provisions on cooperation between the Commission and the competition authorities as well as courts of the Member States and the establishment of an Advisory Committee (Articles 11–15). In addition, the Commission and the national authorities cooperate in the European Competition Network.[51]

---

[48] COM, Case No. IV/32.150 [2000] Eurovision [65]; Case No. 37.576 [2001] UEFA's broadcasting regulations [47].

[49] See, for example, COM, Case No. COMP/M.1439 [1999] Telia/Telenor.

[50] Recital 9 Enforcement Regulation.

[51] See COM, Notice on cooperation within the Network of Competition Authorities (2004), OJ C 101/43.

A restrictive agreement or the abuse of a dominant position is affecting trade between Member States if it is capable of constituting a threat – direct or indirect, actual or potential – to freedom of trade between Member States in a manner that might harm the attainment of the objectives of a single market between states.[52] It is not necessary that the conduct in question should in fact have substantially affected that trade; rather, it is sufficient that the conduct is capable of having such an effect.[53] The European Commission has further elaborated on the notion of 'effect on trade' in a 2004 notice.[54] In particular, the Commission establishes a rule indicating when agreements are unlikely to be capable of appreciably affecting trade between Member States (the 'non-appreciable affectation of trade', or NAAT, rule).

e Enforcement

The Commission's powers to enforce EU antitrust law and the applicable proceedings are set out in Regulation 1/2003, here named 'Enforcement Regulation', and in Regulation 773/2004, here named 'Proceedings Regulation'.[55] The Commission's enforcement procedure can be divided into two stages: the investigation and the decision. A Commission investigation may be triggered in several ways: the Commission may start an investigation on its own initiative or it may act upon a complaint by a third party. Moreover, with a view to multilateral anti-competitive agreements, the Commission has set an incentive for cartel members to obtain 'whistle-blower immunity': the first cartel member informing the European Commission of an anti-competitive agreement generally receives immunity under the Commission's leniency programme. For this purpose, the Commission provides a fax number (+32 2 2994585). Whether a company is the first or the second whistle-blower might be a matter of minutes, and the fax provides the necessary evidence. Undertakings that cooperate with the Commission during the investigation process without having received whistle-blower immunity may still receive a reduction of their fine of up to 50 per cent.[56] The leniency programme is designed to render cartels inherently unstable and thus to prevent their emergence in the first place.

The Enforcement Regulation furnishes the European Commission with considerable powers. The Commission may require undertakings and associations of undertakings to provide all necessary information and impose a fine in case of non-compliance (Articles 17, 18 and 23). The Commission may also conduct interviews

---

[52] ECJ, Case 54/64 [1966] Consten and Grundig, p. 340.

[53] ECJ, Case 322/81 [1983] Michelin v. Commission [104]; Case C-41/90 [1991] Höfner and Elser v. Macrotron [32]; Joined Cases C-241 and 242/91 P [1995] RTE and ITP v. Commission ('Magill') [69].

[54] COM, Notice – Guidelines on the effect on trade concept contained in Articles 81 and 82 of the Treaty (2004), OJ C 101/81.

[55] Council Regulation (EC) No. 1/2003 of 16 December 2002 on the implementation of the rules on competition laid down in Articles 81 and 82 of the Treaty, OJ L 1/1; Commission Regulation (EC) No. 773/2004 of 7 April 2004 relating to the conduct of proceedings by the Commission pursuant to Articles 81 and 82 of the EC Treaty, OJ L 123/18.

[56] COM, Notice on Immunity from fines and reduction of fines in cartel cases (2006), OJ C 298/17.

(Article 19). Furthermore, it may enter and seal business and private premises ('dawn raids'), and examine and seal business records (Articles 20 and 21). Particularly the powers conferred upon the Commission under Articles 20 and 21 may raise fundamental rights concerns under Article 7 EUChFR, as the right to respect for one's 'home' is a concept that also applies to business premises.[57] Moreover, it is subject to debate whether the limited requirement of a prior judicial authorisation codified in Article 20(8) Enforcement Regulation meets the demands established by the Strasbourg Court.[58] In cases in which the European Commission conducts such an investigation against a media company or journalist, it would have to consider the specific privileges of the media as set out in Chapter 2.

Before adopting a decision, the Commission shall hear the undertakings or associations of undertakings that are the subject of the proceedings (Article 27). This provision also has to be applied in light of the fundamental rights involved, such as Article 47 EUChFR.[59] If the Commission finds that undertakings and associations of undertakings have infringed Articles 101 or 102 TFEU, it has several penalties and remedies at its disposal. It may impose fines on them of up to 10 per cent of their total worldwide turnover in the preceding business year (Article 23(2)(a)). Moreover, the Commission may impose on infringing undertakings or associations of undertakings periodic penalty payments of up to 5 per cent of the average daily turnover in the preceding business year per day in order to compel them to put an end to an infringement. Furthermore, the Commission may impose behavioural or structural remedies on infringing undertakings or associations of undertakings (Article 7). These remedies are subject to the principle of proportionality. Article 7 Enforcement Regulation sets out that structural remedies can only be imposed either if there is no equally effective behavioural remedy or if any equally effective behavioural remedy would be more burdensome for the undertaking concerned than the structural remedy. If the undertakings concerned offer commitments to meet the concerns expressed by the Commission, the Commission may by decision make those commitments binding on the undertakings and close the investigation without formally finding an infringement (Article 9). The decisions taken by the European Commission, including those taken during the investigation, may be brought before the General Court.

Complainants in cases under Articles 101 and 102 TFEU enjoy considerable procedural rights. They may receive a copy of the non-confidential version of the statement of objections and make written comments on it (Article 6(2) Proceedings Regulation). They may take part in hearings with the addressees of the statement of objections (Article 11 Proceedings Regulation), they have a (limited) right of access

---

[57] ECtHR, Niemietz v. Germany [1992] App. no. 13710/88 [31].
[58] See ECtHR, Société Colas Est and others v. France [2002] App. no. 37971/97 [49].
[59] See ECtHR, A. Menarini Diagnostics S.R.L. v. Italy [2011] App. no. 43509/08; CJEU, Case C-272/09 P [2011] KME v. Commission.

to information (Article 8 Proceedings Regulation) and they have a right to be heard if the Commission decides not to take the complaint forward (Article 7 Proceedings Regulation).

In addition to Commission action, breaches of EU antitrust law may also be enforced by private parties. In other words, Articles 101 and 102 TFEU have a direct effect between private individuals. For example, private claimants may argue that an agreement is void according to Article 101(2) TFEU, and they may also see compensation for loss they have suffered because of anti-competitive behaviour.[60] The expansion from public to private enforcement of EU antitrust law has long been on the Commission's agenda, and it has also been upheld by the Luxembourg Court.[61] It is now also to a certain extent codified in a Directive.[62] Member States' (contract or tort) law remains applicable to such cases, but it has to be applied in a way that provides full effect of EU competition law.

By contrast, there is no EU policy on the 'private enforcement' of violations of the EU Merger Regulation. It is therefore left to each Member State to decide whether or not it wants to provide a private law remedy for a violation of that Regulation.

2 The Definition of Media Markets

As has been stated before, the Commission itself is aware of the fact that the definition of media markets is particularly complex. What are the reasons for that? The media sector implies several singular features. These include:

- complex supply chains involving a number of stages of production;
- technological change, particularly the phenomenon of media convergence, and change of consumer behaviour in media markets;
- copyright restrictions;
- the distinction between the production of broadcasting content and the distribution of that content in programme schedules by broadcasters as two separate markets;
- concentration of infrastructure ownership;
- the diverging scope of media markets, both product-related and geographic, depending on factors such as languages, regulatory divergences (despite the minimum harmonisation by the AVMS Directive), cultural differences, etc.[63]

---

[60] ECJ, Case C-453/99 [2001] Courage Ltd. v. Crehan [22 ff].

[61] COM, Green Paper: Damages actions for breach of the EC antitrust rules, COM(2005) 672 final; ECJ, Case C-453/99 [2001] Courage Ltd. v. Crehan [25]; Joined Cases C-295/04 to C-298/04 [2006] Manfredi and others [92 ff].

[62] Directive 2014/104/EU of the European Parliament and of the Council of 26 November 2014 on certain rules governing actions for damages under national law for infringements of the competition law provisions of the Member States and of the European Union, OJ L 349/1.

[63] See COM, Case No. COMP/M.2050 [2000] Vivendi/Canal+/Seagram [20]; R. Capito, in Castendyk, Dommering and Scheuer (2008) Article 82 EC paras. 19 ff; Scott (2013).

The European Commission has identified a number of relevant markets along the value chain for the distribution of audiovisual TV content, newspaper publications and the provision of telecommunication services. The following subsections a–d explain several relevant product markets, whereas subsection e deals with the geographic dimension of media markets.[64] Within the media sector, the geographic distinction between media markets is still mostly based on national or regional boundaries.

a TV-Related Markets

As regards the TV-related markets, and with respect to the licensing and distribution of content and channels, the Commission has drawn a distinction between the following market levels:

1 Licensing and acquisition of broadcasting rights for audiovisual content.
2 Wholesale supply of TV channels.
3 Retail supply of TV services.[65]

aa Licensing and Acquisition of Broadcasting Rights   Audiovisual TV content includes products that can be broadcast via TV, such as films, sport events and TV programmes. The rights to broadcast belong, in principle, to the creators of such content. These rights-holders constitute the supply side of the upstream market 'licensing and acquisition of broadcasting rights'. They license their broadcasting rights to, for example, broadcasters or content platform operators. Those audiovisual media services constitute the demand side of this market.

With a view to the supply side – that is, the production of audiovisual content – the European Commission distinguishes, first, between the market for films and other fictional products, on the one hand, and for rights to sports events, on the other hand.[66] The Commission explains this distinction with specific features of sport rights as compared with film and other programme rights: sport programmes covering widely popular sports or major international events are often able to achieve high audience ratings and are particularly suited to carrying advertisements. Moreover, the attractiveness of TV rights for sport events may change considerably

---

[64] See also COM, Market definition in the media sector – Comparative legal analysis (Volume I), Report by Bird & Bird for the European Commission, Directorate-General for Competition, Information, communication and multimedia, December 2002; Media Market Definitions – Comparative Legal Analysis, Final Report (July/October 2003); Media Market Definitions – Comparative Legal Analysis, Final Report (18 July 2005).

[65] See, for example, COM, Case No. COMP/M.6880 [2013] Liberty Global/Virgin Media [29]; Case No. 37.576 [2001] UEFA's broadcasting regulations [22]; Case No. COMP/C.2–38.287 [2003] Telenor/Canal+/Canal Digital [25]; Case No. COMP/M.6990 [2013] Vodafone/Kabel Deutschland [12].

[66] COM, Case No. IV/M.779 [1996] Bertelsmann/CLT [18]; Case No. IV/M.1574 [1999] Kirch/Mediaset [15]; Case No. COMP/M.1958 [2000] Bertelsmann/GBL/Pearson TV [12]; Case No. COMP/M.5932 [2010] News Corp/BSkyB [59].

depending on the actual participation and success of teams or participants appealing to national or regional audiences.[67] The market for sports rights is subdivided into further markets, for example: a market for major international sporting events, such as the Summer and Winter Olympics and the Football World Cup, and a market for broadcasting rights of football matches played almost throughout the year, such as the UEFA Champions League and national football leagues.[68] The Commission has decided that the market for football broadcasting rights should be distinguished from the market for other sports broadcasting rights, because football is the most popular sport across most Member States.[69] The Commission has even considered – but ultimately left open – that the market for football broadcasting rights may be further subdivided in a number of ways, for example, on the basis of the type of event (domestic leagues versus UEFA Champions League, etc.).[70]

Second, the Commission divides the market for premium films into a market of broadcasting rights for films and a market for broadcasting rights for made-for-TV programmes.[71] The market for licensing of rights to TV programmes is distinct from the market for licensing rights of premium films, because the licensing fees for TV programmes are often lower than for premium films.[72] With a view to TV productions, the Commission distinguishes between in-house productions produced by broadcasters and used for captive use, on the one hand, and productions commissioned by a broadcaster to a producer, on the other hand. Only the latter are offered on a market and the relevant product market has, therefore, to be limited to TV productions that are not used for captive use.[73]

Regarding the demand side – that is, linear and non-linear broadcasters – the Commission has frequently emphasised that pay-TV and free access TV (or free-to-air TV, FTA) operate on separate product markets.[74] This is because pay-TV operators are usually financed through subscription, whereas free-TV is usually financed by advertising or by state contributions. But there might be exceptions in those cases

---

[67] COM, Case No. IV/M.779 [1996] Bertelsmann/CLT [18]; Case No. COMP/M.1958 [2000] Bertelsmann/GBL/Pearson TV [12].

[68] COM, Case No. COMP/M.2876 [2003] News Corp/Telepiù [66]; Case No. COMP/C.2–37.398 [2003] UEFA Champions League [77]; Case No. COMP/C-2/37.214 [2005] Bundesliga [17].

[69] COM, Case No. COMP/M.4519 [2007] Lagardère/Sportfive [9]; Case No. COMP/M.5932 [2010] News Corp/BSkyB [61].

[70] COM, Case No. COMP/M.4519 [2007] Lagardère/Sportfive [10]; Case No. COMP/M.2876 [2003] News Corp/Telepiù [64]; Case No. COMP/M.5932 [2010] News Corp/BSkyB [61].

[71] COM, Case No. COMP/M.2050 [2000] Vivendi/Canal+/Seagram [17]; Case No. COMP/M.2876 [2003] News Corp/Telepiù [56]; Case No. COMP/M.5932 [2010] News Corp/BSkyB [59]; Case No. COMP/M.7288 [2014] Viacom/Channel 5 Broadcasting [12].

[72] COM, Case No. COMP/M.3595 [2005] Sony/MGM [20].

[73] See COM, Case No. IV/M.779 [1996] Bertelsmann/CLT [17]; Case No. IV/M.1574 [1999] Kirch/Mediaset [14]; Case No. COMP/M.1958 [2000] Bertelsmann/GBL/Pearson TV [11].

[74] See, for example, COM, Case No. IV/M.110 [1991] ABC/Générale des Eaux/Canal+/W.H. Smith TV [11]; Case No. IV/M.410 [1994] Kirch/Richmond/Telepiù [15]; Case No. COMP/M.2876 [2003] News Corp/Telepiù [41]; Case No. COMP/M.5121 [2008] News Corp/Premiere [15]; Case No. COMP/M.5932 [2010] News Corp/BSkyB [85].

in which pay-TV channels also broadcast advertisements.[75] With regard to services related to pay-TV, the Commission has identified pay-per-view services as a segment of the pay-TV market,[76] whereas digital interactive TV services are complementary to the pay-TV market.[77] Analogue pay-TV and digital pay-TV compete on the same product market, because digital pay-TV is only a further development of analogue pay-TV.[78] The Commission has also subdivided the market for the licensing of broadcasting rights for audio visual TV content into TV content for linear and for non-linear broadcast.[79]

In practice, there are different exhibition windows as regards licensing/acquisition of TV broadcasting rights to content: premium content reaches free-TV often after all other TV-related selling windows have been exploited by suppliers. Therefore, free-TV operators do not always compete with pay-TV operators for the acquisition of the relevant content that makes pay-TV attractive to consumers.[80] The Commission has also even considered a more detailed breakdown based on the different exhibition windows, namely: video-on-demand (VOD), pay-per-view (PPV), first pay-TV window, second pay-TV window and free-TV.[81] Finally, the Commission has frequently indicated that it might apply even narrower standards for TV broadcasting with a view to specialised channels, such as broadcasting of news programmes.[82]

bb Wholesale Supply of TV Channels   As has been shown before, TV broadcasters acquire – or they themselves produce – audiovisual content. On the next step of the supply chain, they package the content into TV channels. These TV channels are then broadcast to end-users via different distribution infrastructures, such as cable, satellite and internet. Hence, the supply side of this market comprises TV broadcasters and its demand side comprises TV retailers (or TV distributors). The latter either confine themselves to transmitting the TV channels and make them available to end-users, or they also act as channel aggregators, which also package TV channels and provide them to end-users.[83]

---

[75] See COM, Case No. COMP/M.1958 [2000] Bertelsmann/GBL/Pearson TV [10].
[76] COM, Case No. COMP M. 2211 [2000] Universal Studio Networks/De Facto 829 (NTL) Studio Channel Ltd. [13].
[77] COM, Case No. COMP/M.2876 [2003] News Corp/Telepiù [43].
[78] COM, Case No. COMP/M.2050 [2000] Vivendi/Canal+/Seagram [20, fn. 20].
[79] COM, Case No. COMP/M.4504 [2007] SFR/Télé 2 France [27].
[80] COM, Case No. COMP/M.3595 [2005] Sony/MGM [15]; Case No. COMP/M.5121 [2008] News Corp/ Premiere [29–32]; Case No. 37.576 [2001] UEFA's broadcasting regulations [25]; see also Di Mauro (2003); Woods (2012) p. 207.
[81] COM, Case No. COMP/M.6369 [2011] HBO/Ziggo/HBO Nederland [18]; Case No. COMP/M.6880 [2013] Liberty Global/Virgin Media [17]; Case No. COMP/M.6990 [2013] Vodafone/Kabel Deutschland [20]; Case No. COMP/M.7288 [2014] Viacom/Channel 5 Broadcasting [13].
[82] COM, Case No. IV/M.1081 [1998] Dow Jones/NBC – CNBC Europe [7].
[83] COM, Case No. COMP/M.6990 [2013] Vodafone/Kabel Deutschland [30].

The Commission identified a wholesale market for the supply of TV channels, in which TV channel broadcasters and retail TV suppliers negotiate the terms and conditions for the distribution of TV channels to end-users.[84] Within this market, the Commission further identified two separate product markets for free-TV channels and for pay-TV channels. The reasoning is the same as for the licensing markets: the differences between the financial models of these channels.[85] This difference influences the negotiations between TV broadcasters on the supply side and the TV distributors on the demand side, as TV distributors have to bear a cost only for distribution of pay TV channels, since distribution of the free channels costs them nothing.[86] Within the market for the wholesale supply of pay-TV channels, the Commission has also previously indicated that there is a differentiation between 'basic' and 'premium' pay-TV channels, such as premium sports and movie channels. However, the Commission left open whether these two categories of pay-TV channels constitute separate product markets.[87] The Commission also examined, but ultimately left open, whether the market should be further segmented by genre or thematic content, such as films, sports, news and youth channels.[88] The Commission has not further distinguished between the different means of infrastructure used for the delivery to the viewer (cable, satellite, DVB-T and IPTV).[89]

cc Retail Supply of TV Services On the retail market for the supply of TV services, the suppliers of linear and non-linear TV services on the supply side serve end-customers who wish to purchase such services on the demand side.[90] The Commission has once more identified separate markets for the retail supply of free-TV and of pay-TV services.[91] Because of the growing convergence of different platforms in terms of content, the Commission has not yet further segmented this market on the basis of the traditional technical means of delivery (cable, satellite, DVB-T or IPTV).[92] The Commission has, however, left open whether the emerging TV services via mobile

---

[84] Case No. COMP/M.5932 [2010] News Corp/BSkyB [76 and 85]; Case No. COMP/M.6369 [2011] HBO/Ziggo/HBO Nederland [22]; Case No. COMP/M.6990 [2013] Vodafone/Kabel Deutschland [33].

[85] COM, Case No. COMP/M.4504 [2007] SFR/Télé 2 France [38]; Case No. COMP/M.6369 [2011] HBO/Ziggo/HBO Nederland [24]; Case No. COMP/M.7288 [2014] Viacom/Channel 5 Broadcasting [20].

[86] COM, Case No. COMP/M.4504 [2007] SFR/Télé 2 France [38].

[87] COM, Case No. COMP/M.2876 [2003] News Corp/Telepiù [74] and [76]; Case No. COMP/M.4504 [2007] SFR/Télé 2 France [41]; Case No. COMP/M.5932 [2010] News Corp/BSkyB [85]; Case No. COMP/M.6369 [2011] HBO/Ziggo/HBO Nederland [24 and 27].

[88] COM, Case No. COMP/M.2876 [2003] News Corp/Telepiù [76]; Case No. COMP/M.4504 [2007] SFR/Télé 2 France [42]; Case No. COMP/M.5932 [2010] News Corp/BSkyB [81]; Case No. COMP/M.6990 [2013] Vodafone/Kabel Deutschland [41].

[89] COM, Case No. COMP/M.4504 [2007] SFR/Télé 2 France [43].

[90] COM, Case No. COMP/M.6990 [2013] Vodafone/Kabel Deutschland [48].

[91] COM, Case No. COMP/M.5121 [2008] News Corp/Premiere [15]; Case No. COMP/M.6990 [2013] Vodafone/Kabel Deutschland [49].

[92] COM, Case No. COMP/M.4504 [2007] SFR/Télé 2 France [46]; Case No. COMP/M.5121 [2008] News Corp/Premiere [22].

telephony platforms form part of this overall market.[93] The Commission has also left open whether linear and non-linear services constitute separate product markets.[94]

b The Transmission Infrastructure

With respect to the infrastructure side (as opposed to the content side) of the TV sector, the Commission has identified the following market levels:

1 Wholesale TV signal transmission market.
2 Intermediary market for signal delivery.
3 Retail supply of signal transmission market.[95]

For the sake of brevity, the intermediary market for signal delivery and the retail signal transmission market shall be left out of account here. The wholesale TV signal transmission market mirrors the above-mentioned market for the wholesale supply of TV channels, but with reversed roles: TV broadcasters, now acting on the demand side, negotiate the terms and conditions of the transmission of the TV signal for their channels with the infrastructure operators – cable, satellite, DVB-T and IPTV operators – on the supply side.[96] The Commission has distinguished quite clearly between different transmission modes.[97] For example, in *Vodafone/Kabel Deutschland*, the Commission had to assess whether the wholesale TV signal transmission via cable (where Kabel Deutschland was active) is in a market separate from the wholesale TV signal transmission via IPTV (where Vodafone was active).[98] The Commission considered that, from the perspective of TV broadcasters, cable and IPTV are complements rather than substitutes. Accordingly, the Commission concluded that the wholesale signal transmission via cable constitutes a separate product market from, at least, the wholesale signal transmission via IPTV.[99] But as with market definitions in general, the exact delineation of the relevant markets in this context is highly dependent on the particular case.

c Newspaper Markets

The Commission distinguishes between (both television and radio) broadcasting markets, on the one side, and newspaper markets, on the other side, with a view to both audience share and advertising revenues. Regarding the audience share,

---

[93] COM, Case No. COMP/M.4504 [2007] SFR/Télé 2 France [47].
[94] COM, Case No. COMP/M.5121 [2008] News Corp/Premiere [21].
[95] COM, Case No. COMP/M.5734 [2010] Liberty Global Europe/Unitymedia [8f]; Case No. COMP/M.5900 [2011] LGI/KBW [18]; Case No. COMP/M.6990 [2013] Vodafone/Kabel Deutschland [13].
[96] COM, Case No. COMP/M.6990 [2013] Vodafone/Kabel Deutschland [57].
[97] For example, the Commission came to the conclusion that in Scandinavian countries the transmission modes constitute separate product markets; see, COM, Case No. COMP/M.2300 [2001] YLE/TDF/Digita/ JV [16]; Case No. IV/M.1439 [1999] Telia/Telenor [279]; but see also, in contrast, COM, Case No. COMP/ C.2–38.287 [2003] Telenor/Canal+/Canal Digital [50].
[98] COM, Case No. COMP/M.6990 [2013] Vodafone/Kabel Deutschland [63].
[99] COM, Case No. COMP/M.6990 [2013] Vodafone/Kabel Deutschland [65.]

broadcasting offers more rapid coverage of news events, but it does usually not match the range and depth of newspaper coverage.[100] Concerning the advertising market, the Commission observed that the consumers targeted through advertising differ considerably because of the different advertising techniques employed.[101] A 2010 market investigation was inconclusive as to the substitutability of print newspapers and online news services. The market investigation was also inconclusive as to the substitutability of print newspapers and paid-for online news services.[102]

Within the newspaper sector, the Commission distinguishes between regional newspapers and national newspapers, as they are not substitutable from a consumer viewpoint.[103] Furthermore, the Commission distinguishes between popular tabloids (such as the *Daily Mirror*), the mid-market titles (such as the *Daily Express*) and the quality segment (such as *The Times*). These segments do not only differ in the depths of their coverage, but also in their price. Therefore, they attract different types of readers and advertisers.[104]

d Other Media Markets

The Commission had to decide on many other media markets. For example, with a view to books, the Commission identified several product markets, such as the market for reproduction rights for images and maps contained in books, markets for publishing rights, markets for marketing and distribution services provided to publishers, markets for book sales and a market for e-books.[105] The Commission has also found that the market for technical services for pay-TV – that is, the infrastructure necessary to operate the conditional access system – is a separate market in its own right.[106] Finally, the Commission has identified separate markets, for example, for printing facilities of catalogues and magazines,[107] mobile operating systems,[108] free access radio broadcasting,[109] the distribution of films to cinemas[110] and for DVD and VHS home entertainment.[111]

---

[100] COM, Case No. IV/M.423 [1994] Newspaper Publishing [13]; Case No. IV/M.553 [1995] RTL/Veronica/Endemol [23]; Case No. COMP/M.5932 [2010] News Corp/BSkyB [211].

[101] COM, Case No. IV/M.779 [1996] Bertelsmann/CLT [14]; see also Case No. IV/M.1574 [1999] Kirch/Mediaset [11].

[102] COM, Case No. COMP/M.5932 [2010] News Corp/BSkyB [211].

[103] COM, Case No. IV/M.423 [1994] Newspaper Publishing [13].

[104] COM, Case No. IV/M.423 [1994] Newspaper Publishing [14–16].

[105] See COM, Case No. COMP/M.2978 [2004] Lagardère/Natexis/VUP [66 ff]; Case No. COMP/AT.39847 [2012] E-Books [93].

[106] COM, Case No. IV/M.993 [1998] Bertelsmann/Kirch/Premiere [19–21]; Case No. COMP/M.5121 [2008] News Corp/Premiere [40]; Case No. IV/36.237 [1999] TPS [41].

[107] COM, Case No. COMP/M.3178 [2005] Bertelsmann/Springer [44].

[108] COM, Case No. COMP/M.6381 [2012] Google/Motorola Mobility [16 ff].

[109] COM, Case No. IV/M.779 [1996] Bertelsmann/CLT [19].

[110] COM, Case No. COMP/M.2050 [2000] Vivendi/Canal+/Seagram [16]; Case No. COMP/M.3595 [2005] Sony/MGM [10].

[111] COM, Case No. COMP/M.3595 [2005] Sony/MGM [12–13].

e The Relevant Geographic Markets

Despite the transnational dimension of media communication, particularly via the internet and satellite broadcasting, the Commission usually views the geographic scope of newspaper and TV-related markets to be national or even regional.[112] The same applies to the relevant geographic market for theatrical distribution of motion pictures.[113] This is for several reasons. Most important are cultural and linguistic reasons. Further factors that have an impact on the geographic scope are copyright restrictions and regulatory differences. As has been shown in Chapter 9, copyright protection is to a large extent still a national issue. The same applies to other exclusive rights. By way of example, although there might be a transnational or even a global interest in international sport events or certain movies (such as the *James Bond* films), broadcasting rights are normally granted for one specific country or language region only.[114] The Commission confirmed the national delineation even after the *Karen Murphy* decision. Although this judgment was presumed to alter the geographic scope for rights negotiations and licensing, the Commission has found that licensing on a multinational basis is still not common.[115]

As we observed in Chapter 5, the AVMS Directive only provides minimum harmonisation, providing Member States opportunities to impose more detailed or stricter rules. For example, despite the common language, the European Commission distinguishes between the Flemish and the Dutch market for TV broadcasting because of regulatory (and also cultural) differences between Belgium and the Netherlands.[116] But the Commission also indicated that all German-speaking regions consisting of Germany, Austria, parts of Switzerland and Belgium, and even Luxembourg, could be regarded as a relevant geographic market for pay-TV and broadcasting rights to premium films.[117] These examples show that market definitions are highly case-specific.

The geographic market definitions for infrastructure services are different, as they are independent of linguistic and cultural aspects and to a large extent harmonised within the EU. Rather than drawing national or regional boundaries, the Commission makes the geographic scope of cable infrastructure services dependent

---

[112] COM, Case No. IV/M.110 [1991] ABC/Générale des Eaux/Canal+/W.H. Smith TV [11]; Case No. IV/M.423 [1994] Newspaper Publishing [17]; Case No. IV/M.410 [1994] Kirch/Richmond/Telepiù [17]; Case No. IV/M.489 [1994] Bertelsmann/News International/Vox [20]; Case No. COMP/M.6990 [2013] Vodafone/Kabel Deutschland [25].

[113] COM, Case No. COMP/M.3595 [2005] Sony/MGM [21].

[114] COM, Case No. IV/M.779 [1996] Bertelsmann/CLT [21]; Case No. IV/M.1574 [1999] Kirch/Mediaset [17]; Case No. COMP/M.1958 [2000] Bertelsmann/GBL/Pearson TV [14]; Case No. COMP/M.5932 [2010] News Corp/BSkyB [70].

[115] COM, Case No. COMP/M.6369 [2011] HBO/Ziggo/HBO Nederland [35]; Case No. COMP/M.6880 [2013] Liberty Global/Virgin Media [24]; Case No. COMP/M.6866 [2013] Time Warner/CME [31]; Case No. COMP/M.7332 [2014] BSkyB/Sky Deutschland/Sky Italia [42].

[116] COM, Case No. IV/M.553 [1995] RTL/Veronica/Endemol [25–26].

[117] COM, Case No. IV/M.993 [1998] Bertelsmann/Kirch/Premiere [22–24]; Case No. COMP/M.5932 [2010] News Corp/BSkyB [73]; but see also Case No. COMP/M.5121 [2008] News Corp/Premiere [27].

on the coverage area of the cable network.[118] The market for *global* internet connectivity is global,[119] whereas the retail market of internet *access services* is national.[120]

3 Anti-Competitive Multilateral Behaviour

Article 101(1) TFEU prohibits agreements between undertakings, decisions by associations of undertakings and concerted practices that may affect trade between Member States and that have as their object or effect the prevention, restriction or distortion of competition within the internal market. Article 101(2) TFEU declares such agreements and decisions void. Article 101(3) TFEU provides exemptions to Article 101(1) and (2).

Until 2004, anti-competitive multilateral behaviour operated under an *ex ante* notification procedure. Undertakings that intended to conclude an agreement, adopt a decision or concert their practices within the meaning of Article 101(1) TFEU had to notify the European Commission prior to this action and wait for the Commission's approval. This provided legal certainty, but it was also a time-consuming administrative procedure for both the undertakings involved and the European Commission. Since 2004, Article 101 TFEU proceedings are based on *ex post* supervision. Undertakings are effectively at liberty to act, unless the Commission suspects anti-competitive behaviour. This reduces the administrative burden, but it creates risks for companies that might be found in violation of EU antitrust law. Article 10 Enforcement Regulation furnishes the European Commission with the authority to adopt declaratory decisions finding that an agreement, a decision or a concerted practice does not violate Article 101 TFEU, if the EU public interest so requires.

a Agreements, Decisions and Concerted Practices

Article 101(1) TFEU encompasses 'all agreements between undertakings, decisions by associations of undertakings and concerted practices'.[121] This provision includes agreements between competitors operating at the same level in the economic process (horizontal agreements) as well as between non-competing persons operating at different levels (vertical agreements). It covers agreements that limit competition between the parties involved and agreements that prevent or restrict the competition that might take place between one of them and third parties. Article 101(1) TFEU names non-exhaustive examples for activities covered by this provision:

---

[118] COM, COMP/M.5734 [2010] Liberty Global Europe/Unitymedia [29]; Case No. COMP/M.5900 [2011] LGI/KBW [119]; Case No. COMP/M.6990 [2013] Vodafone/Kabel Deutschland [67].

[119] COM, Case No. COMP/M.3752 [2005] Verizon/MCI [24].

[120] COM, Case No. COMP/M.6990 [2013] Vodafone/Kabel Deutschland [197].

[121] For the sake of brevity, where the following sections speak of 'agreements', they intend to include decisions and concerted practices as well, unless indicated otherwise.

- direct or indirect fixing of purchase or selling prices or any other trading conditions, so-called 'hardcore cartels';
- limitation or control of production, markets, technical development or investment;
- sharing of markets or sources of supply;
- application of dissimilar conditions to equivalent transactions with other trading parties, thereby placing them at a competitive disadvantage; and
- making the conclusion of contracts subject to acceptance by the other parties of supplementary obligations that, by their nature or according to commercial usage, have no connection with the subject of such contracts.

Finally, a restrictive agreement within the meaning of Article 101(1) TFEU does not necessarily have to constitute an abuse of a dominant position.[122]

b Distortion of Competition

The agreement must have as its 'object or effect the prevention, restriction or distortion of competition within the internal market'. The formula 'object or effect' indicates that the activity does not necessarily have to result in the distortion of competition; it is sufficient that such a distortion is the apparent purpose or very likely result of an agreement.[123] Activities that do not restrict competition to a sufficiently appreciable extent are excluded from the scope of Article 101(1) TFEU.[124] In this context, the European Commission has published a notice on agreements of minor importance.[125] Nevertheless, the cumulative effect of several similar agreements may lift concerted activities outside the scope of this *de minimis* exemption.[126]

c Exemptions

Article 101(3) TFEU allows agreements that contribute to improving the production or distribution of goods or to promoting technical or economic progress, while allowing consumers a fair share of the resulting benefit. In other words, Article 101(3) TFEU provides an exemption from the prohibition of anti-competitive behaviour if the efficiencies gained for the consumer by the activity in question outweigh the anti-competitive disadvantages. However, the agreement must not impose restrictions that are not indispensable to the attainment of these objectives on the undertakings concerned, or afford such undertakings the possibility of eliminating competition in respect of a substantial part of the products in question (Article 101(3)(a) and

---

[122] ECJ, Joined Cases 56 and 58/64 [1966] Consten and Grundig, p. 339.

[123] See ECJ, Case 56/65 [1966] Société Technique Minière v. Maschinenbau Ulm GmbH, p. 249.

[124] See, for example, ECJ, Case C-8/08 [2009] TMobile Netherlands and others [28]; COM, Case No. 37.576 [2001] UEFA's broadcasting regulations [61]; Case No. COMP/C.2–37.398 [2003] UEFA Champions League [132].

[125] COM, Notice on agreements of minor importance which do not appreciably restrict competition under Article 101(1) of the Treaty on the Functioning of the European Union (De Minimis Notice) (2001), OJ C 291/1.

[126] See ECJ, Case C-234/89 [1991] Delimitis [14].

(b) TFEU). Article 2 Enforcement Regulation places the burden of proving the conditions of Article 101(3) TFEU on the undertaking claiming its benefit. Agreements may also benefit from the block exemptions contained in regulations.[127] With a view to the media sector in particular, the Regulation on block exemptions concerning categories of technology transfer agreements may be of interest.[128]

d Application to the Media

An example of anti-competitive multilateral agreements from the Commission's antitrust practice with particular relevance for the media sector is fixed book price agreements. A fixed book price agreement is a vertical agreement or a decision by a publishers' association in which publishers and booksellers set the prices at which books are to be sold to the public. Fixed book pricing agreements amount to straightforward resale price maintenance, which is considered a hardcore restriction. A fixed book price agreement has to be distinguished from the fixing of book prices by law, as is the case, for example, in France and in Germany. Those statutory measures have to be assessed against the free movement of goods, not EU antitrust law.[129] The rationale behind fixed book price agreements is to avoid price competition between booksellers in order to protect cultural diversity in the book market. In *VBVB and VBBB*, the Court of Justice confirmed a Commission decision declaring the fixing of book prices by trade associations in Belgium and the Netherlands to be incompatible with (now) Article 101(1) TFEU.[130] Four years later, the European Commission then declared the British Net Book Agreement incompatible with (now) Article 101(1) TFEU.[131]

The Commission has also frequently found that decisions by collecting agencies restricting the exercise of rights to territories as well as membership restrictions in those societies may fall under Article 101(1) TFEU.[132] Since such agreements may serve to respond to technological developments and thus to promote technical and economic progress, improve the distribution of goods and benefit the consumers, they may be justified under Article 101(3) TFEU.[133]

---

[127] See, for example, Commission Regulation (EU) No. 330/2010 of 20 April 2010 on the application of Article 101(3) of the Treaty on the Functioning of the European Union to categories of vertical agreements and concerted practices, OJ L 102/1.

[128] Commission Regulation (EU) No. 316/2014 of 21 March 2014 on the application of Article 101(3) of the Treaty on the Functioning of the European Union to categories of technology transfer agreements, OJ L 93/17.

[129] See ECJ, Case 229/83 [1985] Association des Centres distributeurs Édouard Leclerc [15]; Case C-531/07 [2009] Fachverband der Buch- und Medienwirtschaft v. LIBRO Handelsgesellschaft mbH.

[130] ECJ, Joined Cases 43 and 63/82 [1984] VBVB and VBBB.

[131] COM, Case No. IV/27.394 [1988] Net Book Agreements.

[132] ECJ, Case C-395/87 [1989] Tournier [26]; COM, Case No. COMP/C2/38.014 [2002] IFPI 'Simulcasting' [60]; Case No. COMP/C2/38.681 [2006] Cannes Extension Agreement; Case No. COMP/C2/38.698 [2008] CISAG.

[133] See COM, Case No. COMP/C2/38.014 [2002] IFPI 'Simulcasting' [84 ff]; Case No. COMP/C2/38.698 [2008] CISAG [229 ff].

Anti-competitive agreements were particularly often found to exist in the exclusive bundled sale or acquisition of rights to broadcast certain content, such as sport or cultural events.[134] Exclusive content licensing agreements may lead to market foreclosure and to divisions between national markets. As the Court of Justice explained in its *Coditel II* decision, the exercise of exclusive rights – in this case copyright in a film – may violate (now) Article 101(1) TFEU '[if] there are economic or legal circumstances the effect of which is to restrict film distribution to an appreciable degree or to distort competition on the cinematographic market, regard being had to the specific characteristics of that market'.[135] The competent authorities need to 'establish whether or not the exercise of the exclusive right', in this case to exhibit a cinematographic film, 'creates barriers which are artificial and unjustifiable ..., or the possibility of charging fees which exceed a fair return on investment, or an exclusivity the duration of which is disproportionate to those requirements, and whether or not, from a general point of view, such exercise within a given geographic area is such as to prevent, restrict or distort competition within the common market'.[136] As a result, exclusive licence agreements that aim at partitioning national markets according to national borders or make the interpenetration of national markets more difficult violate Article 101(1) TFEU.[137]

But the Commission has also considered Article 101(3) TFEU in decisions on anti-competitive agreements in the media sector. For example, the joint and exclusive sales of licence rights have economic advantages, as they lead to a 'one-stop-shop' and thus reduce transaction costs.[138] With a view to football in particular, they allow a common branding of the product, enhance solidarity between the participating clubs and lead to enable consumers to 'one-stop-shop' as well.[139] In order to prevent market foreclosure, the Commission has therefore frequently decided that exclusive licences do not violate Article 101 TFEU under the condition that the rights are offered in several packages that can be acquired by different parties and the licences obtained do not exceed a certain period of time. Undertakings accused of distorting competition with exclusive agreements regularly make commitments in that regard.[140]

---

[134] See, for example, ECJ, Joined Cases T-185/00, T-216/00, T-299/00 and T-300/00 [2002] M6 and others; Case No. COMP/C.2-37.398 [2003] UEFA Champions League; Case No. COMP/C-2/38.173 [2006] FA Premier League; Case No. COMP/C-2/37.214 [2005] Bundesliga.

[135] ECJ, Case 262/81 [1982] Coditel and others v. Ciné Vog Films and others ('Coditel II') [17].

[136] ECJ, Case 262/81 [1982] Coditel and others v. Ciné Vog Films and others ('Coditel II') [19].

[137] CJEU, Joined Cases C-403/08 and C-429/08 [2011] Football Association Premier League Ltd and others v. Karen Murphy and others [139] and [144]; compare COM, Case No. IV/31.734 [1989] Film purchases by German television stations [43 ff].

[138] See COM, Case No. IV/32.150 [2000] Eurovision [84 ff]. The Commission's assessment was subsequently invalidated by the Court of First Instance; see ECJ, Joined Cases T-185/00, T-216/00, T-299/00 and T-300/00 [2002] M6 and others [85]. For more details, see Donders and Van Rompuy (2012, pp. 215 ff).

[139] See COM, Case No. COMP/C.2-37.398 [2003] UEFA Champions League [136 ff].

[140] See, for example, COM, Case No. COMP/C.2-37.398 [2003] UEFA Champions League [197 ff]; Case No. COMP/C-2/38.173 [2006] FA Premier League [32 ff]; Case No. COMP/C-2/37.214 [2005] Bundesliga [27 ff].

Moreover, exclusive agreements made in order to establish new media services and platforms may constitute anti-competitive behaviour.[141] At the same time, such agreements may contribute to technological and economic progress as well as consumer benefits according to Article 101(3) TFEU.[142]

4 *Abuse of a Dominant Position*

Article 102 TFEU prohibits any abuse by an undertaking of a dominant position within the internal market or in a substantial part of it. By contrast to anti-competitive multilateral agreements under Article 101 TFEU, the unilateral distortion of competition by way of an abuse of a dominant position according to Article 102 TFEU plays a less significant role in the Commission's practice. Nevertheless, Article 102 TFEU has, of course, huge significance for those companies that are the subject, or likely to be the subject, of Commission proceedings. The provision thus has a considerable deterring effect. Moreover, it has to be taken into account that domestic law provides rules similar to Article 102 TFEU, which have to be applied in the light of the EU provision. Finally, Commission proceedings under Article 102 TFEU – and equivalent proceedings by the Member States' authorities – have had particular significance in the media sector. Examples are alleged abuses of a dominant position by refusals to grant access to telecommunication network infrastructures, by refusals to reveal information protected by intellectual property rights and in cases against collecting societies. A topical case in which Article 102 TFEU plays the central role is the investigation of the European Commission into Google Inc.'s alleged preferential placement of Google's own services in its search results.[143]

a Dominant Position

A dominant position is such that an undertaking is in a 'position of economic strength which enables it to prevent effective competition being maintained on the relevant market by affording it the power to behave to an appreciable extent independently of its competitors, its customers and ultimately of the consumers'.[144] A dominant position derives from a combination of several factors that are, by themselves, not decisive. Certainly the most influential factor in assessing market power is the undertaking's market share, provided that other factors analysed in the assessment (such as entry barriers, customers' capacity to react, etc.) point in the same direction.[145] The

---

[141] See, for example, COM, Case No. IV/36.539 [1999] British Interactive Broadcasting/Open [140].

[142] COM, Case No. IV/36.539 [1999] British Interactive Broadcasting/Open [159 ff]; Case No. IV/36.237 [1999] TPS [114]; upheld by the Court of First Instance in ECJ, Case T-112/99 [2001] M6.

[143] COM, Antitrust proceedings in cases COMP/C – 3/39.740, COMP/C – 3/39.775 and COMP/C – 3/39.768 – Google Inc., opened on 30 November 2010.

[144] ECJ, Case 85/76 [1979] Hoffmann-La Roche v. Commission [38]; confirmed in subsequent judgments.

[145] COM, Notice on the definition of relevant market for the purposes of Community competition law, para. 10.

higher its market share, the more likely is the dominance of an undertaking.[146] If the market share is for a certain period of time[147] 50 per cent or higher, there is a rebuttable presumption of dominance.[148] In turn, dominance is unlikely if the undertaking's market share is below 40 per cent in the relevant market.[149] Further factors that may be taken into consideration include, for example, the possibility of market access by potential competitors, the bargaining strength of the undertaking's customers, the market position of rivals and the vertical integration of the company in question.[150]

b Abuse

A dominant position alone is not sufficient to take action under Article 102 TFEU.[151] Indeed, undertakings' pursuit of a dominant position in the market is somewhat inherent in the idea of market liberalism as such. Antitrust law merely prohibits the *abuse* of that position. An undertaking abuses its dominant position if it influences the structure of a market by recourse to methods different from those that condition normal competition in a way that competition is weakened, having the effect of hindering the maintenance of the degree of competition still existing in the market or the growth of that competition.[152] Article 102(2) TFEU names examples for an abuse of a dominant position:

1 imposing unfair purchase or selling prices or other unfair trading conditions;
2 limiting production, markets or technical development to the prejudice of consumers;
3 discrimination, that is, applying dissimilar conditions to equivalent transactions with other trading parties, thereby placing them at a competitive disadvantage; or
4 making the conclusion of contracts subject to acceptance by the other parties of supplementary obligations which, by their nature or according to commercial usage, have no connection with the subject of such contracts (so-called tying).

---

[146] COM, Guidance on the Commission's enforcement priorities in applying Article 82 of the EC Treaty to abusive exclusionary conduct by dominant undertakings (2009/C 45/02), para. 15; Jones and Sufrin (2014, p. 337).

[147] The exact period of time that a company needs to have a certain market share is subject to controversy; it arguably ranges between three and five years; see Jones and Sufrin (2014, p. 339, providing further references).

[148] ECJ, Case C-62/86 [1991] AKZO v. Commission [60]; Case T-228/97 [1999] Irish Sugar v. Commission [70]; Case 85/76 [1979] Hoffmann-La Roche v. Commission [41].

[149] COM, Guidance on the Commission's enforcement priorities in applying Article 82 of the EC Treaty to abusive exclusionary conduct by dominant undertakings, para. 14; Case 27/76 [1978] United Brands v. Commission.

[150] See, for example, ECJ, Case 27/76 [1978] United Brands v. Commission [65–66]; [69–81], [85–90]; Case T-30/89 [1991] Hilti v. Commission [93]; COM, Guidance on the Commission's enforcement priorities in applying Article 82 of the EC Treaty to abusive exclusionary conduct by dominant undertakings, para. 12.

[151] See, for example, ECJ, Case C-250/06 [2007] United Pan-Europe Communications Belgium SA and others v. Belgium and others [17].

[152] ECJ, Case 85/76 [1979] Hoffmann-La Roche v. Commission [91]; confirmed in subsequent judgments.

Further categories of abuses of a dominant position developed in case law are, for example, predatory pricing and refusals to deal, especially with a view to intellectual property rights and so-called essential facilities. The notion of 'abuse' can thus be furcated into two categories: exploitative abuse and exclusionary abuse. Exploitative abuse includes the examples mentioned in Articles 102(2)(a) and (b). Exclusionary abuse describes the exclusion of competitors from a market; for example, by way of predatory pricing or refusals to deal.

With particular relevance for the media sector, it is important to note that the abusive behaviour does not have to take place on the same market in which the undertaking in question holds a dominant position. As the Court of Justice decided in *Tetra Pak*, the application of Article 102 TFEU to conduct found on an associated, non-dominated market may be justified 'by special circumstances'.[153] Unfortunately, the Court of Justice did not further explain the nature of those 'special circumstances'. In any case, the Court also established that the markets in question must not be fully independent from each other; instead, they have to be 'closely associated'.[154] The Commission has taken up the notion of 'closely associated' markets and has applied it to interdependent media markets, for example, to the markets for pay-TV and digital interactive television services.

c Application to the Media

The market share in media markets, hence the most important factor for assessing a company's dominant position, is determined, in particular, by audience and advertising revenue.[155] As these aspects are relevant from both an economic and a media-pluralist perspective, even a purely economics-based approach does at least indirectly contribute to safeguarding media pluralism as well. Case examples for the application of (now) Article 102 TFEU to the media include broadcasting monopolies, collecting societies and refusals to deal.

In its early *Sacchi* decision, the Court of Justice held that an undertaking possessing a monopoly in television advertising would abuse its position if it imposed unfair charges or conditions on users of its services, or if it discriminated between national commercial operators or products, on the one hand, and those of other Member States, on the other hand, as regards access to television advertising.[156]

The activities of collecting societies have long been the focus of Commission action under (now) Article 102 TFEU. Collecting societies negotiate, collect and distribute royalties on behalf of copyright holders. We have seen in Chapter 9 that EU legislation – and the same applies to domestic legislation – sometimes even make it mandatory for authors to transfer the exercise of their rights to collecting societies. An

---

[153] ECJ, Case C-333/94 P [1996] Tetra Pak International SA [27].
[154] ECJ, Case C-333/94 P [1996] Tetra Pak International SA [31].
[155] Compare ECJ, Case C-7/97 [1998] Bronner v. Mediaprint Zeitungs- und Zeitschriftenverlag [6]; COM, Case No. IV/M.489 [1994] Bertelsmann/News International/Vox [22].
[156] ECJ, Case 155/73 [1974] Sacchi [17].

example is Article 9 Satellite and Cable Directive. One could thus take the view that collecting societies are 'undertakings entrusted with the operation of services of general economic interest' within the meaning of Article 106(2) TFEU. This provision might exempt them from the application of the antitrust law rules. However, both the Commission and the Court of Justice have regularly emphasised that this is not the case.[157] Collecting societies are neither formally entrusted with the provision of services, nor are the services of general *economic* interest. Instead, the Commission regards the services provided by collecting societies as being of cultural and social interest. This is supported by Recital 36 of the Satellite and Cable Directive, which states that the Directive does not affect the applicability of the antitrust rules in (now) Articles 101 and 102 TFEU. To be sure, a directive – and even less its recitals – may not determine the interpretation of primary law. Nevertheless, it underlines that the Council, when it adopted the Directive, also regarded the antitrust law rules as applicable to collecting societies.

Collecting societies act as intermediaries between rights-holders and users. This 'bottleneck' function of collecting societies has made them prone to the suspicion of having a dominant position – often a monopoly – in the markets for the management of copyrights, and of abusing that position. The European Commission and the Court of Justice have prohibited collecting societies to discriminate on grounds of nationality and to apply unfair trading conditions.[158]

A very broad and important area for the application of (now) Article 102 TFEU in the media sector has been the complex of undertakings' 'refusals to deal'. This category includes refusals to allow the use of 'essential facilities' and of media content protected by intellectual property or other exclusive rights. The 'essential facilities' doctrine describes a type of anti-competitive behaviour in which a firm with market power uses a 'bottleneck resource' in a market to deny competitors entry into that market. It originates from application of Section 2 of the United States Sherman Act[159] and has been applied under into EU law by Commission decisions and ECJ case law.[160] The basic requirements for a legal claim under this doctrine are:

---

[157] ECJ, Case 7/82 [1983] GVL v. Commission [31]; Case 127/73 [1974] BRT v. SABAM [20]; COM, Case No. IV/26.760 [1971] GEMA I.

[158] See ECJ, Case 7/82 [1983] GVL v. Commission [56]; Case 127/73 [1974] BRT v. SABAM [15]; Case C-395/87 [1989] Tournier [46]; COM, Case No. IV/26.760 [1971] GEMA I; Case No. IV/26.760 [1972] GEMA II; Case No. IV/29.971 [1981] GEMA statutes.

[159] See United States v. Terminal Railroad Association, 224 U.S. 383 (1912); Associated Press v. United States, 326 U.S. 1 (1945); Lorain Journal Co. v. United States, 342 U.S. 143, 146–49 (1951); Otter Tail Power Co. v. United States, 410 U.S. 366, 377–79 (1973); Verizon v. Trinko, 540 U.S. 398 (2004); MCI Communications Corp. v. AT&T, 708 F2d 1081 (1132f) (7th Cir. 1982).

[160] ECJ, Cases C-241 P and 242 P/91 [1995] RTE and ITP v. Commission ('Magill'); Case C-7/97 [1998] Bronner v. Mediaprint Zeitungs- und Zeitschriftenverlag; Case C-418/01 [2004] IMS Health GmbH & Co. OHG v. NDC Health GmbH & Co. KG; COM, Case No. IV/34.689 [1993] Sea Containers v. Stena Sealink; Decision 94/119/EC of 21 December 1993, Port of Rødby (Denmark). See also van Rooijen (2008, p. 64).

1 The monopolist controls an essential facility.
2 The competitor is unable to practically or reasonably duplicate the essential facility.
3 The monopolist denies a competitor the use of the facility.
4 It would have been feasible and reasonable for the monopolist to provide the facility to the competitor.

The European framework on electronic communications regulation is based on the essential facility doctrine (see Chapter 7). Telecommunications law is thus sector-specific antitrust law.[161] Closely related to the refusal of providing access to (physical) 'essential facilities', such as telecommunications networks, is the refusal to permit the use of content protected by intellectual property rights or other exclusive rights. In this context, two questions need to be distinguished: first, does the mere ownership of an exclusive right, such as copyright, confer a dominant position; and second, does the exercise of such an exclusive right constitute an abuse of a dominant position? With a view to broadcasting, these questions have to a certain extent already been addressed by Articles 14 and 15 AVMS Directive (see Chapter 5). Nevertheless, these provisions only apply to content to be broadcast via television, and not, for example, to content to be disseminated via the internet or in newspapers.

The seminal *Magill* decision of the Court of Justice concerned the refusal of major Irish broadcasting stations to license their programmer schedule to Magill TV Guide Ltd, a publisher of TV guides. In its decision, the Court of Justice addressed the two questions highlighted above. The Court decided, first, that mere ownership of an intellectual property right does not confer a dominant position.[162] Nevertheless, the Court then observed that the broadcasting stations were 'the only source of … information' relating to the broadcasting schedule. The Court thus held that the broadcasting stations enjoyed 'a *de facto* monopoly over the information used to compile listings for the television programmes'. Hence they were 'in a position to prevent effective competition on the market in weekly television magazines' – by definition a dominant position.[163] Turning to the second question, whether the exercise of their exclusive right to publish the programmer schedule constituted an abuse of their dominant position, the Court indicated that the refusal to provide the information 'prevented the appearance of a new product, a comprehensive weekly guide to television programmes, which the appellants did not offer and for which there was a potential consumer demand'. This, the Court held, constituted an abuse within the meaning of (now) Article 102(b) TFEU.[164]

---

[161] Bavasso (2004, p. 106).
[162] ECJ, Cases C-241 P and 242 P/91 [1995] RTE and ITP v. Commission ('Magill') [46]; see already Case 78/70 [1971] Deutsche Grammophon v. Metro [16]. Reiterated in, for example, Case C-418/01 [2004] IMS Health GmbH & Co. OHG v. NDC Health GmbH & Co. KG [34].
[163] ECJ, Cases C-241 P and 242 P/91 [1995] RTE and ITP v. Commission ('Magill') [47].
[164] ECJ, Cases C-241 P and 242 P/91 [1995] RTE and ITP v. Commission ('Magill') [54].

It appears inconsequential to categorise certain behaviour as 'abusive' if this behaviour consists of the exercise of rights, even protected as human rights. Concerns were also raised regarding the scope, and hence the ramifications, of *Magill*. The Court of Justice alleviated these apprehensions in subsequent decisions. In *IMS Health*, a company tracking sales of pharmaceutical and healthcare products prevented another company from using its copyright-protected database. The Court reiterated that the exercise of an exclusive right by the owner may only 'in exceptional circumstances', such as those in the *Magill* case, constitute an abusive conduct.[165] The Court then summarised the 'exceptional circumstances' of *Magill* as follows:[166]

1 The refusal in question concerned a product the supply of which was indispensable for carrying on the business in question.
2 The refusal prevented the emergence of a new product for which there was a potential consumer demand.
3 The refusal was not justified by objective considerations.
4 The refusal was likely to exclude all competition in the secondary market (that is, the market for weekly TV guides).

Therefore, these four conditions[167] have to be fulfilled to treat the refusal by an undertaking that owns a copyright to give access to a product or service as abusive. In addition, it should be noted that *Magill* was decided before the adoption of the Copyright Directive. This Directive has brought a certain degree of harmonisation of copyright among the Member States (see Chapter 9).

In the case of *Bronner* v. *Mediaprint*, a press undertaking – Mediaprint – held a very large share of the daily newspaper market in a Member State[168] and operated the only nationwide newspaper home-delivery scheme. The undertaking refused to allow Bronner, the publisher of a smaller rival newspaper, which was unable to operate its own home-delivery scheme in economically reasonable conditions, to have access to its own scheme for appropriate remuneration. The Court of Justice had to decide whether this refusal constituted an abuse of a dominant position within the meaning of (now) Article 102 TFEU. In order to do so, the Court would, in principle, have to assess, at first, whether home-delivery schemes for the distribution of daily newspapers constitute a market in its own right. This was because one could also argue that other methods of distributing daily newspapers, such as sale in shops or at kiosks or delivery by post, are sufficiently interchangeable with home-delivery

---

[165] ECJ, Case C-418/01 [2004] IMS Health GmbH & Co. OHG v. NDC Health GmbH & Co. KG [35–36].
[166] ECJ, Case C-418/01 [2004] IMS Health GmbH & Co. OHG v. NDC Health GmbH & Co. KG [37]; see also Case C-7/97 [1998] Bronner v. Mediaprint Zeitungs- und Zeitschriftenverlag [40].
[167] The Court referred to conditions one and two as one condition.
[168] 46.8 per cent of the Austrian daily newspaper market in terms of circulation and 42 per cent in terms of advertising, reaching 53.3 per cent of the population from the age of 14 in private households and 71 per cent of all newspaper readers.

schemes. But the Court left that assessment to the domestic courts.[169] Instead, the Court held that *even if* home-delivery schemes for the distribution of daily newspapers constituted a separate market and Mediaprint was found to have a dominant position in that market, Mediaprint had not abused its dominant position. The Court applied the *IMS Health* and *Magill* criteria: the refusal in question did not concern a service that was indispensable for Bronner to carry out his business; Bronner would have had other methods of distribution at his disposal, such as delivery by post and through sale in shops and at kiosks.[170] Moreover, the refusal was not likely to exclude all competition in the market – if there is such a market – of home-delivery schemes. No technical, legal or economic obstacles made it impossible or even unreasonably difficult for any other newspaper publishers, alone or in cooperation with others, to establish its own nationwide home-delivery scheme.[171] As a result, the Court found that there was no abuse of a dominant position in the *Bronner* case.

A particularly complex example on an undertaking's refusal to deal was the *Microsoft* case. In brief, in 2004 the European Commission had found the software company Microsoft guilty of having abused its dominant position in two ways. First, Microsoft had refused to supply its competitors with information on its 'Windows' operating system software to interoperate with their systems and to authorise the use of that information for the purpose of developing and distributing products competing with Microsoft's own products. Second, Microsoft had tied the sale of Windows with the simultaneous purchase of the Windows Media Player software. The Commission imposed a fine of €497 million on Microsoft, and it required Microsoft to take corrective action.[172] The Court of First Instance confirmed the Commission's decision.[173] In 2008, the European Commission fined Microsoft an additional €899 million for failure to comply with the 2004 decision.[174] The General confirmed the Commission's decision, but reduced the fine due to a miscalculation by the Commission.[175]

It can be presumed that conflicts between exclusive rights, particularly intellectual property rights, and antitrust law will continue to play a major role in the future.[176] Some of the most powerful companies today – Google, Apple, Amazon and Facebook – owe their position to ownership of data, network effects and other scale efficiencies that are often insurmountable for rivals. But their codes and algorithms,

---

[169] ECJ, Case C-7/97 [1998] Bronner v. Mediaprint Zeitungs- und Zeitschriftenverlag [34].

[170] ECJ, Case C-7/97 [1998] Bronner v. Mediaprint Zeitungs- und Zeitschriftenverlag [43].

[171] ECJ, Case C-7/97 [1998] Bronner v. Mediaprint Zeitungs- und Zeitschriftenverlag [44].

[172] COM, Case No. COMP/C-3/37.792 [2004] Microsoft; Decision of 10 November 2005 imposing a periodic penalty payment pursuant to Article 24(1) of Regulation No. 1/2003 on Microsoft Corporation (Case COMP/C-3/37.792 Microsoft).

[173] ECJ, Case T-201/04 [2007] Microsoft v. Commission.

[174] COM, Decision of 27 February 2008 fixing the definitive amount of the periodic penalty payment imposed on Microsoft Corporation by Decision C(2005) 4420 final (Case COMP/C-3/37.792 Microsoft), C(2008) 764 final.

[175] CJEU, Case T-167/08 [2012] Microsoft v. Commission.

[176] See Aplin and Davis (2013, pp. 41 ff); Jones and Sufrin (2014, pp. 558 ff).

which influence what people think and how they decide, are intransparent. Google's search algorithm is one of the best-kept secrets in the world. It is Google's intellectual property, and it is a tool of power. In November 2010 the European Commission opened an antitrust investigation against Google pursuant to Article 102 TFEU.[177] The Commission assesses whether Google has a dominant position in online search and, if it does, whether it abuses this position. The Commission investigates, *inter alia*, whether Google favours its own services over those of competing service providers by placing them more 'prominently' than other results.[178] This raises many interesting questions, some of which will be highlighted in Section VII of this chapter.

5 Mergers, Acquisitions and Joint Ventures in Media Sectors

Mergers, acquisitions and joint ventures play an important role for media law. Such concentrations may occur horizontally and within one media market, for example, between newspapers and between broadcasters. They may also take place across media sectors, such as in a merger between a newspaper company and a broadcaster. Finally, they may also occur vertically; that is, at different stages of the production chain. This would be the case, for instance, if a broadcasting company merged with a film production firm.

As in any other economic sector, concentrations in the media sector may contribute to efficiencies, enhance economies of scope and economies of scale by broadening a media undertaking's audience or lead to consolidation.[179] Nevertheless, concentrations in the media sector pose significant risks to the public interest that are usually absent in other sectors. Concentrations of media control may not only distort competition, but also threaten media pluralism. Concentration of media control needs to be considered with respect to both specific media segments, such as the press or broadcasting, and across different media sectors. Therefore, states have to prevent influential economic or political groups from obtaining a dominant position over the media and interfere with editorial freedom.[180]

a Introduction

Concentrations are not codified under EU primary law. In 1989, the Council adopted the first European Merger Control Regulation, which has subsequently been amended

---

[177] COM, Cases No. COMP/C-3/39.740, COMP/C-3/39.775 & COMP/C-3/39.768 [2010] Google.

[178] An overview over the proceedings can be found at http://ec.europa.eu/competition/elojade/isef/case_details.cfm?proc_code=1_39740.

[179] See Craufurd Smith and Tambini (2012, pp. 38–39).

[180] Human Rights Committee, Concluding observations on the Russian Federation (CCPR/CO/79/RUS), para. 18; Concluding observations on Guyana (CCPR/CO/79/Add.121), para. 19; General Comment no. 34, para. 40; ECtHR, VgT Verein gegen Tierfabriken v. Switzerland (No. 1) [2001] App. no. 24699/94 [73] and [75]; Manole and others v. Moldova [2009] App. no. 13936/02 [98]; Centro Europa 7 S.r.l. and Di Stefano v. Italy [2012] App. no. 38433/09 [133].

and in 2004 replaced by the Merger Regulation 139/2004. The Merger Regulation applies to 'concentrations' with an EU dimension. Unifications of companies that do not constitute a concentration within the meaning of the Merger Regulation are subject to the Member States' legislation. The same applies to concentrations without an EU dimension. The existence of an EU dimension is defined in Article 1(2) and (3) Merger Regulation and essentially depends on the combined aggregate worldwide turnover and the aggregate EU-wide turnover of the undertakings concerned. Article 5 provides the rules for the calculation of turnover. Article 21(3) Merger Regulation bars Member States from applying their national legislation to any concentration that has a EU dimension. However, according to Article 21(4) Merger Regulation, they may take appropriate measures to protect legitimate interests if these measures are compatible with the general principles and other provisions of EU law. The provision then expressly acknowledges 'plurality of the media' as a legitimate interest. Therefore, a Member State may interdict a concentration in its jurisdiction regardless of a positive compatibility decision by the European Commission if it finds that the concentration threatens plurality of the media.

Concentrations are to be distinguished from agreements within the meaning of Article 101 TFEU by reference to the unification of separate undertakings (by contrast to undertakings remaining separate under Article 101 TFEU) and by the permanence of the agreement. Article 3(1) thus defines a concentration as a 'change of control' of one or more undertakings 'on a lasting basis'. The Merger Regulation distinguishes three forms of concentration:

1 The merger of two or more previously independent undertakings or parts of undertakings (Article 3(1)(a)). A merger occurs when two separate undertakings unite into a new entity.[181]
2 The acquisition of an undertaking by one or more persons already controlling at least one other undertaking (Article 3(1)(b)).
3 The creation of a joint venture performing on a lasting basis all the functions of an autonomous economic entity (Article 3(4)).

Article 3(5) explains when a concentration shall not be deemed to arise, for example, in the case of an insolvency trustee.

By contrast to anti-competitive multilateral agreements or unilateral behaviour, concentrations falling within the scope of the Regulation are subject to an *ex ante* control: they have to be notified to the Commission prior to their implementation and following the conclusion of the agreement, the announcement of the public bid or the acquisition of a controlling interest (Article 4). A concentration shall, in principle, not be implemented before it has been declared compatible with the internal market (Article 7). A compatibility decision of the European Commission may include

[181] Whish and Bailey (2015, p. 853); Jones and Sufrin (2014, p. 1129).

conditions and obligations intended to ensure that the undertakings concerned comply with the commitments they have entered into vis-à-vis the Commission (Article 8(2)). In the case of a non-compliance with the Regulation, for example, because the concentration has been implemented in contravention of a condition or without prior notification, the Commission may require the undertakings concerned to dissolve the concentration or take other restorative measures (Article 8(4)). Moreover, the Commission may impose fines of up to 10 per cent of the aggregate turnover of the undertaking concerned (Article 14(2)). In order to prepare its decision, the European Commission and the Member States' authorities have investigatory powers similar to those under Article 101 and 102 TFEU (Articles 11 to 14(1) and 18). The decisions of the Commission are subject to appeal to the General Court.[182]

According to Article 2(1) Merger Regulation, concentrations within the scope of the Regulation shall be appraised with a view to establishing whether or not they are compatible with the common market. The relevant test as to whether a concentration shall be declared compatible with the internal market is the 'significant impediment to competition' test: a concentration shall be declared incompatible with the internal market if it would significantly impede effective competition in the internal market or in a substantial part of it (Article 2(3)). In making this appraisal, the Commission shall take into account:

- the need to maintain and develop effective competition within the common market;
- the market position of the undertakings concerned and their economic and financial power;
- the alternatives available to suppliers and users;
- consumers' and suppliers' access to supplies or markets;
- any legal or other barriers to entry;
- supply and demand trends for the relevant goods and services;
- the interests of the intermediate and ultimate consumers; and
- the development of technical and economic progress provided that it is to consumers' advantage and does not form an obstacle to competition.[183]

Concentrations are presumed to be compatible with the internal market if the market share of the undertakings concerned does not exceed 25 per cent either in the internal market or in a substantial part of it.[184] To the extent that the creation of a joint venture constituting a concentration has as its object or effect the coordination of the competitive behaviour of undertakings that remain independent, such coordination

---

[182] On the scope of judicial review see, for example, ECJ, Case C-413/06 P [2008] Bertelsmann.

[183] Article 2(1) Merger Regulation. With a view to horizontal mergers in particular, see COM, Guidelines on the assessment of horizontal mergers under the Council Regulation on the control of concentrations between undertakings (2004/C 31/03).

[184] Recital 32 Merger Regulation; COM, Guidelines on the assessment of horizontal mergers under the Council Regulation on the control of concentrations between undertakings, para. [18].

shall be appraised in accordance with the criteria of Articles 101(1) and (3) TFEU (Article 2(4)). Article 2(5) names factors the Commission shall take into account in making this appraisal.

b Media Concentrations

The Commission's decision-making on concentrations in media sectors is too voluminous to summarise within the scope of this chapter. This section gives an overview and provides examples of the Commission's practice.

First of all, it is important to recognise whether the undertakings involved operate on media markets at all. This is not always obvious. True, if the concentration involves well-known media companies, such as Kirch, Canal+ or MGM, then it is likely that the relevant markets are media-related. But the same does not apply to, say, a joint venture between private equity firms. Nevertheless, even such cases may involve a media dimension if the firms involved exercise control over broadcasters, newspapers or film producers.[185]

The definition of the relevant market is then of major importance in all cases of concentrations. The Commission often accepts concentrations even of media conglomerates, because the undertakings involved operate on separate product or geographic markets. It is therefore essential to distinguish between concentration in the same media market, on the one hand, and vertical concentration across upstream and downstream markets as well as cross-sector concentration, on the other hand. Given the Commission's detailed and narrow market definitions that have been explained before, which distinguish, for example, pay-TV from free access TV and quality newspapers from tabloid newspapers, concentration in the same media market are relatively rare. Undertakings involved in a merger therefore usually argue that they are operating on different markets. This is somewhat ironic, because, as has been shown before, the narrow market definitions make one or more undertakings more likely to be in violation of Article 102 TFEU. But, on closer inspection, it is logical: Article 102 TFEU relates to specific behaviour of a company that operates on a particular media market. The narrower this market is defined, the more likely it is that an undertaking has a dominant position within the meaning of Article 102 TFEU, which it can abuse with its behaviour. By contrast, the narrower a market is defined, the less likely it is that a concentration between two undertakings leads to a dominant position of the resulting concentration within one and the same market. Yet, *if* the Commission finds that a concentration affects one and the same market, then it is likely that the concentration leads to a dominant position on that market. An example for such a concentration was underlying the 1998 Commission decision *Bertelsmann/Kirch/Premiere*. The European Commission prohibited two major German media groups (Bertelsmann and Kirch) from purchasing shares, and thus acquiring joint control, of

---

[185] See, for example, COM, Case No. COMP/M.4547 [2007] KKR/Permira/ProSiebenSat.1 [2].

a pay-TV supplier (Premiere). Since Kirch also owned a pay-TV channel that it would have transferred to Premiere, the proposed concentration would have led to a near-monopoly of Premiere on the pay-TV market in Germany.[186]

But even if a concentration leads to a dominant position, this does not necessarily mean that it cannot be permitted. The acquisition of control by News Corp of the Italian pay-TV broadcasters Telepiù and Stream, for example, led to the creation of a near-monopoly in the Italian pay-TV market.[187] Nevertheless, the Commission declared the merger to be compatible with the internal market, albeit against substantial commitments. For example, film studios and football clubs could unilaterally terminate contracts entered into with Telepiù without penalties. In addition, News Corp's waived exclusive rights with respect to TV platforms (other than direct-to-home), pay-per-view, video on-demand and near video on-demand. Moreover, News Corp could not subscribe contracts exceeding the duration of two years with football clubs and of three years with film studios. It also had to offer third parties, on a unbundled and non-exclusive basis, the right to distribute premium contents on the basis of the retail price minus the costs which the requesting party saves News Corp (retail minus principle).

In the Commission's practice, concentrations are more often vertical, for example, in cases of TV broadcasters merging with a programme production company. Sometimes concentrations are even entirely cross-sectoral, for instance, in cases of a TV broadcaster merging with a newspaper publisher or with a telecommunication services provider. In cases of vertical and cross-sectoral concentrations that involve separate markets, the European Commission has, at least in most of the more recent decisions,[188] not raised objections, albeit sometimes only following commitments.[189] The reasons for this shift are arguably both economic and political. First, the Commission seems to be more convinced of the economic efficiencies generated by cross-sectoral concentrations, particularly with a view to the need for consolidation in the EU audiovisual industry and the development of new services. Second, with regard to the powerful competition by media conglomerates from third countries, the Commission has become aware of the significance of concentrations for the European media markets.[190]

---

[186] Case No. IV/M.993 [1998] Bertelsmann/Kirch/Premiere [30].

[187] COM, Case No. COMP/M.2876 [2003] News Corp/Telepiù [114].

[188] Earlier decisions in which the Commission declared a concentration incompatible with the internal market were COM, Case No. IV/M.469 [1994] MSG Media Service; Case No. IV/M.993 [1998] Bertelsmann/Kirch/Premiere; Case No. IV/M.1027 [1998] Deutsche Telekom/Beta Research; Case No. IV/M.490 [1995] Nordic Satellite Distribution.

[189] See, for example, COM, Case No. IV/M.110 [1991] ABC/Générale des Eaux/Canal+/W.H. Smith TV; Case No. IV/M.410 [1994] Kirch/Richmond/Telepiù; Case No. IV/M.584 [1995] Kirch/Richemont/Multichoice/Telepiù; Case No. IV/M.779 [1996] Bertelsmann/CLT; Case No. COMP/M.1978 [2000] Telecom Italia/News Television/Stream [23]; Case No. COMP/M.4504 [2007] SFR/Télé 2 France; Case No. COMP/M.6990 [2013] Vodafone/Kabel Deutschland.

[190] See Geradin (2005, pp. 77 f); Bania (2013, pp. 64 ff); Burnley and Bania (2014, pp. 218 f); Van Rompuy and Donders (2014).

Nonetheless, even in cross-sectoral (media) concentrations, the Commission asks whether the markets are interconnected in a way that the position of the new unity in one market has a direct impact on other markets.[191] For example, the audience share in the TV viewers' market is an essential factor for determining the market position in the TV advertising market. Revenues achieved in the advertising market enable the acquisition of more attractive programmes and sports rights, which in turn improves the position in the viewers' market.[192] Therefore, in *RTL/Veronica/Endemol*, the European Commission declared incompatible a joint venture between two TV broadcasters (RTL and Veronica) and a production company (Endemol) in the Netherlands. This was not only because the concentration would lead to the creation of a dominant position in the TV advertising market in the Netherlands, but also because it would strengthen Endemol's dominant position in the market for independent Dutch language TV production.[193] In addition, in the above-mentioned *Bertelsmann/Kirch/ Premiere* case, the pay-TV supplier Premiere would have had 'access to programme resources unparalleled in Germany' through its new parent companies because of their positions on the upstream markets for programme rights.[194] This was another reason for the European Commission to prohibit that concentration.

As has been shown before, Article 21(4) Merger Regulation allows – but does not oblige – a Member State to prohibit a concentration within its jurisdiction if it finds that the concentration threatens plurality of the media. This applies even if the European Commission has already adopted a positive compatibility decision. One may in this context speak of a dualism of a market-based approach and a pluralism-oriented approach.[195] In Germany, for example, the Commission on Concentration in the Media[196] is entrusted with preventing a dominant influence on public opinion in changes in broadcasters' ownership structures. Under Section 26(1) of the German Interstate Broadcasting Treaty, an undertaking may not acquire a 'dominant power of opinion' (*vorherrschende Meinungsmacht*). According to Section 26(2) of the Interstate Broadcasting Treaty, a 'dominant power of opinion' shall be presumed to exist if:

- an undertaking provides[197] services reaching an annual average audience share of 30 per cent of all viewers;[198]

---

[191] See, for example, COM, Case No. IV/M.553 [1995] RTL/Veronica/Endemol [30]; Case No. COMP/ M.2876 [2003] News Corp/Telepiù [115 ff]; Case No. COMP/M.5121 [2008] News Corp/Premiere [59 ff]; Case No. COMP/M.5533 [2009] Bertelsmann/KKR/JV [55 ff].

[192] See, for example, COM, Case No. IV/M.553 [1995] RTL/Veronica/Endemol [30]: TV broadcasting/production; Case No. COMP/M.1978 [2000] Telecom Italia/News Television/Stream [11]: music publishing and recording/TV and radio broadcasting.

[193] See, for example, COM, Case No. IV/M.553 [1995] RTL/Veronica/Endemol [115].

[194] COM, Case No. IV/M.993 [1998] Bertelsmann/Kirch/Premiere [34].

[195] Nehl (2003).

[196] Kommission zur Ermittlung der Konzentration im Medienbereich (KEK).

[197] More precisely, the Treaty speaks of services having to be 'attributable' (*zurechenbar*) to an undertaking; this concept is further explained in Section 28 of the Treaty.

[198] The audience share is to be established in a procedure that is further explained in Section 27 of the Treaty.

- an undertaking provides services reaching an annual average audience share of 25 per cent and holds a dominant position in a media-relevant related market; or
- an overall assessment of an undertaking's activities in television and in media-relevant related markets shows that the influence on the formation of opinion obtained as a result of these activities corresponds to that of an undertaking with a 30 per cent audience share.

By comparison, under Section 67 of the UK Enterprise Act 2002, the Secretary of State may give a 'European intervention notice' if he believes that a public interest consideration within the meaning of Article 21(4) Merger Regulation is relevant to a consideration of the concentration situation concerned. Section 58 Enterprise Act 2002 specifies these public interest considerations. They include the need for, *inter alia*:

- accurate presentation of news and free expression of opinion in specified newspapers (paragraph 2A);
- a sufficient plurality of views in newspapers (paragraph 2B);
- a sufficient plurality of persons with control of the media enterprises serving that audience (paragraph 2C(a));
- the availability throughout the United Kingdom of a wide range of broadcasting which is both of high quality and calculated to appeal to a wide variety of tastes and interests (paragraph 2C(b)); and
- persons carrying on media enterprises, and for those with control of such enterprises, to have a genuine commitment to the attainment in relation to broadcasting of the standards objectives set out in the Communications Act 2003 (paragraph 2C(c)).

Further details concerning the media plurality assessment can be found in Ofcom's 'Guidance for the Public Interest Test for Media Mergers'.[199]

The Secretary of State issued such a European intervention notice in the case of News Corp's proposed acquisition of BSkyB. The US media company News Corp, which is active in a wide range of media fields, including in the UK and Ireland, announced its acquisition of an additional 61 per cent of the shares of the British media holding BSkyB, which would make News Corp the sole shareholder of BSkyB. Relevant markets in this case were, in the audiovisual sector, the market for licensing and acquisition of broadcasting rights, the wholesale supply of TV channels, the retail supply of audiovisual content to end-users and the provision of pay-TV technical services. Further relevant markets concerned the newspaper publishing sector and the advertising sector. Because of its narrow market definitions, the Commission concluded that the proposed transaction did not raise any competition concerns.[200]

---

[199] http://stakeholders.ofcom.org.uk/binaries/broadcast/guidance/pi_test.pdf. From academic literature on the media plurality test in the UK, see Craufurd Smith and Tambini (2012, pp. 43 ff); Arnott (2010).

[200] COM, Case No. COMP/M.5932 [2010] News Corp/BSkyB [66], [107], [216], [268].

As a result, the Commission did not oppose the notified operation and declared it compatible with the internal market. Nevertheless, with its European intervention notice, the Secretary of State made the acquisition subject to a 'media plurality review' by the British authorities.[201]

Both the German and the UK regulatory regimes for ensuring media plurality have their focus on actual influence on public opinion. The core question underlying all legal frameworks regulating media pluralism is therefore: how can influence be measured, and how does this question differ from the question of whether there is sufficient competition?[202] In Germany, market shares stand as a proxy for measuring influence, or 'dominant power of opinion'. However, it has long been argued in academic literature that there is not necessarily a direct relationship between media ownership and diversity of content.[203] And in Germany, the assessment and evaluation of the proxy 'market share' has itself been controversial, as a recent ruling of the highest administrative court in Germany shows.[204] The notion of media influence on public opinion is a complex issue that requires further empirical and interdisciplinary research.[205] The competition framework alone, with its focus on markets and market shares, may well prove to be insufficient to address the contemporary challenges to media pluralism.

A particularly illustrative example to study the judicial review of a media concentration is the case *ARD* v. *Commission*.[206] In this case, the German public broadcaster ARD sought the annulment of the Commission decision approving the joint acquisition of a pay-TV operator (KirchPayTV) by BSkyB after commitments.[207] The Court had to decide, first, whether ARD had standing to bring the claim. Under then-Article 230 EC (similar to Article 263(4) TFEU), '[a]ny natural or legal person may … institute proceedings against a decision addressed to that person or against a decision which, although in the form of a … decision addressed to another person, is of direct and individual concern to the former'. The contested decision was addressed to the parties to the notified concentration, but not to ARD. Yet the Court found that it was 'of direct and individual concern' to it. It was of direct concern because the contested decision brought about 'an immediate change in the situation in the markets concerned, depending solely on the wishes of the parties'.[208] Moreover, ARD was individually concerned by the contested decision within the meaning of

---

[201] See Final decisions by the Secretary of State for Business, Enterprise & Regulatory Reform on British Sky Broadcasting Group's acquisition of a 17.9 per cent shareholding in ITV plc dated 29 January 2008 [20].

[202] See, for example, Craufurd Smith and Tambini (2012, p. 62); Craufurd Smith (2013).

[203] See, for example, Craufurd Smith (2004, p. 653); Bania (2013, p. 66).

[204] German Federal Administrative Court, Case 6 C 2.13 [2014] 'Axel Springer AG'.

[205] See, for example, Valcke et al. (2010).

[206] ECJ, Case T-158/00 [2003] ARD v. Commission.

[207] COM, Case No. COMP/JV.37 [2000] BSkyB/KirchPayTV.

[208] ECJ, Case T-158/00 [2003] ARD v. Commission [60].

the *Plaumann* formula[209] because of its participation in the procedure and the effect on its market position. Upon request by the Commission, ARD participated actively in the procedure. This participation had an effect on the course of the procedure and, at least in part, on the content of the contested decision.[210] The merger in question concerned the pay-TV market, and ARD was not present on that market. However, the fact that ARD cannot be considered to be an actual or potential competitor did not necessarily mean that it is not individually concerned by the decision.[211] KirchPayTV was mostly active in pay-TV, but that market was only one of the three markets on which the Commission found that the merger strengthened its dominant position. Moreover, an action for annulment brought by an operator present only on neighbouring upstream or downstream markets may, in certain circumstances, be admissible. In this case, five factors established that the applicant's position was affected: the existence of some competition between free television and pay-TV, the anticipated convergence between free television and pay-TV due to digitalisation, the effect of the merger on digital interactive television services, the applicant's participation in an interest group whose objective is to impose certain technical solutions for the purpose of operating technical platforms and the acquisition of broadcasting rights.[212] However, the Court of Justice rejected ARD's arguments on the merits, namely that BSkyB should be considered a potential competitor of KirchPayTV, that the Commission was not entitled to approve the merger during the first phase of the examination procedure on the basis of commitments offered by the undertakings concerned, that the commitments were insufficient, that the Commission failed to initiate further proceedings and that the procedure was flawed.

6 *The Case Example*

Our case example concerned a joint central marketing scheme covering all types of broadcasting rights of football matches, administered by the League Association. The European Commission should take action if the scheme violates Article 101 TFEU. First of all, the football clubs or the League Association would have to qualify as 'undertakings' or 'association of undertakings' within the meaning of Article 101(1) TFEU. The football clubs are to be regarded as undertakings, because they engage in a variety of economic activities by selling tickets for the matches, transferring players, selling merchandise, concluding advertising and sponsorship agreements and selling

---

[209] Persons other than those to whom a decision is addressed may claim to be individually concerned if the decision 'affects them by reason of certain attributes peculiar to them or by reason of factual circumstances in which they are distinguished from all other persons, and by virtue of those factors distinguishes them individually in the same way as the person addressed' (ECJ, Case 25/62 [1963] Plaumann v. Commission, p. 107).

[210] ECJ, Case T-158/00 [2003] ARD v. Commission [63–76].

[211] ECJ, Case T-158/00 [2003] ARD v. Commission [78].

[212] ECJ, Case T-158/00 [2003] ARD v. Commission [79–95].

broadcasting rights.[213] The League Association can be regarded both as an association of undertakings (i.e., the football clubs) and as an undertaking in its own right, insofar as it is itself economically active; for example, by negotiating broadcasting rights.[214]

Then, there has to be an agreement between the football clubs, a decision by the Football League as an association of the football clubs or a concerted practice, which may affect trade between Member States and that has as its object or effect the prevention, restriction or distortion of competition within the internal market. The Commission has previously identified the following relevant product markets: the upstream programme procurement market, the downstream media exploitation markets related to programme procurement and, lastly, the emerging upstream and downstream markets in the new media and in particular those for transmission to second- and third-generation mobile phones (for example, GPRS and UMTS) and internet rights.[215] From a geographical viewpoint, the Commission identified national markets.[216] The Commission's competition concerns consisted in the transfer of the media rights on the first and second league matches from the clubs to the League Association and in the subsequent central marketing of those rights.[217] This joint marketing could have an adverse effect on competition in two ways: first, it could potentially restrict competition between the football clubs for the more lucrative marketing of broadcasting rights. A central marketing scheme would be particularly to the disadvantage of more attractive football clubs. Second, it could constitute a vertical restriction, because the broadcasters, when trying to obtain broadcasting rights for football matches, would have only one trading partner, the League Association. Once a broadcaster has concluded an exclusive agreement with the League Association, competitors would not have access to the broadcasting of the matches. Consequently, the decision would not only affect competition on a horizontal level between the football clubs, but also on the relevant downstream television markets and markets in the new media.[218]

The anti-competitive behaviour has to affect trade between Member States. The fact that the relevant market is national does not necessarily mean that the case cannot have a transnational dimension. In this case, the central marketing scheme affected trade between Member States because there was demand for German football league matches in other countries. Here lies a significant difference between antitrust law and unfair competition: as will be shown further below, the notion of 'market' in the law on unfair competition also includes the interests of consumers. By contrast, antitrust law first and foremost serves to protect the competitive process as such. Consumer interests may be considered in the decision-making process, but only the competitive

---

[213] COM, Case No. COMP/C-2/37.214 [2005] Bundesliga [21].
[214] COM, Case No. COMP/C-2/37.214 [2005] Bundesliga [21].
[215] COM, Case No. COMP/C-2/37.214 [2005] Bundesliga [18]. See also Case No. 37.576 [2001] UEFA's broadcasting regulations [23]; Case No. COMP/C-2/38.173 [2006] FA Premier League [20 ff].
[216] COM, Case No. COMP/C-2/37.214 [2005] Bundesliga [19].
[217] COM, Case No. COMP/C-2/37.214 [2005] Bundesliga [22].
[218] COM, Case No. COMP/C-2/37.214 [2005] Bundesliga [23].

process is decisive for the definition of the relevant market. Nevertheless, consumer demand may be – and has to be – taken into account when examining the transnational dimension of the anti-competitive behaviour.

As a result, the central marketing scheme is void according to Article 101(2) TFEU, unless it can be justified according to Article 101(3) TFEU. This would be the case if the efficiencies gained by the decision would outweigh the impediments inflicted on competition. As has been shown before, the central marketing scheme is to the disadvantage of more attractive football clubs. At the same time, by establishing an 'all or nothing' principle and thus avoiding cherry-picking, it creates a solidarity mechanism for the less attractive, usually smaller football clubs. Moreover, it establishes a one-stop-shop for broadcasters interested in purchasing rights and thus lowers transaction costs. Furthermore, it creates efficiencies for consumers: Rather than having to find 'their' football match among a variety of channels, only *one* channel will be enabled to broadcast *all* matches. As a result, the central marketing scheme is to a certain extent more efficient than decentral marketing by the individual football clubs. Nevertheless, Article 101(3)(b) TFEU sets an absolute limit for anti-competitive multilateral behaviour in that the agreement, decision or concerted practice must not eliminate competition 'in respect of a substantial part of the products in question'. In this case one bidder could exclude all competitors from broadcasting the matches. If – as was the case in Germany – a pay-TV broadcaster obtained the rights, consumers would have to pay in order to watch the matches, which would be to the detriment of media pluralism. Therefore, exceptions from the unconfined joint marketing scheme were necessary.

The League Association had to make several commitments under Article 9 Enforcement Regulation by providing certain broadcasting rights 'packages' in order to avoid a prohibition decision by the European Commission. For example, live broadcasts were offered by the League both for free-TV and for pay-TV programme suppliers. Another package entitled the acquirer of the live broadcast to at least two Bundesliga matches and to deferred highlight first coverage on free-TV. Separate packages comprised rights to broadcast matches live and/or near-live on the internet and on mobile phones. Every club was allowed to sell its home games to a free-TV broadcaster 24 hours after the match for one-off free-TV broadcasting of up to the full match.[219]

V Unfair Competition

The rules on unfair completion are significantly fragmented not only on a global stage, but even within the EU itself. While the concept of unfair competition is well-developed in civil law countries,[220] it is a relatively recent phenomenon in common law systems.[221]

---

[219] COM, Case No. COMP/C-2/37.214 [2005] Bundesliga [27 ff].

[220] For example, the German Act Against Unfair Competition (*Gesetz gegen den unlauteren Wettbewerb*) dates back to 1896.

[221] See L'Oréal SA v. Bellure NV [2007] EWCA Civ 968 [161].

1 The International Framework

The law of unfair competition is only to a limited extent harmonised on an international level. A consistent set of rules on unfair competition is missing, but single provisions can be found in international treaties. For example, Article 10*bis*(1) of the Paris Convention for the Protection of Industrial Property obliges its signatories to assure 'effective protection against unfair competition'. Paragraph 2 then defines an 'act of unfair competition' as '[a]ny act of competition contrary to honest practices in industrial or commercial matters'. Paragraph 3 names examples for acts that shall be prohibited:

- All acts of such a nature as to create confusion by any means whatever with the establishment, the goods, or the industrial or commercial activities, of a competitor.
- False allegations in the course of trade of such a nature as to discredit the establishment, the goods, or the industrial or commercial activities, of a competitor.
- Indications or allegations the use of which in the course of trade is liable to mislead the public as to the nature, the manufacturing process, the characteristics, the suitability for their purpose, or the quantity, of the goods.

Article 10*bis* of the Paris Convention applies to members of the WTO via Article 2 of the TRIPS Agreement. In 1994, the WIPO published a comparative analysis of worldwide protection against unfair competition.[222] In 1996, the WIPO subsequently published is 'Model Provisions on Protection Against Unfair Competition'.[223] These provisions implement the obligation contained in Article 10*bis*(1) Paris Convention by defining the principal acts or practices against which protection is to be granted in Articles 2–6, and by providing a basis for protection against any other acts of unfair competition in Article 1.[224] The acts against which protection is to be granted include: causing confusion with respect to another's enterprise or its activities (Article 2), damaging another's goodwill or reputation (Article 3), misleading the public (Article 4), discrediting another's enterprise or its activities (Article 5) and unfair competition in respect of secret information (Article 6).

The EU provides a rather rudimentary and fragmented framework on unfair competition. The provision that comes closest to a definition of the notion of unfair competition is Article 5(2) of the Unfair Commercial Practices Directive. It declares a commercial practice[225] unfair if:

---

[222] WIPO, Protection Against Unfair Competition – Analysis of the Present World Situation, 1994. Available at ftp://ftp.wipo.int/pub/library/ebooks/wipopublications/wipo_pub_725e.pdf.

[223] Available at ftp://ftp.wipo.int/pub/library/ebooks/wipopublications/wipo_pub_832%28e%29.pdf.

[224] See WIPO, Model Provisions on Protection Against Unfair Competition, 1996, Note 1.01.

[225] The term is defined in Article 2(d) of the Directive.

1 it is contrary to the requirements of professional diligence, and
2 it materially distorts or is likely to materially distort the economic behaviour with regard to the product of the average consumer whom it reaches or to whom it is addressed, or of the average member of the group when a commercial practice is directed to a particular group of consumers.

In particular, commercial practices shall be unfair if they are misleading (a notion that will be discussed further below in this section) or aggressive. An Annex to the Directive contains a non-exhaustive list of commercial practices that shall in any circumstances be unfair. These include, for instance, falsely claiming to be a signatory to a code of conduct, falsely stating that a product can legally be sold when it cannot, presenting rights given to consumers in law as a distinctive feature of the trader's offer and informing a consumer that if he does not buy the product or service, the trader's job or livelihood will be in jeopardy. Claims under English law that fall under the notion of unfair competition include, for example, passing off and malicious falsehood in cases of comparative advertising.[226]

2 The Human Rights Dimension

Publications by businesses, even if they would fall under a definition of unfair competition, are basically protected by freedom of expression. The rules on unfair competition have to operate within the framework provided by freedom of expression, and not vice versa (see Chapter 2). However, as has also been shown in Chapter 3, speech published in the context of running a business, so-called 'commercial speech', is often treated as a distinct category of speech, usually receiving less protection than, say, speech on political matters. In Europe, the Strasbourg Court grants a rather broad margin of appreciation to the Member States when interfering with 'commercial speech'. This applies, in particular, in the area of regulation of advertisements. In the seminal case of *Casado Coca* v. *Spain*, the Court held that the near absolute ban on advertising by lawyers based on unfair competition rules did not amount to a violation of Article 10 ECHR. Indicating that the rules governing the profession, particularly in the sphere of advertising, vary from one country to another according to cultural tradition, and with a view to lawyers' central position in the administration of justice as intermediaries between the public and the courts, the Court granted a rather broad margin of appreciation to the Spanish authorities.[227] In *Demuth* v. *Switzerland*, the applicant intended to broadcast 'Car TV AG', a television programme on automobiles, in particular news on cars, car accessories and private-vehicle transport. The Court observed 'that such aspects would have contributed to the ongoing, general debate on the various aspects of a motorised society'. However,

---

[226] Dickinson (2008, para. 6.25).
[227] ECtHR, Casado Coca v. Spain [1994] App. no. 15450/89 [50] and [54].

the Court also found that 'the purpose of Car TV AG was primarily commercial in that it intended to promote cars and, hence, further car sales'.[228] The ECtHR then re-emphasised the Contracting State's broad margin of appreciation in the area of regulation of commercial speech and eventually found that refusal to grant the required broadcasting licence did not breach Article 10 ECHR.

By contrast, the Court held that the domestic courts overstepped their margin of appreciation in *Stambuk* v. *Germany*. Here the Court decided in favour of an ophthalmologist who had been fined for disregarding a ban on advertising under the provisions of rules of professional conduct for medical practitioners. The applicant in this case made the alleged advertising in a newspaper interview on a new laser operation technique, which had taken place on the initiative of the journalist. Consequently, the 'advertising' did not only contain information of the public on a matter of general medical interest, but also participated in the protection of the press.[229]

Although undertakings inevitably expose themselves to close scrutiny of their practices by their competitors and may give rise to criticism by consumers and the specialised press,[230] rules on unfair competition may justifiably limit the right to criticise products or competitors, or both. The ECtHR emphasised that 'there is a competing interest in protecting the commercial success and viability of companies, for the benefit of shareholders and employees, but also for the wider economic good'.[231] If, however, such a critical statement is not 'purely commercial' but pertains to a debate affecting the general interest, the extent of the margin of appreciation afforded to the domestic authorities is reduced. In *Hertel* v. *Switzerland*, the Court found that a publication critical of the effects of microwaves on human health contributed to such a debate.[232] In *Krone Verlag GmbH* v. *Austria (No. 3)*, the applicant's newspaper claimed in an advertisement to be 'the best' local newspaper. Based on the Austrian Unfair Competition Act, a competitor newspaper successfully applied for a court order to refrain from publishing the advertisement. The Strasbourg Court observed that the national courts based their decision 'on the assumption that the two newspapers were not of comparable quality and that a comparison of their prices would therefore be misleading'. However, the domestic courts also held that 'the two newspapers were competitors in the same market and for the same circle of readers'. The Strasbourg Court found these two statements inconsistent.[233] Accordingly, the Court decided that in this case the restriction on comparative advertising breached Article 10 ECHR.

---

228 ECtHR, Demuth v. Switzerland [2002] App. no. 38743/97 [41].
229 ECtHR, Stambuk v. Germany [2002] App. no. 37928/97.
230 See Oster (2011).
231 ECtHR, Steel and Morris v. United Kingdom [2005] App. no. 68416/01 [94]; Heinisch v. Germany [2011] App. no. 28274/08 [89].
232 ECtHR, Hertel v. Switzerland [1998] App. no. 59/1997/843/1049 [47].
233 ECtHR, Krone Verlag GmbH & Co. KG v. Austria (No. 3) [2003] App. no. 39069/97 [32].

3 Misleading Advertising

Apart from certain product-specific and information-specific legislation,[234] the framework for misleading advertising is set out in the Misleading and Comparative Advertising Directive and the Unfair Commercial Practices Directive.[235] Those Directives are in their substance to a large extent overlapping. In particular, both Directives provide standing not only for those who have been harmed by an unfair commercial practice, but also to persons or organisations regarded under national law as having a legitimate interest in combating misleading advertising or regulating comparative advertising or unfair commercial practices, respectively.[236] These are, in particular, consumer associations within the meaning of (now) Directive 2009/22/EC on injunctions for the protection of consumers' interests.[237]

According to Article 2(a) of the Misleading and Comparative Advertising Directive, 'advertising' means 'the making of a representation in any form in connection with a trade, business, craft or profession in order to promote the supply of goods or services, including immovable property, rights and obligations'. Both the Misleading and Comparative Advertising Directive and the Unfair Commercial Practices Directive outrightly prohibit misleading advertising, whereas they allow comparative advertising if it fulfils certain criteria stipulated in the Misleading and Comparative Advertising Directive. 'Misleading advertising' means 'any advertising which in any way, including its presentation, deceives or is likely to deceive the persons to whom it is addressed or whom it reaches and which, by reason of its deceptive nature, is likely to affect their economic behaviour or which, for those reasons, injures or is likely to injure a competitor' (Article 2(b) Misleading and Comparative Advertising Directive). In Article 3, the Misleading and Comparative Advertising Directive establishes minimum criteria for determining whether advertising is misleading.[238] Account shall be taken of all the advertising's features, in particular the characteristics of goods or services, the price or the manner in which the price is

---

[234] See, for example, Regulation (EC) No. 1924/2006 of the European Parliament and of the Council of 20 December 2006 on nutrition and health claims made on foods, OJ L 404/9; Council Regulation (EC) No. 510/2006 of 20 March 2006 on the protection of geographical indications and designations of origin for agricultural products and foodstuffs, OJ L 93/12.

[235] Directive 2006/114/EC of the European Parliament and of the Council of 12 December 2006 concerning misleading and comparative advertising (codified version), OJ L 376/21; Directive 2005/29/EC of the European Parliament and of the Council of 11 May 2005 concerning unfair business-to-consumer commercial practices in the internal market and amending Council Directive 84/450/EEC, Directives 97/7/EC, 98/27/EC and 2002/65/EC of the European Parliament and of the Council and Regulation (EC) No. 2006/2004 of the European Parliament and of the Council ('Unfair Commercial Practices Directive'), OJ L 149/22.

[236] Article 5 Misleading and Comparative Advertising Directive; Article 11 Unfair Commercial Practices Directive.

[237] Directive 2009/22/EC of the European Parliament and of the Council of 23 April 2009 on injunctions for the protection of consumers' interests (Codified version), OJ L 110/30.

[238] Recital 7 of the Misleading and Comparative Advertising Directive.

calculated, the conditions on which the goods are supplied or the services provided and the nature, attributes and rights of the advertiser.[239]

Article 5(4)(a) of the Unfair Commercial Practices Directive prohibits 'misleading commercial practices'. 'Commercial practice' is a concept that includes advertising and marketing.[240] Articles 6 and 7 of the same Directive set out when a 'commercial practice' shall be regarded as misleading. With a view to the general aim of the Directive – consumer protection – it requires that the misleading commercial practice causes or is likely to cause the average consumer to take a transactional decision that he would not have taken otherwise. The concept of misleading commercial practices overlaps to a significant extent with the notion of misleading and unlawful comparative advertising as set out in the Misleading and Comparative Advertising Directive. In addition, the Unfair Commercial Practices Directive includes, for example, untruthful commercial practices, deceit about the extent of the trader's commitments or the consumer's rights and misleading omissions.

4 Comparative Advertising

'Comparative advertising' means any advertising that explicitly or by implication identifies a competitor or goods or services offered by a competitor (Article 2(c) Misleading and Comparative Advertising Directive). Comparative advertising shall, as far as the comparison is concerned, be permitted when the conditions stipulated in Article 4 of the Directive are met:

1 It is not misleading.
2 It compares goods or services meeting the same needs or intended for the same purpose.
3 It objectively compares one or more material, relevant, verifiable and representative features of those goods and services, which may include price.
4 It does not discredit or denigrate the trademarks, trade names, other distinguishing marks, goods, services, activities or circumstances of a competitor.
5 For products with designation of origin, it relates in each case to products with the same designation.
6 It does not take unfair advantage of the reputation of a trademark, trade name or other distinguishing marks of a competitor or of the designation of origin of competing products.
7 It does not present goods or services as imitations or replicas of goods or services bearing a protected trademark or trade name.
8 It does not create confusion among traders, between the advertiser and a competitor or between the advertiser's trademarks, trade names, other distinguishing marks, goods or services and those of a competitor.

---

[239] See Article 3 of the Misleading and Comparative Advertising Directive, which provides several examples for those features.
[240] See Article 2(d) Unfair Commercial Practices Directive.

Notably, Article 4 thus provides an exception from the exclusive rights of the proprietor of a registered trademark to prevent all third parties from using, in the course of trade, any sign that is identical to, or similar to, the trademark in relation to identical goods or services.[241]

VI Jurisdiction and Conflict of Laws

Under EU law, distortions of competition within the meaning of antitrust law and practices of unfair competition are to be classified as torts within the meaning of the Brussels Ia Regulation and the Rome II Regulation. Article 6 Rome II Regulation is a special provision applicable to acts of unfair competition (paragraphs 1 and 2) and anti-competitive behaviour (paragraph 3). The provision is built on several legislative compromises. Not surprisingly, it is therefore quite difficult to interpret and subject to criticism by academic commentators.[242] Although the establishment of jurisdiction and the search for the applicable law are to be strictly distinguished in practice, the following sections will deal with them simultaneously, as the questions arising under jurisdiction as well as the conflict of laws can – and should – receive concerted answers.[243]

1 Unfair Competition

In addition to the general jurisdiction according to Article 4 Brussels Ia Regulation, the establishment of jurisdiction in cases of unfair competition is to be determined according to Article 7(2) Brussels Ia Regulation. Accordingly, the defendant can be sued 'in the courts for the place where the harmful event occurred or may occur'. Hence, according to the *Bier* formula,[244] the claimant may sue at the courts of the place where the defendant has acted – which is usually concordant with the defendant's 'domicile' according to Article 4 in conjunction with Article 63 Brussels Ia Regulation – or at the place where the damage occurred. With a view to the applicable law, Article 6(1) Rome II Regulation states that obligations arising out of an act of unfair competition shall be decided by the law of the country 'where competitive relations or the collective interests of consumers are, or are likely to be, affected'. As Recital 21 Rome II Regulation explains, the provision should not be seen as a derogation from the general *lex loci damni* principle under Article 4(1) Rome II Regulation. Rather, for acts of unfair competition, the country in which competitive relations or consumer interests are affected is 'a clarification' of the 'country in which the damage occurs' within the meaning of Article 4(1) Rome II Regulation.[245] As a result,

---

[241] Article 5 Trade Mark Directive.
[242] See, for example, Dickinson (2008, para. 6.01); Van Calster (2013, pp. 171f).
[243] Compare Dickinson (2008, para. 6.14).
[244] See Chapter 4.
[245] Recital 21 Rome II Regulation.

the country in which the damage occurs within the meaning of the *Bier* interpretation of Article 7(2) Brussels Ia Regulation and the country where competitive relations or the collective interests of consumers are affected under Article 6(1) Rome II Regulation should be one and the same.

This, then, raises the question of what the place in which 'competitive relations or the collective interests of consumers are affected' is. The law on unfair competition is concerned with competition. Competition is a concept that applies to markets. Therefore, Article 6(1) should be read as referring to the country in which the market, on which the interests are affected, is located. Take the following example: a supermarket in Flanders places misleading advertisements in newspapers from the south-east Dutch province of Limburg. It would now have to be established what the relevant country of the market is. One could argue that Flanders, hence Belgium, is the relevant place, because this is the place to which the consumers should be enticed. But the better arguments seem to speak for Limburg, hence the Netherlands, as the relevant place, because this is where the interests of both competitors and consumers are affected. As a result, Dutch courts should have jurisdiction under Article 7(2) Brussels Ia Regulation,[246] and Dutch law on unfair competition shall be applied.

How would the case have to be decided if the supermarket published the misleading advertisements in Flemish newspapers, and as a result of this publication, Flemish customers who usually frequent supermarkets in Limburg switch to the Flemish supermarket? In this case, one could also argue that since the Dutch supermarkets lost customers because of the misleading advertisements, the 'competitive relations' were also 'affected' in the Netherlands. However, it seems more convincing to treat the loss of customers for Dutch supermarkets as a merely *indirect* consequence. The advertisement *directly* affected the interests of Flemish consumers, which is why Belgian courts should have jurisdiction under Article 7(2) Brussels Ia Regulation and Belgian law should apply.

But the application of the 'affected market principle' to Article 6(1) is not entirely uncontroversial, because Article 6(1), unlike Article 6(3), does not include any express reference to the term 'market' – another indicator of the misconception of Article 6.[247] If one applies the 'affected market principle' also to paragraph 1, as is suggested here, it would to a large extent, but not entirely, overlap with the notion of 'market' in paragraph 3.[248] As has been shown before, the aim of antitrust law is, at least to a significant extent, to protect the competitive process as such. By contrast, unfair competition law aims at protecting competitors, consumers and the public at large. This has to be considered when interpreting paragraph 1. Nevertheless, the cases in which the two concepts of 'market' are not fully congruent are rare. They include, for

---

[246] Unless the claimant sues the defendant at its place of 'domicile' within the meaning of Article 4 in conjunction with Article 63 Brussels Ia Regulation.

[247] See Honorati (2006, p. 149).

[248] See M. Illmer, in Huber (2011, Art. 6 Rome II para. 38 ff).

example, cases in which consumers are misled on promotional trips on their holidays and then enter into contracts at their place of domicile.[249]

The localisation of the place where the damage occurred is particularly difficult in so-called multi-state cases; that is, if the interests of competitors and of consumers are equally affected in several countries. This occurs frequently if misleading advertising is published via transnational means of mass communication, such as satellite broadcasting and the internet. For example, a commercial English website operating on a European market for particular goods publishes misleading advertising. Competitors and consumers in Ireland and Sweden are affected. The 'mosaic rule', which we already encountered in Chapter 4, applies: claims for injunctions and damages may be brought in each jurisdiction, and the law of each country applies, in which the publication can be received and affects competitors' or consumers' interests. However, this applies only with a view to the damage caused in this particular country. Hence a Swedish competitor could bring a claim for damages against the website operator in Sweden (Article 7(2) Brussels Ia Regulation), and Swedish law would apply (Article 6(1) Rome II Regulation), but only with a view to the damage suffered in Sweden. If the claimant company also wants to vindicate the damage suffered in, say, Ireland, it would have to bring an action at Irish courts, which would then decide based on Irish law. Only if the Swedish competitor would bring a claim against the website operator at English courts under Article 4 Brussels Ia Regulation could it vindicate the damage it suffered in all countries, but the law of each country in which the damage was suffered would have to be applied to each claim. The English Court would thus have to apply Swedish law with regard to the damage suffered in Sweden, Irish law to the damage suffered in Ireland, etc.

In addition, it should be noted that in cases involving an internet publication or a publication via broadcasting in the EU, the country-of-origin principle according to Article 3 E-commerce Directive and Article 3 AVMS Directive would have to be considered. As a first step, one has to ask whether the publication falls within the scope of the field coordinated by one of these Directives. The AVMS Directive only applies to broadcasters themselves, not to companies producing, editing and commissioning advertisements via broadcasting channels. As has been shown in Chapter 5, the AVMS Directive provides a regulatory regime for audiovisual commercial communication, which also includes several provisions prohibiting what can be considered unfair commercial practices.[250] But these rules are not exhaustive.[251] Therefore, the country-of-origin principle of the AVMS Directive does not have huge relevance for cases of unfair competition. However, it would still have to be examined whether the country-of-origin principle under primary EU law applies, for example, with a view to the freedom to provide services. Moreover, businesses that publish advertisements

---

[249] M. Illmer, in Huber (2011, Art. 6 Rome II para. 40).
[250] See, for example, Article 9(1) AVMS Directive.
[251] ECJ, Joined Cases C-34/95, C-35/95 and C-36/95 [1997] De Agostini (Svenska) Förlag AB and others [38].

(or boycotts or statements defaming their competitors, etc.) on their websites are themselves information society service providers and thus fall within the scope of the E-commerce Directive.

If the country-of-origin principle applies, then one has to decide whether it operates as a conflict of laws rule or as a corrective on the substantive level, a question that has already been discussed in Chapter 6. In any case, with a view to online publications, one has to observe Article 3(4)(a)(i), fourth indent, of the E-commerce Directive. Accordingly, Member States may, under certain conditions, derogate from the country-of-origin principle for the protection of consumers. As a result, insofar as they serve to protect consumers, domestic rules on unfair competition may under certain conditions constitute a justified derogation from the country-of-origin principle.

As has been shown before, the law of unfair competition serves to protect competitors, consumers and the general public alike. Hence Article 6(1) Rome II Regulation declares the law of the country in which those interests are directly affected applicable. But acts of unfair competition can also be targeted against one single competitor. In those cases in which the interests at stake are purely bilateral, it would be unconvincing to use the impact on an entire market as the reference point for the establishment of the applicable law. Instead, there appears to be no need for a derogation from the general principle established in Article 4 Rome II Regulation at all. Article 6(2) Rome II Regulation envisages exactly this scenario. For cases in which an act of unfair competition affects exclusively the interests of a specific competitor, Article 6(2) Rome II Regulation refers to Article 4. As a result, the applicable law shall basically be the law of the country in which the damage occurs (Article 4(1)), unless the person claimed to be liable and the person sustaining damage both have their habitual residence in the same country at the time when the damage occurs; in this case, the law of that country shall apply (Article 4(2)). If it is clear from all the circumstances of the case that the tort or delict is manifestly more closely connected with another country, the law of that other country shall apply. A manifestly closer connection with another country might be based in particular on a pre-existing relationship between the parties, such as a contract, that is closely connected with the tort or delict in question (Article 4(3)).

Article 6(2) Rome II Regulation thus appears as a stringent and convincing provision. However, the problems are again in the detail. When does an act of unfair competition affect *exclusively* the interests of a specific competitor? Once again we need to start from first principles of statutory construction. Article 6(2) Rome II Regulation is an exception to the rule enshrined in Article 6(1) Rome II Regulation. Therefore, it should basically be applied restrictively, unless the legislator's intent or specific rationales of that provision dictate otherwise. But in this case, a restrictive interpretation of that provision appears justified indeed: as we have seen, the rules on unfair competition serve to protect interests of the general public. Hence it would seem inappropriate to apply factors that are in the interest of one specific competitor – the place in which his damage occurs or the country of his 'residence' – as the reference points for the applicable law. As a result, Article 6(2) Rome II Regulation should only apply in cases in which the act has objectively no direct effect on other competitors, consumers or the public.[252] Examples are: enticing away a competitor's staff, corruption, industrial espionage, disclosure of business secrets or inducing breach of contract.[253] But Article 6(2) should not apply, for example, in cases of misleading comparative advertising. Even if only one competitor was the subject of that misleading advertising, potential victims of that advertising are also consumers who might be misled. Therefore, it seems appropriate to apply Article 6(1) here. Finally, which paragraph should apply to defamation of a competitor? If we agree that defamation of competitors falls under Article 6 – we will come back to this in a moment – then we would still have to decide under which paragraph it falls. On the one hand, a competitor would be directly affected by a defamatory publication of another competitor. This speaks for the application of Article 6(2). On the other hand, whether or not he suffers a loss still depends on the consumers' reaction, which weighs in favour of the application of Article 6(1). But then again, defamation serves to protect a (natural or legal) person's reputation, which is a commodity in its own right. Therefore, it appears more convincing to subsume defamatory statements targeted against one single competitor under Article 6(2); but such a case would still have to be decided by the Court of Justice.

As has been stated before, Article 6 Rome II Regulation is a rather controversial provision. This is particularly so because of its unclear scope and its underlying concepts. It is already problematic to determine what is covered by the notion of 'unfair competition' in the first place. First of all, this concept has to be interpreted in an EU-autonomous way. From an international and European perspective, the aspects covered by Article 10*bis* of the Paris Convention and the Unfair Commercial Practices Directive are arguably all covered by Articles 6(1) and (2). But it can be difficult to decide in each individual case whether certain domestic torts fall under this provision or not.[254]

Another problem concerns the distinction between Articles 6(1) and (2) and other provisions of the Rome II Regulation. Two examples that are particularly relevant for media law should be mentioned. First, which provision should apply to defamations of competitors? Should these cases fall under Articles 6(1) or (2), or should they be excluded from the scope of the Regulation altogether by virtue of Article 1(2)(g) Rome II Regulation? Recall that Article 1(2)(g) states that 'non-contractual obligations arising out of violations of privacy and rights relating to personality, including defamation, ... shall be excluded from the scope of this Regulation'. In Chapter 4 it has been argued that this provision applies, albeit slightly awkwardly, also to defamation

---

[252] M. Illmer, in Huber (2011, Art. 6 Rome II para. 3).
[253] COM, Proposal for a Regulation of the European Parliament and the Council on the law applicable to non-contractual obligations ('Rome II'), COM(2003) 427 final, p. 16.
[254] See M. Illmer, in Huber (2011, Art. 6 Rome II para. 11ff).

of companies. However, one exception should apply, and this is in cases in which the defamation of a company would constitute an act of unfair competition within the meaning of Article 6 Rome II Regulation. Article 1(2)(g) Rome II Regulation provides an exception, hence the provision has to be interpreted narrowly. The exception should therefore not apply if there is another rule that is more suitable to cover the phenomenon at hand. This provision would be Article 6, because, as has been shown before, defamation of competitors may constitute an act of unfair competition. Moreover, the legislative history of Article 1(2)(g) reveals that the Member States aimed at protecting their domestic media when including that exception. This rationale does not apply where one company defames a competitor. To be sure, such a case would also have a freedom of expression dimension, but it would merely operate under the category of 'commercial speech' rather than under media freedom. It is therefore submitted that defamatory publications that constitute an act of unfair competition should fall under Article 6 and not under Article 1(2)(g) Rome II Regulation.

The second example to illustrate the difficulty of delineating the scope of Articles 6(1) and (2) Rome II Regulation is the case of allegedly unlawful use of a protected trademark. Should this be covered by Article 6, or should it fall under Article 8 Rome II Regulation? This depends, in the first place, on the basis of the action brought by the claimant. If he bases his claim on a violation of intellectual property, Article 8 applies, and if he bases his claim on unfair competition, then Article 6 applies. If the claim would be brought under both actions, both provisions apply, but restricted to their respective claim.[255] In most cases, Article 8 and Article 6(1) should lead to the application of the same law anyway.

Furthermore, it is questionable as to whether the parties may choose the applicable law in derogation from Articles 6(1) and (2). Article 6(4) unambiguously states that '[t]he law applicable under this Article may not be derogated from by an agreement pursuant to Article 14'. However, there is good reason to argue that this paragraph only applies to Article 6(1), but not to Article 6(2). Article 6(1) does not permit a choice of law by the parties because this would be irreconcilable with its objectives protecting competitors and consumers at large.[256] This rationale does not apply to Article 6(2). Article 6(2) does not envisage the entire market, but only the bilateral relationship between the claimant and the defendant. There is no reason why these two parties should not be able to agree on another applicable law. Yet if one follows such an approach, then it has to be ensured that Article 6(2) is indeed applied narrowly, otherwise the interests of the market in general would be undermined.

The least problematic aspect of Article 6 is the clause 'or are likely to be affected' in Article 6(1), which re-emerges in Article 6(3). That clause merely expresses that the provision applies not only to *ex post* claims, such as claims for damages, but also to injunctive relief.

---

[255] M. Illmer, in Huber (2011, Art. 6 Rome II para. 15).
[256] See M. Illmer, in Huber (2011, Art. 6 Rome II para. 54).

2 Antitrust and Concentration Law

As has been shown before, the European Commission pursues a policy encouraging the 'private enforcement' of EU competition law, meaning that competitors may vindicate their loss because of, or apply for an injunction against, anti-competitive behaviour. With a view to establishing jurisdiction, the general rules of the Brussels Ia Regulation apply, particularly Article 4 on general jurisdiction and Article 7(2) on special jurisdiction. The applicable law is determined by Article 6(3) Rome II Regulation. The notion of 'restrictions of competition' within the meaning of Article 6(3) Rome II Regulation covers infringements of both national law and Articles 101 and 102 TFEU.[257] Claims for damages with regard to unlawful mergers, acquisitions and other concentrations as well as actions against recipients of unlawful state aid also fall under Article 6(3) Rome II Regulation.[258] Being *loi uniforme*, Article 6(3) refers not only to domestic or EU competition law, but it can also declare the competition law of a third country applicable.

According to Article 6(3)(a) Rome II Regulation, the law to be applied to a restriction of competition shall be the law of the country where the market is, or is likely to be, affected. Article 6(3)(a) thus expresses the difference between antitrust law and unfair competition law. While the law on unfair competition protects competitors, consumers and the public, antitrust law serves to protect competition as such. As a result, Article 6(3)(a) declares the law of that country applicable in which the market is affected. 'The market' is in this context congruent with the relevant geographic market that has been described above. In litigation following a Commission action under Articles 101 and 102 TFEU, the domestic courts are bound by the Commission's decision because of Article 16 Enforcement Regulation. Things are more difficult if the claimant files a lawsuit because of alleged anti-competitive behaviour in cases in which no prior market definition has taken place. In such stand-alone actions, domestic courts would have to define the geographic market themselves.

As with Article 6(1), the 'market principle' underlying Article 6(3)(a) Rome II Regulation may lead to a 'competition mosaic' in multi-state cases: if one anti-competitive behaviour leads to immediate damages in more than one jurisdiction, the claimant could sue the defendant under Article 7(2) Brussels Ia Regulation in each jurisdiction in which damage occurred (or will occur), but only for the loss suffered in that jurisdiction. The same would apply with regard to the applicable law. The claimant may sue the defendant at the defendant's place of 'domicile' within the meaning of Article 4, 63 Brussels Ia Regulation for the entire damage. Nevertheless, as under Article 6(1), under Article 6(3)(a) Rome II Regulation the damage would have to be vindicated according to the law of each country with a view to the damage

---

[257] Recitals 22 and 23 Rome II Regulation.
[258] M. Illmer, in Huber (2011, Art. 6 Rome II para. 73f). The success of the action under substantive law depends on whether the state to which Article 6(3) refers provides such a claim or not.

that occurred in that country; hence the 'mosaic rule' would still apply with regard to the applicable law, even if the claimant sues at the place of the defendant. Article 6(3)(b) provides a remedy for this – for the claimant dissatisfying – conundrum. If the market is (or is likely to be) affected in more than one country and the claimant sues the defendant in the latter's country of domicile according to Article 4 Brussels Ia Regulation, he may base his entire claim on the *lex fori* if the market in that Member State is among those directly and substantially affected by the restriction of competition out of which the obligation arises.

That being so, Article 6(3)(b) allows the court of the defendant's jurisdiction to apply the *lex fori* on the entire claim of the claimant. But what if there are several defendants? In cases of Article 102 TFEU, it is likely that there is only one defendant: the company that has abused, or is alleged to have abused, its dominant position. In cases of Article 101 TFEU, however, it is likely that there will be several defendants, namely those undertakings that have collaborated to conduct anti-competitive behaviour. Based on Article 8(1) Brussels Ia Regulation, the claimant may sue several defendants together in one jurisdiction 'where any one of them is domiciled, provided the claims are so closely connected that it is expedient to hear and determine them together to avoid the risk of irreconcilable judgments resulting from separate proceedings'. This provision also encompasses proceedings against several companies involved in an anti-competitive agreement. So which law applies in a lawsuit brought against several defendants in the jurisdiction of only one (or a few) of those defendants? The second clause included in Article 6(3)(b) Brussels Ia Regulation provides the answer: if the claimant sues more than one defendant in the same court (within the meaning of Article 4 Brussels Ia Regulation), he can choose to base his claim on the law of that court if the restriction of competition on which the claim against each of these defendants relies directly and substantially affects also the market in the Member State of that court. This would even include damages suffered in non-EU states.[259]

VII Questions

1 Do you think that the provisions of EU competition law are sufficient to take on board the particularities of media freedom and media pluralism when applied to the media? To what extent does sufficient competition between media companies equal media pluralism? Does single media ownership necessarily conflict with variations in views and opinions?

2. The European Commission's investigation into Google's search engine results raises several interesting questions, many of which go beyond the scope of the Commission's investigation. Google is, in particular, accused of not providing

---

[259] M. Illmer, in Huber (2011, Art. 6 Rome II para. 78).

neutral search results. But which standards should apply to measure a search result as being 'neutral'? What is the legitimate expectation of the public with a view to a Google search result? Does the public have a legitimate expectation as to a search result in the first place? Why should Google not have a right to display its own services more prominently? Moreover, to what extent can algorithms, such as those on which Google's search results are based (with the exception of Google's own services and advertised products), be regarded as biased?

One should also ask for the policy considerations behind the proceedings. What has made Google such a powerful internet search engine, to the extent that 'to google' has even become a synonym for using a search engine? If the European Commission identifies a need for a 'neutral', 'non-biased' search engine, is competition law a proper instrument to address existing deficits? Or should the EU's Member States initiate own steps, for example, by providing a public internet search engine similar to the way they provide public broadcasting?

VIII Further Reading

- A. Fatur, *EU Competition Law and the Information and Communication Technology Network Industries, Economic versus Legal Concepts in Pursuit of (Consumer) Welfare*, 2012
- L. Hitchens, *Broadcasting Pluralism and Diversity: A Comparative Study of Policy and Regulation*, 2006
- N.T. Nikolinakos, *EU Competition Law and Regulation in the Converging Telecommunications, Media and IT Sectors*, 2006
- M. Sükösd, R. Picard and P. Valcke (eds.), *Media Pluralism and Diversity: Concepts, Risks and Global Trends*, 2015

Media Law and State Aid

CASE EXAMPLE

Article 5 of the German Basic Law enshrines the freedom of broadcasting. This requires, according to the case law of the German Federal Constitutional Court, that public broadcasters shall ensure the 'basic provision of broadcasting services'. This also implies adequate financial means allowing public broadcasters to provide this basic provision of broadcasting services and the related 'guarantee of existence and development of public broadcasting'.

The scope of public broadcasters' public service tasks is partly laid down by law and partly left to the public service broadcasters' self-commitments. The fulfilment of the public service mission is subject to internal and external control. Internal control is exercised by the Broadcasting Council, which consists of representatives of the various groups of German society. It establishes the programme guidelines and advises the director of the public broadcasters in programme-related questions. It also checks that public broadcasters respect their programme guidelines as well as the respect their self-commitments. In addition to these internal control mechanisms, the public broadcasters need to inform the parliaments of the federal states every two years, submitting a report about the financial situation and the fulfilment of the public service mission.

The financing of public broadcasters is based partly on a licence fee and partly on incomes from advertisements; the main source of income shall be the television and radio licence fee. The financial needs of public broadcasters are assessed by the independent Commission for the determination of the financial needs of public broadcasters (KEF), which, upon submissions from the public broadcasters, recommends the required revenues level to the state parliaments. The KEF, when assessing the financial needs of public broadcasters, needs to check whether the programme decisions remain within the public service remit, while at the same time respecting the constitutionally guaranteed programme autonomy of public broadcasters. The public service financing is laid down in interstate treaties concluded by the federal states of Germany. The state parliaments have little discretion not to implement the KEF recommendations when fixing the licence fee level. The licence fee is collected on behalf of the individual broadcasting corporations by a joint body established by the public service broadcasters, the GEZ.

In 2005, the German federal states amended the interstate treaties regarding the public service remit of the public broadcasters. The amendments involved, *inter alia*, offering public broadcasters the possibility to offer programme-related and programme-accompanying 'telemedia', a concept that essentially corresponds to information society services. The concept of 'telemedia' includes, *inter alia*, traffic, weather and stock exchange data, news groups, chat rooms, electronic press, TV and radio text, tele-shopping, telegames, online services that provide access to data such as internet search machines as well as the commercial distribution of information via electronic mail such as advertisement mails. Moreover, the public broadcasters were allowed to distribute their programme also via digital technology and to organise – exclusively on the digital platform – six additional channels with a focus on culture, education and information.

Private competitors of the public broadcasters lodged a complaint against the financing of the public broadcasters, especially with a view to their online activities.

(Based on European Commission, State aid E 3/2005 (ex- CP 2/2003, CP 232/2002, CP 43/2003, CP 243/2004 and CP 195/2004) – Financing of public broadcasters in Germany, C (2007)1761 FINAL)

I Introduction

In order to safeguard a pluralistic media, to ensure an informed public debate on matters of general concern or to protect domestic cultural heritage, there can be a legitimate public interest in state support for journalists and media companies in economic difficulties. But such aid may bear considerable risks for both the economy in general and the media in particular. In general terms, subsidies granted by states confer a competitive advantage on the company that benefits from the aid. Hence a state aid can distort competition: operators might reduce capacity or potential operators might decide not to enter into a market. At the same time, if carefully used, state aid measures can also correct market failures by improving the provision of services in areas or sectors where there is no incentive for commercial operators to invest. These are the rationales underlying the WTO rules on subsidies and the EU legal framework on state aid, which apply where state measures distort or threaten to distort competition transnationally.

Yet state aids for media companies include particular risks going beyond the general anti-competitive effects. State aid for the media sector jeopardises the independence of the media, which might be more inclined to report in favour of those institutions that subsidise them, according to the proverb 'He who pays the piper calls the tune'. State subsidies for the media, which are particularly often called for to save the declining newspaper industry, are thus a double-edged sword. As the Human Rights Committee has emphasised, governmental benefits of any kind granted to media undertakings, such as state subsidies, placing of government advertisements and allocation of broadcasting frequencies, must not be used to stifle criticism of the government and media pluralism in general.[1] Given the importance of the media for a democratic society, it is therefore quite unfortunate that the transnational legal environment for scrutinising state subsidies for the media merely consists of the purely competition-focused state subsidy and state aid laws of the WTO and the EU, respectively. By contrast, media-specific legislation, such as the Audiovisual

---

[1] Human Rights Committee, Concluding observations on Ukraine (CCPR/CO/73/UKR), para. 22; Concluding observations on Lesotho (CCPR/CO/79/Add. 106), para. 22.

Media Service Directive, is entirely silent on state aid for broadcasters. To be sure, the 1997 Amsterdam Protocol on the System of Public Broadcasting in the EU Member States (now Protocol No. 29 to the Lisbon Treaty) highlights that 'the system of public broadcasting in the Member States is directly related to the democratic, social and cultural needs of each society and to the need to preserve media pluralism'. Therefore, the Protocol stipulates that the TEU and the TFEU shall apply 'without prejudice to the competence of Member States to provide for the funding of public service broadcasting and in so far as such funding is granted to broadcasting organisations for the fulfilment of the public service remit as conferred, defined and organised by each Member State'. However, this only applies 'in so far as such funding does not affect trading conditions and competition in the Union to an extent which would be contrary to the common interest'. Consequently, state aid granted to public service broadcasting has to operate within the competition law provisions of the TFEU, including Articles 107 and 108 TFEU on state aid, and not independently thereof.

Subsidies and other aids granted to the media are therefore, in the first place, seen through a competition lens. However, those rules need to be conceptualised in a way that they can take on board media-specific concerns. These concerns are:

- media freedom, especially the independence of the media from governmental influence;
- the principle of technology neutrality;
- media pluralism; and
- the need to safeguard the provision of services of public interest by the media.

Since public aids granted to the media are thus scrutinised within the legal framework for subsidies and other state aids, this chapter will go through these rules on a step-by-step basis, thereby highlighting their significance for aids granted to the media. The chapter will show that specific rules, such as Article 106(2) TFEU on services of general economic interest, are conceptualised and applied in a way to take on board the importance of media services for a democratic society, and not just as an economic commodity. In particular, questions relating to the funding of public service broadcasters will reveal the dichotomy of media services as economic activities, on the one hand, and as services beneficial for society in general, on the other hand.

II The Main Areas of Media State Aid

The approach taken in this chapter does not correspond to the sectoral approach by the European Commission, which has published guidelines and recommendations for the operation of state aid rules, in particular media sectors, such as public service broadcasting, film funding and the deployment of communication infrastructure. The distinction between those areas is not as clear-cut as the European Commission's communications seem to suggest. For example, public service broadcasters may also use state aid they received for the production of films and the promotion of cinema productions, thus operating at the interface of state aid for public service broadcast-ers and film funding.[2] Furthermore, funding of the roll-out of a broadband network that remains in public ownership may constitute an aid to electronic communica-tion service providers seeking access to the network,[3] while funding for commercial broadcasters to switch-over from analogue to digital terrestrial television indirectly benefits the network operator.[4] But this chapter will of course have particular regard to those three constellations that have been in the focus of European adjudicators: the financing of public service broadcasting, film funding and public investment in communication infrastructure. At the same time, by taking a horizontal rather than a sectoral approach, the chapter also considers other forms of state aid, such as sub-sidies for the press and other journalistic media undertakings.

1 Funding of Public Service Broadcasters

Public service broadcasting encompasses both public broadcasters, such as ARD and ZDF in Germany, the BBC in Britain or RAI in Italy, and commercial broadcast-ers entrusted with a public service mission, such as ITV in Britain. Public service broadcasting is an important instrument to safeguard media plurality and to pro-mote cultural interests. The importance of public service broadcasting for foster-ing cultural diversity has been recognised by the 2005 UNESCO Convention on the Protection and Promotion of the Diversity of Cultural Expressions.[5] According to Articles 6(1) and (2)(h) of that Convention, each party may adopt 'measures aimed at protecting and promoting the diversity of cultural expressions within its territory'. Such measures may include, among others, 'measures aimed at enhancing diversity of the media, including through public service broadcasting'.

In the EU, according to the Amsterdam Protocol and reiterated in the Council Resolution concerning public service broadcasting, the provisions of the TFEU shall 'be without prejudice to the competence of Member States to provide for the funding of public service broadcasting'.[6] This re-emphasises the principle estab-lished in *Sacchi*, where the Court of Justice recognised that Member States could

---

[2] See COM, Decision 2012/365/EU of 20 December 2011 on the State aid C 85/01 on ad hoc measures implemented by Portugal in favour of RTP [165]; COM, Decision 2005/406/EC of 15 October 2003 on ad hoc measures implemented by Portugal for RTP [168].

[3] COM, Decision C(2011)7285 final of 19 October 2010, State Aid N 330/2010 – France Programme national 'très haut debit' – Volet B [38]; Decision C(2010)888 of 8 February 2010, Italy, State aid N 596/2009 – Italy, Bridging the digital divide in Lombardia [36].

[4] Decision 2006/513/EC of 9 November 2005 on the State Aid which the Federal Republic of Germany has implemented for the introduction of digital terrestrial television (DVB-T) in Berlin-Brandenburg [30]; confirmed by ECJ, Case T-8/06 [2009] FAB v. Commission.

[5] UNESCO Convention on the Protection and Promotion of the Diversity of Cultural Expressions; see Burri (2013). The Convention was approved by Council Decision 2006/515/EC of 18 May 2006 and thus forms part of EU law.

[6] Amsterdam Protocol, now Protocol No. 29 to the Treaty of Lisbon; Resolution of the Council and of the Representatives of the Governments of the Member States, meeting within the Council of 25 January 1999 concerning public service broadcasting, OJ C 30/1.

legitimately define 'services of general economic interests' so as to cover radio and television transmissions for considerations of non-economic public interest as well as activities of an economic nature.[7] As a consequence, both 'single-funding' and 'dual-funding' schemes are permitted under the Treaty. A 'single-funding' scheme is a system in which public service broadcasting is financed exclusively through public funds, such as a licence fee. An example for a single-funding scheme is the financing of the BBC. Dual-funding systems comprise schemes in which public service broadcasting is financed by combinations of state funds and commercial activities, such as the sale of advertising space or programmes and the offering of services against payment.[8] Examples for such schemes are the public broadcasters in Germany and the commercial public service broadcasters in Britain. The European Commission summarised the principles of its policy in applying the state aid rules to public service broadcasting in a Communication in 2009.[9] In practice, the focus on cases involving state funding for public service broadcasting is usually on the (non-)fulfilment of the so-called *Altmark Trans* criteria and the application of Article 106(2) TFEU.[10]

2 Film Funding

Another area of state aid for the media with significant practical importance is the funding of films and other audiovisual works. Such works mirror and shape the cultural diversity of the different traditions and histories of states and regions.[11] However, film production budgets are substantially higher than for other audiovisual content, and they face strong global competition. Left purely to the market, many films would not have been made in the first place. It is therefore generally accepted that aid is important to sustain domestic audiovisual productions or transnational productions with domestic participation.[12]

In the EU, the assessment criteria for state aid for the production of films and other audiovisual works are set out in the Communication of 2013.[13] It includes all aspects of film creation, from story concept to delivery to the audience, and it includes new

---

[7] Case 155/73 [1974] Sacchi [14]; see also ECJ, Joined Cases T-309/04, T-317/04, T-329/04 and T-336/04 [2008] TV 2/Danmark A/S v. Commission [107].

[8] COM, Communication 2009/C 257/01 on the application of State aid rules to public service broadcasting [57]. See ECJ, Case T-442/03 [2008] SIC v. Commission [202].

[9] COM, Communication 2009/C 257/01 on the application of State aid rules to public service broadcasting, OJ C 257/1.

[10] See Section IV.2 in this chapter.

[11] COM, Communication 2013/C 332/01 on State aid for films and other audiovisual works [1].

[12] COM, Communication 2013/C 332/01 on State aid for films and other audiovisual works [4].

[13] COM, Communication 2013/C 332/01 on State aid for films and other audiovisual works. See also Communication 2002/C 43/04 from the Commission to the Council, the European Parliament, the Economic and Social Committee and the Committee of the Regions on certain legal aspects relating to cinematographic and other audiovisual works, OJ C 43/6.

forms of 'transmedia storytelling'.[14] The practical focus, and hence also a focus of this chapter, is the justification of film funding under Article 107(3)(d) TFEU.

3 Public Investment in Communication Infrastructure

Public investment in communication infrastructure, such as wired, wireless or satellite infrastructure, is another phenomenon that will receive particular attention in this chapter.[15] The Europe 2020 Strategy (EU2020) has underlined the importance of broadband deployment as part of the EU's growth strategy.[16] In particular, the Digital Agenda for Europe (DAE)[17] acknowledges the socio-economic benefits of broadband, highlighting its importance for competitiveness, social inclusion and employment. The DAE seeks to ensure that, by 2020, all Europeans have access to internet speeds of above 30 Mbps and 50 per cent or more of European households subscribe to internet connections above 100 Mbps. While hoping that the necessary investments for the broadband deployment shall primarily come from commercial investors, the European Commission acknowledges that the DAE objectives cannot be reached without the support of public funds.[18] In particular, a well-targeted state intervention in the broadband field should contribute to reducing the gap between those areas or regions where individuals and communities have access to information technologies and those where they do not ('digital divide'). The European Commission summarised its guidelines for the application of state aid rules in relation to the rapid deployment of broadband networks in its 2013 Communication.[19] The practical focus of cases involving state aid for the deployment of communication infrastructure is Article 107(3)(c) TFEU.

III International Law

While EU law basically prohibits all forms of state aid, WTO law only applies to subsidies. The concept of 'subsidy' only encompasses 'financial contributions' by a government or public body; that is, a direct transfer of funds or the non-collection

---

[14] COM, Communication 2013/C 332/01 on State aid for films and other audiovisual works [21] and [23]. Transmedia storytelling (also known as multi-platform storytelling or cross-media storytelling) is the technique of telling stories across multiple platforms and formats using digital technologies, such as films and games.

[15] From academic literature, see also Kliemann and Stehmann (2013); Chirico and Gaal (2014).

[16] COM, Communication COM(2010) 2020 final, Europe 2020, A strategy for smart, sustainable and inclusive growth, p. 14.

[17] COM, Communication COM(2010) 245 final to the European Parliament, the Council, the European Economic and Social Committee and the Committee of the Regions, A Digital Agenda for Europe.

[18] COM, Communication 2013/C 25/01: EU Guidelines for the application of State aid rules in relation to the rapid deployment of broadband networks [1].

[19] COM, Communication 2013/C 25/01: EU Guidelines for the application of State aid rules in relation to the rapid deployment of broadband networks. For the purposes of state aid assessment, the guidelines distinguish between basic and NGA networks.

of government revenue, which confers a benefit to a certain enterprise.[20] State subsidies as a positive state intervention – in contrast to the 'negative' barriers on foreign goods or services[21] – are a still largely underdeveloped aspect of multilateral trade law.[22] Within the framework of the GATS, state subsidies are seen as 'measures by Members affecting trade in services' (Article I(1)) and are thus covered by the non-discrimination obligations.[23] Since the GATS obligations only apply to sectors in which a state has made a commitment, EU state aid in the audiovisual services sector does not have to be compatible with the GATS obligations, as the EU has not made a commitment in this sector. Yet the EU has made such commitments in the telecommunications sector. Discriminatory subsidies by the EU or a Member State in this sector disadvantaging foreign competitors are thus open to GATS disciplines. In addition, Article XV of the GATS includes a declaratory statement in which Member States recognise the distortive effects of subsidies on trade in services. Furthermore, the states shall enter into negotiations to develop the multilateral disciplines to avoid such trade-distortive effects.

Yet subsidies granted to media undertakings also have to be compatible with the rules of the GATT and the WTO Agreement on Subsidies and Countervailing Measures (SCM Agreement), if applicable.[24] Subsidies for the domestic film industry or for newspapers are in conflict with the principle of national treatment set out in Article III GATT 1994, which prohibits discriminatory measures against 'like products' from other contracting parties that are intended to protect domestic production. Only the direct payment of subsidies exclusively to domestic producers are justified under Article III(8)(b) GATT 1994. Indirect forms of subsidies, such as tax remittances and fiscal measures, are thus challengeable.[25] For example, in the *Canada – Periodicals* case, the WTO Appellate Body found that state-funded postal rates to protect the domestic magazine industry had not been paid directly to domestic magazine producers and could thus not be justified under Article III(8)(b) GATT 1994.[26]

Moreover, subsidies have to be in accordance with the further reaching SCM Agreement, under which a country can use the WTO's dispute-settlement procedure to seek the withdrawal of the subsidy or the removal of its adverse effects. The SCM Agreement recognises three basic categories of subsidies: those that are prohibited, those that are actionable and those that are not actionable, hence allowed. Article 3 of the SCM Agreement outrightly prohibits export subsidies and subsidies upon the use of domestic over imported goods. By contrast, actionable subsidies are not

---

[20] Articles 1 and 2 of the SCM Agreement.
[21] See Chapter 12.
[22] Keller (2011, p. 174).
[23] Keller (2011, pp. 175, 476).
[24] On the classification of films within the WTO rules, see Chapter 2. With regard to film subsidies in particular, see Pauwels et al. (2007, p. 32).
[25] Pauwels et al. (2007, p. 32).
[26] Canada – Certain measures concerning periodicals [1997] WT/DS31/AB/R.

prohibited *per se*, but they are subject to challenge, either through the WTO's dispute-settlement procedure or through countervailing action. A subsidy is actionable if it causes 'adverse effects to the interests of other Members'. Article 5 distinguishes three kinds of such 'adverse effects'. The first kind is 'injury to the domestic industry of another Member', which is the sole basis for imposing a countervailing duty.[27] This clause plays hardly any particular role for media subsidies; nor does the second kind of adverse effects, the nullification or impairment of benefits accruing directly or indirectly to other Members under GATT 1994. Yet subsidies for the media industry may constitute a 'serious prejudice to the interests of another Member' as the third form of adverse effect. A 'serious prejudice' shall be deemed to exist in those cases mentioned in Article 6 of the SCM Agreement. The main difficulty for a complaining Member will be to establish the facts causing the adverse trade effects arising from subsidisation. This is currently rather unlikely for US productions because of their dominant position on the world market, but more likely for less dominant film-producing countries such as India.[28]

IV EU Law

Within the EU, one needs to distinguish between aid granted by the EU, and aid granted by the Member States (state aid). Articles 107 and 108 TFEU do not apply to aid that is funded exclusively from EU resources; the Articles only apply to aid granted by Member States or through state resources.

1 Aid Granted by the EU

EU aid includes measures such as the European Structural Funds according to Article 175(1) TFEU, agricultural funds according to Article 40(2) TFEU and, with particular relevance for the media, cultural aid within the meaning of Article 167(5) TFEU. Those aids do not have to fulfil the requirements of Articles 107 and 108 TFEU, but have to be compatible only with the relevant provisions of the TFEU as well as with WTO law. An example for EU funding based on Article 167(5) TFEU (ex Article 150(4) EC Treaty) is the Creative Europe Programme (2014 to 2020).[29] This programme offers a variety of funding schemes targeting different areas of the audiovisual sector, such as producers, distributors, operators in new digital technologies and organisers of film festivals. The programme particularly promotes non-national European films.

---

[27] A 'countervailing duty' is 'a special duty levied for the purpose of offsetting any subsidy bestowed directly or indirectly upon the manufacture, production or export of any merchandise, as provided for in [Article VI(3) GATT 1994]' (Article 10 fn. 36 SCM Agreement).

[28] Pauwels et al. (2007, p. 32).

[29] Regulation (EU) No. 1295/2013 of the European Parliament and of the Council of 11 December 2013 establishing the Creative Europe Programme (2014 to 2020) and repealing Decisions No. 1718/2006/EC, No. 1855/2006/EC and No. 1041/2009/EC, OJ L 347/221.

It is possible to cumulate EU and national aids; that is, a project may receive support by both EU and Member State's funds. In those cases of co-financing, the aids will each be subject to their own set of rules: the EU funds to the applicable Treaty provisions, and the state aid to Articles 107 and 108 TFEU and the specific regulations. Furthermore, funding originating from European sources is to be regarded as coming from 'state resources', and thus will be subject to Articles 107 to 109 TFEU, if those monies are allocated under the control and discretion of a Member State.[30]

2 Definition of State Aid

Article 107(1) TFEU provides:

> Save as otherwise provided in the Treaties, any aid granted by a Member State or through State resources in any form whatsoever which distorts or threatens to distort competition by favouring certain undertakings or the production of certain goods shall, in so far as it affects trade between Member States, be incompatible with the internal market.

If the prerequisites of Article 107(1) TFEU are fulfilled, then the state aid has to be notified to the European Commission under Article 108(3) TFEU. The Commission will then decide on the compatibility of the aid with EU law.

a Aid

Article 107(1) does not define the term 'aid' itself, but relies on its interpretation by the European Commission and, eventually, by the Court of Justice. The concept of 'aid' is rather broad, as is indicated by the words 'in any form whatsoever' in Article 107(1) TFEU. It includes 'not only positive benefits, but also measures which, in various forms, mitigate the charges which are normally included in the budget of an undertaking'.[31] The concept of aid is thus wider than that of a subsidy under WTO law. Any economic advantage that a company would not have obtained in the normal course of business under market conditions may constitute an aid.[32] Moreover, Article 107(1) TFEU does not distinguish according to the causes or aims of the measures of state intervention concerned, but defines them according to their effects.[33] An aid may

---

[30] See, for instance, COM, Decision C(2006)5492 final of 22 November 2006, State Aid N 157/2006 – United Kingdom, South Yorkshire Digital Region Broadband Project [29]; Decision C (2010)4862 of 12 July 2010, State aid N 53/2010 – Germany, Federal framework programme on duct support [45].

[31] See, for example, ECJ, Case C-143/99 [2001] Adria-Wien Pipeline and Wietersdorfer & Peggauer Zementwerke [38]; Case C-501/00 [2004] Spain v. Commission [90]; Case C-222/04 [2006] Ministero dell'Economia e delle Finanze v. Cassa di Risparmio di Firenze SpA [131].

[32] See, for example, ECJ, Case C-39/94 [1996] SFEI and others [60]; Case C-342/96 [1999] Spain v. Commission [41] Case T-46/97 [2000] SIC – Sociedade Independente de Comunicação SA v. Commission [78]; COM, Vademecum – Community law on State aid, 30 September 2008, p. 6.

[33] See, for example, Case C-56/93 [1996] Belgium v. Commission [79]; Case T-46/97 [2000] SIC – Sociedade Independente de Comunicação SA v. Commission [83].

consist of, for instance, grants or interest rate rebates, capital injections, loan guarantees, tax exemptions, tax reductions or the postponement of a payment normally due.

Those economic advantages only constitute state aid if they are not receivable in the normal course of business; for example, if a company buys or rents publicly owned land, sells land to the state, enjoys privileged access to public infrastructure or obtains risk capital from the state, on favourable terms. To establish whether the Member State's support confers an advantage, the Commission and the Court of Justice apply the 'market economy investor principle' (MEIP) test. Accordingly, the state action does not confer an advantage on the undertaking if the measure is comparable to the conduct of a private investor, guided by the longer term prospects of profitability of the capital invested.[34] The test is whether, in similar circumstances, a private investor of a size comparable to that of the bodies administering the public sector might have provided capital of such an amount.[35] Although the behaviour of a private investor that is being compared with the public investor's behaviour need not be the conduct of an ordinary investor laying out capital with a view to realising a profit in the relatively short term, it must at least be the behaviour of a private holding company or a private group of undertakings pursuing a structural policy and guided by prospects of profitability in the longer term.[36] This MEIP test must be assessed in relation to the attitude of a private investor at the time when the decision is taken, having regard to the information available and developments foreseeable at that time, and not with the benefit of hindsight.[37]

To illustrate, the following measures have been regarded as aid in the media sector: grants and financial injections to broadcasters and broadband network operators,[38] state guarantees for media companies,[39] exemption of a public service broadcaster from registration charges relating to its transformation into a public limited company,[40] rescheduling of a public service broadcaster's social security debt,[41]

---

[34] See, for example, ECJ, Case C-303/88 [1991] Italy v. Commission [20]; Case C-256/97 [1999] Déménagements-Manutention Transport SA (DMT) [24]. With regard to the application of the market economy investor principle in the broadband field, see, for example, COM, Decision C (2007)6072 final of 11 December 2007, State aid case C 53/2006, Investment by the city of Amsterdam in a fibre-to-the home (FttH) network [87 ff].

[35] See, for example, Case C-261/89 [1991] Italy v. Commission [8]; Joined Cases C-278/92 to C-280/92 [1994] Spain v. Commission [21].

[36] COM, Decision C(2011)2612 of 20 April 2011 on the measures implemented by Denmark (C 2/03) for TV2/Danmark [139].

[37] See, for example, ECJ, Case T-16/96 [1998] Cityflyer [76].

[38] See, for example, COM, Decision C(2011)8121 of 10 November 2011, State aid – SA.33438 (2011/N), SA.33440 (2011/N), SA.33441 (2011/N), SA.33439 (2011/N), SA 30851 (2011/N), Broadband network project in Eastern Poland [56]; State aid N 596/2009 – Italy, Bridging the digital divide in Lombardia [36].

[39] See, for example, CJEU, Joined Cases C-399/10 P and C-401/10 P [2013] Bouygues Télécom SA [107]; COM, Decision C(2007)1761 of 24 April 2007, State aid E 3/2005 (ex-CP 2/2003, CP 232/2002, CP 43/2003, CP 243/2004 and CP 195/2004) – Financing of public service broadcasters in Germany [153].

[40] See, for example, COM, Decision 2012/365/EU of 20 December 2011 on the State aid C 85/01 on ad hoc measures implemented by Portugal in favour of RTP [124].

[41] See, for example, COM, Decision 2012/365/EU of 20 December 2011 on the State aid C 85/01 on ad hoc measures implemented by Portugal in favour of RTP [130].

press subsidies,[42] loans granted to a technically bankrupt public service broadcaster with an interest rate below market conditions and without asset-backed securities,[43] financial assistance for the switch-over from analogue to digital terrestrial television,[44] license fees for public service broadcasters,[45] the acceptance of late payments from a broadcaster by the public broadcasting network operator for using the broadcasting network,[46] grants awarded to selected film productions and tax reductions to films,[47] subsidies to promote the purchase of digital decoders,[48] aid to film distribution or to cinemas[49] and state investments into the broadband network that is subsequently put at the disposal of electronic communication operators selected by a tender procedure.[50]

However, the application of the private investor test is difficult in those cases in which the state provides compensation for an undertaking entrusted with the operation of services of general economic interest that would by themselves not be economically viable. Therefore, the state needs to set an incentive, such as by way of compensation, that somebody provides those services in the first place. Article 106(2) TFEU stipulates that such undertakings are principally subject to the rules contained in the TFEU, including the state aid rules. However, these provisions shall only apply 'in so far as the application of such rules does not obstruct the performance, in law or in fact, of the particular tasks assigned to them'. The seminal question is, therefore, whether the application of the state aid provisions to media undertakings 'obstructs the performance' of the particular tasks assigned to them, namely to provide services of general economic interest (SGEI). For example, the Member States often argue that the deployment of a broadband network or the provision of public service broadcasting constitute SGEI within the meaning of Article 106(2) TFEU.

---

[42] COM, Decision C (2008)1839 final of 20 May 2008, State aid N 537/2007 – Finland; Decision C (2010)4941 final of 20 July2010, State aid E 4/2008 (ex-N 450/2008) – Sweden, Aid to the press. On press subsidies, see Schizer (2010); Psychogiopoulou (2012).

[43] See, for example, COM, Decision 2012/365/EU of 20 December 2011 on the State aid C 85/01 on ad hoc measures implemented by Portugal in favour of RTP [132].

[44] See, for example, COM, Decision 2006/513/EC of 9 November 2005 on the State Aid which the Federal Republic of Germany has implemented for the introduction of digital terrestrial television (DVB-T) in Berlin-Brandenburg; ECJ, Case T-8/06 [2009] FAB v. Commission.

[45] See, for example, COM, Decision C(2003)3371fin of 1 October 2003, State aid No. N 37/2003 – United Kingdom, BBC Digital Curriculum [21]; Decision C(2002)1886fin of 22 May 2002, State aid N 631/2001 – United Kingdom, BBC licence fee [21].

[46] See, for example, COM, Decision 2005/406/EC of 15 October 2003 on ad hoc measures implemented by Portugal for RTP [102]; ECJ, Case T-442/03 [2008] SIC v. Commission [93]. Yet in this case, the economic advantage could not be imputed to the Portuguese Republic.

[47] See COM, Communication 2013/C 332/01 on State aid for films and other audiovisual works [15].

[48] CJEU, Case C-403/10 P [2011] Mediaset v. Commission.

[49] See COM, Communication 2013/C 332/01 on State aid for films and other audiovisual works [16].

[50] See COM, Decision C (2010)4862 of 12 July 2010, State aid N 53/2010 – Germany, Federal framework programme on duct support [45 ff]; Decision C(2011)7285 final of 19 October 2010, State Aid N 330/2010 – France Programme national 'très haut debit' – Volet B [38].

The Court of Justice developed the relevant principles for state measures compensating for the services provided by the recipient undertaking in order to provide SGEI in its seminal *Altmark Trans* judgment. If the criteria established in *Altmark Trans* are met, the measure escapes classification as state aid according to Article 107(1) TFEU and is therefore not subject to prior notification and approval by the Commission. If the *Altmark Trans* criteria are not met, then Article 106(2) TFEU may still serve as a rule *justifying* the state aid, but the state aid would then have to be notified to European Commission. The conditions established in *Altmark Trans* are:

1 The recipient undertaking must have public service obligations to discharge, and the obligations must be clearly defined.
2 The parameters on the basis of which the compensation is calculated must be established in advance in an objective and transparent manner, to avoid it conferring an economic advantage that may favour the recipient undertaking over competing undertakings.
3 The compensation must not exceed what is necessary to cover all or part of the costs incurred in the discharge of the public service obligations, taking into account the relevant receipts and a reasonable profit for discharging those obligations.
4 a) The undertaking that is to discharge public service obligations has to be chosen pursuant to a public procurement procedure which would allow for the selection of the tenderer capable of providing those services at the least cost to the community, or
b) the level of compensation needed must be determined on the basis of an analysis of the costs that a typical undertaking, well run and adequately equipped so as to be able to meet the necessary public service requirements, would have incurred in discharging those obligations, taking into account the relevant receipts and a reasonable profit for discharging the obligations.[51]

The first criterion is whether the recipient undertaking has clearly defined public service obligations to discharge; in other words, whether it is entrusted with an SGEI. The concept of service of general economic interest is nowhere officially defined. The European Commission describes it as 'an evolving notion that depends, among other things, on the needs of citizens, technological and market developments and

---

[51] ECJ, Case C-280/00 [2004] Altmark Trans GmbH [89–93]. The European Commission set out details of its assessment practice regarding Member States' measures to support SGEI in its so-called 'SGEI package': COM, Communication 2012/C 8/02 on the application of the European Union State aid rules to compensation granted for the provision of services of general economic interest; Decision of 20 December 2011 on the application of Article 106(2) of the Treaty on the Functioning of the European Union to State aid in the form of public service compensation granted to certain undertakings entrusted with the operation of services of general economic interest, OJ L 7/3; Communication on a European Union framework for State aid in the form of public service compensation (2011), OJ C 8/15; Commission Regulation (EU) No. 360/2012 of 25 April 2012 on the application of Articles 107 and 108 of the Treaty on the Functioning of the European Union to de minimis aid granted to undertakings providing services of general economic interest, OJ L 114/8.

social and political preferences in the Member State concerned'.[52] The best approach to understanding a concept is usually to start with a literal interpretation of its terms. However, the term 'general economic interest' is actually misleading.

First, a service of general economic interest has to be *economic*. The service itself has to be of an economic nature, not the interest to which it serves. The interest can be of an economic nature, but it can also be of a cultural or other public concern. As the Court of Justice explained in *SIC v. Commission* (2008):

> Although the public service of broadcasting is considered to be an SGEI and not a service of general non-economic interest, it must none the less be pointed out that that classification as an SGEI is explained more by the de facto impact of public service broadcasting on the otherwise competitive and commercial broadcasting sector, than by an alleged commercial dimension to broadcasting.[53]

Instead of 'services of general economic interest', it would thus be more appropriate to speak of an 'economic service of general interest'. The concept of SGEI thus excludes non-economic services.

Second, the concept of SGEI refers to services of an economic nature of a *general interest*. As such, the concept excludes services that are concerned only with managing private interests.[54] Apart from that, Member States enjoy a wide discretion in defining a given service as an SGEI. The Commission's competence in this respect is limited to checking whether the Member State has made a manifest error when defining the service as an SGEI.[55] With a view to the media in particular, the Court of Justice has held that the operation of the public communications network[56] and public service broadcasting[57] fall under the definition of a service of general economic interest. Public service broadcasting is, according to the Court, 'directly related to the democratic, social and cultural needs of each society'.[58]

However, Member States are not allowed to attach public service obligations to services that are already provided or can be provided satisfactorily and under conditions consistent with the public interest by undertakings operating under normal market conditions.[59] Therefore, in media sectors in which private operators already provide competitive media services, a publicly funded media service cannot be

---

[52] COM, Communication 2012/C 8/02 on the application of the European Union State aid rules to compensation granted for the provision of services of general economic interest [45].

[53] ECJ, Case T-442/03 [2008] SIC v. Commission [153].

[54] ECJ, Case 127/73 [1974] BRT v. SABAM [23].

[55] ECJ, Case T-289/03 [2008] BUPA and others v. Commission [166]; Case T-17/02 [2005] Fred Olsen [216].

[56] See ECJ, Case C-18/88 [1991] RTT v. GB-Inno-BM [16].

[57] ECJ,Case 155/73 [1974] Sacchi [14]; Case C-260/89 [1991] ERT v. DEP and others [10]; Case T-69/89 [1991] Radio Telefis Eireann v. Commission [82].

[58] ECJ, Case T-442/03 [2008] SIC v. Commission [153].

[59] COM, Communication 2012/C 8/02 on the application of the European Union State aid rules to compensation granted for the provision of services of general economic interest [48]. Compare ECJ, Case C-205/99 [2001] Analir [71].

entrusted with providing SGEI. For example, if private investors are able to provide adequate broadband coverage, a public service compensation may not be granted to an undertaking entrusted with the operation of a broadband network.[60] Moreover, the provider of a network to be deployed on an SGEI basis will not be able to refuse wholesale access to the infrastructure on a discretionary or discriminatory basis.[61]

For an undertaking to have been *entrusted* with the operation of a service of general economic interest, there must have been an act of public authority,[62] including legislative and administrative acts. Identifying the scope of the 'particular tasks' assigned to the undertaking is important in order to establish which restrictions are necessary for the performance of those tasks. In its decisions on the measures implemented by Denmark for TV2/Danmark and on the financing of public service broadcasters in Germany, the Commission found the licence fees for public service broadcasters lacking a sufficiently clear and precise definition of the public service remit, especially with regard to the offering of new media services and additional digital channels.[63] Consequently, these licence fee schemes could not be excluded from Article 107(1) TFEU by virtue of *Altmark Trans*.

Under the second *Altmark Trans* criterion, the parameters for the compensation by a Member State for the loss incurred by an undertaking must have been established beforehand. In practice, most state aids to public service broadcasters fail to meet this requirement.[64] First, ad hoc investment grants and capital injections granted *a posteriori* to enable media undertakings to cope with the deterioration in their economic situation are *per se* not on the basis of parameters established in advance in an objective and transparent manner.[65] Second, even if the amount of the compensation is set in advance, the second *Altmark Trans* criterion requires that the parameters used to calculate the compensation must themselves be established beforehand. For example, in its second decision on the measures implemented by Denmark for TV2/Danmark, the Commission found that the economic reports prepared by a consultancy firm

---

[60] COM, Communication 2013/C 25/01: EU Guidelines for the application of State aid rules in relation to the rapid deployment of broadband networks [21].

[61] COM, Communication 2013/C 25/01: EU Guidelines for the application of State aid rules in relation to the rapid deployment of broadband networks [22].

[62] See ECJ, Case 127/73 [1974] BRT v. SABAM [20]; Case 66/86 [1989] Ahmed Saeed Flugreisen v. Zentrale zur Bekämpfung unlauteren Wettbewerbs [55].

[63] See, for example, COM, Decision C(2011)2612 of 20 April 2011 on the measures implemented by Denmark (C 2/03) for TV2/Danmark [104]; COM, Decision C(2007)1761 of 24 April 2007, State aid E 3/2005 (ex-CP 2/2003, CP 232/2002, CP 43/2003, CP 243/2004 and CP 195/2004) – Financing of public service broadcasters [163].

[64] See, for example, COM, Decision C(2007)1761 of 24 April 2007, State aid E 3/2005 (ex-CP 2/2003, CP 232/2002, CP 43/2003, CP 243/2004 and CP 195/2004) – Financing of public service broadcasters in Germany [164]; Decision C(2005)1166 fin of 20 April 2005, State Aid E 10/2005 – France Redevance radiodiffusion [24], confirmed by ECJ, Case T-354/05 [2009] TF1 v. Commission [142–146].

[65] See COM, Decision 2004/838/EC of 10 December 2003 on State aid implemented by France for France 2 and France 3 [55]; Decision 2012/365/EU of 20 December 2011 on the State aid C 85/01 on ad hoc measures implemented by Portugal in favour of RTP [146].

only gave estimates of the amount of advertising revenue accruing to TV2 (i.e., the income side). However, they were silent on the cost side of the compensation calculation.[66] In addition, there was no indication of the parameters to be used to calculate the compensation.[67] Therefore, the measures could not meet the second *Altmark Trans* criterion.

According to the third criterion, the compensation must not exceed what is necessary to cover all or part of the costs incurred in the discharge of the public service obligations, taking into account the relevant receipts and a reasonable profit for discharging those obligations. This criterion is an expression of the principle of proportionality. It serves to ensure that the recipient does not receive an advantage that distorts or threatens to distort competition.

The fourth *Altmark Trans* criterion is twofold. Either the undertaking that is to discharge public service obligations has to be chosen pursuant to a public procurement procedure that would allow for the selection of the tenderer capable of providing those services at the least cost to the community. The reason why financing schemes for public service broadcasting usually fail this prong of the fourth *Altmark Trans* criterion is that most public service broadcasters had already been established long before the *Altmark Trans* ruling was issued.[68] Alternatively, the level of compensation needed has to be determined on the basis of an analysis of the costs that a typical undertaking, well run and adequately equipped so as to be able to meet the necessary public service requirements, would have incurred in discharging those obligations, taking into account the relevant receipts and a reasonable profit for discharging the obligations. The Commission is very restrictive in the application of this criterion. With regard to the German licence fee, for example, the Commission decided that the procedure of the independent German commission for the determination of the financial needs of public service broadcasters (KEF) is not equivalent to an analysis of the costs of an efficient operator, in particular since the KEF procedure is based on the financial *needs* of the public service broadcasters, and not their *efficiency*.[69] In particular, the Commission criticised that KEF was not entitled to carry out market comparisons to evaluate the costs of an efficient operator. Germany had argued that the Commission cannot apply the fourth *Altmark Trans* condition in cases where there is no comparable private operator who could be used as a benchmark, since they did not bear the same public service obligations.[70] Yet the Commission did not

[66] COM, Decision C(2011)2612 of 20 April 2011 on the measures implemented by Denmark (C 2/03) for TV2/Danmark [115].

[67] COM, Decision C(2011)2612 of 20 April 2011 on the measures implemented by Denmark (C 2/03) for TV2/Danmark [116].

[68] Harrison and Woods (2007, p. 304).

[69] COM, Decision C(2007)1761 of 24 April 2007, State aid E 3/2005 (ex-CP 2/2003, CP 232/2002, CP 43/2003, CP 243/2004 and CP 195/2004) – Financing of public service broadcasters in Germany [166].

[70] COM, Decision C(2007)1761 of 24 April 2007, State aid E 3/2005 (ex-CP 2/2003, CP 232/2002, CP 43/2003, CP 243/2004 and CP 195/2004) – Financing of public service broadcasters in Germany [58].

agree that it is impossible and purely hypothetical to establish the costs of an efficient operator as a benchmark: the various cost items of the public service broadcaster may 'very well be benchmarked against the costs incurred by other private competitors, while taking into account the specific public service obligations'.[71] Furthermore, as far as the comparison was concerned, the Commission argued in another case that a comparison with a 'typical' broadcaster is necessary, not with another (domestic or foreign) public service broadcaster.[72] Moreover, in its 2011 Decision on the measures implemented by Denmark for TV2/Danmark, the Commission criticised that the reports on which the licence fees were established dealt with the outlook for the advertising market as well as the amount of TV2's future advertising revenue, but included no analysis of the costs that a typical undertaking, well run and adequately provided with means of production, would have incurred in discharging public service obligations.[73]

In practice, financing schemes for public service broadcasters have so far failed to meet the fourth *Altmark Trans* requirement.[74] To be sure, in *TV 2/Danmark A/S v. Commission*, the Court of First Instance found that the Commission's rejection of the *Altmark Trans* criteria lacked a sufficiently 'serious analysis'.[75] Yet the Court's examination only dealt with the Commission's failure to state reasons, as required by (now) Article 296(2) TFEU. In its subsequent decision, the Commission rejected the *Altmark Trans* criteria again.[76]

The deeper reason why state funding for public service broadcasters fails to meet the *Altmark Trans* criteria is arguably that the Member States, for reasons of media independence, *cannot* be sufficiently precise about their public service broadcasters' public service obligations within the narrow scope of *Altmark Trans*. This reveals a significant conflict between media freedom and state aid rules: under state aid rules, it should be the Member States, and not the broadcasters themselves, which

---

[71] COM, Decision C(2007)1761 of 24 April 2007, State aid E 3/2005 (ex-CP 2/2003, CP 232/2002, CP 43/2003, CP 243/2004 and CP 195/2004) – Financing of public service broadcasters in Germany [168]; see also Decision C(2011)2612 of 20 April 2011 on the measures implemented by Denmark (C 2/03) for TV2/Danmark [127].

[72] COM, Decision C(2011)2612 of 20 April 2011 on the measures implemented by Denmark (C 2/03) for TV2/Danmark [132].

[73] COM, Decision C(2011)2612 of 20 April 2011 on the measures implemented by Denmark (C 2/03) for TV2/Danmark [124].

[74] See, for example COM, Decision 2012/365/EU of 20 December 2011 on the State aid C 85/01 on ad hoc measures implemented by Portugal in favour of RTP [145]; Decision C(2007)1761 of 24 April 2007, State aid E 3/2005 (ex-CP 2/2003, CP 232/2002, CP 43/2003, CP 243/2004 and CP 195/2004) – Financing of public service broadcasters in Germany [166]; Decision C(2005)1166 fin of 20 April 2005, State Aid E 10/2005 – France Redevance radiodiffusion [25], confirmed by ECJ, Case T-354/05 [2009] TF1 v. Commission [142–146].

[75] See ECJ, Joined Cases T-309/04, T-317/04, T-329/04 and T-336/04 [2008] TV 2/Danmark A/S v. Commission [228].

[76] COM, Decision C(2011)2612 of 20 April 2011 on the measures implemented by Denmark (C 2/03) for TV2/Danmark.

determine the public service remit; under media freedom, it must be the broadcasters that determine the content of their programme, and not the government. Thus, in order to both escape classification as state aid under the *Altmark Trans* criteria and to avoid violations of media freedom, Member States would have to act in the very narrow margin between eligible determination of the public service remit and prohibited violation of broadcasters' independence; an area that has, as apparent, not yet been found. As a consequence, compensations for public service broadcasters have to be justified under Article 106(2) TFEU – under the auspices of the Commission.

b Granted by a Member State or through State Resources

Article 107 TFEU only covers measures involving a transfer of state resources. The aid does, however, not necessarily need to be granted directly by the state. It may also be granted by a 'state emanation', that is, 'a body, whatever its legal form, which has been made responsible, pursuant to a measure adopted by the state, for providing a public service under the control of the state and has for that purpose special powers beyond that which result from the normal rules applicable in relations between individuals'.[77] A 'state emanation' would thus be, for example, a nationalised private company or a private bank entrusted with the responsibility to manage a state-funded aid scheme. Finally, domestic media authorities acting independently from governmental influence are to be considered 'state' within the meaning of Article 107(1) TFEU.[78]

Depending on the financing modus, it can be particularly problematic whether the financing of public service broadcasting is an aid granted by a Member State or through state resources. In those cases in which a public service broadcaster is financed directly though the state budget, the existence of state aid is uncontroversial. This is however different in licence fee systems in which the contribution levied on the broadcasting recipient is transferred directly to the broadcaster's purse without becoming part of the state's budget. The ECJ's decision *PreussenElektra* seemed to suggest that such a transfer system would not constitute a state aid. In this case, a German law on feeding electricity from renewable energy sources into the public grid required electricity distributors to purchase electricity generated from renewable sources at a fixed minimum price from private companies producing renewable energy. While the Court acknowledged that that the purchase obligation imposed on private electricity supply undertakings confers an advantage on companies producing renewable electricity, the obligation does not involve any direct or indirect transfer of state resources to such companies.[79]

One could thus conclude that a licence fee system in which consumers are under a legal obligation to pay directly to an independent fee collection authority does not

---

[77] ECJ, Case C-188/89 [1990] Foster and others v. British Gas [20].

[78] COM, Decision 2006/513/EC of 9 November 2005 on the State Aid which the Federal Republic of Germany has implemented for the introduction of digital terrestrial television (DVB-T) in Berlin-Brandenburg [52].

[79] ECJ, Case C-379/98 [2001] PreussenElektra AG v. Schleswag AG [59].

involve state resources and hence does not constitute state aid either. But the ECJ's decision in *Bayerischer Rundfunk* then took another route. In this case, the ECJ had to decide whether the German public broadcasters financed not through the state budget but through a licence fee scheme, were 'financed, for the most part, by the State' within the meaning of Article 1(b) third indent of Directive 92/50.[80] Although the case pertained to the interpretation of a directive on public procurement and not to state aid, the Court's conclusions can nonetheless be transferred to state aid, as the concept 'financed by the State' within the meaning of the Directive is functionally equivalent to the notion of 'state resources' under Article 107(1) TFEU. The Court emphasised that the licence fee has its origin in German legislation, here the State Treaty on broadcasting, in other words in a measure of the state. In contrast to *PreussenElektra* (to which the Court did not even refer in its decision), the fee as such and the amount to be paid had been provided for and imposed by statute and were not the result of any contractual arrangement entered into by those bodies and the customers. Liability to pay that fee arose out of the mere fact of possession of a TV receiver and not in consideration of actual use of the services provided by the broadcasters.[81] In addition, there had been a public agency for the collection of fees in place, which enforced the licence fee obligations. Monies from a licence fee system, even if it does not involve a financial burden for the state budget, are thus to be regarded as forming part of state resources.[82] A licence fee levied on private households or broadcasting recipients constitutes a direct cash inflow for the public service broadcaster, similar to commercial revenues, for which the undertaking does not need to compete on the market. Consequently, such a licence fee provides an economic and financial advantage to the beneficiary public service broadcaster compared with other competitors not receiving the same funds, and thus has to be regarded as an economic advantage.[83]

By contrast to licence fee schemes, the *PreussenElektra* jurisprudence is relevant for legal obligations introduced by state legislation but imposed on other market participants. For example, obligations imposed on owners of communication infrastructure to relay public service programmes through their infrastructure ('must-carry' obligations) do not confer any financial advantage to the public service broadcaster

---

[80] Council Directive 92/50/EEC of 18 June 1992 relating to the coordination of procedures for the award of public service contracts, OJ L 209/1.

[81] ECJ, Case C-337/06 [2007] Bayerischer Rundfunk and others v. GEWA [41]; Joined Cases T-309/04, T-317/04, T-329/04 and T-336/04 [2008] TV 2/Danmark A/S v. Commission [158–159]; COM, Decision C(2007)1761 of 24 April 2007, State aid E 3/2005 (ex-CP 2/2003, CP 232/2002, CP 43/2003, CP 243/2004 and CP 195/2004) – Financing of public service broadcasters in Germany [151].

[82] ECJ, Joined Cases T-309/04, T-317/04, T-329/04 and T-336/04 [2008] TV 2/Danmark A/S v. Commission [159]; CJEU, Joined Cases T-231/06 and T-237/06 [2010] Netherlands and Nederlandse Omroep Stichting (NOS) v. Commission [105]; from the Commission, see, for example, COM, Decision C(2007)1761 of 24 April 2007, State aid E 3/2005 (ex-CP 2/2003, CP 232/2002, CP 43/2003, CP 243/2004 and CP 195/2004) – Financing of public service broadcasters in Germany [143 ff].

[83] See COM, Decision SG(99) D/ 10201 of 14 December 1999, State aid No. NN 88/98 of 14 December 1999 – United Kingdom, Financing of a 24-hour advertising-free news channel out of the licence fee by the BBC [24].

from state resources; hence they do not constitute state aid.[84] The same applies to obligations for private network operators to coordinate their civil engineering works and/or to share part of their infrastructure, or for television operators to earmark a percentage of their operating revenue for the pre-funding of European cinematographic films and films made for television.[85]

c Favouring Certain Undertakings

The aid has to favour 'certain undertakings or the production of certain goods', Article 107(1) TFEU. The criterion of 'certain undertakings' consists of two components. First, the beneficiary has to be an undertaking. Second, the aid has to be selective ('*certain* undertakings').

The concept of an 'undertaking' encompasses 'every entity engaged in an economic activity, regardless of the legal status of the entity and the way in which it is financed'.[86] In turn, the concept of 'undertaking' does not cover private individuals, private households or the state itself. Public funding granted to individual journalists would thus not be considered a state aid. Yet since the concept of 'undertakings' only encompasses an economic activity, it is questionable whether public service broadcasters fall under this term. It is even more problematic whether *state* broadcasters entrusted with the provision of public service broadcasting have to be considered 'undertakings', as this concept does not cover the state itself. However, the concept of an undertaking covers any entity engaged in an economic activity *regardless* of the legal status of the entity. Public service broadcasters compete for viewers, which has an impact on advertising and sponsorship revenue for commercial broadcasters. This applies even if the broadcaster does not itself compete for such revenue, as is the case in single-funding schemes.[87] Furthermore, public service broadcasters are engaged in the production of audiovisual programmes and the purchase and sale of programme rights. Thus engaged in economic activities, public service broadcasters, including state broadcasters, have to be considered 'undertakings' within the meaning of Article 107(1) TFEU.[88]

---

[84] COM, Decision of 24 February 1999, Aid No. NN 70/98, 'State aid to public broadcasting channels "Kinderkanal and Phoenix"'; Decision C(2011)2612 of 20 April 2011 on the measures implemented by Denmark (C 2/03) for TV2/Danmark [99]. On 'must carry' obligations, see Chapter 5.

[85] On the former, see COM, Communication 2013/C 25/01: EU Guidelines for the application of State aid rules in relation to the rapid deployment of broadband networks [29]; on the latter, see ECJ, Case C-222/07 [2009] UTECA [43].

[86] See, for example, ECJ, Case C-41/90 [1991] Höfner and Elser v. Macrotron GmbH [21]; Joined Cases C-180/98 to C-184/98 [2000] Pavlov and others [74]; CJEU, Joined Cases T-231/06 and T-237/06 [2010] Netherlands and Nederlandse Omroep Stichting (NOS) v. Commission [92].

[87] COM, Decision C(2003)3371fin of 14 December 1999, State aid NN 88/98 – United Kingdom, Financing of a 24-hour advertising-free news channel out of the licence fee by the BBC [24]; Harrison and Woods (2007, p. 299).

[88] CJEU, Joined Cases T-231/06 and T-237/06 [2010] Netherlands and Nederlandse Omroep Stichting (NOS) v. Commission [105]; See, for example, COM, Decision 2004/339/EC of 15 October 2003 on the measures implemented by Italy for RAI SpA [84]; Decision C(2007)1761 of 24 April 2007, State aid E 3/2005 (ex-CP 2/2003, CP 232/2002, CP 43/2003, CP 243/2004 and CP 195/2004) – Financing of public service broadcasters in Germany [75].

Moreover, the aid has to favour *certain* undertakings. This refers to the selectivity of the measure. An aid is selective if it favours one undertaking over another that is in a comparable situation regarding the aim pursued with the measure.[89] Selectivity thus distinguishes state aid from general measures of tax or economic policy, which apply to all economic operators across the board. The selectivity criterion is also satisfied if the scheme applies to only a single part of the territory of a Member State, as is the case with regional aid schemes, or if it benefits a given sector (sectoral aid schemes).[90] Although undertakings benefiting from a sectoral aid scheme are not in direct competition with another undertaking, they may be in competition with the same sectors from other Member States. Rules that benefit the entire broadcasting sector of a particular Member State would thus be considered state aid.

d Distorting or Threatening to Distort Competition

Article 107(1) TFEU prohibits state aid that distorts 'or threatens to distort competition'. It is therefore not necessary that competition has been distorted; the danger or threat of distorting competition is sufficient. Moreover, it is not necessary that the beneficiaries of the measures used the funds they had received for the distortion of competition. Article 107(1) TFEU does not require anti-competitive *behaviour* of the beneficiary, but merely deals with the *effect* of state aid on competition.[91] Anti-competitive behaviour of the recipient can become relevant for the question of whether the state aid can be justified. Since aid of less than €200,000 is presumed not to significantly distort competition, it is exempted from the requirement to notify the European Commission in advance (*de minimis* rule).[92]

In particular, state aid granted to public service broadcasters has usually been regarded as distorting competition. The Commission set this out most elaborately in its decision on the financing of public service broadcasters in Germany (our case example): first, state aid granted to public service broadcasters distorts the competition for audience. It gives public service broadcasters a financial advantage that strengthens their position towards commercial broadcasters that offer broadcasting services and that need to finance their activities through commercial revenues. The audience are the determining factor for advertisement prices; an increase of the audience share of publicly financed broadcasters to the detriment of private competitors thus has a direct effect on the advertisement revenues of private operators.[93] Second, it distorts the competition for the acquisition of broadcasting rights, such as film or

---

[89] ECJ, Case C-222/04 [2006] Ministero dell'Economia e delle Finanze v. Cassa di Risparmio di Firenze SpA [135].

[90] See ECJ, Case C-172/03 [2005] Heiser [42].

[91] CJEU, Joined Cases T-231/06 and T-237/06 [2010] Netherlands and Nederlandse Omroep Stichting (NOS) v. Commission [121].

[92] See Commission Regulation (EC) No. 1998/2006 of 15 December 2006 on the application of Articles 87 and 88 of the Treaty to *de minimis* aid, OJ L 379/5.

[93] COM, Decision C(2007)1761 of 24 April 2007, State aid E 3/2005 (ex-CP 2/2003, CP 232/2002, CP 43/2003, CP 243/2004 and CP 195/2004) – Financing of public service broadcasters in Germany [184].

sports rights. While commercial operators need to entirely refinance their broadcasting rights through commercial revenues, public service broadcasters are publicly financed without the need to ensure the refinancing of the rights acquired.[94] Third, if public service broadcasters themselves are active in the film production market, they compete with other film producers. Fourth, public service broadcasters that also offer transmission facilities are in competition with other transmission operators. Eventually, public service broadcasters offering online services are in competition with private operators offering similar new media activities.[95]

The breadth of the Commission's notion of competition is most aptly illustrated by its decision on BBC News 24. Here the Commission held that a new news channel may be in competition even with channels that are not dedicated to news, as the presence of a new channel may influence the preferences of viewers to switch from other channels to watch the new news service.[96]

e Affecting Trade between Member States

Finally, state aid is only incompatible with the internal market insofar as it affects trade between Member States. Similar to the free movement provisions and Articles 101 and 102 TFEU, EU state aid law only applies if the case has an interstate trade dimension. For a state measure to be relevant under Article 107(1) TFEU, a direct impact on actual trade between Member States is not necessary. It is, in particular, not necessary that the beneficiary undertaking itself is involved in exporting, as long as it is involved in an economic activity and operates in a market in which there is trade between Member States. This would be the case, for example, if the measures put the recipient in a more favourable position compared with other undertakings that are themselves competing in intra-Union trade,[97] or if undertakings established in other Member States have less chance of exporting their products to the market in the Member State of the subsidised undertaking.[98]

Consequently, even the fact that the media service of a subsidised undertaking is intended solely for nationals of the Member State granting the aid does not prevent an effect on intra-EU trade, if the media service's competitors also sell to other

---

[94] COM, Decision C(2007)1761 of 24 April 2007, State aid E 3/2005 (ex-CP 2/2003, CP 232/2002, CP 43/2003, CP 243/2004 and CP 195/2004) – Financing of public service broadcasters in Germany [185].

[95] COM, Decision C(2007)1761 of 24 April 2007, State aid E 3/2005 (ex-CP 2/2003, CP 232/2002, CP 43/2003, CP 243/2004 and CP 195/2004) – Financing of public service broadcasters in Germany [189].

[96] COM, Decision SG(99) D/ 10201 of 14 December 1999, State aid No. NN 88/98 of 14 December 1999 – United Kingdom, Financing of a 24-hour advertising-free news channel out of the licence fee by the BBC [28].

[97] ECJ, Case C-730/79 [1980] Philip Morris Holland BV v. Commission [11]; C-303/88 [1991] Italy v. Commission [27]. For a media-related case, see COM, Decision SG(99) D/ 10201 of 14 December 1999, State aid No. NN 88/98 of 14 December 1999 – United Kingdom, Financing of a 24-hour advertising-free news channel out of the licence fee by the BBC [31].

[98] ECJ, Case C-75/97 [1999] Belgium v. Commission [47]; COM, Decision 2004/838/EC of 10 December 2003 on State aid implemented by France for France 2 and France 3 [59].

Member State markets or if providers from other Member States want to enter that market.[99] And even if the recipient undertaking is of relatively small size and the aid allocated to that undertaking is of relatively small amount, it does not exclude an effect on competition and trade, if the presence of a large number of small-sized undertakings is a feature of the market structure.[100] Finally, in order to evaluate the impact on trade between Member States, it is not necessary to demonstrate whether the disadvantage of a competitor is a direct consequence of the presence of the state aid. It is sufficient to argue that the *possibility* for an undertaking to offer a service on conditions that cannot be matched by any other commercial operator may put other undertakings in an unfavourable position.[101] In its decision on aid granted by the French state to an audiovisual production company, the Commission could therefore not be convinced by the French government's argument that only 10 per cent of the beneficiary's video production was intended for the international competitive market. This did not, according to the Commission, alter the fact that the financial aid placed the beneficiary in a better position to market its services in other Member States and that the aid made it more difficult for the services provided by foreign audiovisual companies to penetrate the French market.[102]

With regard to state aid to broadcasters in particular, a measure has been found to have a cross-border effect if:

- the markets in the acquisition and sale of programme rights have an international dimension. This is usually the case, even if rights and programmes are acquired for a particular geographic market;[103]
- the beneficiary is a broadcaster that is allowed to sell advertising space (dual-funding system); a subsidy to such a broadcaster has a cross-border effect 'especially for homogeneous linguistic areas across national boundaries';[104]
- the ownership structure of the broadcaster extends to more than one Member State;[105]

---

[99] See COM, Decision C(2003)3371fin of 1 October 2003, State aid No. N 37/2003 – United Kingdom, BBC Digital Curriculum [25]; Decision C(2002)1886fin of 22 May 2002, State aid No. N 631/2001 – United Kingdom, BBC licence fee [22].

[100] ECJ, Case C-298/00 P [2004] Italy v. Commission [55].

[101] COM, Decision SG(99) D/ 10201 of 14 December 1999, State aid No. NN 88/98 of 14 December 1999 – United Kingdom, Financing of a 24-hour advertising-free news channel out of the licence fee by the BBC [30].

[102] COM, Decision 97/238/EC of 2 October 1996 concerning aid granted by the French State to the audio-visual production company Société française de Production.

[103] COM, Decision 2004/838/EC of 10 December 2003 on State aid implemented by France for France 2 and France 3 [61]; COM, Communication 2009/C 257/01 on the application of State aid rules to public service broadcasting [22].

[104] COM, Decision 2004/838/EC of 10 December 2003 on State aid implemented by France for France 2 and France 3 [60].

[105] See CJEU, Joined Cases T-231/06 and T-237/06 [2010] Netherlands and Nederlandse Omroep Stichting (NOS) v. Commission [116]; COM, Decision 2004/838/EC of 10 December 2003 on State aid implemented by France for France 2 and France 3 [60]; Decision C(2007)1761 of 24 April 2007, State aid E 3/ 2005 (ex-CP 2/2003, CP 232/2002, CP 43/2003, CP 243/2004 and CP 195/2004) – Financing of public service broadcasters in Germany [182].

- the programme is distributed internationally;[106]
- services are provided on the internet, as the internet has a global reach;[107]
- the recipient broadcasters is engaged in the production of audiovisual programmes and the purchase and sale of programme rights, which takes place at an international level;[108]
- the broadcaster is not only active on the national broadcasting market but also on European markets, in particular through cooperation with other foreign broadcasters;[109]
- the broadcaster is in competition with private operators with an international ownership structure;[110]
- the broadcaster exchanges television programmes through the European Broadcasting Union and/or participates in the Eurovision system;[111] or
- the broadcaster is in competition with foreign operators that offer their programmes to the domestic market.[112]

Since markets for electronic communications services are open to competition between operators and service providers from different Member States (see Chapter 7), state intervention in the communication network sector affects service providers from other Member States by discouraging their establishment or by providing their services in the Member State in question.

3 The Commission Procedure in State Aid Cases

The EU supervision of state aid is based on a system of advance approval under Article 108(3) TFEU. However, according to Article 109 TFEU, the Council may determine categories of aid that are exempted from this notification requirement. The Commission may then adopt regulations exempting categories of state aid that the Council has determined from the Article 108(3) TFEU procedure (Article

---

[106] COM, Decision C(2005)1479 fin of 7 June 2005, State aid France – Chaîne française d'information internationale [31].

[107] COM, Decision C(2007)1761 of 24 April 2007, State aid E 3/2005 (ex-CP 2/2003, CP 232/2002, CP 43/2003, CP 243/2004 and CP 195/2004) – Financing of public service broadcasters in Germany [189].

[108] COM, Decision 2004/838/EC of 10 December 2003 on State aid implemented by France for France 2 and France 3 [60]; Decision C(2007)1761 of 24 April 2007, State aid E 3/2005 (ex-CP 2/2003, CP 232/2002, CP 43/2003, CP 243/2004 and CP 195/2004) – Financing of public service broadcasters in Germany [182].

[109] COM, Decision C(2007)1761 of 24 April 2007, State aid E 3/2005 (ex-CP 2/2003, CP 232/2002, CP 43/2003, CP 243/2004 and CP 195/2004) – Financing of public service broadcasters in Germany [186].

[110] COM, Decision C(2007)1761 of 24 April 2007, State aid E 3/2005 (ex-CP 2/2003, CP 232/2002, CP 43/2003, CP 243/2004 and CP 195/2004) – Financing of public service broadcasters in Germany [186].

[111] COM, Decision 2012/365/EU of 20 December 2011 on the State aid C 85/01 on ad hoc measures implemented by Portugal in favour of RTP [141].

[112] COM, Decision C(2007)1761 of 24 April 2007, State aid E 3/2005 (ex-CP 2/2003, CP 232/2002, CP 43/2003, CP 243/2004 and CP 195/2004) – Financing of public service broadcasters in Germany [186].

108(4) TFEU). Accordingly, the Council Regulation (EC) No. 994/98[113] has empowered the Commission to declare that certain measures may be exempted from the notification requirement. Among those categories are: aid to small and medium-sized enterprises (SMEs), aid in favour of research and development, certain categories of horizontal state aid, aid for innovation and, with particular relevance for the media, aid for broadband infrastructures as well as aid for culture and heritage conservation. On that basis, the Commission first adopted Commission Regulation (EC) No. 800/2008[114] and, after its expiration, the General Block Exemption Regulation 2014.[115] Where such an exemption does not apply, the Member State must notify the Commission of its plans to grant a new aid[116] or to alter an existing aid.[117] Article 108(3)3 TFEU prevents the Member State from putting the aid into effect before the Commission has authorised it (so-called 'standstill obligation').

Investment aid for broadband network development shall be exempted from the notification requirement of Article 108(3) TFEU if the requirements of Chapter I and of Article 52 of the Regulation are met. In particular:

- the notification threshold of maximum €70 million total costs per project must not be exceeded (Article 4(1)(y));
- the investment shall be located in areas where there is no infrastructure of the same category (either basic broadband or NGA network) and where no such infrastructure is likely to be developed on commercial terms within three years from the moment of publication of the planned aid measure (Article 52(3));
- the aid shall be allocated on the basis of an open, transparent and non-discriminatory competitive selection process respecting the principle of technology neutrality (Article 52(4));

---

[113] Council Regulation (EC) No. 994/98 of 7 May 1998 on the application of Articles 92 and 93 of the Treaty establishing the European Community to certain categories of horizontal State aid, OJ L 142/1; as amended by Council Regulation (EU) No. 733/2013 of 22 July 2013 amending Regulation (EC) No. 994/98 on the application of Articles 92 and 93 of the Treaty establishing the European Community to certain categories of horizontal State aid, OJ L 204/1.

[114] Commission Regulation (EC) No. 800/2008 of 6 August 2008 declaring certain categories of aid compatible with the common market in application of Articles 87 and 88 of the Treaty (General block exemption Regulation), prolonged by Commission Regulation (EU) No. 1224/2013 of 29 November 2013 amending Regulation (EC) No. 800/2008 as regards its period of application, OJ L 320/22.

[115] Commission Regulation (EU) No. 651/2014 of 17 June 2014 declaring certain categories of aid compatible with the internal market in application of Articles 107 and 108 of the Treaty, OJ L 187/1.

[116] Pursuant to Article 1(c) of Regulation 2015/1589, 'new aid' shall mean 'all aid ... which is not existing aid, including alterations to existing aid'.

[117] Article 1(b) of Regulation 2015/1589 defines 'existing aid'. Article 4(1) of Regulation 794/2004 defines an alteration of an existing aid as 'any change, other than a modification of a purely formal or administrative nature, which cannot affect the evaluation of the compatibility of the aid measure'. An increase in the original budget of an existing aid scheme of up to 20 per cent is not considered an alteration (Article 4(1) of Regulation 794/2004). On the alteration to existing aid and the change of existing aid into new aid, see ECJ, Joined Cases T-195/01 and T-207/01 [2002] Gibraltar v. Commission [111].

- the network operator shall offer the widest possible wholesale access under fair and non-discriminatory conditions (Article 52(5));
- the wholesale access price shall be based on the pricing principles set by the national regulatory authority and on benchmarks that prevail in other comparable, more competitive areas of the Member State or the EU taking into account the aid received by the network operator (Article 52(6));[118] and
- Member States shall put in place a monitoring and claw-back mechanism if the amount of aid granted to the project exceeds EUR 10 million (Article 52(7)).[119]

Aid for culture and heritage conservation may include aid schemes for audiovisual works. Such aid schemes may take the form of aid to the production of audiovisual works, pre-production aid and distribution aid (Article 54(3)). Aid schemes for audiovisual work are exempted from the application of Article 108(3) TFEU if:

- they do not exceed €50 million per scheme per year (Article 4(1)(aa));
- they support a cultural product (Article 54(2));
- the thresholds for territorial spending obligations[120] are met (Article 54(4));
- the aid intensity for the production does, subject to certain exceptions, not exceed 50 per cent of the eligible costs ((Article 54(6) to (8));
- the aid is not reserved for specific production activities or individual parts of the production value chain (Article 54(9)); and
- the aid is not discriminatory; this would be the case if it was reserved exclusively for nationals or if beneficiaries were required to have the status of undertaking established under national commercial law (Article 54(10)).

Regulations 2015/1589[121] and 794/2004[122] codify the procedural rules for state aid. In 2009, the Commission also adopted two codes of practice setting out how it would deal in the future with the administration of the state aid regime: the Code of Best Practice for the conduct of state aid control procedures,[123] and its Notice on a simplified procedure for treatment of certain types of state aid.[124] According to those rules,

---

[118] See Chapter 7.
[119] Article 4(1)(y) of the General Block Exemption Regulation 2014. Further general concerns are: Transparency (Article 5), incentive effect (Article 6), eligible costs (Article 7, here to be read in conjunction with Article 52(2)), the cumulation of aids (Article 8), and publication of the relevant information (Article 9).
[120] Territorial spending obligations are obligations imposed by the authorities granting the aid on film producers to spend a certain part of the film production budget in a particular territory.
[121] Council Regulation (EU) 2015/1589 of 13 July 2015 laying down detailed rules for the application of Article 108 of the Treaty on the Functioning of the European Union (codification), OJ L 248/9, repealing Council Regulation (EC) No. 659/1999 of 22 March 1999 laying down detailed rules for the application of Article 93 of the EC Treaty, OJ L 83/1.
[122] Commission Regulation (EC) No. 794/2004 of 21 April 2004 implementing Council Regulation (EU) 2015/1589 laying down detailed rules for the application of Article 108 of the Treaty on the Functioning of the European Union, OJ L 140/1.
[123] OJ C 136/13.
[124] OJ C 136/3.

the Commission must form an opinion on the conformity with the internal market of the measure as notified within two months of the complete notification having been received.[125] At the end of the two-month period the Commission must adopt one of three types of decision:

- The notified measure does not constitute state aid within the meaning of Article 107(1) TFEU (Article 4(2) of Regulation 2015/1589).
- The measure is compatible with the internal market, stating which exception under the Treaty has been applied ('decision not to raise objections', Article 4(3) of Regulation 2015/1589).
- There are doubts as to the compatibility of the measure with the internal market, whereupon the Commission must initiate proceedings under Article 108(2) TFEU ('decision to initiate the formal investigation procedure', Article 4(4) of Regulation 2015/1589).

If the Commission decides to initiate the formal investigation procedure, it shall summarise the relevant issues of fact and law, include a preliminary assessment as to the aid character of the proposed measure and set out the doubts as to its compatibility with the internal market (Article 6(1) of Regulation 2015/1589). The decision shall call upon the Member State concerned and upon 'interested parties' to submit comments within a prescribed period of time. Notably, the state aid procedure itself is opened, and any decision will be addressed, only to the Member State. Consequently, only the Member State has a right to defence. The beneficiary of the aid is only an 'interested party', although the Commission may order the Member State to recover any unlawful and incompatible state aid that the beneficiary has received.[126] The beneficiary must be given the opportunity to participate in the formal investigation procedure, during which they may bring forward their arguments.[127] Furthermore, it is a 'source of information' within the meaning of Article 7 of Regulation 2015/1589 and may thus be subject to an information request by the Commission.[128] However, not only the Member State, but also the beneficiary of the aid has the right to seek the annulment of the decision of the Commission in the General Court under Article 263(4) TFEU.[129] Other 'interested parties' may

---

[125] Article 4(5) of Regulation 2015/1589.

[126] See, for example, CJEU, Joined Cases T-231/06 and T-237/06 [2010] Netherlands and Nederlandse Omroep Stichting (NOS) v. Commission [36].

[127] ECJ, Case T-442/03 [2008] SIC v. Commission [222]; ECJ, Joined Cases T-309/04, T-317/04, T-329/04 and T-336/04 [2008] TV 2/Danmark A/S v. Commission [139]; CJEU, Joined Cases T-231/06 and T-237/06 [2010] Netherlands and Nederlandse Omroep Stichting (NOS) v. Commission [38].

[128] Compare ECJ, Case T-442/03 [2008] SIC v. Commission [222]; Joined Cases T-309/04, T-317/04, T-329/04 and T-336/04 [2008] TV 2/Danmark A/S v. Commission [138].

[129] ECJ, Case C-730/79 [1980] Philip Morris Holland BV v. Commission [5]. With regard to the standing of a competitor in a media state aid case, see CJEU, Case T-193/06 [2010] TF1 v. Commission [70 ff]; ECJ, Joined Cases T-309/04, T-317/04, T-329/04 and T-336/04 [2008] TV 2/Danmark A/S v. Commission [67 ff]. On the scope of judicial review, see Case T-110/97 [1999] Kneissl [45–47].

include the recipient's competitors (Article 1(h) of Regulation 2015/1589). The rights of 'interested parties' are further set out in Article 24 of Regulation 2015/1589.

The Commission must close the formal investigation procedure under Article 108(2) TFEU by adopting within a time limit of usually 18 months[130] one of the following decisions:

- The notified measure does not constitute aid (Article 9(2) of Regulation 2015/1589).
- The aid is compatible with the internal market ('positive decision', Article 9(3) of Regulation 2015/1589), stating which exception under the Treaty has been applied.
- The Commission may attach to a 'positive decision' conditions subject to which an aid may be considered compatible with the internal market and may lay down obligations to enable compliance with the decision to be monitored ('conditional decision', Article 9(4) of Regulation 2015/1589).
- The aid is not compatible with the internal market and thus shall not be put into effect ('negative decision', Article 9(5) of Regulation 2015/1589).
- The measure is existing aid within the meaning of Article 108(1) TFEU and Article 1(b) of Regulation 2015/1589, and thus not subject to the notification requirement in Article 108(3) TFEU (not provided for in Article 9 of Regulation 2015/1589).[131]

If a Member State fails to comply with its obligations under Article 108(3) TFEU to notify the aid, the Commission may, on its own initiative, examine information regarding alleged unlawful aid from whatever source, including newspaper articles or complaints by competitors (Article 12(1) of Regulation 2015/1589). In such cases of a so-called 'unlawful aid', the Commission is not bound by the time-limit set out in Articles 4(5), 9(6) and 9(7) of Regulation 2015/1589.[132] The examination of possible unlawful aid shall result in a decision pursuant to Article 4(2), (3) or (4) of Regulation 2015/1589: the measure is not state aid, or the measure is state aid but it is compatible with the internal market ('decision not to raise objections'), or the Commission has doubts as to the compatibility of the measure with the internal market, in which case the Commission must open the formal investigation ('a decision to initiate the formal procedure').[133] The formal investigation in the case of non-notified aid is initiated in the same way as in the case of notified aid summarised above. However, since the initiation of the Article 108(2) TFEU procedure requires the suspension of the aid, a decision to open the procedure can be challenged in the General Court where

---

[130] See Articles 9(6) and (7) of Regulation 2015/1589.
[131] On the distinction between existing aid and new aid in public service broadcasting funding schemes, see CJEU, Joined Cases T-231/06 and T-237/06 [2010] Netherlands and Nederlandse Omroep Stichting (NOS) v. Commission [159 ff].
[132] Article 15(2) of Regulation 2015/1589.
[133] Article 15(1) of Regulation 2015/1589.

the Member State claims the aid is either existing aid or not state aid at all, and thus would not have required notification in the first place.[134]

Article 11 of Regulation 2015/1589 allows the Commission to revoke its decision approving state aid where the decision was based on incorrect information provided during the procedure, which was a determining factor for the decision. Before revoking a decision and taking a new decision, the Commission shall open the formal investigation procedure.

4 The Compatibility of State Aid with the Internal Market

EU law stipulates four possibilities of compatibility of state aid with the internal market: Article 107(2) TFEU concerns aids that are compatible with the internal market, provided they meet certain conditions. Article 107(3) TFEU enumerates aids that the Commission can declare compatible with the internal market. The difference between paragraphs 2 and 3 is, therefore, that paragraph 3 gives discretion to the Commission in approving the aids. Article 106(2) TFEU provides a justification for compensations granted to undertakings entrusted with SGEI. Finally, Article 108(2)3 TFEU empowers the Council to decide that state aid shall be considered to be compatible with the internal market. But in all those cases the planned aids have to be notified to the Commission for approval in the first place.

Since Article 107(1) TFEU establishes the general principle that state aid is basically incompatible with the internal market, exceptions under Articles 107(2), 107(3) and 106(2) TFEU have to be interpreted restrictively. In particular, a state aid cannot be approved if it violates another provision of the Treaty, such as the free movement provisions or Articles 101 and 102 TFEU. In cases concerning also Articles 101 and 102 TFEU, the Commission is, however, not prevented from first approving the state aid under Article 107 TFEU and later dealing with the agreement under competition law. Thus the Commission, when approving state aid under Article 106(2) TFEU by Germany for the *Kinderkanal and Phoenix* television channels, also took a decision rejecting a complaint alleging that the agreement between the two broadcasters ARD and ZDF to create the two channels infringed now-Articles 101 and 102 TFEU.[135]

a The Compatibility of State Aid under Article 107(2) TFEU

Article 107(2) TFEU provides for three types of aid that *shall be* compatible with the internal market, which means that the Commission *has* to approve them if they meet the conditions set out in the Article. While lit. b) (aid to make good the damage caused by natural disasters or exceptional occurrences) and c) (aid granted to the

---

[134] Case C-400/99 [2005] Italy v. Commission [52]; Joined Cases T-195 and 207/01 [2002] Gibraltar v. Commission [86].

[135] COM, Decision of 24 February 1999, Aid No. NN 70/98, 'State aid to public broadcasting channels "Kinderkanal and Phoenix".'

economy of certain areas of the Federal Republic of Germany affected by the division of Germany) affect media undertakings just as any other industry, lit. a) has been of particular significance with regard to media-related state aid proceedings against Austria: Austria had granted subsidies to low-income consumers and households to help them purchase set-top boxes for digital TV, so that they would have access to digital television with upgraded analogue television sets once analogue television had been phased out. Applying (now) Article 107(2)(a) TFEU, the Commission required that the state aid had to meet three conditions in order to be compatible with the internal market:[136]

1 It has to be granted to individual consumers.
2 It needs to be of a social character.
3 It does not discriminate regarding the origin of the products or the origin of the services concerned.

In this case, the Commission observed that the measure was aimed at citizens with lower incomes to enable them having access to digital television. Without such an upgrade, these citizens would no longer be able to receive television signals with their existing TV sets and, consequently, would be excluded from receiving information from television programmes. Finally, the measure did not discriminate between the origin of the set-top boxes eligible for the subsidy. Therefore, the Commission held the measure to be compatible with the internal market.

While the outcome of the decision is to be welcomed, it shows again the narrow scope of the Commission's analysis. The Commission decided the case entirely within the framework of the EU state aid rules, but ignored what seemed to be of the utmost importance in this scenario: the right to receive information according to Articles 19(2) ICCPR, 10(1) ECHR and 11(1) EUChFR. As has been shown in Chapter 2, the right to receive information even imposes a positive obligation on states to enable potential recipients to receive information. It would have been worrying if the Commission had obliterated this obligation by having recourse to state aid rules only.

b The Compatibility of State Aid under Article 107(3) TFEU

According to Article 107(3) TFEU, the Commission may consider one of the enumerated forms of state aid to be compatible with the internal market. The onus is on the Member State to show that the aid was necessary in the sense that the objective intended to be achieved by the aid would not be achieved without the aid; in short, the recipient of the aid would not undertake the activity in question without the aid.[137] In approving state aid under Article 107(3) TFEU, the Commission has a

---

[136] COM, Decision C (2005)586 fin of 16 March 2005, State aid N 622/03 – Austria: Digitalisierungsfonds [23].
[137] ECJ, Case C-730/79 [1980] Philip Morris Holland BV v. Commission [17].

considerable discretion.[138] The Court has accepted that the Commission may take account of a variety of political, economic and social considerations in exercising its discretion.[139]

Of particular relevance for the media sector are Article 107(3)(c) TFEU for public funding for communication network infrastructure deployment and Article 107(3)(d) TFEU for cultural funding, particularly film funding. However, just as the other derogations in Article 107(3) TFEU, these provisions have to be applied restrictively.

According to Article 107(3)(c) TFEU, aid 'to facilitate the development of certain economic activities or of certain economic areas, where such aid does not adversely affect trading conditions to an extent contrary to the common interest', may be considered compatible with the internal market. An assessment under this provision tests the following cumulative factors with which the aid has to comply:[140]

1 The aid must contribute to the achievement of objectives of common interest;
2. absence of market delivery due to market failures or important inequalities;
3. the aid triggers an incentive effect;
4. the aid is proportionate, in particular:
    a) it is necessary as a policy instrument,
    b) the positive effects of the aid measure in reaching an objective of common interest outweigh the potential negative effects, and
    c) the aid is granted transparently.

As regards the common interest objective (first criterion), the Commission will assess to what extent the planned intervention will contribute to the achievement of the objectives of common interest as further specified in the Digital Agenda for Europe. This is akin to the test of a 'service of general economic interest' under Article 106(2) TFEU.

A 'market failure' according to the second criterion exists if markets, left to their own devices, would fail to deliver an efficient outcome for society without state intervention.[141] In the broadband sector in particular, one form of market failure is related to positive externalities. Positive externalities occur if market participants do not receive the full benefit of their actions. For example, the deployment of broadband networks is generally more profitable in densely populated areas in which demand is higher and concentrated. Because of high fixed costs of investment, costs increase as population densities decrease. Therefore, when deployed on commercial terms,

---

[138] ECJ, Case C-730/79 [1980] Philip Morris Holland BV v. Commission [17]; Case T-21/06 [2009] Germany v. Commission [50].
[139] ECJ, Case T-239/94 [1997] EISA v. Commission [93].
[140] Compare COM, Communication 2013/C 25/01: EU Guidelines for the application of State aid rules in relation to the rapid deployment of broadband networks [32–34].
[141] Niels et al. (2011, p. 384).

broadband networks profitably cover only those parts of the population.[142] However, the availability of broadband networks benefits society in general and not only the immediate investors and subscribers to the network. The market mechanism alone would not generate sufficient private investment in broadband networks.[143] Member States may, therefore, intervene to correct social or regional inequalities generated by a market outcome.[144]

In order to address market failure and equity objectives, the Commission distinguishes three types of geographical areas that may be targeted by broadband subsidies: white, grey and black areas. 'White areas' are those in which there is no broadband infrastructure and it is unlikely to be developed in the near future.[145] The Commission acknowledges that by providing financial support for the provision of communication services in 'white areas', Member States pursue cohesion and economic development objectives and thus their intervention is likely to be in line with the common interest.[146] 'Grey areas' are those in which one network operator is present and another network is unlikely to be developed in the near future. If that operator has a monopoly, it may provide citizens with a suboptimal combination of service quality and prices. At the same time, subsidies in such 'grey areas' could distort market dynamics. Therefore, state support is only justified when it can be clearly demonstrated that a market failure persists.[147] 'Black areas' are geographical areas in which there are or there will be in the near future at least two communication networks of different operators, and services are provided under competitive conditions. In 'black areas' it can be assumed that there is no market failure, hence there 'is very little scope for state intervention to bring further benefits'.[148]

State aid for communication networks need to set incentive effects in the sense that the network investment concerned would not have been undertaken within the same time frame without any state aid (third criterion).[149] If an operator is subject to

[142] COM, Communication 2013/C 25/01: EU Guidelines for the application of State aid rules in relation to the rapid deployment of broadband networks [38].

[143] COM, Communication 2013/C 25/01: EU Guidelines for the application of State aid rules in relation to the rapid deployment of broadband networks [37].

[144] COM, Communication 2013/C 25/01: EU Guidelines for the application of State aid rules in relation to the rapid deployment of broadband networks [39].

[145] COM, Communication 2013/C 25/01: EU Guidelines for the application of State aid rules in relation to the rapid deployment of broadband networks [66].

[146] COM, Communication 2013/C 25/01: EU Guidelines for the application of State aid rules in relation to the rapid deployment of broadband networks [66] and [75].

[147] COM, Communication 2013/C 25/01: EU Guidelines for the application of State aid rules in relation to the rapid deployment of broadband networks [68] and [76].

[148] COM, Communication 2013/C 25/01: EU Guidelines for the application of State aid rules in relation to the rapid deployment of broadband networks [72], [77] and [83].

[149] COM, Communication 2013/C 25/01: EU Guidelines for the application of State aid rules in relation to the rapid deployment of broadband networks [45]. See CJEU, Case C-544/09 P [2011] Germany v. Commission [44–49], regarding COM, Decision 2006/513/EC of 9 November 2005 on the State Aid which the Federal Republic of Germany has implemented for the introduction of digital terrestrial television (DVB-T) in Berlin-Brandenburg.

universal services obligations to cover the target area,[150] state aid is unlikely to have an incentive effect.

Under the proportionality analysis, a state aid has to be, first, a necessary means to address the problem. State aid as a policy to enhance the deployment of communication networks should thus only be envisaged when *ex ante* regulation is insufficient to enable the supply of such services. This might especially be the case in under-served ('white') areas where the inherent profitability of investment is low. In those situations, there may be no alternative to granting public funding to overcome the lack of broadband connectivity. In addition, the aid has to be limited to the minimum necessary. Furthermore, the positive effects of the aid measure in reaching an objective of common interest shall outweigh the potential negative effects. To establish *positive* effects, the aid should lead to at least one of the following achievements:[151]

- The rollout of a new infrastructure that would not have been there otherwise.
- Additional capacity and speed on the market.
- Lower prices.
- Better choice for consumers and more access for consumers to online resources.
- Higher quality and innovation.
- Contribution to the completion of the Digital Single Market.

The *negative* effects of the state aid on competition must be as limited as possible. In particular, national regulatory authorities should ensure effective wholesale access of third parties to the subsidised infrastructure.[152]

In addition to the general requirements of the Transparency Directive and the EU Public Procurement Directive[153] (if applicable), the Member States should clearly identify which geographic areas will be covered by the support measure in question, publish the relevant information of the project and invite to comment.[154]

The Commission considers the cultural exception in Article 107(3)(d) TFEU only in those cases in which the cultural product is clearly identified or identifiable.[155] In particular, the Commission strictly distinguishes between the promotion of culture, on the one hand, and the educational and democratic needs of a Member State, on the other hand. Only the former can be justified under Article 107(3)(d) TFEU, while

---

[150] See Chapter 7.

[151] See COM, Communication 2013/C 25/01: EU Guidelines for the application of State aid rules in relation to the rapid deployment of broadband networks [50].

[152] COM, Communication 2013/C 25/01: EU Guidelines for the application of State aid rules in relation to the rapid deployment of broadband networks [78] and [80].

[153] Directive 2004/18/EC of the European Parliament and of the Council of 31 March 2004 on the coordination of procedures for the award of public works contracts, public supply contracts and public service contracts, OJ L 134/114.

[154] COM, Communication 2013/C 25/01: EU Guidelines for the application of State aid rules in relation to the rapid deployment of broadband networks [78].

[155] COM, Communication 2009/C 257/01 on the application of State aid rules to public service broadcasting [34].

the latter shall seek justification under Article 106(2) TFEU.[156] In practice, state aid to public service broadcasters usually does not, and cannot, differentiate between the cultural and the democratic or educational needs of society. As a consequence of its distinction between the promotion of culture and the educational and democratic needs of a Member State, the Commission regularly reject the financing of public service broadcasters under Article 107(3)(d) TFEU, but has often accepted film subsidies under this provision.

The criteria established by the European Commission for accepting schemes designed to support the scriptwriting, development, production, distribution and promotion of audiovisual works under Article 107(3)(d) TFEU can be summarised as follows:[157]

1 The aid is directed to a cultural product.
2 The aid intensity must in principle be limited to 50 per cent of the production budget.
3 The aid must not be reserved for individual parts of the production value chain, but has to contribute to the overall budget of the production.
4 Territorial spending obligations may not exceed a certain amount of the budget.
5 An eligibility criterion requiring a minimum level of production activity in the territory of the granting Member State shall not exceed 50 per cent of the production budget.[158]
6 The aid has to fulfil the applicable transparency requirements.
7 Member States should encourage and support producers to deposit a copy of the aided film in a designated film heritage institution.

If a Member State can convincingly argue that state aid serves to promote culture and heritage conservation (first criterion), the Commission's discretion *not* to accept the state aid is reduced, for two reasons. First, Article 107(3)(d) TFEU has to be seen in the context of Article 167 TFEU. Article 167(2) TFEU provides that: 'Action by the Union shall be aimed at encouraging cooperation between Member States and, if necessary, supporting and supplementing their action in the following areas: [...] artistic and literary creation, including in the audiovisual sector.' And, according to its fourth paragraph, the EU 'shall take cultural aspects into account in its action under other provisions of the Treaties, in particular in order to respect and to promote the diversity of its cultures'.

---

[156] COM, Communication 2009/C 257/01 on the application of State aid rules to public service broadcasting [34]; see, for example, COM, Decision SG(99) D/ 10201 of 14 December 1999, State aid No. NN 88/98 of 14 December 1999 – United Kingdom, Financing of a 24-hour advertising-free news channel out of the licence fee by the BBC [36]; Decision C(2005)1479 fin of 7 June 2005, State aid France – Chaîne française d'information internationale. Critically on this distinction Harrison and Woods (2007, p. 306).

[157] Compare COM, Communication 2013/C 332/01 on State aid for films and other audiovisual works [52]. From academic literature, see Psychogiopoulou (2006, 2010).

[158] COM, Communication 2013/C 332/01 on State aid for films and other audiovisual works [37].

The Court of Justice has thus found that a Member State's cultural policy, such as the promotion of linguistic diversity, may constitute an overriding requirement relating to the general interest that justifies a restriction on the freedom to provide services.

Second, due to the subsidiarity principle (Article 5 TEU), the definition of cultural activities is primarily a responsibility of the Member States.[159] The Commission thus merely supervises whether a Member State employs a verification mechanism 'to avoid manifest error'. This would be achieved either through the selection of film proposals, for example, by a panel, or by establishing a list of cultural criteria.[160]

The promotion of culture includes, in particular, the promotion of diversity. A cultural objective in the media sector may thus be the promotion of different social, educational, religious, philosophical or linguistic components.[161] Consequently, preserving and promoting the use of minority languages of a Member State is to be regarded as serving the promotion of culture.[162] Hence Member States may require, as condition for the aid, that the film is produced in a certain language, even if this discriminates against the promotion of products that are not in this language.[163]

Furthermore, the fact that a sponsored film or company is commercial does not prevent it from being cultural.[164] According to Article 4(4) of the UNESCO Convention on the Protection and Promotion of the Diversity of Cultural Expressions of 2005: 'Cultural activities, goods and services refers to those activities, goods and services, which ... embody or convey cultural expressions, irrespective of the commercial value they may have.' On the other hand, goods and services that do not refer to cultural activities, but that are purely commercial, cannot be accepted under Article 107(3)(d) TFEU. For example, games do usually not qualify as cultural products.[165]

The aid intensity must in principle be limited to 50 per cent of the production budget in order to stimulate normal commercial initiatives (second criterion).[166] In view of the importance of European works, the Commission considers that a higher aid intensity is justified for co-productions funded by more than one Member State and involving producers from more than one Member State.[167] Consequently, the aid intensity for cross-border productions funded by more than one Member State and involving producers from more than one Member State may amount to up to 60

---

[159] COM, Communication 2013/C 332/01 on State aid for films and other audiovisual works [18] and [25].

[160] COM, Communication 2013/C 332/01 on State aid for films and other audiovisual works [52].

[161] Compare Article 22 EUChFR; see COM, Communication 2013/C 332/01 on State aid for films and other audiovisual works [26]. On education in particular, see COM, Decision C(2003)3371fin of 1 October 2003, State aid No. N 37/2003 – United Kingdom, BBC Digital Curriculum [40].

[162] ECJ, Case C-222/07 [2009] UTECA [27–33]; COM, Decision SG(99) D/ 10201 of 14 December 1999, State aid No. NN 88/98 of 14 December 1999 – United Kingdom, Financing of a 24-hour advertising-free news channel out of the licence fee by the BBC [122].

[163] ECJ, Case C-222/07 [2009] UTECA [36].

[164] COM, Communication 2013/C 332/01 on State aid for films and other audiovisual works [25].

[165] COM, Communication 2013/C 332/01 on State aid for films and other audiovisual works [24].

[166] COM, Communication 2013/C 332/01 on State aid for films and other audiovisual works [52].

[167] COM, Communication 2013/C 332/01 on State aid for films and other audiovisual works [42]; on quotas for European works, see Chapter 5.

per cent of the production budget.[168] Difficult audiovisual works, such as short films, films by first-time and second-time directors, documentaries, low-budget works and co-productions involving countries from the Development Assistance Committee (DAC) List of the OECD[169] are excluded from these limits.

Obligations imposed by the authorities granting the aid on film producers to spend a certain part of the film production budget in a particular territory (territorial spending obligations; fourth criterion) may not exceed:

- 160 per cent of the aid amount in the case of aid awarded as grants;
- 80 per cent of the production budget in the case of aid awarded as a percentage of the expenditure on production activity.[170]

c The Compatibility of State Aid under Article 106(2) TFEU

As shown above, the compensation of undertakings entrusted with the operation of services of general economic interest (SGEI) for the provision of such services may be excluded from the definition of 'aid' according to the *Altmark Trans* formula. If the *Altmark Trans* criteria are, however, not fulfilled, a state aid granted to such undertakings may still be justified under Article 106(2) TFEU, if the application of the state aid rules 'obstruct[s] the performance, in law or in fact, of the particular tasks assigned to them'. Article 106(2) TFEU expresses the insight that there are societal goals that are not directly related to the market and that must, therefore, be added to the market-focused competition law provisions. Article 106(2) TFEU thus provides the gateway for the European Commission to take on board legitimate interests of the EU Member States to compensate public service broadcasters for their services of general interest. The provision needs to be understood against the backdrop of Article 14 TFEU, which provides:

> Without prejudice to Article 4 [TEU] or to Articles 93, 106 and 107 [TFEU], and given the place occupied by services of general economic interest in the shared values of the Union as well as their role in promoting social and territorial cohesion, the Union and the Member States ... shall take care that such services operate on the basis of principles and conditions, particularly economic and financial conditions, which enable them to fulfil their missions.

Furthermore, Article 36 EUChFR provides that the EU 'recognises and respects access to services of general economic interest as provided for in national laws and

---

[168] COM, Communication 2013/C 332/01 on State aid for films and other audiovisual works [52].

[169] The DAC list shows all countries and territories eligible to receive official development assistance. These consist of all low and middle-income countries based on gross national income (GNI) per capita as published by the World Bank, with the exception of G8 members, EU members, and countries with a firm date for entry into the EU. The list also includes all of the Least Developed Countries (LDCs) as defined by the United Nations (www.oecd.org/ document/45/0,3746,en_2649_34447_2093101_1_1_1_1,00.html).

[170] COM, Communication 2013/C 332/01 on State aid for films and other audiovisual works [35–36].

practices, in accordance with the Treaties, in order to promote the social and territorial cohesion of the Union'.

The scope of application of Article 106(2) TFEU as a provision justifying a state aid is rather narrow. Yet it is of major significance with regard to the financing of public service broadcasters. So far, licence fees and other state aid for public service broadcasters have not met the *Altmark Trans* criteria, while many of those measures have been approved under Article 106(2) TFEU. In order to qualify for the Article 106(2) TFEU exemption, the state aid needs to meet the following conditions:[171]

1 The service in question must be a service of general economic interest and clearly defined as such by the Member State (definition).
2 The undertaking in question must be officially entrusted by the Member State with the provision of the service (entrustment).
3 The prohibition in Article 107(1) TFEU would prevent the performance of the entrusted service.
4 The exemption must not affect the development of trade to an extent that would be contrary to the interests of the EU (proportionality).

If those principles are fulfilled, the development of trade is not affected to an extent contrary to the interests of the EU.

The exact relationship between the test under Article 106(2) TFEU and the *Altmark Trans* criteria are controversial and far from being clear.[172] For the purposes of this chapter, it is sufficient to assume that, as far as the legal consequences are concerned, *Altmark Trans* excludes the existence of an 'aid' under Article 107(1) TFEU, whereas Article 106(2) TFEU merely justifies the state aid, but the measure still has to be notified to the European Commission. As far as the legal requirements are concerned, the test established according to Article 106(2) TFEU shares two criteria with *Altmark Trans*: the 'definition' element (no. 1 of *Altmark Trans* and no. 1 of the Article 106(2) TFEU test)[173] and the prohibition of overcompensation (no. 3 of *Altmark Trans* and part of the proportionality analysis under Article 106(2) TFEU). Yet there are also differences to the *Altmark Trans* test, otherwise Article 106(2) TFEU would not have its own field of application. Article 106(2) TFEU does not include a requirement to the effect that the parameters on the basis of which the compensation is calculated

---

[171] See, for example, ECJ, Case T-442/03 [2008] SIC v. Commission [144]; COM, Decision 2005/842/EC of 28 November 2005 on the application of Article 86(2) of the EC Treaty to State aid in the form of public service compensation granted to certain undertakings entrusted with the operation of services of general economic interest, Recitals 9–11.

[172] See, for example, Hancher and Larouche (2011, pp. 761–762).

[173] Although it is again controversial whether the concept of 'service of general economic interest' in Article 106(2) TFEU is equivalent to the notion of 'public service obligations' within the meaing of the first *Altmark Trans* criterion; see the brief remark in ECJ, Case T-289/03 [2008] BUPA and others v. Commission [162]: 'the concept of public service obligation referred to in [*Altmark Trans*] corresponds to that of the SGEI as designated by the contested decision and that it does not differ from that referred to in Article [106(2) TFEU]'.

must be established in advance in an objective and transparent manner (no. 2 of
Altmark Trans), and the Member State neither has to conduct a competitive ten-
dering procedure for the award of the service of general economic interest (no. 4.a)
of *Altmark Trans*)[174] nor to determine the level of compensation on the basis of an
analysis of the costs which a typical undertaking would have incurred in discharging those obligations (no. 4.b) of *Altmark Trans*). Notably, the failure to meet those
two requirements – no. 2 and no. 4 – have induced the Commission to reject an
exclusion of state aid to public broadcasting services from the application of Article
107(1) TFEU.

First, the service in question must be a service of general economic interest and
clearly defined as such by the Member State (definition). The notion of a 'service of
general economic interest' has already been described in the context of the *Altmark
Trans* decision. The service in question must be clearly defined as an SGEI by the
Member State. The definition of the public service mandate by the Member States
has to be as precise as possible.[175] It should be neither too broad, as this might distort
competition, nor too narrow, as this would prevent the provision of SGEI more than
necessary. The definition has to consider various factors:

- Freedom of expression and media freedom. The definition of the public service
  remit has to respect the editorial independence of the public service broadcasters
  from political authorities in the choice of their content.[176]
- Media pluralism, including cultural and linguistic diversity.[177]
- The democratic, social and cultural needs of a particular society.
- Viewers' interest and different viewing habits. Hence the requirement of a 'precise definition' causes problems where the scope or the nature of public services broadcasting changes.[178] This has, most recently, been the case with regard
  the extension of public service broadcasting to the online environment. As the
  Member States expressed in the Council Resolution concerning public service
  broadcasting:

> the ability of public service broadcasting to offer quality programming and
> services to the public must be maintained and enhanced, including the devel-
> opment and diversification of activities in the digital age; ... public service
> broadcasting must be able to continue to provide a wide range of program-
> ming in accordance with its remit as defined by the Member States in order

---

[174] ECJ, Case T-442/03 [2008] SIC v. Commission [145].
[175] COM, Communication 2009/C 257/01 on the application of State aid rules to public service broadcasting [45]. See, for example, ECJ, Joined Cases T-309/04, T-317/04, T-329/04 and T-336/04 [2008] TV 2/
Danmark A/S v. Commission [118].
[176] ECJ, Joined Cases T-309/04, T-317/04, T-329/04 and T-336/04 [2008] TV 2/Danmark A/S v. Commission
[118].
[177] ECJ, Joined Cases T-309/04, T-317/04, T-329/04 and T-336/04 [2008] TV 2/Danmark A/S v. Commission
[117].
[178] Harrison and Woods (2007, p. 307).

to address society as a whole; in this context it is legitimate for public service
broadcasting to seek to reach wide audiences.[179]

Therefore, public service broadcasters must be able to reach all audiences and may
thus extend the provision of their services to new media. At the same time, public services broadcasters are competing with newspaper publishers and other print
media on the internet. The potential negative effects that state aid to public service
broadcasters could have on those commercial media providers have to be taken into
account when extending the public service remit to online services.[180]

When reviewing Member States' public service definition, the Commission
restricts its control to a 'check for manifest errors' of assessment by a Member State
in the definition of its public broadcasting service.[181] The definition of the public
service remit would be in such 'manifest error' if it included 'activities that could
not reasonably be considered to meet ... the "democratic, social and cultural needs
of each society". The Commission sees such a 'manifest error' in the offering of e-
commerce, teleshopping, prize games, sponsoring or merchandising, online games,
online shops, chat rooms, online dating services, online calculators for insurance,
links to external offers, mobile services, the sale of advertising space in order to
obtain revenue or the commercial exploitation of their content by making it available
to telecom operators against remuneration.[182] This corresponds to the approaches
of the ECtHR and the CJEU, which afford generally less protection to 'commercial
speech'.[183] While public service broadcasters are basically not prohibited from performing commercial activities, such activities cannot be viewed as part of the public
service remit. As a consequence, Member States need to ensure that these activities
do not benefit from public funding.[184] Consequently, appropriate separation between
public service activities and non-public service activities include a clear separation of
accounts between public service activities and non-public service activities.[185]

---

[179] Resolution of the Council and of the Representatives of the Governments of the Member States, meeting
within the Council of 25 January 1999 concerning public service broadcasting, OJ C 30/ 1.

[180] COM, Communication 2009/C 257/01 on the application of State aid rules to public service broadcasting [16].

[181] ECJ, Case T-442/03 [2008] SIC v. Commission [195]; ECJ, Joined Cases T-309/04, T-317/04, T-329/
04 and T-336/04 [2008] TV 2/Danmark A/S v. Commission [101]; CJEU, Joined Cases T-231/06 and
T-237/06 [2010] Netherlands and Nederlandse Omroep Stichting (NOS) v. Commission [223]; COM,
Communication 2009/C 257/01 on the application of State aid rules to public service broadcasting [48].

[182] COM, Decision C(2007)1761 of 24 April 2007, State aid E 3/2005 (ex-CP 2/2003, CP 232/2002, CP 43/
2003, CP 243/2004 and CP 195/2004) – Financing of public service broadcasters in Germany [232] and
[239]; Communication 2009/C 257/01 on the application of State aid rules to public service broadcasting
[48]; see also ECJ, Joined Cases T-309/04, T-317/04, T-329/04 and T-336/04 [2008] TV 2/Danmark A/S v.
Commission [173].

[183] See Chapter 3.

[184] ECJ, Joined Cases T-309/04, T-317/04, T-329/04 and T-336/04 [2008] TV 2/Danmark A/S v. Commission
[107–108]; COM, Decision C(2007)1761 of 24 April 2007, State aid E 3/2005 (ex-CP 2/2003, CP 232/2002,
CP 43/2003, CP 243/2004 and CP 195/2004) – Financing of public service broadcasters in Germany [241];
Communication 2009/C 257/01 on the application of State aid rules to public service broadcasting [49].

[185] COM, Communication 2009/C 257/01 on the application of State aid rules to public service
broadcasting [60].

By contrast, the Commission regards the broadcasting of sport events – and thus also the acquisition of rights to broadcast such events – as 'part of a balanced and varied programme'.[186] This is supported by Article 165 TFEU, which emphasises the significance of sports for EU policy. Yet, as with other programming rights, public service broadcasters must not 'structurally outbid private competitors by offering consistently and regularly prices which are significantly higher than what private operators would be able to pay and thus "empty" the market', or to hold back unused exclusive rights.[187]

The establishment of certain quality standards as well as imposing an obligation to provide a wide range of programming and a balanced and varied broadcasting offer, are legitimate under Article 106(2) TFEU.[188] This includes the possibility to define broadcasting SGEI broadly so as to cover the broadcasting of full-spectrum programming, including the sale of advertising space.[189]

Second, the undertaking must be officially entrusted by the Member State with the provision of the service (entrustment). The entrustment act has to specify the precise nature and the duration of the public service obligations, the undertaking and territory concerned, the nature of any exclusive or special rights assigned to the undertaking, the parameters for calculating, controlling and reviewing the compensation, as well as the arrangements for avoiding and repaying any overcompensation.[190] The public service remit has to be entrusted by means of an official act; for example, by legislation, contract or binding terms of reference.[191] Whenever the scope of the public service remit is extended to cover new services, such as online media for public service broadcasters, the definition and the entrusting act have to be modified accordingly.[192]

---

[186] COM, Decision C(2007)1761 of 24 April 2007, State aid E 3/2005 (ex-CP 2/2003, CP 232/2002, CP 43/ 2003, CP 243/2004 and CP 195/2004) – Financing of public service broadcasters in Germany [242] and [289 ff].

[187] COM, Decision C(2007)1761 of 24 April 2007, State aid E 3/2005 (ex-CP 2/2003, CP 232/2002, CP 43/ 2003, CP 243/2004 and CP 195/2004) – Financing of public service broadcasters in Germany [298 ff].

[188] ECJ, Case T-442/03 [2008] SIC v. Commission [211]; Joined Cases T-309/04, T-317/04, T-329/04 and T-336/04 [2008] TV 2/Danmark A/S v. Commission [113]; COM, Communication 2009/C 257/01 on the application of State aid rules to public service broadcasting [47]; Decision C(2007)1761 of 24 April 2007, State aid E 3/2005 (ex-CP 2/2003, CP 232/2002, CP 43/2003, CP 243/2004 and CP 195/2004) – Financing of public service broadcasters in Germany [224].

[189] ECJ, Joined Cases T-309/04, T-317/04, T-329/04 and T-336/04 [2008] TV 2/Danmark A/S v. Commission [107].

[190] Article 4 of the Commission Decision 2005/842/EC of 28 November 2005 on the application of Article 86(2) of the EC Treaty to State aid in the form of public service compensation granted to certain undertakings entrusted with the operation of services of general economic interest; COM, Communication 2009/C 257/01 on the application of State aid rules to public service broadcasting [51]. See, for example, COM, Decision C(2007)1761 of 24 April 2007, State aid E 3/2005 (ex-CP 2/2003, CP 232/2002, CP 43/2003, CP 243/2004 and CP 195/2004) – Financing of public service broadcasters in Germany [247 ff].

[191] COM, Communication 2009/C 257/01 on the application of State aid rules to public service broadcasting [50]; see, for example, COM, Decision C(2003)3371fin of 1 October 2003, State aid No. N 37/2003 – United Kingdom, BBC Digital Curriculum [45]; Decision 2012/365/EU of 20 December 2011 on the State aid C 85/01 on ad hoc measures implemented by Portugal in favour of RTP [171].

[192] COM, Communication 2009/C 257/01 on the application of State aid rules to public service broadcasting [52].

In addition, the Member State in question has to monitor that the public service is actually supplied as provided for in the formal agreement between the state and the entrusted undertaking.[193] This touches one of the most sensitive issues of state aid for public service broadcasters. Due to the principle of subsidiarity, the Commission itself would not be entitled to supervise the adherence of the domestic public service broadcaster to its public service remit. Consequently, the Commission has to scrutinise whether the Member State adhered to a sufficient standard of monitoring, but it is not for the Commission to judge on the compliance with quality standards regarding the programme content.[194] But because of the media freedom principle, which also guarantees the editorial independence of broadcasters from governmental influence (see Chapter 2), the domestic authorities themselves may supervise the broadcasting content only to a very limited extent. Thus, the domestic public service 'watchdog' has to be independent not only from the management of public service broadcasters,[195] but also from governmental influence. At the same time, the public service 'watchdog' would be an obliged addressee of media freedom. As a consequence, the role of such an auditor is essentially restricted to a financial supervision, whereas a content-related supervision is limited by the media freedom principle.[196]

Third, Article 106(2) TFEU requires that the prohibition included in Article 107(1) TFEU would prevent the performance of the entrusted service, namely the ability to provide public service broadcasting. Fourth, the exemption must not affect the development of trade to an extent that would be contrary to the interests of the EU (proportionality). The proportionality assessment to be carried out by the Commission comprises the following aspects:

1 separate accounting;
2 control of the limitation of state funding to the net public service costs; and
3 examination of possible market distortions that are not inherent to the fulfilment of the public service remit.[197]

---

[193] ECJ, Case T-442/03 [2008] SIC v. Commission [209]; Joined Cases T-309/04, T-317/04, T-329/04 and T-336/04 [2008] TV 2/Danmark A/S v. Commission [176]; COM, Communication 2009/C 257/01 on the application of State aid rules to public service broadcasting [53].

[194] ECJ, Case T-442/03 [2008] SIC v. Commission [212]; Joined Cases T-309/04, T-317/04, T-329/04 and T-336/04 [2008] TV 2/Danmark A/S v. Commission [176].

[195] See COM, Communication 2009/C 257/01 on the application of State aid rules to public service broadcasting [54]; Joined Cases T-309/04, T-317/04, T-329/04 and T-336/04 [2008] TV 2/Danmark A/S v. Commission [176].

[196] Compare ECJ, Case T-442/03 [2008] SIC v. Commission [227 ff]; COM, Decision 2012/365/EU of 20 December 2011 on the State aid C 85/01 on ad hoc measures implemented by Portugal in favour of RTP [175 ff]; *mutatis mutandis*, COM, Decision C(2007)1761 of 24 April 2007, State aid E 3/2005 (ex-CP 2/2003, CP 232/2002, CP 43/2003, CP 243/2004 and CP 195/2004) – Financing of public service broadcasters in Germany [251].

[197] COM, Decision C(2007)1761 of 24 April 2007, State aid E 3/2005 (ex-CP 2/2003, CP 232/2002, CP 43/2003, CP 243/2004 and CP 195/2004) – Financing of public service broadcasters in Germany [263]; Decision 2005/406/EC of 15 October 2003 on ad hoc measures implemented by Portugal for RTP [183].

The requirement of separate accounting follows from the Transparency Directive.[198] According to its Article 2(1)(d), an undertaking is required to maintain separate accounts if, *inter alia*, it 'is entrusted with the operation of [an SGEI,] receives public service compensation in any form whatsoever in relation to such service and ... carries on other activities'. 'Such service' refers to the public service remit, 'other activities' describes commercial activities, such as the sale of advertisement.[199]

The compensation must not exceed what is necessary to cover the costs incurred by the undertaking concerned for the operation of the SGEI, taking into account other revenues from commercial activities.[200] This requires, first, the determination of public service costs; second, the determination and subsequent deduction of commercial revenues; and third, the *ex post* control of possible overcompensation.[201] The control mechanisms need to make sure that excess money does not remain at the free disposal of the entrusted undertaking, save for a buffer of 10 per cent against unforeseen fluctuations in revenues and costs.[202] But the compensation for the operation of the SGEI also allows for a reasonable profit. A 'reasonable profit' means 'a rate of return on own capital that takes account of the risk, or absence of risk, incurred by the undertaking by virtue of the intervention by the Member State, particularly if the

---

[198] Commission Directive 2005/81/EC of 28 November 2005 amending Directive 80/723/EEC on the transparency of financial relations between Member States and public undertakings as well as on financial transparency within certain undertakings, OJ L 312/47. See COM, Communication 2009/C 257/01 on the application of State aid rules to public service broadcasting [62 ff]; ECJ, Joined Cases T-309/04, T-317/04, T-329/04 and T-336/04 [2008] TV 2/Danmark A/S v. Commission [179]; COM, Decision C(2007)1761 of 24 April 2007, State aid E 3/2005 (ex-CP 2/2003, CP 232/2002, CP 43/2003, CP 243/2004 and CP 195/2004) – Financing of public service broadcasters in Germany [265 ff].

[199] COM, Decision C(2007)1761 of 24 April 2007, State aid E 3/2005 (ex-CP 2/2003, CP 232/2002, CP 43/2003, CP 243/2004 and CP 195/2004) – Financing of public service broadcasters in Germany [266].

[200] Article 5(1) of the Commission Decision 2005/842/EC of 28 November 2005 on the application of Article 86(2) of the EC Treaty to State aid in the form of public service compensation granted to certain undertakings entrusted with the operation of services of general economic interest. See ECJ, Joined Cases T-309/04, T-317/04, T-329/04 and T-336/04 [2008] TV 2/Danmark A/S v. Commission [181–182]; COM, Decision C(2007)1761 of 24 April 2007, State aid E 3/2005 (ex-CP 2/2003, CP 232/2002, CP 43/2003, CP 243/2004 and CP 195/2004) – Financing of public service broadcasters in Germany [268].

[201] See COM, Decision C(2007)1761 of 24 April 2007, State aid E 3/2005 (ex-CP 2/2003, CP 232/2002, CP 43/2003, CP 243/2004 and CP 195/2004) – Financing of public service broadcasters in Germany [269 ff]; COM, Decision C(2005)1479 fin of 7 June 2005, State aid France – Chaîne française d'information internationale [51 ff].

[202] COM, Decision 2005/842/EC of 28 November 2005 on the application of Article 86(2) of the EC Treaty to State aid in the form of public service compensation granted to certain undertakings entrusted with the operation of services of general economic interest, recital 13; COM, Decision C(2007)1761 of 24 April 2007, State aid E 3/2005 (ex-CP 2/2003, CP 232/2002, CP 43/2003, CP 243/2004 and CP 195/2004) – Financing of public service broadcasters in Germany [317]. A higher annual reserve may be justified, for instance where the surplus is intended to be used for predetermined projects, the costs of which have been certified by an independent body and which are to be carried out at a later stage during the licence fee period, provided that there are satisfactory control mechanisms ensuring that these reserves cannot be used for other purposes.

latter grants exclusive or special rights. This rate shall not normally exceed the average rate for the sector concerned in recent years.'[203] The Member States have to carry out regular checks, or ensure that such checks are carried out, to prevent excessive compensation.[204]

By contrast to the mere anti-competitive *effect* as required by Article 107(1) TFEU, an anti-competitive *behaviour* of the beneficiary undertaking can also become relevant under Article 106(2) TFEU. The public service broadcaster must not distort competition in commercial markets more than is necessary for the fulfilment of the public service mission. A public service broadcaster would distort competition, for instance, if it depresses prices of advertising or of other non-public service activities on the market, so as to reduce the revenue of competitors.[205] Furthermore, while the acquisition of premium content is basically part of the public service mission, public service broadcasters may not maintain exclusive premium rights unused without offering to sublicense them.[206]

As has been stated before, public service broadcasters may basically use state aid to provide their services over new distribution platforms. Yet the expansion to new media must not entail disproportionate effects on the competition with newspaper publishers and other online media, which are 'also important guarantors of an objectively informed public and of democracy'.[207] As a consequence, public service broadcasters have to pursue the same democratic, social and cultural needs of the society in the online as in the offline environment, and they must not include commercial activities that are not necessary for the fulfilment of the public service remit.[208] Therefore, the Commission requires Member States to conduct an evaluation based on an open public consultation as to whether significant new audiovisual services envisaged by public service broadcasters meet the public service requirements by comparing the situation in the presence and in the absence of the planned

---

[203] Article 5(4) of the Commission Decision 2005/842/EC of 28 November 2005 on the application of Article 86(2) of the EC Treaty to State aid in the form of public service compensation granted to certain undertakings entrusted with the operation of services of general economic interest.

[204] Article 6(1) of the Commission Decision 2005/842/EC of 28 November 2005 on the application of Article 86(2) of the EC Treaty to State aid in the form of public service compensation granted to certain undertakings entrusted with the operation of services of general economic interest.

[205] See CJEU, Joined Cases T-231/06 and T-237/06 [2010] Netherlands and Nederlandse Omroep Stichting (NOS) v. Commission [213]; Joined Cases T-309/04, T-317/04, T-329/04 and T-336/04 [2008] TV 2/ Danmark A/S v. Commission [182]; COM, Decision 2004/339/EC of 15 October 2003 on the measures implemented by Italy for RAI SpA [125]; Communication 2009/C 257/01 on the application of State aid rules to public service broadcasting [94].

[206] COM, Communication 2009/C 257/01 on the application of State aid rules to public service broadcasting [92].

[207] COM, Communication 2009/C 257/01 on the application of State aid rules to public service broadcasting [16].

[208] COM, Communication 2009/C 257/01 on the application of State aid rules to public service broadcasting [81]; see, for example, COM, Decision of 14 December 1999, State aid No. NN 88/98 of 14 December 1999 – United Kingdom, Financing of a 24-hour advertising-free news channel out of the licence fee by the BBC [57].

new service.[209] Relevant aspects for this evaluation are the *additional* value of the services in question for society, on the one hand, and the existence of similar or substitutable offers, editorial competition, market structure, market position of the public service broadcaster, level of competition and potential impact on private initiatives, on the other hand.[210] The assessment has to be carried out by a body that is independent from the management of the public service broadcaster.[211] This is drafted along the lines of the 'public value test' (PVT) conducted in the UK.[212]

In addition, the European Commission established the following requirements for the testing of innovative new services by public service broadcasters, such as in the form of pilot projects:

1   The project is on a limited scale in terms of time and audience.
2   The purpose of the project is for the purpose of gathering information on the feasibility of and the value added by the foreseen service.
3   The test phase does not amount to the introduction of a fully fledged, significant new audiovisual service.[213]

d   Aids Approved by the Council under Article 108(2)3 TFEU

The Council may, on application by a Member State, decide that aid which that state is granting or intends to grant shall be considered to be compatible with the internal market, if such a decision is 'justified by exceptional circumstances' (Article 108(2) subpara. 3 TFEU). The decision may derogate from the provisions of Article 107 TFEU or from the regulations provided for in Article 109 TFEU. Consequently, the application to the Council suspends any investigation that the Commission has already initiated according to Article 108(2) TFEU. However, the Council may not take a decision approving an aid if the Commission has already taken a decision closing the Article 108(2) TFEU procedure.[214] In practice, the use by the Council of its power under Article 108(2) TFEU has been very limited outside the field of agriculture, and, more recently, transport and aid for coordination centres.

---

[209]   COM, Communication 2009/C 257/01 on the application of State aid rules to public service broadcasting [84] and [88]. On the definition of 'significant new services', see COM, Communication 2009/C 257/01 on the application of State aid rules to public service broadcasting [85].

[210]   COM, Communication 2009/C 257/01 on the application of State aid rules to public service broadcasting [88]. See, for example, the detailed analysis in COM, Decision C(2007)1761 of 24 April 2007, State aid E 3/2005 (ex-CP 2/2003, CP 232/2002, CP 43/2003, CP 243/2004 and CP 195/2004) – Financing of public service broadcasters in Germany [227 ff].

[211]   COM, Communication 2009/C 257/01 on the application of State aid rules to public service broadcasting [89].

[212]   See www.bbc.co.uk/bbctrust/governance/tools_we_use/public_value_tests.html.

[213]   COM, Communication 2009/C 257/01 on the application of State aid rules to public service broadcasting [90].

[214]   ECJ, Case C-110/02 [2004] Commission v. Council [44–45]; Case C-399/03 [2006] Commission v. Council [28].

5 Recovery of an Unlawful Aid

State aid rules stipulate their own enforcement provisions in derogation from Article 258 TFEU. When the Commission decides that 'unlawful aid' – aid put into effect in contravention of Article 108(3) TFEU – is incompatible with the internal market ('negative decision'), the Member State concerned has to take all necessary measures to recover the aid from the beneficiary.[215] The aid to be recovered shall include interest at an appropriate rate fixed by the Commission, which shall be payable from the date on which the unlawful aid was at the disposal of the beneficiary until the date of its recovery.[216] The recovery of the aid can consist of the repayment of the financial support, the withdrawal of the guarantee, etc. If the Commission's decision is not complied with by the date that it prescribes, the Commission may refer the matter directly to the Court of Justice under Article 108(2) subpara. 2 TFEU. Alternatively, the Commission may bring proceedings in the CJEU against the Member State under Article 258 TFEU.

The aim of the Commission's recovery decision is not the recovery of the state aid as such, but to eliminate the distortion to competition. This distinction can become relevant in cases of insolvency of the beneficiary of the aid. Although in such cases the aid cannot or can only marginally be recovered, the purpose of the recovery decision is nonetheless fulfilled, if and because the recipient of the aid is eliminated from competition.

The Commission shall, however, not issue a recovery decision if this would be contrary to a general principle of EU law.[217] The most significant principle of EU law that may bar a recovery order is that of legitimate expectation. It applies where the Commission's or the Council's action or inaction gave an assurance that the aid has been granted in accordance with EU law.[218] By contrast, practical or domestic legal difficulties in implementing a recovery decision may not prevent such a decision. Furthermore, the conduct of the *Member State* (as opposed to the Commission or the Council), such as the assurance that the state aid is in compliance with EU law or that it will not be recovered, is irrelevant to the recovery of aid.[219] Member States may even be required to adjust the interpretation of their laws in order to enable the enforcement of a recovery decision, such as the national limitation period for the revocation of the administrative act granting the aid.[220]

---

[215] Article 16(1) of Regulation 2015/1589.
[216] Article 16(2) of Regulation 2015/1589, Article 11 of Regulation 794/2004.
[217] Article 16(1) second sentence of Regulation 2015/1589.
[218] See, for example, ECJ, Case 223/85 [1987] RSV v. Commission [17]; Case T-129/96 [1998] Preussag Stahl v. Commission [72]; Case T-21/06 [2009] Germany v. Commission [51].
[219] See ECJ, Case C-148/04 [2005] Unicredito Italiano v. Commission [107].
[220] ECJ, Case C-24/95 [1997] Land Rheinland-Pfalz v. Alcan.

6 The Case Example: Financing of Public Service Broadcasters in Germany

The decision of the European Commission on the financing of public service broadcasters in Germany was a result of a long-lasting legal altercation between Germany and the Commission. The Commission and Germany disagreed on almost every point of the legal assessment. The case example reflects only a part of this controversy, which also included, for example, special tax treatment of commercial activities of public broadcasters and financial guarantees.

The nature of the financing of German public broadcasters[221] as a state aid was already subject to controversy. First, referring to the *Altmark Trans* ruling, Germany denied the existence of a financial advantage. By contrast, the Commission held that the German legal framework on public broadcasting did not give a sufficiently clear and precise definition of the public service remit (first *Altmark Trans* criterion). German legislation allowed public broadcasters to offer certain new media services ('telemedia') 'without the scope and limit of the activities which are covered by the remit being sufficiently clear'. Furthermore, the Commission doubted that the compensation granted to public broadcasters was based on parameters as required by the second *Altmark Trans* criterion, given that it is not the KEF that sets the licence fee level but the parliaments of the federal states. Moreover, the financing regime did not give the necessary guarantees that the compensation granted to public service broadcasters does not exceed the public service costs (third *Altmark Trans* criterion). Finally, the Commission was not convinced that the financing regime ensures – in the absence of a tender procedure – that the compensation amount is limited to the costs of an efficient operator (fourth *Altmark Trans* criterion). As a result, the Commission held that the conditions stipulated in the *Altmark Trans* judgement were not fulfilled.[222]

Then, Germany argued that even if the Commission assumed that there was a financial advantage, the aid was not granted through state resources: The licence fee was paid directly by the owners of radio and TV sets[223] to the public broadcasters and was thus never under the control of the state. However, as has already been indicated above, the Commission held that the licence fee revenues constitute state resources which are under state control.[224] The licence fee is a compulsory levy ultimately imposed by the state legislation on households and the collection of the licence fees follows procedures similar to those of tax collection. That being so, it is irrelevant that the compensation is not directly paid from the state budget.

---

[221] Since all public service broadcasters in Germany are public broadcasters, the latter term will be used here.
[222] COM, Decision C(2007)1761 of 24 April 2007, State aid E 3/2005 (ex-CP 2/2003, CP 232/2002, CP 43/2003, CP 243/2004 and CP 195/2004) – Financing of public service broadcasters in Germany [158 ff].
[223] Now it is paid by households disregarding the availability of a TV or radio set.
[224] COM, Decision C(2007)1761 of 24 April 2007, State aid E 3/2005 (ex-CP 2/2003, CP 232/2002, CP 43/2003, CP 243/2004 and CP 195/2004) – Financing of public service broadcasters in Germany [143 ff].

Next, the Commission also held that the financing regime distorted competition and effected trade between Member States. It referred to the competition for audience and advertisement, the international trade in programmes and programme rights, the cross-border effects of advertisement and the transnational ownership structure of private competitors.[225] The Commission concluded that the licence fee funding constitutes state aid within the meaning of (now) Article 107(1) TFEU, more precisely, an 'existing aid' within the meaning of (now) Article 1(b) of Regulation 2015/1589.

The Commission then had to decide whether the financing regime was compatible with the Treaty. For this purpose, the Commission referred to (now) Article 106(2) TFEU. Despite the freedom of Member States to define the public service remit, the definition of the service (the first Article 106(2) TFEU criterion) must be sufficiently precise and clear. While the Commission regarded this criterion as fulfilled with regard to the general TV programme activities of German public broadcasters, it criticised the lack of precision regarding the additional digital channels. Contrary to the German government, the Commission did not consider the general requirement for additional digital channels to have a focus on 'culture, information and education' as sufficient to clearly describe the public service obligations. Regarding the new media services (the 'telemedia'), the Commission conceded that the public service remit may also comprise new services, provided that they serve the same democratic, social and cultural needs. However, the mere technical possibility to offer new services is not an automatism. Rather, the public service character has to be assessed with regard to each new service that is being offered by public service broadcasters. In this context, the Commission rejected Germany's views that all online activities envisaged by the German public broadcasters, including services such as online games, chat rooms and online dating services, contributed to the process of shaping public opinion. As a result, the Commission considered that Germany did not show that the services covered by the definition of programme-related and programme-accompanying new media could be regarded as services of general economic interest. The inclusion of such purely commercial activities in the public service remit constituted a 'manifest error'.[226]

In order to fulfil the second Article 106(2) TFEU criterion, the public broadcasters had to be officially entrusted by Germany. The Commission observed that there was no official act by which the public broadcasters have been entrusted with the specified new media services and the additional digital channels. Germany had argued that Article 5 of the German Basic Law would not allow for an act of entrustment, as it would interfere with the public broadcasters' independence. However, the

---

[225] COM, Decision C(2007)1761 of 24 April 2007, State aid E 3/2005 (ex-CP 2/2003, CP 232/2002, CP 43/2003, CP 243/2004 and CP 195/2004) – Financing of public service broadcasters in Germany [181ff].

[226] COM, Decision C(2007)1761 of 24 April 2007, State aid E 3/2005 (ex-CP 2/2003, CP 232/2002, CP 43/2003, CP 243/2004 and CP 195/2004) – Financing of public service broadcasters in Germany [227 ff].

Commission held that independence from the state cannot justify an extension of the public service remit without a clear entrustment.[227] Moreover, as has been explained above, Member States have to control that the public service is provided as stipulated in the entrustment. In this context, Germany indicated that there are internal and external control mechanisms in place, such as the Broadcasting Council. However, the Commission doubted that these internal control bodies alone can ensure effective supervision of the fulfilment of the public service with a view to the vaguely defined public service mission. Finally, the Commission also decided that the broadcasting financing regime did not make sure that the state financing is limited to what is necessary for the fulfilment of the public service mission while limiting adverse effects on competition to the necessary minimum. The German public broadcasting financing regime was thus not compatible with EU law.

Consequently, the Commission proposed measures to the German authorities in order to ensure compatibility with EU state aid law.[228] Germany had to make sure, *inter alia*, that the scope of the public broadcasters' obligations in relation to additional channels is further clarified, that the determination of whether new media activities satisfy the same democratic, social and cultural needs of society is based on a set of criteria suitable to assess the public service character of the service in question and that purely commercial activities are not part of the public service remit. The German government subsequently promised to implement a number of measures. In particular, Germany announced the establishment of an evaluation procedure and criteria for all new or modified digital offers of public broadcasters. Public broadcasters shall be obliged for all new or modified digital offers to apply a three-step test. They have to evaluate that each offer (1) serves the democratic, social and cultural needs of society, (2) contributes in a qualitative way to 'editorial competition' and (3) that the public service broadcasters specify the financial impact of such offers.[229] These measures would still respect the editorial responsibility and independence of public broadcasters. The Commission accepted the commitments given by Germany and closed the state aid procedure.

V Questions

1 To what extent is the application of state aid law an instrument to safeguard media pluralism? Do what extent does the application of state aid law pose a threat to media pluralism?

---

[227] COM, Decision C(2007)1761 of 24 April 2007, State aid E 3/2005 (ex-CP 2/2003, CP 232/2002, CP 43/2003, CP 243/2004 and CP 195/2004) – Financing of public service broadcasters in Germany [251].
[228] COM, Decision C(2007)1761 of 24 April 2007, State aid E 3/2005 (ex-CP 2/2003, CP 232/2002, CP 43/2003, CP 243/2004 and CP 195/2004) – Financing of public service broadcasters in Germany [308 ff].
[229] COM, Decision C(2007)1761 of 24 April 2007, State aid E 3/2005 (ex-CP 2/2003, CP 232/2002, CP 43/2003, CP 243/2004 and CP 195/2004) – Financing of public service broadcasters in Germany [328].

2 Are *PreussenElektra* and *Bayerischer Rundfunk* consistent? If not, which decision does not convince you?

3 What should be the role of public (service) broadcasters on the internet? With a view to the powerful and influential role of internet services, such as Google and Facebook, should there be an even broader public service remit, including, for example, a public search engine and a public social network? To what extent would this be compatible with the Commission's decision on the financing of public broadcasters in Germany?

VI Further Reading

- K. Bacon, *European Union Law of State Aid*, 2nd edn, 2013, Chapter 15: Media and Communications
- K. Donders, *Public Service Media and Policy in Europe*, 2011
- L. Hancher, *EU State Aids*, 4th edn, 2011, Chapter 18: Broadcasting
- I. Katsirea, *Public Broadcasting and European Law: A Comparative Examination of Public Service Obligations in Six Member States*, 2008
- P.C. Murschetz, *State Aid for Newspapers, Theories, Cases, Actions*, 2013

REFERENCES

Adamski, D. (2014) 'Access to Documents, Accountability and the Rule of Law – Do Private Watchdogs Matter?' 20 *European Law Journal* 520

Addo, M.K. (1998) 'Are Judges Beyond Criticism Under Article 10 of the European Convention of Human Rights?' 47 *International & Comparative Law Quarterly* 425

Addo, M.K. (ed.) (2000) *Freedom of Expression and the Criticism of Judges: A Comparative Study of European Legal Standards* (Dartmouth: Ashgate)

Ahdar, R. and Leigh, I. (2005) *Religious Freedom in the Liberal State* (Oxford University Press)

Akdeniz, Y. (2008) *Internet Child Pornography and the Law: National and International Responses* (Aldershot: Ashgate)

Albrecht, H.-J., Brunst, P., De Busser, E., Grundies, V., Kilchling, M., Rinceanu, J., Kenzel, B., Nikolova, N., Rotino, S. and Tauschwitz, M. (2012) *Schutzlücken durch Wegfall der Vorratsdatenspeicherung? Eine Untersuchung zu Problemen der Gefahrenabwehr und Strafverfolgung bei Fehlen gespeicherter Telekommunikationsverkehrsdaten* (Berlin: Duncker & Humblot)

Amar, V.D. (1999) 'From Watergate to Kenn Starr: Potter Stewart's "Or of the Press" A Quarter Century Later', 50 *Hastings Law Journal* 711

Anagnostaras, G. (2014) 'Balancing Conflicting Fundamental Rights: The Sky Österreich Paradigm', 1 *European Law Review* 111

Anderson, D.A. (2002) 'Freedom of the Press', 80 *Texas Law Review* 429

Anonymous (2007) 'Developments in the Law: The Law of the Media', 120 *Harvard Law Review* 990

Aplin, T. (2005) *Copyright Law in the Digital Society* (Oxford: Hart Publishing)

Aplin, T. and Davis, J. (2013) *Intellectual Property Law: Text, Cases and Materials* (2nd edn, Oxford University Press)

Arnott, C. (2010) 'Media Mergers and the Meaning of Sufficient Plurality: A Tale of Two Acts', 2 *Journal of Media Law* 245

Austin, J.L. (1962) *How to Do Things with Words* (Oxford University Press)

Baker, C.E. (2007) 'The Independent Significance of the Press Clause Under Existing Law', 35 *Hofstra Law Review* 955

  (2009) 'Viewpoint Diversity and Media Ownership', 60 *Federal Communications Commission Law Journal* 651

  (2011) 'Press Performance, Human Rights, and Private Power as a Threat', 5 *Law & Ethics of Human Rights* 219

Bania, K. (2013) 'European Merger Control in the Broadcasting Sector: Does Media Pluralism Fit?' 9 *Competition Law Review* 49

Barendt, E. (2005) *Freedom of Speech* (2nd edn, Oxford University Press)

  (2005–2006) 'Jurisdiction in Internet Libel Cases', 110 *Penn State Law Review* 727

(2009) 'Bad News for Bloggers', 2 *Journal of Media Law* 141

(2015a) 'An Overlap of Defamation and Privacy?' 7 *Journal of Media Law* 85

(2015b) 'Media Freedom as a Fundamental Right', 7 *Journal of Media Law* 307

Barlow, J.P. (1996) *A Declaration of the Independence of Cyberspace*, available at https://projects. eff.org/~barlow/Declaration-Final.html

Bavasso, A.F. (2004) 'Electronic Communications: A New Paradigm for European Regulation', 41 *Common Market Law Review* 87

Benkler, Y. (2000) 'From Consumers to Users: Shifting the Deeper Structures of Regulation Toward Sustainable Commons and User Access', 52 *Federal Communications Law Journal* 561

Bently, L. and Sherman, B. (2014) *Intellectual Property Law* (4th edn, Oxford University Press)

Berners-Lee, T. (2006) *Net Neutrality: This is Serious*, available at http://dig.csail.mit.edu/breadcrumbs/node/144

Bezanson, R.P. (1977) 'The New Free Press Guarantee', 63 *Virginia Law Review* 731

(2012) 'Whither Freedom of the Press?' 97 *Iowa Law Review* 1259

Blakeney, M. (1996) *Trade Related Aspects of Intellectual Property Rights: A Concise Guide to the TRIPs Agreement* (Andover: Sweet & Maxwell)

Blasi, V. (1977) 'The Checking Value in First Amendment Theory', 1977 *American Bar Foundation Research Journal* 521

Blocher, J. (2012) 'Public Discourse, Expert Knowledge, and the Press', 87 *Washington Law Review* 409

Borghi, M. (2011) 'Chasing Copyright Infringement in the Streaming Landscape', 42 *International Review of Intellectual Property and Competition Law* 316

Bork, R.H. (1971) 'Neutral Principles and Some First Amendment Problems', 47 *Indiana Law Journal* 1

Bradford, A. (2012) 'The Brussels Effect', 107 *Northwestern University Law Review* 1

Bronckers M. and Larouche, P. (1997) 'Telecommunications Services and the World Trade Organization', 31 *Journal of World Trade* 5

Brown, D. (2010) 'Television Sponsorship: An Advertising Opportunity or a Pitfall for the Unwary?' 21 *Entertainment Law Review* 179

Burnley, R. and Bania, K. (2014) 'Co-operation Between Broadcasters in the New Media Age: Rethinking National Competition Policy', 35 *European Competition Law Review* 216

Burri, M. (2013) 'Business as Usual? The Implementation of the UNESCO Convention on Cultural Diversity and EU Media Law and Policies', 3 *European Law Review* 802

Burri Nenova, M. (2007) 'The Law of the World Trade Organization and the Communications Law of the European Community: On a Path of Harmony or Discord?' 41 *Journal of World Trade* 833

Cahn, S. and Schimmel, D. (1997) 'The Cultural Exception: Does it Exist in GATT and GATS Frameworks? How Does it Affect or is it Affected by the Agreement on TRIPS?' 15 *Cardozo Arts and Entertainment Law Journal* 281

Calliess, G.-P. and Zumbansen, P. (2010) *Rough Consensus and Running Code: A Theory of Transnational Law* (Oxford: Hart Publishing)

Carter, S.L. (1992) 'Does the First Amendment Protect More than Free Speech?' 33 *William and Mary Law Review* 871

Castendyk, O. (2006) 'Quotas in Favour of Independent Producers: Article 5 of the "Television Without Frontiers" Directive' 11 *Communications Law* 88

Castendyk, O., Dommering, E. and Scheuer, A. (eds.) (2008) *European Media Law* (Alphen aan den Rijn: Wolters Kluwer)

Chao, T.W. (1996) 'GATT's Cultural Exemption of Audiovisual Trade: The United States May Have Lost the Battle but Not the War', 17 *University of Pennsylvania Journal of International Economic Law* 1127

Chirico, F. and Gaal, N. (2014) 'A Decade of State Aid Control in the Field of Broadband', 13 *European State Aid Law Quarterly* 28

Coase, R.H. (1959) 'The Federal Communications Commission', 2 *Journal of Law and Economics* 1

Cohen, J. (2007) 'Cyberspace as/and Space', 107 *Columbia Law Review* 210

Cooper, J. and Williams, A.M. (1999) 'Hate Speech, Holocaust Denial and International Human Rights Law', 19 *European Human Rights Law Review* 593

Coors, C. (2013) 'Reputations at Stake: The German Federal Court's Decision Concerning Google's Liability for Autocomplete Suggestions in the International Context', 5 *Journal of Media Law* 322

Correa, C.M. (2007) *Trade Related Aspects of Intellectual Property Rights: A Commentary on the TRIPS Agreement* (Oxford University Press)

Craufurd Smith, R. (2004) 'Rethinking European Union Competence in the Field of Media Ownership: The Internal Market, Fundamental Rights and European Citizenship', 29 *European Law Review* 652

    (2007) 'Media Convergence and the Regulation of Audiovisual Content', 60 *Current Legal Problems* 238

    (2011) 'Determining Regulatory Competence for Audiovisual Media Services in the European Union', 3 *Journal of Media Law* 263

    (2013) 'Reviewing Media Ownership Rules in the UK and Europe: Competing or Complementary Investigations?' 5 *Journal of Media Law* 332

Craufurd Smith, R. and Tambini, D. (2012) 'Measuring Media Plurality in the United Kingdom: Policy Choices and Regulatory Challenges', 4 *Journal of Media Law* 35.

Delimatsis, P. (2011) 'Protecting Public Morals in a Digital Age: Revisiting the WTO Rulings in US – Gambling and China – Publications and Audiovisual Products', 14 *Journal of International Economic Law* 257

Derclaye, E. (2010) 'Infopaq International A/S v. Danske Dagblades Forening (C5/08): Wonderful or Worrysome? The Impact of the ECJ Ruling in Infopaq on UK Copyright Law', 32 *European Intellectual Property Review* 247

De Schutter, O. (2010) *International Human Rights Law* (Cambridge University Press)

De Varennes, F. (1993) 'Language and Freedom of Expression in International Law', 15 *Human Rights Quarterly* 163

Dickinson, A. (2008) *The Rome II Regulation: The Law Applicable to Non-Contractual Obligations* (Oxford University Press)

Di Mauro, L. (2003) 'Defining the Retail Market for Audiovisual Products', 8 *European Competition Law Review* 384

Dizon, M.A.C. (2012) 'Looking Beyond the Linear/Non-Linear Horizon: Content Regulation in the Converging Multilayered Contours of the European Audiovisual Media Landscape', 21 *Entertainment Law Review* 185

Dods, D., Brisby, P., Hubbard, R., Ollerenshaw, K. and Ingram, B. (2010) 'Reform of European Electronic Communications Law: A Special Briefing on the Radical Changes of 2009', 16 *Computer and Telecommunications Law Review* 102

Donders, K. and Van Rompuy, B. (2012) 'Competition Law, Sports, and Public Service Broadcasting: The Legal Complexity and Political Sensitivity of Measuring Market Distortion and Public Value', 4 *Journal of Media Law* 213

Drahos, P. (1997) *A Philosophy of Intellectual Property* (Dartmouth: Ashgate)

Drake, W.J. and Noam, E.M. (1997) 'The WTO Deal on Basic Telecommunications: Big Bang or Little Whimper?' 21 *Telecommunications Policy* 799

Edwards, L. (2004) 'The Scotsman, the Greek, the Mauritian Company and the Internet: Where on Earth do Things Happen in Cyberspace?' 8 *Edinburgh Law Review* 99

Edwards, L. and Waelde, C. (eds.) (2009) *Law and the Internet* (3rd edn, Oxford: Hart Publishing)

Ehrenzweig, A.A. (1968) 'Specific Principles of Private Transnational Law', 124 *Collected Courses of the Hague Academy of International Law* 167

El-Agraa, A.M. (2011) *The European Union: Economics and Policies* (9th edn, Cambridge University Press)

Emerson, T.I. (1963) 'Toward a General Theory of the First Amendment', 72 *Yale Law Journal* 877

Erdos, D. (2013) 'Freedom of Expression Turned on its Head? Academic Social Research and Journalism in the European Privacy Framework', 1 *Public Law* 52

European Copyright Society (2015) 'Limitations and Exceptions as Key Elements of the Legal Framework for Copyright in the European Union – Opinion on the Judgment of the CJEU in Case C-201/13 Deckmyn', *European Intellectual Property Review* 130

Fawcett, J. and Carruthers, J.M. (2008) *Cheshire, North & Fawcett Private International Law* (14th edn, Oxford University Press)

Fenwick, H. and Phillipson, G. (2006) *Media Freedom under the Human Rights Act* (Oxford University Press)

Filipek, J. (1992) '"Culture Quotas": The Trade Controversy over the European Community's Broadcasting Directive', 28 *Stanford Journal of International Law* 323

Foucault, M. (1978) *The History of Sexuality: An Introduction*, trans. Robert Hurley (New York: Pantheon Books)

Fried, C. (1968) 'Privacy', 77 *Yale Law Journal* 475

Froomkin, A.M. (2000) 'Wrong Turn in Cyberspace: Using ICANN to Route Around the APA and the Constitution', 50 *Duke Law Journal* 17

Galtung, A. (2001) 'The Rights and Obligations to Access and Interconnect', 12 *European Business Law Review* 210

Garnett, R. and Richardson, M. (2009) 'Libel Tourism or Just Redress? Reconciling the (English) Right to Reputation with the (American) Right to Free Speech in Cross-Border Libel Cases', 5 *Journal of Private International Law* 471

Garry, P. (1989) 'The First Amendment and Freedom of the Press: A Revised Approach to the Marketplace of Ideas Concept', 72 *Marquette Law Review* 187

Gavison, R. (1980) 'Privacy and the Limits of Law', 89 *Yale Law Journal* 421

Geiger, C. (2012) 'Weakening Multilateralism in Intellectual Property Lawmaking: A European Perspective on ACTA', 2012 *WIPO Journal* 166

Geradin, D. (2005) 'Access to Content by New Media Platforms: A Review of the Competition Law Problems', 30 *European Law Review* 68

Gleick, J. (2012) *The Information: A History, A Theory, A Flood* (London: Vintage)

Goldberg, D. (2009) 'Freedom of Information in the 21st Century: Bringing Clarity to Transparency', 14 *Communications Law* 50

Goldsmith, J. and Wu, T. (2008) *Who Controls the Internet? Illusions of a Borderless World* (Oxford University Press)

Grant, J.M. (1995) 'Jurassic' Trade Dispute: The Exclusion of the Audiovisual Sector from the GATT', 70 *Indiana Law Journal* 1333

Greenleaf, G. (2012) 'The Influence of European Data Privacy Standards Outside Europe: Implications for Globalization of Convention 108', 2 *International Data Privacy Law* 68

Griffin, J. (1998) 'Reactions to US Assertions of Extraterritorial Jurisdiction', 19 *European Competition Law Review* 64

Griffiths, J. (2013) 'Constitutionalising or Harmonising? The Court of Justice, the Right to Property and European Copyright Law', 38 *European Law Review* 65

Han, B.-C. (2015) *The Transparency Society* (Stanford University Press, 2015)

Hancher, L. and Larouche, P. (2011) 'The Coming of Age of EU Regulation of Network Industries and Services of General Economic Interest', in P. Craig and G. de Búrca (eds.), *The Evolution of EU Law* (2nd edn, Oxford University Press), 744

Hare, I. (2006) 'Crosses, Crescents and Sacred Cows: Criminalising Incitement to Religious Hatred', 2006 *Public Law* 521

Harrison, J. and Woods, L. (2007) *European Broadcasting Law and Policy* (Cambridge University Press, 2007)

Hartley, T.C. (2010) '"Libel Tourism" and Conflict of Laws', 59 *International & Comparative Law Quarterly* 25

Helfer, L.R. (2008) 'The New Innovation Frontier? Intellectual Property and the European Court of Human Rights', 49 *Harvard International Law Journal* 1

Hettinger, E.C. (1989) 'Justifying Intellectual Property', 18 *Philosophy & Public Affairs* 31

Hins, W. (2014) 'The Freedom to Conduct a Business and the Right to Receive Information for Free: Sky Österreich', 51 *Common Market Law Review* 665

Hon, W.K., Hörnle J. and Millard, C. (2012) 'Data Protection Jurisdiction and Cloud Computing: When are Cloud Users and Providers Subject to EU Data Protection Law? The Cloud of Unknowing', 26 *International Review of Law, Computers & Technology* 129

Honorati, C. (2006) 'The Law Applicable to Unfair Competition', in A. Malatesta (ed.), *The Unification of Choice of Law Rules on Torts and Other Non-Contractual Obligations in Europe* (Milan: CEDAM), 127

Huber, P. (ed.) (2011) *Rome II Regulation Pocket Commentary* (Munich: SELP)

Hughes, J. (1988–1989) 'The Philosophy of Intellectual Property', 77 *Georgetown Law Journal* 287

Hughes, K. (2010) 'No Reasonable Expectation of Anonymity?' 2 *Journal of Media Law* 169
   (2012) 'A Behavioural Understanding of Privacy and its Implications for Privacy Law', 75 *Modern Law Review* 806

Hume, D. (1739) *A Treatise of Human Nature*, available at www.gutenberg.org/files/4705/4705-h/4705-h.htm

Hunter, D. (2003) 'Cyberspace as Place and the Tragedy of the Digital Anticommons', 91 *California Law Review* 439

Hurwitz, J. (2013) 'Trust and Online Interaction', 161 *University of Pennsylvania Law Review* 1579

Hyland, M. (2012) 'The Football Association Premier League ruling – the Bosman of exclusive broadcasting rights?', 17 *Communications Law* 7

Internet Society (2012) *Brief History of the Internet*, available at www.internetsociety.org/sites/default/files/Brief_History_of_the_Internet.pdf

IViR (2007) 'Study on the Implementation and Effect in Member States' Laws of Directive 2001/
29/EC on the Harmonisation of Certain Aspects of Copyright and Related Rights in the
Information Society', available at http://ec.europa.eu/internal_market/copyright/docs/
studies/infosoc-study_en.pdf

Jaoude, P.A. (2003) 'Racist Speech: The Ultimate Challenge for Toleration? A Philosophical
Exploration of Justifications for Hate Speech Protection', 2003 UCL Jurisprudence Review 340

Jessup, P.C. (1956) Transnational Law (New Haven: Yale University Press)

Johnson, D.R. and Post, D. (1996) 'Law and Borders: The Rise of Law in Cyberspace', 48 Stanford
Law Review 1367

Johnson, B.E.H. and Youm, K.H. (2009) 'Commercial Speech and Free Expression: The United
States and Europe Compared', 2 Journal of International Media and Entertainment Law 159

Jones, A. and Sufrin, B. (2014) EU Competition Law – Text, Cases, and Materials (5th edn, Oxford
University Press)

Kahn-Freund, O. (1954) 'Reflections on Public Policy in the English Conflict of Laws', Transactions
for the Year 1953', 39 The Grotius Society 39

Kamecke, U. and Korber, T. (2008) 'Technological Neutrality in the EC Regulatory Framework
for Electronic Communications: A Good Principle Widely Misunderstood', 29 European
Competition Law Review 330

Katsirea, I. (2003) 'Why the European broadcasting quota should be abolished' (2003), 28
European Law Review 190

    (2012) 'Who is Afraid of Public Service Broadcasting? The Digital Future of an Age-Old
Institution Under Threat', 31 Yearbook of European Law 416

Katz, M.L. and Shapiro, C. (1985) 'Network Externalities, Competition and Compatibility', 75
The American Economic Review 424

Keller, H. and Sigron, M. (2010) 'State Security v Freedom of Expression: Legitimate Fight against
Terrorism or Suppression of Political Opposition?' 10 Human Rights Law Review 151

Keller, P. (2011) European and International Media Law (Oxford University Press)

Kelly, C. (2012) 'Current Events and Fair Dealing with Photographs: Time for a Revised
Approach?' 4 Intellectual Property Quarterly 242

Khan, A. (2012) 'A "Right Not to be Offended" Under Article 10(2) ECHR? Concerns in the
Construction of the "Rights of Others"', 2012 European Human Rights Law Review 191

Kliemann, A. and Stehmann, O. (2013) 'EU State Aid Control in the Broadband Sector: The 2013
Broadband Guidelines and Recent Case Practice', 3 European State Aid Law Quarterly 493

Koenig, C., Bartosch, A., Braun, J.-D. and Romes, M. (eds.) (2009) EC Competition and
Telecommunications Law (2nd edn, Alphen aan den Rijn: Wolters Kluwer)

Kohl, U. (2007) Jurisdiction and the Internet (Cambridge University Press)

Komorek, E. (2009) 'Is Media Pluralism a Human Right? The European Court of Human Rights,
the Council of Europe and the Issue of Media Pluralism', 3 European Human Rights Law
Review 395

Kruger, T. (2008) Civil Jurisdiction Rules of the EU and their Impact on Third States (Oxford
University Press)

Kuipers, J-J. (2011) 'Towards a European Approach in the Cross-Border Infringement of
Personality Rights', 8 German Law Journal 1681

Kur, A. and Levin, M. (2011) Intellectual Property Rights in a Fair World Trade System: Proposals
for Reform of TRIPS (Cheltenham: Edward Elgar)

Landes, W.M. and Posner , R.A. (2003) *The Economic Structure of Intellectual Property Law* (Harvard University Press)

Lange, D. (1975) 'The Speech and Press Clauses', 23 *UCLA Law Review* 77

Lefever, K., Cannie, H. and Valcke, P. (2010) 'Watching Live Sport on Television: A Human Right? The Right to Information and the List of Major Events Regime', 4 *European Human Rights Law Review* 396

Le Goueff, S. (2007) 'The Proposed Audiovisual Media Services Directive: Challenges to the Country of Origin Principle', 8 *Computer and Telecommunications Law Review* 232

Lemley, M.A. (2003) 'Place and Cyberspace', 91 *California Law Review* 521

Lessig, L. (1996) 'The Zones of Cyberspace', 48 *Stanford Law Review* 1403

(1999) 'The Law of the Horse: What Cyberlaw Might Teach', 113 *Harvard Law Review* 501

(2006) *Code, Version 2.0* (New York: Basic Books)

Letsas, G. (2012) 'Is There a Right Not to be Offended in One's Religious Beliefs?' in L. Zucca and C. Ungureanu (eds.), *Law, State and Religion in the New Europe* (Cambridge University Press), 239

Lewis, A. (1979) 'A Preferred Position for Journalism?' 7 *Hofstra Law Review* 595

Lindsay, D. (2014) 'The "Right to be Forgotten" by Search Engines Under Data Privacy Law: A Legal Analysis of the Costeja Ruling', 6 *Journal of Media Law* 159

Liu, D. (2013) 'Meltwater Melts Not Water but Principle! The Danger of the Court Adjudicating an Issue Outwith the Ambit of Referral', 35 *European Intellectual Property Review* 327

Lobo, S. (2014) Die digitale Kränkung des Menschen', available at www.faz.net/aktuell/feuilleton/debatten/abschied-von-der-utopie-die-digitale-kraenkung-des-menschen-12747258.html

Locke, J. (1689) *Two Treatises of Government, Second Treatise* (London: A. Millar)

Luhmann, N. (1996) *The Reality of the Mass Media*, trans. K. Cross (Cambridge: Polity Press)

Lust, P. (2003) 'Mobile Interconnection', 7 *International Journal of Communications Law and Policy* 1

Lutz, H. (2006) 'The Distinction Between Linear and Non-Linear Services in the New Proposal for an Audiovisual Media Directive', 12 *Computer and Telecommunications Law Review* 141

Maduro, M., Tuori, K. and Sankari, S. (eds.) (2014) *Transnational Law: Rethinking European Law and Legal Thinking* (Cambridge University Press)

Maier, B. (2010) 'How Has the Law Attempted to Tackle the Borderless Nature of the Internet?' 18 *International Journal of Law and Information Technology* 142

Manners, I. (2002) 'Normative Power Europe: A Contradiction in Terms?' 40 *Journal of Common Market Studies* 235

Marsden, C.T. (2010) *Net Neutrality: Towards a Co-regulatory Solution* (London: Bloomsbury Publishing)

(2011) *Internet Co-Regulation: European Law, Regulatory Governance and Legitimacy in Cyberspace* (Cambridge University Press)

Marshall, G. (1992) 'Press Freedom and Free Speech Theory', 40 *Public Law* 51

Maxwell, W.J. and Bourreau, M. (2015) 'Technology Neutrality in Internet, Telecoms and Data Protection Regulation', 21 *Computer and Telecommunications Law Review* 1

Mayer-Schönberger, V. (2008) 'Demystifying Lessig', 2008 *Wisconsin Law Review* 713

(2009) *Delete: The Virtue of Forgetting in the Digital Age* (Princeton University Press)

Mayer-Schönberger, V. and Cukier, K. (2013) *Big Data: A Revolution That Will Transform How We Live, Work and Think* (London: John Murray)

McEvedy, V. (2013) 'Defamation and Intermediaries: ISP Defences', 19 *Computer & Telecommunications Law Review* 108

McLuhan, M. (1964) *Understanding Media* (republished London and New York: Routledge, 2001)

McManis, C.R. (2009–2010) 'Proposed Anti-Counterfeiting Trade Agreement (ACTA): Two Tales of a Treaty', 46 *Houston Law Review* 1235

Meiklejohn, A. (1948) *Free Speech and its Relation to Self-Government* (New York: Harper Brother Publishers)

(1961) 'The First Amendment is an Absolute', 1961 *Supreme Court Review* 245

Mensching, C. (2010) 'Limitless or Limited International Internet Jurisdiction within the European Union?' 21 *Entertainment Law Review* 281

Michel, R. (2012/2013) 'Jurisdiction in Case of Personality Torts Committed over the Internet: A Proposal for a Targeting Test', 14 *Yearbook of Private International Law* 205

Mill, J.S. (1869) *On Liberty* (republished London and Felling-on-Tyne: The Walter Scott Publishing Co., 1989)

Mills, A. (2014) 'Rethinking Jurisdiction in International Law', 84 *The British Yearbook of International Law* 187

Milton, J. (1644) *Areopagitica; A Speech of Mr. John Milton for the Liberty of Unlicenc'd Printing, to the Parliament of England* (London, 1644)

Monti, M. (2004) 'A Reformed Competition Policy: Achievements and Challenges for the Future', 3 *Competition Policy Newsletter* 1

Moore, V. (2005) 'Free Speech and the Right to Self-Realisation', 12 *UCL Jurisprudence Review* 95

Moosavian, R. (2014) 'Deconstructing "Public Interest" in the Article 8 vs Article 10 Balancing Exercise', 6 *Journal of Media Law* 234

Moreham, N.A. (2006) 'Privacy in Public Places', 65 *Cambridge Law Journal* 606

Munro, C.R. (2003) 'The Value of Commercial Speech', 62 *Cambridge Law Journal* 134

Murray, A. (2013) *Information Technology Law* (2nd edn, Oxford University Press)

Murray, D. (2009) 'Freedom of Expression, Counter-Terrorism and the Internet in Light of the UK Terrorist Act 2006 and the Jurisprudence of the European Court of Human Rights', 27 *Netherlands Quarterly of Human Rights* 331

Nehaluddin, A. (2010) 'A Viewpoint on the Regulation of Converging Technologies', 16 *Computer and Telecommunications Law Review* 27

Nehl, H.P. (2003) 'Rechtsschutz im Bereich grenzüberschreitender Medienzusammenschlüsse', available at http://ec.europa.eu/competition/speeches/text/sp2003_041_de.pdf

Newman, J.L. (2008) 'Keeping the Internet Neutral: Net Neutrality and its Role in Protecting Political Expression on the Internet', 31 *Hastings Communications & Entertainment Law Journal* 153

Nicol, A., Millar, G. and Sharland, A. (2009) *Media Law & Human Rights* (2nd edn, Oxford University Press)

Niels, G., Jenkins, H. and Kavanagh, J. (2011) *Economics for Competition Lawyers* (Oxford University Press)

Nielsen, P.A. (2013) 'Libel Tourism: English and EU Private International Law', 9 *Journal of Private International Law* 269

Nikolinakos, N.T. (2006) *EU Competition Law and Regulation in the Converging Telecommunications Media and IT Sectors* (Amsterdam: Wolters Kluwer)

Nimmer, M.B. (1975) 'Introduction: Is Freedom of the Press a Redundancy: What Does it Add to Freedom of Speech?' 26 *Hastings Law Journal* 639

Nowak, M. (2005) *UN Covenant on Civil and Political Rights Commentary* (2nd edn, Kehl am Rhein: Engel)

Ó Fathaigh, R. (2012) 'The Recognition of a Right of Reply under the European Convention', 4 *Journal of Media Law* 322

Oliva, J.G. (2007) 'The Legal Protection of Believers and Beliefs in the United Kingdom', 9 *Ecclesiastical Law Journal* 66

Oster, J. (2011) 'The Criticism of Trading Corporations and their Right to Sue for Defamation', 2 *Journal of European Tort Law* 255

  (2012a) 'Rethinking Shevill: Conceptualising the EU Private International Law of Internet Torts Against Personality Rights', 26 *International Review of Law, Computers & Technology* 113

  (2012b) 'The Commission Proposal to Amend the Regulation on Credit Rating Agencies', 19 *Maastricht Journal of European and Comparative Law* 206

  (2013) 'Theory and Doctrine of "Media Freedom" as a Legal Concept', 5 *Journal of Media Law* 57

  (2015a) 'Communication, Defamation, and Liability of Intermediaries', 35 *Legal Studies* 348

  (2015b) *Media Freedom as a Fundamental Right* (Cambridge University Press)

  (2015c) 'Public Policy and Human Rights', 11 *Journal of Private International Law* 542

Oswald, M. (2012) 'Freedom of Information in Cyberspace: What Now for Copyright?' 26 *International Review of Law, Computers & Technology* 245

Parmar, S. (2009) 'The Challenge of "Defamation of Religions" to Freedom of Expression and the International Human Rights', 3 *European Human Rights Law Review* 353

Pasqualucci, J.M. (2006) 'Criminal Defamation and the Evolution of the Doctrine of Freedom of Expression in International Law: Comparative Jurisprudence of the Inter-American Court of Human Rights', 39 *Vanderbilt Journal of Transnational Law* 379

Pauwels, C., De Vinck, S. and Van Rompuy, B. (2007) 'Can State Aid in the Film Sector Stand the Proof of EU and WTO Liberalisation Efforts?' 24 *European Studies* 23

Peers, S. (2011) *EU Justice and Home Affairs Law* (3rd edn, Oxford University Press)

Peng, S. (2007) 'Trade in Telecommunications Services: Doha and Beyond' (2007), 41 *Journal of World Trade* 293

Post, D.G. (2000) 'What Larry Doesn't Get: Code, Law, and Liberty in Cyberspace', 52 *Stanford Law Review* 1439

  (2008) 'Governing Cyberspace: Law', 24 *Santa Clara Computer & High Tech. Law Journal* 883

Post, R.C. (1991) 'Racist Speech, Democracy, and the First Amendment', 32 *William and Mary Law Review* 267

  (2001) 'Three Concepts of Privacy', 89 *Georgetown Law Journal* 2087

Prosser, W.L. (1960) 'Privacy', 48 *California Law Review* 383

Psychogiopoulou, E. (2006) 'The Cultural Mainstreaming Clause of Article 151(4) EC: Protection and Promotion of Cultural Diversity or Hidden Cultural Agenda?' 12 *European Law Journal* 575

  (2010) 'The "Cultural" Criterion in the European Commission's Assessment of State Aids to the Audiovisual Sector', 37 *Legal Issues of Economic Integration* 273

  (2012) 'State Aids to the Press: The EU's Perspective', 11 *European State Aid Law Quarterly* 57

Rahmatian, A. (2013) 'Originality in UK Copyright Law: The Old "Skill and Labour" Doctrine Under Pressure', 44 *International Review of Intellectual Property and Competition Law*, 4

Ramsay, M. (2012) 'The Status of Hearers' Rights in Freedom of Expression', 18 *Legal Theory* 31

Randall, M.H. (2006) 'Commercial Speech under the European Convention on Human Rights: Subordinate or Equal?' 6 *Human Rights Law Review* 53

Reed, C. (2004) *Internet Law* (2nd edn, Cambridge University Press)

Reidenberg, J.R. (1998) 'Lex Informatica: The Formation of Information Policy Rules Through Technology', 76 *Texas Law Review* 553

(2000) 'Resolving Conflicting International Data Privacy Rules in Cyberspace', 52 *Stanford Law Review* 1315

(2001) 'E-Commerce and Trans-Atlantic Privacy', 38 *Houston Law Review* 717

Ridgway, S. (2008) 'The Audiovisual Media Services Directive: What Does it Mean, is it Necessary and What Are the Challenges to its Implementation?' 14 *Computer and Telecommunications Law Review* 108

Rogers, E.M. (1994) *A History of Communication Study* (New York: The Free Press)

Rooney, M.J. (1983) 'Freedom of the Press: An Emerging Privilege', 67 *Marquette Law Review* 34

Rosati, E. (2011) 'Originality in a Work, or a Work of Originality: The Effects of the Infopaq Decision', 33 *European Intellectual Property Review* 746

(2013) 'Towards an EU-Wide Copyright? (Judicial) Pride and (Legislative) Prejudice', 1 *Intellectual Property Quarterly* 47

Saltzer, J.H., Reed, D.P. and Clark, D.D. (1984) 'End-to-End Arguments in System Design', available at http://web.mit.edu/Saltzer/www/publications/endtoend/endtoend.txt

Sandeen, S.K. (2002) 'In for a Calf is Not Always in for a Cow: An Analysis of the Constitutional Right of Anonymity as Applied to Anonymous E-Commerce', 29 *Hastings Constitutional Law Quarterly* 527

Sartor, G. (2015) 'The Right to be Forgotten in the Draft Data Protection Regulation', 5 *International Data Privacy Law* 64

Scanlon, T.M. (1972) 'A Theory of Freedom of Expression', 1 *Philosophy & Public Affairs* 204

Schauer, F. (1982) *Free Speech: a Philosophical Enquiry* (Cambridge University Press)

(2005) 'Towards an Institutional First Amendment', 89 *Minnesota Law Review* 1256

Schiff Berman, P. (2012) *Global Legal Pluralism: A Jurisprudence of Law Beyond Borders* (Cambridge University Press)

Schizer, D.M. (2010) 'Subsidizing the Press', 3 *Journal of Legal Analysis* 1

Schultz, T. (2008) 'Carving Up the Internet: Jurisdiction, Legal Orders, and the Private/Public International Law Interface', 19 *European Journal of International Law* 799

Schwartz, P.M. (1999) 'Privacy and Democracy in Cyberspace', 52 *Vanderbilt Law Review* 1609

(2013) 'The EU–US Privacy Collision: A Turn to Institutions and Procedures', 126 *Harvard Law Review* 1966

Scott, A. (2013) 'Editorial – Media Markets: A Crucible for Assessing the Intrinsic and Extrinsic Challenges for Competition Law and Policy', 9 *The Competition Law Review* 1

Scott, J. (2014) 'The New EU "Extraterritoriality"', 51 *Common Market Law Review* 1343

Senftleben, M. (2004) *Copyright, Limitations and the Three-Step Test: An Analysis of the Three-Step Test in International and EC Copyright Law* (Alphen aan den Rijn: Wolters Kluwer)

Shannon, C.E. (1948) 'A Mathematical Theory of Communication', 27 *The Bell System Technical Journal* 379

Shannon, C.E. and Weaver, W. (1949) *The Mathematical Theory of Communication* (Champaign, IL: University of Illinois Press)

Shy, O. (2010) *The Economics of Network Industries* (Cambridge University Press)

Simpson, E. (2006) 'Responsibilities for Hateful Speech', 12 *Legal Theory* 157

Slaughter, A.-M. (2004) *A New World Order* (Princeton University Press)

Smith, G.J.H. (2007a) 'Here, There or Everywhere? Cross-border Liability on the Internet', 13 *Computer and Telecommunications Law Review* 41

   (2007b) *Internet Law and Regulation* (4th edn, London: Sweet & Maxwell)

Solove, D.J. (2002) 'Conceptualizing Privacy', 90 *California Law Review* 1087

Solove, D.J. and Schwartz, P.M. (2011) *Information Privacy Law* (4th edn, New York: Wolters Kluwer)

Sottiaux, S. (2011) '"Bad Tendencies" in the ECtHR's "Hate Speech" Jurisprudence', 7 *European Constitutional Law Review* 40

Stein, A.R. (1998) 'The Unexceptional Problem of Jurisdiction in Cyberspace', 32 *The International Lawyer* 1167

Stewart, P. (1975) 'Or of the Press', 26 *Hastings Law Journal* 631

Stone, P. (2010) *EU Private International Law* (2nd edn, Cheltenham: Edward Elgar)

Sunstein, C.R. (1986) 'Pornography and the First Amendment', 35 *Duke Law Journal* 589

   (1992) 'Free Speech Now', 59 *University of Chicago Law Review* 255

   (2000) 'Television and the Public Interest', 88 *California Law Review* 499

   (2007) *Republic.com 2.0* (Princeton University Press)

Svantesson, D.J.B. (2012) *Private International Law and the Internet* (2nd edn, Alphen aan den Rijn: Wolters Kluwer)

   (2015) 'Limitless Borderless Forgetfulness? Limiting the Geographical Reach of the "Right to be Forgotten"', 2 *Oslo Law Review* 116

Swire, P.P. (1998) 'Of Elephants, Mice, and Privacy: International Choice of Law and the Internet', 32 *International Law* 991

Swire, P.P. and Litan, R.E. (1998) 'None of Your Business: World Data Flows, Electronic Commerce, and the European Privacy Directive', 12 *Harvard Journal of Law & Technology* 683

Tamura, Y. (2009) 'Rethinking Copyright Institution for the Digital Age', 1 *WIPO Journal* 63

Temperman, J. (2008) 'Blasphemy, Defamation of Religions and Human Rights Law', 26 *Netherlands Quarterly of Human Rights* 517

Tiilikka, P. (2013) 'Access to Information as a Human Right in the Case Law of the European Court of Human Rights', 5 *Journal of Media Law* 79

Tinbergen, J. (1954) *International Economic Integration* (Amsterdam: Elsevier)

Ugland, E. (2008) 'Demarcating the Right to Gather News: A Sequential Interpretation of the First Amendment', 3 *Duke Journal of Constitutional Law and Public Policy* 118

Valcke, P., Picard, R., Sükösd, M., Klimkiewicz, B., Petkovic, B., dal Zotto, C. and Kerremans, R. (2010) 'The European Media Pluralism Monitor: Bridging Law, Economics and Media Studies as a First Step towards Risk-Based Regulation in Media Markets', 2 *Journal of Media Law* 85

Van Calster, G. (2013) *European Private International Law* (Oxford: Hart Publishing)

van Gerven, W. (1989) 'EC Jurisdiction in Antitrust Matters: The Wood Pulp Judgment', 1989 *Fordham Corporate Law Institute* 451

Van Rompuy, B. and Donders, K. (2014) 'Competition Law Scrutiny of Horizontal Cooperation between Broadcasters: Is there a Mismatch between Theory and Commercial Reality?' 6 *Journal of Media Law* 269

van Rooijen, A. (2008) 'The Role of Investments in Refusals to Deal', 31 *World Competition* 63

Volokh, E. (2000) 'Freedom of Speech and Information Privacy: The Troubling Implications of a Right to Stop People From Speaking About You', 52 *Stanford Law Review* 1049

(2003a) 'Freedom of Speech and Intellectual Property: Some Thoughts after *Eldred*, *44 Liquormart*, and *Bartnicki*', 40 *Houston Law Review* 697

(2003b) 'Freedom of Speech and the Right of Publicity', 40 *Houston Law Review* 903

(2012) 'Freedom for the Press as an Industry, or For the Press as a Technology? From the Framing to Today', 160 *University of Pennsylvania Law Review* 459

Volokh, E. and Falk, D.M. (2012) 'Google First Amendment Protection for Search Engine Search Results', 8 *Journal of Law, Economics & Policy* 883

von Lewinski, S. and Walter, M.M. (eds.) (2010) *European Copyright Law: A Commentary* (Oxford University Press)

Voorhoof, D. and Humblet, P. (2014) 'Human Rights and the Employment Relation – The Right to Freedom of Expression at Work', 2014 *Les e-publi de l'Europe en mutation – La CEDH et la relation auf travail*

Vousden, S. (2010) 'Infopaq and the Europeanisation of Copyright Law', 2 *WIPO Journal* 197

Wagner, M.A. (2014) 'Revisiting the Country-of-Origin Principle in the AVMS Directive', 6 *Journal of Media Law* 286

Warren, S. and Brandeis, L. (1890) 'The Right to Privacy', 4 *Harvard Law Review* 193

Weatherall, K. (2011) 'ACTA as a New Kind of International IP Lawmaking', 26 *American University International Law Review* 839

Weber, A. (2009) *Manual on Hate Speech* (Strasbourg: Council of Europe Publishing)

Weinberg, J. (2000) 'ICANN and the Problem of Legitimacy', 50 *Duke Law Journal* 187

Weinstein, J. (2011) 'Participatory Democracy as the Central Value of American Free Speech Doctrine', 97 *Virginia Law Review* 491

Wells, C.E. (1997) 'Reinvigorating Autonomy: Freedom and Responsibility in the Supreme Court's First Amendment Jurisprudence', 32 *Harvard Civil Rights – Civil Liberties Law Journal* 159

Wells Branscomb, A. (1995) 'Anonymity, Autonomy, and Accountability: Challenges to the First Amendment in Cyberspaces', 104 *Yale Law Journal* 1639

West, S.R. (2011) 'Awakening the Press Clause', 58 *UCLA Law Review* 1025

Whish, R. and Bailey, D. (2015) *Competition Law* (8th edn, Oxford University Press)

Whitman, J.Q. (2004) 'The Two Western Cultures of Privacy: Dignity Versus Liberty', 113 *Yale Law Journal* 1151

Wolf, C. (2014) 'Delusions of Adequacy? Examining the Case for Finding the United States Adequate for Cross-Border EU-U.S. Data Transfers', 43 *Washington University Journal of Law & Policy* 227

Wood, A. (2012) 'The CJEU's Ruling in the Premier League Pub TV Cases: The Final Whistle Beckons: Joined Cases Football Association Premier League Ltd v. QC Leisure (C-403/08) and Murphy v. Media Protection Services Ltd (C-429/08)', 34 *European Intellectual Property Review* 203

Woods, L. (2012) 'Beyond *Murphy*, Films and Football: Audiovisual Content in Europe', 4 *Journal of Media Law* 189

Wragg, P. (2013) 'Mill's Dead Dogma: The Value of Truth to Free Speech Jurisprudence', 2013 *Public Law* 363

Wu, T. (2003) 'Network Neutrality, Broadband Discrimination', 2 *Journal of Telecommunication and High Technology Law* 141

Wu, T. and Yoo, C. (2007) 'Keeping the Internet Neutral? Tim Wu and Christopher Yoo Debate', 59 *Federal Communications Law Journal* 575

Yoo, C. (2006) 'Network Neutrality and the Economics of Congestion', 94 *Georgetown Law Journal* 1847

Zalnieriute, M. and Schneider, T. (2014) 'ICANN's Procedures and Policies in the Light of Human Rights, Fundamental Freedoms and Democratic Values', *Council of Europe Document GI*, 12

Zumbansen, P. (2012) 'Transnational Law: Evolving', in J. Smits (ed.), *Encyclopedia of Comparative Law* (2nd edn, Cheltenham: Edward Elgar) 899

INDEX

abuse of dominant positions 470–77
academic expression 44
access
 to information, data subject's right
  of 343–45
 to information, right to 59–64
 to networks 194–99, 290–94
accountability 193–94
accounting separation in telecommunications
 296–97
accreditation schemes for journalists 109
accuracy of data 334–35
acquisitions 477–87, 499–500
actor sequitur forum rei principle 121
adjudicative jurisdiction 114
advertising 105, 170–72
 comparative advertising 492–93
 and human rights 489–90
 misleading advertising 491–92
 product-related restrictions 173–74
 restrictions on 35
 time and timing of 176–79
 transparency requirements 172–73
affected market principle 493–97
Africa
 receive information, right to 59
aggressive practices 175
aid, state *see* state aid
Altmark Trans criteria for state aid 513–18,
 536
anonymity
 freedom of expression 46–50
 internet service providers (ISPs) 50
 journalistic media 48–49
 and privacy 47
 social media 49–50
 United States 47–48
anti-trust law
 aims of 447–49
 case example 485–87
 European

abuse of dominant positions 470–77
agreements, decisions and concerted
 practices 466–67
anti-competitive multilateral behaviour
 466–70
collecting societies 472–73
definition of media markets 458–66
demand substitutability 453–54
distortion of competition 467
dominant positions 470–71
enforcement 456–58
essential facilities doctrine 473–74
exclusive licensing agreements 469
exemptions 467–68
fixed book price agreements 468
jurisdiction 450–52
licensing and acquisition of broadcasting
 rights 459–61
market definition 452–54
mergers, acquisitions and joint
 ventures 477–87
newspaper markets 463–64
refusal to deal 473–74
relevant geographic market 454, 465–66
relevant product market 453–54
retail supply of TV services 462–63
supply-side substitutability 454
trade between members 455–56
transmission infrastructure 463
TV-related markets 459–63
undertaking 454–55
whistle-blower immunity 456
wholesale supply of TV channels 461–62
international 449–50
jurisdiction 499–500
media pluralism 447–49
media relevance 446
mergers, acquisitions and joint ventures
 499–500
as part of competition law 445–46
Article 29 Working Party 324

artistic expression 43–44
audiovisual media services
    anti-trust law and TV-related markets
        459–63
    case example 144
    cultural policy/free trade conflict 145
    Europe/US differences 145
    European Union
        access to networks 194–99
        accountability 193–94
        additional rules from member
            states 165–68
        advertising 170–72
        co-/self-regulation 160
        commercial communications 168–79
        companies, establishment of and invest-
            ment in 160–62
        content-based restrictions 173–75
        content quotas 191, 192–93
        content regulation 179–81
        content/transmission distinction 160
        country of origin principle 162–65
        country-of-origin principle 158
        cultural interests, protection of 158
        definitions 150–51, 168–72
        disseminate/receive information,
            right to 157
        editorial content as obligatory 154
        editorial independence from
            advertising 175–76
        editorial responsibilities of providers 154
        electronic communication
            networks 154–55
        European productions, promotion
            of 190–93
        events of major importance for
            society 184–87
        exclusive rights, restrictions on 181–89
        filtering systems 189–90
        foreign decoding devices, use of 182–84
        framework 150–57
        free movement provisions 158
        general public as intended
            recipient 153–54
        influences, factors and actors 148–49
        internal market of EU 158
        licensing 161
        media pluralism 157
        minors, protection of 189–90
        misleading/aggressive practices 175
        must carry obligations 194–98

        on-demand services 152–53, 155–56,
            163–64
        and other provisions 156
        principle purpose, programmes as 153
        principles of 157–60
        private/public broadcasting 158–60
        product placement 170, 175
        programmes defined 151–53
        prohibition of content, right of 197–99
        public procurement law, privileges under
            199–200
        separation, principle of 175–76
        services defined 151
        short news reports 187–88
        sponsorship 169
        state aid 534–36
        territorially applicable exclusive
            rights 181–84
        transparency requirements 161, 172–73
        video clips 152–53
    film funding 506–7
    international law 145–48
    licensing and acquisition of broadcasting
        rights 459–61
    retail supply of TV services 462–63
    state aid 526
    wholesale supply of TV channels 461–62
authenticity of information published 79–87
automated decision-making 346–47

Barlow, John Perry 207
behaviour, modalities regulating 209
Big Data 307–9, 334
Body of European Regulators for Electronic
        Communications (BEREC) 270–71
broadband network development 525–26,
        531–33
broadcasters/broadcasting
    anti-trust law and TV-related
        markets 459–63
    case example 144
    cultural policy/free trade conflict 145
    Europe/US differences 145
    European Union
        access to networks 194–99
        accountability 193–94
        additional rules from member
            states 165–68
        advertising 170–72
        co-/self-regulation 160
        commercial communications 168–79

companies, establishment of and investment in 160–62
content-based restrictions 173–75
content quotas 191, 192–93
content regulation 179–81
content/transmission distinction 160
country-of-origin principle 158, 162–65
cultural interests, protection of 158
definition of 261n. 61
definitions 150–51, 168–72
disseminate/receive information, right to 157
editorial content as obligatory 154
editorial independence from advertising 175–76
editorial responsibilities of providers 154
electronic communication networks 154–55
European productions, promotion of 190–93
events of major importance for society 184–87
exclusive rights, restrictions on 181–89
filtering systems 189–90
foreign decoding devices, use of 182–84
framework 150–57
free movement provisions 158
general public as intended recipient 153–54
incitement to hatred 179–81
influences, factors and actors 148–49
internal market of EU 158
licensing 161
media pluralism 157
minors, protection of 189–90
misleading/aggressive practices 175
must carry obligations 194–98
on-demand services 152–53, 155–56, 163–64
and other provisions 156
principle purpose, programmes as 153
principles of 157–60
private/public broadcasting 158–60
product placement 170, 175
programmes defined 151–53
prohibition of content, right of 197–99
public procurement law, privileges under 199–200
separation, principle of 175–76
services defined 151
short news reports 187–88

sponsorship 169
state aid 534–36
territorially applicable exclusive rights 181–84
time and timing of advertising 176–79
transparency requirements 161, 172–73
video clips 152–53
international law 145–48
licensing and acquisition of rights 459–61
licensing of 109–10
location of, jurisdiction at 121–23
separation from transmission infrastructure 3–4
wholesale supply of TV channels 461–62 *see also* communication intermediaries
business confidential information, disclosure of 118–19

cable and satellite transmission 387–88, 400–1
caricature and satire 87
centre of gravity of the conflict analysis of jurisdiction 135–37
centre of interests analysis 132–33
child pornography 97
citizen journalists
   freedom of expression 45–46
   freedom of the press 5–12
classified information, disclosure of 93–95
code
   and data protection 306
   and internet governance and regulation 209–11
collecting societies 472–73
commercial communications
   advertising 35, 105, 170–72
   audiovisual media services 168–79
   comparative advertising 492–93
   content-based restrictions 173–75
   editorial independence 175–76
   forms of 169–72
   general rules for 169
   and human rights 489–90
   internet-based 227
   justification for limitations 168
   misleading advertising 491–92
   misleading/aggressive practices 175
   non-discrimination in 174–75
   product placement 170, 175
   product-related restrictions 173–74
   restrictions 105

commercial communications (*cont.*)
  separation, principle of 175–76
  sponsorship 169
  teleshopping 170–72
  terminology 168–72
  time and timing of 176–79
  transparency requirements 172–73, 227
communication
  factual/opinion 16–18
  media law as linked to 2
communication infrastructure, state
        investment in 507
communication intermediaries
  active role of 231
  automatically generated content 229–30
  and content providers, distinction between
        5, 13–15, 18–20
  duties of care under EU legal order 235–36
  editorial control 13–15, 230
  harmonisation *vs.* one-sided 236–37
  immunity, requirements for 232–34
  internet intermediaries, liability of 227–41
  location of, jurisdiction at 121–23
  media as 3
  monitoring obligations, lack of 234–36
  own/third-party content 229–30
  rights of 64–67
  search engines 230
  storage of information 232–34
competition law
  anti-trust law
    abuse of dominant positions 470–77
    agreements, decisions and concerted
          practices 466–67
    aims of 447–49
    anti-competitive multilateral
          behaviour 466–70
    case example 485–87
    collecting societies 472–73
    definition of media markets 458–66
    demand substitutability 453–54
    distortion of competition 467
    dominant positions 470–71
    enforcement 456–58
    essential facilities doctrine 473–74
    European 450–66
    exclusive licensing agreements 469
    exemptions 467–68
    fixed book price agreements 468
    international 449–50
    jurisdiction 499–500

licensing and acquisition of broadcasting
        rights 459–61
  market definition 452–54
  media pluralism 447–49
  media relevance 446
  mergers, acquisitions and joint ventures
        477–87, 499–500
  newspaper markets 463–64
  as part of competition law 445–46
  refusal to deal 473–74
  relevant geographic markets 454, 465–66
  relevant product market 453–54
  retail supply of TV services 462–63
  supply-side substitutability 454
  trade between EU members 455–56
  transmission infrastructure 463
  TV-related markets 459–63
  undertaking 454–55
  whistle-blower immunity 456
  wholesale supply of TV channels 461–62
case example 445
European 450–52
  public service broadcasters 521–22
  and state aid 521–22
mosaic formula 130
non-discrimination, principle of 276
telecommunications law distinction 274–75
unfair competition
  affected market principle 493–97
  comparative advertising 492–93
  country-of-origin principle 495–96
  and human rights 489–90
  international framework 488–89
  jurisdiction 493–98
  media relevance 446–47
  misleading advertising 491–92
  objectives of 446
  against single competitor 496–97*see also*
        market power
competitive safeguards 259
concentrations in the media sector 477–87,
        499–500
Conference of Postal and Telecommunications
        Administrations (CEPT) 301
confidentiality
  of communication process 43
  data processing 340–41
  disclosure of confidential
        information, 118–19
  protection of 305
consent of data subjects 335–39

consequences of publication 79
content providers
  automatically generated content 229–30
  and communication intermediaries, dis-
      tinction between 5, 13–15, 18–20
  editorial control 13–15
  freedom of expression
    academic expression 44
    anonymity 46–50
    artistic expression 43–44
    as content-neutral 42
    democracy, argument based on 39–40
    direct/indirect horizontal effects of
        human rights 49–50
    fundamental importance of 41
    individual autonomy, argument based
        on 40–41
    of information and ideas 42
    internet, communication via 44–46
    journalists/non-journalists 45–46
    justification of restriction 42
    marketplace of ideas rationale 39, 40, 49
    means and forms of expression 42
    media freedom distinction 39
    'regardless of frontiers' clause 39
    symbolic expression 43
    theory 39–41
    truth, argument based on 40
  location of, jurisdiction at 121–23
  own/third-party content 229–30
  separation from transmission infrastructure
      3–4 see also freedom of the media
content quotas 191, 192–93
convergence, media 4
cookies 328
copyright
  case examples 370–71, 431–36
  conflicting interests, balancing 372
  Council of Europe 381–82
  Cybercrime Convention 382
  digital information, impact of 372–73
  economic analysis of intellectual
      property 374–76
  economic rights 398–408
  European Union
    approximation and
        harmonisation 385–89
    balanced approach of 375
    Copyright Directive 386, 388
    current developments 389
    exhaustion doctrine 384–85

free movement provisions 383–85
  making available 402, 403–4
  public, communication to 387–88,
      399–407
  rental and lending rights 386–87
  rights of owners 400–3
  satellite and cable transmission 387–88,
      400–1
ideas and expression, distinction
    between 371
international framework
  Anti-Counterfeiting Trade Agreement
      (ACTA) 380–81
  Beijing Treaty 379
  Berne Convention 377–78
  dispute settlement 378
  human rights 379
  lex loci protectionis principle 378
  minimum rights, principle of 378
  national treatment, principle of 378
  Performances and Phonograms
      Treaty 379
  rights of owners 400
  Rome Convention 379
  United International Bureaux for
      the Protection of Intellectual
      Property 376
  World Intellectual Property Organization
      (WIPO) 377
jurisdiction
  choice of applicable law 439–43
  country-of-origin principle 439, 442
  distribution 443
  establishment of 437–39
  lex loci protectionis principle 436, 439,
      440–42
  territoriality principle 436
labour rationale 373–74
moral rights 375–76, 397
mosaic formula 130
personality rationale 374
reasons for protecting 373–76
transnational framework
  author, notion of 396
  authors' rights and related rights
      distinction 391–92
  beneficiaries of protection 395–97
  distribution of works 407–8
  economic rights 398–408
  enforcement 422–31
  exceptions and limitations 409–22

copyright (*cont.*)
    fixation 395, 398
    infringements 408–9
    internet intermediaries 427–31
    licensing 397–98
    literary and artistic works, concept of 390
    moral rights 397
    originality of work 394–95
    ownership of rights 424
    personal data, protection of 425–27
    personality rights 398
    public, communication to 399–408
    qualification of author 395
    reproduction 398–99, 409–14
    rights of owners 397–408, 424
    sui generis rights 392
    temporary acts of reproduction 409–14
    term of protection 422
    terminology 390–92
    three-step test 421–22
    works protected 393–94
   utilitarian argument 374
   WTO TRIPS Agreement 380
correlation 308
cost recovery in telecommunications 294–95
Council of Europe
   copyright 381–82
   data protection 318–22
   as source of media law 23–24
   telecommunications legal
       framework 261–63
country-of-origin principle
   audiovisual media services 123–25, 137–38,
       158, 162–65
   copyright 439, 442
   data protection 358
   discrimination due to 34
   internet governance and regulation 224–27
   jurisdiction 123–25, 137–38
   short news reports 187–88
   unfair competition 495–96
country-of-reception principle 125–32
cultural interests
   European audiovisual works, promotion
       of 190–93
   free trade/cultural policy conflict 145
   as justifying restriction 35, 36–37
   protection of,and audiovisual media
       services 158
   public service broadcasters 505
   state aid 533–36

Cyberidealism 207–8, 212–13
Cyberrealism 208–13

data controllers/processors 330–32
data processing 329–30, 333–43
data protection
   access to protected information 306
   Big Data 307–9, 334
   case examples 304–5
   code, important role of 306
   communicators, protection of 305
   conclusions, drawing of from data 308
   confidentiality, protection of 305
   and copyright enforcement 425–27
   data processing 329–30
   datafication of information 307, 308
   European Union
      absence of consent, data processing
         in 337–39
      access to information, data subject's right
         of 343–45
      accuracy of data 334–35
      aims of regulations 318
      Article 29 Working Party 324
      automated decision-making 346–47
      case examples 361–67
      conflicting interests, balancing 350–51
      consent 335–39
      content of messages 341
      cookies 328
      Council of Europe 318–22
      country-of-origin principle 358
      data controllers/processors 330–32
      data processing principles 333–43
      Data Protection Supervisor (EDPS) 324
      development of regulations 317–18
      equipment, location of 359–60
      establishment 357–60
      European Union
         traffic data 328–29
      exceptions and derogations 347
      human rights 348–51
      international applicability of law 356–60
      internet 327–29
      IP addresses 327–28
      journalistic media 348–49
      jurisdiction 356–60
      lawfulness of data processing 333
      legal framework 322–25
      legitimate interest notion 338
      limitation principle 335

location data 329, 341–42
objection to personal data processing 346
obligation to notify 332
personal data 325–29
principles of data processing 333–43
proportionality, principle of 350–51
public information, right of access to 349–50
purpose specification, principle of 334
quality of data 334–35
rectification/erasure of data 345–46
retention of data 342–43
rights of data subjects 343–47
security and confidentiality 340–41
third countries, transfer of data to 351–56
traffic data 341–42
transparency 343–45
Guidelines for the Regulation of
    Computerized Personal Data Files
    (UN) 313
Guidelines on the Protection of Privacy and
    Transborder Flows of Personal Data
    (OECD) 312
and human communication 305–6
metadata, protection of 305–6
personal nature of data 308
privacy, postmodern philosophies
    of 316–17
privacy of communication 308
probability and correlation 308
public-private dimensions of 309–12, 315
purpose specification, principle of 308
Special Rapporteur on the Right to
    Privacy 313
storage and processing of information 307
surveillance, government 309–12
transaction commodity, data as 315–16
transnational developments 312–13
UN level 312–13
US and EU comparison 313–17
datafication of information 307, 308
decency and morality, law on 95–97
decision-making, automated 346–47
'Declaration of the Independence of
    Cyberspace' (Barlow) 207
defamation 73–74
of religions 100–1
demand substitutability 453–54
democracy
    freedom of expression argument based
        on 39–40
    freedom of the media 51

Digital Agenda for Europe (DAE) 507
direct/indirect horizontal effects of human
    rights 32–33, 49–50
dispute settlement in telecommunications 255
distortion of competition 467
distribution of works 407–8, 443
Domain Name System (DNS) 215–16

e-books and Big Data 309
economic rights framework
    advertising, restrictions on 35
    copyright 398–408
    country of origin, discrimination due to 34
    economic rights as human rights 36
    EU/WTO comparison 33–34
    European Union 34–37
    free movement provisions 29, 34–37
    human rights integration 28–29
    internal market of EU 34–37
    public interest, restriction due to 34–35
    World Trade Organization (WTO) 37–39
editorial control
    content providers/communication
        intermediaries 13–15
    decisions, location of 124–25
    independence from advertising 175–76
    responsibilities of providers 154
    third party statements 230
electronic communication
    broadband network development 525–26,
        531–33
    networks 154–55
    privatisation/liberalisation in 3–4, see also
        audiovisual media services; inter-
        net governance and regulation;
        telecommunications
end-to-end principle 204–5
enforcement
    anti-trust law 456–58
    copyright 422–31
    foreign judgements, recognition and
        enforcement of 140–43
    jurisdiction 114
equality, and freedom of the media 55–56
equipment, location of 359–60
equivalence model 5
erasure/rectification of data 345–46
essential facilities doctrine 473–74
establishment, freedom of 160–62
European Commission, role regarding
    telecommunications, 270

European Court of Justice
  freedom of expression 24
  as source of media law 24–25
European media law
  Council of Europe 23–24
  European Union 24–25
  sources of 23–25
European productions, promotion of 190–93
European Union
  access to information, right to 60, 61–64
  anti-trust law
    abuse of dominant positions 470–77
    anti-competitive multilateral
        behaviour 466–70
    collecting societies 472–73
    definition of media markets 458–66
    demand substitutability 453–54
    distortion of competition 467
    dominant positions 470–71
    enforcement 456–58
    essential facilities doctrine 473–74
    exclusive licensing agreements 469
    exemptions 467–68
    fixed book price agreements 468
    jurisdiction 450–52
    licensing and acquisition of broadcasting
        rights 459–61
    market definition 452–54
    mergers, acquisitions and joint
        ventures 477–87
    newspaper markets 463–64
    refusal to deal 473–74
    relevant geographic markets 454, 465–66
    relevant product market 453–54
    retail supply of TV services 462–63
    supply-side substitutability 454
    trade between members 455–56
    transmission infrastructure 463
    TV-related markets 459–63
    undertaking 454–55
    whistle-blower immunity 456
    wholesale supply of TV channels 461–62
  audiovisual media services
    access to networks 194–99
    accountability 193–94
    additional rules from member
        states 165–68
    co-/self-regulation 160
    commercial communications 168–79
    companies, establishment of and
        investment in 160–62

content quotas 191, 192–93
content regulation 179–81
content/transmission distinction 160
country-of-origin principle 158
cultural interests, protection of 158
definitions 150–51
editorial content as obligatory 154
editorial independence from
    advertising 175–76
electronic communication
    networks 154–55
European productions, promotion
    of 190–93
events of major importance for
    society 184–87
exclusive rights, restrictions on 181–89
foreign decoding devices, use of 182–84
free movement provisions 158
general public as intended
    recipient 153–54
incitement to hatred 179–81
influences, factors and actors 148–49
legal framework 150–57
licensing 161
minors, protection of 189–90
must carry obligations 194–98
on-demand services 152–53, 155–56,
    163–64
principle purpose, programmes as 153
principles of 157–60
principles of EU order 157–60
private/public broadcasting 158–60
programmes defined 151–53
prohibition of content, right of 197–99
public procurement law, privileges under
    199–200
separation, principle of 175–76
services defined 151
short news reports 187–88
state aid 534–36
territorially applicable exclusive
    rights 181–84
time and timing of advertising 176–79
transparency requirements 161
and the US 145
balance between public order and freedom
    of expression 91–93
broadcasting definition 261n. 61
centre of gravity of the conflict analysis of
    jurisdiction 135–37
centre of interests analysis 132–33

commercial communications
  forms of 169–72
  general rules for 169
  product placement 170
  sponsorship 169
communication intermediaries, rights
  of 64–67
copyright
  approximation and
    harmonisation 385–89
  Copyright Directive 386, 388
  exhaustion doctrine 384–85
  free movement provisions 383–85
  making available 402, 403–4
  public, communication to 387–88,
    399–407
  rental and lending rights 386–87
  rights of owners 400–3
  satellite and cable transmission 387–88,
    400–1
country-of-reception principle 126,
  127–28
data protection
  absence of consent, data processing
    in 337–39
  access to information, data subject's right
    of 343–45
  accuracy of data 334–35
  aims of regulations 318
  Article 29 Working Party 324
  automated decision-making 346–47
  case examples 361–67
  conflicting interests, balancing 350–51
  consent 335–39
  content of messages 341
  Council of Europe 318–22
  country-of-origin principle 358
  data controllers/processors 330–32
  data processing principles 333–43
  Data Protection Supervisor (EDPS) 324
  development of regulations 317–18
  equipment, location of 359–60
  establishment 357–60
  exceptions and derogations 347
  human rights 348–51
  international applicability of law 356–60
  journalistic media 348–49
  jurisdiction 356–60
  lawfulness of data processing 333
  legal framework 322–25
  legitimate interest notion 338

limitation principle 335
  location data 329, 341–42
  objection to personal data processing 346
  obligation to notify 332
  personal data 325–29
  principles of data processing 333–43
  proportionality, principle of 350–51
  public information, right of access
    to 349–50
  purpose specification, principle of 334
  quality of data 334–35
  rectification/erasure of data 345–46
  retention of data 342–43
  rights of data subjects 343–47
  security and confidentiality 340–41
  third countries, transfer of data
    to 351–56
  traffic data 328–29, 341–42
  transparency 343–45
  US comparison 313–17
economic rights framework 34–37
film funding 506–7
foreign judgements, recognition and
  enforcement of 140, 142–43
freedom of the media 50–51
hate speech 98–100
human rights legal framework 29–30
information as goods or service 34
integration of human rights and
  economics 28–29
intellectual property rights 89
internal market of 34–37
internet governance and regulation 219–21
jurisdiction, and place of
  establishment 121–23
media pluralism 107
morality and decency, law on 95–97
original place of publication and jurisdiction 123–25, 137–38
personality rights 71–89
public order as interference
  justification 89–91
public service broadcasters 505–6
receive information, right to 58
as source of media law 24–25
state aid
  Altmark Trans criteria 513–18, 536
  broadband network development
    525–26, 531–33
  and competition 521–22
  culture and heritage related 526, 533–36

European Union (*cont.*)
    definition of state aid 510–24
    EU, aid granted by 509–10
    exceptional circumstances 544
    favouring of certain undertakings 520–21
    and the internal market 526–44
    investigation procedure 526–29
    licence fee systems 518–19
    market economy investor principle
        test 511–12
    member states, aid granted by 518–20
    national/EU co-funding 510
    necessity for as key factor 530–36
    notification requirement 524–26
    procedure 524–29
    public service broadcasters 521–22,
        538–44
    recovery of unlawful aid 545
    right to receive information 530
    services of general economic interest
        512–15, 538–44
    state emanations 518
    state obligations placed on private
        sector 519–20
    trade between member states 522–24
    undertakings, concept of 520
    unlawful aid 528–29, 544
targeted approach to jurisdiction 134
telecommunications
    access regulation 290–94
    accounting separation 296–97
    actors in 269–71
    Body of European Regulators for
        Electronic Communications
        (BEREC) 270–71
    Commission's role 270
    competition law distinction 274–75
    Conference of Postal and
        Telecommunications
        Administrations (CEPT) 301
    conflicting interests, balancing 276–77
    cost recovery 294–95
    development phases 265–69
    domestic markets, access to 279–80
    ex ante regulation 280–99
    excluded equipment 274
    frequency allocation and management
        299–302
    functional separation 297
    government responsibility, changes
        in 263–64

    harmonisation 264, 265
    imposition of specific obligations 289–99
    independence from significant market
        power, 279–80
    Independent Regulators Group
        (IRG) 271
    internet freedom provision 298
    internet neutrality 277–78
    liberalisation 264–67
    market definition and analysis 282–89
    market failure as reason for law 275
    national regulatory authorities
        (NRAs) 271
    neutrality of technology and service 277
    non-discrimination 276, 296
    objectives and principles of law 275–78
    payment, services provided for 274
    price control 294–95
    proportionality, principle of 277
    public services as focus 273
    Radio Spectrum Committee 300
    Radio Spectrum Policy Group
        (RSPG) 300–1
    retail services 297–98
    scope of regulatory framework 271–75
    significant market power, obligations
        requiring 281–99
    terminology 263n. 79
    transmission services, not content
        provision 272–73
    transparency requirements 296
untrue/unproven statements of fact 84–86
value judgements 86–87
World Trade Organisation (WTO)
    comparison with 33–34
    and EU telecommunications law 260–61
events of major importance for
    society 184–87
exclusive rights, restrictions on 181–89
exhaustion doctrine 384–85

factual information, distinguished from
    opinion 16–18
factual statements, categories of 79–87
films *see* audiovisual media services
filtering systems 189–90
fixed book price agreements 468
foreign decoding devices, use of 182–84
forms of expression 42
forum non conveniens doctrine 127, 127n. 56
free movement provisions 29, 34–37

audiovisual media services 158
and copyright 383–85
and freedom of expression 36
free trade/cultural policy conflict 145
freedom of establishment 160–62
freedom of expression
    academic expression 44
    access to information 60–61
    anonymity 46–50
    artistic expression 43–44
    authority and impartiality of the
        judiciary 104–5
    balance with public order 91–93
    case examples 87–89
    consequences of publication 79
    content and form of publication 78–79
    as content-neutral 42
    defining 'journalist' 9–12
    democracy, argument based on 39–40
    direct/indirect horizontal effects of human
        rights 49–50
    duties and responsibilities 78–79
    ECJ case law 24–25
    European Court of Justice 24
    and free movement provisions 36
    and freedom of the media 7–9, 51–52
    fundamental importance of 41
    hate speech 98–100
    individual autonomy, argument based
        on 40–41
    of information and ideas 42
    internet, communication via 44–46
    journalists/non-journalists 45–46
    justification of restriction 42
    knowingly false statements of fact 83
    marketplace of ideas rationale 39, 40, 49
    means and forms of expression 42
    media freedom distinction 39
    media pluralism 105–8
    morality and decency, law on 95–97
    prior conduct of person concerned 77–78
    public concern, matters of 74–76
    public/private individuals 76–78
    'regardless of frontiers' clause 39
    religiously offensive speech 100–3
    restrictions, case examples 68–69
    severity of sanctions 87
    state secrets, disclosure of 93–95
    statements of facts, categories of 79–87
    symbolic expression 43
    truth, argument based on 40

untrue/unproven statements 83–86
value judgements 86–87
veracity of the publication 79–87 see also
    restrictions
freedom of the media 3
    acknowledgement of importance 50–51
    case example 56–57
    citizen journalists 5–12, 45–46
    as equality right 55–56
    equivalence model 5
    and freedom of expression 7–9, 51–52
    freedom of expression distinction 39
    functional understanding of 12
    independence of the media 52
    intensity of protection 8–9
    journalists/non-journalists 5–12, 45–46
    lex specialis approach 7–9
    and media pluralism 106–7
    neutrality doctrine 5–6
    political discourse and democracy 51
    press-as-technology model 6
    professionalism of journalists 10–11
    in the public interest 11–12
    research and investigation, protection of 52–53
    restrictions case examples 68–69
    search and seizure of material 54
    sources, protection of 53–54, 56–57
    state action, entitlements to 54–55 see also
        restrictions
frequency allocation and management
    253–55, 299–302
functional separation in
    telecommunications 297
funding see state aid

Germany, funding of public service
    broadcasters 546–48
global media law
    International Covenant on Civil and
        Political Rights (ICCPR) 25
    Universal Declaration of Human Rights
        (UDHR) 25
    World Trade Organization 26
Global Multistakeholder Meeting on the
    Future of Internet Governance
    (GMMFIG) 218
goods, information as 34, 37
government
    public-private dimension of data
        protection 309–12
    surveillance 309–12 see also state aid

Guidelines for the Regulation of
          Computerized Personal Data Files
          (UN) 313
Guidelines on the Protection of Privacy and
          Transborder Flows of Personal Data
          (OECD) 312

harmful interference, prohibition of 252–53
hate speech 98–100, 179–81
honour, protection of 71–72
human behaviour, modalities regulating 209
human rights
     access to information 60–61
     as binding on states 30–31
     copyright 379
     data protection 348–51
     direct/indirect horizontal effects of 32–33,
          49–50
     economic rights as 36
     between individuals 32–33
     integration of with economics 28–29
     interference with 31
     legal framework 29–33
     protection from interference 31–32
     and unfair competition 489–90
     Universal Declaration of Human Rights
          (UDHR) 25

idealism concerning internet governance and
          regulation 207–8, 212–13
incitement to hatred 98–100, 179–81
independence of the media 52
Independent Regulators Group (IRG) 271
indirect/direct horizontal effects of human
          rights 32–33
individual autonomy, freedom of expression
          argument based on 40–41
information
     access to information, right to 59–64,
          343–45
     classified, disclosure of 93–95
     datafication of 307
     factual/opinion 16–18
     as goods or service 34, 37
     right to receive 530
     storage and processing of 307
     taxonomy of 16–18 see also data protection
information society services defined 222–24
          see also internet governance and
          regulation
informed consent 336
infrastructure
     internet 205–6

state investment in 507
state investment in communication 507
transmission
     anti-trust law 463
     information as goods or service 34, 37
     separation from broadcasters/
          broadcasting 3–4
infringements of copyright 408–9
intellectual property rights
     restrictions 89 see also copyright
interference with rights
     human rights 31
     protection from interference 31–32
intermediaries see communication
          intermediaries
internal market of EU
     audiovisual media services 158
     economic rights framework 34–37
     state aid 526–44
international law
     anti-trust law 449–50
     audiovisual media services 145–48
     broadcasters/broadcasting 145–48
     International Covenant on Civil and
          Political Rights (ICCPR) 25
     state aid 507–9
     unfair competition 488–89
     Universal Declaration of Human Rights
          (UDHR) 25
     World Trade Organization 26 see also
          copyright; European Union; internet
          governance and regulation
International Telecommunications
          Union (ITU)
     Council of 248
     dispute settlement 255
     EU influence in 246
     freedom and equality of
          correspondence 251–52
     General Secretariat 248
     harmful interference, prohibition of 252–53
     history 246
     legal framework and scope 246–47
     membership 246
     organs of 248
     Plenipotentiary Conference 248
     prior consent, principle of 251
     purposes of 247–48
     radio-frequency management 253–55
     Radiocommunication Sector
          (ITU-R) 249–50
     secrecy of telecommunications 252
     sectors of 248–51

substantive law 251–55
technical efficiency, principle of 252–55
Telecommunication Development Sector
    (ITU-D) 251
Telecommunication Standardization Sector
    (ITU-T) 250–51
Internet Corporation for Assigned Names and
    Numbers (ICANN) 215–16
Internet Engineering Task Force
    (IETF) 214–15
internet governance and regulation
  anonymity 46–50
  and Big Data 308–9
  broadband network development 525–26,
    531–33
  CAPTCHA test 210
  case example 202, 212–13
  code as key to 209–11
  communication intermediaries,
    rights of 65
  cookies 328
  and copyright 372–73
  copyright enforcement 427–31
  Council of Europe 219–21
  country-of-reception principle 128–29
  Cyberidealism 207–8, 212–13
  Cyberrealism 208–13
  data protection 327–29
  debate over methods of 212
  development of 203
  Domain Name System (DNS) 215–16
  end-to-end principle 204–5
  European Union
    active role of ISPs 231
    aims of e-commerce Directive 221–22
    automatically generated content 229–30
    becoming a information society service
      provider 227
    case example 238–41
    commercial communications 227
    country-of-origin principle 224–27
    current developments 237–38
    duties of care 235–36
    editorial control over third party
      statements 230
    harmonisation *vs.* one-sided 236–37
    immunity, requirements for 232–34
    information society services
      defined 222–24
    liability of internet intermediaries 227–41
    monitoring obligations, lack of 234–36
    own/third-party content 229–30
    scope of e-commerce Directive 222–24

  search engines 230
    storage of information 232–34
  evolution of 4
  freedom of expression 44–46
  Global Multistakeholder Meeting on the
    Future of Internet Governance
    (GMMFIG) 218
  governments' role 217
  HTTP 206
  idealism 207–8, 212–13
  infrastructure of the internet 205–6
  intermediaries, liability of 227–41
  international
    as decentralised hybrid 214
    ICANN 215–16
    Internet Society (ISOC) 214–15
    self-regulating organisations 214–15
  Internet Engineering Task Force
    (IETF) 214–15
  internet freedom provision 298
  Internet Governance Forum (IGF) 218
  IP addresses 327–28
  key components of internet 203–6
  legitimacy of regulators 211–12
  modalities regulating behaviour 209
  morality and decency, law on 95–97
  mosaic formula 131–32
  NETmundial Initiative 218
  neutrality of the internet 277–78
  on-demand audiovisual services 152–53,
    155–56
  open architecture networking 204
  packet switching 203–4
  private sector dominance of 211–12
  quantitative criteria, application of to
    jurisdiction 134–35
  realism 208–13
  schools of thought on 206–14
  traceability of users 210
  traffic data 328–29
  Transmission Control Protocol/Internet
    Protocol (TCP/IP) 204, 205
  UN level 216–18
  video clips 152–53
  Working Group on Internet Governance
    (WGIG) 217–18
  World Summit on the Information Society
    (WSIS) 217–18
  World Wide Web 206
  World Wide Web Consortium (W3C)
    215 *see also* internet service
    providers (ISPs)
Internet Governance Forum (IGF) 218

internet service providers (ISPs)
  active role of 231
  and anonymity 50
  automatically generated content 229–30
  editorial control over third party
     statements 230
  EU legal order
    duties of care 235–36
  harmonisation *vs.* one-sided 236–37
  immunity, requirements for 232–34
  liability of 227–41
  monitoring obligations, lack of 234–36
  own/third-party content 229–30
  search engines 230
  storage of information 232–34
  United States 228 *see also* internet govern-
     ance and regulation
Internet Society (ISOC) 214–15
investigation, protection of 52–53
investment in audiovisual media
     companies 161–62

joint ventures 477–87, 499–500
journalistic media
  anonymity 48–49
  authority and impartiality of the
     judiciary 104–5
  balance between public order and freedom
     of expression 92–93
  and Big Data 308–9
  data processing of personal data 339
  data protection 348–49
  defining 'journalist' 9–12
  journalists/non-journalists 5–12, 45–46
  licensing of journalist/media
     companies 108–10
  privileges of 3
  professionalism of journalists 10–11 *see*
    also freedom of the media
judiciary
  authority and impartiality of 104–5
  personality rights 77
jurisdiction
  adjudicative 114
  anti-trust law 499–500
    European 450–52
  application of principles to cases 138–40
  case examples 112
  categories of 114
  centre of gravity of the conflict
     analysis 135–37

centre of interests analysis 132–33
communication media, location of 124–25
competition law 450–52
confidential information, disclosure
    of 118–19
conflicting interests, balance between 113
copyright
  choice of applicable law 439–43
  country-of-origin principle 439, 442
  distribution 443
  establishment of jurisdiction 437–39
  lex loci protectionis principle 436, 439,
    440–42
  territoriality principle 436
data protection 356–60
divergences globally 112–13
editorial decisions, location of 124–25
enforcement 114
equipment, location of 359–60
establishment 357–60
foreign judgements, recognition and
    enforcement of 140–43
forum non conveniens doctrine 127,127n. 56
legal framework 116–20
mosaic formula 499–500
multiple publication rule 137–38
nationality principle 115
objective 115
passive personality principle 115
personal 114
prescriptive 114
principles of 114–16
private law cases 116–19
protective principle 115
public law cases 119–20
quantitative criteria, application
    of 134–35
reception country principle 125–32
single publication rule 138
subject-matter 114
subjective 115
targeted approach 134
territorial principle 115–16
transnational cases
  actor sequitur forum rei principle 121
  challenges of 120–21
  locus actus principle 123–24
  original place of publication 123–25,
    137–38
  place of establishment 121–23
  ubiquity principle 120

and transnational media law 22–23
ubiquity principle 125, 137
unfair competition 493–98
universality principle 115, 125

knowingly false statements of fact 83

labour rationale for copyright 373–74
lawfulness of data processing 333
legal frameworks
  economic rights framework 33–39
  free movement provisions 29, 34–37
  human rights framework 29–33
  integration of human rights and
    economics 28–29
  jurisdiction 116–20
legislative jurisdiction *see* prescriptive
    jurisdiction
legitimate interest notion 338
length of copyright protection 422
Lessig, Lawrence 209, 210–11
lex loci protectionis principle 378, 436, 439,
    440–42
liability of internet intermediaries 227–41
liberalisation in electronic
    communication 3–4
licence fee systems 518–19
licensing
  audiovisual media services 161
  broadcasting rights 459–61
  copyright 397–98
  exclusive agreements 469
  of journalist/media companies 108–10
limitation principle 335
location data 329, 341–42
location of providers
  jurisdiction at 121–23
  original place of publication and jurisdic-
    tion 123–25, 137–38
Locke, John 373–74
locus actus principle 123–24

margin of appreciation 69–70, 103–4
market definition
  and analysis in telecommunications 282–89
  anti-trust law 452–54, 458–66
  concentrations in the media sector 480–82
  newspaper markets 463–64
  relevant geographic markets 454, 465–66
  relevant product market 453–54
  retail supply of TV services 462–63

transmission infrastructure 463
  TV-related markets 459–63
  wholesale supply of TV channels 461–62
market power
  independence from significant 279–80
  significant, obligations requiring 281–99
marketplace of ideas rationale 39, 40, 49
mass communication media 3, 44–46 *see also*
    audiovisual media services; com-
    mercial communications; content
    providers; data protection; inter-
    net governance and regulation;
    journalistic media
McLuhan, Marshall 2
means and forms of expression 42
media, defining 2–3
media convergence 4
media freedom *see* freedom of the media
media in a technological sense *see* communi-
    cation intermediaries
media law
  as cross-sectoral area 1–2
  European 23–25
  international 25–26
  internet, evolution of 4
  Jersild case example 1
  privatisation/liberalisation in electronic
    communication 3–4
  transnational 20–22
media pluralism
  anti-trust law 447–49
  audiovisual media services 157
  concentrations in the media sector 478,
    482–84
  defined 106
  and freedom of the media 106–7
  internal/external 107–8
  legislation 105–6
  policy areas 107–8
  safeguarding 107–8
mergers, acquisitions and joint ventures
    477–87, 499–500
messages
  factual/opinion 16–18
  taxonomy of 16–18
metadata, protection of 305–6
minimum rights, principle of 378
minors, protection of 189–90
misleading/aggressive practices 175
  advertising 491–92
monitoring obligations, lack of 234–36

moral rights in copyright 397
morality and decency, law on 95–97
mosaic formula 129–32, 499–500
most favoured nation (MFN) principle 37–38
multiple publication rule 137–38
must carry obligations 194–98

national regulatory authorities (NRAs)
        (telecoms) 271
national treatment, principle of 378
national treatment obligation 38
nationality principle of jurisdiction 115
net neutrality 277–78 *see also* internet govern-
        ance and regulation
NETmundial Initiative 218
networks, communication
    access to 194–99
    broadband network development 525–26,
        531–33
    telecommunications 244–45
neutrality
    doctrine of 5–6
    of technology and service 277
newsgathering activities, protection of 52–53
newspaper markets 463–64
non-discrimination
    freedom of the media 55–56
    principle of 276
    telecommunications 296

objective jurisdiction 115
obscene materials 95–97
old media 3
on-demand services 152–53, 155–56, 163–64
online publications *see* internet governance
        and regulation
open architecture networking 204
opinion distinguished from factual
        information 16–18
original place of publication
    audiovisual media services 158
    and jurisdiction 123–25, 137–38
others, rights of 71–73
own/third-party content 229–30
    distinction between 5
    and media convergence 4

packet switching 203–4
passive personality principle of
        jurisdiction 115
personal jurisdiction 114

personality rationale for copyright 374
personality rights
    case examples 87–89
    consequences of publication 79
    content and form of publication 78–79
    copyright 398
    crimes and criminals 81–82
    criteria for cases 73–87
    defamation 73–74
    duties and responsibilities 78–79
    honour, protection of 71–72
    judiciary 77
    jurisdiction 117–18
    knowingly false statements of fact 83
    mosaic formula 130
    photos/videos 80–81
    prior conduct of person concerned 77–78
    privacy cases 73–74
    private life, respect for 71–73
    public concern, matters of 74–76
    public/private individuals 76–78
    reputation, protection of 71–72
    satire and caricature 87
    severity of sanctions 87
    statements of facts, categories of 79–87
    taxonomy of 71–73
    true statements of fact 80–82
    untrue/unproven statements 83–86
    value judgements 86–87
    veracity of the publication 79–87
place of establishment, jurisdiction at 121–23
place of publication, original, and jurisdiction
        123–25, 137–38
pluralism of the media
    anti-trust law 447–49
    audiovisual media services 157
    concentrations in the media sector 478,
        482–84
    defined 106
    and freedom of the media 106–7
    internal/external 107–8
    legislation 105–6
    policy areas 107–8
    safeguarding 107–8
political discourse
    freedom of expression argument based
        on 39–40
    freedom of the media 51
pornography 95–97
prescriptive jurisdiction 114
press-as-technology model 6

price control in telecommunications 294–95
prior consent, principle of 251
privacy 73–74
  and anonymity 47
  and consent 81–82
  crimes and criminals 81–82
  locus actus principle 124
  photos/videos 80–81
  postmodern philosophies of 316–17
  protection of 72–73
  true statements of fact 80–82 *see also* data
    protection
private life, respect for 71–73
private/public dimension
  audiovisual media services 158–60
  data protection 315
  matters of concern 75–76
privatisation in electronic
    communication 3–4
probability and correlation 308
processing of information 307
procurement law, privileges under 199–200
product placement 170, 175
professionalism of journalists 10–11
programmes
  defined 151–53
  as principle purpose of audiovisual
    services 153
proportionality, principle of 277, 350–51
proportionality test 69
protective principle of jurisdiction 115
pseudonymous speech 46–50
public, communication to 399–408
public information, right of access to 349–50
public interest
  matters of, and personality rights 74–76
  restriction due to 34–35
  secrets of state, disclosure of 93–95
public order
  balance with freedom of expression 91–93
  exception 38
  legislation 89–91
  religiously offensive speech 103
  state secrets, disclosure of 93–95
public/private dimension
  audiovisual media services 158–60
  data protection 309–12, 315
public procurement law, privileges under
    199–200
public service broadcasters 505–6
  case examples 546–48

single/dual funding schemes 506
  state aid 521–22, 538–44
purpose specification, principle of 308, 334

quality of data 334–35
quantitative criteria, application of to
    jurisdiction 134–35
quotas, content 191, 192–93

radio *see* telecommunications
Radio Spectrum Committee 300
Radio Spectrum Policy Group (RSPG) 300–1
Radiocommunication Sector of the ITU
    (ITU-R) 249–50
realism concerning internet governance and
    regulation 208–13
reception country principle 125–32
recipients, rights of
  access to information, right to 59–64
  receive information, right to 58–59
rectification/erasure of data 345–46
refusal to deal 473–74
registration of journalist/media
    companies 108–10
religiously offensive speech
  defamation of religions 100–1
  margin of appreciation 103–4
  public order 103
  right to respect for religious feelings 101–3
reputation, protection of 71–72
research and investigation, protection
    of 52–53
restrictions
  advertising 35
  allowable 69–70
  authority and impartiality of the
    judiciary 104–5
  case examples 68–69
  child pornography 97
  commercial speech 105
  cultural aspects as justifying 35, 36–37
  duties and responsibilities of content
    providers 70
  exclusive rights 181–89
  hate speech 98–100
  intellectual property rights 89
  justification of, and freedom of
    expression 42
  licensing of journalist/media
    companies 108–10
  margin of appreciation 69–70, 74

restrictions (*cont.*)
  media pluralism 105–8
  morality and decency, law on 95–97
  personality rights
    balance with freedom of
        expression 73–89
    case examples 87–89
    consequences of publication 79
    content and form of publication 78–79
    crimes and criminals 81–82
    criteria for cases 73–87
    defamation 73–74
    duties and responsibilities 78–79
    judiciary 77
    knowingly false statements of fact 83
    margin of appreciation 74
    photos/videos 80–81
    prior conduct of person concerned 77–78
    privacy cases 73–74
    private life, respect for 71–73
    public concern, matters of 74–76
    public/private individuals 76–78
    reputation, protection of 71–72
    satire and caricature 87
    severity of sanctions 87
    statements of facts, categories of 79–87
    taxonomy of 71–73
    true statements of fact 80–82
    untrue/unproven statements 83–86
    value judgements 86–87
    veracity of the publication 79–87
  public order
    balance with freedom of
        expression 91–93
    legislation 89–91
    state secrets, disclosure of 93–95
  religiously offensive speech 100–3
retail services in telecommunications 297–98
rights and freedoms
  as binding on states 30–31
  case example 27
  content providers
    freedom of expression 39–50
    freedom of expression/media freedom
        distinction 39
  data subjects 343–47
  between individuals 32–33
  interference with 31
  intermediaries, rights of 64–67
  journalistic media 3, 45–46
  legal frameworks
    economic rights framework 33–39

  human rights framework 29–33
  integration of human rights and
      economics 28–29
  protection from interference 31–32
  rights of others 71–73 (*see also* personal-
      ity rights) *see also* freedom of the
      media; recipients, rights of

sanctions, severity of 87
satellite and cable transmission 387–88,
    400–1
satire and caricature 87
search engines 230
secrets of state, disclosure of 93–95
security of data processing 340–41
separation, principle of 175–76
service, information as 34, 37
severity of sanctions 87
single publication rule 138
social media and anonymity 49–50
sources, journalistic
  protection of 53–54, 56–57 *see also* freedom
      of the media; journalistic media
Special Rapporteur on the Right to
    Privacy 313
speech act theory 16–18
speech intermediaries *see* communication
    intermediaries
sponsorship 169
standards, telecommunication 250–51
state aid
  case examples 502–3, 546–48
  cultural diversity 505
  European Union
    aid granted by 509–10
    Altmark Trans criteria 513–18, 536
    broadband network development
        525–26, 531–33
    and competition 521–22
    culture and heritage related 526, 533–36
    definition of state aid 510–24
    exceptional circumstances 544
    favouring of certain undertakings 520–21
    and the internal market 526–44
    investigation procedure 526–29
    licence fee systems 518–19
    market economy investor principle
        test 511–12
    member states, aid granted by 518–20
    national/EU co-funding 510
    necessity for as key factor 530–36
    notification requirement 524–26

procedure 524–29
public service broadcasters 521–22, 538–44
recovery of unlawful aid 544
right to receive information 530
services of general economic interest 536, 538–44
social character of aid 530
state emanations 518
state obligations placed on private sector 519–20
trade between member states 522–24
undertakings, concept of 520
unlawful aid 528–29, 544
film funding 506–7
international law 507–9
investment in communication infrastructure 507
public service broadcasters 505–6
risks and benefits of 503
single/dual funding schemes 506
transnational framework 503–4
state secrets, disclosure of 93–95
statements of facts, categories of 79–87
storage of information 232–34, 307
subject-matter jurisdiction 114
subjective jurisdiction 115
supply-side substitutability 454
surveillance, government 309–12
symbolic expression 43

targeted approach to jurisdiction 134
technical efficiency, principle of 252–55
Telecommunication Development Sector (ITU-D) of the ITU 251
Telecommunication Standardization Sector (ITU-T) of the ITU 250–51
telecommunications
  case example 242–43, 261–63
  Conference of Postal and Telecommunications Administrations (CEPT) 301
  Council of Europe legal framework 261–63
  economics of 244–45
  European Union
    access regulation 290–94
    accounting separation 296–97
    actors in 269–71
    Body of European Regulators for Electronic Communications (BEREC) 270–71
    Commission's role 270

competition law distinction 274–75
conflicting interests, balancing 276–77
cost recovery 294–95
development phases 265–69
domestic markets, access to 279–80
ex ante regulation 280–99
excluded equipment 274
frequency allocation and management 299–302
functional separation 297
government responsibility, changes in 263–64
harmonisation 264, 265
imposition of specific obligations 289–99
independence from significant market power, 279–80
Independent Regulators Group (IRG) 271
internet freedom provision 298
internet neutrality 277–78
liberalisation 264–67
market definition and analysis 282–89
market failure as reason for 275
national regulatory authorities (NRAs) 271
neutrality of technology and service 277
non-discrimination 296
non-discrimination, principle of 276
objectives and principles 275–78
payment, services provided for 274
price control 294–95
proportionality, principle of 277
public services as focus 273
retail services 297–98
scope of 271–75
significant market power, obligations requiring 281–99
substantive regulation 279–302
terminology 263n. 79
transmission services, not content provision 272–73
transparency requirements 296
frequency allocation and management 253–55, 299–302
International Telecommunications Union
  Council of 248
  dispute settlement 255
  EU influence in 246
  freedom and equality of correspondence 251–52
  General Secretariat 248

telecommunications (*cont.*)
    harmful interference, prohibition of 252–53
    history 246
    legal framework and scope 246–47
    membership 246
    organs of 248
    Plenipotentiary Conference 248
    prior consent, principle of 251
    priority of certain
        correspondence 251–52
    purposes of 247–48
    radio-frequency management 253–55,
        299–302
    Radiocommunication Sector
        (ITU-R) 249–50
    secrecy of telecommunications 252
    sectors of 248–51
    substantive law 251–55
    technical efficiency, principle of 252–55
    Telecommunication Development Sector
        (ITU-D) 251
    Telecommunication Standardization
        Sector (ITU-T) 250–51
  as network-based 244–45
  Radio Spectrum Committee 300
  Radio Spectrum Policy Group
    (RSPG) 300–1
  role in media law 243–44
  United States 264
  World Trade Organization (WTO)
    access to and use of networks and
        services 257–58
    allocation and use of scarce resources 260
    Annex on Telecommunications 256–58
    competitive safeguards 259
    definitions 256–57
    and EU telecommunications law 260–61
    interconnection with major suppliers
        260, 260n. 56
    Reference Paper 258–60
    transparency requirements 257
    universal services 260
teleshopping 170–72, 176–79
television services *see* audiovisual media services
term of copyright protection 422
territorial principle of jurisdiction 115–16
territorially applicable exclusive rights 181–84
third countries, transfer of data to 351–56
third-party/own content 229–30
  distinction between 5
  and media convergence 4

three-step test 421–22
time and timing of advertising 176–79
traceability of internet users 210
traditional media 3
traffic data 328–29, 341–42
transaction commodity, data as 315–16
Transmission Control Protocol/Internet
    Protocol (TCP/IP) 204, 205
transmission infrastructure 463
  information as goods or service 34, 37
  separation from content providers 3–4
transnational media law
  concept of 20–22
  and jurisdiction 22–23
  need for 21–22
transparency requirements
  audiovisual media services 161
  commercial communications 172–73
  data protection 343–45
  internet-based commercial
    communications 227
  and licensing 108
  telecommunications 296
  WTO and telecommunications 257
true statements of fact 80–82
truth, freedom of expression argument
    based on 40

ubiquity principle 120, 125, 137
undertakings 454–55
  concept of 520
  state favouring of certain 520
unfair commercial practices 175
unfair competition
  affected market principle 493–97
  comparative advertising 492–93
  country-of-origin principle 495–96
  and human rights 489–90
  international framework 488–89
  jurisdiction 493–98
  media relevance 446–47
  misleading advertising 491–92
  objectives of 446
  against single competitor 496–97
United International Bureaux for the Protection
    of Intellectual Property 376
United States
  anonymity 47–48
  audiovisual media services, and the EU 145
  data protection
    EU comparison 313–17

foreign judgements, recognition and
enforcement of 141–42
hate speech 98–99
internet service providers (ISPs) 228
single publication rule 138
telecommunications 264n. 80
untrue/unproven statements of fact
83–86
utilitarian argument for copyright 375
universality principle 125
of jurisdiction 115
unjustifiable 70
unproven statements of fact 83–86
untrue/unproven statements of fact 83–86
utilitarian argument for copyright 374

value judgements
distinguished from factual
information 16–18
restrictions 86–87
satire and caricature 87
veracity of the publication 79–87
video clips 152–53

web-based publications *see* internet
governance and regulation
Westphalian model 20
whistle-blower immunity 456
Working Group on Internet Governance
(WGIG) 217–18
World Intellectual Property Organization
(WIPO) 377

World Summit on the Information Society
(WSIS) 217–18
World Trade Organization (WTO)
copyright 380
economic rights framework 37–39
EU comparison 33–34
and global media law 26
information as goods or service 37
integration of human rights and
economics 29
most favoured nation (MFN)
principle 37–38
national treatment obligation 38
public order exception 38
state aid 507–9
telecommunications
access to and use of networks and
services 257–58
allocation and use of scarce resources 260
Annex on Telecommunications 256–58
competitive safeguards 259
definitions 256–57
EU telecommunications law 260–61
interconnection with major suppliers
260, 260n. 56
Reference Paper 258–60
transparency requirements 257
universal services 260
TRIPS Agreement 380
World Wide Web 206 *see also* internet
governance and regulation
World Wide Web Consortium (W3C) 215